American Map

Business Control Atlas

The Basic Business Bible

The information shown on this map has been obtained from various authoritative sources. Nevertheless, a work of this scope may contain some inaccuracies. Any errors and omissions called to our attention will be greatly appreciated.

Cover photo by Phil Cantor, Superstock

Printed in Canada

Business Control Atlas
CONTENTS

The Business Control Atlas is the single, most comprehensive source of basic marketing data for all North American markets, including the United States, Canada, and Puerto Rico. Its information-packed pages constitute an indispensable business tool for anyone involved in market analysis, advertising, sales planning, distribution, transportation, and traffic control.

Features of the Business Control Atlas

Maps of the Individual States/Provinces:

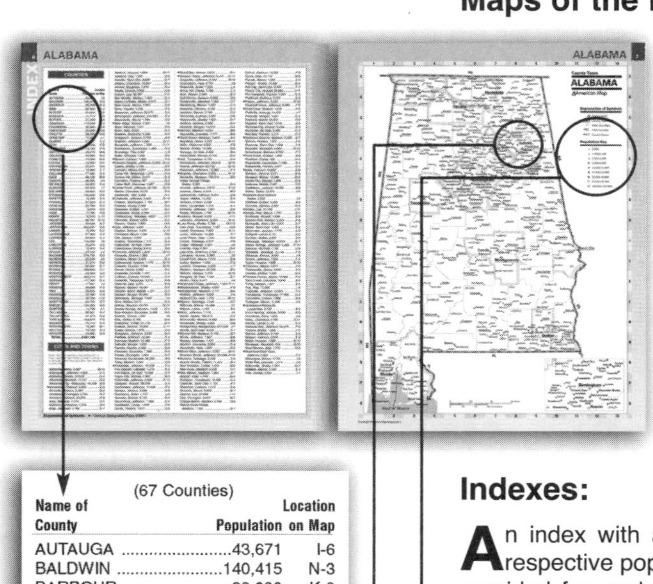

The Business Control Atlas offers clear, accurate, easy-to-read maps, showing county outlines of every state and province, accompanied by a corresponding index. All places of 1,000 population or more are shown on the maps and listed in the indexes. Where room permits, selected places under 1,000 are also shown, but these do not appear in the index. County seats are always shown and identified as such, regardless of size. City/town population categories are shown by special symbols explained in the map key.

For improved readability, areas containing a great number of places in close proximity are shown in enlarged insets. Areas covered by these insets are indicated by green, numbered boxes on the main maps. Where insets were not sufficient to enhance clarity, states have been accommodated on two pages.

(67 Counties)

Name of County	Population	Location on Map
AUTAUGA	43,671	I-6
BALDWIN	140,415	N-3
BARBOUR	29,038	K-9
BIBB	20,826	G-5
BLOUNT	51,024	D-6
BULLOCK	11,714	K-8
BUTLER	21,399	K-6
CALHOUN	112,249	E-8
CHAMBERS	36,583	H-9
CHEROKEE	23,988	D-9
CHILTON	39,593	H-6
CHOCTAW	15,922	J-1
CLARKE	27,867	L-2
CLAY	14,254	F-8
CLEBURNE	[illegible]	[illegible]
COFFEE	[illegible]	[illegible]
COLBERT	[illegible]	[illegible]

Boaz
Sardis City
Mountainboro
Douglas
106 ETOWAH
Walnut Grove
Reece City
Attalla
Gadsden
Altoona
Rainbow City
Hokes
Glencoe
Steele
Southside
CALHOUN

Explanation of Symbols

- State Capital
- Vernon County Seat
- MSA Boundary
- 192 MSA Number
- DALE County Name

Population Key

- 0-999
- 1,000-2,499
- 2,500-4,999
- 5,000-9,999
- 10,000-19,999
- 20,000-24,999
- 25,000-49,999
- 50,000-99,999
- 100,000-249,999

Indexes:

An index with alphabetical listings of counties/divisions, and towns, their respective populations and status, and a key to their location on the map is provided for each state or province. Wherever possible, the entire index is located on the facing page of the corresponding map.

MSA/NECMA Boundaries:

The latest (1999) boundary definitions of Metropolitan Statistical Areas (MSAs) and New England County Metropolitan Areas (NECMAs) are indicated on each map by blue outlines and reference numbers. With these numbers, official names of MSAs/NECMAs may be found on page 179.

NOTE: MSAs are constituted of entire counties in all but the New England states (Connecticut, Maine, Massachusetts, New Hampshire, Rhode Island, Vermont). New England MSAs consist of cities and towns, and boundaries may include parts of several counties. NECMAs, on the other hand, are constituted of entire counties. In order to provide data that are consistently county-based throughout the U.S., we provide data for New England by NECMA, and for the rest of the country by MSA.

Metro Market Statistical Data:

Ranks all year 2000 Metro Market Areas by a variety of categories important to business users. These include population, median and average household incomes, retail sales figures for automotive sales, etc. See table of contents for list. The data for each category are based on year 2000 estimates.

Daily Planning Section:

Offers the user helpful business information, including: Major U.S. cities air and road mileage chart; U.S. standard time zones; area codes, national zip code regions, and international direct dial codes.

Explanation of Symbols Used in the Indexes:

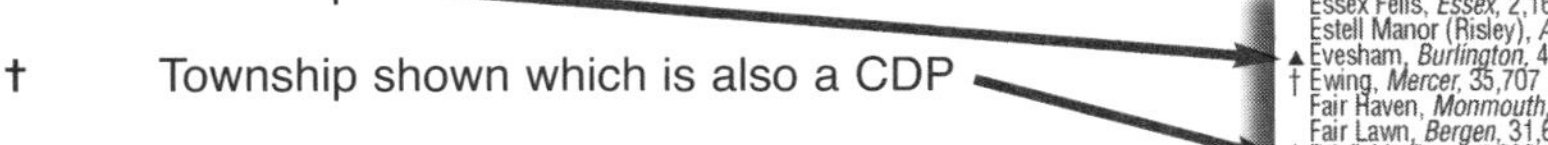

▲ Township

† Township shown which is also a CDP

● Census Designated Place (CDP)

Italics County names

Essex Fells, *Essex*, 2,162 ....Gg-4
Estell Manor (Risley), *Atlantic*, 1,585 .....V-8
▲ Evesham, *Burlington*, 42,275 ....Q-7
† Ewing, *Mercer*, 35,707 ....L-9
Fair Haven, *Monmouth*, 5,937 ....K-15
Fair Lawn, *Bergen*, 31,637 ....Dd-7
† Fairfield, *Essex*, 7,063 ....Ff-4
▲ Fairfield, *Essex*, 7,063 ....V-4
● Fairton, *Cumberland*, 2,253 ....V-5
Fairview, *Bergen*, 13,255 ....Hh-10
● Fairview, *Monmouth*, 3,942 ....K-14
Fanwood, *Union*, 7,174 ....Ll-2
Farmingdale, *Monmouth*, 1,587 ....M-14
Flemington, *Hunterdon*, 4,200 ....J-8
▲ Florence, *Burlington*, 10,746 ....N-8
● Florence-Roebling, *Burlington*, 8,200 .....N-8
Florham Park, *Morris*, 8,857 ....Hh-2

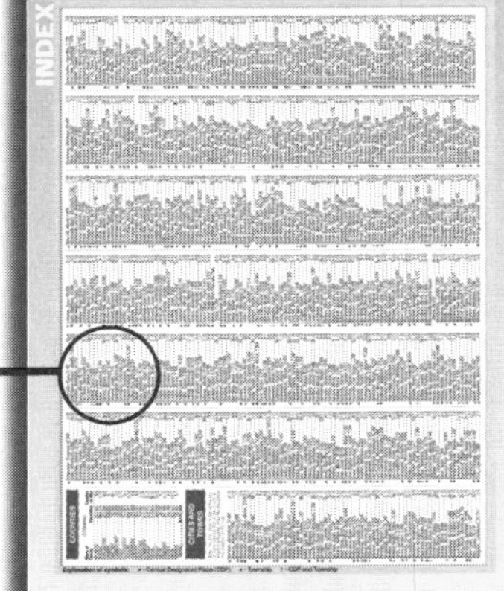

(For symbols used on maps see explanation on individual map pages.)

Notes on Places Shown on the Maps

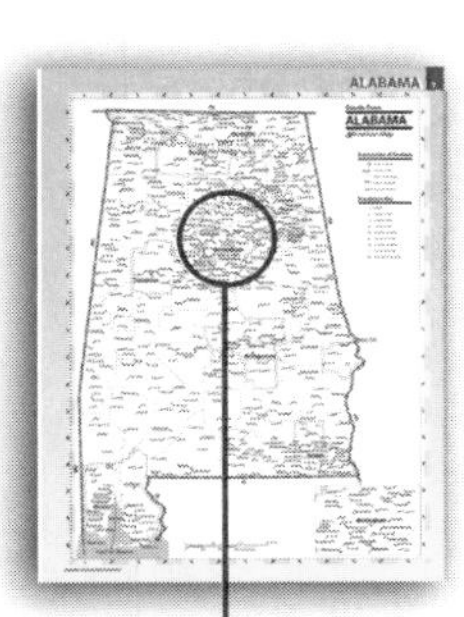

State map section, actual scale

1. Incorporated Places:

Those places which are incorporated under the laws of their respective states as cities, boroughs, towns, and villages.

2. Unincorporated Places:

a. CDPs (Census Designated Places) are closely settled population centers without corporate limits.

b. Additional population centers not classified by the Census as CDPs because they do not meet specific requirements but recognized by American Map as separate entities due to their significant population. Those places whose population is estimated to be above 1,000 are included in the index.

3. Townships:

In Pennsylvania, New Jersey, New York, and the New England states, many government functions are delegated to divisions within the counties called "towns" or "townships," recognized by the Bureau of the Census. Townships which contain other localities within them are not shown on the map. Nevertheless, these have been included in the index and are preceded by a triangle to identify them. In many cases they have a significant population not accounted for by the localities contained within their borders. Grid coordinates give approximate location of these townships.

4. Independent Cities:

Cities such as St. Louis, Missouri; Baltimore, Maryland; Carson City, Nevada; and 40 cities in Virginia are administered independently of their surrounding counties. These independent cities are listed in the index following the state's other counties. The population counts of the independent cities are not included in the population counts of their surrounding counties. Though independent, some of these cities serve as county seats for neighboring counties. In the index to cities and towns, independent city entries are followed by a repetition of their respective independent city names in place of county names.

5. Locations that Fall in Two States:

Where this occurs, the total population count for that location is given. However, state population figures will reflect only that area of the community within the state's borders.

Note:
Population-specific information on the state maps is based on 2000 census statistical data provided by the U.S. Department of Commerce Bureau of the Census. Canadian information is based on the 1996 census provided by Statistics Canada.

The Metro Market statistical data used for MSAs/NECMAs on pages 179 through 199 are based on year 2000 estimates. The data are copyrighted by Claritas, a national demographic company located in San Diego, California, and are reproduced here by permission. For information on statistical data, call Claritas (Toll Free 1-800-866-6520). Direct all other questions to the American Map Corporation at 718-784-0055.

ALABAMA

COUNTIES

(67 Counties)

Name of County	Population	Location on Map
AUTAUGA	43,671	I-6
BALDWIN	140,415	N-3
BARBOUR	29,038	K-9
BIBB	20,826	G-5
BLOUNT	51,024	D-6
BULLOCK	11,714	K-8
BUTLER	21,399	K-6
CALHOUN	112,249	E-8
CHAMBERS	36,583	H-9
CHEROKEE	23,988	D-9
CHILTON	39,593	H-6
CHOCTAW	15,922	J-1
CLARKE	27,867	L-2
CLAY	14,254	F-8
CLEBURNE	14,123	F-9
COFFEE	43,615	M-8
COLBERT	54,984	B-2
CONECUH	14,089	M-5
COOSA	12,202	H-7
COVINGTON	37,631	N-6
CRENSHAW	13,665	L-7
CULLMAN	77,483	D-5
DALE	49,129	M-9
DALLAS	46,365	J-4
DE KALB	64,452	C-8
ELMORE	65,874	I-7
ESCAMBIA	38,440	N-3
ETOWAH	103,459	D-8
FAYETTE	18,495	E-3
FRANKLIN	31,223	C-3
GENEVA	25,764	N-8
GREENE	9,974	H-2
HALE	17,185	H-3
HENRY	16,310	L-10
HOUSTON	88,787	N-10
JACKSON	53,926	A-7
JEFFERSON	662,047	E-5
LAMAR	15,904	E-2
LAUDERDALE	87,966	A-2
LAWRENCE	34,803	C-4
LEE	115,092	I-9
LIMESTONE	65,676	A-5
LOWNDES	13,473	K-6
MACON	24,105	J-8
MADISON	276,700	B-6
MARENGO	22,539	J-2
MARION	31,214	D-2
MARSHALL	82,231	C-7
MOBILE	399,843	O-1
MONROE	24,324	L-4
MONTGOMERY	223,510	K-7
MORGAN	111,064	C-5
PERRY	11,861	I-4
PICKENS	20,949	F-2
PIKE	29,605	K-8
RANDOLPH	22,380	F-9
RUSSELL	49,756	J-10
SAINT CLAIR	64,742	E-7
SHELBY	143,293	G-5
SUMTER	14,798	J-1
TALLADEGA	80,321	F-7
TALLAPOOSA	41,475	H-8
TUSCALOOSA	164,875	F-3
WALKER	70,713	E-4
WASHINGTON	18,097	M-1
WILCOX	13,183	K-3
WINSTON	24,843	D-3
TOTAL	**4,447,100**	

CITIES AND TOWNS

Note: The first name is that of the city or town, second, that of the county in which it is located, then the population and location on the map.

Abbeville, *Henry,* 2,987 ....M-10
Adamsville, *Jefferson,* 4,965 ....F-5
Alabaster, *Shelby,* 22,619 ....G-6
Albertville, *Marshall,* 17,247 ....D-8
Alexander City, *Tallapoosa,* 15,008 ..H-8
• Alexandria, *Calhoun,* 3,692 ....E-8
Aliceville, *Pickens,* 2,567 ....G-2
Andalusia, *Covington,* 8,794 ....N-7
Anniston, *Calhoun,* 24,276 ....F-9
Arab, *Marshall,* 7,174 ....C-7
Ardmore, *Limestone,* 1,034 ....A-6
Argo, *Jefferson,* 1,780 ....E-7
Ashford, *Houston,* 1,853 ....N-11
Ashland, *Clay,* 1,965 ....G-9
Ashville, *Saint Clair,* 2,260 ....E-7
Athens, *Limestone,* 18,967 ....B-5
Atmore, *Escambia,* 7,676 ....N-4
Attalla, *Etowah,* 6,592 ....D-8
Auburn, *Lee,* 42,987 ....I-10
Bay Minette, *Baldwin,* 7,820 ....O-3
Bayou La Batre, *Mobile,* 2,313 ....Q-1
Bear Creek, *Marion,* 1,053 ....C-3
Berry, *Fayette,* 1,238 ....F-3
Bessemer, *Jefferson,* 29,672 ....F-5
Birmingham, *Jefferson,* 242,820 ....F-6
Blountsville, *Blount,* 1,768 ....D-6
• Blue Ridge, *Elmore,* 1,331 ....I-8
Boaz, *Marshall,* 7,411 ....D-8
Brent, *Bibb,* 4,024 ....H-5
Brewton, *Escambia,* 5,498 ....N-5
Bridgeport, *Jackson,* 2,728 ....A-9
Brighton, *Jefferson,* 3,640 ....Q-11
Brookside, *Jefferson,* 1,393 ....O-11
Brookwood, *Tuscaloosa,* 1,483 ....G-4
Brundidge, *Pike,* 2,341 ....L-9
Butler, *Choctaw,* 1,952 ....K-2
• Bynum, *Calhoun,* 1,863 ....F-8
• Cahaba Heights, *Jefferson,* 5,203 ..Q-12
Calera, *Shelby,* 3,158 ....G-6
Camden, *Wilcox,* 2,257 ....K-4
Camp Hill, *Tallapoosa,* 1,273 ....H-9
Carbon Hill, *Walker,* 2,071 ....E-4
Carrollton, *Pickens,* 987 ....G-2
Cedar Bluff, *Cherokee,* 1,467 ....D-9
• Center Point, *Jefferson,* 22,784 ....O-13
Centre, *Cherokee,* 3,216 ....D-9
Centreville, *Bibb,* 2,466 ....H-5
• Chalkville, *Jefferson,* 3,829 ....O-13
Chatom, *Washington,* 1,193 ....M-1
Chelsea, *Shelby,* 2,949 ....G-6
Cherokee, *Colbert,* 1,237 ....B-2
Chickasaw, *Mobile,* 6,364 ....O-2
Childersburg, *Talladega,* 4,927 ....G-7
Citronelle, *Mobile,* 3,659 ....N-2
Clanton, *Chilton,* 7,800 ....H-6
• Clay, *Jefferson,* 4,947 ....E-6
Clayton, *Barbour,* 1,475 ....L-10
Cleveland, *Blount,* 1,241 ....D-6
Clio, *Barbour,* 2,206 ....L-9
Coaling, *Tuscaloosa,* 1,115 ....G-4
Collinsville, *De Kalb,* 1,644 ....D-9
Columbiana, *Shelby,* 3,316 ....G-6
• Concord, *Jefferson,* 1,809 ....Q-10
Coosada, *Elmore,* 1,382 ....I-7
Cordova, *Walker,* 2,423 ....E-5
Cottonwood, *Houston,* 1,170 ....N-10
Cowarts, *Houston,* 1,546 ....N-10
Creola, *Mobile,* 2,002 ....O-2
Crossville, *De Kalb,* 1,431 ....C-8
Cullman, *Cullman,* 13,995 ....D-6
Dadeville, *Tallapoosa,* 3,212 ....H-9
Daleville, *Dale,* 4,653 ....M-9
Daphne, *Baldwin,* 16,581 ....P-2
Dauphin Island, *Mobile,* 1,371 ....Q-2
Decatur, *Morgan,* 53,929 ....B-5
Demopolis, *Marengo,* 7,540 ....I-3
Dora, *Walker,* 2,413 ....E-5
Dothan, *Houston,* 57,737 ....N-10
Double Springs, *Winston,* 1,003 ....D-4
East Brewton, *Escambia,* 2,496 ....N-5
Eclectic, *Elmore,* 1,037 ....I-8
Elba, *Coffee,* 4,185 ....M-8
Enterprise, *Coffee,* 21,178 ....M-9
Eufaula, *Barbour,* 13,908 ....L-11
Eutaw, *Greene,* 1,878 ....H-3
Evergreen, *Conecuh,* 3,630 ....M-5
Fairfield, *Jefferson,* 12,381 ....F-5
Fairhope, *Baldwin,* 12,480 ....P-2
Falkville, *Morgan,* 1,202 ....C-6
Fayette, *Fayette,* 4,922 ....E-3
Flomaton, *Escambia,* 1,588 ....N-4
Florala, *Covington,* 1,964 ....N-7
Florence, *Lauderdale,* 36,264 ....B-3
Foley, *Baldwin,* 7,590 ....Q-3
• Forestdale, *Jefferson,* 10,509 ....F-5
Fort Deposit, *Lowndes,* 1,270 ....K-6
Fort Payne, *De Kalb,* 12,938 ....C-9
Frisco City, *Monroe,* 1,460 ....M-4
Fultondale, *Jefferson,* 6,595 ....P-12
Gadsden, *Etowah,* 38,978 ....D-8
Gardendale, *Jefferson,* 11,626 ....F-6
Geneva, *Geneva,* 4,388 ....N-9
Georgiana, *Butler,* 1,737 ....L-6
Glencoe, *Etowah,* 5,152 ....E-8
Good Hope, *Jefferson,* 1,966 ....D-6
Goodwater, *Coosa,* 1,633 ....H-8
Gordo, *Pickens,* 1,677 ....G-3
• Grand Bay, *Mobile,* 3,918 ....P-1
• Grayson Valley, *Jefferson,* 5,447 ....O-13
Graysville, *Jefferson,* 2,344 ....O-10
Greensboro, *Hale,* 2,731 ....I-3
Greenville, *Butler,* 7,228 ....L-6
Grove Hill, *Clarke,* 1,438 ....L-3
Guin, *Marion,* 2,389 ....E-3
Gulf Shores, *Baldwin,* 5,044 ....Q-3
Guntersville, *Marshall,* 7,395 ....C-7
Hackleburg, *Marion,* 1,527 ....C-3
Haleyville, *Winston,* 4,182 ....D-3
Hamilton, *Marion,* 6,786 ....D-2
Hanceville, *Cullman,* 2,951 ....D-6
Harpersville, *Shelby,* 1,620 ....G-7
Hartford, *Geneva,* 2,369 ....N-9
Hartselle, *Morgan,* 12,019 ....C-5
• Harvest, *Madison,* 3,054 ....B-6
Hayneville, *Lowndes,* 1,177 ....K-6
• Hazel Green, *Madison,* 3,805 ....A-6
Headland, *Henry,* 3,523 ....M-10
Heflin, *Cleburne,* 3,002 ....F-9
Helena, *Shelby,* 10,296 ....G-6
Henagar, *De Kalb,* 2,400 ....B-9
Hokes Bluff, *Etowah,* 4,149 ....D-9
• Holt, *Tuscaloosa,* 4,103 ....G-4
Homewood, *Jefferson,* 25,043 ....Q-12
Hoover, *Jefferson,* 62,742 ....Q-12
Hueytown, *Jefferson,* 15,364 ....F-5
• Huguley, *Chambers,* 2,953 ....H-10
Huntsville, *Madison,* 158,216 ....B-6
Indian Springs Village, *Shelby,* 2,225 ....G-6
Irondale, *Jefferson,* 9,813 ....P-12
Jackson, *Clarke,* 5,419 ....M-3
Jacksonville, *Calhoun,* 8,404 ....E-9
Jasper, *Walker,* 14,052 ....E-4
Jemison, *Chilton,* 2,248 ....H-6
Killen, *Lauderdale,* 1,119 ....A-4
Kimberly, *Jefferson,* 1,801 ....E-6
Kinsey, *Houston,* 1,796 ....M-10
• Ladonia, *Russell,* 3,229 ....I-11
Lafayette, *Chambers,* 3,234 ....H-10
• Lake Purdy, *Shelby,* 5,799 ....Q-713
Lake View, *Tuscaloosa,* 1,357 ....G-5
Lanett, *Chambers,* 7,897 ....H-11
Leeds, *Jefferson,* 10,455 ....F-7
Level Plains, *Dale,* 1,544 ....N-9
Lincoln, *Talladega,* 4,577 ....F-8
Linden, *Marengo,* 2,424 ....J-3
Lineville, *Clay,* 2,401 ....G-9
Lipscomb, *Jefferson,* 2,458 ....Q-11
Livingston, *Sumter,* 3,297 ....I-2
Locust Fork, *Blount,* 1,016 ....E-6
Loxley, *Baldwin,* 1,348 ....P-3
Luverne, *Crenshaw,* 2,635 ....L-7
Madison, *Madison,* 29,329 ....B-6
Malvern, *Geneva,* 1,215 ....N-10
Margaret, *St. Clair,* 1,169 ....E-7
Marion, *Perry,* 3,511 ....I-4
• McDonald Chapel, *Jefferson,* 1,054 P-11
• Meadowbrook, *Shelby,* 4,697 ....F-9
• Meridianville, *Madison,* 4,117 ....B-6
Midfield, *Jefferson,* 5,626 ....F-6
Midland City, *Dale,* 1,703 ....M-10
• Mignon, *Talladega,* 1,348 ....G-7
Millbrook, *Elmore,* 10,386 ....I-7
Millport, *Lamar,* 1,160 ....F-2
• Minor, *Jefferson,* 1,116 ....I-5
Mobile, *Mobile,* 198,915 ....P-2
Monroeville, *Monroe,* 6,862 ....M-4
Montevallo, *Shelby,* 4,825 ....G-6
Montgomery, *Montgomery,* 201,568 ..J-7
Moody, *Saint Clair,* 8,053 ....F-7
• Moores Mill, *Madison,* 5,178 ....B-7
Morris, *Jefferson,* 1,827 ....E-6
Mosses, *Lowndes,* 1,101 ....K-6
Moulton, *Lawrence,* 3,260 ....C-4
Moundville, *Hale,* 1,809 ....H-3
• Mount Olive, *Jefferson,* 3,957 ....O-11
Mountain Brook, *Jefferson,* 20,604 .P-12
• Munford, *Talladega,* 2,446 ....F-8
Muscle Shoals, *Colbert,* 11,924 ....B-3
New Brockton, *Coffee,* 1,250 ....M-8
New Hope, *Madison,* 2,539 ....C-7
• New Market, *Madison,* 1,864 ....A-7
Newton, *Dale,* 1,708 ....M-9
Northport, *Tuscaloosa,* 19,435 ....G-4
Odenville, *Saint Clair,* 1,131 ....F-7
Ohatchee, *Calhoun,* 1,215 ....E-8
Oneonta, *Blount,* 5,576 ....E-7
Opelika, *Lee,* 23,498 ....I-10
Opp, *Covington,* 6,607 ....N-7
Orange Beach, *Baldwin,* 3,784 ....Q-3
Owens Cross Roads, *Madison,* 1,124 ....B-7
Oxford, *Calhoun,* 14,592 ....F-9
Ozark, *Dale,* 15,119 ....M-9
Parrish, *Walker,* 1,268 ....E-4
Pelham, *Shelby,* 14,369 ....G-6
Pell City, *Saint Clair,* 9,565 ....F-7
Phenix City, *Russell,* 28,265 ....I-11
Phil Campbell, *Franklin,* 1,091 ....C-3
Piedmont, *Calhoun,* 5,120 ....E-9
• Pinson, *Jefferson,* 5,033 ....O-12
Pleasant Grove, *Jefferson,* 9,983 ....F-5
• Point Clear, *Baldwin,* 1,876 ....P-2
Prattville, *Autauga,* 24,303 ....J-7
Priceville, *Morgan,* 1,631 ....C-6
Prichard, *Mobile,* 28,633 ....O-2
Ragland, *Saint Clair,* 1,918 ....E-8
Rainbow City, *Etowah,* 8,428 ....E-8
Rainsville, *De Kalb,* 4,499 ....C-9
Red Bay, *Franklin,* 3,374 ....C-2
• Redstone Arsenal, *Madison,* 2,365 ...A-7
Reform, *Pickens,* 1,978 ....F-2
Riverside, *Saint Clair,* 1,564 ....F-8
Roanoke, *Randolph,* 6,563 ....G-10
Robertsdale, *Baldwin,* 3,782 ....P-3
• Rock Creek, *Colbert,* 1,495 ....B-3
Rockford, *Coosa,* 428 ....H-8
Rogersville, *Lauderdale,* 1,199 ....B-4
Russellville, *Franklin,* 8,971 ....C-3
• Saks, *Calhoun,* 10,698 ....E-9
Samson, *Geneva,* 2,071 ....N-8
Saraland, *Mobile,* 12,288 ....O-2
Sardis City, *Etowah,* 1,438 ....D-8
Satsuma, *Mobile,* 5,687 ....O-2
Scottsboro, *Jackson,* 14,762 ....B-8
Selma, *Dallas,* 20,512 ....J-5
• Selmont-West Selmont, *Dallas,* 3,502 ....J-5
Sheffield, *Colbert,* 9,652 ....B-3
Slocomb, *Geneva,* 2,052 ....N-9
• Smiths, *Lee,* 21,756 ....I-11
• Smoke Rise, *Blount,* 1,750 ....E-6
Southside, *Etowah,* 7,036 ....E-8
Spanish Fort, *Baldwin,* 5,423 ....P-3
Springville, *Saint Clair,* 2,521 ....E-7
Steele, *Saint Clair,* 1,093 ....E-8
Stevenson, *Jackson,* 1,770 ....A-9
Sulligent, *Lamar,* 2,151 ....E-2
Sumiton, *Walker,* 2,665 ....E-5
Sylacauga, *Talladega,* 12,616 ....G-7
Sylvan Springs, *Jefferson,* 1,465 ....P-10
Sylvania, *De Kalb,* 1,186 ....C-9
Talladega, *Talladega,* 15,143 ....F-8
Tallassee, *Elmore,* 4,934 ....I-8
Tarrant, *Jefferson,* 7,022 ....F-6
Taylor, *Houston,* 1,898 ....N-10
• Theodore, *Mobile,* 6,811 ....P-2
Thomasville, *Clarke,* 4,649 ....K-3
Thorsby, *Chilton,* 1,820 ....H-6
• Tillmans Corner, *Mobile,* 15,685 ....P-2
Town Creek, *Lawrence,* 1,216 ....B-4
Trinity, *Morgan,* 1,841 ....B-5
Troy, *Pike,* 13,935 ....L-8
Trussville, *Jefferson,* 12,924 ....F-6
Tuscaloosa, *Tuscaloosa,* 77,906 ....G-4
Tuscumbia, *Colbert,* 7,856 ....B-3
Tuskegee, *Macon,* 11,846 ....J-9
• Underwood-Petersville, *Lauderdale,* 3,137 ....B-3
Union Springs, *Bullock,* 3,670 ....K-9
Uniontown, *Perry,* 1,636 ....J-4
Valley, *Chambers,* 9,198 ....H-11
Vernon, *Lamar,* 2,143 ....E-2
Vestavia Hills, *Jefferson,* 24,476 ....F-6
Vincent, *Shelby,* 1,853 ....F-7
Warrior, *Jefferson,* 3,169 ....E-6
Weaver, *Calhoun,* 2,619 ....E-9
Webb, *Houston,* 1,298 ....N-10
Wedowee, *Randolph,* 818 ....G-10
West Blocton, *Bibb,* 1,372 ....G-5
• West End-Cobb Town, *Calhoun,* 3,924 ....F-9
Wetumpka, *Elmore,* 5,726 ....I-8
White Hall, *Lowndes,* 1,014 ....J-6
Wilsonville, *Shelby,* 1,551 ....G-7
Winfield, *Marion,* 4,540 ....E-3
York, *Sumter,* 2,854 ....I-1

Explanation of symbols: • - Census Designated Place (CDP)

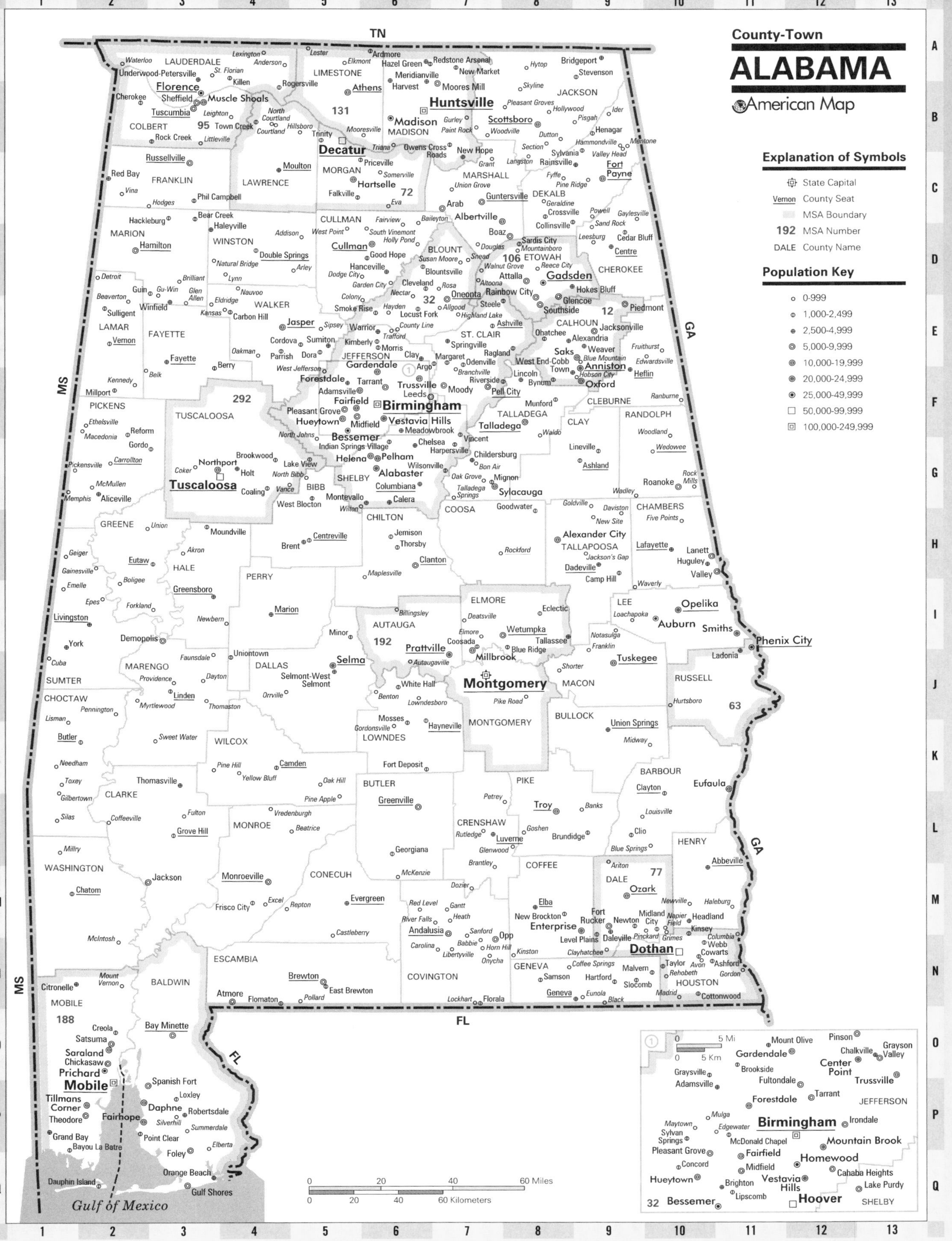

County-Town
ALABAMA
American Map
Explanation of Symbols
State Capital
Vernon County Seat
MSA Boundary
192 MSA Number
DALE County Name
Population Key
0-999
1,000-2,499
2,500-4,999
5,000-9,999
10,000-19,999
20,000-24,999
25,000-49,999
50,000-99,999
100,000-249,999
TN
GA
MS
FL
Gulf of Mexico
LAUDERDALE
LIMESTONE
MADISON
JACKSON
COLBERT
LAWRENCE
MORGAN
MARSHALL
DEKALB
FRANKLIN
MARION
WINSTON
CULLMAN
BLOUNT
ETOWAH
CHEROKEE
LAMAR
FAYETTE
WALKER
JEFFERSON
ST. CLAIR
CALHOUN
CLEBURNE
PICKENS
TUSCALOOSA
TALLADEGA
CLAY
RANDOLPH
SHELBY
BIBB
COOSA
TALLAPOOSA
CHAMBERS
GREENE
HALE
PERRY
CHILTON
ELMORE
LEE
SUMTER
MARENGO
DALLAS
AUTAUGA
MACON
RUSSELL
CHOCTAW
WILCOX
LOWNDES
MONTGOMERY
BULLOCK
CLARKE
BUTLER
PIKE
BARBOUR
MONROE
CRENSHAW
WASHINGTON
CONECUH
COFFEE
DALE
HENRY
ESCAMBIA
COVINGTON
GENEVA
HOUSTON
MOBILE
BALDWIN
131
95
72
106
32
12
292
192
63
77
188
Florence
Huntsville
Decatur
Birmingham
Montgomery
Tuscaloosa
Mobile
Dothan
Gadsden
Anniston
Athens
Scottsboro
Cullman
Jasper
Selma
Opelika
Auburn
Phenix City
Eufaula
Enterprise
Troy
Hoover
0 20 40 60 Miles
0 20 40 60 Kilometers
0 5 Mi
0 5 Km

ALASKA

BOROUGHS AND CENSUS AREAS

(25 Boroughs and Census Areas)

Name of Borough or Census Area	Population	Location on Map
ALEUTIANS EAST Borough	2,464	L-3
ALEUTIANS WEST Borough	9,478	M-1
ANCHORAGE Borough	226,338	H-9
BETHEL Census Area	13,656	H-4
BRISTOL BAY Borough	1,410	J-6
DENALI Borough	1,783	F-9
DILLINGHAM Census Area	4,012	I-6
FAIRBANKS NORTH STAR Borough	77,720	F-10
HAINES Borough	2,117	I-14
JUNEAU Borough	26,751	J-15
KENAI PENINSULA Borough	40,802	I-8
KETCHIKAN GATEWAY Borough	13,828	K-17
KODIAK ISLAND Borough	13,309	K-7
LAKE AND PENINSULA Borough	1,668	K-6
MATANUSKA-SUSITNA Borough	1,668	G-9
NOME Census Area	8,288	D-4
NORTH SLOPE Borough	5,979	B-8
NORTHWEST ARCTIC Borough	6,113	C-6
PRINCE OF WALES-OUTER KETCHIKAN Census Area	6,278	M-16
SITKA Borough	8,588	K-14
SKAGWAY-HOONAH-ANGOON Census Area	4,385	J-13
SOUTHEAST FAIRBANKS Census Area	5,913	F-11
VALDEZ-CORDOVA Census Area	9,952	I-11
WADE HAMPTON Census Area	5,791	G-5
WRANGELL-PETERSBURG Census Area	7,042	K-16
YUKON-KOYUKUK Census Area	8,478	C-8
TOTAL	**626,932**	

CITIES AND TOWNS

Note: The first name is that of the city or town, second, that of the borough or census area in which it is located, then the population and location on the map.

Explanation of symbols: • - Census Designated Place (CDP)

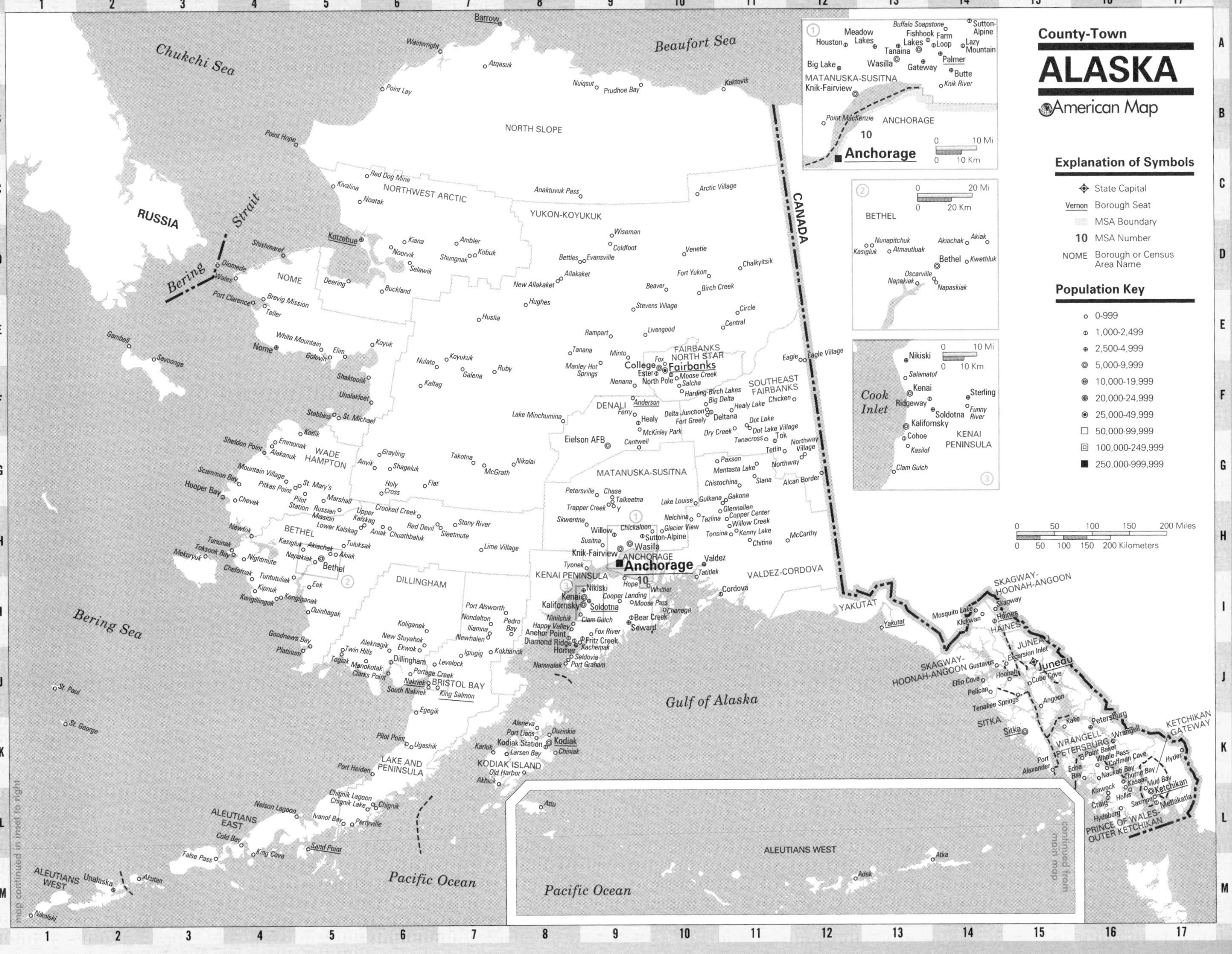
County-Town
ALASKA
American Map
Explanation of Symbols
State Capital
Vernon Borough Seat
MSA Boundary
10 MSA Number
NOME Borough or Census Area Name
Population Key
0-999
1,000-2,499
2,500-4,999
5,000-9,999
10,000-19,999
20,000-24,999
25,000-49,999
50,000-99,999
100,000-249,999
250,000-999,999
0 50 100 150 200 Miles
0 50 100 150 200 Kilometers
Beaufort Sea
Chukchi Sea
Bering Strait
Bering Sea
Gulf of Alaska
Pacific Ocean
CANADA
RUSSIA
NORTH SLOPE
NORTHWEST ARCTIC
YUKON-KOYUKUK
NOME
WADE HAMPTON
BETHEL
DILLINGHAM
BRISTOL BAY
LAKE AND PENINSULA
KODIAK ISLAND
KENAI PENINSULA
ANCHORAGE
MATANUSKA-SUSITNA
DENALI
FAIRBANKS NORTH STAR
SOUTHEAST FAIRBANKS
VALDEZ-CORDOVA
YAKUTAT
SKAGWAY-HOONAH-ANGOON
HAINES
JUNEAU
SITKA
WRANGELL-PETERSBURG
KETCHIKAN GATEWAY
PRINCE OF WALES-OUTER KETCHIKAN
ALEUTIANS EAST
ALEUTIANS WEST
Anchorage
Fairbanks
Juneau
Cook Inlet
continued from main map
map continued in inset to right

COUNTIES

(15 Counties)

Name of County	Population	Location on Map
APACHE	69,423	A-11
COCHISE	117,755	L-10
COCONINO	116,320	A-6
GILA	51,335	G-8
GRAHAM	33,489	I-11
GREENLEE	8,547	I-12
LA PAZ	19,715	H-3
MARICOPA	3,072,149	H-4
MOHAVE	155,032	A-3
NAVAJO	97,470	A-9
PIMA	843,746	L-4
PINAL	179,727	J-7
SANTA CRUZ	38,381	N-9
YAVAPAI	167,517	E-4
YUMA	160,026	I-2
TOTAL	**5,130,632**	

CITIES AND TOWNS

Note: The first name is that of the city or town, second, that of the county in which it is located, then the population and location on the map.

•Ajo, *Pima,* 3,705 .... L-5
•Arizona City, *Pinal,* 4,385 .... K-7
Avondale, *Maricopa,* 35,883 .... P-8
•Avra Valley, *Pima,* 5,038 .... L-8
•Bagdad, *Yavapai,* 1,578 .... G-4
Benson, *Cochise,* 4,711 .... M-10
•Big Park, *Yavapai,* 5,245 .... F-7
Bisbee, *Cochise,* 6,090 .... N-11
•Black Canyon City, *Yavapai,* 2,697 .... H-7
Buckeye, *Maricopa,* 6,537 .... J-6
Bullhead City, *Mohave,* 33,769 .... E-2
Camp Verde, *Yavapai,* 9,451 .... G-7
•Canyon Day, *Gila,* 1,092 .... I-11
Carefree, *Maricopa,* 2,927 .... H-7
Casa Grande, *Pinal,* 25,224 .... K-7
•Casas Adobes, *Pima,* 54,011 .... L-9
•Catalina, *Pima,* 7,025 .... L-9
•Catalina Foothills, *Pima,* 53,794 .... L-9
Cave Creek, *Maricopa,* 3,728 .... H-7
•Central Heights-Midland City, *Gila,* 2,694 .... I-9
Chandler, *Maricopa,* 176,581 .... J-7
•Chinle, *Apache,* 5,366 .... C-12
Chino Valley, *Yavapai,* 7,835 .... F-6
•Cibecue, *Navajo,* 1,331 .... H-10
Clarkdale, *Yavapai,* 3,422 .... F-7
•Claypool, *Gila,* 1,794 .... I-9
Clifton, *Greenlee,* 2,596 .... J-12
Colorado City, *Mohave,* 3,334 .... A-5
•Congress, *Yavapai,* 1,717 .... H-5
Coolidge, *Pinal,* 7,786 .... J-8
•Cordes Lakes, *Yavapai,* 2,058 .... G-7
•Cornville, *Yavapai,* 3,335 .... F-7
•Cottonwood-Verde Village, *Yavapai,* 10,610 .... F-7
•Desert Hills, *Mohave,* 2,183 .... G-2
•Dewey-Humboldt, *Yavapai,* 6,295 .... G-6
•Dilkon, *Navajo,* 1,265 .... E-10
•Dolan Springs, *Mohave,* 1,867 .... D-2
Douglas, *Cochise,* 14,312 .... N-12
•Drexel Heights, *Pima,* 23,849 .... L-9
Drexel-Alvernon, *Pima,* 4,192 .... Q-12
•Dudleyville, *Pinal,* 1,323 .... K-9
Eagar, *Apache,* 4,033 .... H-12
East Sahuarita, *Pima,* 1,419 .... M-9
•Ehrenberg, *La Paz,* 1,357 .... I-2
El Mirage, *Maricopa,* 7,609 .... P-8
Eloy, *Pinal,* 10,375 .... K-8
•First Mesa, *Navajo,* 1,124 .... D-10
Flagstaff, *Coconino,* 52,894 .... E-8
Florence, *Pinal,* 17,054 .... J-8
•Flowing Wells, *Pima,* 15,050 .... P-12
•Fort Defiance, *Apache,* 4,061 .... D-13
•Fortuna Foothills, *Yuma,* 20,478 .... K-2
Fountain Hills, *Maricopa,* 20,235 .... P-10
Fredonia, *Mohave,* 1,036 .... A-6
•Ganado, *Apache,* 1,505 .... D-12
Gila Bend, *Maricopa,* 1,980 .... K-5
Gilbert, *Maricopa,* 109,697 .... J-7
Glendale, *Maricopa,* 218,812 .... I-6
Globe, *Gila,* 7,486 .... I-9
Gold Camp, *Pinal,* 6,029 .... J-8
•Golden Valley, *Mohave,* 4,515 .... E-2
Goodyear, *Maricopa,* 18,911 .... P-8
•Grand Canyon Village, *Coconino,* 1,460 .... C-7
•Green Valley, *Pima,* 17,283 .... M-9
Guadalupe, *Maricopa,* 5,228 .... Q-9
•Heber-Overgaard, *Navajo,* 2,722 .... G-10
Holbrook, *Navajo,* 4,917 .... F-10
•Houck, *Apache,* 1,087 .... E-12
Huachuca City, *Cochise,* 1,751 .... N-10
•Kachina Village, *Coconino,* 2,664 .... F-7
•Kaibito, *Coconino,* 1,607 .... B-9
•Kayenta, *Navajo,* 4,922 .... B-10
Kearny, *Pinal,* 2,249 .... J-9
Kingman, *Mohave,* 20,069 .... E-3
Lake Havasu City, *Mohave,* 41,938 .... G-2
•Lake Montezuma, *Yavapai,* 3,344 .... G-7
•Lechee, *Coconino,* 1,606 .... F-9
Litchfield Park, *Maricopa,* 3,810 .... I-6
Littletown, *Pima,* 1,010 .... Q-12
•Lukachukai, *Apache,* 1,565 .... B-12
Mammoth, *Pinal,* 1,762 .... K-10
•Many Farms, *Apache,* 1,548 .... C-11
Marana, *Pima,* 13,556 .... L-8
•Maricopa, *Pinal,* 1,040 .... J-7
•Mayer, *Yavapai,* 1,408 .... G-6
Mesa, *Maricopa,* 396,375 .... I-7
Miami, *Gila,* 1,936 .... I-9
•Mohave Valley, *Mohave,* 13,694 .... F-2
•Morenci, *Greenlee,* 1,879 .... J-12
•Mountainaire, *Coconino,* 1,014 .... F-7
•Munds Park, *Coconino,* 1,250 .... F-8
•New Kingman-Butler, *Mohave,* 14,810 .... E-3
•New River, *Maricopa,* 10,740 .... H-7
Nogales, *Santa Cruz,* 20,878 .... N-9
•Oracle, *Pinal,* 3,563 .... K-9
Oro Valley, *Pima,* 29,700 .... L-9
Page, *Coconino,* 6,809 .... A-8
Paradise Valley, *Maricopa,* 13,664 .... P-9
Parker, *La Paz,* 3,140 .... H-2
•Parks, *Coconino,* 1,137 .... E-7
•Paulden, *Yavapai,* 3,420 .... F-6
Payson, *Gila,* 13,620 .... H-8
Peoria, *Maricopa,* 108,364 .... I-6
•Peridot, *Gila,* 1,266 .... J-10
Phoenix, *Maricopa,* 1,321,045 .... P-9
•Picture Rocks, *Pima,* 8,139 .... L-8
Pima, *Graham,* 1,989 .... K-11
•Pine, *Gila,* 1,931 .... G-8
Pinetop-Lakeside, *Navajo,* 3,582 .... H-11
•Pinon, *Navajo,* 1,190 .... C-10
•Pirtleville, *Cochise,* 1,550 .... N-12
Prescott, *Yavapai,* 33,938 .... G-6
Prescott Valley, *Yavapai,* 23,535 .... G-6
•Quartzsite, *La Paz,* 3,354 .... I-2
Queen Creek, *Maricopa,* 4,316 .... J-8
•Rio Rico Northeast, *Santa Cruz,* 3,164 .... N-9
•Rio Rico Northwest, *Santa Cruz,* 2,882 .... N-9
•Rio Rico Southeast, *Santa Cruz,* 1,590 .... N-9
•Rio Rico Southwest, *Santa Cruz,* 2,777 .... N-9
•Rio Verde, *Maricopa,* 1,419 .... I-7
•Sacaton, *Pinal,* 1,584 .... J-7
Safford, *Graham,* 9,232 .... K-12
Sahuarita, *Pima,* 3,242 .... M-9
•Saint David, *Cochise,* 1,744 .... M-10
Saint Johns, *Apache,* 3,269 .... G-12
•Saint Michaels, *Apache,* 1,295 .... D-13
•Salome, *La Paz,* 1,690 .... I-4
•San Carlos, *Gila,* 3,716 .... J-10
San Luis, *Yuma,* 15,322 .... L-1
•San Manuel, *Pinal,* 4,375 .... K-10
Scottsdale, *Maricopa,* 202,705 .... I-7
Sedona, *Coconino,* 10,192 .... F-7
•Sells, *Pima,* 2,799 .... M-7
Show Low, *Navajo,* 7,695 .... G-11
Sierra Vista, *Cochise,* 37,775 .... N-10
•Sierra Vista Southeast, *Cochise,* 14,348 .... N-10
Snowflake, *Navajo,* 4,460 .... G-11
Somerton, *Yuma,* 7,266 .... K-1
South Tucson, *Pima,* 5,490 .... P-12
•Spring Valley, *Yavapai,* 1,019 .... G-7
Springerville, *Apache,* 1,972 .... H-12
•Strawberry, *Gila,* 1,028 .... G-8
Summit, *Pima,* 3,702 .... M-9
•Sun City, *Maricopa,* 38,309 .... P-8
•Sun City West, *Maricopa,* 26,344 .... O-8
•Sun Lakes, *Maricopa,* 11,936 .... J-7
•Sun Valley, *Navajo,* 1,536 .... F-11
Superior, *Pinal,* 3,254 .... J-9
Surprise, *Maricopa,* 30,848 .... P-8
•Swift Trail Junction, *Graham,* 2,195 .... K-11
•Tanque Verde, *Pima,* 16,195 .... P-13
Taylor, *Navajo,* 3,176 .... G-11
Tempe, *Maricopa,* 158,625 .... I-7
Thatcher, *Graham,* 4,022 .... K-11
•Three Points, *Pima,* 5,273 .... M-8
Tolleson, *Maricopa,* 4,974 .... P-8
Tombstone, *Cochise,* 1,504 .... M-11
Tortolita, *Pima,* 3,740 .... O-12
•Tsaile, *Apache,* 1,078 .... C-12
•Tuba City, *Coconino,* 8,225 .... C-8
Tucson, *Pima,* 486,699 .... L-9
•Tucson Estates, *Pima,* 9,755 .... L-9
•Vail, *Pima,* 2,484 .... M-9
Wellton, *Yuma,* 1,829 .... K-2
•Whetstone, *Cochise,* 2,354 .... M-10
•Whiteriver, *Navajo,* 5,220 .... H-11
Wickenburg, *Maricopa,* 5,082 .... H-5
Willcox, *Cochise,* 3,733 .... L-11
Williams, *Coconino,* 2,842 .... E-6
•Williamson, *Yavapai,* 3,776 .... F-6
•Window Rock, *Apache,* 3,059 .... D-13
Winslow, *Navajo,* 9,520 .... F-9
Youngtown, *Maricopa,* 3,010 .... I-6
Yuma, *Yuma,* 77,515 .... K-1

Explanation of symbols: • - Census Designated Place (CDP)

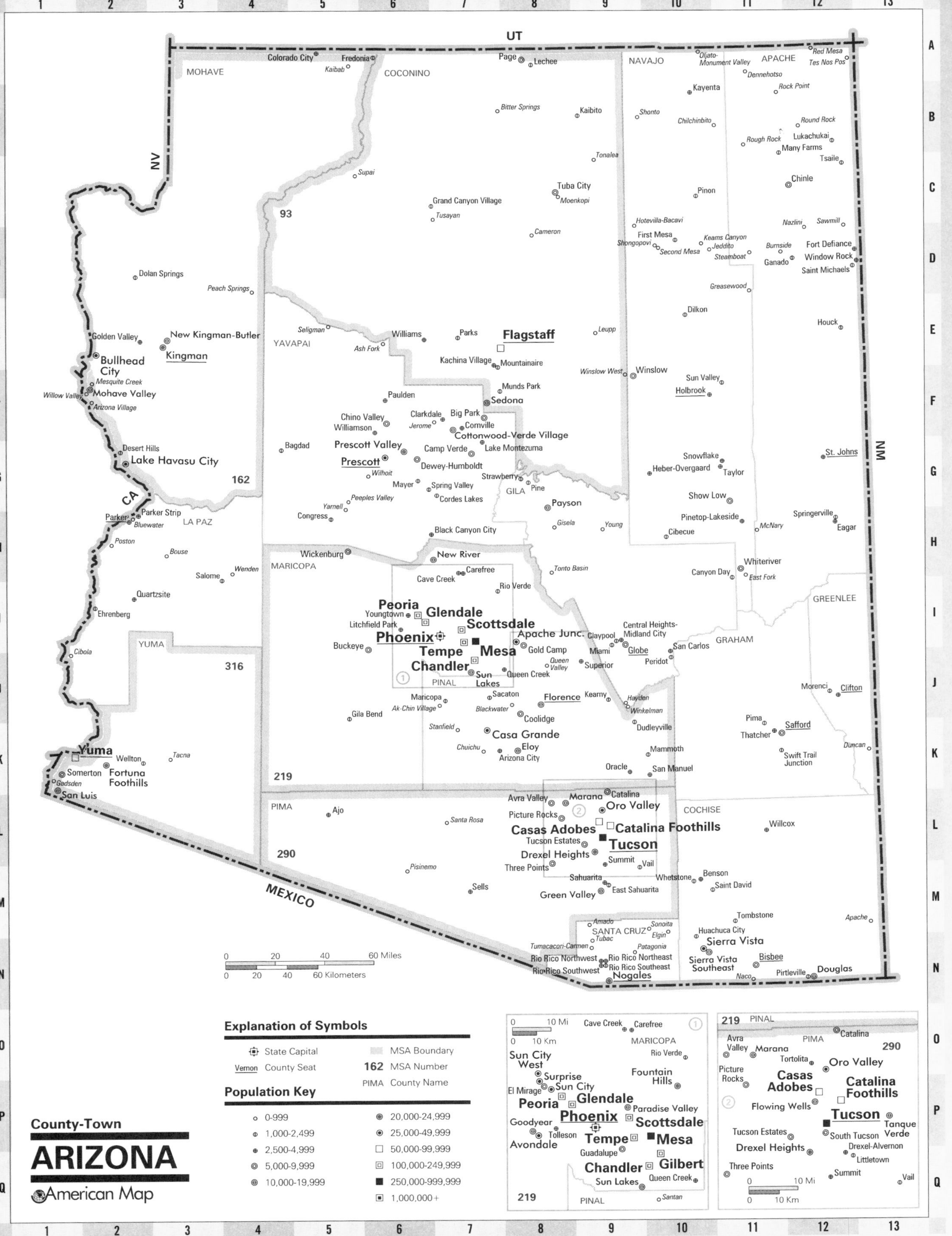

UT
NV
CA
NM
MEXICO
MOHAVE
COCONINO
NAVAJO
APACHE
YAVAPAI
GILA
LA PAZ
MARICOPA
YUMA
PINAL
PIMA
GRAHAM
GREENLEE
COCHISE
SANTA CRUZ
93
162
316
219
290
Colorado City
Fredonia
Kaibab
Page
Lechee
Oljato-Monument Valley
Red Mesa
Tes Nos Pos
Dennehotso
Kayenta
Rock Point
Bitter Springs
Kaibito
Shonto
Chilchinbito
Round Rock
Rough Rock
Lukachukai
Many Farms
Tsaile
Tonalea
Supai
Tuba City
Moenkopi
Pinon
Chinle
Grand Canyon Village
Tusayan
Cameron
Hotevilla-Bacavi
First Mesa
Shongopovi
Second Mesa
Keams Canyon
Jeddito
Steamboat
Nazlini
Sawmill
Burnside
Ganado
Fort Defiance
Window Rock
Saint Michaels
Dolan Springs
Peach Springs
Greasewood
Dilkon
Houck
Golden Valley
New Kingman-Butler
Kingman
Seligman
Ash Fork
Williams
Parks
Flagstaff
Leupp
Bullhead City
Mesquite Creek
Willow Valley
Mohave Valley
Arizona Village
Kachina Village
Mountainaire
Winslow West
Winslow
Sun Valley
Holbrook
Munds Park
Paulden
Sedona
Chino Valley
Williamson
Clarkdale
Jerome
Big Park
Cornville
Cottonwood-Verde Village
Lake Montezuma
Desert Hills
Lake Havasu City
Bagdad
Prescott Valley
Prescott
Camp Verde
Dewey-Humboldt
Wilhoit
Snowflake
Heber-Overgaard
Taylor
St. Johns
Mayer
Spring Valley
Cordes Lakes
Strawberry
Pine
Peeples Valley
Yarnell
Congress
Payson
Show Low
Parker Strip
Parker
Bluewater
Gisela
Young
Pinetop-Lakeside
Springerville
Eagar
McNary
Cibecue
Black Canyon City
Poston
Bouse
Wickenburg
New River
Carefree
Cave Creek
Rio Verde
Tonto Basin
Whiteriver
Canyon Day
East Fork
Salome
Wenden
Quartzsite
Ehrenberg
Peoria
Youngtown
Glendale
Litchfield Park
Scottsdale
Phoenix
Apache Junc.
Claypool
Central Heights-Midland City
Globe
Miami
San Carlos
Peridot
Buckeye
Tempe
Mesa
Gold Camp
Queen Valley
Superior
Cibola
Chandler
Sun Lakes
Queen Creek
Morenci
Clifton
Maricopa
Sacaton
Florence
Kearny
Hayden
Winkelman
Ak-Chin Village
Blackwater
Coolidge
Gila Bend
Dudleyville
Stanfield
Casa Grande
Pima
Safford
Thatcher
Chuichu
Eloy
Arizona City
Mammoth
Duncan
Swift Trail Junction
Yuma
Wellton
Tacna
Somerton
Gadsden
Fortuna Foothills
San Luis
Oracle
San Manuel
Avra Valley
Marana
Catalina
Oro Valley
Ajo
Picture Rocks
Santa Rosa
Casas Adobes
Catalina Foothills
Willcox
Tucson Estates
Tucson
Drexel Heights
Summit
Vail
Three Points
Pisinemo
Sahuarita
Whetstone
Benson
Saint David
Sells
Green Valley
East Sahuarita
Tombstone
Apache
Amado
Sonoita
Tubac
Elgin
Huachuca City
Sierra Vista
Tumacacori-Carmen
Patagonia
Rio Rico Northwest
Rio Rico Northeast
Rio Rico Southeast
Rio Rico Southwest
Sierra Vista Southeast
Bisbee
Nogales
Naco
Pirtleville
Douglas
0 20 40 60 Miles
0 20 40 60 Kilometers
Explanation of Symbols
State Capital
MSA Boundary
Vernon County Seat
162 MSA Number
PIMA County Name
Population Key
0-999
1,000-2,499
2,500-4,999
5,000-9,999
10,000-19,999
20,000-24,999
25,000-49,999
50,000-99,999
100,000-249,999
250,000-999,999
1,000,000+
County-Town
ARIZONA
American Map
0 10 Mi
0 10 Km
Cave Creek
Carefree
MARICOPA
Rio Verde
Sun City West
Surprise
Fountain Hills
El Mirage
Sun City
Peoria
Glendale
Paradise Valley
Goodyear
Phoenix
Scottsdale
Tolleson
Avondale
Tempe
Mesa
Guadalupe
Chandler
Gilbert
Sun Lakes
Queen Creek
219
PINAL
Santan
219 PINAL
Catalina
Avra Valley
Marana
PIMA
290
Tortolita
Oro Valley
Picture Rocks
Casas Adobes
Catalina Foothills
Flowing Wells
Tucson
Tanque Verde
Tucson Estates
South Tucson
Drexel Heights
Drexel-Alvernon
Littletown
Three Points
Summit
Vail
0 10 Mi
0 10 Km

COUNTIES

(75 Counties)

Name of County	Population	Location on Map
ARKANSAS	20,749	H-12
ASHLEY	24,209	L-11
BAXTER	38,386	A-9
BENTON	153,406	A-4
BOONE	33,948	B-7
BRADLEY	12,600	K-10
CALHOUN	5,744	K-9
CARROLL	25,357	A-6
CHICOT	14,117	K-12
CLARK	23,546	I-7
CLAY	17,609	A-14
CLEBURNE	24,046	D-10
CLEVELAND	8,571	J-10
COLUMBIA	25,603	L-7
CONWAY	20,336	E-9
CRAIGHEAD	82,148	C-14
CRAWFORD	53,247	D-4
CRITTENDEN	50,866	E-15
CROSS	19,526	E-13
DALLAS	9,210	I-8
DESHA	15,341	J-12
DREW	18,723	K-11
FAULKNER	86,014	E-9
FRANKLIN	17,771	D-6
FULTON	11,642	A-10
GARLAND	88,068	G-7
GRANT	16,464	H-9
GREENE	37,331	B-14
HEMPSTEAD	23,587	K-6
HOT SPRING	30,353	H-7
HOWARD	14,300	I-5
INDEPENDENCE	34,233	D-11
IZARD	13,249	B-10
JACKSON	18,418	E-12
JEFFERSON	84,278	H-10
JOHNSON	22,781	D-6
LAFAYETTE	8,559	L-6
LAWRENCE	17,774	C-12
LEE	12,580	G-13
LINCOLN	14,492	J-11
LITTLE RIVER	13,628	J-4
LOGAN	22,486	E-6
LONOKE	52,828	G-11
MADISON	14,243	B-6
MARION	16,140	A-9
MILLER	40,443	K-5
MISSISSIPPI	51,979	D-15
MONROE	10,254	H-13
MONTGOMERY	9,245	G-6
NEVADA	9,955	K-7
NEWTON	8,608	C-7
OUACHITA	28,790	K-8
PERRY	10,209	G-8
PHILLIPS	26,445	H-13
PIKE	11,303	I-6
POINSETT	25,614	D-13
POLK	20,229	G-4
POPE	54,469	D-8
PRAIRIE	9,539	G-11
PULASKI	361,474	G-9
RANDOLPH	18,195	A-12
SAINT FRANCIS	29,329	G-14
SALINE	83,529	G-8
SCOTT	10,996	G-4
SEARCY	8,261	C-8
SEBASTIAN	115,071	E-4
SEVIER	15,757	I-4
SHARP	17,119	B-12
STONE	11,499	C-10
UNION	45,629	L-8
VAN BUREN	16,192	D-9
WASHINGTON	157,715	C-4
WHITE	67,165	E-11
WOODRUFF	8,741	F-12
YELL	21,139	F-7
TOTAL	**2,673,400**	

CITIES AND TOWNS

Note: The first name is that of the city or town, second, that of the county in which it is located, then the population and location on the map.

Alma, *Crawford*, 4,160 ... E-5
Altheimer, *Jefferson*, 1,192 ... I-11
Arkadelphia, *Clark*, 10,912 ... I-8
Arkansas City, *Desha*, 589 ... K-13
Ash Flat, *Sharp*, 977 ... B-12
Ashdown, *Little River*, 4,781 ... K-5
Atkins, *Pope*, 2,878 ... F-8
Augusta, *Woodruff*, 2,665 ... E-12
Bald Knob, *White*, 3,210 ... E-12
Barling, *Sebastian*, 4,176 ... E-5
Batesville, *Independence*, 9,445 ... D-12
Bay, *Craighead*, 1,800 ... D-15
Bearden, *Ouachita*, 1,125 ... K-9
Beebe, *White*, 4,930 ... F-11
• Bella Vista, *Benton*, 16,582 ... B-5
Benton, *Saline*, 21,906 ... H-9
Bentonville, *Benton*, 19,730 ... B-5
Berryville, *Carroll*, 4,433 ... B-7
Blytheville, *Mississippi*, 18,272 ... C-16
Booneville, *Logan*, 4,117 ... F-6
Brinkley, *Monroe*, 3,940 ... G-13
Brookland, *Craighead*, 1,332 ... C-14
Bryant, *Saline*, 9,764 ... H-9
Bull Shoals, *Marion*, 2,000 ... B-9
Cabot, *Lonoke*, 15,261 ... K-17
Camden, *Ouachita*, 13,154 ... K-8
Caraway, *Craighead*, 1,349 ... D-15
Carlisle, *Lonoke*, 2,304 ... G-11
Cave City, *Sharp*, 1,946 ... C-12
Cave Springs, *Benton*, 1,103 ... B-5
Cedarville, *Crawford*, 1,133 ... D-4
Centerton, *Benton*, 2,146 ... B-5
Charleston, *Franklin*, 2,965 ... E-5
Cherokee Village-Hidden Valley, *Sharp*, 4,648 ... B-12
Clarendon, *Monroe*, 1,960 ... G-13
Clarksville, *Johnson*, 7,719 ... E-7
Clinton, *Van Buren*, 2,283 ... D-9
Coal Hill, *Johnson*, 1,001 ... E-6
Conway, *Faulkner*, 43,167 ... F-9
Corning, *Clay*, 3,679 ... B-14
Crossett, *Ashley*, 6,097 ... M-11
Danville, *Yell*, 2,392 ... F-7
Dardanelle, *Yell*, 4,228 ... F-8
De Queen, *Sevier*, 5,765 ... J-4
De Valls Bluff, *Prairie*, 783 ... G-12
De Witt, *Arkansas*, 3,552 ... I-12
Decatur, *Benton*, 1,314 ... B-4
Dermott, *Chicot*, 3,292 ... K-12
Des Arc, *Prairie*, 1,933 ... F-12
Diaz, *Jackson*, 1,284 ... D-13
Dierks, *Howard*, 1,230 ... I-5
Dover, *Pope*, 1,329 ... E-8
Dumas, *Desha*, 5,238 ... J-12
Earle, *Crittenden*, 3,036 ... E-15
• East End, *Saline*, 5,623 ... H-10
El Dorado, *Union*, 21,530 ... L-9
Elkins, *Washington*, 1,251 ... C-5
Elm Springs, *Washington*, 1,044 ... B-5
England, *Lonoke*, 2,972 ... M-17
Eudora, *Chicot*, 2,819 ... M-13
Eureka Springs, *Carroll*, 2,278 ... B-6
Fairfield Bay, *Van Buren*, 2,460 ... D-10
Farmington, *Washington*, 3,605 ... C-5
Fayetteville, *Washington*, 58,047 ... C-5
Flippin, *Marion*, 1,357 ... B-9
Fordyce, *Dallas*, 4,799 ... J-10
Foreman (New Rocky Comfort), *Little River*, 1,267 ... K-4
Forrest City, *Saint Francis*, 14,774 ... F-14
Fort Smith, *Sebastian*, 80,268 ... E-4
Gassville, *Baxter*, 1,706 ... B-9
Gentry, *Benton*, 2,165 ... B-4
• Gibson, *Pulaski*, 4,678 ... G-10
Glenwood, *Pike*, 1,751 ... I-7
Gosnell, *Mississippi*, 3,968 ... C-16
Gould, *Lincoln*, 1,305 ... J-12
• Gravel Ridge, *Pulaski*, 3,232 ... K-16
Gravette, *Benton*, 1,810 ... A-4
Green Forest, *Carroll*, 2,717 ... B-7
Greenbrier, *Faulkner*, 3,042 ... F-10
Greenwood, *Sebastian*, 7,112 ... F-5
Gurdon, *Clark*, 2,276 ... J-8
Hamburg, *Ashley*, 3,039 ... L-11
Hampton, *Calhoun*, 1,579 ... K-9
Harrisburg, *Poinsett*, 2,192 ... D-14
Harrison, *Boone*, 12,152 ... B-8
Haskell, *Saline*, 2,645 ... H-9
Hazen, *Prairie*, 1,637 ... G-12
Heber Springs, *Cleburne*, 6,432 ... E-11
Helena, *Phillips*, 6,323 ... H-14
Hope, *Hempstead*, 10,616 ... K-6
Horseshoe Bend, *Izard*, 2,278 ... B-11
Hot Springs, *Garland*, 35,750 ... H-8
• Hot Springs Village, *Garland*, 8,397 ... G-8
Hoxie, *Lawrence*, 2,817 ... C-13
Hughes, *Saint Francis*, 1,867 ... F-15
Huntsville, *Madison*, 1,931 ... C-6
Jacksonville, *Pulaski*, 29,916 ... G-10
Jasper, *Newton*, 498 ... C-8
Johnson, *Washington*, 2,319 ... B-5
Jonesboro, *Craighead*, 55,515 ... D-14
Judsonia, *White*, 1,982 ... E-12
Kensett, *White*, 1,791 ... F-12
Lake City, *Craighead*, 1,956 ... D-15
• Lake Hamilton, *Garland*, 1,609 ... H-8
Lake Village, *Chicot*, 2,823 ... L-13
Lamar, *Johnson*, 1,415 ... E-7
Lavaca, *Sebastian*, 1,825 ... E-5
Leachville, *Mississippi*, 1,981 ... C-15
Lepanto, *Poinsett*, 2,133 ... D-15
Lewisville, *Lafayette*, 1,285 ... L-6
Lincoln, *Washington*, 1,752 ... C-4
Little Flock, *Benton*, 2,585 ... B-5
Little Rock, *Pulaski*, 183,133 ... G-10
Lonoke, *Lonoke*, 4,287 ... G-11
Lowell, *Benton*, 5,013 ... B-5
Luxora, *Mississippi*, 1,317 ... D-16
Magnolia, *Columbia*, 10,858 ... L-7
Malvern, *Hot Spring*, 9,021 ... H-8
Mammoth Spring, *Fulton*, 1,147 ... A-12
Manila, *Mississippi*, 3,055 ... C-16
Mansfield, *Sebastian*, 1097 ... F-5
Marianna, *Lee*, 5,181 ... G-14
Marion, *Crittenden*, 8,901 ... F-15
Marked Tree, *Poinsett*, 2,800 ... E-15
Marmaduke, *Greene*, 1,158 ... B-15
Marshall, *Searcy*, 1,313 ... C-9
Marvell, *Phillips*, 1,395 ... H-14
Maumelle, *Pulaski*, 10,557 ... G-10
Mayflower, *Faulkner*, 1,631 ... K-15
• McAlmont, *Pulaski*, 1,922 ... G-10
McCrory, *Woodruff*, 1,850 ... E-13
McGehee, *Desha*, 4,570 ... K-12
Melbourne, *Izard*, 1,673 ... C-11
Mena, *Polk*, 5,637 ... H-5
Mineral Springs, *Howard*, 1,264 ... J-5
Monette, *Craighead*, 1,179 ... C-15
Monticello, *Drew*, 9,146 ... K-11
Morrilton, *Conway*, 6,550 ... F-9
Mount Ida, *Montgomery*, 981 ... H-6
Mountain Home, *Baxter*, 11,012 ... B-10
Mountain View, *Stone*, 2,876 ... C-10
Mulberry, *Crawford*, 1,627 ... E-5
Murfreesboro, *Pike*, 1,764 ... I-6
Nashville, *Howard*, 4,878 ... J-6
Newark, *Independence*, 1,219 ... D-12
Newport, *Jackson*, 7,811 ... D-13
• North Crossett, *Ashley*, 3,581 ... M-11
North Little Rock, *Pulaski*, 60,433 ... G-10
Ola, *Yell*, 1,204 ... F-7
Osceola, *Mississippi*, 8,875 ... D-16
Ozark, *Franklin*, 3,525 ... E-6
Paragould, *Greene*, 22,017 ... C-15
Paris, *Logan*, 3,707 ... E-6
• Parkers-Iron Springs, *Pulaski*, 3,499 ... H-10
Parkin, *Cross*, 1,602 ... E-15
Pea Ridge, *Benton*, 2,346 ... A-5
Perryville, *Perry*, 1,458 ... F-9
Piggott, *Clay*, 3,894 ... B-15
Pine Bluff, *Jefferson*, 55,085 ... I-11
• Piney, *Johnson*, 3,988 ... E-7
Pocahontas, *Randolph*, 6,518 ... B-13
Pottsville, *Pope*, 1,271 ... F-8
• Prairie Creek, *Benton*, 1,849 ... B-5
Prairie Grove, *Washington*, 2,540 ... C-5
Prescott, *Nevada*, 3,686 ... J-7
Rector, *Clay*, 2,017 ... B-15
Redfield, *Jefferson*, 1,157 ... H-10
Rison, *Cleveland*, 1,271 ... J-10
• Rockwell, *Garland*, 3,024 ... H-8
Rogers, *Benton*, 38,829 ... B-5
Russellville, *Pope*, 23,682 ... E-8
Salem, *Fulton*, 1,591 ... B-11
• Salem, *Saline*, 2,789 ... H-9
Searcy, *White*, 18,928 ... F-11
Shannon Hills, *Saline*, 2,005 ... H-10
Sheridan, *Grant*, 3,872 ... I-10
Sherwood, *Pulaski*, 21,511 ... G-10
Siloam Springs, *Benton*, 10,843 ... B-4
Smackover, *Union*, 2,005 ... L-9
Springdale, *Washington*, 45,798 ... B-5
Stamps, *Lafayette*, 2,131 ... L-7
Star City, *Lincoln*, 2,471 ... J-11
Stephens, *Ouachita*, 1,152 ... L-8
Stuttgart, *Arkansas*, 9,745 ... H-12
• Sweet Home, *Pulaski*, 1,070 ... G-10
Texarkana, *Miller*, 26,448 ... L-5
Trumann, *Poinsett*, 6,889 ... D-15
Tuckerman, *Jackson*, 1,757 ... D-13
Van Buren, *Crawford*, 18,986 ... E-4
Vilonia, *Faulkner*, 2,106 ... F-10
Waldo, *Columbia*, 1,594 ... L-7
Waldron, *Scott*, 3,508 ... G-5
Walnut Ridge, *Lawrence*, 4,925 ... C-13
Ward, *Lonoke*, 2,580 ... F-11
Warren, *Bradley*, 6,442 ... K-11
• West Crossett, *Ashley*, 1,664 ... M-11
West Fork, *Washington*, 2,042 ... C-5
West Helena, *Phillips*, 8,689 ... H-14
West Memphis, *Crittenden*, 27,666 ... F-16
White Hall, *Jefferson*, 4,732 ... I-10
Wrightsville, *Pulaski*, 1,368 ... H-10
Wynne, *Cross*, 8,615 ... F-14
Yellville, *Marion*, 1,312 ... B-9

Explanation of symbols: • - Census Designated Place (CDP)

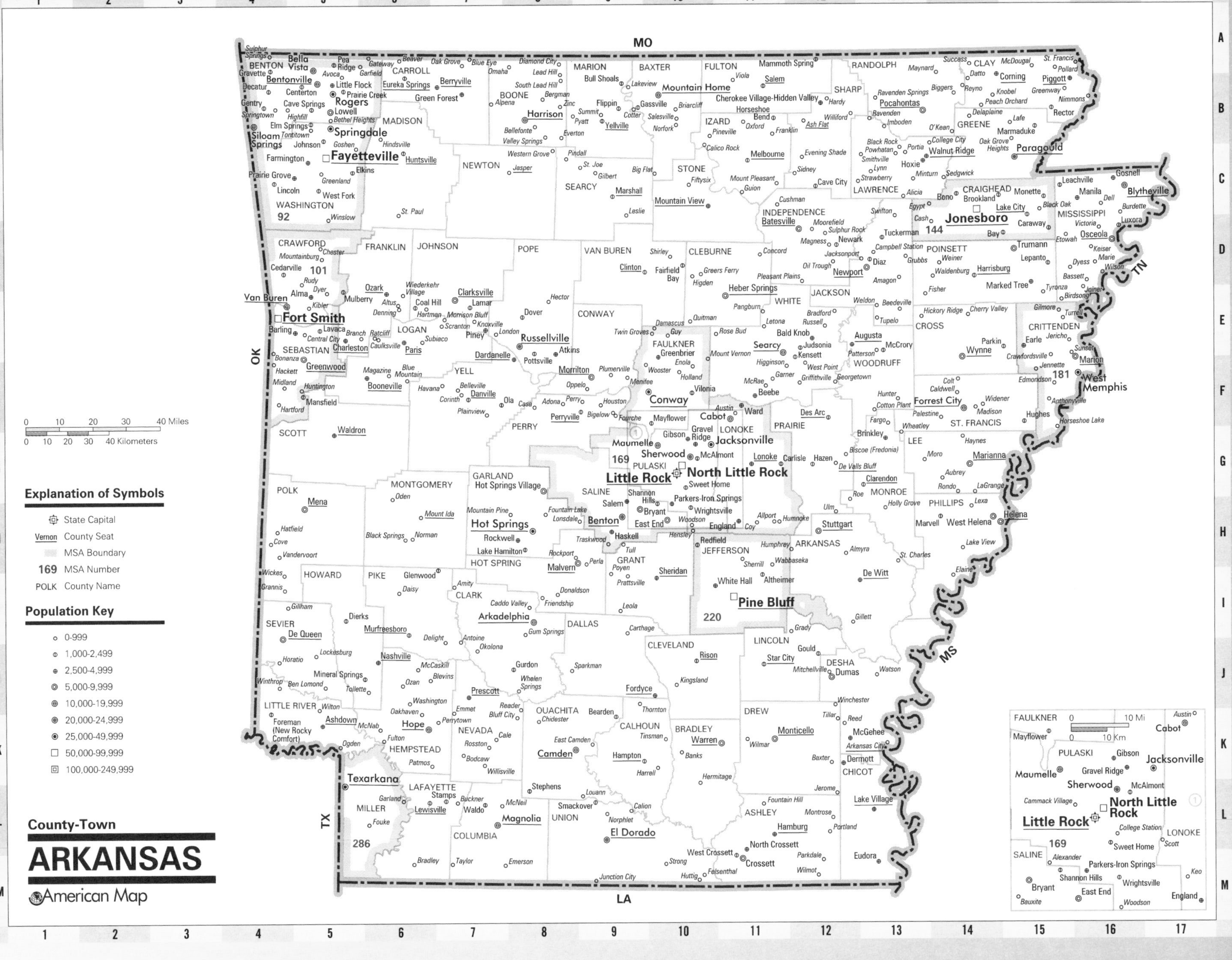
County-Town
ARKANSAS
American Map
Explanation of Symbols
State Capital
Vernon County Seat
MSA Boundary
169 MSA Number
POLK County Name
Population Key
0-999
1,000-2,499
2,500-4,999
5,000-9,999
10,000-19,999
20,000-24,999
25,000-49,999
50,000-99,999
100,000-249,999
0 10 20 30 40 Miles
0 10 20 30 40 Kilometers
MO
OK
TX
LA
MS
TN
BENTON
CARROLL
BOONE
MARION
BAXTER
FULTON
SHARP
RANDOLPH
CLAY
GREENE
LAWRENCE
CRAIGHEAD
MISSISSIPPI
POINSETT
CRITTENDEN
CROSS
ST. FRANCIS
LEE
PHILLIPS
MONROE
WOODRUFF
JACKSON
INDEPENDENCE
IZARD
STONE
SEARCY
NEWTON
MADISON
WASHINGTON
CRAWFORD
FRANKLIN
JOHNSON
POPE
VAN BUREN
CLEBURNE
WHITE
PRAIRIE
LONOKE
FAULKNER
CONWAY
LOGAN
SEBASTIAN
SCOTT
YELL
PERRY
PULASKI
SALINE
GARLAND
MONTGOMERY
POLK
HOWARD
SEVIER
LITTLE RIVER
PIKE
HOT SPRING
CLARK
GRANT
JEFFERSON
ARKANSAS
DESHA
LINCOLN
CLEVELAND
DALLAS
OUACHITA
CALHOUN
BRADLEY
DREW
CHICOT
ASHLEY
UNION
COLUMBIA
NEVADA
HEMPSTEAD
LAFAYETTE
MILLER
Little Rock
North Little Rock
Fort Smith
Fayetteville
Springdale
Rogers
Bentonville
Jonesboro
Pine Bluff
Hot Springs
Conway
Jacksonville
Texarkana
El Dorado
Blytheville
West Memphis
Russellville
Searcy
Paragould
Camden
Magnolia
Arkadelphia
Malvern
Benton
Batesville
Harrison
Mountain Home
Helena
Forrest City
Stuttgart
Monticello
Hope
Van Buren
Osceola
Newport
Wynne
Marianna
Mena
De Queen
92
101
144
169
181
220
286
FAULKNER
PULASKI
SALINE
LONOKE
10 Mi
10 Km

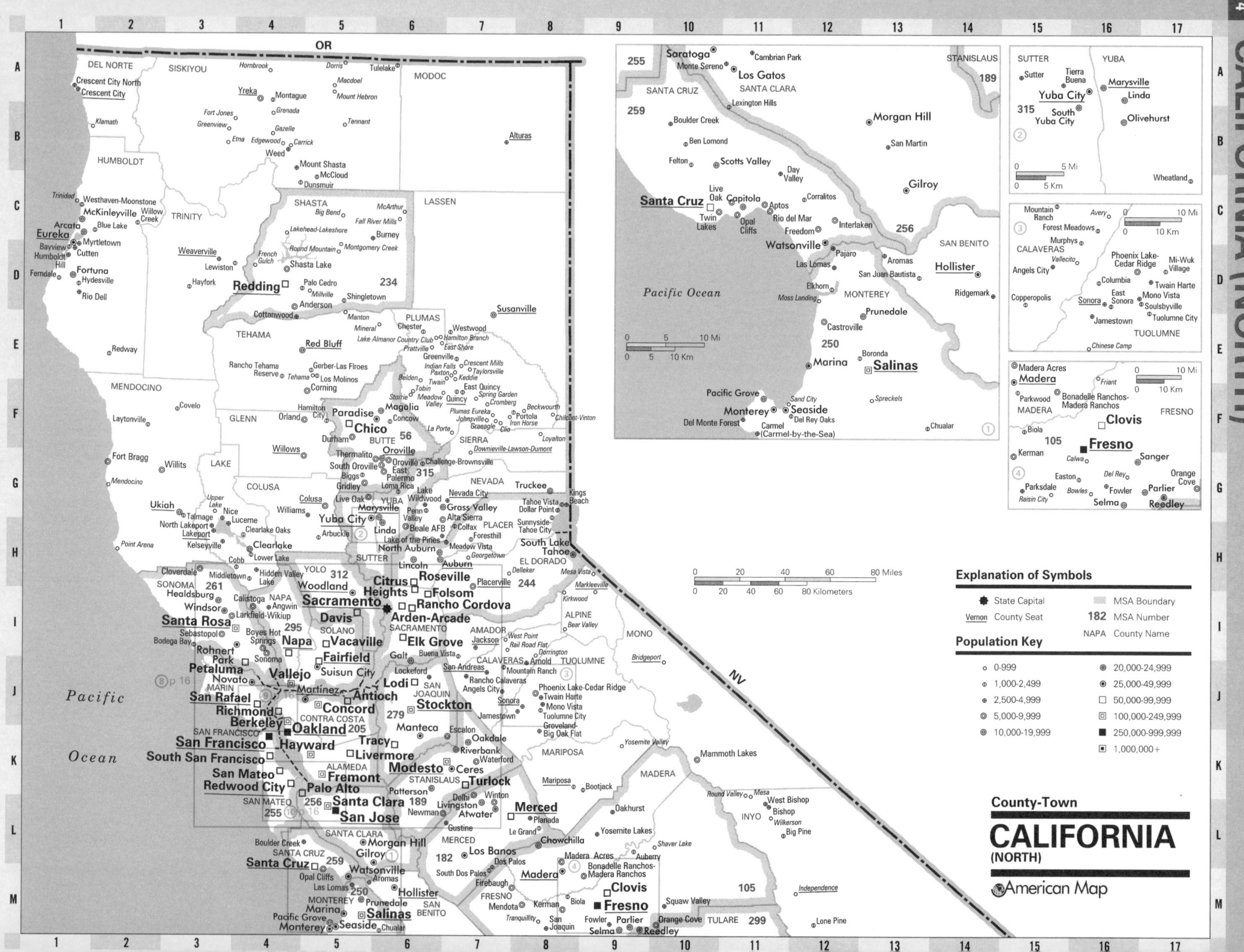

OR
NV
Pacific Ocean
DEL NORTE
SISKIYOU
MODOC
HUMBOLDT
TRINITY
SHASTA
LASSEN
TEHAMA
PLUMAS
MENDOCINO
GLENN
BUTTE
SIERRA
NEVADA
LAKE
COLUSA
YUBA
SUTTER
PLACER
EL DORADO
ALPINE
SONOMA
NAPA
YOLO
SACRAMENTO
AMADOR
CALAVERAS
TUOLUMNE
MONO
MARIN
SOLANO
SAN JOAQUIN
CONTRA COSTA
SAN FRANCISCO
ALAMEDA
STANISLAUS
MARIPOSA
MADERA
SAN MATEO
SANTA CLARA
MERCED
SANTA CRUZ
SAN BENITO
MONTEREY
FRESNO
INYO
TULARE
Crescent City
Yreka
Alturas
Eureka
Weaverville
Redding
Susanville
Red Bluff
Quincy
Willows
Oroville
Chico
Colusa
Yuba City
Marysville
Ukiah
Lakeport
Santa Rosa
Napa
Woodland
Sacramento
Auburn
Placerville
South Lake Tahoe
Fairfield
Vacaville
Martinez
San Rafael
San Francisco
Oakland
Stockton
Jackson
San Andreas
Sonora
Modesto
Merced
Mariposa
Madera
Fresno
San Jose
Hollister
Salinas
Santa Cruz
Monterey
Bridgeport
Markleeville
Independence
Pacific Grove
Watsonville
Gilroy
Morgan Hill
Los Gatos
Saratoga
Capitola
Scotts Valley
Marina
Seaside
Castroville
Prunedale
Clovis
Sanger
Reedley
Selma
Fowler
Kerman
Linda
Olivehurst
Wheatland
0 20 40 60 80 Miles
0 20 40 60 80 Kilometers
Explanation of Symbols
State Capital
Vernon County Seat
MSA Boundary
182 MSA Number
NAPA County Name
Population Key
0-999
1,000-2,499
2,500-4,999
5,000-9,999
10,000-19,999
20,000-24,999
25,000-49,999
50,000-99,999
100,000-249,999
250,000-999,999
1,000,000+
County-Town
CALIFORNIA
(NORTH)
American Map

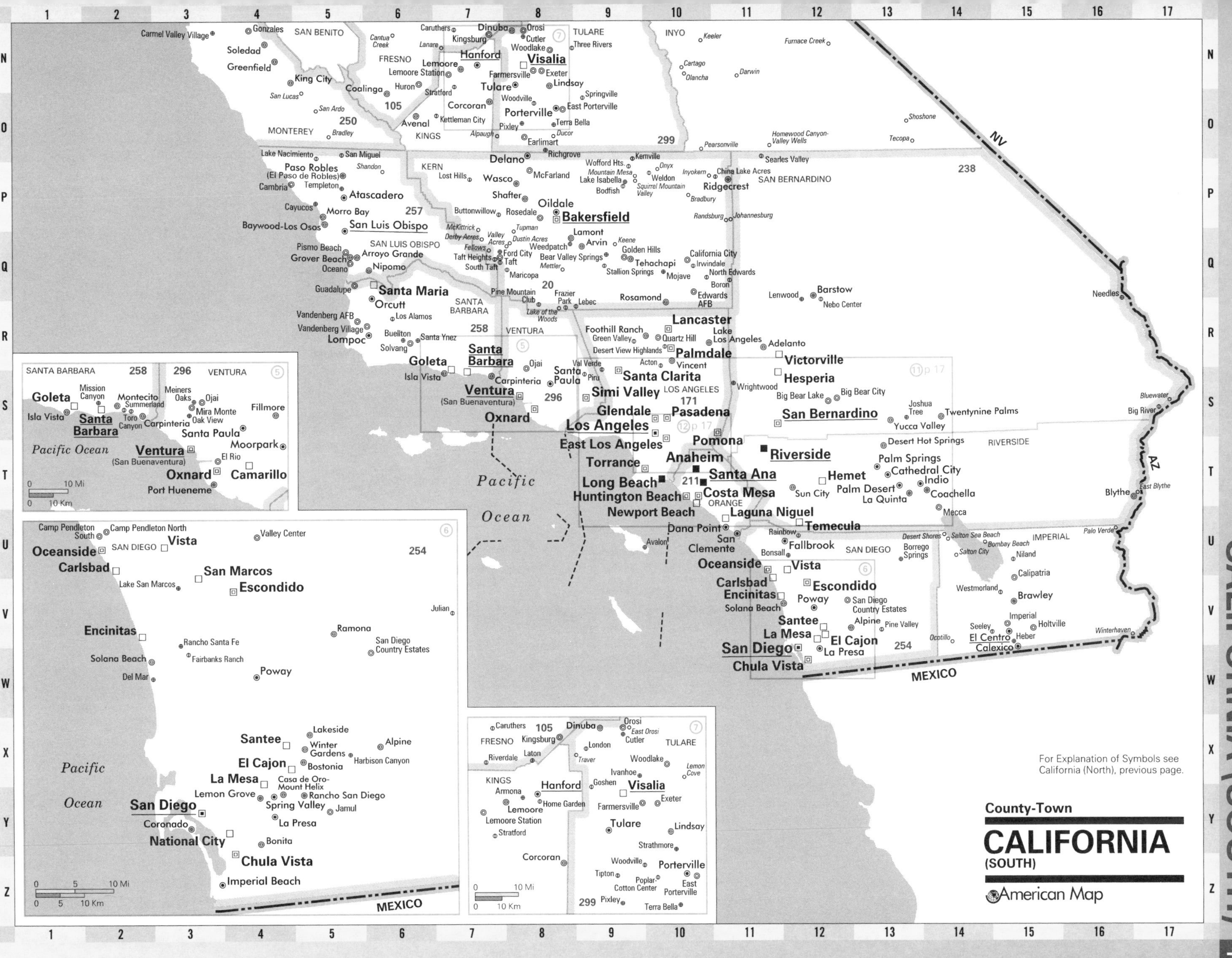
County-Town
CALIFORNIA
(SOUTH)
American Map
For Explanation of Symbols see California (North), previous page.
NV
AZ
MEXICO
Pacific Ocean
INYO
TULARE
KINGS
FRESNO
SAN BENITO
MONTEREY
KERN
SAN LUIS OBISPO
SANTA BARBARA
VENTURA
LOS ANGELES
SAN BERNARDINO
RIVERSIDE
ORANGE
SAN DIEGO
IMPERIAL
Los Angeles
San Diego
Bakersfield
Santa Barbara
San Bernardino
Riverside
Anaheim
Santa Ana
Long Beach
Huntington Beach
Costa Mesa
Newport Beach
Pasadena
Glendale
Torrance
Pomona
Santa Clarita
Simi Valley
Oxnard
Ventura
Lancaster
Palmdale
Victorville
Hesperia
Palm Springs
Escondido
Oceanside
Carlsbad
Encinitas
Chula Vista
El Cajon
La Mesa
Santee
Visalia
Hanford
Tulare
Porterville
Delano
San Luis Obispo
Santa Maria
Lompoc
Goleta
Barstow
Ridgecrest
Needles
Blythe
El Centro
Calexico
Brawley
Temecula
Hemet
Laguna Niguel
Copyright American Map Corporation

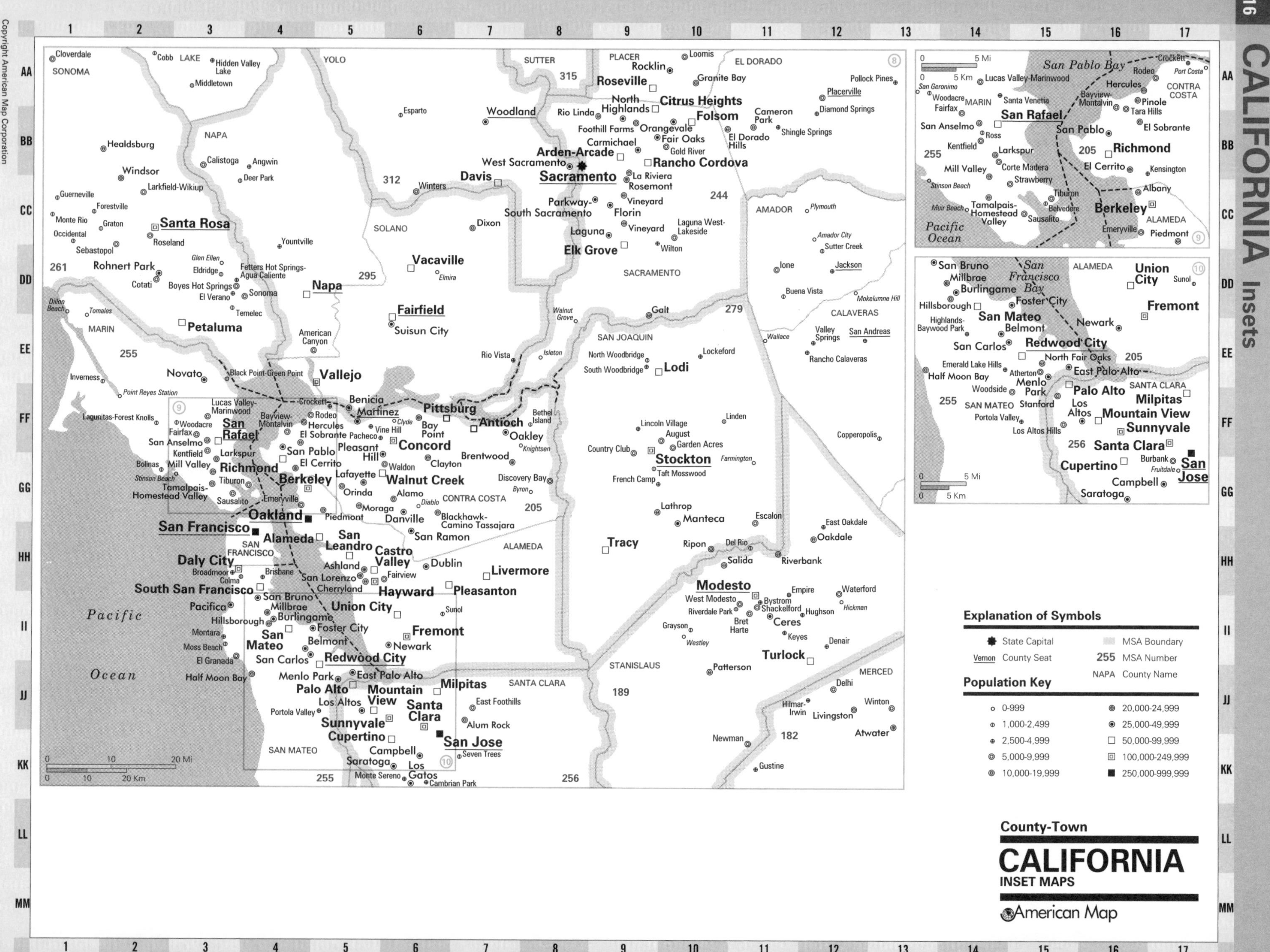
County-Town
CALIFORNIA
INSET MAPS
American Map
Explanation of Symbols
State Capital
Vernon County Seat
MSA Boundary
255 MSA Number
NAPA County Name
Population Key
0-999
1,000-2,499
2,500-4,999
5,000-9,999
10,000-19,999
20,000-24,999
25,000-49,999
50,000-99,999
100,000-249,999
250,000-999,999
Pacific Ocean
Sacramento
San Francisco
Oakland
San Jose
Stockton
Modesto
Santa Rosa
Vallejo
Berkeley
Richmond
Concord
Hayward
Fremont

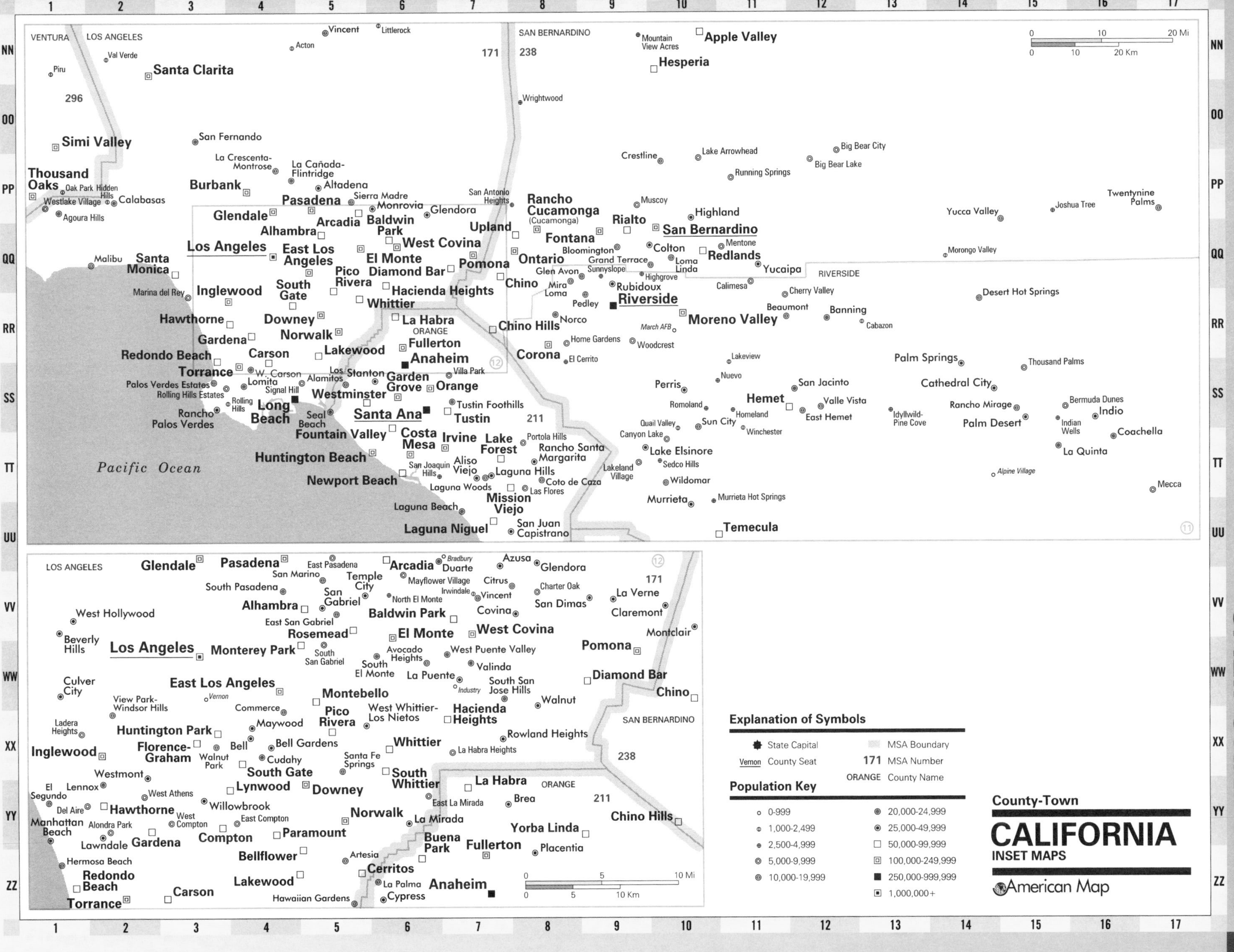
VENTURA
LOS ANGELES
SAN BERNARDINO
RIVERSIDE
ORANGE
Pacific Ocean
Santa Clarita
Simi Valley
Thousand Oaks
Calabasas
Agoura Hills
San Fernando
Burbank
Pasadena
Glendale
Alhambra
Arcadia
Baldwin Park
West Covina
Los Angeles
East Los Angeles
El Monte
Pomona
Upland
Rancho Cucamonga
Fontana
Ontario
Rialto
San Bernardino
Colton
Redlands
Yucaipa
Chino
Riverside
Moreno Valley
Chino Hills
Corona
Norco
Inglewood
Santa Monica
Hawthorne
Downey
Norwalk
Gardena
Carson
Lakewood
Redondo Beach
Torrance
Long Beach
La Habra
Fullerton
Anaheim
Garden Grove
Orange
Westminster
Santa Ana
Tustin
Fountain Valley
Costa Mesa
Irvine
Lake Forest
Huntington Beach
Newport Beach
Laguna Hills
Mission Viejo
Laguna Niguel
San Juan Capistrano
Perris
Hemet
San Jacinto
Lake Elsinore
Murrieta
Temecula
Palm Springs
Cathedral City
Rancho Mirage
Palm Desert
Indio
La Quinta
Coachella
Mecca
Yucca Valley
Twentynine Palms
Apple Valley
Hesperia
Banning
Beaumont
Explanation of Symbols
State Capital
Vernon County Seat
MSA Boundary
171 MSA Number
ORANGE County Name
Population Key
0-999
1,000-2,499
2,500-4,999
5,000-9,999
10,000-19,999
20,000-24,999
25,000-49,999
50,000-99,999
100,000-249,999
250,000-999,999
1,000,000+
County-Town
CALIFORNIA
INSET MAPS
American Map

CALIFORNIA

COUNTIES

(58 Counties)

Name of County	Population	Location on Map
ALAMEDA	1,443,741	K-5
ALPINE	1,208	I-8
AMADOR	35,100	I-7
BUTTE	203,171	F-5
CALAVERAS	40,554	J-7
COLUSA	18,804	G-4
CONTRA COSTA	948,816	J-4
DEL NORTE	27,507	A-1
EL DORADO	156,299	H-8
FRESNO	799,407	M-7
GLENN	26,453	F-3
HUMBOLDT	126,518	B-2
IMPERIAL	142,361	U-15
INYO	17,945	L-11
KERN	661,645	P-6
KINGS	129,461	O-6
LAKE	58,309	G-3
LASSEN	33,828	C-6
LOS ANGELES	9,519,338	R-9
MADERA	123,109	K-9
MARIN	247,289	J-3
MARIPOSA	17,130	K-8
MENDOCINO	86,265	F-2
MERCED	210,554	L-6
MODOC	9,449	A-6
MONO	12,853	I-9
MONTEREY	401,762	M-5
NAPA	124,279	I-4
NEVADA	92,033	G-7
ORANGE	2,846,289	U-10
PLACER	248,399	H-7
PLUMAS	20,824	E-6
RIVERSIDE	1,545,387	T-14
SACRAMENTO	1,223,499	I-6
SAN BENITO	53,234	M-6
SAN BERNARDINO	1,709,434	P-11
SAN DIEGO	2,813,833	U-12
SAN FRANCISCO (CITY COUNTY)	776,733	K-3
SAN JOAQUIN	563,598	J-6
SAN LUIS OBISPO	246,681	Q-6
SAN MATEO	707,161	L-4
SANTA BARBARA	399,347	R-7
SANTA CLARA	1,682,585	L-5
SANTA CRUZ	255,602	L-4
SHASTA	163,256	C-4
SIERRA	3,555	F-7
SISKIYOU	44,301	A-3
SOLANO	394,542	I-5
SONOMA	458,614	I-2
STANISLAUS	446,997	K-6
SUTTER	78,930	H-5
TEHAMA	56,039	E-4
TRINITY	13,022	C-3
TULARE	368,021	M-10
TUOLUMNE	54,501	J-8
VENTURA	753,197	R-8
YOLO	168,660	H-4
YUBA	60,219	G-6
TOTAL	**33,871,648**	

CITIES AND TOWNS

Note: The first name is that of the city or town, second, that of the county in which it is located, then the population and location on the map.

• Acton, *Los Angeles,* 2,390 ....R-10
Adelanto, *San Bernardino,* 18,130 ....R-11
Agoura Hills, *Los Angeles,* 20,537 ....PP-1
Alameda, *Alameda,* 72,259 ....HH-5
• Alamo, *Contra Costa,* 15,626 ....GG-6
Albany, *Alameda,* 16,444 ....CC-16
Alhambra, *Los Angeles,* 85,804 ....QQ-5
• Aliso Viejo, *Orange,* 40,166 ....TT-7
• Alondra Park, *Contra Costa,* 8,622 ....YY-2
• Alpine, *San Diego,* 13,143 ....V-12
• Alta Sierra, *Nevada,* 6,522 ....H-7
• Altadena, *Los Angeles,* 42,610 ....PP-5
Alturas, *Modoc,* 2,892 ....B-7
• Alum Rock, *Santa Clara,* 13,479 ....JJ-7
American Canyon, *Napa,* 9,774 ....EE-5
Anaheim, *Orange,* 328,014 ....T-10
Anderson, *Shasta,* 9,022 ....D-4
Angels City, *Calaveras,* 3,004 ....J-7
• Angwin, *Napa,* 3,148 ....I-4
Antioch, *Contra Costa,* 90,532 ....J-5
Apple Valley, *San Bernardino,* 54,239 ...NN-10
• Aptos, *Santa Cruz,* 9,396 ....C-11
• Arbuckle, *Colusa,* 2,332 ....H-5
Arcadia, *Los Angeles,* 53,054 ....PP-5
Arcata, *Humboldt,* 16,651 ....C-1
• Arden-Arcade, *Alameda,* 96,025 ....I-6
• Armona, *Kings,* 3,239 ....Y-8
• Arnold, *Calaveras,* 4,218 ....J-8
• Aromas, *San Benito,* 2,797 ....M-5
Arroyo Grande, *San Luis Obispo,* 15,851 ..Q-5
Artesia, *Los Angeles,* 16,380 ....ZZ-5
Arvin, *Kern,* 12,956 ....Q-9
• Ashland, *Sacramento,* 20,793 ....HH-5
Atascadero, *San Luis Obispo,* 26,411 ....P-5
Atherton, *Sacramento,* 7,194 ....EE-15
Atwater, *Merced,* 23,113 ....L-7
• Auberry, *Fresno,* 2,053 ....L-9
Auburn, *Placer,* 12,462 ....H-6
• August, *San Joaquin,* 7,808 ....FF-10
Avalon, *Los Angeles,* 3,127 ....U-10
Avenal, *Kings,* 14,674 ....O-6
• Avocado Heights, *Riverside,* 15,148 ....WW-6
Azusa, *Los Angeles,* 44,712 ....UU-7
Bakersfield, *Kern,* 247,057 ....P-8
Baldwin Park, *Los Angeles,* 75,837 ....QQ-6
Banning, *Riverside,* 23,562 ....RR-12
Barstow, *San Bernardino,* 21,119 ....Q-12
• Bay Point, *Contra Costa,* 21,534 ....FF-6
• Bayview, *Humboldt,* 2,359 ....D-1
• Bayview-Montalvin, *Contra Costa,* 5,004 .FF-4
• Baywood-Los Osos,
San Luis Obispo, 14,351 ....P-5
• Beale AFB, *Yuba,* 5,115 ....H-6
• Bear Valley Springs, *Kern,* 4,232 ....Q-9
Beaumont, *Riverside,* 11,384 ....RR-12
Bell, *Los Angeles,* 36,664 ....XX-4
Bell Gardens, *Los Angeles,* 44,054 ....XX-4
Bellflower, *Los Angeles,* 72,878 ....ZZ-5
Belmont, *San Mateo,* 25,123 ....II-4
Belvedere, *Marin,* 2,125 ....CC-15
• Ben Lomond, *Santa Cruz,* 2,364 ....B-10
Benicia, *Solano,* 26,865 ....FF-5
Berkeley, *Alameda,* 102,743 ....J-4
• Bermuda Dunes, *Riverside,* 6,229 ....SS-16
• Bethel Island, *Contra Costa,* 2,312 ....FF-8
Beverly Hills, *Los Angeles,* 33,784 ....VV-1
• Big Bear City, *San Bernardino,* 5,779 ....S-12
Big Bear Lake, *San Bernardino,* 5,438 ....S-12
• Big Pine, *Inyo,* 1,350 ....L-11
Biggs, *Butte,* 1,793 ....G-5
• Biola, *Fresno,* 1,037 ....M-8
Bishop, *Inyo,* 3,575 ....L-11
• Blackhawk-Camino Tassajara,
Contra Costa, 10,048 ....GG-6
• Bloomington, *San Bernardino,* 19,318 ....QQ-9
Blue Lake, *Humboldt,* 1,135 ....C-2
Blythe, *Riverside,* 12,155 ....T-17
• Bodega Bay, *Sonoma,* 1,423 ....I-3
• Bodfish, *Kern,* 1,823 ....P-9
• Bolinas, *Marin,* 1,246 ....GG-2
• Bonadelle Ranchos-Madera Ranchos,
Madera, 7,300 ....M-9
• Bonita, *San Diego,* 12,401 ....Y-4
• Bonsall, *San Diego,* 3,401 ....U-12
• Bootjack, *Mariposa,* 1,588 ....K-9
• Boron, *Kern,* 2,025 ....Q-11
• Borrego Springs, *San Diego,* 2,535 ....U-13
• Bostonia, *San Diego,* 15,169 ....X-5
• Boulder Creek, *Santa Cruz,* 4,081 ....L-5
• Boyes Hot Springs, *Sonoma,* 6,665 ....I-4
Brawley, *Imperial,* 22,052 ....V-15
Brea, *Orange,* 35,410 ....YY-8
Brentwood, *Contra Costa,* 23,302 ....GG-7
Bridgeport, *Mono,* 525 ....J-10
Brisbane, *San Bernardino,* 3,597 ....HH-4
• Broadmoor, *San Mateo,* 4,026 ....HH-3
Buellton, *Santa Barbara,* 3,828 ....R-6
Buena Park, *Orange,* 78,282 ....ZZ-6
• Buena Vista, *Amador,* 1,704 ....I-7
Burbank, *Los Angeles,* 100,316 ....PP-4
• Burbank, *Santa Clara,* 5,239 ....GG-17
Burlingame, *San Mateo,* 28,158 ....II-4
• Burney, *Shasta,* 3,217 ....C-5
• Buttonwillow, *Kern,* 1,266 ....P-7
Bystrom, *Stanislaus,* 4,518 ....II-11
• Cabazon, *Riverside,* 2,229 ....RR-13
Calabasas, *Los Angeles,* 20,033 ....PP-2
Calexico, *Imperial,* 27,109 ....W-15
California City, *Kern,* 8,385 ....Q-10
Calimesa, *Riverside,* 7,139 ....QQ-11
Calipatria, *Imperial,* 7,289 ....V-15
Calistoga, *Napa,* 5,190 ....I-4
Camarillo, *Ventura,* 57,077 ....T-4
• Cambria, *San Luis Obispo,* 6,232 ....P-5
• Cambrian Park, *Santa Clara,* 3,258 ....A-11
Campbell, *Santa Clara,* 38,138 ....KK-6
Canyon Lake, *Riverside,* 9,952 ....TT-10
Capitola, *Santa Cruz,* 10,033 ....C-11
Carlsbad, *San Diego,* 78,247 ....V-11
Carmel (Carmel-By-The-Sea),
Monterey, 4,081 ....F-11
• Carmel Valley Village, *Monterey,* 4,700 ....N-3
Carpinteria, *Santa Barbara,* 14,194 ....S-7
Carson, *Los Angeles,* 89,730 ....ZZ-3
• Caruthers, *Fresno,* 2,103 ....N-7
• Casa De Oro-Mount Helix,
San Diego, 18,874 ....Y-4
• Castro Valley, *Alameda,* 57,292 ....HH-5
• Castroville, *Monterey,* 6,724 ....E-12
Cathedral City, *Riverside,* 42,647 ....T-13
• Cayucos, *San Luis Obispo,* 2,943 ....P-5
Ceres, *Stanislaus,* 34,609 ....K-7
Cerritos, *Los Angeles,* 51,488 ....ZZ-5
• Charter Oak, *Orange,* 9,027 ....VV-8
• Cherry Valley, *Riverside,* 5,891 ....RR-12
• Cherryland, *Alameda,* 13,837 ....HH-5
• Chester, *Plumas,* 2,316 ....E-6
Chico, *Butte,* 59,954 ....F-5
Chino, *San Bernardino,* 67,168 ....QQ-7
Chino Hills, *San Bernardino,* 66,787 ....RR-7
Chowchilla, *Madera,* 11,127 ....L-8
• Chualar, *Monterey,* 1,444 ....M-6
Chula Vista, *San Diego,* 173,556 ....W-12
• Citrus, *Orange,* 10,581 ....VV-8
Citrus Heights, *Sacramento,* 85,071 ....I-6
Claremont, *Los Angeles,* 33,998 ....VV-10
Clayton, *Contra Costa,* 10,762 ....GG-6
Clearlake, *Lake,* 13,142 ....H-4
• Clearlake Oaks, *Lake,* 2,402 ....H-4
Cloverdale, *Sonoma,* 6,831 ....H-3
Clovis, *Fresno,* 68,468 ....M-9
Coachella, *Riverside,* 22,724 ....T-14
Coalinga, *Fresno,* 11,668 ....O-6
• Cobb, *Lake,* 1,638 ....AA-2
Colfax, *Placer,* 1,496 ....H-7
Colma, *San Mateo,* 1,191 ....HH-3
Colton, *San Bernardino,* 47,662 ....QQ-10
• Columbia, *Tuolumne,* 2,405 ....D-16
Colusa, *Colusa,* 5,402 ....G-5
Commerce, *Los Angeles,* 12,568 ....XX-4
Compton, *Los Angeles,* 93,493 ....YY-3
Concord, *Contra Costa,* 121,780 ....J-5
• Copperopolis, *Calaveras,* 2,363 ....D-15
Corcoran, *Kings,* 14,458 ....O-7
Corning, *Tehama,* 6,741 ....F-5
Corona, *Riverside,* 124,966 ....RR-8
Coronado, *San Diego,* 24,100 ....Y-3
• Corralitos, *Santa Cruz,* 2,431 ....C-12
Costa Mesa, *Orange,* 108,724 ....T-10
Cotati, *Sonoma,* 6,471 ....DD-2
• Coto De Caza, *Orange,* 13,057 ....TT-8
• Cottonwood, *Shasta,* 2,960 ....E-4
• Country Club, *San Joaquin,* 9,462 ....GG-9
• Covelo, *Mendocino,* 1,175 ....F-3
Covina, *Los Angeles,* 46,837 ....VV-8
Crescent City, *Del Norte,* 4,006 ....A-1
• Crestline, *San Bernardino,* 10,218 ....PP-10
• Crockett, *Contra Costa,* 3,194 ....FF-5
Cudahy, *Inyo,* 24,208 ....XX-4
Culver City, *Los Angeles,* 38,816 ....WW-1
Cupertino, *Santa Clara,* 50,546 ....KK-6
• Cutler, *Tulare,* 4,491 ....N-8
• Cutten, *Humboldt,* 2,933 ....D-1
Cypress, *Orange,* 46,229 ....ZZ-6
Daly City, *San Mateo,* 103,621 ....HH-3
Dana Point, *Orange,* 35,110 ....U-11
Danville, *Contra Costa,* 41,715 ....GG-6
Davis, *Yolo,* 60,308 ....I-5
• Day Valley, *Santa Cruz,* 3,587 ....C-11
• Deer Park, *Napa,* 1,433 ....CC-3
• Del Aire, *Orange,* 9,012 ....YY-2
Del Mar, *San Diego,* 4,389 ....W-3
• Del Monte Forest, *Monterey,* 4,531 ....F-11
Del Rey Oaks, *Monterey,* 1,650 ....F-12
Delano, *Kern,* 38,824 ....O-8
• Delhi, *Merced,* 8,022 ....K-7
• Denair, *Stanislaus,* 3,446 ....II-12
Desert Hot Springs, *Riverside,* 16,582 ....T-13
• Desert View Highlands,
Los Angeles, 2,337 ....R-10
Diamond Bar, *Los Angeles,* 56,287 ....RR-7
Dinuba, *Tulare,* 16,844 ....N-8
• Discovery Bay, *Santa Clara,* 8,981 ....GG-8
Dixon, *Solano,* 16,103 ....CC-7
Dos Palos, *Merced,* 4,581 ....M-7
Downey, *Los Angeles,* 107,323 ....RR-5
Downieville-Lawson-Dumont, *Sierra,* 500 .G-7
Duarte, *Los Angeles,* 21,486 ....UU-7
Dublin, *Alameda,* 29,973 ....HH-6
Dunsmuir, *Siskiyou,* 1,923 ....C-4
• Durham, *Butte,* 5,220 ....F-5
• Earlimart, *Tulare,* 6,583 ....O-8
• East Compton, *Orange,* 9,286 ....YY-4
• East Foothills, *Santa Clara,* 8,133 ....JJ-7
• East Hemet, *Riverside,* 14,823 ....SS-12
• East La Mirada, *Los Angeles,* 9,538 ....YY-6
• East Los Angeles, *Los Angeles,* 124,283 .T-10
• East Oakdale, *Stanislaus,* 2,742 ....HH-12
East Palo Alto, *San Mateo,* 29,506 ....JJ-5
• East Pasadena, *Los Angeles,* 6,045 ....UU-5
• East Porterville, *Tulare,* 6,730 ....O-8
• East Quincy, *Plumas,* 2,398 ....F-7
• East San Gabriel, *Los Angeles,* 14,512 ...VV-5
• East Sonora, *Tuolumne,* 2,078 ....D-16
• Easton, *Fresno,* 1,966 ....G-16
• Edwards AFB, *Kern,* 5,909 ....Q-10
El Cajon, *San Diego,* 94,869 ....V-12
El Centro, *Imperial,* 37,835 ....V-15
El Cerrito, *Contra Costa,* 23,171 ....GG-4
• El Cerrito, *Riverside,* 4,590 ....SS-8
• El Granada, *San Mateo,* 5,724 ....II-3
El Monte, *Los Angeles,* 115,965 ....QQ-6
• El Rio, *Ventura,* 6,193 ....T-3
El Segundo, *Los Angeles,* 16,033 ....YY-1
• El Sobrante, *San Mateo,* 12,260 ....FF-4
• El Verano, *Sonoma,* 3,954 ....DD-3
• Eldridge, *Santa Cruz,* 1,534 ....DD-3
• Elk Grove, *Sacramento,* 59,984 ....I-6
• Elkhorn, *Sacramento,* 1,591 ....D-12
• Emerald Lake Hills, *San Mateo,* 3,899 ...EE-14
Emeryville, *Orange,* 6,882 ....GG-4
• Empire, *Stanislaus,* 3,903 ....II-11
Encinitas, *San Diego,* 58,014 ....V-11
Escalon, *San Joaquin,* 5,963 ....K-7
Escondido, *San Diego,* 133,559 ....V-12
Eureka, *Humboldt,* 26,128 ....D-1
Exeter, *Tulare,* 9,168 ....N-8
Fairbanks Ranch, *San Diego,* 2,244 ....W-3
Fairfax, *Marin,* 7,319 ....FF-3
Fairfield, *Solano,* 96,178 ....J-5
• Fairview, *Marin,* 9,470 ....HH-6
• Fallbrook, *San Diego,* 29,100 ....U-12
Farmersville, *Tulare,* 8,737 ....N-8
• Felton, *Santa Cruz,* 1,051 ....B-10
Ferndale, *Humboldt,* 1,382 ....D-1
• Fetters Hot Springs-Agua Caliente,
Sonoma, 2,505 ....DD-3
Fillmore, *Ventura,* 13,643 ....S-4
Firebaugh, *Fresno,* 5,743 ....M-8
• Florence-Graham, *Los Angeles,* 60,197 ..XX-3
• Florin, *Sacramento,* 27,653 ....CC-9
Folsom, *Sacramento,* 51,884 ....I-6
Fontana, *San Bernardino,* 128,929 ....QQ-9
• Foothill Ranch, *Orange,* 10,899 ....R-10
• Ford City, *Kern,* 3,512 ....Q-7
• Foresthill, *Placer,* 1,791 ....H-7
• Forestville, *Sonoma,* 2,370 ....CC-1
Fort Bragg, *Mendocino,* 7,026 ....G-2
Fortuna, *Humboldt,* 10,497 ....D-1
Foster City, *Monterey,* 28,803 ....II-5
Fountain Valley, *Orange,* 54,978 ....TT-6
Fowler, *Fresno,* 3,979 ....M-9
• Frazier Park, *Kern,* 2,348 ....R-8
• Freedom, *Santa Cruz,* 6,000 ....C-12
Fremont, *Alameda,* 203,413 ....K-5
• French Camp, *San Joaquin,* 4,109 ....GG-9
Fresno, *Fresno,* 427,652 ....M-9
Fullerton, *Orange,* 126,003 ....RR-6
Galt, *Sacramento,* 19,472 ....J-6
• Garden Acres, *San Joaquin,* 9,747 ....FF-10
Garden Grove, *Orange,* 165,196 ....SS-6
Gardena, *Los Angeles,* 57,746 ....RR-4
Gilroy, *Santa Clara,* 41,464 ....L-6
• Glen Avon, *Riverside,* 14,853 ....QQ-9
Glendale, *Los Angeles,* 194,973 ....S-10
Glendora, *Los Angeles,* 49,415 ....PP-6
• Golden Hills, *Kern,* 7,434 ....Q-9
• Goleta, *Santa Barbara,* 55,204 ....S-7
Gonzales, *Monterey,* 7,525 ....N-4
• Goshen, *Tulare,* 2,394 ....X-9
Grand Terrace,
San Bernardino, 11,626 ....QQ-10
• Granite Bay, *Placer,* 19,388 ....AA-10
Grass Valley, *Nevada,* 10,922 ....G-6
• Graton, *Sonoma,* 1,815 ....CC-1
• Grayson, *Stanislaus,* 1,077 ....II-10
• Green Valley, *Los Angeles,* 1,859 ....R-9
Greenfield, *Monterey,* 12,583 ....N-4
• Greenville, *Plumas,* 1,160 ....E-7
Gridley, *Butte,* 5,382 ....G-5
• Groveland-Big Oak Flat, *Tuolumne,* 3,388 .K-8
Grover Beach, *San Luis Obispo,* 13,067 ...Q-5
Guadalupe, *Santa Barbara,* 5,659 ....Q-5
• Guerneville, *Sonoma,* 2,441 ....CC-1
Gustine, *Merced,* 4,698 ....L-7
• Hacienda Heights, *Los Angeles,* 53,122 .QQ-6
Half Moon Bay, *San Mateo,* 11,842 ....JJ-4
• Hamilton City, *Glenn,* 1,903 ....F-5
Hanford, *Kings,* 41,686 ....N-7
• Harbison Canyon, *San Diego,* 3,645 ....X-5
Hawaiian Gardens, *Los Angeles,* 14,779 .ZZ-5
Hawthorne, *Los Angeles,* 84,112 ....RR-4
• Hayfork, *Trinity,* 2,315 ....D-3
Hayward, *Alameda,* 140,030 ....K-5
Healdsburg, *Sonoma,* 10,722 ....I-3
• Heber, *Imperial,* 2,988 ....V-15
Hemet, *Riverside,* 58,812 ....T-12
Hercules, *Contra Costa,* 19,488 ....FF-4
Hermosa Beach, *Los Angeles,* 18,566 ....ZZ-1
Hesperia, *San Bernardino,* 62,582 ....S-11
Hidden Hills, *Los Angeles,* 1,875 ....PP-2
• Hidden Valley Lake, *Lake,* 3,777 ....H-4
• Highgrove, *Riverside,* 3,445 ....QQ-10
Highland, *San Bernardino,* 44,605 ....QQ-10
• Highlands-Baywood Park,
San Mateo, 4,210 ....EE-14
Hillsborough, *San Mateo,* 10,825 ....II-4
• Hilmar-Irwin, *Merced,* 4,807 ....JJ-12
Hollister, *San Benito,* 34,413 ....M-6
Holtville, *Imperial,* 5,612 ....V-15
• Home Garden, *Kings,* 1,702 ....Y-8
• Home Gardens, *Riverside,* 9,461 ....RR-8
• Homeland, *Riverside,* 3,710 ....SS-11
Hughson, *Stanislaus,* 3,980 ....II-12
• Humboldt Hill, *Humboldt,* 3,246 ....D-1
Huntington Beach, *Orange,* 189,594 ....T-10
Huntington Park, *Los Angeles,* 61,348 ....XX-3
Huron, *Fresno,* 6,306 ....N-6
• Hydesville, *Humboldt,* 1,209 ....D-1
• Idyllwild-Pine Cove, *Riverside,* 3,504 ....SS-13
Imperial, *Imperial,* 7,560 ....V-15
Imperial Beach, *San Diego,* 26,992 ....Z-4
Independence, *Inyo,* 574 ....M-12
Indian Wells, *Riverside,* 3,816 ....SS-15
Indio, *Riverside,* 49,116 ....T-14
Inglewood, *Los Angeles,* 112,580 ....RR-4
• Interlaken, *Santa Cruz,* 7,328 ....C-12
• Inverness, *Marin,* 1,421 ....EE-2
Ione, *Amador,* 7,129 ....DD-11
Irvine, *Orange,* 143,072 ....TT-7
Irwindale, *Los Angeles,* 1,446 ....Q-10
• Isla Vista, *Santa Barbara,* 18,344 ....S-7
• Ivanhoe, *Tulare,* 4,474 ....X-9
Jackson, *Amador,* 3,989 ....I-7
• Jamestown, *Tuolumne,* 3,017 ....J-8
• Jamul, *San Diego,* 5,920 ....Y-5
• Joshua Tree, *San Bernardino,* 4,207 ....S-13
• Julian, *San Diego,* 1,621 ....V-7
• Kelseyville, *Lake,* 2,928 ....H-3
• Kentfield, *Marin,* 6,351 ....FF-3
Kerman, *Fresno,* 8,551 ....M-8
• Kernville, *Kern,* 1,736 ....O-9
• Kettleman City, *Kings,* 1,499 ....O-7
• Keyes, *Stanislaus,* 4,575 ....II-11
King City, *Monterey,* 11,094 ....N-4
• Kings Beach, *Placer,* 4,037 ....G-8
Kingsburg, *Fresno,* 9,199 ....N-7
La Cañada-Flintridge,
Los Angeles, 20,318 ....PP-5
La Crescenta-Montrose,
Los Angeles, 18,532 ....PP-4
La Habra, *Orange,* 58,974 ....RR-6
La Habra Heights, *Los Angeles,* 5,712 ....XX-7
La Mesa, *San Diego,* 54,749 ....V-12
La Mirada, *Los Angeles,* 46,783 ....YY-6
La Palma, *Los Angeles,* 15,408 ....YY-6
• La Presa, *San Diego,* 32,721 ....W-12
La Puente, *Los Angeles,* 41,063 ....WW-7
La Quinta, *Riverside,* 23,694 ....T-13
La Verne, *Los Angeles,* 31,638 ....VV-9
• Ladera Heights, *Los Angeles,* 6,568 ....XX-1
Lafayette, *Contra Costa,* 23,908 ....GG-5
• Laguna, *Monterey,* 34,309 ....CC-9
Laguna Beach, *Orange,* 23,727 ....UU-7
Laguna Hills, *Orange,* 31,178 ....TT-7
Laguna Niguel, *Orange,* 61,891 ....U-11
Laguna West-Lakeside,
Sacramento, 8,414 ....CC-10
Laguna Woods, *Orange,* 16,507 ....TT-7
• Lagunitas-Forest Knolls, *Marin,* 1,835 ....FF-2
• Lake Arrowhead,
San Bernardino, 8,934 ....PP-10
Lake Elsinore, *Riverside,* 28,928 ....TT-10
Lake Forest, *Orange,* 58,707 ....TT-7
• Lake Isabella, *Kern,* 3,315 ....P-9
• Lake Los Angeles, *Los Angeles,* 11,523 ..R-10
• Lake Nacimiento, *San Luis Obispo,* 2,176 O-5
• Lake of The Pines, *Nevada,* 3,956 ....H-7
• Lake San Marcos, *San Diego,* 4,138 ....V-3
Lake Wildwood, *Nevada,* 4,868 ....G-6
• Lakeland Village, *Riverside,* 5,626 ....TT-9
Lakeport, *Lake,* 4,820 ....H-3
• Lakeside, *San Diego,* 19,560 ....X-5
• Lakeview, *Riverside,* 1,619 ....SS-11

Explanation of symbols: • - Census Designated Place (CDP)

Lakewood, *Los Angeles*, 79,345 ... RR-5
• Lamont, *Kern*, 13,296 ... Q-8
Lancaster, *Los Angeles*, 118,718 ... R-10
• Larkfield-Wikiup, *Sonoma*, 7,479 ... I-4
Larkspur, *Marin*, 12,014 ... GG-3
• Las Flores, *Orange*, 5,625 ... TT-8
• Las Lomas, *Orange*, 3,078 ... M-5
Lathrop, *San Joaquin*, 10,445 ... GG-9
• Laton, *Fresno*, 1,236 ... X-8
Lawndale, *Los Angeles*, 31,711 ... YY-2
• Laytonville, *Mendocino*, 1,301 ... F-2
• Le Grand, *Merced*, 1,760 ... L-8
• Lebec, *Kern*, 1,285 ... R-9
Lemon Grove, *San Diego*, 24,918 ... Y-4
Lemoore, *Kings*, 19,712 ... N-7
• Lemoore Station, *Kings*, 5,749 ... N-7
• Lennox, *Los Angeles*, 22,950 ... YY-2
• Lenwood, *San Bernardino*, 3,222 ... R-12
• Lewiston, *Trinity*, 1,305 ... D-4
• Lexington Hills, *Santa Clara*, 2,454 ... B-11
Lincoln, *Placer*, 11,205 ... H-6
• Lincoln Village, *San Joaquin*, 4,216 ... FF-9
• Linda, *Yuba*, 13,474 ... H-6
• Linden, *San Joaquin*, 1,103 ... FF-10
Lindsay, *Tulare*, 10,297 ... N-8
• Littlerock, *Los Angeles*, 1,402 ... NN-6
• Live Oak, *Santa Cruz*, 16,628 ... C-11
Live Oak, *Sutter*, 6,229 ... G-5
Livermore, *Alameda*, 73,345 ... K-5
Livingston, *Merced*, 10,473 ... L-7
• Lockeford, *San Joaquin*, 3,179 ... J-6
Lodi, *San Joaquin*, 56,999 ... J-6
Loma Linda, *San Bernardino*, 18,681 ... QQ-10
• Loma Rica, *Yuba*, 2,075 ... G-6
Lomita, *Los Angeles*, 20,046 ... SS-4
Lompoc, *Santa Barbara*, 41,103 ... R-6
• London, *Tulare*, 1,848 ... X-9
• Lone Pine, *Inyo*, 1,655 ... M-12
Long Beach, *Los Angeles*, 461,522 ... T-10
Loomis, *Placer*, 6,260 ... AA-10
Los Alamitos, *Orange*, 11,536 ... SS-5
• Los Alamos, *Santa Barbara*, 1,372 ... R-6
Los Altos, *Santa Clara*, 27,693 ... JJ-5
Los Altos Hills, *Orange*, 7,902 ... FF-15
Los Angeles, *Los Angeles*, 3,694,820 ... S-10
Los Banos, *Merced*, 25,869 ... L-7
Los Gatos, *Santa Clara*, 28,592 ... KK-6
• Los Molinos, *Tehama*, 1,952 ... E-5
• Lost Hills, *Kern*, 1,938 ... P-7
• Lower Lake, *Lake*, 1,755 ... H-4
• Lucas Valley-Marinwood, *Marin*, 6,357 ... FF-3
• Lucerne, *Lake*, 2,870 ... H-3
Lynwood, *Los Angeles*, 69,845 ... YY-4
Madera, *Madera*, 43,207 ... M-8
• Madera Acres, *Madera*, 7,741 ... L-8
• Magalia, *Butte*, 10,569 ... F-6
Malibu, *Los Angeles*, 12,575 ... QQ-2
Mammoth Lakes, *Mono*, 7,093 ... K-10
Manhattan Beach, *Los Angeles*, 33,852 ... YY-1
Manteca, *San Joaquin*, 49,258 ... K-6
Maricopa, *Kern*, 1,111 ... Q-8
Marina, *Monterey*, 25,101 ... M-5
• Marina Del Rey, *Los Angeles*, 8,176 ... RR-3
• Mariposa, *Mariposa*, 1,373 ... K-8
Markleeville, *Alpine*, 197 ... I-9
Martinez, *Contra Costa*, 35,866 ... J-5
Marysville, *Yuba*, 12,268 ... G-6
• Mayflower Village, *Los Angeles*, 5,081 ... VV-6
Maywood, *Los Angeles*, 28,083 ... XX-4
• McCloud, *Siskiyou*, 1,343 ... C-5
McFarland, *Kern*, 9,618 ... P-8
• McKinleyville, *Humboldt*, 13,599 ... C-1
• Meadow Vista, *Placer*, 3,096 ... H-7
• Mecca, *Riverside*, 5,402 ... U-14
• Meiners Oaks, *Ventura*, 3,750 ... S-3
Mendota, *Fresno*, 7,890 ... M-8
Menlo Park, *San Mateo*, 30,785 ... JJ-5
• Mentone, *San Bernardino*, 7,803 ... QQ-11
Merced, *Merced*, 63,893 ... L-8
• Middletown, *Lake*, 1,020 ... H-4
Mill Valley, *Marin*, 13,600 ... GG-3
Millbrae, *San Mateo*, 20,718 ... II-4
Milpitas, *Santa Clara*, 62,698 ... JJ-6
• Mira Loma, *Riverside*, 17,617 ... QQ-8
• Mira Monte, *Ventura*, 7,177 ... S-3
Mission Canyon, *Santa Barbara*, 2,610 ... S-2
Mission Viejo, *Orange*, 93,102 ... TT-8
• Mi-Wuk Village, *Tuolumne*, 1,485 ... D-17
Modesto, *Stanislaus*, 188,856 ... K-7
• Mojave, *Kern*, 3,836 ... Q-10
• Mono Vista, *Tuolumne*, 3,072 ... J-8
Monrovia, *Los Angeles*, 36,929 ... PP-6
Montague, *Siskiyou*, 1,456 ... A-4
• Montara, *San Mateo*, 2,950 ... II-3
Montclair, *San Bernardino*, 33,049 ... VV-10
• Monte Rio, *Sonoma*, 1,104 ... CC-1
Monte Sereno, *Santa Clara*, 3,483 ... KK-6
Montebello, *Los Angeles*, 62,150 ... WW-5
• Montecito, *Santa Barbara*, 10,000 ... S-2
Monterey, *Monterey*, 29,674 ... M-5
Monterey Park, *Los Angeles*, 60,051 ... WW-5
Moorpark, *Ventura*, 31,415 ... T-4
Moraga, *Contra Costa*, 16,290 ... GG-5
Moreno Valley, *Riverside*, 142,381 ... RR-10
Morgan Hill, *Santa Clara*, 33,556 ... L-5
• Morongo Valley,
San Bernardino, 1,929 ... QQ-14
Morro Bay, *San Luis Obispo*, 10,350 ... P-5
• Moss Beach, *San Mateo*, 1,953 ... II-3
Mount Shasta, *Siskiyou*, 3,621 ... B-4
• Mountain Ranch, *Calaveras*, 1,557 ... J-7
Mountain View, *Santa Clara*, 70,708 ... JJ-5
Mountain View Acres,
San Bernardino, 2,521 ... NN-10
• Murphys, *Calaveras*, 2,061 ... D-16
Murrieta, *Riverside*, 44,282 ... UU-10
• Murrieta Hot Springs, *Riverside*, 2,948 UU-11
• Muscoy, *San Bernardino*, 8,919 ... PP-9
• Myrtletown, *Humboldt*, 4,459 ... D-1
Napa, *Napa*, 72,585 ... I-4
National City, *San Diego*, 54,260 ... Y-4
Needles, *San Bernardino*, 4,830 ... Q-16
Nevada City, *Nevada*, 3,001 ... G-7
Newark, *Alameda*, 42,471 ... II-6
Newman, *Stanislaus*, 7,093 ... L-7
Newport Beach, *Orange*, 70,032 ... T-10
• Nice, *Lake*, 2,509 ... H-3
• Niland, *Imperial*, 1,143 ... U-15
• Nipomo, *San Luis Obispo*, 12,626 ... Q-6
Norco, *Riverside*, 24,157 ... RR-8
• North Auburn, *Placer*, 11,847 ... H-6
• North Edwards, *Kern*, 1,227 ... Q-10
• North El Monte, *San Diego*, 3,703 ... VV-6
• North Fair Oaks, *San Mateo*, 15,440 ... EE-15
• North Lakeport, *Lake*, 2,879 ... H-3
Norwalk, *Los Angeles*, 103,298 ... RR-5
Novato, *Marin*, 47,630 ... J-4
• Nuevo, *Riverside*, 4,135 ... SS-11
• Oak Park, *Ventura*, 2,320 ... OO-1
• Oak View, *Ventura*, 4,199 ... S-3
Oakdale, *Stanislaus*, 15,503 ... K-7
• Oakhurst, *Madera*, 2,868 ... L-9
Oakland, *Alameda*, 399,484 ... K-4
Oakley, *Contra Costa*, 25,619 ... FF-7
• Occidental, *Sonoma*, 1,272 ... CC-1
• Oceano, *San Luis Obispo*, 7,260 ... Q-5
Oceanside, *San Diego*, 161,029 ... U-11
• Oildale, *Kern*, 27,885 ... P-8
Ojai, *Ventura*, 7,862 ... S-8
• Olivehurst, *Yuba*, 11,061 ... B-16
Ontario, *San Bernardino*, 158,007 ... QQ-8
• Opal Cliffs, *Santa Cruz*, 6,458 ... M-5
Orange, *Orange*, 128,821 ... SS-7
Orange Cove, *Fresno*, 7,722 ... M-10
• Orcutt, *Santa Barbara*, 28,830 ... R-6
Orinda, *Contra Costa*, 17,599 ... GG-5
Orland, *Glenn*, 6,281 ... F-5
• Orosi, *Tulare*, 7,318 ... N-8
Oroville, *Butte*, 13,004 ... G-6
Oxnard, *Ventura*, 170,358 ... S-8
• Pacheco, *San Mateo*, 3,562 ... FF-5
Pacific Grove, *Monterey*, 15,522 ... M-5
Pacifica, *San Mateo*, 38,390 ... II-3
• Pajaro, *Orange*, 3,384 ... D-12
• Palermo, *Butte*, 5,720 ... G-6
Palm Desert, *Riverside*, 41,155 ... T-13
Palm Springs, *Riverside*, 42,807 ... T-13
Palmdale, *Los Angeles*, 116,670 ... R-10
Palo Alto, *Santa Clara*, 58,598 ... K-5
• Palo Cedro, *Shasta*, 1,247 ... D-4
Palos Verdes Estates,
Los Angeles, 13,340 ... SS-3
Paradise, *Butte*, 26,408 ... F-6
Paramount, *Los Angeles*, 55,266 ... YY-4
• Parkway-South Sacramento,
Los Angeles, 36,468 ... CC-9
Parlier, *Fresno*, 11,145 ... M-9
Pasadena, *Los Angeles*, 133,936 ... S-10
Paso Robles (El Paso De Robles),
San Luis Obispo, 24,297 ... P-5
Patterson, *Stanislaus*, 11,606 ... K-6
• Pedley, *Riverside*, 11,207 ... RR-9
Perris, *Riverside*, 36,189 ... SS-10
Petaluma, *Sonoma*, 54,548 ... J-4
• Phoenix Lake-Cedar Ridge,
Tuolumne, 5,123 ... J-8
Pico Rivera, *Los Angeles*, 63,428 ... RR-5
Piedmont, *Alameda*, 10,952 ... GG-5
• Pine Valley, *San Diego*, 1,501 ... V-13
Pinole, *Contra Costa*, 19,039 ... AA-16
• Piru, *Ventura*, 1,196 ... S-9
Pismo Beach, *San Luis Obispo*, 8,551 ... Q-5
Pittsburg, *Contra Costa*, 56,769 ... FF-6
• Pixley, *Tulare*, 2,586 ... O-8
Placentia, *Orange*, 46,488 ... ZZ-8
Placerville, *El Dorado*, 9,610 ... H-7
• Planada, *Merced*, 4,369 ... L-8
Pleasant Hill, *Contra Costa*, 32,837 ... GG-6
Pleasanton, *Alameda*, 63,654 ... HH-6
• Pollock Pines, *El Dorado*, 4,728 ... AA-13
Pomona, *Los Angeles*, 149,473 ... S-11
• Poplar-Cotton Center, *Tulare*, 1,496 ... Z-10
Port Hueneme, *Ventura*, 21,845 ... T-3
Porterville, *Tulare*, 39,615 ... O-8
Portola, *Plumas*, 2,227 ... F-8
• Portola Hills, *Orange*, 6,391 ... TT-8
Portola Valley, *Contra Costa*, 4,462 ... JJ-4
Poway, *San Diego*, 48,044 ... V-12
• Prunedale, *Monterey*, 16,432 ... M-5
• Quartz Hill, *Los Angeles*, 9,890 ... R-10
• Quincy, *Plumas*, 1,879 ... F-7
• Rainbow, *San Diego*, 2,026 ... U-12
• Ramona, *San Diego*, 15,691 ... V-5
Rancho Calaveras, *Calaveras*, 4,182 ... J-7
• Rancho Cordova, *Sacramento*, 55,060 ... I-6
Rancho Cucamonga (Cucamonga),
San Bernardino, 127,743 ... QQ-8
Rancho Mirage, *Riverside*, 13,249 ... SS-15
Rancho Palos Verdes,
Los Angeles, 41,145 ... SS-3
• Rancho San Diego, *San Diego*, 20,155 ... Y-5
• Rancho Santa Fe, *San Diego*, 3,252 ... V-3
Rancho Santa Margarita,
Orange, 47,214 ... TT-8
Red Bluff, *Tehama*, 13,147 ... E-4
Redding, *Shasta*, 80,865 ... D-4
Redlands, *San Bernardino*, 63,591 ... QQ-10
Redondo Beach, *Los Angeles*, 63,261 ... SS-3
• Redway, *Humboldt*, 1,188 ... E-2
Redwood City, *San Mateo*, 75,402 ... K-4
Reedley, *Fresno*, 20,756 ... M-9
Rialto, *San Bernardino*, 91,873 ... QQ-9
• Richgrove, *Tulare*, 2,723 ... O-8
Richmond, *Contra Costa*, 99,216 ... J-4
Ridgecrest, *Kern*, 24,927 ... P-11
• Rio del Mar, *Siskiyou*, 9,198 ... C-11
Rio Dell, *Humboldt*, 3,174 ... D-1
Rio Vista, *Solano*, 4,571 ... EE-7
Ripon, *San Joaquin*, 10,146 ... HH-10
Riverbank, *Stanislaus*, 15,826 ... K-7
• Riverdale, *Fresno*, 2,416 ... X-7
Riverside, *Riverside*, 255,166 ... T-11
Rocklin, *Placer*, 36,330 ... AA-10
• Rodeo, *Contra Costa*, 8,717 ... FF-4
Rohnert Park, *Sonoma*, 42,236 ... I-4
Rolling Hills, *Contra Costa*, 1,871 ... SS-4
Rolling Hills Estates, *Los Angeles*, 7,676 SS-4
• Romoland, *Riverside*, 2,764 ... SS-10
• Rosamond, *Kern*, 14,349 ... R-10
• Rosedale, *Kern*, 8,445 ... P-8
• Roseland, *Sonoma*, 6,369 ... CC-2
Rosemead, *Los Angeles*, 53,505 ... VV-5
• Rosemont, *Sacramento*, 22,904 ... CC-9
Roseville, *Placer*, 79,921 ... H-6
• Rossmoor, *Orange*, 10,298 ... T-10
• Rowland Heights, *Los Angeles*, 48,553 ... XX-7
• Rubidoux, *Riverside*, 29,180 ... QQ-9
• Running Springs,
San Bernardino, 5,125 ... PP-11
Sacramento, *Sacramento*, 407,018 ... I-6
• Salida, *Stanislaus*, 12,560 ... HH-10
Salinas, *Monterey*, 151,060 ... M-5
• San Andreas, *Calaveras*, 2,615 ... J-7
San Anselmo, *Marin*, 12,378 ... FF-3
• San Antonio Heights,
San Bernardino, 3,122 ... PP-8
San Bernardino,
San Bernardino, 185,401 ... S-11
San Bruno, *San Mateo*, 40,165 ... II-4
San Carlos, *San Mateo*, 27,718 ... II-4
San Clemente, *Orange*, 49,936 ... U-11
San Diego, *San Diego*, 1,223,400 ... W-12
• San Diego Country Estates,
San Diego, 9,262 ... V-12
San Dimas, *Los Angeles*, 34,980 ... VV-9
San Fernando, *Los Angeles*, 23,564 ... OO-3
San Francisco, *San Francisco*, 776,733 ... K-4
San Gabriel, *Los Angeles*, 39,804 ... VV-5
San Jacinto, *Riverside*, 23,779 ... SS-12
San Joaquin, *Fresno*, 3,270 ... M-8
San Joaquin Hills, *Orange*, 2,959 ... TT-7
San Jose, *Santa Clara*, 894,943 ... L-5
San Juan Bautista, *San Benito*, 1,549 ... D-13
San Juan Capistrano, *Orange*, 33,826 ... UU-8
San Leandro, *Alameda*, 79,452 ... HH-5
• San Lorenzo, *Alameda*, 21,898 ... HH-5
San Luis Obispo,
San Luis Obispo, 44,174 ... Q-5
San Marcos, *San Diego*, 54,977 ... V-3
San Marino, *Los Angeles*, 12,945 ... VV-5
• San Martin, *Santa Clara*, 4,230 ... L-5
San Mateo, *San Mateo*, 92,482 ... K-4
• San Miguel, *San Luis Obispo*, 1,427 ... O-5
San Pablo, *Contra Costa*, 30,215 ... J-4
San Rafael, *Marin*, 56,063 ... J-4
San Ramon, *Contra Costa*, 44,722 ... HH-6
Sanger, *Fresno*, 18,931 ... G-16
Santa Ana, *Orange*, 337,977 ... T-10
Santa Barbara, *Santa Barbara*, 92,325 ... S-7
Santa Clara, *Santa Clara*, 102,361 ... L-5
Santa Clarita, *Los Angeles*, 151,088 ... S-9
Santa Cruz, *Santa Cruz*, 54,593 ... M-5
Santa Fe Springs, *Los Angeles*, 17,438 ... XX-5
Santa Maria, *Santa Barbara*, 77,423 ... Q-6
Santa Monica, *Los Angeles*, 84,084 ... QQ-3
Santa Paula, *Ventura*, 28,598 ... S-8
Santa Rosa, *Sonoma*, 147,595 ... I-4
• Santa Venetia, *Alameda*, 4,298 ... AA-14
• Santa Ynez, *Santa Barbara*, 4,584 ... R-6
Santee, *San Diego*, 52,975 ... V-12
Saratoga, *Santa Clara*, 29,843 ... A-10
Sausalito, *Marin*, 7,330 ... GG-3
Scotts Valley, *Santa Cruz*, 11,385 ... B-10
Seal Beach, *Orange*, 24,157 ... SS-5
• Searles Valley, *San Bernardino*, 1,885 ... O-11
Seaside, *Monterey*, 31,696 ... M-5
Sebastopol, *Sonoma*, 7,774 ... I-3
• Sedco Hills, *Riverside*, 3,078 ... TT-10
• Seeley, *Imperial*, 1,624 ... V-15
Selma, *Fresno*, 19,444 ... M-9
Shackelford, *Stanislaus*, 5,170 ... II-11
Shafter, *Kern*, 12,736 ... P-8
Shasta Lake, *Shasta*, 9,008 ... D-4
• Shingletown, *Shasta*, 2,222 ... D-5
Sierra Madre, *Los Angeles*, 10,578 ... PP-5
Signal Hill, *Los Angeles*, 9,333 ... SS-5
Simi Valley, *Ventura*, 111,351 ... S-9
Solana Beach, *San Diego*, 12,979 ... V-12
Soledad, *Monterey*, 11,263 ... N-4
Solvang, *Santa Barbara*, 5,332 ... R-6
Sonoma, *Sonoma*, 9,128 ... I-4
Sonora, *Tuolumne*, 4,423 ... J-8
• Soquel, *Santa Cruz*, 5,081 ... L-5
• Soulsbyville, *Tuolumne*, 1,729 ... D-17
• South Dos Palos, *Merced*, 1,385 ... M-7
South El Monte, *Los Angeles*, 21,144 ... WW-6
South Gate, *Los Angeles*, 96,375 ... RR-5
South Lake Tahoe, *El Dorado*, 23,609 ... H-8
• South Oroville, *Butte*, 7,695 ... G-6
South Pasadena, *Los Angeles*, 24,292 ... VV-4
South San Francisco, *San Mateo*, 60,552 ... K-4
• South San Gabriel, *San Mateo*, 7,595 ... WW-6
• South San Jose Hills,
Monterey, 20,218 ... WW-7
• South Taft, *Kern*, 1,898 ... Q-7
• South Whittier, *Los Angeles*, 55,193 ... XX-6
• South Woodbridge, *San Joaquin*, 2,825 ... EE-9
• South Yuba City, *Sutter*, 12,651 ... B-16
• Spring Valley, *San Diego*, 26,663 ... Y-4
• Springville, *Tulare*, 1,109 ... O-9
• Squaw Valley, *Fresno*, 2,691 ... M-10
• Stanford, *Santa Clara*, 13,315 ... FF-15
Stanton, *Orange*, 37,403 ... SS-6
Stockton, *San Joaquin*, 243,771 ... J-6
• Stratford, *Kings*, 1,264 ... N-7
• Strathmore, *Tulare*, 2,584 ... Y-10
• Strawberry, *Marin*, 5,302 ... CC-15
Suisun City, *Solano*, 26,118 ... J-5
• Summerland, *Santa Barbara*, 1,545 ... S-2
• Sun City, *Riverside*, 17,773 ... T-12
• Sunnyside-Tahoe City, *Placer*, 1,761 ... G-8
• Sunnyslope, *Riverside*, 4,437 ... QQ-9
Sunnyvale, *Santa Clara*, 131,760 ... JJ-6
• Sunol, *Alameda*, 1,332 ... II-6
Susanville, *Lassen*, 13,541 ... E-7
• Sutter, *Sutter*, 2,885 ... A-15
Sutter Creek, *Amador*, 2,303 ... DD-12
Taft, *Kern*, 6,400 ... Q-7
• Taft Heights, *Kern*, 1,865 ... Q-7
• Tahoe Vista, *Placer*, 1,668 ... G-8
• Talmage, *Mendocino*, 1,141 ... G-3
• Tamalpais-Homestead Valley,
Marin, 10,691 ... GG-3
• Tara Hills, *Contra Costa*, 5,332 ... AA-16
Tehachapi, *Kern*, 10,957 ... Q-9
Temecula, *Riverside*, 57,716 ... U-12
Temple City, *Los Angeles*, 33,377 ... VV-6
• Templeton, *San Luis Obispo*, 4,687 ... P-5
• Terra Bella, *Tulare*, 3,466 ... O-8
• Thermalito, *Butte*, 6,045 ... G-6
Thousand Oaks, *Ventura*, 117,005 ... PP-1
• Thousand Palms, *Riverside*, 5,120 ... SS-15
• Three Rivers, *Tulare*, 2,248 ... N-9
Tiburon, *Marin*, 8,666 ... GG-4
• Tierra Buena, *Sutter*, 4,587 ... A-15
• Tipton, *Tulare*, 1,790 ... Z-9
Torrance, *Los Angeles*, 137,946 ... T-10
Tracy, *San Joaquin*, 56,929 ... K-6
Truckee, *Nevada*, 13,864 ... G-8
Tulare, *Tulare*, 43,994 ... N-8
Tulelake, *Siskiyou*, 1,020 ... A-6
• Tuolumne City, *Tuolumne*, 1,865 ... J-8
Turlock, *Stanislaus*, 55,810 ... K-7
Tustin, *Orange*, 67,504 ... SS-7
• Tustin Foothills, *Los Angeles*, 24,044 ... SS-7
• Twain Harte, *Tuolumne*, 2,586 ... J-8
Twentynine Palms,
San Bernardino, 14,764 ... S-14
• Twin Lakes, *Orange*, 5,533 ... C-10
Ukiah, *Mendocino*, 15,497 ... G-3
Union City, *Alameda*, 66,869 ... II-6
Upland, *Los Angeles*, 68,393 ... QQ-8
Vacaville, *Solano*, 88,625 ... I-5
• Val Verde, *Los Angeles*, 1,472 ... S-9
• Valinda, *Madera*, 21,776 ... WW-7
• Valle Vista, *Riverside*, 10,488 ... SS-12
Vallejo, *Solano*, 116,760 ... J-4
• Valley Center, *San Diego*, 7,323 ... U-4
• Valley Springs, *Calaveras*, 2,560 ... EE-12
• Vandenberg AFB, *Santa Barbara*, 6,151 ... R-5
• Vandenberg Village, *Santa Barbara*, 5,802 R-6
Ventura (San Buenaventura),
Ventura, 100,916 ... S-8
Victorville, *San Bernardino*, 64,029 ... R-11
• View Park-Windsor Hills,
Los Angeles, 10,958 ... XX-2
Villa Park, *Orange*, 5,999 ... SS-7
• Vincent, *Los Angeles*, 15,097 ... R-10
• Vine Hill, *Contra Costa*, 3,260 ... FF-5
• Vineyard, *Sacramento*, 10,109 ... CC-9
Visalia, *Tulare*, 91,565 ... N-8
Vista, *San Diego*, 89,857 ... U-12
Waldon, *Contra Costa*, 5,133 ... GG-6
Walnut, *Los Angeles*, 30,004 ... WW-8
Walnut Creek, *Contra Costa*, 64,296 ... GG-5
• Walnut Park, *Los Angeles*, 16,180 ... XX-3
Wasco, *Kern*, 21,263 ... P-8
Waterford, *Stanislaus*, 6,924 ... K-7
Watsonville, *Santa Cruz*, 44,265 ... M-5
• Weaverville, *Trinity*, 3,554 ... D-3
Weed, *Siskiyou*, 2,978 ... B-4
• Weedpatch, *Kern*, 2,726 ... Q-8
• Weldon, *Kern*, 2,387 ... P-10
• West Athens, *Contra Costa*, 9,101 ... YY-2
• West Bishop, *Inyo*, 2,807 ... L-11
• West Carson, *Contra Costa*, 21,138 ... ZZ-2
• West Compton, *Orange*, 5,435 ... YY-3
West Covina, *Los Angeles*, 105,080 ... QQ-6
West Hollywood, *Los Angeles*, 35,716 ... VV-1
• West Puente Valley, *Alameda*, 22,589 ... WW-6
• West Whittier-Los Nietos,
Los Angeles, 25,129 ... XX-6
Westlake Village, *Los Angeles*, 8,368 ... PP-1
Westminster, *Orange*, 88,207 ... SS-6
• Westmont, *San Mateo*, 31,623 ... XX-2
Westmorland, *Imperial*, 2,131 ... V-15
• Westwood, *Lassen*, 1,998 ... E-7
Wheatland, *Yuba*, 2,275 ... C-17
Whittier, *Los Angeles*, 83,680 ... RR-5
• Wildomar, *Riverside*, 14,064 ... TT-10
Williams, *Colusa*, 3,670 ... G-5
Willits, *Mendocino*, 5,073 ... G-3
• Willow Creek, *Humboldt*, 1,743 ... C-2
• Willowbrook, *Los Angeles*, 34,138 ... YY-3
Willows, *Glenn*, 6,220 ... G-5
• Wilton, *Sacramento*, 4,551 ... CC-9
• Winchester, *Riverside*, 2,155 ... TT-11
Windsor, *Sonoma*, 22,744 ... I-3
• Winter Gardens, *San Diego*, 19,771 ... X-5
Winters, *Yolo*, 6,125 ... CC-6
• Winton, *Merced*, 8,832 ... L-7
• Wofford Heights, *Kern*, 2,276 ... P-9
• Woodacre, *Marin*, 1,393 ... FF-3
• Woodcrest, *Riverside*, 8,342 ... RR-9
Woodlake, *Tulare*, 6,651 ... N-8
Woodland, *Yolo*, 49,151 ... I-5
Woodside, *San Mateo*, 5,352 ... FF-15
• Woodville, *Tulare*, 1,678 ... O-8
• Wrightwood, *San Bernardino*, 3,837 ... S-11
Yorba Linda, *Orange*, 58,918 ... YY-9
• Yosemite Lakes, *Madera*, 4,160 ... L-9
Yountville, *Napa*, 2,916 ... DD-4
Yreka, *Siskiyou*, 7,290 ... A-4
Yuba City, *Sutter*, 36,758 ... H-6
Yucaipa, *San Bernardino*, 41,207 ... QQ-11
Yucca Valley, *San Bernardino*, 16,865 ... S-13

COLORADO

COUNTIES

(63 Counties)

Name of County	Population	Location on Map
ADAMS	363,857	F-13
ALAMOSA	14,966	K-9
ARAPAHOE	487,967	F-13
ARCHULETA	9,898	L-7
BACA	4,517	L-15
BENT	5,998	J-15
BOULDER	291,288	E-10
CHAFFEE	16,242	H-8
CHEYENNE	2,231	H-15
CLEAR CREEK	9,322	F-10
CONEJOS	8,400	L-8
COSTILLA	3,663	L-10
CROWLEY	5,518	I-13
CUSTER	3,503	J-10
DELTA	27,834	H-6
DENVER	554,636	F-11
DOLORES	1,844	K-4
DOUGLAS	175,766	H-11
EAGLE	41,659	F-7
EL PASO	516,929	I-13
ELBERT	19,872	G-13
FREMONT	46,145	I-10
GARFIELD	43,791	F-6
GILPIN	4,757	F-10
GRAND	12,442	E-8
GUNNISON	13,956	H-7
HINSDALE	790	J-7
HUERFANO	7,862	K-11
JACKSON	1,577	C-8
JEFFERSON	527,056	G-11
KIOWA	1,622	I-15
KIT CARSON	8,011	G-15
LA PLATA	43,941	L-6
LAKE	7,812	H-9
LARIMER	251,494	C-9
LAS ANIMAS	15,207	K-12
LINCOLN	6,087	G-14
LOGAN	20,504	C-14
MESA	116,255	G-4
MINERAL	558	K-7
MOFFAT	13,184	C-4
MONTEZUMA	23,830	L-4
MONTROSE	33,432	I-4
MORGAN	27,171	D-13
OTERO	20,311	K-13
OURAY	3,742	J-6
PARK	14,523	G-10
PHILLIPS	4,480	D-16
PITKIN	14,872	G-7
PROWERS	14,483	J-16
PUEBLO	141,472	I-13
RIO BLANCO	5,986	E-4
RIO GRANDE	12,413	L-8
ROUTT	19,690	C-7
SAGUACHE	5,917	J-8
SAN JUAN	558	K-6
SAN MIGUEL	6,594	J-4
SEDGWICK	2,747	C-16
SUMMIT	23,548	F-9
TELLER	20,555	I-11
WASHINGTON	4,926	D-14
WELD	180,936	C-12
YUMA	9,841	D-16
TOTAL	**4,301,261**	

CITIES AND TOWNS

Note: The first name is that of the city or town, second, that of the county in which it is located, then the population and location on the map.

Acres Green, *Douglas*, 3,205 .... E-3
●Air Force Academy, *El Paso*, 7,526 .... H-12
Akron, *Washington*, 1,711 .... E-15
Alamosa, *Alamosa*, 7,960 .... L-10
●Alamosa East, *Alamosa*, 1,528 .... L-10
●Applewood, *Jefferson*, 7,123 .... C-1
Arvada, *Jefferson*, 102,153 .... F-11
Aspen, *Pitkin*, 5,914 .... G-8
Ault, *Weld*, 1,432 .... D-12
Aurora, *Adams*, 276,393 .... F-12
Avon, *Eagle*, 5,561 .... F-9
Basalt, *Eagle*, 2,681 .... G-8
●Battlement Mesa, *Garfield*, 3,497 .... G-6
Bayfield, *La Plata*, 1,549 .... L-6
Bennett, *Adams*, 2,021 .... F-13
●Berkley, *Adams*, 10,743 .... C-2
Berthoud, *Larimer*, 4,839 .... E-11
●Beulah Valley, *Pueblo*, 1,164 .... J-12
●Black Forest, *El Paso*, 13,247 .... H-12
Boulder, *Boulder*, 94,673 .... E-11
Breckenridge, *Summit*, 2,408 .... G-9
Brighton, *Adams*, 20,905 .... E-12
Broomfield, *Boulder*, 38,272 .... B-2
Brush, *Morgan*, 5,117 .... E-14
Buena Vista, *Chaffee*, 2,195 .... H-9
Burlington, *Kit Carson*, 3,678 .... G-17
●Byers, *Arapahoe*, 1,233 .... F-13
Cañon City, *Fremont*, 15,431 .... I-11
●Campion, *Larimer*, 1,832 .... E-11
Carbondale, *Garfield*, 5,196 .... G-7
Carriage Club, *Douglas*,1,002 .... E-3
●Cascade-Chipita Park, *El Paso*, 1,709 .... H-12
Castle Pines, *Douglas*, 5,958 .... G-12
Castle Rock, *Douglas*, 20,224 .... G-12
●Castlewood, *Arapahoe*, 25,567 .... F-12
Cedaredge, *Delta*, 1,854 .... H-6
Center, *Saguache*, 2,392 .... K-9
Central City, *Gilpin*, 515 .... F-10
Cherry Hills Village, *Arapahoe*, 5,958 .... D-3
Cheyenne Wells, *Cheyenne*, 1,010 .... H-17
●Cimarron Hills, *El Paso*, 15,194 .... H-12
●Clifton, *Mesa*, 17,345 .... H-5
●Colorado City, *Pueblo*, 2,018 .... K-12
Colorado Springs, *El Paso*, 360,890 .... H-12
●Columbine, *Routt*, 24,095 .... F-9
Columbine Valley, *Arapahoe*, 1,132 .... D-2
Commerce City, *Adams*, 20,991 .... C-3
Conejos, *Conejos*, 200 .... M-9
Cortez, *Montezuma*, 7,977 .... L-4
Craig, *Moffat*, 9,189 .... D-7
Creede, *Mineral*, 377 .... K-8
Crested Butte, *Gunnison*, 1,529 .... H-8
Cripple Creek, *Teller*, 1,115 .... I-11
Dacono, *Weld*, 3,015 .... A-3
Del Norte, *Rio Grande*, 1,705 .... K-9
Delta, *Delta*, 6,400 .... I-6
Denver, *Denver*, 554,636 .... F-12
●Derby, *Adams*, 6,423 .... B-3
Dove Creek, *Dolores*, 698 .... K-4
Durango, *La Plata*, 13,922 .... L-6
Eads, *Kiowa*, 747 .... I-16
Eagle, *Eagle*, 3,032 .... F-8
Eaton, *Weld*, 2,690 .... D-12
Edgewater, *Jefferson*, 5,445 .... C-2
●Edwards, *Eagle*, 8,257 .... F-8
●El Jebel, *Eagle*, 4,488 .... G-7
Elizabeth, *Elbert*, 1,434 .... G-12
Englewood, *Arapahoe*, 31,727 .... D-2
Erie, *Boulder*, 6,291 .... A-2
Estes Park, *Larimer*, 5,413 .... D-10
Evans, *Weld*, 9,514 .... D-12
●Evergreen, *Jefferson*, 9,216 .... F-11
Fairplay, *Park*, 610 .... G-10
Federal Heights, *Adams*, 12,065 .... B-2
Firestone, *Weld*, 1,908 .... E-12
Florence, *Fremont*, 3,653 .... I-11
●Fort Carson, *El Paso*, 10,566 .... I-12
Fort Collins, *Larimer*, 118,652 .... D-11
Fort Lupton, *Weld*, 6,787 .... A-3
Fort Morgan, *Morgan*, 11,034 .... E-14
Fountain, *El Paso*, 15,197 .... I-12
Fowler, *Otero*, 1,206 .... J-13
Frederick, *Weld*, 2,467 .... A-3
Frisco, *Summit*, 2,443 .... F-9
Fruita, *Mesa*, 6,478 .... G-4
●Fruitvale, *Mesa*, 6,936 .... H-5
●Genesee, *Jefferson*, 3,699 .... C-1
Georgetown, *Clear Creek*, 1,088 .... F-10
Gilcrest, *Weld*, 1,162 .... E-12
Glendale, *Arapahoe*, 4,547 .... C-3
●Gleneagle, *El Paso*, 4,246 .... H-12
Glenwood Springs, *Garfield*, 7,736 .... G-7
Golden, *Jefferson*, 17,159 .... C-1
Granby, *Grand*, 1,525 .... E-10
Grand Junction, *Mesa*, 41,986 .... H-5
Greeley, *Weld*, 76,930 .... D-12
Greenwood Village, *Custer*, 11,035 .... D-3
●Gunbarrel, *Boulder*, 9,435 .... A-1
Gunnison, *Gunnison*, 5,409 .... I-8
Gypsum, *Eagle*, 3,654 .... F-8
Hayden, *Routt*, 1,634 .... D-7
●Highlands Ranch, *Douglas*, 70,931 .... D-2
Holly, *Prowers*, 1,048 .... J-17
Holyoke, *Phillips*, 2,261 .... D-17
Hot Sulphur Springs, *Grand*, 521 .... E-9
Hudson, *Weld*, 1,565 .... E-12
Hugo, *Lincoln*, 885 .... H-14
Idaho Springs, *Clear Creek*, 1,889 .... F-10
●Indian Hills, *Jefferson*, 1,197 .... D-1
Johnstown, *Weld*, 3,827 .... E-12
Julesburg, *Sedgwick*, 1,467 .... C-17
●Ken Caryl, *Jefferson*, 30,887 .... D-2
Kersey, *Weld*, 1,389 .... D-12
Kiowa, *Elbert*, 581 .... G-12
Kremmling, *Grand*, 1,578 .... E-9
La Junta, *Otero*, 7,568 .... K-14
La Salle, *Weld*, 1,849 .... E-12
Lafayette, *Boulder*, 23,197 .... A-2
Lake City, *Hinsdale*, 375 .... J-7
Lakewood, *Jefferson*, 144,126 .... C-2
Lamar, *Prowers*, 8,869 .... J-16
●Laporte, *Larimer*, 2,691 .... D-11
Las Animas, *Bent*, 2,758 .... J-15
Leadville, *Lake*, 2,821 .... G-9
●Leadville North, *Lake*, 1,942 .... G-9
Limon, *Lincoln*, 2,071 .... G-14
●Lincoln Park, *Fremont*, 3,904 .... I-11
Littleton, *Arapahoe*, 40,340 .... F-11
Lochbuie, *Weld*, 2,049 .... E-12
Log Lane Village, *Morgan*, 1,006 .... E-14
Lone Tree, *Douglas*, 4,873 .... D-3
Longmont, *Boulder*, 71,093 .... E-11
Louisville, *Boulder*, 18,937 .... E-11
Loveland, *Larimer*, 50,608 .... D-11
Lyons, *Boulder*, 1,585 .... E-11
Manassa, *Conejos*, 1,042 .... M-10
Mancos, *Montezuma*, 1,119 .... L-5
Manitou Springs, *El Paso*, 4,980 .... H-12
Mead, *Weld*, 2,017 .... E-11
Meeker, *Rio Blanco*, 2,242 .... E-6
Milliken, *Weld*, 2,888 .... E-12
Minturn, *Eagle*, 1,068 .... F-9
Monte Vista, *Rio Grande*, 4,529 .... L-9
Montrose, *Montrose*, 12,344 .... I-6
Monument, *El Paso*, 1,971 .... H-12
Nederland, *Boulder*, 1,394 .... E-10
New Castle, *Garfield*, 1,984 .... F-7
●Niwot, *Boulder*, 4,160 .... E-11
Northglenn, *Adams*, 31,575 .... B-2
Olathe, *Montrose*, 1,573 .... I-6
Orchard City, *Delta*, 2,880 .... H-6
●Orchard Mesa, *Mesa*, 6,456 .... H-5
Ordway, *Crowley*, 1,248 .... J-14
Ouray, *Ouray*, 813 .... J-6
Pagosa Springs, *Archuleta*, 1,591 .... L-8
Palisade, *Mesa*, 2,579 .... H-5
Palmer Lake, *El Paso*, 2,179 .... H-12
Paonia, *Delta*, 1,497 .... H-6
Parachute, *Garfield*, 1,006 .... G-6
Parker, *Douglas*, 23,558 .... G-12
●Penrose, *Fremont*, 4,070 .... I-11
Perry Park, *Douglas*, 1,180 .... G-11
Platteville, *Weld*, 2,370 .... E-12
●Ponderosa Park, *Elbert*, 3,112 .... G-12
Pueblo, *Pueblo*, 102,121 .... J-12
●Pueblo West, *Pueblo*, 16,899 .... J-12
Rangely, *Rio Blanco*, 2,096 .... E-4
●Redlands, *Mesa*, 8,043 .... H-4
Rifle, *Garfield*, 6,784 .... G-6
Rocky Ford, *Otero*, 4,286 .... J-14
●Roxborough Park, *Douglas*, 4,446 .... E-2
Saguache, *Saguache*, 578 .... J-9
Salida, *Chaffee*, 5,504 .... I-10
San Luis, *Costilla*, 739 .... M-11
●Security-Widefield, *El Paso*, 29,845 .... I-12
Sheridan, *Arapahoe*, 5,600 .... D-2
●Sherrelwood, *Adams*, 17,657 .... B-2
Silt, *Garfield*, 1,740 .... G-6
Silverthorne, *Summit*, 3,196 .... F-9
Silverton, *San Juan*, 531 .... K-6
Snowmass Village, *Pitkin*, 1,822 .... G-8
●Southglenn, *Arapahoe*, 43,520 .... D-2
Springfield, *Baca*, 1,562 .... L-16
Steamboat Springs, *Routt*, 9,815 .... D-8
Sterling, *Logan*, 11,360 .... D-15
●Stonegate, *Douglas*, 6,284 .... E-3
●Strasburg, *Adams*, 1,402 .... F-13
●Stratmoor, *El Paso*, 6,650 .... I-12
Superior, *Boulder*, 9,011 .... B-1
Telluride, *San Miguel*, 2,221 .... K-6
●The Pinery, *Douglas*, 7,253 .... G-12
Thornton, *Adams*, 82,384 .... F-11
●Towaoc, *Montezuma*, 1,097 .... L-4
Trinidad, *Las Animas*, 9,078 .... M-12
●Twin Lakes, *Lake*, 6,301 .... H-9
Vail, *Eagle*, 4,531 .... F-9
Walden, *Jackson*, 734 .... D-9
Walsenburg, *Huerfano*, 4,182 .... K-12
●Welby, *Adams*, 12,973 .... B-2
Wellington, *Larimer*, 2,672 .... D-11
Westcliffe, *Custer*, 417 .... J-11
Westminster, *Adams*, 100,940 .... F-11
West Pleasant View, *Jefferson*,3,932 .... C-1
Wheat Ridge, *Jefferson*, 32,913 .... C-2
Windsor, *Weld*, 9,896 .... D-12
Woodland Park, *Teller*, 6,515 .... H-11
●Woodmoor, *El Paso*, 7,177 .... H-12
Wray, *Yuma*, 2,187 .... E-17
Yuma, *Yuma*, 3,285 .... E-16

Explanation of symbols: ● - Census Designated Place (CDP)

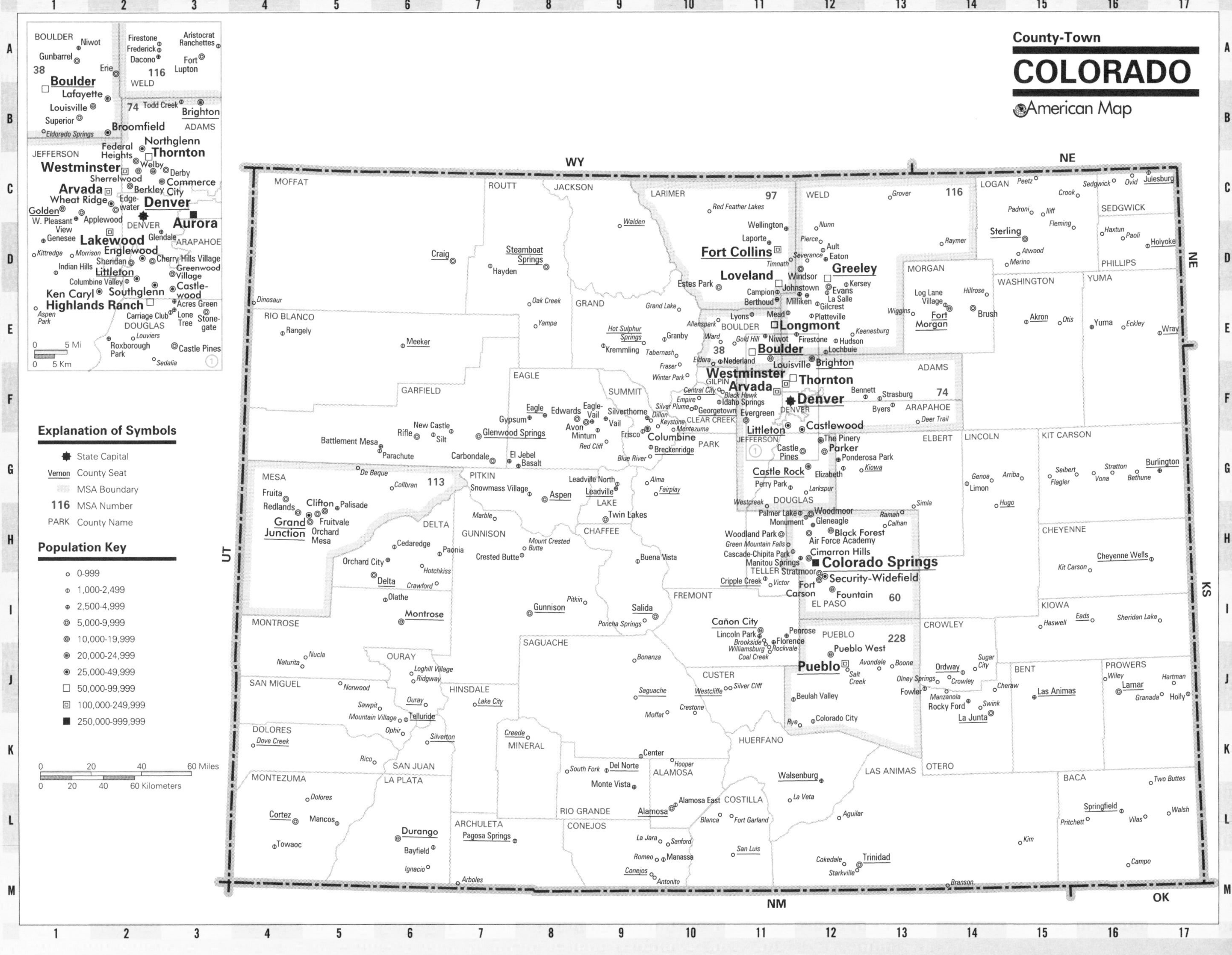
County-Town
COLORADO
American Map
Explanation of Symbols
State Capital
Vernon County Seat
MSA Boundary
116 MSA Number
PARK County Name
Population Key
0-999
1,000-2,499
2,500-4,999
5,000-9,999
10,000-19,999
20,000-24,999
25,000-49,999
50,000-99,999
100,000-249,999
250,000-999,999
0 20 40 60 Miles
0 20 40 60 Kilometers
0 5 Mi
0 5 Km
WY
NE
KS
OK
NM
UT

COUNTIES

(8 Counties)

Name of County	Population	Location on Map
FAIRFIELD	882,567	G-3
HARTFORD	857,183	A-7
LITCHFIELD	182,193	A-3
MIDDLESEX	155,071	F-9
NEW HAVEN	824,008	G-4
NEW LONDON	259,088	E-13
TOLLAND	136,364	A-11
WINDHAM	109,091	A-14
TOTAL	**3,405,565**	

CITIES AND TOWNS

Note: The first name is that of the city or town, second, that of the county in which it is located, then the population and location on the map.

▲Andover, *Tolland*, 3,036 .... E-12
Ansonia, *New Haven*, 18,554 .... I-6
▲Ashford, *Windham*, 4,098 .... C-14
▲Avon, *Hartford*, 15,832 .... D-8
▲Beacon Falls, *New Haven*, 5,246 .... H-6
▲Berlin, *Hartford*, 18,215 .... F-9
▲Bethany, *New Haven*, 5,040 .... H-7
●Bethel, *Fairfield*, 9,137 .... I-4
▲Bethel, *Fairfield*, 18,067 .... I-4
▲Bethlehem, *Litchfield*, 3,422 .... F-5
●Bethlehem Village, *Litchfield*, 2,022 .... F-5
▲Bloomfield, *Hartford*, 19,587 .... D-9
●Blue Hills, *Hartford*, 3,020 .... D-9
▲Bozrah, *New London*, 2,357 .... G-14
▲Bolton, *Tolland*, 5,017 .... D-12
▲Branford, *New Haven*, 28,683 .... J-8
●Branford Center, *New Haven*, 5,735 .... J-8
Bridgeport, *Fairfield*, 139,529 .... K-5
▲Bridgewater, *Litchfield*, 1,824 .... G-4
Bristol, *Hartford*, 60,062 .... E-7
●Broad Brook, *Hartford*, 3,469 .... C-11
▲Brookfield, *Fairfield*, 15,664 .... G-4
▲Brooklyn, *Windham*, 7,173 .... D-15
▲Burlington, *Hartford*, 8,190 .... D-7
Canaan, *Litchfield*, 1,288 .... A-4
▲Canaan, *Litchfield*, 1,081 .... B-4
▲Canterbury, *Windham*, 4,692 .... E-15
▲Canton, *Hartford*, 8,840 .... D-8
●Canton Valley, *Hartford*, 1,565 .... D-8
●Central Manchester, *Hartford*, 30,595 .... D-11
●Central Somers, *Tolland*, 1,626 .... B-11
●Central Waterford, *New London*, 2,935 .... I-14
▲Chaplin, *Windham*, 2,250 .... D-14
▲Cheshire, *New Haven*, 28,543 .... G-8
●Cheshire Village, *New Haven*, 5,789 .... G-8
▲Chester, *Middlesex*, 3,743 .... H-11
●Chester Center, *Middlesex*, 1,546 .... H-11
▲Clinton, *Middlesex*, 13,094 .... J-11
●Clinton, *Middlesex*, 3,516 .... J-11
▲Colchester, *New London*, 14,551 .... F-12
▲Colebrook, *Litchfield*, 1,471 .... B-6
●Collinsville, *Hartford*, 2,686 .... D-8
▲Columbia, *Tolland*, 4,971 .... E-13
●Conning Towers-Nautilus Park, *New London*, 10,241 ..I-15
▲Cornwall, *Litchfield*, 1,434 .... C-4
▲Coventry, *Tolland*, 11,504 .... D-13
●Coventry Lake, *Tolland*, 2,914 .... D-12
▲Cromwell, *Middlesex*, 12,871 .... F-10
●Crystal Lake, *Tolland*, 1,459 .... B-12
Danbury, *Fairfield*, 74,848 .... H-3
Danielson, *Windham*, 4,265 .... D-16
Darien, *Fairfield*, 19,607 .... L-3
▲Deep River, *Middlesex*, 4,610 .... H-12
●Deep River Center, *Middlesex*, 2,470 .... I-11
Derby, *New Haven*, 12,391 .... I-6
●Durham, *Middlesex*, 6,627 .... G-10
●East Brooklyn, *Windham*, 1,473 .... D-15
▲East Granby, *Hartford*, 4,745 .... B-9
▲East Haddam, *Middlesex*, 8,333 .... H-11
●East Hampton, *Middlesex*, 2,254 .... F-11
▲East Hampton, *Middlesex*, 13,352 .... F-11
East Hartford, *Hartford*, 49,575 .... D-10
East Haven, *New Haven*, 28,189 .... J-8
▲East Lyme, *New London*, 18,118 .... I-13
▲East Windsor, *Hartford*, 9,818 .... C-11
▲Eastford, *Windham*, 1,618 .... C-14
▲Easton, *Fairfield*, 7,272 .... J-4
▲Ellington, *Tolland*, 12,921 .... C-11
▲Enfield, *Hartford*, 45,212 .... B-10
▲Essex, *Middlesex*, 6,505 .... I-12
●Essex Village, *Middlesex*, 2,573 .... I-12
Fairfield, *Fairfield*, 57,340 .... K-5
Farmington, *Hartford*, 23,641 .... E-8
▲Franklin, *New London*, 1,835 .... F-14
●Georgetown, *Fairfield*, 1,650 .... J-3
▲Glastonbury, *Hartford*, 31,876 .... E-10
●Glastonbury Center, *Hartford*, 7,157 .... E-10
▲Goshen, *Litchfield*, 2,697 .... C-5
▲Granby, *Hartford*, 10,347 .... B-9
Greenwich, *Fairfield*, 61,101 .... L-2
▲Griswold, *New London*, 10,807 .... F-16
▲Groton, *New London*, 39,907 .... I-14
Groton, *New London*, 10,010 .... I-14
▲Guilford, *New Haven*, 21,398 .... J-10
●Guilford Center, *New Haven*, 2,603 .... J-9
▲Haddam, *Middlesex*, 7,157 .... G-11
Hamden, *New Haven*, 56,913 .... H-8
▲Hampton, *Windham*, 1,758 .... D-15
Hartford, *Hartford*, 121,578 .... D-10
▲Hartland, *Hartford*, 2,012 .... A-7
▲Harwinton, *Litchfield*, 5,283 .... D-6
●Hazardville, *Hartford*, 4,900 .... B-11
▲Hebron, *Tolland*, 8,610 .... E-12
●Heritage Village, *New Haven*, 3,435 .... G-5
●Higganum, *Middlesex*, 1,671 .... G-11
Jewett City, *New London*, 3,053 .... F-15
●Kensington, *Hartford*, 8,541 .... F-9
▲Kent, *Litchfield*, 2,858 .... E-3
▲Killingly, *Windham*, 16,472 .... C-16
▲Killingworth, *Middlesex*, 6,018 .... I-10
●Lake Pocotopaug, *Middlesex*, 3,169 .... F-11
▲Lebanon, *New London*, 6,907 .... F-13
▲Ledyard, *New London*, 14,687 .... H-15
▲Lisbon, *New London*, 4,069 .... F-15
▲Litchfield, *Litchfield*, 8,316 .... D-5
Litchfield, *Litchfield*, 1,328 .... D-5
●Long Hill, *Fairfield*, 3,534 .... J-5
▲Lyme, *New London*, 2,016 .... H-13
▲Madison, *New Haven*, 17,858 .... J-10
●Madison Center, *New Haven*, 2,222 .... J-10
Manchester, *Hartford*, 54,740 .... D-11
▲Mansfield, *Tolland*, 20,720 .... D-13
▲Marlborough, *Hartford*, 5,709 .... F-11
Meriden, *New Haven*, 58,244 .... G-8
▲Middlebury, *New Haven*, 6,451 .... G-6
▲Middlefield, *Middlesex*, 4,203 .... G-9
Middletown, *Middlesex*, 43,167 .... G-10
Milford, *New Haven*, 52,305 .... J-6
▲Monroe, *Fairfield*, 19,247 .... I-5
●Moodus, *Middlesex*, 1,263 .... G-11
●Moosup, *Windham*, 3,237 .... E-16
▲Morris, *Litchfield*, 2,301 .... E-5
●Mystic, *New London*, 4,001 .... I-15
Naugatuck, *New Haven*, 30,989 .... G-6
New Britain, *Hartford*, 71,538 .... E-9
New Canaan, *Fairfield*, 19,395 .... K-3
▲New Fairfield, *Fairfield*, 13,953 .... G-3
▲New Hartford, *Litchfield*, 6,088 .... C-7
●New Hartford Center, *Litchfield*, 1,049 .... C-7
New Haven, *New Haven*, 123,626 .... I-8
New London, *New London*, 25,671 .... I-14
New Milford, *Litchfield*, 27,121 .... F-4
●New Preston, *Litchfield*, 1,110 .... E-4
Newington, *Hartford*, 29,306 .... E-9
Newtown, *Fairfield*, 25,031 .... H-4
●Niantic, *New London*, 3,085 .... I-13
●Noank, *New London*, 1,830 .... I-15
▲Norfolk, *Litchfield*, 1,660 .... B-5
▲North Branford, *New Haven*, 13,906 .... I-9
●North Granby, *Hartford*, 1,720 .... B-8
●North Grosvenor Dale, *Windham*, 1,424 .... B-16
North Haven, *New Haven*, 23,035 .... H-8
▲North Stonington, *New London*, 4,991 .... H-16
●Northwest Harwinton, *Litchfield*, 3,242 .... D-6
Norwalk, *Fairfield*, 82,951 .... K-3
Norwich, *New London*, 36,117 .... G-14
●Oakville, *Litchfield*, 8,618 .... F-6
▲Old Lyme, *New London*, 7,406 .... I-12
●Old Mystic, *New London*, 3,205 .... H-15
▲Old Saybrook, *Middlesex*, 10,367 .... J-12
●Old Saybrook Center, *Middlesex*, 1,962 .... J-12
Orange, *New Haven*, 13,233 .... J-7
▲Oxford, *New Haven*, 9,821 .... H-6
●Oxoboxo River, *New London*, 2,938 .... H-14
●Pawcatuck, *New London*, 5,474 .... I-16
▲Plainfield, *Windham*, 14,619 .... E-16
●Plainfield Village, *Windham*, 2,638 .... E-16
▲Plainville, *Hartford*, 17,328 .... E-8
▲Plymouth, *Litchfield*, 11,634 .... E-7
▲Pomfret, *Windham*, 3,798 .... C-15
●Poquonock Bridge, *New London*, 1,592 .... I-15
▲Portland, *Middlesex*, 8,732 .... F-10
●Portland, *Middlesex*, 5,534 .... F-10
▲Preston, *New London*, 4,688 .... G-16
▲Prospect, *New Haven*, 8,707 .... G-7
▲Putnam, *Windham*, 9,002 .... B-16
●Putnam District, *Windham*, 6,746 .... C-16
●Quinebaug, *Windham*, 1,122 .... A-15
▲Redding, *Fairfield*, 8,270 .... I-4
●Ridgefield, *Fairfield*, 7,212 .... J-3
▲Ridgefield, *Fairfield*, 23,643 .... J-3
●Rockville, *Tolland*, 7,708 .... C-11
▲Rocky Hill, *Hartford*, 17,966 .... E-10
▲Roxbury, *Litchfield*, 2,136 .... G-4
▲Salem, *New London*, 3,858 .... G-13
▲Salisbury, *Litchfield*, 3,977 .... B-3
●Salmon Brook, *Hartford*, 2,453 .... B-9
●Saybrook Manor, *Middlesex*, 1,133 .... J-12
▲Scotland, *Windham*, 1,556 .... E-14
Seymour, *New Haven*, 15,454 .... H-6
▲Sharon, *Litchfield*, 2,968 .... C-3
Shelton, *Fairfield*, 38,101 .... I-6
▲Sherman, *Fairfield*, 3,827 .... F-3
●Sherwood Manor, *Hartford*, 5,689 .... A-10
▲Simsbury, *Hartford*, 23,234 .... C-8
●Simsbury Center, *Hartford*, 5,603 .... C-8
▲Somers, *Tolland*, 10,417 .... B-11
●South Coventry, *Tolland*, 1,381 .... D-12
●South Windham, *Windham*, 1,278 .... E-14
▲South Windsor, *Hartford*, 24,412 .... D-10
●South Woodstock, *Windham*, 1,211 .... B-15
▲Southbury, *New Haven*, 18,567 .... G-5
▲Southington, *Hartford*, 39,728 .... F-8
●Southwood Acres, *Hartford*, 8,067 .... B-10
▲Sprague, *New London*, 2,971 .... F-15
▲Stafford, *Tolland*, 11,307 .... B-13
Stamford, *Fairfield*, 117,083 .... L-2
▲Sterling, *Windham*, 3,099 .... E-16
▲Stonington, *New London*, 17,906 .... I-16
Stonington, *New London*, 1,032 .... I-16
●Storrs, *Tolland*, 10,996 .... D-13
Stratford, *Fairfield*, 49,976 .... K-6
▲Suffield, *Hartford*, 13,552 .... B-10
●Suffield Depot, *Hartford*, 1,244 .... B-10
●Tariffville, *Hartford*, 1,371 .... C-9
●Terramuggus, *Hartford*, 1,048 .... F-11
●Terryville, *Litchfield*, 5,360 .... E-7
▲Thomaston, *Litchfield*, 7,503 .... E-6
▲Thompson, *Windham*, 8,878 .... B-16
●Thompsonville, *Hartford*, 8,125 .... B-10
▲Tolland, *Tolland*, 13,146 .... C-12
Torrington, *Litchfield*, 35,202 .... D-6
Trumbull, *Fairfield*, 34,243 .... J-5
▲Vernon, *Tolland*, 28,063 .... D-11
▲Voluntown, *New London*, 2,528 .... F-16
▲Wallingford, *New Haven*, 43,026 .... H-8
●Wallingford Center, *New Haven*, 17,509 .... H-8
▲Warren, *Litchfield*, 1,254 .... D-4
▲Washington, *Litchfield*, 3,596 .... F-4
Waterbury, *New Haven*, 107,271 .... G-6
▲Waterford, *New London*, 19,152 .... I-14
▲Watertown, *Litchfield*, 21,661 .... F-6
●Wauregan, *Windham*, 1,085 .... D-16
●Weatogue, *Hartford*, 2,805 .... C-8
●West Hartford, *Hartford*, 63,589 .... D-9
West Haven, *New Haven*, 52,360 .... J-7
●West Simsbury, *Hartford*, 2,395 .... C-8
▲Westbrook, *Middlesex*, 6,292 .... J-11
●Westbrook Center, *Middlesex*, 2,238 .... J-11
▲Weston, *Fairfield*, 10,037 .... K-4
Westport, *Fairfield*, 25,749 .... K-4
Wethersfield, *Hartford*, 26,271 .... E-10
●Willimantic, *Windham*, 15,823 .... E-13
▲Willington, *Tolland*, 5,959 .... C-13
▲Wilton, *Fairfield*, 17,633 .... K-3
▲Winchester, *Litchfield*, 10,664 .... C-6
▲Windham, *Windham*, 22,857 .... E-14
▲Windsor, *Hartford*, 28,237 .... C-10
Windsor Locks, *Hartford*, 12,043 .... B-10
●Winsted, *Litchfield*, 7,321 .... B-6
▲Wolcott, *New Haven*, 15,215 .... F-7
▲Woodbridge, *New Haven*, 8,983 .... I-7
▲Woodbury, *Litchfield*, 9,198 .... G-5
Woodmont, *New Haven*, 1,711 .... J-7
▲Woodstock, *Windham*, 7,221 .... B-15

Explanation of symbols: ● - Census Designated Place (CDP) ▲ - Township

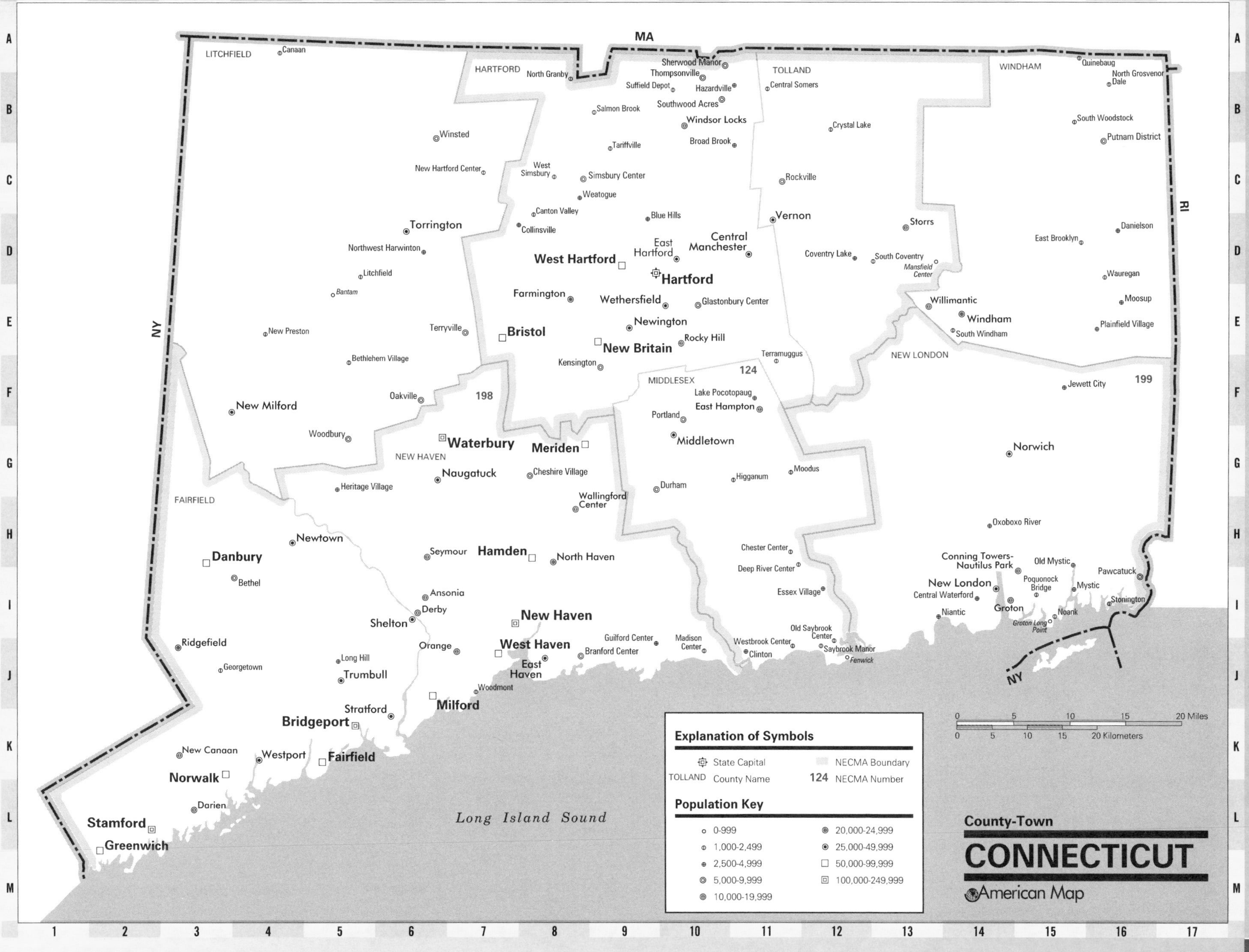
County-Town
CONNECTICUT
American Map
Explanation of Symbols
State Capital
TOLLAND County Name
NECMA Boundary
124 NECMA Number
Population Key
0-999
1,000-2,499
2,500-4,999
5,000-9,999
10,000-19,999
20,000-24,999
25,000-49,999
50,000-99,999
100,000-249,999
0 5 10 15 20 Miles
0 5 10 15 20 Kilometers
Long Island Sound
MA
RI
NY
LITCHFIELD
HARTFORD
TOLLAND
WINDHAM
NEW LONDON
MIDDLESEX
NEW HAVEN
FAIRFIELD
124
198
199
Canaan
North Granby
Sherwood Manor
Thompsonville
Suffield Depot
Hazardville
Central Somers
Quinebaug
North Grosvenor Dale
Southwood Acres
Salmon Brook
Windsor Locks
Crystal Lake
South Woodstock
Winsted
Broad Brook
Putnam District
Tariffville
New Hartford Center
West Simsbury
Simsbury Center
Rockville
Weatogue
Canton Valley
Collinsville
Blue Hills
Vernon
Storrs
Danielson
Torrington
East Brooklyn
East Hartford
Central Manchester
Northwest Harwinton
Coventry Lake
South Coventry
Mansfield Center
West Hartford
Hartford
Litchfield
Wauregan
Bantam
Farmington
Wethersfield
Glastonbury Center
Willimantic
Moosup
Windham
Newington
New Preston
Terryville
South Windham
Plainfield Village
Bristol
Rocky Hill
New Britain
Bethlehem Village
Terramuggus
Kensington
New London
Jewett City
Lake Pocotopaug
Oakville
New Milford
East Hampton
Portland
Woodbury
Waterbury
Meriden
Middletown
Norwich
Naugatuck
Cheshire Village
Moodus
Higganum
Heritage Village
Durham
Wallingford Center
Oxoboxo River
Newtown
Danbury
Seymour
Hamden
North Haven
Chester Center
Conning Towers-Nautilus Park
Old Mystic
Deep River Center
Pawcatuck
Bethel
Poquonock Bridge
Mystic
Ansonia
Essex Village
Central Waterford
Groton
Stonington
Derby
Niantic
Noank
New Haven
Shelton
Groton Long Point
Old Saybrook Center
Guilford Center
Madison Center
Ridgefield
Orange
West Haven
Westbrook Center
Saybrook Manor
Branford Center
Clinton
Long Hill
Georgetown
East Haven
Fenwick
Trumbull
Woodmont
Stratford
Milford
Bridgeport
New Canaan
Westport
Fairfield
Norwalk
Darien
Stamford
Greenwich

COUNTIES

(3 Counties)

Name of County	Population	Location on Map
KENT	126,697	H-5
NEW CASTLE	500,265	B-6
SUSSEX	156,638	M-5
TOTAL	**783,600**	

CITIES AND TOWNS

Note: The first name is that of the city or town, second, that of the county in which it is located, then the population and location on the map.

•Bear, *New Castle,* 17,593 ....C-5
Bellefonte, *New Castle,* 1,249 ....B-7
Bridgeville, *Sussex,* 1,436 ....N-6
•Brookside, *New Castle,* 14,806 ....C-5
Camden, *Kent,* 2,100 ....I-6
•Claymont, *New Castle,* 9,220 ....B-7
Clayton, *Kent,* 1,273 ....G-6
Delaware City, *New Castle,* 1,453 ....D-6
Delmar, *Sussex,* 1,407 ....Q-6
Dover, *Kent,* 32,135 ....I-7
•Edgemoor, *New Castle,* 5,992 ....B-7
Elsmere, *New Castle,* 5,800 ....B-6
Georgetown, *Sussex,* 4,643 ....N-8
•Glasgow, *New Castle,* 12,840 ....D-5
•Greenville, *New Castle,* 2,332 ....B-6
Harrington, *Kent,* 3,174 ....K-6
•Highland Acres, *Kent,* 3,379 ....I-7
•Hockessin, *New Castle,* 12,902 ....B-5
•Kent Acres, *Kent,* 1,637 ....I-7
Laurel, *Sussex,* 3,668 ....P-6
Lewes, *Sussex,* 2,932 ....M-10
•Long Neck, *Sussex,* 1,629 ....O-10
Middletown, *New Castle,* 6,161 ....F-5
Milford, *Sussex,* 6,732 ....L-7
Millsboro, *Sussex,* 2,360 ....O-9
Milton, *Sussex,* 1,657 ....M-9
New Castle, *New Castle,* 4,862 ....C-6
Newark, *New Castle,* 28,547 ....C-5
Newport, *New Castle,* 1,122 ....C-6
•North Star, *New Castle,* 8,277 ....B-5
Ocean View, *Sussex,* 1,006 ....P-11
•Pike Creek, *New Castle,* 19,751 ....B-5
Rehoboth Beach, *Sussex,* 1,495 ....N-11
•Rising Sun-Lebanon, *Kent,* 2,458 ....I-7
•Riverview, *Kent,* 1,583 ....J-7
•Rodney, *Kent,* 1,602 ....I-7
Seaford, *Sussex,* 6,699 ....O-6
Selbyville, *Sussex,* 1,645 ....Q-9
Smyrna, *Kent,* 5,679 ....G-6
Wilmington, *New Castle,* 72,664 ....B-6
•Wilmington Manor, *New Castle,* 8,262 ....C-6
Wyoming, *Kent,* 1,141 ....I-6

Explanation of symbols: • - Census Designated Place (CDP)

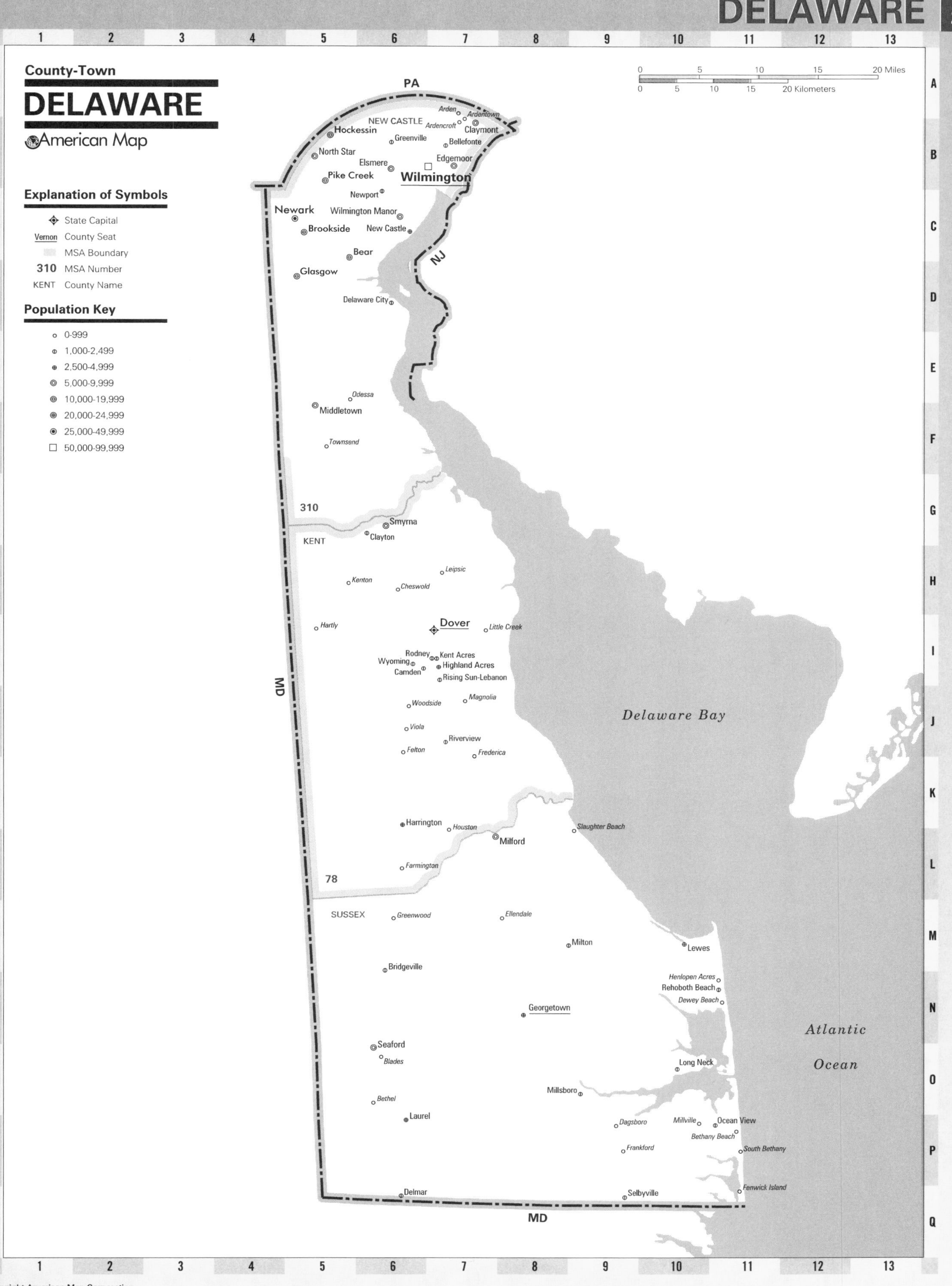
County-Town
DELAWARE
American Map
Explanation of Symbols
State Capital
Vernon County Seat
MSA Boundary
310 MSA Number
KENT County Name
Population Key
0-999
1,000-2,499
2,500-4,999
5,000-9,999
10,000-19,999
20,000-24,999
25,000-49,999
50,000-99,999
0 5 10 15 20 Miles
0 5 10 15 20 Kilometers
PA
NJ
MD
NEW CASTLE
KENT
SUSSEX
310
78
Arden
Ardentown
Ardencroft
Claymont
Hockessin
Greenville
Bellefonte
North Star
Elsmere
Edgemoor
Pike Creek
Wilmington
Newport
Newark
Wilmington Manor
Brookside
New Castle
Bear
Glasgow
Delaware City
Odessa
Middletown
Townsend
Smyrna
Clayton
Leipsic
Kenton
Cheswold
Hartly
Dover
Little Creek
Rodney
Kent Acres
Wyoming
Highland Acres
Camden
Rising Sun-Lebanon
Woodside
Magnolia
Viola
Riverview
Felton
Frederica
Delaware Bay
Harrington
Houston
Milford
Slaughter Beach
Farmington
Greenwood
Ellendale
Milton
Lewes
Bridgeville
Henlopen Acres
Rehoboth Beach
Dewey Beach
Georgetown
Atlantic Ocean
Seaford
Blades
Long Neck
Millsboro
Bethel
Laurel
Dagsboro
Millville
Ocean View
Bethany Beach
Frankford
South Bethany
Delmar
Selbyville
Fenwick Island
1 2 3 4 5 6 7 8 9 10 11 12 13
A B C D E F G H I J K L M N O P Q

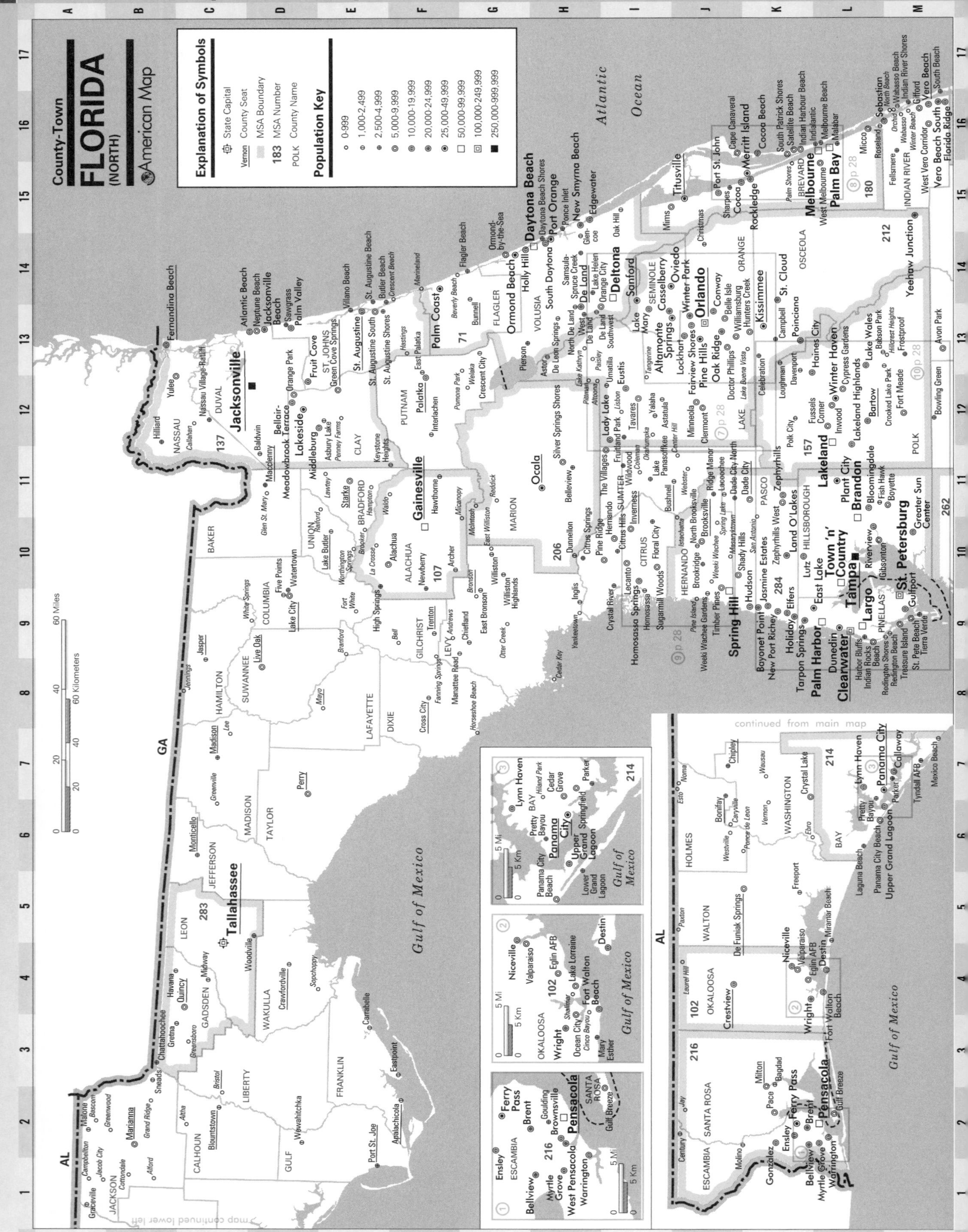
County-Town
FLORIDA
(NORTH)
American Map
Explanation of Symbols
State Capital
Vernon County Seat
MSA Boundary
183 MSA Number
POLK County Name
Population Key
0-999
1,000-2,499
2,500-4,999
5,000-9,999
10,000-19,999
20,000-24,999
25,000-49,999
50,000-99,999
100,000-249,999
250,000-999,999
Atlantic Ocean
Gulf of Mexico
continued from main map
map continued lower left

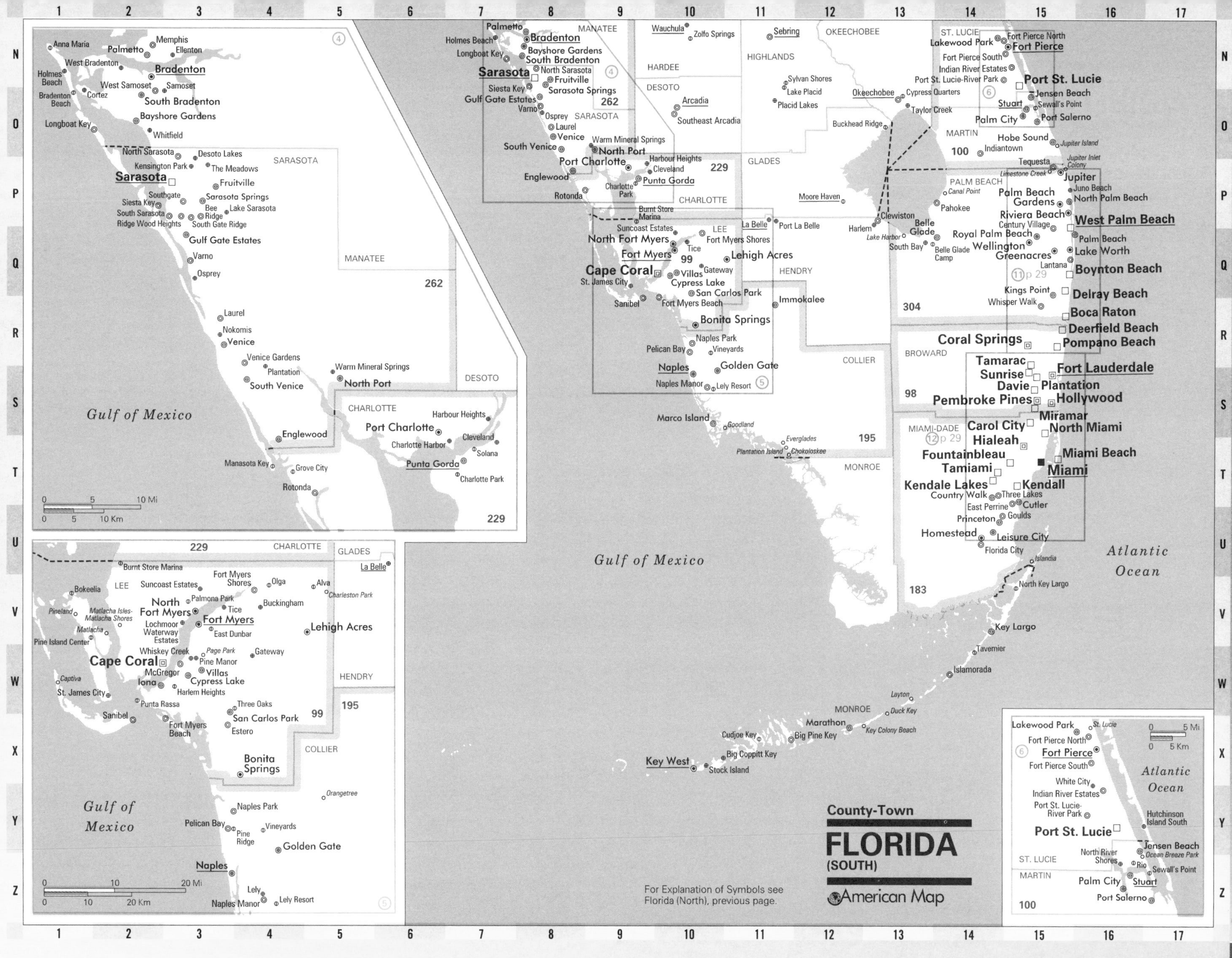
County-Town
FLORIDA
(SOUTH)
American Map
For Explanation of Symbols see Florida (North), previous page.
Atlantic Ocean
Gulf of Mexico
ST. LUCIE
MARTIN
PALM BEACH
OKEECHOBEE
HIGHLANDS
GLADES
HENDRY
BROWARD
MIAMI-DADE
COLLIER
MONROE
LEE
CHARLOTTE
DESOTO
HARDEE
MANATEE
SARASOTA
Fort Pierce
Port St. Lucie
Stuart
Jupiter
West Palm Beach
Boynton Beach
Delray Beach
Boca Raton
Deerfield Beach
Pompano Beach
Fort Lauderdale
Coral Springs
Hollywood
Miramar
North Miami
Miami Beach
Miami
Hialeah
Kendall
Homestead
Key Largo
Islamorada
Marathon
Key West
Okeechobee
Sebring
Immokalee
Lehigh Acres
Cape Coral
Fort Myers
North Fort Myers
Bonita Springs
Naples
Golden Gate
Marco Island
Punta Gorda
Port Charlotte
North Port
Englewood
Venice
Sarasota
Bradenton
Palmetto
Arcadia
Wauchula
La Belle
Clewiston
Belle Glade
Pahokee
Palm City
Port Salerno
Jensen Beach
Wellington
Royal Palm Beach
Palm Beach Gardens
Riviera Beach
Greenacres
Tamarac
Sunrise
Plantation
Davie
Pembroke Pines
Carol City
Fountainbleau
Tamiami
Kendale Lakes
Sanibel
Longboat Key
Siesta Key
Gulf Gate Estates
South Venice
Osprey
Laurel
Rotonda
Copyright American Map Corporation

Explanation of Symbols

- State Capital
- Vernon — County Seat
- MSA Boundary
- 157 — MSA Number
- POLK — County Name

Population Key

- 0-999
- 1,000-2,499
- 2,500-4,999
- 5,000-9,999
- 10,000-19,999
- 20,000-24,999
- 25,000-49,999
- 50,000-99,999
- 100,000-249,999
- 250,000-999,999

County-Town
FLORIDA
INSET MAPS

American Map

Explanation of Symbols

- State Capital
- Vernon — County Seat
- MSA Boundary
- 183 — MSA Number
- POLK — County Name

Population Key

- 0-999
- 1,000-2,499
- 2,500-4,999
- 5,000-9,999
- 10,000-19,999
- 20,000-24,999
- 25,000-49,999
- 50,000-99,999
- 100,000-249,999
- 250,000-999,999

County-Town FLORIDA INSET MAPS

American Map

(11)

0 5 10 Mi
0 5 10 Km

PALM BEACH
Jupiter
Juno Beach
Juno Ridge
North Palm Beach
Palm Beach Gardens
Lake Park
Riviera Beach
Palm Beach Shores
Magnonia Park
Lakeside Green
Cypress Lakes
Schall Circle
Century Village
West Palm Beach
Plantation Mobile Home Park
Stacey Street
Westgate-Belvedere Homes
Palm Beach
Golden Lakes
Lake Belvedere Estates
Haverhill
Royal Palm Beach
Royal Palm Estates
Gun Club Estates
Cloud Lake
Glen Ridge
Wellington
Lake Clarke Shores
Palm Springs
Lake Worth
Greenacres
Lake Worth Corridor
Atlantis
Lantana
South Palm Beach
Seminole Manor
Manalapan
Hypoluxo
Atlantic Ocean
Boynton Beach
Ocean Ridge
Briny Breezes
Golf
Dunes Road
Gulf Stream
Villages of Oriole
High Point
Delray Beach
Kings Point
Highland Beach
Whisper Walk
Hamptons at Boca Raton
Mission Bay
Boca Raton
304
Sandalfoot Cove
Boca Del Mar
Boca Pointe
BROWARD
Parkland
Hillsboro Pines
Hillsboro Ranches
Deerfield Beach
Hillsboro Beach
Godfrey Road
Ramblewood East
Tedder
Pompano Beach Highlands
Bonnie Lock-Woodstetter North
Loch Lomond
Pompano Estates
Lighthouse Point
Coral Springs
Coconut Creek
Leisureville
Collier Manor-Cresthaven
Kendall Green
Margate
Pompano Beach
Tamarac
North Lauderdale
Terra Mar
98
Broadview-Pompano Park
Palm Aire
Sea Ranch Lakes

(12)

BROWARD
Village Park
Twin Lakes
N. Andrews Gardens
Lauderdale-by-the-Sea
Lauderdale Lakes
Oakland Park
Tamarac
Rock Island
Wilton Manors
West Ken-Lark
Lazy Lake
Lauderhill
Golden Hts.
Sunrise
Roosevelt Gardens
St. George
Franklin Park
Plantation
Washington Park
Broward Estates
Boulevard Gardens
Fort Lauderdale
Melrose Park
Weston
Chula Vista
Pine Island Ridge
Broadview Park
Riverland Village
Ivanhoe Estates
Sunshine Acres
Davie
Green Meadow
Ivanhoe Estates
Country Estates
Cooper City
Dania Beach
Rolling Oaks
Sunshine Ranches
Chambers Estates
Ravenswood Estates
Royal Palm Ranches
Oak Point
Estates of Fort Lauderdale
Hollywood
Pembroke Pines
Carver Ranches
Hallandale
Miramar
Utopia
Pembroke Park
98
Miami Gardens
Lake Forest
Sunny Isles Beach
Lake Lucerne
Andover
Ives Estates
Golden Beach
Country Club
Norland
Ojus
Aventura
MIAMI-DADE
Carol City
Scott Lake
Palm Springs North
Opa-locka North
North Miami Beach
Bunche Park
Miami Lakes
Opa-Locka
Golden Glades
North Miami
Biscayne Park
Bal Harbour
Bay Harbor Islands
Westview
Indian Creek
Surfside
Hialeah Gardens
Hialeah
Pinewood
Miami Shores
West Little River
El Portal
North Bay Village
Medley
Gladeview
Doral
Miami Springs
Virginia Gardens
Fountainbleau
Miami
Miami Beach
Sweetwater
Westchester
West Miami
Fisher Island
Tamiami
Coral Terrace
University Park
Westwood Lakes
Olympia Heights
Coral Gables
Glenvar Heights
Kendall West
Sunset
South Miami
Kendale Lakes
Key Biscayne
Kendall
The Hammocks
The Crossings
Pinecrest
Three Lakes
Country Walk
Richmond Heights
Palmetto Estates
Cutler
Richmond West
West Perrine
East Perrine
Atlantic Ocean
South Miami Heights
Cutler Ridge
Lakes by the Bay
Goulds
Princeton
Naranja
Homestead Base
Leisure City
183
Homestead

0 5 10 Mi
0 5 10 Km

COUNTIES

(67 Counties)

Name of County	Population	Location on Map
ALACHUA	217,955	F-9
BAKER	22,259	C-10
BAY	148,217	L-6
BRADFORD	26,088	E-10
BREVARD	476,230	K-15
BROWARD	1,623,018	S-13
CALHOUN	13,017	C-1
CHARLOTTE	141,627	P-10
CITRUS	118,085	I-10
CLAY	140,814	E-11
COLLIER	251,377	R-12
COLUMBIA	56,513	D-9
DE SOTO	32,209	O-9
DIXIE	13,827	F-7
DUVAL	778,879	C-12
ESCAMBIA	294,410	J-1
FLAGLER	49,832	G-13
FRANKLIN	11,057	E-2
GADSDEN	45,087	C-3
GILCHRIST	14,437	F-8
GLADES	10,576	P-11
GULF	13,332	D-1
HAMILTON	13,327	C-8
HARDEE	26,938	N-9
HENDRY	36,210	Q-11
HERNANDO	130,802	J-9
HIGHLANDS	87,366	N-11
HILLSBOROUGH	998,948	K-10
HOLMES	18,564	J-6
INDIAN RIVER	112,947	M-15
JACKSON	46,755	B-1
JEFFERSON	12,902	C-5
LAFAYETTE	7,022	E-7
LAKE	210,528	J-12
LEE	440,888	Q-10
LEON	239,452	C-4
LEVY	34,450	F-9
LIBERTY	7,021	D-2
MADISON	18,733	D-6
MANATEE	264,002	N-8
MARION	258,916	H-10
MARTIN	126,731	O-14
MIAMI-DADE	2,253,362	S-13
MONROE	79,589	T-12
NASSAU	57,663	C-11
OKALOOSA	170,498	J-3
OKEECHOBEE	35,910	N-12
ORANGE	896,344	K-14
OSCEOLA	172,493	L-13
PALM BEACH	1,131,184	P-14
PASCO	344,765	K-11
PINELLAS	921,482	M-9
POLK	483,924	K-12
PUTNAM	70,423	F-12
SAINT JOHNS	123,135	D-13
SAINT LUCIE	192,695	N-14
SANTA ROSA	117,743	J-2
SARASOTA	325,957	O-8
SEMINOLE	365,196	I-14
SUMTER	53,345	I-11
SUWANNEE	34,844	D-8
TAYLOR	19,256	D-6
UNION	13,442	D-10
VOLUSIA	443,343	G-12
WAKULLA	22,863	D-3
WALTON	40,601	J-5
WASHINGTON	20,973	K-6
TOTAL	**15,982,378**	

CITIES AND TOWNS

Note: The first name is that of the city or town, second, that of the county in which it is located, then the population and location on the map.

Alachua, *Alachua*, 6,098 ....F-10
Altamonte Springs, *Seminole*, 41,200 ....J-13
•Alva, *Lee*, 2,182 ....V-5
•Andover, *Miami-Dade*, 8,489 ....RR-14
Anna Maria, *Manatee*, 1,814 ....N-1
Apalachicola, *Franklin*, 2,334 ....F-2
•Apollo Beach, *Hillsborough*, 7,444 ....LL-5
Apopka, *Orange*, 26,642 ....DD-4
Arcadia, *De Soto*, 6,604 ....O-10
Archer, *Alachua*, 1,289 ....G-10
•Asbury Lake, *Clay*, 2,228 ....E-12
Astatula, *Lake*, 1,298 ....I-12
•Astor, *Lake*, 1,487 ....H-13
Atlantic Beach, *Duval*, 13,368 ....D-13
Atlantis, *Palm Beach*, 2,005 ....TT-7
Auburndale, *Polk*, 11,032 ....II-9
Aventura, *Miami-Dade*, 25,267 ....RR-16
Avon Park, *Highlands*, 8,542 ....M-13
•Azalea Park, *Orange*, 11,073 ....EE-5
•Babson Park, *Polk*, 1,182 ....M-13
•Bagdad, *Santa Rosa*, 1,490 ....K-3
Bal Harbour, *Miami-Dade*, 3,305 ....RR-16
Baldwin, *Duval*, 1,634 ....D-11
Bartow, *Polk*, 15,340 ....L-12
Bay Harbor Islands,
Miami-Dade, 5,146 ....SS-16
•Bay Hill, *Orange*, 5,177 ....EE-4
•Bay Pines, *Pinellas*, 3,065 ....KK-2
•Bayonet Point, *Pasco*, 23,577 ....K-9
Bayshore Gardens, *Manatee*, 17,350 ....N-8
•Beacon Square, *Pasco*, 7,263 ....HH-2
•Bee Ridge, *Sarasota*, 8,744 ....P-3
•Bellair-Meadowbrook Terrace,
Clay, 16,539 ....D-12
Belle Glade, *Palm Beach*, 14,906 ....Q-13
•Belle Glade Camp, *Palm Beach*, 1,141 .Q-13
Belle Isle, *Orange*, 5,531 ....J-13
Belleair, *Pinellas*, 4,067 ....JJ-2
Belleair Beach, *Pinellas*, 1,751 ....KK-2
Belleair Bluffs, *Pinellas*, 2,243 ....KK-2
Belleview, *Marion*, 3,478 ....H-11
•Bellview, *Escambia*, 21,201 ....K-2
•Beverly Hills, *Citrus*, 8,317 ....I-10
•Big Coppitt Key, *Monroe*, 2,595 ....X-10
•Big Pine Key, *Monroe*, 5,032 ....X-11
Biscayne Park, *Miami-Dade*, 3,269 ....SS-15
•Bithlo, *Orange*, 4,626 ....EE-7
•Bloomingdale, *Hillsborough*, 19,839 ....L-11
Blountstown, *Calhoun*, 2,444 ....C-2
•Boca Del Mar, *Palm Beach*, 21,832 ....XX-7
•Boca Pointe, *Palm Beach*, 3,302 ....XX-6
Boca Raton, *Palm Beach*, 74,764 ....R-15
•Bokeelia, *Lee*, 1,997 ....V-1
Bonifay, *Holmes*, 4,078 ....J-7
Bonita Springs, *Lee*, 32,797 ....R-10
•Bonnie Lock-Woodstetter North,
Broward, 4,275 ....YY-7
•Boulevard Gardens, *Broward*, 1,415 ...OO-15
Bowling Green, *Hardee*, 2,892 ....M-12
•Boyette, *Hillsborough*, 5,895 ....M-11
Boynton Beach, *Palm Beach*, 60,389 ....Q-15
Bradenton, *Manatee*, 49,504 ....N-8
Bradenton Beach, *Manatee*, 1,482 ....O-1
•Brandon, *Hillsborough*, 77,895 ....L-10
•Brent, *Escambia*, 22,257 ....K-2
Bristol, *Liberty*, 845 ....C-2
•Broadview Park, *Broward*, 6,798 ....OO-14
•Broadview-Pompano Park,
Broward, 5,314 ....ZZ-6
Bronson, *Levy*, 964 ....G-9
•Brookridge, *Hernando*, 3,279 ....J-10
Brooksville, *Hernando*, 7,264 ....J-10
•Broward Estates, *Broward*, 3,416 ....OO-15
•Brownsville, *Escambia*, 14,393 ....H-2
•Buckhead Ridge, *Glades*, 1,390 ....O-13
•Buckingham, *Lee*, 3,742 ....V-4
•Bunche Park, *Miami-Dade*, 3,972 ....RR-14
Bunnell, *Flagler*, 2,122 ....G-14
•Burnt Store Marina, *Lee*, 1,271 ....P-9
Bushnell, *Sumter*, 2,050 ....J-11
•Butler Beach, *St. Johns*, 4,436 ....F-13
Callaway, *Bay*, 14,233 ....M-7
•Campbell, *Osceola*, 2,677 ....K-13
Cape Canaveral, *Brevard*, 8,829 ....K-16
Cape Coral, *Lee*, 102,286 ....Q-10
•Carol City, *Miami-Dade*, 59,443 ....S-15
Carrabelle, *Franklin*, 1,303 ....E-3
•Carver Ranches, *Broward*, 4,299 ....QQ-15
Casselberry, *Seminole*, 22,629 ....J-13
Cedar Grove, *Bay*, 5,367 ....H-7
•Celebration, *Osceola*, 2,736 ....K-13
Century, *Escambia*, 1,714 ....J-2
•Century Village, *Palm Beach*, 7,616 ....Q-15
•Charlotte Harbor, *Charlotte*, 3,647 ....T-7
•Charlotte Park, *Charlotte*, 2,182 ....P-9
Chattahoochee, *Gadsden*, 3,287 ....B-3
•Cheval, *Hillsborough*, 7,602 ....II-4
Chiefland, *Levy*, 1,993 ....G-9
Chipley, *Washington*, 3,592 ....J-7
•Christmas, *Orange*, 1,162 ....J-14
•Chuluota, *Seminole*, 1,921 ....DD-7
•Citrus Hills, *Citrus*, 4,029 ....I-10
•Citrus Park, *Hillsborough*, 20,226 ....II-4
•Citrus Springs, *Citrus*, 4,157 ....H-10
Clearwater, *Pinellas*, 108,787 ....L-9
Clermont, *Lake*, 9,333 ....J-12
•Cleveland, *Charlotte*, 3,268 ....P-9
Clewiston, *Hendry*, 6,460 ....P-13
Cocoa, *Brevard*, 16,412 ....K-15
Cocoa Beach, *Brevard*, 12,482 ....K-16
•Cocoa West, *Brevard*, 5,921 ....BB-8
•Coconut Creek, *Brevard*, 43,566 ....ZZ-6
•Collier Manor-Cresthaven,
Broward, 7,741 ....YY-7
•Combee Settlement, *Polk*, 5,436 ....II-8
•Conway, *Orange*, 14,394 ....J-13
Cooper City, *Broward*, 27,939 ....PP-14
Coral Gables, *Miami-Dade*, 42,249 ....UU-14
Coral Springs, *Washington*, 117,549 ....R-15
•Coral Terrace, *Miami-Dade*, 24,380 ....UU-13
•Cortez, *Manatee*, 4,491 ....O-1
•Country Club, *Miami-Dade*, 36,310 ....RR-13
•Country Walk, *Miami-Dade*, 10,653 ....T-14
Crawfordville, *Wakulla*, 1,110 ....D-4
Crescent City, *Putnam*, 1,776 ....G-13
Crestview, *Okaloosa*, 14,766 ....J-4
•Crooked Lake Park, *Polk*, 1,682 ....M-13
Cross City, *Dixie*, 1,775 ....F-8
•Crystal Lake, *Washington*, 5,341 ....K-7
Crystal River, *Citrus*, 3,485 ....I-10
•Crystal Springs, *Pasco*, 1,175 ....HH-7
•Cudjoe Key, *Monroe*, 1,695 ....X-11
•Cutler, *Miami-Dade*, 17,390 ....U-15
•Cutler Ridge, *Miami-Dade*, 24,781 ....XX-12
•Cypress Gardens, *Polk*, 8,844 ....L-12
•Cypress Lake, *Lee*, 12,072 ....Q-10
•Cypress Lakes, *Palm Beach*, 1,468 ....QQ-7
•Cypress Quarters, *Okeechobee*, 1,150 ..O-13
Dade City, *Pasco*, 6,188 ....K-11
•Dade City North, *Pasco*, 3,319 ....J-11
Dania Beach, *Broward*, 20,061 ....PP-15
Davenport, *Polk*, 1,924 ....K-13
Davie, *Broward*, 75,720 ....S-15
Daytona Beach, *Volusia*, 64,112 ....H-14
Daytona Beach Shores, *Volusia*, 4,299 ..H-14
De Bary, *Volusia*, 15,559 ....BB-5
De Funiak Springs, *Walton*, 5,089 ....J-5
De Land, *Volusia*, 20,904 ....H-13
•De Land Southwest, *Volusia*, 1,169 ....I-13
•De Leon Springs, *Volusia*, 2,358 ....H-13
Deerfield Beach, *Broward*, 64,583 ....R-15
Delray Beach, *Palm Beach*, 60,020 ....Q-15
Deltona, *Volusia*, 69,543 ....I-14
•Desoto Lakes, *Sarasota*, 3,198 ....P-3
Destin, *Okaloosa*, 11,119 ....I-4
•Doctor Phillips, *Orange*, 9,548 ....J-13
•Doral, *Miami-Dade*, 20,438 ....TT-12
•Dover, *Hillsborough*, 2,798 ....JJ-6
Dundee, *Polk*, 2,912 ....JJ-10
Dunedin, *Pinellas*, 35,691 ....L-9
Dunnellon, *Marion*, 1,898 ....H-10
Eagle Lake, *Polk*, 2,496 ....JJ-9
•East Bronson, *Levy*, 1,075 ....G-9
•East Lake, *Pinellas*, 29,394 ....L-9
•East Lake-Orient Park,
Hillsborough, 5,703 ....JJ-5
•East Palatka, *Putnam*, 1,707 ....F-12
•East Perrine, *Miami-Dade*, 7,079 ....U-15
•Eastpoint, *Franklin*, 2,158 ....F-3
Eatonville, *Orange*, 2,432 ....DD-5
Edgewater, *Volusia*, 18,668 ....H-15
Edgewood, *Orange*, 1,901 ....EE-5
•Eglin AFB, *Okaloosa*, 8,082 ....K-4
•Egypt Lake-Leto, *Hillsborough*, 32,782 ....JJ-4
•El Portal, *Miami-Dade*, 2,505 ....TT-15
•Elfers, *Pasco*, 13,161 ....K-9
•Ellenton, *Manatee*, 3,142 ....N-3
•Englewood, *Sarasota*, 16,196 ....P-8
•Ensley, *Escambia*, 18,752 ....K-2
•Estero, *Lee*, 9,503 ....X-3
Eustis, *Lake*, 15,106 ....I-12
•Fairview Shores, *Orange*, 13,898 ....J-13
•Feather Sound, *Pinellas*, 3,597 ....II-3
Fellsmere, *Indian River*, 3,813 ....M-16
•Fern Park, *Seminole*, 8,318 ....DD-5
Fernandina Beach, *Nassau*, 10,549 ....B-13
•Ferry Pass, *Escambia*, 27,176 ....K-2
•Fish Hawk, *Hillsborough*, 1,991 ....M-11
•Five Points, *Columbia*, 1,362 ....D-9
Flagler Beach, *Flagler*, 4,954 ....G-14
•Floral City, *Citrus*, 4,989 ....I-10
Florida City, *Miami-Dade*, 7,843 ....U-14
•Florida Ridge, *Indian River*, 15,217 ....M-16
•Forest City, *Seminole*, 12,612 ....DD-5
Fort Lauderdale, *Broward*, 152,397 ....S-15
Fort Meade, *Polk*, 5,691 ....M-12
Fort Myers, *Lee*, 48,208 ....Q-10
Fort Myers Beach, *Lee*, 6,561 ....R-10
•Fort Myers Shores, *Lee*, 5,793 ....Q-10
Fort Pierce, *Saint Lucie*, 37,516 ....N-15
•Fort Pierce North, *St. Lucie*, 7,386 ....N-14
•Fort Pierce South, *St. Lucie*, 5,672 ....N-14
Fort Walton Beach, *Okaloosa*, 19,973 ....H-4
•Fountainbleau, *Miami-Dade*, 59,549 ....T-15
Freeport, *Walton*, 1,190 ....K-5
Frostproof, *Polk*, 2,975 ....M-13
•Fruit Cove, *St. Johns*, 16,077 ....D-12
Fruitland Park, *Lake*, 3,186 ....I-12
•Fruitville, *Sarasota*, 12,741 ....N-8
•Fussels Corner, *Polk*, 5,313 ....L-12
Gainesville, *Alachua*, 95,447 ....F-10
•Gandy, *Pinellas*, 2,031 ....KK-3
•Gateway, *Lee*, 2,943 ....Q-10
•Geneva, *Seminole*, 2,601 ....CC-7
•Gibsonia, *Polk*, 4,507 ....II-8
•Gibsonton, *Hillsborough*, 8,752 ....L-10
•Gifford, *Indian River*, 7,599 ....M-16
•Gladeview, *Miami-Dade*, 14,468 ....TT-14
•Glencoe, *Volusia*, 2,485 ....H-14
•Glenvar Heights,
Miami-Dade, 16,243 ....VV-13
•Golden Gate, *Collier*, 20,951 ....S-10
•Golden Glades, *Miami-Dade*, 32,623 ...SS-15
•Golden Lakes, *Palm Beach*, 6,694 ....RR-6
•Goldenrod, *Seminole*, 12,871 ....DD-5
•Gonzalez, *Escambia*, 11,365 ....K-2
•Goulding, *Escambia*, 4,484 ....H-2
•Goulds, *Miami-Dade*, 7,453 ....U-14
Graceville, *Jackson*, 2,402 ....A-1
•Greater Carrollwood,
Hillsborough, 33,519 ....JJ-4
•Greater Northdale, *Hillsborough*, 20,461 ..II-5
•Greater Sun Center,
Hillsborough, 16,321 ....M-10
Green Cove Springs, *Clay*, 5,378 ....E-12
Greenacres, *Palm Beach*, 27,569 ....Q-15
Gretna, *Gadsden*, 1,709 ....C-3
•Grove City, *Charlotte*, 2,092 ....T-4
Groveland, *Lake*, 2,360 ....EE-2
Gulf Breeze, *Santa Rosa*, 5,665 ....L-2
•Gulf Gate Estates, *Sarasota*, 11,647 ....O-8
Gulfport, *Pinellas*, 12,527 ....M-9
Haines City, *Polk*, 13,174 ....L-13
Hallandale, *Broward*, 34,282 ....QQ-16
•Hamptons At Boca Raton,
Palm Beach, 11,306 ....WW-6
•Harbor Bluffs, *Pinellas*, 2,807 ....L-9
•Harbour Heights, *Charlotte*, 2,873 ....P-9
•Harlem, *Hendry*, 2,730 ....Q-13
•Harlem Heights, *Lee*, 1,065 ....W-3
Havana, *Gadsden*, 1,713 ....C-4
Haverhill, *Palm Beach*, 1,454 ....RR-7
Hawthorne, *Alachua*, 1,415 ....F-11
•Heathrow, *Seminole*, 4,068 ....CC-5
•Hernando, *Citrus*, 8,253 ....I-10
•Hernando Beach, *Hernando*, 2,185 ....DD-13
Hialeah, *Miami-Dade*, 226,419 ....T-15
Hialeah Gardens,
Miami-Dade, 19,297 ....TT-13
•High Point, *Palm Beach*, 2,191 ....VV-7
High Springs, *Alachua*, 3,863 ....E-9
Highland Beach, *Palm Beach*, 3,775 ....WW-8
•Highland City, *Polk*, 2,051 ....JJ-9
Hilliard, *Nassau*, 2,702 ....B-12
Hillsboro Beach, *Broward*, 2,163 ....YY-7
•Hobe Sound, *Martin*, 11,376 ....O-15
•Holden Heights, *Orange*, 3,856 ....EE-5
•Holiday, *Pasco*, 21,904 ....HH-3
•Holiday, *Pasco*, 21,904 ....K-9
Holly Hill, *Volusia*, 12,119 ....H-14
Hollywood, *Broward*, 139,357 ....S-15
Holmes Beach, *Manatee*, 4,966 ....N-7
Homestead, *Miami-Dade*, 31,909 ....U-14
•Homosassa, *Citrus*, 2,294 ....I-9
•Homosassa Springs, *Citrus*, 12,458 ....I-10
•Hudson, *Pasco*, 12,765 ....K-9
•Hunters Creek, *Orange*, 9,369 ....K-13
•Hutchinson Island South,
St. Lucie, 4,846 ....Y-16
Hypoluxo, *Palm Beach*, 2,015 ....TT-8
•Immokalee, *Collier*, 19,763 ....R-11
Indialantic, *Brevard*, 2,944 ....L-16
Indian Harbour Beach, *Brevard*, 8,152 ....K-16
•Indian River Estates, *St. Lucie*, 5,793 ....N-15
Indian River Shores,
Indian River, 3,448 ....M-16
Indian Rocks Beach, *Pinellas*, 5,072 ....L-9
Indian Shores, *Pinellas*, 1,705 ....KK-2
•Indiantown, *Martin*, 5,588 ....P-14
Inglis, *Levy*, 1,491 ....H-9
Interlachen, *Putnam*, 1,475 ....F-12
Inverness, *Citrus*, 6,789 ....I-10
•Inverness Highlands South,
Citrus, 5,781 ....AA-15
•Inwood, *Polk*, 6,925 ....L-12
•Iona, *Lee*, 11,756 ....W-2
Islamorada, *Monroe*, 6,846 ....W-14
•Ives Estates, *Miami-Dade*, 17,586 ....RR-15
Jacksonville, *Duval*, 735,617 ....D-12
Jacksonville Beach, *Duval*, 20,990 ....D-13
•Jasmine Estates, *Pasco*, 18,213 ....K-9
Jasper, *Hamilton*, 1,780 ....C-8
•Jensen Beach, *Martin*, 11,100 ....O-15
•June Park, *Brevard*, 4,367 ....FF-9
Juno Beach, *Palm Beach*, 3,262 ....P-15
Jupiter, *Palm Beach*, 39,328 ....P-15
•Kathleen, *Polk*, 3,280 ....II-8
•Kendale Lakes, *Miami-Dade*, 56,901 ....T-14
•Kendall, *Miami-Dade*, 75,226 ....T-15
•Kendall Green, *Broward*, 3,084 ....YY-7
•Kendall West, *Miami-Dade*, 38,034 ....WW-11
Kenneth City, *Pinellas*, 4,400 ....LL-3
•Kensington Park, *Sarasota*, 3,720 ....P-3
•Key Biscayne, *Miami-Dade*, 10,507 ....VV-15
•Key Largo, *Monroe*, 11,886 ....V-14
Key West, *Monroe*, 25,478 ....X-10
•Keystone, *Hillsborough*, 14,627 ....II-3
Keystone Heights, *Clay*, 1,349 ....F-11
•Kings Point, *Palm Beach*, 12,207 ....R-15
Kissimmee, *Osceola*, 47,814 ....K-13
La Belle, *Hendry*, 2,703 ....P-11
•Lacoochee, *Pasco*, 1,345 ....J-11
Lady Lake, *Lake*, 11,828 ....I-12
•Laguna Beach, *Bay*, 2,909 ....L-6
Lake Alfred, *Polk*, 3,890 ....II-10
•Lake Belvedere Estates,
Palm Beach, 1,525 ....RR-7
Lake Butler, *Union*, 1,927 ....E-10
•Lake Butter, *Orange*, 7,062 ....EE-4
Lake City, *Columbia*, 9,980 ....D-9
Lake Clarke Shores,
Palm Beach, 3,451 ....SS-8
•Lake Forest, *Broward*, 4,994 ....RR-15
Lake Hamilton, *Polk*, 1,304 ....JJ-10
Lake Helen, *Volusia*, 2,743 ....H-14
•Lake Lorraine, *Okaloosa*, 7,106 ....H-4
•Lake Lucerne, *Miami-Dade*, 9,132 ....RR-14
•Lake Magdalene, *Hillsborough*, 28,755 ....II-4
Lake Mary, *Seminole*, 11,458 ....I-13
•Lake Panasoffkee, *Sumter*, 3,413 ....I-11
Lake Park, *Palm Beach*, 8,721 ....PP-8
Lake Placid, *Highlands*, 1,668 ....O-11

Explanation of symbols: • - Census Designated Place (CDP)

•Lake Sarasota, *Sarasota*, 4,458 ....P-3
Lake Wales, *Polk*, 10,194 ....L-13
Lake Worth, *Palm Beach*, 35,133 ....Q-15
•Lake Worth Corridor,
Palm Beach, 18,663 ....SS-7
Lakeland, *Polk*, 78,452 ....L-12
•Lakeland Highlands, *Polk*, 12,557 ....L-11
•Lakes By The Bay,
Miami-Dade, 9,055 ....XX-13
•Lakeside, *Clay*, 30,927 ....D-12
•Lakeside Green, *Palm Beach*, 3,311 ....QQ-7
•Lakewood Park, *St. Lucie*, 10,458 ....N-14
•Land O'Lakes, *Pasco*, 20,971 ....K-10
Lantana, *Palm Beach*, 9,437 ....Q-15
Largo, *Pinellas*, 69,371 ....L-9
Lauderdale Lakes, *Broward*, 31,705 ....NN-15
•Lauderdale-By-The-Sea,
Broward, 2,563 ....NN-16
Lauderhill, *Broward*, 57,585 ....OO-14
•Laurel, *Sarasota*, 8,393 ....O-8
•Lecanto, *Citrus*, 5,161 ....I-10
Leesburg, *Lake*, 15,956 ....I-12
•Lehigh Acres, *Lee*, 33,430 ....Q-11
•Leisure City, *Miami-Dade*, 22,152 ....U-14
•Leisureville, *Broward*, 1,147 ....YY-7
•Lely, *Collier*, 3,857 ....Z-4
•Lely Resort, *Collier*, 1,426 ....S-10
Lighthouse Point, *Broward*, 10,767 ....YY-8
Live Oak, *Suwannee*, 6,480 ....D-8
•Lochmoor Waterway Estates, *Lee*, 3,858 .V-3
•Lockhart, *Orange*, 12,944 ....J-13
Longboat Key, *Manatee*, 7,603 ....N-7
Longwood, *Seminole*, 13,745 ....CC-5
•Loughman, *Polk*, 1,385 ....K-13
•Lower Grand Lagoon, *Bay*, 4,082 ....H-5
•Lutz, *Hillsborough*, 17,081 ....K-10
Lynn Haven, *Bay*, 12,451 ....L-7
Macclenny, *Baker*, 4,459 ....D-11
Madeira Beach, *Pinellas*, 4,511 ....LL-2
Madison, *Madison*, 3,061 ....C-7
•Magnonia Park, *Palm Beach*, 1,283 ....QQ-8
Maitland, *Orange*, 12,019 ....DD-5
Malabar, *Brevard*, 2,622 ....L-16
Malone, *Jackson*, 2,007 ....A-2
•Manasota Key, *Charlotte*, 1,345 ....T-4
•Manattee Road, *Levy*, 1,937 ....G-9
•Mango, *Hillsborough*, 8,842 ....JJ-6
Marathon, *Monroe*, 10,255 ....X-12
Marco Island, *Collier*, 14,879 ....S-10
Margate, *Broward*, 53,909 ....ZZ-6
Marianna, *Jackson*, 6,230 ....B-2
Mary Esther, *Okaloosa*, 4,055 ....L-4
Mascotte, *Lake*, 2,687 ....DD-1
Mayo, *Lafayette*, 988 ....E-8
•McGregor, *Lee*, 7,136 ....W-3
•Meadow Woods, *Orange*, 11,286 ....EE-5
Medley, *Miami-Dade*, 1,098 ....TT-13
•Medulla, *Polk*, 6,637 ....JJ-8
Melbourne, *Brevard*, 71,382 ....L-16
Melbourne Beach, *Brevard*, 3,335 ....L-16
•Melrose Park, *Broward*, 7,114 ....OO-15
•Memphis, *Manatee*, 7,264 ....N-2
•Merritt Island, *Brevard*, 36,090 ....K-15
Mexico Beach, *Bay*, 1,017 ....M-7
Miami, *Miami-Dade*, 362,470 ....T-15
Miami Beach, *Miami-Dade*, 87,933 ....T-15
•Miami Gardens, *Broward*, 2,706 ....QQ-15
•Miami Lakes, *Miami-Dade*, 22,676 ....SS-13
Miami Shores, *Miami-Dade*, 10,380 ....TT-15
Miami Springs, *Miami-Dade*, 13,712 ....TT-13
•Micco, *Brevard*, 9,498 ....L-16
•Middleburg, *Clay*, 10,338 ....E-12
Midway, *Gadsden*, 1,446 ....C-4
•Midway, *Seminole*, 1,714 ....CC-6
Milton, *Santa Rosa*, 7,045 ....K-3
•Mims, *Brevard*, 9,147 ....J-15
Minneola, *Lake*, 5,435 ....J-12
Miramar, *Broward*, 72,739 ....S-15
•Miramar Beach, *Walton*, 2,435 ....L-5
•Mission Bay, *Palm Beach*, 2,926 ....WW-6
•Molino, *Escambia*, 1,312 ....J-2
Monticello, *Jefferson*, 2,533 ....C-6
Moore Haven, *Glades*, 1,635 ....P-12
Mount Dora, *Lake*, 9,418 ....CC-3
•Mount Plymouth, *Lake*, 2,814 ....CC-4
Mulberry, *Polk*, 3,230 ....KK-8
•Myrtle Grove, *Escambia*, 17,211 ....L-2
Naples, *Collier*, 20,976 ....S-10
•Naples Manor, *Collier*, 5,186 ....S-10
•Naples Park, *Collier*, 6,741 ....R-10
•Naranja, *Miami-Dade*, 4,034 ....YY-11
•Nassau Village-Ratliff, *Nassau*, 4,633 ....C-12
Neptune Beach, *Duval*, 7,270 ....D-13
New Port Richey, *Pasco*, 16,117 ....K-9
•New Port Richey East, *Pasco*, 9,916 ....HH-3
New Smyrna Beach, *Volusia*, 20,048 ....H-15
Newberry, *Alachua*, 3,316 ....F-9
Niceville, *Okaloosa*, 11,684 ....K-4
•Nokomis, *Sarasota*, 3,334 ....R-3
•Norland, *Miami-Dade*, 22,995 ....RR-14
•North Andrews Gardens,
Broward, 9,656 ....NN-15
North Bay Village, *Miami-Dade*, 6,733 ..TT-15
•North Brooksville, *Hernando*, 1,461 ....J-10
•North De Land, *Volusia*, 1,327 ....H-13
•North Fort Myers, *Lee*, 40,214 ....Q-10
•North Key Largo, *Monroe*, 1,049 ....V-15
North Lauderdale, *Broward*, 32,264 ....ZZ-5
North Miami, *Miami-Dade*, 59,880 ....T-15
North Miami Beach,
Miami-Dade, 40,786 ....RR-15
North Palm Beach,
Palm Beach, 12,064 ....P-15
North Port, *Sarasota*, 22,797 ....O-9
North Redington Beach, *Pinellas*, 1,474 KK-2
•North River Shores, *Martin*, 3,101 ....Z-16
•North Sarasota, *Sarasota*, 6,738 ....N-8
•North Weeki Wachee,
Hernando, 4,253 ....CC-14
Oak Hill, *Volusia*, 1,378 ....I-15
•Oak Ridge, *Orange*, 22,349 ....J-13
Oakland Park, *Broward*, 30,966 ....NN-16
Ocala, *Marion*, 45,943 ....H-11
•Ocean City, *Okaloosa*, 5,594 ....H-3
Ocean Ridge, *Palm Beach*, 1,636 ....UU-8
Ocoee, *Orange*, 24,391 ....EE-4
•Odessa, *Pasco*, 3,173 ....HH-4
•Ojus, *Miami-Dade*, 16,642 ....RR-15
Okeechobee, *Okeechobee*, 5,376 ....O-13
Oldsmar, *Pinellas*, 11,910 ....JJ-3
•Olga, *Lee*, 1,398 ....V-4
•Olympia Heights, *Miami-Dade*, 13,452 .VV-12
Opa-Locka, *Miami-Dade*, 14,951 ....SS-14
•Opa-Locka North, *Miami-Dade*, 6,224 .RR-14
Orange City, *Volusia*, 6,604 ....I-13
Orange Park, *Clay*, 9,081 ....D-12
Orlando, *Orange*, 185,951 ....J-13
•Orlovista, *Orange*, 6,047 ....EE-4
Ormond Beach, *Volusia*, 36,301 ....G-14
•Ormond-By-The-Sea, *Volusia*, 8,430 ....G-14
•Osprey, *Sarasota*, 4,143 ....O-8
Oviedo, *Seminole*, 26,316 ....J-14
•Pace, *Santa Rosa*, 7,393 ....K-2
Pahokee, *Palm Beach*, 5,985 ....P-13
Palatka, *Putnam*, 10,033 ....F-12
•Palm Aire, *Broward*, 1,539 ....ZZ-6
Palm Bay, *Brevard*, 79,413 ....L-16
Palm Beach, *Palm Beach*, 10,468 ....Q-15
Palm Beach Gardens,
Palm Beach, 35,058 ....P-15
Palm Beach Shores,
Palm Beach, 1,269 ....PP-8
•Palm City, *Martin*, 20,097 ....O-15
Palm Coast, *Flagler*, 32,732 ....F-14
•Palm Harbor, *Pinellas*, 59,248 ....L-9
•Palm River-Claire Mel,
Hillsborough, 17,589 ....JJ-5
Palm Springs, *Palm Beach*, 11,699 ....SS-7
•Palm Springs North,
Miami-Dade, 5,460 ....RR-13
•Palm Valley, *St. Johns*, 19,860 ....D-13
Palmetto, *Manatee*, 12,571 ....N-8
•Palmetto Estates,
Miami-Dade, 13,675 ....XX-12
•Palmona Park, *Lee*, 1,353 ....V-3
Panama City, *Bay*, 36,417 ....L-7
Panama City Beach, *Bay*, 7,671 ....L-6
•Paradise Heights, *Orange*, 1,310 ....DD-4
Parker, *Bay*, 4,623 ....M-7
Parkland, *Broward*, 13,835 ....YY-5
•Pebble Creek, *Hillsborough*, 4,824 ....II-5
•Pelican Bay, *Collier*, 5,686 ....R-10
Pembroke Park, *Broward*, 6,299 ....QQ-15
Pembroke Pines, *Broward*, 137,427 ....S-15
Pensacola, *Escambia*, 56,255 ....L-2
Perry, *Taylor*, 6,847 ....D-7
Pierson, *Volusia*, 2,596 ....H-13
•Pine Castle, *Orange*, 8,803 ....EE-5
•Pine Hills, *Orange*, 41,764 ....J-13
•Pine Island Center, *Lee*, 1,721 ....V-1
•Pine Island Ridge, *Broward*, 5,199 ....PP-14
•Pine Manor, *Lee*, 3,785 ....W-3
•Pine Ridge, *Citrus*, 5,490 ....I-10
Pinecrest, *Miami-Dade*, 19,055 ....WW-13
Pinellas Park, *Pinellas*, 45,658 ....KK-3
•Pinewood, *Miami-Dade*, 16,523 ....SS-14
•Placid Lakes, *Highlands*, 3,054 ....O-11
Plant City, *Hillsborough*, 29,915 ....L-11
Plantation, *Broward*, 82,934 ....S-15
Plantation, *Sarasota*, 4,168 ....S-4
•Plantation Mobile Home Park,
Palm Beach, 1,218 ....RR-7
•Poinciana, *Osceola*, 13,647 ....K-13
Polk City, *Polk*, 1,516 ....K-12
Pompano Beach, *Broward*, 78,191 ....R-15
•Pompano Beach Highlands,
Broward, 6,505 ....YY-7
Ponce Inlet, *Volusia*, 2,513 ....H-15
•Port Charlotte, *Charlotte*, 46,451 ....P-9
•Port La Belle, *Hendry*, 3,050 ....P-11
Port Orange, *Volusia*, 45,823 ....H-14
Port Richey, *Pasco*, 3,021 ....HH-3
Port Saint Joe, *Gulf*, 3,644 ....E-1
•Port Saint John, *Brevard*, 12,112 ....J-15
Port Saint Lucie, *Saint Lucie*, 88,769 ....N-15
•Port Saint Lucie-River Park,
St. Lucie, 5,175 ....N-14
•Port Salerno, *Martin*, 10,141 ....O-15
•Pretty Bayou, *Pinellas*, 3,519 ....L-7
•Princeton, *Miami-Dade*, 10,090 ....U-14
•Progress Village, *Hillsborough*, 2,482 ....KK-5
Punta Gorda, *Charlotte*, 14,344 ....P-9
•Punta Rassa, *Lee*, 1,731 ....W-2
Quincy, *Gadsden*, 6,982 ....C-4
Redington Beach, *Pinellas*, 1,539 ....M-9
Redington Shores, *Pinellas*, 2,338 ....M-9
•Richmond Heights,
Miami-Dade, 8,479 ....WW-12
•Richmond West, *Miami-Dade*, 28,082 ..XX-11
•Ridge Manor, *Hernando*, 4,108 ....J-11
•Ridge Wood Heights, *Sarasota*, 5,028 ....P-3
•Ridgecrest, *Pinellas*, 2,453 ....KK-2
•Rio, *Martin*, 1,028 ....Z-16
•Riverview, *Hillsborough*, 12,035 ....L-10
Riviera Beach, *Palm Beach*, 29,884 ....P-15
•Rock Island, *Broward*, 3,076 ....NN-15
Rockledge, *Brevard*, 20,170 ....K-15
•Roseland, *Indian River*, 1,775 ....M-16
•Rotonda, *Charlotte*, 6,574 ....P-8
Royal Palm Beach,
Palm Beach, 21,523 ....Q-15
•Royal Palm Estates,
Palm Beach, 3,583 ....RR-7
•Ruskin, *Hillsborough*, 8,321 ....LL-5
Safety Harbor, *Pinellas*, 17,203 ....JJ-3
Saint Augustine, *Saint Johns*, 11,592 ....E-13
Saint Augustine Beach,
Saint Johns, 4,683 ....E-13
•Saint Augustine Shores,
St. Johns, 4,922 ....F-13
•Saint Augustine South,
St. Johns, 5,035 ....E-13
Saint Cloud, *Osceola*, 20,074 ....K-13
•Saint George, *Broward*, 2,450 ....NN-15
Saint James City, *Lee*, 4,105 ....Q-9
Saint Pete Beach, *Pinellas*, 9,929 ....M-9
Saint Petersburg, *Pinellas*, 248,232 ....M-9
•Samoset, *Manatee*, 3,440 ....O-2
•Samsula-Spruce Creek, *Volusia*, 4,877 ..H-14
•San Carlos Park, *Lee*, 16,317 ....Q-10
•Sandalfoot Cove, *Palm Beach*, 16,582 ..XX-6
Sanford, *Seminole*, 38,291 ....I-14
Sanibel, *Lee*, 6,064 ....R-9
Sarasota, *Sarasota*, 52,715 ....N-8
•Sarasota Springs, *Sarasota*, 15,875 ....O-8
Satellite Beach, *Brevard*, 9,577 ....K-16
•Sawgrass, *St. Johns*, 4,942 ....D-13
•Scott Lake, *Miami-Dade*, 14,401 ....RR-14
Sea Ranch Lakes, *Broward*, 1,392 ....ZZ-7
Sebastian, *Indian River*, 16,181 ....M-16
Sebring, *Highlands*, 9,667 ....N-11
•Seffner, *Hillsborough*, 5,467 ....JJ-6
Seminole, *Pinellas*, 10,890 ....KK-2
•Seminole Manor, *Palm Beach*, 2,546 ....TT-7
Sewall's Point, *Martin*, 1,946 ....O-15
•Shady Hills, *Pasco*, 7,798 ....K-10
•Sharpes, *Brevard*, 3,415 ....J-15
•Siesta Key, *Sarasota*, 7,150 ....O-8
•Silver Lake, *Lake*, 1,882 ....BB-2
•Silver Springs Shores, *Marion*, 6,690 ....H-11
•Sky Lake, *Orange*, 5,651 ....EE-5
Sneads, *Jackson*, 1,919 ....B-3
•Solana, *Charlotte*, 1,011 ....T-7
•South Apopka, *Orange*, 5,800 ....DD-4
South Bay, *Palm Beach*, 3,859 ....Q-13
•South Beach, *Indian River*, 3,457 ....M-16
•South Bradenton, *Manatee*, 21,587 ....N-8
•South Brooksville, *Hernando*, 1,376 ....CC-15
South Daytona, *Volusia*, 13,177 ....H-14
•South Gate Ridge, *Sarasota*, 5,655 ....P-3
•South Highpoint, *Pinellas*, 8,839 ....KK-3
South Miami, *Miami-Dade*, 10,741 ....VV-13
•South Miami Heights,
Miami-Dade, 33,522 ....XX-12
South Pasadena, *Pinellas*, 5,778 ....LL-2
•South Patrick Shores, *Brevard*, 8,913 ....K-16
•South Sarasota, *Sarasota*, 5,314 ....P-3
•South Venice, *Sarasota*, 13,539 ....O-8
•Southchase, *Orange*, 4,633 ....FF-5
•Southeast Arcadia, *Desoto*, 6,064 ....O-10
•Southgate, *Sarasota*, 7,455 ....P-3
•Spring Hill, *Hernando*, 69,078 ....J-9
Springfield, *Bay*, 8,810 ....H-7
Starke, *Bradford*, 5,593 ....E-11
•Stock Island, *Monroe*, 4,410 ....X-10
Stuart, *Martin*, 14,633 ....O-15
•Sugarmill Woods, *Citrus*, 6,409 ....I-10
•Suncoast Estates, *Lee*, 4,867 ....Q-10
•Sunny Isles Beach,
Miami-Dade, 15,315 ....RR-16
Sunrise, *Broward*, 85,779 ....S-15
•Sunset, *Miami-Dade*, 17,150 ....VV-12
•Sunshine Ranches, *Broward*, 1,704 ....PP-13
Surfside, *Miami-Dade*, 4,909 ....SS-16
Sweetwater, *Miami-Dade*, 14,226 ....UU-12
•Sylvan Shores, *Highlands*, 2,424 ....N-11
•Taft, *Orange*, 1,938 ....FF-5
Tallahassee, *Leon*, 150,624 ....C-5
Tamarac, *Broward*, 55,588 ....R-15
•Tamiami, *Miami-Dade*, 54,788 ....T-14
Tampa, *Hillsborough*, 303,447 ....L-10
•Tangelo Park, *Orange*, 2,430 ....EE-4
Tarpon Springs, *Pinellas*, 21,003 ....K-9
Tavares, *Lake*, 9,700 ....CC-2
•Tavernier, *Monroe*, 2,173 ....W-14
•Taylor Creek, *Okeechobee*, 4,289 ....O-13
•Tedder, *Broward*, 2,079 ....YY-7
Temple Terrace, *Hillsborough*, 20,918 ....JJ-5
Tequesta, *Palm Beach*, 5,273 ....P-15
•Terra Mar, *Broward*, 2,631 ....ZZ-7
•The Crossings, *Miami-Dade*, 23,557 ..WW-12
•The Hammocks,
Miami-Dade, 47,379 ....WW-11
•The Meadows, *Sarasota*, 4,423 ....P-3
•The Villages, *Sumter*, 8,333 ....I-11
•Thonotosassa, *Hillsborough*, 6,091 ....II-6
•Three Lakes, *Miami-Dade*, 6,955 ....T-14
•Three Oaks, *Lee*, 2,255 ....W-3
•Tice, *Lee*, 4,538 ....Q-10
•Tierra Verde, *Pinellas*, 3,574 ....M-9
•Timber Pines, *Hernando*, 5,840 ....J-9
Titusville, *Brevard*, 40,670 ....J-15
•Town 'N' Country, *Hillsborough*, 72,523 ..L-10
Treasure Island, *Pinellas*, 7,450 ....M-9
Trenton, *Gilchrist*, 1,617 ....F-9
•Trinity, *Pasco*, 4,279 ....HH-3
•Twin Lakes, *Broward*, 1,875 ....NN-15
•Tyndall AFB, *Bay*, 2,757 ....M-7
Umatilla, *Lake*, 2,214 ....I-12
•Union Park, *Orange*, 10,191 ....EE-6
•University, *Hillsborough*, 30,736 ....JJ-5
•University Park, *Miami-Dade*, 26,538 ..UU-12
•Upper Grand Lagoon, *Bay*, 10,889 ....L-6
Valparaiso, *Okaloosa*, 6,408 ....K-4
•Valrico, *Hillsborough*, 6,582 ....JJ-6
•Varno, *Sarasota*, 5,285 ....O-8
Venice, *Sarasota*, 17,764 ....O-8
•Venice Gardens, *Sarasota*, 7,466 ....S-4
Vero Beach, *Indian River*, 17,705 ....M-16
•Vero Beach South,
Indian River, 20,362 ....M-16
•Villages of Oriole, *Palm Beach*, 4,758 ....VV-7
•Villano Beach, *St. Johns*, 2,533 ....E-13
•Villas, *Lee*, 11,346 ....Q-10
•Vineyards, *Collier*, 2,232 ....R-10
Virginia Gardens, *Miami-Dade*, 2,348 ...TT-13
•Wabasso Beach, *Indian River*, 1,075 ....M-16
•Wahneta, *Polk*, 4,731 ....JJ-10
•Warm Mineral Springs, *Sarasota*, 4,811 ...O-9
•Warrington, *Escambia*, 15,207 ....L-2
•Washington Park, *Broward*, 1,257 ....OO-15
•Watertown, *Columbia*, 2,837 ....D-9
Wauchula, *Hardee*, 4,368 ....N-10
•Waverly, *Polk*, 1,927 ....JJ-11
•Wedgefield, *Orange*, 2,700 ....EE-7
•Weeki Wachee Gardens,
Hernando, 1,140 ....J-9
•Wekiwa Springs, *Seminole*, 23,169 ....CC-5
Wellington, *Palm Beach*, 38,216 ....Q-15
•Wesley Chapel, *Pasco*, 5,691 ....HH-5
•Wesley Chapel South, *Pasco*, 3,245 ....HH-5
•West and East Lealman,
Pinellas, 21,753 ....KK-3
•West Bradenton, *Manatee*, 4,444 ....N-2
•West Chase, *Hillsborough*, 11,116 ....JJ-3
•West De Land, *Volusia*, 3,424 ....H-13
•West Little River, *Miami-Dade*, 32,498 .TT-14
West Melbourne, *Brevard*, 9,824 ....L-16
West Miami, *Miami-Dade*, 5,863 ....UU-13
West Palm Beach,
Palm Beach, 82,103 ....Q-15
•West Pensacola, *Escambia*, 21,939 ....H-2
•West Perrine, *Miami-Dade*, 8,600 ....XX-12
•West Samoset, *Manatee*, 5,507 ....O-2
•West Vero Corridor, *Indian River*, 7,695 .M-16
•Westchester, *Miami-Dade*, 30,271 ....UU-13
•Westgate-Belvedere Homes,
Palm Beach, 8,134 ....RR-7
Weston, *Broward*, 49,286 ....OO-12
•Westview, *Miami-Dade*, 9,692 ....SS-14
•Westwood Lakes,
Miami-Dade, 12,005 ....VV-12
Wewahitchka, *Gulf*, 1,722 ....D-2
•Whiskey Creek, *Lee*, 4,806 ....W-3
•Whisper Walk, *Palm Beach*, 5,135 ....R-15
•White City, *St. Lucie*, 4,221 ....Y-16
•Whitfield, *Manatee*, 2,984 ....O-2
Wildwood, *Sumter*, 3,924 ....I-11
•Williamsburg, *Orange*, 6,736 ....K-13
Williston, *Levy*, 2,297 ....G-10
•Williston Highlands, *Levy*, 1,386 ....G-10
•Willow Oak, *Polk*, 4,917 ....KK-8
Wilton Manors, *Broward*, 12,697 ....NN-16
•Wimauma, *Hillsborough*, 4,246 ....LL-6
Windermere, *Orange*, 1,897 ....EE-4
•Winston, *Polk*, 9,024 ....JJ-8
Winter Garden, *Orange*, 14,351 ....EE-3
Winter Haven, *Polk*, 26,487 ....L-12
Winter Park, *Orange*, 24,090 ....J-13
Winter Springs, *Seminole*, 31,666 ....CC-5
•Woodville, *Leon*, 3,006 ....D-5
•Wright, *Okaloosa*, 21,697 ....K-4
•Yalaha, *Lake*, 1,175 ....I-12
•Yeehaw Junction, *Osceola*, 21,778 ....M-15
•Yulee, *Nassau*, 8,392 ....C-12
•Zellwood, *Orange*, 2,540 ....CC-3
Zephyrhills, *Pasco*, 10,833 ....K-11
•Zephyrhills North, *Pasco*, 2,544 ....HH-6
•Zephyrhills South, *Pasco*, 4,435 ....HH-6
•Zephyrhills West, *Pasco*, 5,242 ....K-11
Zolfo Springs, *Hardee*, 1,641 ....N-10

COUNTIES

(159 Counties)

Name of County	Population	Location on Map
APPLING	17,419	K-9
ATKINSON	7,609	M-7
BACON	10,103	L-8
BAKER	4,074	L-3
BALDWIN	44,700	G-6
BANKS	14,422	C-6
BARROW	46,144	D-5
BARTOW	76,019	C-2
BEN HILL	17,484	K-6
BERRIEN	16,235	L-6
BIBB	153,887	H-5
BLECKLEY	11,666	I-6
BRANTLEY	14,629	M-10
BROOKS	16,450	M-6
BRYAN	23,417	J-11
BULLOCH	55,983	J-10
BURKE	22,243	H-9
BUTTS	19,522	G-5
CALHOUN	6,320	L-3
CAMDEN	43,664	M-10
CANDLER	9,577	I-10
CARROLL	87,268	F-1
CATOOSA	53,282	B-2
CHARLTON	10,282	N-9
CHATHAM	232,048	J-12
CHATTAHOOCHEE	14,882	J-2
CHATTOOGA	25,470	C-1
CHEROKEE	141,903	C-3
CLARKE	101,489	D-6
CLAY	3,357	K-2
CLAYTON	236,517	F-4
CLINCH	6,878	M-8
COBB	607,751	D-3
COFFEE	37,413	L-7
COLQUITT	42,053	M-5
COLUMBIA	89,288	E-9
COOK	15,771	M-6
COWETA	89,215	F-3
CRAWFORD	12,495	H-4
CRISP	21,996	J-5
DADE	15,154	B-1
DAWSON	15,999	C-4
DECATUR	28,240	M-3
DEKALB	665,865	E-4
DODGE	19,171	J-7
DOOLY	11,525	J-5
DOUGHERTY	96,065	L-4
DOUGLAS	92,174	E-3
EARLY	12,354	L-2
ECHOLS	3,754	N-7
EFFINGHAM	37,535	I-11
ELBERT	20,511	D-7
EMANUEL	21,837	H-9
EVANS	10,495	J-10
FANNIN	19,798	B-3
FAYETTE	91,263	F-3
FLOYD	90,565	D-1
FORSYTH	98,407	D-4
FRANKLIN	20,285	C-7
FULTON	816,006	F-3
GILMER	23,456	C-3
GLASCOCK	2,556	G-8
GLYNN	67,568	L-11
GORDON	44,104	C-2
GRADY	23,659	M-4
GREENE	14,406	E-6
GWINNETT	588,448	D-5
HABERSHAM	35,902	B-6
HALL	139,277	C-5
HANCOCK	10,076	F-7
HARALSON	25,690	E-1
HARRIS	23,695	H-2
HART	22,997	C-7
HEARD	11,012	G-2
HENRY	119,341	F-4
HOUSTON	110,765	I-5
IRWIN	9,931	K-6
JACKSON	41,589	D-6
JASPER	11,426	F-5
JEFF DAVIS	12,684	K-8
JEFFERSON	17,266	G-8
JENKINS	8,575	H-10
JOHNSON	8,560	H-8
JONES	23,639	G-5
LAMAR	15,912	G-4
LANIER	7,241	N-7
LAURENS	44,874	H-7
LEE	24,757	K-4
LIBERTY	61,610	J-11
LINCOLN	8,348	E-9
LONG	10,304	L-11
LOWNDES	92,115	N-6
LUMPKIN	21,016	C-4
MACON	14,074	I-4
MADISON	25,730	D-7
MARION	7,144	I-3
MCDUFFIE	21,231	F-9
MCINTOSH	10,847	L-11
MERIWETHER	22,534	G-3
MILLER	6,383	M-2
MITCHELL	23,932	M-4
MONROE	21,757	H-5
MONTGOMERY	8,270	J-8
MORGAN	15,457	F-6
MURRAY	36,506	B-3
MUSCOGEE	186,291	I-2
NEWTON	62,001	F-5
OCONEE	26,225	E-6
OGLETHORPE	12,635	E-7
PAULDING	81,678	D-2
PEACH	23,668	I-5
PICKENS	22,983	C-3
PIERCE	15,636	L-9
PIKE	13,688	G-4
POLK	38,127	D-1
PULASKI	9,588	J-6
PUTNAM	18,812	F-6
QUITMAN	2,598	K-2
RABUN	15,050	B-6
RANDOLPH	7,791	K-2
RICHMOND	199,775	F-9
ROCKDALE	70,111	F-5
SCHLEY	3,766	J-4
SCREVEN	15,374	H-11
SEMINOLE	9,369	M-2
SPALDING	58,417	G-4
STEPHENS	25,435	C-6
STEWART	5,252	J-2
SUMTER	33,200	J-4
TALBOT	6,498	H-3
TALIAFERRO	2,077	F-7
TATTNALL	22,305	J-10
TAYLOR	8,815	H-4
TELFAIR	11,794	K-7
TERRELL	10,970	K-3
THOMAS	42,737	N-5
TIFT	38,407	L-6
TOOMBS	26,067	J-9
TOWNS	9,319	B-5
TREUTLEN	6,854	I-8
TROUP	58,779	G-2
TURNER	9,504	K-5
TWIGGS	10,590	H-6
UNION	17,289	B-5
UPSON	27,597	H-4
WALKER	61,053	B-1
WALTON	60,687	E-5
WARE	35,483	L-9
WARREN	6,336	F-8
WASHINGTON	21,176	G-8
WAYNE	26,565	K-10
WEBSTER	2,390	J-3
WHEELER	6,179	J-8
WHITE	19,944	B-5
WHITFIELD	83,525	B-2
WILCOX	8,577	J-6
WILKES	10,687	E-8
WILKINSON	10,220	H-7
WORTH	21,967	K-5
TOTAL	**8,186,453**	

CITIES AND TOWNS

Note: The first name is that of the city or town, second, that of the county in which it is located, then the population and location on the map.

Abbeville, *Wilcox,* 2,298 ....J-7
Acworth, *Cobb,* 13,422 ....D-3
Adairsville, *Bartow,* 2,542 ....C-2
Adel, *Cook,* 5,307 ....M-6
Alamo, *Wheeler,* 1,943 ....J-8
Albany, *Dougherty,* 76,939 ....L-4
Alma, *Bacon,* 3,236 ....L-9
Alpharetta, *Fulton,* 34,854 ....D-4
Americus, *Sumter,* 17,013 ....J-4
Appling, *Columbia,* 150 ....F-9
Aragon, *Polk,* 1,039 ....D-2
Arcade, *Jackson,* 1,643 ....D-6
Arlington, *Calhoun,* 1,602 ....L-3
Ashburn, *Turner,* 4,419 ....K-6
Athens, *Clarke,* 101,489 ....D-7
Atlanta, *Fulton,* 416,474 ....E-4
Atlanta, *Fulton,* 416,474 ....E-4
Auburn, *Barrow,* 6,904 ....D-5
Augusta, *Richmond,* 199,775 ..F-10
Austell, *Cobb,* 5,359 ....B-9
Avondale Estates, *DeKalb,* 2,609 ....C-11
Bainbridge, *Decatur,* 11,722 ....N-3
Baldwin, *Habersham,* 2,425 ....C-6
Barnesville, *Lamar,* 5,972 ....G-4
Baxley, *Appling,* 4,150 ....K-9
• Belvedere Park, *DeKalb,* 18,945 ....C-11
Berkeley Lake, *Gwinnett,* 1,695 ....A-12
Blackshear, *Pierce,* 3,283 ....L-10
Blairsville, *Union,* 659 ....B-5
Blakely, *Early,* 5,696 ....L-2
Bloomingdale, *Chatham,* 2,665 ....J-12
Blue Ridge, *Fannin,* 1,210 ....B-4
Bogart, *Oconee,* 1,049 ....E-6
• Bonanza, *Clayton,* 2,904 ....E-11
Boston, *Thomas,* 1,417 ....N-5
Bowdon, *Carroll,* 1,959 ....F-2
Braselton, *Jackson,* 1,206 ....D-5
Bremen, *Haralson,* 4,579 ....E-2
Brooklet, *Bulloch,* 1,113 ....I-11
Broxton, *Coffee,* 1,428 ....L-8
Brunswick, *Glynn,* 15,600 ....M-12
Buchanan, *Haralson,* 941 ....E-2
Buena Vista, *Marion,* 1,664 ....I-3
Buford, *Gwinnett,* 10,668 ....D-5
Butler, *Taylor,* 1,907 ....I-4
Byron, *Peach,* 2,887 ....H-5
Cairo, *Grady,* 9,239 ....N-4
Calhoun, *Gordon,* 10,667 ....C-2
Camilla, *Mitchell,* 5,669 ....M-4
• Candler-McAfee, *DeKalb,* 28,294 ....C-11
Canton, *Cherokee,* 7,709 ....D-4
Carnesville, *Franklin,* 541 ....C-7
Carrollton, *Carroll,* 19,843 ....F-2
Cartersville, *Bartow,* 15,925 ....D-3
Cedartown, *Polk,* 9,470 ....D-2
Centerville, *Houston,* 4,278 ....H-6
Chamblee, *DeKalb,* 9,552 ....B-11
Chatsworth, *Murray,* 3,531 ....B-3
• Chattanooga Valley, *Walker,* 4,065 ....A-1
Chickamauga, *Walker,* 2,245 ....B-2
Clarkesville, *Habersham,* 1,248 C-6
Clarkston, *DeKalb,* 7,231 ....B-11
Claxton, *Evans,* 2,276 ....J-10
Clayton, *Rabun,* 2,019 ....B-6
Cleveland, *White,* 1,907 ....C-6
Cochran, *Bleckley,* 4,455 ....I-7
College Park, *Fulton,* 20,382 ...D-10
Colquitt, *Miller,* 1,939 ....M-3
Columbus, *Muscogee,* 186,291 .I-2
Comer, *Madison,* 1,052 ....D-7
Commerce, *Jackson,* 5,292 ....D-6
• Conley, *Clayton,* 6,188 ....D-11
Conyers, *Rockdale,* 10,689 ....E-5
Cordele, *Crisp,* 11,608 ....J-5
Cornelia, *Habersham,* 3,674 ....C-6
• Country Club Estates, *Glynn,* 7,594 ....M-12
Covington, *Newton,* 11,547 ....F-5
Crawfordville, *Taliaferro,* 572 ....F-8
Cumming, *Forsyth,* 4,220 ....D-5
Cusseta, *Chattahoochee,* 1,196 ..I-3
Cuthbert, *Randolph,* 3,731 ....K-3
Dacula, *Gwinnett,* 3,848 ....A-13
Dahlonega, *Lumpkin,* 3,638 ....C-5
Dallas, *Paulding,* 5,056 ....E-3
Dalton, *Whitfield,* 27,912 ....B-2
Danielsville, *Madison,* 457 ....D-7
Darien, *McIntosh,* 1,719 ....L-12
Davisboro, *Washington,* 1,544 .G-9
Dawson, *Terrell,* 5,058 ....K-4
Dawsonville, *Dawson,* 619 ....C-5
Decatur, *DeKalb,* 18,147 ....C-11
• Deenwood, *Ware,* 1,836 ....M-9
Demorest, *Habersham,* 1,465 ...C-6
• Dock Junction, *Glynn,* 6,951 ..M-11
Donalsonville, *Seminole,* 2,796 ....M-2
Doraville, *DeKalb,* 9,862 ....B-11
Douglas, *Coffee,* 10,639 ....L-8
Douglasville, *Douglas,* 20,065 ...E-3
• Druid Hills, *DeKalb,* 12,741 ....C-11
Dublin, *Laurens,* 15,857 ....I-8
Duluth, *Gwinnett,* 22,122 ....D-5
• Dunwoody, *DeKalb,* 32,808 ....A-11
East Dublin, *Laurens,* 2,484 ....I-8
• East Griffin, *Spalding,* 1,635 ....G-4
• East Newnan, *Coweta,* 1,305 ....F-3
East Point, *Fulton,* 39,595 ....E-4
Eastman, *Dodge,* 5,440 ....J-7
Eatonton, *Putnam,* 6,764 ....F-6
Edison, *Calhoun,* 1,340 ....L-3
Elberton, *Elbert,* 4,743 ....D-8
Ellaville, *Schley,* 1,609 ....J-4
Ellijay, *Gilmer,* 1,584 ....B-4
Emerson, *Bartow,* 1,092 ....D-3
Euharlee, *Bartow,* 3,208 ....D-2
• Evans, *Columbia,* 17,727 ....F-10
• Experiment, *Spalding,* 3,233 ....G-4
• Fair Oaks, *Cobb,* 8,443 ....B-9
Fairburn, *Fulton,* 5,464 ....D-9
• Fairview, *Walker,* 6,601 ....A-2
Fayetteville, *Fayette,* 11,148 ....F-4
Fitzgerald, *Ben Hill,* 8,758 ....K-7
Flowery Branch, *Hall,* 1,806 ....D-5
Folkston, *Charlton,* 2,178 ....N-10
Forest Park, *Clayton,* 21,447 ....E-4
Forsyth, *Monroe,* 3,776 ....G-5
• Fort Benning South, *Chattahoochee,* 11,737 ....I-2
Fort Gaines, *Clay,* 1,110 ....L-2
Fort Oglethorpe, *Catoosa,* 6,940 ....A-2
• Fort Stewart, *Liberty,* 11,205 ..K-11
Fort Valley, *Peach,* 8,005 ....I-5
Franklin, *Heard,* 902 ....F-2
Gainesville, *Hall,* 25,578 ....C-5
Garden City, *Chatham,* 11,289 J-12
• Georgetown, *Quitman,* 10,599 ..K-2
Gibson, *Glascock,* 694 ....G-9
Glennville, *Tattnall,* 3,641 ....K-10
Gordon, *Wilkinson,* 2,152 ....H-7
Grantville, *Coweta,* 1,309 ....G-3
Gray, *Jones,* 1,811 ....G-6
Greensboro, *Greene,* 3,238 ....F-7
Greenville, *Meriwether,* 946 ....G-3
• Gresham Park, *DeKalb,* 9,215 .C-11
Griffin, *Spalding,* 23,451 ....G-4
Grovetown, *Columbia,* 6,089 ...F-10
• Gumlog, *Franklin,* 2,025 ....C-7
Hahira, *Lowndes,* 1,626 ....M-6
Hamilton, *Harris,* 307 ....H-3
Hampton, *Henry,* 3,857 ....F-4
• Hannahs Mill, *Upson,* 3,267 ....H-4
Hapeville, *Fulton,* 6,180 ....C-10
Harlem, *Columbia,* 1,814 ....F-9
Hartwell, *Hart,* 4,188 ....C-8
Hawkinsville, *Pulaski,* 3,280 ....J-6
Hazlehurst, *Jeff Davis,* 3,787 ....K-9
Helena, *Telfair,* 2,307 ....J-8
Hephzibah, *Richmond,* 3,880 ..F-10
Hiawassee, *Towns,* 808 ....A-6
Hinesville, *Liberty,* 30,392 ....K-11
Hiram, *Paulding,* 1,361 ....E-3
Hogansville, *Troup,* 2,774 ....G-2
Holly Springs, *Cherokee,* 3,195 D-4
Homer, *Banks,* 950 ....C-6
Homerville, *Clinch,* 2,803 ....M-8
Hoschton, *Jackson,* 1,070 ....D-6
• Indian Springs, *Butts,* 1,982 ....G-5
• Irondale, *Clayton,* 7,727 ....E-10
Irwinton, *Wilkinson,* 587 ....H-7
• Isle of Hope-Dutch Island, *Chatham,* 2,605 ....Q-12
Ivey, *Wilkinson,* 1,100 ....H-7
Jackson, *Butts,* 3,934 ....F-5
Jasper, *Pickens,* 2,167 ....C-4
Jefferson, *Jackson,* 3,825 ....D-6
Jeffersonville, *Twiggs,* 1,209 ....H-7
Jesup, *Wayne,* 9,279 ....L-10
Jonesboro, *Clayton,* 3,829 ....D-10
Kennesaw, *Cobb,* 21,675 ....A-9
• Kings Bay Base, *Camden,* 2,599 ....N-11
Kingsland, *Camden,* 10,506 ....N-11
Knoxville, *Crawford,* 75 ....H-5
La Fayette, *Walker,* 6,702 ....B-2
La Grange, *Troup,* 25,998 ....G-2
Lake City, *Clayton,* 2,886 ....D-11
Lakeland, *Lanier,* 2,730 ....M-7
• Lakeview, *Catoosa,* 4,820 ....A-2
• Lakeview Estates, *Rockdale,* 2,637 ....C-12
Lavonia, *Franklin,* 1,827 ....C-7
Lawrenceville, *Gwinnett,* 22,397 ....D-5
Leesburg, *Lee,* 2,633 ....K-4
Lexington, *Oglethorpe,* 239 ....E-7
Lilburn, *Gwinnett,* 11,307 ....B-12
• Lincoln Park, *Upson,* 1,122 ....H-4
Lincolnton, *Lincoln,* 1,595 ....E-9
• Lindale, *Floyd,* 4,088 ....D-2
Lithia Springs, *Douglas,* 2,072 ..E-3
Lithonia, *DeKalb,* 2,187 ....C-12
Locust Grove, *Henry,* 2,322 ....F-5
Loganville, *Walton,* 5,435 ....B-13
Lookout Mountain, *Walker,* 1,617 ....A-1
Louisville, *Jefferson,* 2,712 ....G-9
Lovejoy, *Clayton,* 2,495 ....F-4
Ludowici, *Long,* 1,440 ....K-11
Lula, *Hall,* 1,438 ....C-6
Lumber City, *Telfair,* 1,247 ....K-8
Lumpkin, *Stewart,* 1,369 ....J-3
Lyons, *Toombs,* 4,169 ....J-9
• Mableton, *Cobb,* 29,733 ....E-3
Macon, *Bibb,* 97,255 ....H-6
Madison, *Morgan,* 3,636 ....F-6
Manchester, *Meriwether,* 3,988 H-3
Marietta, *Cobb,* 58,748 ....D-3
Marshallville, *Macon,* 1,335 ....I-5
• Martinez, *Columbia,* 27,749 ....F-10
Maysville, *Jackson,* 1,247 ....D-6
McCaysville, *Fannin,* 1,071 ....A-4
McDonough, *Henry,* 8,493 ....F-4
McRae, *Telfair,* 2,682 ....J-8
Meigs, *Thomas,* 1,090 ....M-5
Metter, *Candler,* 3,879 ....I-10
• Midway, *Liberty,* 1,100 ....K-12
Midway-Hardwick, *Baldwin,* 5,135 ....G-7
Milan, *Telfair,* 1,012 ....J-7
Milledgeville, *Baldwin,* 18,757 ..G-7
Millen, *Jenkins,* 3,492 ....H-10
Monroe, *Walton,* 11,407 ....E-6
Montezuma, *Macon,* 3,999 ....I-5
• Montgomery, *Chatham,* 4,134 ....Q-12
Monticello, *Jasper,* 2,428 ....F-6
Morgan, *Calhoun,* 1,464 ....L-3
Morrow, *Clayton,* 4,882 ....D-11
Moultrie, *Colquitt,* 14,387 ....M-5
Mount Vernon, *Montgomery,* 2,082 ....J-9
Mount Zion, *Carroll,* 1,275 ....E-2
Mountain Park, *Gwinnett,* 11,753 ....B-12
Nahunta, *Brantley,* 930 ....M-10
Nashville, *Berrien,* 4,697 ....M-7
Newnan, *Coweta,* 16,242 ....F-3
Newton, *Baker,* 851 ....L-4
Nicholls, *Coffee,* 1,008 ....L-8
Nicholson, *Jackson,* 1,247 ....D-6
Norcross, *Gwinnett,* 8,410 ....B-11
• North Atlanta, *DeKalb,* 38,579 ...E-4
• North Decatur, *DeKalb,* 15,270 ....C-11
• North Druid Hills, *DeKalb,* 18,852 ....B-11
Oakwood, *Hall,* 2,689 ....D-5
Ocilla, *Irwin,* 3,270 ....L-7
Oglethorpe, *Macon,* 1,200 ....I-5
Omega, *Tift,* 1,340 ....L-6
Oxford, *Newton,* 1,892 ....E-5
Palmetto, *Fulton,* 3,400 ....F-3
• Panthersville, *DeKalb,* 11,791 .C-11
Peachtree City, *Fayette,* 31,580 .F-3
Pearson, *Atkinson,* 1,805 ....L-8
Pelham, *Mitchell,* 4,126 ....M-4
Pembroke, *Bryan,* 2,379 ....J-11
Perry, *Houston,* 9,602 ....I-6
Pine Mountain (Chipley), *Harris,* 1,141 ....H-3
Pooler, *Chatham,* 6,239 ....J-12
Port Wentworth, *Chatham,* 3,276 ....P-12
Porterdale, *Newton,* 1,281 ....F-5
Powder Springs, *Cobb,* 12,481 .E-3
Preston, *Webster,* 453 ....J-3
• Putney, *Dougherty,* 2,998 ....L-5
Quitman, *Brooks,* 4,638 ....N-6
• Raoul, *Habersham,* 1,816 ....B-6
• Redan, *DeKalb,* 33,841 ....E-5
• Reed Creek, *Hart,* 2,148 ....C-8
Reidsville, *Tattnall,* 2,235 ....J-10
Reynolds, *Taylor,* 1,036 ....I-5
Richland, *Stewart,* 1,794 ....J-3
Richmond Hill, *Bryan,* 6,959 ...K-12
Rincon, *Effingham,* 4,376 ....I-12
Ringgold, *Catoosa,* 2,422 ....B-2
Riverdale, *Clayton,* 12,478 ....D-10
• Robins AFB, *Houston,* 3,949 ....H-6
Rochelle, *Wilcox,* 1,415 ....K-6
Rockmart, *Polk,* 3,870 ....D-2
Rome, *Floyd,* 34,980 ....D-2
Rossville, *Walker,* 3,511 ....A-2
Roswell, *Fulton,* 79,334 ....D-4
Royston, *Franklin,* 2,493 ....C-7
Saint Marys, *Camden,* 13,761 N-11
Saint Simons Island, *Glynn,* 13,381 ....M-12
Sandersville, *Washington,* 6,144 ....G-8
• Sandy Springs, *Fulton,* 85,781 ..E-4
Sardis, *Burke,* 1,171 ....G-11
Savannah, *Chatham,* 131,510 .J-13
• Scottdale, *DeKalb,* 9,803 ....C-11
Senoia, *Coweta,* 1,738 ....F-3
• Shannon, *Floyd,* 1,682 ....C-2
Shellman, *Randolph,* 1,166 ....K-3
• Skidaway Island, *Chatham,* 6,914 ....J-13
Smyrna, *Cobb,* 40,999 ....E-4
Snellville, *Gwinnett,* 15,351 ....B-13
Social Circle, *Walton,* 3,379 ....E-6
Soperton, *Treutlen,* 2,824 ....I-9
Sparks, *Cook,* 1,755 ....M-6
Sparta, *Hancock,* 1,522 ....G-8
Springfield, *Effingham,* 1,821 ..I-12
Statenville, *Echols,* 700 ....N-7
Statesboro, *Bulloch,* 22,698 ....I-11
Statham, *Barrow,* 2,040 ....D-6
Stockbridge, *Henry,* 9,853 ....F-4
Stone Mountain, *DeKalb,* 7,145 ....B-12
Sugar Hill, *Gwinnett,* 11,399 ....D-5
Summerville, *Chattooga,* 4,556 C-1
• Sunnyside, *Ware,* 1,385 ....M-9
Suwanee, *Gwinnett,* 8,725 ....A-12
Swainsboro, *Emanuel,* 6,943 ....I-9
Sylvania, *Screven,* 2,675 ....H-11
Sylvester, *Worth,* 5,990 ....L-5
Talbotton, *Talbot,* 1,019 ....H-3
Tallapoosa, *Haralson,* 2,789 ....E-2
Temple, *Carroll,* 2,383 ....E-2
Tennille, *Washington,* 1,505 ....H-8
Thomaston, *Upson,* 9,411 ....H-4
Thomasville, *Thomas,* 18,162 ...N-5
Thomson, *Mcduffie,* 6,828 ....F-9
Thunderbolt, *Chatham,* 2,340 ..J-13
Tifton, *Tift,* 15,060 ....L-6
Toccoa, *Stephens,* 9,323 ....C-7
Trenton, *Dade,* 1,942 ....B-1
Trion, *Chattooga,* 1,993 ....C-2
• Tucker, *DeKalb,* 26,532 ....B-11
Tunnel Hill, *Whitfield,* 1,209 ....B-2
Twin City, *Emanuel,* 1,752 ....I-10
Tybee Island, *Chatham,* 3,392 P-13
Tyrone, *Fayette,* 3,916 ....F-3
Unadilla, *Dooly,* 2,772 ....J-6
Union City, *Fulton,* 11,621 ....F-3
Union Point, *Greene,* 1,669 ....F-7
• Unionville, *Tift,* 2,074 ....L-6
Valdosta, *Lowndes,* 43,724 ....N-7
Varnell, *Whitfield,* 1,491 ....B-2
Vidalia, *Toombs,* 10,491 ....J-9
Vienna, *Dooly,* 2,973 ....J-5
Villa Rica, *Carroll,* 4,134 ....E-2
• Vinings, *Cobb,* 9,677 ....B-10
Wadley, *Jefferson,* 2,088 ....H-9
Walnut Grove, *Walton,* 1,241 ....E-5
Walthourville, *Liberty,* 4,030 ...K-11
Warner Robins, *Houston,* 48,804 ....I-6
Warrenton, *Warren,* 2,013 ....F-8
Washington, *Wilkes,* 4,295 ....E-8
Watkinsville, *Oconee,* 2,097 ....E-6
Waycross, *Ware,* 15,333 ....M-9
Waynesboro, *Burke,* 5,813 ....G-10
West Point, *Troup,* 3,382 ....H-2
• Whitemarsh Island, *Chatham,* 5,824 ....J-13
Willacoochee, *Atkinson,* 1,434 ..L-7
• Wilmington Island, *Chatham,* 14,213 ....J-13
Winder, *Barrow,* 10,201 ....D-6
Winterville, *Clarke,* 1,068 ....D-7
Woodbine, *Camden,* 1,218 ....M-11
Woodbury, *Meriwether,* 1,184 ..G-3
Woodstock, *Cherokee,* 10,050 ..D-4
Wrens, *Jefferson,* 2,314 ....G-9
Wrightsville, *Johnson,* 2,223 ....H-8
Zebulon, *Pike,* 1,181 ....G-4

Explanation of symbols: • - Census Designated Place (CDP)

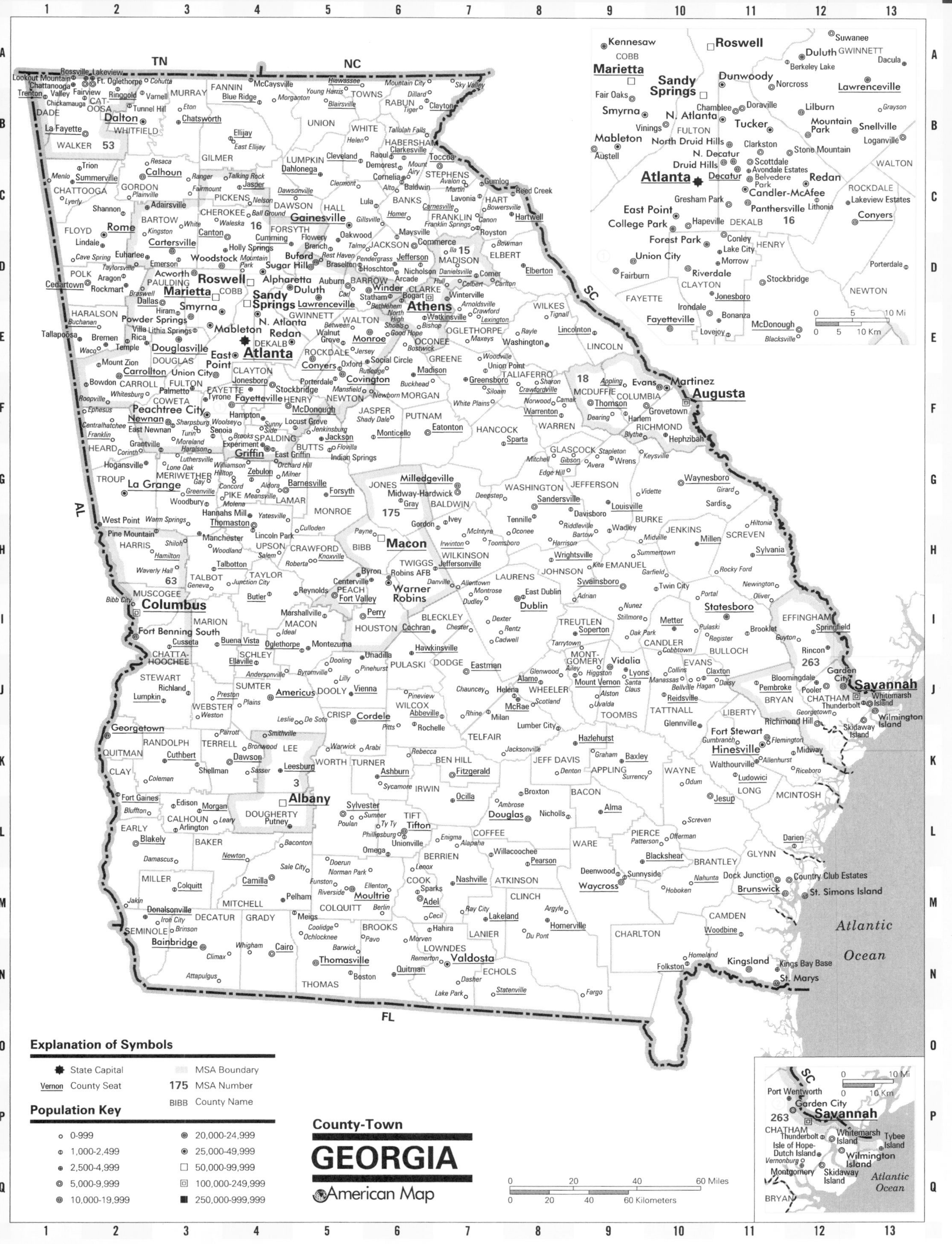

TN
NC
SC
AL
FL
Atlantic Ocean
Atlanta
Savannah
Augusta
Columbus
Macon
Albany
Athens
Roswell
Marietta
Sandy Springs
Valdosta
Warner Robins
Dalton
Rome
Gainesville
La Grange
Peachtree City
Newnan
Griffin
Carrollton
Douglasville
Smyrna
Mableton
Redan
Alpharetta
Duluth
Lawrenceville
Conyers
Covington
Milledgeville
Dublin
Statesboro
Hinesville
Brunswick
Waycross
Thomasville
Tifton
Americus
Cordele
Bainbridge
Douglas
Kingsland
St. Marys
WALKER
CATOOSA
WHITFIELD
MURRAY
FANNIN
UNION
TOWNS
RABUN
GILMER
LUMPKIN
WHITE
HABERSHAM
STEPHENS
FLOYD
GORDON
PICKENS
DAWSON
HALL
BANKS
FRANKLIN
HART
BARTOW
CHEROKEE
FORSYTH
JACKSON
MADISON
ELBERT
POLK
PAULDING
COBB
GWINNETT
BARROW
CLARKE
OCONEE
OGLETHORPE
WILKES
LINCOLN
HARALSON
DOUGLAS
FULTON
DEKALB
ROCKDALE
WALTON
MORGAN
GREENE
TALIAFERRO
MCDUFFIE
COLUMBIA
RICHMOND
CARROLL
COWETA
FAYETTE
CLAYTON
HENRY
NEWTON
JASPER
PUTNAM
HANCOCK
WARREN
GLASCOCK
HEARD
MERIWETHER
SPALDING
BUTTS
PIKE
LAMAR
MONROE
JONES
BALDWIN
WASHINGTON
JEFFERSON
BURKE
TROUP
HARRIS
TALBOT
UPSON
CRAWFORD
BIBB
TWIGGS
WILKINSON
JOHNSON
EMANUEL
JENKINS
SCREVEN
MUSCOGEE
MARION
TAYLOR
PEACH
HOUSTON
BLECKLEY
LAURENS
TREUTLEN
CANDLER
BULLOCH
EFFINGHAM
CHATTAHOOCHEE
SCHLEY
MACON
DOOLY
PULASKI
DODGE
MONTGOMERY
EVANS
BRYAN
CHATHAM
STEWART
WEBSTER
SUMTER
WILCOX
TELFAIR
WHEELER
TOOMBS
TATTNALL
LIBERTY
QUITMAN
RANDOLPH
TERRELL
LEE
CRISP
TURNER
BEN HILL
JEFF DAVIS
APPLING
WAYNE
LONG
MCINTOSH
CLAY
CALHOUN
DOUGHERTY
WORTH
IRWIN
COFFEE
BACON
PIERCE
EARLY
BAKER
MITCHELL
COLQUITT
TIFT
BERRIEN
ATKINSON
WARE
BRANTLEY
GLYNN
MILLER
SEMINOLE
DECATUR
GRADY
THOMAS
BROOKS
COOK
LANIER
LOWNDES
ECHOLS
CLINCH
CHARLTON
CAMDEN
53
16
15
18
175
63
3
263
Explanation of Symbols
State Capital
Vernon County Seat
MSA Boundary
175 MSA Number
BIBB County Name
Population Key
0-999
1,000-2,499
2,500-4,999
5,000-9,999
10,000-19,999
20,000-24,999
25,000-49,999
50,000-99,999
100,000-249,999
250,000-999,999
County-Town
GEORGIA
American Map
0 20 40 60 Miles
0 20 40 60 Kilometers
0 5 10 Mi
0 5 10 Km

COUNTIES

(5 Counties)

Name of County	Population	Location on Map
HAWAII	148,677	H-13
HONOLULU	876,156	C-7
KALAWAO	147	D-11
KAUAI	58,463	A-2
MAUI	128,094	G-12
TOTAL	**1,211,537**	

CITIES AND TOWNS

Note: The first name is that of the city or town, second, that of the county in which it is located, then the population and location on the map.

•Ahuimanu, *Honolulu,* 8,506 ....G-3
•Aiea, *Honolulu,* 9,019 ....D-8
•Ainaloa, *Hawaii,* 1,910 ....J-17
•Anahola, *Kauai,* 1,932 ....A-4
•Captain Cook, *Hawaii,* 3,206 ....J-14
•Eleele, *Kauai,* 2,040 ....B-3
•Ewa Beach, *Honolulu,* 14,650 ....H-2
•Ewa Gentry, *Honolulu,* 4,939 ....H-2
•Ewa Villages, *Honolulu,* 4,741 ....H-1
•Haiku-Pauwela, *Maui,* 6,578 ....E-13
•Halawa, *Honolulu,* 13,891 ....G-3
•Haleiwa, *Honolulu,* 2,225 ....C-7
•Hanamaulu, *Kauai,* 3,272 ....B-4
•Hanapepe, *Kauai,* 2,153 ....B-3
•Hauula, *Honolulu,* 3,651 ....C-8
•Hawaiian Acres, *Hawaii,* 1,776 ....M-11
•Hawaiian Beaches, *Hawaii,* 3,709 ....J-17
•Hawaiian Ocean View, *Hawaii,* 2,178 ....K-14
•Hawaiian Paradise Park, *Hawaii,* 7,051 ....J-17
•Heeia, *Honolulu,* 4,944 ....G-3
•Hickam Housing, *Honolulu,* 5,471 ....H-2
•Hilo, *Hawaii,* 40,759 ....I-16
•Holualoa, *Hawaii,* 6,107 ....I-14
•Honalo, *Hawaii,* 1,987 ....J-14
•Honaunau-Napoopoo, *Hawaii,* 2,414 ....J-14
•Honokaa, *Hawaii,* 2,233 ....H-15
•Honolulu, *Honolulu,* 371,657 ....D-8
•Iroquois Point, *Honolulu,* 2,462 ....H-2
•Kaaawa, *Honolulu,* 1,324 ....C-8
•Kaanapali, *Maui,* 1,375 ....E-12
•Kahaluu, *Honolulu,* 2,935 ....D-8
•Kahaluu-Keauhou, *Hawaii,* 2,414 ....J-14
•Kahuku, *Honolulu,* 2,097 ....C-8
•Kahului, *Maui,* 20,146 ....E-12
•Kailua, *Hawaii,* 9,870 ....I-14
•Kailua, *Honolulu,* 36,513 ....D-8
•Kalaheo, *Kauai,* 3,913 ....B-3
•Kalaoa, *Hawaii,* 6,794 ....I-14
Kalaupapa, *Kalawao,* 120 ....E-11
•Kaneohe, *Honolulu,* 34,970 ....D-8
•Kaneohe Station, *Honolulu,* 11,827 ....G-4
•Kapaa, *Kauai,* 9,472 ....B-4
•Kapaau, *Hawaii,* 1,159 ....H-14
•Kapaau, *Hawaii,* 1,159 ....J-17
•Kaunakakai, *Maui,* 2,726 ....E-11
•Keaau, *Hawaii,* 2,010 ....I-16
•Kealakekua, *Hawaii,* 1,645 ....J-14
•Kekaha, *Kauai,* 3,175 ....B-3
•Kihei, *Maui,* 16,749 ....F-12
•Kilauea, *Kauai,* 2,092 ....A-4
•Koloa, *Kauai,* 1,942 ....B-3
•Kualapuu, *Maui,* 1,936 ....E-11
•Kurtistown, *Hawaii,* 1,157 ....J-16
•Lahaina, *Maui,* 9,118 ....E-12
•Laie, *Honolulu,* 4,585 ....C-8
•Lanai City, *Maui,* 3,164 ....F-11
•Lawai, *Kauai,* 1,984 ....D-2
•Leilani Estates, *Hawaii,* 1,046 ....J-17
•Lihue, *Kauai,* 5,674 ....B-4
•Maili, *Honolulu,* 5,943 ....D-7
•Makaha, *Honolulu,* 7,753 ....D-7
•Makaha Valley, *Honolulu,* 1,289 ....C-7
•Makakilo City, *Honolulu,* 13,156 ....H-1
•Makawao, *Maui,* 6,327 ....F-13
•Maunawili, *Honolulu,* 4,869 ....G-4
•Mililani Town, *Honolulu,* 28,608 ....D-8
•Mokuleia, *Honolulu,* 1,839 ....C-7
•Mountain View, *Hawaii,* 2,799 ....J-16
•Nanakuli, *Honolulu,* 10,814 ....D-7
•Nanawale Estates, *Hawaii,* 1,073 ....M-12
•Napili-Honokowai, *Maui,* 6,788 ....E-12
•Omao, *Kauai,* 1,221 ....D-2
•Orchidlands Estates, *Hawaii,* 1,731 ....M-11
•Pahala, *Hawaii,* 1,378 ....K-15
•Paia, *Maui,* 2,499 ....E-12
•Papaikou, *Hawaii,* 1,414 ....I-16
•Pearl City, *Honolulu,* 30,976 ....G-2
•Pepeekeo, *Hawaii,* 1,697 ....I-16
•Poipu, *Kauai,* 1,075 ....B-3
•Princeville, *Kauai,* 1,698 ....A-3
•Puhi, *Kauai,* 1,186 ....D-2
•Pukalani, *Maui,* 7,380 ....F-13
•Pupukea, *Honolulu,* 4,250 ....C-8
•Schofield Barracks, *Honolulu,* 14,428 ....F-1
•Village Park, *Honolulu,* 9,625 ....G-2
•Volcano, *Hawaii,* 2,231 ....J-16
•Wahiawa, *Honolulu,* 16,151 ....F-2
•Waialua, *Honolulu,* 3,761 ....C-7
•Waianae, *Honolulu,* 10,506 ....D-7
•Waihee-Waiehu, *Maui,* 7,310 ....E-12
•Waikapu, *Maui,* 1,115 ....E-12
•Waikoloa Village, *Hawaii,* 4,806 ....I-14
•Wailea-Makena, *Hawaii,* 5,671 ....F-12
•Wailua, *Kauai,* 2,083 ....B-4
•Wailua Homesteads, *Kauai,* 4,567 ....B-4
•Wailuku, *Maui,* 12,296 ....E-12
•Waimalu, *Honolulu,* 29,371 ....G-2
•Waimanalo, *Honolulu,* 3,664 ....H-4
•Waimanalo Beach, *Honolulu,* 4,271 ....H-4
•Waimea, *Honolulu,* 7,028 ....C-8
•Waimea, *Kauai,* 1,787 ....B-3
•Wainaku, *Hawaii,* 1,227 ....I-16
•Waipahu, *Honolulu,* 33,108 ....D-8
•Waipio, *Honolulu,* 11,672 ....H-15
•Waipio Acres, *Honolulu,* 5,298 ....F-2
•Wheeler AFB, *Honolulu,* 2,829 ....F-1
•Whitmore Village, *Honolulu,* 4,057 ....F-2

Explanation of symbols: • - Census Designated Place (CDP)

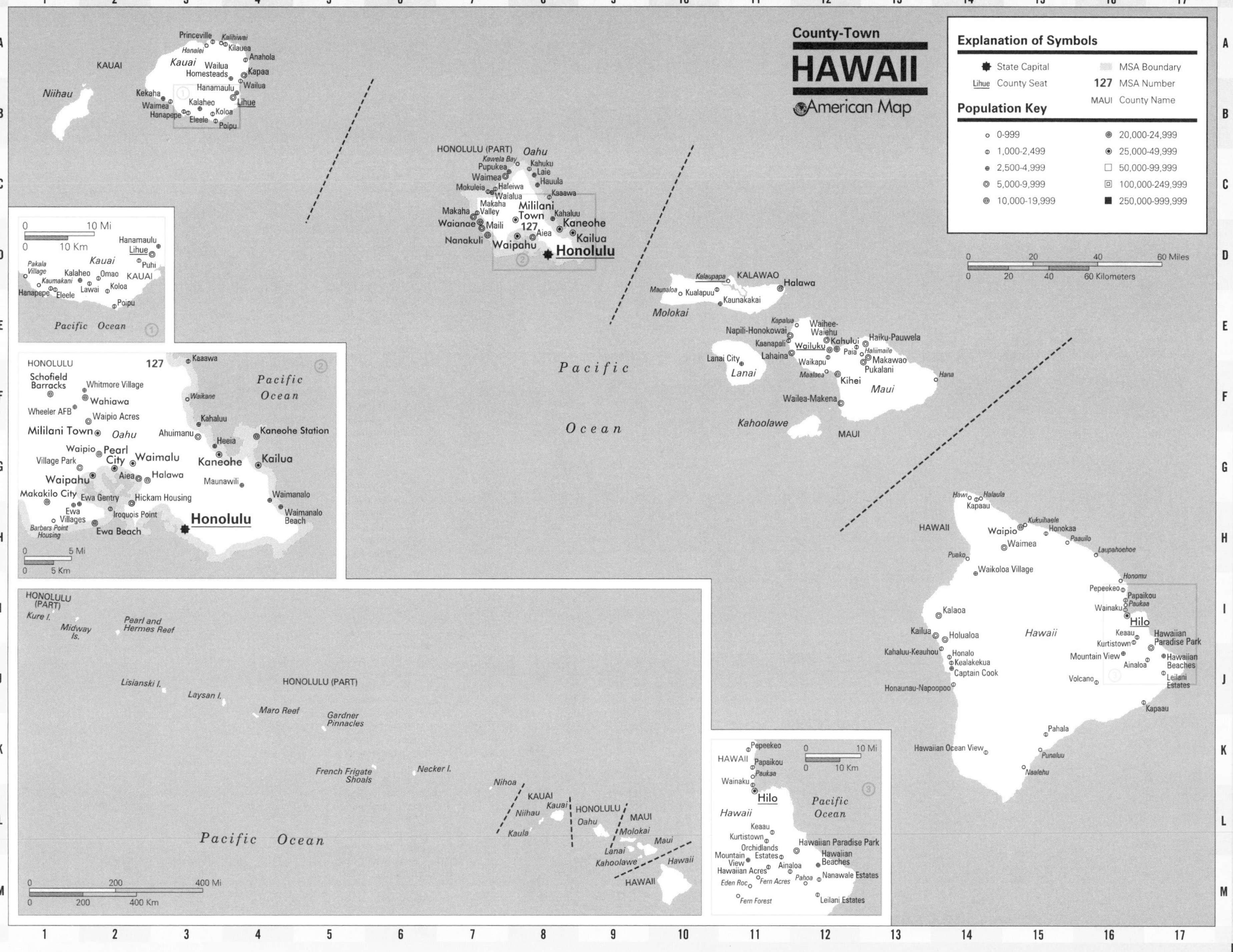
County-Town
HAWAII
American Map
Explanation of Symbols
State Capital
Lihue County Seat
MSA Boundary
127 MSA Number
MAUI County Name
Population Key
0-999
1,000-2,499
2,500-4,999
5,000-9,999
10,000-19,999
20,000-24,999
25,000-49,999
50,000-99,999
100,000-249,999
250,000-999,999
0 20 40 60 Miles
0 20 40 60 Kilometers
KAUAI
Niihau
Kauai
Princeville
Hanalei
Kalihiwai
Kilauea
Anahola
Kapaa
Wailua
Wailua Homesteads
Hanamaulu
Lihue
Kekaha
Waimea
Kalaheo
Hanapepe
Eleele
Koloa
Poipu
HONOLULU (PART)
Oahu
Kawela Bay
Pupukea
Waimea
Kahuku
Laie
Hauula
Mokuleia
Haleiwa
Waialua
Kaaawa
Makaha Valley
Makaha
Mililani Town
127
Kahaluu
Waianae
Maili
Kaneohe
Aiea
Kailua
Nanakuli
Waipahu
Honolulu
KALAWAO
Kalaupapa
Maunaloa
Kualapuu
Halawa
Kaunakakai
Molokai
Kapalua
Napili-Honokowai
Waihee-Waiehu
Kaanapali
Kahului
Haiku-Pauwela
Wailuku
Paia
Haliimaile
Makawao
Lahaina
Waikapu
Pukalani
Lanai City
Lanai
Maalaea
Kihei
Hana
Maui
Wailea-Makena
Kahoolawe
MAUI
Pacific Ocean
HAWAII
Hawi
Halaula
Kapaau
Waipio
Kukuihaele
Honokaa
Waimea
Paauilo
Laupahoehoe
Puako
Waikoloa Village
Honomu
Pepeekeo
Papaikou
Paukaa
Wainaku
Hilo
Kalaoa
Kailua
Holualoa
Hawaii
Keaau
Kurtistown
Hawaiian Paradise Park
Kahaluu-Keauhou
Honalo
Kealakekua
Captain Cook
Mountain View
Ainaloa
Hawaiian Beaches
Leilani Estates
Honaunau-Napoopoo
Volcano
Kapaau
Pahala
Hawaiian Ocean View
Punaluu
Naalehu
0 10 Mi
0 10 Km
Hanamaulu
Lihue
Kauai
Pakala Village
Kalaheo
Omao
KAUAI
Puhi
Kaumakani
Lawai
Koloa
Hanapepe
Eleele
Poipu
Pacific Ocean
HONOLULU
127
Kaaawa
Schofield Barracks
Whitmore Village
Wahiawa
Pacific Ocean
Waikane
Wheeler AFB
Waipio Acres
Kahaluu
Mililani Town
Oahu
Ahuimanu
Kaneohe Station
Heeia
Waipio
Pearl City
Waimalu
Kaneohe
Kailua
Village Park
Waipahu
Aiea
Halawa
Maunawili
Makakilo City
Ewa Gentry
Hickam Housing
Waimanalo
Ewa
Ewa Villages
Iroquois Point
Waimanalo Beach
Barbers Point Housing
Ewa Beach
Honolulu
0 5 Mi
0 5 Km
HONOLULU (PART)
Kure I.
Midway Is.
Pearl and Hermes Reef
Lisianski I.
Laysan I.
HONOLULU (PART)
Maro Reef
Gardner Pinnacles
French Frigate Shoals
Necker I.
Nihoa
KAUAI
Kauai
Niihau
Kaula
HONOLULU
Oahu
MAUI
Molokai
Lanai
Maui
Kahoolawe
Hawaii
HAWAII
Pacific Ocean
0 200 400 Mi
0 200 400 Km
Pepeekeo
HAWAII
Papaikou
Paukaa
Wainaku
Hilo
Hawaii
Pacific Ocean
Keaau
Kurtistown
Orchidlands Estates
Hawaiian Paradise Park
Mountain View
Ainaloa
Hawaiian Beaches
Hawaiian Acres
Eden Roc
Fern Acres
Pahoa
Nanawale Estates
Fern Forest
Leilani Estates

COUNTIES

(44 Counties)

Name of County	Population	Location on Map
ADA	300,904	N-3
ADAMS	3,476	J-3
BANNOCK	75,565	O-10
BEAR LAKE	6,411	P-11
BENEWAH	9,171	E-2
BINGHAM	41,735	N-9
BLAINE	18,991	M-6
BOISE	6,670	L-3
BONNER	36,835	B-2
BONNEVILLE	82,522	N-11
BOUNDARY	9,871	A-2
BUTTE	2,899	L-8
CAMAS	991	M-5
CANYON	131,441	M-2
CARIBOU	7,304	O-11
CASSIA	21,416	P-7
CLARK	1,022	L-9
CLEARWATER	8,930	F-3
CUSTER	4,342	K-5
ELMORE	29,130	M-4
FRANKLIN	11,329	Q-11
FREMONT	11,819	L-11
GEM	15,181	M-3
GOODING	14,155	O-5
IDAHO	15,511	H-2
JEFFERSON	19,155	M-9
JEROME	18,342	P-6
KOOTENAI	108,685	D-2
LATAH	34,935	E-2
LEMHI	7,806	I-6
LEWIS	3,747	G-3
LINCOLN	4,044	O-6
MADISON	27,467	M-11
MINIDOKA	20,174	O-8
NEZ PERCE	37,410	G-2
ONEIDA	4,125	Q-9
OWYHEE	10,644	N-2
PAYETTE	20,578	L-2
POWER	7,538	P-9
SHOSHONE	13,771	E-3
TETON	5,999	M-12
TWIN FALLS	64,284	P-5
VALLEY	7,651	J-4
WASHINGTON	9,977	L-2
TOTAL	**1,293,953**	

CITIES AND TOWNS

Note: The first name is that of the city or town, second, that of the county in which it is located, then the population and location on the map.

Aberdeen, *Bingham,* 1,840 ....O-9
American Falls, *Power,* 4,111 ....O-9
Ammon, *Bonneville,* 6,187 ....N-11
Arco, *Butte,* 1,026 ....M-8
Ashton, *Fremont,* 1,129 ....L-12
Bellevue, *Blaine,* 1,876 ....N-7
Blackfoot, *Bingham,* 10,419 ....N-10
Boise, *Ada,* 185,787 ....N-3
Bonners Ferry, *Boundary,* 2,515 ....A-3
Buhl, *Twin Falls,* 3,985 ....P-6
Burley, *Cassia,* 9,316 ....P-8
Caldwell, *Canyon,* 25,967 ....M-2
Chubbuck, *Bannock,* 9,700 ....O-10
Coeur D'Alene, *Kootenai,* 34,514 ....D-3
Dalton Gardens, *Kootenai,* 2,278 ....D-3
Driggs, *Teton,* 1,100 ....M-12
Eagle, *Ada,* 11,085 ....D-8
Emmett, *Gem,* 5,490 ....M-3
Filer, *Twin Falls,* 1,620 ....P-6
•Fort Hall, *Bingham,* 3,193 ....O-10
Fruitland, *Payette,* 3,805 ....L-2
Garden City, *Ada,* 10,624 ....M-3
Glenns Ferry, *Elmore,* 1,611 ....O-5
Gooding, *Gooding,* 3,384 ....O-6
Grangeville, *Idaho,* 3,228 ....H-3
Hailey, *Blaine,* 6,200 ....N-7
Hayden, *Kootenai,* 9,159 ....D-2
Heyburn, *Minidoka,* 2,899 ....P-8
Homedale, *Owyhee,* 2,528 ....M-2
Idaho Falls, *Bonneville,* 50,730 ....N-11
Iona, *Bonneville,* 1,201 ....N-11
Jerome, *Jerome,* 7,780 ....P-6
Kamiah, *Lewis,* 1,160 ....G-4
Kellogg, *Shoshone,* 2,395 ....B-8
Ketchum, *Blaine,* 3,003 ....M-6
Kimberly, *Twin Falls,* 2,614 ....P-6
Kuna, *Ada,* 5,382 ....N-3
Lapwai, *Nez Perce,* 1,134 ....G-2
Lewiston, *Nez Perce,* 30,904 ....G-2
Malad City, *Oneida,* 2,158 ....Q-10
McCall, *Valley,* 2,084 ....J-3
Meridian, *Ada,* 34,919 ....D-8
Middleton, *Canyon,* 2,978 ....D-7
Montpelier, *Bear Lake,* 2,785 ....P-12
Moscow, *Latah,* 21,291 ....F-2
Mountain Home, *Elmore,* 11,143 ....O-4
•Mountain Home AFB, *Elmore,* 8,894 ....O-4
Nampa, *Canyon,* 51,867 ....N-3
New Plymouth, *Payette,* 1,400 ....M-2
Orofino, *Clearwater,* 3,247 ....G-3
Osburn, *Shoshone,* 1,545 ....D-4
Parma, *Canyon,* 1,771 ....M-2
Payette, *Payette,* 7,054 ....L-2
Pinehurst, *Shoshone,* 1,661 ....B-8
Pocatello, *Bannock,* 51,466 ....O-10
Post Falls, *Kootenai,* 17,247 ....D-2
Preston, *Franklin,* 4,682 ....Q-11
Priest River, *Bonner,* 1,754 ....C-2
Rathdrum, *Kootenai,* 4,816 ....C-2
Rexburg, *Madison,* 17,257 ....M-11
Rigby, *Jefferson,* 2,998 ....M-11
Rupert, *Minidoka,* 5,645 ....P-8
Saint Anthony, *Fremont,* 3,342 ....M-11
Saint Maries, *Benewah,* 2,652 ....E-3
Salmon, *Lemhi,* 3,122 ....J-7
Sandpoint, *Bonner,* 6,835 ....B-3
Shelley, *Bingham,* 3,813 ....N-10
Shoshone, *Lincoln,* 1,398 ....O-6
Soda Springs, *Caribou,* 3,381 ....P-11
Spirit Lake, *Kootenai,* 1,376 ....C-2
Star, *Ada,* 1,795 ....D-7
Sugar City, *Madison,* 1,242 ....M-11
Sun Valley, *Blaine,* 1,427 ....M-6
Twin Falls, *Twin Falls,* 34,469 ....P-6
Weiser, *Washington,* 5,343 ....L-2
Wendell, *Gooding,* 2,338 ....O-6
Wilder, *Canyon,* 1,462 ....M-2

Explanation of symbols: • - Census Designated Place (CDP)

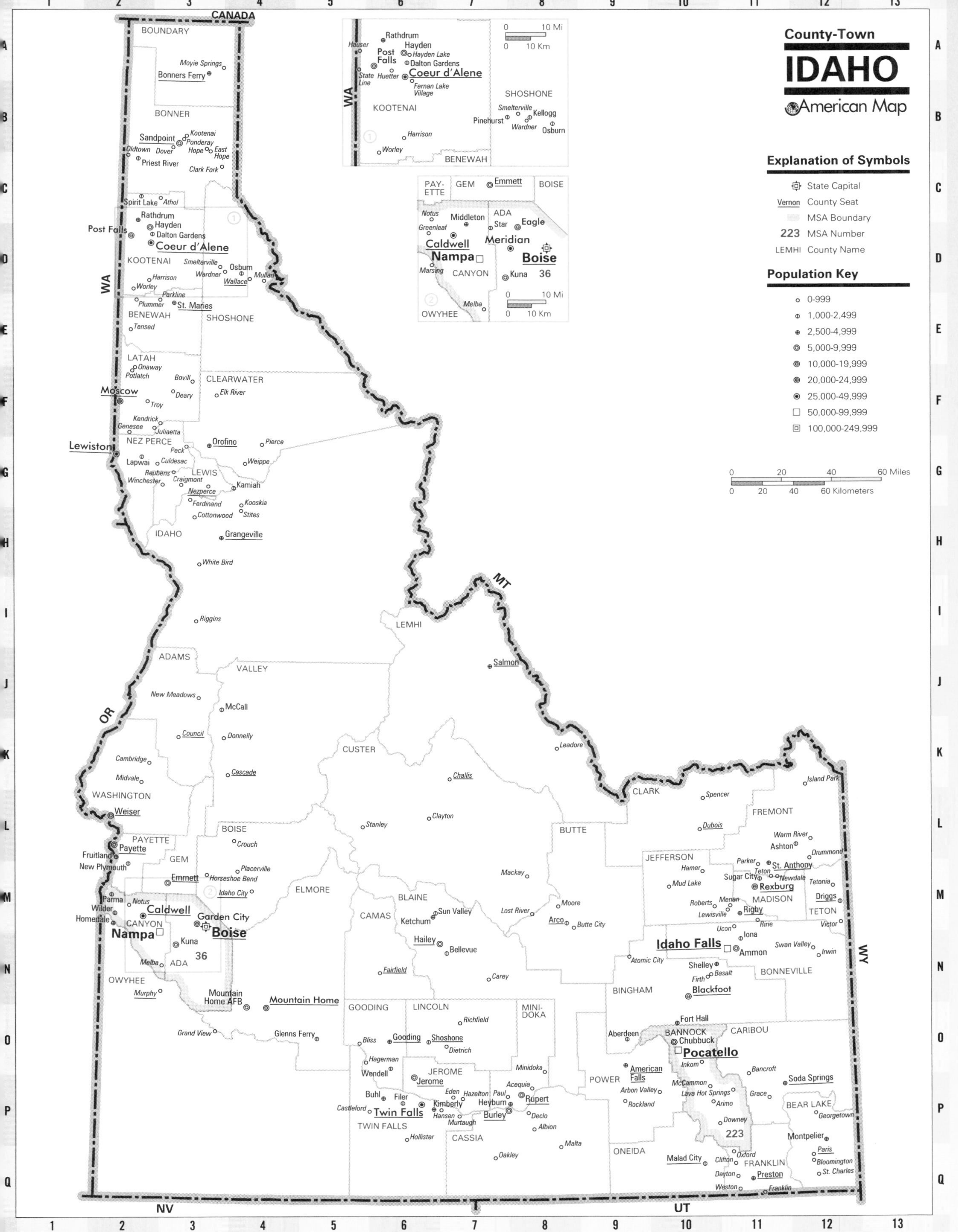
County-Town
IDAHO
American Map
Explanation of Symbols
State Capital
Vernon County Seat
MSA Boundary
223 MSA Number
LEMHI County Name
Population Key
0-999
1,000-2,499
2,500-4,999
5,000-9,999
10,000-19,999
20,000-24,999
25,000-49,999
50,000-99,999
100,000-249,999
0 20 40 60 Miles
0 20 40 60 Kilometers
CANADA
WA
OR
MT
WY
NV
UT
BOUNDARY
Moyie Springs
Bonners Ferry
BONNER
Sandpoint
Kootenai
Ponderay
Oldtown
Dover
Hope
East Hope
Priest River
Clark Fork
Spirit Lake
Athol
Rathdrum
Post Falls
Hayden
Dalton Gardens
Coeur d'Alene
KOOTENAI
Smelterville
Osburn
Wardner
Wallace
Mullan
Harrison
Worley
Parkline
Plummer
St. Maries
BENEWAH
SHOSHONE
Tensed
LATAH
Onaway
Potlatch
Bovill
CLEARWATER
Moscow
Deary
Elk River
Troy
Kendrick
Genesee
Juliaetta
NEZ PERCE
Lewiston
Peck
Orofino
Pierce
Lapwai
Culdesac
Weippe
Reubens
Winchester
Craigmont
LEWIS
Kamiah
Nezperce
Ferdinand
Cottonwood
Kooskia
Stites
IDAHO
Grangeville
White Bird
Riggins
LEMHI
Salmon
ADAMS
VALLEY
New Meadows
McCall
Council
Donnelly
Leadore
CUSTER
Cambridge
Midvale
Cascade
Challis
WASHINGTON
Weiser
Island Park
CLARK
Spencer
Stanley
Clayton
FREMONT
Dubois
BOISE
Crouch
BUTTE
Warm River
Ashton
PAYETTE
Fruitland
Payette
Drummond
New Plymouth
GEM
JEFFERSON
Hamer
Parker
Teton
St. Anthony
Placerville
Emmett
Horseshoe Bend
Mackay
Mud Lake
Sugar City
Newdale
Tetonia
Rexburg
Idaho City
ELMORE
Parma
Notus
Wilder
Homedale
Caldwell
CANYON
Nampa
Garden City
Boise
Kuna
36
Melba
ADA
OWYHEE
Murphy
BLAINE
Sun Valley
CAMAS
Ketchum
Lost River
Moore
Arco
Butte City
Roberts
Menan
Lewisville
MADISON
Rigby
Driggs
TETON
Victor
Ririe
Ucon
Iona
Idaho Falls
Ammon
Swan Valley
Irwin
Hailey
Bellevue
Atomic City
Fairfield
Carey
Shelley
Basalt
Firth
BONNEVILLE
Blackfoot
BINGHAM
Mountain Home AFB
Mountain Home
GOODING
LINCOLN
MINI-DOKA
Richfield
Fort Hall
Grand View
Glenns Ferry
Bliss
Gooding
Shoshone
Dietrich
Aberdeen
BANNOCK
Chubbuck
CARIBOU
Pocatello
Hagerman
Wendell
JEROME
Jerome
Minidoka
Inkom
American Falls
POWER
Bancroft
Soda Springs
Arbon Valley
McCammon
Lava Hot Springs
Buhl
Filer
Eden
Hazelton
Paul
Acequia
Rupert
Heyburn
Castleford
Twin Falls
Kimberly
Hansen
Murtaugh
Burley
Declo
Rockland
Arimo
Grace
BEAR LAKE
Georgetown
TWIN FALLS
Albion
Downey
223
Hollister
CASSIA
Malta
Montpelier
Oakley
ONEIDA
Malad City
Clifton
Oxford
FRANKLIN
Paris
Bloomington
St. Charles
Dayton
Preston
Weston
Franklin
Hauser
State Line
Huetter
Fernan Lake Village
Hayden Lake
SHOSHONE
Kellogg
Pinehurst
Osburn
PAY-ETTE
GEM
Emmett
BOISE
Middleton
Star
Eagle
Greenleaf
Meridian
Marsing
Melba
0 10 Mi
0 10 Km

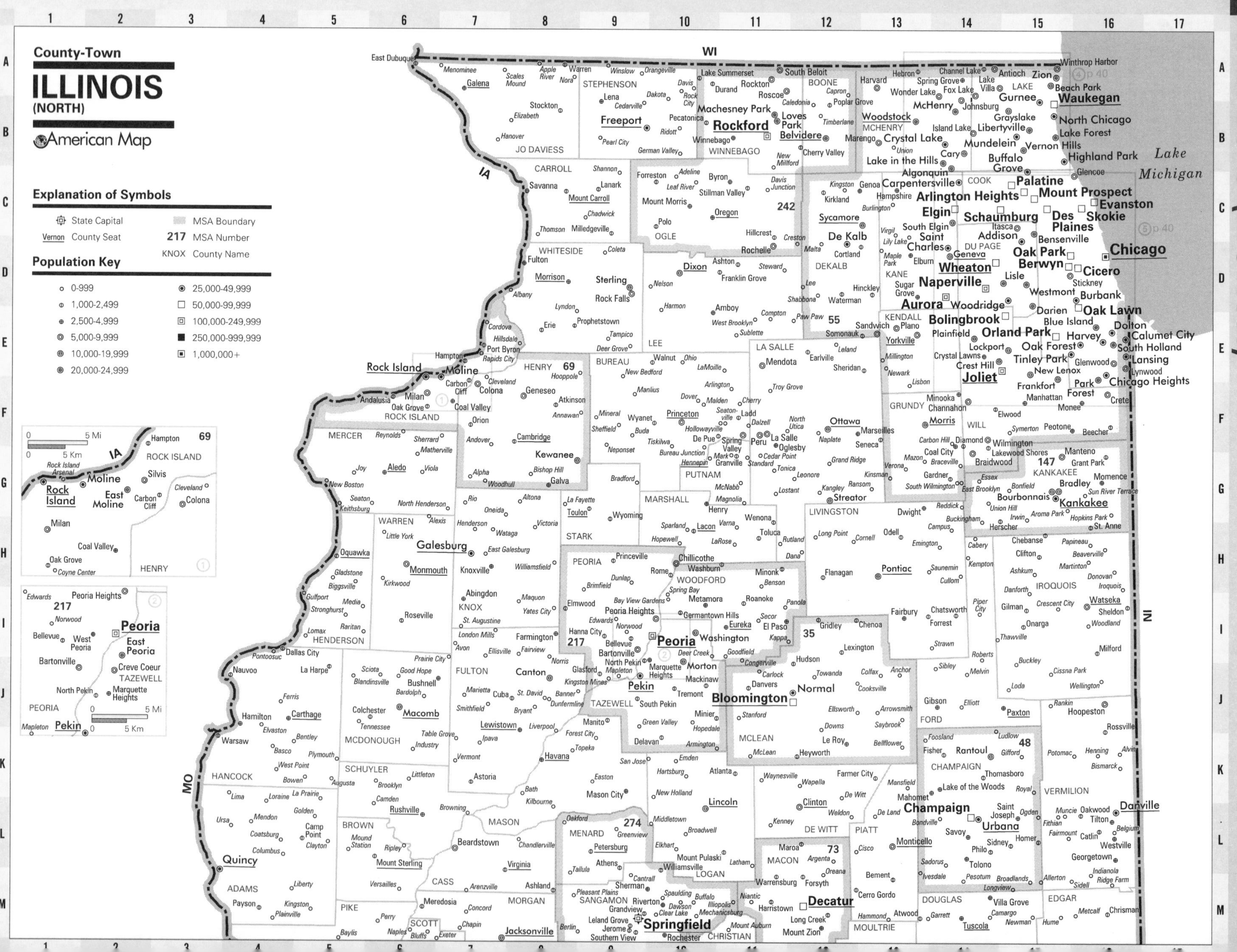

County-Town
ILLINOIS
(NORTH)
American Map
Explanation of Symbols
State Capital
Vernon County Seat
MSA Boundary
217 MSA Number
KNOX County Name
Population Key
0-999
1,000-2,499
2,500-4,999
5,000-9,999
10,000-19,999
20,000-24,999
25,000-49,999
50,000-99,999
100,000-249,999
250,000-999,999
1,000,000+
Lake Michigan
WI
IN
IA
MO
Chicago
Rockford
Peoria
Springfield
Joliet
Aurora
Naperville
Bloomington
Champaign
Decatur
Kankakee
Galesburg
Quincy
Moline
Rock Island
Danville
Hampton
ROCK ISLAND
Silvis
Carbon Cliff
East Moline
Coal Valley
Milan
Oak Grove
Coyne Center
Cleveland
Colona
HENRY
69
5 Mi
5 Km
Peoria Heights
East Peoria
Creve Coeur
TAZEWELL
Marquette Heights
North Pekin
Pekin
West Peoria
Bellevue
Bartonville
Norwood
Edwards
Mapleton
PEORIA
217

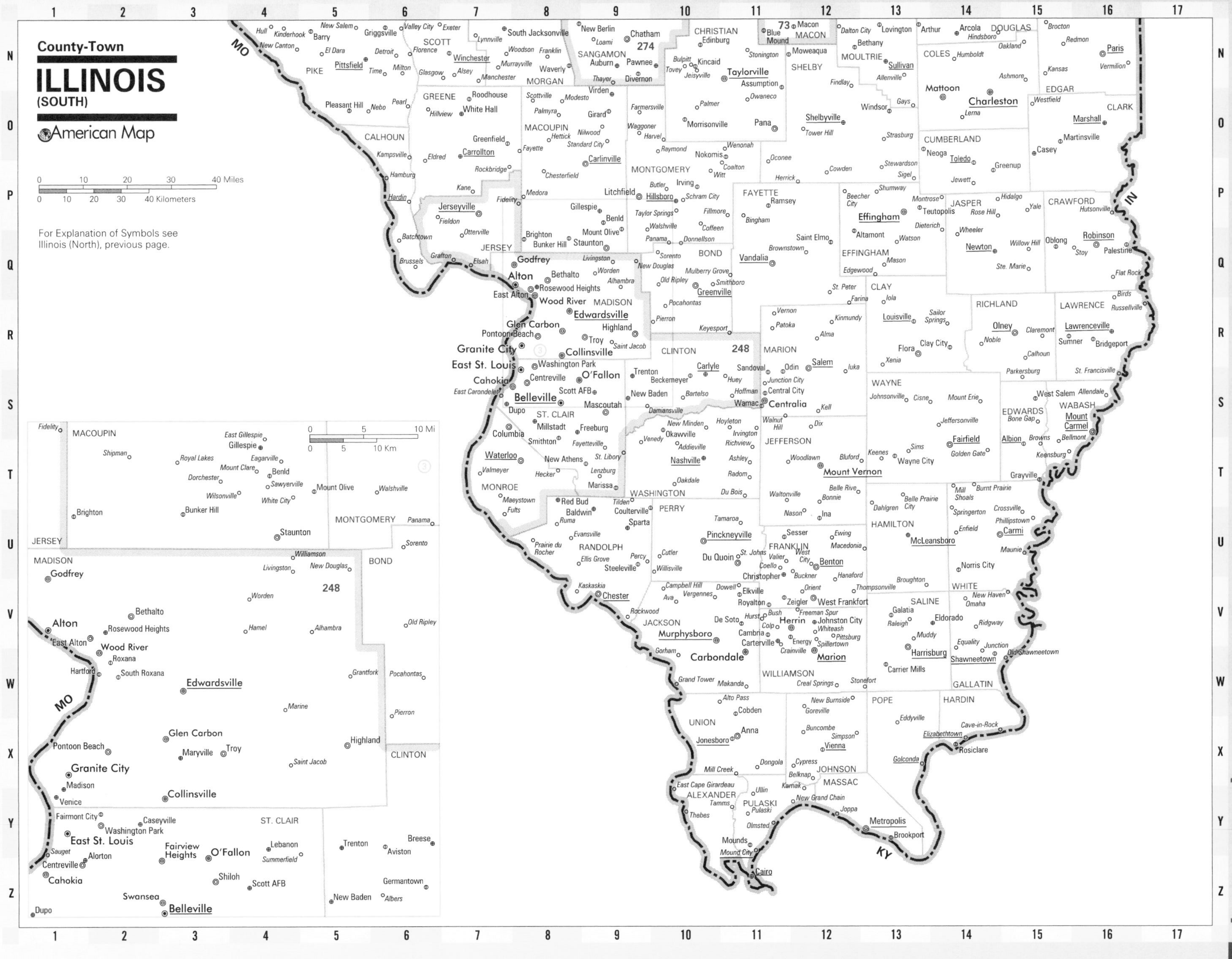
County-Town
ILLINOIS
(SOUTH)
American Map
40 Miles
40 Kilometers
For Explanation of Symbols see Illinois (North), previous page.
10 Mi
10 Km
MO
IN
KY
PIKE
SCOTT
MORGAN
SANGAMON
CHRISTIAN
MACON
MOULTRIE
SHELBY
COLES
DOUGLAS
EDGAR
CLARK
GREENE
CALHOUN
MACOUPIN
MONTGOMERY
FAYETTE
EFFINGHAM
CUMBERLAND
JASPER
CRAWFORD
JERSEY
MADISON
BOND
CLINTON
MARION
CLAY
RICHLAND
LAWRENCE
WAYNE
EDWARDS
WABASH
ST. CLAIR
MONROE
WASHINGTON
JEFFERSON
HAMILTON
WHITE
RANDOLPH
PERRY
FRANKLIN
SALINE
GALLATIN
JACKSON
WILLIAMSON
UNION
JOHNSON
POPE
HARDIN
ALEXANDER
PULASKI
MASSAC
Springfield
Chatham
Taylorville
Pana
Mattoon
Charleston
Paris
Marshall
Effingham
Robinson
Vandalia
Greenville
Carlinville
Litchfield
Hillsboro
Jerseyville
Godfrey
Alton
Wood River
Edwardsville
Granite City
East St. Louis
Collinsville
O'Fallon
Belleville
Cahokia
Carlyle
Salem
Centralia
Olney
Lawrenceville
Mount Carmel
Fairfield
Mount Vernon
Nashville
Waterloo
Chester
Pinckneyville
Du Quoin
Benton
West Frankfort
Murphysboro
Carbondale
Marion
Harrisburg
Shawneetown
Carmi
Anna
Vienna
Metropolis
Cairo

County-Town ILLINOIS INSET MAPS

American Map

Explanation of Symbols

- State Capital
- Vernon County Seat
- MSA Boundary
- 55 MSA Number
- COOK County Name

Population Key

- 0-999
- 1,000-2,499
- 2,500-4,999
- 5,000-9,999
- 10,000-19,999
- 20,000-24,999
- 25,000-49,999
- 50,000-99,999
- 100,000-249,999
- 250,000-999,999
- 1,000,000+

COUNTIES

(102 Counties)

Name of County	Population	Location on Map
ADAMS	68,277	M-4
ALEXANDER	9,590	Y-10
BOND	17,633	Q-10
BOONE	41,786	A-12
BROWN	6,950	L-5
BUREAU	35,503	E-9
CALHOUN	5,084	O-5
CARROLL	16,674	C-8
CASS	13,695	M-6
CHAMPAIGN	179,669	K-14
CHRISTIAN	35,372	M-10
CLARK	17,008	O-16
CLAY	14,560	Q-13
CLINTON	35,535	R-10
COLES	53,196	N-13
COOK	5,376,741	C-14
CRAWFORD	20,452	P-15
CUMBERLAND	11,253	O-13
DE KALB	88,969	D-12
DE WITT	16,798	L-12
DOUGLAS	19,922	M-13
DU PAGE	904,161	D-14
EDGAR	19,704	M-15
EDWARDS	6,971	S-15
EFFINGHAM	34,264	Q-12
FAYETTE	21,802	P-11
FORD	14,241	J-13
FRANKLIN	39,018	U-11
FULTON	38,250	J-7
GALLATIN	6,445	W-14
GREENE	14,761	O-6
GRUNDY	37,535	F-13
HAMILTON	8,621	U-13
HANCOCK	20,121	K-3
HARDIN	4,800	W-14
HENDERSON	8,213	I-5
HENRY	51,020	E-8
IROQUOIS	31,334	H-15
JACKSON	59,612	V-9
JASPER	10,117	P-14
JEFFERSON	40,045	T-11
JERSEY	21,668	Q-7
JO DAVIESS	22,289	B-8
JOHNSON	12,878	X-12
KANE	404,119	D-13
KANKAKEE	103,833	G-15
KENDALL	54,544	E-13
KNOX	55,836	I-7
LA SALLE	111,509	E-11
LAKE	644,356	A-15
LAWRENCE	15,452	R-15
LEE	36,062	E-10
LIVINGSTON	39,678	G-12
LOGAN	31,183	M-10
MACON	114,706	L-11
MACOUPIN	49,019	O-8
MADISON	258,941	R-9
MARION	41,691	R-11
MARSHALL	13,180	G-9
MASON	16,038	L-7
MASSAC	15,161	Y-12
MCDONOUGH	32,913	K-5
MCHENRY	260,077	B-13
MCLEAN	150,433	K-11
MENARD	12,486	L-8
MERCER	16,957	F-5
MONROE	27,619	T-7
MONTGOMERY	30,652	P-9
MORGAN	36,616	M-8
MOULTRIE	14,287	M-12
OGLE	51,032	D-10
PEORIA	183,433	H-8
PERRY	23,094	U-10
PIATT	16,365	L-12
PIKE	17,384	M-5
POPE	4,413	W-13
PULASKI	7,348	Y-11
PUTNAM	6,086	G-10
RANDOLPH	33,893	U-8
RICHLAND	16,149	R-14
ROCK ISLAND	149,374	F-6
SAINT CLAIR	256,082	S-8
SALINE	26,733	V-13
SANGAMON	188,951	M-9
SCHUYLER	7,189	K-5
SCOTT	5,537	M-6
SHELBY	22,893	N-12
STARK	6,332	H-8
STEPHENSON	48,979	A-9
TAZEWELL	128,485	J-9
UNION	18,293	X-10
VERMILION	83,919	K-15
WABASH	12,937	S-15
WARREN	18,735	H-6
WASHINGTON	15,148	T-9
WAYNE	17,151	S-13
WHITE	15,371	V-14
WHITESIDE	60,653	D-8
WILL	502,266	F-14
WILLIAMSON	61,296	W-11
WINNEBAGO	278,418	B-10
WOODFORD	35,469	H-10
TOTAL	**12,419,293**	

CITIES AND TOWNS

Note: The first name is that of the city or town, second, that of the county in which it is located, then the population and location on the map.

Abingdon, *Knox*, 3,612	I-7
Addison, *Du Page*, 35,914	D-15
Albion, *Edwards*, 1,933	T-15
Aledo, *Mercer*, 3,613	G-6
Algonquin, *McHenry*, 23,276	C-14
Alorton, *Saint Clair*, 2,749	Z-1
Alsip, *Cook*, 19,725	II-15
Altamont, *Effingham*, 2,283	Q-12
Alton, *Madison*, 30,496	Q-8
Amboy, *Lee*, 2,561	E-10
Andalusia, *Rock Island*, 1,050	F-6
Anna, *Union*, 5,136	X-11
Antioch, *Lake*, 8,788	A-14
Arcola, *Douglas*, 2,652	N-14
Arlington Heights, *Cook*, 76,031	C-15
Arthur, *Douglas*, 2,203	N-13
Ashland, *Cass*, 1,361	M-8
Ashton, *Lee*, 1,142	D-11
Assumption, *Christian*, 1,261	O-11
Astoria, *Fulton*, 1,193	K-7
Athens, *Menard*, 1,726	L-9
Atkinson, *Henry*, 1,001	F-8
Atlanta, *Logan*, 1,649	K-11
Atwood, *Douglas*, 1,290	M-13
Auburn, *Sangamon*, 4,317	N-9
Aurora, *Kane*, 142,990	D-14
Aviston, *Clinton*, 1,231	Y-6
Baldwin, *Randolph*, 3,627	U-9
Bannockburn, *Lake*, 1,429	MM-6
Barrington, *Cook*, 10,168	AA-10
Barrington Hills, *Cook*, 3,915	AA-10
Barry, *Pike*, 1,368	N-5
Bartlett, *Cook*, 36,706	DD-9
Bartonville, *Peoria*, 6,310	I-9
Batavia, *Kane*, 23,866	FF-8
Beach Park, *Lake*, 10,072	A-15
Beardstown, *Cass*, 5,766	L-7
Beckemeyer, *Clinton*, 1,043	S-10
Beecher, *Will*, 2,033	F-16
Belleville, *Saint Clair*, 41,410	S-8
Bellevue, *Peoria*, 1,887	I-9
Bellwood, *Cook*, 20,535	FF-13
Belvidere, *Boone*, 20,820	B-12
Bement, *Piatt*, 1,784	M-13
Benld, *Macoupin*, 1,541	P-9
Bensenville, *Du Page*, 20,703	C-15
Benton, *Franklin*, 6,880	U-12
Berkeley, *Cook*, 5,245	FF-13
Berwyn, *Cook*, 54,016	D-15
Bethalto, *Madison*, 9,454	Q-8
Bethany, *Moultrie*, 1,287	N-12
Bloomingdale, *Du Page*, 21,675	DD-11
Bloomington, *McLean*, 64,808	J-12
Blue Island, *Cook*, 23,463	E-16
Blue Mound, *Macon*, 1,129	N-11
Bolingbrook, *Will*, 56,321	E-15
•Boulder Hill, *Kendall*, 8,169	HH-7
Bourbonnais, *Kankakee*, 15,256	G-15
Bradley, *Kankakee*, 12,784	G-15
Braidwood, *Will*, 5,203	G-14
Breese, *Clinton*, 4,048	Y-6
Bridgeport, *Lawrence*, 2,168	R-16
Bridgeview, *Cook*, 15,335	HH-14
Brighton, *Macoupin*, 2,196	Q-8
Broadview, *Cook*, 8,264	FF-13
Brookfield, *Cook*, 19,085	GG-13
Brookport, *Massac*, 1,054	Y-13
Buffalo Grove, *Cook*, 42,909	C-15
Bunker Hill, *Macoupin*, 1,801	Q-8
Burbank, *Cook*, 27,902	D-16
Burnham, *Cook*, 4,170	JJ-17
Burr Ridge, *Du Page*, 10,408	HH-12
Bushnell, *McDonough*, 3,221	J-7
Byron, *Ogle*, 2,917	C-11
Cahokia, *Saint Clair*, 16,391	S-8
Cairo, *Alexander*, 3,632	Z-11
Calumet City, *Cook*, 39,071	E-16
Calumet Park, *Cook*, 8,516	II-16
Cambria, *Williamson*, 1,330	V-11
Cambridge, *Henry*, 2,180	F-8
Camp Point, *Adams*, 1,244	L-5
Canton, *Fulton*, 15,288	J-8
Carbon Cliff, *Rock Island*, 1,689	F-7
Carbondale, *Jackson*, 20,681	W-11
Carlinville, *Macoupin*, 5,685	P-9
Carlyle, *Clinton*, 3,406	S-10
Carmi, *White*, 5,422	U-15
Carol Stream, *Du Page*, 40,438	EE-10
Carpentersville, *Kane*, 30,586	C-14
Carrier Mills, *Saline*, 1,886	W-13
Carrollton, *Greene*, 2,605	O-7
Carterville, *Williamson*, 4,616	V-11
Carthage, *Hancock*, 2,725	J-4
Cary, *McHenry*, 15,531	B-14
Casey, *Clark*, 2,942	O-15
Caseyville, *Saint Clair*, 4,310	Y-2
Catlin, *Vermilion*, 2,087	L-16
Central City, *Marion*, 1,371	S-11
Centralia, *Marion*, 14,136	S-11
Centreville, *Saint Clair*, 5,951	S-8
Cerro Gordo, *Piatt*, 1,436	M-12
Champaign, *Champaign*, 67,518	L-14
Channahon, *Will*, 7,344	F-14
•Channel Lake, *Lake*, 1,785	A-14
Charleston, *Coles*, 21,039	O-14
Chatham, *Sangamon*, 8,583	N-9
Chatsworth, *Livingston*, 1,265	I-14
Chebanse, *Kankakee*, 1,148	H-15
Chenoa, *McLean*, 1,845	I-12
Cherry Valley, *Winnebago*, 2,191	B-12
Chester, *Randolph*, 5,185	V-9
Chicago, *Cook*, 2,896,016	D-16
Chicago Heights, *Cook*, 32,776	E-16
Chicago Ridge, *Cook*, 14,127	II-14
Chillicothe, *Peoria*, 5,996	H-10
Chrisman, *Edgar*, 1,318	M-16
Christopher, *Franklin*, 2,836	U-11
Cicero, *Cook*, 85,616	D-16
Clarendon Hills, *Du Page*, 7,610	GG-12
Clay City, *Clay*, 1,000	R-14
Clifton, *Iroquois*, 1,317	H-15
Clinton, *Dewitt*, 7,485	L-12
Coal City, *Grundy*, 4,797	F-14
Coal Valley, *Rock Island*, 3,606	F-7
Cobden, *Union*, 1,116	W-11
Colchester, *McDonough*, 1,493	J-6
Collinsville, *Madison*, 24,707	R-8
Colona, *Henry*, 5,173	F-7
Columbia, *Monroe*, 7,922	S-7
Cortland, *De Kalb*, 2,066	D-13
Coulterville, *Randolph*, 1,230	U-10
Country Club Hills, *Cook*, 16,169	KK-15
Countryside, *Cook*, 5,991	GG-13
Crest Hill, *Will*, 13,329	E-14
Crestwood, *Cook*, 11,251	II-14
Crete, *Will*, 7,346	F-16
Creve Coeur, *Tazewell*, 5,448	J-2
Crystal Lake, *McHenry*, 38,000	B-14
•Crystal Lawns, *Will*, 2,933	E-14
Cuba, *Fulton*, 1,418	J-8
Dallas City, *Hancock*, 1,055	I-4
Danvers, *McLean*, 1,183	J-11
Danville, *Vermilion*, 33,904	L-16
Darien, *Du Page*, 22,860	D-15
De Kalb, *De Kalb*, 39,018	D-12
De Pue, *Bureau*, 1,842	F-11
De Soto, *Jackson*, 1,653	V-11
Decatur, *Macon*, 81,860	M-12
Deer Park, *Lake*, 3,102	MM-4
Deerfield, *Lake*, 18,420	MM-6
Delavan, *Tazewell*, 1,825	K-10
Des Plaines, *Cook*, 58,720	C-15
Diamond, *Grundy*, 1,393	F-14
Divernon, *Sangamon*, 1,201	N-9
Dixmoor, *Cook*, 3,934	JJ-16
Dixon, *Lee*, 15,941	D-10
Dolton, *Cook*, 25,614	E-16
Downers Grove, *Du Page*, 48,724	GG-11
Du Quoin, *Perry*, 6,448	U-11
Dupo, *Saint Clair*, 3,933	S-7
Durand, *Winnebago*, 1,081	A-10
Dwight, *Livingston*, 4,363	G-13
Earlville, *La Salle*, 1,778	E-12

Explanation of symbols: • - Census Designated Place (CDP)

North Barrington, *Lake,* 2,918 .... MM-3
North Chicago, *Lake,* 35,918 .... B-15
North Pekin, *Tazewell,* 1,574 .... J-9
North Riverside, *Cook,* 6,688 .... FF-14
Northbrook, *Cook,* 33,435 .... BB-14
Northfield, *Cook,* 5,389 .... BB-14
Northlake, *Cook,* 11,878 .... EE-13
O'Fallon, *St. Clair,* 21,910 .... S-8
Oak Brook, *Du Page,* 8,702 .... GG-12
Oak Forest, *Cook,* 28,051 .... E-16
Oak Grove, *Rock Island,* 1,318 .... F-6
Oak Lawn, *Cook,* 55,245 .... D-16
Oak Park, *Cook,* 52,524 .... D-15
Oakbrook Terrace, *Du Page,* 2,300 .... FF-12
Oakwood, *Vermilion,* 1,502 .... L-16
Oakwood Hills, *McHenry,* 2,194 .... LL-3
Oblong, *Crawford,* 1,580 .... Q-15
Odell, *Livingston,* 1,014 .... H-13
Odin, *Marion,* 1,122 .... S-11
Oglesby, *La Salle,* 3,647 .... F-11
Okawville, *Washington,* 1,355 .... S-10
Olney, *Richland,* 8,631 .... R-15
Olympia Fields, *Cook,* 4,732 .... LL-15
Onarga, *Iroquois,* 1,438 .... I-15
Oquawka, *Henderson,* 1,539 .... H-5
Oregon, *Ogle,* 4,060 .... C-10
Orion, *Henry,* 1,713 .... F-7
Orland Hills, *Cook,* 6,779 .... KK-13
Orland Park, *Cook,* 51,077 .... E-15
Oswego, *Kendall,* 13,326 .... II-7
Ottawa, *La Salle,* 18,307 .... F-12
Palatine, *Cook,* 65,479 .... C-15
Palestine, *Crawford,* 1,366 .... Q-16
Palos Heights, *Cook,* 11,260 .... II-14
Palos Hills, *Cook,* 17,665 .... II-14
Palos Park, *Cook,* 4,689 .... II-13
Pana, *Christian,* 5,614 .... O-11
Paris, *Edgar,* 9,077 .... N-16
Park City, *Lake,* 6,637 .... KK-6
Park Forest, *Will,* 23,462 .... F-16
Park Ridge, *Cook,* 37,775 .... DD-13
Pawnee, *Sangamon,* 2,647 .... N-10
Paxton, *Ford,* 4,525 .... J-15
Payson, *Adams,* 1,066 .... M-4
Pecatonica, *Winnebago,* 1,997 .... B-10
Pekin, *Tazewell,* 33,857 .... J-9
Peoria, *Peoria,* 112,936 .... I-10
Peoria Heights, *Peoria,* 6,635 .... I-10
Peotone, *Will,* 3,385 .... F-16
Peru, *La Salle,* 9,835 .... F-11
Petersburg, *Menard,* 2,299 .... L-9
Philo, *Champaign,* 1,314 .... L-14
Phoenix, *Cook,* 2,157 .... JJ-16
Pinckneyville, *Perry,* 5,464 .... U-10
• Pistakee Highlands, *McHenry,* 3,812 .... JJ-3
Pittsfield, *Pike,* 4,211 .... N-5
Plainfield, *Will,* 13,038 .... E-14
Plano, *Kendall,* 5,633 .... E-13
Pleasant Hill, *Pike,* 1,047 .... O-5
Polo, *Ogle,* 2,477 .... C-10
Pontiac, *Livingston,* 11,864 .... H-13
Pontoon Beach, *Madison,* 5,620 .... R-8
Poplar Grove, *Boone,* 1,368 .... B-12
Port Byron, *Rock Island,* 1,535 .... E-7
Posen, *Cook,* 4,730 .... JJ-15
• Preston Heights, *Will,* 2,527 .... LL-10
Princeton, *Bureau,* 7,501 .... F-10
Princeville, *Peoria,* 1,621 .... H-9
Prophetstown, *Whiteside,* 2,023 .... E-8
Prospect Heights, *Cook,* 17,081 .... BB-12

Quincy, *Adams,* 40,366 .... M-4
Ramsey, *Fayette,* 1,056 .... P-11
Rantoul, *Champaign,* 12,857 .... K-14
Red Bud, *Randolph,* 3,422 .... T-8
Richmond, *McHenry,* 1,091 .... II-2
Richton Park, *Cook,* 12,533 .... LL-15
River Forest, *Cook,* 11,635 .... EE-14
River Grove, *Cook,* 10,668 .... EE-13
Riverdale, *Cook,* 15,055 .... JJ-16
Riverton, *Sangamon,* 3,048 .... M-10
Riverwoods, *Lake,* 3,843 .... MM-6
Roanoke, *Woodford,* 1,994 .... I-11
Robbins, *Cook,* 6,635 .... JJ-15
Robinson, *Crawford,* 6,822 .... Q-16
Rochelle, *Ogle,* 9,424 .... D-11
Rochester, *Sangamon,* 2,893 .... M-10
Rock Falls, *Whiteside,* 9,580 .... D-9
Rock Island, *Rock Island,* 39,684 .... E-6
Rockdale, *Will,* 1,888 .... LL-10
Rockford, *Winnebago,* 150,115 .... B-11
Rockton, *Winnebago,* 5,296 .... A-11
Rolling Meadows, *Cook,* 24,604 .... BB-11
• Rome, *Peoria,* 1,776 .... H-10
Romeoville, *Will,* 21,153 .... JJ-10
Roodhouse, *Greene,* 2,214 .... O-7
Roscoe, *Winnebago,* 6,244 .... A-11
Roselle, *Du Page,* 23,115 .... DD-11
Rosemont, *Cook,* 4,224 .... DD-13
Roseville, *Warren,* 1,083 .... I-6
• Rosewood Heights, *Madison,* 4,262 .... Q-8
Rosiclare, *Hardin,* 1,213 .... X-14
Rossville, *Vermilion,* 1,217 .... K-16
Round Lake, *Lake,* 5,842 .... KK-4
Round Lake Beach, *Lake,* 25,859 .... KK-4
Round Lake Heights, *Lake,* 1,347 .... KK-4
Round Lake Park, *Lake,* 6,038 .... KK-4
Roxana, *Madison,* 1,547 .... W-2
Royalton, *Franklin,* 1,130 .... V-11
Rushville, *Schuyler,* 3,212 .... L-6
Saint Anne, *Kankakee,* 1,212 .... H-16
Saint Charles, *Kane,* 27,896 .... D-14
Saint Elmo, *Fayette,* 1,456 .... Q-12
Saint Joseph, *Champaign,* 2,912 .... L-15
Salem, *Marion,* 7,909 .... S-12
Sandoval, *Marion,* 1,434 .... S-11
Sandwich, *De Kalb,* 6,509 .... E-13
Sauk Village, *Cook,* 10,411 .... LL-17
Savanna, *Carroll,* 3,542 .... C-8
Savoy, *Champaign,* 4,476 .... L-14
Schaumburg, *Cook,* 75,386 .... C-15
Schiller Park, *Cook,* 11,850 .... EE-13
• Scott AFB, *St. Clair,* 2,707 .... S-9
Seneca, *La Salle,* 2,053 .... F-13
Sesser, *Franklin,* 2,128 .... U-11
Shawneetown, *Gallatin,* 1,410 .... W-14
Shelbyville, *Shelby,* 4,971 .... O-12
Sheldon, *Iroquois,* 1,232 .... I-16
Sheridan, *La Salle,* 2,411 .... E-13
Sherman, *Sangamon,* 2,871 .... M-10
Shiloh, *Saint Clair,* 7,643 .... Z-3
Shorewood, *Will,* 7,686 .... LL-9
Sidney, *Champaign,* 1,062 .... L-15
Silvis, *Rock Island,* 7,269 .... G-2
Skokie, *Cook,* 63,348 .... C-16
Sleepy Hollow, *Kane,* 3,553 .... BB-8
Smithton, *Saint Clair,* 2,248 .... T-8
Somonauk, *De Kalb,* 1,295 .... E-13
South Barrington, *Cook,* 3,760 .... BB-10
South Beloit, *Winnebago,* 5,397 .... A-11
South Chicago Heights, *Cook,* 3,970 .... LL-16

South Elgin, *Kane,* 16,100 .... C-14
South Holland, *Cook,* 22,147 .... E-16
South Jacksonville, *Morgan,* 3,475 .... N-7
South Pekin, *Tazewell,* 1,162 .... J-9
South Roxana, *Madison,* 1,888 .... W-2
Southern View, *Sangamon,* 1,695 .... M-9
Sparta, *Randolph,* 4,486 .... U-9
Spring Grove, *McHenry,* 3,880 .... A-14
Spring Valley, *Bureau,* 5,398 .... F-11
Springfield, *Sangamon,* 111,454 .... M-9
Staunton, *Macoupin,* 5,030 .... Q-9
Steeleville, *Randolph,* 2,077 .... U-9
Steger, *Cook,* 9,682 .... LL-16
Sterling, *Whiteside,* 15,451 .... D-9
Stickney, *Cook,* 6,148 .... D-16
Stillman Valley, *Ogle,* 1,048 .... C-11
Stockton, *Jo Daviess,* 1,926 .... B-8
Stone Park, *Cook,* 5,127 .... EE-13
Streamwood, *Cook,* 36,407 .... CC-9
Streator, *La Salle,* 14,190 .... G-12
Sugar Grove, *Kane,* 3,909 .... D-13
Sullivan, *Moultrie,* 4,326 .... N-13
Summit, *Cook,* 10,637 .... GG-14
Sumner, *Lawrence,* 1,022 .... R-15
Swansea, *Saint Clair,* 10,579 .... Z-3
Sycamore, *De Kalb,* 12,020 .... C-13
Taylorville, *Christian,* 11,427 .... N-11
Teutopolis, *Effingham,* 1,559 .... P-13
Third Lake, *Lake,* 1,355 .... KK-5
Thomasboro, *Champaign,* 1,233 .... K-14
Thornton, *Cook,* 2,582 .... KK-16
Tilton, *Vermilion,* 2,976 .... L-16
Tinley Park, *Cook,* 48,401 .... E-16
Toledo, *Cumberland,* 1,166 .... P-14
Tolono, *Champaign,* 2,700 .... L-14
Toluca, *Marshall,* 1,339 .... H-11
Toulon, *Stark,* 1,400 .... G-9
Tower Lakes, *Lake,* 1,310 .... LL-3
Tremont, *Tazewell,* 2,029 .... J-10
Trenton, *Clinton,* 2,610 .... S-9
Troy, *Madison,* 8,524 .... R-9
Tuscola, *Douglas,* 4,448 .... M-14
University Park, *Will,* 6,662 .... JJ-15
Urbana, *Champaign,* 36,395 .... L-14
Vandalia, *Fayette,* 6,975 .... Q-11
• Venetian Village, *Lake,* 3,082 .... JJ-4
Venice, *Madison,* 2,528 .... Y-1
Vernon Hills, *Lake,* 20,120 .... B-15
Vienna, *Johnson,* 1,234 .... X-12
Villa Grove, *Douglas,* 2,553 .... M-14
Villa Park, *Du Page,* 22,075 .... FF-12
Virden, *Macoupin,* 3,488 .... O-9
Virginia, *Cass,* 1,728 .... M-8
Wadsworth, *Lake,* 3,083 .... JJ-5
Walnut, *Bureau,* 1,461 .... E-10
Wamac, *Clinton,* 1,378 .... S-11
Warren, *Jo Daviess,* 1,496 .... A-8
Warrensburg, *Macon,* 1,289 .... M-11
Warrenville, *Du Page,* 13,363 .... GG-9
Warsaw, *Hancock,* 1,793 .... K-3
Washburn, *Woodford,* 1,147 .... H-11
Washington, *Tazewell,* 10,841 .... I-10
Washington Park, *Saint Clair,* 5,345 .... S-8
Waterloo, *Monroe,* 7,614 .... T-8
Waterman, *De Kalb,* 1,224 .... D-12
Watseka, *Iroquois,* 5,670 .... I-16
Wauconda, *Lake,* 9,448 .... LL-4
Waukegan, *Lake,* 87,901 .... B-15
Waverly, *Morgan,* 1,346 .... N-8
Wayne, *Du Page,* 2,137 .... EE-9

Wayne City, *Wayne,* 1,089 .... T-13
Wenona, *Marshall,* 1,065 .... H-11
West Chicago, *Du Page,* 23,469 .... FF-9
West Dundee, *Kane,* 5,428 .... BB-8
West Frankfort, *Franklin,* 8,196 .... V-12
West Peoria, *Peoria,* 4,762 .... I-2
West Salem, *Edwards,* 1,001 .... S-15
Westchester, *Cook,* 16,824 .... FF-13
Western Springs, *Cook,* 12,493 .... GG-13
Westmont, *Du Page,* 24,554 .... D-15
Westville, *Vermilion,* 3,175 .... L-16
Wheaton, *Du Page,* 55,416 .... D-14
Wheeling, *Cook,* 34,496 .... AA-12
White Hall, *Greene,* 2,629 .... O-7
Williamsville, *Sangamon,* 1,439 .... M-10
Willow Springs, *Cook,* 5,027 .... HH-13
Willowbrook, *Du Page,* 8,967 .... HH-12
Wilmette, *Cook,* 27,651 .... CC-15
Wilmington, *Will,* 5,134 .... F-14
Winchester, *Scott,* 1,650 .... N-7
Windsor, *Shelby,* 1,125 .... O-13
Winfield, *Du Page,* 8,718 .... FF-10
Winnebago, *Winnebago,* 2,958 .... B-11
Winnetka, *Cook,* 12,419 .... BB-15
Winthrop Harbor, *Lake,* 6,670 .... A-15
• Wonder Lake, *McHenry,* 7,463 .... A-14
Wood Dale, *Du Page,* 13,535 .... DD-12
Wood River, *Madison,* 11,296 .... R-8
Woodridge, *Du Page,* 30,934 .... D-15
Woodstock, *McHenry,* 20,151 .... B-13
Worth, *Cook,* 11,047 .... II-14
Wyanet, *Bureau,* 1,028 .... F-10
Wyoming, *Stark,* 1,424 .... H-9
Yorkville, *Kendall,* 6,189 .... E-13
Zeigler, *Franklin,* 1,669 .... V-11
Zion, *Lake,* 22,866 .... A-15

Explanation of symbols: • - Census Designated Place (CDP)

COUNTIES

(92 Counties)

Name of County	Population	Location on Map
ADAMS	33,625	E-12
ALLEN	331,849	D-12
BARTHOLOMEW	71,435	L-9
BENTON	9,421	F-5
BLACKFORD	14,048	F-11
BOONE	46,107	H-7
BROWN	14,957	K-8
CARROLL	20,165	F-8
CASS	40,930	E-8
CLARK	96,472	N-11
CLAY	26,556	K-6
CLINTON	33,866	G-7
CRAWFORD	29,820	O-7
DAVIESS	29,820	M-6
DE KALB	40,285	C-12
DEARBORN	46,109	K-12
DECATUR	24,555	K-11
DELAWARE	118,769	G-11
DUBOIS	39,674	N-6
ELKHART	182,791	B-9
FAYETTE	25,588	I-12
FLOYD	70,823	O-10
FOUNTAIN	17,954	H-5
FRANKLIN	22,151	J-12
FULTON	20,511	D-8
GIBSON	32,500	O-4
GRANT	73,403	F-10
GREENE	33,157	L-6
HAMILTON	182,740	H-9
HANCOCK	55,391	I-10
HARRISON	34,325	P-9
HENDRICKS	104,093	I-7
HENRY	48,508	I-11
HOWARD	84,964	F-8
HUNTINGTON	38,075	E-11
JACKSON	41,335	L-9
JASPER	30,043	D-5
JAY	21,806	F-12
JEFFERSON	31,705	M-11
JENNINGS	27,554	L-10
JOHNSON	115,209	J-9
KNOX	39,256	N-4
KOSCIUSKO	74,057	C-9
LAGRANGE	34,909	A-11
LAKE	484,564	C-5
LAPORTE	110,106	B-6
LAWRENCE	45,922	L-7
MADISON	133,358	H-10
MARION	860,454	I-8
MARSHALL	45,128	C-8
MARTIN	10,369	M-7
MIAMI	36,082	E-9
MONROE	120,563	L-7
MONTGOMERY	37,629	H-6
MORGAN	66,689	J-7
NEWTON	14,566	D-5
NOBLE	46,275	B-11
OHIO	5,623	L-13
ORANGE	19,306	N-7
OWEN	21,786	J-7
PARKE	17,241	I-5
PERRY	18,899	O-7
PIKE	12,837	N-6
PORTER	146,798	C-6
POSEY	27,061	P-3
PULASKI	13,755	D-7
PUTNAM	36,019	I-6
RANDOLPH	27,401	H-12
RIPLEY	26,523	L-11
RUSH	18,261	I-11
SAINT JOSEPH	265,559	B-8
SCOTT	22,960	M-10
SHELBY	43,445	J-10
SPENCER	20,391	P-6
STARKE	23,556	C-7
STEUBEN	33,214	B-12
SULLIVAN	21,751	L-4
SWITZERLAND	9,065	M-12
TIPPECANOE	148,955	F-6
TIPTON	16,577	G-9
UNION	7,349	I-13
VANDERBURGH	171,922	P-4
VERMILLION	16,788	I-5
VIGO	105,848	J-5
WABASH	34,960	D-10
WARREN	8,419	G-5
WARRICK	52,383	P-5
WASHINGTON	27,223	M-9
WAYNE	71,097	H-12
WELLS	27,600	E-11
WHITE	25,267	E-6
WHITLEY	30,707	D-11
TOTAL	**6,080,485**	

CITIES AND TOWNS

Note: The first name is that of the city or town, second, that of the county in which it is located, then the population and location on the map.

Akron, *Fulton,* 1,076 ....D-9
Albany, *Delaware,* 2,368 ....G-12
Albion, *Noble,* 2,284 ....C-11
Alexandria, *Madison,* 6,260 ....G-10
Anderson, *Madison,* 59,734 ....H-10
Andrews, *Huntington,* 1,290 ....E-11
Angola, *Steuben,* 7,344 ....B-12
Arcadia, *Hamilton,* 1,747 ....H-9
Argos, *Marshall,* 1,613 ....A-9
Ashley, *De Kalb,* 1,010 ....B-12
Attica, *Fountain,* 3,491 ....G-5
Auburn, *De Kalb,* 12,074 ....C-12
Aurora, *Dearborn,* 3,965 ....L-13
Austin, *Scott,* 4,724 ....M-10
Avilla, *Noble,* 2,049 ....C-12
Avon, *Hendricks,* 6,248 ....I-8
Bargersville, *Johnson,* 2,120 ....J-9
• Bass Lake, *Starke,* 1,249 ....C-8
Batesville, *Ripley,* 6,033 ....K-12
Battle Ground, *Tippecanoe,* 1,323 ....F-7
Bedford, *Lawrence,* 13,768 ....M-8
Beech Grove, *Marion,* 14,880 ....I-9
Berne, *Adams,* 4,150 ....F-13
Bicknell, *Knox,* 3,378 ....M-5
Bloomfield, *Greene,* 2,542 ....L-6
Bloomington, *Monroe,* 69,291 ....L-8
Bluffton, *Wells,* 9,536 ....E-12
Boonville, *Warrick,* 6,834 ....P-5
Bourbon, *Marshall,* 1,691 ....C-9
Brazil, *Clay,* 8,188 ....J-6
Bremen, *Marshall,* 4,486 ....B-9
• Bright, *Dearborn,* 5,405 ....K-13
Bristol, *Elkhart,* 1,382 ....A-10
Brook, *Newton,* 1,062 ....E-5
Brooklyn, *Morgan,* 1,545 ....J-8
Brookston, *White,* 1,717 ....F-7
Brookville, *Franklin,* 2,652 ....J-13
Brownsburg, *Hendricks,* 14,520 ....I-8
Brownstown, *Jackson,* 2,978 ....M-9
Butler, *De Kalb,* 2,725 ....B-13
Cambridge City, *Wayne,* 2,121 ....I-12
Cannelton, *Perry,* 1,209 ....Q-7
Carlisle, *Sullivan,* 2,660 ....L-5
Carmel, *Hamilton,* 37,733 ....H-9
Cayuga, *Vermillion,* 1,109 ....H-5
Cedar Lake, *Lake,* 9,279 ....C-5
Centerville, *Wayne,* 2,427 ....I-13
Chandler, *Warrick,* 3,094 ....P-5
Charlestown, *Clark,* 5,993 ....N-11
Chesterfield, *Madison,* 2,969 ....H-11
Chesterton, *Porter,* 10,488 ....B-6
Churubusco, *Whitley,* 1,666 ....C-12
Cicero, *Hamilton,* 4,303 ....H-9
Clarksville, *Clark,* 21,400 ....O-10
Clay City, *Clay,* 1,019 ....K-6
Clermont, *Marion,* 1,477 ....H-1
Clinton, *Vermillion,* 5,126 ....J-5
Cloverdale, *Putnam,* 2,243 ....J-7
Columbia City, *Whitley,* 7,077 ....D-11
Columbus, *Bartholomew,* 39,059 ....K-10
Connersville, *Fayette,* 15,411 ....J-12
Converse, *Blackford,* 1,137 ....G-12
Converse, *Miami,* 1,137 ....F-10
Corydon, *Harrison,* 2,715 ....O-9
Covington, *Fountain,* 2,565 ....H-5
Crawfordsville,
Montgomery, 15,243 ....H-7
Crothersville, *Jackson,* 1,570 ....M-10
Crown Point, *Lake,* 19,806 ....C-5
Culver, *Marshall,* 1,539 ....C-8
Cumberland, *Marion,* 5,500 ....L-3
Dale, *Spencer,* 1,568 ....O-6
Daleville, *Delaware,* 1,658 ....H-11
Danville, *Hendricks,* 6,418 ....I-8
Darmstadt, *Vanderburgh,* 1,313 ....P-4
Dayton, *Tippecanoe,* 1,120 ....G-7
Decatur, *Adams,* 9,528 ....E-13
Delphi, *Carroll,* 3,015 ....F-7
Demotte (De Motte), *Jasper,* 3,234 ..C-6
Dillsboro, *Dearborn,* 1,436 ....L-12
Dunkirk, *Jay,* 2,646 ....G-12
• Dunlap, *Elkhart,* 5,887 ....B-10
Dyer, *Lake,* 13,895 ....B-5
East Chicago, *Lake,* 32,414 ....B-5
Eaton, *Delaware,* 1,603 ....G-11
Edgewood, *Madison,* 1,988 ....H-10
Edinburgh, *Johnson,* 4,505 ....K-10
Elkhart, *Elkhart,* 51,874 ....A-10
Ellettsville, *Monroe,* 5,078 ....K-7
Elwood, *Madison,* 9,737 ....G-10
English, *Crawford,* 673 ....O-8
Evansville, *Vanderburgh,* 121,582 .....P-4
• Fairland, *Shelby,* 1,276 ....J-10
Fairmount, *Grant,* 2,992 ....G-11
Fairview Park, *Vermillion,* 1,496 ....I-5
Farmersburg, *Sullivan,* 1,180 ....K-5
Farmland, *Randolph,* 1,456 ....G-12
Ferdinand, *Dubois,* 2,277 ....O-7
Fishers, *Hamilton,* 37,835 ....H-9
Flora, *Carroll,* 2,227 ....F-8
Fort Branch, *Gibson,* 2,320 ....O-4
Fort Wayne, *Allen,* 205,727 ....D-12
Fortville, *Hancock,* 3,444 ....H-10
Fowler, *Benton,* 2,415 ....F-5
Frankfort, *Clinton,* 16,662 ....G-8
Franklin, *Johnson,* 19,463 ....J-9
Frankton, *Madison,* 1,905 ....G-10
Fremont, *Steuben,* 1,696 ....A-13
French Lick, *Orange,* 1,941 ....N-7
• Galena, *Floyd,* 1,831 ....O-10
Galveston, *Cass,* 1,532 ....F-9
Garrett, *De Kalb,* 5,803 ....C-12
Gary, *Lake,* 102,746 ....B-5
Gas City, *Grant,* 5,940 ....F-11
Gaston, *Delaware,* 1,010 ....G-11
Geneva, *Adams,* 1,368 ....F-13
Georgetown, *Floyd,* 2,227 ....O-10
• Georgetown, *St. Joseph,* 4,497 ....A-9
Goodland, *Newton,* 1,096 ....E-5
Goshen, *Elkhart,* 29,383 ....B-10
Grabill, *Allen,* 1,113 ....C-13
• Granger, *St. Joseph,* 28,284 ....A-9
Greencastle, *Putnam,* 9,880 ....J-7
Greendale, *Dearborn,* 4,296 ....L-13
Greenfield, *Hancock,* 14,600 ....I-10
Greensburg, *Decatur,* 10,260 ....K-11
Greentown, *Howard,* 2,546 ....F-10
Greenwood, *Johnson,* 36,037 ....J-9
Griffith, *Lake,* 17,334 ....B-5
• Grissom AFB, *Miami,* 1,652 ....F-9
• Gulivoire Park, *St. Joseph,* 2,974 .....B-9
Hagerstown, *Wayne,* 1,768 ....I-12
Hamilton, *Steuben,* 1,233 ....B-13
Hammond, *Lake,* 83,048 ....B-5
Hanover, *Jefferson,* 2,834 ....M-11
Hartford City, *Blackford,* 6,928 ....F-11
Haubstadt, *Gibson,* 1,529 ....O-4
Hebron, *Porter,* 3,596 ....C-6
• Henryville, *Clark,* 1,545 ....N-10
• Hidden Valley, *Dearborn,* 4,417 ......K-13
Highland, *Lake,* 23,546 ....B-5
Hobart, *Lake,* 25,363 ....B-6
Hope, *Bartholomew,* 2,140 ....K-10
Huntertown, *Allen,* 1,771 ....C-12
Huntingburg, *Dubois,* 5,598 ....O-6
Huntington, *Huntington,* 17,450 ......E-11
• Indian Heights, *Howard,* 3,274 ....G-9
Indianapolis, *Marion,* 791,926 ....I-9
Ingalls, *Madison,* 1,168 ....H-10
Jasonville, *Greene,* 2,490 ....L-6
Jasper, *Dubois,* 12,100 ....O-6
Jeffersonville, *Clark,* 27,362 ....O-10
Johnson, *Gibson,* 4,186 ....O-4
Jonesboro, *Grant,* 1,887 ....F-11
Kendallville, *Noble,* 9,616 ....B-12
Kentland, *Newton,* 1,822 ....E-5
Kingsford Heights, *La Porte,* 1,453 ...B-7
Knightstown, *Henry,* 2,148 ....I-11
Knox, *Starke,* 3,721 ....C-7
Kokomo, *Howard,* 46,113 ....F-9
• Koontz Lake, *Starke,* 1,554 ....C-8
Kouts, *Porter,* 1,698 ....C-6
La Porte, *La Porte,* 21,621 ....B-7
Ladoga, *Montgomery,* 1,047 ....I-7
Lafayette, *Tippecanoe,* 56,397 ....G-7
Lagrange, *Lagrange,* 2,919 ....B-11
• Lake Dalecarlia, *Lake,* 1,285 ....C-5
Lake Station, *Lake,* 13,948 ....H-3
• Lakes Of The Four Seasons,
Porter, 7,291 ....C-6
Lapel, *Madison,* 1,855 ....H-10
Lawrence, *Marion,* 38,915 ....I-9
Lawrenceburg, *Dearborn,* 4,685 .....L-13
Lebanon, *Boone,* 14,222 ....H-8
Leo-Cedarville, *Adams,* 2,782 ....C-12
Liberty, *Union,* 2,061 ....J-13
Ligonier, *Noble,* 4,357 ....B-11
Linton, *Greene,* 5,774 ....L-6
Logansport, *Cass,* 19,684 ....E-8
Long Beach, *La Porte,* 1,559 ....A-7
Loogootee, *Martin,* 2,741 ....M-7
Lowell, *Lake,* 7,505 ....C-5
Lynn, *Randolph,* 1,143 ....H-13
Madison, *Jefferson,* 12,004 ....M-11
Marion, *Grant,* 31,320 ....F-10
Markle, *Wells,* 1,102 ....E-11
Martinsville, *Morgan,* 11,698 ....J-8
McCordsville, *Hancock,* 1,134 ....I-10
• Melody Hill, *Vanderburgh,* 3,066 ......O-5
Meridian Hills, *Marion,* 1,713 ....I-9
Merrillville, *Lake,* 30,560 ....B-5
Michigan City, *La Porte,* 32,900 ....A-7
Middlebury, *Elkhart,* 2,956 ....B-10
Middletown, *Henry,* 2,488 ....H-11
Milan, *Ripley,* 1,816 ....L-12
Mishawaka, *St. Joseph,* 46,557 ....B-9
Mitchell, *Lawrence,* 4,567 ....M-8
Monon, *White,* 1,733 ....E-7
Monroeville, *Allen,* 1,236 ....D-13
Montezuma, *Parke,* 1,179 ....I-5
Monticello, *White,* 5,723 ....E-7
Montpelier, *Blackford,* 1,929 ....F-12
Mooresville, *Morgan,* 9,273 ....J-8
Morocco, *Newton,* 1,127 ....D-5
Morristown, *Shelby,* 1,133 ....I-10
Mount Vernon, *Posey,* 7,478 ....P-3
Mulberry, *Clinton,* 1,387 ....G-7
Muncie, *Delaware,* 67,430 ....G-11
Munster, *Lake,* 21,511 ....I-1
Nappanee, *Elkhart,* 6,710 ....B-9
Nashville, *Brown,* 825 ....K-9
New Albany, *Floyd,* 37,603 ....O-10
New Carlisle, *St. Joseph,* 1,505 ....A-8
New Castle, *Henry,* 17,780 ....H-11
New Chicago, *Lake,* 2,063 ....I-2
New Haven, *Allen,* 12,406 ....D-12
New Palestine, *Hancock,* 1,264 ....I-10
• New Paris, *Elkhart,* 1,006 ....B-10
New Pekin, *Washington,* 1,334 ....N-9
New Whiteland, *Johnson,* 4,579 ....J-9
Newburgh, *Warrick,* 3,088 ....P-5
Newport, *Vermillion,* 578 ....I-5
Noblesville, *Hamilton,* 28,590 ....H-9
North Judson, *Starke,* 1,675 ....C-7
North Liberty, *St. Joseph,* 1,402 ....B-8
North Manchester, *Wabash,* 6,260 .D-10
• North Terre Haute, *Vigo,* 4,606 ....J-5
North Vernon, *Jennings,* 6,515 ....L-11
North Webster, *Kosciusko,* 1,067 ...C-10
• Oak Park, *Clark,* 5,379 ....O-10
Oakland City, *Gibson,* 2,588 ....O-5
Odon, *Daviess,* 1,376 ....M-6
Ogden Dunes, *Porter,* 1,313 ....K-3
Oolitic, *Lawrence,* 1,152 ....M-8
Orleans, *Orange,* 2,273 ....N-8
Osceola, *St. Joseph,* 1,859 ....B-9
Osgood, *Ripley,* 1,669 ....L-12
Ossian, *Wells,* 2,943 ....E-12
Otterbein, *Benton,* 1,312 ....F-6
Owensville, *Gibson,* 1,322 ....O-4
Oxford, *Benton,* 1,271 ....F-6
Paoli, *Orange,* 3,844 ....N-8
Parker City, *Randolph,* 1,416 ....G-12
Pendleton, *Madison,* 3,873 ....H-10
Peru, *Miami,* 12,994 ....E-9
Petersburg, *Pike,* 2,570 ....N-5
Pittsboro, *Hendricks,* 1,588 ....I-8
Plainfield, *Hendricks,* 18,396 ....I-8
Plymouth, *Marshall,* 9,840 ....C-8
Portage, *Porter,* 33,496 ....B-6
Porter, *Porter,* 4,972 ....B-6
Portland, *Jay,* 6,437 ....F-13
Poseyville, *Posey,* 1,187 ....O-4
Princes Lakes, *Johnson,* 1,506 ....K-9
Princeton, *Gibson,* 8,175 ....O-4
Redkey, *Jay,* 1,427 ....G-12
Remington, *Jasper,* 1,323 ....E-6
Rensselaer, *Jasper,* 5,294 ....D-6
Richmond, *Wayne,* 39,124 ....I-13
Ripley, *Pulaski,* 4,723 ....D-7
Rising Sun, *Ohio,* 2,470 ....L-13
Roanoke, *Huntington,* 1,495 ....D-11
Rochester, *Fulton,* 6,414 ....D-9
Rockport, *Spencer,* 2,160 ....Q-6
Rockville, *Parke,* 2,765 ....I-6
Rome City, *Noble,* 1,615 ....B-11
Roseland, *St. Joseph,* 1,809 ....A-9
• Roselawn, *Newton,* 3,933 ....D-5
Rossville, *Clinton,* 1,513 ....G-8
Rushville, *Rush,* 5,995 ....J-11
Russiaville, *Howard,* 1,092 ....G-9
Saint John, *Lake,* 8,382 ....I-1
Saint Paul, *Shelby,* 1,022 ....J-11
Salem, *Washington,* 6,172 ....N-9
Santa Claus, *Spencer,* 2,041 ....P-7
Schererville, *Lake,* 24,851 ....I-1
Scottsburg, *Scott,* 6,040 ....M-10
Seelyville, *Vigo,* 1,182 ....J-5
Sellersburg, *Clark,* 6,071 ....O-10
Seymour, *Jackson,* 18,101 ....L-10
Shadeland, *Tippecanoe,* 1,682 ....G-6
Shelburn, *Sullivan,* 1,268 ....K-5
Shelbyville, *Shelby,* 17,951 ....J-10
Sheridan, *Hamilton,* 2,520 ....H-9
Shoals, *Martin,* 807 ....N-7
• Simonton Lake, *Elkhart,* 4,053 ....A-9
South Bend, *St. Joseph,* 107,789 .....B-9
• South Haven, *Porter,* 5,619 ....B-6
South Whitley, *Whitley,* 1,782 ....D-11
Southport, *Marion,* 1,852 ....J-9
Speedway, *Marion,* 12,881 ....I-9
Spencer, *Owen,* 2,508 ....K-7
Sullivan, *Sullivan,* 4,617 ....L-5
Summitville, *Madison,* 1,090 ....G-11
Swayzee, *Grant,* 1,011 ....F-10
Syracuse, *Kosciusko,* 3,038 ....C-10
Tell City, *Perry,* 7,845 ....P-7
Terre Haute, *Vigo,* 59,614 ....J-5
Thorntown, *Boone,* 1,562 ....H-8
Tipton, *Tipton,* 5,251 ....G-9
Topeka, *Lagrange,* 1,159 ....B-11
Trail Creek, *La Porte,* 2,296 ....A-7
• Tri-Lakes, *Whitley,* 3,925 ....C-11
Union City, *Randolph,* 3,622 ....G-13
Upland, *Grant,* 3,803 ....F-11
Valparaiso, *Porter,* 27,428 ....B-6
Veedersburg, *Fountain,* 2,299 ....H-5
Vernon, *Jennings,* 330 ....L-11
Versailles, *Ripley,* 1,784 ....L-12
Vevay, *Switzerland,* 1,735 ....M-12
Vincennes, *Knox,* 18,701 ....M-5
Wabash, *Wabash,* 11,743 ....E-10
Wakarusa, *Elkhart,* 1,618 ....B-9
Walkerton, *St. Joseph,* 2,274 ....B-8
Walton, *Cass,* 1,069 ....F-9
Wanatah, *La Porte,* 1,013 ....C-7
Warren, *Huntington,* 1,272 ....E-11
Warren Park, *Marion,* 1,656 ....L-3
Warsaw, *Kosciusko,* 12,415 ....C-10
Washington, *Daviess,* 11,380 ....N-6
Waterloo, *De Kalb,* 2,200 ....B-12
West Lafayette,
Tippecanoe, 28,778 ....G-7
West Terre Haute, *Vigo,* 2,330 ....J-5
Westfield, *Hamilton,* 9,293 ....H-9
Westport, *Decatur,* 1,515 ....K-11
Westville, *La Porte,* 2,116 ....B-7
Whiteland, *Johnson,* 3,958 ....J-9
Whiting, *Lake,* 5,137 ....B-5
Williamsport, *Warren,* 1,935 ....G-5
Winamac, *Pulaski,* 2,418 ....D-8
Winchester, *Randolph,* 5,037 ....G-13
Winfield, *Lake,* 2,298 ....C-5
Winona Lake, *Kosciusko,* 3,987 .....C-10
Woodburn, *Allen,* 1,579 ....D-13
Worthington, *Greene,* 1,481 ....L-6
Yorktown, *Delaware,* 4,785 ....G-11
Zionsville, *Boone,* 8,775 ....H-9

Explanation of symbols: • - Census Designated Place (CDP)

County-Town INDIANA

American Map

Explanation of Symbols

✹	State Capital
Vernon	County Seat
(shading)	MSA Boundary
132	MSA Number
RUSH	County Name

Population Key

Symbol	Population
○	0-999
⦶	1,000-2,499
⊕	2,500-4,999
◎	5,000-9,999
◎	10,000-19,999
◉	20,000-24,999
◉	25,000-49,999
□	50,000-99,999
▣	100,000-249,999
■	250,000-999,999

COUNTIES

(99 Counties)

Name of County	Population	Location on Map
ADAIR	8,243	I-6
ADAMS	4,482	I-5
ALLAMAKEE	14,675	A-13
APPANOOSE	13,721	J-10
AUDUBON	6,830	G-5
BENTON	25,308	F-12
BLACK HAWK	128,012	E-11
BOONE	26,224	F-7
BREMER	23,325	D-11
BUCHANAN	21,093	D-12
BUENA VISTA	20,411	D-4
BUTLER	15,305	D-10
CALHOUN	11,115	E-5
CARROLL	21,421	F-5
CASS	14,684	H-4
CEDAR	18,187	G-14
CERRO GORDO	46,447	C-9
CHEROKEE	13,035	D-3
CHICKASAW	13,095	B-11
CLARKE	9,133	I-7
CLAY	17,372	B-4
CLAYTON	18,678	C-13
CLINTON	50,149	F-15
CRAWFORD	16,942	G-3
DALLAS	40,750	G-7
DAVIS	8,541	J-11
DECATUR	8,689	K-7
DELAWARE	18,404	E-14
DES MOINES	42,351	J-14
DICKINSON	16,424	B-4
DUBUQUE	89,143	E-15
EMMET	11,027	A-5
FAYETTE	22,008	C-12
FLOYD	16,900	B-10
FRANKLIN	10,704	C-9
FREMONT	8,010	K-3
GREENE	10,366	F-6
GRUNDY	12,369	E-10
GUTHRIE	11,353	H-5
HAMILTON	16,438	E-8
HANCOCK	12,100	B-7
HARDIN	18,812	E-9
HARRISON	15,666	G-3
HENRY	20,336	J-13
HOWARD	9,932	B-11
HUMBOLDT	10,381	D-6
IDA	7,837	D-3
IOWA	15,671	G-12
JACKSON	20,296	F-15
JASPER	37,213	G-10
JEFFERSON	16,181	J-12
JOHNSON	111,006	H-13
JONES	20,221	E-14
KEOKUK	11,400	I-11
KOSSUTH	17,163	A-6
LEE	38,052	K-14
LINN	191,701	F-13
LOUISA	12,183	I-14
LUCAS	9,422	I-8
LYON	11,763	B-2
MADISON	14,019	H-7
MAHASKA	22,335	H-10
MARION	32,052	H-10
MARSHALL	39,311	F-10
MILLS	14,547	I-3
MITCHELL	10,874	A-10
MONONA	10,020	F-2
MONROE	8,016	J-10
MONTGOMERY	11,771	J-4
MUSCATINE	41,722	H-15
OÕBRIEN	15,102	B-3
OSCEOLA	7,003	A-3
PAGE	16,976	J-4
PALO ALTO	10,147	B-5
PLYMOUTH	24,849	D-1
POCAHONTAS	8,662	D-5
POLK	374,601	H-8
POTTAWATTAMIE	87,704	I-3
POWESHIEK	18,815	G-11
RINGGOLD	5,469	K-6
SAC	11,529	D-4
SCOTT	158,668	H-16
SHELBY	13,173	H-4
SIOUX	31,589	B-1
STORY	79,981	F-9
TAMA	18,103	F-10
TAYLOR	6,958	J-5
UNION	12,309	I-6
VAN BUREN	7,809	K-12
WAPELLO	36,051	J-11
WARREN	40,671	I-8
WASHINGTON	20,670	H-13
WAYNE	6,730	K-8
WEBSTER	40,235	E-6
WINNEBAGO	11,723	B-7
WINNESHIEK	21,310	A-12
WOODBURY	103,877	E-2
WORTH	7,909	A-9
WRIGHT	14,334	C-7
TOTAL	**2,926,324**	

CITIES AND TOWNS

Note: The first name is that of the city or town, second, that of the county in which it is located, then the population and location on the map.

Ackley, *Hardin,* 1,809 ....D-10
Adel, *Dallas,* 3,435 ....H-7
Akron, *Plymouth,* 1,489 ....C-1
Albia, *Monroe,* 3,706 ....J-10
Algona, *Kossuth,* 5,741 ....C-7
Allison, *Butler,* 1,006 ....D-10
Alta, *Buena Vista,* 1,865 ....D-4
Alton, *Sioux,* 1,095 ....C-2
Altoona, *Polk,* 10,345 ....H-9
Ames, *Story,* 50,731 ....F-8
Anamosa, *Jones,* 5,494 ....F-14
Anita, *Cass,* 1,049 ....H-5
Ankeny, *Polk,* 27,117 ....G-8
Aplington, *Butler,* 1,054 ....D-10
Arnolds Park, *Dickinson,* 1,162 ....A-5
Asbury, *Dubuque,* 2,450 ....D-16
Atlantic, *Cass,* 7,257 ....H-5
Audubon, *Audubon,* 2,382 ....G-5
Aurelia, *Cherokee,* 1,062 ....D-4
Avoca, *Pottawattamie,* 1,610 ....H-4
Baxter, *Jasper,* 1,052 ....G-10
Bedford, *Taylor,* 1,620 ....K-5
Belle Plaine, *Benton,* 2,878 ....G-12
Bellevue, *Jackson,* 2,350 ....E-16
Belmond, *Wright,* 2,560 ....C-8
Bettendorf, *Scott,* 31,275 ....H-16
Bloomfield, *Davis,* 2,601 ....K-11
Blue Grass, *Scott,* 1,169 ....H-16
Bondurant, *Polk,* 1,846 ....G-9
Boone, *Boone,* 12,803 ....F-8
Britt, *Hancock,* 2,052 ....B-8
Brooklyn, *Poweshiek,* 1,367 ....G-11
Buffalo, *Scott,* 1,321 ....H-16
Burlington,
Des Moines, 26,839 ....J-15
Calmar, *Winneshiek,* 1,058 ....B-13
Camanche, *Clinton,* 4,215 ....G-17
Carlisle, *Warren,* 3,497 ....H-9
Carroll, *Carroll,* 10,106 ....F-5
Carter Lake,
Pottawattamie, 3,248 ....I-2
Cascade, *Dubuque,* 1,958 ....E-15
Cedar Falls,
Black Hawk, 36,145 ....D-11
Cedar Rapids, *Linn,* 120,758 ....F-13
Center Point, *Linn,* 2,007 ....F-13
Centerville, *Appanoose,* 5,924 ....K-10
Central City, *Linn,* 1,157 ....F-14
Chariton, *Lucas,* 4,573 ....J-9
Charles City, *Floyd,* 7,812 ....C-11
Cherokee, *Cherokee,* 5,369 ....D-3
Clarence, *Cedar,* 1,008 ....G-15
Clarinda, *Page,* 5,690 ....K-5
Clarion, *Wright,* 2,968 ....D-8
Clarksville, *Butler,* 1,441 ....D-11
Clear Lake, *Cerro Gordo,* 8,161 ....B-9
Clinton, *Clinton,* 27,772 ....G-17
Clive, *Polk,* 12,855 ....H-8
Colfax, *Jasper,* 2,223 ....G-9
Columbus Junction,
Louisa, 1,900 ....I-14
Conrad, *Grundy,* 1,055 ....F-10
Coon Rapids, *Carroll,* 1,305 ....G-6
Coralville, *Johnson,* 15,123 ....G-14
Corning, *Adams,* 1,783 ....J-5
Corydon, *Wayne,* 1,591 ....K-9
Council Bluffs,
Pottawattamie, 58,268 ....I-3
Cresco, *Howard,* 3,905 ....A-12
Creston, *Union,* 7,597 ....J-6
Dakota City, *Humboldt,* 911 ....D-7
Dallas Center, *Dallas,* 1,595 ....G-7
Davenport, *Scott,* 98,359 ....H-16
De Soto, *Dallas,* 1,009 ....H-7
De Witt, *Clinton,* 5,049 ....G-16
Decorah, *Winneshiek,* 8,172 ....B-13
Denison, *Crawford,* 7,339 ....F-4
Denver, *Bremer,* 1,627 ....D-12
Des Moines, *Polk,* 198,682 ....H-8
Dubuque, *Dubuque,* 57,686 ....D-16
Dunlap, *Harrison,* 1,139 ....G-3
Durant, *Cedar,* 1,677 ....H-15
Dyersville, *Dubuque,* 4,035 ....E-15
Dysart, *Tama,* 1,303 ....F-12
Eagle Grove, *Wright,* 3,712 ....D-8
Earlham, *Madison,* 1,298 ....H-7
Eddyville, *Wapello,* 1,064 ....I-11
Eldora, *Hardin,* 3,035 ....E-10
Eldridge, *Scott,* 4,159 ....G-16
Elk Run Heights,
Black Hawk, 1,052 ....E-12
Elkader, *Clayton,* 1,465 ....C-14
Ely, *Linn,* 1,149 ....G-14
Emmetsburg, *Palo Alto,* 3,958 ....B-6
Epworth, *Dubuque,* 1,428 ....E-15
Estherville, *Emmet,* 6,656 ....A-5
Evansdale, *Black Hawk,* 4,526 ....E-12
Fairbank, *Buchanan,* 1,041 ....D-12
Fairfield, *Jefferson,* 9,509 ....J-13
Farley, *Dubuque,* 1,334 ....E-15
Fayette, *Fayette,* 1,300 ....C-13
Forest City, *Winnebago,* 4,362 ....B-8
Fort Dodge, *Webster,* 25,136 ....E-7
Fort Madison, *Lee,* 10,715 ....K-14
Garner, *Hancock,* 2,922 ....B-8
George, *Lyon,* 1,051 ....A-2
Gladbrook, *Tama,* 1,015 ....F-11
Glenwood, *Mills,* 5,358 ....J-3
Glidden, *Carroll,* 1,253 ....F-5
Gowrie, *Webster,* 1,038 ....E-7
Greene, *Butler,* 1,099 ....C-10
Greenfield, *Adair,* 2,129 ....I-6
Grimes, *Polk,* 5,098 ....G-8
Grinnell, *Poweshiek,* 9,105 ....G-11
Griswold, *Cass,* 1,039 ....I-4
Grundy Center, *Grundy,* 2,596 ....E-10
Guthrie Center, *Guthrie,* 1,668 ....G-6
Guttenberg, *Clayton,* 1,987 ....C-15
Hamburg, *Fremont,* 1,240 ....K-3
Hampton, *Franklin,* 4,218 ....D-9
Harlan, *Shelby,* 5,282 ....H-4
Hartley, *O'Brien,* 1,733 ....B-4
Hawarden, *Sioux,* 2,478 ....C-1
Hiawatha, *Linn,* 6,480 ....F-13
Holstein, *Ida,* 1,470 ....E-3
Hudson, *Black Hawk,* 2,117 ....E-11
Hull, *Sioux,* 1,960 ....B-2
Humboldt, *Humboldt,* 4,452 ....D-7
Huxley, *Story,* 2,316 ....G-8
Ida Grove, *Ida,* 2,350 ....E-4
Independence,
Buchanan, 6,014 ....E-13
Indianola, *Warren,* 12,998 ....I-8
Iowa City, *Johnson,* 62,220 ....G-14
Iowa Falls, *Hardin,* 5,193 ....D-9
Jefferson, *Greene,* 4,626 ....F-6
Jesup, *Buchanan,* 2,212 ....E-12
Jewell Junction, *Hamilton,* 1,239 ....E-8
Johnston, *Polk,* 8,649 ....G-8
Kalona, *Washington,* 2,293 ....H-13
Keokuk, *Lee,* 11,427 ....L-14
Keosauqua, *Van Buren,* 1,066 ....K-13
Keota, *Keokuk,* 1,025 ....I-13
Kingsley, *Plymouth,* 1,245 ....D-2
Knoxville, *Marion,* 7,731 ....I-10
La Porte City,
Black Hawk, 2,275 ....E-12
Lake City, *Calhoun,* 1,787 ....E-5
Lake Mills, *Winnebago,* 2,140 ....A-9
Lake Park, *Dickinson,* 1,023 ....A-4
Lake View, *Sac,* 1,278 ....E-5
Lamoni, *Decatur,* 2,444 ....K-7
Lansing, *Allamakee,* 1,012 ....A-14
Laurens, *Pocahontas,* 1,476 ....C-5
Le Claire, *Scott,* 2,847 ....H-17
Le Mars, *Plymouth,* 9,237 ....C-2
Lenox, *Taylor,* 1,401 ....J-6
Leon, *Decatur,* 1,983 ....K-8
Lisbon, *Linn,* 1,898 ....G-14
Logan, *Harrison,* 1,545 ....G-3
Lone Tree, *Johnson,* 1,151 ....H-14
Madrid, *Boone,* 2,264 ....G-8
Malvern, *Mills,* 1,256 ....J-3
Manchester, *Delaware,* 5,257 ....E-14
Manly, *Worth,* 1,342 ....B-9
Manning, *Carroll,* 1,490 ....G-5
Manson, *Calhoun,* 1,893 ....D-6
Mapleton, *Monona,* 1,416 ....F-3
Maquoketa, *Jackson,* 6,112 ....F-16
Marcus, *Cherokee,* 1,139 ....C-3
Marengo, *Iowa,* 2,535 ....G-12
Marion, *Linn,* 26,294 ....F-14
Marshalltown, *Marshall,* 26,009 ....F-10
Mason City,
Cerro Gordo, 29,172 ....B-9
Mechanicsville, *Cedar,* 1,173 ....G-14
Mediapolis, *Des Moines,* 1,644 ....J-15
Melcher-Dallas, *Marion,* 1,298 ....I-9
Milford, *Dickinson,* 2,474 ....B-4
Missouri Valley, *Harrison,* 2,992 ....H-2
Mitchellville, *Polk,* 1,715 ....A-17
Monona, *Clayton,* 1,550 ....C-14
Monroe, *Jasper,* 1,808 ....H-10
Montezuma, *Poweshiek,* 1,440 ....H-11
Monticello, *Jones,* 3,607 ....E-15
Mount Ayr, *Ringgold,* 1,822 ....K-7
Mount Pleasant, *Henry,* 8,751 ....J-14
Mount Vernon, *Linn,* 3,390 ....G-14
Moville, *Woodbury,* 1,583 ....D-2
Muscatine, *Muscatine,* 22,697 ....H-15
Nashua, *Chickasaw,* 1,618 ....C-11
Nevada, *Story,* 6,658 ....F-9
New Hampton,
Chickasaw, 3,692 ....C-12
New London, *Henry,* 1,937 ....J-14
New Sharon, *Mahaska,* 1,301 ....H-11
Newton, *Jasper,* 15,579 ....G-10
Nora Springs, *Floyd,* 1,532 ....B-10
North Liberty, *Johnson,* 5,367 ....G-14
Northwood, *Worth,* 2,050 ....A-9
Norwalk, *Warren,* 6,884 ....H-8
Oakland, *Pottawattamie,* 1,487 ....I-4
Odebolt, *Sac,* 1,153 ....E-4
Oelwein, *Fayette,* 6,692 ....D-13
Ogden, *Boone,* 2,023 ....F-7
Onawa, *Monona,* 3,091 ....F-2
Orange City, *Sioux,* 5,582 ....C-2
Osage, *Mitchell,* 3,451 ....B-10
Osceola, *Clarke,* 4,659 ....J-8
Oskaloosa, *Mahaska,* 10,938 ....I-11
Ottumwa, *Wapello,* 24,998 ....J-11
Panora, *Guthrie,* 1,175 ....G-6
• Park View, *Scott,* 2,169 ....G-16
Parkersburg, *Butler,* 1,889 ....D-10
Paullina, *O'Brien,* 1,124 ....C-3
Pella, *Marion,* 9,832 ....H-10
Perry, *Dallas,* 7,633 ....G-7
Pleasant Hill, *Polk,* 5,070 ....B-17
Pleasantville, *Marion,* 1,539 ....H-9
Pocahontas, *Pocahontas,* 1,970 ....D-6
Polk City, *Polk,* 2,344 ....G-8
Postville, *Allamakee,* 2,273 ....B-13
Prairie City, *Jasper,* 1,365 ....H-9
Primghar, *O'Brien,* 891 ....B-3
Red Oak, *Montgomery,* 6,197 ....J-4
Reinbeck, *Grundy,* 1,751 ....E-11
Remsen, *Plymouth,* 1,762 ....C-2
Robins, *Linn,* 1,806 ....F-13
Rock Rapids, *Lyon,* 2,573 ....A-2
Rock Valley, *Sioux,* 2,702 ....B-2
Rockwell City, *Calhoun,* 2,264 ....E-6
Roland, *Story,* 1,324 ....F-9
Sac City, *Sac,* 2,368 ....E-5
Saint Ansgar, *Mitchell,* 1,031 ....A-10
Sanborn, *O'Brien,* 1,353 ....B-3
• Saylorville, *Polk,* 3,238 ....A-16
Sergeant Bluff, *Woodbury,* 3,321 E-1
Sheldon, *O'Brien,* 4,914 ....B-3
Shell Rock, *Butler,* 1,298 ....D-11
Shenandoah, *Page,* 5,546 ....K-4
Sibley, *Osceola,* 2,796 ....A-3
Sidney, *Fremont,* 1,300 ....K-3
Sigourney, *Keokuk,* 2,209 ....I-12
Sioux Center, *Sioux,* 6,002 ....B-2
Sioux City, *Woodbury,* 85,013 ....D-1
Slater, *Story,* 1,306 ....G-8
Sloan, *Woodbury,* 1,032 ....E-2
Solon, *Johnson,* 1,177 ....G-14
Spencer, *Clay,* 11,317 ....B-5
Spirit Lake, *Dickinson,* 4,261 ....A-5
Springville, *Linn,* 1,091 ....F-14
State Center, *Marshall,* 1,349 ....F-9
Storm Lake,
Buena Vista, 10,076 ....D-4
Story City, *Story,* 3,228 ....F-8
Strawberry Point,
Clayton, 1,386 ....D-14
Stuart, *Guthrie,* 1,712 ....H-7
Sumner, *Bremer,* 2,106 ....C-12
Tama, *Tama,* 2,731 ....F-11
Tipton, *Cedar,* 3,155 ....G-15
Toledo, *Tama,* 2,539 ....F-11
Traer, *Tama,* 1,594 ....F-11
Tripoli, *Bremer,* 1,310 ....C-12
Urbana, *Benton,* 1,019 ....E-13
Urbandale, *Polk,* 29,072 ....B-16
Villisca, *Montgomery,* 1,344 ....J-5
Vinton, *Benton,* 5,102 ....F-12
Walcott, *Scott,* 1,528 ....H-16
Walford, *Benton,* 1,224 ....G-13
Wapello, *Louisa,* 2,124 ....I-15
Washington, *Washington,* 7,047 ....I-13
Waterloo, *Black Hawk,* 68,747 ....E-12
Waukee, *Dallas,* 5,126 ....H-8
Waukon, *Allamakee,* 4,131 ....B-14
Waverly, *Bremer,* 8,968 ....D-11
Webster City, *Hamilton,* 8,176 ....E-8
Wellman, *Washington,* 1,393 ....H-13
West Branch, *Cedar,* 2,188 ....G-14
West Burlington,
Des Moines, 3,161 ....J-15
West Des Moines,
Polk, 46,403 ....B-16
West Liberty, *Muscatine,* 3,332 ....H-14
West Union, *Fayette,* 2,549 ....C-13
Williamsburg, *Iowa,* 2,622 ....G-12
Wilton, *Muscatine,* 2,829 ....H-15
Windsor Heights, *Polk,* 4,805 ....B-16
Winfield, *Henry,* 1,131 ....I-14
Winterset, *Madison,* 4,768 ....I-7
Woodbine, *Harrison,* 1,564 ....G-3
Woodward, *Dallas,* 1,200 ....G-8

Explanation of symbols: • - Census Designated Place (CDP)

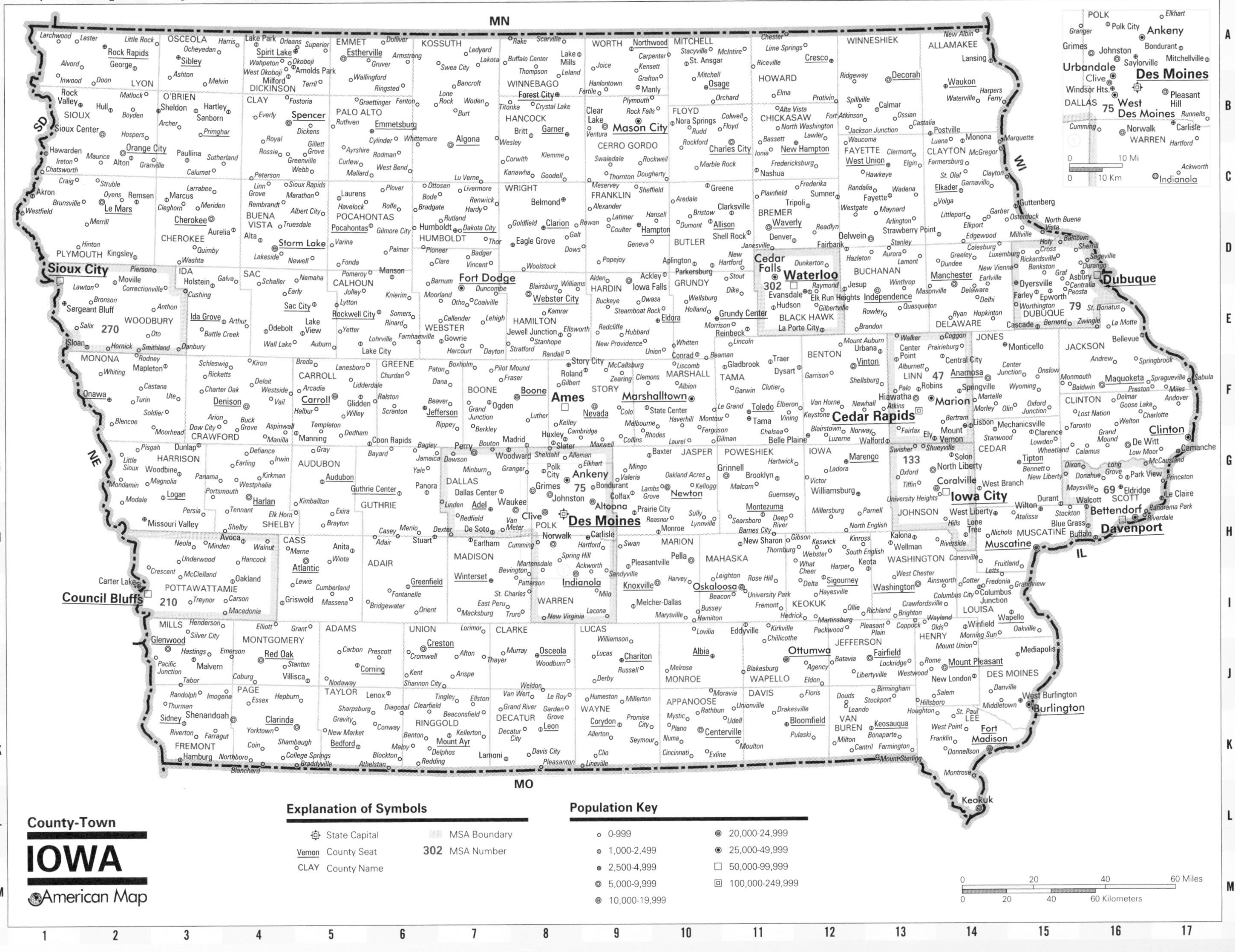
County-Town
IOWA
American Map
Explanation of Symbols
State Capital
Vernon County Seat
CLAY County Name
MSA Boundary
302 MSA Number
Population Key
0-999
1,000-2,499
2,500-4,999
5,000-9,999
10,000-19,999
20,000-24,999
25,000-49,999
50,000-99,999
100,000-249,999
0 20 40 60 Miles
0 20 40 60 Kilometers
MN
WI
IL
MO
NE
SD
Des Moines
Cedar Rapids
Davenport
Sioux City
Waterloo
Dubuque
Iowa City
Council Bluffs
Ames

KANSAS

COUNTIES

(105 Counties)

Name of County	Population	Location on Map
ALLEN	14,385	G-15
ANDERSON	8,110	F-15
ATCHISON	16,774	C-15
BARBER	5,307	I-7
BARTON	28,205	E-7
BOURBON	15,379	H-16
BROWN	10,724	B-14
BUTLER	59,482	G-12
CHASE	3,030	F-12
CHAUTAUQUA	4,359	I-13
CHEROKEE	22,605	I-16
CHEYENNE	3,165	A-1
CLARK	2,390	I-5
CLAY	8,822	C-11
CLOUD	10,268	C-10
COFFEY	8,865	F-14
COMANCHE	1,967	I-6
COWLEY	36,291	I-11
CRAWFORD	38,242	H-16
DECATUR	3,472	A-4
DICKINSON	19,344	E-11
DONIPHAN	8,249	B-15
DOUGLAS	99,962	D-15
EDWARDS	3,449	H-6
ELK	3,261	H-13
ELLIS	27,507	D-6
ELLSWORTH	6,525	E-9
FINNEY	40,523	F-3
FORD	32,458	G-5
FRANKLIN	24,784	E-15
GEARY	27,947	D-12
GOVE	3,068	E-4
GRAHAM	2,946	C-5
GRANT	7,909	H-2
GRAY	5,904	G-4
GREELEY	1,534	E-1
GREENWOOD	1,534	G-13
HAMILTON	2,670	F-1
HARPER	6,536	I-9
HARVEY	32,869	G-10
HASKELL	4,307	H-3
HODGEMAN	2,085	F-5
JACKSON	12,657	C-14
JEFFERSON	18,426	D-15
JEWELL	3,791	A-9
JOHNSON	451,086	D-16
KEARNY	4,531	F-2
KINGMAN	8,673	H-9
KIOWA	3,278	H-6
LABETTE	22,835	I-15
LANE	2,155	E-4
LEAVENWORTH	68,691	C-16
LINCOLN	3,578	D-9
LINN	9,570	F-16
LOGAN	3,046	D-2
LYON	35,935	F-13
MARION	13,361	F-11
MARSHALL	10,965	B-12
MCPHERSON	29,554	F-10
MEADE	4,631	H-4
MIAMI	28,351	E-16
MITCHELL	6,932	C-9
MONTGOMERY	36,252	I-14
MORRIS	6,104	E-12
MORTON	3,496	I-1
NEMAHA	10,717	B-13
NEOSHO	16,997	H-15
NESS	3,454	E-5
NORTON	5,953	A-5
OSAGE	16,712	E-14
OSBORNE	4,452	C-7
OTTAWA	6,163	C-10
PAWNEE	7,233	F-6
PHILLIPS	6,001	B-7
POTTAWATOMIE	18,209	C-13
PRATT	9,647	H-8
RAWLINS	2,966	A-2
RENO	64,790	G-9
REPUBLIC	5,835	B-10
RICE	10,761	F-9
RILEY	62,843	C-12
ROOKS	5,685	C-6
RUSH	3,551	E-6
RUSSELL	7,370	D-7
SALINE	53,597	E-10
SCOTT	5,120	E-3
SEDGWICK	452,869	H-10
SEWARD	22,510	I-3
SHAWNEE	169,871	D-14
SHERIDAN	2,813	C-4
SHERMAN	6,760	C-1
SMITH	4,536	A-7
STAFFORD	4,789	G-7
STANTON	2,406	H-1
STEVENS	5,463	I-2
SUMNER	25,946	I-10
THOMAS	8,180	C-2
TREGO	3,319	E-5
WABAUNSEE	6,885	D-13
WALLACE	1,749	D-1
WASHINGTON	6,483	B-11
WICHITA	2,531	E-2
WILSON	10,332	H-14
WOODSON	3,788	H-14
WYANDOTTE	157,882	D-16
TOTAL	**2,688,418**	

CITIES AND TOWNS

Note: The first name is that of the city or town, second, that of the county in which it is located, then the population and location on the map.

Abilene, *Dickinson*, 6,543 ... D-11
Alma, *Wabaunsee*, 797 ... D-13
Altamont, *Labette*, 1,092 ... I-16
Andover, *Butler*, 6,698 ... H-11
Anthony, *Harper*, 2,440 ... I-10
Arkansas City, *Cowley*, 11,963 ... I-12
Arma, *Crawford*, 1,529 ... H-17
Ashland, *Clark*, 975 ... I-6
Atchison, *Atchison*, 10,232 ... B-16
Atwood, *Rawlins*, 1,279 ... B-3
Auburn, *Shawnee*, 1,121 ... D-14
Augusta, *Butler*, 8,423 ... H-12
Baldwin City, *Douglas*, 3,400 ... E-16
Basehor, *Leavenworth*, 2,238 ... C-16
Baxter Springs, *Cherokee*, 4,602 ... I-17
Bel Aire, *Sedgwick*, 5,836 ... L-14
Belle Plaine, *Sumner*, 1,708 ... I-11
Belleville, *Republic*, 2,239 ... B-10
Beloit, *Mitchell*, 4,019 ... C-9
Blue Rapids, *Marshall*, 1,088 ... B-12
Bonner Springs, *Wyandotte*, 6,768 ... D-16
Buhler, *Reno*, 1,358 ... F-10
Burlingame, *Osage*, 1,017 ... E-14
Burlington, *Coffey*, 2,790 ... F-14
Caldwell, *Sumner*, 1,284 ... J-10
Caney, *Montgomery*, 2,092 ... J-14
Carbondale, *Osage*, 1,478 ... D-15
Chanute, *Neosho*, 9,411 ... H-15
Chapman, *Dickinson*, 1,241 ... D-12
Cheney, *Sedgwick*, 1,783 ... H-10
Cherryvale, *Montgomery*, 2,386 ... I-15
Chetopa, *Labette*, 1,281 ... I-16
Cimarron, *Gray*, 1,934 ... G-5
Clay Center, *Clay*, 4,564 ... C-11
Clearwater, *Sedgwick*, 2,178 ... H-11
Coffeyville, *Montgomery*, 11,021 ... I-15
Colby, *Thomas*, 5,450 ... C-3
Coldwater, *Comanche*, 792 ... I-7
Columbus, *Cherokee*, 3,396 ... I-16
Colwich, *Sedgwick*, 1,229 ... G-11
Concordia, *Cloud*, 5,714 ... B-10
Conway Springs, *Sumner*, 1,322 ... I-10
Cottonwood Falls, *Chase*, 966 ... F-13
Council Grove, *Morris*, 2,321 ... E-13
De Soto, *Johnson*, 4,561 ... D-16
Derby, *Sedgwick*, 17,807 ... M-14
Dighton, *Lane*, 1,261 ... E-4
Dodge City, *Ford*, 25,176 ... H-5
Douglass, *Butler*, 1,813 ... H-12
Downs, *Osborne*, 1,038 ... C-8
Edgerton, *Johnson*, 1,440 ... E-16
Edwardsville, *Wyandotte*, 4,146 ... L-15
El Dorado, *Butler*, 12,057 ... G-12
Elkhart, *Morton*, 2,233 ... I-1
Ellinwood, *Barton*, 2,164 ... F-8
Ellis, *Ellis*, 1,873 ... D-6
Ellsworth, *Ellsworth*, 2,965 ... E-9
Elwood, *Doniphan*, 1,145 ... B-16
Emporia, *Lyon*, 26,760 ... F-14
Erie, *Neosho*, 1,211 ... H-16
Eudora, *Douglas*, 4,307 ... D-16
Eureka, *Greenwood*, 2,914 ... G-13
Fairway, *Johnson*, 3,952 ... D-17
• Fort Riley North, *Geary*, 8,114 ... D-12
Fort Scott, *Bourbon*, 8,297 ... G-17
Fredonia, *Wilson*, 2,600 ... H-14
Frontenac, *Crawford*, 2,996 ... H-17
Galena, *Cherokee*, 3,287 ... I-17
Garden City, *Finney*, 28,451 ... G-3
Gardner, *Johnson*, 9,396 ... D-16
Garnett, *Anderson*, 3,368 ... F-16
Girard, *Crawford*, 2,773 ... H-16
Goddard, *Sedgwick*, 2,037 ... H-11
Goodland, *Sherman*, 4,948 ... C-2
Gove, *Gove*, 105 ... D-4
Grandview Plaza, *Geary*, 1,184 ... D-12
Great Bend, *Barton*, 15,345 ... F-8
Greensburg, *Kiowa*, 1,574 ... H-7
Halstead, *Harvey*, 1,873 ... G-11
Harper, *Harper*, 1,567 ... I-10
Haven, *Reno*, 1,175 ... G-10
Hays, *Ellis*, 20,013 ... D-7
Haysville, *Sedgwick*, 8,502 ... H-11
Herington, *Dickinson*, 2,563 ... E-12
Hesston, *Harvey*, 3,509 ... F-11
Hiawatha, *Brown*, 3,417 ... B-15
Hill City, *Graham*, 1,604 ... C-6
Hillsboro, *Marion*, 2,854 ... F-11
Hoisington, *Barton*, 2,975 ... E-8
Holcomb, *Finney*, 2,026 ... G-3
Holton, *Jackson*, 3,353 ... C-14
Horton, *Brown*, 1,967 ... B-15
Howard, *Elk*, 808 ... H-13
Hoxie, *Sheridan*, 1,244 ... C-4
Hugoton, *Stevens*, 3,708 ... I-2
Humboldt, *Allen*, 1,999 ... G-15
Hutchinson, *Reno*, 40,787 ... G-10
Independence, *Montgomery*, 9,846 ... I-15
Inman, *McPherson*, 1,142 ... F-10
Iola, *Allen*, 6,302 ... G-15
Jetmore, *Hodgeman*, 903 ... G-6
Johnson (Johnson City), *Stanton*, 1,528 ... H-1
Junction City, *Geary*, 18,886 ... D-12
Kansas City, *Wyandotte*, 146,866 ... D-17
Kechi, *Sedgwick*, 1,038 ... G-11
Kingman, *Kingman*, 3,387 ... H-9
Kinsley, *Edwards*, 1,658 ... G-7
Kiowa, *Barber*, 1,055 ... J-9
La Crosse, *Rush*, 1,376 ... E-7
La Cygne, *Linn*, 1,115 ... F-17
Lakin, *Kearny*, 2,316 ... G-3
Lansing, *Leavenworth*, 9,199 ... C-16
Larned, *Pawnee*, 4,236 ... F-7
Lawrence, *Douglas*, 80,098 ... D-15
Leavenworth, *Leavenworth*, 35,420 ... C-16
Leawood, *Johnson*, 27,656 ... D-17
Lenexa, *Johnson*, 40,238 ... L-16
Leoti, *Wichita*, 1,598 ... E-2
Liberal, *Seward*, 19,666 ... I-3
Lincoln (Lincoln Center), *Lincoln*, 1,349 ... D-9
Lindsborg, *McPherson*, 3,321 ... E-10
Louisburg, *Miami*, 2,576 ... E-17
Lyndon, *Osage*, 1,038 ... E-15
Lyons, *Rice*, 3,732 ... F-9
Maize, *Sedgwick*, 1,868 ... L-13
Manhattan, *Riley*, 44,831 ... C-13
Mankato, *Jewell*, 976 ... B-9
Marion, *Marion*, 2,110 ... F-12
Marysville, *Marshall*, 3,271 ... B-12
McPherson, *McPherson*, 13,770 ... F-10
Meade, *Meade*, 1,672 ... I-5
Medicine Lodge, *Barber*, 2,193 ... I-8
Merriam, *Johnson*, 11,008 ... L-16
Minneapolis, *Ottawa*, 2,046 ... D-10
Mission, *Johnson*, 9,727 ... L-16
Mission Hills, *Johnson*, 3,593 ... L-17
Mound City, *Linn*, 821 ... F-16
Moundridge, *McPherson*, 1,593 ... F-11
Mulvane, *Sumner*, 5,155 ... H-11
Neodesha, *Wilson*, 2,848 ... H-15
Ness City, *Ness*, 1,534 ... F-6
Newton, *Harvey*, 17,190 ... K-14
Nickerson, *Reno*, 1,194 ... F-9
North Newton, *Harvey*, 1,522 ... G-11
Norton, *Norton*, 3,012 ... B-6
• Oaklawn-Sunview, *Sedgwick*, 3,135 ... M-14
Oakley, *Logan*, 2,173 ... D-4
Oberlin, *Decatur*, 1,994 ... B-4
Ogden, *Riley*, 1,762 ... D-12
Olathe, *Johnson*, 92,962 ... D-16
Osage City, *Osage*, 3,034 ... E-14
Osawatomie, *Miami*, 4,645 ... E-16
Osborne, *Osborne*, 1,607 ... C-8
Oskaloosa, *Jefferson*, 1,165 ... C-15
Oswego, *Labette*, 2,046 ... I-16
Ottawa, *Franklin*, 11,921 ... E-15
Overland Park, *Johnson*, 149,080 ... L-16
Oxford, *Sumner*, 1,173 ... I-11
Paola, *Miami*, 5,011 ... E-16
Park City, *Sedgwick*, 5,814 ... L-14
Parsons, *Labette*, 11,514 ... I-16
Peabody, *Marion*, 1,384 ... F-12
Phillipsburg, *Phillips*, 2,668 ... B-7
Pittsburg, *Crawford*, 19,243 ... H-17
Plains (West Plains), *Meade*, 1,163 ... I-4
Plainville, *Rooks*, 2,029 ... C-7
Pleasanton, *Linn*, 1,387 ... F-17
Prairie Village, *Johnson*, 22,072 ... L-17
Pratt, *Pratt*, 6,570 ... H-8
Roeland Park, *Johnson*, 6,817 ... D-17
Rose Hill, *Butler*, 3,432 ... H-11
Rossville, *Shawnee*, 1,014 ... D-14
Russell, *Russell*, 4,696 ... D-8
Sabetha, *Nemaha*, 2,589 ... A-14
Saint Francis, *Cheyenne*, 1,497 ... B-2
Saint John, *Stafford*, 1,318 ... G-8
Saint Marys, *Pottawatomie*, 2,198 ... C-14
Salina, *Saline*, 45,679 ... D-10
Satanta, *Haskell*, 1,239 ... H-3
Scott City, *Scott*, 3,855 ... E-3
Sedan, *Chautauqua*, 1,342 ... I-14
Sedgwick, *Harvey*, 1,537 ... G-11
Seneca, *Nemaha*, 2,122 ... B-14
Sharon Springs, *Wallace*, 835 ... D-2
Shawnee, *Johnson*, 47,996 ... L-16
Silver Lake, *Shawnee*, 1,358 ... D-14
Smith Center, *Smith*, 1,931 ... B-8
Solomon, *Dickinson*, 1,072 ... D-11
South Hutchinson, *Reno*, 2,539 ... G-10
Spring Hill, *Johnson*, 2,727 ... E-16
Stafford, *Stafford*, 1,161 ... G-8
Sterling, *Rice*, 2,642 ... F-9
Stockton, *Rooks*, 1,558 ... C-7
Sublette, *Haskell*, 1,592 ... H-3
Syracuse, *Hamilton*, 1,824 ... G-2
Tonganoxie, *Leavenworth*, 2,728 ... D-16
Topeka, *Shawnee*, 122,377 ... D-15
Towanda, *Butler*, 1,338 ... G-12
Tribune, *Greeley*, 835 ... E-2
Troy, *Doniphan*, 1,054 ... B-16
Ulysses, *Grant*, 5,960 ... H-2
Valley Center, *Sedgwick*, 4,883 ... G-11
Valley Falls, *Jefferson*, 1,254 ... C-15
Victoria, *Ellis*, 1,208 ... D-7
Wakeeney, *Trego*, 1,924 ... D-6
Wamego, *Pottawatomie*, 4,246 ... C-13
Washington, *Washington*, 1,223 ... B-12
Wathena, *Doniphan*, 1,348 ... B-16
Wellington, *Sumner*, 8,647 ... I-11
Wellsville, *Franklin*, 1,606 ... E-16
Westmoreland, *Pottawatomie*, 631 ... C-13
Westwood, *Johnson*, 1,533 ... L-17
Wichita, *Sedgwick*, 344,284 ... H-11
Winfield, *Cowley*, 12,206 ... I-12
Yates Center, *Woodson*, 1,599 ... G-14

Explanation of symbols: • - Census Designated Place (CDP)

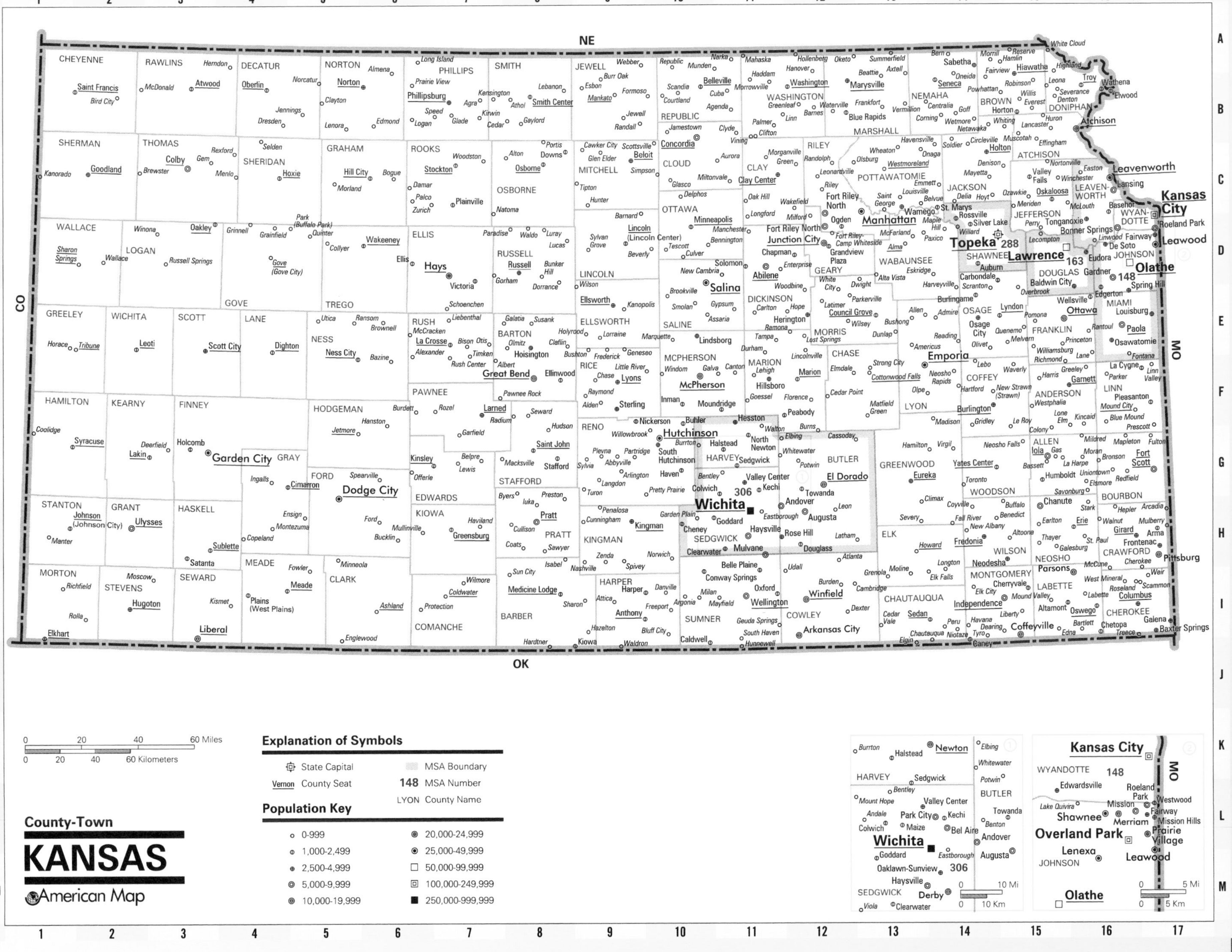
County-Town
KANSAS
American Map
Explanation of Symbols
State Capital
Vernon County Seat
MSA Boundary
148 MSA Number
LYON County Name
Population Key
0-999
1,000-2,499
2,500-4,999
5,000-9,999
10,000-19,999
20,000-24,999
25,000-49,999
50,000-99,999
100,000-249,999
250,000-999,999
60 Miles
60 Kilometers
Kansas City
Wichita
NE
MO
OK
CO

KENTUCKY

COUNTIES

(120 Counties)

Name of County	Population	Location on Map
ADAIR	17,244	H-8
ALLEN	17,800	I-5
ANDERSON	19,111	E-8
BALLARD	8,286	K-13
BARREN	38,033	I-5
BATH	11,085	D-12
BELL	30,060	I-13
BOONE	85,991	B-9
BOURBON	19,360	D-10
BOYD	49,752	D-15
BOYLE	27,697	G-9
BRACKEN	8,279	B-11
BREATHITT	16,100	F-13
BRECKINRIDGE	18,648	F-4
BULLITT	61,236	E-6
BUTLER	13,010	G-4
CALDWELL	13,060	K-16
CALLOWAY	34,177	L-15
CAMPBELL	88,616	B-10
CARLISLE	5,351	L-13
CARROLL	10,155	C-8
CARTER	26,889	C-14
CASEY	15,447	G-9
CHRISTIAN	72,265	I-1
CLARK	33,144	E-11
CLAY	24,556	H-12
CLINTON	9,634	J-8
CRITTENDEN	9,384	J-16
CUMBERLAND	7,147	I-7
DAVIESS	91,545	F-2
EDMONSON	11,644	H-5
ELLIOTT	6,748	D-14
ESTILL	15,307	F-11
FAYETTE	260,512	E-10
FLEMING	13,792	D-12
FLOYD	42,441	F-14
FRANKLIN	47,687	D-9
FULTON	7,752	M-13
GALLATIN	7,870	B-9
GARRARD	14,792	F-9
GRANT	22,384	B-9
GRAVES	37,028	L-14
GRAYSON	24,053	G-4
GREEN	11,518	G-7
GREENUP	36,891	C-14
HANCOCK	8,392	F-3
HARDIN	94,174	F-5
HARLAN	33,202	I-13
HARRISON	17,983	C-10
HART	17,445	G-6
HENDERSON	44,829	F-1
HENRY	15,060	C-8
HICKMAN	5,262	L-13
HOPKINS	46,519	G-1
JACKSON	13,495	G-11
JEFFERSON	693,604	D-6
JESSAMINE	39,041	E-9
JOHNSON	23,445	E-14
KENTON	151,464	B-10
KNOTT	17,649	G-14
KNOX	31,795	I-11
LARUE	13,373	F-6
LAUREL	52,715	H-11
LAWRENCE	15,569	E-14
LEE	7,916	F-12
LESLIE	12,401	H-13
LETCHER	25,277	H-14
LEWIS	14,092	C-12
LINCOLN	23,361	G-9
LIVINGSTON	9,804	J-15
LOGAN	26,573	I-3
LYON	8,080	L-16
MADISON	70,872	F-10
MAGOFFIN	13,332	F-14
MARION	18,212	F-7
MARSHALL	30,125	L-15
MARTIN	12,578	F-15
MASON	16,800	C-11
MCCRACKEN	65,514	K-14
MCCREARY	17,080	I-10
MCLEAN	9,938	F-2
MEADE	26,349	E-5
MENIFEE	6,556	E-12
MERCER	20,817	F-9
METCALFE	10,037	I-7
MONROE	11,756	I-6
MONTGOMERY	22,554	E-11
MORGAN	13,948	E-13
MUHLENBERG	31,839	H-2
NELSON	37,477	F-7
NICHOLAS	6,813	D-11
OHIO	22,916	G-3
OLDHAM	46,178	D-7
OWEN	10,547	C-9
OWSLEY	4,858	G-12
PENDLETON	14,390	B-10
PERRY	29,390	G-13
PIKE	68,736	F-16
POWELL	13,237	F-12
PULASKI	56,217	I-9
ROBERTSON	2,266	C-11
ROCKCASTLE	16,582	G-10
ROWAN	22,094	D-13
RUSSELL	16,315	I-8
SCOTT	33,061	D-9
SHELBY	33,337	D-8
SIMPSON	16,405	I-4
SPENCER	11,766	E-7
TAYLOR	22,927	G-7
TODD	11,971	I-2
TRIGG	12,597	L-16
TRIMBLE	8,125	C-7
UNION	15,637	I-16
WARREN	92,522	H-4
WASHINGTON	10,916	F-8
WAYNE	19,923	I-9
WEBSTER	14,120	G-1
WHITLEY	35,865	I-11
WOLFE	7,065	F-12
WOODFORD	23,208	E-9
TOTAL	**4,041,769**	

CITIES AND TOWNS

Note: The first name is that of the city or town, second, that of the county in which it is located, then the population and location on the map.

Albany, *Clinton,* 2,220 ....J-8
Alexandria, *Campbell,* 8,286 ....A-10
Anchorage, *Jefferson,* 2,264 ....B-4
Ashland, *Boyd,* 21,981 ....C-15
Auburn, *Logan,* 1,444 ....I-4
Audubon Park, *Jefferson,* 1,545 ..B-3
Augusta, *Bracken,* 1,204 ....B-11
Barbourmeade, *Jefferson,* 1,260 .A-4
Barbourville, *Knox,* 3,589 ....I-12
Bardstown, *Nelson,* 10,374 ....F-7
Bardwell, *Carlisle,* 799 ....L-14
Beattyville, *Lee,* 1,193 ....F-12
Beaver Dam, *Ohio,* 3,033 ....G-3
Bedford, *Trimble,* 677 ....C-8
Beechwood Village, *Jefferson,* 1,173 ....B-3
Bellevue, *Campbell,* 6,480 ....K-10
Benton, *Marshall,* 4,197 ....L-16
Berea, *Madison,* 9,851 ....G-11
Booneville, *Owsley,* 111 ....G-12
Bowling Green, *Warren,* 49,296 ...I-5
Brandenburg, *Meade,* 2,049 ....E-5
• Breckinridge Center, *Union,* 1,874 ....I-17
Brodhead, *Rockcastle,* 1,193 ....G-10
• Brooks, *Bullitt,* 2,678 ....E-7
Brooksville, *Bracken,* 589 ....B-11
Brownsville, *Edmonson,* 921 ....H-5
• Buckner, *Oldham,* 4,000 ....D-7
• Buechel, *Jefferson,* 7,272 ....C-3
Burkesville, *Cumberland,* 1,756 ....I-8
• Burlington, *Boone,* 10,779 ....A-9
Cadiz, *Trigg,* 2,373 ....L-17
Calhoun, *McLean,* 836 ....G-2
Calvert City, *Marshall,* 2,701 ....K-16
Campbellsville, *Taylor,* 10,498 ....G-8
Campton, *Wolfe,* 424 ....F-13
Carlisle, *Nicholas,* 1,917 ....D-11
Carrollton, *Carroll,* 3,846 ....B-8
Catlettsburg, *Boyd,* 1,960 ....C-15
Cave City, *Barren,* 1,880 ....H-6
Central City, *Muhlenberg,* 5,893 .H-3
• Claryville, *Campbell,* 2,588 ....M-11
Clay, *Webster,* 1,179 ....G-1
Clay City, *Powell,* 1,303 ....E-12
Clinton, *Hickman,* 1,415 ....L-14
Cloverport, *Breckinridge,* 1,256 ...F-4
Cold Spring, *Campbell,* 3,806 ....L-11
Columbia, *Adair,* 4,014 ....H-8
Corbin, *Whitley,* 7,742 ....I-11
Covington, *Kenton,* 43,370 ....A-10
Crescent Springs, *Kenton,* 3,931 .L-9
Crestview Hills, *Kenton,* 2,889 ....L-9
Crestwood, *Oldham,* 1,999 ....D-7
Crittenden, *Grant,* 2,401 ....B-10
Cumberland, *Harlan,* 2,611 ....I-14
Cynthiana, *Harrison,* 6,258 ....D-11
Danville, *Boyle,* 15,477 ....F-9
Dawson Springs, *Hopkins,* 2,980 H-1
Dayton, *Campbell,* 5,966 ....A-10
Dixon, *Webster,* 632 ....G-1
Douglass Hills, *Jefferson,* 5,718 .D-7
Dry Ridge, *Grant,* 1,995 ....B-10
Earlington, *Hopkins,* 1,649 ....H-2
Eddyville, *Lyon,* 2,350 ....K-16
Edgewood, *Kenton,* 9,400 ....L-9
Edmonton, *Metcalfe,* 1,586 ....I-7
Elizabethtown, *Hardin,* 22,542 ....F-6
Elkhorn City, *Pike,* 1,060 ....G-16
Elkton, *Todd,* 1,984 ....I-3
Elsmere, *Kenton,* 8,139 ....L-9
Eminence, *Henry,* 2,231 ....D-8
Erlanger, *Kenton,* 16,676 ....L-9
Evarts, *Harlan,* 1,101 ....I-14
• Fairdale, *Jefferson,* 7,658 ....E-7
Falmouth, *Pendleton,* 2,058 ....B-10
• Fern Creek, *Jefferson,* 17,870 ....C-4
Flatwoods, *Greenup,* 7,605 ....C-15
Flemingsburg, *Fleming,* 3,010 ..C-12
Florence, *Boone,* 23,551 ....A-10
• Fort Campbell North, *Christian,* 14,338 ....J-2
• Fort Knox, *Hardin,* 12,377 ....E-6
Fort Mitchell, *Kenton,* 8,089 ....K-10
Fort Thomas, *Campbell,* 16,495 A-10
Fort Wright, *Kenton,* 5,681 ....L-10
Frankfort, *Franklin,* 27,741 ....D-9
Franklin, *Simpson,* 7,996 ....J-4
Frenchburg, *Menifee,* 551 ....E-13
Fulton, *Fulton,* 2,775 ....M-14
Georgetown, *Scott,* 18,080 ....D-10
Glasgow, *Barren,* 13,019 ....I-6
Graymoor-Devondale, *Jefferson,* 2,925 ....B-3
Grayson, *Carter,* 3,877 ....D-14
Greensburg, *Green,* 2,396 ....H-7
Greenup, *Greenup,* 1,198 ....C-15
Greenville, *Muhlenberg,* 4,398 ....H-3
Guthrie, *Todd,* 1,469 ....J-3
Hardinsburg, *Breckinridge,* 2,345 F-5
Harlan, *Harlan,* 2,081 ....I-13
Harrodsburg, *Mercer,* 8,014 ....F-9
Hartford, *Ohio,* 2,571 ....G-3
Hawesville, *Hancock,* 971 ....E-4
Hazard, *Perry,* 4,806 ....H-14
Hebron Estates, *Bullitt,* 1,104 ....D-3
Henderson, *Henderson,* 27,373 ..F-1
• Hendron, *McCracken,* 4,239 ....A-16
Hickman, *Fulton,* 2,560 ....M-13
Highland Heights, *Campbell,* 6,554 ....A-10
• Highview, *Jefferson,* 15,161 ....C-3
Hillview, *Bullitt,* 7,037 ....D-3
Hindman, *Knott,* 787 ....G-14
Hodgenville, *Larue,* 2,874 ....G-7
Hopkinsville, *Christian,* 30,089 ....I-2
Horse Cave, *Hart,* 2,252 ....H-6
Hurstbourne, *Jefferson,* 3,884 ....B-4
Hurstbourne Acres, *Jefferson,* 1,504 ....B-4
Hyden, *Leslie,* 204 ....H-13
Independence, *Kenton,* 14,982 .B-10
Indian Hills, *Jefferson,* 2,882 ....B-3
Inez, *Martin,* 466 ....E-16
Irvine, *Estill,* 2,843 ....F-12
Irvington, *Breckinridge,* 1,257 ....E-5
Jackson, *Breathitt,* 2,490 ....G-13
Jamestown, *Russell,* 1,624 ....I-9
Jeffersontown, *Jefferson,* 26,633 C-4
Jeffersonville, *Montgomery,* 1,804 ....E-12
Jenkins, *Letcher,* 2,401 ....H-15
Junction City, *Boyle,* 2,184 ....F-9
La Center, *Ballard,* 1,038 ....K-14
La Grange, *Oldham,* 5,676 ....C-8
Lakeside Park, *Kenton,* 2,869 ...L-10
Lancaster, *Garrard,* 3,734 ....F-10
Lawrenceburg, *Anderson,* 9,014 .E-9
Lebanon, *Marion,* 5,718 ....G-8
Lebanon Junction, *Bullitt,* 1,801 ..F-7
• Ledbetter, *Livingston,* 1,700 ....K-15
Leitchfield, *Grayson,* 6,139 ....G-5
Lewisport, *Hancock,* 1,639 ....E-3
Lexington, *Fayette,* 260,512 ....E-10
Liberty, *Casey,* 1,850 ....G-9
Livermore, *McLean,* 1,482 ....G-3
London, *Laurel,* 5,692 ....H-11
Louisa, *Lawrence,* 2,018 ....D-15
Louisville, *Jefferson,* 256,231 ....D-7
Ludlow, *Kenton,* 4,409 ....K-10
Lyndon, *Jefferson,* 9,369 ....D-7
Madisonville, *Hopkins,* 19,307 ....G-2
Manchester, *Clay,* 1,738 ....H-12
Marion, *Crittenden,* 3,196 ....J-16
• Masonville, *Daviess,* 1,075 ....F-3
• Massac, *McCracken,* 3,888 ....K-14
Mayfield, *Graves,* 10,349 ....L-15
Maysville, *Mason,* 8,993 ....C-12
McKee, *Jackson,* 878 ....G-12
Middlesboro, *Bell,* 10,384 ....J-12
Middletown, *Jefferson,* 5,744 ....B-4
Midway, *Woodford,* 1,620 ....D-10
Minor Lane Heights, *Jefferson,* 1,435 ....C-3
Monticello, *Wayne,* 5,981 ....I-9
Morehead, *Rowan,* 5,914 ....D-13
Morganfield, *Union,* 3,494 ....I-17
Morgantown, *Butler,* 2,544 ....H-4
Mount Olivet, *Robertson,* 289 ...C-11
Mount Sterling, *Montgomery,* 5,876 ....E-12
Mount Vernon, *Rockcastle,* 2,592 ....G-11
Mount Washington, *Bullitt,* 8,485 E-7
Muldraugh, *Meade,* 1,298 ....E-6
Munfordville, *Hart,* 1,563 ....H-6
Murray, *Calloway,* 14,950 ....M-16
New Castle, *Henry,* 919 ....C-8
• Newburg, *Jefferson,* 20,636 ....C-3
Newport, *Campbell,* 17,048 ....K-10
Nicholasville, *Jessamine,* 19,680 ....E-10
• North Corbin, *Whitley,* 1,662 ....I-11
Nortonville, *Hopkins,* 1,264 ....H-2
Oak Grove, *Christian,* 7,064 ....J-2
• Oakbrook, *Boone,* 7,726 ....A-10
• Okolona, *Jefferson,* 17,807 ....C-3
Olive Hill, *Carter,* 1,813 ....D-14
Orchard Grass Hills, *Oldham,* 1,031 ....A-4
Owensboro, *Daviess,* 54,067 ....F-3
Owenton, *Owen,* 1,387 ....C-9
Owingsville, *Bath,* 1,488 ....D-12
Paducah, *McCracken,* 26,307 ...K-15
Paintsville, *Johnson,* 4,132 ....F-15
Paris, *Bourbon,* 9,183 ....D-11
Park Hills, *Kenton,* 2,977 ....K-10
Pewee Valley, *Oldham,* 1,436 ....D-7
• Phelps, *Pike,* 1,053 ....G-17
Pikeville, *Pike,* 6,295 ....G-16
• Pine Knot, *McCreary,* 1,680 ....J-10
Pineville, *Bell,* 2,093 ....I-12
Pioneer Village, *Bullitt,* 2,555 ....D-3
• Pleasure Ridge Park, *Jefferson,* 25,776 ....C-1
Prestonsburg, *Floyd,* 3,612 ....F-15
Princeton, *Caldwell,* 6,536 ....K-17
Prospect, *Jefferson,* 4,657 ....D-7
Providence, *Webster,* 3,611 ....G-1
Raceland, *Greenup,* 2,355 ....C-15
Radcliff, *Hardin,* 21,961 ....F-6
• Reidland, *McCracken,* 4,353 ....K-15
Richmond, *Madison,* 27,152 ....F-11
Russell, *Greenup,* 3,645 ....C-15
Russell Springs, *Russell,* 2,399 ..H-8
Russellville, *Logan,* 7,149 ....I-3
• Saint Dennis, *Jefferson,* 9,177 ....C-1
Saint Matthews, *Jefferson,* 15,852 ....B-3
Saint Regis Park, *Jefferson,* 1,520 ....B-4
Salyersville, *Magoffin,* 1,604 ....F-14
Sandy Hook, *Elliott,* 678 ....E-14
Scottsville, *Allen,* 4,327 ....J-5
Sebree, *Webster,* 1,558 ....F-2
Shelbyville, *Shelby,* 10,085 ....D-8
Shepherdsville, *Bullitt,* 8,334 ....E-7
Shively, *Jefferson,* 15,157 ....D-6
Silver Grove, *Campbell,* 1,215 ...L-11
Simpsonville, *Shelby,* 1,281 ....D-8
Smithland, *Livingston,* 401 ....K-15
Somerset, *Pulaski,* 11,352 ....H-10
South Shore, *Greenup,* 1,226 ..B-14
Southgate, *Campbell,* 3,472 ....K-10
Springfield, *Washington,* 2,634 ....F-8
Stanford, *Lincoln,* 3,430 ....G-10
Stanton, *Powell,* 3,029 ....E-12
• Stearns, *McCreary,* 1,586 ....J-10
Sturgis, *Union,* 2,030 ....I-17
Taylor Mill, *Kenton,* 6,913 ....L-10
Taylorsville, *Spencer,* 1,009 ....E-8
Tompkinsville, *Monroe,* 2,660 ....J-7
Union, *Boone,* 2,893 ....M-8
Uniontown, *Union,* 1,064 ....H-17
• Valley Station, *Jefferson,* 22,946 .E-6
Vanceburg, *Lewis,* 1,731 ....C-13
Versailles, *Woodford,* 7,511 ....E-9
Villa Hills, *Kenton,* 7,948 ....A-10
Vine Grove, *Hardin,* 4,169 ....F-6
Walton, *Boone,* 2,450 ....B-10
Warsaw, *Gallatin,* 1,811 ....B-9
West Buechel, *Jefferson,* 1,301 ..C-3
West Liberty, *Morgan,* 3,277 ....E-14
West Point, *Hardin,* 1,100 ....E-6
• Westwood, *Boyd,* 4,888 ....C-15
Wheelwright, *Floyd,* 1,042 ....G-15
Whitesburg, *Letcher,* 1,600 ....H-15
• Whitley City, *McCreary,* 1,111 ....J-10
Wickliffe, *Ballard,* 794 ....K-13
Wilder, *Campbell,* 2,624 ....L-10
Williamsburg, *Whitley,* 5,143 ....J-11
Williamstown, *Grant,* 3,227 ....C-10
Wilmore, *Jessamine,* 5,905 ....E-10
Winchester, *Clark,* 16,724 ....E-11
Windy Hills, *Jefferson,* 2,480 ....B-3
Woodlawn Park, *Jefferson,* 1,033 ....B-3
• Woodlawn-Oakdale, *McCracken,* 4,937 ....A-16
Worthington, *Greenup,* 1,673 ....C-15
Worthington Hills, *Jefferson,* 1,594 ....A-4
Wurtland, *Greenup,* 1,049 ....C-15

Explanation of symbols: • - Census Designated Place (CDP)

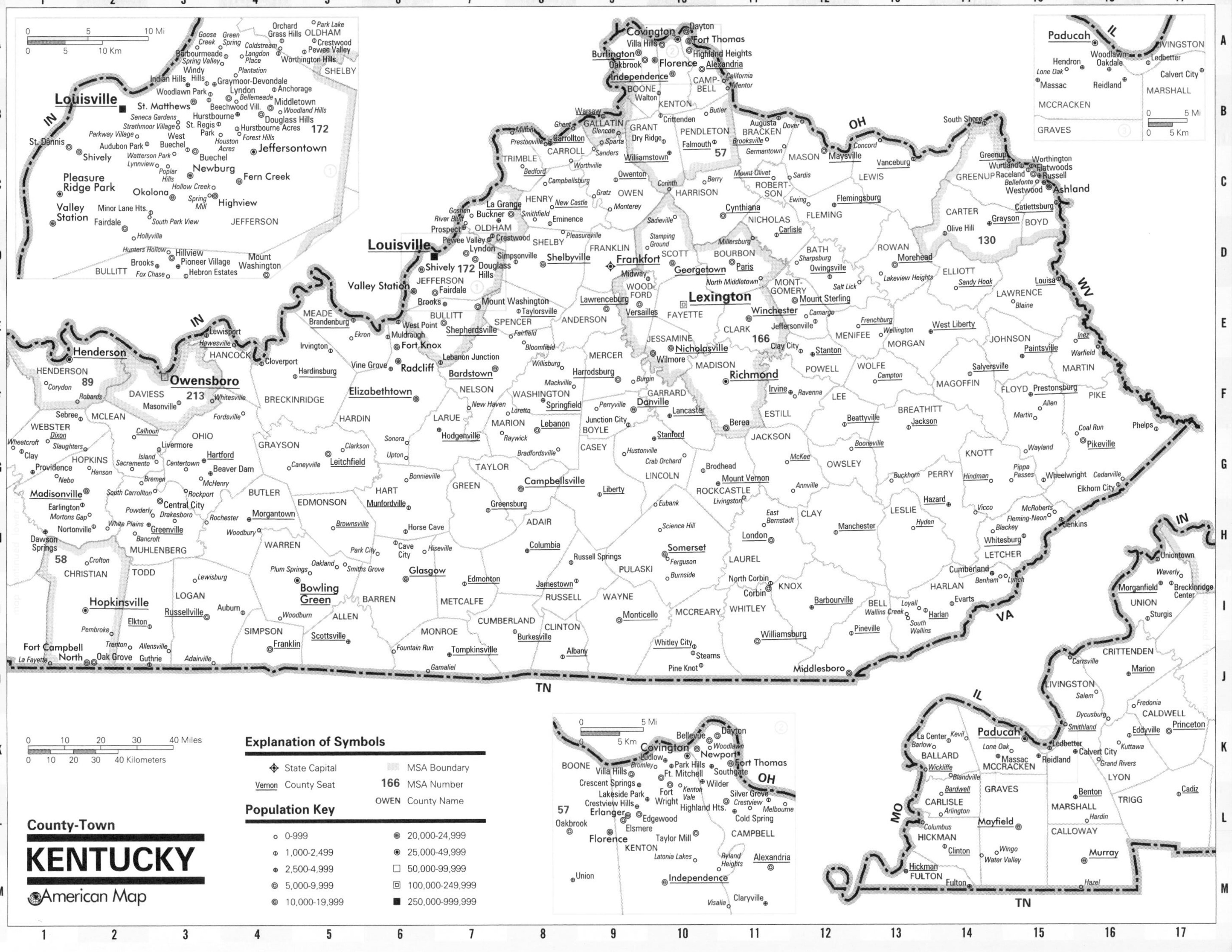
County-Town
KENTUCKY
American Map
Explanation of Symbols
State Capital
Vernon County Seat
MSA Boundary
166 MSA Number
OWEN County Name
Population Key
0-999
1,000-2,499
2,500-4,999
5,000-9,999
10,000-19,999
20,000-24,999
25,000-49,999
50,000-99,999
100,000-249,999
250,000-999,999
40 Miles
40 Kilometers
OH
WV
VA
TN
IN
IL
MO
Louisville
Lexington
Frankfort
Owensboro
Bowling Green
Paducah
Covington
Ashland
Hopkinsville
Henderson
Middlesboro

PARISHES

(64 Parishes)

Name of Parish	Population	Location on Map
ACADIA	58,861	I-5
ALLEN	25,440	H-4
ASCENSION	76,627	J-9
ASSUMPTION	23,388	J-9
AVOYELLES	41,481	F-6
BEAUREGARD	32,986	H-2
BIENVILLE	15,752	C-3
BOSSIER	98,310	B-2
CADDO	252,161	A-1
CALCASIEU	183,577	I-2
CALDWELL	10,560	C-6
CAMERON	9,991	J-2
CATAHOULA	10,920	E-7
CLAIBORNE	16,851	A-3
CONCORDIA	20,247	F-7
DE SOTO	25,494	D-1
EAST BATON ROUGE	412,852	H-9
EAST CARROLL	9,421	B-8
EAST FELICIANA	21,360	H-9
EVANGELINE	35,434	H-5
FRANKLIN	21,263	D-7
GRANT	18,698	E-5
IBERIA	73,266	J-8
IBERVILLE	33,320	I-8
JACKSON	15,397	C-5
JEFFERSON	455,466	L-11
JEFFERSON DAVIS	31,435	I-4
LA SALLE	14,282	E-6
LAFAYETTE	190,503	I-6
LAFOURCHE	89,974	K-10
LINCOLN	42,509	B-4
LIVINGSTON	91,814	H-9
MADISON	13,728	B-8
MOREHOUSE	31,021	A-6
NATCHITOCHES	39,080	E-3
ORLEANS	484,674	J-12
OUACHITA	147,250	C-6
PLAQUEMINES	26,757	L-12
POINTE COUPEE	22,763	H-7
RAPIDES	126,337	F-5
RED RIVER	9,622	D-3
RICHLAND	20,981	B-7
SABINE	23,459	E-2
SAINT BERNARD	67,229	K-12
SAINT CHARLES	48,072	K-11
SAINT HELENA	10,525	G-9
SAINT JAMES	21,216	J-9
SAINT JOHN THE BAPTIST	43,044	J-10
SAINT LANDRY	87,700	H-6
SAINT MARTIN	48,583	K-8
SAINT MARTIN	48,583	J-7
SAINT MARY	53,500	K-8
SAINT TAMMANY	191,268	H-11
TANGIPAHOA	100,588	H-10
TENSAS	6,618	C-8
TERREBONNE	104,503	L-9
UNION	22,803	A-5
VERMILION	53,807	J-5
VERNON	52,531	F-3
WASHINGTON	43,926	G-11
WEBSTER	41,831	B-3
WEST BATON ROUGE	21,601	I-8
WEST CARROLL	12,314	A-8
WEST FELICIANA	15,111	G-8
WINN	16,894	D-4
TOTAL	**4,468,976**	

CITIES AND TOWNS

Note: The first name is that of the city or town, second, that of the parish in which it is located, then the population and location on the map.

Explanation of symbols: • - Census Designated Place (CDP)

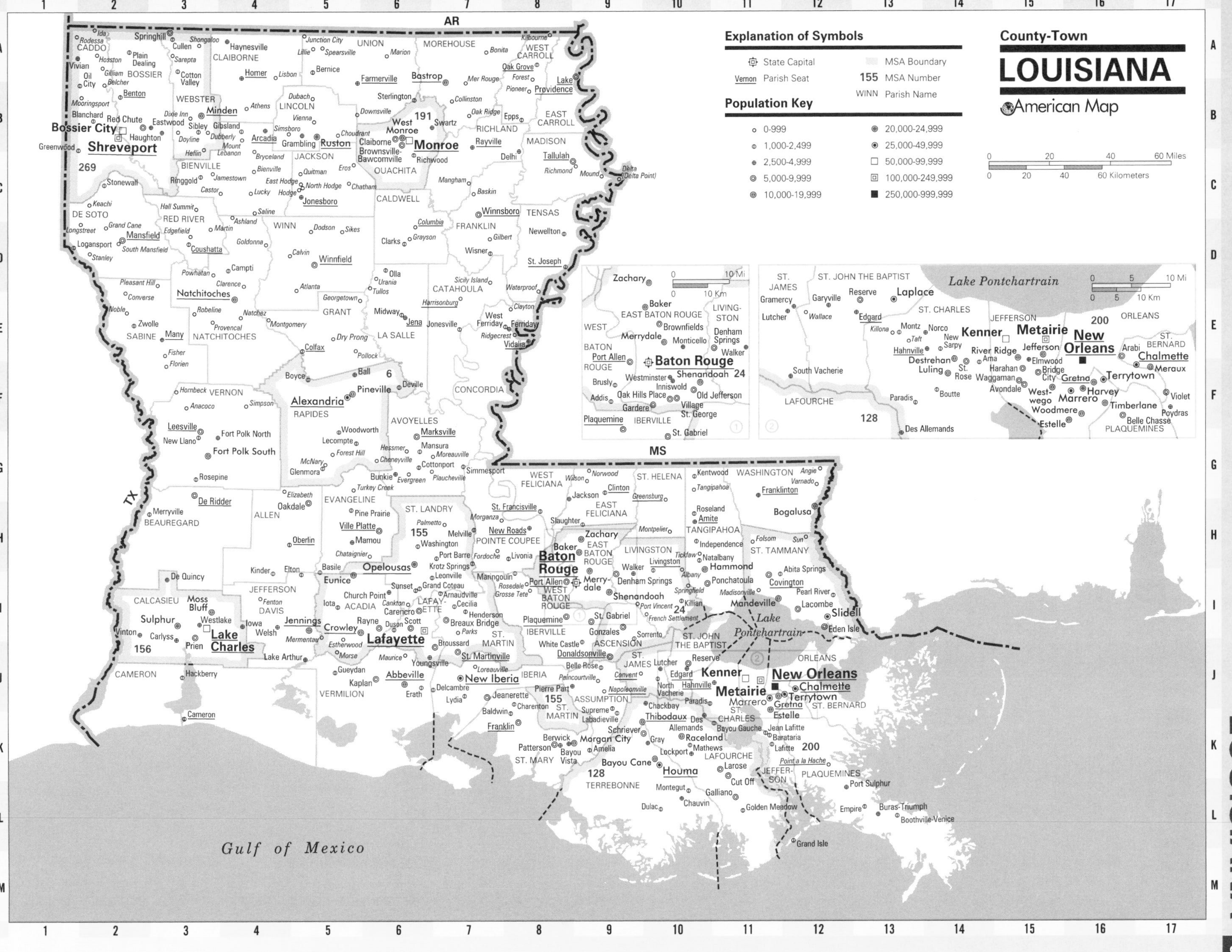
County-Town
LOUISIANA
American Map
Explanation of Symbols
State Capital
Vernon Parish Seat
MSA Boundary
155 MSA Number
WINN Parish Name
Population Key
0-999
1,000-2,499
2,500-4,999
5,000-9,999
10,000-19,999
20,000-24,999
25,000-49,999
50,000-99,999
100,000-249,999
250,000-999,999
0 20 40 60 Miles
0 20 40 60 Kilometers
AR
MS
TX
Gulf of Mexico
Lake Pontchartrain
Shreveport
Bossier City
Monroe
Alexandria
Lake Charles
Lafayette
Baton Rouge
New Orleans
Metairie
Kenner
Houma

MAINE

COUNTIES

(16 Counties)

Name of County	Population	Location on Map
ANDROSCOGGIN	103,793	M-3
AROOSTOOK	73,938	B-6
CUMBERLAND	265,612	N-2
FRANKLIN	29,467	I-2
HANCOCK	51,791	I-9
KENNEBEC	117,114	L-4
KNOX	39,618	M-6
LINCOLN	33,616	M-5
OXFORD	54,755	J-1
PENOBSCOT	144,919	E-8
PISCATAQUIS	17,235	D-5
SAGADAHOC	35,214	N-4
SOMERSET	50,888	E-4
WALDO	36,280	K-6
WASHINGTON	33,941	H-10
YORK	186,742	O-2
TOTAL	**1,274,923**	

CITIES AND TOWNS

Note: The first name is that of the city or town, second, that of the county in which it is located, then the population and location on the map.

▲Acton, *York,* 2,145 ....O-2
▲Addison, *Washington,* 1,209 ....K-10
▲Albion, *Kennebec,* 1,946 ....L-6
▲Alfred, *York,* 2,497 ....P-2
▲Anson, *Somerset,* 2,583 ....K-4
▲Appleton, *Knox,* 1,271 ....M-6
▲Arundel, *York,* 3,571 ....P-3
▲Ashland, *Aroostook,* 1,474 ....D-9
Auburn, *Androscoggin,* 23,203 ....M-4
Augusta, *Kennebec,* 18,560 ....M-5
▲Baileyville, *Washington,* 1,686 ....I-11
▲Baldwin, *Cumberland,* 1,290 ....N-3
Bangor, *Penobscot,* 31,473 ....K-8
▲Bar Harbor, *Hancock,* 4,820 ....L-9
●Bar Harbor, *Hancock,* 2,680 ....L-9
Bath, *Sagadahoc,* 9,266 ....N-5
Belfast, *Waldo,* 6,381 ....L-7
▲Belgrade, *Kennebec,* 2,978 ....L-5
▲Benton, *Kennebec,* 2,557 ....K-5
▲Berwick, *York,* 6,353 ....P-2
●Berwick, *York,* 1,993 ....P-2
▲Bethel, *Oxford,* 2,411 ....L-2
Biddeford, *York,* 20,942 ....P-3
▲Blue Hill, *Hancock,* 2,390 ....L-8
▲Boothbay, *Lincoln,* 2,960 ....N-5
▲Boothbay Harbor, *Lincoln,* 2,334 ....N-5
●Boothbay Harbor, *Lincoln,* 1,237 ....N-5
▲Bowdoin, *Sagadahoc,* 2,727 ....N-5
▲Bowdoinham, *Sagadahoc,* 2,612 ....N-4
▲Bradford, *Penobscot,* 1,186 ....J-7
▲Bradley, *Penobscot,* 1,242 ....J-8
Brewer, *Penobscot,* 8,987 ....K-8
▲Bridgton, *Cumberland,* 4,883 ....M-2
●Bridgton, *Cumberland,* 2,359 ....M-2
▲Bristol, *Lincoln,* 2,644 ....N-6
▲Brooks, *Waldo,* 1,022 ....L-7
▲Brownfield, *Oxford,* 1,251 ....N-2
▲Brownville, *Piscataquis,* 1,259 ....I-7
▲Brunswick, *Cumberland,* 21,172 ....N-4
●Brunswick, *Cumberland,* 14,816 ....N-4
●Brunswick Station, *Cumberland,* 1,511 ....N-4
▲Buckfield, *Oxford,* 1,723 ....M-3
▲Bucksport, *Hancock,* 4,908 ....L-8
●Bucksport, *Hancock,* 2,970 ....L-8
▲Burnham, *Waldo,* 1,142 ....K-6
▲Buxton, *York,* 7,452 ....O-3
Calais, *Washington,* 3,447 ....I-12
▲Camden, *Knox,* 5,254 ....M-7
●Camden, *Knox,* 3,934 ....M-7
▲Canaan, *Somerset,* 2,017 ....K-5
▲Canton, *Oxford,* 1,121 ....L-3
Cape Elizabeth, *Cumberland,* 9,068 O-4
●Cape Neddick, *York,* 2,997 ....Q-2
Caribou, *Aroostook,* 8,312 ....C-10
▲Carmel, *Penobscot,* 2,416 ....K-7
▲Casco, *Cumberland,* 3,469 ....N-3
▲Castine, *Hancock,* 1,343 ....L-8
▲Charleston, *Penobscot,* 1,397 ....J-7
▲Chelsea, *Kennebec,* 2,559 ....M-5
▲Cherryfield, *Washington,* 1,157 ....K-10
▲Chesterville, *Franklin,* 1,170 ....L-4
▲China, *Kennebec,* 4,106 ....L-6
●Chisholm, *Franklin,* 1,399 ....L-4
▲Clinton, *Kennebec,* 3,340 ....K-6
●Clinton, *Kennebec,* 1,305 ....K-6
▲Corinna, *Penobscot,* 2,145 ....J-6
▲Corinth, *Penobscot,* 2,511 ....J-7
▲Cornish, *York,* 1,269 ....N-2
▲Cornville, *Somerset,* 1,208 ....K-5
▲Cumberland, *Cumberland,* 7,159 ....O-4
●Cumberland Center, *Cumberland,* 2,596 ....N-3
▲Cushing, *Knox,* 1,322 ....N-6
▲Damariscotta, *Lincoln,* 2,041 ....N-6
●Damariscotta-Newcastle, *Lincoln,* 1,751 ....M-6
▲Dayton, *York,* 1,805 ....O-3
▲Dedham, *Hancock,* 1,422 ....K-8
▲Deer Isle, *Hancock,* 1,876 ....M-8
▲Denmark, *Oxford,* 1,004 ....N-2
▲Dexter, *Penobscot,* 3,890 ....J-6
●Dexter, *Penobscot,* 2,201 ....J-6
▲Dixfield, *Oxford,* 2,514 ....L-3
●Dixfield, *Oxford,* 1,137 ....L-3
▲Dixmont, *Penobscot,* 1,065 ....K-7
▲Dover-Foxcroft, *Piscataquis,* 4,211 ....I-5
●Dover-Foxcroft, *Piscataquis,* 2,592 ....I-6
▲Dresden, *Lincoln,* 1,625 ....M-5
▲Durham, *Androscoggin,* 3,381 ....N-4
▲East Machias, *Washington,* 1,298 ..K-11
▲East Millinocket, *Penobscot,* 1,828 ..H-8
●East Millinocket, *Penobscot,* 1,701 ..H-8
▲Easton, *Aroostook,* 1,249 ....D-10
Eastport, *Washington,* 1,640 ....J-12
▲Eddington, *Penobscot,* 2,052 ....K-8
▲Edgecomb, *Lincoln,* 1,090 ....N-5
▲Eliot, *York,* 5,954 ....Q-2
Ellsworth, *Hancock,* 6,456 ....L-9
▲Enfield, *Penobscot,* 1,616 ....I-8
▲Etna, *Penobscot,* 1,012 ....K-7
▲Fairfield, *Somerset,* 6,573 ....K-5
●Fairfield, *Somerset,* 2,569 ....K-5
▲Falmouth, *Cumberland,* 10,310 ....O-3
Falmouth Foreside, *Cumberland,* 1,964 ....O-4
Farmingdale, *Kennebec,* 1,935 ....M-5
▲Farmingdale, *Kennebec,* 2,804 ....M-5
▲Farmington, *Franklin,* 7,410 ....K-4
●Farmington, *Franklin,* 4,098 ....K-4
▲Fayette, *Kennebec,* 1,040 ....L,,5
▲Fort Fairfield, *Aroostook,* 3,579 ....C-10
●Fort Fairfield, *Aroostook,* 1,600 ....C-10
▲Fort Kent, *Aroostook,* 4,233 ....B-8
●Fort Kent, *Aroostook,* 1,978 ....B-8
▲Frankfort, *Waldo,* 1,041 ....K-7
▲Franklin, *Hancock,* 1,370 ....K-9
▲Freeport, *Cumberland,* 7,800 ....N-4
●Freeport, *Cumberland,* 1,813 ....N-4
▲Frenchville, *Aroostook,* 1,225 ....A-9
▲Friendship, *Knox,* 1,204 ....N-6
▲Fryeburg, *Oxford,* 3,083 ....N-1
●Fryeburg, *Oxford,* 1,549 ....N-1
Gardiner, *Kennebec,* 6,198 ....M-5
▲Georgetown, *Sagadahoc,* 1,020 ....N-5
▲Glenburn, *Penobscot,* 3,964 ....J-7
▲Gorham, *Cumberland,* 14,141 ....O-3
●Gorham, *Cumberland,* 4,164 ....O-3
▲Gouldsboro, *Hancock,* 1,941 ....L-10
▲Gray, *Cumberland,* 6,820 ....N-3
▲Greenbush, *Penobscot,* 1,421 ....J-8
▲Greene, *Androscoggin,* 4,076 ....M-4
▲Greenville, *Piscataquis,* 1,623 ....H-5
●Greenville, *Piscataquis,* 1,319 ....H-5
▲Guilford, *Piscataquis,* 1,531 ....I-6
Hallowell, *Kennebec,* 2,467 ....M-5
▲Hampden, *Penobscot,* 6,327 ....K-7
●Hampden, *Penobscot,* 4,126 ....K-7
▲Hancock, *Hancock,* 2,147 ....L-9
▲Harpswell, *Cumberland,* 5,239 ....N-4
▲Harrison, *Cumberland,* 2,315 ....M-2
▲Hartland, *Somerset,* 1,816 ....J-6
▲Hebron, *Oxford,* 1,053 ....M-3
▲Hermon, *Penobscot,* 4,437 ....K-7
▲Hiram, *Oxford,* 1,423 ....N-2
▲Hodgdon, *Aroostook,* 1,240 ....F-10
▲Holden, *Penobscot,* 2,827 ....K-8
▲Hollis, *York,* 4,114 ....O-3
Hollis Center, *York,* 4,114 ....O-3
Hope, *Knox,* 1,310 ....M-7
▲Houlton, *Aroostook,* 6,476 ....F-10
●Houlton, *Aroostook,* 5,270 ....F-10
▲Howland, *Penobscot,* 1,362 ....I-8
●Howland, *Penobscot,* 1,210 ....I-8
▲Hudson, *Penobscot,* 1,393 ....J-7
▲Jay, *Franklin,* 4,985 ....L-4
▲Jefferson, *Lincoln,* 2,388 ....M-6
▲Jonesport, *Washington,* 1,408 ....L-11
▲Kenduskeag, *Penobscot,* 1,171 ....J-7
▲Kennebunk, *York,* 10,476 ....P-3
●Kennebunk, *York,* 4,804 ....P-3
▲Kennebunkport, *York,* 3,720 ....P-3
●Kennebunkport, *York,* 1,376 ....P-3
▲Kingfield, *Franklin,* 1,103 ....J-4
▲Kittery, *York,* 9,543 ....Q-2
●Kittery, *York,* 4,884 ....Q-2
●Kittery Point, *York,* 1,135 ....Q-2
●Lake Arrowhead, *York,* 2,264 ....O-2
▲Lamoine, *Hancock,* 1,495 ....L-9
▲Lebanon, *York,* 5,083 ....P-2
▲Leeds, *Androscoggin,* 2,001 ....M-4
▲Levant, *Penobscot,* 2,171 ....J-7
Lewiston, *Androscoggin,* 35,690 ....M-4
▲Limerick, *York,* 2,240 ....O-2
▲Limestone, *Aroostook,* 2,361 ....C-10
●Limestone, *Aroostook,* 1,453 ....C-10
▲Limington, *York,* 3,403 ....O-2
▲Lincoln, *Penobscot,* 5,221 ....I-8
●Lincoln, *Penobscot,* 2,933 ....I-8
▲Lincolnville, *Waldo,* 2,042 ....M-7
▲Lisbon, *Androscoggin,* 9,077 ....N-4
●Lisbon Falls, *Androscoggin,* 4,420 ...N-4
▲Litchfield, *Kennebec,* 3,110 ....M-4
●Little Falls-South Windham, *Cumberland,* 1,792 ....O-3
▲Livermore, *Androscoggin,* 2,106 ....L-4
▲Livermore Falls, *Androscoggin,* 3,227 ....L-4
●Livermore Falls, *Androscoggin,* 1,626 ....L-4
▲Lubec, *Washington,* 1,652 ....J-12
▲Lyman, *York,* 3,795 ....O-2
▲Machias, *Washington,* 2,353 ....K-11
●Machias, *Washington,* 1,376 ....K-11
▲Machiasport, *Washington,* 1,160 ....K-11
▲Madawaska, *Aroostook,* 4,534 ....A-9
●Madawaska, *Aroostook,* 3,326 ....A-9
▲Madison, *Somerset,* 4,523 ....K-5
●Madison, *Somerset,* 2,733 ....K-5
▲Manchester, *Kennebec,* 2,465 ....L-5
▲Mapleton, *Aroostook,* 1,889 ....D-9
▲Mars Hill, *Aroostook,* 1,480 ....D-10
●Mars Hill-Blaine, *Aroostook,* 1,428 .D-10
▲Mechanic Falls, *Androscoggin,* 3,138 ....M-3
●Mechanic Falls, *Androscoggin,* 2,450 ....M-3
▲Medway, *Penobscot,* 1,489 ....H-8
▲Mexico, *Oxford,* 2,959 ....K-3
●Mexico, *Oxford,* 1,946 ....K-3
▲Milbridge, *Washington,* 1,279 ....L-10
▲Milford, *Penobscot,* 2,950 ....J-8
●Milford, *Penobscot,* 2,197 ....J-8
▲Millinocket, *Penobscot,* 5,203 ....G-8
●Millinocket, *Penobscot,* 5,190 ....G-8
▲Milo, *Piscataquis,* 2,383 ....I-7
●Milo, *Piscataquis,* 1,898 ....I-7
▲Minot, *Androscoggin,* 2,248 ....M-3
▲Monmouth, *Kennebec,* 3,785 ....M-4
▲Montville, *Waldo,* 1,002 ....L-6
▲Mount Desert, *Hancock,* 2,109 ....L-9
▲Mount Vernon, *Kennebec,* 1,524 ....L-4
▲Naples, *Cumberland,* 3,274 ....N-2
▲New Gloucester, *Cumberland,* 4,803 N-3
▲New Sharon, *Franklin,* 1,297 ....K-4
▲Newburgh, *Penobscot,* 1,394 ....K-7
▲Newcastle, *Lincoln,* 1,748 ....M-5
▲Newfield, *York,* 1,328 ....O-2
▲Newport, *Penobscot,* 3,017 ....K-6
●Newport, *Penobscot,* 1,754 ....K-6
▲Nobleboro, *Lincoln,* 1,626 ....M-6
▲Norridgewock, *Somerset,* 3,294 ....K-5
●Norridgewock, *Somerset,* 1,557 ....K-5
▲North Berwick, *York,* 4,293 ....P-2
●North Berwick, *York,* 1,580 ....P-2
●North Windham, *Cumberland,* 4,568 N-3
▲North Yarmouth, *Cumberland,* 3,210 N-4
▲Northport, *Waldo,* 1,331 ....L-7
▲Norway, *Oxford,* 4,611 ....M-3
●Norway, *Oxford,* 2,623 ....M-3
▲Oakland, *Kennebec,* 5,959 ....L-5
●Oakland, *Kennebec,* 2,758 ....L-5
Ogunquit, *York,* 1,226 ....P-2
†Old Orchard Beach, *York,* 8,856 ....O-3
Old Town, *Penobscot,* 8,130 ....J-8
▲Orland, *Hancock,* 2,134 ....L-8
▲Orono, *Penobscot,* 9,112 ....J-8
●Orono, *Penobscot,* 8,253 ....J-8
▲Orrington, *Penobscot,* 3,526 ....K-8
▲Otisfield, *Oxford,* 1,560 ....M-3
▲Owls Head, *Knox,* 1,601 ....M-7
▲Oxford, *Oxford,* 3,960 ....M-3
●Oxford, *Oxford,* 1,300 ....M-3
▲Palermo, *Waldo,* 1,220 ....L-6
▲Palmyra, *Somerset,* 1,953 ....K-6
▲Paris, *Oxford,* 4,793 ....M-3
▲Parsonsfield, *York,* 1,584 ....O-2
▲Patten, *Penobscot,* 1,111 ....F-8
▲Penobscot, *Hancock,* 1,344 ....L-8
▲Peru, *Oxford,* 1,515 ....L-3
▲Phippsburg, *Sagadahoc,* 2,106 ....N-5
▲Pittsfield, *Somerset,* 4,214 ....K-6
●Pittsfield, *Somerset,* 3,217 ....K-6
▲Plymouth, *Penobscot,* 1,257 ....K-6
▲Poland, *Androscoggin,* 4,866 ....M-3
▲Porter, *Oxford,* 1,438 ....N-2
Portland, *Cumberland,* 64,249 ....O-3
▲Pownal, *Cumberland,* 1,491 ....N-4
Presque Isle, *Aroostook,* 9,511 ....D-10
†Randolph, *Kennebec,* 1,911 ....M-5
▲Rangeley, *Franklin,* 1,052 ....J-2
▲Raymond, *Cumberland,* 4,299 ....N-3
▲Readfield, *Kennebec,* 2,360 ....L-4
▲Richmond, *Sagadahoc,* 3,298 ....M-5
●Richmond, *Sagadahoc,* 1,864 ....M-5
Rockland, *Knox,* 7,609 ....M-7
▲Rockport, *Knox,* 3,209 ....M-7
▲Rumford, *Oxford,* 6,472 ....L-3
●Rumford, *Oxford,* 4,795 ....L-3
▲Sabattus, *Androscoggin,* 4,486 ....M-4
Saco, *York,* 16,822 ....O-3
▲Saint Albans, *Somerset,* 1,836 ....J,,6
▲Saint George, *Knox,* 2,580 ....N,,6
▲Sanford, *York,* 20,806 ....P-2
●Sanford, *York,* 10,133 ....P-2
▲Sangerville, *Piscataquis,* 1,270 ....I-6
▲Scarborough, *Cumberland,* 16,970 ..O-3
●Scarborough, *Cumberland,* 3,867 ....O-3
▲Searsmont, *Waldo,* 1,174 ....L-6
▲Searsport, *Waldo,* 2,641 ....L-7
●Searsport, *Waldo,* 1,102 ....L-7
▲Sebago, *Cumberland,* 1,433 ....N-2
▲Sedgwick, *Hancock,* 1,102 ....M-8
▲Shapleigh, *York,* 2,326 ....O-2
▲Sidney, *Kennebec,* 3,514 ....L-5
▲Skowhegan, *Somerset,* 8,824 ....K-5
●Skowhegan, *Somerset,* 6,696 ....K-5
▲South Berwick, *York,* 6,671 ....P-2
●South Eliot, *York,* 3,445 ....Q-2
●South Paris, *Oxford,* 2,237 ....M-3
South Portland, *Cumberland,* 23,324 O-4
●South Sanford, *York,* 4,173 ....P-2
▲South Thomaston, *Knox,* 1,416 ....M-7
▲Southwest Harbor, *Hancock,* 1,966 .M-9
●Springvale, *York,* 3,488 ....P-2
▲Standish, *Cumberland,* 9,285 ....O-3
▲Steuben, *Washington,* 1,126 ....L-10
▲Stockton Springs, *Waldo,* 1,481 ....L-7
▲Stonington, *Hancock,* 1,152 ....M-8
▲Strong, *Franklin,* 1,259 ....K-4
▲Sullivan, *Hancock,* 1,185 ....L-9
▲Surry, *Hancock,* 1,361 ....L-8
▲Swanville, *Waldo,* 1,357 ....L-7
●Thomaston, *Knox,* 2,714 ....M-7
▲Thomaston, *Knox,* 3,748 ....M-6
▲Topsham, *Sagadahoc,* 9,100 ....N-4
●Topsham, *Sagadahoc,* 6,271 ....N-4
▲Trenton, *Hancock,* 1,370 ....L-9
▲Turner, *Androscoggin,* 4,972 ....M-3
▲Union, *Knox,* 2,209 ....M-6
▲Unity, *Waldo,* 1,889 ....K-6
▲Van Buren, *Aroostook,* 2,631 ....B-10
●Van Buren, *Aroostook,* 2,369 ....B-10
▲Vassalboro, *Kennebec,* 4,047 ....L-5
Veazie, *Penobscot,* 1,744 ....J-8
▲Vinalhaven, *Knox,* 1,235 ....M-7
▲Waldoboro, *Lincoln,* 4,916 ....M-6
●Waldoboro, *Lincoln,* 1,291 ....M-6
▲Wales, *Androscoggin,* 1,322 ....M-4
▲Warren, *Knox,* 3,794 ....M-6
▲Washburn, *Aroostook,* 1,627 ....C-9
▲Washington, *Knox,* 1,345 ....M-6
▲Waterboro, *York,* 6,214 ....O-2
▲Waterford, *Oxford,* 1,455 ....M-2
Waterville, *Kennebec,* 15,605 ....L-5
▲Wayne, *Kennebec,* 1,112 ....L-4
▲Wells, *York,* 9,400 ....P-3
▲West Bath, *Sagadahoc,* 1,798 ....N-5
▲West Gardiner, *Kennebec,* 2,902 ....M-5
▲West Paris, *Oxford,* 1,722 ....L-3
Westbrook, *Cumberland,* 16,142 ....O-3
▲Whitefield, *Lincoln,* 2,273 ....M-5
▲Wilton, *Franklin,* 4,123 ....K-4
●Wilton, *Franklin,* 2,290 ....K-4
▲Windham, *Cumberland,* 14,904 ....N-3
▲Windsor, *Kennebec,* 2,204 ....M-5
†Winslow, *Kennebec,* 7,743 ....L-5
▲Winterport, *Waldo,* 3,602 ....K-7
●Winterport, *Waldo,* 1,307 ....K-7
●Winthrop, *Kennebec,* 2,893 ....L-4
▲Winthrop, *Kennebec,* 6,232 ....M-4
▲Wiscasset, *Lincoln,* 3,603 ....N-5
●Wiscasset, *Lincoln,* 1,203 ....N-5
●Woodland, *Washington,* 1,044 ....I-11
▲Woodstock, *Oxford,* 1,307 ....L-3
▲Woolwich, *Sagadahoc,* 2,810 ....N-5
▲Yarmouth, *Cumberland,* 8,360 ....N-4
●Yarmouth, *Cumberland,* 3,560 ....N-4
▲York, *York,* 12,854 ....Q-2
●York Harbor, *York,* 3,321 ....Q-2

Explanation of symbols: ● - Census Designated Place (CDP) ▲ - Township † - CDP and Township

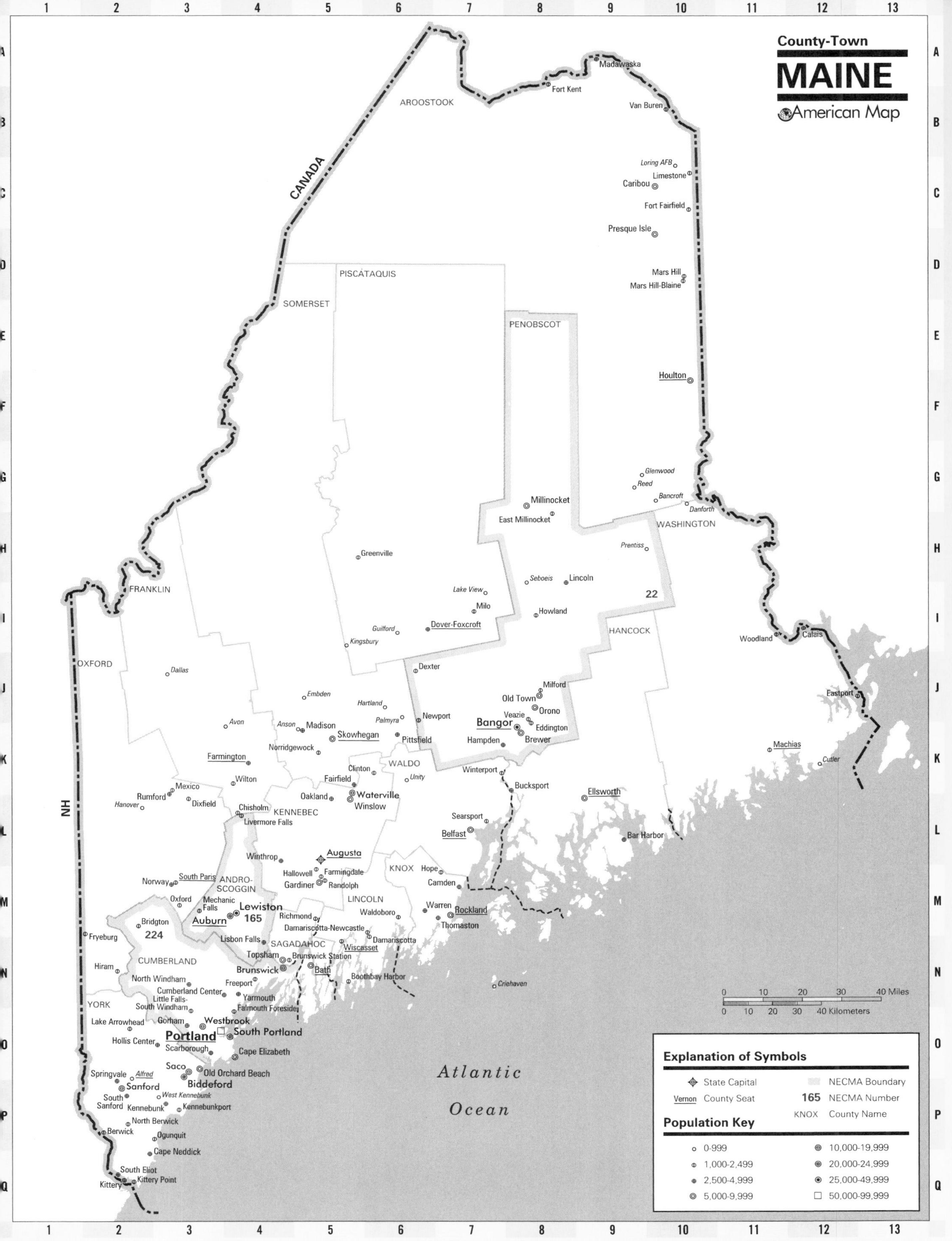
County-Town
MAINE
American Map
1 2 3 4 5 6 7 8 9 10 11 12 13
A B C D E F G H I J K L M N O P Q
CANADA
NH
AROOSTOOK
PISCATAQUIS
SOMERSET
PENOBSCOT
FRANKLIN
OXFORD
WASHINGTON
HANCOCK
WALDO
KENNEBEC
ANDRO-SCOGGIN
KNOX
LINCOLN
SAGADAHOC
CUMBERLAND
YORK
22
165
224
Madawaska
Fort Kent
Van Buren
Loring AFB
Limestone
Caribou
Fort Fairfield
Presque Isle
Mars Hill
Mars Hill-Blaine
Houlton
Glenwood
Reed
Bancroft
Danforth
Millinocket
East Millinocket
Prentiss
Greenville
Seboeis
Lincoln
Lake View
Milo
Howland
Guilford
Dover-Foxcroft
Kingsbury
Woodland
Calais
Dallas
Dexter
Milford
Old Town
Orono
Embden
Hartland
Palmyra
Newport
Veazie
Bangor
Eddington
Brewer
Hampden
Avon
Anson
Madison
Skowhegan
Pittsfield
Norridgewock
Eastport
Machias
Cutler
Farmington
Clinton
Unity
Winterport
Bucksport
Ellsworth
Wilton
Fairfield
Mexico
Rumford
Dixfield
Hanover
Oakland
Waterville
Winslow
Chisholm
Livermore Falls
Searsport
Belfast
Bar Harbor
Winthrop
Augusta
Hallowell
Farmingdale
Gardiner
Randolph
Hope
Camden
Norway
South Paris
Oxford
Mechanic Falls
Lewiston
Auburn
Warren
Rockland
Thomaston
Waldoboro
Richmond
Damariscotta-Newcastle
Damariscotta
Bridgton
Fryeburg
Lisbon Falls
Wiscasset
Topsham
Brunswick Station
Brunswick
Bath
Boothbay Harbor
Hiram
North Windham
Freeport
Cumberland Center
Yarmouth
Little Falls-South Windham
Falmouth Foreside
Criehaven
Lake Arrowhead
Gorham
Westbrook
Portland
South Portland
Hollis Center
Scarborough
Cape Elizabeth
Saco
Old Orchard Beach
Springvale
Alfred
Sanford
Biddeford
South Sanford
West Kennebunk
Kennebunk
Kennebunkport
North Berwick
Berwick
Ogunquit
Cape Neddick
South Eliot
Kittery
Kittery Point
Atlantic Ocean
0 10 20 30 40 Miles
0 10 20 30 40 Kilometers
Explanation of Symbols
State Capital
Vernon County Seat
NECMA Boundary
165 NECMA Number
KNOX County Name
Population Key
0-999
1,000-2,499
2,500-4,999
5,000-9,999
10,000-19,999
20,000-24,999
25,000-49,999
50,000-99,999

COUNTIES

(24 Counties)

Name of County	Population	Location on Map
ALLEGANY	74,930	A-1
ANNE ARUNDEL	489,656	F-10
BALTIMORE	692,134	A-9
BALTIMORE (Independent City)	754,292	A-9
CALVERT	74,563	G-10
CAROLINE	29,772	F-13
CARROLL	150,897	A-7
CECIL	85,951	A-12
CHARLES	120,546	I-7
DORCHESTER	30,674	I-12
FREDERICK	195,277	B-6
GARRETT	29,846	F-2
HARFORD	218,590	A-10
HOWARD	247,842	C-8
KENT	19,197	C-12
MONTGOMERY	873,341	D-6
PRINCE GEORGES	801,515	F-8
QUEEN ANNES	40,563	E-12
SAINT MARYS	86,211	I-9
SOMERSET	24,747	K-14
TALBOT	33,812	F-12
WASHINGTON	131,923	A-3
WICOMICO	84,644	I-14
WORCESTER	46,543	J-15
TOTAL	**5,296,486**	

CITIES AND TOWNS

Note: The first name is that of the city or town, second, that of the county in which it is located, then the population and location on the map.

Explanation of symbols: • - Census Designated Place (CDP)

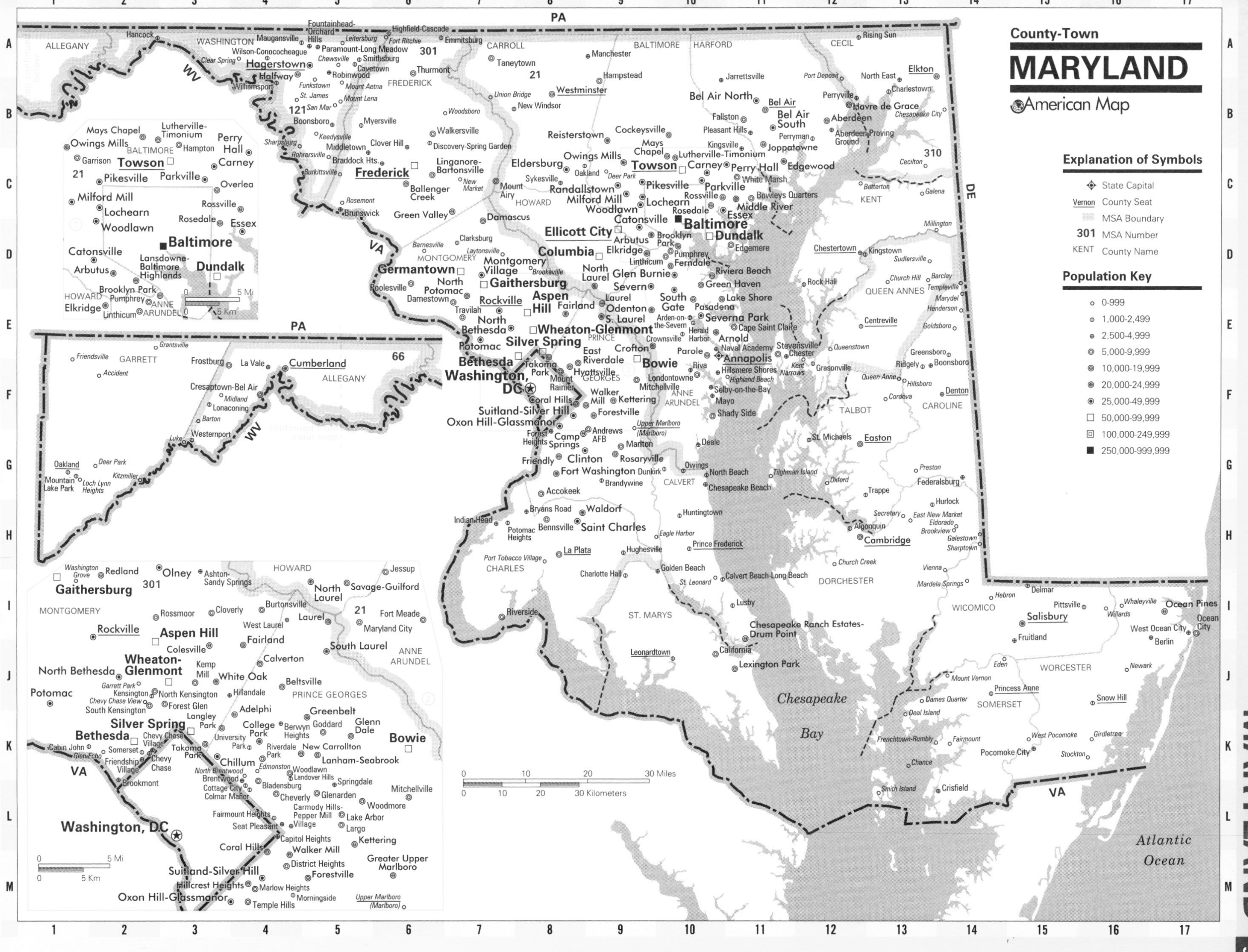

County-Town
MARYLAND
American Map
Explanation of Symbols
State Capital
Vernon County Seat
MSA Boundary
301 MSA Number
KENT County Name
Population Key
0-999
1,000-2,499
2,500-4,999
5,000-9,999
10,000-19,999
20,000-24,999
25,000-49,999
50,000-99,999
100,000-249,999
250,000-999,999
PA
DE
VA
WV
Chesapeake Bay
Atlantic Ocean
ALLEGANY
GARRETT
WASHINGTON
FREDERICK
CARROLL
BALTIMORE
HARFORD
CECIL
KENT
QUEEN ANNES
CAROLINE
TALBOT
DORCHESTER
WICOMICO
WORCESTER
SOMERSET
HOWARD
MONTGOMERY
PRINCE GEORGES
ANNE ARUNDEL
CALVERT
CHARLES
ST. MARYS
Baltimore
Annapolis
Washington, DC
30 Miles
30 Kilometers

COUNTIES

(14 Counties)

Name of County	Population	Location on Map
BARNSTABLE	222,230	I-15
BERKSHIRE	134,953	C-2
BRISTOL	534,678	H-11
DUKES	14,987	K-14
ESSEX	723,419	C-12
FRANKLIN	71,535	B-4
HAMPDEN	456,228	E-3
HAMPSHIRE	152,251	D-3
MIDDLESEX	1,465,396	D-10
NANTUCKET	9,520	K-16
NORFOLK	650,308	F-10
PLYMOUTH	472,822	F-13
SUFFOLK	689,807	E-12
WORCESTER	750,963	C-7
TOTAL	**6,349,097**	

CITIES AND TOWNS

Note: The first name is that of the city or town, second, that of the county in which it is located, then the population and location on the map.

•Abington, *Plymouth*, 14,605 ... F-13
▲Acton, *Middlesex*, 20,331 ... D-10
▲Acushnet, *Bristol*, 10,161 ... I-13
•Acushnet Center, *Bristol*, 3,171 ... I-13
•Adams, *Berkshire*, 5,784 ... C-3
▲Adams, *Berkshire*, 8,809 ... C-3
Agawam, *Hampden*, 28,144 ... F-5
•Amesbury, *Essex*, 12,327 ... A-13
▲Amesbury, *Essex*, 16,450 ... A-13
▲Amherst, *Hampshire*, 34,874 ... D-5
•Amherst Center, *Hampshire*, 17,050 ... D-5
•Andover, *Essex*, 7,900 ... B-12
▲Andover, *Essex*, 31,247 ... B-12
†Arlington, *Middlesex*, 42,389 ... J-2
▲Ashburnham, *Worcester*, 5,546 ... C-8
▲Ashby, *Middlesex*, 2,845 ... B-8
▲Ashfield, *Franklin*, 1,800 ... C-4
Ashland, *Middlesex*, 14,674 ... E-10
▲Athol, *Worcester*, 8,370 ... C-7
•Athol, *Worcester*, 8,370 ... C-7
Attleboro, *Bristol*, 42,068 ... G-11
Auburn, *Worcester*, 15,901 ... E-8
Avon, *Norfolk*, 4,443 ... M-3
•Ayer, *Middlesex*, 2,960 ... C-10
•Baldwinville, *Worcester*, 1,852 ... C-7
Barnstable, *Barnstable*, 47,821 ... I-16
•Barre, *Worcester*, 1,150 ... D-7
▲Barre, *Worcester*, 5,113 ... D-7
▲Becket, *Berkshire*, 1,755 ... E-3
Bedford, *Middlesex*, 12,595 ... I-1
•Belchertown, *Hampshire*, 2,626 ... E-6
▲Belchertown, *Hampshire*, 12,968 ... E-6
•Bellingham, *Norfolk*, 4,497 ... F-10
▲Bellingham, *Norfolk*, 15,314 ... F-10
†Belmont, *Middlesex*, 24,194 ... J-2
▲Berkley, *Bristol*, 5,749 ... H-12
▲Berlin, *Worcester*, 2,380 ... D-9
▲Bernardston, *Franklin*, 2,155 ... B-5
Beverly, *Essex*, 39,862 ... C-13
▲Billerica, *Middlesex*, 38,981 ... C-11
▲Blackstone, *Worcester*, 8,804 ... G-10
▲Blandford, *Hampden*, 1,214 ... F-3
•Bliss Corner, *Bristol*, 5,466 ... I-13
▲Bolton, *Worcester*, 4,148 ... D-9
•Bondsville, *Hampden*, 1,876 ... E-6
Boston, *Suffolk*, 589,141 ... D-12
•Bourne, *Barnstable*, 1,443 ... H-14
▲Bourne, *Barnstable*, 18,721 ... H-14
▲Boxborough, *Middlesex*, 4,868 ... D-10
•Boxford, *Essex*, 2,340 ... B-12
▲Boxford, *Essex*, 7,921 ... B-12
▲Boylston, *Worcester*, 4,008 ... D-9
†Braintree, *Norfolk*, 33,828 ... E-12
•Brewster, *Barnstable*, 2,212 ... H-17
▲Brewster, *Barnstable*, 10,094 ... H-17
•Bridgewater, *Plymouth*, 6,664 ... G-12
▲Bridgewater, *Plymouth*, 25,185 ... G-12
▲Brimfield, *Hampden*, 3,339 ... F-7
Brockton, *Plymouth*, 94,304 ... F-12
▲Brookfield, *Worcester*, 3,051 ... E-7
†Brookline, *Norfolk*, 57,107 ... E-12
▲Buckland, *Franklin*, 1,991 ... C-4
†Burlington, *Middlesex*, 22,876 ... C-11
•Buzzards Bay, *Barnstable*, 3,549 ... H-14
Cambridge, *Middlesex*, 101,355 ... D-12
▲Canton, *Norfolk*, 20,775 ... F-12
Canton, *Norfolk*, 20,775 ... F-12
▲Carlisle, *Middlesex*, 4,717 ... C-11
▲Carver, *Plymouth*, 11,163 ... G-13
▲Charlemont, *Franklin*, 1,358 ... C-4
▲Charlton, *Worcester*, 11,263 ... F-8
•Chatham, *Barnstable*, 1,667 ... I-17
▲Chatham, *Barnstable*, 6,625 ... I-17
▲Chelmsford, *Middlesex*, 33,858 ... C-11
Chelmsford, *Middlesex*, 33,858 ... C-11
Chelsea, *Suffolk*, 35,080 ... D-12
▲Cheshire, *Berkshire*, 3,401 ... C-2
▲Chester, *Hampden*, 1,308 ... E-3
▲Chesterfield, *Hampshire*, 1,201 ... D-4
Chicopee, *Hampden*, 54,653 ... F-5
▲Clarksburg, *Berkshire*, 1,686 ... B-3
•Clinton, *Worcester*, 7,884 ... D-9
▲Clinton, *Worcester*, 13,435 ... D-9
•Cochituate, *Middlesex*, 6,768 ... E-11
▲Cohasset, *Norfolk*, 7,261 ... E-13
▲Colrain, *Franklin*, 1,813 ... B-4
▲Concord, *Middlesex*, 16,993 ... D-11
▲Conway, *Franklin*, 1,809 ... C-4
•Cordaville, *Worcester*, 2,515 ... E-10
Dalton, *Berkshire*, 6,892 ... D-2
†Danvers, *Essex*, 25,212 ... C-13
▲Dartmouth, *Bristol*, 30,666 ... J-12
†Dedham, *Norfolk*, 23,464 ... E-11
▲Deerfield, *Franklin*, 4,750 ... C-5
•Dennis, *Barnstable*, 2,798 ... H-16
▲Dennis, *Barnstable*, 15,973 ... H-16
•Dennis Port, *Barnstable*, 3,612 ... I-16
▲Dighton, *Bristol*, 6,175 ... H-12
▲Douglas, *Worcester*, 7,045 ... F-9
▲Dover, *Norfolk*, 5,558 ... E-11
•Dover, *Norfolk*, 2,216 ... L-1
Dracut, *Middlesex*, 28,562 ... B-11
Dudley, *Worcester*, 10,036 ... F-8
▲Dunstable, *Middlesex*, 2,829 ... B-10
•Duxbury, *Plymouth*, 1,426 ... F-14
▲Duxbury, *Plymouth*, 14,248 ... F-14
▲East Bridgewater, *Plymouth*, 12,974 ... G-12
▲East Brookfield, *Worcester*, 2,097 ... E-7
•East Dennis, *Barnstable*, 3,299 ... H-16
•East Douglas, *Worcester*, 2,319 ... F-9
•East Falmouth, *Barnstable*, 6,615 ... I-14
•East Harwich, *Barnstable*, 4,744 ... I-17
East Longmeadow, *Hampden*, 14,100 ... F-5
•East Pepperell, *Middlesex*, 2,034 ... B-10
•East Sandwich, *Barnstable*, 3,720 ... H-15
▲Eastham, *Barnstable*, 5,453 ... H-17
Easthampton, *Hampshire*, 15,994 ... E-5
▲Easton, *Bristol*, 22,299 ... G-12
Edgartown, *Dukes*, 3,779 ... K-15
▲Egremont, *Berkshire*, 1,345 ... F-1
▲Erving, *Franklin*, 1,467 ... C-6
•Essex, *Essex*, 1,426 ... C-13
▲Essex, *Essex*, 3,267 ... C-13
Everett, *Middlesex*, 38,037 ... J-3
Fairhaven, *Bristol*, 16,159 ... I-13
Fall River, *Bristol*, 91,938 ... I-12
•Falmouth, *Barnstable*, 4,115 ... J-14
▲Falmouth, *Barnstable*, 32,660 ... J-14
•Fiskdale, *Worcester*, 2,156 ... F-7
Fitchburg, *Worcester*, 39,102 ... C-9
•Forestdale, *Barnstable*, 3,992 ... I-15
•Fort Devens, *Worcester*, 1,017 ... C-9
▲Foxborough, *Norfolk*, 16,246 ... F-11
†Framingham, *Middlesex*, 66,910 ... E-10
Franklin, *Norfolk*, 29,560 ... F-10
▲Freetown, *Bristol*, 8,472 ... H-12
Gardner, *Worcester*, 20,770 ... C-8
▲Georgetown, *Essex*, 7,377 ... B-12
▲Gill, *Franklin*, 1,363 ... C-5
Gloucester, *Essex*, 30,273 ... C-14
▲Grafton, *Worcester*, 14,894 ... E-9
▲Granby, *Hampshire*, 6,132 ... E-5
▲Granville, *Hampden*, 1,521 ... F-4
•Great Barrington, *Berkshire*, 2,459 ... E-1
▲Great Barrington, *Berkshire*, 7,527 ... E-1
•Green Harbor-Cedar Crest, *Plymouth*, 2,397 ... F-14
•Greenfield, *Franklin*, 13,716 ... C-5
▲Greenfield, *Franklin*, 18,168 ... C-5
•Groton, *Middlesex*, 1,113 ... C-10
▲Groton, *Middlesex*, 9,547 ... C-10
▲Groveland, *Essex*, 6,038 ... B-12
▲Hadley, *Hampshire*, 4,793 ... E-5
▲Halifax, *Plymouth*, 7,500 ... G-13
▲Hamilton, *Essex*, 8,315 ... C-13
▲Hampden, *Hampden*, 5,171 ... F-6
▲Hanover, *Plymouth*, 13,164 ... F-13
•Hanson, *Plymouth*, 2,044 ... F-13
▲Hanson, *Plymouth*, 9,495 ... F-13
▲Hardwick, *Worcester*, 2,622 ... D-7
▲Harvard, *Worcester*, 5,981 ... D-10
▲Harwich, *Barnstable*, 12,386 ... I-17
•Harwich Center, *Barnstable*, 1,832 ... M-15
•Harwich Port, *Barnstable*, 1,809 ... M-15
•Hatfield, *Hampshire*, 1,298 ... D-5
▲Hatfield, *Hampshire*, 3,249 ... D-5
Haverhill, *Essex*, 58,969 ... B-12
▲Hingham, *Plymouth*, 19,882 ... E-13
•Hingham, *Plymouth*, 5,352 ... L-4
▲Hinsdale, *Berkshire*, 1,872 ... D-2
†Holbrook, *Norfolk*, 10,785 ... M-3
▲Holden, *Worcester*, 15,621 ... D-8
•Holland, *Hampden*, 1,444 ... F-7
▲Holland, *Hampden*, 2,407 ... F-7
Holliston, *Middlesex*, 13,801 ... E-10
Holyoke, *Hampden*, 39,838 ... E-5
•Hopedale, *Worcester*, 4,158 ... F-10
▲Hopedale, *Worcester*, 5,907 ... F-10
•Hopkinton, *Middlesex*, 2,628 ... E-10
▲Hopkinton, *Middlesex*, 13,346 ... E-10
•Housatonic, *Berkshire*, 1,335 ... E-1
▲Hubbardston, *Worcester*, 3,909 ... D-8
•Hudson, *Middlesex*, 14,388 ... D-10
▲Hudson, *Middlesex*, 18,113 ... D-10
▲Hull, *Plymouth*, 11,050 ... E-13
•Hull, *Plymouth*, 11,050 ... E-13
▲Huntington, *Hampshire*, 2,174 ... E-4
•Ipswich, *Essex*, 4,161 ... B-13
▲Ipswich, *Essex*, 12,987 ... B-13
•Kingston, *Plymouth*, 5,380 ... G-14
▲Kingston, *Plymouth*, 11,780 ... G-14
▲Lakeville, *Plymouth*, 9,821 ... H-13
▲Lancaster, *Worcester*, 7,380 ... D-9
▲Lanesborough, *Berkshire*, 2,990 ... C-2
Lawrence, *Essex*, 72,043 ... B-11
•Lee, *Berkshire*, 2,021 ... E-2
▲Lee, *Berkshire*, 5,985 ... E-2
▲Leicester, *Worcester*, 10,471 ... E-8
•Lenox, *Berkshire*, 1,667 ... D-2
▲Lenox, *Berkshire*, 5,077 ... D-2
Leominster, *Worcester*, 41,303 ... C-9
▲Leverett, *Franklin*, 1,663 ... D-5
†Lexington, *Middlesex*, 30,355 ... D-11
▲Lincoln, *Middlesex*, 8,056 ... D-11
▲Littleton, *Middlesex*, 8,184 ... C-10
•Littleton Common, *Middlesex*, 2,816 ... C-10
†Longmeadow, *Hampden*, 15,633 ... F-5
Lowell, *Middlesex*, 105,167 ... C-11
Ludlow, *Hampden*, 21,209 ... F-5
•Lunenburg, *Worcester*, 1,695 ... C-9
▲Lunenburg, *Worcester*, 9,401 ... C-9
Lynn, *Essex*, 89,050 ... D-12
†Lynnfield, *Essex*, 11,542 ... C-12
Malden, *Middlesex*, 56,340 ... D-12
Manchester-by-the-Sea, *Essex*, 5,228 ... C-13
▲Mansfield, *Bristol*, 22,414 ... G-11
•Mansfield Center, *Bristol*, 7,320 ... G-11
†Marblehead, *Essex*, 20,377 ... D-13
•Marion, *Plymouth*, 1,202 ... I-13
▲Marion, *Plymouth*, 5,123 ... I-13
Marlborough, *Middlesex*, 36,255 ... E-10
▲Marshfield, *Plymouth*, 24,324 ... F-14
•Marshfield, *Plymouth*, 4,246 ... F-14
•Marshfield Hills, *Plymouth*, 2,369 ... F-13
▲Mashpee, *Barnstable*, 12,946 ... I-15
▲Mattapoisett, *Plymouth*, 6,268 ... I-13
•Mattapoisett Center, *Plymouth*, 2,966 ... I-13
†Maynard, *Middlesex*, 10,433 ... D-10
•Medfield, *Norfolk*, 6,670 ... F-11
▲Medfield, *Norfolk*, 12,273 ... F-11
Medford, *Middlesex*, 55,765 ... D-12
▲Medway, *Norfolk*, 12,448 ... F-10
▲Melrose, *Middlesex*, 27,134 ... D-12
▲Mendon, *Worcester*, 5,286 ... F-10
▲Merrimac, *Essex*, 6,138 ... A-12
Methuen, *Essex*, 43,789 ... B-11
•Middleboro Center, *Plymouth*, 6,913 ... G-13
▲Middleborough, *Plymouth*, 19,941 ... G-13
▲Middleton, *Essex*, 7,744 ... C-12
•Milford, *Worcester*, 24,230 ... F-10
▲Milford, *Worcester*, 26,799 ... F-10
▲Millbury, *Worcester*, 12,784 ... E-9
•Millers Falls, *Franklin*, 1,072 ... C-5
▲Millis, *Norfolk*, 7,902 ... F-11
•Millis-Clicquot, *Norfolk*, 4,607 ... F-11
Millville, *Worcester*, 2,724 ... G-10
†Milton, *Norfolk*, 26,062 ... E-12
▲Monson, *Hampden*, 8,359 ... F-6
•Monson Center, *Hampden*, 2,103 ... F-6
▲Montague, *Franklin*, 8,489 ... C-5
•Monument Beach, *Barnstable*, 2,438 ... H-14
†Nahant, *Essex*, 3,632 ... D-13
•Nantucket, *Nantucket*, 3,830 ... K-17
▲Nantucket, *Nantucket*, 9,520 ... K-17
Natick, *Middlesex*, 32,170 ... E-11
†Needham, *Norfolk*, 28,911 ... E-11
New Bedford, *Bristol*, 93,768 ... I-13
▲New Marlborough, *Berkshire*, 1,494 ... F-2
▲Newbury, *Essex*, 6,717 ... B-13
Newburyport, *Essex*, 17,189 ... A-13
Newton, *Middlesex*, 83,829 ... E-11
▲Norfolk, *Norfolk*, 10,460 ... F-11
North Adams, *Berkshire*, 14,681 ... B-3
•North Amherst, *Hampshire*, 6,019 ... D-5
North Andover, *Essex*, 27,202 ... B-12
▲North Attleborough, *Bristol*, 27,143 ... G-11
•North Brookfield, *Worcester*, 2,527 ... E-7
▲North Brookfield, *Worcester*, 4,683 ... E-7
•North Eastham, *Barnstable*, 1,915 ... H-17
•North Falmouth, *Barnstable*, 3,355 ... I-14
•North Lakeville, *Plymouth*, 2,233 ... H-13
•North Pembroke, *Plymouth*, 2,913 ... M-5
•North Plymouth, *Plymouth*, 3,593 ... G-14
North Reading, *Middlesex*, 13,837 ... C-12
•North Scituate, *Plymouth*, 5,065 ... L-5
•North Seekonk, *Bristol*, 2,598 ... G-11
•North Westport, *Bristol*, 4,533 ... I-12
Northampton, *Hampshire*, 28,978 ... E-5
•Northborough, *Worcester*, 6,257 ... E-9
▲Northborough, *Worcester*, 14,013 ... E-9
▲Northbridge, *Worcester*, 13,182 ... F-9
•Northfield, *Franklin*, 1,141 ... B-6
▲Northfield, *Franklin*, 2,951 ... B-6
•Northwest Harwich, *Barnstable*, 4,001 ... I-16
▲Norton, *Bristol*, 18,036 ... G-11
•Norton Center, *Bristol*, 2,618 ... G-11
▲Norwell, *Plymouth*, 9,765 ... F-13
†Norwood, *Norfolk*, 28,587 ... E-11
▲Oak Bluffs, *Dukes*, 3,713 ... J-14
▲Oakham, *Worcester*, 1,673 ... D-7
•Ocean Bluff-Brant Rock, *Plymouth*, 5,100 ... F-14
•Ocean Grove, *Bristol*, 3,012 ... H-11
•Onset, *Plymouth*, 1,292 ... H-14
▲Orange, *Franklin*, 7,518 ... C-6
•Orange, *Franklin*, 3,945 ... D-6
•Orleans, *Barnstable*, 1,716 ... H-17
▲Orleans, *Barnstable*, 6,341 ... H-17
▲Otis, *Berkshire*, 1,365 ... E-3
•Oxford, *Worcester*, 5,899 ... F-8
▲Oxford, *Worcester*, 13,352 ... F-8
•Palmer, *Hampden*, 3,900 ... F-6
▲Palmer, *Hampden*, 12,497 ... F-6
▲Paxton, *Worcester*, 4,386 ... E-8
Peabody, *Essex*, 48,129 ... I-4
▲Pelham, *Hampshire*, 1,403 ... D-6
▲Pembroke, *Plymouth*, 16,927 ... F-13
•Pepperell, *Middlesex*, 2,517 ... B-10
▲Pepperell, *Middlesex*, 11,142 ... B-9
▲Petersham, *Worcester*, 1,180 ... D-7
▲Phillipston, *Worcester*, 1,621 ... C-7
•Pinehurst, *Middlesex*, 6,941 ... C-11
Pittsfield, *Berkshire*, 45,793 ... D-2
Plainville, *Norfolk*, 7,683 ... G-11
•Plymouth, *Plymouth*, 7,658 ... G-14
▲Plymouth, *Plymouth*, 51,701 ... G-14
▲Plympton, *Plymouth*, 2,637 ... G-13
•Pocasset, *Barnstable*, 2,671 ... I-14
▲Princeton, *Worcester*, 3,353 ... D-8
•Provincetown, *Barnstable*, 3,192 ... F-16
▲Provincetown, *Barnstable*, 3,431 ... F-16
Quincy, *Norfolk*, 88,025 ... E-12
†Randolph, *Norfolk*, 30,963 ... F-12
▲Raynham, *Bristol*, 11,739 ... G-12
•Raynham Center, *Bristol*, 3,633 ... G-12
†Reading, *Middlesex*, 23,708 ... C-12
▲Rehoboth, *Bristol*, 10,172 ... H-11
Revere, *Suffolk*, 47,283 ... J-3
▲Richmond, *Berkshire*, 1,604 ... D-1
▲Rochester, *Plymouth*, 4,581 ... H-13
Rockland, *Plymouth*, 17,670 ... F-13
•Rockport, *Essex*, 5,606 ... B-14
▲Rockport, *Essex*, 7,767 ... B-14
•Rowley, *Essex*, 1,434 ... B-13
▲Rowley, *Essex*, 5,500 ... B-13
▲Royalston, *Worcester*, 1,254 ... B-7
▲Russell, *Hampden*, 1,657 ... E-4
•Rutland, *Worcester*, 2,205 ... D-8
▲Rutland, *Worcester*, 6,353 ... D-8
•Sagamore, *Barnstable*, 3,544 ... H-14
Salem, *Essex*, 40,407 ... C-13
•Salisbury, *Essex*, 4,484 ... A-13
▲Salisbury, *Essex*, 7,827 ... A-13
•Sandwich, *Barnstable*, 3,058 ... H-15
▲Sandwich, *Barnstable*, 20,136 ... H-15
†Saugus, *Essex*, 26,078 ... D-12
•Scituate, *Plymouth*, 5,069 ... E-14
▲Scituate, *Plymouth*, 17,863 ... E-14
Seekonk, *Bristol*, 13,425 ... H-11
•Sharon, *Norfolk*, 5,941 ... F-11
▲Sharon, *Norfolk*, 17,408 ... F-11
▲Sheffield, *Berkshire*, 3,335 ... F-1
▲Shelburne, *Franklin*, 2,058 ... C-4
•Shelburne Falls, *Franklin*, 1,951 ... C-4
▲Sherborn, *Middlesex*, 4,200 ... E-11
•Shirley, *Middlesex*, 1,427 ... C-9
▲Shirley, *Middlesex*, 6,373 ... C-9
Shrewsbury, *Worcester*, 31,640 ... E-9
▲Shutesbury, *Franklin*, 1,810 ... D-6
•Smith Mills, *Bristol*, 4,432 ... I-12
†Somerset, *Bristol*, 18,234 ... H-12
Somerville, *Middlesex*, 77,478 ... D-12
•South Amherst, *Hampshire*, 5,039 ... E-5
•South Ashburnham, *Worcester*, 1,013 ... C-8
•South Deerfield, *Franklin*, 1,868 ... D-5
•South Dennis, *Barnstable*, 3,679 ... M-15
•South Duxbury, *Plymouth*, 3,062 ... G-14
▲South Hadley, *Hampshire*, 17,196 ... E-5
•South Lancaster, *Worcester*, 1,742 ... D-9
•South Yarmouth, *Barnstable*, 11,603 ... M-14
▲Southampton, *Hampshire*, 5,387 ... E-4
▲Southborough, *Worcester*, 8,781 ... E-10
•Southbridge, *Worcester*, 12,878 ... F-8
▲Southbridge, *Worcester*, 17,214 ... F-7
▲Southwick, *Hampden*, 8,835 ... F-4
•Spencer, *Worcester*, 6,032 ... E-8
▲Spencer, *Worcester*, 11,691 ... E-8
Springfield, *Hampden*, 152,082 ... F-5
▲Sterling, *Worcester*, 7,257 ... D-9
▲Stockbridge, *Berkshire*, 2,276 ... E-2
†Stoneham, *Middlesex*, 22,219 ... I-2
Stoughton, *Norfolk*, 27,149 ... F-12
▲Stow, *Middlesex*, 5,902 ... D-10
•Sturbridge, *Worcester*, 2,047 ... F-7
▲Sturbridge, *Worcester*, 7,837 ... F-7
▲Sudbury, *Middlesex*, 16,841 ... D-11
▲Sunderland, *Franklin*, 3,777 ... D-5
▲Sutton, *Worcester*, 8,250 ... F-9
†Swampscott, *Essex*, 14,412 ... D-13
▲Swansea, *Bristol*, 15,901 ... H-11
Taunton, *Bristol*, 55,976 ... G-12
•Teaticket, *Barnstable*, 1,907 ... I-14
▲Templeton, *Worcester*, 6,799 ... C-7
▲Tewksbury, *Middlesex*, 28,851 ... C-11
•Three Rivers, *Hampden*, 2,939 ... F-6
▲Tisbury, *Dukes*, 3,755 ... J-14
•Topsfield, *Essex*, 2,826 ... C-12
▲Topsfield, *Essex*, 6,141 ... C-12
•Townsend, *Middlesex*, 1,043 ... B-9
▲Townsend, *Middlesex*, 9,198 ... B-9
▲Truro, *Barnstable*, 2,087 ... G-17
•Turners Falls, *Franklin*, 4,441 ... C-5
▲Upton, *Worcester*, 5,642 ... F-10
•Upton-West Upton, *Worcester*, 2,326 ... F-9
▲Uxbridge, *Worcester*, 11,156 ... F-9
•Vineyard Haven, *Dukes*, 2,048 ... J-14
†Wakefield, *Middlesex*, 24,804 ... C-12
▲Wales, *Hampden*, 1,737 ... F-7
•Walpole, *Norfolk*, 5,867 ... F-11
▲Walpole, *Norfolk*, 22,824 ... F-11
Waltham, *Middlesex*, 59,226 ... J-1
•Ware, *Hampshire*, 6,174 ... E-7
▲Ware, *Hampshire*, 9,707 ... E-7
▲Wareham, *Plymouth*, 20,335 ... H-14
•Wareham Center, *Plymouth*, 2,874 ... H-14
•Warren, *Worcester*, 1,452 ... E-7
▲Warren, *Worcester*, 4,776 ... E-7
Watertown, *Middlesex*, 32,986 ... J-2
▲Wayland, *Middlesex*, 13,100 ... D-11
•Webster, *Worcester*, 11,600 ... F-8
▲Webster, *Worcester*, 16,415 ... F-8
†Wellesley, *Norfolk*, 26,613 ... E-11
▲Wellfleet, *Barnstable*, 2,749 ... G-17
Wenham, *Essex*, 4,440 ... C-13
▲West Boylston, *Worcester*, 7,481 ... D-9
▲West Bridgewater, *Plymouth*, 6,634 ... G-12
•West Brookfield, *Worcester*, 1,610 ... E-7
▲West Brookfield, *Worcester*, 3,804 ... E-7
•West Chatham, *Barnstable*, 1,446 ... I-17
•West Concord, *Middlesex*, 5,632 ... D-10
•West Dennis, *Barnstable*, 2,570 ... M-14
•West Falmouth, *Barnstable*, 1,867 ... I-14
▲West Newbury, *Essex*, 4,149 ... B-12
†West Springfield, *Hampden*, 27,899 ... F-5
▲West Stockbridge, *Berkshire*, 1,416 ... D-1
▲West Tisbury, *Dukes*, 2,467 ... K-14
•West Wareham, *Plymouth*, 1,908 ... H-13
•West Yarmouth, *Barnstable*, 6,460 ... I-16
•Westborough, *Worcester*, 3,983 ... E-9
▲Westborough, *Worcester*, 17,997 ... E-9
Westfield, *Hampden*, 40,072 ... F-4
▲Westford, *Middlesex*, 20,754 ... C-10
▲Westhampton, *Hampshire*, 1,468 ... E-4
▲Westminster, *Worcester*, 6,907 ... C-8
Weston, *Middlesex*, 11,469 ... J-1
▲Westport, *Bristol*, 14,183 ... I-12
▲Westwood, *Norfolk*, 14,117 ... E-11
•Weweantic, *Plymouth*, 1,903 ... H-14
•Weymouth, *Norfolk*, 53,988 ... E-13
▲Weymouth, *Norfolk*, 53,988 ... E-13
▲Whately, *Franklin*, 1,573 ... D-5
•White Island Shores, *Plymouth*, 2,133 ... H-14
•Whitinsville, *Worcester*, 6,340 ... F-9
Whitman, *Plymouth*, 13,882 ... F-13
•Wilbraham, *Hampden*, 3,544 ... F-6
▲Wilbraham, *Hampden*, 13,473 ... F-6
▲Williamsburg, *Hampshire*, 2,427 ... D-4
•Williamstown, *Berkshire*, 4,754 ... B-2
▲Williamstown, *Berkshire*, 8,424 ... B-2
†Wilmington, *Middlesex*, 21,363 ... C-11
•Winchendon, *Worcester*, 4,246 ... B-7
▲Winchendon, *Worcester*, 9,611 ... B-7
†Winchester, *Middlesex*, 20,810 ... I-2
•Winthrop, *Suffolk*, 18,303 ... J-3
Woburn, *Middlesex*, 37,258 ... D-12
Worcester, *Worcester*, 172,648 ... E-9
▲Worthington, *Hampshire*, 1,270 ... D-3
▲Wrentham, *Norfolk*, 10,554 ... F-11
▲Yarmouth, *Barnstable*, 24,807 ... I-16
•Yarmouth Port, *Barnstable*, 5,395 ... I-16

Explanation of symbols: • - Census Designated Place (CDP) ▲ - Township † - CDP and Township

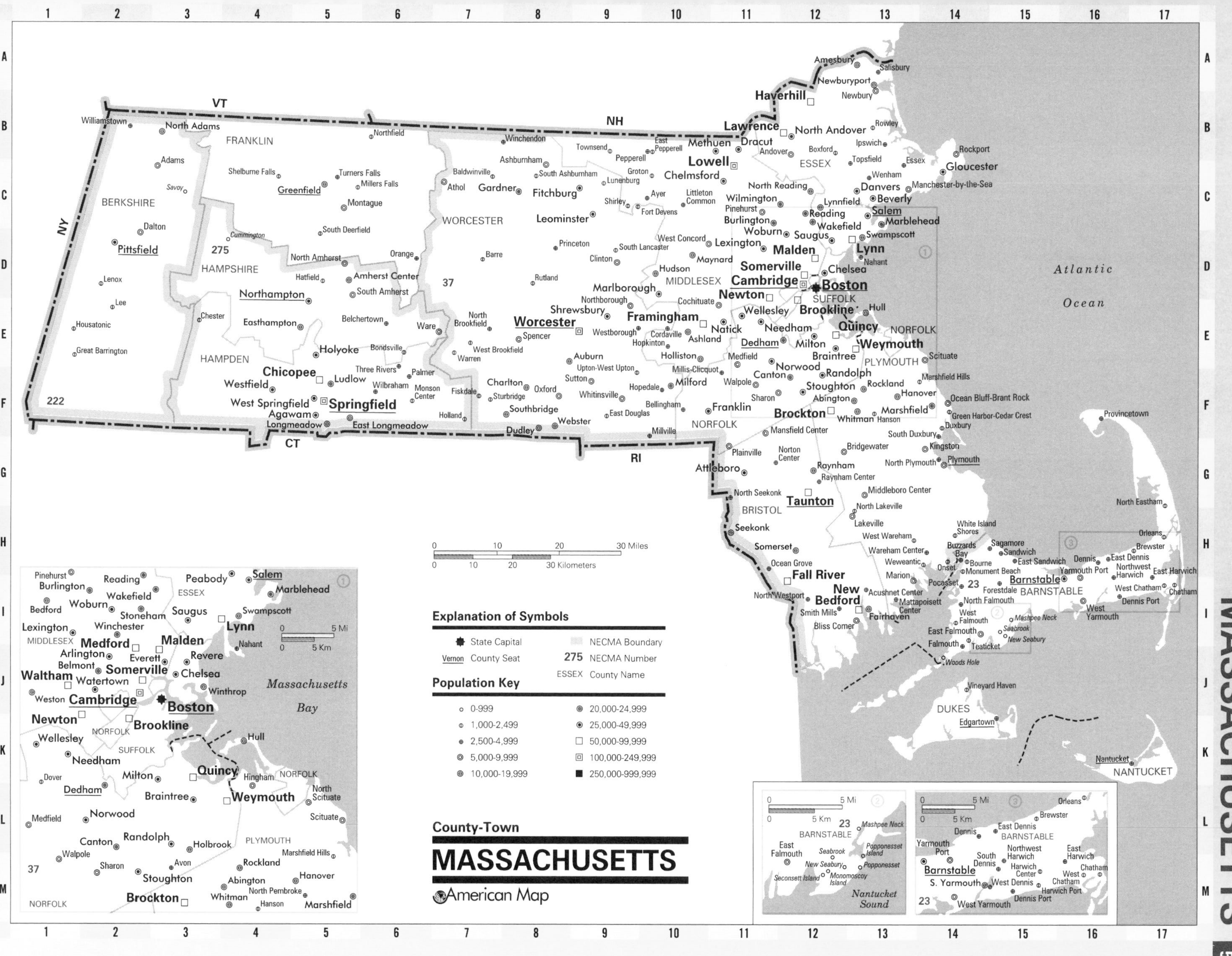
County-Town
MASSACHUSETTS
American Map
Explanation of Symbols
State Capital
Vernon County Seat
NECMA Boundary
275 NECMA Number
ESSEX County Name
Population Key
0-999
1,000-2,499
2,500-4,999
5,000-9,999
10,000-19,999
20,000-24,999
25,000-49,999
50,000-99,999
100,000-249,999
250,000-999,999
30 Miles
30 Kilometers
Atlantic Ocean
Massachusetts Bay
Nantucket Sound
VT
NH
NY
CT
RI
BERKSHIRE
FRANKLIN
HAMPSHIRE
HAMPDEN
WORCESTER
MIDDLESEX
ESSEX
SUFFOLK
NORFOLK
PLYMOUTH
BRISTOL
BARNSTABLE
DUKES
NANTUCKET
Boston
Springfield
Worcester
Pittsfield
Greenfield
Northampton
Cambridge
Salem
Dedham
Plymouth
Taunton
Barnstable
Edgartown
Nantucket

MICHIGAN (UPPER)

1 2 3 4 5 6 7 8 9 10 11 12 13

A B C D E F G H I J K L M N O P Q

Lake Superior
Eagle River
KEWEENAW
Ahmeek
Calumet
Copper City
Laurium
Lake Linden
Hancock
Hubbell
South Range
Mason
Houghton
HOUGHTON
Ontonagon
ONTONAGON
Big Bay
Baraga
L'Anse
BARAGA
MARQUETTE
GOGEBIC
Bessemer
Wakefield
Ironwood
Michigamme
Trowbridge Park
Ishpeming
Marquette
West Ishpeming
Negaunee
Harvey
Palmer
Republic
K.I. Sawyer AFB
ALGER
Chatham
Munising
LUCE
Newberry
CHIPPEWA
Sault Ste. Marie
CANADA
IRON
Gwinn
SCHOOLCRAFT
continued from Lower Michigan map opposite page
DICKINSON
Turner
MACKINAC
Mineral Hills
Iron River
Crystal Falls
WI
Stambaugh
Gaastra
Caspian
Alpha
DELTA
Manistique
De Tour Village
Iron Mountain
Quinnesec
Norway
Kingsford
Gladstone
Escanaba
Garden
St. Ignace
Mackinac Island
Lake Huron
Cheboygan
Powers
CHARLEVOIX
Lake Michigan
EMMET
Carney
MENOMINEE
Daggett
Stephenson
continued from Lower Michigan map
CHEBOYGAN
Rogers City
Petoskey
PRESQUE ISLE
Charlevoix
CHARLEVOIX
Menominee
LEELANAU
ANTRIM
OTSEGO
MONT-MORENCY
ALPENA
Alpena

County-Town

MICHIGAN
(UPPER)

American Map

0 20 40 60 Miles
0 20 40 60 Kilometers

Explanation of Symbols

State Capital
Vernon County Seat
MSA Boundary
114 MSA Number
IRON County Name

Population Key

0-999	20,000-24,999
1,000-2,499	25,000-49,999
2,500-4,999	50,000-99,999
5,000-9,999	100,000-249,999
10,000-19,999	250,000-999,999

1
CLINTON
Grand Ledge
Edgemont Park
East Lansing
Waverly
Lansing
Haslett
EATON
Okemos
INGHAM
Dimondale
Potterville
159
0 5 Mi
0 5 Km

2
Coopersville
OTTAWA
Comstock Park
Northview
KENT
114
Walker
Allendale
Grand Rapids
Forest Hills
East Grand Rapids
Grandville
Wyoming
Jenison
Kentwood
Hudsonville
Cutlerville
Byron Center
Caledonia
0 5 Mi
0 5 Km

3
MIDLAND
Freeland
245
BAY
Zilwaukee
SAGINAW
Saginaw Township North
Carrollton
Robin Glen-Indiantown
Saginaw
Merrill
Hemlock
Shields
Buena Vista
Saginaw Township South
Bridgeport
Frankenmuth
0 5 Mi
0 5 Km
St. Charles

4
114 Plainwell
ALLEGAN
BARRY
KALAMAZOO
South Gull Lake
146
CALHOUN
Richland
Level Park-Oak Park
Parchment
Augusta
Springfield
Brownlee Park
Westwood
Eastwood
Greater Galesburg
Battle Creek
Comstock Northwest
Galesburg
Kalamazoo
Climax
Portage
0 5 Mi
0 5 Km

5
OAKLAND
Clarkston
MACOMB
New Haven
Waterford
Lake Angelus
Auburn Hills
Rochester
Shelby
Pontiac
Rochester Hills
Utica
Keego Harbor
Sylvan Lake
Troy
Milford
Orchard Lake Village
West Bloomfield Township
Bloomfield Hills
Clinton
Mount Clemens
Harrison
Wolverine Lake
Bloomfield Township
Sterling Heights
Birmingham
Wixom
Walled Lake
Beverly Hills
Fraser
Franklin
Clawson
Bingham Farms
Royal Oak
Warren
Farmington Hills
Berkley
Lathrup Village
Madison Hts.
Roseville
St. Clair Shores
Novi
Huntington Woods
Center Line
LIVINGSTON
South Lyon
Farmington
Southfield
Pleasant Ridge
Eastpointe (East Detroit)
Oak Park
Ferndale
Hazel Park
Grosse Pointe Woods
Northville
76
WAYNE
Harper Woods
Grosse Pointe Shores
WASHTENAW
11
Livonia
Highland Park
Grosse Pointe Farms
Plymouth Township
Redford
Hamtramck
Grosse Pointe
Plymouth
Grosse Pointe Park
Lake St. Clair
Garden City
Dearborn Heights
Detroit
Westland
Dearborn
CANADA
Canton
Ann Arbor
Inkster
Melvindale
River Rouge
Wayne
Allen Park
Lincoln Park
Ypsilanti
Taylor
Ecorse
Romulus
Southgate
Wyandotte
Belleville
Riverview
Trenton
Woodhaven
Grosse Ile
Flat Rock
Gibraltar
Milan
Rockwood
MONROE
Carleton
South Rockwood
0 5 10 Mi
0 5 10 Km

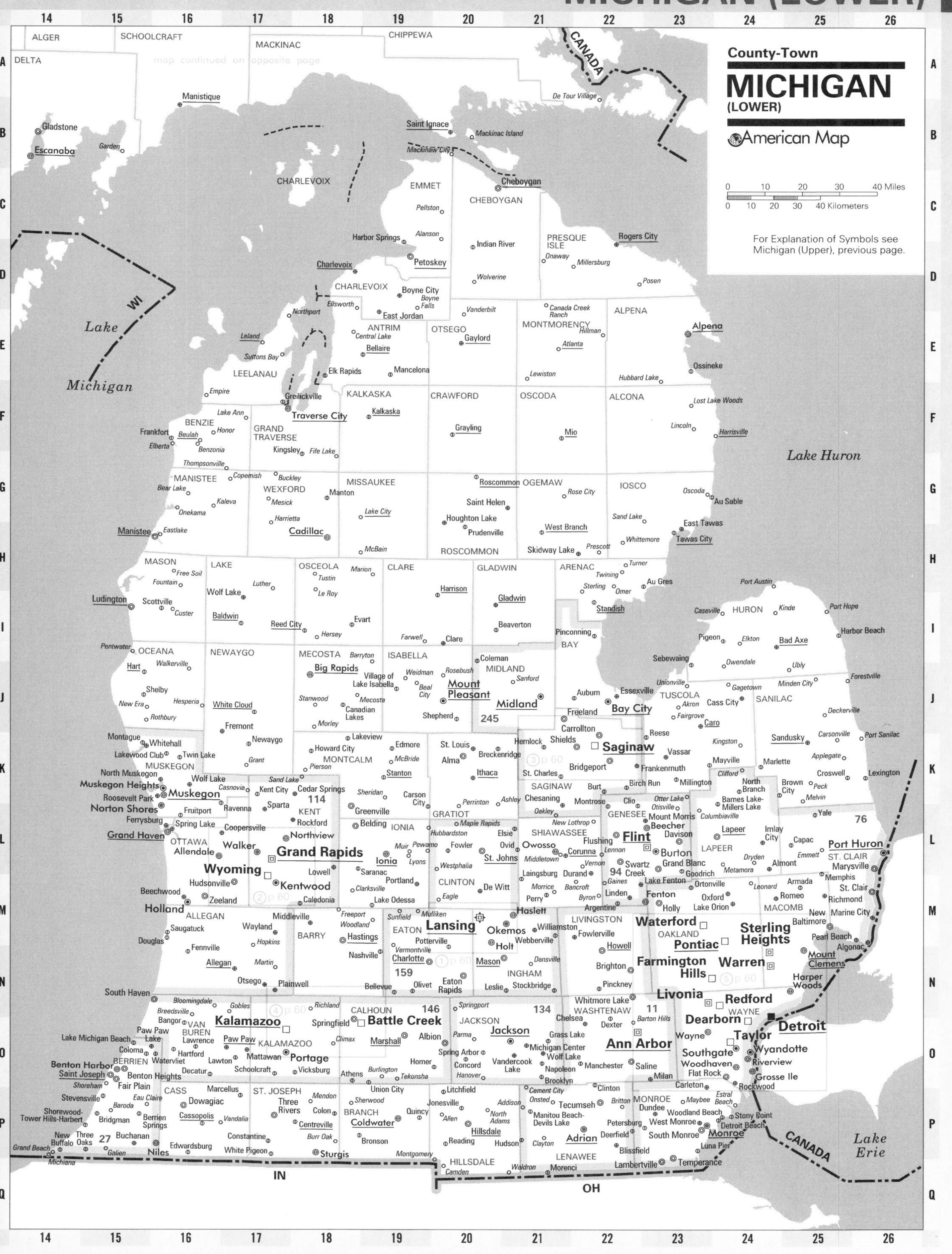
County-Town
MICHIGAN
(LOWER)
American Map
0 10 20 30 40 Miles
0 10 20 30 40 Kilometers
For Explanation of Symbols see Michigan (Upper), previous page.
map continued on opposite page
ALGER
SCHOOLCRAFT
MACKINAC
CHIPPEWA
DELTA
CANADA
EMMET
CHEBOYGAN
PRESQUE ISLE
CHARLEVOIX
ANTRIM
OTSEGO
MONTMORENCY
ALPENA
LEELANAU
KALKASKA
CRAWFORD
OSCODA
ALCONA
BENZIE
GRAND TRAVERSE
MANISTEE
WEXFORD
MISSAUKEE
ROSCOMMON
OGEMAW
IOSCO
MASON
LAKE
OSCEOLA
CLARE
GLADWIN
ARENAC
OCEANA
NEWAYGO
MECOSTA
ISABELLA
MIDLAND
BAY
HURON
TUSCOLA
SANILAC
MUSKEGON
MONTCALM
GRATIOT
SAGINAW
KENT
OTTAWA
IONIA
CLINTON
SHIAWASSEE
GENESEE
LAPEER
ST. CLAIR
ALLEGAN
BARRY
EATON
INGHAM
LIVINGSTON
OAKLAND
MACOMB
VAN BUREN
KALAMAZOO
CALHOUN
JACKSON
WASHTENAW
WAYNE
BERRIEN
CASS
ST. JOSEPH
BRANCH
HILLSDALE
LENAWEE
MONROE
IN
OH
WI
Lake Michigan
Lake Huron
Lake Erie
Traverse City
Cadillac
Alpena
Midland
Bay City
Saginaw
Flint
Mount Pleasant
Muskegon
Grand Rapids
Wyoming
Kentwood
Holland
Lansing
Kalamazoo
Portage
Battle Creek
Jackson
Ann Arbor
Pontiac
Waterford
Sterling Heights
Warren
Farmington Hills
Livonia
Redford
Dearborn
Taylor
Detroit
Port Huron
Monroe

COUNTIES

(83 Counties)

Name of County	Population	Location on Map
ALCONA	11,719	F-22
ALGER	9,862	D-7
ALLEGAN	105,665	M-16
ALPENA	31,314	G-13
ANTRIM	23,110	G-10
ARENAC	17,269	H-21
BARAGA	8,746	C-4
BARRY	56,755	M-18
BAY	110,157	I-21
BENZIE	15,998	F-16
BERRIEN	162,453	O-15
BRANCH	45,787	P-18
CALHOUN	137,985	N-18
CASS	51,104	P-16
CHARLEVOIX	26,090	F-10
CHEBOYGAN	26,448	F-11
CHIPPEWA	38,543	D-10
CLARE	31,252	H-19
CLINTON	64,753	M-20
CRAWFORD	14,273	F-19
DELTA	38,520	D-6
DICKINSON	27,472	D-5
EATON	103,655	M-19
EMMET	31,437	F-10
GENESEE	436,141	L-22
GLADWIN	26,023	H-20
GOGEBIC	17,370	C-1
GRAND TRAVERSE	77,654	F-17
GRATIOT	42,285	L-20
HILLSDALE	46,527	Q-20
HOUGHTON	36,016	B-3
HURON	36,079	I-24
INGHAM	279,320	N-21
IONIA	61,518	L-19
IOSCO	27,339	G-22
IRON	13,138	D-3
ISABELLA	63,351	I-19
JACKSON	158,422	N-20
KALAMAZOO	238,603	O-17
KALKASKA	16,571	F-18
KENT	574,335	L-18
KEWEENAW	2,301	A-5
LAKE	11,333	H-16
LAPEER	87,904	L-23
LEELANAU	21,119	G-9
LENAWEE	98,890	Q-21
LIVINGSTON	156,951	M-21
LUCE	7,024	C-9
MACKINAC	11,943	D-9
MACOMB	788,149	M-24
MANISTEE	24,527	G-16
MARQUETTE	64,634	C-5
MASON	28,274	H-15
MECOSTA	40,553	I-18
MENOMINEE	25,326	F-6
MIDLAND	82,874	I-20
MISSAUKEE	14,478	G-18
MONROE	145,945	P-22
MONTCALM	61,266	K-18
MONTMORENCY	10,315	G-12
MUSKEGON	170,200	K-15
NEWAYGO	47,874	I-16
OAKLAND	1,194,156	M-23
OCEANA	26,873	I-15
OGEMAW	21,645	G-21
ONTONAGON	7,818	C-2
OSCEOLA	23,197	H-18
OSCODA	9,418	F-21
OTSEGO	23,301	G-11
OTTAWA	238,314	L-16
PRESQUE ISLE	14,411	F-12
ROSCOMMON	25,469	H-20
SAGINAW	210,039	K-21
SAINT CLAIR	164,235	L-25
SAINT JOSEPH	62,422	P-17
SANILAC	44,547	J-24
SCHOOLCRAFT	8,903	D-8
SHIAWASSEE	71,687	L-21
TUSCOLA	58,266	J-23
VAN BUREN	76,263	O-16
WASHTENAW	322,895	N-22
WAYNE	2,061,162	N-24
WEXFORD	30,484	G-17
TOTAL	**9,938,444**	

CITIES AND TOWNS

Note: The first name is that of the city or town, second, that of the county in which it is located, then the population and location on the map.

Adrian, *Lenawee,* 21,574 ....P-22
Albion, *Calhoun,* 9,144 ....O-20
Algonac, *Saint Clair,* 4,613 ....M-26
Allegan, *Allegan,* 4,838 ....N-17
Allen Park, *Wayne,* 29,376 ....O-10
• Allendale, *Ottawa,* 11,555 ....L-16
Alma, *Gratiot,* 9,275 ....K-20
Almont, *Lapeer,* 2,803 ....L-24
Alpena, *Alpena,* 11,304 ....E-23
Ann Arbor, *Washtenaw,* 114,024 ....O-5
• Argentine, *Genesee,* 2,285 ....M-22
Armada, *Macomb,* 1,573 ....M-25
Athens, *Calhoun,* 1,111 ....O-18
Atlanta, *Montmorency,* 757 ....E-21
Au Gres, *Arenac,* 1,028 ....H-23
• Au Sable, *Iosco,* 1,533 ....G-24
Auburn, *Bay,* 2,011 ....J-22
Auburn Hills, *Oakland,* 19,837 ....K-10
Bad Axe, *Huron,* 3,462 ....I-24
Baldwin, *Lake,* 1,107 ....I-17
Bangor, *Van Buren,* 1,933 ....O-16
Baraga, *Baraga,* 1,285 ....C-4
• Barnes Lake-Millers Lake, *Lapeer,* 1,187 ....L-24
Battle Creek, *Calhoun,* 53,364 ....O-19
Bay City, *Bay,* 36,817 ....J-22
Beaverton, *Gladwin,* 1,106 ....I-20
• Beecher, *Genesee,* 12,793 ....L-23
• Beechwood, *Ottawa,* 2,963 ....M-16
Belding, *Ionia,* 5,877 ....L-18
Bellaire, *Antrim,* 1,164 ....E-19
Belleville, *Wayne,* 3,997 ....P-8
Bellevue, *Eaton,* 1,365 ....N-19
Benton Harbor, *Berrien,* 11,182 ....O-15
• Benton Heights, *Berrien,* 5,458 ....O-15
Berkley, *Oakland,* 15,531 ....M-10
Berrien Springs, *Berrien,* 1,862 ....P-15
Bessemer, *Gogebic,* 2,148 ....C-1
Beulah, *Benzie,* 363 ....F-16
Beverly Hills, *Oakland,* 10,437 ....M-10
Big Rapids, *Mecosta,* 10,849 ....J-18
Bingham Farms, *Oakland,* 1,030 ....M-9
Birch Run, *Saginaw,* 1,653 ....K-22
Birmingham, *Oakland,* 19,291 ....L-10
Blissfield, *Lenawee,* 3,223 ....P-22
Bloomfield Hills, *Oakland,* 3,940 ....L-9
• Bloomfield Township, *Oakland,* 43,021 ....L-9
Boyne City, *Charlevoix,* 3,503 ....D-19
Breckenridge, *Gratiot,* 1,339 ....K-20
• Bridgeport, *Saginaw,* 7,849 ....K-22
Bridgman, *Berrien,* 2,428 ....P-15
Brighton, *Livingston,* 6,701 ....N-22
Bronson, *Branch,* 2,421 ....P-19
Brooklyn, *Jackson,* 1,176 ....O-21
Brown City, *Sanilac,* 1,334 ....K-24
• Brownlee Park, *Calhoun,* 2,588 ....P-5
Buchanan, *Berrien,* 4,681 ....P-15
• Buena Vista, *Saginaw,* 7,845 ....N-4
• Burt, *Saginaw,* 1,122 ....K-22
Burton, *Genesee,* 30,308 ....L-23
• Byron Center, *Kent,* 3,777 ....L-3
Cadillac, *Wexford,* 10,000 ....H-18
Caledonia, *Kent,* 1,102 ....M-18
• Canadian Lakes, *Mecosta,* 1,922 ....J-18
• Canton, *Wayne,* 76,366 ....O-8
Capac, *Saint Clair,* 1,775 ....L-25
Carleton, *Monroe,* 2,562 ....P-23
Caro, *Tuscola,* 4,145 ....J-23
• Carrollton, *Saginaw,* 6,602 ....K-22
Carson City, *Montcalm,* 1,190 ....L-19
Cass City, *Tuscola,* 2,643 ....J-24
Cassopolis, *Cass,* 1,740 ....P-16
Cedar Springs, *Kent,* 3,112 ....K-18
Center Line, *Macomb,* 8,531 ....M-11
Centreville, *Saint Joseph,* 1,579 ....P-18
Charlevoix, *Charlevoix,* 2,994 ....D-18
Charlotte, *Eaton,* 8,389 ....N-20
Cheboygan, *Cheboygan,* 5,295 ....C-20
Chelsea, *Washtenaw,* 4,398 ....O-22
Chesaning, *Saginaw,* 2,548 ....L-21
Clare, *Clare,* 3,173 ....I-20
Clawson, *Oakland,* 12,732 ....M-10
Clinton, *Lenawee,* 2,293 ....O-22
• Clinton, *Macomb,* 95,648 ....L-11
Clio, *Genesee,* 2,483 ....L-22
Coldwater, *Branch,* 12,697 ....P-19
Coleman, *Midland,* 1,296 ....J-20
Coloma, *Berrien,* 1,595 ....O-15
Colon, *Saint Joseph,* 1,227 ....P-18
• Comstock Northwest, *Kalamazoo,* 4,472 ....P-2
• Comstock Park, *Kent,* 10,674 ....J-3
Concord, *Jackson,* 1,101 ....O-20
Constantine, *Saint Joseph,* 2,095 ....P-17
Coopersville, *Ottawa,* 3,910 ....L-17
Corunna, *Shiawassee,* 3,381 ....L-21
Croswell, *Sanilac,* 2,467 ....K-25
Crystal Falls, *Iron,* 1,791 ....D-4
• Cutlerville, *Kent,* 15,114 ....L-3
Davison, *Genesee,* 5,536 ....L-23
De Witt, *Clinton,* 4,702 ....M-20
Dearborn, *Wayne,* 97,775 ....O-24
Dearborn Heights, *Wayne,* 58,264 ....O-9
Decatur, *Van Buren,* 1,838 ....O-16
Deerfield, *Lenawee,* 1,005 ....P-22
Detroit, *Wayne,* 951,270 ....O-24
• Detroit Beach, *Monroe,* 2,289 ....P-24
Dexter, *Washtenaw,* 2,338 ....O-22
Dimondale, *Eaton,* 1,342 ....I-2
Douglas, *Allegan,* 1,214 ....M-16
Dowagiac, *Cass,* 6,147 ....P-16
Dundee, *Monroe,* 3,522 ....P-23
Durand, *Shiawassee,* 3,933 ....M-22
Eagle River, *Keweenaw,* 20 ....A-5
East Grand Rapids, *Kent,* 10,764 ....K-4
East Jordan, *Charlevoix,* 2,507 ....E-19
East Lansing, *Ingham,* 46,525 ....I-3
East Tawas, *Iosco,* 2,951 ....H-23
Eastpointe (East Detroit), *Macomb,* 34,077 ....M-12
• Eastwood, *Kalamazoo,* 6,265 ....P-2
Eaton Rapids, *Eaton,* 5,330 ....N-20
Ecorse, *Wayne,* 11,229 ....P-10
• Edgemont Park, *Isabella,* 2,442 ....I-2
Edmore, *Montcalm,* 1,244 ....K-19
Edwardsburg, *Cass,* 1,147 ....P-16
Elk Rapids, *Antrim,* 1,700 ....E-18
Elsie, *Clinton,* 1,055 ....L-21
Escanaba, *Delta,* 13,140 ....B-14
Essexville, *Bay,* 3,766 ....J-22
Evart, *Osceola,* 1,738 ....I-18
• Fair Plain, *Berrien,* 7,828 ....O-15
Farmington, *Oakland,* 10,423 ....M-8
Farmington Hills, *Oakland,* 82,111 ....N-24
Fennville, *Allegan,* 1,459 ....N-16
Fenton, *Genesee,* 10,582 ....M-23
Ferndale, *Oakland,* 22,105 ....M-10
Ferrysburg, *Ottawa,* 3,040 ....L-16
Flat Rock, *Wayne,* 8,488 ....O-24
Flint, *Genesee,* 124,943 ....L-23
Flushing, *Genesee,* 8,348 ....L-22
• Forest Hills, *Kent,* 20,942 ....K-5
Fowler, *Clinton,* 1,136 ....L-20
Fowlerville, *Livingston,* 2,972 ....M-22
Frankenmuth, *Saginaw,* 4,838 ....K-22
Frankfort, *Benzie,* 1,513 ....F-16
Franklin, *Oakland,* 2,937 ....M-9
Fraser, *Macomb,* 15,297 ....M-12
• Freeland, *Saginaw,* 5,147 ....J-21
Fremont, *Newaygo,* 4,224 ....K-17
Fruitport, *Muskegon,* 1,124 ....L-16
Galesburg, *Kalamazoo,* 1,988 ....Q-3
Garden City, *Wayne,* 30,047 ....O-9
Gaylord, *Otsego,* 3,681 ....E-20
Gibraltar, *Wayne,* 4,264 ....Q-10
Gladstone, *Delta,* 5,032 ....B-14
Gladwin, *Gladwin,* 3,001 ....I-20
Goodrich, *Genesee,* 1,353 ....L-23
Grand Blanc, *Genesee,* 8,242 ....L-23
Grand Haven, *Ottawa,* 11,168 ....L-16
Grand Ledge, *Eaton,* 7,813 ....H-1
Grand Rapids, *Kent,* 197,800 ....L-17
Grandville, *Kent,* 16,263 ....K-3
Grass Lake, *Jackson,* 1,082 ....O-21
Grayling, *Crawford,* 1,952 ....F-20
• Greater Galesburg, *Kalamazoo,* 1,631 ....P-3
Greenville, *Montcalm,* 7,935 ....L-18
• Greilickville, *Leelanau,* 1,415 ....F-17
• Grosse Ile, *Wayne,* 10,894 ....O-24
Grosse Pointe, *Wayne,* 5,670 ....N-12
Grosse Pointe Farms, *Wayne,* 9,764 ....N-12
Grosse Pointe Park, *Wayne,* 12,443 ....N-12
Grosse Pointe Shores, *Wayne,* 2,823 ....N-12
Grosse Pointe Woods, *Wayne,* 17,080 ....M-12
• Gwinn, *Marquette,* 1,965 ....D-6
Hamtramck, *Wayne,* 22,976 ....N-11
Hancock, *Houghton,* 4,323 ....B-4
Harbor Beach, *Huron,* 1,837 ....I-25
Harbor Springs, *Emmet,* 1,567 ....D-19
Harper Woods, *Wayne,* 14,254 ....N-25
Harrison, *Clare,* 2,108 ....I-20

Explanation of symbols: • - Census Designated Place (CDP)

•Harrison, *Macomb,* 24,461 ... L-13
Harrisville, *Alcona,* 514 ... F-24
Hart, *Oceana,* 1,950 ... J-15
Hartford, *Van Buren,* 2,476 ... O-16
•Harvey, *Marquette,* 1,321 ... C-6
•Haslett, *Ingham,* 11,283 ... M-21
Hastings, *Barry,* 7,095 ... M-18
Hazel Park, *Oakland,* 18,963 ... M-11
•Hemlock, *Saginaw,* 1,585 ... K-21
Highland Park, *Wayne,* 16,746 ... N-11
Hillsdale, *Hillsdale,* 8,233 ... P-20
Holland, *Ottawa,* 35,048 ... M-16
Holly, *Oakland,* 6,135 ... M-23
•Holt, *Ingham,* 11,315 ... M-20
Homer, *Calhoun,* 1,851 ... O-20
Houghton, *Houghton,* 7,010 ... B-4
•Houghton Lake, *Roscommon,* 3,749 ... H-20
Howard City, *Montcalm,* 1,585 ... K-18
Howell, *Livingston,* 9,232 ... N-22
•Hubbell, *Houghton,* 1,105 ... B-4
Hudson, *Lenawee,* 2,499 ... P-21
Hudsonville, *Ottawa,* 7,160 ... M-17
Huntington Woods, *Oakland,* 6,151 ... M-10
Imlay City, *Lapeer,* 3,869 ... L-24
•Indian River, *Cheboygan,* 2,008 ... D-20
Inkster, *Wayne,* 30,115 ... O-9
Ionia, *Ionia,* 10,569 ... L-19
Iron Mountain, *Dickinson,* 8,154 ... E-5
Iron River, *Iron,* 1,929 ... D-4
Ironwood, *Gogebic,* 6,293 ... C-1
Ishpeming, *Marquette,* 6,686 ... C-6
Ithaca, *Gratiot,* 3,098 ... K-20
Jackson, *Jackson,* 36,316 ... O-21
•Jenison, *Ottawa,* 17,211 ... K-2
Jonesville, *Hillsdale,* 2,337 ... P-20
•K.I. Sawyer Afb, *Marquette,* 1,443 ... D-6
Kalamazoo, *Kalamazoo,* 77,145 ... O-17
Kalkaska, *Kalkaska,* 2,226 ... F-19
Keego Harbor, *Oakland,* 2,769 ... L-9
Kent City, *Kent,* 1,061 ... K-17
Kentwood, *Kent,* 45,255 ... M-17
Kingsford, *Dickinson,* 5,549 ... E-5
Kingsley, *Grand Traverse,* 1,469 ... G-18
L'anse, *Baraga,* 2,151 ... C-4
Laingsburg, *Shiawassee,* 1,223 ... M-21
Lake City, *Missaukee,* 923 ... G-19
•Lake Fenton, *Genesee,* 4,876 ... M-23
Lake Linden, *Houghton,* 1,081 ... B-4
•Lake Michigan Beach, *Berrien,* 1,509 ... O-15
Lake Odessa, *Ionia,* 2,272 ... M-19
Lake Orion, *Oakland,* 2,715 ... M-24
Lakeview, *Montcalm,* 1,112 ... K-18
Lakewood Club, *Muskegon,* 1,006 ... K-16
•Lambertville, *Monroe,* 9,299 ... Q-23
Lansing, *Ingham,* 119,128 ... M-20
Lapeer, *Lapeer,* 9,072 ... L-24
Lathrup Village, *Oakland,* 4,236 ... M-10
Laurium, *Houghton,* 2,126 ... A-4
Lawrence, *Van Buren,* 1,059 ... O-16
Lawton, *Van Buren,* 1,859 ... O-17
Leland, *Leelanau,* 776 ... E-17
Leslie, *Ingham,* 2,044 ... N-21
•Level Park-Oak Park, *Calhoun,* 3,605 ... P-4
Lexington, *Sanilac,* 1,104 ... K-26
Lincoln Park, *Wayne,* 40,008 ... O-10
Linden, *Genesee,* 2,861 ... M-22
Litchfield, *Hillsdale,* 1,458 ... P-20
Livonia, *Wayne,* 100,545 ... N-23
Lowell, *Kent,* 4,013 ... L-18
Ludington, *Mason,* 8,357 ... I-15
Luna Pier, *Monroe,* 1,483 ... P-23
Madison Heights, *Oakland,* 31,101 ... M-10
Mancelona, *Antrim,* 1,408 ... E-19
Manchester, *Washtenaw,* 2,160 ... O-22
Manistee, *Manistee,* 6,586 ... H-16
Manistique, *Schoolcraft,* 3,583 ... B-16
•Manitou Beach-Devils Lake, *Lenawee,* 2,080 ... P-21
Manton, *Wexford,* 1,221 ... G-18
Marcellus, *Cass,* 1,162 ... P-17
Marine City, *Saint Clair,* 4,652 ... M-26
Marlette, *Sanilac,* 2,104 ... K-24
Marquette, *Marquette,* 19,661 ... C-6
Marshall, *Calhoun,* 7,459 ... O-19
Marysville, *Saint Clair,* 9,684 ... L-26
Mason, *Ingham,* 6,714 ... N-21
Mattawan, *Van Buren,* 2,536 ... O-17
Mayville, *Tuscola,* 1,055 ... K-23
Melvindale, *Wayne,* 10,735 ... O-10
Memphis, *Macomb,* 1,129 ... M-25
Menominee, *Menominee,* 9,131 ... G-6
•Michigan Center, *Jackson,* 4,641 ... O-21
Middleville, *Barry,* 2,721 ... M-18
Midland, *Midland,* 41,685 ... J-21
Milan, *Washtenaw,* 4,775 ... O-23
Milford, *Oakland,* 6,272 ... L-7
Millington, *Tuscola,* 1,137 ... K-23
•Mio, *Oscoda,* 2,016 ... F-21
Monroe, *Monroe,* 22,076 ... P-23
Montague, *Muskegon,* 2,407 ... K-15
Montrose, *Genesee,* 1,619 ... L-22
Morenci, *Lenawee,* 2,398 ... Q-21
Mount Clemens, *Macomb,* 17,312 ... N-25
Mount Morris, *Genesee,* 3,194 ... L-23
Mount Pleasant, *Isabella,* 25,946 ... J-20
Munising, *Alger,* 2,539 ... C-7
Muskegon, *Muskegon,* 40,105 ... K-16
Muskegon Heights, *Muskegon,* 12,049 ... K-16
•Napoleon, *Jackson,* 1,254 ... O-21
Nashville, *Barry,* 1,684 ... N-19
Negaunee, *Marquette,* 4,576 ... C-6
New Baltimore, *Macomb,* 7,405 ... M-25
New Buffalo, *Berrien,* 2,200 ... P-14
New Haven, *Macomb,* 3,071 ... K-13
Newaygo, *Newaygo,* 1,670 ... K-17
Newberry, *Luce,* 2,686 ... D-9
Niles, *Berrien,* 12,204 ... P-16
North Branch, *Lapeer,* 1,027 ... K-24
North Muskegon, *Muskegon,* 4,031 ... K-16
•Northview, *Kent,* 14,730 ... L-17
Northville, *Wayne,* 6,459 ... N-7
Norton Shores, *Muskegon,* 22,527 ... L-16
Norway, *Dickinson,* 2,959 ... E-5
Novi, *Oakland,* 47,386 ... M-8
Oak Park, *Oakland,* 29,793 ... M-10
•Okemos, *Ingham,* 22,805 ... M-21
Olivet, *Eaton,* 1,758 ... N-19
Ontonagon, *Ontonagon,* 1,769 ... B-3
Orchard Lake Village, *Oakland,* 2,215 ... L-9
Ortonville, *Oakland,* 1,535 ... M-23
•Ossineke, *Alpena,* 1,059 ... E-23
Otsego, *Allegan,* 3,933 ... N-17
Ovid, *Clinton,* 1,514 ... L-21
Owosso, *Shiawassee,* 15,713 ... L-21
Oxford, *Oakland,* 3,540 ... M-24
Parchment, *Kalamazoo,* 1,936 ... P-2
Paw Paw, *Van Buren,* 3,363 ... O-17
•Paw Paw Lake, *Berrien,* 3,944 ... O-16
•Pearl Beach, *Saint Clair,* 3,224 ... M-26
Perry, *Shiawassee,* 2,065 ... M-21
Petersburg, *Monroe,* 1,157 ... P-23
Petoskey, *Emmet,* 6,080 ... D-19
Pigeon, *Huron,* 1,207 ... I-24
Pinckney, *Livingston,* 2,141 ... N-22
Pinconning, *Bay,* 1,386 ... I-22
Plainwell, *Allegan,* 3,933 ... N-17
Pleasant Ridge, *Oakland,* 2,594 ... M-10
Plymouth, *Wayne,* 9,022 ... N-8
•Plymouth Township, *Wayne,* 27,798 ... N-7
Pontiac, *Oakland,* 66,337 ... M-24
Port Huron, *Saint Clair,* 32,338 ... L-26
Portage, *Kalamazoo,* 44,897 ... O-17
Portland, *Ionia,* 3,789 ... M-19
Potterville, *Eaton,* 2,168 ... N-20
•Prudenville, *Roscommon,* 1,737 ... H-20
Quincy, *Branch,* 1,701 ... P-19
•Quinnesec, *Dickinson,* 1,187 ... E-5
Ravenna, *Muskegon,* 1,206 ... L-17
Reading, *Hillsdale,* 1,134 ... P-20
•Redford, *Wayne,* 51,622 ... N-24
Reed City, *Osceola,* 2,430 ... I-18
Reese, *Tuscola,* 1,375 ... K-23
Richmond, *Macomb,* 4,897 ... M-25
River Rouge, *Wayne,* 9,917 ... O-10
Riverview, *Wayne,* 13,272 ... O-24
•Robin Glen-Indiantown, *Saginaw,* 1,158 ... M-4
Rochester, *Oakland,* 10,467 ... K-10
Rochester Hills, *Oakland,* 68,825 ... K-10
Rockford, *Kent,* 4,626 ... L-18
Rockwood, *Wayne,* 3,442 ... O-24
Rogers City, *Presque Isle,* 3,322 ... D-22
Romeo, *Macomb,* 3,721 ... M-24
Romulus, *Wayne,* 22,979 ... P-8
Roosevelt Park, *Muskegon,* 3,890 ... K-16
Roscommon, *Roscommon,* 1,133 ... G-20
Roseville, *Macomb,* 48,129 ... M-12
Royal Oak, *Oakland,* 60,062 ... M-10
Saginaw, *Saginaw,* 61,799 ... K-22
•Saginaw Township North, *Saginaw,* 24,994 ... N-3
•Saginaw Township South, *Saginaw,* 13,801 ... N-3
Saint Charles, *Saginaw,* 2,215 ... K-21
Saint Clair, *Saint Clair,* 5,802 ... M-26
Saint Clair Shores, *Macomb,* 63,096 ... M-12
Saint Helen, *Roscommon,* 2,993 ... G-21
Saint Ignace, *Mackinac,* 2,678 ... B-20
Saint Johns, *Clinton,* 7,485 ... L-20
Saint Joseph, *Berrien,* 8,789 ... O-15
Saint Louis, *Gratiot,* 4,494 ... K-20
Saline, *Washtenaw,* 8,034 ... O-22
Sand Lake, *Kent,* 1,914 ... K-18
Sandusky, *Sanilac,* 2,745 ... K-25
Saranac, *Ionia,* 1,326 ... L-18
Saugatuck, *Allegan,* 1,065 ... M-16
Sault Ste. Marie, *Chippewa,* 16,542 ... C-12
Schoolcraft, *Kalamazoo,* 1,587 ... O-17
Scottville, *Mason,* 1,266 ... I-16
Sebewaing, *Huron,* 1,974 ... J-23
•Shelby, *Macomb,* 65,159 ... K-11
Shelby, *Oceana,* 1,914 ... J-15
Shepherd, *Isabella,* 1,536 ... J-20
•Shields, *Saginaw,* 6,590 ... K-22
•Shorewood-Tower Hills-Harbert, *Berrien,* 1,619 ... P-15
•Skidway Lake, *Ogemaw,* 3,147 ... H-22
•South Gull Lake, *Kalamazoo,* 1,526 ... P-3
South Haven, *Van Buren,* 5,021 ... N-16
South Lyon, *Oakland,* 10,036 ... M-6
•South Monroe, *Monroe,* 6,370 ... P-23
South Rockwood, *Monroe,* 1,284 ... Q-9
Southfield, *Oakland,* 78,296 ... M-9
Southgate, *Wayne,* 30,136 ... O-24
Sparta, *Kent,* 4,159 ... L-17
•Spring Arbor, *Jackson,* 2,188 ... O-20
Spring Lake, *Ottawa,* 2,514 ... L-16
Springfield, *Calhoun,* 5,189 ... O-18
Stambaugh, *Iron,* 1,243 ... D-4
Standish, *Arenac,* 1,581 ... I-22
Stanton, *Montcalm,* 1,504 ... K-19
Sterling Heights, *Macomb,* 124,471 ... N-24
Stevensville, *Berrien,* 1,191 ... P-15
Stockbridge, *Ingham,* 1,260 ... N-21
•Stony Point, *Monroe,* 1,775 ... P-24
Sturgis, *Saint Joseph,* 11,285 ... P-18
Swartz Creek, *Genesee,* 5,102 ... L-22
Sylvan Lake, *Oakland,* 1,735 ... L-9
Tawas City, *Iosco,* 2,005 ... H-23
Taylor, *Wayne,* 65,868 ... O-24
Tecumseh, *Lenawee,* 8,574 ... P-22
•Temperance, *Monroe,* 7,757 ... Q-23
Three Oaks, *Berrien,* 1,829 ... P-15
Three Rivers, *Saint Joseph,* 7,328 ... P-17
Traverse City, *Grand Traverse,* 14,532 ... F-17
Trenton, *Wayne,* 19,584 ... Q-10
•Trowbridge Park, *Marquette,* 2,012 ... C-6
Troy, *Oakland,* 80,959 ... L-10
•Twin Lake, *Muskegon,* 1,613 ... K-16
Union City, *Branch,* 1,804 ... O-19
Utica, *Macomb,* 4,577 ... L-11
•Vandercook Lake, *Jackson,* 4,809 ... O-21
Vassar, *Tuscola,* 2,823 ... K-23
Vicksburg, *Kalamazoo,* 2,320 ... O-18
Village Of Lake Isabella, *Marquette,* 1,243 ... J-19
Wakefield, *Gogebic,* 2,085 ... C-2
Walker, *Kent,* 21,842 ... L-17
Walled Lake, *Oakland,* 6,713 ... M-7
Warren, *Macomb,* 138,247 ... N-24
•Waterford, *Oakland,* 73,150 ... M-23
Watervliet, *Berrien,* 1,843 ... O-16
•Waverly, *Eaton,* 16,194 ... I-2
Wayland, *Allegan,* 3,939 ... M-17
Wayne, *Wayne,* 19,051 ... O-23
Webberville, *Ingham,* 1,503 ... M-21
•West Bloomfield Township, *Oakland,* 64,862 ... L-8
West Branch, *Ogemaw,* 1,926 ... H-21
•West Ishpeming, *Marquette,* 2,792 ... C-6
•West Monroe, *Monroe,* 3,893 ... P-23
Westland, *Wayne,* 86,602 ... O-8
•Westwood, *Kalamazoo,* 9,122 ... P-1
White Cloud, *Newaygo,* 1,420 ... J-17
White Pigeon, *Saint Joseph,* 1,627 ... P-17
Whitehall, *Muskegon,* 2,884 ... K-15
•Whitmore Lake, *Washtenaw,* 6,574 ... N-22
Williamston, *Ingham,* 3,441 ... M-21
Wixom, *Oakland,* 13,263 ... M-7
•Wolf Lake, *Muskegon,* 4,455 ... K-16
Wolverine Lake, *Oakland,* 4,415 ... L-8
Woodhaven, *Wayne,* 12,530 ... O-24
•Woodland Beach, *Monroe,* 2,179 ... P-24
Wyandotte, *Wayne,* 28,006 ... O-24
Wyoming, *Kent,* 69,368 ... M-17
Yale, *Saint Clair,* 2,063 ... L-25
Ypsilanti, *Washtenaw,* 22,362 ... P-6
Zeeland, *Ottawa,* 5,805 ... M-16
Zilwaukee, *Saginaw,* 1,799 ... M-4

County-Town
MINNESOTA
(NORTH)
American Map
0 20 40 60 Miles
0 20 40 60 Kilometers
Explanation of Symbols
State Capital
Vernon County Seat
MSA Boundary
186 MSA Number
CASS County Name
Population Key
0-999
1,000-2,499
2,500-4,999
5,000-9,999
10,000-19,999
20,000-24,999
25,000-49,999
50,000-99,999
100,000-249,999
250,000-999,999
CANADA
ND
WI
Lake Superior
KITTSON
ROSEAU
LAKE OF THE WOODS
KOOCHICHING
ST. LOUIS
LAKE
COOK
MARSHALL
PENNINGTON
RED LAKE
POLK
BELTRAMI
CLEARWATER
ITASCA
CASS
HUBBARD
MAHNOMEN
NORMAN
International Falls
Baudette
Warroad
Roseau
Hallock
Thief River Falls
Red Lake Falls
Crookston
East Grand Forks
Warren
Ada
Bagley
Bemidji
Hibbing
Virginia
Ely
Grand Marais
Minneapolis
St. Paul
CHISAGO
WASHINGTON
ISANTI
ANOKA
SHERBURNE
WRIGHT
HENNEPIN
RAMSEY
CARVER
SCOTT
DAKOTA
10 Mi
10 Km

County-Town
MINNESOTA
(SOUTH)

American Map

For Explanation of Symbols see Minnesota (North), previous page.

COUNTIES

(87 Counties)

Name of County	Population	Location on Map
AITKIN	15,301	O-8
ANOKA	298,084	T-9
BECKER	30,000	N-4
BELTRAMI	39,650	J-4
BENTON	34,226	S-7
BIG STONE	5,820	T-2
BLUE EARTH	55,941	X-7
BROWN	26,911	X-6
CARLTON	31,671	P-10
CARVER	70,205	V-8
CASS	27,150	M-7
CHIPPEWA	13,088	U-4
CHISAGO	41,101	S-9
CLAY	51,229	O-2
CLEARWATER	8,423	L-4
COOK	5,168	K-14
COTTONWOOD	12,167	Y-4
CROW WING	55,099	Q-7
DAKOTA	355,904	V-9
DODGE	17,731	X-10
DOUGLAS	32,821	S-4
FARIBAULT	16,181	Y-7
FILLMORE	21,122	Y-11
FREEBORN	32,584	Z-9
GOODHUE	44,127	W-10
GRANT	6,289	R-3
HENNEPIN	1,116,200	U-8
HOUSTON	19,718	Y-13
HUBBARD	18,376	M-5
ISANTI	31,287	S-9
ITASCA	43,992	L-7
JACKSON	11,268	Z-4
KANABEC	14,996	R-9
KANDIYOHI	41,203	T-5
KITTSON	5,285	H-2
KOOCHICHING	14,355	I-7
LAC QUI PARLE	8,067	V-2
LAKE	11,058	K-12
LAKE OF THE WOODS	4,522	I-5
LE SUEUR	25,426	W-8
LINCOLN	6,429	W-2
LYON	25,425	W-3
MAHNOMEN	5,190	M-3
MARSHALL	10,155	J-1
MARTIN	21,802	Y-6
MCLEOD	34,898	V-6
MEEKER	22,644	U-6
MILLE LACS	22,330	R-8
MORRISON	31,712	R-6
MOWER	38,603	Z-10
MURRAY	9,165	X-3
NICOLLET	29,771	W-6
NOBLES	20,832	Y-3
NORMAN	7,442	M-2
OLMSTED	124,277	Y-11
OTTER TAIL	57,159	P-3
PENNINGTON	13,584	K-3
PINE	26,530	Q-11
PIPESTONE	9,895	X-2
POLK	31,369	K-1
POPE	11,236	T-4
RAMSEY	511,035	U-9
RED LAKE	4,299	L-3
REDWOOD	16,815	W-5
RENVILLE	17,154	V-5
RICE	56,665	W-9
ROCK	9,721	Y-2
ROSEAU	16,338	H-3
SAINT LOUIS	200,528	J-10
SCOTT	89,498	V-8
SHERBURNE	64,417	T-8
SIBLEY	15,356	W-6
STEARNS	133,166	T-6
STEELE	33,680	Y-9
STEVENS	10,053	S-3
SWIFT	11,956	T-3
TODD	24,426	Q-5
TRAVERSE	4,134	S-2
WABASHA	21,610	W-11
WADENA	13,713	P-5
WASECA	19,526	Y-8
WASHINGTON	201,130	U-10
WATONWAN	11,876	X-6
WILKIN	7,138	P-2
WINONA	49,985	Y-12
WRIGHT	89,986	U-8
YELLOW MEDICINE	11,080	V-2
TOTAL	**4,919,479**	

CITIES AND TOWNS

Note: The first name is that of the city or town, second, that of the county in which it is located, then the population and location on the map.

Ada, *Norman,* 1,657 ... M-2
Adrian, *Nobles,* 1,234 ... Z-3
Afton, *Washington,* 2,839 ... F-16
Aitkin, *Aitkin,* 1,984 ... P-8
Albany, *Stearns,* 1,796 ... S-6
Albert Lea, *Freeborn,* 18,356 ... Z-9
Albertville, *Wright,* 3,621 ... C-11
Alexandria, *Douglas,* 8,820 ... R-5
Andover, *Anoka,* 26,588 ... C-13
Annandale, *Wright,* 2,684 ... T-7
Anoka, *Anoka,* 18,076 ... U-9
Apple Valley, *Dakota,* 45,527 ... G-13
Appleton, *Swift,* 2,871 ... T-3
Arden Hills, *Ramsey,* 9,652 ... D-14
Arlington, *Sibley,* 2,048 ... W-7
• Arnold, *St. Louis,* 3,032 ... O-12
Atwater, *Kandiyohi,* 1,079 ... U-6
Aurora, *Saint Louis,* 1,850 ... M-11
Austin, *Mower,* 23,314 ... Z-10
Avon, *Stearns,* 1,242 ... S-7
Babbitt, *Saint Louis,* 1,670 ... L-12
Bagley, *Clearwater,* 1,235 ... M-5
Barnesville, *Clay,* 2,173 ... P-2
Baudette, *Lake of the Woods,* 1,104 ... I-6
Baxter, *Crow Wing,* 5,555 ... Q-7
Bayport, *Washington,* 3,162 ... E-16
Becker, *Sherburne,* 2,673 ... T-8
Belle Plaine, *Scott,* 3,789 ... V-8
Bemidji, *Beltrami,* 11,917 ... M-6
Benson, *Swift,* 3,376 ... T-4
Big Lake, *Sherburne,* 6,063 ... T-8
Bird Island, *Renville,* 1,195 ... V-6
Blaine, *Anoka,* 44,942 ... C-13
Blooming Prairie, *Steele,* 1,933 ... Y-10
Bloomington, *Hennepin,* 85,172 ... V-9
Blue Earth, *Faribault,* 3,621 ... Z-7
Braham, *Isanti,* 1,276 ... S-9
Brainerd, *Crow Wing,* 13,178 ... Q-7
Breckenridge, *Wilkin,* 3,559 ... Q-2
Brooklyn Center, *Hennepin,* 29,172 ... D-13
Brooklyn Park, *Hennepin,* 67,388 ... D-13
Buffalo, *Wright,* 10,097 ... U-8
Burnsville, *Dakota,* 60,220 ... G-13
Byron, *Olmsted,* 3,500 ... X-11
Caledonia, *Houston,* 2,965 ... Z-13
Cambridge, *Isanti,* 5,520 ... S-9
Canby, *Yellow Medicine,* 1,903 ... V-2
Cannon Falls, *Goodhue,* 3,795 ... W-10
Carlton, *Carlton,* 810 ... P-11
Carver, *Carver,* 1,266 ... G-11
Center City, *Chisago,* 582 ... A-16
Centerville, *Anoka,* 3,202 ... C-14
Champlin, *Hennepin,* 22,193 ... C-12
Chanhassen, *Carver,* 20,321 ... F-11
Chaska, *Carver,* 17,449 ... V-8
Chatfield, *Fillmore,* 2,394 ... Y-12
Chisago City, *Chisago,* 2,622 ... T-10
Chisholm, *Saint Louis,* 4,960 ... M-10
Circle Pines, *Anoka,* 4,663 ... D-14
Clara City, *Chippewa,* 1,393 ... U-4
Cloquet, *Carlton,* 11,201 ... P-11
Cohasset, *Itasca,* 2,481 ... N-8
Cokato, *Wright,* 2,727 ... U-7
Cold Spring, *Stearns,* 2,975 ... T-7
Coleraine, *Itasca,* 1,110 ... N-9
Cologne, *Carver,* 1,012 ... G-10
Columbia Heights, *Anoka,* 18,520 ... E-13
Coon Rapids, *Anoka,* 61,607 ... U-9
Corcoran, *Hennepin,* 5,630 ... D-11
Cottage Grove, *Washington,* 30,582 ... G-15
Cottonwood, *Lyon,* 1,148 ... V-4
Crookston, *Polk,* 8,192 ... L-2
Crosby, *Crow Wing,* 2,299 ... Q-8
Crosslake, *Crow Wing,* 1,893 ... P-7
Crystal, *Hennepin,* 22,698 ... E-13
Dassel, *Meeker,* 1,233 ... U-7
Dawson, *Lac Qui Parle,* 1,539 ... U-3
Dayton, *Hennepin,* 4,699 ... C-12
Deephaven, *Hennepin,* 3,853 ... F-11
Delano, *Wright,* 3,837 ... E-10
Dellwood, *Washington,* 1,033 ... D-15
Detroit Lakes, *Becker,* 7,348 ... O-4
Dilworth, *Clay,* 3,001 ... O-2
Dodge Center, *Dodge,* 2,226 ... X-10
Duluth, *Saint Louis,* 86,918 ... O-12
Eagan, *Dakota,* 63,557 ... G-14
Eagle Lake, *Blue Earth,* 1,787 ... X-8
East Bethel, *Anoka,* 10,941 ... T-9
East Grand Forks, *Polk,* 7,501 ... K-1
Eden Prairie, *Hennepin,* 54,901 ... F-12
Edgerton, *Pipestone,* 1,033 ... Y-3
Edina, *Hennepin,* 47,425 ... F-13
Elbow Lake, *Grant,* 1,275 ... R-3
Elk River, *Sherburne,* 16,447 ... T-9
Ely, *Saint Louis,* 3,724 ... L-12
Eveleth, *Saint Louis,* 3,865 ... M-11
Excelsior, *Hennepin,* 2,393 ... F-11
Eyota, *Olmsted,* 1,644 ... Y-12
Fairfax, *Renville,* 1,295 ... W-6
Fairmont, *Martin,* 10,889 ... Z-6
Falcon Heights, *Ramsey,* 5,572 ... E-14
Faribault, *Rice,* 20,818 ... X-9
Farmington, *Dakota,* 12,365 ... V-9
Fergus Falls, *Otter Tail,* 13,471 ... Q-3
Foley, *Benton,* 2,154 ... S-8
Forest Lake, *Washington,* 6,798 ... T-10
Fosston, *Polk,* 1,575 ... M-4
Frazee, *Becker,* 1,377 ... O-4
Fridley, *Anoka,* 27,449 ... D-13
Fulda, *Murray,* 1,283 ... Y-4
Gaylord, *Sibley,* 2,279 ... W-7
Gilbert, *Saint Louis,* 1,847 ... M-11
Glencoe, *McLeod,* 5,453 ... V-7
Glenwood, *Pope,* 2,594 ... S-4
Glyndon, *Clay,* 1,049 ... O-2
Golden Valley, *Hennepin,* 20,281 ... E-13
Goodview, *Winona,* 3,373 ... X-13
Grand Marais, *Cook,* 1,353 ... L-15
Grand Rapids, *Itasca,* 7,764 ... N-9
Granite Falls, *Yellow Medicine,* 3,070 ... V-4

Explanation of symbols: • - Census Designated Place (CDP)

Grant, *Washington,* 4,026 .... D-15
Greenfield, *Hennepin,* 2,544 .... D-10
Hallock, *Kittson,* 1,196 .... I-1
Ham Lake, *Anoka,* 12,710 .... C-13
Hanover, *Wright,* 1,355 .... C-11
Harmony, *Fillmore,* 1,080 .... Z-12
Harris, *Chisago,* 1,121 .... S-10
Hastings, *Dakota,* 18,204 .... V-10
Hawley, *Clay,* 1,882 .... O-3
Hayfield, *Dodge,* 1,325 .... Y-10
Hector, *Renville,* 1,166 .... V-6
Hermantown, *St. Louis,* 7,448 .... O-11
Hibbing, *Saint Louis,* 17,071 .... M-10
Hinckley, *Pine,* 1,291 .... R-10
Hopkins, *Hennepin,* 17,145 .... F-12
Houston, *Houston,* 1,020 .... Y-13
Howard Lake, *Wright,* 1,853 .... U-7
Hoyt Lakes, *Saint Louis,* 2,082 .... M-12
Hugo, *Washington,* 6,363 .... C-15
Hutchinson, *McLeod,* 13,080 .... V-7
Independence, *Hennepin,* 3,236 .... E-10
International Falls, *Koochiching,* 6,703 .... I-9
Inver Grove Heights, *Dakota,* 29,751 .... F-15
Isanti, *Isanti,* 2,324 .... T-9
Ivanhoe, *Lincoln,* 679 .... W-2
Jackson, *Jackson,* 3,501 .... Z-5
Janesville, *Waseca,* 2,109 .... X-8
Jordan, *Scott,* 3,833 .... V-8
Kasson, *Dodge,* 4,398 .... X-10
Keewatin, *Itasca,* 1,164 .... M-10
Kenyon, *Goodhue,* 1,661 .... X-10
La Crescent, *Houston,* 4,923 .... Y-14
Lake City, *Wabasha,* 4,950 .... W-11
Lake Crystal, *Blue Earth,* 2,420 .... X-7
Lake Elmo, *Washington,* 6,863 .... E-16
Lake Saint Croix Beach, *Washington,* 1,140 .... F-16
Lakefield, *Jackson,* 1,721 .... Z-5
Lakeland, *Washington,* 1,917 .... E-16
Lakeville, *Dakota,* 43,128 .... V-9
Lauderdale, *Ramsey,* 2,364 .... E-13
Le Center, *Le Sueur,* 2,240 .... W-8
Le Sueur, *Le Sueur,* 3,922 .... W-8
Lester Prairie, *McLeod,* 1,377 .... V-7
Lewiston, *Winona,* 1,484 .... Y-12
Lexington, *Anoka,* 2,214 .... W-8
Lindstrom, *Chisago,* 3,015 .... A-16
Lino Lakes, *Anoka,* 16,791 .... D-14
Litchfield, *Meeker,* 6,562 .... U-6
Little Canada, *Ramsey,* 9,771 .... E-14
Little Falls, *Morrison,* 7,719 .... R-7
•Little Rock, *Beltrami,* 1,055 .... L-5
Long Lake, *Hennepin,* 1,842 .... E-11
Long Prairie, *Todd,* 3,040 .... R-6
Lonsdale, *Rice,* 1,491 .... W-9
Luverne, *Rock,* 4,617 .... Z-2
Madelia, *Watonwan,* 2,340 .... X-7
Madison, *Lac Qui Parle,* 1,768 .... U-3
Mahnomen, *Mahnomen,* 1,202 .... M-3
Mahtomedi, *Washington,* 7,563 .... D-15
Mankato, *Blue Earth,* 32,427 .... X-8
Mantorville, *Dodge,* 1,054 .... X-10
Maple Grove, *Hennepin,* 50,365 .... U-9
Maple Lake, *Wright,* 1,633 .... T-8
Maple Plain, *Hennepin,* 2,088 .... E-11
Mapleton, *Blue Earth,* 1,678 .... Y-8
Maplewood, *Ramsey,* 34,947 .... E-15
Marshall, *Lyon,* 12,735 .... W-3
Medina, *Hennepin,* 4,005 .... E-11
Melrose, *Stearns,* 3,091 .... S-6
Menahga, *Wadena,* 1,220 .... O-5
Mendota Heights, *Dakota,* 11,434 .... F-14
Milaca, *Mille Lacs,* 2,580 .... S-8
Minneapolis, *Hennepin,* 382,618 .... U-9
Minneota, *Lyon,* 1,449 .... W-3
Minnetonka, *Hennepin,* 51,301 .... F-12
Minnetrista, *Hennepin,* 4,358 .... E-10
Montevideo, *Chippewa,* 5,346 .... U-4
Montgomery, *Le Sueur,* 2,794 .... W-8
Monticello, *Wright,* 7,868 .... T-8
Montrose, *Wright,* 1,143 .... D-9
Moorhead, *Clay,* 32,177 .... O-2
Moose Lake, *Carlton,* 2,239 .... P-10
Mora, *Kanabec,* 3,193 .... R-9
Morris, *Stevens,* 5,068 .... S-3
Mound, *Hennepin,* 9,435 .... F-11
Mounds View, *Ramsey,* 12,738 .... D-13
Mountain Iron, *Saint Louis,* 2,999 .... M-11
Mountain Lake, *Cottonwood,* 2,082 .... Y-5
New Brighton, *Ramsey,* 22,206 .... D-14
New Hope, *Hennepin,* 20,873 .... E-12
New London, *Kandiyohi,* 1,066 .... T-5
New Prague, *Le Sueur,* 4,559 .... W-9
New Richland, *Waseca,* 1,197 .... Y-9
New Ulm, *Brown,* 13,594 .... W-6
New York Mills, *Otter Tail,* 1,158 .... P-5
Newport, *Washington,* 3,715 .... F-15
Nisswa, *Crow Wing,* 1,953 .... P-7
North Branch, *Chisago,* 8,023 .... T-10
North Mankato, *Nicollet,* 11,798 .... X-7
North Oaks, *Ramsey,* 3,883 .... D-14
North Saint Paul, *Ramsey,* 11,929 .... E-15
Northfield, *Rice,* 17,147 .... W-9
Norwood Young America, *Carver,* 3,108 .... G-9
Oak Grove, *Anoka,* 6,903 .... T-9
Oak Park Heights, *Washington,* 3,957 .... E-16
Oakdale, *Washington,* 26,653 .... E-15
•Oakport, *Clay,* 1,334 .... O-2
Olivia, *Renville,* 2,570 .... V-5
Orono, *Hennepin,* 7,538 .... U-8
Ortonville, *Big Stone,* 2,158 .... T-2
Osakis, *Douglas,* 1,567 .... R-5
Osseo, *Hennepin,* 2,434 .... D-12
Otsego, *Wright,* 6,389 .... B-11
Owatonna, *Steele,* 22,434 .... X-9
Park Rapids, *Hubbard,* 3,276 .... O-5
Paynesville, *Stearns,* 2,267 .... T-6
Pelican Rapids, *Otter Tail,* 2,374 .... P-3
Perham, *Otter Tail,* 2,559 .... P-4
Pierz, *Morrison,* 1,277 .... R-7
Pine City, *Pine,* 3,043 .... S-10
Pine Island, *Goodhue,* 2,337 .... X-11
Pipestone, *Pipestone,* 4,280 .... X-2
Plainview, *Wabasha,* 3,190 .... X-12
Plymouth, *Hennepin,* 65,894 .... U-9
Preston, *Fillmore,* 1,426 .... Z-12
Princeton, *Mille Lacs,* 3,933 .... S-8
Prior Lake, *Scott,* 15,917 .... H-12
Proctor, *St. Louis,* 2,852 .... O-11
Ramsey, *Anoka,* 18,510 .... C-12
•Red Lake, *Beltrami,* 1,430 .... L-5
Red Lake Falls, *Red Lake,* 1,590 .... L-3
Red Wing, *Goodhue,* 16,116 .... W-11
Redwood Falls, *Redwood,* 5,459 .... W-5
Renville, *Renville,* 1,323 .... V-5
Richfield, *Hennepin,* 34,439 .... F-13
Richmond, *Stearns,* 1,213 .... T-6
Robbinsdale, *Hennepin,* 14,123 .... E-13
Rochester, *Olmsted,* 85,806 .... X-11
Rock Creek, *Pine,* 1,119 .... S-10
Rockford, *Hennepin,* 3,484 .... D-10
Rogers, *Hennepin,* 3,588 .... C-11
Roseau, *Roseau,* 2,756 .... H-4
Rosemount, *Dakota,* 14,619 .... V-10
Roseville, *Ramsey,* 33,690 .... U-10
Rush City, *Chisago,* 2,102 .... S-10
Rushford, *Fillmore,* 1,696 .... Y-13
Saint Anthony, *Hennepin,* 8,012 .... E-13
Saint Bonifacius, *Hennepin,* 1,873 .... F-10
Saint Charles, *Winona,* 3,295 .... Y-12
Saint Cloud, *Stearns,* 59,107 .... S-7
Saint Francis, *Anoka,* 4,910 .... T-9
Saint James, *Watonwan,* 4,695 .... Y-6
Saint Joseph, *Stearns,* 4,681 .... S-7
Saint Louis Park, *Hennepin,* 44,126 .... E-13
Saint Michael, *Wright,* 9,099 .... C-11
Saint Paul, *Ramsey,* 287,151 .... U-10
Saint Paul Park, *Washington,* 5,070 .... F-15
Saint Peter, *Nicollet,* 9,747 .... W-8
Sandstone, *Pine,* 1,549 .... R-10
Sartell, *Stearns,* 9,641 .... S-7
Sauk Centre, *Stearns,* 3,930 .... S-5
Sauk Rapids, *Benton,* 10,213 .... S-7
Savage, *Scott,* 21,115 .... G-13
Shakopee, *Scott,* 20,568 .... V-9
Sherburn, *Martin,* 1,082 .... Z-6
Shoreview, *Ramsey,* 25,924 .... D-14
Shorewood, *Hennepin,* 7,400 .... F-11
Silver Bay, *Lake,* 2,068 .... N-14
Slayton, *Murray,* 2,072 .... X-4
Sleepy Eye, *Brown,* 3,515 .... X-6
South Saint Paul, *Dakota,* 20,167 .... F-15
Spicer, *Kandiyohi,* 1,126 .... T-5
Spring Grove, *Houston,* 1,304 .... Z-13
Spring Lake Park, *Anoka,* 6,772 .... D-13
Spring Park, *Hennepin,* 1,717 .... F-11
Spring Valley, *Fillmore,* 2,518 .... Z-11
Springfield, *Brown,* 2,215 .... X-5
Stacy, *Chisago,* 1,278 .... T-10
Staples, *Todd,* 3,104 .... Q-6
Starbuck, *Pope,* 1,314 .... S-4
Stewartville, *Olmsted,* 5,411 .... Y-11
Stillwater, *Washington,* 15,143 .... U-10
Thief River Falls, *Pennington,* 8,410 .... K-3
Tonka Bay, *Hennepin,* 1,547 .... F-11
Tracy, *Lyon,* 2,268 .... X-4
Truman, *Martin,* 1,259 .... Y-7
Two Harbors, *Lake,* 3,613 .... O-13
Tyler, *Lincoln,* 1,218 .... W-3
Vadnais Heights, *Ramsey,* 13,069 .... D-14
Victoria, *Carver,* 4,025 .... F-11
Virginia, *Saint Louis,* 9,157 .... M-11
Wabasha, *Wabasha,* 2,599 .... W-12
Waconia, *Carver,* 6,814 .... F-10
Wadena, *Wadena,* 4,294 .... P-5
Waite Park, *Stearns,* 6,568 .... S-7
Walker, *Cass,* 1,069 .... N-6
Wanamingo, *Goodhue,* 1,007 .... W-10
Warren, *Marshall,* 1,678 .... K-2
Warroad, *Roseau,* 1,722 .... H-5
Waseca, *Waseca,* 8,493 .... X-9
Watertown, *Carver,* 3,029 .... U-8
Waterville, *Le Sueur,* 1,833 .... X-9
Wayzata, *Hennepin,* 4,113 .... E-12
Wells, *Faribault,* 2,494 .... Y-8
West Saint Paul, *Dakota,* 19,405 .... F-14
Wheaton, *Traverse,* 1,619 .... R-2
White Bear Lake, *Ramsey,* 24,325 .... U-10
Willmar, *Kandiyohi,* 18,351 .... U-5
Windom, *Cottonwood,* 4,490 .... Y-5
Winnebago, *Faribault,* 1,487 .... Y-7
Winona, *Winona,* 27,069 .... X-13
Winsted, *McLeod,* 2,094 .... U-7
Winthrop, *Sibley,* 1,367 .... W-7
Woodbury, *Washington,* 46,463 .... F-15
Worthington, *Nobles,* 11,283 .... Z-4
Wyoming, *Chisago,* 3,048 .... T-10
Zimmerman, *Sherburne,* 2,851 .... T-8
Zumbrota, *Goodhue,* 2,789 .... X-11

COUNTIES

(82 Counties)

Name of County	Population	Location on Map
ADAMS	34,340	M-3
ALCORN	34,558	A-11
AMITE	13,599	M-5
ATTALA	19,661	G-8
BENTON	8,026	A-9
BOLIVAR	40,633	E-5
CALHOUN	15,069	D-9
CARROLL	10,769	F-7
CHICKASAW	19,440	D-10
CHOCTAW	9,758	F-9
CLAIBORNE	11,831	K-4
CLARKE	17,955	K-11
CLAY	21,979	E-11
COAHOMA	30,622	C-5
COPIAH	28,757	K-5
COVINGTON	19,407	L-8
DE SOTO	107,199	A-8
FORREST	72,604	M-9
FRANKLIN	8,448	M-4
GEORGE	19,144	O-11
GREENE	13,299	M-11
GRENADA	23,263	E-7
HANCOCK	42,967	P-9
HARRISON	189,601	P-10
HINDS	250,800	J-6
HOLMES	21,609	G-7
HUMPHREYS	11,206	G-5
ISSAQUENA	2,274	I-4
ITAWAMBA	22,770	C-12
JACKSON	131,420	P-11
JASPER	18,149	J-10
JEFFERSON	9,740	L-4
JEFFERSON DAVIS	13,962	M-8
JONES	64,958	L-10
KEMPER	10,453	H-11
LAFAYETTE	38,744	C-8
LAMAR	39,070	M-9
LAUDERDALE	78,161	I-11
LAWRENCE	13,258	M-7
LEAKE	20,940	H-8
LEE	75,755	C-11
LEFLORE	37,947	E-6
LINCOLN	33,166	L-5
LOWNDES	61,586	F-12
MADISON	74,674	H-8
MARION	25,595	M-7
MARSHALL	34,993	A-9
MONROE	38,014	E-11
MONTGOMERY	12,189	F-8
NESHOBA	28,684	H-10
NEWTON	21,838	I-10
NOXUBEE	12,548	G-11
OKTIBBEHA	42,902	F-11
PANOLA	34,274	B-7
PEARL RIVER	48,621	O-8
PERRY	12,138	M-10
PIKE	38,940	N-6
PONTOTOC	26,726	D-10
PRENTISS	25,556	B-11
QUITMAN	10,117	D-6
RANKIN	115,327	J-8
SCOTT	28,423	I-8
SHARKEY	6,580	G-5
SIMPSON	27,639	K-7
SMITH	16,182	J-9
STONE	13,622	O-10
SUNFLOWER	34,369	F-5
TALLAHATCHIE	14,903	E-6
TATE	25,370	B-7
TIPPAH	20,826	A-10
TISHOMINGO	19,163	B-12
TUNICA	9,227	B-6
UNION	25,362	B-10
WALTHALL	15,156	N-7
WARREN	49,644	I-5
WASHINGTON	62,977	G-4
WAYNE	21,216	L-11
WEBSTER	10,294	E-9
WILKINSON	10,312	N-3
WINSTON	20,160	G-10
YALOBUSHA	13,051	D-8
YAZOO	28,149	H-6
TOTAL	**2,844,658**	

CITIES AND TOWNS

Note: The first name is that of the city or town, second, that of the county in which it is located, then the population and location on the map.

Aberdeen, *Monroe,* 6,415 ..... E-12
Ackerman, *Choctaw,* 1,696 ..... G-10
Amory, *Monroe,* 6,956 ..... D-12
Ashland, *Benton,* 577 ..... A-10
Baldwyn, *Lee,* 3,321 ..... B-11
Batesville, *Panola,* 7,113 ..... C-8
Bay Saint Louis, *Hancock,* 8,209 ..... Q-10
Bay Springs, *Jasper,* 2,097 ..... K-10
Belmont, *Tishomingo,* 1,961 ..... B-13
Belzoni, *Humphreys,* 2,663 ..... G-6
Biloxi, *Harrison,* 50,644 ..... Q-11
Booneville, *Prentiss,* 8,625 ..... B-12
Brandon, *Rankin,* 16,436 ..... J-7
Brookhaven, *Lincoln,* 9,861 ..... M-6
Brooksville, *Noxubee,* 1,182 ..... G-12
Bruce, *Calhoun,* 2,097 ..... D-9
Bude, *Franklin,* 1,037 ..... M-5
Burnsville, *Tishomingo,* 1,034 ..... A-12
●Byram, *Hinds,* 7,386 ..... J-7
Caledonia, *Lowndes,* 1,015 ..... E-12
Calhoun City, *Calhoun,* 1,872 ..... E-9
Canton, *Madison,* 12,911 ..... I-7
Carrollton, *Carroll,* 408 ..... F-8
Carthage, *Leake,* 4,637 ..... I-9
Centreville, *Wilkinson,* 1,680 ..... N-4
Charleston, *Tallahatchie,* 2,198 ..... D-7
Clarksdale, *Coahoma,* 20,645 ..... D-6
Cleveland, *Bolivar,* 13,841 ..... E-5
Clinton, *Hinds,* 23,347 ..... J-6
Coffeeville, *Yalobusha,* 930 ..... D-8
Coldwater, *Tate,* 1,674 ..... B-7
Collins, *Covington,* 2,683 ..... L-9
●Collinsville, *Lauderdale,* 1,823 ..... I-11
Columbia, *Marion,* 6,603 ..... N-8
Columbus, *Lowndes,* 25,944 ..... F-12
●Columbus AFB, *Lowndes,* 2,060 ..... F-12
Como, *Panola,* 1,310 ..... B-8
Corinth, *Alcorn,* 14,054 ..... A-12
Crystal Springs, *Copiah,* 5,873 ..... K-6
D'Iberville, *Harrison,* 7,608 ..... P-4
De Kalb, *Kemper,* 972 ..... H-11
Decatur, *Newton,* 1,426 ..... J-10
Derma, *Calhoun,* 1,023 ..... E-10
●Diamondhead, *Hancock,* 5,912 ..... Q-9
Drew, *Sunflower,* 2,434 ..... E-6
Durant, *Holmes,* 2,932 ..... G-8
Edwards, *Hinds,* 1,347 ..... J-6
Ellisville, *Jones,* 3,465 ..... L-10
●Escatawpa, *Jackson,* 3,566 ..... P-6
Eupora, *Webster,* 2,326 ..... F-10
Farmington, *Alcorn,* 1,810 ..... A-12
Fayette, *Jefferson,* 2,242 ..... L-4
Flora, *Madison,* 1,546 ..... I-7
Florence, *Rankin,* 2,396 ..... K-7
Flowood, *Rankin,* 4,750 ..... J-7
Forest, *Scott,* 5,987 ..... J-9
Friars Point, *Coahoma,* 1,480 ..... C-6
Fulton, *Itawamba,* 3,882 ..... C-12
Gautier, *Jackson,* 11,681 ..... Q-12
Gloster, *Amite,* 1,073 ..... N-4
Goodman, *Holmes,* 1,252 ..... H-8
Greenville, *Washington,* 41,633 ..... F-4
Greenwood, *Leflore,* 18,425 ..... F-7
Grenada, *Grenada,* 14,879 ..... E-8
●Gulf Hills, *Jackson,* 5,900 ..... P-11
●Gulf Park Estates, *Jackson,* 4,272 ..... Q-4
Gulfport, *Harrison,* 71,127 ..... Q-10
Guntown, *Lee,* 1,183 ..... C-11
Hattiesburg, *Forrest,* 44,779 ..... M-10
Hazlehurst, *Copiah,* 4,400 ..... L-6
Hernando, *De Soto,* 6,812 ..... A-7
●Hickory Hills, *Jackson,* 3,046 ..... P-5
Hollandale, *Washington,* 3,437 ..... G-5
Holly Springs, *Marshall,* 7,957 ..... B-9
Horn Lake, *De Soto,* 14,099 ..... A-7
Houston, *Chickasaw,* 4,079 ..... E-10
Indianola, *Sunflower,* 12,066 ..... F-5
Inverness, *Sunflower,* 1,153 ..... F-6
Itta Bena, *Leflore,* 2,208 ..... F-6
Iuka, *Tishomingo,* 3,059 ..... A-13
Jackson, *Hinds,* 184,256 ..... J-7
Jonestown, *Coahoma,* 1,701 ..... C-6
●Kiln, *Hancock,* 2,040 ..... Q-9
Kosciusko, *Attala,* 7,372 ..... G-9
Lambert, *Quitman,* 1,967 ..... D-7
●Latimer, *Jackson,* 4,288 ..... P-11
Laurel, *Jones,* 18,393 ..... L-10
Leakesville, *Greene,* 1,026 ..... N-12
Leland, *Washington,* 5,502 ..... F-5
Lexington, *Holmes,* 2,025 ..... G-7
Liberty, *Amite,* 633 ..... N-5
Long Beach, *Harrison,* 17,320 ..... Q-2
Louisville, *Winston,* 7,006 ..... G-10
Lucedale, *George,* 2,458 ..... O-12
Lumberton, *Lamar,* 2,228 ..... O-9
●Lyman, *Harrison,* 1,081 ..... P-10
●Lynchburg, *Desoto,* 2,959 ..... A-7
Macon, *Noxubee,* 2,461 ..... G-12
Madison, *Madison,* 14,692 ..... J-7
Magee, *Simpson,* 4,200 ..... L-8
Magnolia, *Pike,* 2,071 ..... N-6
Mantachie, *Itawamba,* 1,107 ..... C-12
Marion, *Lauderdale,* 1,305 ..... J-12
Marks, *Quitman,* 1,551 ..... C-7
Mayersville, *Issaquena,* 795 ..... H-4
McComb, *Pike,* 13,337 ..... N-6
Meadville, *Franklin,* 519 ..... M-5
Mendenhall, *Simpson,* 2,555 ..... K-8
Meridian, *Lauderdale,* 39,968 ..... J-11
●Meridian Station, *Lauderdale,* 1,849 ..... I-12
Metcalfe, *Washington,* 1,109 ..... F-4
Monticello, *Lawrence,* 1,726 ..... M-7
Moorhead, *Sunflower,* 2,573 ..... F-6
Morton, *Scott,* 3,482 ..... J-8
Moss Point, *Jackson,* 15,851 ..... Q-12
Mound Bayou, *Bolivar,* 2,102 ..... E-5
Natchez, *Adams,* 18,464 ..... M-3
●Nellieburg, *Lauderdale,* 1,354 ..... J-11
Nettleton, *Lee,* 1,932 ..... D-12
New Albany, *Union,* 7,607 ..... C-10
New Augusta, *Perry,* 715 ..... N-10
●New Hope, *Lowndes,* 1,964 ..... F-12
Newton, *Newton,* 3,699 ..... J-10
●North Tunica, *Tunica,* 1,450 ..... B-6
Ocean Springs, *Jackson,* 17,225 ..... Q-11
Okolona, *Chickasaw,* 3,056 ..... D-11
Olive Branch, *De Soto,* 21,054 ..... A-8
Oxford, *Lafayette,* 11,756 ..... C-9
Pascagoula, *Jackson,* 26,200 ..... Q-12
Pass Christian, *Harrison,* 6,579 ..... Q-1
Paulding, *Jasper,* 630 ..... K-10
Pearl, *Rankin,* 21,961 ..... J-7
●Pearl River, *Neshoba,* 3,156 ..... H-10
●Pearlington, *Hancock,* 1,684 ..... Q-9
Pelahatchie, *Rankin,* 1,461 ..... J-8
Petal, *Forrest,* 7,579 ..... M-10
Philadelphia, *Neshoba,* 7,303 ..... H-10
Picayune, *Pearl River,* 10,535 ..... P-8
Pickens, *Holmes,* 1,325 ..... H-8
Pittsboro, *Calhoun,* 212 ..... D-9
Plantersville, *Lee,* 1,144 ..... C-11
Pontotoc, *Pontotoc,* 5,253 ..... C-10
Poplarville, *Pearl River,* 2,601 ..... O-9
Port Gibson, *Claiborne,* 1,840 ..... K-4
Prentiss, *Jefferson Davis,* 1,158 ..... L-8
Purvis, *Lamar,* 2,164 ..... N-9
Quitman, *Clarke,* 2,463 ..... K-11
Raleigh, *Smith,* 1,255 ..... K-9
Raymond, *Hinds,* 1,664 ..... J-6
Richland, *Rankin,* 6,027 ..... H-7
Richton, *Perry,* 1,038 ..... M-11
Ridgeland, *Madison,* 20,173 ..... J-7
Ripley, *Tippah,* 5,478 ..... B-11
Rolling Fork, *Sharkey,* 2,486 ..... H-5
Rosedale, *Bolivar,* 2,414 ..... E-4
Ruleville, *Sunflower,* 3,234 ..... E-6
●Saint Martin, *Jackson,* 6,676 ..... P-11
Saltillo, *Lee,* 3,393 ..... C-11
Sardis, *Panola,* 2,038 ..... C-8
●Saucier, *Harrison,* 1,303 ..... P-10
Senatobia, *Tate,* 6,682 ..... B-8
Shannon, *Lee,* 1,657 ..... D-11
Shaw, *Bolivar,* 2,312 ..... F-5
Shelby, *Bolivar,* 2,926 ..... D-5
●Shoreline Park, *Hancock,* 4,058 ..... Q-9
Southaven, *De Soto,* 28,977 ..... A-7
Starkville, *Oktibbeha,* 21,869 ..... F-11
Stonewall, *Clarke,* 1,149 ..... K-11
Summit, *Pike,* 1,428 ..... N-6
Sumner, *Tallahatchie,* 407 ..... D-6
Sumrall, *Lamar,* 1,005 ..... M-9
Taylorsville, *Smith,* 1,341 ..... L-9
Tchula, *Holmes,* 2,332 ..... G-7
Tunica, *Tunica,* 1,132 ..... B-6
Tupelo, *Lee,* 34,211 ..... C-11
Tutwiler, *Tallahatchie,* 1,364 ..... D-6
Tylertown, *Walthall,* 1,910 ..... N-7
Union, *Newton,* 2,021 ..... I-10
Vaiden, *Carroll,* 840 ..... G-8
●Vancleave, *Jefferson,* 4,910 ..... P-11
Vardaman, *Calhoun,* 1,065 ..... E-10
Verona, *Lee,* 3,334 ..... D-11
Vicksburg, *Warren,* 26,407 ..... J-5
Walthall, *Webster,* 170 ..... F-10
Water Valley, *Yalobusha,* 3,677 ..... D-9
Waveland, *Hancock,* 6,674 ..... Q-9
Waynesboro, *Wayne,* 5,197 ..... L-12
Wesson, *Copiah,* 1,693 ..... L-6
●West Hattiesburg, *Lamar,* 6,305 ..... M-9
West Point, *Clay,* 12,145 ..... F-11
Wiggins, *Stone,* 3,849 ..... O-10
Winona, *Montgomery,* 5,482 ..... F-8
Woodville, *Wilkinson,* 1,192 ..... N-3
Yazoo City, *Yazoo,* 14,550 ..... H-6

Explanation of symbols: ● - Census Designated Place (CDP)

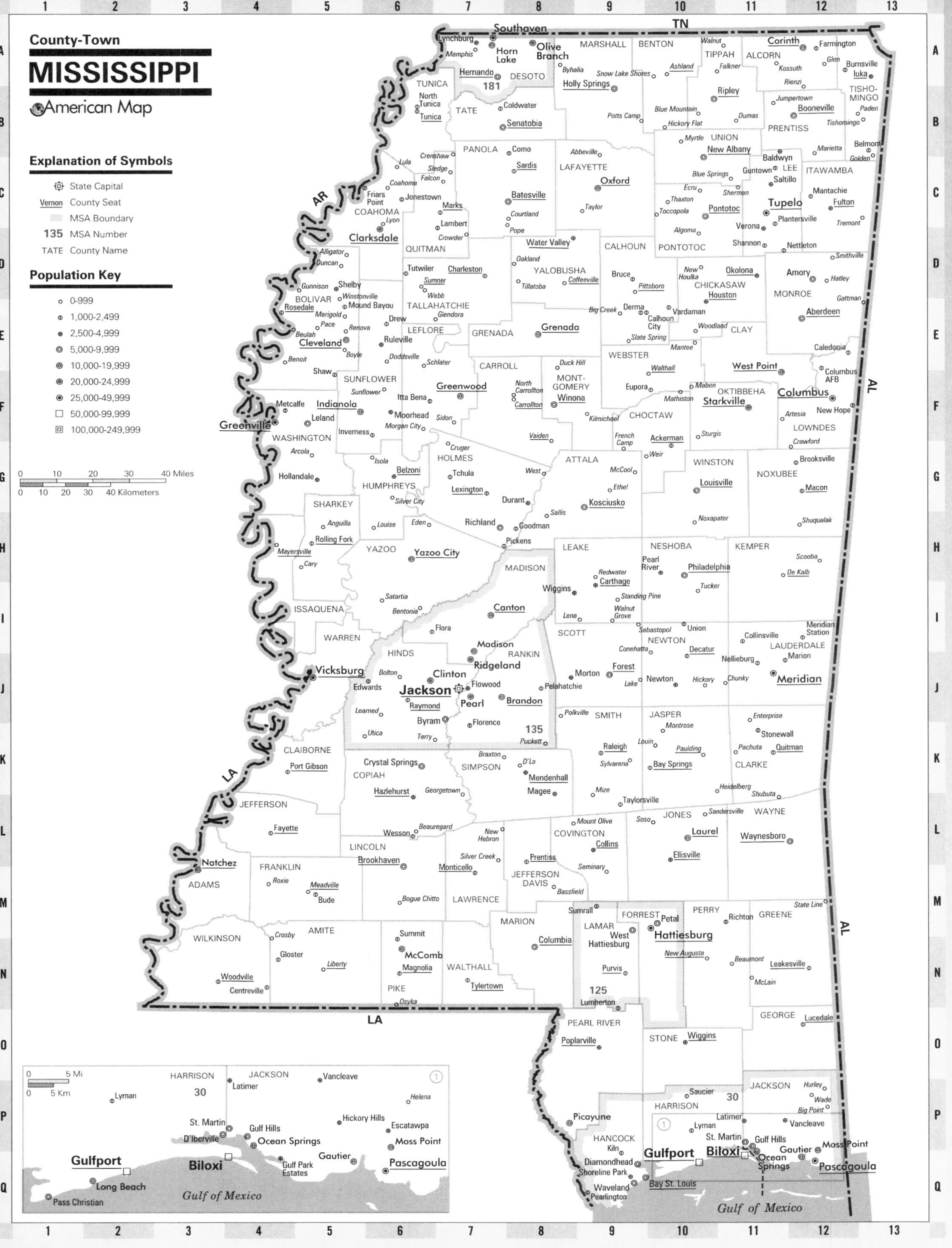
County-Town
MISSISSIPPI
American Map
Explanation of Symbols
State Capital
Vernon County Seat
MSA Boundary
135 MSA Number
TATE County Name
Population Key
0-999
1,000-2,499
2,500-4,999
5,000-9,999
10,000-19,999
20,000-24,999
25,000-49,999
50,000-99,999
100,000-249,999
0 10 20 30 40 Miles
0 10 20 30 40 Kilometers
TN
AR
LA
AL
Southaven
Olive Branch
Horn Lake
Hernando
181
DESOTO
TUNICA
Tunica
TATE
Senatobia
MARSHALL
Holly Springs
BENTON
TIPPAH
Ripley
ALCORN
Corinth
TISHOMINGO
Iuka
Booneville
PRENTISS
UNION
New Albany
PANOLA
Batesville
Sardis
LAFAYETTE
Oxford
PONTOTOC
Pontotoc
LEE
Tupelo
ITAWAMBA
Fulton
COAHOMA
Clarksdale
QUITMAN
Marks
YALOBUSHA
Water Valley
Coffeeville
CALHOUN
Pittsboro
CHICKASAW
Houston
Okolona
MONROE
Aberdeen
Amory
BOLIVAR
Cleveland
Rosedale
TALLAHATCHIE
Charleston
Sumner
GRENADA
Grenada
CLAY
West Point
LEFLORE
Greenwood
CARROLL
Vaiden
Carrollton
MONTGOMERY
Winona
WEBSTER
Walthall
OKTIBBEHA
Starkville
LOWNDES
Columbus
Columbus AFB
SUNFLOWER
Indianola
WASHINGTON
Greenville
HOLMES
Lexington
ATTALA
Kosciusko
CHOCTAW
Ackerman
WINSTON
Louisville
NOXUBEE
Macon
HUMPHREYS
Belzoni
SHARKEY
Rolling Fork
YAZOO
Yazoo City
LEAKE
Carthage
NESHOBA
Philadelphia
KEMPER
De Kalb
MADISON
Canton
Madison
Ridgeland
ISSAQUENA
Mayersville
WARREN
Vicksburg
HINDS
Jackson
Clinton
Raymond
RANKIN
Brandon
Pearl
SCOTT
Forest
NEWTON
Decatur
LAUDERDALE
Meridian
135
CLAIBORNE
Port Gibson
COPIAH
Hazlehurst
SIMPSON
Mendenhall
SMITH
Raleigh
JASPER
Bay Springs
Paulding
CLARKE
Quitman
JEFFERSON
Fayette
LINCOLN
Brookhaven
LAWRENCE
Monticello
JEFFERSON DAVIS
Prentiss
COVINGTON
Collins
JONES
Laurel
Ellisville
WAYNE
Waynesboro
ADAMS
Natchez
FRANKLIN
Meadville
WILKINSON
Woodville
AMITE
Liberty
PIKE
Magnolia
McComb
WALTHALL
Tylertown
MARION
Columbia
LAMAR
Purvis
FORREST
Hattiesburg
PERRY
New Augusta
GREENE
Leakesville
125
PEARL RIVER
Poplarville
Picayune
STONE
Wiggins
GEORGE
Lucedale
HANCOCK
Bay St. Louis
HARRISON
Gulfport
Biloxi
30
JACKSON
Pascagoula
Gulf of Mexico
HARRISON
JACKSON
30
Vancleave
Latimer
Lyman
Helena
St. Martin
D'Iberville
Gulf Hills
Ocean Springs
Hickory Hills
Escatawpa
Moss Point
Gautier
Gulf Park Estates
Long Beach
Pass Christian
0 5 Mi
0 5 Km

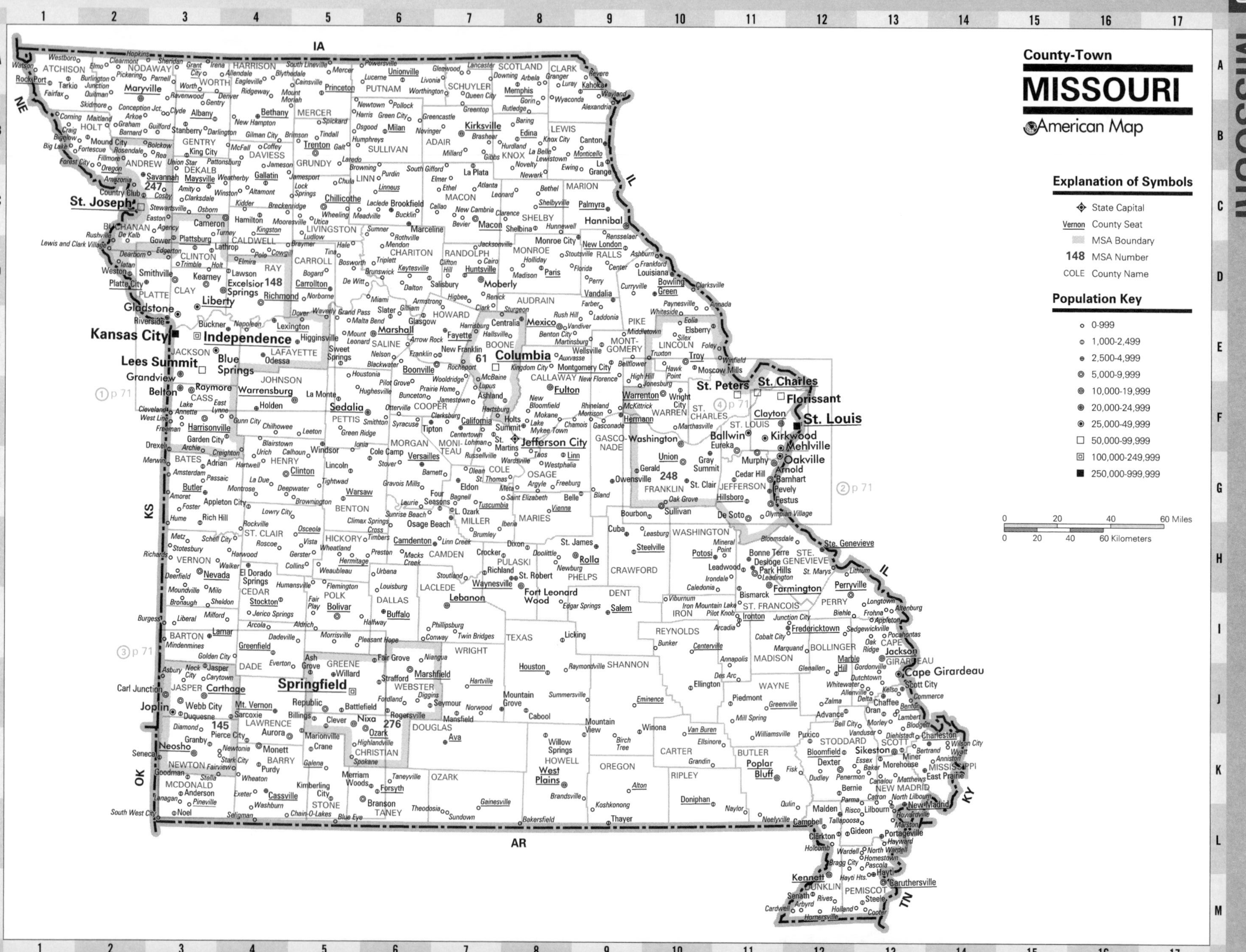

County-Town
MISSOURI
American Map
Explanation of Symbols
State Capital
Vernon County Seat
MSA Boundary
148 MSA Number
COLE County Name
Population Key
0-999
1,000-2,499
2,500-4,999
5,000-9,999
10,000-19,999
20,000-24,999
25,000-49,999
50,000-99,999
100,000-249,999
250,000-999,999
0 20 40 60 Miles
0 20 40 60 Kilometers

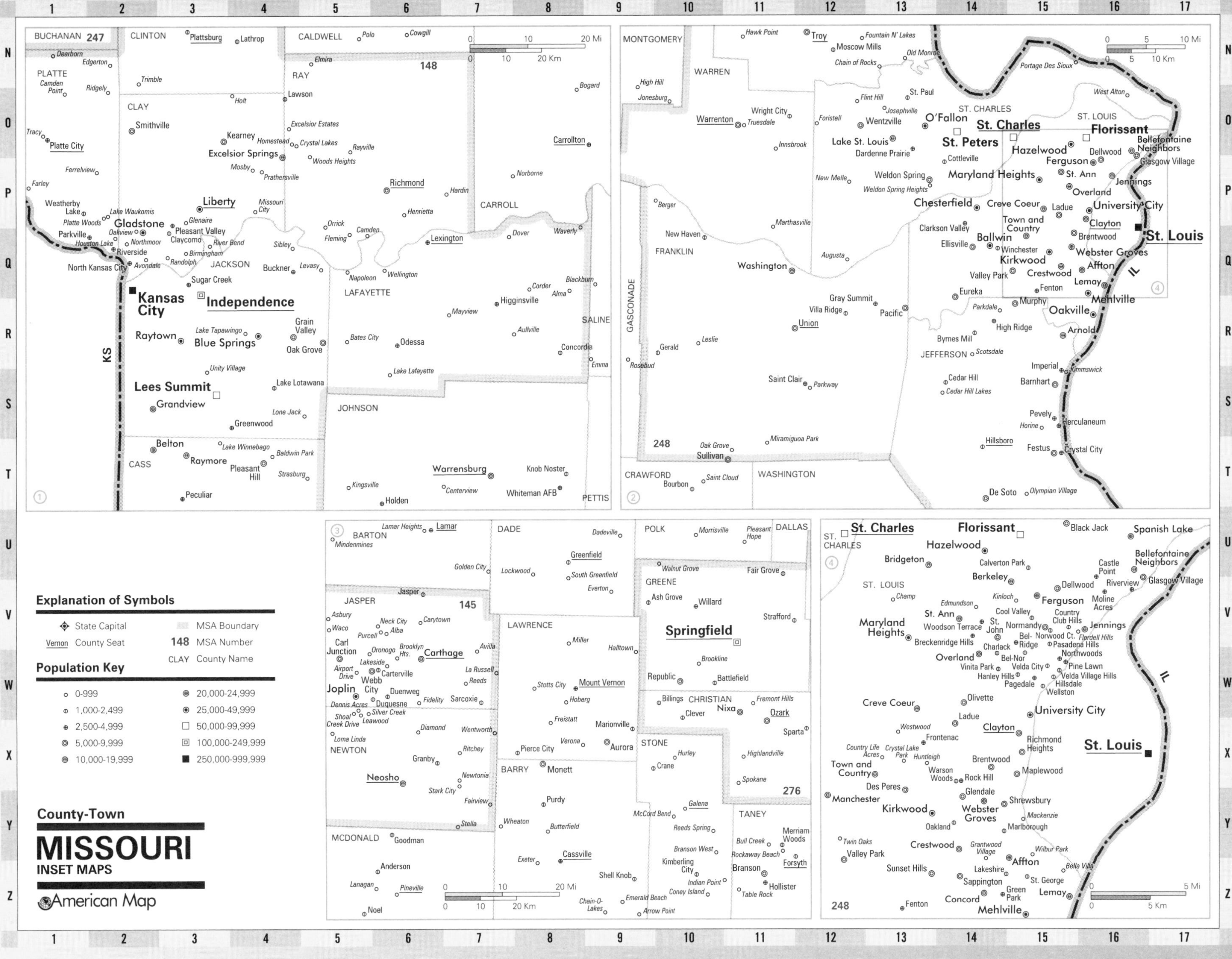
Explanation of Symbols
State Capital
Vernon County Seat
MSA Boundary
148 MSA Number
CLAY County Name
Population Key
0-999
1,000-2,499
2,500-4,999
5,000-9,999
10,000-19,999
20,000-24,999
25,000-49,999
50,000-99,999
100,000-249,999
250,000-999,999
County-Town
MISSOURI
INSET MAPS
American Map
Kansas City
Independence
Lees Summit
Liberty
Gladstone
Raytown
Blue Springs
Grandview
Belton
Raymore
Excelsior Springs
Lexington
Richmond
Carrollton
Warrensburg
Whiteman AFB
Knob Noster
Odessa
Oak Grove
Grain Valley
Holden
St. Louis
St. Charles
St. Peters
O'Fallon
Florissant
Hazelwood
Chesterfield
Ballwin
Kirkwood
Webster Groves
University City
Clayton
Oakville
Mehlville
Affton
Maryland Heights
Creve Coeur
Ferguson
Washington
Union
Sullivan
Troy
Warrenton
Wentzville
Lake St. Louis
Springfield
Joplin
Carthage
Neosho
Webb City
Monett
Aurora
Mount Vernon
Nixa
Ozark
Branson
Cassville
Lamar
Republic
Forsyth
BUCHANAN 247
CLINTON
CALDWELL
CARROLL
SALINE
PETTIS
PLATTE
CLAY
RAY
JACKSON
LAFAYETTE
JOHNSON
CASS
MONTGOMERY
WARREN
ST. CHARLES
ST. LOUIS
FRANKLIN
JEFFERSON
WASHINGTON
CRAWFORD
GASCONADE
BARTON
DADE
LAWRENCE
JASPER
NEWTON
BARRY
MCDONALD
POLK
DALLAS
GREENE
CHRISTIAN
STONE
TANEY
148
248
145
276
KS
IL
0 10 20 Mi
0 10 20 Km
0 5 10 Mi
0 5 10 Km
0 5 Mi
0 5 Km

COUNTIES

(115 Counties)

Name of County	Population	Location on Map
ADAIR	24,977	B-6
ANDREW	16,492	C-2
ATCHISON	6,430	A-1
AUDRAIN	25,853	D-8
BARRY	34,010	K-4
BARTON	12,541	I-3
BATES	16,653	G-3
BENTON	17,180	G-5
BOLLINGER	12,029	I-12
BOONE	135,454	E-7
BUCHANAN	85,998	C-2
BUTLER	40,867	K-11
CALDWELL	8,969	D-4
CALLAWAY	40,766	F-8
CAMDEN	37,051	H-6
CAPE GIRARDEAU	68,693	J-13
CARROLL	10,285	D-5
CARTER	5,941	K-10
CASS	82,092	F-3
CEDAR	13,733	I-4
CHARITON	8,438	D-6
CHRISTIAN	54,285	K-5
CLARK	7,416	A-8
CLAY	184,006	D-3
CLINTON	18,979	D-3
COLE	71,397	G-7
COOPER	16,670	F-6
CRAWFORD	22,804	H-9
DADE	7,923	J-4
DALLAS	15,661	I-6
DAVIESS	8,016	B-4
DE KALB	11,597	C-3
DENT	14,927	I-9
DOUGLAS	13,084	K-6
DUNKLIN	33,155	M-12
FRANKLIN	93,807	G-9
GASCONADE	15,342	G-9
GENTRY	6,861	B-3
GREENE	240,391	J-5
GRUNDY	10,432	C-5
HARRISON	8,850	A-4
HENRY	21,997	G-4
HICKORY	8,940	H-5
HOLT	5,351	B-1
HOWARD	10,212	E-6
HOWELL	37,238	K-8
IRON	10,697	I-10
JACKSON	654,880	E-3
JASPER	104,686	J-3
JEFFERSON	198,099	G-11
JOHNSON	48,258	F-4
KNOX	4,361	B-7
LACLEDE	32,513	I-6
LAFAYETTE	32,960	E-4
LAWRENCE	35,204	K-4
LEWIS	10,494	B-8
LINCOLN	38,944	E-10
LINN	13,754	C-5
LIVINGSTON	14,558	C-5
MACON	15,762	C-7
MADISON	11,800	J-11
MARIES	8,903	H-8
MARION	28,289	C-8
MCDONALD	21,681	K-3
MERCER	3,757	B-5
MILLER	23,564	H-7
MISSISSIPPI	13,427	K-14
MONITEAU	14,827	G-7
MONROE	9,311	D-8
MONTGOMERY	12,136	E-9
MORGAN	19,309	G-6
NEW MADRID	19,760	K-13
NEWTON	52,636	K-3
NODAWAY	21,912	A-2
OREGON	10,344	K-9
OSAGE	13,062	G-8
OZARK	9,542	K-6
PEMISCOT	20,047	M-12
PERRY	18,132	I-12
PETTIS	39,403	F-5
PHELPS	39,825	H-8
PIKE	18,351	E-9
PLATTE	73,781	D-2
POLK	26,992	I-5
PULASKI	41,165	H-7
PUTNAM	5,223	A-6
RALLS	9,626	D-9
RANDOLPH	24,663	D-7
RAY	23,354	D-4
REYNOLDS	6,689	I-10
RIPLEY	13,509	K-10
SAINT CHARLES	283,883	F-10
SAINT CLAIR	9,652	H-4
SAINT FRANCOIS	55,641	I-11
SAINT LOUIS	1,016,315	F-11
SAINT LOUIS (Independent City)	348,189	F-11
SAINTE GENEVIEVE	17,842	H-12
SALINE	23,756	E-6
SCHUYLER	4,170	A-7
SCOTLAND	4,983	A-7
SCOTT	40,422	J-13
SHANNON	8,324	J-9
SHELBY	6,799	C-8
STODDARD	29,705	K-12
STONE	28,658	L-5
SULLIVAN	7,219	B-6
TANEY	39,703	L-6
TEXAS	23,003	I-8
VERNON	20,454	H-3
WARREN	24,525	F-10
WASHINGTON	23,344	H-10
WAYNE	13,259	J-11
WEBSTER	31,045	I-6
WORTH	2,382	A-3
WRIGHT	17,955	I-7
TOTAL	**5,595,211**	

CITIES AND TOWNS

Note: The first name is that of the city or town, second, that of the county in which it is located, then the population and location on the map.

Adrian, *Bates,* 1,780 ..... G-3
Advance, *Stoddard,* 1,244 ..... J-12
•Affton, *Saint Louis,* 20,535 ..... Q-16
Albany, *Gentry,* 1,937 ..... B-3
Alton, *Oregon,* 668 ..... K-9
Anderson, *McDonald,* 1,856 ..... K-3
Appleton City, *Saint Clair,* 1,314 ..... G-4
Arnold, *Jefferson,* 19,965 ..... R-15
Ash Grove, *Greene,* 1,430 ..... J-5
Ashland, *Boone,* 1,869 ..... F-7
Aurora, *Lawrence,* 7,014 ..... K-4
Ava, *Douglas,* 3,021 ..... K-7
Ballwin, *Saint Louis,* 31,283 ..... F-11
•Barnhart, *Jefferson,* 6,108 ..... G-11
Battlefield, *Greene,* 2,385 ..... J-5
Belle, *Maries,* 1,344 ..... G-9
Bellefontaine Neighbors, *Saint Louis,* 11,271 ..... P-16
Bel-Nor, *Saint Louis,* 1,598 ..... W-15
Bel-Ridge, *Saint Louis,* 3,082 ..... V-15
Belton, *Cass,* 21,730 ..... F-3
Benton, *Scott,* 732 ..... J-13
Berkeley, *Saint Louis,* 10,063 ..... V-15
Bernie, *Stoddard,* 1,777 ..... K-12
Bethany, *Harrison,* 3,087 ..... B-4
Billings, *Christian,* 1,091 ..... J-5
Bismarck, *Saint Francois,* 1,470 ..... I-11
Black Jack, *Saint Louis,* 6,792 ..... U-15
Bloomfield, *Stoddard,* 1,952 ..... K-12
Blue Springs, *Jackson,* 48,080 ..... E-3
Bolivar, *Polk,* 9,143 ..... I-5
Bonne Terre, *Saint Francois,* 4,039 ..... H-11
Boonville, *Cooper,* 8,202 ..... E-7
Bourbon, *Crawford,* 1,348 ..... H-10
Bowling Green, *Pike,* 3,260 ..... D-10
Branson, *Taney,* 6,050 ..... L-5
Breckenridge Hills, *Saint Louis,* 4,817 ..... V-14
Brentwood, *Saint Louis,* 7,693 ..... Q-15
Bridgeton, *Saint Louis,* 15,550 ..... U-13
Brookfield, *Linn,* 4,769 ..... C-6
Buckner, *Jackson,* 2,725 ..... E-4
Buffalo, *Dallas,* 2,781 ..... I-6
Butler, *Bates,* 4,209 ..... G-3
Byrnes Mill, *Jefferson,* 2,376 ..... R-14
Cabool, *Texas,* 2,168 ..... J-8
California, *Moniteau,* 4,005 ..... F-7
Calverton Park, *Saint Louis,* 1,322 ..... U-15
Camdenton, *Camden,* 2,779 ..... H-7
Cameron, *Clinton,* 8,312 ..... C-4
Campbell, *Dunklin,* 1,883 ..... L-12
Canton, *Lewis,* 2,557 ..... B-9
Cape Girardeau, *Cape Girardeau,* 35,349 ..... J-13
Carl Junction, *Jasper,* 5,294 ..... J-3
Carrollton, *Carroll,* 4,122 ..... D-5
Carterville, *Jasper,* 1,850 ..... W-6
Carthage, *Jasper,* 12,668 ..... J-3
Caruthersville, *Pemiscot,* 6,760 ..... M-13
Cassville, *Barry,* 2,890 ..... K-4
•Castle Point, *Saint Louis,* 4,559 ..... V-16
•Cedar Hill, *Jefferson,* 1,703 ..... G-11
Centerville, *Reynolds,* 171 ..... I-10
Centralia, *Boone,* 3,774 ..... E-8
Chaffee, *Scott,* 3,044 ..... J-13
Charlack, *Saint Louis,* 1,431 ..... W-14
Charleston, *Mississippi,* 4,732 ..... K-14
Chesterfield, *Saint Louis,* 46,802 ..... P-14
Chillicothe, *Livingston,* 8,968 ..... C-5
Clarkson Valley, *Saint Louis,* 2,675 ..... Q-14
Clarkton, *Dunklin,* 1,330 ..... L-12
Claycomo, *Clay,* 1,267 ..... Q-3
Clayton, *Saint Louis,* 12,825 ..... F-11
Clever, *Christian,* 1,010 ..... K-5
Clinton, *Henry,* 9,311 ..... G-4
Cole Camp, *Benton,* 1,028 ..... G-6
Columbia, *Boone,* 84,531 ..... E-7
•Concord, *Saint Louis,* 16,689 ..... Z-14
Concordia, *Lafayette,* 2,360 ..... R-8
Cool Valley, *Saint Louis,* 1,081 ..... V-15
Cottleville, *Saint Charles,* 1,928 ..... P-14
Country Club, *Andrew,* 1,846 ..... C-2
Country Club Hills, *Saint Louis,* 1,381 ..... V-15
Crane, *Stone,* 1,390 ..... K-5
Crestwood, *Saint Louis,* 11,863 ..... Q-15
Creve Coeur, *Saint Louis,* 16,500 ..... P-15
Crocker, *Pulaski,* 1,033 ..... H-7
Crystal City, *Jefferson,* 4,247 ..... T-15
Cuba, *Crawford,* 3,230 ..... H-9
Dardenne Prairie, *Saint Charles,* 4,384 ..... O-13
De Soto, *Jefferson,* 6,375 ..... H-11
Dellwood, *Saint Louis,* 5,255 ..... P-16
Des Peres, *Saint Louis,* 8,592 ..... Y-13
Desloge, *Saint Francois,* 4,802 ..... H-11
Dexter, *Stoddard,* 7,356 ..... K-12
Dixon, *Pulaski,* 1,570 ..... H-8
Doniphan, *Ripley,* 1,932 ..... L-10
Drexel, *Cass,* 1,090 ..... G-3
Duenweg, *Jasper,* 1,034 ..... W-6
Duquesne, *Jasper,* 1,640 ..... J-3
East Prairie, *Mississippi,* 3,227 ..... K-13
Edina, *Knox,* 1,233 ..... B-8
El Dorado Springs, *Cedar,* 3,775 ..... H-4
Eldon, *Miller,* 4,895 ..... G-7
Ellington, *Reynolds,* 1,045 ..... J-10
Ellisville, *Saint Louis,* 9,104 ..... Q-14
Elsberry, *Lincoln,* 2,047 ..... E-10
Eminence, *Shannon,* 548 ..... J-9
Eureka, *Saint Louis,* 7,676 ..... G-11
Excelsior Springs, *Clay,* 10,847 ..... D-4
Fair Grove, *Greene,* 1,107 ..... J-6
Farmington, *Saint Francois,* 13,924 ..... I-11
Fayette, *Howard,* 2,793 ..... E-7
Fenton, *Saint Louis,* 4,360 ..... Q-15
Ferguson, *Saint Louis,* 22,406 ..... P-16
Festus, *Jefferson,* 9,660 ..... G-11
Florissant, *Saint Louis,* 50,497 ..... F-11
Forsyth, *Taney,* 1,686 ..... K-6
•Fort Leonard Wood, *Pulaski,* 13,666 ..... I-8
Four Seasons, *Camden,* 1,493 ..... G-7
Fredericktown, *Madison,* 3,928 ..... I-12
Frontenac, *Saint Louis,* 3,483 ..... X-13
Fulton, *Callaway,* 12,128 ..... F-8
Gainesville, *Ozark,* 632 ..... L-7
Galena, *Stone,* 451 ..... K-5
Gallatin, *Daviess,* 1,789 ..... C-4
Garden City, *Cass,* 1,500 ..... F-4
Gerald, *Franklin,* 1,171 ..... G-9
Gideon, *New Madrid,* 1,113 ..... L-12
Gladstone, *Clay,* 26,365 ..... E-3
Glasgow, *Howard,* 1,263 ..... E-6
•Glasgow Village, *Saint Louis,* 5,234 ..... P-16
Glendale, *Saint Louis,* 5,767 ..... Y-14
Goodman, *McDonald,* 1,183 ..... K-3
Gower, *Clinton,* 1,399 ..... D-3
Grain Valley, *Jackson,* 5,160 ..... R-4
Granby, *Newton,* 2,121 ..... K-3
Grandview, *Jackson,* 24,881 ..... F-3
Grant City, *Worth,* 926 ..... A-3
•Gray Summit, *Franklin,* 2,640 ..... G-10
Green Park, *Saint Louis,* 2,666 ..... Z-14

Explanation of symbols: • - Census Designated Place (CDP)

Greenfield, *Dade,* 1,358 ..... I-4
Greenville, *Wayne,* 451 ..... J-11
Greenwood, *Jackson,* 3,952 ..... S-4
Hamilton, *Caldwell,* 1,813 ..... C-4
Hanley Hills, *Saint Louis,* 2,124 ..... W-15
Hannibal, *Marion,* 17,757 ..... C-9
Harrisonville, *Cass,* 8,946 ..... F-3
Hartville, *Wright,* 607 ..... J-7
Hayti, *Pemiscot,* 3,207 ..... M-13
Hazelwood, *Saint Louis,* 26,206 ..... O-15
Herculaneum, *Jefferson,* 2,805 ..... S-15
Hermann, *Gasconade,* 2,674 ..... F-9
Hermitage, *Hickory,* 406 ..... H-5
Higginsville, *Lafayette,* 4,682 ..... E-5
•High Ridge, *Jefferson,* 4,236 ..... R-14
Hillsboro, *Jefferson,* 1,675 ..... G-11
Hillsdale, *Saint Louis,* 1,477 ..... W-15
Holden, *Johnson,* 2,510 ..... F-4
Hollister, *Taney,* 3,867 ..... Z-11
Holts Summit, *Callaway,* 2,935 ..... F-8
Houston, *Texas,* 1,992 ..... J-8
Huntsville, *Randolph,* 1,553 ..... D-7
•Imperial, *Jefferson,* 4,373 ..... S-15
Independence, *Jackson,* 113,288 ..... E-3
Ironton, *Iron,* 1,471 ..... I-11
Jackson, *Cape Girardeau,* 11,947 ..... J-13
Jasper, *Jasper,* 1,011 ..... J-3
Jefferson City, *Cole,* 39,636 ..... F-8
Jennings, *Saint Louis,* 15,469 ..... P-16
Joplin, *Jasper,* 45,504 ..... J-3
Kahoka, *Clark,* 2,241 ..... A-9
Kansas City, *Jackson,* 441,545 ..... E-3
Kearney, *Clay,* 5,472 ..... D-3
Kennett, *Dunklin,* 11,260 ..... M-12
Keytesville, *Chariton,* 533 ..... D-6
Kimberling City, *Stone,* 2,253 ..... L-5
King City, *Gentry,* 1,012 ..... B-3
Kingston, *Caldwell,* 287 ..... D-4
Kirksville, *Adair,* 16,988 ..... B-7
Kirkwood, *Saint Louis,* 27,324 ..... F-11
Knob Noster, *Johnson,* 2,462 ..... T-8
La Grange, *Lewis,* 1,000 ..... B-9
La Monte, *Pettis,* 1,064 ..... F-5
La Plata, *Macon,* 1,486 ..... C-7
Ladue, *Saint Louis,* 8,645 ..... P-15
Lake Lotawana, *Jackson,* 1,872 ..... S-4
Lake Ozark, *Miller,* 1,489 ..... G-7
Lake Saint Louis, *Saint Charles,* 10,169 ..... O-13
Lakeshire, *Saint Louis,* 1,375 ..... Z-14
Lamar, *Barton,* 4,425 ..... I-3
Lancaster, *Schuyler,* 737 ..... A-7
Lathrop, *Clinton,* 2,092 ..... D-3
Lawson, *Ray,* 2,336 ..... D-4
Leadwood, *Saint Francois,* 1,160 ..... H-11
Lebanon, *Laclede,* 12,155 ..... I-7
Lees Summit, *Jackson,* 70,700 ..... F-3
•Lemay, *Saint Louis,* 17,215 ..... Q-16
Lexington, *Lafayette,* 4,453 ..... E-4
Liberty, *Clay,* 26,232 ..... E-3
Licking, *Texas,* 1,471 ..... I-8
Lilbourn, *New Madrid,* 1,303 ..... L-13
Lincoln, *Benton,* 1,026 ..... G-5
Linn, *Osage,* 1,354 ..... G-8
Linneus, *Linn,* 369 ..... C-6
Louisiana, *Pike,* 3,863 ..... D-10
Macon, *Macon,* 5,538 ..... C-7
Malden, *Dunklin,* 4,782 ..... L-12
Manchester, *Saint Louis,* 19,161 ..... Y-12
Mansfield, *Wright,* 1,349 ..... J-7
Maplewood, *Saint Louis,* 9,228 ..... X-15
Marble Hill, *Bollinger,* 1,502 ..... J-12
Marceline, *Linn,* 2,558 ..... C-6
Marionville, *Lawrence,* 2,113 ..... K-5
Marlborough, *Saint Louis,* 2,235 ..... Y-14
Marshall, *Saline,* 12,433 ..... E-6
Marshfield, *Webster,* 5,720 ..... J-6
Maryland Heights, *Saint Louis,* 25,756 ..... P-15
Maryville, *Nodaway,* 10,581 ..... B-2
Maysville, *DeKalb,* 1,212 ..... C-3
•Mehlville, *Saint Louis,* 28,822 ..... G-11
Memphis, *Scotland,* 2,061 ..... A-8
Merriam Woods, *Taney,* 1,142 ..... K-6
Mexico, *Audrain,* 11,320 ..... E-8
Milan, *Sullivan,* 1,958 ..... B-6
Miner, *Scott,* 1,056 ..... K-13
Moberly, *Randolph,* 11,945 ..... D-7
Moline Acres, *Saint Louis,* 2,662 ..... V-16
Monett, *Barry,* 7,396 ..... K-4
Monroe City, *Monroe,* 2,588 ..... D-9
Montgomery City, *Montgomery,* 2,442 ..... E-9
Monticello, *Lewis,* 126 ..... B-9
Morehouse, *New Madrid,* 1,015 ..... K-13
Moscow Mills, *Lincoln,* 1,742 ..... E-10
Mound City, *Holt,* 1,193 ..... B-2
Mount Vernon, *Lawrence,* 4,017 ..... J-4
Mountain Grove, *Wright,* 4,574 ..... J-7
Mountain View, *Howell,* 2,430 ..... K-9
•Murphy, *Jefferson,* 9,048 ..... G-11
Neosho, *Newton,* 10,505 ..... K-3
Nevada, *Vernon,* 8,607 ..... H-3
New Franklin, *Howard,* 1,145 ..... E-7
New Haven, *Franklin,* 1,867 ..... Q-10
New London, *Ralls,* 1,001 ..... D-9
New Madrid, *New Madrid,* 3,334 ..... L-13
Nixa, *Christian,* 12,124 ..... K-5
Noel, *McDonald,* 1,480 ..... L-3
Normandy, *Saint Louis,* 5,153 ..... V-15
North Kansas City, *Clay,* 4,714 ..... Q-2
Northwoods, *Saint Louis,* 4,643 ..... W-15
Norwood Court, *Saint Louis,* 1,061 ..... V-15
O'Fallon, *Saint Charles,* 46,169 ..... O-13
Oak Grove, *Jackson,* 5,535 ..... R-5
Oakland, *Saint Louis,* 1,540 ..... Y-14
•Oakville, *Saint Louis,* 35,309 ..... G-11
Odessa, *Lafayette,* 4,818 ..... E-4
Olivette, *Saint Louis,* 7,438 ..... W-14
Oran, *Scott,* 1,264 ..... J-13
Oregon, *Holt,* 935 ..... C-2
Osage Beach, *Camden,* 3,662 ..... H-7
Osceola, *Saint Clair,* 835 ..... H-5
Overland, *Saint Louis,* 16,838 ..... P-15
Owensville, *Gasconade,* 2,500 ..... G-9
Ozark, *Christian,* 9,665 ..... K-6
Pacific, *Franklin,* 5,482 ..... R-13
Pagedale, *Saint Louis,* 3,616 ..... W-15
Palmyra, *Marion,* 3,467 ..... C-9
Paris, *Monroe,* 1,529 ..... D-8
Park Hills, *Saint Francois,* 7,861 ..... H-11
Parkville, *Platte,* 4,059 ..... Q-2
Pasadena Hills, *Saint Louis,* 1,267 ..... W-15
Peculiar, *Cass,* 2,604 ..... T-3
Perryville, *Perry,* 7,667 ..... I-12
Pevely, *Jefferson,* 3,768 ..... G-11
Piedmont, *Wayne,* 1,992 ..... J-11
Pierce City, *Lawrence,* 1,385 ..... K-4
Pine Lawn, *Saint Louis,* 4,204 ..... W-15
Pineville, *McDonald,* 768 ..... L-3
Platte City, *Platte,* 3,866 ..... D-2
Plattsburg, *Clinton,* 2,354 ..... D-3
Pleasant Hill, *Cass,* 5,582 ..... T-4
Pleasant Valley, *Clay,* 3,321 ..... Q-3
Poplar Bluff, *Butler,* 16,651 ..... K-11
Portageville, *New Madrid,* 3,295 ..... L-13
Potosi, *Washington,* 2,662 ..... H-10
Princeton, *Mercer,* 1,047 ..... B-5
Purdy, *Barry,* 1,103 ..... K-4
Puxico, *Stoddard,* 1,145 ..... K-12
Raymore, *Cass,* 11,146 ..... F-3
Raytown, *Jackson,* 30,388 ..... R-3
Republic, *Greene,* 8,438 ..... J-5
Rich Hill, *Bates,* 1,461 ..... H-3
Richland, *Pulaski,* 1,805 ..... H-7
Richmond, *Ray,* 6,116 ..... E-4
Richmond Heights, *Saint Louis,* 9,602 ..... X-15
Riverside, *Platte,* 2,979 ..... E-3
Riverview, *Saint Louis,* 3,146 ..... V-16
Rock Hill, *Saint Louis,* 4,765 ..... X-14
Rock Port, *Atchison,* 1,395 ..... A-1
Rogersville, *Webster,* 1,508 ..... J-6
Rolla, *Phelps,* 16,367 ..... H-8
Saint Ann, *Saint Louis,* 13,607 ..... P-15
Saint Charles, *Saint Charles,* 60,321 ..... O-15
Saint Clair, *Franklin,* 4,390 ..... G-10
Saint George, *Saint Louis,* 1,288 ..... Z-15
Saint James, *Phelps,* 3,704 ..... H-9
Saint John, *Saint Louis,* 6,871 ..... V-14
Saint Joseph, *Buchanan,* 73,990 ..... C-2
Saint Louis, *Saint Louis City,* 348,189 ..... F-12
Saint Martins, *Cole,* 1,023 ..... F-7
Saint Paul, *Saint Charles,* 1,634 ..... O-13
Saint Peters, *Saint Charles,* 51,381 ..... O-14
Saint Robert, *Pulaski,* 2,760 ..... H-8
Sainte Genevieve, *Sainte Genevieve,* 4,476 ..... H-12
Salem, *Dent,* 4,854 ..... I-9
Salisbury, *Chariton,* 1,726 ..... D-6
•Sappington, *Saint Louis,* 7,287 ..... Z-14
Sarcoxie, *Jasper,* 1,354 ..... J-4
Savannah, *Andrew,* 4,762 ..... C-2
Scott City, *Scott,* 4,591 ..... J-13
Sedalia, *Pettis,* 20,339 ..... F-6
Senath, *Dunklin,* 1,650 ..... M-12
Seneca, *Newton,* 2,135 ..... K-3
Seymour, *Webster,* 1,834 ..... J-6
Shelbina, *Shelby,* 1,943 ..... C-8
Shelbyville, *Shelby,* 682 ..... C-8
•Shell Knob, *Barry,* 1,393 ..... Z-9
Shrewsbury, *Saint Louis,* 6,644 ..... Y-14
Sikeston, *Scott,* 16,992 ..... K-13
Slater, *Saline,* 2,083 ..... E-6
Smithville, *Clay,* 5,514 ..... D-3
•Spanish Lake, *Saint Louis,* 21,337 ..... U-16
Sparta, *Christian,* 1,144 ..... X-12
Springfield, *Greene,* 151,580 ..... J-5
Stanberry, *Gentry,* 1,243 ..... B-3
Steele, *Pemiscot,* 2,263 ..... M-13
Steelville, *Crawford,* 1,429 ..... H-9
Stockton, *Cedar,* 1,960 ..... I-4
Strafford, *Greene,* 1,845 ..... J-6
Sugar Creek, *Jackson,* 3,839 ..... Q-3
Sullivan, *Franklin,* 6,351 ..... G-10
Sunset Hills, *Saint Louis,* 8,267 ..... Z-13
Sweet Springs, *Saline,* 1,628 ..... E-5
Tarkio, *Atchison,* 1,935 ..... A-1
Thayer, *Oregon,* 2,201 ..... L-9
Tipton, *Moniteau,* 3,261 ..... F-6
Town and Country, *Saint Louis,* 10,894 ..... Q-15
Trenton, *Grundy,* 6,216 ..... B-5
Troy, *Lincoln,* 6,737 ..... E-10
Tuscumbia, *Miller,* 218 ..... G-7
Union, *Franklin,* 7,757 ..... G-10
Unionville, *Putnam,* 2,041 ..... A-6
University City, *Saint Louis,* 37,428 ..... P-16
Valley Park, *Saint Louis,* 6,518 ..... Q-15
Van Buren, *Carter,* 845 ..... K-10
Vandalia, *Audrain,* 2,529 ..... D-9
Velda City, *Saint Louis,* 1,616 ..... W-15
Velda Village Hills, *Saint Louis,* 1,090 ..... W-15
Versailles, *Morgan,* 2,565 ..... G-6
Vienna, *Maries,* 628 ..... G-8
•Villa Ridge, *Franklin,* 2,417 ..... R-12
Vinita Park, *Saint Louis,* 1,924 ..... W-14
Warrensburg, *Johnson,* 16,340 ..... F-5
Warrenton, *Warren,* 5,281 ..... F-10
Warsaw, *Benton,* 2,070 ..... G-5
Warson Woods, *Saint Louis,* 1,983 ..... X-14
Washington, *Franklin,* 13,243 ..... F-10
Waynesville, *Pulaski,* 3,507 ..... H-8
Weatherby Lake, *Platte,* 1,873 ..... P-1
Webb City, *Jasper,* 9,812 ..... J-3
Webster Groves, *Saint Louis,* 23,230 ..... Q-15
Weldon Spring, *Saint Charles,* 5,270 ..... P-13
Wellston, *Saint Louis,* 2,460 ..... W-15
Wellsville, *Montgomery,* 1,423 ..... E-9
Wentzville, *Saint Charles,* 6,896 ..... O-12
West Plains, *Howell,* 10,866 ..... K-8
Weston, *Platte,* 1,631 ..... D-2
•Whiteman AFB, *Johnson,* 3,814 ..... T-8
Willard, *Greene,* 3,193 ..... J-5
Willow Springs, *Howell,* 2,147 ..... K-8
Winchester, *Saint Louis,* 1,651 ..... Q-14
Windsor, *Henry,* 3,087 ..... G-5
Winona, *Shannon,* 1,290 ..... K-9
Woodson Terrace, *Saint Louis,* 4,189 ..... V-14
Wright City, *Warren,* 1,532 ..... F-10

MONTANA

COUNTIES

(56 Counties)

Name of County	Population	Location on Map
BEAVERHEAD	9,202	H-3
BIG HORN	12,671	H-12
BLAINE	7,009	A-10
BROADWATER	4,385	G-6
CARBON	9,552	I-9
CARTER	1,360	G-16
CASCADE	80,357	E-6
CHOUTEAU	5,970	C-7
CUSTER	11,696	F-14
DANIELS	2,017	A-14
DAWSON	9,059	D-15
DEER LODGE	9,417	G-4
FALLON	2,837	F-16
FERGUS	11,893	D-9
FLATHEAD	74,471	A-3
GALLATIN	67,831	G-7
GARFIELD	1,279	D-12
GLACIER	13,247	A-4
GOLDEN VALLEY	1,042	G-10
GRANITE	2,830	F-4
HILL	16,673	A-8
JEFFERSON	10,049	H-6
JUDITH BASIN	2,329	E-8
LAKE	26,507	C-3
LEWIS AND CLARK	55,716	E-5
LIBERTY	2,158	A-7
LINCOLN	18,837	A-1
MADISON	6,851	H-5
MCCONE	1,977	C-14
MEAGHER	1,932	F-7
MINERAL	3,884	E-2
MISSOULA	95,802	E-4
MUSSELSHELL	4,497	F-10
PARK	15,694	G-8
PETROLEUM	493	E-11
PHILLIPS	4,601	A-11
PONDERA	6,424	C-5
POWDER RIVER	1,858	H-14
POWELL	7,180	E-4
PRAIRIE	1,199	E-14
RAVALLI	36,070	G-3
RICHLAND	9,667	C-15
ROOSEVELT	10,620	B-15
ROSEBUD	9,383	F-12
SANDERS	10,227	D-1
SHERIDAN	4,105	A-15
SILVER BOW	34,606	H-5
STILLWATER	8,195	H-10
SWEET GRASS	3,609	G-8
TETON	6,445	C-5
TOOLE	5,267	A-7
TREASURE	861	G-12
VALLEY	7,675	A-13
WHEATLAND	2,259	F-9
WIBAUX	1,068	F-16
YELLOWSTONE	129,352	G-11
TOTAL	**902,195**	

CITIES AND TOWNS

Note: The first name is that of the city or town, second, that of the county in which it is located, then the population and location on the map.

•Absarokee, *Stillwater,* 1,234	I-10
Anaconda, *Deer Lodge,* 9,417	G-5
Baker, *Fallon,* 1,695	F-17
Belgrade, *Gallatin,* 5,728	H-7
•Big Sky, *Gallatin,* 1,221	I-7
Big Timber, *Sweet Grass,* 1,650	H-9
•Bigfork, *Flathead,* 1,421	C-3
Billings, *Yellowstone,* 89,847	H-11
•Bonner-West Riverside, *Missoula,* 1,693	F-3
Boulder, *Jefferson,* 1,300	G-6
Bozeman, *Gallatin,* 27,509	H-7
Broadus, *Powder River,* 451	I-15
Browning, *Glacier,* 1,065	B-5
Butte, *Silver Bow,* 33,892	G-5
Chester, *Liberty,* 871	B-8
Chinook, *Blaine,* 1,386	B-10
Choteau, *Teton,* 1,781	D-6
Circle, *McCone,* 644	D-15
•Clancy, *Jefferson,* 1,406	F-6
Colstrip, *Rosebud,* 2,346	H-14
Columbia Falls, *Flathead,* 3,645	B-3
Columbus, *Stillwater,* 1,748	H-10
Conrad, *Pondera,* 2,753	C-6
•Crow Agency, *Big Horn,* 1,552	H-12
Cut Bank, *Glacier,* 3,105	B-6
Deer Lodge, *Powell,* 3,421	G-5
Dillon, *Beaverhead,* 3,752	I-5
East Helena, *Lewis and Clark,* 1,642	L-2
•East Missoula, *Lewis and Clark,* 2,070	F-3
Ekalaka, *Carter,* 410	G-16
Eureka, *Lincoln,* 1,017	A-2
•Evergreen, *Flathead,* 6,215	C-3
Forsyth, *Rosebud,* 1,944	G-13
•Fort Belknap Agency, *Blaine,* 1,262	B-10
Fort Benton, *Chouteau,* 1,594	D-8
•Four Corners, *Lewis and Clark,* 1,828	H-7
Glasgow, *Valley,* 3,253	C-13
Glendive, *Dawson,* 4,729	E-16
Great Falls, *Cascade,* 56,690	D-7
Hamilton, *Ravalli,* 3,705	G-3
Hardin, *Big Horn,* 3,384	H-12
Harlowton, *Wheatland,* 1,062	G-9
Havre, *Hill,* 9,621	B-9
Helena, *Lewis and Clark,* 25,780	F-6
•Helena Valley Northeast, *Lewis and Clark,* 2,122	F-6
•Helena Valley Northwest, *Lewis and Clark,* 2,082	F-6
•Helena Valley Southwest, *Lewis and Clark,* 7,141	L-2
•Helena Valley West Central, *Lewis and Clark,* 6,983	L-2
•Helena West Side, *Lewis and Clark,* 1,711	L-2
Hysham, *Treasure,* 330	G-13
Jordan, *Garfield,* 364	E-13
Kalispell, *Flathead,* 14,223	C-3
•Lakeside, *Flathead,* 1,679	C-3
•Lame Deer, *Rosebud,* 2,018	H-13
Laurel, *Yellowstone,* 6,255	H-11
Lewistown, *Fergus,* 5,813	E-10
Libby, *Lincoln,* 2,626	B-1
•Lincoln, *Lewis and Clark,* 1,100	E-5
Livingston, *Park,* 6,851	H-8
•Lockwood, *Yellowstone,* 4,306	H-11
•Lolo, *Missoula,* 3,388	F-3
•Malmstrom AFB, *Cascade,* 4,544	D-7
Malta, *Phillips,* 2,120	C-12
Manhattan, *Gallatin,* 1,396	H-7
Miles City, *Custer,* 8,487	G-15
Missoula, *Missoula,* 57,053	F-3
•Montana City, *Jefferson,* 2,094	M-2
•North Browning, *Glacier,* 2,200	B-5
•Orchard Homes, *Missoula,* 5,199	F-3
•Pablo, *Lake,* 1,814	D-3
Philipsburg, *Granite,* 914	G-4
Plains, *Sanders,* 1,126	D-2
Plentywood, *Sheridan,* 2,061	B-16
Polson, *Lake,* 4,041	D-3
Red Lodge, *Carbon,* 2,177	I-10
Ronan, *Lake,* 1,812	D-3
Roundup, *Musselshell,* 1,931	G-11
Ryegate, *Golden Valley,* 268	G-10
Scobey, *Daniels,* 1,082	B-15
•Seeley Lake, *Missoula,* 1,436	E-4
Shelby, *Toole,* 3,216	B-6
Sidney, *Richland,* 4,774	D-17
•South Browning, *Glacier,* 1,677	B-5
Stanford, *Judith Basin,* 454	E-8
Stevensville, *Ravalli,* 1,553	F-3
•Sun Prairie, *Cascade,* 1,772	D-7
Superior, *Mineral,* 893	E-2
Terry, *Prairie,* 611	F-15
Thompson Falls, *Sanders,* 1,321	D-2
Three Forks, *Gallatin,* 1,728	H-7
Townsend, *Broadwater,* 1,867	G-7
Virginia City, *Madison,* 130	I-6
•West Glendive, *Dawson,* 1,833	E-16
West Yellowstone, *Gallatin,* 1,177	J-7
White Sulphur Springs, *Meagher,* 984	F-8
Whitefish, *Flathead,* 5,032	B-3
Whitehall, *Jefferson,* 1,044	H-6
Wibaux, *Wibaux,* 567	E-17
Winnett, *Petroleum,* 185	E-11
Wolf Point, *Roosevelt,* 2,663	C-15

Explanation of symbols: • - Census Designated Place (CDP)

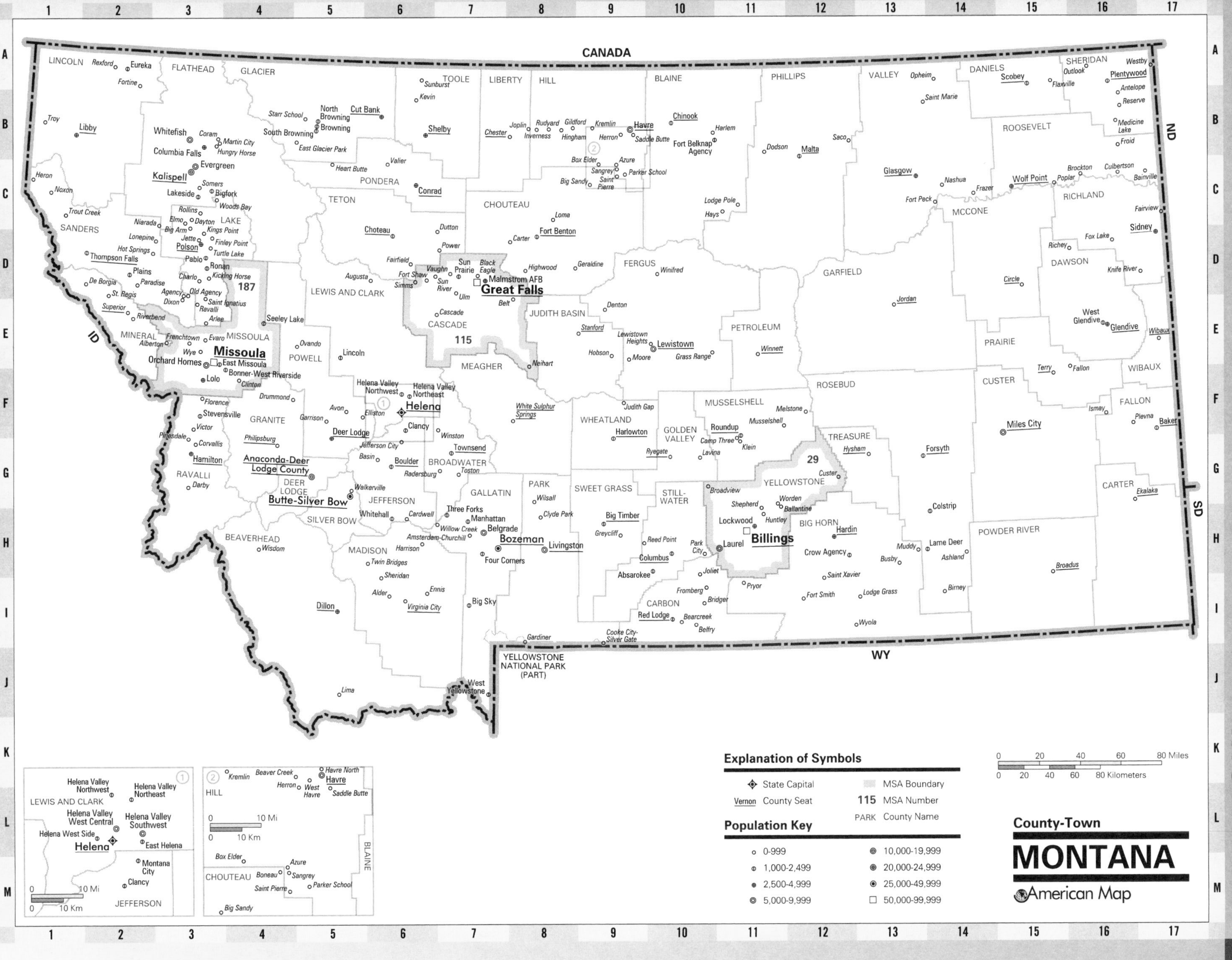
CANADA
ND
SD
WY
ID
YELLOWSTONE NATIONAL PARK (PART)
Explanation of Symbols
State Capital
Vernon County Seat
MSA Boundary
115 MSA Number
PARK County Name
Population Key
0-999
1,000-2,499
2,500-4,999
5,000-9,999
10,000-19,999
20,000-24,999
25,000-49,999
50,000-99,999
0 20 40 60 80 Miles
0 20 40 60 80 Kilometers
County-Town
MONTANA
American Map

COUNTIES

(93 Counties)

Name of County	Population	Location on Map
ADAMS	31,151	H-11
ANTELOPE	7,452	D-12
ARTHUR	444	E-5
BANNER	819	E-1
BLAINE	583	D-8
BOONE	6,259	E-12
BOX BUTTE	12,158	C-2
BOYD	2,438	B-10
BROWN	3,525	B-8
BUFFALO	42,259	G-10
BURT	7,791	D-15
BUTLER	8,767	F-14
CASS	24,334	G-15
CEDAR	9,615	B-13
CHASE	4,068	H-5
CHERRY	6,148	B-5
CHEYENNE	9,830	F-2
CLAY	7,039	H-12
COLFAX	10,441	E-14
CUMING	10,203	D-14
CUSTER	11,793	E-8
DAKOTA	20,253	C-15
DAWES	9,060	B-2
DAWSON	24,365	G-9
DEUEL	2,098	F-3
DIXON	6,339	C-14
DODGE	36,160	E-14
DOUGLAS	463,585	F-15
DUNDY	2,292	I-5
FILLMORE	6,634	H-13
FRANKLIN	3,574	I-10
FRONTIER	3,099	H-7
FURNAS	5,324	I-8
GAGE	22,993	I-15
GARDEN	2,292	D-3
GARFIELD	1,902	D-10
GOSPER	2,143	H-8
GRANT	747	D-5
GREELEY	2,714	F-11
HALL	53,534	G-11
HAMILTON	9,403	G-12
HARLAN	3,786	I-9
HAYES	1,068	H-6
HITCHCOCK	3,111	I-6
HOLT	11,551	B-10
HOOKER	783	D-6
HOWARD	6,567	F-11
JEFFERSON	8,333	I-13
JOHNSON	4,488	I-15
KEARNEY	6,882	H-10
KEITH	8,875	F-5
KEYA PAHA	983	B-8
KIMBALL	4,089	F-1
KNOX	9,374	B-12
LANCASTER	250,291	G-14
LINCOLN	34,632	F-6
LOGAN	774	E-7
LOUP	712	D-9
MADISON	35,226	E-12
MCPHERSON	533	E-6
MERRICK	8,204	F-12
MORRILL	5,440	D-2
NANCE	4,038	F-12
NEMAHA	7,576	I-16
NUCKOLLS	5,057	I-12
OTOE	15,396	G-16
PAWNEE	3,087	I-15
PERKINS	3,200	G-5
PHELPS	9,747	H-9
PIERCE	7,857	D-13
PLATTE	31,662	E-13
POLK	5,639	F-13
RED WILLOW	11,448	I-7
RICHARDSON	9,531	I-16
ROCK	1,756	C-9
SALINE	13,843	H-14
SARPY	122,595	G-15
SAUNDERS	19,830	F-14
SCOTTS BLUFF	36,951	E-1
SEWARD	16,496	G-13
SHERIDAN	6,198	B-3
SHERMAN	3,318	F-10
SIOUX	1,475	B-1
STANTON	6,455	E-13
THAYER	6,055	I-13
THOMAS	729	E-7
THURSTON	7,171	D-15
VALLEY	4,647	E-10
WASHINGTON	18,780	E-15
WAYNE	9,851	D-14
WEBSTER	4,061	I-11
WHEELER	886	D-11
YORK	14,598	G-13
TOTAL	**1,711,263**	

CITIES AND TOWNS

Note: The first name is that of the city or town, second, that of the county in which it is located, then the population and location on the map.

Ainsworth, *Brown*, 1,862 .... C-9
Albion, *Boone*, 1,797 .... E-12
Alliance, *Box Butte*, 8,959 .... D-3
Alma, *Harlan*, 1,214 .... I-10
Arapahoe, *Furnas*, 1,028 .... I-9
Arlington, *Washington*, 1,197 .... F-15
Arthur, *Arthur*, 145 .... E-5
Ashland, *Saunders*, 2,262 .... G-15
Atkinson, *Holt*, 1,244 .... C-10
Auburn, *Nemaha*, 3,350 .... H-16
Aurora, *Hamilton*, 4,225 .... G-12
Bartlett, *Wheeler*, 128 .... E-11
Bassett, *Rock*, 743 .... C-9
Battle Creek, *Madison*, 1,158 .... D-13
Bayard, *Morrill*, 1,247 .... E-2
Beatrice, *Gage*, 12,496 .... I-15
Beaver City, *Furnas*, 641 .... I-9
Bellevue, *Sarpy*, 44,382 .... F-16
Benkelman, *Dundy*, 1,006 .... I-5
Blair, *Washington*, 7,512 .... E-16
Bloomfield, *Knox*, 1,126 .... C-13
Brewster, *Blaine*, 29 .... E-9
Bridgeport, *Morrill*, 1,594 .... E-3
Broken Bow, *Custer*, 3,491 .... F-9
Burwell, *Garfield*, 1,130 .... E-10
Butte, *Boyd*, 366 .... B-11
Cambridge, *Furnas*, 1,041 .... I-8
Center, *Knox*, 90 .... C-12
Central City, *Merrick*, 2,998 .... G-12
Chadron, *Dawes*, 5,634 .... B-3
•Chalco, *Sarpy*, 10,736 .... F-16
Chappell, *Deuel*, 983 .... G-4
Clay Center, *Clay*, 861 .... H-12
Columbus, *Platte*, 20,971 .... F-13
Cozad, *Dawson*, 4,163 .... G-8
Crawford, *Dawes*, 1,107 .... B-2
Creighton, *Knox*, 1,270 .... C-12
Crete, *Saline*, 6,028 .... H-14
Dakota City, *Dakota*, 1,821 .... C-15
David City, *Butler*, 2,597 .... F-14
Eagle, *Cass*, 1,105 .... G-15
Elkhorn, *Douglas*, 6,062 .... F-16
Elwood, *Gosper*, 761 .... H-9
Fairbury, *Jefferson*, 4,262 .... I-14
Falls City, *Richardson*, 4,671 .... I-17
Franklin, *Franklin*, 1,026 .... I-10
Fremont, *Dodge*, 25,174 .... F-15
Friend, *Saline*, 1,174 .... H-14
Fullerton, *Nance*, 1,378 .... F-12
Geneva, *Fillmore*, 2,226 .... H-13
Gering, *Scotts Bluff*, 7,751 .... E-2
Gibbon, *Buffalo*, 1,759 .... H-11
Gordon, *Sheridan*, 1,756 .... B-4
Gothenburg, *Dawson*, 3,619 .... G-8
Grand Island, *Hall*, 42,940 .... G-12
Grant, *Perkins*, 1,225 .... G-5
Greeley (Greeley Center), *Greeley*, 531 .... E-11
Gretna, *Sarpy*, 2,355 .... L-16
Harrisburg, *Banner*, 75 .... E-1
Harrison, *Sioux*, 279 .... B-1
Hartington, *Cedar*, 1,640 .... C-13
Hastings, *Adams*, 24,064 .... H-11
Hayes Center, *Hayes*, 240 .... H-6
Hebron, *Thayer*, 1,565 .... I-13
Hickman, *Lancaster*, 1,084 .... H-15
Holdrege, *Phelps*, 5,636 .... H-10
Hyannis, *Grant*, 287 .... D-5
Imperial, *Chase*, 1,982 .... H-5
Kearney, *Buffalo*, 27,431 .... H-10
Kimball, *Kimball*, 2,559 .... F-1
La Vista, *Sarpy*, 11,699 .... F-16
Lexington, *Dawson*, 10,011 .... H-9
Lincoln, *Lancaster*, 225,581 .... G-15
Louisville, *Cass*, 1,046 .... G-16
Loup City, *Sherman*, 996 .... F-10
Madison, *Madison*, 2,367 .... E-13
McCook, *Red Willow*, 7,994 .... I-7
Milford, *Seward*, 2,070 .... G-14
Minden, *Kearney*, 2,964 .... H-10
Mitchell, *Scotts Bluff*, 1,831 .... D-1
Mullen, *Hooker*, 491 .... D-6
Nebraska City, *Otoe*, 7,228 .... H-16
Neligh, *Antelope*, 1,651 .... D-12
Nelson, *Nuckolls*, 587 .... I-12
Norfolk, *Madison*, 23,516 .... D-13
North Bend, *Dodge*, 1,213 .... K-14
North Platte, *Lincoln*, 23,878 .... G-7
Oakland, *Burt*, 1,367 .... E-15
•Offutt AFB, *Sarpy*, 8,901 .... L-17
Ogallala, *Keith*, 4,930 .... G-5
Omaha, *Douglas*, 390,007 .... F-16
O'Neill, *Holt*, 3,733 .... C-11
Ord, *Valley*, 2,269 .... E-10
Osceola, *Polk*, 921 .... F-13
Oshkosh, *Garden*, 887 .... F-4
Papillion, *Sarpy*, 16,363 .... F-16
Pawnee City, *Pawnee*, 1,033 .... I-16
Pender, *Thurston*, 1,148 .... D-15
Pierce, *Pierce*, 1,774 .... D-13
Plainview, *Pierce*, 1,353 .... C-12
Plattsmouth, *Cass*, 6,887 .... G-16
Ponca, *Dixon*, 1,062 .... C-14
Ralston, *Douglas*, 6,314 .... F-16
Ravenna, *Buffalo*, 1,341 .... G-10
Red Cloud, *Webster*, 1,131 .... I-11
Rushville, *Sheridan*, 999 .... B-4
Saint Paul, *Howard*, 2,218 .... F-11
Schuyler, *Colfax*, 5,371 .... F-14
Scottsbluff, *Scotts Bluff*, 14,732 .... E-2
Seward, *Seward*, 6,319 .... G-14
Shelton, *Buffalo*, 1,140 .... G-11
Sidney, *Cheyenne*, 6,282 .... F-3
South Sioux City, *Dakota*, 11,925 .... C-15
Springfield, *Sarpy*, 1,450 .... L-16
Springview, *Keya Paha*, 244 .... B-9
Stanton, *Stanton*, 1,627 .... D-14
Stapleton, *Logan*, 301 .... F-7
Stockville, *Frontier*, 36 .... H-8
Stromsburg, *Polk*, 1,232 .... G-13
Superior, *Nuckolls*, 2,055 .... I-12
Sutherland, *Lincoln*, 1,129 .... G-6
Sutton, *Clay*, 1,447 .... H-12
Syracuse, *Otoe*, 1,762 .... H-16
Taylor, *Loup*, 207 .... E-10
Tecumseh, *Johnson*, 1,716 .... H-16
Tekamah, *Burt*, 1,892 .... E-15
Thedford, *Thomas*, 211 .... D-7
Tilden, *Madison*, 1,078 .... D-12
Trenton, *Hitchcock*, 507 .... I-6
Tryon, *McPherson*, 139 .... F-7
Valentine, *Cherry*, 2,820 .... B-7
Valley, *Douglas*, 1,788 .... F-15
Wahoo, *Saunders*, 3,942 .... F-15
Wakefield, *Dixon*, 1,411 .... D-14
Waverly, *Lancaster*, 2,448 .... G-15
Wayne, *Wayne*, 5,583 .... D-14
Weeping Water, *Cass*, 1,103 .... G-16
West Point, *Cuming*, 3,660 .... E-15
Wilber, *Saline*, 1,761 .... H-14
Wisner, *Cuming*, 1,270 .... D-14
Wood River, *Hall*, 1,204 .... G-11
Wymore, *Gage*, 1,656 .... I-15
York, *York*, 8,081 .... G-13
Yutan, *Saunders*, 1,216 .... F-15

Explanation of symbols: • - Census Designated Place (CDP)

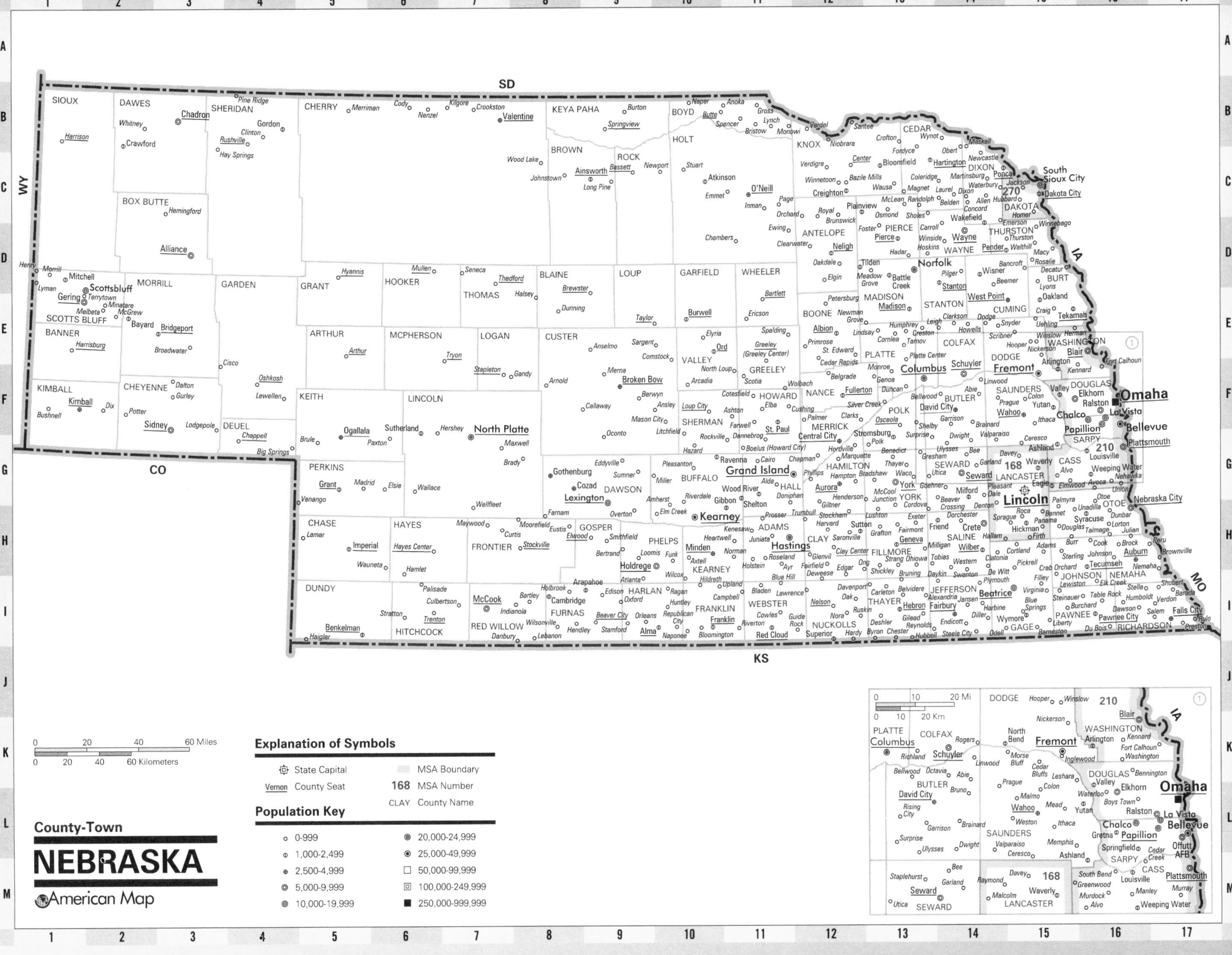
County-Town
NEBRASKA
American Map
0 20 40 60 Miles
0 20 40 60 Kilometers
Explanation of Symbols
State Capital
Vernon County Seat
MSA Boundary
168 MSA Number
CLAY County Name
Population Key
0-999
1,000-2,499
2,500-4,999
5,000-9,999
10,000-19,999
20,000-24,999
25,000-49,999
50,000-99,999
100,000-249,999
250,000-999,999
SD
IA
MO
KS
CO
WY

INDEX

COUNTIES

(17 Counties)

Name of County	Population	Location on Map
CARSON CITY (Independent City)	52,457	G-2
CHURCHILL	23,982	F-3
CLARK	1,375,765	M-9
DOUGLAS	41,259	H-2
ELKO	45,291	A-7
ESMERALDA	971	J-5
EUREKA	1,651	C-8
HUMBOLDT	16,106	A-3
LANDER	5,794	C-7
LINCOLN	4,165	I-11
LYON	34,501	G-3
MINERAL	5,071	H-3
NYE	32,485	H-6
PERSHING	6,693	D-3
STOREY	3,399	G-2
WASHOE	339,486	A-2
WHITE PINE	9,181	E-9
TOTAL	**1,998,257**	

CITIES AND TOWNS

Note: The first name is that of the city or town, second, that of the county in which it is located, then the population and location on the map.

•Battle Mountain, *Lander,* 2,871 ....D-7
•Beatty, *Nye,* 1,154 ....M-7
Boulder City, *Clark,* 14,966 ....Q-9
•Bunkerville, *Clark,* 1,014 ....M-12
Caliente, *Lincoln,* 1,123 ....K-11
Carlin, *Elko,* 2,161 ....D-8
Carson City, *Carson City,* 52,457 ....G-2
•Cold Springs, *Churchill,* 3,834 ....G-5
•Dayton, *Lyon,* 5,907 ....G-2
Elko, *Elko,* 16,708 ....D-9
Ely, *White Pine,* 4,041 ....G-11
•Enterprise, *Clark,* 14,676 ....O-10
Eureka, *Eureka,* 300 ....G-9
Fallon, *Churchill,* 7,536 ....G-3
•Fallon Station, *Churchill,* 1,265 ....G-4
•Fernley, *Lyon,* 8,543 ....F-3
•Gardnerville, *Douglas,* 3,357 ....H-2
•Gardnerville Ranchos, *Douglas,* 11,054 ....H-2
Goldfield, *Esmeralda,* 500 ....K-6
•Hawthorne, *Mineral,* 3,311 ....I-4
Henderson, *Clark,* 175,381 ....N-11
•Incline Village-Crystal Bay, *Washoe,* 9,952 ....G-1
•Indian Hills, *Douglas,* 4,407 ....H-2
•Indian Springs, *Clark,* 1,302 ....M-9
•Johnson Lane, *Douglas,* 4,837 ....H-2
•Kingsbury, *Douglas,* 2,624 ....H-1
Las Vegas, *Clark,* 478,434 ....N-10
•Laughlin, *Clark,* 7,076 ....P-11
•Lemmon Valley-Golden Valley, *Washoe,* 6,855 ....F-2
Lovelock, *Pershing,* 2,003 ....E-4
•McGill, *White Pine,* 1,054 ....G-11
Mesquite, *Clark,* 9,389 ....M-12
•Minden, *Douglas,* 2,836 ....H-2
•Moapa Valley, *Clark,* 5,784 ....M-11
•Nellis AFB, *Clark,* 8,896 ....P-8
North Las Vegas, *Clark,* 115,488 ....P-7
•Owyhee, *Elko,* 1,017 ....A-8
•Pahrump, *Nye,* 24,631 ....N-9
•Paradise, *Clark,* 186,070 ....N-10
Pioche, *Lincoln,* 850 ....J-11
Reno, *Washoe,* 180,480 ....G-2
•Sandy Valley, *Clark,* 1,804 ....O-9
•Silver Springs, *Lyon,* 4,708 ....G-3
•Smith Valley, *Lyon,* 1,425 ....H-2
•Spanish Springs, *Washoe,* 9,018 ....F-2
Sparks, *Washoe,* 66,346 ....G-2
•Spring Creek, *Elko,* 10,548 ....D-9
•Spring Valley, *Clark,* 117,390 ....N-10
•Stateline, *Clark,* 1,215 ....H-1
•Summerlin South, *Clark,* 3,735 ....P-7
•Sun Valley, *Washoe,* 19,461 ....F-2
•Sunrise Manor, *Clark,* 156,120 ....P-8
•Tonopah, *Nye,* 2,627 ....J-6
•Verdi-Mogul, *Washoe,* 2,949 ....G-1
Virginia City, *Storey,* 750 ....G-2
Wells, *Elko,* 1,346 ....C-10
West Wendover, *Elko,* 4,721 ....D-12
•Whitney, *Clark,* 18,273 ....Q-7
•Winchester, *Clark,* 26,958 ....P-7
Winnemucca, *Humboldt,* 7,174 ....C-5
Yerington, *Lyon,* 2,883 ....H-3
•Zephyr Cove-Round Hill Village, *Douglas,* 1,649 ....H-1

Explanation of symbols: • - Census Designated Place (CDP)

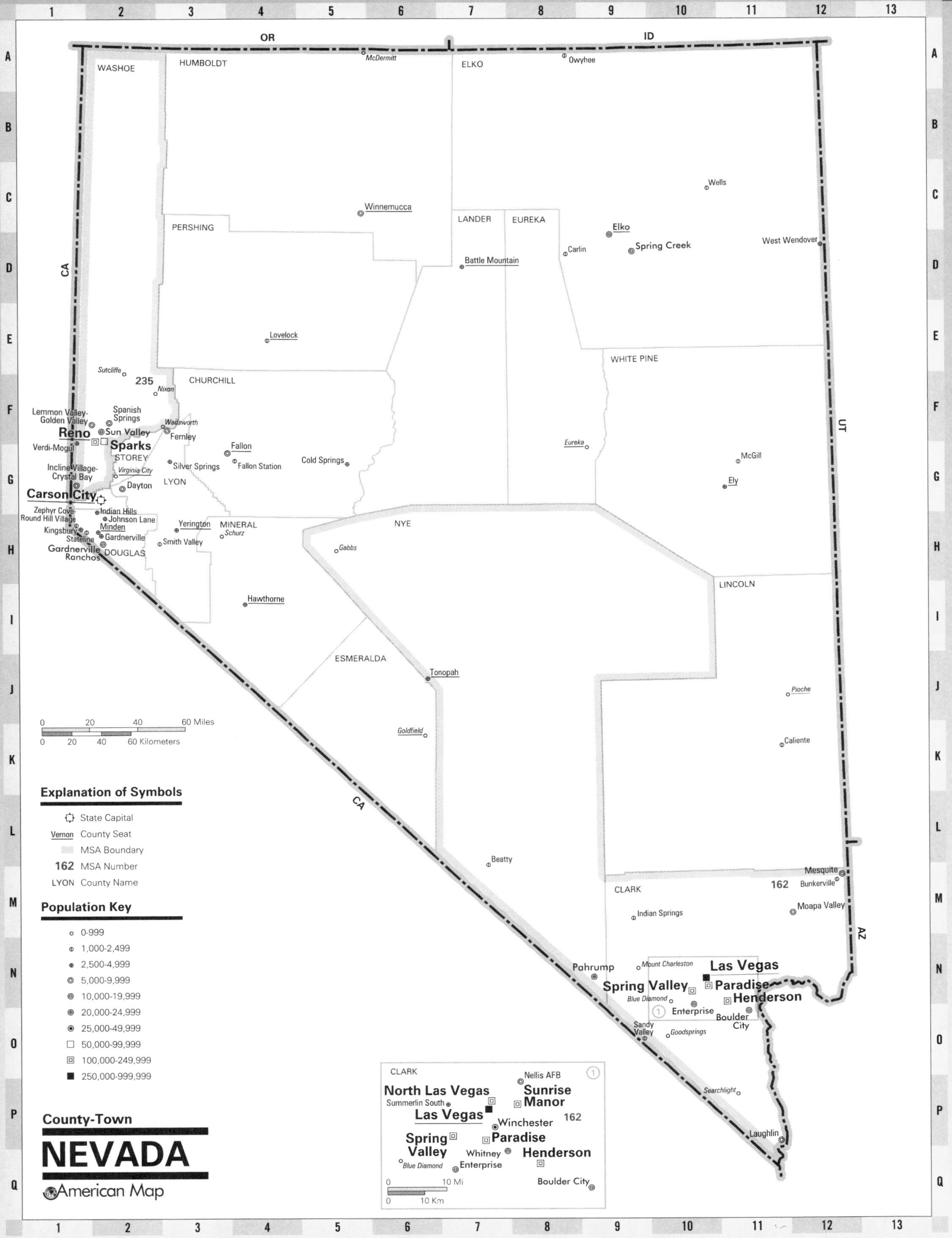

OR
ID
CA
UT
AZ

WASHOE
HUMBOLDT
ELKO
PERSHING
LANDER
EUREKA
CHURCHILL
WHITE PINE
STOREY
LYON
MINERAL
NYE
DOUGLAS
LINCOLN
ESMERALDA
CLARK

McDermitt
Owyhee
Wells
Winnemucca
Elko
Spring Creek
Carlin
West Wendover
Battle Mountain
Lovelock
Sutcliffe
235
Nixon
Lemmon Valley-Golden Valley
Spanish Springs
Wadsworth
Reno
Sun Valley
Fernley
Verdi-Mogul
Sparks
Fallon
Eureka
McGill
Incline Village-Crystal Bay
Virginia City
Silver Springs
Fallon Station
Cold Springs
Ely
Carson City
Dayton
Zephyr Cove-Round Hill Village
Indian Hills
Johnson Lane
Kingsbury
Minden
Yerington
Schurz
Stateline
Gardnerville
Smith Valley
Gabbs
Gardnerville Ranchos
Hawthorne
Tonopah
Pioche
Goldfield
Caliente
Beatty
Mesquite
162
Bunkerville
Indian Springs
Moapa Valley
Pahrump
Mount Charleston
Las Vegas
Spring Valley
Paradise
Blue Diamond
Henderson
1
Enterprise
Boulder City
Sandy Valley
Goodsprings
Searchlight
Laughlin

0 20 40 60 Miles
0 20 40 60 Kilometers

Explanation of Symbols

State Capital
Vernon County Seat
MSA Boundary
162 MSA Number
LYON County Name

Population Key

0-999
1,000-2,499
2,500-4,999
5,000-9,999
10,000-19,999
20,000-24,999
25,000-49,999
50,000-99,999
100,000-249,999
250,000-999,999

CLARK
1
Nellis AFB
North Las Vegas
Sunrise Manor
Summerlin South
Las Vegas
Winchester
162
Spring Valley
Paradise
Whitney
Henderson
Blue Diamond
Enterprise
0 10 Mi
0 10 Km
Boulder City

County-Town

NEVADA

American Map

COUNTIES

(10 Counties)

Name of County	Population	Location on Map
BELKNAP	56,325	L-5
CARROLL	43,666	H-7
CHESHIRE	73,825	O-2
COOS	33,111	A-7
GRAFTON	81,743	G-4
HILLSBOROUGH	380,841	O-4
MERRIMACK	136,225	L-4
ROCKINGHAM	277,359	N-7
STRAFFORD	112,233	M-8
SULLIVAN	40,458	L-2
TOTAL	**1,235,786**	

CITIES AND TOWNS

Note: The first name is that of the city or town, second, that of the county in which it is located, then the population and location on the map.

▲Alexandria, *Grafton,* 1,329 ... L-4
▲Allenstown, *Merrimack,* 4,843 ... N-6
▲Alstead, *Cheshire,* 1,944 ... N-2
▲Alton, *Belknap,* 4,502 ... M-7
▲Amherst, *Hillsborough,* 10,769 ... P-5
▲Andover, *Merrimack,* 2,109 ... M-4
▲Antrim, *Hillsborough,* 2,449 ... O-4
●Antrim, *Hillsborough,* 1,389 ... O-4
▲Ashland, *Grafton,* 1,955 ... K-5
▲Atkinson, *Rockingham,* 6,178 ... P-8
▲Auburn, *Rockingham,* 4,682 ... O-7
▲Barnstead, *Belknap,* 3,886 ... M-7
▲Barrington, *Strafford,* 7,475 ... N-8
▲Bartlett, *Carroll,* 2,705 ... I-7
▲Bedford, *Hillsborough,* 18,274 ... P-6
▲Belmont, *Belknap,* 6,716 ... M-6
▲Bennington, *Hillsborough,* 1,401 ... O-4
Berlin, *Coos,* 10,331 ... F-7
▲Bethlehem, *Grafton,* 2,199 ... G-5
▲Boscawen, *Merrimack,* 3,672 ... M-5
▲Bow, *Merrimack,* 7,138 ... O-6
▲Bradford, *Merrimack,* 1,454 ... N-4
▲Brentwood, *Rockingham,* 3,197 ... P-8
●Bristol, *Grafton,* 1,670 ... L-5
▲Bristol, *Grafton,* 3,033 ... L-5
▲Brookline, *Hillsborough,* 4,181 ... Q-5
▲Campton, *Grafton,* 2,719 ... J-5
▲Canaan, *Grafton,* 3,319 ... K-3
▲Candia, *Rockingham,* 3,911 ... O-7
▲Canterbury, *Merrimack,* 1,979 ... M-6
▲Charlestown, *Sullivan,* 4,749 ... N-1
●Charlestown, *Sullivan,* 1,145 ... N-1
▲Chester, *Rockingham,* 3,792 ... P-7
▲Chesterfield, *Cheshire,* 3,542 ... P-1
▲Chichester, *Merrimack,* 2,236 ... N-6
Claremont, *Sullivan,* 13,151 ... M-2
▲Colebrook, *Coos,* 2,321 ... C-6
Concord, *Merrimack,* 40,687 ... N-6
●Contoocook, *Merrimack,* 1,444 ... N-5
●Conway, *Carroll,* 1,692 ... I-8
▲Conway, *Carroll,* 8,604 ... I-8
▲Cornish, *Sullivan,* 1,661 ... L-2
▲Danbury, *Merrimack,* 1,071 ... L-4
▲Danville, *Rockingham,* 4,023 ... P-8
▲Deerfield, *Rockingham,* 3,678 ... O-7
▲Deering, *Hillsborough,* 1,875 ... O-4
●Derry, *Rockingham,* 22,661 ... P-7
▲Derry, *Rockingham,* 34,021 ... P-7
Dover, *Strafford,* 26,884 ... N-9
▲Dublin, *Cheshire,* 1,476 ... P-3
▲Dunbarton, *Merrimack,* 2,226 ... O-5
▲Durham, *Strafford,* 12,664 ... O-9
●Durham, *Strafford,* 9,024 ... O-9
▲East Kingston, *Rockingham,* 1,784 ... P-8
●East Merrimack, *Hillsborough,* 3,784 ... P-6
▲Effingham, *Carroll,* 1,273 ... K-8
●Enfield, *Grafton,* 1,698 ... K-3
▲Enfield, *Grafton,* 4,618 ... L-3
●Epping, *Rockingham,* 1,673 ... O-8
▲Epping, *Rockingham,* 5,476 ... O-8
▲Epsom, *Merrimack,* 4,021 ... N-7
▲Exeter, *Rockingham,* 14,058 ... O-8
●Exeter, *Rockingham,* 9,759 ... P-9
●Farmington, *Strafford,* 3,468 ... M-8
▲Farmington, *Strafford,* 5,774 ... M-8
▲Fitzwilliam, *Cheshire,* 2,141 ... Q-3
▲Francestown, *Hillsborough,* 1,480 ... P-4
Franklin, *Merrimack,* 8,405 ... M-5
▲Freedom, *Carroll,* 1,303 ... J-8
▲Fremont, *Rockingham,* 3,510 ... O-8
▲Gilford, *Belknap,* 6,803 ... L-6
▲Gilmanton, *Belknap,* 3,060 ... M-6
▲Goffstown, *Hillsborough,* 16,929 ... O-5
●Gorham, *Coos,* 1,773 ... G-7
▲Gorham, *Coos,* 2,895 ... G-7
▲Grafton, *Grafton,* 1,138 ... L-4
▲Grantham, *Sullivan,* 2,167 ... L-3
▲Greenfield, *Hillsborough,* 1,657 ... P-4
▲Greenland, *Rockingham,* 3,208 ... O-9
●Greenville, *Hillsborough,* 1,131 ... Q-4
▲Greenville, *Hillsborough,* 2,224 ... Q-4
●Groveton, *Coos,* 1,197 ... E-6
▲Hampstead, *Rockingham,* 8,297 ... P-7
●Hampton, *Rockingham,* 9,126 ... P-9
▲Hampton, *Rockingham,* 14,937 ... P-9
▲Hampton Falls, *Rockingham,* 1,880 ... P-9
Hancock, *Hillsborough,* 1,739 ... P-4
●Hanover, *Grafton,* 8,162 ... K-2
▲Hanover, *Grafton,* 10,850 ... K-3
▲Harrisville, *Cheshire,* 1,075 ... P-3
▲Haverhill, *Grafton,* 4,416 ... I-3
●Henniker, *Merrimack,* 1,627 ... N-4
▲Henniker, *Merrimack,* 4,433 ... N-4
▲Hillsborough, *Hillsborough,* 4,928 ... N-4
●Hillsborough, *Hillsborough,* 1,842 ... N-4
●Hinsdale, *Cheshire,* 1,713 ... Q-1
▲Hinsdale, *Cheshire,* 4,082 ... Q-1
▲Holderness, *Grafton,* 1,930 ... K-5
▲Hollis, *Hillsborough,* 7,015 ... Q-5
●Hooksett, *Merrimack,* 3,609 ... O-6
▲Hooksett, *Merrimack,* 11,721 ... O-6
▲Hopkinton, *Merrimack,* 5,399 ... N-5
●Hudson, *Hillsborough,* 7,814 ... Q-6
▲Hudson, *Hillsborough,* 22,928 ... Q-6
●Jaffrey, *Cheshire,* 2,802 ... Q-3
▲Jaffrey, *Cheshire,* 5,476 ... Q-3
▲Jefferson, *Coos,* 1,006 ... F-6
Keene, *Cheshire,* 22,563 ... P-2
▲Kensington, *Rockingham,* 1,893 ... P-9
▲Kingston, *Rockingham,* 5,862 ... P-8
Laconia, *Belknap,* 16,411 ... L-6
●Lancaster, *Coos,* 1,695 ... F-6
▲Lancaster, *Coos,* 3,280 ... F-6
Lebanon, *Grafton,* 12,568 ... K-2
▲Lee, *Strafford,* 4,145 ... O-8
▲Lincoln, *Grafton,* 1,271 ... I-5
●Lisbon, *Grafton,* 1,070 ... H-4
▲Lisbon, *Grafton,* 1,587 ... H-4
▲Litchfield, *Hillsborough,* 7,360 ... P-6
●Littleton, *Grafton,* 4,431 ... G-5
▲Littleton, *Grafton,* 5,845 ... G-4
●Londonderry, *Rockingham,* 11,417 ... P-6
▲Londonderry, *Rockingham,* 23,236 ... P-6
▲Loudon, *Merrimack,* 4,481 ... N-6
▲Lyme, *Grafton,* 1,679 ... J-3
▲Lyndeborough, *Hillsborough,* 1,585 ... P-5
▲Madbury, *Strafford,* 1,509 ... N-9
▲Madison, *Carroll,* 1,984 ... J-8
Manchester, *Hillsborough,* 107,006 ... O-6
●Marlborough, *Cheshire,* 1,089 ... P-2
▲Marlborough, *Cheshire,* 2,009 ... P-3
▲Mason, *Hillsborough,* 1,147 ... Q-5
▲Meredith, *Belknap,* 5,943 ... K-6
●Meredith, *Belknap,* 1,739 ... K-6
▲Merrimack, *Hillsborough,* 25,119 ... P-6
▲Middleton, *Strafford,* 1,440 ... M-7
▲Milan, *Coos,* 1,331 ... E-7
●Milford, *Hillsborough,* 8,293 ... P-5
▲Milford, *Hillsborough,* 13,535 ... Q-5
▲Milton, *Strafford,* 3,910 ... M-8
▲Mont Vernon, *Hillsborough,* 2,034 ... P-5
▲Moulton Borough, *Carroll,* 4,484 ... K-7
Nashua, *Hillsborough,* 86,605 ... Q-6
▲New Boston, *Hillsborough,* 4,138 ... P-5
▲New Castle, *Rockingham,* 1,010 ... O-10
▲New Durham, *Strafford,* 2,220 ... M-7
▲New Hampton, *Belknap,* 1,950 ... L-5
▲New Ipswich, *Hillsborough,* 4,289 ... Q-4
▲New London, *Merrimack,* 4,116 ... M-4
▲Newbury, *Merrimack,* 1,702 ... M-3
▲Newfields, *Rockingham,* 1,551 ... O-9
●Newmarket, *Rockingham,* 5,124 ... O-9
▲Newmarket, *Rockingham,* 8,027 ... O-8
●Newport, *Sullivan,* 4,008 ... M-3
▲Newport, *Sullivan,* 6,269 ... M-3
▲Newton, *Rockingham,* 4,289 ... P-8
●North Conway, *Carroll,* 2,069 ... I-8
▲North Hampton, *Rockingham,* 4,259 ... P-9
▲Northfield, *Merrimack,* 4,548 ... M-6
▲Northumberland, *Coos,* 2,438 ... F-6
▲Northwood, *Rockingham,* 3,640 ... N-8
▲Nottingham, *Rockingham,* 3,701 ... O-8
▲Orford, *Grafton,* 1,091 ... J-3
▲Ossipee, *Carroll,* 4,211 ... K-8
▲Pelham, *Hillsborough,* 10,914 ... Q-7
▲Pembroke, *Merrimack,* 6,897 ... N-6
●Peterborough, *Hillsborough,* 2,944 ... P-4
▲Peterborough, *Hillsborough,* 5,883 ... P-4
●Pinardville, *Hillsborough,* 5,779 ... O-6
●Pittsfield, *Merrimack,* 1,669 ... M-7
▲Pittsfield, *Merrimack,* 3,931 ... N-7
▲Plainfield, *Sullivan,* 2,241 ... L-2
▲Plaistow, *Rockingham,* 7,747 ... P-8
●Plymouth, *Grafton,* 3,528 ... K-5
▲Plymouth, *Grafton,* 5,892 ... K-5
Portsmouth, *Rockingham,* 20,784 ... O-9
●Raymond, *Rockingham,* 2,839 ... O-7
▲Raymond, *Rockingham,* 9,674 ... O-7
▲Richmond, *Cheshire,* 1,077 ... Q-2
▲Rindge, *Cheshire,* 5,451 ... Q-3
Rochester, *Strafford,* 28,461 ... M-8
▲Rollinsford, *Strafford,* 2,648 ... N-9
▲Rumney, *Grafton,* 1,480 ... J-4
▲Rye, *Rockingham,* 5,182 ... O-9
▲Salem, *Rockingham,* 28,112 ... Q-7
▲Salisbury, *Merrimack,* 1,137 ... M-5
▲Sanbornton, *Belknap,* 2,581 ... L-5
▲Sandown, *Rockingham,* 5,143 ... P-7
▲Sandwich, *Carroll,* 1,286 ... J-6
▲Seabrook, *Rockingham,* 7,934 ... P-9
Somersworth, *Strafford,* 11,477 ... N-9
●South Hooksett, *Merrimack,* 5,282 ... O-6
▲Stewartstown, *Coos,* 1,012 ... E-6
▲Strafford, *Strafford,* 3,626 ... M-7
▲Stratham, *Rockingham,* 6,355 ... O-9
▲Sunapee, *Sullivan,* 3,055 ... M-3
●Suncook, *Merrimack,* 5,362 ... O-6
▲Sutton, *Merrimack,* 1,544 ... M-4
▲Swanzey, *Cheshire,* 6,800 ... P-2
▲Tamworth, *Carroll,* 2,510 ... J-7
▲Temple, *Hillsborough,* 1,297 ... Q-4
▲Thornton, *Grafton,* 1,843 ... I-5
●Tilton-Northfield, *Belknap,* 3,231 ... M-5
▲Titton, *Belknap,* 3,477 ... L-6
▲Troy, *Cheshire,* 1,962 ... Q-3
▲Tuftonboro, *Carroll,* 2,148 ... K-7
▲Unity, *Sullivan,* 1,530 ... M-2
▲Wakefield, *Carroll,* 4,252 ... L-8
▲Walpole, *Cheshire,* 3,594 ... O-1
▲Warner, *Merrimack,* 2,760 ... N-4
▲Weare, *Hillsborough,* 7,776 ... O-5
▲Webster, *Merrimack,* 1,579 ... M-5
●West Swanzey, *Cheshire,* 1,118 ... P-2
▲Westmoreland, *Cheshire,* 1,747 ... P-1
●Whitefield, *Coos,* 1,089 ... G-5
▲Whitefield, *Coos,* 2,038 ... G-5
▲Wilmot, *Merrimack,* 1,144 ... M-4
●Wilton, *Hillsborough,* 1,236 ... P-5
▲Wilton, *Hillsborough,* 3,743 ... Q-5
●Winchester, *Cheshire,* 1,832 ... Q-2
▲Winchester, *Cheshire,* 4,144 ... Q-2
▲Windham, *Rockingham,* 10,709 ... Q-7
●Wolfeboro, *Carroll,* 2,979 ... L-7
▲Wolfeboro, *Carroll,* 6,083 ... L-7
▲Woodstock, *Grafton,* 1,139 ... I-5
●Woodsville, *Grafton,* 1,081 ... H-3

Explanation of symbols: ● - Census Designated Place (CDP) ▲ - Township

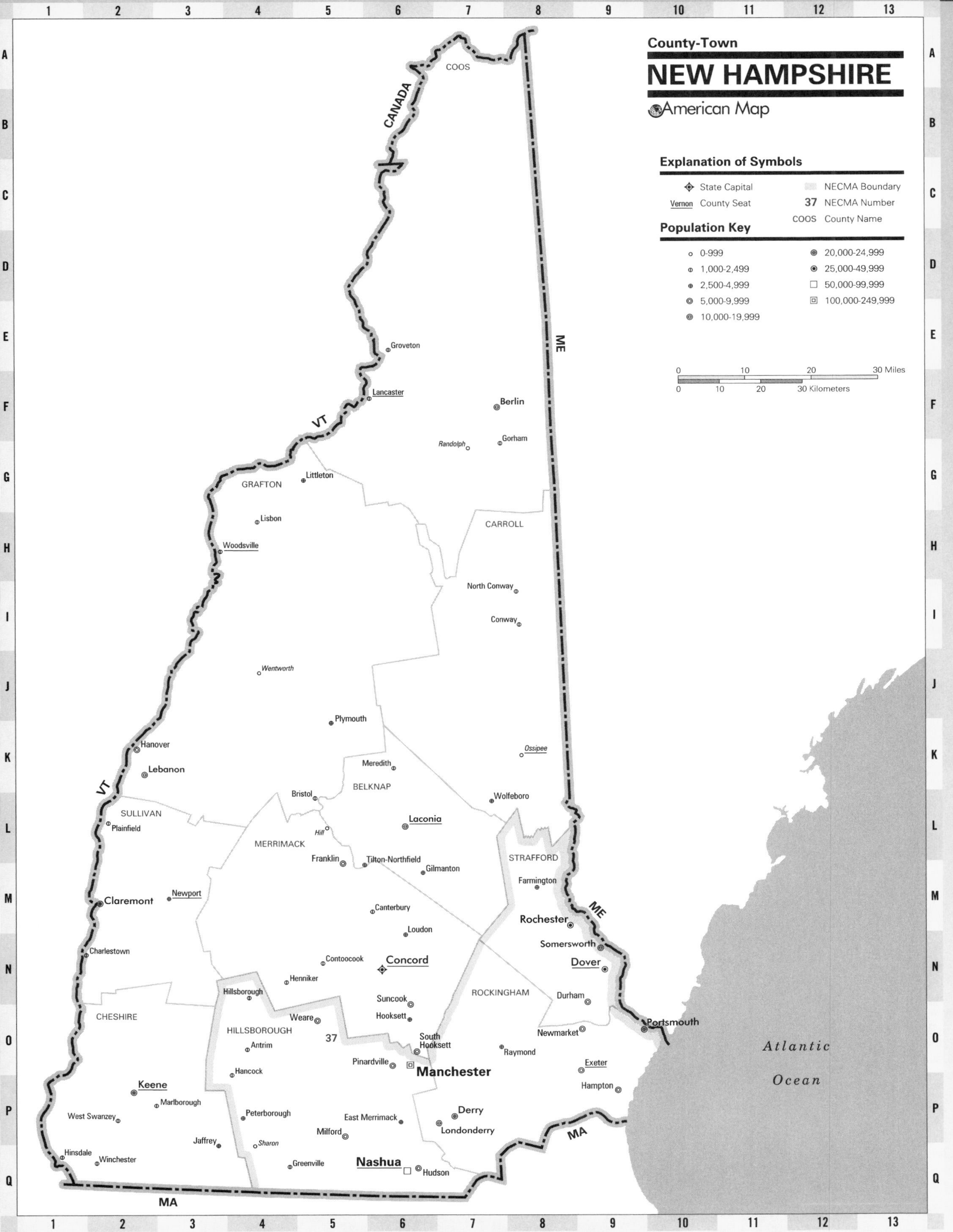
County-Town
NEW HAMPSHIRE
American Map
Explanation of Symbols
State Capital
Vernon County Seat
NECMA Boundary
37 NECMA Number
COOS County Name
Population Key
0-999
1,000-2,499
2,500-4,999
5,000-9,999
10,000-19,999
20,000-24,999
25,000-49,999
50,000-99,999
100,000-249,999
0 10 20 30 Miles
0 10 20 30 Kilometers
CANADA
VT
ME
MA
COOS
GRAFTON
CARROLL
BELKNAP
SULLIVAN
MERRIMACK
STRAFFORD
CHESHIRE
HILLSBOROUGH
ROCKINGHAM
Groveton
Lancaster
Berlin
Randolph
Gorham
Littleton
Lisbon
Woodsville
North Conway
Conway
Wentworth
Plymouth
Hanover
Lebanon
Ossipee
Meredith
Bristol
Wolfeboro
Plainfield
Laconia
Hill
Franklin
Tilton-Northfield
Gilmanton
Farmington
Claremont
Newport
Canterbury
Rochester
Loudon
Somersworth
Charlestown
Contoocook
Concord
Dover
Henniker
Hillsborough
Suncook
Durham
Weare
Hooksett
Portsmouth
37
Antrim
South Hooksett
Newmarket
Raymond
Atlantic Ocean
Pinardville
Manchester
Exeter
Hancock
Keene
Hampton
Marlborough
West Swanzey
Peterborough
Derry
East Merrimack
Londonderry
Milford
Jaffrey
Sharon
Hinsdale
Winchester
Greenville
Nashua
Hudson

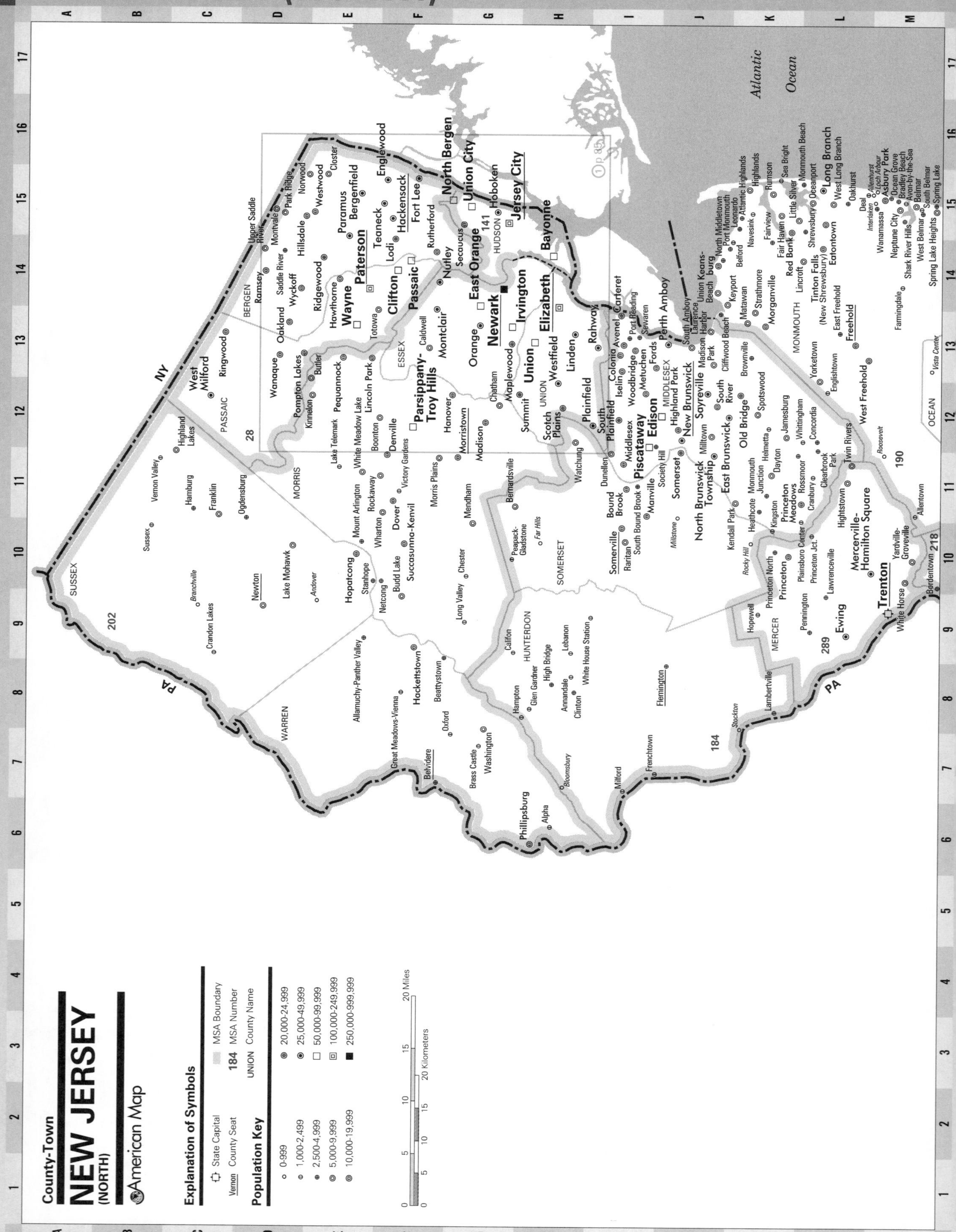
County-Town
NEW JERSEY
(NORTH)
American Map
Explanation of Symbols
State Capital
Vernon County Seat
MSA Boundary
184 MSA Number
UNION County Name
Population Key
0-999
1,000-2,499
2,500-4,999
5,000-9,999
10,000-19,999
20,000-24,999
25,000-49,999
50,000-99,999
100,000-249,999
250,000-999,999
0 5 10 15 20 Miles
0 5 10 15 20 Kilometers
Atlantic Ocean
NY
PA
SUSSEX
PASSAIC
BERGEN
MORRIS
ESSEX
HUDSON
UNION
WARREN
HUNTERDON
SOMERSET
MIDDLESEX
MONMOUTH
MERCER
OCEAN
202
28
141
184
190
218
289
Newark
Jersey City
Paterson
Elizabeth
Trenton
Edison
Clifton
Camden
Passaic
East Orange
Union City
North Bergen
Bayonne
Irvington
Hoboken
Hackensack
Morristown
Newton
Flemington
Belvidere
Somerville
Freehold
Phillipsburg
Hackettstown
New Brunswick
Perth Amboy
Long Branch
Asbury Park
Princeton
Ewing
Mercerville-Hamilton Square
Parsippany-Troy Hills
Piscataway
Sayreville
Old Bridge
East Brunswick
North Brunswick Township
Plainfield
Linden
Rahway
Woodbridge
Wayne
Montclair
Orange
Union
Westfield
Summit
Teaneck
Englewood
Fort Lee
Bergenfield
Ridgewood
Paramus
Kearny
Nutley
Bloomfield
West Milford
Ringwood
Hopatcong
Dover
Vista Center

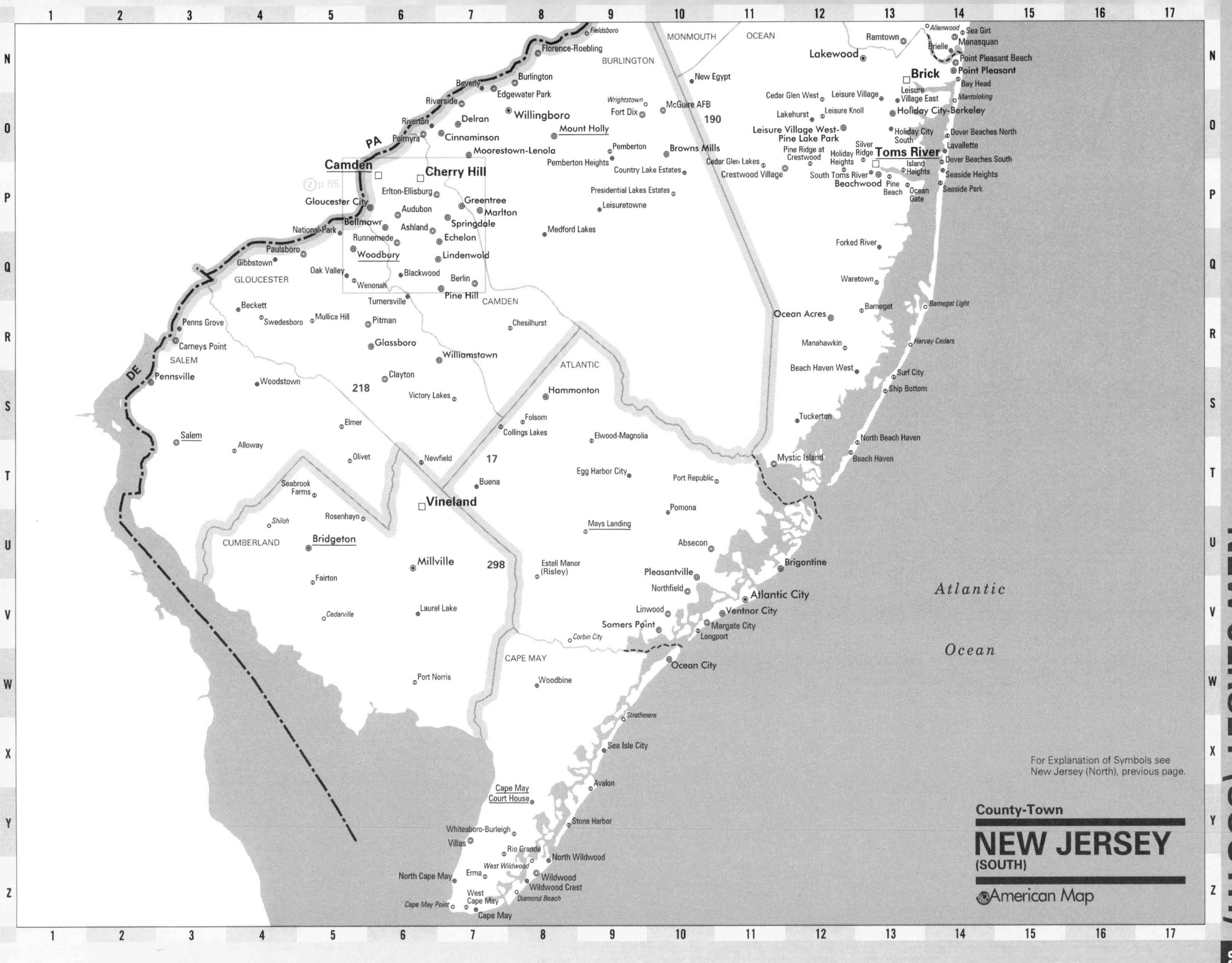
County-Town
NEW JERSEY
(SOUTH)
American Map
For Explanation of Symbols see New Jersey (North), previous page.
Atlantic
Ocean
MONMOUTH
OCEAN
BURLINGTON
CAMDEN
GLOUCESTER
SALEM
ATLANTIC
CUMBERLAND
CAPE MAY
PA
DE
Fieldsboro
Florence-Roebling
Burlington
Beverly
Edgewater Park
Riverside
Willingboro
Delran
Riverton
Palmyra
Cinnaminson
Moorestown-Lenola
Mount Holly
Camden
Cherry Hill
p 85
Erlton-Ellisburg
Gloucester City
Greentree
Marlton
Audubon
Springdale
Bellmawr
Ashland
Echelon
National Park
Runnemede
Paulsboro
Woodbury
Lindenwold
Gibbstown
Oak Valley
Blackwood
Berlin
Wenonah
Pine Hill
Turnersville
Beckett
Swedesboro
Mullica Hill
Pitman
Chesilhurst
Penns Grove
Carneys Point
Glassboro
Williamstown
Pennsville
Woodstown
Clayton
218
Victory Lakes
Hammonton
Folsom
Collings Lakes
Elmer
Salem
Alloway
Elwood-Magnolia
Olivet
Newfield
17
Egg Harbor City
Port Republic
Seabrook Farms
Buena
Vineland
Rosenhayn
Pomona
Shiloh
Mays Landing
Bridgeton
Absecon
Millville
298
Estell Manor (Risley)
Pleasantville
Fairton
Northfield
Laurel Lake
Linwood
Cedarville
Somers Point
Corbin City
Port Norris
Woodbine
Strathmere
Sea Isle City
Avalon
Cape May Court House
Stone Harbor
Whitesboro-Burleigh
Villas
Rio Grande
West Wildwood
North Wildwood
North Cape May
Erma
Wildwood
Wildwood Crest
West Cape May
Diamond Beach
Cape May Point
Cape May
New Egypt
Wrightstown
Fort Dix
McGuire AFB
190
Pemberton
Pemberton Heights
Browns Mills
Country Lake Estates
Cedar Glen Lakes
Crestwood Village
Presidential Lakes Estates
Leisuretowne
Medford Lakes
Ramtown
Lakewood
Allenwood
Sea Girt
Manasquan
Brielle
Point Pleasant Beach
Brick
Point Pleasant
Bay Head
Cedar Glen West
Leisure Village
Leisure Village East
Mantoloking
Lakehurst
Leisure Knoll
Holiday City-Berkeley
Leisure Village West-Pine Lake Park
Holiday City South
Dover Beaches North
Pine Ridge at Crestwood
Holiday Heights
Silver Ridge
Toms River
Lavallette
Island Heights
Dover Beaches South
South Toms River
Beachwood
Seaside Heights
Pine Beach
Ocean Gate
Seaside Park
Forked River
Waretown
Barnegat
Barnegat Light
Ocean Acres
Manahawkin
Harvey Cedars
Beach Haven West
Surf City
Ship Bottom
Tuckerton
North Beach Haven
Mystic Island
Beach Haven
Brigantine
Atlantic City
Ventnor City
Margate City
Longport
Ocean City
1 2 3 4 5 6 7 8 9 10 11 12 13 14 15 16 17
N O P Q R S T U V W X Y Z

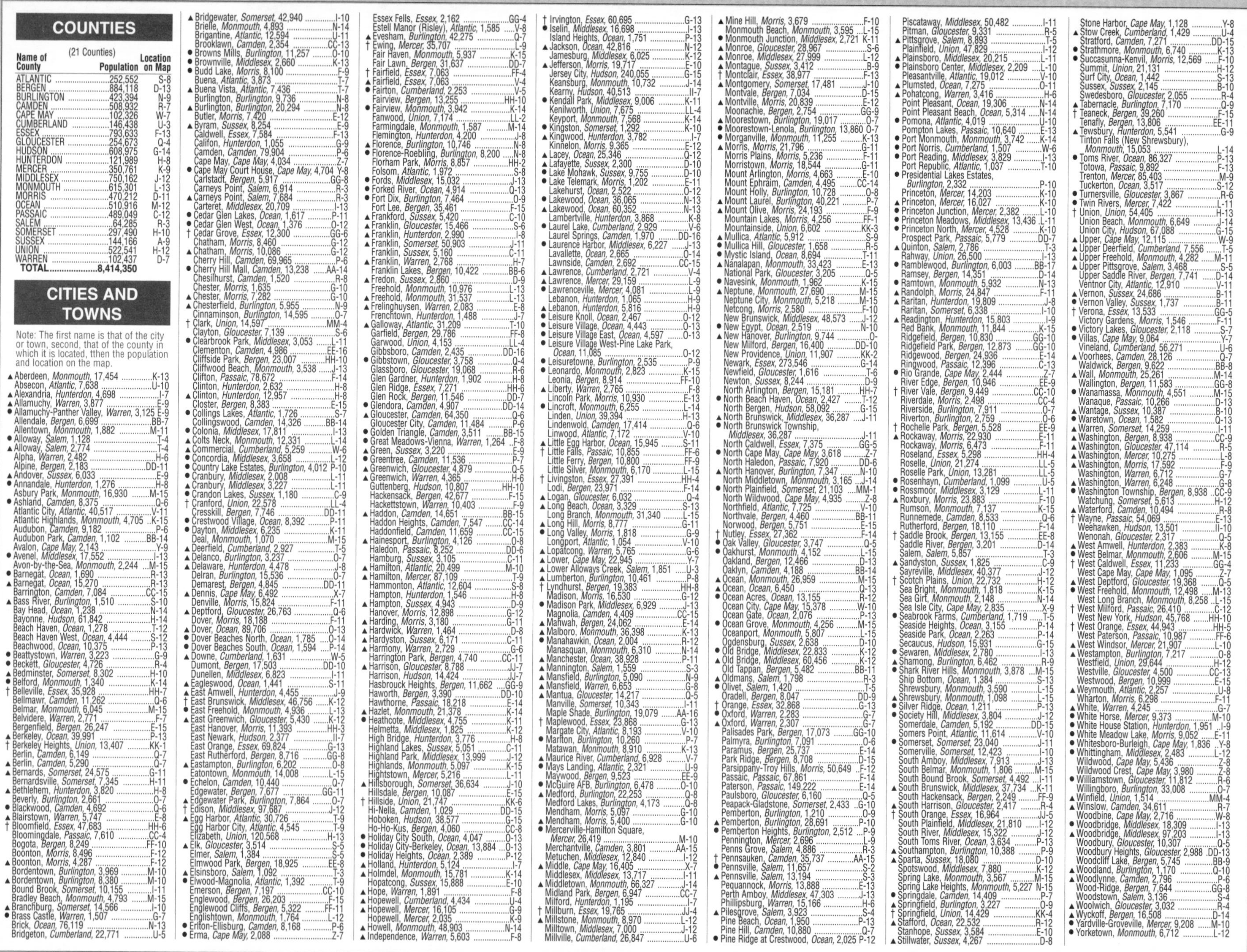

COUNTIES

(21 Counties)

Name of County	Population	Location on Map
ATLANTIC	252,552	S-8
BERGEN	884,118	D-13
BURLINGTON	423,394	N-9
CAMDEN	508,932	R-7
CAPE MAY	102,326	W-7
CUMBERLAND	146,438	U-3
ESSEX	793,633	F-13
GLOUCESTER	254,673	Q-4
HUDSON	608,975	G-14
HUNTERDON	121,989	H-8
MERCER	350,761	K-9
MIDDLESEX	750,162	J-12
MONMOUTH	615,301	L-13
MORRIS	470,212	D-11
OCEAN	510,916	M-12
PASSAIC	489,049	C-12
SALEM	64,285	R-3
SOMERSET	297,490	H-10
SUSSEX	144,166	A-9
UNION	522,541	H-12
WARREN	102,437	D-7
TOTAL	**8,414,350**	

CITIES AND TOWNS

Note: The first name is that of the city or town, second, that of the county in which it is located, then the population and location on the map.

Explanation of symbols: • - Census Designated Place (CDP) ▲ - Township † - CDP and Township

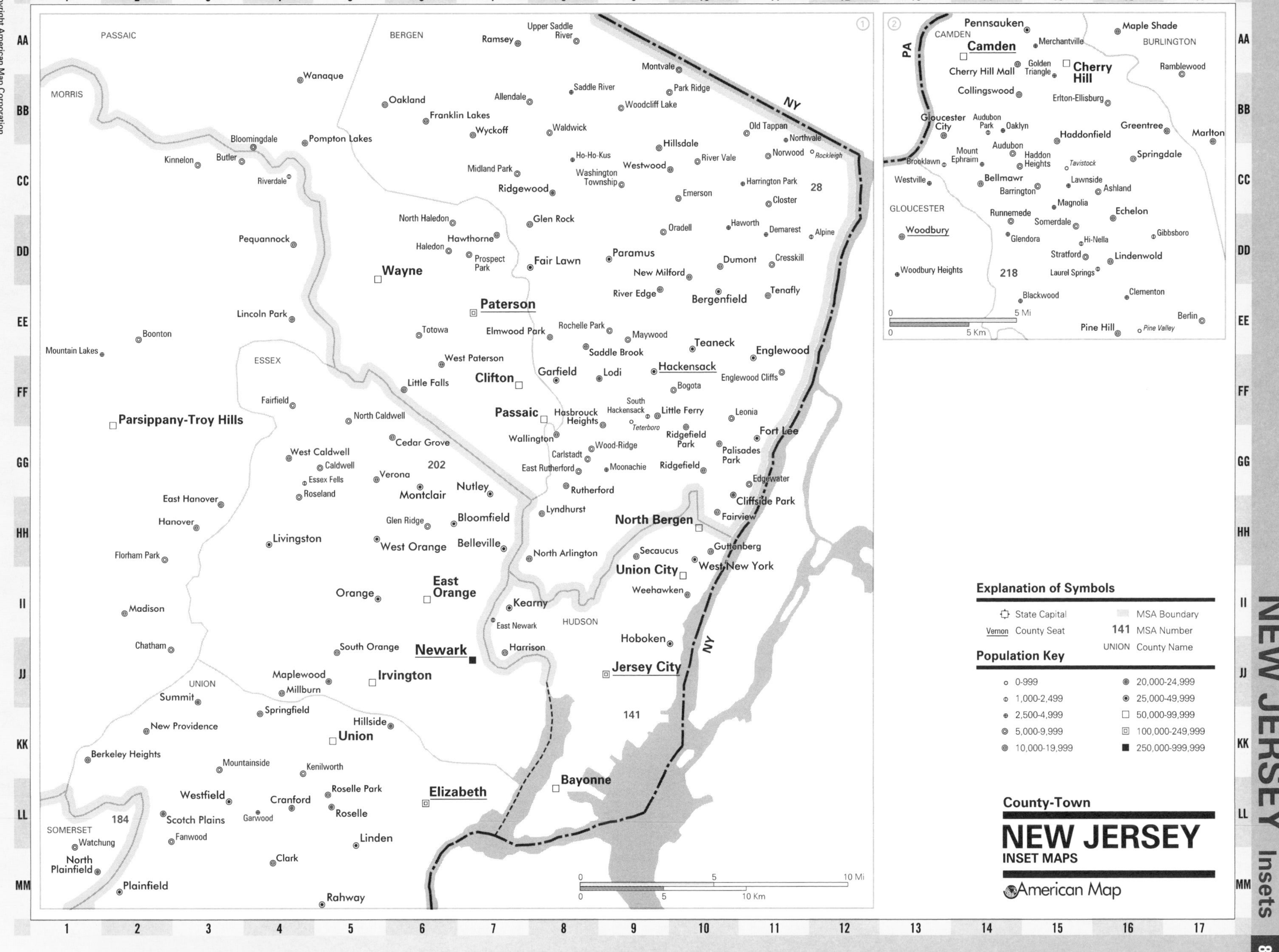
Explanation of Symbols
State Capital
Vernon County Seat
MSA Boundary
141 MSA Number
UNION County Name
Population Key
0-999
1,000-2,499
2,500-4,999
5,000-9,999
10,000-19,999
20,000-24,999
25,000-49,999
50,000-99,999
100,000-249,999
250,000-999,999
County-Town
NEW JERSEY
INSET MAPS
American Map
PA
NY
CAMDEN
BURLINGTON
GLOUCESTER
Pennsauken
Camden
Merchantville
Maple Shade
Cherry Hill Mall
Golden Triangle
Cherry Hill
Ramblewood
Collingswood
Erlton-Ellisburg
Gloucester City
Audubon Park
Oaklyn
Haddonfield
Greentree
Marlton
Brooklawn
Mount Ephraim
Audubon
Haddon Heights
Tavistock
Springdale
Westville
Bellmawr
Barrington
Lawnside
Ashland
Magnolia
Runnemede
Somerdale
Echelon
Woodbury
Glendora
Hi-Nella
Gibbsboro
Stratford
Lindenwold
Woodbury Heights
218
Laurel Springs
Blackwood
Clementon
Pine Hill
Pine Valley
Berlin
PASSAIC
BERGEN
MORRIS
ESSEX
HUDSON
UNION
SOMERSET
Ramsey
Upper Saddle River
Montvale
Wanaque
Saddle River
Park Ridge
Oakland
Allendale
Woodcliff Lake
Franklin Lakes
Wyckoff
Waldwick
Old Tappan
Northvale
Hillsdale
Bloomingdale
Pompton Lakes
Kinnelon
Butler
Ho-Ho-Kus
River Vale
Norwood
Rockleigh
Westwood
Washington Township
Midland Park
Riverdale
Harrington Park
28
Ridgewood
Emerson
Closter
North Haledon
Glen Rock
Haworth
Oradell
Demarest
Alpine
Pequannock
Hawthorne
Haledon
Prospect Park
Paramus
Fair Lawn
Dumont
Cresskill
New Milford
Wayne
River Edge
Bergenfield
Tenafly
Paterson
Lincoln Park
Boonton
Totowa
Elmwood Park
Rochelle Park
Maywood
Teaneck
Englewood
Mountain Lakes
Saddle Brook
West Paterson
Hackensack
Englewood Cliffs
Clifton
Garfield
Lodi
Little Falls
Bogota
Fairfield
Passaic
Hasbrouck Heights
South Hackensack
Little Ferry
Leonia
North Caldwell
Teterboro
Parsippany-Troy Hills
Cedar Grove
Wallington
Ridgefield Park
Fort Lee
West Caldwell
Carlstadt
Wood-Ridge
Palisades Park
Caldwell
202
East Rutherford
Moonachie
Ridgefield
Verona
Essex Fells
Montclair
Nutley
Roseland
Rutherford
Edgewater
East Hanover
Cliffside Park
Lyndhurst
Glen Ridge
Bloomfield
North Bergen
Hanover
Fairview
Livingston
West Orange
Belleville
Secaucus
Guttenberg
Florham Park
North Arlington
Union City
West New York
East Orange
Orange
Weehawken
Kearny
Madison
East Newark
Hoboken
Chatham
South Orange
Newark
Harrison
Jersey City
Maplewood
Irvington
Summit
Millburn
Springfield
141
New Providence
Hillside
Union
Berkeley Heights
Mountainside
Kenilworth
Bayonne
Roselle Park
Westfield
Elizabeth
Cranford
184
Scotch Plains
Garwood
Roselle
Watchung
Fanwood
Linden
North Plainfield
Clark
Plainfield
Rahway
0 5 10 Mi
0 5 10 Km
0 5 Mi
0 5 Km

COUNTIES

(33 Counties)

Name of County	Population	Location on Map
BERNALILLO	556,678	F-6
CATRON	3,543	G-1
CHAVES	61,382	H-10
CIBOLA	25,595	F-1
COLFAX	14,189	A-9
CURRY	45,044	F-12
DE BACA	2,240	G-10
DONA ANA	174,682	K-5
EDDY	51,658	K-10
GRANT	31,002	J-1
GUADALUPE	4,680	F-9
HARDING	810	C-10
HIDALGO	5,932	L-1
LEA	55,511	I-12
LINCOLN	55,511	H-8
LOS ALAMOS	18,343	D-6
LUNA	25,016	L-3
MCKINLEY	74,798	D-1
MORA	5,180	C-8
OTERO	62,298	J-7
QUAY	10,155	D-12
RIO ARRIBA	41,190	A-4
ROOSEVELT	18,018	I-12
SAN JUAN	113,801	A-1
SAN MIGUEL	30,126	D-8
SANDOVAL	89,908	C-4
SANTA FE	129,292	E-7
SIERRA	13,270	J-3
SOCORRO	18,078	G-4
TAOS	29,979	A-7
TORRANCE	16,911	F-8
UNION	4,174	A-11
VALENCIA	66,152	F-5
TOTAL	**1,819,046**	

CITIES AND TOWNS

Note: The first name is that of the city or town, second, that of the county in which it is located, then the population and location on the map.

•Agua Fria, *Santa Fe,* 2,051 ....D-7
•Alamo, *Socorro,* 1,183 ....G-4
Alamogordo, *Otero,* 35,582 ....K-7
Albuquerque, *Bernalillo,* 448,607 ....E-6
Angel Fire, *Colfax,* 1,048 ....C-9
•Anthony, *Dona Ana,* 7,904 ....M-6
Artesia, *Eddy,* 10,692 ....K-10
Aztec, *San Juan,* 6,378 ....A-3
Bayard, *Grant,* 2,534 ....K-3
Belen, *Valencia,* 6,901 ....F-6
Bernalillo, *Sandoval,* 6,611 ....E-6
•Black Rock, *McKinley,* 1,252 ....E-2
Bloomfield, *San Juan,* 6,417 ....B-3
•Boles Acres, *Otero,* 1,172 ....K-7
Bosque Farms, *Valencia,* 3,931 ....P-11
•Cannon AFB, *Curry,* 2,557 ....G-12
Capitan, *Lincoln,* 1,443 ....I-8
Carlsbad, *Eddy,* 25,625 ....L-11
•Carlsbad North, *Eddy,* 1,245 ....L-11
Carrizozo, *Lincoln,* 1,036 ....I-7
•Cedar Crest, *Bernalillo,* 1,060 ....N-13
Chama, *Rio Arriba,* 1,199 ....A-6
•Chaparral, *Dona Ana,* 6,117 ....M-6
•Chimayo, *Rio Arriba,* 2,924 ....C-7
•Church Rock, *McKinley,* 1,077 ....D-2
Clayton, *Union,* 2,524 ....B-13
Clovis, *Curry,* 32,667 ....G-13
Columbus, *Luna,* 1,765 ....M-4
Corrales, *Sandoval,* 7,334 ....E-6
•Crownpoint, *McKinley,* 2,630 ....D-3
Deming, *Luna,* 14,116 ....L-4
Dexter, *Chaves,* 1,235 ....J-10
•Doña Ana, *Dona Ana,* 1,379 ....L-5
•Dulce, *Rio Arriba,* 2,623 ....A-5
Edgewood, *Santa Fe,* 1,893 ....F-7
•El Cerro-Monterey Park, *Valencia,* 5,483 ....G-6
•El Valle de Arroyo Seco, *Santa Fe,* 1,149 ....D-7
•Eldorado at Santa Fe, *Santa Fe,* 5,799 ....E-7
Elephant Butte, *Sierra,* 1,390 ....J-5
Española, *Rio Arriba,* 9,688 ....D-7
Estancia, *Torrance,* 1,584 ....F-7
Eunice, *Lea,* 2,562 ....L-13
Farmington, *San Juan,* 37,844 ....B-3
•Flora Vista, *San Juan,* 1,383 ....B-3
Fort Sumner, *De Baca,* 1,249 ....G-11
Gallup, *McKinley,* 20,209 ....D-2
Grants, *Cibola,* 8,806 ....E-3
Hagerman, *Chaves,* 1,168 ....J-11
Hatch, *Dona Ana,* 1,673 ....K-5
Hobbs, *Lea,* 28,657 ....K-13
•Holloman AFB, *Otero,* 2,076 ....K-7
Hurley, *Grant,* 1,464 ....K-3
Jal, *Lea,* 1,996 ....L-13
•Jarales, *Valencia,* 1,434 ....G-6
•Jemez Pueblo, *Sandoval,* 1,953 ....D-6
•Kirtland, *San Juan,* 6,190 ....B-2
•La Cienega, *Santa Fe,* 3,007 ....D-7
•La Luz, *Otero,* 1,615 ....K-7
•La Puebla, *Santa Fe,* 1,296 ....C-7
Las Cruces, *Dona Ana,* 74,267 ....L-6
Las Vegas, *San Miguel,* 14,565 ....D-9
Logan, *Quay,* 1,094 ....E-12
Lordsburg, *Hidalgo,* 3,379 ....L-2
•Los Alamos, *Los Alamos,* 11,909 ....D-6
•Los Chaves, *Valencia,* 5,033 ....F-6
Los Lunas, *Valencia,* 10,034 ....F-6
Los Ranchos de Albuquerque, *Bernalillo,* 5,092 ....N-11
•Los Trujillos-Gabaldon, *Valencia,* 2,166 ....Q-11
Loving, *Eddy,* 1,326 ....L-11
Lovington, *Lea,* 9,471 ....K-13
•Meadow Lake, *Valencia,* 4,491 ....P-12
•Mescalero, *Otero,* 1,233 ....J-8
Mesilla, *Dona Ana,* 2,180 ....L-6
Milan, *Cibola,* 1,891 ....E-3
Moriarty, *Torrance,* 1,765 ....F-7
Mosquero, *Harding,* 120 ....D-10
Mountainair, *Torrance,* 1,116 ....G-7
•Navajo, *McKinley,* 2,097 ....D-1
•North Valley, *Bernalillo,* 11,923 ....E-6
Pecos, *San Miguel,* 1,441 ....D-8
•Peralta, *Valencia,* 3,750 ....P-11
•Placitas, *Sandoval,* 3,452 ....M-13
•Pojoaque, *Santa Fe,* 1,261 ....D-7
Portales, *Roosevelt,* 11,131 ....H-13
Questa, *Taos,* 1,864 ....B-8
•Radium Springs, *Dona Ana,* 1,518 ....L-5
•Ranchos De Taos, *Taos,* 2,390 ....C-8
Raton, *Colfax,* 7,282 ....A-10
Reserve, *Catron,* 387 ....I-1
•Rio Communities, *Dona Ana,* 4,213 ....Q-11
•Rio Communities North, *Valencia,* 1,588 ....D-6
Rio Rancho, *Sandoval,* 51,765 ....E-6
Roswell, *Chaves,* 45,293 ....J-10
Ruidoso, *Lincoln,* 7,698 ....J-8
Ruidoso Downs, *Lincoln,* 1,824 ....J-8
•San Felipe Pueblo, *Sandoval,* 2,080 ....E-6
•Santa Clara, *Grant,* 1,944 ....K-3
Santa Fe, *Santa Fe,* 62,203 ....D-7
Santa Rosa, *Guadalupe,* 2,744 ....F-10
•Santa Teresa, *Dona Ana,* 2,607 ....M-6
•Santo Domingo Pueblo, *Sandoval,* 2,550 ....E-6
•Shiprock, *San Juan,* 8,156 ....A-2
Silver City, *Grant,* 10,545 ....K-2
•Skyline-Ganipa, *Cibola,* 1,035 ....F-4
Socorro, *Socorro,* 8,877 ....H-5
•South Valley, *Bernalillo,* 39,060 ....F-6
Springer, *Colfax,* 1,285 ....C-10
Sunland Park, *Dona Ana,* 13,309 ....M-6
Taos, *Taos,* 4,700 ....B-8
•Taos Pueblo, *Taos,* 1,264 ....B-8
Texico, *Curry,* 1,065 ....G-13
•Thoreau, *McKinley,* 1,863 ....E-3
Tierra Amarilla, *Rio Arriba,* 850 ....B-6
•Tohatchi, *McKinley,* 1,037 ....D-2
•Tome-Adelino, *Valencia,* 2,211 ....Q-11
Truth or Consequences, *Sierra,* 7,289 ....J-4
Tucumcari, *Quay,* 5,989 ....E-12
Tularosa, *Otero,* 2,864 ....J-7
•Twin Lakes, *McKinley,* 1,069 ....D-2
•University Park, *Dona Ana,* 2,732 ....L-6
•Upper Fruitland, *San Juan,* 1,664 ....B-3
•Vado, *Dona Ana,* 3,003 ....M-6
•Valencia, *Valencia,* 4,500 ....P-11
•White Rock, *Los Alamos,* 6,045 ....D-7
•White Sands, *Dona Ana,* 1,323 ....L-6
•Zuni Pueblo, *McKinley,* 6,367 ....D-2

Explanation of symbols: • - Census Designated Place (CDP)

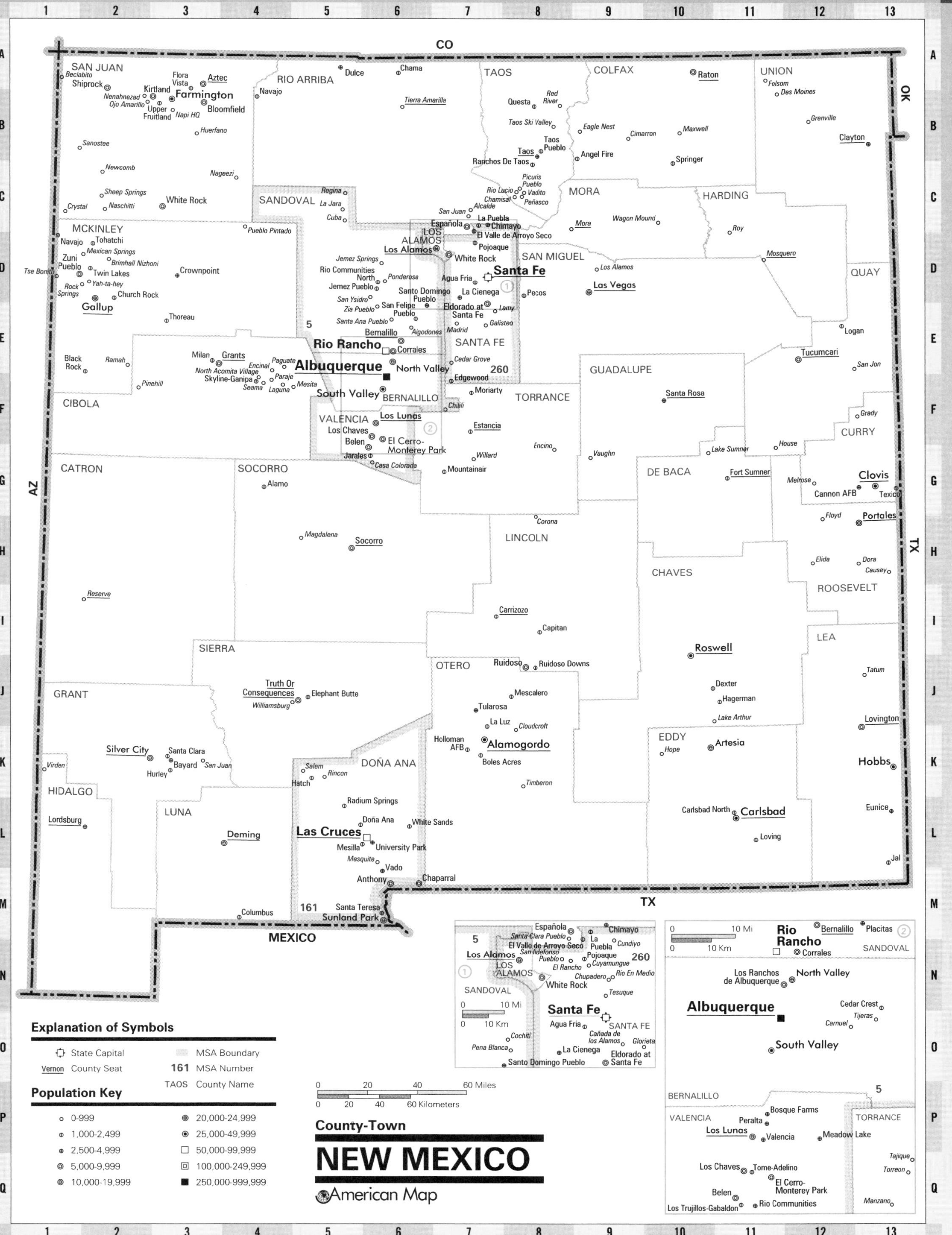

CO
OK
TX
AZ
MEXICO
SAN JUAN
Beclabito
Shiprock
Flora Vista
Aztec
Kirtland
Farmington
Nenahnezad
Ojo Amarillo
Upper Fruitland
Napi HQ
Bloomfield
Huerfano
Sanostee
Newcomb
Nageezi
Sheep Springs
Naschitti
Crystal
White Rock
RIO ARRIBA
Dulce
Chama
Navajo
Tierra Amarilla
TAOS
Questa
Red River
Taos Ski Valley
Taos Pueblo
Taos
Ranchos De Taos
Picuris Pueblo
Rio Lucio
Vadito
Chamisal
Peñasco
Alcalde
San Juan
La Puebla
Española
Chimayo
El Valle de Arroyo Seco
Pojoaque
COLFAX
Raton
Eagle Nest
Cimarron
Maxwell
Angel Fire
Springer
UNION
Folsom
Des Moines
Grenville
Clayton
MORA
Mora
Wagon Mound
HARDING
Roy
Mosquero
SANDOVAL
Regina
La Jara
Cuba
Pueblo Pintado
LOS ALAMOS
Los Alamos
White Rock
Jemez Springs
Rio Communities North
Ponderosa
Jemez Pueblo
Santo Domingo Pueblo
San Ysidro
Zia Pueblo
San Felipe Pueblo
Santa Ana Pueblo
Algodones
Bernalillo
Rio Rancho
Corrales
SAN MIGUEL
Santa Fe
Agua Fria
La Cienega
Eldorado at Santa Fe
Lamy
Galisteo
Madrid
Pecos
Los Alamos
Las Vegas
QUAY
Logan
Tucumcari
San Jon
MCKINLEY
Navajo
Tohatchi
Mexican Springs
Brimhall Nizhoni
Tse Bonito
Zuni Pueblo
Twin Lakes
Yah-ta-hey
Rock Springs
Church Rock
Gallup
Crownpoint
Thoreau
Black Rock
Ramah
Milan
Grants
North Acomita Village
Skyline-Ganipa
Seama
Encinal
Paguate
Paraje
Laguna
Mesita
Pinehill
CIBOLA
Albuquerque
North Valley
South Valley
BERNALILLO
SANTA FE
Cedar Grove
Edgewood
Moriarty
Chilili
TORRANCE
GUADALUPE
Santa Rosa
VALENCIA
Los Lunas
Los Chaves
Belen
El Cerro-Monterey Park
Jarales
Casa Colorada
Estancia
Encino
Willard
Mountainair
Vaughn
Lake Sumner
House
Grady
CURRY
DE BACA
Fort Sumner
Melrose
Clovis
Cannon AFB
Texico
CATRON
SOCORRO
Alamo
Corona
Magdalena
Socorro
LINCOLN
Floyd
Portales
Elida
Dora
Causey
CHAVES
ROOSEVELT
Reserve
Carrizozo
Capitan
SIERRA
Ruidoso
Ruidoso Downs
OTERO
Roswell
LEA
Tatum
GRANT
Truth Or Consequences
Williamsburg
Elephant Butte
Mescalero
Tularosa
Dexter
Hagerman
La Luz
Cloudcroft
Lake Arthur
Lovington
Holloman AFB
Alamogordo
Boles Acres
EDDY
Hope
Artesia
Silver City
Santa Clara
Bayard
San Juan
Hurley
Virden
Salem
Hatch
Rincon
DOÑA ANA
HIDALGO
Timberon
Hobbs
Radium Springs
Doña Ana
White Sands
Lordsburg
LUNA
Deming
Las Cruces
Mesilla
University Park
Mesquite
Vado
Anthony
Chaparral
Carlsbad North
Carlsbad
Eunice
Loving
Jal
Columbus
Santa Teresa
Sunland Park
161
5
260
Santa Clara Pueblo
Cundiyo
San Ildefonso Pueblo
Cuyamungue
El Rancho
Chupadero
Rio En Medio
Tesuque
0 10 Mi
0 10 Km
SANTA FE
Cañada de los Alamos
Glorieta
Cochiti
Pena Blanca
Santo Domingo Pueblo
Placitas
Los Ranchos de Albuquerque
Cedar Crest
Tijeras
Carnuel
Bosque Farms
Peralta
Valencia
Meadow Lake
Tajique
Torreon
Tome-Adelino
Los Trujillos-Gabaldon
Rio Communities
Manzano
Explanation of Symbols
State Capital
Vernon County Seat
MSA Boundary
161 MSA Number
TAOS County Name
Population Key
0-999
1,000-2,499
2,500-4,999
5,000-9,999
10,000-19,999
20,000-24,999
25,000-49,999
50,000-99,999
100,000-249,999
250,000-999,999
0 20 40 60 Miles
0 20 40 60 Kilometers
County-Town
NEW MEXICO
American Map

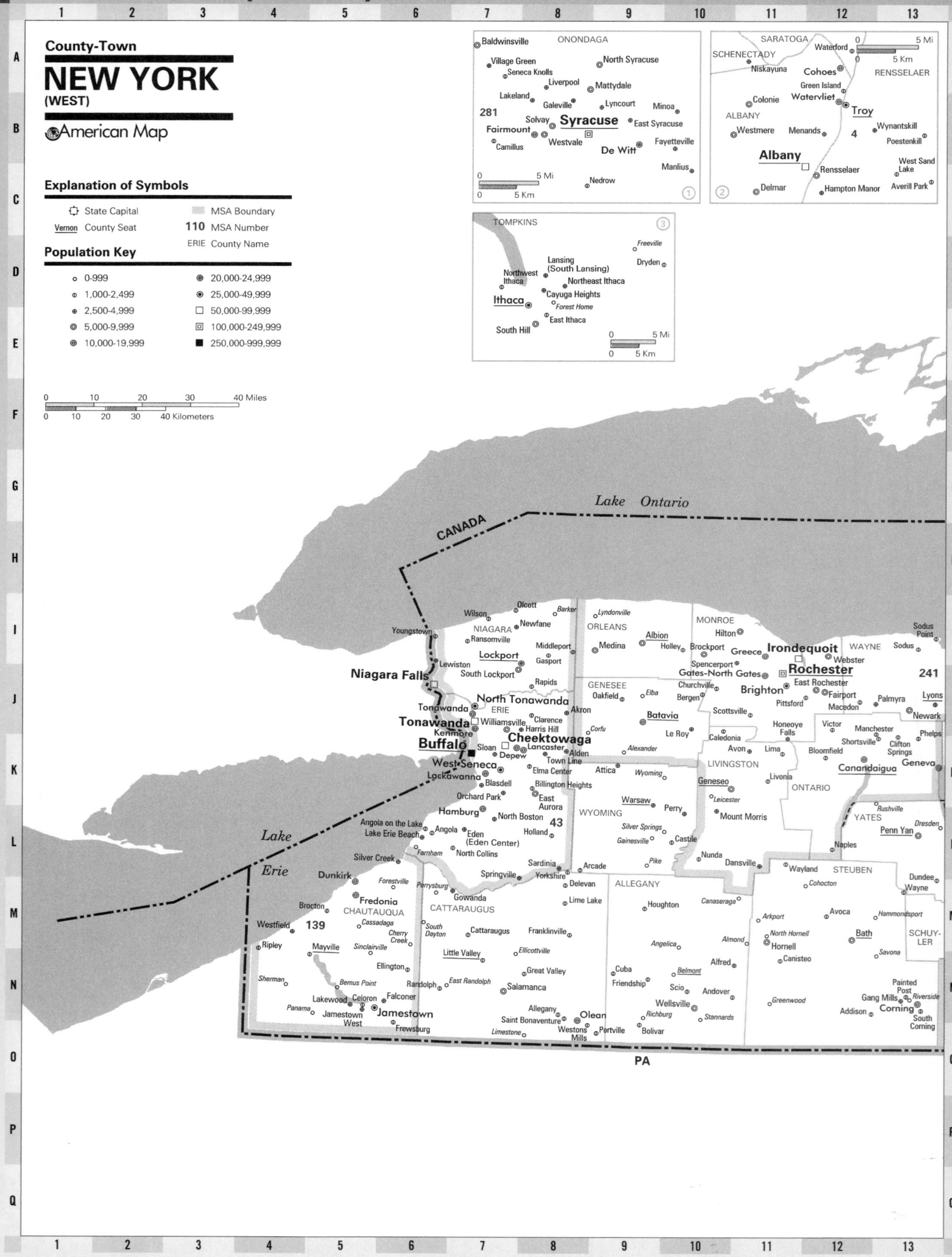
County-Town
NEW YORK
(WEST)
American Map
Explanation of Symbols
State Capital
Vernon County Seat
MSA Boundary
110 MSA Number
ERIE County Name
Population Key
0-999
1,000-2,499
2,500-4,999
5,000-9,999
10,000-19,999
20,000-24,999
25,000-49,999
50,000-99,999
100,000-249,999
250,000-999,999
0 10 20 30 40 Miles
0 10 20 30 40 Kilometers
Baldwinsville
ONONDAGA
Village Green
Seneca Knolls
North Syracuse
Liverpool
Mattydale
Lakeland
Galeville
Lyncourt
Minoa
281
Solvay
Syracuse
East Syracuse
Fairmount
Westvale
Camillus
De Witt
Fayetteville
Manlius
Nedrow
0 5 Mi
0 5 Km
1
SARATOGA
Waterford
SCHENECTADY
Niskayuna
Cohoes
RENSSELAER
Green Island
Colonie
Watervliet
Troy
ALBANY
Westmere
Menands
4
Wynantskill
Poestenkill
Albany
Rensselaer
West Sand Lake
Delmar
Hampton Manor
Averill Park
2
TOMPKINS
3
Freeville
Lansing (South Lansing)
Dryden
Northwest Ithaca
Northeast Ithaca
Cayuga Heights
Ithaca
Forest Home
East Ithaca
South Hill
Lake Ontario
CANADA
Olcott
Barker
Wilson
Lyndonville
Newfane
Youngstown
NIAGARA
Ransomville
ORLEANS
Albion
MONROE
Hilton
Sodus Point
Middleport
Medina
Holley
Brockport
Greece
Irondequoit
WAYNE
Sodus
Lockport
Gasport
Spencerport
Webster
Lewiston
Gates-North Gates
Rochester
241
Niagara Falls
South Lockport
Rapids
GENESEE
Churchville
Brighton
East Rochester
Oakfield
Elba
Bergen
Fairport
Pittsford
Palmyra
Lyons
North Tonawanda
Macedon
Newark
Tonawanda
ERIE
Akron
Scottsville
Tonawanda
Williamsville
Clarence
Batavia
Honeoye Falls
Victor
Manchester
Phelps
Kenmore
Harris Hill
Corfu
Le Roy
Caledonia
Shortsville
Clifton Springs
Cheektowaga
Buffalo
Sloan
Lancaster
Alexander
Avon
Lima
Bloomfield
Depew
Alden
Town Line
LIVINGSTON
Canandaigua
Geneva
West Seneca
Elma Center
Attica
Wyoming
Livonia
Lackawanna
Blasdell
Billington Heights
Geneseo
ONTARIO
Orchard Park
East Aurora
Leicester
Warsaw
Perry
Rushville
Hamburg
WYOMING
Mount Morris
YATES
North Boston
43
Dresden
Angola on the Lake
Angola
Eden (Eden Center)
Holland
Silver Springs
Penn Yan
Lake Erie Beach
Gainesville
Castile
Lake
Farnham
North Collins
Naples
Erie
Silver Creek
Nunda
Dansville
Pike
Sardinia
Arcade
Wayland
STEUBEN
Dunkirk
Forestville
Springville
Yorkshire
Dundee
Perrysburg
Delevan
ALLEGANY
Cohocton
Wayne
Fredonia
Gowanda
Lime Lake
Canaseraga
Brocton
CHAUTAUQUA
CATTARAUGUS
Houghton
Avoca
Hammondsport
Westfield
139
Cassadaga
South Dayton
Cattaraugus
Franklinville
Arkport
North Hornell
Bath
SCHUY-LER
Cherry Creek
Almond
Ripley
Mayville
Sinclairville
Little Valley
Ellicottville
Angelica
Hornell
Canisteo
Savona
Ellington
Alfred
Sherman
Bemus Point
Randolph
East Randolph
Great Valley
Cuba
Belmont
Friendship
Painted Post
Lakewood
Celoron
Falconer
Salamanca
Scio
Andover
Greenwood
Gang Mills
Riverside
Wellsville
Panama
Jamestown West
Jamestown
Allegany
Olean
Richburg
Stannards
Addison
Corning
South Corning
Saint Bonaventure
Frewsburg
Limestone
Westons Mills
Portville
Bolivar
PA

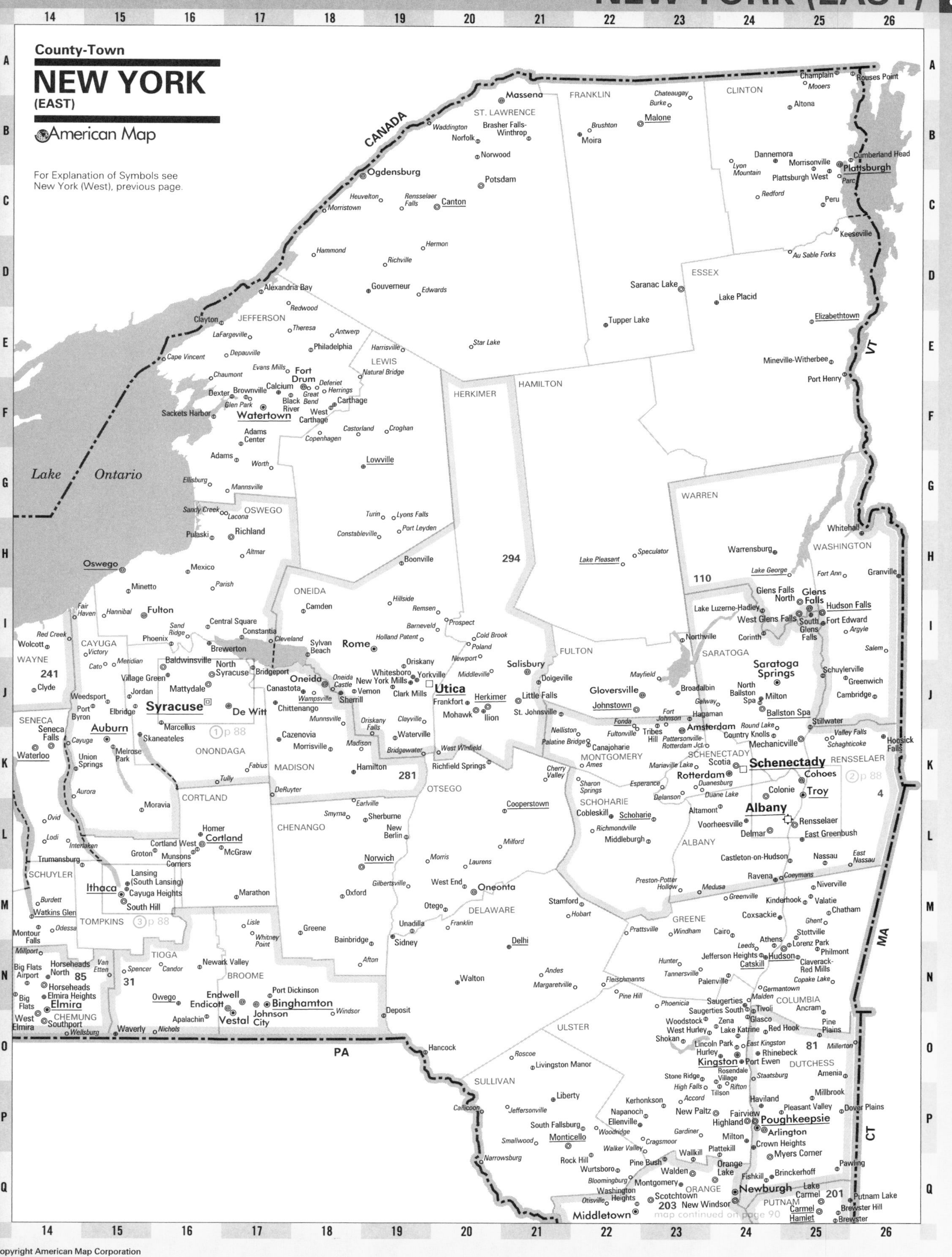

map continued on page 90

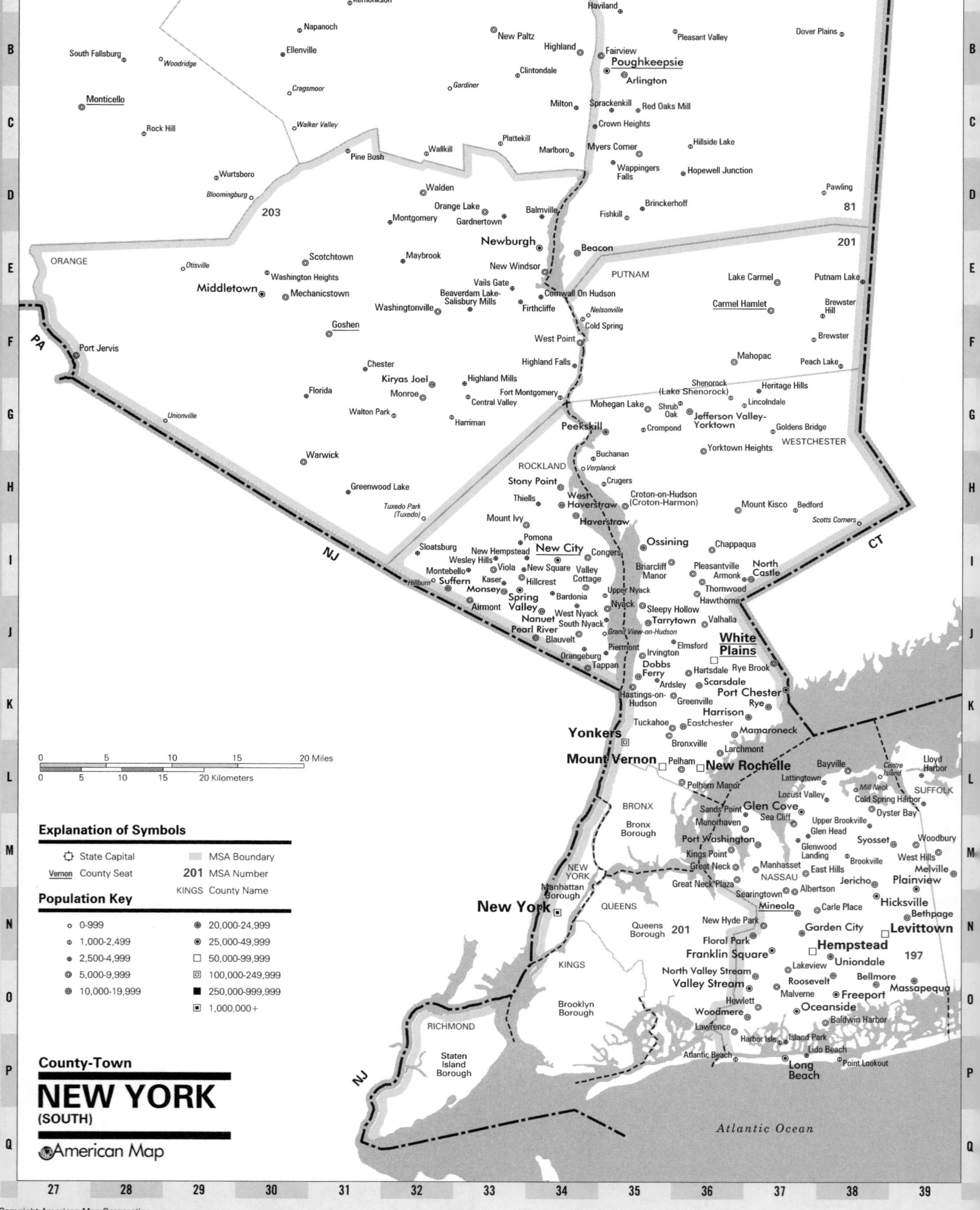
27 28 29 30 31 32 33 34 35 36 37 38 39
A B C D E F G H I J K L M N O P Q
continued from main map page 89
SULLIVAN
ULSTER
DUTCHESS
ORANGE
PUTNAM
ROCKLAND
WESTCHESTER
BRONX
NEW YORK
QUEENS
KINGS
RICHMOND
NASSAU
SUFFOLK
PA
NJ
CT
Atlantic Ocean
203
81
201
197
Liberty
Rosendale Village
Rifton
High Falls
Tillson
Accord
Kerhonkson
Haviland
Millbrook
Napanoch
New Paltz
Pleasant Valley
Dover Plains
South Fallsburg
Woodridge
Ellenville
Highland
Fairview
Poughkeepsie
Arlington
Clintondale
Cragsmoor
Gardiner
Monticello
Milton
Spackenkill
Red Oaks Mill
Crown Heights
Rock Hill
Walker Valley
Plattekill
Hillside Lake
Pine Bush
Wallkill
Marlboro
Myers Corner
Wappingers Falls
Hopewell Junction
Wurtsboro
Bloomingburg
Walden
Pawling
Orange Lake
Balmville
Brinckerhoff
Montgomery
Gardnertown
Fishkill
Newburgh
Beacon
Scotchtown
Maybrook
New Windsor
Otisville
Washington Heights
Lake Carmel
Putnam Lake
Middletown
Mechanicstown
Vails Gate
Beaverdam Lake-Salisbury Mills
Cornwall On Hudson
Washingtonville
Firthcliffe
Nelsonville
Carmel Hamlet
Brewster Hill
Goshen
Cold Spring
Brewster
Port Jervis
West Point
Mahopac
Highland Falls
Peach Lake
Chester
Kiryas Joel
Highland Mills
Shenorock (Lake Shenorock)
Heritage Hills
Florida
Monroe
Fort Montgomery
Central Valley
Mohegan Lake
Shrub Oak
Lincolndale
Walton Park
Jefferson Valley-Yorktown
Unionville
Harriman
Peekskill
Crompond
Goldens Bridge
Buchanan
Yorktown Heights
Warwick
Verplanck
Stony Point
Crugers
Greenwood Lake
Thiells
West Haverstraw
Croton-on-Hudson (Croton-Harmon)
Mount Kisco
Bedford
Tuxedo Park (Tuxedo)
Mount Ivy
Haverstraw
Scotts Corners
Pomona
Ossining
Sloatsburg
New Hempstead
New City
Congers
Chappaqua
Wesley Hills
Viola
New Square
Valley Cottage
Briarcliff Manor
Pleasantville
North Castle
Montebello
Armonk
Hillburn
Suffern
Kaser
Hillcrest
Upper Nyack
Thornwood
Monsey
Spring Valley
Bardonia
Hawthorne
Airmont
Nyack
Sleepy Hollow
West Nyack
Nanuet
Tarrytown
Valhalla
South Nyack
Pearl River
Grand View-on-Hudson
Blauvelt
White Plains
Elmsford
Piermont
Orangeburg
Irvington
Dobbs Ferry
Tappan
Hartsdale
Rye Brook
Ardsley
Scarsdale
Port Chester
Hastings-on-Hudson
Greenville
Rye
Harrison
Tuckahoe
Eastchester
Yonkers
Mamaroneck
Bronxville
Larchmont
Mount Vernon
Pelham
New Rochelle
Bayville
Centre Island
Lloyd Harbor
Lattingtown
Pelham Manor
Mill Neck
Locust Valley
Cold Spring Harbor
Sands Point
Glen Cove
Oyster Bay
Bronx Borough
Manorhaven
Sea Cliff
Upper Brookville
Glen Head
Port Washington
Syosset
Woodbury
Kings Point
Glenwood Landing
Brookville
West Hills
Great Neck
Manhasset
East Hills
Melville
Great Neck Plaza
Jericho
Plainview
Manhattan Borough
Albertson
Searingtown
Hicksville
New York
Mineola
Carle Place
Bethpage
New Hyde Park
Queens Borough
Garden City
Levittown
Floral Park
Franklin Square
Hempstead
Uniondale
North Valley Stream
Lakeview
Valley Stream
Roosevelt
Bellmore
Malverne
Freeport
Massapequa
Hewlett
Brooklyn Borough
Oceanside
Woodmere
Baldwin Harbor
Lawrence
Harbor Isle
Island Park
Lido Beach
Atlantic Beach
Long Beach
Point Lookout
Staten Island Borough
0 5 10 15 20 Miles
0 5 10 15 20 Kilometers
Explanation of Symbols
State Capital
MSA Boundary
Vernon County Seat
201 MSA Number
KINGS County Name
Population Key
0-999
1,000-2,499
2,500-4,999
5,000-9,999
10,000-19,999
20,000-24,999
25,000-49,999
50,000-99,999
100,000-249,999
250,000-999,999
1,000,000+
County-Town
NEW YORK
(SOUTH)
American Map

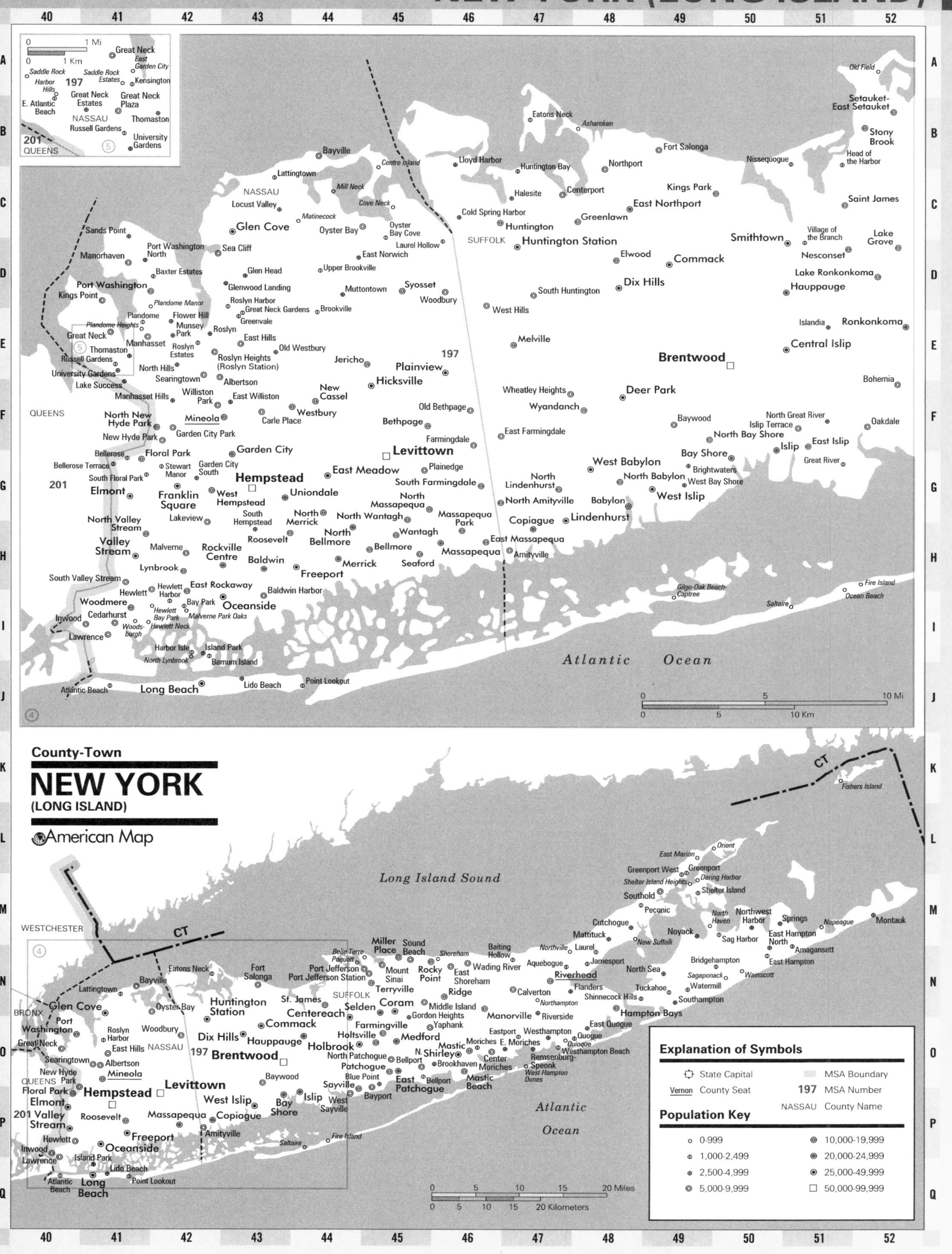
County-Town
NEW YORK
(LONG ISLAND)
American Map
Long Island Sound
Atlantic Ocean
Explanation of Symbols
State Capital
MSA Boundary
Vernon County Seat
197 MSA Number
NASSAU County Name
Population Key
0-999
1,000-2,499
2,500-4,999
5,000-9,999
10,000-19,999
20,000-24,999
25,000-49,999
50,000-99,999

COUNTIES

(62 Counties)

Name of County	Population	Location on Map
ALBANY	294,565	L-23
ALLEGANY	49,927	M-9
BRONX	1,332,650	L-35
BROOME	200,536	N-17
CATTARAUGUS	83,955	M-6
CAYUGA	81,963	I-14
CHAUTAUQUA	139,750	M-5
CHEMUNG	91,070	O-14
CHENANGO	51,401	L-17
CLINTON	79,894	A-24
COLUMBIA	63,094	N-24
CORTLAND	48,599	L-16
DELAWARE	48,055	M-20
DUTCHESS	280,150	O-25
ERIE	950,265	J-7
ESSEX	38,851	D-23
FRANKLIN	51,134	B-21
FULTON	55,073	I-21
GENESEE	60,370	J-8
GREENE	48,195	M-23
HAMILTON	5,379	F-21
HERKIMER	64,427	F-20
JEFFERSON	111,738	E-17
KINGS	2,465,326	O-34
LEWIS	26,944	E-19
LIVINGSTON	64,328	K-10
MADISON	69,441	K-17
MONROE	735,343	I-10
MONTGOMERY	49,708	K-22
NASSAU	1,334,544	M-37
NEW YORK	1,537,195	M-34
NIAGARA	219,846	I-7
ONEIDA	235,469	I-18
ONONDAGA	458,336	K-16
ONTARIO	100,224	K-11
ORANGE	341,367	Q-23
ORLEANS	44,171	I-8
OSWEGO	122,377	G-17
OTSEGO	61,676	K-19
PUTNAM	95,745	Q-24
QUEENS	2,229,379	N-35
RENSSELAER	152,538	K-25
RICHMOND	443,728	O-32
ROCKLAND	286,753	H-33
SAINT LAWRENCE	111,931	B-20
SARATOGA	200,635	I-23
SCHENECTADY	146,555	K-23
SCHOHARIE	31,582	L-22
SCHUYLER	19,224	M-13
SENECA	33,342	J-14
STEUBEN	98,726	L-12
SUFFOLK	1,419,369	L-39
SULLIVAN	73,966	P-20
TIOGA	51,784	N-16
TOMPKINS	96,501	M-14
ULSTER	177,749	O-21
WARREN	63,303	G-23
WASHINGTON	61,042	H-25
WAYNE	93,765	I-12
WESTCHESTER	923,459	G-37
WYOMING	43,424	L-8
YATES	24,621	L-12
TOTAL	**18,976,457**	

CITIES AND TOWNS

Note: The first name is that of the city or town, second, that of the county in which it is located, then the population and location on the map.

Explanation of symbols: ● - Census Designated Place (CDP) ▲ - Township

▲Leon, *Cattaraugus*, 1,380 ...N-6
● Levittown, *Nassau*, 53,067 ...N-38
▲Lewis, *Essex*, 1,200 ...D-25
▲Lewisboro, *Westchester*, 12,324 ...H-38
Lewiston, *Niagara*, 2,781 ...J-6
▲Leyden, *Lewis*, 1,792 ...H-19
Liberty, *Sullivan*, 3,975 ...P-21
▲Liberty, *Sullivan*, 9,632 ...P-21
● Lido Beach, *Nassau*, 2,825 ...J-43
Lima, *Livingston*, 2,459 ...K-11
▲Lima, *Livingston*, 4,541 ...K-11
● Lime Lake, *Cattaraugus*, 1,422 ...M-8
▲Lincoln, *Madison*, 1,818 ...J-18
● Lincoln Park, *Ulster*, 2,337 ...O-24
● Lincolndale, *Westchester*, 2,018 ...G-36
Lindenhurst, *Suffolk*, 27,819 ...H-47
▲Lindley, *Steuben*, 1,913 ...O-13
▲Lisbon, *Saint Lawrence*, 4,047 ...C-19
▲Lisle, *Broome*, 2,707 ...M-17
▲Litchfield, *Herkimer*, 1,453 ...K-20
Little Falls, *Herkimer*, 5,188 ...J-21
▲Little Falls, *Herkimer*, 1,544 ...J-21
Little Valley, *Cattaraugus*, 1,130 ...N-7
▲Little Valley, *Cattaraugus*, 1,788 ...N-7
Liverpool, *Onondaga*, 2,505 ...A-8
▲Livingston, *Columbia*, 3,424 ...N-25
● Livingston Manor, *Sullivan*, 1,355 ...O-21
Livonia, *Livingston*, 1,373 ...K-11
▲Livonia, *Livingston*, 7,286 ...K-11
▲Lloyd, *Ulster*, 9,941 ...P-24
Lloyd Harbor, *Suffolk*, 3,675 ...L-39
Lockport, *Niagara*, 22,279 ...J-7
▲Lockport, *Niagara*, 19,653 ...J-7
● Locust Valley, *Nassau*, 3,521 ...L-38
▲Lodi, *Seneca*, 1,476 ...L-14
Long Beach, *Nassau*, 35,462 ...P-37
● Lorenz Park, *Columbia*, 1,981 ...N-25
▲Louisville, *Lawrence*, 3,195 ...B-20
Lowville, *Lewis*, 3,476 ...G-18
▲Lowville, *Lewis*, 4,548 ...G-18
▲Lumberland, *Sullivan*, 1,939 ...Q-21
▲Lyme, *Jefferson*, 2,015 ...F-16
Lynbrook, *Nassau*, 19,911 ...H-42
● Lyncourt, *Onondaga*, 4,268 ...B-9
Lyons, *Wayne*, 3,695 ...J-13
▲Lyons, *Wayne*, 5,831 ...J-13
▲Lyonsdale, *Lewis*, 1,273 ...H-19
▲Lysander, *Onondaga*, 19,285 ...J-15
Macedon, *Wayne*, 1,496 ...J-12
▲Macedon, *Wayne*, 8,688 ...J-12
▲Machias, *Cattaraugus*, 2,482 ...M-8
▲Madison, *Madison*, 2,801 ...K-18
▲Madrid, *Saint Lawrence*, 1,828 ...B-20
● Mahopac, *Putnam*, 8,478 ...F-36
▲Maine, *Broome*, 5,459 ...N-17
Malone, *Franklin*, 6,075 ...B-22
▲Malone, *Franklin*, 14,981 ...B-22
▲Malta, *Saratoga*, 13,005 ...J-24
Malverne, *Nassau*, 8,934 ...O-37
▲Mamakating, *Sullivan*, 11,002 ...Q-22
Mamaroneck, *Westchester*, 18,752 ...L-36
▲Mamaroneck, *Westchester*, 28,967 ...L-36
Manchester, *Ontario*, 1,475 ...K-12
▲Manchester, *Ontario*, 9,258 ...K-12
● Manhasset, *Nassau*, 8,362 ...M-37
● Manhasset Hills, *Nassau*, 3,661 ...F-42
▲Manheim, *Herkimer*, 3,171 ...J-21
▲Manlius, *Onondaga*, 31,872 ...C-10
Manlius, *Onondaga*, 4,819 ...C-10
Manorhaven, *Nassau*, 6,138 ...M-36
● Manorville, *Suffolk*, 11,131 ...N-46
Marathon, *Cortland*, 1,063 ...M-17
▲Marathon, *Cortland*, 2,189 ...M-17
▲Marbletown, *Ulster*, 5,854 ...O-23
Marcellus, *Onondaga*, 1,826 ...J-16
▲Marcellus, *Onondaga*, 6,319 ...J-16
▲Marcy, *Oneida*, 9,469 ...J-19
▲Marilla, *Erie*, 5,709 ...K-8
▲Marion, *Wayne*, 4,974 ...J-13
▲Marlboro, *Ulster*, 2,339 ...D-34
▲Marlborough, *Ulster*, 8,263 ...P-24
▲Marshall, *Oneida*, 2,127 ...K-19
▲Martinsburg, *Lewis*, 1,249 ...G-19
▲Maryland, *Otsego*, 1,920 ...L-21
▲Masonville, *Delaware*, 1,405 ...N-19
● Massapequa, *Nassau*, 22,652 ...O-39
Massapequa Park, *Nassau*, 17,499 ...H-46
Massena, *Saint Lawrence*, 11,209 ...B-20
▲Massena, *Saint Lawrence*, 13,121 ...B-20
▲Mastic, *Suffolk*, 15,436 ...O-46
● Mastic Beach, *Suffolk*, 11,543 ...O-46
● Mattituck, *Suffolk*, 4,198 ...M-48
▲Mattydale, *Onondaga*, 6,367 ...J-16
Maybrook, *Orange*, 3,084 ...E-32
▲Mayfield, *Fulton*, 6,432 ...J-23
Mayville, *Chautauqua*, 1,756 ...N-5
McGraw, *Cortland*, 1,000 ...L-16
● Mechanicstown, *Orange*, 6,061 ...E-30
Mechanicville, *Saratoga*, 5,019 ...K-25
● Medford, *Suffolk*, 21,985 ...O-45
Medina, *Orleans*, 6,415 ...I-9
● Melrose Park, *Cayuga*, 2,359 ...K-15
● Melville, *Suffolk*, 14,533 ...M-39
Menands, *Albany*, 3,910 ...B-12
▲Mendon, *Monroe*, 8,370 ...J-12
▲Mentz, *Cayuga*, 2,446 ...J-15
▲Meredith, *Delaware*, 1,588 ...M-20
● Merrick, *Nassau*, 22,764 ...H-44
Mexico, *Oswego*, 1,572 ...H-16
▲Mexico, *Oswego*, 5,181 ...H-16
● Middle Island, *Suffolk*, 9,702 ...N-45
Middleburgh, *Schoharie*, 1,398 ...L-23
▲Middleburgh, *Schoharie*, 3,515 ...L-23
▲Middlebury, *Wyoming*, 1,508 ...K-9
▲Middlefield, *Otsego*, 2,249 ...L-21
Middleport, *Niagara*, 1,917 ...I-8
▲Middlesex, *Yates*, 1,345 ...L-12
▲Middletown, *Delaware*, 4,051 ...N-21
Middletown, *Orange*, 25,388 ...Q-22
▲Milan, *Dutchess*, 4,559 ...O-25
▲Milford, *Otsego*, 2,938 ...L-20
Millbrook, *Dutchess*, 1,429 ...A-37
● Miller Place, *Suffolk*, 10,580 ...N-45
▲Milo, *Yates*, 7,026 ...L-13
▲Milton, *Saratoga*, 2,692 ...J-24
▲Milton, *Saratoga*, 17,103 ...J-24
● Milton, *Ulster*, 1,251 ...P-24
▲Mina, *Chautauqua*, 1,176 ...N-4
▲Minden, *Montgomery*, 4,202 ...K-21
Mineola, *Nassau*, 19,234 ...N-37
● Minetto, *Oswego*, 1,086 ...I-15
▲Minetto, *Oswego*, 1,663 ...I-15
● Mineville-Witherbee, *Essex*, 1,747 ...E-25
▲Minisink, *Orange*, 3,585 ...G-28
Minoa, *Onondaga*, 3,348 ...B-10
Mohawk, *Herkimer*, 2,660 ...J-20
▲Mohawk, *Montgomery*, 3,902 ...J-22
Mohegan Lake, *Westchester*, 5,979 ...G-35
▲Moira, *Franklin*, 2,857 ...B-22
Monroe, *Orange*, 7,780 ...G-32
▲Monroe, *Orange*, 31,407 ...G-32
● Monsey, *Rockland*, 14,504 ...J-33
● Montauk, *Suffolk*, 3,851 ...M-52
Montebello, *Rockland*, 3,688 ...I-33
▲Montezuma, *Cayuga*, 1,431 ...J-14
Montgomery, *Orange*, 3,636 ...Q-23
▲Montgomery, *Orange*, 20,891 ...Q-23
Monticello, *Sullivan*, 6,512 ...P-21
▲Montour, *Schuyler*, 2,446 ...M-14
Montour Falls, *Schuyler*, 1,797 ...M-14
▲Mooers, *Clinton*, 3,404 ...A-25
Moravia, *Cayuga*, 1,363 ...L-15
▲Moravia, *Cayuga*, 4,040 ...L-15
▲Moreau, *Saratoga*, 13,826 ...I-25
▲Moriah, *Essex*, 4,879 ...F-25
● Moriches, *Suffolk*, 2,319 ...O-46
▲Morris, *Otsego*, 1,867 ...L-19
● Morrisonville, *Clinton*, 1,702 ...C-25
▲Morristown, *Saint Lawrence*, 2,050 ...C-18
Morrisville, *Madison*, 2,148 ...K-18
▲Mount Hope, *Orange*, 6,639 ...Q-22
▲Mount Ivy, *Rockland*, 6,536 ...I-33
Mount Kisco, *Westchester*, 9,983 ...H-36
Mount Morris, *Livingston*, 3,266 ...L-10
▲Mount Morris, *Livingston*, 4,567 ...L-10
● Mount Sinai, *Suffolk*, 8,734 ...N-45
Mount Vernon, *Westchester*, 68,381 ...L-35
Munsey Park, *Nassau*, 2,632 ...E-42
● Munsons Corners, *Cortland*, 2,426 ...L-16
▲Murray, *Orleans*, 6,259 ...I-10
Muttontown, *Nassau*, 3,412 ...D-44
Myers Corner, *Dutchess*, 5,546 ...Q-24
▲Nanticoke, *Broome*, 1,790 ...N-14
● Nanuet, *Rockland*, 16,707 ...J-34
● Napanoch, *Ulster*, 1,168 ...P-23
Naples, *Ontario*, 1,072 ...L-12
▲Naples, *Ontario*, 2,441 ...L-12
▲Napoli, *Cattaraugus*, 1,159 ...N-7
Nassau, *Rensselaer*, 1,161 ...L-25
▲Nassau, *Rensselaer*, 4,818 ...L-25
● Nedrow, *Onondaga*, 2,265 ...C-8
▲Nelson, *Madison*, 1,964 ...K-18
● Nesconset, *Suffolk*, 11,992 ...D-51
▲Neversink, *Sullivan*, 3,553 ...P-22
▲New Albion, *Cattaraugus*, 2,068 ...M-7
▲New Baltimore, *Greene*, 3,417 ...M-24
New Berlin, *Chenango*, 1,129 ...L-19
▲New Berlin, *Chenango*, 2,803 ...L-19
▲New Bremen, *Lewis*, 2,722 ...F-19
● New Cassel, *Nassau*, 13,298 ...F-44
▲New Castle, *Westchester*, 17,491 ...I-36
▲New City, *Rockland*, 34,038 ...I-34
New Hartford, *Oneida*, 1,886 ...J-19
▲New Hartford, *Oneida*, 21,172 ...J-19
▲New Haven, *Oswego*, 2,930 ...H-16
New Hempstead, *Rockland*, 4,767 ...I-33
New Hyde Park, *Nassau*, 9,523 ...N-37
▲New Lebanon, *Columbia*, 2,454 ...M-26
▲New Lisbon, *Otsego*, 1,116 ...L-20
New Paltz, *Ulster*, 6,034 ...P-24
▲New Paltz, *Ulster*, 12,830 ...P-24
New Rochelle, *Westchester*, 72,182 ...L-36
▲New Scotland, *Albany*, 8,626 ...L-23
● New Square, *Rockland*, 4,624 ...I-33
▲New Windsor, *Orange*, 9,077 ...Q-24
▲New Windsor, *Orange*, 22,866 ...Q-24
New York, *New York*, 8,008,278 ...N-34
New York Mills, *Oneida*, 3,191 ...J-19
Newark, *Wayne*, 9,682 ...J-13
Newark Valley, *Tioga*, 1,071 ...N-16
▲Newark Valley, *Tioga*, 4,097 ...N-16
Newburgh, *Orange*, 28,259 ...Q-24
▲Newburgh, *Orange*, 27,568 ...Q-24
● Newfane, *Niagara*, 3,129 ...I-7
▲Newfane, *Niagara*, 9,657 ...I-7
▲Newfield, *Tompkins*, 5,108 ...M-15
▲Newport, *Herkimer*, 2,192 ...J-20
▲Newstead, *Erie*, 8,404 ...J-8
▲Niagara, *Niagara*, 8,978 ...J-6
Niagara Falls, *Erie*, 55,593 ...J-6
▲Nichols, *Tioga*, 2,584 ...O-15
▲Niles, *Cayuga*, 1,208 ...K-15
● Niskayuna, *Schenectady*, 4,892 ...A-11
▲Niskayuna, *Schenectady*, 20,295 ...K-24
Nissequogue, *Suffolk*, 1,543 ...C-51
● Niverville, *Columbia*, 1,737 ...M-25
● Norfolk, *Saint Lawrence*, 1,334 ...B-20
▲Norfolk, *Saint Lawrence*, 4,565 ...B-20
● North Amityville, *Nassau*, 16,572 ...G-46
● North Babylon, *Nassau*, 17,877 ...G-48
● North Ballston Spa, *Saratoga*, 1,237 ...J-24
● North Bay Shore, *Suffolk*, 14,992 ...F-49
● North Bellmore, *Nassau*, 20,079 ...H-44
● North Bellport, *Suffolk*, 9,007 ...O-45
● North Boston, *Erie*, 2,680 ...L-7
▲North Castle, *Westchester*, 10,849 ...I-37
North Collins, *Erie*, 1,079 ...L-7
▲North Collins, *Erie*, 3,376 ...L-7
▲North Danville, *Livingston*, 5,738 ...L-10
▲North East, *Dutchess*, 3,002 ...O-25
▲North Elba, *Essex*, 8,661 ...D-24
● North Great River, *Suffolk*, 3,929 ...F-51
● North Greenbush, *Rensselaer*, 10,805 ...L-25
▲North Harmony, *Chautauqua*, 2,521 ...N-5
▲North Hempstead, *Nassau*, 222,611 ...E-43
North Hills, *Nassau*, 4,301 ...E-42
● North Lindenhurst, *Suffolk*, 11,767 ...G-47
● North Massapequa, *Nassau*, 19,152 ...G-45
● North Merrick, *Nassau*, 11,844 ...G-44
● North New Hyde Park, *Nassau*, 14,542 ...F-42
▲North Norwich, *Chenango*, 1,966 ...L-19
● North Patchogue, *Suffolk*, 7,825 ...O-45
▲North Salem, *Westchester*, 5,173 ...G-38
● North Sea, *Suffolk*, 4,493 ...N-49
North Syracuse, *Onondaga*, 6,862 ...J-16
North Tonawanda, *Niagara*, 33,262 ...J-7
● North Valley Stream, *Nassau*, 15,789 ...O-37
● North Wantagh, *Nassau*, 12,156 ...H-45
▲Northampton, *Fulton*, 2,760 ...I-23
● Northeast Ithaca, *Tompkins*, 2,655 ...D-8
● Northport, *Suffolk*, 7,606 ...C-48
▲Northumberland, *Saratoga*, 4,603 ...I-25
Northville, *Fulton*, 1,139 ...I-23
● Northwest Harbor, *Suffolk*, 3,059 ...M-50
● Northwest Ithaca, *Tompkins*, 1,115 ...D-7
Norwich, *Chenango*, 7,355 ...M-18
▲Norwich, *Chenango*, 3,836 ...M-18
Norwood, *Saint Lawrence*, 1,685 ...B-20
● Noyack, *Suffolk*, 2,696 ...M-49
Nunda, *Livingston*, 1,330 ...L-10
▲Nunda, *Livingston*, 3,017 ...L-10
Nyack, *Rockland*, 6,737 ...J-35
● Oakdale, *Suffolk*, 8,075 ...F-52
Oakfield, *Genesee*, 1,805 ...J-9
▲Oakfield, *Genesee*, 3,203 ...J-9
● Oceanside, *Nassau*, 32,733 ...O-37
▲Ogden, *Monroe*, 18,492 ...I-11
Ogdensburg, *Saint Lawrence*, 12,364 ...C-18
● Olcott, *Niagara*, 1,156 ...I-7
● Old Bethpage, *Nassau*, 5,400 ...F-46
Old Westbury, *Nassau*, 4,228 ...E-43
Olean, *Cattaraugus*, 15,347 ...O-8
▲Olean, *Cattaraugus*, 2,029 ...O-8
▲Olive, *Ulster*, 4,579 ...O-23
Oneida, *Madison*, 10,987 ...J-18
Oneonta, *Otsego*, 13,292 ...M-20
▲Oneonta, *Otsego*, 4,994 ...M-20
▲Onondaga, *Onondaga*, 21,063 ...J-16
▲Ontario, *Wayne*, 9,778 ...I-12
▲Oppenheim, *Fulton*, 1,774 ...J-22
▲Orange, *Schuyler*, 1,752 ...M-14
● Orange Lake, *Orange*, 6,085 ...Q-24
● Orangeburg, *Rockland*, 3,388 ...J-34
▲Orangetown, *Rockland*, 47,711 ...J-34
▲Orangeville, *Wyoming*, 1,301 ...K-9
Orchard Park, *Erie*, 3,294 ...K-7
▲Orchard Park, *Erie*, 27,637 ...K-7
Oriskany, *Oneida*, 1,459 ...J-19
▲Orleans, *Jefferson*, 2,465 ...E-17
▲Orwell, *Oswego*, 1,254 ...H-17
Ossining, *Westchester*, 24,010 ...I-35
▲Ossining, *Westchester*, 36,534 ...I-35
▲Oswegatchie, *Saint Lawrence*, 4,370 ...E-20
Oswego, *Oswego*, 17,954 ...H-15
▲Oswego, *Oswego*, 7,287 ...H-15
Otego, *Otsego*, 1,052 ...M-20
▲Otego, *Otsego*, 3,183 ...M-20
▲Otisco, *Onondaga*, 2,561 ...K-16
▲Otsego, *Otsego*, 3,904 ...L-20
▲Ovid, *Seneca*, 2,757 ...L-14
▲Owasco, *Cayuga*, 3,755 ...K-15
Owego, *Tioga*, 3,911 ...N-16
▲Owego, *Tioga*, 20,365 ...N-16
Oxford, *Chenango*, 1,584 ...M-18
▲Oxford, *Chenango*, 3,992 ...M-18
● Oyster Bay, *Nassau*, 6,826 ...M-38
Oyster Bay Cove, *Nassau*, 2,262 ...D-45
Painted Post, *Steuben*, 1,842 ...N-13
▲Palatine, *Montgomery*, 3,070 ...K-22
▲Palenville, *Greene*, 1,120 ...N-24
▲Palermo, *Oswego*, 3,686 ...I-16
Palmyra, *Wayne*, 3,490 ...J-12
▲Palmyra, *Wayne*, 7,672 ...J-12
▲Pamelia, *Jefferson*, 2,897 ...F-17
▲Paris, *Oneida*, 4,609 ...J-19
▲Parish, *Oswego*, 2,694 ...I-16
▲Parishville, *Saint Lawrence*, 2,049 ...C-21
▲Parma, *Monroe*, 14,822 ...I-10
Patchogue, *Suffolk*, 11,919 ...O-45
▲Patterson, *Putnam*, 11,306 ...Q-25
▲Pavilion, *Genesee*, 2,467 ...K-10
Pawling, *Dutchess*, 2,233 ...Q-25
▲Pawling, *Dutchess*, 7,521 ...Q-25
● Peach Lake, *Putnam*, 1,671 ...F-38
● Pearl River, *Rockland*, 15,553 ...J-34
● Peconic, *Suffolk*, 1,081 ...M-48
Peekskill, *Westchester*, 22,441 ...G-35
Pelham, *Westchester*, 6,400 ...L-36
▲Pelham, *Westchester*, 11,866 ...L-36
Pelham Manor, *Westchester*, 5,466 ...L-36
▲Pembroke, *Genesee*, 4,530 ...J-8
▲Pendleton, *Niagara*, 6,050 ...J-7
▲Penfield, *Monroe*, 34,645 ...J-12
Penn Yan, *Yates*, 5,219 ...L-13
▲Perinton, *Monroe*, 46,090 ...J-12
Perry, *Wyoming*, 3,945 ...L-10
▲Perry, *Wyoming*, 6,654 ...L-10
▲Perrysburg, *Cattaraugus*, 1,771 ...M-6
▲Persia, *Cattaraugus*, 2,512 ...M-6
▲Perth, *Fulton*, 3,638 ...J-23
● Peru, *Clinton*, 1,514 ...C-25
▲Peru, *Clinton*, 6,370 ...C-25
▲Petersburgh, *Rensselaer*, 1,563 ...K-26
Phelps, *Ontario*, 1,969 ...K-13
▲Phelps, *Ontario*, 7,017 ...K-13
Philadelphia, *Jefferson*, 1,519 ...E-18
▲Philadelphia, *Jefferson*, 2,140 ...E-18
▲Philipstown, *Putnam*, 9,422 ...Q-24
Philmont, *Columbia*, 1,480 ...N-25
Phoenix, *Oswego*, 2,251 ...I-16
Piermont, *Rockland*, 2,607 ...J-35
▲Pierrepont, *Saint Lawrence*, 2,674 ...C-20
▲Pike, *Wyoming*, 1,086 ...L-9
● Pine Bush, *Orange*, 1,539 ...Q-23
● Pine Plains, *Dutchess*, 1,412 ...O-25
▲Pine Plains, *Dutchess*, 2,569 ...O-25
▲Pittsfield, *Otsego*, 1,295 ...L-20
Pittsford, *Monroe*, 1,418 ...J-12
▲Pittsford, *Monroe*, 27,219 ...J-12
▲Pittstown, *Rensselaer*, 5,644 ...K-25
● Plainedge, *Nassau*, 9,195 ...G-45
● Plainview, *Nassau*, 25,637 ...N-39
Plandome, *Nassau*, 1,272 ...E-41
● Plattekill, *Ulster*, 1,050 ...Q-24
▲Plattekill, *Ulster*, 9,892 ...Q-24
Plattsburgh, *Clinton*, 18,816 ...C-25
▲Plattsburgh, *Clinton*, 11,190 ...C-25
● Plattsburgh West, *Clinton*, 1,289 ...C-25
● Pleasant Valley, *Dutchess*, 1,839 ...P-24
▲Pleasant Valley, *Dutchess*, 9,066 ...P-24
Pleasantville, *Westchester*, 7,172 ...I-36
▲Plymouth, *Chenango*, 2,049 ...L-18
▲Poestenkill, *Rensselaer*, 4,054 ...B-13
● Poestenkill, *Rensselaer*, 1,024 ...B-13
● Point Lookout, *Nassau*, 1,472 ...P-38
▲Poland, *Chautauqua*, 2,467 ...N-6
▲Pomfret, *Chautauqua*, 14,703 ...M-5
Pomona, *Rockland*, 2,726 ...I-33
▲Pompey, *Onondaga*, 6,159 ...K-17
Port Byron, *Cayuga*, 1,297 ...J-15
Port Chester, *Westchester*, 27,867 ...K-37
Port Dickinson, *Broome*, 1,697 ...N-17
● Port Ewen, *Ulster*, 3,650 ...O-24
Port Henry, *Essex*, 1,152 ...E-25
Port Jefferson, *Suffolk*, 7,837 ...N-44
● Port Jefferson Station, *Suffolk*, 7,527 ...N-45
Port Jervis, *Orange*, 8,860 ...F-27
● Port Washington, *Nassau*, 15,215 ...M-37
● Port Washington North, *Nassau*, 2,700 ...D-41
▲Porter, *Niagara*, 6,920 ...I-6
▲Portland, *Chautauqua*, 5,502 ...M-5
Portville, *Cattaraugus*, 1,024 ...O-9
▲Portville, *Cattaraugus*, 3,952 ...O-9
Potsdam, *Saint Lawrence*, 9,425 ...C-20
▲Potsdam, *Saint Lawrence*, 15,957 ...C-20
▲Potter, *Yates*, 1,830 ...L-13
Poughkeepsie, *Dutchess*, 29,871 ...P-24
▲Poughkeepsie, *Dutchess*, 42,777 ...P-24
▲Pound Ridge, *Westchester*, 4,726 ...L-41
▲Prattsburgh, *Steuben*, 2,064 ...M-12
▲Preble, *Cortland*, 1,582 ...L-16
▲Princetown, *Schenectady*, 2,132 ...K-23
▲Providence, *Saratoga*, 1,841 ...J-23
Pulaski, *Oswego*, 2,398 ...H-16
● Putnam Lake, *Putnam*, 3,855 ...Q-25
● Putnam Valley, *Putnam*, 10,686 ...G-35
▲Queensbury, *Warren*, 25,441 ...I-25
Quogue, *Suffolk*, 1,018 ...O-47
▲Ramapo, *Rockland*, 108,905 ...I-32
Randolph, *Cattaraugus*, 1,316 ...N-6
▲Randolph, *Cattaraugus*, 2,681 ...N-6
▲Ransomville, *Niagara*, 1,488 ...I-7
● Rapids, *Niagara*, 1,356 ...J-8
▲Rathbone, *Steuben*, 1,080 ...N-12
Ravena, *Albany*, 3,369 ...M-24
▲Reading, *Schuyler*, 1,786 ...M-14
Red Hook, *Dutchess*, 1,805 ...O-24
▲Red Hook, *Dutchess*, 10,408 ...O-24
● Red Oaks Mill, *Dutchess*, 4,930 ...C-35
▲Remsen, *Oneida*, 1,958 ...I-20
● Remsenburg-Speonk, *Suffolk*, 2,675 ...O-47
Rensselaer, *Rensselaer*, 7,761 ...L-25
▲Rensselaerville, *Albany*, 1,915 ...M-23
Rhinebeck, *Dutchess*, 3,077 ...O-24
▲Rhinebeck, *Dutchess*, 7,762 ...O-24
▲Richfield, *Otsego*, 2,423 ...K-20
Richfield Springs, *Otsego*, 1,255 ...K-20
▲Richford, *Tioga*, 1,170 ...M-16
▲Richland, *Oswego*, 5,824 ...H-17
▲Richmond, *Ontario*, 3,452 ...K-11
▲Richmondville, *Schoharie*, 2,412 ...L-22
● Ridge, *Suffolk*, 13,380 ...N-46
▲Ridgeway, *Orleans*, 6,886 ...I-8
▲Riga, *Monroe*, 5,437 ...J-10
▲Rilteney, *Steuben*, 1,405 ...L-13
▲Ripley, *Chautauqua*, 1,030 ...N-4
▲Ripley, *Chautauqua*, 2,636 ...N-4
▲Riverhead, *Suffolk*, 10,513 ...N-47
▲Riverhead, *Suffolk*, 27,680 ...N-47
● Riverside, *Suffolk*, 2,875 ...O-18
Rochester, *Monroe*, 219,773 ...J-11
▲Rochester, *Ulster*, 7,018 ...P-23
● Rock Hill, *Sullivan*, 1,056 ...Q-22
▲Rockland, *Sullivan*, 3,913 ...O-21
Rockville Centre, *Nassau*, 24,568 ...H-42
● Rocky Point, *Suffolk*, 10,185 ...N-45
▲Rodman, *Jefferson*, 1,147 ...G-17
Rome, *Oneida*, 34,950 ...I-19
▲Romulus, *Seneca*, 2,036 ...L-14
● Ronkonkoma, *Suffolk*, 20,029 ...E-52
● Roosevelt, *Nassau*, 15,854 ...O-38
▲Root, *Montgomery*, 1,752 ...K-22
▲Rose, *Wayne*, 2,442 ...J-14
● Rosendale Village, *Ulster*, 1,374 ...P-24
Roslyn, *Nassau*, 2,570 ...E-42
Roslyn Estates, *Nassau*, 1,210 ...E-42
Roslyn Harbor, *Nassau*, 1,023 ...O-41
● Roslyn Heights (Roslyn Station), *Nassau*, 6,295 ...E-42
● Rotterdam, *Schenectady*, 20,536 ...K-24
▲Rotterdam, *Schenectady*, 28,316 ...K-24
Rouses Point, *Clinton*, 2,277 ...A-25
▲Roxbury, *Delaware*, 2,509 ...N-22
▲Royalton, *Niagara*, 7,710 ...J-8
▲Rush, *Monroe*, 3,603 ...J-11
▲Rushford, *Allegany*, 1,259 ...M-9
▲Russell, *Saint Lawrence*, 1,801 ...D-20
Russell Gardens, *Nassau*, 1,074 ...E-41
▲Russia, *Herkimer*, 2,487 ...I-20
▲Rutland, *Jefferson*, 2,959 ...F-17
Rye, *Westchester*, 14,955 ...K-37
▲Rye, *Westchester*, 43,880 ...K-37
Rye Brook, *Westchester*, 8,602 ...K-37
Sackets Harbor, *Jefferson*, 1,386 ...F-16
Sag Harbor, *Suffolk*, 2,313 ...M-50
▲Saint Armand, *Essex*, 1,321 ...D-23
● Saint Bonaventure, *Chautauqua*, 2,127 ...O-8
Saint James, *Suffolk*, 13,268 ...N-44
Saint Johnsville, *Montgomery*, 1,685 ...J-21
▲Saint Johnsville, *Montgomery*, 2,565 ...J-21
Salamanca, *Cattaraugus*, 6,097 ...N-7
▲Salem, *Washington*, 2,702 ...I-26
▲Salina, *Onondaga*, 33,290 ...J-16
● Salisbury, *Herkimer*, 12,341 ...J-21
▲Salisbury, *Herkimer*, 1,953 ...J-21
▲Sand Lake, *Rensselaer*, 7,987 ...L-25
Sands Point, *Nassau*, 2,786 ...M-36
▲Sandy Creek, *Oswego*, 3,863 ...H-16
▲Sanford, *Broome*, 2,477 ...O-19
▲Sangerfield, *Oneida*, 2,610 ...K-19
▲Saranac, *Clinton*, 4,165 ...C-24
Saranac Lake, *Franklin*, 5,041 ...D-23
▲Saratoga, *Saratoga*, 5,141 ...J-24
Saratoga Springs, *Saratoga*, 26,186 ...J-24
▲Sardinia, *Erie*, 2,692 ...L-8
Saugerties, *Ulster*, 4,955 ...N-24
▲Saugerties, *Ulster*, 19,868 ...N-24
● Saugerties South, *Ulster*, 2,285 ...O-24
▲Savannah, *Wayne*, 1,838 ...J-14
● Sayville, *Suffolk*, 16,735 ...P-44
Scarsdale, *Westchester*, 17,823 ...K-36
▲Schaghticoke, *Rensselaer*, 7,456 ...K-25
Schenectady, *Schenectady*, 61,821 ...K-24
▲Schodack, *Rensselaer*, 12,536 ...L-24
Schoharie, *Schoharie*, 1,030 ...L-23
▲Schoharie, *Schoharie*, 3,299 ...L-23
▲Schroeppel, *Oswego*, 8,566 ...I-16
▲Schroon, *Essex*, 1,759 ...F-24
▲Schuyler, *Herkimer*, 3,385 ...J-20
▲Schuyler Falls, *Clinton*, 5,128 ...C-25
Schuylerville, *Saratoga*, 1,197 ...J-25
Scio, *Allegany*, 1,914 ...N-10
▲Scipio, *Cayuga*, 1,537 ...K-15
● Scotchtown, *Orange*, 8,954 ...Q-23
Scotia, *Schenectady*, 7,957 ...K-24
▲Scott, *Cortland*, 1,193 ...L-16
Scottsville, *Monroe*, 2,128 ...J-11
▲Scriba, *Oswego*, 7,331 ...H-15
Sea Cliff, *Nassau*, 5,066 ...M-37
● Seaford, *Nassau*, 15,791 ...H-45
● Searingtown, *Nassau*, 5,034 ...N-37
● Selden, *Suffolk*, 21,861 ...O-45
▲Seneca, *Ontario*, 2,731 ...K-13
Seneca Falls, *Seneca*, 6,861 ...K-14
▲Seneca Falls, *Seneca*, 9,347 ...K-14
● Seneca Knolls, *Onondaga*, 2,138 ...A-7
▲Sennett, *Cayuga*, 3,244 ...J-15
● Setauket-East Setauket, *Suffolk*, 15,931 ...B-52
▲Seward, *Schoharie*, 1,637 ...L-22
▲Shandaken, *Ulster*, 3,235 ...N-22
▲Sharon, *Schoharie*, 1,843 ...K-21
▲Shawangunk, *Ulster*, 12,022 ...P-23
▲Shelby, *Orleans*, 5,420 ...J-9
▲Sheldon, *Wyoming*, 2,561 ...L-8
● Shelter Island, *Suffolk*, 1,234 ...M-49
▲Shelter Island, *Suffolk*, 2,228 ...M-49
● Shenorock (Lake Shenorock), *Westchester*, 1,887 ...G-36
▲Sherburne, *Chenango*, 3,979 ...L-18
Sherburne, *Chenango*, 1,455 ...L-19
▲Sheridan, *Chautauqua*, 2,838 ...M-5
▲Sherman, *Chautauqua*, 1,553 ...N-4
Sherrill, *Oneida*, 3,147 ...J-18
● Shinnecock Hills, *Suffolk*, 1,749 ...N-48
● Shirley, *Suffolk*, 25,395 ...O-46
▲Shokan, *Ulster*, 1,252 ...O-23
Shortsville, *Ontario*, 1,320 ...K-13
● Shrub Oak, *Westchester*, 1,812 ...G-36
Sidney, *Delaware*, 4,068 ...N-19
▲Sidney, *Delaware*, 6,109 ...N-19
Silver Creek, *Chautauqua*, 2,896 ...L-6
▲Skaneateles, *Onondaga*, 7,323 ...K-13
Skaneateles, *Onondaga*, 2,616 ...K-15
Sleepy Hollow, *Westchester*, 9,212 ...J-35
Sloan, *Erie*, 3,775 ...K-7
Sloatsburg, *Rockland*, 3,117 ...I-32
▲Smithfield, *Madison*, 1,205 ...K-18
▲Smithtown, *Suffolk*, 115,715 ...D-50
● Smithtown, *Suffolk*, 26,901 ...D-50
▲Smithville, *Chenango*, 1,347 ...M-18
▲Smyrna, *Chenango*, 1,418 ...L-18
Sodus, *Wayne*, 1,735 ...I-13
▲Sodus, *Wayne*, 8,949 ...I-13
Sodus Point, *Wayne*, 1,160 ...I-13
▲Solon, *Cortland*, 1,108 ...L-17
Solvay, *Onondaga*, 6,845 ...B-8
▲Somers, *Westchester*, 18,346 ...G-37
● Sound Beach, *Suffolk*, 9,807 ...N-45
▲South Bristol, *Ontario*, 1,645 ...L-12
South Corning, *Steuben*, 1,147 ...N-13
● South Fallsburg, *Sullivan*, 2,061 ...P-22
● South Farmingdale, *Nassau*, 15,061 ...G-46
South Floral Park, *Nassau*, 1,578 ...G-41
South Glens Falls, *Saratoga*, 3,368 ...I-25
● South Hempstead, *Nassau*, 3,188 ...H-43
● South Hill, *Tompkins*, 6,003 ...M-15
● South Huntington, *Suffolk*, 9,465 ...D-47
● South Lockport, *Niagara*, 8,552 ...J-7
South Nyack, *Rockland*, 3,473 ...J-35
● South Valley Stream, *Nassau*, 5,638 ...H-41
Southampton, *Suffolk*, 3,965 ...N-49
▲Southampton, *Suffolk*, 54,712 ...N-49
▲Southeast, *Putnam*, 17,316 ...F-37
● Southold, *Suffolk*, 5,465 ...M-49
▲Southold, *Suffolk*, 20,599 ...M-49
● Southport, *Chemung*, 7,396 ...O-14
● Spackenkill, *Dutchess*, 4,756 ...C-35
▲Spafford, *Onondaga*, 1,661 ...K-16
▲Sparta, *Livingston*, 1,627 ...L-11
▲Spencer, *Tioga*, 2,979 ...N-15
Spencerport, *Monroe*, 3,559 ...J-11
Spring Valley, *Rockland*, 25,464 ...J-33
▲Springfield, *Otsego*, 1,350 ...K-21
▲Springport, *Cayuga*, 2,256 ...K-14
● Springs, *Suffolk*, 4,950 ...M-50
Springville, *Erie*, 4,252 ...M-7
▲Springwater, *Livingston*, 2,322 ...L-11
▲Stafford, *Genesee*, 2,409 ...J-10
Stamford, *Delaware*, 1,265 ...M-22
▲Stamford, *Delaware*, 1,943 ...M-22
▲Stanford, *Dutchess*, 3,544 ...P-25
▲Starkey, *Yates*, 3,465 ...M-13
▲Stephentown, *Rensselaer*, 2,873 ...L-26
▲Sterling, *Cayuga*, 3,432 ...I-15
▲Steuben, *Oneida*, 1,172 ...I-19
Stewart Manor, *Nassau*, 1,935 ...G-42
Stillwater, *Saratoga*, 1,644 ...K-25
▲Stillwater, *Saratoga*, 7,522 ...K-25
▲Stockbridge, *Madison*, 2,080 ...J-18
▲Stockholm, *Saint Lawrence*, 3,592 ...C-20
▲Stockport, *Columbia*, 2,933 ...M-24
▲Stockton, *Chautauqua*, 2,331 ...M-5
● Stone Ridge, *Ulster*, 1,173 ...P-23
● Stony Brook, *Suffolk*, 13,727 ...B-52
● Stony Point, *Rockland*, 11,744 ...H-34
▲Stony Point, *Rockland*, 14,244 ...H-34
▲Stottville, *Columbia*, 1,355 ...N-25
▲Stuyvesant, *Columbia*, 2,188 ...M-24
Suffern, *Rockland*, 11,006 ...I-32
▲Sullivan, *Madison*, 14,991 ...J-18
▲Summit, *Schoharie*, 1,123 ...L-22
▲Sweden, *Monroe*, 13,716 ...J-10
Sylvan Beach, *Oneida*, 1,071 ...J-18
● Syosset, *Nassau*, 18,544 ...M-39
Syracuse, *Onondaga*, 147,306 ...J-16
▲Taghkanic, *Columbia*, 1,118 ...N-25
● Tappan, *Rockland*, 6,757 ...K-34
Tarrytown, *Westchester*, 11,090 ...J-35
● Terryville, *Suffolk*, 10,589 ...N-45
▲Theresa, *Jefferson*, 2,414 ...E-17
● Thiells, *Rockland*, 4,758 ...H-34
Thomaston, *Nassau*, 2,607 ...E-41
▲Thompson, *Sullivan*, 14,189 ...P-21
● Thornwood, *Westchester*, 5,980 ...I-36
▲Throop, *Cayuga*, 1,824 ...K-15
▲Thurman, *Warren*, 1,199 ...H-24
▲Thurston, *Steuben*, 1,309 ...N-12
▲Ticonderoga, *Essex*, 5,167 ...F-26
● Tillson, *Ulster*, 1,709 ...P-24
▲Tioga, *Tioga*, 4,840 ...O-15
Tivoli, *Dutchess*, 1,163 ...O-24
▲Tompkins, *Delaware*, 1,105 ...N-20
● Tonawanda, *Erie*, 16,136 ...J-7
▲Tonawanda, *Erie*, 78,155 ...J-7
● Tonawanda, *Erie*, 61,729 ...J-7
▲Torrey, *Yates*, 1,307 ...L-13
● Town Line, *Erie*, 2,521 ...K-8
▲Trenton, *Oneida*, 4,670 ...J-20
▲Triangle, *Broome*, 3,032 ...N-17
● Tribes Hill, *Montgomery*, 1,024 ...K-23
▲Troupsburg, *Steuben*, 1,126 ...O-11
Troy, *Rensselaer*, 49,170 ...K-25
Trumansburg, *Tompkins*, 1,581 ...L-14
▲Truxton, *Cortland*, 1,225 ...L-17
▲Tuckahoe, *Suffolk*, 1,741 ...N-49
Tuckahoe, *Westchester*, 6,211 ...K-35
▲Tully, *Onondaga*, 2,709 ...K-17
Tupper Lake, *Franklin*, 3,935 ...E-22
▲Tuscarora, *Livingston*, 1,400 ...L-10
▲Tusten, *Sullivan*, 1,415 ...Q-20
▲Tuxedo, *Orange*, 3,334 ...H-32
▲Tyrone, *Schuyler*, 1,714 ...M-13
▲Ulster, *Ulster*, 12,544 ...O-24
▲Ulysses, *Tompkins*, 4,775 ...M-15
Unadilla, *Otsego*, 1,127 ...M-19
▲Unadilla, *Otsego*, 4,548 ...M-19
▲Union, *Broome*, 56,298 ...N-17
Union Springs, *Cayuga*, 1,074 ...K-14
▲Union Vale, *Dutchess*, 4,546 ...P-25
● Uniondale, *Nassau*, 23,011 ...O-38
● University Gardens, *Nassau*, 4,138 ...E-41
Upper Brookville, *Nassau*, 1,801 ...D-44
Upper Nyack, *Rockland*, 1,863 ...J-35
▲Urbana, *Steuben*, 2,546 ...M-12
Utica, *Oneida*, 60,651 ...J-19
● Vails Gate, *Orange*, 3,319 ...E-33
Valatie, *Columbia*, 1,712 ...M-25
● Valhalla, *Westchester*, 5,379 ...J-36
● Valley Cottage, *Rockland*, 9,269 ...I-34
Valley Stream, *Nassau*, 36,368 ...O-37
▲Van Buren, *Onondaga*, 12,667 ...I-13
▲Van Etten, *Chemung*, 1,518 ...N-15
▲Varick, *Seneca*, 1,729 ...L-14
▲Venice, *Cayuga*, 1,286 ...L-15
Vernon, *Oneida*, 1,155 ...J-18
▲Vernon, *Oneida*, 5,335 ...J-18
▲Verona, *Oneida*, 6,425 ...J-18
Vestal, *Broome*, 26,535 ...O-17
Victor, *Ontario*, 2,433 ...J-12
▲Victor, *Ontario*, 9,977 ...K-12
▲Victory, *Cayuga*, 1,838 ...J-15
▲Vienna, *Oneida*, 5,819 ...I-18
● Village Green, *Onondaga*, 3,945 ...J-16
Village of the Branch, *Suffolk*, 1,895 ...D-51
▲Villenova, *Chautauqua*, 1,121 ...M-6
● Viola, *Rockland*, 5,931 ...I-33
▲Virgil, *Cortland*, 2,287 ...M-16
▲Volney, *Oswego*, 6,094 ...I-16
Voorheesville, *Albany*, 2,705 ...L-24
▲Waddington, *Saint Lawrence*, 2,212 ...B-19
● Wading River, *Suffolk*, 6,668 ...N-46
Walden, *Orange*, 6,164 ...Q-23
▲Wales, *Erie*, 2,960 ...L-8
▲Wallkill, *Orange*, 24,659 ...Q-22
● Wallkill, *Ulster*, 2,143 ...Q-23
Walton, *Delaware*, 3,070 ...N-20
▲Walton, *Delaware*, 5,607 ...N-20
● Walton Park, *Orange*, 2,330 ...G-32
▲Walworth, *Wayne*, 8,402 ...J-12
Wampsville, *Madison*, 561 ...J-18
● Wantagh, *Nassau*, 18,971 ...H-45
▲Wappinger, *Dutchess*, 26,274 ...Q-24
Wappingers Falls, *Dutchess*, 4,929 ...D-35
▲Warren, *Herkimer*, 1,136 ...K-20
▲Warrensburg, *Warren*, 3,208 ...H-24
▲Warrensburg, *Warren*, 4,255 ...H-24
Warsaw, *Wyoming*, 3,814 ...L-9
▲Warsaw, *Wyoming*, 5,423 ...L-9
Warwick, *Orange*, 6,412 ...H-30
▲Warwick, *Orange*, 30,764 ...H-30
▲Washington, *Dutchess*, 4,742 ...P-25
● Washington Heights, *Orange*, 1,318 ...Q-22
Washingtonville, *Orange*, 5,851 ...F-32
▲Waterford, *Saratoga*, 8,515 ...A-12
Waterford, *Saratoga*, 2,204 ...A-12
Waterloo, *Seneca*, 5,111 ...K-14
▲Waterloo, *Seneca*, 7,866 ...K-14
● Watermill, *Suffolk*, 1,724 ...N-49
Watertown, *Jefferson*, 26,705 ...F-17
▲Watertown, *Jefferson*, 4,482 ...F-17
Waterville, *Oneida*, 1,721 ...K-19
Watervliet, *Albany*, 10,207 ...B-12
Watkins Glen, *Schuyler*, 2,149 ...M-14
▲Watson, *Lewis*, 1,987 ...G-19
▲Waverly, *Franklin*, 1,118 ...C-22
Waverly, *Tioga*, 4,607 ...O-15
▲Wawarsing, *Ulster*, 12,889 ...P-23
▲Wawayanda, *Orange*, 6,273 ...F-29
Wayland, *Steuben*, 1,893 ...L-11
▲Wayland, *Steuben*, 4,314 ...L-11
▲Wayne, *Steuben*, 1,165 ...M-13
▲Webb, *Herkimer*, 1,912 ...F-20
Webster, *Monroe*, 5,216 ...I-12
▲Webster, *Monroe*, 37,926 ...I-12
Weedsport, *Cayuga*, 2,017 ...J-15
Wellsville, *Allegany*, 5,171 ...N-10
▲Wellsville, *Allegany*, 7,678 ...N-10
Wesley Hills, *Rockland*, 4,848 ...I-33
▲West Babylon, *Suffolk*, 43,452 ...G-48
● West Bay Shore, *Suffolk*, 4,775 ...G-49
▲West Bloomfield, *Ontario*, 2,549 ...K-11
West Carthage, *Jefferson*, 2,102 ...F-18
● West Elmira, *Chemung*, 5,136 ...O-14
● West End, *Otsego*, 1,813 ...M-20
● West Glens Falls, *Warren*, 6,721 ...I-25
West Haverstraw, *Rockland*, 10,295 ...H-34
● West Hempstead, *Nassau*, 18,713 ...G-42
● West Hills, *Nassau*, 5,607 ...M-39
● West Hurley, *Ulster*, 2,105 ...O-23
● West Islip, *Suffolk*, 28,907 ...P-43
● West Monroe, *Oswego*, 4,428 ...I-17
● West Nyack, *Rockland*, 3,282 ...J-34
● West Point, *Orange*, 7,138 ...F-34
● West Sand Lake, *Rensselaer*, 2,439 ...C-13
● West Sayville, *Suffolk*, 5,003 ...P-44
▲West Seneca, *Erie*, 45,943 ...K-7
● West Seneca, *Erie*, 45,920 ...K-7
▲West Sparta, *Livingston*, 1,244 ...L-11
▲West Turin, *Lewis*, 1,674 ...H-18
Westbury, *Nassau*, 14,263 ...F-43
▲Westerlo, *Albany*, 3,466 ...M-24
▲Western, *Oneida*, 2,029 ...I-19
Westfield, *Chautauqua*, 3,481 ...M-4
▲Westfield, *Chautauqua*, 5,232 ...M-4
● Westhampton, *Suffolk*, 2,869 ...O-47
Westhampton Beach, *Suffolk*, 1,902 ...O-47
● Westmere, *Albany*, 7,188 ...B-10
▲Westmoreland, *Oneida*, 6,207 ...J-19
● Westons Mills, *Cattaraugus*, 1,608 ...O-8
▲Westport, *Essex*, 1,362 ...E-25
● Westvale, *Onondaga*, 5,166 ...B-8
▲Westville, *Otsego*, 1,823 ...L-21
▲Wheatfield, *Niagara*, 14,086 ...J-7
▲Wheatland, *Monroe*, 5,149 ...J-11
● Wheatley Heights, *Suffolk*, 5,013 ...F-47
▲Wheeler, *Steuben*, 1,263 ...M-12
▲White Creek, *Washington*, 3,411 ...J-26
White Plains, *Westchester*, 53,077 ...J-36
Whitehall, *Washington*, 2,667 ...H-26
▲Whitehall, *Washington*, 4,035 ...H-26
Whitesboro, *Oneida*, 3,943 ...J-19
▲Whitestown, *Oneida*, 18,635 ...J-19
▲Willet, *Cortland*, 1,011 ...M-17
▲Williamson, *Wayne*, 6,777 ...I-13
▲Williamstown, *Oswego*, 1,350 ...I-17
Williamsville, *Erie*, 5,573 ...K-7
▲Willing, *Allegany*, 1,371 ...O-10
Williston Park, *Nassau*, 7,261 ...F-42
▲Willsboro, *Essex*, 1,903 ...D-26
▲Wilmington, *Essex*, 1,131 ...D-24
▲Wilna, *Jefferson*, 6,235 ...F-18
Wilson, *Niagara*, 1,213 ...I-7
▲Wilson, *Niagara*, 5,840 ...I-7
▲Wilton, *Saratoga*, 12,511 ...I-25
▲Windham, *Greene*, 1,660 ...M-23
▲Windsor, *Broome*, 6,421 ...O-18
▲Winfield, *Herkimer*, 2,202 ...L-20
▲Wirt, *Allegany*, 1,215 ...N-9
Wolcott, *Wayne*, 1,712 ...I-14
▲Wolcott, *Wayne*, 4,692 ...I-14
● Woodbury, *Nassau*, 9,010 ...M-39
▲Woodbury, *Orange*, 9,460 ...G-33
▲Woodhull, *Steuben*, 1,528 ...O-12
● Woodmere, *Nassau*, 16,447 ...O-37
● Woodstock, *Ulster*, 2,187 ...O-23
▲Woodstock, *Ulster*, 6,241 ...O-23
▲Worcester, *Otsego*, 2,207 ...L-21
▲Wright, *Schoharie*, 1,547 ...L-23
Wurtsboro, *Sullivan*, 1,234 ...Q-22
● Wyandanch, *Suffolk*, 10,546 ...F-48
● Wynantskill, *Rensselaer*, 3,018 ...B-12
● Yaphank, *Suffolk*, 5,025 ...O-45
▲Yates, *Orleans*, 2,510 ...I-9
Yonkers, *Westchester*, 196,086 ...L-35
▲York, *Livingston*, 3,219 ...K-10
● Yorkshire, *Cattaraugus*, 1,403 ...L-8
▲Yorkshire, *Cattaraugus*, 4,210 ...L-8
▲Yorktown, *Westchester*, 36,318 ...G-36
● Yorktown Heights, *Westchester*, 7,972 ...H-36
Yorkville, *Oneida*, 2,675 ...J-19
Youngstown, *Niagara*, 1,957 ...I-6
● Zena, *Ulster*, 1,119 ...O-24

COUNTIES

(100 Counties)

Name of County	Population	Location on Map
ALAMANCE	130,800	B-7
ALEXANDER	33,603	C-2
ALLEGHANY	10,677	A-2
ANSON	25,275	F-5
ASHE	24,384	A-2
AVERY	17,167	B-1
BEAUFORT	44,958	D-13
BERTIE	19,773	B-13
BLADEN	32,278	G-9
BRUNSWICK	73,143	I-9
BUNCOMBE	206,330	I-15
BURKE	89,148	D-1
CABARRUS	131,063	E-4
CALDWELL	77,415	C-1
CAMDEN	6,885	A-15
CARTERET	59,383	F-14
CASWELL	23,501	A-7
CATAWBA	141,685	D-2
CHATHAM	49,329	D-7
CHEROKEE	24,298	K-11
CHOWAN	14,526	B-14
CLAY	8,775	K-12
CLEVELAND	96,287	E-1
COLUMBUS	54,749	I-9
CRAVEN	91,436	E-13
CUMBERLAND	302,963	F-9
CURRITUCK	18,190	A-15
DARE	29,967	C-16
DAVIDSON	147,246	C-5
DAVIE	34,835	C-4
DUPLIN	49,063	F-11
DURHAM	223,314	C-8
EDGECOMBE	55,606	C-11
FORSYTH	306,067	C-5
FRANKLIN	47,260	B-10
GASTON	190,365	E-2
GATES	10,516	A-14
GRAHAM	7,993	J-12
GRANVILLE	48,498	A-9
GREENE	18,974	D-12
GUILFORD	421,048	C-6
HALIFAX	57,370	B-11
HARNETT	91,025	E-8
HAYWOOD	54,033	I-14
HENDERSON	89,173	K-15
HERTFORD	22,601	B-13
HOKE	33,646	F-8
HYDE	5,826	D-14
IREDELL	122,660	C-3
JACKSON	33,121	K-14
JOHNSTON	121,965	E-10
JONES	10,381	F-12
LEE	49,040	D-8
LENOIR	59,648	E-11
LINCOLN	63,780	D-2
MACON	29,811	K-12
MADISON	19,635	I-15
MARTIN	25,593	D-13
MCDOWELL	42,151	D-1
MECKLENBURG	695,454	E-3
MITCHELL	15,687	H-16
MONTGOMERY	26,822	E-5
MOORE	74,769	E-7
NASH	87,420	C-10
NEW HANOVER	160,307	H-11
NORTHAMPTON	22,086	B-12
ONSLOW	150,355	F-12
ORANGE	118,227	B-8
PAMLICO	12,934	F-14
PASQUOTANK	34,897	B-15
PENDER	41,082	H-10
PERQUIMANS	11,368	B-15
PERSON	35,623	A-8
PITT	133,798	D-13
POLK	18,324	K-16
RANDOLPH	130,454	D-6
RICHMOND	46,564	F-6
ROBESON	123,339	G-8
ROCKINGHAM	91,928	B-6
ROWAN	130,340	D-5
RUTHERFORD	62,899	D-1
SAMPSON	60,161	F-9
SCOTLAND	35,998	G-7
STANLY	58,100	E-5
STOKES	44,711	A-5
SURRY	71,219	B-3
SWAIN	12,968	J-12
TRANSYLVANIA	29,334	K-14
TYRRELL	4,149	C-15
UNION	123,677	G-4
VANCE	42,954	A-9
WAKE	627,846	D-9
WARREN	19,972	A-10
WASHINGTON	13,723	D-14
WATAUGA	42,695	B-1
WAYNE	113,329	E-10
WILKES	65,632	B-2
WILSON	73,814	D-10
YADKIN	36,348	B-4
YANCEY	17,774	I-16
TOTAL	**8,049,313**	

CITIES AND TOWNS

Note: The first name is that of the city or town, second, that of the county in which it is located, then the population and location on the map.

Aberdeen, *Moore*, 3,400 F-7
Ahoskie, *Hertford*, 4,523 B-13
Albemarle, *Stanly*, 15,680 E-5
Andrews, *Cherokee*, 1,602 K-12
Angier, *Harnett*, 3,419 D-9
Apex, *Wake*, 20,212 D-9
Archdale, *Randolph*, 9,014 K-2
Asheboro, *Randolph*, 21,672 D-6
Asheville, *Buncombe*, 68,889 J-15
Atlantic Beach, *Carteret*, 1,781 G-14
• Avery Creek, *Buncombe*, 1,405 J-15
Ayden, *Pitt*, 4,622 D-12
Badin, *Stanly*, 1,154 E-5
Bakersville, *Mitchell*, 357 H-16
• Balfour, *Henderson*, 1,200 J-16
• Barker Heights, *Henderson*, 1,237 K-16
Bayboro, *Pamlico*, 741 E-14
• Bayshore, *New Hanover*, 2,512 K-6
Beaufort, *Carteret*, 3,771 G-14
Belhaven, *Beaufort*, 1,968 D-14
Belmont, *Gaston*, 8,705 E-3
Benson, *Johnston*, 2,923 E-9
• Bent Creek, *Buncombe*, 1,389 J-15
Bermuda Run, *Davie*, 1,431 C-5
Bessemer City, *Gaston*, 5,119 L-1
Bethel, *Pitt*, 1,681 C-12
• Bethlehem, *Alexander*, 3,713 C-2
Beulaville, *Duplin*, 1,067 F-11
Biltmore Forest, *Buncombe*, 1,440 J-15
Biscoe, *Montgomery*, 1,700 E-6
Black Mountain, *Buncombe*, 7,511 J-16
Bladenboro, *Bladen*, 1,718 H-9
Blowing Rock, *Watauga*, 1,418 B-1
Boiling Spring Lakes, *Brunswick*, 2,972 I-11
Boiling Springs, *Cleveland*, 3,866 E-1
Bolivia, *Brunswick*, 148 I-10
Boone, *Watauga*, 13,472 B-1
Boonville, *Yadkin*, 1,138 B-4
Brevard, *Transylvania*, 6,789 K-15
• Brices Creek, *Craven*, 2,060 F-13
Broadway, *Lee*, 1,015 E-8
• Brogden, *Wayne*, 2,907 E-11
Bryson City, *Swain*, 1,411 J-13
• Buies Creek, *Harnett*, 2,215 E-9
Burgaw, *Pender*, 3,337 G-11
Burlington, *Alamance*, 44,917 C-7
Burnsville, *Yancey*, 1,623 I-16
• Butner, *Granville*, 5,792 B-9
Cajah's Mountain, *Caldwell*, 2,683 C-2
Camden, *Camden*, 300 B-15
Canton, *Haywood*, 4,029 J-15
Cape Carteret, *Carteret*, 1,214 G-13
Carolina Beach, *New Hanover*, 4,701 I-11
Carolina Shores, *Brunswick*, 1,482 J-9
Carrboro, *Orange*, 16,782 C-8
Carthage, *Moore*, 1,871 E-7
Cary, *Wake*, 94,536 D-9
• Castle Hayne, *New Hanover*, 1,116 H-11
Chadbourn, *Columbus*, 2,129 H-9
Chapel Hill, *Orange*, 48,715 C-8
Charlotte, *Mecklenburg*, 540,828 E-3
Cherryville, *Gaston*, 5,361 E-2
China Grove, *Rowan*, 3,616 D-4
Claremont, *Catawba*, 1,038 D-3
Clayton, *Johnston*, 6,973 D-10
Clemmons, *Forsyth*, 13,827 C-5
Clinton, *Sampson*, 8,600 F-10
Clyde, *Haywood*, 1,324 J-14
Coats, *Harnett*, 1,845 E-9
Columbia, *Tyrrell*, 819 C-15
Columbus, *Polk*, 992 K-16
Concord, *Cabarrus*, 55,977 E-4
Connelly Springs, *Burke*, 1,814 I-2
Conover, *Catawba*, 6,604 D-2
Cornelius, *Mecklenburg*, 11,969 E-3
Cramerton, *Gaston*, 2,976 M-3
Creedmoor, *Granville*, 2,232 B-9
• Cricket, *Wilkes*, 2,053 B-3
• Cullowhee, *Jackson*, 3,579 K-14
Currituck, *Currituck*, 700 A-16
Dallas, *Gaston*, 3,402 L-2
Danbury, *Stokes*, 108 A-5
Davidson, *Mecklenburg*, 7,139 D-3
Denton, *Davidson*, 1,450 D-5
Dobson, *Surry*, 1,457 A-4
Drexel, *Burke*, 1,938 I-1
Dunn, *Harnett*, 9,196 E-9
Durham, *Durham*, 187,035 C-8
• East Flat Rock, *Henderson*, 4,151 K-16
• East Rockingham, *Richmond*, 3,885 F-6
East Spencer, *Rowan*, 1,755 D-5
• Eastover, *Cumberland*, 1,376 F-9
Eden, *Rockingham*, 15,908 A-6
Edenton, *Chowan*, 5,394 B-14
Elizabeth City, *Pasquotank*, 17,188 B-15
Elizabethtown, *Bladen*, 3,698 G-9
Elkin, *Surry*, 4,109 B-3
Ellerbe, *Richmond*, 1,021 F-6
Elm City, *Wilson*, 1,165 C-11
Elon College, *Alamance*, 6,738 B-7
• Elroy, *Wayne*, 3,896 E-11
Emerald Isle, *Carteret*, 3,488 G-14
Enfield, *Halifax*, 2,347 B-12
• Enochville, *Rowan*, 2,851 D-4
Erwin, *Harnett*, 4,537 E-9
• Etowah, *Henderson*, 2,766 K-15
Fair Bluff, *Columbus*, 1,181 H-8
• Fairfield Harbour, *Craven*, 1,983 F-13
Fairmont, *Robeson*, 2,604 H-8
• Fairplains, *Wilkes*, 2,051 B-3
• Fairview, *Buncombe*, 2,495 J-16
Farmville, *Pitt*, 4,302 D-12
Fayetteville, *Cumberland*, 121,015 F-8
Flat Rock, *Henderson*, 2,565 K-16
• Flat Rock, *Surry*, 1,690 A-4
Fletcher, *Henderson*, 4,185 J-15
Forest City, *Rutherford*, 7,549 K-17
• Forest Oaks, *Guilford*, 3,241 K-3
• Fort Bragg, *Cumberland*, 29,183 F-8
Four Oaks, *Johnston*, 1,424 E-10
Franklin, *Macon*, 3,490 K-13
Franklinton, *Franklin*, 1,745 B-10
Franklinville, *Randolph*, 1,258 D-6
Fremont, *Wayne*, 1,463 D-11
Fuquay-Varina, *Wake*, 7,898 D-9
Gamewell, *Caldwell*, 3,644 C-2
Garner, *Wake*, 17,757 D-9
Garysburg, *Northampton*, 1,254 A-12
Gastonia, *Gaston*, 66,277 E-3
Gatesville, *Gates*, 281 A-14
Gibsonville, *Guilford*, 4,372 J-4
Glen Alpine, *Burke*, 1,090 D-1
• Glen Raven, *Alamance*, 2,750 J-5
Goldsboro, *Wayne*, 39,043 E-11
• Gorman, *Durham*, 1,002 C-9
Graham, *Alamance*, 12,833 C-7
Granite Falls, *Caldwell*, 4,612 C-2
Granite Quarry, *Rowan*, 2,175 D-4
Green Level, *Alamance*, 2,042 J-6
Greensboro, *Guilford*, 223,891 C-6
Greenville, *Pitt*, 60,476 D-12
Grifton, *Pitt*, 2,073 E-12
• Half Moon, *Onslow*, 6,645 G-12
Halifax, *Halifax*, 344 B-12
Hamlet, *Richmond*, 6,018 F-6
• Harkers Island, *Carteret*, 1,525 G-15
Harrisburg, *Cabarrus*, 4,493 E-4
Havelock, *Craven*, 22,442 F-14
Haw River, *Alamance*, 1,908 J-5
Hayesville, *Clay*, 297 K-12
• Hays, *Wilkes*, 1,731 B-3
Henderson, *Vance*, 16,095 B-10
Hendersonville, *Henderson*, 10,420 K-16
Hertford, *Perquimans*, 2,070 B-15
Hickory, *Catawba*, 37,222 D-2
High Point, *Guilford*, 85,839 C-6
Hildebran, *Burke*, 1,472 I-2
Hillsborough, *Orange*, 5,446 C-8
Holly Springs, *Wake*, 9,192 D-9
Hope Mills, *Cumberland*, 11,237 F-8
Hudson, *Caldwell*, 3,078 H-2
Huntersville, *Mecklenburg*, 24,960 E-3
• Icard, *Burke*, 2,734 I-2
Indian Trail, *Union*, 11,905 F-4
Jackson, *Northampton*, 695 A-12
Jacksonville, *Onslow*, 66,715 G-12
• James City, *Craven*, 5,420 F-13
Jamestown, *Guilford*, 3,088 K-2
Jefferson, *Ashe*, 1,422 A-2
Jonesville, *Yadkin*, 1,464 B-3
Kannapolis, *Cabarrus*, 36,910 D-4
Kenansville, *Duplin*, 1,149 F-11
Kenly, *Johnston*, 1,569 D-10
Kernersville, *Forsyth*, 17,126 J-2
Kill Devil Hills, *Dare*, 5,897 C-17
King, *Stokes*, 5,952 B-5
• Kings Grant, *New Hanover*, 7,738 H-11
Kings Mountain, *Cleveland*, 9,693 M-1
Kinston, *Lenoir*, 23,688 E-12
Kitty Hawk, *Dare*, 2,991 B-17
Knightdale, *Wake*, 5,958 C-9
Kure Beach, *New Hanover*, 1,507 I-11
La Grange, *Lenoir*, 2,844 E-11
• Lake Junaluska, *Haywood*, 2,675 J-14
Lake Lure, *Rutherford*, 1,027 J-16
• Lake Norman of Catawba, *Catawba*, 4,744 D-3
Lake Park, *Union*, 2,093 G-1
Lake Waccamaw, *Columbus*, 1,411 H-9
Landis, *Rowan*, 2,996 D-4
Laurel Park, *Henderson*, 1,835 K-15
Laurinburg, *Scotland*, 15,874 G-7
Leland, *Brunswick*, 1,938 H-11
Lenoir, *Caldwell*, 16,793 C-2
Lewisville, *Forsyth*, 8,826 B-5
Lexington, *Davidson*, 19,953 C-5
Liberty, *Randolph*, 2,661 C-7
Lillington, *Harnett*, 2,915 E-9
Lincolnton, *Lincoln*, 9,965 E-2
Locust, *Stanly*, 2,416 E-5
Long View, *Catawba*, 4,722 I-2
Louisburg, *Franklin*, 3,111 B-10
Lowell, *Gaston*, 2,662 M-3
• Lowesville, *Lincoln*, 1,440 E-3
Lumberton, *Robeson*, 20,795 G-8
Madison, *Rockingham*, 2,262 B-6
Maiden, *Catawba*, 3,282 D-2
Manteo, *Dare*, 1,052 C-17
Marion, *McDowell*, 4,943 I-17
• Mar-Mac, *Wayne*, 3,004 E-11
Mars Hill, *Madison*, 1,764 I-15
Marshall, *Madison*, 840 I-15
Marshville, *Union*, 2,360 F-5
Marvin, *Union*, 1,039 F-3
• Masonboro, *New Hanover*, 11,812 M-5
Matthews, *Mecklenburg*, 22,127 F-4
Maxton, *Robeson*, 2,551 G-7
Mayodan, *Rockingham*, 2,417 A-6
Maysville, *Jones*, 1,002 F-13
• McLeansville, *Guilford*, 1,080 J-4
Mebane, *Alamance*, 7,284 J-6
• Millers Creek, *Wilkes*, 2,071 B-2
Mineral Springs, *Union*, 1,370 F-4
Mint Hill, *Mecklenburg*, 14,922 E-4
Mocksville, *Davie*, 4,178 C-4
Monroe, *Union*, 26,228 F-4
Mooresville, *Iredell*, 18,823 D-4
• Moravian Falls, *Wilkes*, 1,440 B-3
Morehead City, *Carteret*, 7,691 G-14
Morganton, *Burke*, 17,310 D-1
Morrisville, *Wake*, 5,208 C-9
Mount Airy, *Surry*, 8,484 A-4
Mount Gilead, *Montgomery*, 1,389 E-6
Mount Holly, *Gaston*, 9,618 E-3
Mount Olive, *Wayne*, 4,567 E-11
Mount Pleasant, *Cabarrus*, 1,259 E-4
• Mountain Home, *Henderson*, 2,169 J-15
• Mountain View, *Catawba*, 3,768 J-2
• Mulberry, *Wilkes*, 2,269 B-3
Murfreesboro, *Hertford*, 2,045 A-13
Murphy, *Cherokee*, 1,568 K-11
• Murraysville, *New Hanover*, 7,279 H-11
• Myrtle Grove, *New Hanover*, 7,125 I-11
Nags Head, *Dare*, 2,700 C-17
Nashville, *Nash*, 4,309 C-11
• Neuse Forest, *Craven*, 1,426 F-14
New Bern, *Craven*, 23,128 F-13
Newland, *Avery*, 704 B-1
Newport, *Carteret*, 3,349 G-14
Newton, *Catawba*, 12,560 D-2
Norlina, *Warren*, 1,107 A-10
North Wilkesboro, *Wilkes*, 4,116 B-3
• Northlakes, *Caldwell*, 1,390 I-2
Norwood, *Stanly*, 2,216 E-5
Oak Island, *Brunswick*, 6,571 J-10
Oak Ridge, *Guilford*, 3,988 J-2
Oakboro, *Stanly*, 1,198 E-5
• Ogden, *New Hanover*, 5,481 L-6
Oxford, *Granville*, 8,338 B-9
Pembroke, *Robeson*, 2,399 G-8
Pilot Mountain, *Surry*, 1,281 B-4
Pine Knoll Shores, *Carteret*, 1,524 G-14
Pine Level, *Johnston*, 1,313 D-10
Pinebluff, *Moore*, 1,109 F-7
Pinehurst, *Moore*, 9,706 E-7
Pinetops, *Edgecombe*, 1,419 C-12
Pineville, *Mecklenburg*, 3,449 F-3
• Piney Green, *Onslow*, 11,658 G-13
Pittsboro, *Chatham*, 2,226 D-8
• Plain View, *Sampson*, 1,820 E-9
Pleasant Garden, *Guilford*, 4,714 C-6
• Pleasant Hill, *Wilkes*, 1,109 B-3
Plymouth, *Washington*, 4,107 C-14
Polkton, *Anson*, 1,195 F-5
• Pope AFB, *Cumberland*, 2,583 E-8
Princeton, *Johnston*, 1,066 D-10
• Pumpkin Center, *Onslow*, 2,228 G-12
Raeford, *Hoke*, 3,386 F-8
Raleigh, *Wake*, 276,093 D-9
Ramseur, *Randolph*, 1,588 D-7
Randleman, *Randolph*, 3,557 C-6
Ranlo, *Gaston*, 2,198 L-2
Red Oak, *Nash*, 2,723 C-11
Red Springs, *Robeson*, 3,493 G-8
Reidsville, *Rockingham*, 14,485 B-6
River Bend, *Craven*, 2,923 F-13
• River Road, *Beaufort*, 4,094 D-13
Roanoke Rapids, *Halifax*, 16,957 A-12
Robbins, *Moore*, 1,195 E-7
Robbinsville, *Graham*, 747 K-12
Robersonville, *Martin*, 1,731 C-13
• Rockfish, *Hoke*, 2,353 F-8
Rockingham, *Richmond*, 9,672 F-6
Rockwell, *Rowan*, 1,971 D-5
Rocky Mount, *Nash*, 55,893 C-11
Rose Hill, *Duplin*, 1,330 G-11
Roseboro, *Sampson*, 1,267 F-9
Rowland, *Robeson*, 1,146 H-7
Roxboro, *Person*, 8,696 B-8
• Royal Pines, *Buncombe*, 5,334 J-15
Rural Hall, *Forsyth*, 2,464 B-5
Rutherford College, *Burke*, 1,293 I-1
Rutherfordton, *Rutherford*, 4,131 J-17
Saint Pauls, *Robeson*, 2,137 G-8
• Saint Stephens, *Catawba*, 9,439 I-3
• Salem, *Burke*, 2,923 D-1
Salisbury, *Rowan*, 26,462 D-4
Sanford, *Lee*, 23,220 E-8
Sawmills, *Caldwell*, 4,921 H-2
• Saxapahaw, *Alamance*, 1,418 C-7
Scotland Neck, *Halifax*, 2,362 B-12
• Sea Breeze, *New Hanover*, 1,312 I-11
• Seagate, *New Hanover*, 4,590 L-5
Selma, *Johnston*, 5,914 D-10
• Seven Lakes, *Moore*, 3,214 E-7
Shallotte, *Brunswick*, 1,381 I-10
Sharpsburg, *Nash*, 2,421 C-11
Shelby, *Cleveland*, 19,477 E-2
Siler City, *Chatham*, 6,966 D-7
• Silver City, *Hoke*, 1,146 F-8
• Silver Lake, *New Hanover*, 5,788 I-11
• Skippers Corner, *New Hanover*, 1,246 H-11
Smithfield, *Johnston*, 11,510 D-10
• Sneads Ferry, *Onslow*, 2,248 G-12
Snow Hill, *Greene*, 1,514 E-12
• South Gastonia, *Gaston*, 5,433 M-2
• South Henderson, *Vance*, 1,220 B-10
• South Rosemary, *Halifax*, 2,843 A-12
• South Weldon, *Halifax*, 1,414 A-12
Southern Pines, *Moore*, 10,918 F-7
Southern Shores, *Dare*, 2,201 B-16
Southport, *Brunswick*, 2,351 J-11
Sparta, *Alleghany*, 1,817 A-3
Spencer, *Rowan*, 3,355 D-5
Spindale, *Rutherford*, 4,022 J-17
Spring Hope, *Nash*, 1,261 C-10
Spring Lake, *Cumberland*, 8,098 F-8
Spruce Pine, *Mitchell*, 2,030 I-17
Stallings, *Union*, 3,189 G-1
Stanfield, *Stanly*, 1,113 E-5
Stanley, *Gaston*, 3,053 L-3
Statesville, *Iredell*, 23,320 D-3
Stokesdale, *Guilford*, 3,267 B-6
Stoneville, *Rockingham*, 1,002 A-6
• Stony Point, *Alexander*, 1,380 C-3
Summerfield, *Guilford*, 7,018 B-6
Sunset Beach, *Brunswick*, 1,824 J-10
Surf City, *Pender*, 1,393 H-12
• Swannanoa, *Buncombe*, 4,132 J-16
Swanquarter, *Hyde*, 550 E-15
Swansboro, *Onslow*, 1,426 G-13
Sylva, *Jackson*, 2,435 J-14
Tabor City, *Columbus*, 2,509 I-9
Tarboro, *Edgecombe*, 11,138 C-12
Taylorsville, *Alexander*, 1,799 C-3
Thomasville, *Davidson*, 19,788 C-5
• Toast, *Surry*, 1,922 A-4
Tobaccoville, *Forsyth*, 2,209 B-5
Trent Woods, *Craven*, 4,192 F-13
Trenton, *Jones*, 206 F-12
Trinity, *Randolph*, 6,690 K-2
Troutman, *Iredell*, 1,592 D-3
Troy, *Montgomery*, 3,430 E-6
Tryon, *Polk*, 1,760 K-16
Unionville, *Union*, 4,797 F-4
Valdese, *Burke*, 4,485 D-2
• Valley Hill, *Henderson*, 2,137 K-15
• Vander, *Cumberland*, 1,204 F-9
Wadesboro, *Anson*, 3,552 F-5
Wake Forest, *Wake*, 12,588 C-9
Walkertown, *Forsyth*, 4,009 J-2
Wallace, *Duplin*, 3,344 G-11
Walnut Cove, *Stokes*, 1,465 B-5
• Wanchese, *Dare*, 1,527 C-17
Warrenton, *Warren*, 811 A-10
Warsaw, *Duplin*, 3,051 F-11
Washington, *Beaufort*, 9,583 D-13
Waxhaw, *Union*, 2,625 F-4
Waynesville, *Haywood*, 9,232 J-14
Weaverville, *Buncombe*, 2,416 I-15
Weddington, *Union*, 6,696 F-4
• Welcome, *Davidson*, 3,538 C-5
Weldon, *Halifax*, 1,374 A-12
Wendell, *Wake*, 4,247 C-10
Wentworth, *Rockingham*, 2,779 A-6
Wesley Chapel, *Union*, 2,549 G-1
• West Canton, *Haywood*, 1,156 J-14
West Jefferson, *Ashe*, 1,081 A-2
• West Marion, *McDowell*, 1,556 I-17
• Westport, *Lincoln*, 2,006 D-3
Whispering Pines, *Moore*, 2,090 E-7
• White Plains, *Surry*, 1,049 A-4
Whiteville, *Columbus*, 5,148 H-9
Wilkesboro, *Wilkes*, 3,159 B-3
Williamston, *Martin*, 5,843 C-13
Wilmington, *New Hanover*, 75,838 I-11
Wilson, *Wilson*, 44,405 D-11
Wilsons Mills, *Johnston*, 1,291 D-10
Windsor, *Bertie*, 2,283 C-13
Wingate, *Union*, 2,406 H-3
Winston-Salem, *Forsyth*, 185,776 C-5
Winterville, *Pitt*, 4,791 D-12
Winton, *Hertford*, 956 A-13
Woodfin, *Buncombe*, 3,162 J-15
• Woodlawn, *McDowell*, 1,051 I-17
• Wrightsboro, *New Hanover*, 4,496 K-5
• Wrightsville Beach, *New Hanover*, 2,593 L-6
Yadkinville, *Yadkin*, 2,818 B-4
Yanceyville, *Caswell*, 2,091 A-7
Zebulon, *Wake*, 4,046 C-10

Explanation of symbols: • - Census Designated Place (CDP)

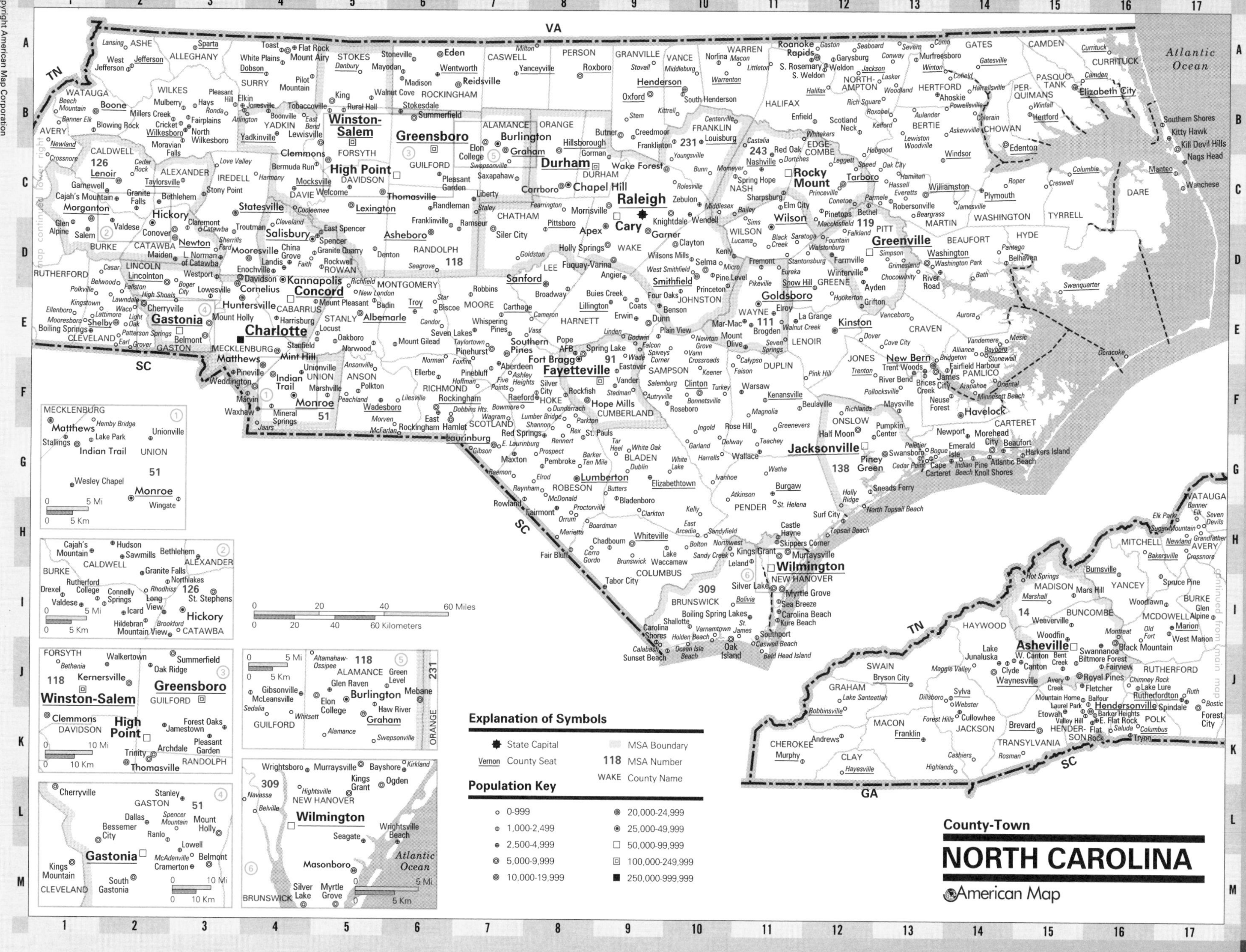
County-Town
NORTH CAROLINA
American Map
Explanation of Symbols
State Capital
Vernon County Seat
MSA Boundary
118 MSA Number
WAKE County Name
Population Key
0-999
1,000-2,499
2,500-4,999
5,000-9,999
10,000-19,999
20,000-24,999
25,000-49,999
50,000-99,999
100,000-249,999
250,000-999,999
60 Miles
60 Kilometers
continued from main map
continued lower right
Atlantic Ocean
VA
SC
TN
GA
Raleigh
Charlotte
Greensboro
Winston-Salem
Durham
Fayetteville
Wilmington
Asheville
Greenville
Jacksonville
High Point
Cary
Gastonia
Concord
Rocky Mount
Wilson
Goldsboro
Kinston
New Bern
Hickory
MECKLENBURG
Matthews
Indian Trail
Monroe
Wesley Chapel
Unionville
Wingate
5 Mi
5 Km
10 Mi
10 Km

COUNTIES

(53 Counties)

Name of County	Population	Location on Map
ADAMS	2,593	J-3
BARNES	11,775	G-13
BENSON	6,964	E-10
BILLINGS	888	G-2
BOTTINEAU	7,149	A-8
BOWMAN	3,242	J-1
BURKE	2,242	A-4
BURLEIGH	69,416	G-8
CASS	123,138	G-15
CAVALIER	4,831	A-13
DICKEY	5,757	J-12
DIVIDE	2,283	A-1
DUNN	3,600	F-3
EDDY	2,757	E-12
EMMONS	4,331	I-8
FOSTER	3,759	F-11
GOLDEN VALLEY	1,924	G-1
GRAND FORKS	66,109	D-14
GRANT	2,841	I-5
GRIGGS	2,754	F-13
HETTINGER	2,715	I-3
KIDDER	2,753	G-9
LAMOURE	4,701	I-12
LOGAN	2,308	I-10
MCHENRY	5,987	C-7
MCINTOSH	3,390	J-10
MCKENZIE	5,737	D-3
MCLEAN	9,311	E-5
MERCER	8,644	F-5
MORTON	25,303	H-5
MOUNTRAIL	6,631	C-4
NELSON	3,715	D-13
OLIVER	2,065	G-6
PEMBINA	8,585	A-14
PIERCE	4,675	C-9
RAMSEY	12,066	C-12
RANSOM	5,890	I-15
RENVILLE	2,610	A-6
RICHLAND	17,998	I-15
ROLETTE	13,674	A-9
SARGENT	4,366	J-14
SHERIDAN	1,710	E-8
SIOUX	4,044	J-8
SLOPE	767	I-2
STARK	22,636	H-3
STEELE	2,258	F-14
STUTSMAN	21,908	G-11
TOWNER	2,876	A-11
TRAILL	8,477	F-15
WALSH	12,389	C-15
WARD	58,795	C-6
WELLS	5,102	E-10
WILLIAMS	19,761	C-1
TOTAL	**642,200**	

CITIES AND TOWNS

Note: The first name is that of the city or town, second, that of the county in which it is located, then the population and location on the map.

Explanation of symbols: • - Census Designated Place (CDP)

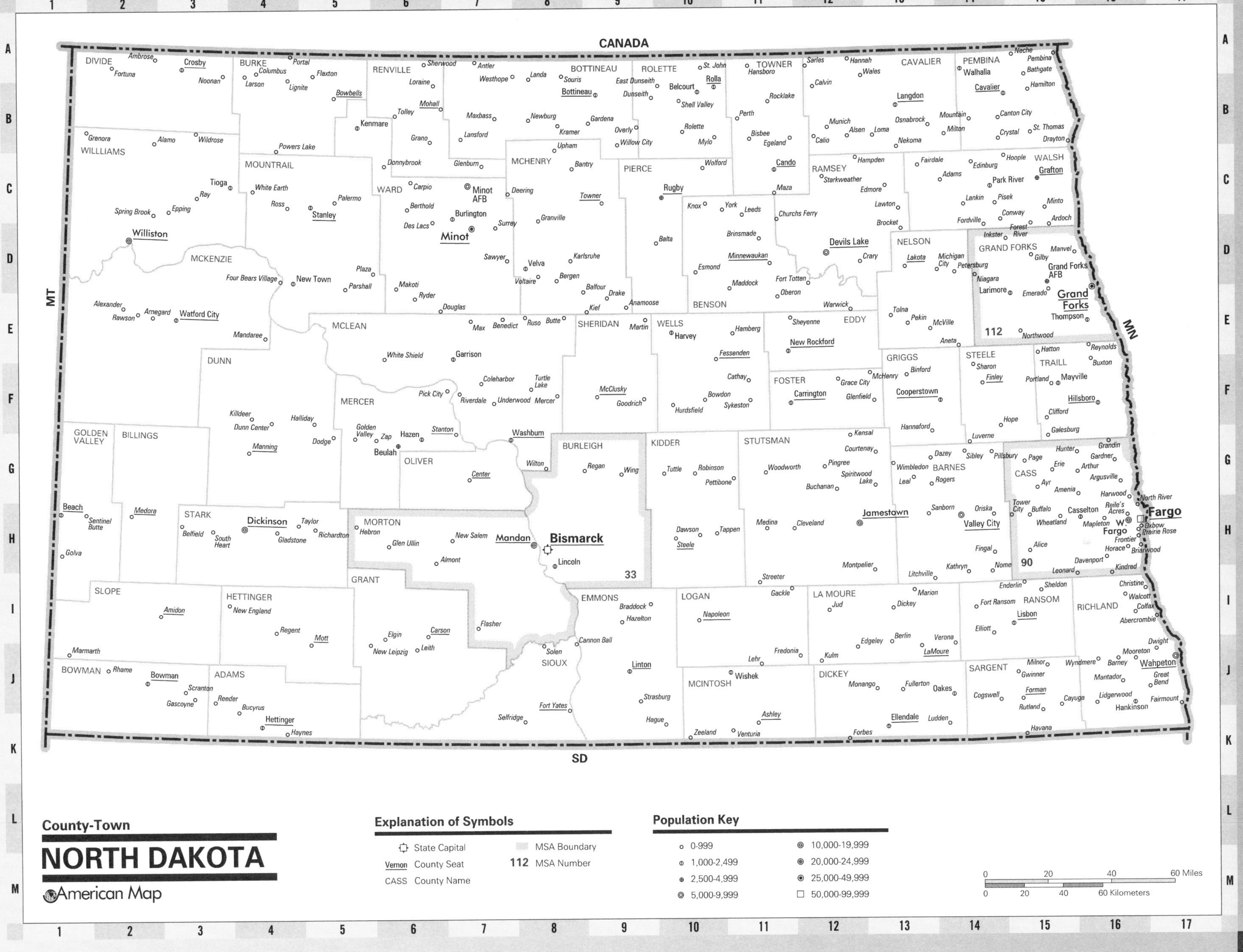
CANADA
MT
MN
SD
DIVIDE
BURKE
RENVILLE
BOTTINEAU
ROLETTE
TOWNER
CAVALIER
PEMBINA
WILLIAMS
MOUNTRAIL
WARD
MCHENRY
PIERCE
RAMSEY
WALSH
MCKENZIE
NELSON
GRAND FORKS
BENSON
MCLEAN
SHERIDAN
WELLS
EDDY
GRIGGS
STEELE
TRAILL
DUNN
MERCER
FOSTER
GOLDEN VALLEY
BILLINGS
OLIVER
BURLEIGH
KIDDER
STUTSMAN
BARNES
CASS
STARK
MORTON
SLOPE
HETTINGER
GRANT
EMMONS
LOGAN
LA MOURE
RANSOM
RICHLAND
BOWMAN
ADAMS
SIOUX
MCINTOSH
DICKEY
SARGENT
Williston
Minot
Minot AFB
Devils Lake
Grand Forks
Grand Forks AFB
Dickinson
Mandan
Bismarck
Jamestown
Valley City
Fargo
West Fargo
Wahpeton
112
33
90
County-Town
NORTH DAKOTA
American Map
Explanation of Symbols
State Capital
Vernon County Seat
CASS County Name
MSA Boundary
112 MSA Number
Population Key
0-999
1,000-2,499
2,500-4,999
5,000-9,999
10,000-19,999
20,000-24,999
25,000-49,999
50,000-99,999
0 20 40 60 Miles
0 20 40 60 Kilometers

Explanation of Symbols

- State Capital
- Vernon: County Seat
- MSA Boundary
- 177: MSA Number
- PIKE: County Name

Population Key

- 0-999
- 1,000-2,499
- 2,500-4,999
- 5,000-9,999
- 10,000-19,999
- 20,000-24,999
- 25,000-49,999
- 50,000-99,999
- 100,000-249,999
- 250,000-999,999

0 20 40 60 Miles

0 20 40 60 Kilometers

County-Town

OHIO

American Map

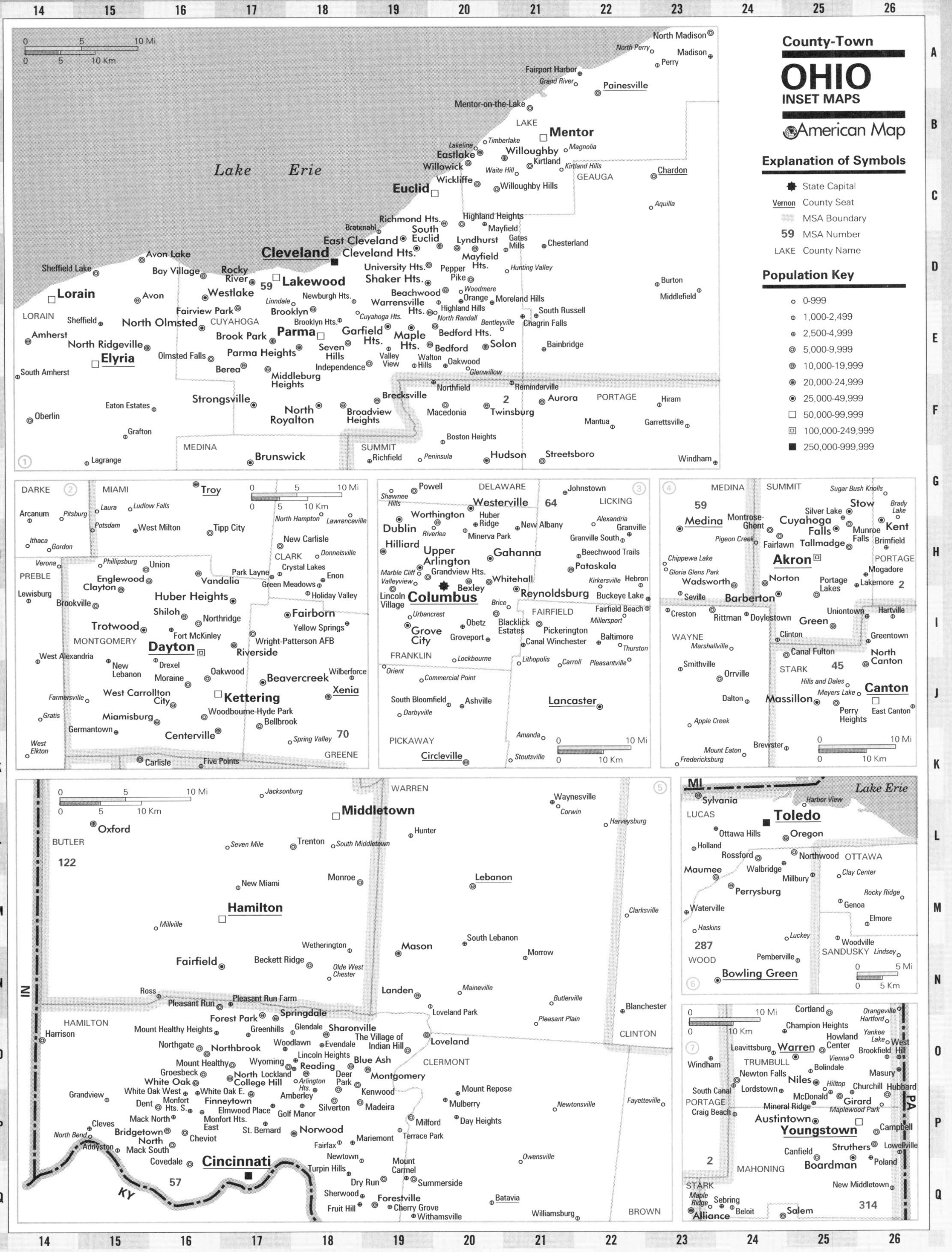
County-Town
OHIO
INSET MAPS
American Map
Explanation of Symbols
State Capital
Vernon County Seat
MSA Boundary
59 MSA Number
LAKE County Name
Population Key
0-999
1,000-2,499
2,500-4,999
5,000-9,999
10,000-19,999
20,000-24,999
25,000-49,999
50,000-99,999
100,000-249,999
250,000-999,999
Lake Erie
North Madison
North Perry
Madison
Perry
Fairport Harbor
Grand River
Painesville
Mentor-on-the-Lake
LAKE
Mentor
Lakeline
Timberlake
Eastlake
Willoughby
Magnolia
Willowick
Kirtland
Kirtland Hills
Waite Hill
Wickliffe
GEAUGA
Chardon
Euclid
Willoughby Hills
Aquilla
Richmond Hts.
Bratenahl
Highland Heights
South Euclid
Mayfield
East Cleveland
Lyndhurst
Gates Mills
Chesterland
Cleveland
Cleveland Hts.
Mayfield Hts.
Avon Lake
University Hts.
Pepper Pike
Hunting Valley
Sheffield Lake
Bay Village
Rocky River
Shaker Hts.
Burton
59
Lakewood
Woodmere
Orange
Moreland Hills
Middlefield
Lorain
Avon
Westlake
Newburgh Hts.
Beachwood
Linndale
Warrensville Hts.
Highland Hills
South Russell
Fairview Park
Brooklyn
Cuyahoga Hts.
North Randall
LORAIN
Sheffield
North Olmsted
CUYAHOGA
Brooklyn Hts.
Bentleyville
Chagrin Falls
Garfield Hts.
Maple Hts.
Bedford Hts.
Amherst
Brook Park
Parma
North Ridgeville
Seven Hills
Bedford
Solon
Bainbridge
Elyria
Olmsted Falls
Parma Heights
Valley View
Walton Hills
Oakwood
Independence
Glenwillow
South Amherst
Berea
Middleburg Heights
Northfield
Reminderville
Brecksville
Strongsville
2
Aurora
PORTAGE
Hiram
Eaton Estates
North Royalton
Broadview Heights
Macedonia
Twinsburg
Oberlin
Mantua
Garrettsville
Grafton
Boston Heights
MEDINA
SUMMIT
Brunswick
Hudson
Streetsboro
Lagrange
Richfield
Peninsula
Windham
DARKE
MIAMI
Troy
Arcanum
Pitsburg
Laura
Ludlow Falls
North Hampton
Lawrenceville
Potsdam
West Milton
Tipp City
Ithaca
Gordon
New Carlisle
CLARK
Donnelsville
Verona
Phillipsburg
Union
Crystal Lakes
PREBLE
Park Layne
Englewood
Vandalia
Enon
Clayton
Green Meadows
Lewisburg
Holiday Valley
Brookville
Huber Heights
Fairborn
Shiloh
Northridge
Yellow Springs
Trotwood
Fort McKinley
Wright-Patterson AFB
MONTGOMERY
Dayton
Riverside
West Alexandria
New Lebanon
Drexel
Oakwood
Wilberforce
Moraine
Beavercreek
Xenia
Farmersville
West Carrollton City
Kettering
Woodbourne-Hyde Park
Gratis
Miamisburg
Bellbrook
Germantown
Centerville
Spring Valley
70
West Elkton
GREENE
Carlisle
Five Points
Powell
DELAWARE
Johnstown
Shawnee Hills
Westerville
64
LICKING
Worthington
Huber Ridge
Alexandria
Dublin
Riverlea
New Albany
Granville
Minerva Park
Granville South
Hilliard
Upper Arlington
Gahanna
Beechwood Trails
Marble Cliff
Valleyview
Grandview Hts.
Pataskala
Whitehall
Kirkersville
Hebron
Lincoln Village
Bexley
Columbus
Reynoldsburg
Buckeye Lake
Brice
FAIRFIELD
Fairfield Beach
Urbancrest
Millersport
Obetz
Blacklick Estates
Grove City
Groveport
Pickerington
Baltimore
Canal Winchester
Thurston
FRANKLIN
Lockbourne
Lithopolis
Carroll
Pleasantville
Orient
Commercial Point
South Bloomfield
Ashville
Lancaster
Darbyville
PICKAWAY
Amanda
Circleville
Stoutsville
MEDINA
SUMMIT
Sugar Bush Knolls
59
Stow
Brady Lake
Silver Lake
Medina
Montrose-Ghent
Cuyahoga Falls
Kent
Pigeon Creek
Munroe Falls
Fairlawn
Tallmadge
Brimfield
Chippewa Lake
Akron
PORTAGE
Gloria Glens Park
Mogadore
Wadsworth
Norton
Portage Lakes
Lakemore
2
Seville
Barberton
Creston
Rittman
Doylestown
Uniontown
Hartville
Green
WAYNE
Clinton
Greentown
Marshallville
Canal Fulton
North Canton
Smithville
STARK
45
Orrville
Hills and Dales
Meyers Lake
Canton
Dalton
Massillon
Perry Heights
East Canton
Apple Creek
Brewster
Mount Eaton
Fredericksburg
WARREN
Jacksonburg
Waynesville
Corwin
Oxford
Middletown
Harveysburg
Hunter
BUTLER
Trenton
Seven Mile
South Middletown
122
Monroe
Lebanon
New Miami
Hamilton
Clarksville
Millville
South Lebanon
Wetherington
Mason
Morrow
Fairfield
Beckett Ridge
Olde West Chester
Maineville
Landen
Ross
Butlerville
Pleasant Run
Pleasant Run Farm
Blanchester
Springdale
Loveland Park
Pleasant Plain
HAMILTON
Forest Park
Harrison
Mount Healthy Heights
Greenhills
Glendale
Sharonville
The Village of Indian Hill
CLINTON
Northgate
Northbrook
Woodlawn
Evendale
Loveland
Lincoln Heights
Mount Healthy
Wyoming
Reading
Blue Ash
CLERMONT
Groesbeck
North College Hill
Lockland
Arlington Hts.
Deer Park
Montgomery
White Oak
Grandview
White Oak West
White Oak E.
Amberley
Kenwood
Mount Repose
Monfort Hts. S.
Finneytown
Dent
Elmwood Place
Silverton
Madeira
Mulberry
Newtonsville
Fayetteville
Golf Manor
Mack North
Monfort Hts.
Milford
Day Heights
Cleves
East
Bridgetown
North Bend
St. Bernard
Norwood
Terrace Park
Mariemont
Cheviot
Addyston
North
Fairfax
Mack South
Owensville
Covedale
Cincinnati
Newtown
Mount Carmel
Turpin Hills
57
Dry Run
Summerside
KY
Sherwood
Forestville
Batavia
Fruit Hill
Cherry Grove
Withamsville
Williamsburg
BROWN
IN
MI
Lake Erie
Sylvania
Harbor View
LUCAS
Toledo
Ottawa Hills
Oregon
Holland
Rossford
Northwood
OTTAWA
Maumee
Walbridge
Millbury
Clay Center
Perrysburg
Rocky Ridge
Genoa
Waterville
Elmore
Haskins
Luckey
287
Woodville
WOOD
SANDUSKY
Lindsey
Pemberville
Bowling Green
Cortland
Orangeville
Hartford
Champion Heights
Yankee Lake
Howland Center
West Hill
Leavittsburg
Warren
Brookfield
Windham
TRUMBULL
Vienna
Bolindale
Masury
Newton Falls
Niles
Hilltop
Churchill
Hubbard
South Canal
Lordstown
McDonald
PORTAGE
Mineral Ridge
Girard
PA
Craig Beach
Maplewood Park
Austintown
Youngstown
Campbell
Struthers
Lowellville
Canfield
2
MAHONING
Boardman
Poland
STARK
New Middletown
Maple Ridge
Sebring
314
Alliance
Beloit
Salem

COUNTIES

(88 Counties)

Name of County	Population	Location on Map
ADAMS	27,330	L-4
ALLEN	108,473	F-3
ASHLAND	52,523	E-8
ASHTABULA	102,728	C-12
ATHENS	62,223	K-8
AUGLAIZE	46,611	G-3
BELMONT	70,226	I-11
BROWN	42,285	M-4
BUTLER	332,807	K-2
CARROLL	28,836	F-11
CHAMPAIGN	38,890	H-3
CLARK	144,742	I-4
CLERMONT	177,977	L-2
CLINTON	40,543	J-3
COLUMBIANA	112,075	F-12
COSHOCTON	36,655	G-9
CRAWFORD	46,966	E-6
CUYAHOGA	1,393,978	C-10
DARKE	53,309	G-1
DEFIANCE	39,500	C-1
DELAWARE	109,989	H-6
ERIE	79,551	D-7
FAIRFIELD	122,759	J-7
FAYETTE	28,433	K-4
FRANKLIN	1,068,978	I-5
FULTON	42,084	B-2
GALLIA	31,069	M-8
GEAUGA	90,895	C-11
GREENE	147,886	I-3
GUERNSEY	40,792	H-10
HAMILTON	845,303	K-2
HANCOCK	71,295	E-4
HARDIN	31,945	F-4
HARRISON	15,856	G-11
HENRY	29,210	D-3
HIGHLAND	40,875	L-4
HOCKING	28,241	K-7
HOLMES	38,943	F-9
HURON	59,487	D-7
JACKSON	32,641	L-7
JEFFERSON	73,894	G-12
KNOX	54,500	G-8
LAKE	227,511	C-10
LAWRENCE	62,319	M-7
LICKING	145,491	H-7
LOGAN	46,005	G-4
LORAIN	284,664	D-8
LUCAS	455,054	C-4
MADISON	40,213	I-5
MAHONING	257,555	E-12
MARION	66,217	F-5
MEDINA	151,095	D-9
MEIGS	23,072	L-8
MERCER	40,924	F-1
MIAMI	98,868	H-3
MONROE	15,180	J-11
MONTGOMERY	559,062	J-2
MORGAN	14,897	I-9
MORROW	31,628	F-7
MUSKINGUM	84,585	H-8
NOBLE	14,058	I-10
OTTAWA	40,985	C-5
PAULDING	20,293	D-1
PERRY	34,078	I-8
PICKAWAY	52,727	J-5
PIKE	27,695	L-5
PORTAGE	152,061	E-11
PREBLE	42,337	I-1
PUTNAM	34,726	E-2
RICHLAND	128,852	F-7
ROSS	73,345	J-5
SANDUSKY	61,792	C-6
SCIOTO	79,195	L-6
SENECA	58,683	E-5
SHELBY	47,910	H-3
STARK	378,098	E-11
SUMMIT	542,899	E-10
TRUMBULL	225,116	C-12
TUSCARAWAS	90,914	G-10
UNION	40,909	G-5
VAN WERT	29,659	E-2
VINTON	12,806	K-7
WARREN	158,383	K-3
WASHINGTON	63,251	K-9
WAYNE	111,564	F-9
WILLIAMS	39,188	B-1
WOOD	121,065	D-4
WYANDOT	22,908	F-5
TOTAL	**11,353,140**	

CITIES AND TOWNS

Note: The first name is that of the city or town, second, that of the county in which it is located, then the population and location on the map.

Aberdeen, *Brown,* 1,603 ....M-4
Ada, *Hardin,* 5,582 ....F-4
Addyston, *Hamilton,* 1,010 ....P-15
Akron, *Summit,* 217,074 ....E-10
Alliance, *Stark,* 23,253 ....E-11
Amberley, *Hamilton,* 3,425 ....P-18
Amelia, *Clermont,* 2,752 ....L-2
Amherst, *Lorain,* 11,797 ....C-8
Andover, *Ashtabula,* 1,269 ....C-13
Anna, *Shelby,* 1,319 ....G-3
Ansonia, *Darke,* 1,145 ....H-1
Antwerp, *Paulding,* 1,740 ....D-1
Arcanum, *Darke,* 2,076 ....H-2
Archbold, *Fulton,* 4,290 ....C-2
Arlington, *Hancock,* 1,351 ....E-4
Ashland, *Ashland,* 21,249 ....E-8
Ashley, *Delaware,* 1,216 ....G-6
Ashtabula, *Ashtabula,* 20,962 ....B-12
Ashville, *Pickaway,* 3,174 ....I-6
Athens, *Athens,* 21,342 ....K-9
Aurora, *Portage,* 13,556 ....D-11
•Austintown, *Mahoning,* 31,627 ....D-12
Avon, *Lorain,* 11,446 ....E-15
Avon Lake, *Lorain,* 18,145 ....D-15
•Bainbridge, *Geauga,* 3,417 ....E-21
•Bainbridge, *Ross,* 1,012 ....K-5
•Ballville, *Sandusky,* 3,255 ....D-6
Baltimore, *Fairfield,* 2,881 ....I-7
Barberton, *Summit,* 27,899 ....E-10
Barnesville, *Belmont,* 4,225 ....H-11
Batavia, *Clermont,* 1,617 ....L-3
Bay Village, *Cuyahoga,* 16,087 ....D-16
Beach City, *Stark,* 1,137 ....F-10
Beachwood, *Cuyahoga,* 12,186 ....D-20
Beavercreek, *Greene,* 37,984 ....J-17
•Beckett Ridge, *Butler,* 8,663 ....N-18
Bedford, *Cuyahoga,* 14,214 ....E-19
Bedford Heights,
Cuyahoga, 11,375 ....E-20
•Beechwood Trails, *Licking,* 2,258 ....H-22
Bellaire, *Belmont,* 4,892 ....H-13
Bellbrook, *Greene,* 7,009 ....J-3
Bellefontaine, *Logan,* 13,069 ....G-4
Bellevue, *Huron,* 8,193 ....D-7
Bellville, *Richland,* 1,773 ....F-7
Beloit, *Mahoning,* 1,024 ....Q-24
Belpre, *Washington,* 6,660 ....K-10
Berea, *Cuyahoga,* 18,970 ....D-9
Bethel, *Clermont,* 2,637 ....L-3
Bethesda, *Belmont,* 1,413 ....H-12
Beverly, *Washington,* 1,282 ....J-10
Bexley, *Franklin,* 13,203 ....I-20
•Blacklick Estates, *Franklin,* 9,518 ....I-20
Blanchester, *Clinton,* 4,220 ....K-3
Bloomville, *Seneca,* 1,045 ....E-6
Blue Ash, *Hamilton,* 12,513 ....K-2
Bluffton, *Allen,* 3,896 ....E-4
•Boardman, *Mahoning,* 37,215 ....E-13
•Bolindale, *Trumbull,* 2,489 ....O-25
Boston Heights, *Summit,* 1,186 ....F-20
Botkins, *Shelby,* 1,205 ....G-3
Bowling Green, *Wood,* 29,636 ....C-4
Bradford, *Miami,* 1,859 ....H-2
Bradner, *Wood,* 1,171 ....D-5
Bratenahl, *Cuyahoga,* 1,337 ....D-19
Brecksville, *Cuyahoga,* 13,382 ....D-10
Bremen, *Fairfield,* 1,265 ....J-8
Brewster, *Stark,* 2,324 ....F-10
Bridgeport, *Belmont,* 2,186 ....H-13
•Bridgetown North,
Hamilton, 12,569 ....P-16
•Brimfield, *Portage,* 3,248 ....H-26
Broadview Heights,
Cuyahoga, 15,967 ....F-18
Brook Park, *Cuyahoga,* 21,218 ....C-9
•Brookfield, *Trumbull,* 1,288 ....O-26
Brooklyn, *Cuyahoga,* 11,586 ....E-18
Brooklyn Heights, *Cuyahoga,* 1,558 E-18
Brookville, *Montgomery,* 5,289 ....I-2
Brunswick, *Medina,* 33,388 ....D-9
Bryan, *Williams,* 8,333 ....C-2
Buckeye Lake, *Licking,* 3,049 ....I-23
Bucyrus, *Crawford,* 13,224 ....F-6
•Burlington, *Lawrence,* 2,794 ....N-7
Burton, *Geauga,* 1,450 ....D-23
Byesville, *Guernsey,* 2,574 ....I-10
Cadiz, *Harrison,* 3,308 ....G-12
•Calcutta, *Columbiana,* 3,491 ....F-13
Caldwell, *Noble,* 1,956 ....I-10
Cambridge, *Guernsey,* 11,520 ....H-10
Camden, *Preble,* 2,302 ....J-1
Campbell, *Mahoning,* 9,460 ....P-26
Canal Fulton, *Stark,* 5,061 ....E-10
Canal Winchester, *Fairfield,* 4,478 ....I-7
Canfield, *Mahoning,* 7,374 ....Q-25
Canton, *Stark,* 80,806 ....F-11
Cardington, *Morrow,* 1,849 ....G-6
Carey, *Wyandot,* 3,901 ....E-5
Carlisle, *Warren,* 5,121 ....J-2
Carrollton, *Carroll,* 3,190 ....F-12
Cedarville, *Greene,* 3,828 ....I-4
Celina, *Mercer,* 10,303 ....F-2
Centerburg, *Knox,* 1,432 ....G-7
Centerville, *Montgomery,* 23,024 ....J-3
Chagrin Falls, *Cuyahoga,* 4,024 ....E-21
•Champion Heights, *Trumbull,* 4,727 O-24
Chardon, *Geauga,* 5,156 ....C-11
Chauncey, *Athens,* 1,067 ....K-9
•Cherry Grove, *Hamilton,* 4,555 ....Q-19
•Chesterland, *Geauga,* 2,646 ....D-21
Cheviot, *Hamilton,* 9,015 ....P-16
Chillicothe, *Ross,* 21,796 ....K-6
•Choctaw Lake, *Madison,* 1,562 ....I-5
•Churchill, *Trumbull,* 2,601 ....P-25
Cincinnati, *Hamilton,* 331,285 ....L-2
Circleville, *Pickaway,* 13,485 ....J-6
Clayton, *Montgomery,* 13,347 ....I-2
Cleveland, *Cuyahoga,* 478,403 ....C-10
Cleveland Heights,
Cuyahoga, 49,958 ....D-19
Cleves, *Hamilton,* 2,790 ....P-15
Clinton, *Summit,* 1,337 ....I-24
Clyde, *Sandusky,* 6,064 ....D-6
Coal Grove, *Lawrence,* 2,027 ....N-7
Coldwater, *Mercer,* 4,482 ....G-1
Columbiana, *Columbiana,* 5,635 ....E-13
Columbus, *Franklin,* 711,470 ....I-6
Columbus Grove, *Putnam,* 2,200 ....E-3
Conneaut, *Ashtabula,* 12,485 ....A-13
Continental, *Putnam,* 1,188 ....D-2
Convoy, *Van Wert,* 1,110 ....E-1
Cortland, *Trumbull,* 6,830 ....D-13
Coshocton, *Coshocton,* 11,682 ....G-9
•Covedale, *Hamilton,* 6,360 ....L-1
Covington, *Miami,* 2,559 ....H-2
Craig Beach, *Mahoning,* 1,254 ....P-24
Crestline, *Crawford,* 5,088 ....F-7
Creston, *Wayne,* 2,161 ....I-23
Cridersville, *Auglaize,* 1,817 ....F-3
Crooksville, *Perry,* 2,483 ....I-9
•Crystal Lakes, *Clark,* 1,411 ....H-17
Cuyahoga Falls, *Summit,* 49,374 ....D-10
Dalton, *Wayne,* 1,605 ....J-24
Danville, *Knox,* 1,104 ....G-8
•Day Heights, *Clermont,* 2,823 ....P-20
Dayton, *Montgomery,* 166,179 ....I-3
De Graff, *Logan,* 1,212 ....G-3
Deer Park, *Hamilton,* 5,982 ....P-18
Defiance, *Defiance,* 16,465 ....D-2
Delaware, *Delaware,* 25,243 ....G-6
Delphos, *Allen,* 6,944 ....E-2
Delta, *Fulton,* 2,930 ....C-3
Dennison, *Tuscarawas,* 2,992 ....G-11
•Dent, *Hamilton,* 7,612 ....P-16
Deshler, *Henry,* 1,831 ....D-4
•Devola, *Washington,* 2,771 ....J-11
•Dillonvale, *Jefferson,* 3,716 ....H-12
Dover, *Tuscarawas,* 12,210 ....G-10
Doylestown, *Wayne,* 2,799 ....I-24
Dresden, *Muskingum,* 1,423 ....H-9
•Drexel, *Montgomery,* 2,057 ....J-16
•Dry Run, *Hamilton,* 6,553 ....Q-19
Dublin, *Franklin,* 31,392 ....H-6
East Canton, *Stark,* 1,629 ....F-11
East Cleveland, *Cuyahoga,* 27,217 .D-19
East Liverpool, *Columbiana,* 13,089 F-13
East Palestine, *Columbiana,* 4,917 .E-13
Eastlake, *Lake,* 20,255 ....B-20
Eaton, *Preble,* 8,133 ....I-1
•Eaton Estates, *Lorain,* 1,409 ....F-16
Edgerton, *Williams,* 2,117 ....C-1
•Edgewood, *Ashtabula,* 4,762 ....B-12
Elida, *Allen,* 1,917 ....F-3
Elmore, *Ottawa,* 1,426 ....C-5
Elmwood Place, *Hamilton,* 2,681 ....P-17
Elyria, *Lorain,* 55,953 ....D-9
Englewood, *Montgomery,* 12,235 ....H-15
Enon, *Clark,* 2,638 ....H-18
Euclid, *Cuyahoga,* 52,717 ....C-10
Evendale, *Hamilton,* 3,090 ....O-18
Fairborn, *Greene,* 32,052 ....I-3
Fairfax, *Hamilton,* 1,938 ....P-18
Fairfield, *Butler,* 42,097 ....K-1
•Fairfield Beach, *Fairfield,* 1,163 ....I-23
Fairlawn, *Summit,* 7,307 ....D-10
Fairport Harbor, *Lake,* 3,180 ....A-22
•Fairview Lanes, *Erie,* 1,015 ....C-7
Fairview Park, *Cuyahoga,* 17,572 ....E-17
Fayette, *Fulton,* 1,340 ....B-2
Findlay, *Hancock,* 38,967 ....E-4
•Finneytown, *Hamilton,* 13,492 ....P-17
•Five Points, *Warren,* 2,191 ....K-16
Forest, *Hardin,* 1,488 ....F-5
Forest Park, *Hamilton,* 19,463 ....O-17
•Forestville, *Hamilton,* 10,978 ....L-2
Fort Loramie, *Shelby,* 1,344 ....G-2
•Fort McKinley, *Montgomery,* 3,989 ....I-16
Fort Recovery, *Mercer,* 1,273 ....G-1
Fort Shawnee, *Allen,* 3,855 ....F-3
Fostoria, *Seneca,* 13,931 ....D-5
Frankfort, *Ross,* 1,011 ....K-6
Franklin, *Warren,* 11,396 ....J-2
•Franklin Furnace, *Scioto,* 1,537 ....M-6
Frazeysburg, *Muskingum,* 1,201 ....H-9
Fredericktown, *Knox,* 2,428 ....G-7
Fremont, *Sandusky,* 17,375 ....D-6
•Fruit Hill, *Hamilton,* 3,945 ....Q-18
Gahanna, *Franklin,* 32,636 ....H-20
Galion, *Crawford,* 11,341 ....F-7
Gallipolis, *Gallia,* 4,180 ....M-8
Gambier, *Knox,* 1,871 ....G-8
Garfield Heights,
Cuyahoga, 30,734 ....E-19
Garrettsville, *Portage,* 2,262 ....D-11
Gates Mills, *Cuyahoga,* 2,493 ....D-21
Geneva, *Ashtabula,* 6,595 ....B-12
•Geneva-On-The-Lake,
Ashtabula, 1,545 ....B-12
Genoa, *Ottawa,* 2,230 ....C-5
Georgetown, *Brown,* 3,691 ....M-3
Germantown, *Montgomery,* 4,884 ....K-15
Gibsonburg, *Sandusky,* 2,506 ....C-5
Girard, *Trumbull,* 10,902 ....P-25
Glendale, *Hamilton,* 2,188 ....O-17
•Glenmoor, *Columbiana,* 2,192 ....F-13
Glouster, *Athens,* 1,972 ....J-9
Gnadenhutten, *Tuscarawas,* 1,280 .G-11
Golf Manor, *Hamilton,* 3,999 ....P-18
Grafton, *Lorain,* 2,302 ....F-15
Grand Rapids, *Wood,* 1,002 ....C-4
•Grandview, *Hamilton,* 1,391 ....P-15
Grandview Heights, *Franklin,* 6,695 .H-19
Granville, *Licking,* 3,167 ....H-7
•Granville South, *Licking,* 1,194 ....H-22
Green, *Summit,* 22,817 ....E-10
•Green Meadows, *Clark,* 2,318 ....I-18
Green Springs, *Seneca,* 1,247 ....D-6
Greenfield, *Highland,* 4,906 ....K-5
Greenhills, *Hamilton,* 4,103 ....O-17
•Greentown, *Stark,* 3,154 ....I-26
Greenville, *Darke,* 13,294 ....H-1
Greenwich, *Huron,* 1,525 ....E-7
•Groesbeck, *Hamilton,* 7,202 ....O-16
Grove City, *Franklin,* 27,075 ....I-6
Groveport, *Franklin,* 3,865 ....I-6
Hamilton, *Butler,* 60,690 ....K-2
•Harbor Hills, *Licking,* 1,303 ....I-8
Harrison, *Hamilton,* 7,487 ....O-14
Hartville, *Stark,* 2,174 ....I-26
Heath, *Licking,* 8,527 ....H-8
Hebron, *Licking,* 2,034 ....I-22
Hicksville, *Defiance,* 3,649 ....D-1
Highland Heights, *Cuyahoga,* 8,082 C-20
Highland Hills, *Cuyahoga,* 1,618 ....E-20
Hilliard, *Franklin,* 24,230 ....H-6
Hillsboro, *Highland,* 6,368 ....K-4
Hiram, *Portage,* 1,242 ....D-11
Holgate, *Henry,* 1,194 ....D-3
•Holiday Valley, *Clark,* 1,712 ....I-18
Holland, *Lucas,* 1,306 ....C-4
•Howland Center, *Trumbull,* 6,481 ....O-25
Hubbard, *Trumbull,* 8,284 ....P-26
Huber Heights, *Montgomery,* 38,212 .I-17
•Huber Ridge, *Franklin,* 4,883 ....H-20
Hudson, *Summit,* 22,439 ....D-11
•Hunter, *Warren,* 1,737 ....L-19
Huron, *Erie,* 7,958 ....C-7
Independence, *Cuyahoga,* 7,109 ....E-19
Ironton, *Lawrence,* 11,211 ....N-7
Jackson, *Jackson,* 6,184 ....L-7
Jackson Center, *Shelby,* 1,369 ....G-3
Jamestown, *Greene,* 1,917 ....J-4
Jefferson, *Ashtabula,* 3,572 ....B-12
Jeffersonville, *Fayette,* 1,288 ....J-4
Johnstown, *Licking,* 3,440 ....H-7
Kalida, *Putnam,* 1,031 ....E-3
Kent, *Portage,* 27,906 ....D-11
Kenton, *Hardin,* 8,336 ....F-4

Explanation of symbols: • - Census Designated Place (CDP)

COUNTIES

(77 Counties)

Name of County	Population	Location on Map
ADAIR	21,038	D-16
ALFALFA	6,105	A-7
ATOKA	13,879	H-13
BEAVER	5,857	A-1
BECKHAM	19,799	F-3
BLAINE	11,976	D-7
BRYAN	36,534	J-12
CADDO	30,150	F-7
CANADIAN	87,697	E-7
CARTER	45,621	J-10
CHEROKEE	42,521	D-15
CHOCTAW	15,342	J-14
CIMARRON	3,148	L-4
CLEVELAND	208,016	G-9
COAL	6,031	H-12
COMANCHE	114,996	H-6
COTTON	6,614	I-7
CRAIG	14,950	A-15
CREEK	67,367	E-12
CUSTER	26,142	E-5
DELAWARE	37,077	C-16
DEWEY	4,743	D-5
ELLIS	4,075	B-3
GARFIELD	57,813	D-8
GARVIN	27,210	H-9
GRADY	45,516	G-8
GRANT	5,144	A-8
GREER	6,061	G-4
HARMON	3,283	H-3
HARPER	3,562	A-3
HASKELL	11,792	F-15
HUGHES	14,154	G-13
JACKSON	28,439	H-4
JEFFERSON	6,818	J-8
JOHNSTON	10,513	I-11
KAY	48,080	A-10
KINGFISHER	13,926	D-8
KIOWA	10,227	G-5
LATIMER	10,692	G-15
LE FLORE	48,109	G-16
LINCOLN	32,080	D-10
LOGAN	33,924	D-9
LOVE	8,831	K-9
MAJOR	7,545	C-6
MARSHALL	13,184	J-11
MAYES	38,369	C-15
MCCLAIN	27,740	H-9
MCCURTAIN	34,402	I-16
MCINTOSH	19,456	G-13
MURRAY	12,623	I-10
MUSKOGEE	69,451	E-14
NOBLE	11,411	B-10
NOWATA	10,569	A-14
OKFUSKEE	11,814	E-12
OKLAHOMA	660,448	E-9
OKMULGEE	39,685	E-13
OSAGE	44,437	A-12
OTTAWA	33,194	B-16
PAWNEE	16,612	C-11
PAYNE	68,190	D-10
PITTSBURG	43,953	G-13
PONTOTOC	35,143	H-11
POTTAWATOMIE	65,521	F-11
PUSHMATAHA	11,667	I-14
ROGER MILLS	3,436	E-3
ROGERS	70,641	B-14
SEMINOLE	24,894	F-11
SEQUOYAH	38,972	F-16
STEPHENS	43,182	I-8
TEXAS	20,107	L-7
TILLMAN	9,287	I-5
TULSA	563,299	C-13
WAGONER	57,491	D-14
WASHINGTON	48,996	A-13
WASHITA	11,508	F-6
WOODS	9,089	A-5
WOODWARD	18,486	B-5
TOTAL	**3,450,654**	

CITIES AND TOWNS

Note: The first name is that of the city or town, second, that of the county in which it is located, then the population and location on the map.

Explanation of symbols: • - Census Designated Place (CDP)

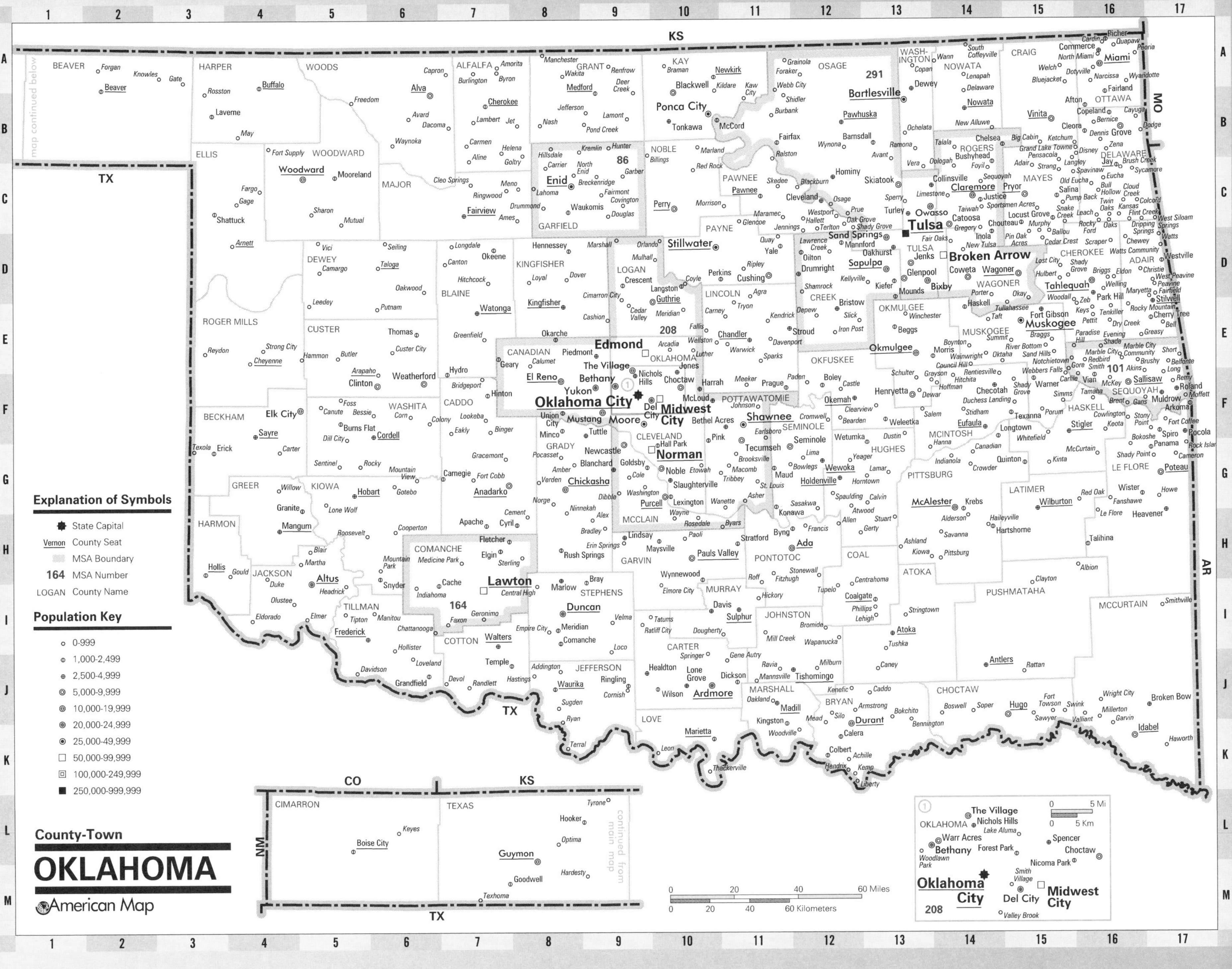
Explanation of Symbols
State Capital
Vernon County Seat
MSA Boundary
164 MSA Number
LOGAN County Name
Population Key
0-999
1,000-2,499
2,500-4,999
5,000-9,999
10,000-19,999
20,000-24,999
25,000-49,999
50,000-99,999
100,000-249,999
250,000-999,999
County-Town
OKLAHOMA
American Map
continued from main map
map continued below
0 20 40 60 Miles
0 20 40 60 Kilometers

COUNTIES

(36 Counties)

Name of County	Population	Location on Map
BAKER	16,741	F-14
BENTON	78,153	G-5
CLACKAMAS	338,391	F-7
CLATSOP	35,630	D-5
COLUMBIA	43,560	D-6
COOS	62,779	I-4
CROOK	19,182	G-10
CURRY	21,137	K-4
DESCHUTES	115,367	I-8
DOUGLAS	100,399	I-5
GILLIAM	1,915	D-11
GRANT	7,935	F-12
HARNEY	7,609	I-12
HOOD RIVER	20,411	E-8
JACKSON	181,269	L-6
JEFFERSON	19,009	G-9
JOSEPHINE	75,726	L-5
KLAMATH	63,775	J-8
LAKE	7,422	J-9
LANE	322,959	H-5
LINCOLN	44,479	G-5
LINN	103,069	G-7
MALHEUR	31,615	G-15
MARION	284,834	F-8
MORROW	10,995	D-12
MULTNOMAH	660,486	E-8
POLK	62,380	F-5
SHERMAN	1,934	E-10
TILLAMOOK	24,262	E-5
UMATILLA	70,548	D-13
UNION	24,530	D-15
WALLOWA	7,226	D-15
WASCO	23,791	F-9
WASHINGTON	445,342	E-6
WHEELER	1,547	F-11
YAMHILL	84,992	E-6
TOTAL	**3,421,399**	

CITIES AND TOWNS

Note: The first name is that of the city or town, second, that of the county in which it is located, then the population and location on the map.

Albany, *Linn*, 40,852 ..... G-6
•Aloha, *Washington*, 41,741 ..... A-9
•Altamont, *Klamath*, 19,603 ..... M-8
Amity, *Yamhill*, 1,478 ..... F-6
Ashland, *Jackson*, 19,522 ..... M-7
Astoria, *Clatsop*, 9,813 ..... C-5
Athena, *Umatilla*, 1,221 ..... D-14
Aumsville, *Marion*, 3,003 ..... B-14
Baker City, *Baker*, 9,860 ..... F-15
Bandon, *Coos*, 2,833 ..... J-4
Banks, *Washington*, 1,286 ..... D-6
•Barview, *Coos*, 1,872 ..... J-4
Bay City, *Tillamook*, 1,149 ..... E-5
Beaverton, *Washington*, 76,129 ..... A-9
Bend, *Deschutes*, 52,029 ..... H-9
Boardman, *Morrow*, 2,855 ..... D-12
Brookings, *Curry*, 5,447 ..... M-4
Brownsville, *Linn*, 1,449 ..... G-6
•Bunker Hill, *Coos*, 1,462 ..... J-4
Burns, *Harney*, 3,064 ..... I-13
Canby, *Clackamas*, 12,790 ..... C-10
Cannon Beach, *Clatsop*, 1,588 ..... D-5
Canyon City, *Grant*, 669 ..... G-13
Canyonville, *Douglas*, 1,293 ..... K-6
Carlton, *Yamhill*, 1,514 ..... E-6
Cascade Locks, *Hood River*, 1,115 ..... D-8
Cave Junction, *Josephine*, 1,363 ..... M-5
•Cedar Hills, *Washington*, 8,949 ..... A-9
•Cedar Mill, *Washington*, 12,597 ..... A-9
Central Point, *Jackson*, 12,493 ..... L-6
•Chenoweth, *Wasco*, 3,412 ..... D-9
•Clackamas, *Clackamas*, 5,177 ..... B-11
Clatskanie, *Columbia*, 1,528 ..... C-6
Columbia City, *Columbia*, 1,571 ..... D-7
Condon, *Gilliam*, 759 ..... E-11
Coos Bay, *Coos*, 15,374 ..... J-4
Coquille, *Coos*, 4,184 ..... J-4
Cornelius, *Washington*, 9,652 ..... A-8
Corvallis, *Benton*, 49,322 ..... G-6
Cottage Grove, *Lane*, 8,445 ..... I-6
Creswell, *Lane*, 3,579 ..... I-6
Dallas, *Polk*, 12,459 ..... F-6
Dayton, *Yamhill*, 2,119 ..... D-8
Depoe Bay, *Lincoln*, 1,174 ..... F-5
•Deschutes River Woods, *Deschutes*, 4,631 ..... H-9
Drain, *Douglas*, 1,021 ..... I-6
Dundee, *Yamhill*, 2,598 ..... C-8
Dunes City, *Lane*, 1,241 ..... I-4
Durham, *Washington*, 1,382 ..... B-10
Eagle Point, *Jackson*, 4,797 ..... L-7
Elgin, *Union*, 1,654 ..... E-15
Enterprise, *Wallowa*, 1,895 ..... E-16
Estacada, *Clackamas*, 2,371 ..... E-7
Eugene, *Lane*, 137,893 ..... H-6
Fairview, *Multnomah*, 7,561 ..... A-11
Florence, *Lane*, 7,263 ..... H-4
Forest Grove, *Washington*, 17,708 ..... A-7
Fossil, *Wheeler*, 469 ..... F-11
•Four Corners, *Marion*, 13,922 ..... F-6
•Garden Home-Whitford, *Washington*, 6,931 ..... B-9
Gervais, *Marion*, 2,009 ..... A-13
Gladstone, *Clackamas*, 11,438 ..... B-10
•Glide, *Douglas*, 1,690 ..... J-6
Gold Beach, *Curry*, 1,897 ..... L-4
Gold Hill, *Jackson*, 1,073 ..... L-6
Grants Pass, *Josephine*, 23,003 ..... L-6
•Green, *Douglas*, 6,174 ..... J-6
Gresham, *Multnomah*, 90,205 ..... E-7
Happy Valley, *Clackamas*, 4,519 ..... B-11
•Harbeck-Fruitdale, *Josephine*, 3,780 ..... L-6
•Harbor, *Curry*, 2,622 ..... M-4
Harrisburg, *Linn*, 2,795 ..... H-6
•Hayesville, *Marion*, 18,222 ..... A-13
Heppner, *Morrow*, 1,395 ..... E-12
Hermiston, *Umatilla*, 13,154 ..... D-13
Hillsboro, *Washington*, 70,186 ..... E-6
Hines, *Harney*, 1,623 ..... I-13
Hood River, *Hood River*, 5,831 ..... D-9
Hubbard, *Marion*, 2,483 ..... E-7
Independence, *Polk*, 6,035 ..... B-12
Irrigon, *Morrow*, 1,702 ..... D-12
Jacksonville, *Jackson*, 2,235 ..... L-6
Jefferson, *Marion*, 2,487 ..... G-6
•Jennings Lodge, *Clackamas*, 7,036 ..... B-10
John Day, *Grant*, 1,821 ..... G-13
Joseph, *Wallowa*, 1,054 ..... E-16
Junction City, *Lane*, 4,721 ..... H-6
Keizer, *Marion*, 32,203 ..... A-13
King City, *Washington*, 1,949 ..... B-9
Klamath Falls, *Klamath*, 19,462 ..... M-8
La Grande, *Union*, 12,327 ..... E-15
•La Pine, *Deschutes*, 5,799 ..... I-9
Lafayette, *Yamhill*, 2,586 ..... D-7
Lake Oswego, *Clackamas*, 35,278 ..... B-10
Lakeside, *Coos*, 1,371 ..... I-4
Lakeview, *Lake*, 2,474 ..... M-11
Lebanon, *Linn*, 12,950 ..... G-6
•Lincoln Beach, *Lincoln*, 2,078 ..... F-5
Lincoln City, *Lincoln*, 7,437 ..... F-5
Lyons, *Linn*, 1,008 ..... B-14
Madras, *Jefferson*, 5,078 ..... G-9
McMinnville, *Yamhill*, 26,499 ..... E-6
Medford, *Jackson*, 63,154 ..... L-6
•Metzger, *Washington*, 3,354 ..... B-9
Mill City, *Linn*, 1,537 ..... G-7
Milton-Freewater, *Umatilla*, 6,470 ..... D-14
Milwaukie, *Clackamas*, 20,490 ..... B-10
•Mission, *Umatilla*, 1,019 ..... D-14
Molalla, *Clackamas*, 5,647 ..... F-7
Monmouth, *Polk*, 7,741 ..... F-6
Moro, *Sherman*, 337 ..... E-10
Mount Angel, *Marion*, 3,121 ..... A-14
•Mount Hood Village, *Hood River*, 3,306 ..... E-9
Myrtle Creek, *Douglas*, 3,419 ..... K-6
Myrtle Point, *Coos*, 2,451 ..... K-4
Newberg, *Yamhill*, 18,064 ..... C-8
Newport, *Lincoln*, 9,532 ..... G-5
North Bend, *Coos*, 9,544 ..... J-4
North Plains, *Washington*, 1,605 ..... D-6
Nyssa, *Malheur*, 3,163 ..... I-17
•Oak Grove, *Clackamas*, 12,808 ..... B-10
•Oak Hills, *Washington*, 9,050 ..... A-9
Oakridge, *Lane*, 3,148 ..... I-7
•Oatfield, *Clackamas*, 15,750 ..... B-10
•Odell, *Hood River*, 1,849 ..... D-9
Ontario, *Malheur*, 10,985 ..... H-17
Oregon City, *Clackamas*, 25,754 ..... E-7
•Pacific City, *Tillamook*, 1,027 ..... E-5
Pendleton, *Umatilla*, 16,354 ..... D-13
Philomath, *Benton*, 3,838 ..... G-6
Phoenix, *Jackson*, 4,060 ..... M-6
Pilot Rock, *Umatilla*, 1,532 ..... E-13
Port Orford, *Curry*, 1,153 ..... K-4
Portland, *Multnomah*, 529,121 ..... E-7
Prairie City, *Grant*, 1,080 ..... G-14
Prineville, *Crook*, 7,356 ..... H-10
Rainier, *Columbia*, 1,687 ..... C-7
•Raleigh Hills, *Washington*, 5,865 ..... A-9
Redmond, *Deschutes*, 13,481 ..... H-9
•Redwood, *Josephine*, 5,844 ..... L-5
Reedsport, *Douglas*, 4,378 ..... I-4
Riddle, *Douglas*, 1,014 ..... K-6
Rockaway Beach, *Tillamook*, 1,267 ..... D-5
•Rockcreek, *Washington*, 9,404 ..... E-7
Rogue River, *Jackson*, 1,847 ..... L-6
•Rose Lodge, *Lincoln*, 1,708 ..... F-5
Roseburg, *Douglas*, 20,017 ..... J-6
•Roseburg North, *Douglas*, 5,473 ..... J-6
Saint Helens, *Columbia*, 10,019 ..... D-7
Salem, *Marion*, 136,924 ..... F-6
Sandy, *Clackamas*, 5,385 ..... E-8
Scappoose, *Columbia*, 4,976 ..... D-7
Seaside, *Clatsop*, 5,900 ..... C-5
Shady Cove, *Jackson*, 2,307 ..... L-7
Sheridan, *Yamhill*, 3,570 ..... F-6
Sherwood, *Washington*, 11,791 ..... C-9
Siletz, *Lincoln*, 1,133 ..... G-5
Silverton, *Marion*, 7,414 ..... F-7
•South Lebanon, *Linn*, 1,155 ..... G-6
Springfield, *Lane*, 52,864 ..... H-6
Stanfield, *Umatilla*, 1,979 ..... D-13
Stayton, *Marion*, 6,816 ..... F-7
Sublimity, *Marion*, 2,148 ..... B-14
•Sunnyside, *Clackamas*, 6,791 ..... B-11
Sutherlin, *Douglas*, 6,669 ..... J-6
Sweet Home, *Linn*, 8,016 ..... G-7
Talent, *Jackson*, 5,589 ..... M-7
•Terrebonne, *Deschutes*, 1,469 ..... H-9
The Dalles, *Wasco*, 12,156 ..... E-9
•Three Rivers, *Deschutes*, 2,445 ..... I-9
Tigard, *Washington*, 41,223 ..... B-9
Tillamook, *Tillamook*, 4,352 ..... E-5
Toledo, *Lincoln*, 3,472 ..... G-5
•Tri-City, *Douglas*, 3,519 ..... K-6
Troutdale, *Multnomah*, 13,777 ..... A-12
Tualatin, *Washington*, 22,791 ..... B-9
Turner, *Marion*, 1,199 ..... B-13
Umatilla, *Umatilla*, 4,978 ..... D-12
Union, *Union*, 1,926 ..... E-15
Vale, *Malheur*, 1,976 ..... H-16
Veneta, *Lane*, 2,755 ..... H-6
Vernonia, *Columbia*, 2,228 ..... D-6
Waldport, *Lincoln*, 2,050 ..... G-5
•Warm Springs, *Jefferson*, 2,431 ..... G-9
Warrenton, *Clatsop*, 4,096 ..... C-5
•West Haven-Sylvan, *Washington*, 7,147 ..... A-9
West Linn, *Clackamas*, 22,261 ..... B-10
•West Slope, *Washington*, 6,442 ..... A-9
•White City, *Jackson*, 5,466 ..... L-6
Willamina, *Yamhill*, 1,844 ..... F-6
Wilsonville, *Clackamas*, 13,991 ..... C-9
Winston, *Douglas*, 4,613 ..... J-6
Wood Village, *Multnomah*, 2,860 ..... A-11
Woodburn, *Marion*, 20,100 ..... F-7
Yoncalla, *Douglas*, 1,052 ..... I-6

Explanation of symbols: • - Census Designated Place (CDP)

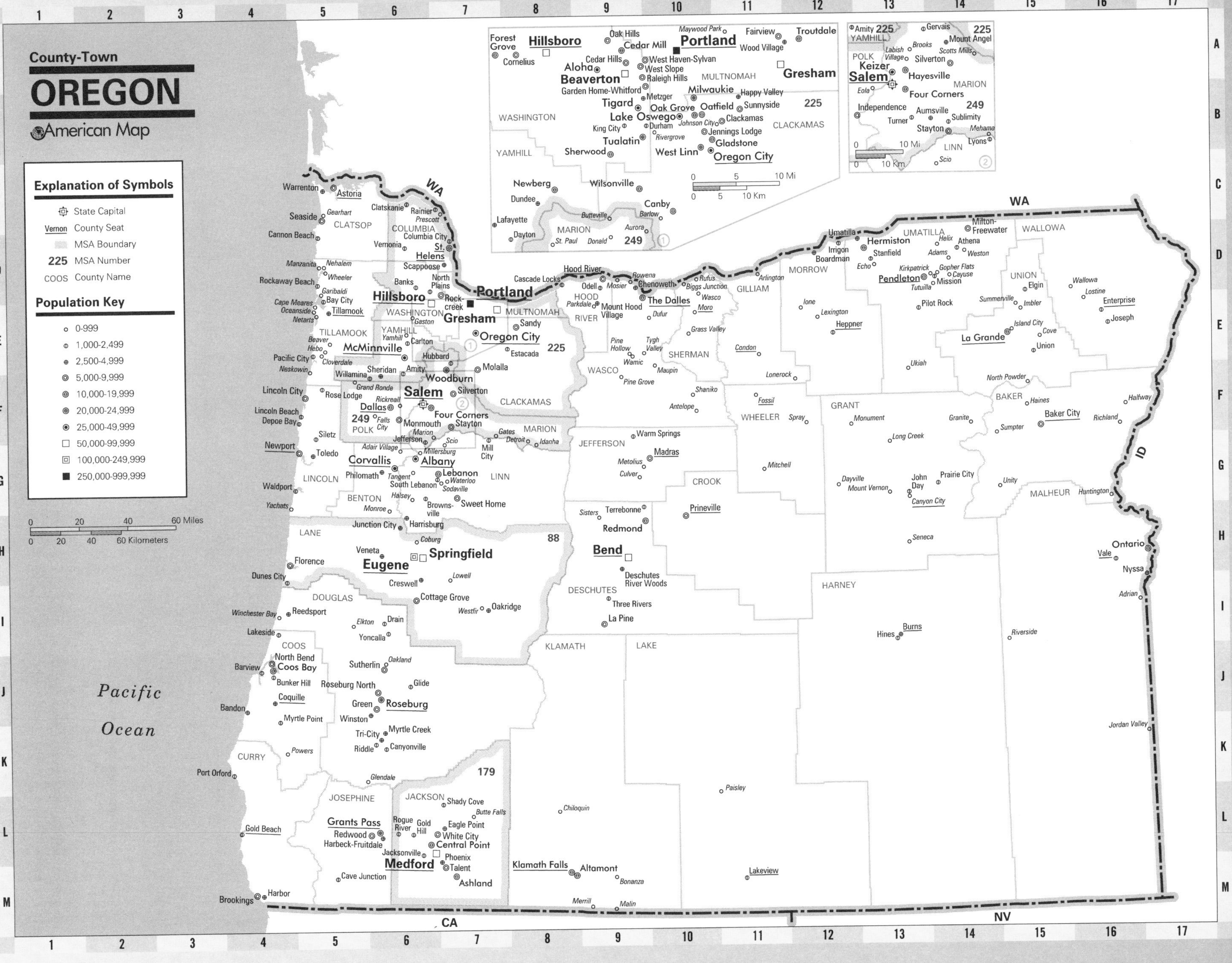
County-Town
OREGON
American Map
Explanation of Symbols
State Capital
Vernon County Seat
MSA Boundary
225 MSA Number
COOS County Name
Population Key
0-999
1,000-2,499
2,500-4,999
5,000-9,999
10,000-19,999
20,000-24,999
25,000-49,999
50,000-99,999
100,000-249,999
250,000-999,999
0 20 40 60 Miles
0 20 40 60 Kilometers
Pacific Ocean
WA
ID
NV
CA
CLATSOP
COLUMBIA
TILLAMOOK
WASHINGTON
MULTNOMAH
YAMHILL
CLACKAMAS
POLK
MARION
LINCOLN
BENTON
LINN
LANE
DOUGLAS
COOS
CURRY
JOSEPHINE
JACKSON
KLAMATH
LAKE
DESCHUTES
JEFFERSON
CROOK
WASCO
HOOD RIVER
SHERMAN
GILLIAM
WHEELER
MORROW
UMATILLA
UNION
WALLOWA
BAKER
GRANT
HARNEY
MALHEUR
Portland
Salem
Eugene
Springfield
Gresham
Hillsboro
Beaverton
Medford
Corvallis
Bend
Albany
Grants Pass
Roseburg
Klamath Falls
Pendleton
La Grande
Baker City
Ontario
Astoria
Newport
Coos Bay
The Dalles
Hood River
Burns
Lakeview
Prineville
Madras
Ashland
Oregon City
McMinnville
Tillamook
Brookings

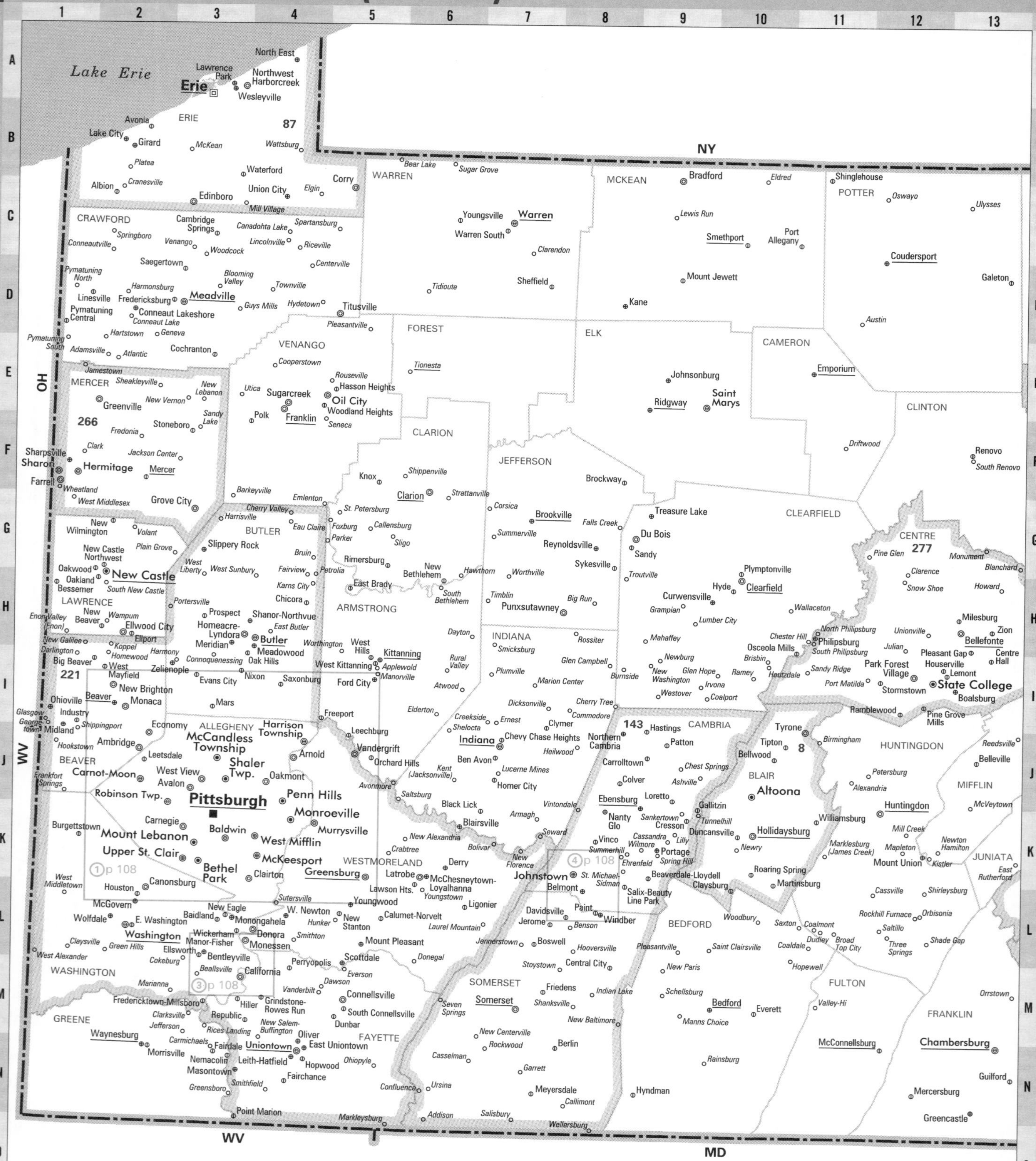

1 2 3 4 5 6 7 8 9 10 11 12 13

A B C D E F G H I J K L M N O P Q

Lake Erie
North East
Lawrence Park
Erie
Northwest Harborcreek
Wesleyville
ERIE
87
Avonia
Lake City
Girard
McKean
Wattsburg
Platea
Waterford
Albion
Cranesville
Union City
Elgin
Corry
Edinboro
Mill Village
NY
Bear Lake
Sugar Grove
WARREN
MCKEAN
Bradford
Eldred
Shinglehouse
POTTER
Oswayo
Ulysses
CRAWFORD
Cambridge Springs
Canadohta Lake
Spartansburg
Springboro
Conneautville
Venango
Lincolnville
Riceville
Woodcock
Youngsville
Warren
Warren South
Lewis Run
Smethport
Port Allegany
Clarendon
Coudersport
Saegertown
Centerville
Pymatuning North
Blooming Valley
Harmonsburg
Townville
Linesville
Fredericksburg
Meadville
Pymatuning Central
Conneaut Lakeshore
Conneaut Lake
Guys Mills
Hydetown
Titusville
Tidioute
Sheffield
Mount Jewett
Galeton
Kane
Pleasantville
Hartstown
Geneva
Pymatuning South
FOREST
ELK
CAMERON
Austin
Adamsville
Atlantic
Cochranton
VENANGO
Cooperstown
Tionesta
Emporium
Jamestown
MERCER
Sheakleyville
New Lebanon
Rouseville
Johnsonburg
OH
Greenville
New Vernon
Utica
Sugarcreek
Hasson Heights
Oil City
Woodland Heights
Ridgway
Saint Marys
CLINTON
266
Stoneboro
Sandy Lake
Polk
Franklin
Seneca
Fredonia
CLARION
Clark
Jackson Center
Sharpsville
Sharon
Hermitage
Mercer
Driftwood
Renovo
South Renovo
JEFFERSON
Farrell
Wheatland
West Middlesex
Grove City
Barkeyville
Emlenton
Knox
Shippenville
Clarion
Strattanville
Brockway
Cherry Valley
Harrisville
St. Petersburg
Corsica
Brookville
Falls Creek
Treasure Lake
CLEARFIELD
New Wilmington
Volant
BUTLER
Eau Claire
Foxburg
Callensburg
Parker
Sligo
Summerville
Du Bois
CENTRE
277
New Castle Northwest
Plain Grove
Slippery Rock
Reynoldsville
Sandy
Pine Glen
Monument
Bruin
Rimersburg
West Liberty
West Sunbury
Fairview
Petrolia
Oakwood
New Castle
Oakland
Bessemer
South New Castle
Karns City
New Bethlehem
Hawthorn
Worthville
Sykesville
Troutville
Plymptonville
Clarence
Blanchard
Snow Shoe
Howard
LAWRENCE
Portersville
Chicora
East Brady
South Bethlehem
Timblin
Punxsutawney
Big Run
Hyde
Clearfield
Curwensville
Grampian
Lumber City
Wallaceton
Enon Valley
(Enon)
New Beaver
Wampum
Ellwood City
Prospect
Shanor-Northvue
East Butler
ARMSTRONG
Homeacre-Lyndora
Butler
Meridian
Worthington
Dayton
INDIANA
Smicksburg
Rossiter
Mahaffey
North Philipsburg
Chester Hill
Philipsburg
South Philipsburg
Osceola Mills
Unionville
Milesburg
Zion
Bellefonte
Julian
Pleasant Gap
Centre Hall
New Galilee
Ellport
Koppel
Darlington
Homewood
Harmony
Connoquenessing
Meadowood
Oak Hills
West Hills
Kittanning
Rural Valley
Glen Campbell
Burnside
Newburg
New Washington
Glen Hope
Brisbin
Ramey
Houtzdale
Sandy Ridge
Park Forest Village
Houserville
Lemont
Big Beaver
West Mayfield
Zelienople
221
Evans City
Nixon
Saxonburg
West Kittanning
Applewold
Manorville
Ford City
Plumville
Marion Center
Irvona
Coalport
Port Matilda
Stormstown
State College
Boalsburg
New Brighton
Beaver
Monaca
Ohioville
Mars
Atwood
Westover
Glasgow
Georgetown
Industry
Midland
Shippingport
Economy
ALLEGHENY
Harrison Township
Freeport
Elderton
Dicksonville
Cherry Tree
Commodore
Ramblewood
Pine Grove Mills
Tyrone
143
Hastings
CAMBRIA
Creekside
Ernest
Shelocta
Clymer
Chevy Chase Heights
Indiana
Heilwood
Northern Cambria
Patton
Birmingham
HUNTINGDON
Reedsville
Tipton
8
Belleville
Hookstown
Ambridge
McCandless Township
Leechburg
Vandergrift
BEAVER
Leetsdale
Arnold
Shaler Twp.
WV
Carnot-Moon
West View
Orchard Hills
Ben Avon
Kent (Jacksonville)
Lucerne Mines
Carrolltown
Chest Springs
Bellwood
Petersburg
Frankfort Springs
Avalon
Oakmont
Avonmore
Homer City
Colver
Ashville
BLAIR
Alexandria
MIFFLIN
Robinson Twp.
Pittsburgh
Penn Hills
Saltsburg
Ebensburg
Loretto
Altoona
McVeytown
Monroeville
Black Lick
Vintondale
Nanty Glo
Sankertown
Gallitzin
Huntingdon
Carnegie
Armagh
Cresson
Tunnelhill
Williamsburg
Burgettstown
Mount Lebanon
Baldwin
Murrysville
Blairsville
Seward
Vinco
Cassandra
Lilly
Duncansville
Hollidaysburg
Mill Creek
West Mifflin
New Alexandria
Wilmore
Summerhill
Portage
Newry
Newton Hamilton
Crabtree
Bolivar
Marklesburg (James Creek)
Mapleton
Upper St. Clair
New Florence
Ehrenfeld
Spring Hill
JUNIATA
1 p 108
Bethel Park
McKeesport
WESTMORELAND
Derry
4 p 108
Mount Union
Kistler
West Middletown
Clairton
Greensburg
Latrobe
McChesneytown-Loyalhanna
Johnstown
St. Michael-Sidman
Beaverdale-Lloydell
Roaring Spring
East Rutherford
Houston
Canonsburg
Lawson Hts.
Youngstown
Belmont
Claysburg
Martinsburg
Cassville
Shirleysburg
McGovern
Sutersville
Youngwood
Ligonier
Davidsville
Salix-Beauty Line Park
New Eagle
W. Newton
Paint
Wolfdale
E. Washington
Baidland
Monongahela
Calumet-Norvelt
Jerome
Windber
Woodbury
Rockhill Furnace
Orbisonia
Hunker
New Stanton
Laurel Mountain
Benson
BEDFORD
Saxton
Coalmont
Washington
Wickerham Manor-Fisher
Donora
Smithton
Saltillo
Claysville
Green Hills
Monessen
Mount Pleasant
Jennerstown
Boswell
Hooversville
Pleasantville
Saint Clairsville
Coaldale
Dudley
Broad Top City
Three Springs
Shade Gap
West Alexander
Ellsworth
Bentleyville
Donegal
Cokeburg
Perryopolis
Scottdale
Stoystown
Central City
Hopewell
WASHINGTON
Beallsville
California
Everson
New Paris
SOMERSET
FULTON
Marianna
Dawson
Friedens
Indian Lake
Vanderbilt
3 p 108
Connellsville
Seven Springs
Somerset
Schellsburg
Orrstown
Fredericktown-Millsboro
Hiller
Grindstone-Rowes Run
Shanksville
Bedford
Valley-Hi
Everett
Clarksville
Republic
South Connellsville
New Baltimore
GREENE
Jefferson
New Salem-Buffington
Dunbar
Manns Choice
FRANKLIN
Rices Landing
Oliver
New Centerville
Waynesburg
Carmichaels
FAYETTE
Rockwood
Berlin
Fairdale
Uniontown
East Uniontown
McConnellsburg
Chambersburg
Morrisville
Casselman
Nemacolin
Leith-Hatfield
Ohiopyle
Rainsburg
Masontown
Hopwood
Garrett
Guilford
Fairchance
Greensboro
Smithfield
Confluence
Ursina
Meyersdale
Hyndman
Mercersburg
Callimont
Point Marion
Addison
Salisbury
Greencastle
Markleysburg
Wellersburg
WV
MD

County-Town

PENNSYLVANIA
(WEST)

American Map

For Explanation of Symbols see Pennsylvania (East), next page.

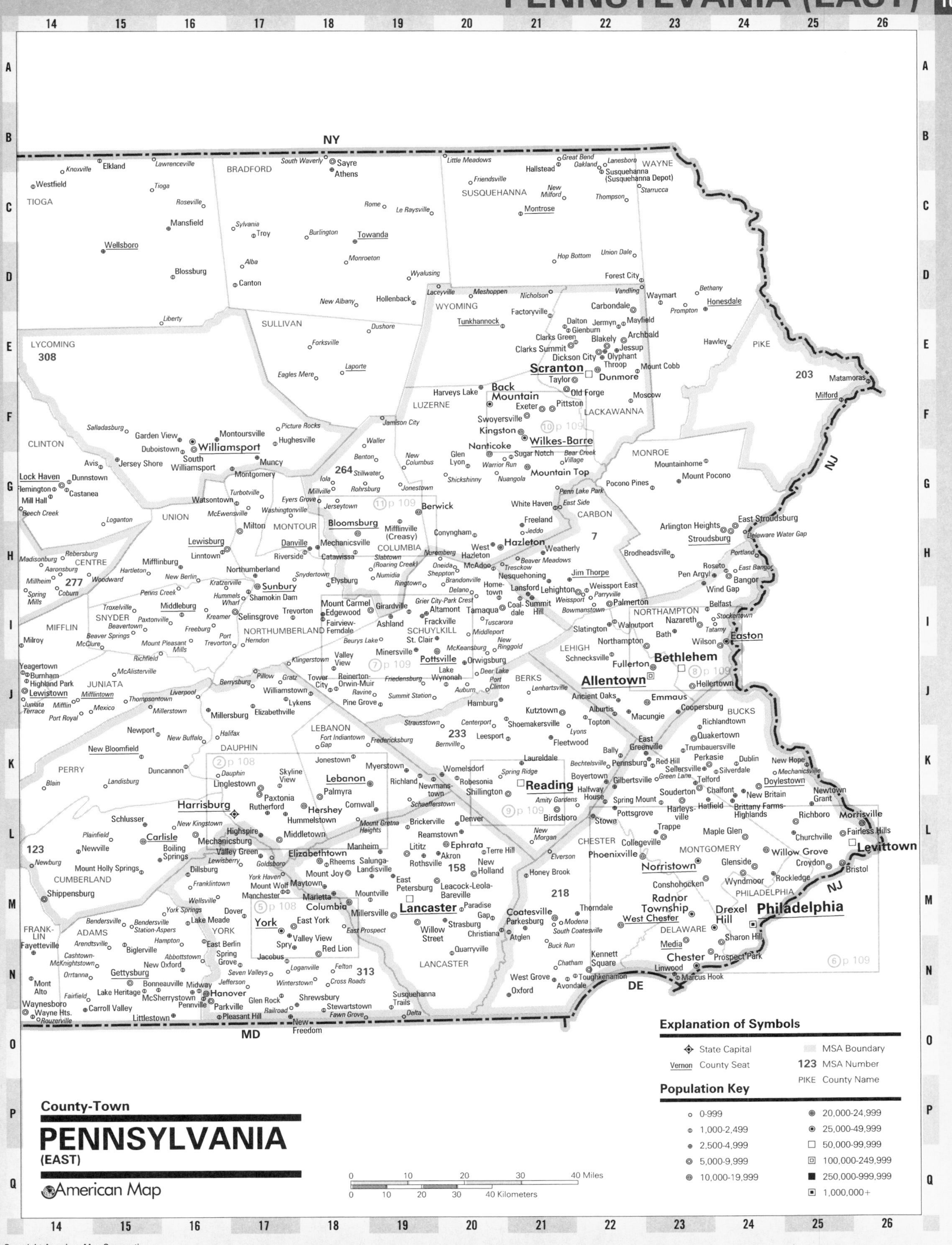
NY
TIOGA
Knoxville
Elkland
Lawrenceville
Westfield
Tioga
Roseville
Mansfield
Wellsboro
Blossburg
Liberty
BRADFORD
South Waverly
Sayre
Athens
Rome
Le Raysville
Sylvania
Troy
Burlington
Towanda
Monroeton
Alba
Canton
Wyalusing
New Albany
Hollenback
SULLIVAN
Dushore
Forksville
Laporte
Eagles Mere
SUSQUEHANNA
Little Meadows
Friendsville
Hallstead
Great Bend
Oakland
Lanesboro
Susquehanna (Susquehanna Depot)
New Milford
Thompson
Starrucca
Montrose
Hop Bottom
Union Dale
Forest City
WAYNE
Vandling
Waymart
Bethany
Prompton
Honesdale
Hawley
PIKE
203
Matamoras
Milford
WYOMING
Laceyville
Meshoppen
Nicholson
Factoryville
Tunkhannock
Carbondale
Dalton
Jermyn
Mayfield
Glenburn
Archbald
Clarks Green
Blakely
Clarks Summit
Jessup
Dickson City
Olyphant
Throop
Scranton
Dunmore
Mount Cobb
Taylor
Old Forge
Moscow
Harveys Lake
Back Mountain
Exeter
Pittston
LACKAWANNA
LUZERNE
Swoyersville
Kingston
Wilkes-Barre
10 p 109
Nanticoke
Sugar Notch
Bear Creek Village
Glen Lyon
Warrior Run
Mountain Top
Shickshinny
Nuangola
New Columbus
Jamison City
LYCOMING
308
CLINTON
Salladasburg
Garden View
Montoursville
Picture Rocks
Duboistown
Williamsport
Hughesville
Avis
Jersey Shore
South Williamsport
Muncy
Lock Haven
Dunnstown
Flemington
Castanea
Mill Hall
Beech Creek
Montgomery
Waller
Benton
264
Stillwater
Iola
Millville
Rohrsburg
Jonestown
Turbotville
Eyers Grove
Jerseytown
Watsontown
Washingtonville
McEwensville
UNION
Loganton
11 p 109
Berwick
Bloomsburg
Mifflinville (Creasy)
Conyngham
Milton
MONTOUR
Danville
Mechanicsville
COLUMBIA
Lewisburg
Linntown
Riverside
Catawissa
Nuremberg
Hazleton
West Hazleton
White Haven
Penn Lake Park
East Side
Freeland
Jeddo
CARBON
Weatherly
Beaver Meadows
McAdoo
Tresckow
Nesquehoning
Jim Thorpe
Lansford
Lehighton
Weissport East
Weissport
Parryville
Summit Hill
Coaldale
Palmerton
Bowmanstown
MONROE
Mountainhome
Mount Pocono
Pocono Pines
Arlington Heights
East Stroudsburg
Stroudsburg
Delaware Water Gap
7
NJ
Brodheadsville
Portland
Roseto
East Bangor
Pen Argyl
Bangor
Wind Gap
Belfast
NORTHAMPTON
Stockertown
Nazareth
Tatamy
Bath
Easton
Wilson
Walnutport
Slatington
Northampton
LEHIGH
Schnecksville
Fullerton
Bethlehem
8 p 109
Allentown
Hellertown
Ancient Oaks
Emmaus
Alburtis
Macungie
Coopersburg
BUCKS
Richlandtown
Topton
Quakertown
Trumbauersville
East Greenville
Pennsburg
Red Hill
Perkasie
Dublin
New Hope
Sellersville
Silverdale
Mechanicsville
Green Lane
Telford
Doylestown
Gilbertsville
Souderton
Chalfont
New Britain
Newtown Grant
Harleysville
Hatfield
Brittany Farms-Highlands
Richboro
Morrisville
Fairless Hills
Levittown
Bristol
Croydon
Willow Grove
Glenside
Rockledge
Wyndmoor
MONTGOMERY
Maple Glen
Churchville
Norristown
Conshohocken
Radnor Township
West Chester
Drexel Hill
Philadelphia
PHILADELPHIA
DELAWARE
Media
Sharon Hill
Chester
Prospect Park
Linwood
Marcus Hook
6 p 109
DE
Kennett Square
Toughkenamon
Avondale
Chatham
West Grove
Oxford
Buck Run
Coatesville
South Coatesville
Modena
Thorndale
Parkesburg
Atglen
218
Honey Brook
Elverson
Phoenixville
Collegeville
Trappe
Pottsgrove
Spring Mount
Stowe
Halfway House
Boyertown
Bechtelsville
CHESTER
New Morgan
Birdsboro
Amity Gardens
Reading
9 p 109
Spring Ridge
Shillington
Robesonia
Laureldale
Fleetwood
Lyons
Kutztown
Shoemakersville
Leesport
Centerport
Hamburg
BERKS
Lenhartsville
Port Clinton
Auburn
Deer Lake
Lake Wynonah
Orwigsburg
McKeansburg
New Ringgold
Middleport
Tuscarora
Tamaqua
Pottsville
Minersville
St. Clair
Frackville
Altamont
Grier City-Park Crest
Delano
Hometown
Brandonville
Shepton
Oneida
Ringtown
Numidia
Slabtown (Roaring Creek)
Elysburg
Snydertown
SCHUYLKILL
Ashland
Girardville
Mount Carmel
Edgewood
Fairview-Ferndale
Beurys Lake
Valley View
7 p 109
Klingerstown
Tower City
Reinerton-Orwin-Muir
Friedensburg
Ravine
Pine Grove
Summit Station
Strausstown
Bernville
233
Fredericksburg
Jonestown
Myerstown
Richland
Womelsdorf
Newmanstown
Schaefferstown
Brickerville
Denver
Reamstown
Ephrata
Akron
Terre Hill
Lititz
Rothsville
158
New Holland
Leacock-Leola-Bareville
East Petersburg
Lancaster
Paradise
Gap
Strasburg
Christiana
Quarryville
LANCASTER
Willow Street
Millersville
Mountville
Columbia
Marietta
Maytown
Mount Joy
Rheems
Manheim
Elizabethtown
Salunga-Landisville
Mount Gretna Heights
Cornwall
LEBANON
Fort Indiantown Gap
Lebanon
Palmyra
Hershey
Hummelstown
Middletown
Highspire
Paxtonia
Linglestown
Skyline View
Rutherford
Harrisburg
Dauphin
DAUPHIN
2 p 108
Halifax
Elizabethville
Lykens
Williamstown
Millersburg
Gratz
Pillow
Berrysburg
Herndon
Trevorton
NORTHUMBERLAND
Shamokin Dam
Selinsgrove
Hummels Wharf
Kratzerville
Sunbury
Northumberland
Kreamer
Freeburg
Port Trevorton
Middleburg
SNYDER
Troxelville
Paxtonville
Beavertown
Beaver Springs
McClure
Mount Pleasant Mills
Penns Creek
New Berlin
Mifflinburg
Hartleton
CENTRE
Rebersburg
Madisonburg
Aaronsburg
Millheim
277
Woodward
Spring Mills
Coburn
MIFFLIN
Milroy
Richfield
McAlisterville
JUNIATA
Yeagertown
Burnham
Highland Park
Lewistown
Juniata Terrace
Mifflin
Mifflintown
Mexico
Port Royal
Thompsontown
Liverpool
Millerstown
Newport
New Buffalo
New Bloomfield
PERRY
Duncannon
Blain
Landisburg
Schlusser
New Kingstown
Mechanicsburg
Lemoyne
Plainfield
Carlisle
Boiling Springs
Newville
123
Newburg
Mount Holly Springs
Dillsburg
Goldsboro
Lewisberry
Valley Green
CUMBERLAND
Shippensburg
Franklintown
York Haven
Mount Wolf
Manchester
Wellsville
York Springs
Dover
Lake Meade
5 p 108
York
East York
Valley View
Spry
Red Lion
East Prospect
Jacobus
Loganville
Felton
313
Cross Roads
Winterstown
Seven Valleys
Shrewsbury
Stewartstown
Fawn Grove
Railroad
New Freedom
Delta
Susquehanna Trails
Glen Rock
Jefferson
Hanover
Pennville
Parkville
Pleasant Hill
McSherrystown
Midway
Bonneauville
Abbottstown
New Oxford
Gettysburg
East Berlin
Spring Grove
Hampton
YORK
ADAMS
Bendersville
Bendersville Station-Aspers
Arendtsville
Biglerville
Cashtown-McKnightstown
Orrtanna
Fairfield
Lake Heritage
Carroll Valley
Littlestown
FRANKLIN
Fayetteville
Mont Alto
Waynesboro
Wayne Hts.
Rouzerville
MD
Explanation of Symbols
State Capital
Vernon County Seat
MSA Boundary
123 MSA Number
PIKE County Name
Population Key
0-999
1,000-2,499
2,500-4,999
5,000-9,999
10,000-19,999
20,000-24,999
25,000-49,999
50,000-99,999
100,000-249,999
250,000-999,999
1,000,000+
County-Town
PENNSYLVANIA
(EAST)
American Map
0 10 20 30 40 Miles
0 10 20 30 40 Kilometers

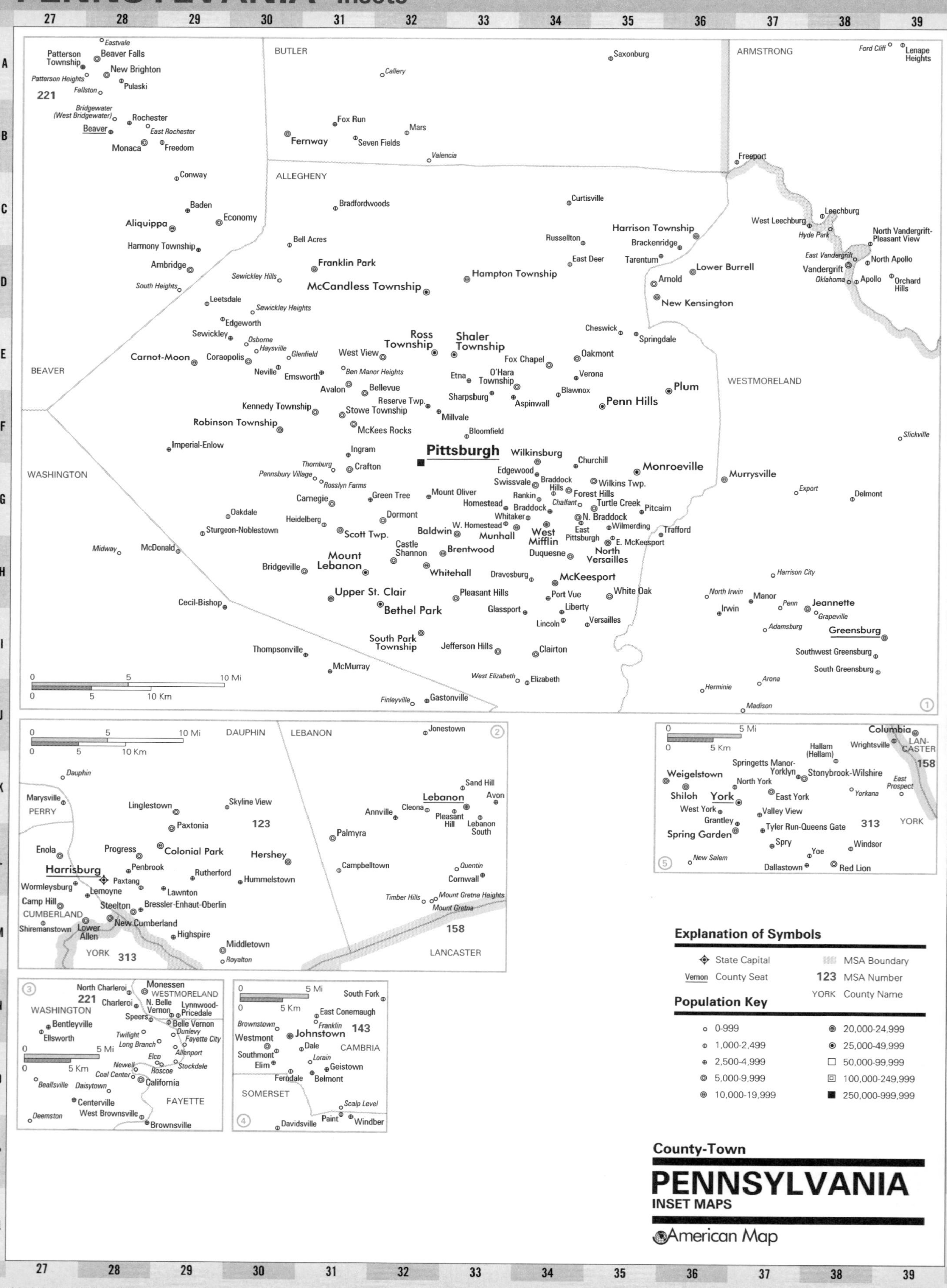
27 28 29 30 31 32 33 34 35 36 37 38 39
A B C D E F G H I J K L M N O P Q
Eastvale
Patterson Township
Beaver Falls
New Brighton
Patterson Heights
Pulaski
221
Fallston
Bridgewater (West Bridgewater)
Rochester
Beaver
East Rochester
Monaca
Freedom
BUTLER
Callery
Fox Run
Mars
Fernway
Seven Fields
Valencia
Saxonburg
ARMSTRONG
Ford Cliff
Lenape Heights
Freeport
ALLEGHENY
Conway
Baden
Economy
Aliquippa
Harmony Township
Ambridge
South Heights
Sewickley Hills
Leetsdale
Sewickley Heights
Edgeworth
Sewickley
Osborne
Haysville
Glenfield
Carnot-Moon
Coraopolis
Neville
Emsworth
BEAVER
Bradfordwoods
Bell Acres
Franklin Park
McCandless Township
Hampton Township
Curtisville
Russellton
East Deer
Harrison Township
Brackenridge
Tarentum
Arnold
Lower Burrell
New Kensington
West Leechburg
Leechburg
Hyde Park
North Vandergrift-Pleasant View
East Vandergrift
North Apollo
Vandergrift
Oklahoma
Apollo
Orchard Hills
Cheswick
Springdale
West View
Ross Township
Shaler Township
Fox Chapel
Oakmont
Ben Manor Heights
Avalon
Bellevue
Etna
O'Hara Township
Verona
Blawnox
Plum
Penn Hills
WESTMORELAND
Kennedy Township
Reserve Twp.
Stowe Township
Sharpsburg
Aspinwall
Millvale
Robinson Township
McKees Rocks
Bloomfield
Slickville
Imperial-Enlow
Ingram
Pittsburgh
Wilkinsburg
Churchill
Monroeville
Thornburg
Crafton
Pennsbury Village
Rosslyn Farms
Edgewood
Swissvale
Braddock Hills
Wilkins Twp.
Forest Hills
Murrysville
WASHINGTON
Carnegie
Green Tree
Mount Oliver
Homestead
Rankin
Chalfant
Turtle Creek
Braddock
Pitcairn
Export
Delmont
Oakdale
Heidelberg
Dormont
Whitaker
N. Braddock
Sturgeon-Noblestown
Scott Twp.
Baldwin
W. Homestead
Munhall
West Mifflin
East Pittsburgh
Wilmerding
Trafford
E. McKeesport
Midway
McDonald
Castle Shannon
Brentwood
Duquesne
North Versailles
Mount Lebanon
Bridgeville
Whitehall
Dravosburg
McKeesport
Harrison City
Upper St. Clair
Pleasant Hills
White Oak
North Irwin
Manor
Port Vue
Penn
Jeanneatte
Cecil-Bishop
Bethel Park
Glassport
Liberty
Irwin
Grapeville
Lincoln
Versailles
Adamsburg
Greensburg
South Park Township
Jefferson Hills
Clairton
Southwest Greensburg
Thompsonville
McMurray
South Greensburg
West Elizabeth
Elizabeth
Arona
Herminie
Finleyville
Gastonville
Madison
0 5 10 Mi
0 5 10 Km
1
0 5 10 Mi
0 5 10 Km
DAUPHIN
LEBANON
Jonestown
2
Dauphin
Sand Hill
Marysville
PERRY
Linglestown
Skyline View
Lebanon
Avon
Annville
Cleona
Paxtonia
123
Pleasant Hill
Lebanon South
Palmyra
Enola
Progress
Colonial Park
Hershey
Harrisburg
Penbrook
Rutherford
Campbelltown
Quentin
Paxtang
Hummelstown
Cornwall
Wormleysburg
Lemoyne
Lawnton
Camp Hill
Steelton
Bressler-Enhaut-Oberlin
Timber Hills
Mount Gretna Heights
Mount Gretna
CUMBERLAND
New Cumberland
Shiremanstown
Lower Allen
Highspire
158
YORK
313
Middletown
Royalton
LANCASTER
0 5 Mi
0 5 Km
Columbia
Hallam (Hellam)
Wrightsville
LAN-CASTER
158
Springetts Manor-Yorklyn
Weigelstown
North York
Stonybrook-Wilshire
East Prospect
Shiloh
York
East York
Yorkana
West York
Valley View
Grantley
313
YORK
Spring Garden
Tyler Run-Queens Gate
Spry
Windsor
New Salem
Yoe
Dallastown
Red Lion
5
3
North Charleroi
Monessen
221
WESTMORELAND
Charleroi
N. Belle Vernon
Lynnwood-Pricedale
WASHINGTON
Speers
Bentleyville
Belle Vernon
Dunlevy
Ellsworth
Twilight
Fayette City
Long Branch
0 5 Mi
Allenport
Elco
0 5 Km
Newell
Roscoe
Stockdale
Coal Center
California
Beallsville
Daisytown
Centerville
FAYETTE
Deemston
West Brownsville
Brownsville
0 5 Mi
0 5 Km
South Fork
East Conemaugh
Brownstown
Franklin
Westmont
Johnstown
143
Dale
CAMBRIA
Southmont
Lorain
Elim
Geistown
Ferndale
Belmont
SOMERSET
Scalp Level
Paint
Windber
Davidsville
4
Explanation of Symbols
State Capital
MSA Boundary
Vernon County Seat
123 MSA Number
YORK County Name
Population Key
0-999
20,000-24,999
1,000-2,499
25,000-49,999
2,500-4,999
50,000-99,999
5,000-9,999
100,000-249,999
10,000-19,999
250,000-999,999
County-Town
PENNSYLVANIA
INSET MAPS
American Map

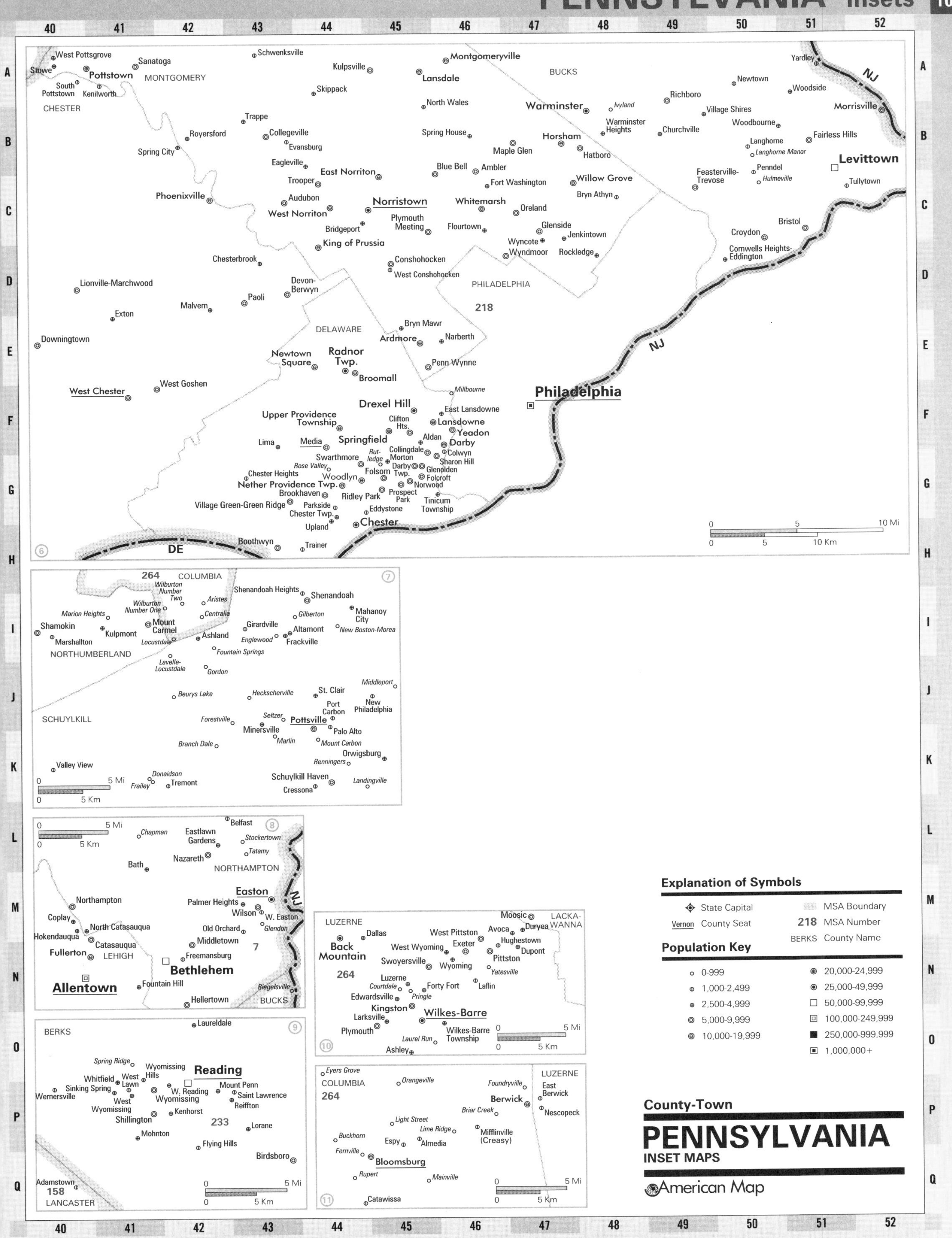

West Pottsgrove
Stowe
Pottstown
Sanatoga
MONTGOMERY
South Pottstown
Kenilworth
CHESTER
Schwenksville
Kulpsville
Skippack
Lansdale
Montgomeryville
BUCKS
North Wales
Warminster
Ivyland
Warminster Heights
Richboro
Newtown
Yardley
Woodside
NJ
Village Shires
Woodbourne
Morrisville
Churchville
Langhorne
Langhorne Manor
Fairless Hills
Trappe
Royersford
Collegeville
Evansburg
Spring City
Spring House
Horsham
Maple Glen
Hatboro
Eagleville
East Norriton
Trooper
Blue Bell
Ambler
Fort Washington
Willow Grove
Feasterville-Trevose
Penndel
Hulmeville
Levittown
Tullytown
Phoenixville
Audubon
West Norriton
Norristown
Whitemarsh
Oreland
Bryn Athyn
Plymouth Meeting
Flourtown
Glenside
Jenkintown
Bridgeport
King of Prussia
Wyncote
Wyndmoor
Rockledge
Bristol
Croydon
Cornwells Heights-Eddington
Chesterbrook
Conshohocken
West Conshohocken
Lionville-Marchwood
Devon-Berwyn
Paoli
Malvern
PHILADELPHIA
218
Exton
Bryn Mawr
DELAWARE
Downingtown
Ardmore
Narberth
Newtown Square
Radnor Twp.
Penn Wynne
Broomall
West Goshen
West Chester
Millbourne
Philadelphia
Drexel Hill
Upper Providence Township
Clifton Hts.
East Lansdowne
Lansdowne
Yeadon
Aldan
Darby
Lima
Media
Springfield
Swarthmore
Rutledge
Collingdale
Colwyn
Morton
Sharon Hill
Rose Valley
Darby Twp.
Glenolden
Chester Heights
Folsom
Woodlyn
Folcroft
Nether Providence Twp.
Norwood
Brookhaven
Ridley Park
Prospect Park
Tinicum Township
Village Green-Green Ridge
Parkside
Chester Twp.
Eddystone
Chester
Upland
Boothwyn
Trainer
DE
0 5 10 Mi
0 5 10 Km
6
264
COLUMBIA
Wilburton Number Two
Wilburton Number One
Aristes
Centralia
Shenandoah Heights
Shenandoah
Marion Heights
Shamokin
Kulpmont
Mount Carmel
Marshallton
Locustdale
Ashland
Girardville
Englewood
Gilberton
Altamont
Frackville
Mahanoy City
New Boston-Morea
NORTHUMBERLAND
Fountain Springs
Lavelle-Locustdale
Gordon
Beurys Lake
Heckscherville
St. Clair
Middleport
Port Carbon
New Philadelphia
SCHUYLKILL
Forestville
Seltzer
Pottsville
Minersville
Palo Alto
Marlin
Mount Carbon
Branch Dale
Orwigsburg
Renningers
Valley View
Donaidson
Frailey
Tremont
Schuylkill Haven
Landingville
Cressona
0 5 Mi
0 5 Km
7
0 5 Mi
0 5 Km
Belfast
Chapman
Eastlawn Gardens
Stockertown
Tatamy
Nazareth
Bath
NORTHAMPTON
Northampton
Easton
Palmer Heights
Wilson
W. Easton
Glendon
Coplay
North Catasauqua
Old Orchard
Hokendauqua
Middletown
Catasauqua
Fullerton
LEHIGH
Freemansburg
Bethlehem
Allentown
Fountain Hill
Riegelsville
Hellertown
BUCKS
8
Laureldale
BERKS
9
Spring Ridge
Wyomissing Hills
Reading
Whitfield
West Lawn
Sinking Spring
Wernersville
W. Reading
Mount Penn
Saint Lawrence
Reiffton
West Wyomissing
Wyomissing
Kenhorst
Shillington
233
Lorane
Mohnton
Flying Hills
Birdsboro
Adamstown
158
LANCASTER
0 5 Mi
0 5 Km
LUZERNE
Moosic
LACKAWANNA
Dallas
West Pittston
Avoca
Duryea
Back Mountain
Hughestown
West Wyoming
Exeter
Dupont
Pittston
Swoyersville
Wyoming
Yatesville
264
Luzerne
Courtdale
Forty Fort
Laflin
Edwardsville
Pringle
Kingston
Wilkes-Barre
Larksville
Wilkes-Barre Township
Plymouth
Laurel Run
Ashley
10
0 5 Mi
0 5 Km
Eyers Grove
COLUMBIA
264
Orangeville
Foundryville
LUZERNE
East Berwick
Berwick
Briar Creek
Nescopeck
Light Street
Lime Ridge
Mifflinville (Creasy)
Buckhorn
Espy
Almedia
Fernville
Bloomsburg
Rupert
Mainville
Catawissa
11
0 5 Mi
0 5 Km
Explanation of Symbols
State Capital
Vernon County Seat
MSA Boundary
218 MSA Number
BERKS County Name
Population Key
0-999
1,000-2,499
2,500-4,999
5,000-9,999
10,000-19,999
20,000-24,999
25,000-49,999
50,000-99,999
100,000-249,999
250,000-999,999
1,000,000+
County-Town
PENNSYLVANIA
INSET MAPS
American Map

COUNTIES

(67 Counties)

Name of County	Population	Location on Map
ADAMS	91,292	N-14
ALLEGHENY	1,281,666	J-3
ARMSTRONG	72,392	H-5
BEAVER	181,412	J-1
BEDFORD	49,984	L-9
BERKS	373,638	J-21
BLAIR	129,144	J-10
BRADFORD	62,761	C-17
BUCKS	597,635	J-24
BUTLER	174,083	G-3
CAMBRIA	152,598	J-9
CAMERON	5,974	E-10
CARBON	58,802	H-22
CENTRE	135,758	G-12
CHESTER	433,501	L-22
CLARION	41,765	F-6
CLEARFIELD	83,382	G-10
CLINTON	37,914	E-12
COLUMBIA	64,151	H-19
CRAWFORD	90,366	C-2
CUMBERLAND	213,674	M-14
DAUPHIN	251,798	K-16
DELAWARE	550,864	M-23
ELK	35,112	E-8
ERIE	280,843	B-3
FAYETTE	148,644	N-5
FOREST	4,946	D-6
FRANKLIN	129,313	M-12
FULTON	14,261	M-11
GREENE	40,672	M-1
HUNTINGDON	45,586	J-12
INDIANA	89,605	H-7
JEFFERSON	45,932	F-7
JUNIATA	22,821	K-13
LACKAWANNA	213,295	F-22
LANCASTER	470,658	N-19
LAWRENCE	94,643	H-1
LEBANON	120,327	K-18
LEHIGH	312,090	I-21
LUZERNE	319,250	F-19
LYCOMING	120,044	E-14
MCKEAN	45,936	C-8
MERCER	120,293	E-1
MIFFLIN	46,486	J-13
MONROE	138,687	G-22
MONTGOMERY	750,097	L-23
MONTOUR	18,236	H-17
NORTHAMPTON	267,066	I-22
NORTHUMBERLAND	94,556	I-17
PERRY	43,602	K-14
PHILADELPHIA	1,517,550	M-24
PIKE	46,302	E-24
POTTER	18,080	C-11
SCHUYLKILL	150,336	I-19
SNYDER	37,546	I-15
SOMERSET	80,023	M-6
SULLIVAN	6,556	E-17
SUSQUEHANNA	42,238	C-20
TIOGA	41,373	C-14
UNION	41,624	H-16
VENANGO	57,565	E-4
WARREN	43,863	C-5
WASHINGTON	202,897	M-1
WAYNE	47,722	B-23
WESTMORELAND	369,993	K-5
WYOMING	28,080	E-20
YORK	381,751	M-16
TOTAL	**12,281,054**	

CITIES AND TOWNS

Note: The first name is that of the city or town, second, that of the county in which it is located, then the population and location on the map.

▲Abington, *Lackawanna*, 1,616 ....E-22
▲Abington, *Montgomery*, 56,103 ....M-24
▲Adams, *Butler*, 6,774 ....I-3
▲Adams, *Cambria*, 6,495 ....J-9
Adamstown, *Lancaster*, 1,203 ....O-40
▲Addison, *Somerset*, 1,019 ....O-6
Akron, *Lancaster*, 4,046 ....L-20
▲Albany, *Berks*, 1,662 ....J-21
Albion, *Erie*, 1,607 ....C-2
Alburtis, *Lehigh*, 2,117 ....J-22
Aldan, *Delaware*, 4,313 ....F-45
▲Aleppo, *Allegheny*, 1,039 ....J-2
Aliquippa, *Beaver*, 11,734 ....C-29
▲Allegheny, *Blair*, 6,965 ....K-9
▲Allegheny, *Cambria*, 2,498 ....K-9
▲Allegheny, *Westmoreland*, 8,002 ....J-5
▲Allen, *Northampton*, 2,630 ....I-22
Allentown, *Lehigh*, 106,632 ....J-23
●Almedia, *Columbia*, 1,056 ....P-45
▲Alsace, *Berks*, 3,689 ....K-21
●Altamont, *Schuylkill*, 2,689 ....I-19
Altoona, *Blair*, 49,523 ....J-10
Ambler, *Montgomery*, 6,426 ....C-46
Ambridge, *Beaver*, 7,769 ....J-2
▲Amity, *Berks*, 8,867 ....L-21
▲Amity, *Erie*, 1,140 ....B-4
●Amity Gardens, *Berks*, 3,370 ....L-22
▲Amwell, *Washington*, 3,960 ....L-2
●Ancient Oaks, *Lehigh*, 3,161 ....J-22
†Annville, *Lebanon*, 4,518 ....K-32
▲Anthony, *Montour*, 1,388 ....G-17
▲Antis, *Blair*, 6,328 ....J-10
▲Antrim, *Franklin*, 12,504 ....O-13
Apollo, *Armstrong*, 1,765 ....D-38
Archbald, *Lackawanna*, 6,220 ....E-22
●Ardmore, *Montgomery*, 12,616 ....E-45
●Arlington Heights, *Monroe*, 5,132 ....H-24
▲Armagh, *Mifflin*, 3,988 ....I-13
▲Armstrong, *Indiana*, 3,090 ....J-6
Arnold, *Westmoreland*, 5,667 ....J-4
▲Ashland, *Clarion*, 1,081 ....F-5
Ashland, *Schuylkill*, 3,283 ....I-19
Ashley, *Luzerne*, 2,866 ....O-45
Aspinwall, *Allegheny*, 2,960 ....F-33
▲Aston, *Delaware*, 16,203 ....N-23
▲Asylum, *Bradford*, 1,097 ....D-19
Atglen, *Chester*, 1,217 ....M-21
Athens, *Bradford*, 3,415 ....C-18
▲Athens, *Bradford*, 5,058 ....C-18
▲Auburn, *Susquehanna*, 1,816 ....D-20
●Audubon, *Montgomery*, 6,549 ....C-43
Avalon, *Allegheny*, 5,294 ....J-3
Avis, *Clinton*, 1,492 ....G-15
Avoca, *Luzerne*, 2,851 ....M-47
●Avon, *Lebanon*, 2,856 ....K-33
Avondale, *Chester*, 1,108 ....N-21
●Avonia, *Erie*, 1,331 ....B-2
▲Ayr, *Fulton*, 1,982 ....N-12
●Back Mountain, *Luzerne*, 26,690 ....F-20
Baden, *Beaver*, 4,377 ....C-29
●Baidland, *Washington*, 1,576 ....L-3
▲Bald Eagle, *Blair*, 1,898 ....I-11
Baldwin, *Allegheny*, 19,999 ....K-3
▲Baldwin, *Allegheny*, 2,244 ....K-3
Bally, *Berks*, 1,062 ....K-22
Bangor, *Northampton*, 5,319 ....H-24
▲Banks, *Carbon*, 1,359 ....H-21
▲Barr, *Cambria*, 2,175 ....J-8
▲Barrett, *Monroe*, 3,880 ....G-24
▲Bart, *Lancaster*, 3,003 ....N-20
Bath, *Northampton*, 2,678 ....I-23
▲Bear Creek, *Luzerne*, 2,580 ....G-21
Beaver, *Beaver*, 4,775 ....I-2
▲Beaver, *Clarion*, 1,753 ....G-5
Beaver Falls, *Beaver*, 9,920 ....A-28
●Beaverdale-Lloydell, *Cambria*, 1,230 ....K-9
▲Beccaria, *Clearfield*, 1,835 ....I-10
Bedford, *Bedford*, 3,141 ....M-9
▲Bedford, *Bedford*, 5,417 ....M-9
▲Bedminster, *Bucks*, 4,804 ....K-24
▲Beech Creek, *Clinton*, 1,010 ....G-13
▲Belfast, *Fulton*, 1,341 ....N-11
●Belfast, *Northampton*, 1,301 ....I-23
▲Bell, *Jefferson*, 2,029 ....H-8
▲Bell, *Westmoreland*, 2,458 ....K-5
Bell Acres, *Allegheny*, 1,382 ....D-30
Belle Vernon, *Fayette*, 1,211 ....N-29
Bellefonte, *Centre*, 6,395 ....H-13
●Belleville, *Mifflin*, 1,386 ....J-13
Bellevue, *Allegheny*, 8,770 ....F-31
Bellwood, *Blair*, 2,016 ....J-10
●Belmont, *Cambria*, 2,846 ....L-8
Ben Avon, *Allegheny*, 1,917 ....J-7
▲Benner, *Centre*, 5,217 ....I-12
▲Bensalem, *Bucks*, 58,434 ....M-25
Bentleyville, *Washington*, 2,502 ....L-3
▲Benton, *Columbia*, 1,216 ....G-19
▲Benton, *Lackawanna*, 1,881 ....E-21
Berlin, *Somerset*, 2,192 ....N-7
▲Berlin, *Wayne*, 2,188 ....D-24
▲Bern, *Berks*, 6,758 ....K-20
▲Berwick, *Adams*, 1,818 ....N-16
Berwick, *Columbia*, 10,774 ....G-19
Bessemer, *Lawrence*, 1,172 ....H-1
▲Bethel, *Armstrong*, 1,290 ....I-5
▲Bethel, *Berks*, 4,166 ....K-19
▲Bethel, *Delaware*, 6,421 ....N-23
▲Bethel, *Fulton*, 1,420 ....O-11
▲Bethel, *Lebanon*, 4,526 ....K-18
Bethel Park, *Allegheny*, 33,556 ....K-3
Bethlehem, *Northampton*, 71,329 ....J-23
▲Bethlehem, *Northampton*, 21,171 ....J-23
Big Beaver, *Beaver*, 2,186 ....I-2
▲Bigler, *Clearfield*, 1,368 ....H-10
Biglerville, *Adams*, 1,101 ....N-15
Birdsboro, *Berks*, 5,064 ....L-21
▲Birmingham, *Chester*, 4,221 ....N-22
▲Black Creek, *Luzerne*, 2,132 ....H-20
●Black Lick, *Indiana*, 1,438 ....K-7
▲Black Lick, *Indiana*, 1,317 ....K-6
▲Blacklick, *Cambria*, 2,200 ....J-8
▲Blair, *Blair*, 4,587 ....K-10
Blairsville, *Indiana*, 3,607 ....K-6
Blakely, *Lackawanna*, 7,027 ....E-22
Blawnox, *Allegheny*, 1,550 ....F-34
▲Bloomfield, *Crawford*, 2,051 ....C-4
▲Blooming Grove, *Pike*, 3,621 ....F-24
Bloomsburg, *Columbia*, 12,375 ....H-18
Blossburg, *Tioga*, 1,480 ....D-16
●Blue Bell, *Montgomery*, 6,395 ....C-46
●Boalsburg, *Centre*, 3,578 ....I-13
▲Boggs, *Centre*, 2,834 ....H-13
▲Boggs, *Clearfield*, 1,837 ....H-10
●Boiling Springs, *Cumberland*, 2,769 ....L-15
Bonneauville, *Adams*, 1,378 ....N-15
●Boothwyn, *Delaware*, 5,206 ....H-43
Boswell, *Somerset*, 1,364 ....L-7
Boyertown, *Berks*, 3,940 ....K-22
Brackenridge, *Allegheny*, 3,543 ....D-36
Braddock, *Allegheny*, 2,912 ....G-34
Braddock Hills, *Allegheny*, 1,998 ....G-34
▲Bradford, *Clearfield*, 3,314 ....H-10
▲Bradford, *McKean*, 4,816 ....C-9
Bradford, *McKean*, 9,175 ....C-9
Bradfordwoods, *Allegheny*, 1,149 ....C-31
▲Brady, *Butler*, 1,452 ....H-3
▲Brady, *Clearfield*, 2,010 ....H-8
▲Brady, *Huntingdon*, 1,035 ....K-12
▲Branch, *Schuylkill*, 1,871 ....J-19
▲Bratton, *Mifflin*, 1,259 ....K-13
▲Brecknock, *Berks*, 4,459 ....L-20
▲Brecknock, *Lancaster*, 6,699 ....L-20
Brentwood, *Allegheny*, 10,466 ....H-32
●Bressler-Enhaut-Oberlin, *Dauphin*, 2,809 ....M-28
▲Briar Creek, *Columbia*, 3,061 ....G-19
●Brickerville, *Lancaster*, 1,287 ....L-19
Bridgeport, *Montgomery*, 4,371 ....C-44
▲Bridgeton, *York*, 1,408 ....N-19
Bridgeville, *Allegheny*, 5,341 ....H-31
▲Bridgewater, *Susquehanna*, 2,668 ....C-21
▲Brighton, *Beaver*, 8,024 ....I-2
▲Bristol, *Bucks*, 55,521 ....L-25
Bristol, *Bucks*, 9,923 ....M-25
Bristol, *Bucks*, 9,923 ....M-25
●Brittany Farms-Highlands, *Bucks*, 3,268 ....L-24
▲Broad Top, *Bedford*, 1,827 ....M-11
Brockway, *Jefferson*, 2,182 ....F-8
●Brodheadsville, *Monroe*, 1,637 ....H-23
▲Brokenstraw, *Warren*, 2,068 ....C-6
Brookhaven, *Delaware*, 7,985 ....G-44
Brookville, *Jefferson*, 4,230 ....G-7
●Broomall, *Delaware*, 11,046 ....E-44
▲Brothersvalley, *Somerset*, 4,184 ....N-7
▲Brown, *Mifflin*, 3,852 ....J-13
Brownsville, *Fayette*, 2,804 ....P-28
▲Brush Valley, *Indiana*, 1,881 ....J-7
Bryn Athyn, *Montgomery*, 1,351 ....C-48
●Bryn Mawr, *Montgomery*, 4,382 ....E-45
▲Buckingham, *Bucks*, 16,442 ....K-24
▲Buffalo, *Butler*, 6,827 ....I-4
▲Buffalo, *Perry*, 1,128 ....J-16
▲Buffalo, *Union*, 3,207 ....H-16
▲Buffalo, *Washington*, 2,100 ....L-1
▲Buffington, *Indiana*, 1,275 ....K-7
▲Bullskin, *Fayette*, 7,782 ....M-5
Burgettstown, *Washington*, 1,576 ....K-1
Burnham, *Mifflin*, 2,144 ....J-14
▲Burnside, *Clearfield*, 1,128 ....I-8
▲Burrell, *Indiana*, 3,746 ....K-6
▲Bushkill, *Pike*, 6,982 ....G-25
▲Butler, *Adams*, 2,678 ....N-15
Butler, *Butler*, 15,121 ....H-4
▲Butler, *Butler*, 17,185 ....I-3
▲Butler, *Luzerne*, 7,166 ....H-20
▲Butler, *Schuylkill*, 3,588 ....I-19
▲Caernarvon, *Berks*, 2,312 ....L-21
▲Caernarvon, *Lancaster*, 4,278 ....L-21
California, *Washington*, 5,274 ....M-3
▲Caln, *Chester*, 11,916 ....M-21
●Calumet-Norvelt, *Westmoreland*, 1,682 ....L-5
▲Cambria, *Luzerne*, 6,323 ....G-19
▲Cambridge, *Chester*, 1,486 ....M-21
Cambridge Springs, *Crawford*, 2,363 ....C-3
Camp Hill, *Cumberland*, 7,636 ....M-27
●Campbelltown, *Lebanon*, 2,415 ....L-31
▲Canaan, *Wayne*, 1,916 ....E-23
▲Canal, *Venango*, 1,008 ....E-3
▲Canoe, *Indiana*, 1,670 ....H-8
Canonsburg, *Washington*, 8,607 ....L-2
Canton, *Bradford*, 1,807 ....D-17
▲Canton, *Bradford*, 2,084 ....D-17
▲Canton, *Washington*, 8,826 ....L-2
Carbondale, *Lackawanna*, 9,804 ....E-22
▲Carbondale, *Lackawanna*, 1,008 ....E-22
Carlisle, *Cumberland*, 17,970 ....L-15
Carnegie, *Allegheny*, 8,389 ....K-3
●Carnot-Moon, *Allegheny*, 10,637 ....J-2
▲Carroll, *Perry*, 5,095 ....K-15
▲Carroll, *Washington*, 5,677 ....L-3
▲Carroll, *York*, 4,715 ....M-16
Carroll Valley, *Adams*, 3,291 ....O-14
Carrolltown, *Cambria*, 1,049 ....J-9
▲Cass, *Huntingdon*, 1,062 ....L-12
▲Cass, *Schuylkill*, 2,383 ....I-19
●Castanea, *Clinton*, 1,189 ....G-14
▲Castanea, *Clinton*, 1,233 ....G-14
Castle Shannon, *Allegheny*, 8,556 ....H-32
Catasauqua, *Lehigh*, 6,588 ....N-40
Catawissa, *Columbia*, 1,589 ....H-18
▲Cecil, *Washington*, 9,756 ....K-2
●Cecil-Bishop, *Washington*, 2,585 ....I-29
▲Center, *Beaver*, 11,492 ....J-2
▲Center, *Butler*, 8,182 ....H-3
▲Center, *Greene*, 1,393 ....N-2
▲Center, *Indiana*, 4,876 ....K-7
▲Center, *Snyder*, 2,162 ....I-15
Centerville, *Washington*, 3,390 ....O-27
Central City, *Somerset*, 1,258 ....M-8
▲Centre, *Berks*, 3,631 ....J-20
▲Centre, *Perry*, 2,209 ....K-15
Centre Hall, *Centre*, 1,079 ....I-13
▲Ceres, *McKean*, 1,003 ....C-11
▲Chadds Ford, *Delaware*, 3,170 ....N-22
Chalfont, *Bucks*, 3,900 ....L-24
Chambersburg, *Franklin*, 17,862 ....N-13
▲Chanceford, *York*, 5,973 ....N-18
▲Chapman, *Snyder*, 1,426 ....J-16
Charleroi, *Washington*, 4,871 ....N-28
▲Charleston, *Tioga*, 3,233 ....D-15
▲Charlestown, *Chester*, 4,051 ....M-22
▲Chartiers, *Washington*, 7,154 ....L-2
▲Cheltenham, *Montgomery*, 36,875 ....M-24
▲Cherry, *Butler*, 1,053 ....G-3
▲Cherry, *Sullivan*, 1,718 ....E-19
▲Cherry Ridge, *Wayne*, 1,817 ....E-23
▲Cherryhill, *Indiana*, 2,842 ....J-7
▲Cherrytree, *Venango*, 1,543 ....E-4
Chester, *Delaware*, 36,854 ....N-23
▲Chester, *Delaware*, 4,604 ....N-23
Chester Heights, *Delaware*, 2,481 ....G-43
Chester Township, *Delaware*, 4,604 ....G-44
●Chesterbrook, *Chester*, 4,625 ....D-43
▲Chestnuthill, *Monroe*, 14,418 ....H-23
Cheswick, *Allegheny*, 1,899 ....E-35
●Chevy Chase Heights, *Indiana*, 1,511 ....J-7
Chicora, *Butler*, 1,021 ....H-4
▲Chippewa, *Beaver*, 7,021 ....I-1
Christiana, *Lancaster*, 1,124 ....M-20
Churchill, *Allegheny*, 3,566 ....G-34
●Churchville, *Bucks*, 4,469 ....L-25
Clairton, *Allegheny*, 8,491 ....L-4
Clarion, *Clarion*, 6,185 ....G-6
▲Clarion, *Clarion*, 3,273 ....G-6
Clarks Green, *Lackawanna*, 1,630 ....E-22
Clarks Summit, *Lackawanna*, 5,126 ....E-21
▲Clay, *Butler*, 2,628 ....H-4
▲Clay, *Lancaster*, 5,173 ....L-19
●Claysburg, *Blair*, 1,503 ....L-10
▲Clearfield, *Butler*, 2,705 ....J-4
▲Clearfield, *Cambria*, 1,680 ....J-9
Clearfield, *Clearfield*, 6,631 ....H-10
Cleona, *Lebanon*, 2,148 ....K-32
▲Cleveland, *Columbia*, 1,004 ....H-18
▲Clifford, *Susquehanna*, 2,381 ....D-22
▲Clifton, *Lackawanna*, 1,139 ....F-22
Clifton Heights, *Delaware*, 6,779 ....F-45
▲Clinton, *Butler*, 2,779 ....I-4
▲Clinton, *Lycoming*, 3,947 ....G-16
▲Clinton, *Wayne*, 1,926 ....D-23
▲Clinton, *Wyoming*, 1,343 ....E-21
Clymer, *Indiana*, 1,547 ....I-7
▲Coal, *Northumberland*, 10,628 ....I-18
Coaldale, *Schuylkill*, 2,295 ....I-21
Coatesville, *Chester*, 10,838 ....M-21
Cochranton, *Crawford*, 1,148 ....E-3
▲Codorus, *York*, 3,646 ....O-17
▲Colebrookdale, *Berks*, 5,270 ....K-22
▲Colerain, *Bedford*, 1,147 ....N-9
▲Colerain, *Lancaster*, 3,261 ....N-20
▲College, *Centre*, 8,489 ....I-12
Collegeville, *Montgomery*, 8,032 ....L-23
▲Collier, *Allegheny*, 5,265 ....K-2
Collingdale, *Delaware*, 8,664 ....G-45
●Colonial Park, *Dauphin*, 13,259 ....L-29
▲Columbia, *Bradford*, 1,162 ....C-16
Columbia, *Lancaster*, 10,311 ....M-18
▲Columbus, *Warren*, 1,741 ....C-5
●Colver, *Cambria*, 1,035 ....J-8
Colwyn, *Delaware*, 2,453 ....G-46
▲Concord, *Butler*, 1,493 ....H-4
▲Concord, *Delaware*, 9,933 ....N-23
▲Concord, *Erie*, 1,361 ....C-4
▲Conemaugh, *Cambria*, 2,145 ....K-8
▲Conemaugh, *Indiana*, 2,437 ....K-6
▲Conemaugh, *Somerset*, 7,452 ....L-7
▲Conestoga, *Lancaster*, 3,749 ....N-19
▲Conewago, *Adams*, 5,709 ....N-16
▲Conewago, *Dauphin*, 2,847 ....L-18
▲Conewago, *York*, 5,278 ....M-17
▲Conewango, *Warren*, 3,915 ....C-6
▲Conneaut, *Crawford*, 1,550 ....D-1
▲Conneaut, *Erie*, 3,908 ....C-2
●Conneaut Lakeshore, *Crawford*, 2,502 ....D-2
Connellsville, *Fayette*, 9,146 ....M-5
▲Connellsville, *Fayette*, 2,483 ....M-5
▲Connoquenessing, *Butler*, 3,653 ....H-3
▲Conoy, *Lancaster*, 3,067 ....M-17
Conshohocken, *Montgomery*, 7,589 ....M-23
Conway, *Beaver*, 2,290 ....C-29
▲Conyngham, *Luzerne*, 1,385 ....G-20
Conyngham, *Luzerne*, 1,958 ....H-20
▲Cook, *Westmoreland*, 2,403 ....M-6
▲Coolbaugh, *Monroe*, 15,205 ....G-22
▲Coolspring, *Mercer*, 2,287 ....F-2
▲Cooper, *Clearfield*, 2,731 ....H-11
Coopersburg, *Lehigh*, 2,582 ....J-23
Coplay, *Lehigh*, 3,387 ....M-40
Coraopolis, *Allegheny*, 6,131 ....E-30
▲Cornplanter, *Venango*, 2,687 ....E-5
Cornwall, *Lebanon*, 3,486 ....L-19
●Cornwells Heights-Eddington, *Bucks*, 3,406 .D-50
Corry, *Erie*, 6,834 ....C-5
Coudersport, *Potter*, 2,650 ....D-12
▲Covington, *Lackawanna*, 1,994 ....F-22
▲Covington, *Tioga*, 1,047 ....D-15
▲Cowanshannock, *Armstrong*, 3,006 ....I-6
Crafton, *Allegheny*, 6,706 ....G-31
▲Cranberry, *Butler*, 23,625 ....I-3
▲Cranberry, *Venango*, 7,014 ....F-4
▲Crescent, *Allegheny*, 2,314 ....J-2
Cresson, *Cambria*, 1,631 ....K-9
▲Cresson, *Cambria*, 4,055 ....K-9
Cressona, *Schuylkill*, 1,635 ....K-44
▲Cromwell, *Huntingdon*, 1,632 ....L-12
▲Cross Creek, *Washington*, 1,685 ....K-1
●Croydon, *Bucks*, 9,993 ....M-25
▲Croyle, *Cambria*, 2,233 ....K-8
▲Cumberland, *Adams*, 5,718 ....O-15
▲Cumberland, *Greene*, 6,564 ....N-3
▲Cumberland Valley, *Bedford*, 1,494 ....N-9
▲Cumru, *Berks*, 13,816 ....L-21
●Curtisville, *Allegheny*, 1,173 ....C-34
Curwensville, *Clearfield*, 2,650 ....H-9
▲Cussewago, *Crawford*, 1,597 ....C-2
Dale, *Cambria*, 1,503 ....O-31
▲Dallas, *Luzerne*, 8,179 ....F-20
Dallas, *Luzerne*, 2,557 ....N-44
Dallastown, *York*, 4,087 ....L-38
Dalton, *Lackawanna*, 1,294 ....E-21
▲Damascus, *Wayne*, 3,662 ....D-24
Danville, *Montour*, 4,897 ....H-18
Darby, *Delaware*, 10,299 ....F-46
▲Darby, *Delaware*, 9,622 ....G-45
●Darby Township, *Delaware*, 9,622 ....G-45
▲Darlington, *Beaver*, 1,974 ....I-1
▲Daugherty, *Beaver*, 3,441 ....I-2
●Davidsville, *Somerset*, 1,119 ....L-8
▲Decatur, *Clearfield*, 2,974 ....H-11
▲Decatur, *Mifflin*, 3,021 ....I-14
▲Delaware, *Juniata*, 1,464 ....J-15
▲Delaware, *Mercer*, 2,159 ....F-2
▲Delaware, *Northumberland*, 4,341 ....G-17
▲Delaware, *Pike*, 6,319 ....F-25
▲Delmar, *Union*, 2,893 ....D-14
Delmont, *Westmoreland*, 2,497 ....G-38
Denver, *Lancaster*, 3,332 ....L-20
▲Derry, *Dauphin*, 21,273 ....L-18
▲Derry, *Mifflin*, 7,256 ....J-14
▲Derry, *Montour*, 1,215 ....H-18
Derry, *Westmoreland*, 2,991 ....K-6
▲Derry, *Westmoreland*, 14,726 ....K-6
●Devon-Berwyn, *Chester*, 5,067 ....D-43
▲Dickinson, *Cumberland*, 4,702 ....M-15
Dickson City, *Lackawanna*, 6,205 ....E-22
Dillsburg, *York*, 2,063 ....M-16
▲Dimock, *Susquehanna*, 1,398 ....D-21
▲Dingman, *Pike*, 8,788 ....F-25
▲District, *Berks*, 1,449 ....K-22
▲Donegal, *Butler*, 1,722 ....H-4
▲Donegal, *Washington*, 2,428 ....L-1
▲Donegal, *Westmoreland*, 2,442 ....M-6
Donora, *Washington*, 5,653 ....L-4
Dormont, *Allegheny*, 9,305 ....G-32
▲Dorrance, *Luzerne*, 2,109 ....G-20
▲Douglass, *Berks*, 3,327 ....L-22
▲Douglass, *Montgomery*, 9,104 ....K-22
Dover, *York*, 1,815 ....M-17
▲Dover, *York*, 18,074 ....M-17
Downingtown, *Chester*, 7,589 ....E-40
Doylestown, *Bucks*, 8,227 ....K-24
▲Doylestown, *Bucks*, 17,619 ....L-24
Dravosburg, *Allegheny*, 2,015 ....H-34
▲Dreher, *Wayne*, 1,280 ....F-23
●Drexel Hill, *Delaware*, 29,364 ....M-23
▲Drumore, *Lancaster*, 2,243 ....N-20
Du Bois, *Clearfield*, 8,123 ....G-8
Dublin, *Bucks*, 2,083 ....K-24
▲Dublin, *Fulton*, 1,277 ....M-12
▲Dublin, *Huntingdon*, 1,280 ....M-12
Duboistown, *Lycoming*, 1,280 ....G-16
Dunbar, *Fayette*, 1,219 ....M-5
▲Dunbar, *Fayette*, 7,562 ....M-5
Duncannon, *Perry*, 1,508 ....K-16
Duncansville, *Blair*, 1,238 ....K-10
▲Dunkard, *Greene*, 2,358 ....O-3
Dunmore, *Lackawanna*, 14,018 ....E-22
●Dunnstown, *Clinton*, 1,365 ....G-14
Dupont, *Luzerne*, 2,719 ....N-47
Duquesne, *Allegheny*, 7,332 ....H-34
▲Durham, *Bucks*, 1,313 ....J-24
Duryea, *Luzerne*, 4,634 ....M-47
▲Dyberry, *Wayne*, 1,353 ....D-23
●Eagleville, *Montgomery*, 4,458 ....B-44
▲Earl, *Berks*, 3,050 ....K-22
▲Earl, *Lancaster*, 6,183 ....M-20
▲East Allen, *Northampton*, 4,903 ....I-23
East Berlin, *Adams*, 1,365 ....N-16
East Berwick, *Luzerne*, 1,998 ....P-47
▲East Bethlehem, *Washington*, 2,524 ....M-3
▲East Bradford, *Chester*, 9,405 ....M-22
East Brady, *Clarion*, 1,038 ....H-5
▲East Brandywine, *Chester*, 5,822 ....M-21
▲East Brunswick, *Schuylkill*, 1,601 ....J-21
▲East Buffalo, *Union*, 5,730 ....H-17
▲East Caln, *Chester*, 2,857 ....M-22
▲East Carroll, *Cambria*, 1,798 ....J-8
▲East Cocalico, *Lancaster*, 9,954 ....L-20
East Conemaugh, *Cambria*, 1,291 ....N-31
▲East Coventry, *Chester*, 4,566 ....L-22
▲East Deer, *Allegheny*, 1,362 ....J-4
▲East Donegal, *Lancaster*, 5,405 ....M-18

Explanation of symbols: ● - Census Designated Place (CDP) ▲ - Township † - CDP and Township

▲East Drumore, *Lancaster,* 3,535 ... N-20
▲East Earl, *Lancaster,* 5,723 ... M-20
▲East Fallowfield, *Chester,* 5,157 ... N-21
▲East Fallowfield, *Crawford,* 1,434 ... E-2
▲East Finley, *Washington,* 1,489 ... M-1
▲East Franklin, *Armstrong,* 3,900 ... H-5
▲East Goshen, *Chester,* 16,824 ... M-22
East Greenville, *Montgomery,* 3,103 ... K-23
▲East Hanover, *Dauphin,* 5,322 ... K-17
▲East Hanover, *Lebanon,* 2,858 ... K-18
▲East Hempfield, *Lancaster,* 21,399 ... M-19
▲East Hopewell, *York,* 2,209 ... N-18
▲East Huntingdon, *Westmoreland,* 7,781 ... M-5
▲East Lackawannock, *Mercer,* 1,701 ... G-2
▲East Lampeter, *Lancaster,* 13,556 ... M-19
East Lansdowne, *Delaware,* 2,586 ... F-46
▲East Mahoning, *Indiana,* 1,196 ... I-7
▲East Manchester, *York,* 5,078 ... M-17
▲East Marlborough, *Chester,* 6,317 ... N-22
East McKeesport, *Allegheny,* 2,343 ... H-35
▲East Mead, *Crawford,* 1,485 ... D-3
▲East Nantmeal, *Chester,* 1,787 ... L-22
† East Norriton, *Montgomery,* 13,211 ... C-45
▲East Nottingham, *Chester,* 5,516 ... O-20
▲East Penn, *Carbon,* 2,461 ... I-21
▲East Pennsboro, *Cumberland,* 18,254 ... L-16
East Petersburg, *Lancaster,* 4,450 ... M-19
▲East Pikeland, *Chester,* 6,551 ... M-22
East Pittsburgh, *Allegheny,* 2,017 ... G-34
▲East Providence, *Bedford,* 1,858 ... N-10
▲East Rockhill, *Bucks,* 5,199 ... K-23
▲East Saint Clair, *Bedford,* 3,123 ... M-9
East Stroudsburg, *Monroe,* 9,888 ... H-24
▲East Taylor, *Cambria,* 2,726 ... K-8
▲East Union, *Schuylkill,* 1,419 ... H-20
● East Uniontown, *Fayette,* 2,760 ... N-4
▲East Vincent, *Chester,* 5,493 ... L-22
East Washington, *Washington,* 1,930 ... L-2
▲East Wheatfield, *Indiana,* 2,607 ... K-7
▲East Whiteland, *Chester,* 9,333 ... M-22
● East York, *York,* 8,782 ... M-17
● Eastlawn Gardens, *Northampton,* 2,832 ... L-42
Easton, *Northampton,* 26,263 ... I-24
▲Easttown, *Chester,* 10,270 ... M-23
▲Eaton, *Wyoming,* 1,644 ... E-20
Ebensburg, *Cambria,* 3,091 ... K-9
Economy, *Beaver,* 9,363 ... J-2
Eddystone, *Delaware,* 2,442 ... G-44
▲Eden, *Lancaster,* 1,856 ... N-20
Edgewood, *Allegheny,* 3,311 ... G-34
● Edgewood, *Northumberland,* 2,619 ... I-18
Edgeworth, *Allegheny,* 1,730 ... E-29
▲Edgmont, *Delaware,* 3,918 ... M-23
Edinboro, *Erie,* 6,950 ... C-3
Edwardsville, *Luzerne,* 4,984 ... N-45
▲Eldred, *Jefferson,* 1,277 ... F-11
▲Eldred, *Lycoming,* 2,178 ... F-16
▲Eldred, *McKean,* 1,696 ... C-10
▲Eldred, *Monroe,* 2,665 ... H-23
● Elim, *Cambria,* 4,175 ... O-30
▲Elizabeth, *Allegheny,* 13,839 ... J-34
Elizabeth, *Allegheny,* 1,609 ... J-34
▲Elizabeth, *Lancaster,* 3,833 ... L-19
Elizabethtown, *Lancaster,* 11,887 ... L-18
Elizabethville, *Dauphin,* 1,344 ... J-17
▲Elk, *Chester,* 1,485 ... O-21
▲Elk, *Clarion,* 1,519 ... F-5
▲Elk Creek, *Erie,* 1,800 ... C-2
▲Elk Lick, *Somerset,* 2,293 ... O-7
Elkland, *Tioga,* 1,786 ... B-15
Ellport, *Lawrence,* 1,148 ... H-2
Ellsworth, *Washington,* 1,083 ... M-3
Ellwood City, *Lawrence,* 8,688 ... H-2
● Elysburg, *Northumberland,* 2,067 ... I-18
Emmaus, *Lehigh,* 11,313 ... J-23
Emporium, *Cameron,* 2,526 ... E-11
Emsworth, *Allegheny,* 2,598 ... E-31
● Enola, *Cumberland,* 5,627 ... L-27
Ephrata, *Lancaster,* 13,213 ... L-20
▲Ephrata, *Lancaster,* 8,026 ... L-20
Erie, *Erie,* 103,717 ... B-3
● Espy, *Columbia,* 1,428 ... Q-45
Etna, *Allegheny,* 3,924 ... E-33
Evans City, *Butler,* 2,009 ... I-3
● Evansburg, *Montgomery,* 1,536 ... B-43
Everett, *Bedford,* 1,905 ... M-10
▲Exeter, *Berks,* 21,161 ... L-21
Exeter, *Luzerne,* 5,955 ... F-21
▲Exeter, *Luzerne,* 2,557 ... F-21
● Exton, *Chester,* 4,267 ... E-41
Factoryville, *Wyoming,* 1,144 ... E-21
Fairchance, *Fayette,* 2,174 ... N-4
● Fairdale, *Greene,* 1,955 ... N-3
▲Fairfield, *Crawford,* 1,104 ... E-3
▲Fairfield, *Lycoming,* 2,659 ... F-17
▲Fairfield, *Westmoreland,* 2,536 ... K-7
● Fairless Hills, *Bucks,* 8,365 ... L-25
▲Fairmount, *Lancaster,* 1,226 ... M-20
▲Fairview, *Butler,* 2,061 ... H-4
▲Fairview, *Erie,* 10,140 ... B-3
▲Fairview, *Luzerne,* 3,995 ... G-21
▲Fairview, *Mercer,* 1,036 ... F-2
▲Fairview, *York,* 14,321 ... L-17
● Fairview-Ferndale, *Northumberland,* 2,411 ... I-18
▲Fallowfield, *Washington,* 4,461 ... L-3
▲Falls, *Bucks,* 34,865 ... L-21
▲Falls, *Wyoming,* 1,997 ... E-21
▲Fannett, *Franklin,* 2,370 ... L-13
▲Farmington, *Clarion,* 1,986 ... F-6
▲Farmington, *Warren,* 1,353 ... C-7
Farrell, *Mercer,* 6,050 ... F-1
▲Fawn, *Allegheny,* 2,504 ... J-4
▲Fawn, *York,* 2,727 ... O-18
▲Fayette, *Juniata,* 3,252 ... J-15
● Fayetteville, *Franklin,* 2,774 ... N-14
● Feasterville-Trevose, *Bucks,* 6,525 ... C-49
▲Fell, *Lackawanna,* 2,331 ... D-22
▲Ferguson, *Centre,* 14,063 ... I-12
▲Fermanagh, *Juniata,* 2,544 ... J-14
Ferndale, *Cambria,* 1,834 ... O-30
● Fernway, *Butler,* 12,188 ... B-30
▲Findlay, *Allegheny,* 5,145 ... K-2
▲Findley, *Mercer,* 2,305 ... G-2
▲Fishing Creek, *Columbia,* 1,393 ... G-19
Fleetwood, *Berks,* 4,018 ... K-21
Flemington, *Clinton,* 1,319 ... G-14
● Flourtown, *Montgomery,* 4,669 ... C-46
● Flying Hills, *Berks,* 1,191 ... Q-42
Folcroft, *Delaware,* 6,978 ... G-45
● Folsom, *Delaware,* 8,072 ... G-45
Ford City, *Armstrong,* 3,451 ... I-5
Forest City, *Susquehanna,* 1,855 ... D-22
Forest Hills, *Allegheny,* 6,831 ... G-34
▲Forest Lake, *Susquehanna,* 1,194 ... C-20

▲Forks, *Northampton,* 8,419 ... I-24
● Fort Washington, *Montgomery,* 3,680 ... C-46
Forty Fort, *Luzerne,* 4,579 ... N-45
▲Forward, *Allegheny,* 3,771 ... L-3
▲Forward, *Butler,* 2,687 ... I-3
▲Foster, *Luzerne,* 3,323 ... H-21
▲Foster, *McKean,* 4,566 ... C-9
▲Foster, *Schuylkill,* 1,124 ... J-19
Fountain Hill, *Lehigh,* 4,614 ... N-41
▲Fox, *Elk,* 3,734 ... F-9
Fox Chapel, *Allegheny,* 5,436 ... E-34
● Fox Run, *Butler,* 3,044 ... B-31
Frackville, *Schuylkill,* 4,361 ... I-19
▲Franconia, *Montgomery,* 11,523 ... L-23
▲Franklin, *Adams,* 4,590 ... N-14
▲Franklin, *Beaver,* 4,307 ... I-2
▲Franklin, *Butler,* 2,292 ... H-3
▲Franklin, *Carbon,* 4,243 ... I-22
▲Franklin, *Chester,* 3,850 ... N-21
▲Franklin, *Erie,* 1,609 ... C-2
▲Franklin, *Fayette,* 2,628 ... M-4
▲Franklin, *Greene,* 7,694 ... N-2
▲Franklin, *Luzerne,* 1,601 ... F-21
▲Franklin, *Snyder,* 2,094 ... I-16
Franklin, *Venango,* 7,212 ... F-4
▲Franklin, *York,* 4,515 ... M-16
Franklin Park, *Allegheny,* 11,364 ... D-31
▲Frankstown, *Blair,* 7,694 ... K-10
▲Frazer, *Chester,* 1,286 ... M-22
● Fredericksburg, *Crawford,* 1,140 ... D-2
● Fredericktown-Millsboro, *Washington,* 1,094 ... M-3
Freedom, *Beaver,* 1,763 ... B-29
▲Freedom, *Blair,* 3,261 ... K-10
▲Freehold, *Warren,* 1,402 ... C-6
Freeland, *Luzerne,* 3,643 ... H-21
Freemansburg, *Northampton,* 1,897 ... N-42
Freeport, *Armstrong,* 1,962 ... I-4
▲Frenchcreek, *Venango,* 1,605 ... F-3
● Friedens, *Somerset,* 1,673 ... M-7
● Fullerton, *Lehigh,* 14,268 ... J-23
▲Fulton, *Lancaster,* 2,826 ... N-19
Galeton, *Potter,* 1,325 ... D-13
▲Gallitzin, *Cambria,* 1,310 ... J-9
Gallitzin, *Cambria,* 1,756 ... K-9
● Gap, *Lancaster,* 1,611 ... M-20
● Garden View, *Lycoming,* 2,679 ... F-16
● Gastonville, *Washington,* 3,002 ... J-32
Geistown, *Cambria,* 2,555 ... O-31
▲Georges, *Fayette,* 6,752 ... N-4
▲German, *Fayette,* 5,595 ... N-4
▲Germany, *Adams,* 2,269 ... O-16
Gettysburg, *Adams,* 7,490 ... N-15
▲Gibson, *Susquehanna,* 1,129 ... D-22
● Gilbertsville, *Montgomery,* 4,242 ... K-22
▲Gilpin, *Armstrong,* 2,587 ... J-5
Girard, *Erie,* 3,164 ... B-2
▲Girard, *Erie,* 5,133 ... B-2
Girardville, *Schuylkill,* 1,742 ... I-19
▲Glade, *Warren,* 2,319 ... C-7
Glassport, *Allegheny,* 4,993 ... I-34
● Glen Lyon, *Luzerne,* 1,881 ... G-20
Glen Rock, *York,* 1,809 ... N-17
† Glenburn, *Lackawanna,* 1,212 ... E-21
Glenolden, *Delaware,* 7,476 ... G-45
● Glenside, *Montgomery,* 7,914 ... M-24
▲Graham, *Clearfield,* 1,236 ... H-11
● Grantley, *York,* 3,580 ... L-37
▲Granville, *Mifflin,* 4,895 ... J-13
▲Great Bend, *Susquehanna,* 1,890 ... C-21
▲Green, *Indiana,* 3,995 ... I-7
Green Tree, *Allegheny,* 4,719 ... G-31
Greencastle, *Franklin,* 3,722 ... N-13
▲Greene, *Beaver,* 2,705 ... J-1
▲Greene, *Clinton,* 1,464 ... H-15
▲Greene, *Erie,* 4,768 ... B-3
▲Greene, *Franklin,* 12,284 ... M-13
▲Greene, *Mercer,* 1,153 ... E-1
▲Greene, *Pike,* 3,149 ... F-23
▲Greenfield, *Blair,* 3,904 ... L-10
▲Greenfield, *Erie,* 1,909 ... B-4
Greensburg, *Westmoreland,* 15,889 ... L-5
Greenville, *Mercer,* 6,380 ... E-2
▲Greenwich, *Berks,* 3,386 ... J-21
▲Greenwood, *Columbia,* 1,932 ... G-18
▲Greenwood, *Crawford,* 1,487 ... E-2
▲Greenwood, *Perry,* 1,010 ... J-16
▲Gregg, *Centre,* 2,119 ... H-13
▲Gregg, *Union,* 4,687 ... G-16
● Grindstone-Rowes Run, *Fayette,* 1,141 ... M-4
Grove City, *Mercer,* 8,024 ... G-3
▲Guilford, *Franklin,* 13,100 ... N-13
● Guilford, *Franklin,* 1,835 ... N-13
▲Gulich, *Clearfield,* 1,275 ... I-10
▲Haines, *Centre,* 1,479 ... H-14
▲Halfmoon, *Centre,* 2,357 ... I-12
● Halfway House, *Montgomery,* 1,823 ... L-22
▲Halifax, *Dauphin,* 3,329 ... J-16
Hallam (Hellam), *York,* 1,532 ... K-38
Hallstead, *Susquehanna,* 1,216 ... B-21
Hamburg, *Berks,* 4,114 ... J-20
▲Hamilton, *Adams,* 2,044 ... N-16
▲Hamilton, *Franklin,* 8,949 ... N-13
▲Hamilton, *Monroe,* 8,235 ... H-23
▲Hamiltonban, *Adams,* 2,216 ... N-14
▲Hampden, *Cumberland,* 24,135 ... L-16
● Hampton Township, *Allegheny,* 17,526 ... D-33
▲Hanover, *Beaver,* 3,529 ... J-1
▲Hanover, *Lehigh,* 1,913 ... J-23
▲Hanover, *Luzerne,* 11,488 ... G-21
▲Hanover, *Northampton,* 9,563 ... I-23
▲Hanover, *Washington,* 2,795 ... K-1
Hanover, *York,* 14,535 ... N-16
▲Harborcreek, *Erie,* 15,178 ... A-3
▲Harford, *Susquehanna,* 1,301 ... C-21
● Harleysville, *Montgomery,* 8,795 ... L-23
▲Harmar, *Allegheny,* 3,242 ... J-4
▲Harmony, *Beaver,* 3,373 ... D-29
● Harmony Township, *Beaver,* 3,373 ... D-29
▲Harris, *Centre,* 4,657 ... I-13
Harrisburg, *Dauphin,* 48,950 ... L-17
▲Harrison, *Allegheny,* 10,934 ... J-4
▲Harrison, *Bedford,* 1,007 ... N-9
▲Harrison, *Potter,* 1,093 ... C-13
● Harrison Township, *Allegheny,* 10,934 ... J-4
▲Hartley, *Union,* 1,714 ... H-15
Harveys Lake, *Luzerne,* 2,888 ... F-20
● Hasson Heights, *Venango,* 1,495 ... E-5
Hastings, *Cambria,* 1,398 ... J-9
Hatboro, *Montgomery,* 7,393 ... B-48
Hatfield, *Montgomery,* 2,605 ... L-23
▲Hatfield, *Montgomery,* 16,712 ... L-23
▲Haverford, *Delaware,* 48,498 ... M-23
Hawley, *Wayne,* 1,303 ... E-24
▲Haycock, *Bucks,* 2,191 ... K-24

▲Hayfield, *Crawford,* 3,092 ... D-2
▲Hazle, *Luzerne,* 9,000 ... H-21
Hazleton, *Luzerne,* 23,329 ... H-20
▲Hegins, *Schuylkill,* 3,519 ... J-18
Heidelberg, *Allegheny,* 1,225 ... G-31
▲Heidelberg, *Berks,* 1,636 ... K-11
▲Heidelberg, *Lebanon,* 3,832 ... L-19
▲Heidelberg, *Lehigh,* 3,279 ... I-21
▲Heidelberg, *York,* 2,970 ... N-16
▲Hellam, *York,* 5,930 ... M-18
Hellertown, *Northampton,* 5,606 ... J-23
▲Hemlock, *Columbia,* 1,874 ... H-18
▲Hempfield, *Mercer,* 4,004 ... E-2
▲Hempfield, *Westmoreland,* 40,721 ... K-5
▲Henderson, *Jefferson,* 1,727 ... H-8
▲Henry Clay, *Fayette,* 1,984 ... N-6
▲Hepburn, *Lycoming,* 2,836 ... F-16
▲Hereford, *Berks,* 3,174 ... K-22
Hermitage, *Mercer,* 16,157 ... F-1
● Hershey, *Dauphin,* 12,771 ... L-18
▲Hickory, *Lawrence,* 2,356 ... G-2
▲Highland, *Chester,* 1,125 ... N-21
● Highland Park, *Mifflin,* 1,446 ... J-14
Highspire, *Dauphin,* 2,720 ... L-17
● Hiller, *Fayette,* 1,234 ... M-3
▲Hilltown, *Bucks,* 12,102 ... K-24
● Hokendauqua, *Lehigh,* 3,411 ... M-40
▲Hollenback, *Luzerne,* 1,243 ... H-20
Hollidaysburg, *Blair,* 5,368 ... K-10
● Homeacre-Lyndora, *Butler,* 6,685 ... H-3
Homer City, *Indiana,* 1,844 ... J-7
Homestead, *Allegheny,* 3,569 ... G-33
● Hometown, *Schuylkill,* 1,399 ... I-20
Honesdale, *Wayne,* 4,874 ... E-23
Honey Brook, *Chester,* 1,287 ... M-21
▲Honey Brook, *Chester,* 6,278 ... M-21
▲Hopewell, *Beaver,* 13,254 ... J-2
▲Hopewell, *Bedford,* 1,894 ... M-10
▲Hopewell, *Cumberland,* 2,096 ... M-14
▲Hopewell, *York,* 5,062 ... O-18
● Hopwood, *Fayette,* 2,006 ... N-4
● Horsham, *Montgomery,* 14,779 ... B-47
▲Horsham, *Montgomery,* 24,232 ... L-24
▲Horton, *Elk,* 1,574 ... F-9
● Houserville, *Centre,* 1,809 ... I-12
Houston, *Washington,* 1,314 ... L-2
Hughestown, *Luzerne,* 1,541 ... N-46
Hughesville, *Lycoming,* 2,220 ... F-17
Hummelstown, *Dauphin,* 4,360 ... L-17
▲Hunlock, *Luzerne,* 2,568 ... G-20
Huntingdon, *Huntingdon,* 6,918 ... K-12
▲Huntington, *Adams,* 2,233 ... M-16
▲Huntington, *Luzerne,* 2,104 ... G-19
▲Huston, *Blair,* 1,262 ... K-11
▲Huston, *Centre,* 1,311 ... H-12
▲Huston, *Clearfield,* 1,468 ... G-10
● Hyde, *Clearfield,* 1,491 ... H-10
Hyndman, *Bedford,* 1,005 ... N-9
● Imperial-Enlow, *Allegheny,* 3,514 ... F-29
▲Independence, *Beaver,* 2,802 ... J-2
▲Independence, *Washington,* 1,676 ... L-1
▲Indiana, *Allegheny,* 6,809 ... J-4
Indiana, *Indiana,* 14,895 ... J-7
Industry, *Beaver,* 1,921 ... J-1
Ingram, *Allegheny,* 3,712 ... F-31
▲Irwin, *Venango,* 1,309 ... F-3
Irwin, *Westmoreland,* 4,366 ... I-36
▲Jackson, *Butler,* 3,645 ... I-3
▲Jackson, *Cambria,* 4,925 ... K-8
▲Jackson, *Dauphin,* 1,728 ... J-17
▲Jackson, *Lebanon,* 6,338 ... K-19
▲Jackson, *Luzerne,* 4,453 ... F-20
▲Jackson, *Mercer,* 1,206 ... F-3
▲Jackson, *Monroe,* 5,979 ... H-23
▲Jackson, *Snyder,* 1,276 ... H-16
▲Jackson, *Tioga,* 2,054 ... C-16
▲Jackson, *Venango,* 1,168 ... E-4
▲Jackson, *York,* 6,095 ... N-16
Jacobus, *York,* 1,203 ... N-17
▲Jay, *Elk,* 2,094 ... F-9
Jeannette, *Westmoreland,* 10,654 ... I-37
▲Jefferson, *Berks,* 1,604 ... K-20
▲Jefferson, *Butler,* 5,690 ... I-4
▲Jefferson, *Fayette,* 2,259 ... M-4
▲Jefferson, *Greene,* 2,528 ... N-3
▲Jefferson, *Lackawanna,* 3,592 ... E-22
▲Jefferson, *Mercer,* 2,416 ... F-2
▲Jefferson, *Somerset,* 1,375 ... M-6
▲Jefferson, *Washington,* 1,218 ... K-1
Jefferson Hills, *Allegheny,* 9,666 ... I-33
▲Jenkins, *Luzerne,* 4,584 ... N-46
Jenkintown, *Montgomery,* 4,478 ... D-47
▲Jenks, *Forest,* 1,261 ... E-7
▲Jenner, *Somerset,* 4,054 ... L-7
Jermyn, *Lackawanna,* 2,287 ... E-22
● Jerome, *Somerset,* 1,068 ... L-7
Jersey Shore, *Lycoming,* 4,482 ... G-15
Jessup, *Lackawanna,* 4,718 ... E-22
Jim Thorpe, *Carbon,* 4,804 ... H-21
Johnsonburg, *Elk,* 3,003 ... E-9
Johnstown, *Cambria,* 23,906 ... K-8
▲Jones, *Elk,* 1,721 ... D-10
Jonestown, *Lebanon,* 1,028 ... K-18
▲Juniata, *Bedford,* 1,016 ... M-9
▲Juniata, *Blair,* 1,115 ... K-9
▲Juniata, *Perry,* 1,359 ... J-15
Kane, *McKean,* 4,126 ... D-8
▲Keating, *McKean,* 3,087 ... C-10
▲Kelly, *Union,* 4,502 ... H-17
Kenhorst, *Berks,* 2,679 ... P-42
● Kenilworth, *Chester,* 1,576 ... A-41
▲Kennedy, *Allegheny,* 7,504 ... F-31
● Kennedy Township, *Allegheny,* 7,504 ... F-31
▲Kennett, *Chester,* 6,451 ... N-22
Kennett Square, *Chester,* 5,273 ... N-22
▲Kidder, *Carbon,* 1,185 ... H-22
▲Kimmel, *Bedford,* 1,609 ... L-9
▲King, *Bedford,* 1,264 ... L-10
● King of Prussia, *Montgomery,* 18,511 ... D-44
Kingston, *Luzerne,* 13,855 ... F-21
▲Kingston, *Luzerne,* 7,145 ... F-21
▲Kiskiminetas, *Armstrong,* 4,950 ... J-5
Kittanning, *Armstrong,* 4,787 ... I-5
▲Kittanning, *Armstrong,* 2,359 ... I-5
▲Kline, *Schuylkill,* 1,591 ... H-20
Knox, *Clarion,* 1,176 ... F-5
▲Knox, *Clarion,* 1,045 ... F-6
▲Knox, *Jefferson,* 1,056 ... G-7
Kulpmont, *Northumberland,* 2,985 ... I-41
● Kulpsville, *Montgomery,* 8,005 ... A-45
Kutztown, *Berks,* 5,067 ... J-21
▲Lackawannock, *Mercer,* 2,561 ... G-2
▲Lackawaxen, *Pike,* 4,154 ... E-25
▲Lafayette, *McKean,* 2,337 ... C-9

Laflin, *Luzerne,* 1,502 ... N-46
▲Lake, *Luzerne,* 2,110 ... F-20
▲Lake, *Wayne,* 4,361 ... E-23
Lake City, *Erie,* 2,811 ... B-2
● Lake Heritage, *Adams,* 1,136 ... N-15
● Lake Meade, *Adams,* 1,832 ... M-16
● Lake Wynonah, *Schuylkill,* 1,961 ... J-20
▲Lamar, *Clinton,* 2,450 ... H-14
▲Lancaster, *Butler,* 2,511 ... H-3
Lancaster, *Lancaster,* 56,348 ... M-19
▲Lancaster, *Lancaster,* 13,944 ... M-19
Langhorne, *Bucks,* 1,981 ... B-50
Lansdale, *Montgomery,* 16,071 ... A-45
Lansdowne, *Delaware,* 11,044 ... F-45
Lansford, *Carbon,* 4,230 ... I-21
Laporte, *Sullivan,* 290 ... E-18
Larksville, *Luzerne,* 4,694 ... O-45
▲Latimore, *Adams,* 2,528 ... M-16
Latrobe, *Westmoreland,* 8,994 ... L-6
Laureldale, *Berks,* 3,759 ... K-21
● Lawnton, *Dauphin,* 3,787 ... L-29
▲Lawrence, *Clearfield,* 7,712 ... G-10
▲Lawrence, *Tioga,* 1,721 ... C-15
† Lawrence Park, *Erie,* 4,048 ... A-3
● Lawson Heights, *Westmoreland,* 2,339 ... L-6
▲Leacock, *Lancaster,* 4,878 ... M-20
● Leacock-Leola-Bareville, *Lancaster,* 6,625 ... M-19
Lebanon, *Lebanon,* 24,461 ... K-19
● Lebanon South, *Lebanon,* 2,145 ... K-33
▲Leboeuf, *Erie,* 1,680 ... C-3
Leechburg, *Armstrong,* 2,386 ... J-5
Leesport, *Berks,* 1,805 ... K-21
▲Leet, *Allegheny,* 1,568 ... J-2
Leetsdale, *Allegheny,* 1,232 ... J-2
▲Lehigh, *Northampton,* 9,728 ... I-22
▲Lehigh, *Wayne,* 1,639 ... F-22
Lehighton, *Carbon,* 5,537 ... I-22
▲Lehman, *Luzerne,* 3,206 ... F-20
▲Lehman, *Pike,* 7,515 ... G-24
● Leith-Hatfield, *Fayette,* 2,820 ... N-4
▲Lemon, *Wyoming,* 1,189 ... D-21
● Lemont, *Centre,* 2,116 ... I-12
Lemoyne, *Cumberland,* 3,995 ... M-28
● Lenape Heights, *Armstrong,* 1,212 ... A-39
▲Lenox, *Susquehanna,* 1,832 ... D-22
▲Letterkenny, *Franklin,* 2,074 ... M-13
● Levittown, *Bucks,* 53,966 ... L-25
▲Lewis, *Lycoming,* 1,139 ... F-16
▲Lewis, *Northumberland,* 1,862 ... G-17
▲Lewis, *Union,* 1,405 ... H-15
Lewisburg, *Union,* 5,620 ... H-16
Lewistown, *Mifflin,* 8,998 ... J-14
▲Liberty, *Adams,* 1,063 ... O-15
Liberty, *Allegheny,* 2,670 ... I-34
▲Liberty, *Bedford,* 1,477 ... L-11
▲Liberty, *Centre,* 1,830 ... G-13
▲Liberty, *McKean,* 1,726 ... C-11
▲Liberty, *Mercer,* 1,276 ... G-3
▲Liberty, *Montour,* 1,476 ... H-17
▲Liberty, *Susquehanna,* 1,266 ... B-21
▲Licking Creek, *Fulton,* 1,532 ... M-11
Ligonier, *Westmoreland,* 1,695 ... L-6
▲Ligonier, *Westmoreland,* 6,973 ... L-6
● Lima, *Delaware,* 3,225 ... F-43
▲Limerick, *Montgomery,* 13,534 ... L-22
▲Limestone, *Clarion,* 1,773 ... G-6
▲Limestone, *Lycoming,* 2,136 ... G-15
▲Limestone, *Montour,* 1,004 ... G-17
▲Limestone, *Union,* 1,572 ... I-16
Lincoln, *Allegheny,* 1,218 ... I-34
▲Lincoln, *Somerset,* 1,669 ... M-7
Linesville, *Crawford,* 1,155 ... D-1
● Linglestown, *Dauphin,* 6,414 ... K-17
● Linntown, *Union,* 1,542 ... H-16
● Linwood, *Delaware,* 3,374 ... N-23
● Lionville-Marchwood, *Chester,* 6,298 ... D-40
▲Litchfield, *Bradford,* 1,307 ... C-18
Lititz, *Lancaster,* 9,029 ... L-19
▲Little Beaver, *Lawrence,* 1,310 ... H-1
▲Little Britain, *Lancaster,* 3,514 ... N-20
Littlestown, *Adams,* 3,947 ... O-16
Lock Haven, *Clinton,* 9,149 ... G-14
▲Locust, *Columbia,* 1,410 ... H-18
▲Logan, *Blair,* 11,925 ... J-9
▲London Britain, *Chester,* 2,797 ... O-21
▲London Grove, *Chester,* 5,265 ... N-21
▲Londonderry, *Bedford,* 1,760 ... O-8
▲Londonderry, *Chester,* 1,632 ... N-21
▲Londonderry, *Dauphin,* 5,224 ... L-17
▲Longswamp, *Berks,* 5,608 ... J-22
● Lorane, *Berks,* 2,994 ... P-43
Loretto, *Cambria,* 1,190 ... J-9
▲Lower Allen, *Cumberland,* 17,437 ... L-17
● Lower Allen, *Cumberland,* 6,619 ... M-28
▲Lower Alsace, *Berks,* 4,478 ... K-21
▲Lower Augusta, *Northumberland,* 1,079 ... I-17
Lower Burrell, *Westmoreland,* 12,608 ... D-36
▲Lower Chanceford, *York,* 2,899 ... N-19
▲Lower Chichester, *Delaware,* 3,591 ... N-23
▲Lower Frankford, *Cumberland,* 1,823 ... L-15
▲Lower Frederick, *Montgomery,* 4,795 ... L-23
▲Lower Gwynedd, *Montgomery,* 10,422 ... L-23
▲Lower Heidelberg, *Berks,* 4,150 ... K-20
▲Lower Macungie, *Lehigh,* 19,220 ... J-22
▲Lower Mahanoy, *Northumberland,* 1,586 ... J-17
▲Lower Makefield, *Bucks,* 32,681 ... L-25
▲Lower Merion, *Montgomery,* 59,850 ... M-24
▲Lower Mifflin, *Cumberland,* 1,620 ... L-14
▲Lower Milford, *Lehigh,* 3,617 ... J-23
▲Lower Moreland, *Montgomery,* 11,281 ... M-25
▲Lower Mount Bethel, *Northampton,* 3,228 ... I-24
▲Lower Nazareth, *Northampton,* 5,259 ... I-23
▲Lower Oxford, *Chester,* 4,319 ... N-21
▲Lower Paxton, *Dauphin,* 44,424 ... K-17
▲Lower Pottsgrove, *Montgomery,* 11,213 ... L-22
▲Lower Providence, *Montgomery,* 22,390 ... L-23
▲Lower Salford, *Montgomery,* 12,893 ... L-23
▲Lower Saucon, *Northampton,* 9,884 ... J-23
▲Lower Southampton, *Bucks,* 19,276 ... L-25
▲Lower Swatara, *Dauphin,* 8,149 ... L-17
▲Lower Towamensing, *Carbon,* 3,173 ... I-22
▲Lower Tyrone, *Fayette,* 1,171 ... M-4
▲Lower Windsor, *York,* 7,405 ... N-18
▲Lower Yoder, *Cambria,* 3,029 ... K-7
▲Lowhill, *Lehigh,* 1,869 ... J-22
▲Loyalhanna, *Westmoreland,* 2,301 ... K-6
▲Loyalsock, *Lycoming,* 10,876 ... F-16
▲Lurgan, *Franklin,* 2,014 ... M-13
▲Luzerne, *Fayette,* 4,683 ... M-3
Luzerne, *Luzerne,* 2,952 ... N-45
▲Lycoming, *Lycoming,* 1,606 ... F-15
Lykens, *Dauphin,* 1,937 ... J-17
▲Lykens, *Dauphin,* 1,095 ... J-17
▲Lynn, *Susquehanna,* 3,849 ... D-20

Explanation of symbols: ● - Census Designated Place (CDP) ▲ - Township † - CDP and Township

● Salix-Beauty Line Park, *Cambria*, 1,259 ... L-8
▲ Saltlick, *Fayette*, 3,715 ... M-6
● Salunga-Landisville, *Lancaster*, 4,771 ... M-19
● Sanatoga, *Montgomery*, 7,734 ... A-41
● Sand Hill, *Lebanon*, 2,345 ... K-33
▲ Sandy, *Clearfield*, 11,556 ... G-9
● Sandy, *Clearfield*, 1,687 ... G-8
▲ Sandy Lake, *Mercer*, 1,248 ... F-3
▲ Sandycreek, *Venango*, 2,406 ... F-4
▲ Saville, *Perry*, 2,204 ... K-14
Saxonburg, *Butler*, 1,629 ... I-4
Sayre, *Bradford*, 5,813 ... B-18
Schlusser, *Cumberland*, 4,750 ... L-15
● Schnecksville, *Lehigh*, 1,989 ... J-22
▲ Schuylkill, *Chester*, 6,960 ... M-23
▲ Schuylkill, *Schuylkill*, 1,123 ... I-20
Schuylkill Haven, *Schuylkill*, 5,548 ... K-44
Schwenksville, *Montgomery*, 1,693 ... A-43
▲ Scott, *Allegheny*, 17,288 ... G-31
▲ Scott, *Columbia*, 4,768 ... H-19
▲ Scott, *Lackawanna*, 4,931 ... E-22
▲ Scott, *Lawrence*, 2,235 ... G-2
● Scott Township, *Allegheny*, 17,288 ... G-31
Scottdale, *Westmoreland*, 4,772 ... M-5
Scranton, *Lackawanna*, 76,415 ... F-22
Selinsgrove, *Snyder*, 5,383 ... I-17
Sellersville, *Bucks*, 4,564 ... K-23
Seven Fields, *Butler*, 1,986 ... B-31
Sewickley, *Allegheny*, 3,902 ... E-29
▲ Sewickley, *Westmoreland*, 6,230 ... L-4
▲ Shade, *Somerset*, 2,886 ... M-8
▲ Shaler, *Allegheny*, 29,757 ... J-3
● Shaler Township, *Allegheny*, 29,757 ... J-3
▲ Shamokin, *Northumberland*, 2,159 ... I-40
Shamokin, *Northumberland*, 8,009 ... I-40
Shamokin Dam, *Snyder*, 1,502 ... I-17
● Shanor-Northvue, *Butler*, 4,825 ... H-3
Sharon, *Mercer*, 16,328 ... F-1
Sharon Hill, *Delaware*, 5,468 ... N-24
Sharpsburg, *Allegheny*, 3,594 ... F-33
Sharpsville, *Mercer*, 4,500 ... F-1
● Sheffield, *Warren*, 1,268 ... D-7
▲ Sheffield, *Warren*, 2,346 ... D-8
Shenandoah, *Schuylkill*, 5,624 ... I-44
● Shenandoah Heights, *Schuylkill*, 1,298 ... I-44
▲ Shenango, *Lawrence*, 7,633 ... H-2
▲ Shenango, *Mercer*, 4,037 ... G-1
▲ Sheshequin, *Bradford*, 1,300 ... C-18
Shillington, *Berks*, 5,059 ... L-21
● Shiloh, *York*, 10,192 ... K-36
Shinglehouse, *Potter*, 1,250 ... C-11
▲ Shippen, *Cameron*, 2,495 ... E-11
Shippensburg, *Cumberland*, 5,586 ... M-14
▲ Shippensburg, *Cumberland*, 4,504 ... M-14
Shiremanstown, *Cumberland*, 1,521 ... M-27
▲ Shirley, *Huntingdon*, 2,526 ... K-13
Shoemakersville, *Berks*, 2,124 ... J-21
▲ Shohola, *Pike*, 2,088 ... E-25
Shrewsbury, *York*, 3,378 ... O-17
▲ Shrewsbury, *York*, 5,947 ... O-17
● Silver Lake, *Susquehanna*, 1,729 ... C-21
▲ Silver Spring, *Lancaster*, 10,592 ... M-18
Silverdale, *Bucks*, 1,001 ... K-24
Sinking Spring, *Berks*, 2,639 ... P-41
▲ Skippack, *Montgomery*, 6,516 ... A-44
● Skippack, *Montgomery*, 2,889 ... A-44
● Skyline View, *Dauphin*, 2,307 ... K-17
Slatington, *Lehigh*, 4,434 ... I-22
Slippery Rock, *Butler*, 3,068 ... G-3
▲ Slippery Rock, *Butler*, 5,251 ... G-3
▲ Slippery Rock, *Lawrence*, 3,179 ... H-2
▲ Slocum, *Luzerne*, 1,112 ... G-20
Smethport, *McKean*, 1,684 ... C-10
▲ Smith, *Washington*, 4,567 ... K-1
▲ Smithfield, *Bedford*, 1,538 ... C-18
▲ Smithfield, *Huntingdon*, 4,466 ... K-12
▲ Smithfield, *Monroe*, 5,672 ... H-24
▲ Snake Spring, *Bedford*, 1,482 ... M-10
▲ Snow Shoe, *Centre*, 1,760 ... H-12
▲ Snyder, *Blair*, 3,358 ... I-11
▲ Snyder, *Jefferson*, 2,432 ... F-8
▲ Solebury, *Bucks*, 7,743 ... K-25
Somerset, *Somerset*, 6,762 ... M-7
▲ Somerset, *Somerset*, 9,319 ... M-7
▲ Somerset, *Washington*, 2,701 ... L-3
Souderton, *Montgomery*, 6,730 ... K-23
▲ South Abington, *Lackawanna*, 8,638 ... E-22
▲ South Annville, *Lebanon*, 2,946 ... L-18
▲ South Beaver, *Beaver*, 2,974 ... I-1
▲ South Bend, *Armstrong*, 1,259 ... J-6
▲ South Buffalo, *Armstrong*, 2,785 ... I-5
▲ South Canaan, *Wayne*, 1,666 ... E-23
▲ South Centre, *Columbia*, 1,972 ... M-19
South Connellsville, *Fayette*, 2,281 ... M-5
▲ South Coventry, *Chester*, 1,895 ... L-22
▲ South Creek, *Bradford*, 1,261 ... C-17
▲ South Fayette, *Allegheny*, 12,271 ... K-2
South Fork, *Cambria*, 1,138 ... N-32
▲ South Franklin, *Washington*, 3,796 ... M-2
South Greensburg, *Westmoreland*, 2,280 ... I-38
▲ South Hanover, *Dauphin*, 4,793 ... L-17
▲ South Heidelberg, *Berks*, 5,491 ... L-20
▲ South Huntingdon, *Westmoreland*, 6,175 ... M-4
▲ South Lebanon, *Lebanon*, 8,383 ... L-19
▲ South Londonderry, *Lebanon*, 5,458 ... L-18
▲ South Mahoning, *Indiana*, 1,852 ... I-7
▲ South Manheim, *Schuylkill*, 2,191 ... J-20
▲ South Middleton, *Cumberland*, 12,939 ... M-15
▲ South Newton, *Cumberland*, 1,290 ... M-14
▲ South Park, *Allegheny*, 14,340 ... I-32
● South Park Township, *Allegheny*, 14,340 ... I-32
● South Pottstown, *Chester*, 2,135 ... A-40
▲ South Pymatuning, *Mercer*, 2,857 ... F-1
▲ South Shenango, *Crawford*, 2,047 ... E-1
▲ South Strabane, *Washington*, 7,987 ... L-2
▲ South Union, *Fayette*, 11,337 ... N-4
▲ South Whitehall, *Lehigh*, 18,028 ... J-22
South Williamsport, *Lycoming*, 6,412 ... G-16
▲ South Woodbury, *Bedford*, 2,000 ... L-10
▲ Southampton, *Bedford*, 1,010 ... O-9
▲ Southampton, *Cumberland*, 4,787 ... M-14
▲ Southampton, *Franklin*, 6,138 ... M-14
Southmont, *Cambria*, 2,262 ... O-30
Southwest Greensburg, *Westmoreland*, 2,398 ... I-38
▲ Sparta, *Crawford*, 1,740 ... C-4
Speers, *Washington*, 1,241 ... N-28
▲ Spring, *Berks*, 21,805 ... K-21
▲ Spring, *Centre*, 6,117 ... H-13
▲ Spring, *Crawford*, 1,571 ... C-2
▲ Spring, *Perry*, 2,021 ... K-15
▲ Spring, *Snyder*, 1,563 ... I-15
▲ Spring Brook, *Lackawanna*, 2,367 ... F-22
Spring City, *Chester*, 3,305 ... B-42
▲ Spring Garden, *York*, 11,974 ... N-17
Spring Grove, *York*, 2,050 ... N-17
● Spring House, *Montgomery*, 3,290 ... B-46
● Spring Mount, *Montgomery*, 2,205 ... L-23
Springdale, *Allegheny*, 3,828 ... E-35
▲ Springdale, *Allegheny*, 1,802 ... J-4
● Springetts Manor-Yorklyn, *York*, 4,156 ... K-37
▲ Springettsbury, *York*, 23,883 ... M-17
▲ Springfield, *Bradford*, 1,167 ... C-17
▲ Springfield, *Bucks*, 4,963 ... J-23
† Springfield, *Delaware*, 23,677 ... F-45
▲ Springfield, *Erie*, 3,378 ... B-1
▲ Springfield, *Fayette*, 3,111 ... M-5
▲ Springfield, *Mercer*, 1,972 ... G-2
▲ Springfield, *Montgomery*, 19,533 ... M-24
▲ Springfield, *York*, 3,889 ... N-17
▲ Springhill, *Fayette*, 2,974 ... N-3
▲ Springville, *Susquehanna*, 1,555 ... D-21
● Spry, *York*, 4,903 ... N-17
State College, *Centre*, 38,420 ... I-12
Steelton, *Dauphin*, 5,858 ... M-28
▲ Sterling, *Wayne*, 1,251 ... F-23
Stewartstown, *York*, 1,752 ... O-18
Stoneboro, *Mercer*, 1,104 ... F-3
● Stonybrook-Wilshire, *York*, 5,414 ... K-37
▲ Stonycreek, *Cambria*, 3,204 ... L-8
▲ Stonycreek, *Somerset*, 2,221 ... M-8
● Stormstown, *Centre*, 1,602 ... I-12
▲ Stowe, *Allegheny*, 6,706 ... F-31
▲ Stowe, *Montgomery*, 3,585 ... L-22
● Stowe Township, *Allegheny*, 6,706 ... F-31
▲ Straban, *Adams*, 4,539 ... N-15
Strasburg, *Lancaster*, 2,800 ... M-20
▲ Strasburg, *Lancaster*, 4,021 ... N-20
▲ Stroud, *Monroe*, 13,978 ... H-24
Stroudsburg, *Monroe*, 5,756 ... H-24
● Sturgeon-Noblestown, *Allegheny*, 1,764 ... H-29
▲ Sugar Grove, *Warren*, 1,870 ... B-6
Sugar Notch, *Luzerne*, 1,023 ... G-21
▲ Sugarcreek, *Armstrong*, 1,557 ... H-5
Sugarcreek, *Venango*, 5,331 ... E-4
▲ Sugarloaf, *Luzerne*, 3,652 ... H-20
▲ Sullivan, *Tioga*, 1,322 ... D-16
▲ Summerhill, *Cambria*, 2,724 ... K-9
▲ Summerhill, *Crawford*, 1,350 ... D-2
▲ Summit, *Butler*, 4,728 ... H-4
▲ Summit, *Crawford*, 2,172 ... D-2
▲ Summit, *Erie*, 5,529 ... B-3
▲ Summit, *Somerset*, 2,368 ... N-7
Summit Hill, *Carbon*, 2,974 ... I-21
Sunbury, *Northumberland*, 10,610 ... I-17
▲ Susquehanna, *Cambria*, 2,198 ... J-8
▲ Susquehanna, *Dauphin*, 21,895 ... K-17
▲ Susquehanna, *Juniata*, 1,261 ... J-16
Susquehanna (Susquehanna Depot),
Susquehanna, 1,690 ... C-22
● Susquehanna Trails, *York*, 2,134 ... O-19
Swarthmore, *Delaware*, 6,170 ... G-44
▲ Swatara, *Dauphin*, 22,611 ... L-17
▲ Swatara, *Lebanon*, 3,941 ... J-18
Swissvale, *Allegheny*, 9,653 ... G-34
Swoyersville, *Luzerne*, 5,157 ... F-21
Sykesville, *Jefferson*, 1,246 ... G-8
Tamaqua, *Schuylkill*, 7,174 ... I-20
Tarentum, *Allegheny*, 4,993 ... D-35
▲ Taylor, *Blair*, 2,239 ... L-10
▲ Taylor, *Fulton*, 1,237 ... M-11
Taylor, *Lackawanna*, 6,475 ... F-21
▲ Taylor, *Lawrence*, 1,198 ... H-1
Telford, *Montgomery*, 4,680 ... K-23
Terre Hill, *Lancaster*, 1,237 ... L-20
▲ Texas, *Wayne*, 2,501 ... E-23
● Thompsonville, *Washington*, 3,592 ... I-31
▲ Thornbury, *Chester*, 2,678 ... N-22
▲ Thornbury, *Delaware*, 7,093 ... N-23
● Thorndale, *Chester*, 3,561 ... M-22
Throop, *Lackawanna*, 4,010 ... E-22
▲ Tilden, *York*, 3,553 ... N-18
▲ Tinicum, *Bucks*, 4,206 ... J-24
▲ Tinicum Township, *Delaware*, 4,353 ... G-46
● Tinicum Township, *Delaware*, 4,353 ... G-46
Tionesta, *Forest*, 615 ... E-6
● Tipton, *Blair*, 1,225 ... J-10
Titusville, *Crawford*, 6,146 ... D-5
▲ Toby, *Elk*, 1,166 ... F-9
▲ Tobyhanna, *Monroe*, 6,152 ... G-23
▲ Todd, *Fulton*, 1,488 ... M-12
▲ Todd, *Huntingdon*, 1,004 ... L-11
Topton, *Berks*, 1,948 ... J-22
● Toughkenamon, *Chester*, 1,375 ... N-21
▲ Towamencin, *Montgomery*, 17,597 ... L-23
▲ Towamensing, *Carbon*, 3,475 ... H-22
Towanda, *Bradford*, 3,024 ... D-18
▲ Towanda, *Bradford*, 1,131 ... D-18
Tower City, *Schuylkill*, 1,396 ... J-18
Trafford, *Westmoreland*, 3,236 ... H-35
Trainer, *Delaware*, 1,901 ... H-44
Trappe, *Montgomery*, 3,210 ... L-23
● Treasure Lake, *Clearfield*, 4,507 ... G-9
▲ Tredyffrin, *Chester*, 29,062 ... D-43
Tremont, *Schuylkill*, 1,784 ... K-42
● Trevorton, *Northumberland*, 2,010 ... I-17
● Trooper, *Montgomery*, 6,061 ... C-44
Troy, *Bradford*, 1,508 ... C-17
▲ Troy, *Bradford*, 1,645 ... C-17
▲ Troy, *Crawford*, 1,339 ... D-4
Trumbauersville, *Bucks*, 1,059 ... K-23
Tullytown, *Bucks*, 2,031 ... C-51
▲ Tulpehocken, *Berks*, 3,290 ... K-19
▲ Tunkhannock, *Monroe*, 4,983 ... H-22
Tunkhannock, *Wyoming*, 1,911 ... E-20
▲ Tunkhannock, *Wyoming*, 4,298 ... E-20
▲ Turbot, *Northumberland*, 1,677 ... H-17
Turtle Creek, *Allegheny*, 6,076 ... G-35
▲ Tuscarora, *Bradford*, 1,072 ... D-20
▲ Tuscarora, *Juniata*, 1,159 ... K-14
▲ Tuscarora, *Perry*, 1,122 ... J-15
● Tyler Run-Queens Gate, *York*, 2,926 ... L-37
▲ Tyrone, *Adams*, 2,273 ... M-15
Tyrone, *Blair*, 5,528 ... J-11
▲ Tyrone, *Blair*, 1,800 ... J-11
▲ Tyrone, *Perry*, 1,863 ... L-14
▲ Ulster, *Bradford*, 1,340 ... C-18
▲ Union, *Adams*, 2,989 ... O-16
▲ Union, *Berks*, 3,453 ... L-21
▲ Union, *Centre*, 1,200 ... H-12
▲ Union, *Crawford*, 1,049 ... E-3
▲ Union, *Erie*, 1,663 ... C-4
▲ Union, *Huntingdon*, 1,005 ... K-12
▲ Union, *Lawrence*, 5,103 ... G-2
▲ Union, *Lebanon*, 2,590 ... K-18
▲ Union, *Luzerne*, 2,100 ... G-20
▲ Union, *Mifflin*, 3,313 ... J-13
▲ Union, *Schuylkill*, 1,308 ... H-19
▲ Union, *Snyder*, 1,519 ... I-16
▲ Union, *Union*, 1,427 ... H-17
▲ Union, *Washington*, 5,599 ... L-3
Union City, *Erie*, 3,463 ... C-4
Uniontown, *Fayette*, 12,422 ... N-4
▲ Unity, *Westmoreland*, 21,137 ... L-6
Upland, *Delaware*, 2,977 ... H-44
▲ Upper Allen, *Cumberland*, 15,338 ... L-16
▲ Upper Augusta, *Northumberland*, 2,556 ... H-17
▲ Upper Bern, *Berks*, 1,479 ... K-20
▲ Upper Burrell, *Westmoreland*, 2,240 ... J-4
▲ Upper Chichester, *Delaware*, 16,842 ... N-23
▲ Upper Darby, *Delaware*, 81,821 ... M-23
▲ Upper Dublin, *Montgomery*, 25,878 ... L-24
▲ Upper Fairfield, *Lycoming*, 1,654 ... F-16
▲ Upper Frankford, *Cumberland*, 1,807 ... L-14
▲ Upper Frederick, *Montgomery*, 3,141 ... K-23
▲ Upper Gwynedd, *Montgomery*, 14,243 ... L-23
▲ Upper Hanover, *Montgomery*, 4,885 ... K-23
▲ Upper Leacock, *Lancaster*, 8,229 ... M-20
▲ Upper Macungie, *Lehigh*, 13,895 ... J-22
▲ Upper Makefield, *Bucks*, 7,180 ... L-25
▲ Upper Merion, *Montgomery*, 26,863 ... M-23
▲ Upper Mifflin, *Cumberland*, 1,347 ... L-14
▲ Upper Milford, *Lehigh*, 6,889 ... J-23
▲ Upper Moreland, *Montgomery*, 24,993 ... L-24
▲ Upper Mount Bethel, *Northampton*, 6,063 ... H-24
▲ Upper Nazareth, *Northampton*, 4,426 ... I-23
▲ Upper Oxford, *Chester*, 2,095 ... N-21
▲ Upper Paxton, *Dauphin*, 3,930 ... J-16
▲ Upper Pottsgrove, *Montgomery*, 4,192 ... L-22
▲ Upper Providence, *Delaware*, 10,509 ... M-23
▲ Upper Providence, *Montgomery*, 15,398 ... M-23
● Upper Providence Township,
Delaware, 10,509 ... F-44
† Upper Saint Clair, *Allegheny*, 20,053 ... K-3
▲ Upper Salford, *Montgomery*, 3,024 ... K-23
▲ Upper Saucon, *Lehigh*, 11,939 ... J-23
▲ Upper Southampton, *Bucks*, 15,764 ... L-25
▲ Upper Tulpehocken, *Berks*, 1,495 ... J-20
▲ Upper Turkeyfoot, *Somerset*, 1,232 ... N-6
▲ Upper Tyrone, *Fayette*, 2,244 ... M-5
▲ Upper Uwchlan, *Chester*, 6,850 ... C-40
▲ Upper Yoder, *Cambria*, 5,862 ... L-7
▲ Uwchlan, *Chester*, 16,576 ... M-22
▲ Valley, *Chester*, 5,116 ... M-21
▲ Valley, *Montour*, 2,093 ... H-18
● Valley Green, *York*, 3,550 ... L-17
● Valley View, *Schuylkill*, 1,677 ... J-18
● Valley View, *York*, 2,743 ... N-17
Vandergrift, *Westmoreland*, 5,455 ... J-5
▲ Vanport, *Beaver*, 1,451 ... I-2
▲ Venango, *Erie*, 2,277 ... B-4
▲ Vernon, *Crawford*, 5,499 ... E-20
Verona, *Allegheny*, 3,124 ... E-34
Versailles, *Allegheny*, 1,724 ... I-34
● Village Green-Green Ridge, *Delaware*, 8,279 G-43
● Village Shires, *Bucks*, 4,137 ... B-49
● Vinco, *Cambria*, 1,429 ... K-8
▲ Walker, *Centre*, 3,299 ... H-13
▲ Walker, *Huntingdon*, 1,747 ... K-11
▲ Walker, *Juniata*, 2,598 ... J-14
▲ Wallace, *Chester*, 3,240 ... M-21
Walnutport, *Northampton*, 2,043 ... I-22
Warminster, *Bucks*, 31,383 ... B-48
● Warminster Heights, *Bucks*, 4,191 ... B-48
▲ Warren, *Bradford*, 1,025 ... C-19
Warren, *Warren*, 10,259 ... C-7
● Warren South, *Warren*, 1,651 ... C-7
▲ Warrington, *Bucks*, 17,580 ... L-24
▲ Warrington, *York*, 4,435 ... M-16
▲ Warriors Mark, *Huntingdon*, 1,635 ... I-11
▲ Warsaw, *Jefferson*, 1,346 ... G-8
▲ Warwick, *Bucks*, 11,977 ... L-24
▲ Warwick, *Chester*, 2,556 ... L-21
▲ Warwick, *Lancaster*, 15,475 ... L-19
▲ Washington, *Armstrong*, 1,029 ... H-5
▲ Washington, *Berks*, 3,354 ... K-22
▲ Washington, *Butler*, 1,419 ... G-4
▲ Washington, *Clarion*, 2,037 ... F-6
▲ Washington, *Dauphin*, 2,047 ... J-17
▲ Washington, *Erie*, 4,526 ... C-3
▲ Washington, *Fayette*, 4,461 ... L-4
▲ Washington, *Franklin*, 11,559 ... O-13
▲ Washington, *Greene*, 1,106 ... M-2
▲ Washington, *Indiana*, 1,805 ... I-7
▲ Washington, *Jefferson*, 1,931 ... G-8
▲ Washington, *Lehigh*, 6,588 ... I-22
▲ Washington, *Lycoming*, 1,613 ... G-15
▲ Washington, *Northampton*, 4,152 ... I-24
▲ Washington, *Schuylkill*, 2,750 ... J-19
▲ Washington, *Snyder*, 1,532 ... I-16
Washington, *Washington*, 15,268 ... L-2
▲ Washington, *Westmoreland*, 7,384 ... J-5
▲ Washington, *Wyoming*, 1,306 ... E-20
▲ Washington, *York*, 2,460 ... M-16
Waterford, *Erie*, 1,449 ... C-3
▲ Waterford, *Erie*, 3,878 ... C-3
Watsontown, *Northumberland*, 2,255 ... G-17
▲ Watts, *Perry*, 1,196 ... K-16
Waymart, *Wayne*, 1,429 ... D-23
▲ Wayne, *Armstrong*, 1,117 ... H-6
▲ Wayne, *Clinton*, 1,363 ... G-15
▲ Wayne, *Crawford*, 1,558 ... E-3
▲ Wayne, *Dauphin*, 1,184 ... K-17
▲ Wayne, *Erie*, 1,766 ... B-4
▲ Wayne, *Greene*, 1,223 ... N-2
▲ Wayne, *Lawrence*, 2,328 ... H-2
▲ Wayne, *Mifflin*, 2,414 ... K-12
▲ Wayne, *Schuylkill*, 4,721 ... J-19
● Wayne Heights, *Franklin*, 1,805 ... O-14
Waynesboro, *Franklin*, 9,614 ... O-14
Waynesburg, *Greene*, 4,184 ... N-2
Weatherly, *Carbon*, 2,612 ... H-21
● Weigelstown, *York*, 10,117 ... K-36
▲ Weisenberg, *Lehigh*, 4,144 ... J-21
● Weissport East, *Carbon*, 1,936 ... I-22
▲ Wells, *Bradford*, 1,278 ... C-16
Wellsboro, *Tioga*, 3,328 ... D-15
Wernersville, *Berks*, 2,150 ... P-40
Wesleyville, *Erie*, 3,617 ... A-3
▲ West Beaver, *Snyder*, 1,124 ... I-15
▲ West Bethlehem, *Washington*, 1,432 ... M-2
▲ West Bradford, *Chester*, 10,775 ... M-22
▲ West Brandywine, *Chester*, 7,153 ... M-21
West Brownsville, *Washington*, 1,075 ... P-28
▲ West Brunswick, *Schuylkill*, 3,428 ... J-20
▲ West Buffalo, *Union*, 2,795 ... I-16
▲ West Caln, *Chester*, 7,054 ... M-21
▲ West Carroll, *Cambria*, 1,445 ... J-8
West Chester, *Chester*, 17,861 ... M-22
▲ West Chillisquaque, *Northumberland*, 2,846 ... H-17
▲ West Cocalico, *Lancaster*, 6,967 ... L-20
West Conshohocken, *Montgomery*, 1,446 ... D-45
▲ West Cornwall, *Lebanon*, 1,909 ... L-18
▲ West Deer, *Allegheny*, 11,563 ... J-4
▲ West Donegal, *Lancaster*, 6,539 ... M-18
▲ West Earl, *Lancaster*, 6,766 ... M-20
West Easton, *Northampton*, 1,152 ... M-43
▲ West Fallowfield, *Chester*, 2,485 ... N-21
▲ West Franklin, *Armstrong*, 1,935 ... D-18
● West Goshen, *Chester*, 8,472 ... F-41
▲ West Goshen, *Chester*, 20,495 ... M-22
West Grove, *Chester*, 2,652 ... N-21
▲ West Hanover, *Dauphin*, 6,505 ... K-17
West Hazleton, *Luzerne*, 3,542 ... H-20
▲ West Hempfield, *Lancaster*, 15,128 ... M-18
● West Hills, *Armstrong*, 1,229 ... I-5
West Homestead, *Allegheny*, 2,197 ... G-33
West Kittanning, *Armstrong*, 1,199 ... I-5
▲ West Lampeter, *Lancaster*, 13,145 ... M-19
West Lawn, *Berks*, 1,597 ... P-41
West Leechburg, *Westmoreland*, 1,290 ... C-38
▲ West Mahanoy, *Schuylkill*, 6,166 ... I-19
▲ West Mahoning, *Indiana*, 1,128 ... H-7
▲ West Manchester, *York*, 17,035 ... N-17
▲ West Manheim, *York*, 4,865 ... O-16
West Mayfield, *Beaver*, 1,187 ... I-2
▲ West Mead, *Crawford*, 5,227 ... D-3
West Mifflin, *Allegheny*, 22,464 ... K-4
▲ West Nantmeal, *Chester*, 2,031 ... M-21
West Newton, *Westmoreland*, 3,083 ... L-4
† West Norriton, *Montgomery*, 14,901 ... C-44
▲ West Nottingham, *Chester*, 2,634 ... O-20
▲ West Penn, *Schuylkill*, 3,852 ... I-21
▲ West Pennsboro, *Cumberland*, 5,263 ... L-15
▲ West Perry, *Snyder*, 1,038 ... I-16
▲ West Pike Run, *Washington*, 1,925 ... M-3
▲ West Pikeland, *Chester*, 3,551 ... M-22
West Pittston, *Luzerne*, 5,072 ... N-46
▲ West Pottsgrove, *Montgomery*, 3,815 ... L-22
▲ West Providence, *Bedford*, 3,323 ... N-10
West Reading, *Berks*, 4,049 ... P-42
▲ West Rockhill, *Bucks*, 4,233 ... K-23
▲ West Sadsbury, *Chester*, 2,444 ... M-21
▲ West Saint Clair, *Bedford*, 1,647 ... M-9
▲ West Salem, *Mercer*, 3,565 ... E-1
West View, *Allegheny*, 7,277 ... J-3
▲ West Vincent, *Chester*, 3,170 ... M-22
▲ West Wheatfield, *Indiana*, 2,375 ... K-7
▲ West Whiteland, *Chester*, 16,499 ... M-22
West Wyoming, *Luzerne*, 2,833 ... N-46
● West Wyomissing, *Berks*, 3,016 ... P-41
West York, *York*, 4,321 ... K-36
▲ Westfall, *Pike*, 2,430 ... E-26
Westfield, *Tioga*, 1,190 ... C-14
Westmont, *Cambria*, 5,523 ... O-30
▲ Westtown, *Chester*, 10,352 ... N-22
▲ Wetmore, *McKean*, 1,721 ... D-8
▲ Wharton, *Fayette*, 4,145 ... N-5
▲ Wheatfield, *Perry*, 3,329 ... K-16
Whitaker, *Allegheny*, 1,338 ... G-34
▲ White, *Beaver*, 1,434 ... I-2
▲ White, *Indiana*, 14,034 ... J-7
▲ White Deer, *Union*, 4,273 ... G-17
White Haven, *Luzerne*, 1,182 ... G-21
White Oak, *Allegheny*, 8,437 ... H-35
Whitehall, *Allegheny*, 14,444 ... H-32
▲ Whitehall, *Lehigh*, 24,896 ... J-22
Whitemarsh, *Montgomery*, 16,702 ... C-46
● Whitfield, *Berks*, 2,952 ... P-41
▲ Whitpain, *Montgomery*, 18,572 ... L-23
● Wickerham Manor-Fisher, *Washington*, 1,783 . L-3
▲ Wiconisco, *Dauphin*, 1,168 ... J-17
▲ Wilkes-Barre, *Luzerne*, 3,235 ... F-21
Wilkes-Barre, *Luzerne*, 43,123 ... F-21
● Wilkes-Barre Township, *Luzerne*, 3,235 ... O-46
▲ Wilkins, *Allegheny*, 6,917 ... K-4
● Wilkins Township, *Allegheny*, 6,917 ... G-35
Wilkinsburg, *Allegheny*, 19,196 ... G-34
▲ Williams, *Dauphin*, 1,135 ... J-18
▲ Williams, *Northampton*, 4,470 ... J-24
Williamsburg, *Blair*, 1,345 ... K-11
Williamsport, *Lycoming*, 30,706 ... F-16
Williamstown, *Dauphin*, 1,433 ... J-18
▲ Willistown, *Chester*, 10,011 ... M-23
● Willow Grove, *Montgomery*, 16,234 ... L-24
● Willow Street, *Lancaster*, 7,258 ... M-19
Wilmerding, *Allegheny*, 2,145 ... G-35
▲ Wilmington, *Lawrence*, 2,760 ... G-2
▲ Wilmington, *Mercer*, 1,105 ... G-2
▲ Wilmot, *Bradford*, 1,177 ... D-19
Wilson, *Northampton*, 7,682 ... I-24
Wind Gap, *Northampton*, 2,812 ... I-23
Windber, *Somerset*, 4,395 ... L-8
▲ Windsor, *Berks*, 2,392 ... J-20
▲ Windsor, *York*, 12,807 ... L-38
Windsor, *York*, 1,331 ... L-38
▲ Winfield, *Union*, 3,585 ... H-17
▲ Winslow, *Jefferson*, 2,591 ... G-8
▲ Wolf, *Lycoming*, 2,707 ... G-17
● Wolfdale, *Washington*, 2,873 ... L-2
Womelsdorf, *Berks*, 2,599 ... K-20
● Woodbourne, *Bucks*, 3,512 ... B-50
▲ Woodbury, *Bedford*, 1,198 ... L-10
▲ Woodbury, *Blair*, 1,637 ... K-11
▲ Woodcock, *Crawford*, 2,976 ... D-3
● Woodland Heights, *Venango*, 1,402 ... E-4
● Woodlyn, *Delaware*, 10,036 ... G-44
● Woodside, *Bucks*, 2,575 ... A-51
▲ Woodward, *Clearfield*, 3,550 ... I-10
▲ Woodward, *Clinton*, 2,296 ... G-14
▲ Woodward, *Lycoming*, 2,397 ... G-15
▲ Worcester, *Montgomery*, 7,789 ... L-23
Wormleysburg, *Cumberland*, 2,607 ... L-27
▲ Worth, *Butler*, 1,331 ... H-3
▲ Wright, *Luzerne*, 5,593 ... G-21
▲ Wrightstown, *Bucks*, 2,839 ... L-25
Wrightsville, *York*, 2,223 ... J-39
▲ Wyalusing, *Bradford*, 1,341 ... D-19
● Wyncote, *Montgomery*, 3,046 ... D-47
● Wyndmoor, *Montgomery*, 5,601 ... M-24
Wyoming, *Luzerne*, 3,221 ... N-46
Wyomissing, *Berks*, 8,587 ... P-41
Wyomissing Hills, *Berks*, 2,568 ... P-41
▲ Wysox, *Bradford*, 1,763 ... D-19
Yardley, *Bucks*, 2,498 ... A-51
Yeadon, *Delaware*, 11,762 ... F-46
● Yeagertown, *Mifflin*, 1,035 ... J-14
Yoe, *York*, 1,022 ... L-38
▲ York, *York*, 23,637 ... M-17
York, *York*, 40,862 ... M-17
▲ Young, *Indiana*, 1,744 ... J-6
▲ Young, *Jefferson*, 1,800 ... H-7
Youngsville, *Warren*, 1,834 ... C-6
Youngwood, *Westmoreland*, 4,138 ... L-5
Zelienople, *Butler*, 4,123 ... I-3
▲ Zerbe, *Northumberland*, 2,021 ... I-18
● Zion, *Centre*, 2,054 ... H-13

COUNTIES

(5 Counties)

Name of County	Population	Location on Map
BRISTOL	50,648	F-9
KENT	167,090	F-3
NEWPORT	85,433	G-8
PROVIDENCE	621,602	A-3
WASHINGTON	123,546	H-3
TOTAL	**1,048,319**	

CITIES AND TOWNS

Note: The first name is that of the city or town, second, that of the county in which it is located, then the population and location on the map.

●Ashaway, *Washington,* 1,537 ....L-2
†Barrington, *Bristol,* 16,819 ....F-9
Block Island (New Shoreham), *Washington,* 1,010 ....P-6
●Bradford, *Washington,* 1,497 ....L-3
†Bristol, *Bristol,* 22,469 ....G-9
▲Burrillville, *Providence,* 15,796 ....C-3
Central Falls, *Providence,* 18,928 ....C-8
▲Charlestown, *Washington,* 7,859 ....L-4
▲Coventry, *Kent,* 33,668 ....G-4
Cranston, *Providence,* 79,269 ....E-7
▲Cumberland, *Providence,* 31,840 ....B-7
●Cumberland Hill, *Providence,* 7,738 ....A-7
East Greenwich, *Kent,* 12,948 ....G-7
East Providence, *Providence,* 48,688 ....D-8
▲Exeter, *Washington,* 6,045 ....I-6
▲Foster, *Providence,* 4,274 ....E-3
▲Glocester, *Providence,* 9,948 ....C-5
●Greenville, *Providence,* 8,626 ....C-6
●Harrisville, *Providence,* 1,561 ....B-4
●Hope Valley, *Washington,* 1,649 ....J-3
▲Hopkinton, *Washington,* 7,836 ....K-2
Jamestown, *Newport,* 5,622 ....J-8
▲Johnston, *Providence,* 28,195 ....D-6
●Kingston, *Washington,* 5,446 ....J-6
▲Lincoln, *Providence,* 20,898 ....C-7
Little Compton, *Newport,* 3,593 ....J-11
●Melville, *Newport,* 2,325 ....I-9
▲Middletown, *Newport,* 17,334 ....J-9
▲Narragansett, *Washington,* 16,361 ....K-7
●Narragansett Pier, *Washington,* 3,671 ....K-7
▲New Shoreham, *Washington,* 1,010 ....P-5
Newport, *Newport,* 26,475 ....J-9
●Newport East, *Newport,* 11,463 ....J-9
▲North Kingstown, *Washington,* 26,326 ....I-7
†North Providence, *Providence,* 32,411 ....D-7
▲North Smithfield, *Providence,* 10,618 ....B-6
●Pascoag, *Providence,* 4,742 ....B-4
Pawtucket, *Providence,* 72,958 ....C-8
▲Portsmouth, *Newport,* 17,149 ....H-10
Providence, *Providence,* 173,618 ....D-8
▲Richmond, *Washington,* 7,222 ....J-4
▲Scituate, *Providence,* 10,324 ....D-5
▲Smithfield, *Providence,* 20,613 ....C-6
▲South Kingstown, *Washington,* 27,921 ....L-6
●Tiverton, *Newport,* 7,282 ....H-10
▲Tiverton, *Newport,* 15,260 ....H-10
●Valley Falls, *Providence,* 11,599 ....C-8
●Wakefield-Peacedale, *Washington,* 8,468 ....K-6
Warren, *Bristol,* 11,360 ....F-9
Warwick, *Kent,* 85,808 ....G-8
▲West Greenwich, *Kent,* 5,085 ....H-5
†West Warwick, *Kent,* 29,581 ....F-6
●Westerly, *Washington,* 17,682 ....L-2
▲Westerly, *Washington,* 22,966 ....L-2
Woonsocket, *Providence,* 43,224 ....A-6

Explanation of symbols: ● - Census Designated Place (CDP) ▲ - Township † - CDP and Township

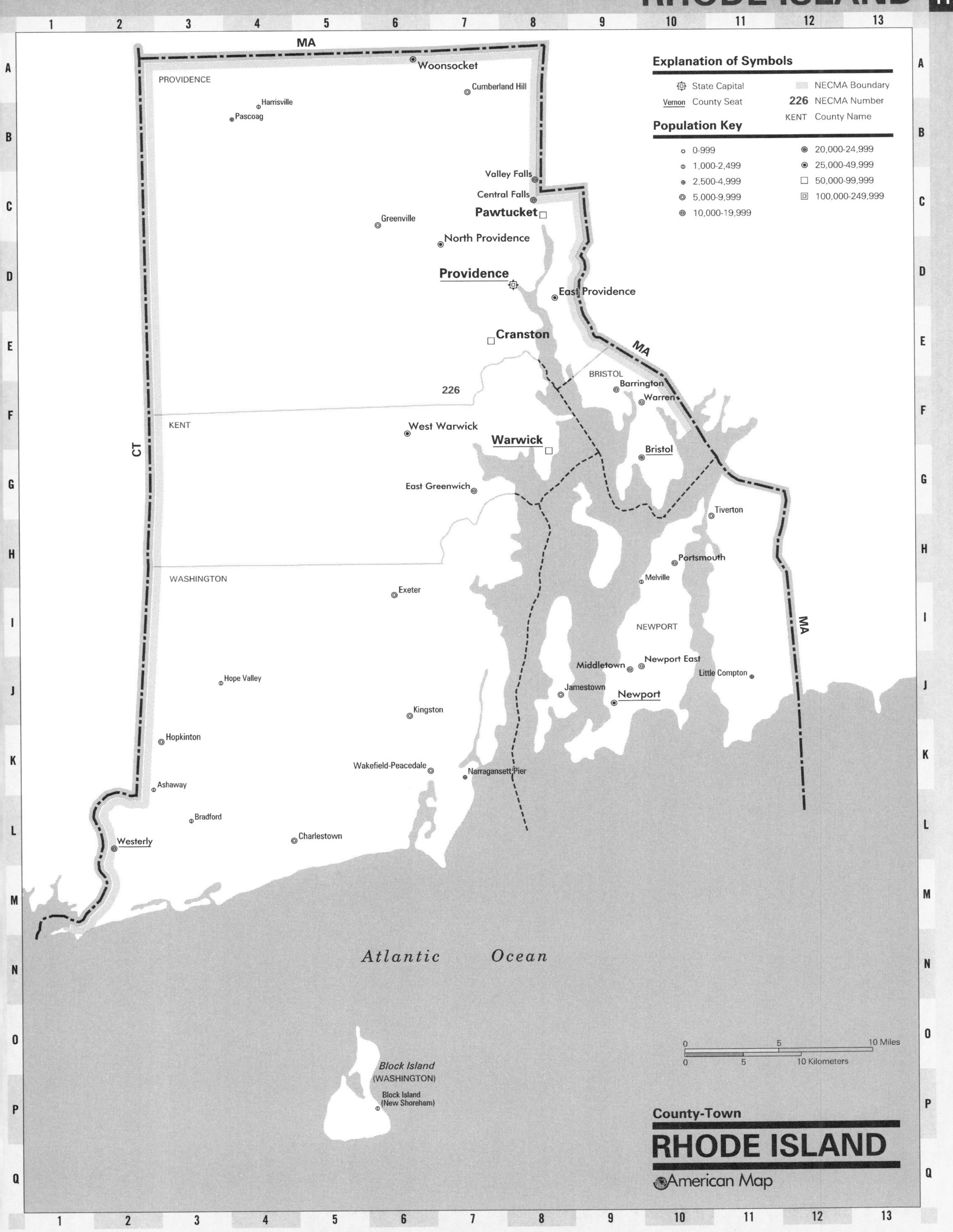

County-Town
RHODE ISLAND
American Map

COUNTIES

(46 Counties)

Name of County	Population	Location on Map
ABBEVILLE	26,167	E-3
AIKEN	142,552	F-6
ALLENDALE	11,211	I-6
ANDERSON	165,740	D-2
BAMBERG	16,658	I-7
BARNWELL	23,478	H-6
BEAUFORT	120,937	L-8
BERKELEY	142,651	H-10
CALHOUN	15,185	G-8
CHARLESTON	309,969	K-10
CHEROKEE	52,537	A-5
CHESTER	34,068	C-7
CHESTERFIELD	42,768	C-10
CLARENDON	32,502	F-10
COLLETON	38,264	I-8
DARLINGTON	67,394	D-11
DILLON	30,722	D-12
DORCHESTER	96,413	I-9
EDGEFIELD	24,595	F-4
FAIRFIELD	23,454	D-7
FLORENCE	125,761	E-11
GEORGETOWN	55,797	G-13
GREENVILLE	379,616	A-3
GREENWOOD	66,271	E-4
HAMPTON	21,386	J-7
HORRY	196,629	E-13
JASPER	20,678	K-7
KERSHAW	52,647	D-9
LANCASTER	61,351	C-8
LAURENS	69,567	C-4
LEE	20,119	D-10
LEXINGTON	216,014	F-6
MARION	35,466	E-12
MARLBORO	28,818	C-11
MCCORMICK	9,958	F-3
NEWBERRY	36,108	D-6
OCONEE	66,215	B-1
ORANGEBURG	91,582	G-7
PICKENS	110,757	B-2
RICHLAND	320,677	E-7
SALUDA	19,181	E-5
SPARTANBURG	253,791	B-4
SUMTER	104,646	E-9
UNION	29,881	B-6
WILLIAMSBURG	37,217	F-11
YORK	164,614	A-7
TOTAL	**4,012,012**	

CITIES AND TOWNS

Note: The first name is that of the city or town, second, that of the county in which it is located, then the population and location on the map.

Abbeville, *Abbeville*, 5,840 ....E-4
Aiken, *Aiken*, 25,337 ....G-6
Allendale, *Allendale*, 4,052 ....I-7
Anderson, *Anderson*, 25,514 ....D-3
Andrews, *Georgetown*, 3,068 ....H-12
•Arial, *Pickens*, 2,607 ....B-3
Awendaw, *Charleston*, 1,195 ....I-12
Bamberg, *Bamberg*, 3,733 ....H-8
Barnwell, *Barnwell*, 5,035 ....H-7
Batesburg-Leesville, *Lexington*, 5,517 ....F-6
Beaufort, *Beaufort*, 12,950 ....K-9
Belton, *Anderson*, 4,461 ....C-3
•Belvedere, *Aiken*, 5,631 ....G-5
Bennettsville, *Marlboro*, 9,425 ....C-12
•Berea, *Greenville*, 14,158 ....B-3
Bishopville, *Lee*, 3,670 ....E-10
Blacksburg, *Cherokee*, 1,880 ....A-6
Blackville, *Barnwell*, 2,973 ....H-7
Bluffton, *Beaufort*, 1,275 ....L-8
•Boiling Springs, *Spartanburg*, 4,544 ....A-5
Bowman, *Orangeburg*, 1,198 ....H-9
Branchville, *Orangeburg*, 1,083 ....H-8
•Brookdale, *Orangeburg*, 4,724 ....G-8
•Bucksport, *Horry*, 1,117 ....G-14
•Buffalo, *Union*, 1,426 ....C-6
Burnettown, *Aiken*, 2,720 ....G-5
•Burton, *Beaufort*, 7,180 ....K-9
Calhoun Falls, *Abbeville*, 2,303 ....E-3
Camden, *Kershaw*, 6,682 ....E-9
•Cane Savannah, *Sumter*, 1,452 ....G-1
Cayce, *Lexington*, 12,150 ....F-8
•Centerville, *Anderson*, 5,181 ....C-3
Central, *Pickens*, 3,522 ....C-2
Charleston, *Charleston*, 96,650 ....J-11
Cheraw, *Chesterfield*, 5,524 ....C-11
•Cherryvale, *Sumter*, 2,461 ....F-9
Chesnee, *Spartanburg*, 1,003 ....A-5
Chester, *Chester*, 6,476 ....C-7
Chesterfield, *Chesterfield*, 1,318 ....C-11
•City View, *Greenville*, 1,254 ....L-1
•Clearwater, *Aiken*, 4,199 ....G-5
Clemson, *Pickens*, 11,939 ....C-2
Clinton, *Laurens*, 8,091 ....D-5
Clover, *York*, 4,014 ....A-7
Columbia, *Richland*, 116,278 ....E-8
Conway, *Horry*, 11,788 ....F-14
Cowpens, *Spartanburg*, 2,279 ....B-5
•Dalzell, *Sumter*, 2,260 ....E-10
Darlington, *Darlington*, 6,720 ....D-11
Denmark, *Bamberg*, 3,328 ....H-7
•Dentsville, *Richland*, 13,009 ....E-8
Dillon, *Dillon*, 6,316 ....D-13
Due West, *Abbeville*, 1,209 ....D-4
Duncan, *Spartanburg*, 2,870 ....K-3
•Dunean, *Greenville*, 4,158 ....L-1
Easley, *Pickens*, 17,754 ....B-3
•East Gaffney, *Cherokee*, 3,349 ....A-6
•East Sumter, *Sumter*, 1,220 ....G-3
Edgefield, *Edgefield*, 4,449 ....F-5
•Edisto, *Orangeburg*, 2,632 ....G-8
•Elgin, *Lancaster*, 2,426 ....C-9
Estill, *Hampton*, 2,425 ....J-7
•Eureka Mill, *Chester*, 1,737 ....C-7
Fairfax, *Allendale*, 3,206 ....I-7
•Five Forks, *Greenville*, 8,064 ....D-13
Florence, *Florence*, 30,248 ....E-12
Folly Beach, *Charleston*, 2,116 ....K-11
Forest Acres, *Richland*, 10,558 ....I-2
•Forestbrook, *Horry*, 3,391 ....F-14
Fort Mill, *York*, 7,587 ....B-8
Fountain Inn, *Greenville*, 6,017 ....C-4
Gaffney, *Cherokee*, 12,968 ....A-6
•Gantt, *Greenville*, 13,962 ....B-4
•Garden City, *Horry*, 9,357 ....G-14
Gaston, *Lexington*, 1,304 ....F-7
•Gayle Mill, *Chester*, 1,094 ....C-7
Georgetown, *Georgetown*, 8,950 ....H-13
•Gloverville, *Aiken*, 2,805 ....G-5
•Golden Grove, *Greenville*, 2,348 ....M-1
Goose Creek, *Berkeley*, 29,208 ....I-11
Gray Court, *Laurens*, 1,021 ....C-4
Great Falls, *Chester*, 2,194 ....C-8
Greenville, *Greenville*, 56,002 ....B-4
Greenwood, *Greenwood*, 22,071 ....E-4
Greer, *Greenville*, 16,843 ....K-3
Hampton, *Hampton*, 2,837 ....J-7
Hanahan, *Berkeley*, 12,937 ....J-11
Hardeeville, *Jasper*, 1,793 ....L-8
Hartsville, *Darlington*, 7,556 ....D-11
Hilton Head Island, *Beaufort*, 33,862 ....L-9
Holly Hill, *Orangeburg*, 1,281 ....H-10
Hollywood, *Charleston*, 3,946 ....J-10
•Homeland Park, *Anderson*, 6,337 ....D-3
Honea Path, *Anderson*, 3,504 ....D-4
•India Hook, *York*, 1,614 ....B-8
Inman, *Spartanburg*, 1,884 ....A-5
•Inman Mills, *Spartanburg*, 1,151 ....A-4
Irmo, *Lexington*, 11,039 ....E-7
•Irwin, *Lancaster*, 1,343 ....C-8
Isle of Palms, *Charleston*, 4,583 ....J-12
Iva, *Anderson*, 1,156 ....D-3
Jackson, *Aiken*, 1,625 ....H-5
•Joanna, *Laurens*, 1,609 ....D-5
Johnsonville, *Florence*, 1,418 ....F-13
Johnston, *Edgefield*, 2,336 ....F-5
•Judson, *Greenville*, 2,456 ....L-1
Kershaw, *Lancaster*, 1,645 ....C-9
•Kiawah Island, *Charleston*, 1,163 ....K-11
Kingstree, *Williamsburg*, 3,496 ....G-11
•Ladson, *Charleston*, 13,264 ....I-11
Lake City, *Florence*, 6,478 ....F-12
•Lake Murray of Richland, *Richland*, 3,526 ....H-1
•Lake Wylie, *York*, 3,061 ....A-8
•Lakewood, *Sumter*, 2,603 ....H-2
Lamar, *Darlington*, 1,015 ....E-11
Lancaster, *Lancaster*, 8,177 ....C-8
•Lancaster Mill, *Lancaster*, 2,109 ....C-8
Landrum, *Spartanburg*, 2,472 ....A-4
Latta, *Dillon*, 1,410 ....D-13
•Laurel Bay, *Beaufort*, 6,625 ....K-8
Laurens, *Laurens*, 9,916 ....D-5
•Lesslie, *York*, 2,268 ....B-8
Lexington, *Lexington*, 9,793 ....F-7
Liberty, *Pickens*, 3,009 ....B-3
•Little River, *Horry*, 7,027 ....F-15
Loris, *Horry*, 2,079 ....E-14
•Lugoff, *Kershaw*, 6,278 ....E-9
Lyman, *Spartanburg*, 2,659 ....K-4
Manning, *Clarendon*, 4,025 ....G-10
Marion, *Marion*, 7,042 ....E-13
Mauldin, *Greenville*, 15,224 ....B-4
Mayesville, *Sumter*, 1,001 ....E-10
•Mayo, *Spartanburg*, 1,842 ....A-5
McColl, *Marlboro*, 2,498 ....C-12
McCormick, *McCormick*, 1,489 ....F-4
Meggett, *Charleston*, 1,230 ....J-10
•Monarch Mill, *Union*, 1,930 ....C-6
Moncks Corner, *Berkeley*, 5,952 ....I-11
Mount Pleasant, *Charleston*, 47,609 ....J-11
Mullins, *Marion*, 5,029 ....E-13
•Murphys Estates, *Edgefield*, 1,518 ....G-5
•Murrells Inlet, *Georgetown*, 5,519 ....G-14
Myrtle Beach, *Horry*, 22,759 ....G-14
New Ellenton, *Aiken*, 2,250 ....H-6
Newberry, *Newberry*, 10,580 ....D-6
•Newport, *York*, 4,033 ....B-8
Ninety Six, *Greenwood*, 1,936 ....E-5
North Augusta, *Aiken*, 17,574 ....G-5
North Charleston, *Charleston*, 79,641 ....J-11
•North Hartsville, *Darlington*, 3,136 ....D-11
North Myrtle Beach, *Horry*, 10,974 ....F-15
•Northlake, *Anderson*, 3,659 ....C-3
•Oak Grove, *Lexington*, 8,183 ....J-1
•Oakland, *Sumter*, 1,272 ....F-9
Orangeburg, *Orangeburg*, 12,765 ....G-8
Pacolet, *Spartanburg*, 2,690 ....B-6
Pageland, *Chesterfield*, 2,521 ....B-10
Pamplico, *Florence*, 1,139 ....E-12
•Parker, *Greenville*, 10,760 ....L-1
•Parris Island, *Beaufort*, 4,841 ....L-9
Pendleton, *Anderson*, 2,966 ....C-2
Pickens, *Pickens*, 3,012 ....B-3
•Piedmont, *Anderson*, 4,684 ....C-3
Pineridge, *Lexington*, 1,593 ....J-1
Port Royal, *Beaufort*, 3,950 ....L-9
•Powderville, *Anderson*, 5,362 ....M-1
•Privateer, *Sumter*, 2,118 ....F-10
Prosperity, *Newberry*, 1,047 ....E-6
Ravenel, *Charleston*, 2,214 ....J-10
•Red Bank, *Lexington*, 8,811 ....F-7
•Red Hill, *Horry*, 10,509 ....F-14
Ridgeland, *Jasper*, 2,518 ....K-8
Ridgeville, *Dorchester*, 1,690 ....I-10
Rock Hill, *York*, 49,765 ....B-8
•Roebuck, *Spartanburg*, 1,725 ....B-5
•Saint Andrews, *Richland*, 21,814 ....E-8
Saint George, *Dorchester*, 2,092 ....I-9
Saint Matthews, *Calhoun*, 2,107 ....G-8
Saint Stephen, *Berkeley*, 1,776 ....H-11
Saluda, *Saluda*, 3,066 ....E-5
•Sans Souci, *Greenville*, 7,836 ....L-1
•Saxon, *Spartanburg*, 3,707 ....B-5
Seabrook Island, *Charleston*, 1,250 ....K-10
Seneca, *Oconee*, 7,652 ....C-2
•Seven Oaks, *Lexington*, 15,755 ....I-1
•Shell Point, *Beaufort*, 2,856 ....L-9
Simpsonville, *Greenville*, 14,352 ....M-3
•Slater-Marietta, *Greenville*, 2,228 ....B-3
•Socastee, *Horry*, 14,295 ....G-14
South Congaree, *Lexington*, 2,266 ....J-1
•South Sumter, *Sumter*, 3,365 ....F-10
•Southern Shops, *Spartanburg*, 3,707 ....B-5
Spartanburg, *Spartanburg*, 39,673 ....B-5
•Springdale, *Lancaster*, 2,864 ....C-8
Springdale, *Lexington*, 2,877 ....J-1
•Stateburg, *Sumter*, 1,264 ....G-1
Sullivans Island, *Charleston*, 1,911 ....J-11
Summerton, *Clarendon*, 1,061 ....G-10
Summerville, *Dorchester*, 27,752 ....I-10
Sumter, *Sumter*, 39,643 ....F-10
Surfside Beach, *Horry*, 4,425 ....G-14
•Taylors, *Greenville*, 20,125 ....B-4
Tega Cay, *York*, 4,044 ....B-8
Timmonsville, *Florence*, 2,315 ....E-11
Travelers Rest, *Greenville*, 4,099 ....K-1
Union, *Union*, 8,793 ....C-6
•Utica, *Oconee*, 1,322 ....C-2
•Valley Falls, *Spartanburg*, 3,990 ....B-5
Varnville, *Hampton*, 2,074 ....J-8
•Wade Hampton, *Greenville*, 20,458 ....L-2
Walhalla, *Oconee*, 3,801 ....B-2
Walterboro, *Colleton*, 5,153 ....J-9
Ware Shoals, *Greenwood*, 2,363 ....D-4
•Watts Mills, *Laurens*, 1,479 ....C-5
•Wedgewood, *Sumter*, 1,544 ....H-1
•Welcome, *Greenville*, 6,390 ....L-1
Wellford, *Spartanburg*, 2,030 ....K-4
West Columbia, *Lexington*, 13,064 ....J-2
Westminster, *Oconee*, 2,743 ....C-1
Whitmire, *Newberry*, 1,512 ....D-6
•Wilkinson Heights, *Orangeburg*, 3,068 ....G-8
Williamston, *Anderson*, 3,791 ....C-3
Williston, *Barnwell*, 3,307 ....H-7
Winnsboro, *Fairfield*, 3,599 ....D-8
•Winnsboro Mills, *Fairfield*, 2,263 ....D-8
•Woodfield, *Richland*, 9,238 ....I-3
Woodruff, *Spartanburg*, 4,229 ....C-5
York, *York*, 6,985 ....B-7

Explanation of symbols: • - Census Designated Place (CDP)

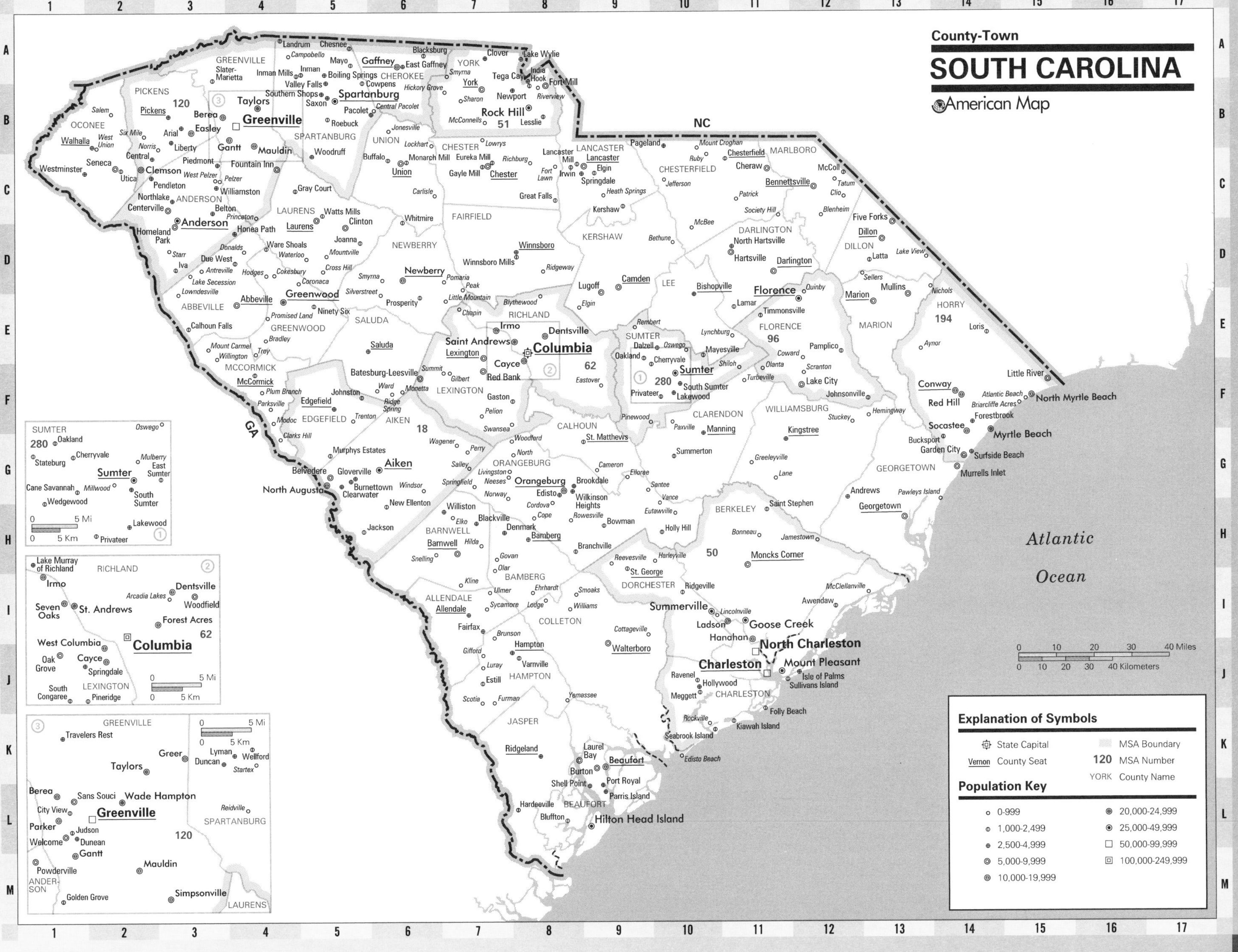
County-Town
SOUTH CAROLINA
American Map
Explanation of Symbols
State Capital
Vernon County Seat
MSA Boundary
120 MSA Number
YORK County Name
Population Key
0-999
1,000-2,499
2,500-4,999
5,000-9,999
10,000-19,999
20,000-24,999
25,000-49,999
50,000-99,999
100,000-249,999
Atlantic Ocean
NC
GA
0 10 20 30 40 Miles
0 10 20 30 40 Kilometers

SOUTH DAKOTA

COUNTIES

(66 Counties)

Name of County	Population	Location on Map
AURORA	3,058	G-12
BEADLE	17,023	E-12
BENNETT	3,574	I-5
BON HOMME	7,260	J-14
BROOKINGS	28,220	F-16
BROWN	35,460	A-12
BRULE	5,364	G-11
BUFFALO	2,032	G-11
BUTTE	9,094	D-1
CAMPBELL	1,782	B-9
CHARLES MIX	9,350	I-12
CLARK	4,143	D-14
CLAY	13,537	J-16
CODINGTON	25,897	D-15
CORSON	4,181	A-5
CUSTER	7,275	H-1
DAVISON	18,741	H-13
DEUEL	4,498	D-16
DEWEY	5,972	C-6
DOUGLAS	3,458	I-13
EDMUNDS	4,367	C-10
FALL RIVER	7,453	I-1
FAULK	2,640	C-10
GRANT	7,847	C-15
GREGORY	4,792	I-11
HAAKON	2,196	F-5
HAMLIN	5,540	E-15
HAND	3,741	E-11
HANSON	3,139	H-14
HARDING	1,353	A-1
HUGHES	16,481	F-8
HUTCHINSON	8,075	I-14
HYDE	1,671	E-10
JACKSON	2,930	H-5
JERAULD	2,295	G-12
JONES	1,193	G-7
KINGSBURY	5,815	F-14
LAKE	11,276	G-15
LAWRENCE	21,802	E-1
LINCOLN	24,131	I-16
LYMAN	3,895	G-9
MARSHALL	4,576	A-14
MCCOOK	5,832	H-15
MCPHERSON	2,904	B-10
MEADE	24,253	D-3
MELLETTE	2,083	H-7
MINER	2,884	G-14
MINNEHAHA	148,281	H-16
MOODY	6,595	G-16
PENNINGTON	88,565	G-1
PERKINS	3,363	A-4
POTTER	2,693	D-9
ROBERTS	10,016	A-15
SANBORN	2,675	G-13
SHANNON	12,466	H-4
SPINK	7,454	C-12
SPINK	7,454	B-14
STANLEY	2,772	E-7
SULLY	1,556	E-9
TODD	9,050	I-7
TRIPP	6,430	H-9
TURNER	8,849	I-15
UNION	12,584	J-16
WALWORTH	5,974	B-9
YANKTON	21,652	J-15
ZIEBACH	2,519	C-5
TOTAL	**754,844**	

CITIES AND TOWNS

Note: The first name is that of the city or town, second, that of the county in which it is located, then the population and location on the map.

Aberdeen, *Brown*, 24,658 ....C-13
Alexandria, *Hanson*, 563 ....H-14
Armour, *Douglas*, 782 ....I-13
Belle Fourche, *Butte*, 4,565 ....E-1
Beresford, *Union*, 2,006 ....J-16
Bison, *Perkins*, 373 ....B-4
•Blackhawk, *Meade*, 2,432 ....G-2
Box Elder, *Pennington*, 2,841 ....G-3
Brandon, *Minnehaha*, 5,693 ....H-17
Britton, *Marshall*, 1,328 ....B-14
Brookings, *Brookings*, 18,504 ....F-16
Buffalo, *Harding*, 380 ....B-2
Burke, *Gregory*, 676 ....J-11
Canton, *Lincoln*, 3,110 ....I-17
Chamberlain, *Brule*, 2,338 ....H-11
Clark, *Clark*, 1,285 ....D-14
Clear Lake, *Deuel*, 1,335 ....E-16
•Colonial Pine Hills, *Pennington*, 2,561 ....G-2
Custer, *Custer*, 1,860 ....H-2
De Smet, *Kingsbury*, 1,164 ....F-15
Deadwood, *Lawrence*, 1,380 ....F-2
Dell Rapids, *Minnehaha*, 2,980 ....H-16
Dupree, *Ziebach*, 434 ....D-6
Elk Point, *Union*, 1,714 ....K-17
•Ellsworth AFB, *Meade*, 4,165 ....G-3
Eureka, *McPherson*, 1,101 ....B-10
Faulkton, *Faulk*, 785 ....D-11
Flandreau, *Moody*, 2,376 ....G-17
Fort Pierre, *Stanley*, 1,991 ....F-9
•Fort Thompson, *Buffalo*, 1,375 ....G-11
Freeman, *Hutchinson*, 1,317 ....I-15
Garretson, *Minnehaha*, 1,165 ....H-17
Gettysburg, *Potter*, 1,352 ....D-10
Gregory, *Gregory*, 1,342 ....J-11
Groton, *Brown*, 1,356 ....C-13
Hartford, *Minnehaha*, 1,844 ....H-16
Hayti, *Hamlin*, 367 ....E-15
Highmore, *Hyde*, 851 ....F-11
Hot Springs, *Fall River*, 4,129 ....I-2
Howard, *Miner*, 1,071 ....G-15
Huron, *Beadle*, 11,893 ....F-13
Ipswich, *Edmunds*, 943 ....C-11
Kadoka, *Jackson*, 706 ....H-6
Kennebec, *Lyman*, 286 ....G-10
Lake Andes, *Charles Mix*, 819 ....J-13
Lead, *Lawrence*, 3,027 ....F-2
Lemmon, *Perkins*, 1,398 ....A-5
Lennox, *Lincoln*, 2,037 ....I-16
Leola, *McPherson*, 462 ....B-12
Madison, *Lake*, 6,540 ....G-16
Martin, *Bennett*, 1,106 ....J-6
McIntosh, *Corson*, 217 ....A-7
Milbank, *Grant*, 3,640 ....C-16
Miller, *Hand*, 1,530 ....F-12
Mitchell, *Davison*, 14,558 ....H-14
Mobridge, *Walworth*, 3,574 ....B-9
Mound City, *Campbell*, 84 ....B-9
Murdo, *Jones*, 612 ....H-8
•North Eagle Butte, *Dewey*, 2,163 ....D-7
North Sioux City, *Union*, 2,288 ....K-17
•North Spearfish, *Lawrence*, 2,306 ....E-1
•Oglala, *Shannon*, 1,229 ....J-4
Olivet, *Hutchinson*, 70 ....I-14
Onida, *Sully*, 740 ....E-9
Parker, *Turner*, 1,031 ....I-16
Parkston, *Hutchinson*, 1,674 ....I-14
Philip, *Haakon*, 885 ....G-6
Pierre, *Hughes*, 13,876 ....F-9
•Pine Ridge, *Shannon*, 3,171 ....J-4
Plankinton, *Aurora*, 601 ....H-13
Platte, *Charles Mix*, 1,367 ....I-12
Rapid City, *Pennington*, 59,607 ....G-3
•Rapid Valley, *Pennington*, 7,043 ....G-3
Redfield, *Spink*, 2,897 ....D-13
•Rosebud, *Todd*, 1,557 ....I-8
Salem, *McCook*, 1,371 ....H-15
Selby, *Walworth*, 736 ....C-9
Sioux Falls, *Minnehaha*, 123,975 ....H-16
Sisseton, *Roberts*, 2,572 ....B-16
Spearfish, *Lawrence*, 8,606 ....F-1
Sturgis, *Meade*, 6,442 ....F-2
Tea, *Lincoln*, 1,742 ....I-16
Timber Lake, *Dewey*, 443 ....C-7
Tyndall, *Bon Homme*, 1,239 ....J-14
Vermillion, *Clay*, 9,765 ....K-16
Volga, *Brookings*, 1,435 ....F-16
Wagner, *Charles Mix*, 1,675 ....J-13
Watertown, *Codington*, 20,237 ....D-15
Webster, *Day*, 1,952 ....C-15
Wessington Springs, *Jerauld*, 1,011 ....G-13
White River, *Mellette*, 598 ....H-8
Winner, *Tripp*, 3,137 ....I-10
Woonsocket, *Sanborn*, 720 ....G-13
Yankton, *Yankton*, 13,528 ....J-15

Explanation of symbols: • - Census Designated Place (CDP)

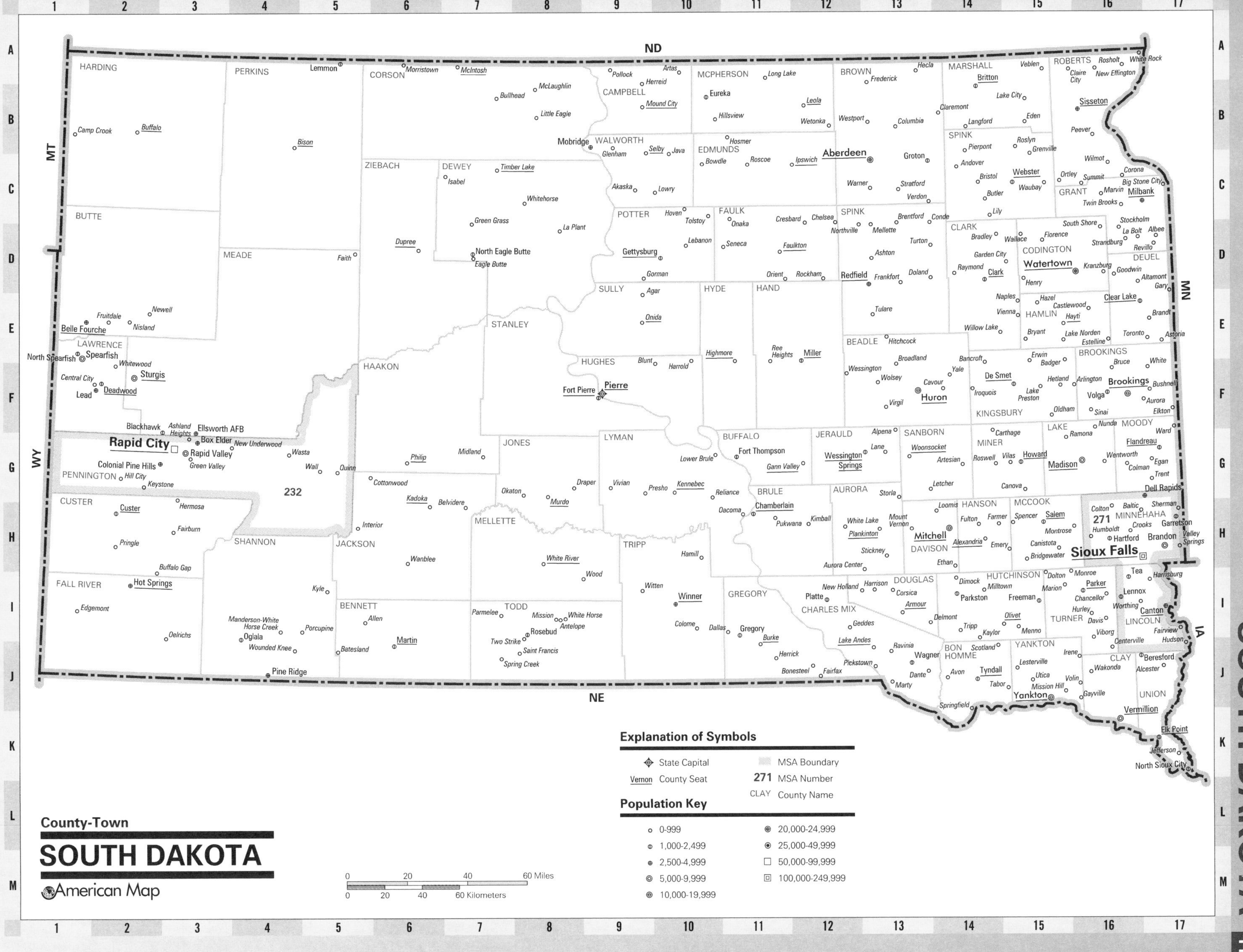
County-Town
SOUTH DAKOTA
American Map
Explanation of Symbols
State Capital
Vernon County Seat
MSA Boundary
271 MSA Number
CLAY County Name
Population Key
0-999
1,000-2,499
2,500-4,999
5,000-9,999
10,000-19,999
20,000-24,999
25,000-49,999
50,000-99,999
100,000-249,999
0 20 40 60 Miles
0 20 40 60 Kilometers
ND
MN
IA
NE
WY
MT
HARDING
PERKINS
CORSON
CAMPBELL
MCPHERSON
BROWN
MARSHALL
ROBERTS
BUTTE
MEADE
ZIEBACH
DEWEY
WALWORTH
EDMUNDS
SPINK
GRANT
LAWRENCE
POTTER
FAULK
CLARK
CODINGTON
DEUEL
SULLY
HYDE
HAND
HAMLIN
STANLEY
HUGHES
BEADLE
BROOKINGS
HAAKON
KINGSBURY
MOODY
PENNINGTON
JONES
LYMAN
BUFFALO
JERAULD
SANBORN
MINER
LAKE
CUSTER
MELLETTE
BRULE
AURORA
HANSON
MCCOOK
MINNEHAHA
SHANNON
JACKSON
TRIPP
DAVISON
FALL RIVER
BENNETT
TODD
GREGORY
CHARLES MIX
DOUGLAS
HUTCHINSON
TURNER
LINCOLN
BON HOMME
YANKTON
CLAY
UNION
Pierre
Fort Pierre
Rapid City
Sioux Falls
Aberdeen
Watertown
Brookings
Huron
Mitchell
Yankton
232
271

TENNESSEE

COUNTIES

(95 Counties)

Name of County	Population	Location on Map
ANDERSON	71,330	C-17
BEDFORD	37,586	E-11
BENTON	16,537	C-7
BLEDSOE	12,367	E-15
BLOUNT	105,823	K-2
BRADLEY	87,965	G-15
CAMPBELL	39,854	B-17
CANNON	12,826	D-12
CARROLL	29,475	C-5
CARTER	56,742	I-7
CHEATHAM	35,912	B-9
CHESTER	15,540	F-5
CLAIBORNE	29,862	H-2
CLAY	7,976	B-14
COCKE	33,565	J-4
COFFEE	48,014	F-12
CROCKETT	14,532	D-3
CUMBERLAND	46,802	C-15
DAVIDSON	569,891	C-10
DE KALB	17,423	D-13
DECATUR	11,731	D-7
DICKSON	43,156	D-8
DYER	37,279	C-3
FAYETTE	28,806	F-3
FENTRESS	16,625	B-15
FRANKLIN	39,270	G-12
GIBSON	48,152	C-4
GILES	29,447	F-9
GRAINGER	20,659	I-3
GREENE	62,909	I-5
GRUNDY	14,332	E-13
HAMBLEN	58,128	I-3
HAMILTON	307,896	F-15
HANCOCK	6,786	H-3
HARDEMAN	28,105	F-4
HARDIN	25,578	F-7
HAWKINS	53,563	H-4
HAYWOOD	19,797	E-3
HENDERSON	25,522	E-6
HENRY	31,115	B-6
HICKMAN	22,295	D-8
HOUSTON	8,088	C-7
HUMPHREYS	17,929	C-7
JACKSON	10,984	B-13
JEFFERSON	44,294	J-3
JOHNSON	17,499	H-7
KNOX	382,032	J-2
LAKE	7,954	B-3
LAUDERDALE	27,101	E-2
LAWRENCE	39,926	F-8
LEWIS	11,367	E-8
LINCOLN	31,340	F-10
LOUDON	39,086	E-17
MACON	20,386	B-12
MADISON	91,837	E-4
MARION	27,776	F-13
MARSHALL	26,767	F-10
MAURY	69,498	E-9
MCMINN	49,015	F-16
MCNAIRY	24,653	F-5
MEIGS	11,086	F-15
MONROE	38,961	E-17
MONTGOMERY	134,768	B-8
MOORE	5,740	F-11
MORGAN	19,757	C-16
OBION	32,450	B-4
OVERTON	20,118	B-14
PERRY	7,631	E-7
PICKETT	4,945	B-15
POLK	16,050	F-16
PUTNAM	62,315	C-14
RHEA	28,400	E-15
ROANE	51,910	D-16
ROBERTSON	54,433	B-10
RUTHERFORD	182,023	D-11
SCOTT	21,127	B-16
SEQUATCHIE	11,370	F-14
SEVIER	71,170	K-3
SHELBY	897,472	F-2
SMITH	17,712	C-12
STEWART	12,370	B-7
SULLIVAN	153,048	H-5
SUMNER	130,449	B-11
TIPTON	51,271	E-3
TROUSDALE	7,259	B-12
UNICOI	17,667	I-6
UNION	17,808	I-2
VAN BUREN	5,508	E-14
WARREN	38,276	D-13
WASHINGTON	107,198	I-5
WAYNE	16,842	F-7
WEAKLEY	34,895	B-5
WHITE	23,102	C-14
WILLIAMSON	126,638	D-9
WILSON	88,809	C-12
TOTAL	**5,689,283**	

CITIES AND TOWNS

Note: The first name is that of the city or town, second, that of the county in which it is located, then the population and location on the map.

Adamsville, *McNairy,* 1,983 ... F-6
Alamo, *Crockett,* 2,392 ... D-4
Alcoa, *Blount,* 7,734 ... K-2
Algood, *Putnam,* 2,942 ... C-14
Altamont, *Grundy,* 1,136 ... F-13
Ardmore, *Giles,* 1,082 ... G-10
Arlington, *Shelby,* 2,569 ... F-2
Ashland City, *Cheatham,* 3,641 ... C-10
Athens, *McMinn,* 13,220 ... E-16
Atoka, *Tipton,* 3,235 ... E-2
Atwood, *Carroll,* 1,000 ... D-5
•Banner Hill, *Unicoi,* 1,053 ... I-6
Bartlett, *Shelby,* 40,543 ... F-2
Baxter, *Putnam,* 1,279 ... C-13
Belle Meade, *Davidson,* 2,943 ... C-10
Bells, *Crockett,* 2,171 ... E-4
Benton, *Polk,* 1,138 ... F-16
Blaine, *Grainger,* 1,585 ... I-3
•Bloomingdale, *Sullivan,* 10,350 ... H-6
•Blountville, *Sullivan,* 2,959 ... H-6
Bluff City, *Sullivan,* 1,559 ... H-6
Bolivar, *Hardeman,* 5,802 ... F-4
Bradford, *Gibson,* 1,113 ... C-5
Brentwood, *Williamson,* 23,445 ... C-10
Brighton, *Tipton,* 1,719 ... E-2
Bristol, *Sullivan,* 24,821 ... H-7
Brownsville, *Haywood,* 10,748 ... E-4
Bruceton, *Carroll,* 1,554 ... C-6
Burns, *Dickson,* 1,366 ... C-9
Byrdstown, *Pickett,* 903 ... B-15
Camden, *Benton,* 3,828 ... C-7
Carthage, *Smith,* 2,251 ... C-13
Caryville, *Campbell,* 2,243 ... B-17
Celina, *Clay,* 1,379 ... B-14
Centerville, *Hickman,* 3,793 ... D-9
•Central, *Carter,* 2,717 ... I-6
Charlotte, *Dickson,* 1,153 ... C-9
Chattanooga, *Hamilton,* 155,554 ... G-14
Church Hill, *Hawkins,* 5,916 ... H-5
Clarksville, *Montgomery,* 103,455 ... B-9
Cleveland, *Bradley,* 37,192 ... F-16
Clifton, *Wayne,* 2,699 ... F-7
Clinton, *Anderson,* 9,409 ... I-1
Collegedale, *Hamilton,* 6,514 ... G-15
Collierville, *Shelby,* 31,872 ... G-2
Collinwood, *Wayne,* 1,024 ... F-8
•Colonial Heights, *Sullivan,* 7,067 ... L-7
Columbia, *Maury,* 33,055 ... E-10
Cookeville, *Putnam,* 23,923 ... C-14
Coopertown, *Robertson,* 3,027 ... B-10
Covington, *Tipton,* 8,463 ... E-3
Cowan, *Franklin,* 1,770 ... F-13
Cross Plains, *Robertson,* 1,381 ... B-11
Crossville, *Cumberland,* 8,981 ... D-15
Crump, *Hardin,* 1,521 ... F-6
Dandridge, *Jefferson,* 2,078 ... J-3
Dayton, *Rhea,* 6,180 ... E-15
Decatur, *Meigs,* 1,395 ... E-16
Decaturville, *Decatur,* 859 ... E-7
Decherd, *Franklin,* 2,246 ... F-12
Dickson, *Dickson,* 12,244 ... C-9
Dover, *Stewart,* 1,442 ... B-8
Dresden, *Weakley,* 2,855 ... C-5
Dunlap, *Sequatchie,* 4,173 ... F-14
Dyer, *Gibson,* 2,406 ... C-4
Dyersburg, *Dyer,* 17,452 ... C-3
•Eagleton Village, *Blount,* 4,883 ... J-2
•East Brainerd, *Hamilton,* 14,132 ... G-15
•East Cleveland, *Bradley,* 1,729 ... F-16
East Ridge, *Hamilton,* 20,640 ... M-9
Elizabethton, *Carter,* 13,372 ... I-7
Englewood, *McMinn,* 1,590 ... E-17
Erin, *Houston,* 1,490 ... B-8
Erwin, *Unicoi,* 5,610 ... I-6
Estill Springs, *Franklin,* 2,152 ... F-12
Etowah, *McMinn,* 3,663 ... F-17
•Fairfield Glade, *Cumberland,* 4,885 ... D-16
•Fairmount, *Hamilton,* 2,600 ... K-9
Fairview, *Williamson,* 5,800 ... D-9
•Fall Branch, *Washington,* 1,313 ... H-5
Farragut, *Knox,* 17,720 ... J-1
Fayetteville, *Lincoln,* 6,994 ... G-11
Forest Hills, *Davidson,* 4,710 ... C-10
Franklin, *Williamson,* 41,842 ... D-10
Gainesboro, *Jackson,* 879 ... B-13
Gallatin, *Sumner,* 23,230 ... B-11
Gatlinburg, *Sevier,* 3,382 ... K-3
Germantown, *Shelby,* 37,348 ... G-2
Gleason, *Weakley,* 1,463 ... C-5
Goodlettsville, *Davidson,* 13,780 ... B-11
Gordonsville, *Smith,* 1,066 ... C-13
•Gray, *Washington,* 1,273 ... H-6
Graysville, *Rhea,* 1,411 ... E-15
•Green Hill, *Wilson,* 7,068 ... C-11
Greenbrier, *Robertson,* 4,940 ... B-10
Greeneville, *Greene,* 15,198 ... I-5
Greenfield, *Weakley,* 2,208 ... C-5
Gruetli-Laager, *Grundy,* 1,867 ... F-14
Halls, *Lauderdale,* 2,311 ... D-3
Harriman, *Roane,* 6,744 ... D-16
•Harrison, *Hamilton,* 7,630 ... L-10
•Harrogate-Shawanee, *Claiborne,* 2,865 ... H-3
Hartsville, *Trousdale,* 2,395 ... B-12
Henderson, *Chester,* 5,670 ... F-5
Hendersonville, *Sumner,* 40,620 ... C-11
Hickory Withe, *Fayette,* 2,574 ... F-3
Hohenwald, *Lewis,* 3,754 ... E-8
•Hopewell, *Bradley,* 1,815 ... F-16
Humboldt, *Gibson,* 9,467 ... D-5
•Hunter, *Carter,* 1,566 ... H-7
Huntingdon, *Carroll,* 4,349 ... D-6
Huntsville, *Scott,* 981 ... B-17
Jacksboro, *Campbell,* 1,887 ... B-17
Jackson, *Madison,* 59,643 ... E-5
Jamestown, *Fentress,* 1,839 ... B-15
Jasper, *Marion,* 3,214 ... G-14
Jefferson City, *Jefferson,* 7,760 ... I-3
Jellico, *Campbell,* 2,448 ... H-1
Johnson City, *Washington,* 55,469 ... I-6
Jonesborough, *Washington,* 4,168 ... I-6
Kenton, *Obion,* 1,306 ... C-4
Kimball, *Marion,* 1,312 ... G-13
Kingsport, *Sullivan,* 44,905 ... H-6
Kingston, *Roane,* 5,264 ... D-17
Kingston Springs, *Cheatham,* 2,773 ... C-9
Knoxville, *Knox,* 173,890 ... J-2
La Follette, *Campbell,* 7,926 ... H-1
La Vergne, *Rutherford,* 18,687 ... D-11
Lafayette, *Macon,* 3,885 ... B-12
Lake City, *Anderson,* 1,888 ... I-1
•Lake Tansi, *Cumberland,* 2,621 ... D-15
Lakeland, *Shelby,* 6,862 ... F-2
Lakesite, *Hamilton,* 1,845 ... F-15
Lakewood, *Davidson,* 2,341 ... C-11
Lawrenceburg, *Lawrence,* 10,796 ... F-9
Lebanon, *Wilson,* 20,235 ... C-12
Lenoir City, *Loudon,* 6,819 ... D-17
Lewisburg, *Marshall,* 10,413 ... F-10
Lexington, *Henderson,* 7,393 ... E-6
Linden, *Perry,* 1,015 ... E-7
Livingston, *Overton,* 3,498 ... B-14
Lookout Mountain, *Hamilton,* 2,000 ... M-8
Loretto, *Lawrence,* 1,665 ... G-9
Loudon, *Loudon,* 4,476 ... D-17
Louisville, *Blount,* 2,001 ... J-2
Lynchburg, *Moore,* 5,740 ... F-12
Madisonville, *Monroe,* 3,939 ... E-17
Manchester, *Coffee,* 8,294 ... E-12
Martin, *Weakley,* 10,515 ... B-5
Maryville, *Blount,* 23,120 ... K-2
•Mascot, *Knox,* 2,119 ... J-2
Mason, *Tipton,* 1,089 ... F-3
Maynardville, *Union,* 1,782 ... I-2
McEwen, *Humphreys,* 1,702 ... C-8
McKenzie, *Carroll,* 5,295 ... C-6
McMinnville, *Warren,* 12,749 ... E-13
Memphis, *Shelby,* 650,100 ... F-1
•Middle Valley, *Hamilton,* 11,854 ... K-10
Midtown, *Roane,* 1,306 ... D-16
•Midway, *Washington,* 2,491 ... M-8
Milan, *Gibson,* 7,664 ... D-5
Millersville, *Sumner,* 5,308 ... B-11
Millington, *Shelby,* 10,433 ... F-2
Monteagle, *Marion,* 1,238 ... F-13
Monterey, *Putnam,* 2,717 ... C-15
Morristown, *Hamblen,* 24,965 ... I-4
Mosheim, *Greene,* 1,749 ... I-5
Mount Carmel, *Hawkins,* 4,795 ... H-5
Mount Juliet, *Wilson,* 12,366 ... C-11
Mount Pleasant, *Maury,* 4,491 ... E-9
Mountain City, *Johnson,* 2,383 ... H-8
Munford, *Tipton,* 4,708 ... E-2
Murfreesboro, *Rutherford,* 68,816 ... D-11
Nashville, *Davidson,* 569,891 ... C-10
New Hope, *Marion,* 1,043 ... G-14
New Johnsonville, *Humphreys,* 1,905 ... D-7
New Market, *Jefferson,* 1,234 ... I-3
New Tazewell, *Claiborne,* 2,871 ... H-3
Newbern, *Dyer,* 2,988 ... C-4
Newport, *Cocke,* 7,242 ... J-4
Nolensville, *Williamson,* 3,099 ... D-11
Norris, *Anderson,* 1,446 ... I-2
•Oak Grove, *Sumner,* 4,072 ... L-8
Oak Hill, *Davidson,* 4,493 ... C-10
Oak Ridge, *Anderson,* 27,387 ... C-17
Oakland, *Fayette,* 1,279 ... F-3
Obion, *Obion,* 1,134 ... C-4
Oliver Springs, *Roane,* 3,303 ... C-17
Oneida, *Scott,* 3,615 ... B-17
•Ooltewah, *Hamilton,* 5,681 ... G-15
Paris, *Henry,* 9,763 ... C-6
Parsons, *Decatur,* 2,452 ... E-7
Pegram, *Cheatham,* 2,146 ... C-10
Pigeon Forge, *Sevier,* 5,083 ... K-3
Pikeville, *Bledsoe,* 1,781 ... E-15
•Pine Crest, *Carter,* 2,872 ... I-6
Plainview, *Union,* 1,866 ... I-2
Pleasant View, *Cheatham,* 2,934 ... B-10
Portland, *Sumner,* 8,458 ... B-11
Powells Crossroads, *Marion,* 1,286 ... F-14
Pulaski, *Giles,* 7,871 ... F-10
Red Bank, *Hamilton,* 12,418 ... L-9
Red Boiling Springs, *Macon,* 1,023 ... B-13
Ridgely, *Lake,* 1,667 ... C-3
Ridgetop, *Robertson,* 1,083 ... B-10
Ripley, *Lauderdale,* 7,844 ... D-3
•Roan Mountain, *Carter,* 1,160 ... I-7
Rockwood, *Roane,* 5,774 ... D-16
Rogersville, *Hawkins,* 4,240 ... H-4
•Rural Hill, *Wilson,* 2,032 ... C-11
Rutherford, *Gibson,* 1,272 ... C-4
Rutledge, *Grainger,* 1,187 ... I-3
Savannah, *Hardin,* 6,917 ... F-6
Selmer, *McNairy,* 4,541 ... F-5
Sevierville, *Sevier,* 11,757 ... J-3
•Sewanee, *Franklin,* 2,361 ... F-13
•Seymour, *Sevier,* 8,850 ... J-2
Shelbyville, *Bedford,* 16,105 ... E-11
Signal Mountain, *Hamilton,* 7,429 ... L-8
Smithville, *Dekalb,* 3,994 ... D-13
Smyrna, *Rutherford,* 25,569 ... D-11
Sneedville, *Hancock,* 1,257 ... H-4
Soddy-Daisy, *Hamilton,* 11,530 ... F-15
Somerville, *Fayette,* 2,519 ... F-3
South Carthage, *Smith,* 1,302 ... C-13
•South Cleveland, *Bradley,* 6,216 ... G-16
South Fulton, *Obion,* 2,517 ... B-5
South Pittsburg, *Marion,* 3,295 ... G-13
Sparta, *White,* 4,599 ... D-14
Spencer, *Van Buren,* 1,713 ... D-14
Spring City, *Rhea,* 2,025 ... E-16
Spring Hill, *Maury,* 7,715 ... D-10
Springfield, *Robertson,* 14,329 ... B-10
•Spurgeon, *Washington,* 3,460 ... H-6
Surgoinsville, *Hawkins,* 1,484 ... H-5
Sweetwater, *Monroe,* 5,586 ... E-17
Tazewell, *Claiborne,* 2,165 ... H-3
Tennessee Ridge, *Houston,* 1,334 ... B-8
Thompsons Station, *Williamson,* 1,283 ... D-10
Three Way, *Madison,* 1,375 ... D-5
Tiptonville, *Lake,* 2,439 ... B-3
Tracy City, *Grundy,* 1,679 ... F-13
Trenton, *Gibson,* 4,683 ... D-4
Troy, *Obion,* 1,273 ... B-4
Tullahoma, *Coffee,* 17,994 ... F-12
Tusculum, *Greene,* 2,004 ... I-5
Unicoi, *Unicoi,* 3,519 ... I-6
Union City, *Obion,* 10,876 ... B-4
Vonore, *Monroe,* 1,162 ... E-17
Walden, *Hamilton,* 1,960 ... L-9
•Walnut Hill, *Sullivan,* 2,756 ... H-6
•Walterhill, *Rutherford,* 1,523 ... D-11
Wartburg, *Morgan,* 890 ... C-16
Watertown, *Wilson,* 1,358 ... C-12
Waverly, *Humphreys,* 4,028 ... C-8
Waynesboro, *Wayne,* 2,228 ... F-8
Westmoreland, *Sumner,* 2,093 ... B-12
White Bluff, *Dickson,* 2,142 ... C-9
White House, *Sumner,* 7,220 ... B-11
White Pine, *Jefferson,* 1,997 ... I-4
Whiteville, *Hardeman,* 3,148 ... F-4
Whitwell, *Marion,* 1,660 ... F-14
•Wildwood Lake, *Bradley,* 3,050 ... L-12
Winchester, *Franklin,* 7,329 ... F-12
Woodbury, *Cannon,* 2,428 ... D-12

Explanation of symbols: • - Census Designated Place (CDP)

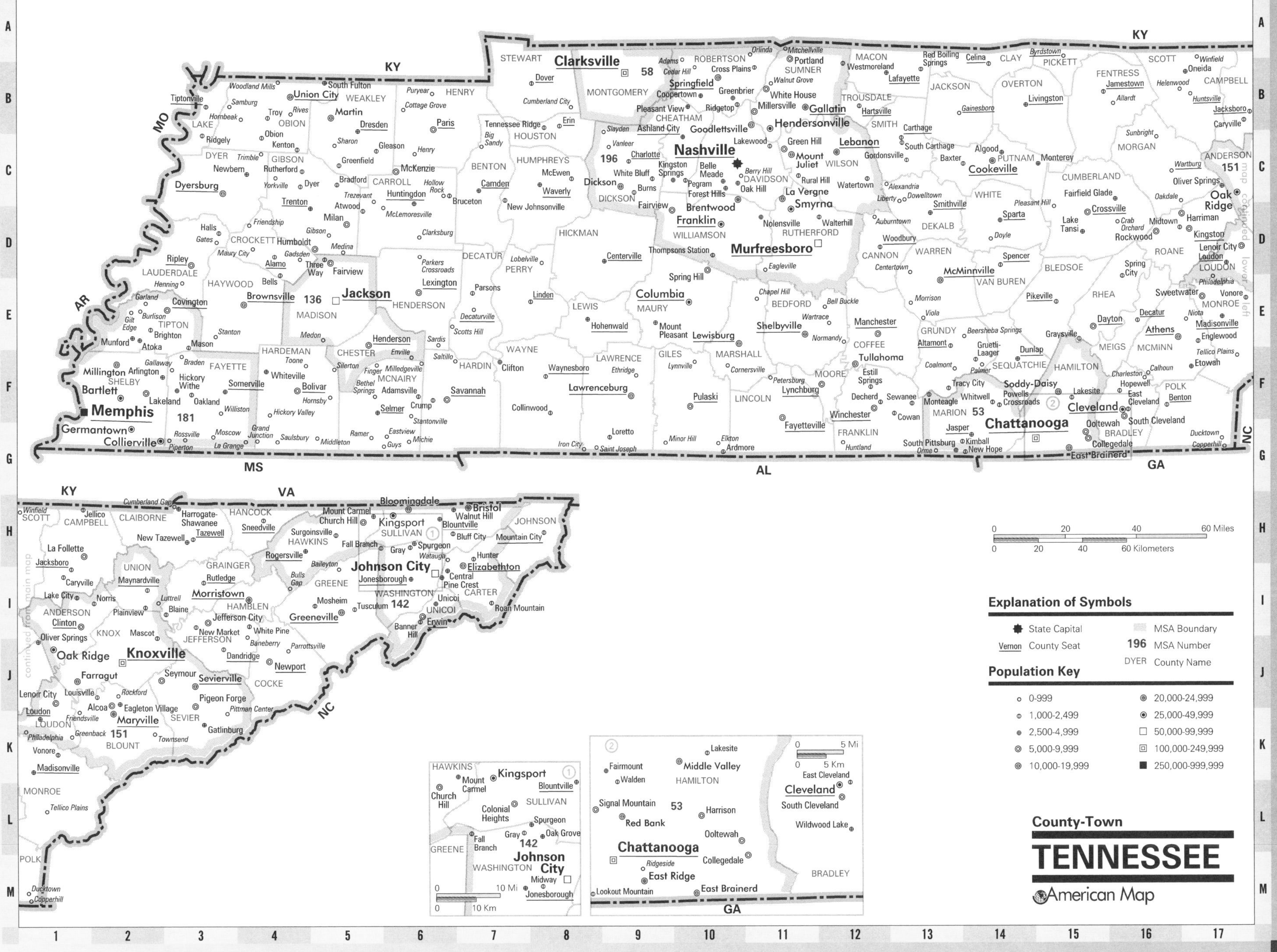
County-Town
TENNESSEE
American Map
Explanation of Symbols
State Capital
Vernon County Seat
MSA Boundary
196 MSA Number
DYER County Name
Population Key
0-999
1,000-2,499
2,500-4,999
5,000-9,999
10,000-19,999
20,000-24,999
25,000-49,999
50,000-99,999
100,000-249,999
250,000-999,999
0 20 40 60 Miles
0 20 40 60 Kilometers
map continued lower left
continued from main map

1 2 3 4 5 6 7 8 9 10 11 12 13

A B C D E F G H I J K L M N O P Q

OK
NM
DALLAM Texline
Texhoma Stratford SHERMAN
HANSFORD Gruver Spearman
Perryton Booker Darrouzett Follett
LIPSCOMB Lipscomb Higgins
Dalhart
Morse OCHILTREE
HARTLEY Hartley Channing
Cactus Sunray Dumas MOORE
HUTCHIN-SON Stinnett
ROBERTS
HEMPHILL Canadian
Sanford Fritch Borger Miami
OLDHAM
POTTER 9
Skellytown CARSON White Deer Panhandle
Pampa Lefors
WHEELER Mobeetie Wheeler
Adrian Vega Bishop Hills Amarillo Groom GRAY McLean Shamrock
DEAF SMITH Lake Tanglewood Timbercreek Canyon Palisades
Claude DONLEY Howardwick Clarendon Hedley
COLLINGS-WORTH Samnorwood Quail Wellington Dodson
Canyon Hereford RANDALL ARMSTRONG
PARMER Friona Bovina Farwell
CASTRO Dimmitt Nazareth
Happy Tulia SWISHER Kress Hart
BRISCOE Silverton Quitaque
Lakeview HALL Turkey Memphis Estelline
CHILD-RESS Childress
continued from main map

Friona CASTRO PARMER Bovina Dimmitt Farwell
map continued top left
Nazareth Tulia BRISCOE Silverton Quitaque
Hart SWISHER Kress
HALL Lakeview CHILDRESS Estelline Turkey Childress
Earth Springlake Edmonson
Muleshoe BAILEY
LAMB Olton Sudan Amherst Littlefield
HALE Plainview Seth Ward Hale Center
FLOYD Lockney Floydada
MOTLEY Matador Roaring Springs
COTTLE Paducah
COCHRAN Morton Whiteface
Anton HOCKLEY Shallowater Levelland Sundown
Abernathy Petersburg LUBBOCK Idalou Lorenzo CROSBY Ralls Crosbyton
Wolfforth Lubbock 173 Slaton 1
DICKENS Dickens Spur
KING Guthrie
YOAKUM Plains TERRY Brownfield Tahoka Post
Denver City Wellman LYNN O'Donnell GARZA
KENT Girard Jayton
STONEWALL Aspermont
GAINES Seagraves Seminole
DAWSON Lamesa Los Ybanez Ackerly
BORDEN Gail
SCURRY Snyder Hermleigh
Rotan Roby Hamlin
FISHER
ANDREWS Andrews
MARTIN Stanton
HOWARD Big Spring Coahoma Forsan Westbrook
Loraine Sweetwater Roscoe Colorado City Trent Merkel
NOLAN Blackwell MITCHELL
Anthony EL PASO 83 Canutillo Fort Bliss El Paso Socorro Horizon City San Elizario Fabens Tornillo 2
Dell City
CULBERSON
HUDSPETH
Fort Hancock
Sierra Blanca
Van Horn
LOVING Mentone
WINKLER Kermit Wink
Gardendale Goldsmith ECTOR West Odessa
207 Midland MIDLAND Odessa
GLASSCOCK Garden City
STERLING Sterling City
Robert Lee COKE
Winters Bronte
REEVES Pecos Toyah Lindsay Balmorhea
WARD Wickett Barstow Pyote Monahans Thorntonville Grandfalls
Crane CRANE Imperial Coyanosa
UPTON Rankin McCamey
REAGAN Big Lake
IRION Mertzon
Grape Creek 252 San Angelo TOM GREEN Christoval Miles
JEFF DAVIS
PECOS Fort Stockton
CROCKETT Iraan Ozona
SCHLEICHER Eldorado
SUTTON Sonora
Valentine Fort Davis
PRESIDIO Marfa
Alpine BREWSTER Marathon
TERRELL Sanderson
VAL VERDE
EDWARDS Rocksprings
Camp Wood
Presidio Redford
Study Butte-Terlingua
MEXICO
Box Canyon-Amistad Lake View
Cienegas Terrace Val Verde Park Del Rio Laughlin AFB
KINNEY Brackettville Spofford
MAVERICK Quemado Radar Base
Elm Creek Las Quintas Fonterizas Eagle Pass Rosita North Eidson Road Rosita South El Indio

Spade Littlefield HALE Petersburg FLOYD 1
LAMB
Anton Abernathy HOCKLEY LUBBOCK New Deal CROSBY
Shallowater Idalou Ralls Lorenzo Crosbyton
Opdyke West Smyer Reese Village Lubbock Levelland
Ransom Canyon Wolfforth
Ropesville 173 Slaton
Meadow TERRY LYNN New Home Wilson GARZA Pleasant Valley
Brownfield Tahoka Post
0 10 Mi
0 10 Km

NM
Anthony Vinton Westway 83 EL PASO 2 Canutillo
Homestead Meadows North HUDSPETH
Prado Verde Butterfield
Fort Bliss El Paso Homestead Meadows South
MEXICO Horizon City Socorro Agua Dulce
San Elizario Clint Morning Glory Fabens Tornillo
0 10 Mi
0 10 Km

County-Town
TEXAS
(WEST)
American Map

0 20 40 60 80 Miles
0 20 40 60 80 Kilometers

Explanation of Symbols

State Capital
Vernon County Seat
MSA Boundary
129 MSA Number
HOOD County Name

Population Key

0-999
1,000-2,499
2,500-4,999
5,000-9,999
10,000-19,999
20,000-24,999
25,000-49,999
50,000-99,999
100,000-249,999
250,000-999,999
1,000,000+

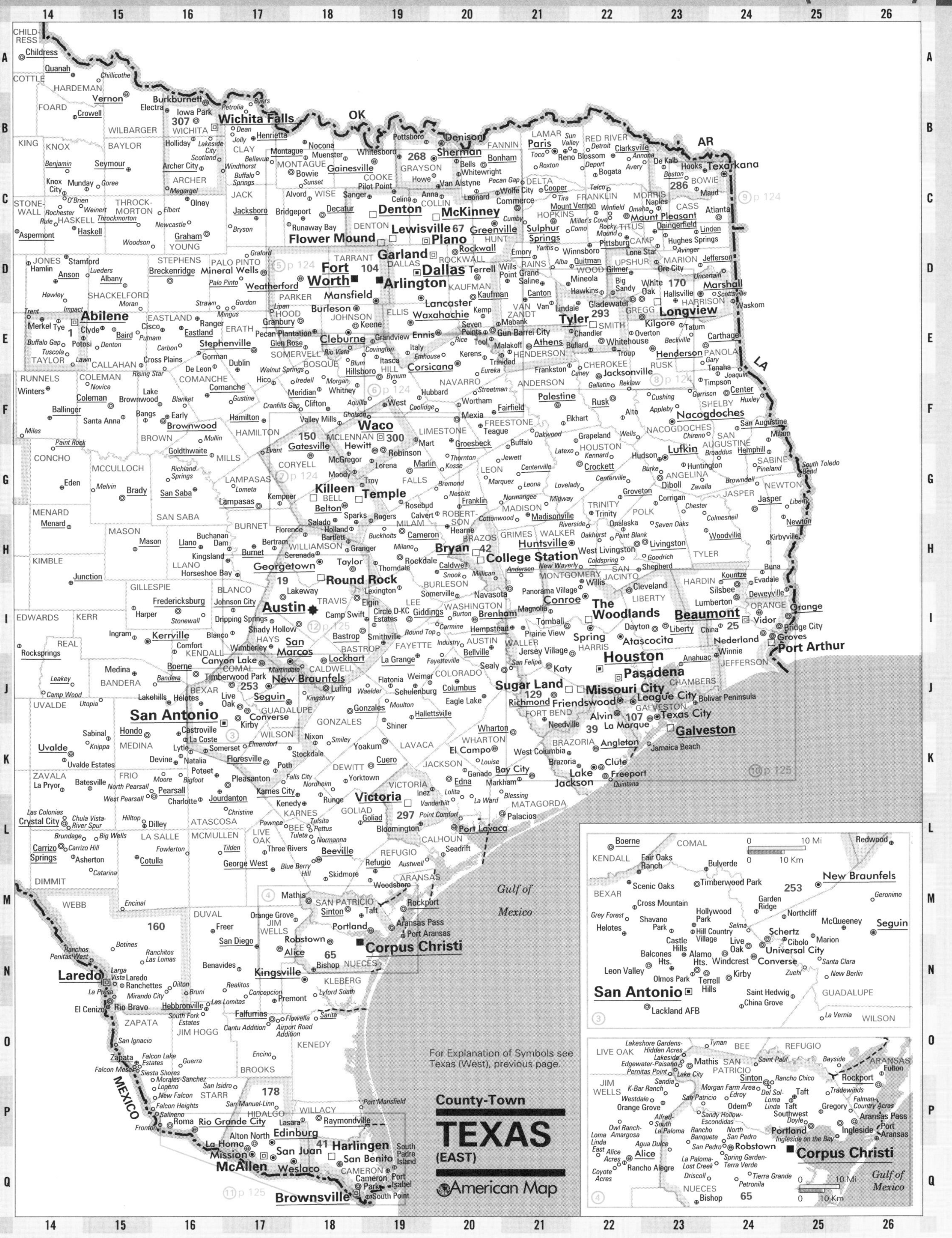
County-Town
TEXAS
(EAST)
American Map
For Explanation of Symbols see Texas (West), previous page.
OK
AR
LA
MEXICO
Gulf of Mexico
Wichita Falls
Sherman
Denison
Paris
Texarkana
Denton
McKinney
Lewisville
Plano
Flower Mound
Garland
Fort Worth
Dallas
Arlington
Mansfield
Lancaster
Waxahachie
Tyler
Longview
Marshall
Abilene
Cleburne
Corsicana
Palestine
Nacogdoches
Lufkin
Waco
Killeen
Temple
Belton
Bryan
College Station
Huntsville
Georgetown
Round Rock
Austin
San Marcos
New Braunfels
Seguin
San Antonio
Conroe
The Woodlands
Beaumont
Port Arthur
Orange
Houston
Pasadena
Baytown
Sugar Land
Missouri City
League City
Texas City
Galveston
Victoria
Port Lavaca
Corpus Christi
Kingsville
Laredo
McAllen
Edinburg
Mission
Harlingen
San Benito
Brownsville
South Padre Island
Port Isabel
San Juan
Weslaco
Rio Grande City
Beeville
Alice
Uvalde
Kerrville
Fredericksburg
Bastrop
Lockhart
Gonzales
Brenham
Navasota
Angleton
Freeport
Lake Jackson
Bay City
El Campo
Wharton
Rockport
Aransas Pass
Portland
Robstown
Sinton
Boerne
Schertz
Universal City
Converse
Lackland AFB
Jasper
Newton
Livingston
Woodville
Crockett
Jacksonville
Athens
Kaufman
Terrell
Rockwall
Greenville
Sulphur Springs
Mount Pleasant
Gainesville
Decatur
Weatherford
Granbury
Stephenville
Brownwood
Lampasas
Gatesville
Hillsboro
Mexia
Fairfield
Seguin
Hondo
Pleasanton
Cotulla
Carrizo Springs
Crystal City
Del Rio
Eagle Pass
Zapata
Hebbronville
Falfurrias
Raymondville
Port Mansfield
Jamaica Beach
Bolivar Peninsula
Lake Sabine

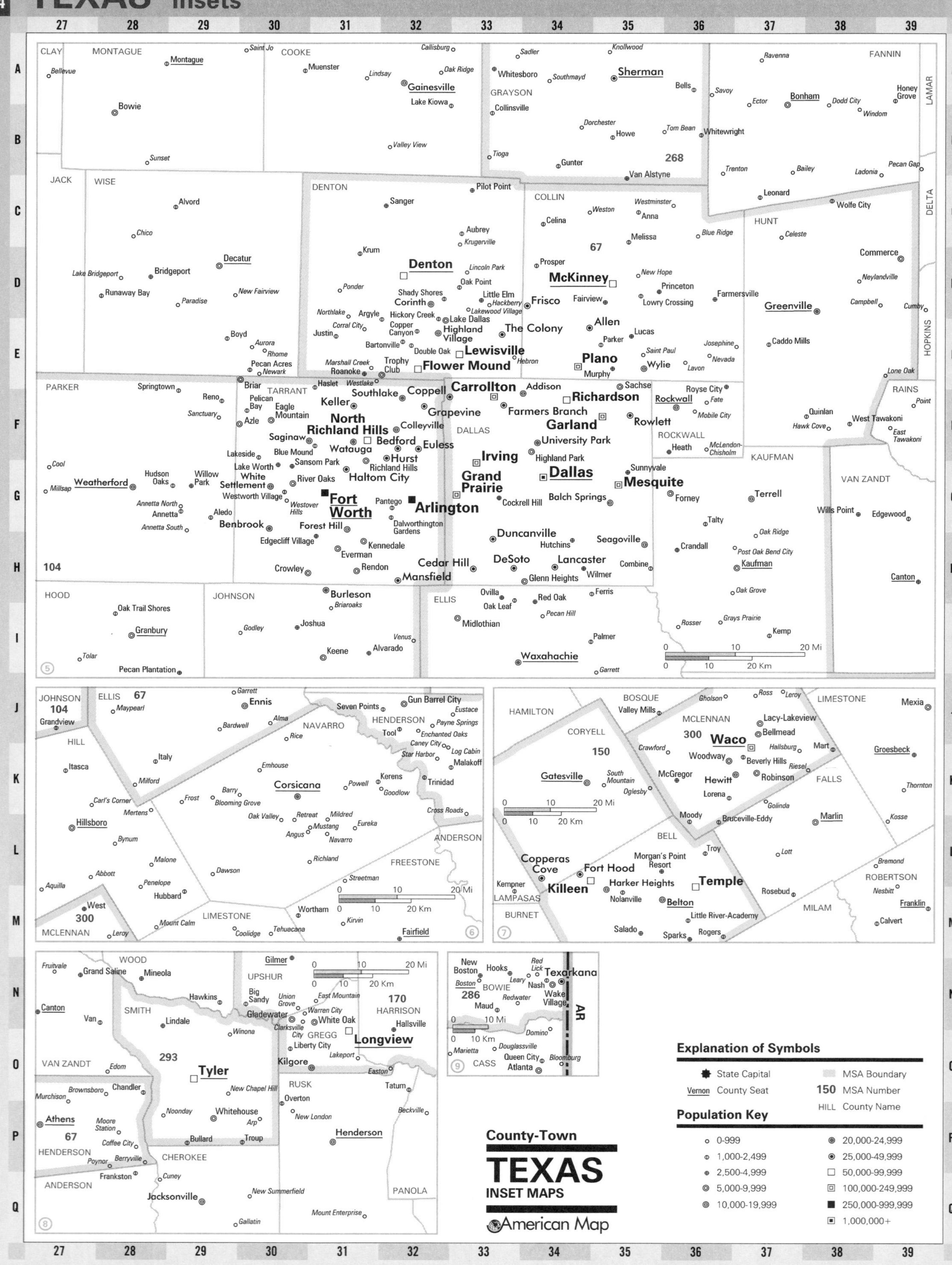
27 28 29 30 31 32 33 34 35 36 37 38 39
A B C D E F G H I J K L M N O P Q
CLAY
MONTAGUE
Bellevue
Montague
Saint Jo
COOKE
Muenster
Callisburg
Lindsay
Oak Ridge
Gainesville
Lake Kiowa
Bowie
Valley View
Sunset
Sadler
Knollwood
Whitesboro
Southmayd
Sherman
GRAYSON
Collinsville
Bells
Dorchester
Howe
Tom Bean
Whitewright
Tioga
Gunter
268
Van Alstyne
Ravenna
FANNIN
Savoy
Ector
Bonham
Dodd City
Honey Grove
Windom
LAMAR
Trenton
Bailey
Ladonia
Pecan Gap
Leonard
Wolfe City
DELTA
JACK
WISE
Alvord
Chico
Decatur
Lake Bridgeport
Bridgeport
Runaway Bay
Paradise
New Fairview
Boyd
Aurora
Rhome
Pecan Acres
Newark
DENTON
Pilot Point
Sanger
Aubrey
Krugerville
Krum
Denton
Lincoln Park
Oak Point
Ponder
Shady Shores
Corinth
Little Elm
Hackberry
Lakewood Village
Frisco
Northlake
Argyle
Hickory Creek
Lake Dallas
Corral City
Copper Canyon
Highland Village
The Colony
Justin
Bartonville
Double Oak
Lewisville
Hebron
Marshall Creek
Roanoke
Trophy Club
Flower Mound
COLLIN
Weston
Westminster
Anna
Celina
Melissa
Blue Ridge
67
Prosper
McKinney
New Hope
Princeton
Fairview
Lowry Crossing
Farmersville
Allen
Lucas
Parker
Saint Paul
Josephine
Nevada
Plano
Wylie
Lavon
Murphy
HUNT
Celeste
Commerce
Neylandville
Greenville
Campbell
Cumby
Caddo Mills
HOPKINS
Lone Oak
PARKER
Springtown
Reno
Sanctuary
Briar
TARRANT
Haslet
Westlake
Pelican Bay
Eagle Mountain
Azle
Keller
Southlake
Coppell
Carrollton
Addison
Sachse
Richardson
Grapevine
Farmers Branch
North Richland Hills
Colleyville
DALLAS
Garland
Rowlett
Rockwall
Royse City
Fate
Mobile City
ROCKWALL
Heath
McLendon-Chisholm
RAINS
Point
Quinlan
Hawk Cove
West Tawakoni
East Tawakoni
Saginaw
Bedford
Euless
Watauga
University Park
Blue Mound
Lakeside
Lake Worth
Sansom Park
Hurst
Richland Hills
Irving
Highland Park
Cool
Millsap
Weatherford
Hudson Oaks
Willow Park
White Settlement
River Oaks
Haltom City
Grand Prairie
Dallas
Sunnyvale
Mesquite
KAUFMAN
VAN ZANDT
Westworth Village
Westover Hills
Fort Worth
Pantego
Arlington
Cockrell Hill
Balch Springs
Forney
Terrell
Wills Point
Edgewood
Annetta North
Annetta
Aledo
Annetta South
Benbrook
Forest Hill
Dalworthington Gardens
Talty
Edgecliff Village
Kennedale
Everman
Duncanville
Hutchins
Seagoville
Crandall
Oak Ridge
Post Oak Bend City
104
Crowley
Rendon
Cedar Hill
DeSoto
Lancaster
Wilmer
Combine
Kaufman
Mansfield
Glenn Heights
Canton
HOOD
JOHNSON
Burleson
Briaroaks
ELLIS
Ovilla
Oak Leaf
Red Oak
Ferris
Pecan Hill
Oak Grove
Oak Trail Shores
Granbury
Godley
Joshua
Midlothian
Rosser
Grays Prairie
Kemp
Venus
Palmer
Tolar
Keene
Alvarado
Waxahachie
Pecan Plantation
Garrett
0 10 20 Mi
0 10 20 Km
5
JOHNSON
104
Grandview
ELLIS
67
Maypearl
Garrett
Ennis
Seven Points
Gun Barrel City
Eustace
HENDERSON
Payne Springs
Bardwell
Alma
NAVARRO
Tool
Enchanted Oaks
Rice
Caney City
Log Cabin
Star Harbor
Malakoff
HILL
Itasca
Italy
Emhouse
Kerens
Trinidad
Milford
Corsicana
Powell
Goodlow
Carl's Corner
Frost
Barry
Blooming Grove
Mertens
Oak Valley
Retreat
Mildred
Eureka
Cross Roads
Hillsboro
Angus
Mustang
Navarro
ANDERSON
Bynum
Richland
Malone
FREESTONE
Abbott
Dawson
Streetman
Aquilla
Penelope
Hubbard
West
300
Wortham
Kirvin
MCLENNAN
Mount Calm
LIMESTONE
Coolidge
Tehuacana
Leroy
Fairfield
6
HAMILTON
BOSQUE
Valley Mills
Gholson
Ross
Leroy
LIMESTONE
Mexia
CORYELL
MCLENNAN
Lacy-Lakeview
Bellmead
300
Waco
150
Crawford
Woodway
Hallsburg
Mart
Groesbeck
Beverly Hills
Riesel
Gatesville
South Mountain
McGregor
Hewitt
Robinson
FALLS
Oglesby
Lorena
Thornton
Golinda
Moody
Bruceville-Eddy
Marlin
Kosse
BELL
Troy
Lott
Copperas Cove
Morgan's Point Resort
Fort Hood
Bremond
Kempner
Killeen
Harker Heights
Temple
ROBERTSON
LAMPASAS
Nolanville
Rosebud
Nesbitt
Belton
MILAM
Franklin
BURNET
Little River-Academy
Calvert
Salado
Sparks
Rogers
7
WOOD
Fruitvale
Grand Saline
Mineola
Gilmer
UPSHUR
Canton
Hawkins
Big Sandy
Union Grove
East Mountain
170
SMITH
Van
Gladewater
Warren City
HARRISON
Lindale
Clarksville City
White Oak
Hallsville
Winona
GREGG
Longview
Liberty City
VAN ZANDT
293
Lakeport
Edom
Kilgore
Tyler
Easton
RUSK
Tatum
Murchison
Brownsboro
Chandler
New Chapel Hill
Overton
Noonday
Whitehouse
Beckville
Athens
Moore Station
Arp
New London
67
Coffee City
Bullard
Troup
Henderson
HENDERSON
Poynor
Berryville
CHEROKEE
Frankston
Cuney
ANDERSON
New Summerfield
PANOLA
Jacksonville
Mount Enterprise
Gallatin
8
New Boston
Hooks
Red Lick
Texarkana
Boston
Leary
BOWIE
Nash
286
Redwater
Wake Village
Maud
AR
Domino
0 10 Mi
0 10 Km
Marietta
Douglassville
Queen City
Bloomburg
CASS
Atlanta
9
Explanation of Symbols
State Capital
MSA Boundary
Vernon County Seat
150 MSA Number
HILL County Name
Population Key
0-999
1,000-2,499
2,500-4,999
5,000-9,999
10,000-19,999
20,000-24,999
25,000-49,999
50,000-99,999
100,000-249,999
250,000-999,999
1,000,000+
County-Town
TEXAS
INSET MAPS
American Map

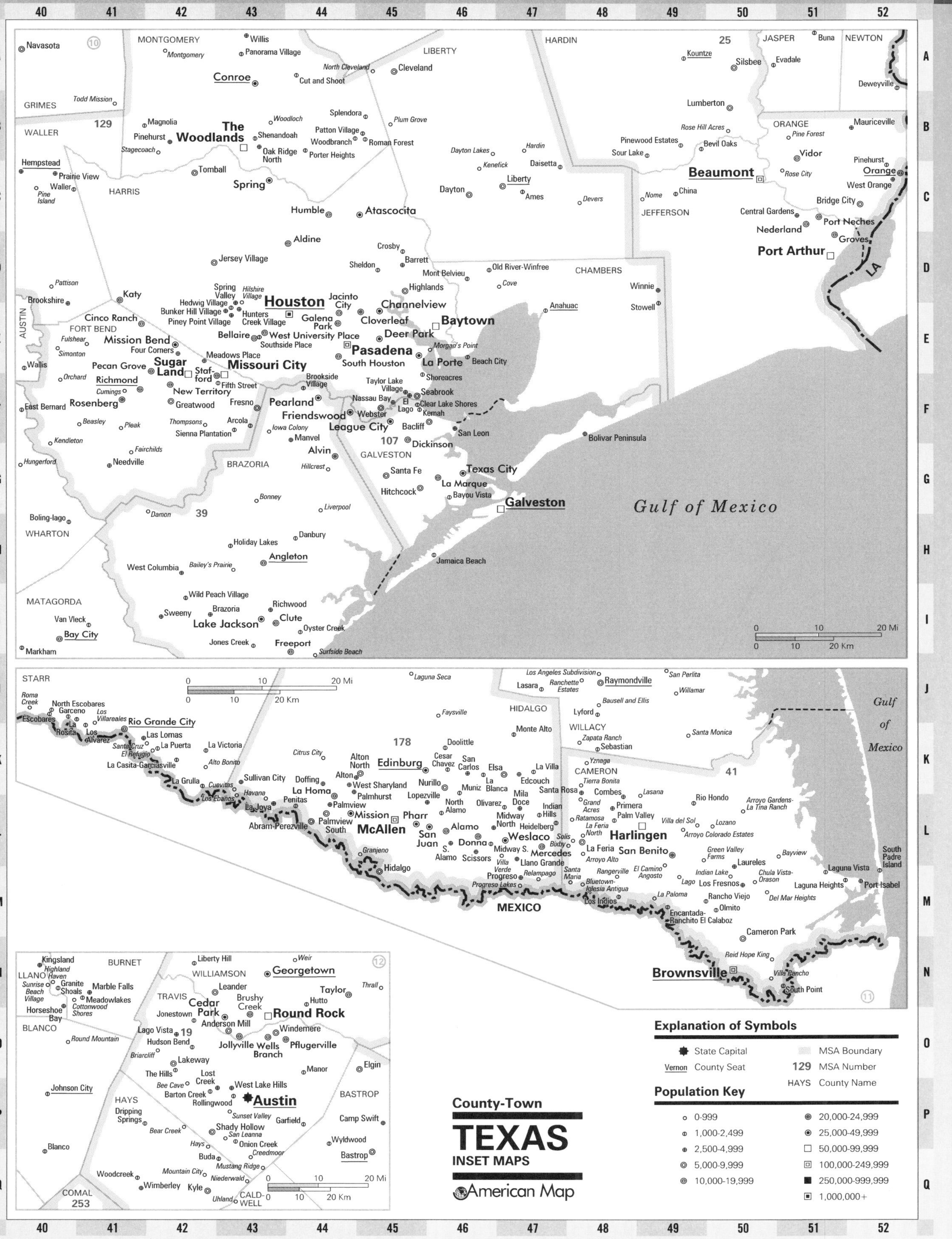
40
41
42
43
44
45
46
47
48
49
50
51
52
A
B
C
D
E
F
G
H
I
J
K
L
M
N
O
P
Q
Navasota
10
MONTGOMERY
Montgomery
Willis
Panorama Village
Conroe
North Cleveland
Cleveland
Cut and Shoot
LIBERTY
HARDIN
25
Kountze
Silsbee
JASPER
Buna
NEWTON
Evadale
Deweyville
GRIMES
Todd Mission
Lumberton
WALLER
129
Magnolia
Pinehurst
The Woodlands
Stagecoach
Woodloch
Shenandoah
Oak Ridge North
Splendora
Patton Village
Woodbranch
Roman Forest
Porter Heights
Plum Grove
Dayton Lakes
Hardin
Kenefick
Daisetta
Rose Hill Acres
Pinewood Estates
Sour Lake
Bevil Oaks
ORANGE
Pine Forest
Mauriceville
Vidor
Rose City
Pinehurst
Orange
West Orange
Hempstead
Prairie View
Waller
Pine Island
HARRIS
Tomball
Spring
Liberty
Ames
Dayton
Devers
Beaumont
Nome
China
JEFFERSON
Bridge City
Humble
Atascocita
Central Gardens
Port Neches
Nederland
Groves
Aldine
Crosby
Barrett
Port Arthur
Jersey Village
Sheldon
Mont Belvieu
Old River-Winfree
CHAMBERS
LA
Pattison
Cove
Winnie
Spring Valley
Hilshire Village
Highlands
Brookshire
Katy
Hedwig Village
Bunker Hill Village
Houston
Jacinto City
Channelview
Anahuac
Stowell
AUSTIN
Cinco Ranch
Piney Point Village
Hunters Creek Village
Galena Park
Cloverleaf
Baytown
FORT BEND
Bellaire
West University Place
Deer Park
Fulshear
Mission Bend
Southside Place
Morgan's Point
Simonton
Four Corners
Pasadena
Meadows Place
La Porte
Beach City
Wallis
Pecan Grove
Sugar Land
Missouri City
South Houston
Stafford
Orchard
Richmond
Brookside Village
Shoreacres
Cumings
Fifth Street
Taylor Lake Village
New Territory
Seabrook
East Bernard
Rosenberg
Greatwood
Fresno
Pearland
Nassau Bay
El Lago
Clear Lake Shores
Friendswood
Webster
Kemah
Beasley
Pleak
Thompsons
Arcola
League City
Iowa Colony
Bacliff
San Leon
Sienna Plantation
Bolivar Peninsula
Kendleton
Manvel
107
Dickinson
Fairchilds
Alvin
GALVESTON
Hungerford
Needville
BRAZORIA
Hillcrest
Texas City
Santa Fe
La Marque
Hitchcock
Bayou Vista
Bonney
Galveston
Gulf of Mexico
Liverpool
Damon
39
Boling-Iago
WHARTON
Danbury
Holiday Lakes
Angleton
Jamaica Beach
West Columbia
Bailey's Prairie
MATAGORDA
Wild Peach Village
Richwood
Brazoria
Sweeny
Clute
Van Vleck
Lake Jackson
Oyster Creek
Bay City
Jones Creek
Freeport
Markham
Surfside Beach
0 10 20 Mi
0 10 20 Km
STARR
Laguna Seca
Los Angeles Subdivision
Lasara
Ranchette Estates
Raymondville
San Perlita
Willamar
Roma Creek
North Escobares
Garceno
Los Villareales
Escobares
Rio Grande City
Faysville
HIDALGO
Lyford
Bausell and Ellis
Gulf of Mexico
Rosita
Las Lomas
Alvarez
Santa Cruz
El Refugio
La Puerta
La Victoria
Monte Alto
WILLACY
Zapata Ranch
Sebastian
Santa Monica
178
Doolittle
La Casita-Garciasville
Alto Bonito
Citrus City
Alton North
Edinburg
Cesar Chavez
San Carlos
Elsa
La Villa
Yznaga
CAMERON
41
La Grulla
Cuevitas
Sullivan City
Doffing
Alton
West Sharyland
Nurillo
La Blanca
Edcouch
Tierra Bonita
Los Ebanos
Havana
Penitas
La Homa
Palmhurst
Lopezville
Muniz
Mila Doce
Santa Rosa
Combes
Lasana
Rio Hondo
Arroyo Gardens-La Tina Ranch
La Joya
Palmview
North Alamo
Olivarez
Indian Hills
Grand Acres
Primera
Abram-Perezville
Palmview South
Mission
Pharr
Midway North
Ratamosa
Palm Valley
Villa del Sol
Lozano
McAllen
San Juan
Alamo
Heidelberg
La Feria North
Harlingen
Arroyo Colorado Estates
Weslaco
Solis
Bixby
Granjeno
S. Alamo
Donna
Scissors
Midway S.
Mercedes
La Feria
San Benito
Green Valley Farms
Bayview
South Padre Island
Hidalgo
Villa Verde
Llano Grande
Arroyo Alto
Laureles
Laguna Vista
Progreso
Relampago
Santa Maria
Rangerville
El Camino Angosto
Indian Lake
Chula Vista-Orason
Port Isabel
Progreso Lakes
Bluetown-Iglesia Antigua
Lago
Los Fresnos
Laguna Heights
MEXICO
Los Indios
La Paloma
Rancho Viejo
Del Mar Heights
Encantada-Ranchito El Calaboz
Olmito
Cameron Park
Reid Hope King
Brownsville
Villa Rancho
South Point
11
Kingsland
Highland Haven
BURNET
Liberty Hill
Weir
12
LLANO
WILLIAMSON
Georgetown
Sunrise Beach Village
Granite Shoals
Marble Falls
Thrall
Meadowlakes
Leander
Taylor
Horseshoe Bay
Cottonwood Shores
TRAVIS
Cedar Park
Brushy Creek
Hutto
Jonestown
Round Rock
BLANCO
Anderson Mill
Lago Vista
19
Windemere
Round Mountain
Hudson Bend
Jollyville
Wells Branch
Pflugerville
Briarcliff
Lakeway
Manor
Elgin
The Hills
Lost Creek
Bee Cave
West Lake Hills
Johnson City
Barton Creek
Rollingwood
Austin
BASTROP
HAYS
Dripping Springs
Sunset Valley
Garfield
Camp Swift
Bear Creek
Shady Hollow
San Leanna
Blanco
Hays
Onion Creek
Wyldwood
Creedmoor
Bastrop
Buda
Mustang Ridge
Woodcreek
Mountain City
Niederwald
Wimberley
Kyle
COMAL
253
Uhland
CALDWELL
0 10 20 Mi
0 10 20 Km
County-Town
TEXAS
INSET MAPS
American Map
Explanation of Symbols
State Capital
MSA Boundary
Vernon County Seat
129 MSA Number
HAYS County Name
Population Key
0-999
1,000-2,499
2,500-4,999
5,000-9,999
10,000-19,999
20,000-24,999
25,000-49,999
50,000-99,999
100,000-249,999
250,000-999,999
1,000,000+

COUNTIES

(256 Counties)

Name of County	Population	Location on Map
ANDERSON	55,109	F-21
ANDREWS	13,004	E-9
ANGELINA	80,130	G-23
ARANSAS	22,497	M-19
ARCHER	8,854	C-16
ARCHER	8,854	B-16
ARMSTRONG	2,148	D-3
ATASCOSA	38,628	L-16
AUSTIN	23,590	I-20
BAILEY	6,594	B-9
BANDERA	17,645	J-15
BASTROP	57,733	J-18
BAYLOR	4,093	B-15
BEE	32,359	L-17
BELL	237,974	G-18
BEXAR	1,392,931	J-16
BLANCO	8,418	I-16
BORDEN	729	D-11
BOSQUE	17,204	E-18
BOWIE	89,306	C-23
BRAZORIA	241,767	K-21
BRAZOS	152,415	H-20
BREWSTER	8,866	I-7
BRISCOE	1,790	A-11
BROOKS	7,976	P-17
BROWN	37,674	F-15
BURLESON	16,470	I-19
BURNET	34,147	H-17
CALDWELL	32,194	J-18
CALHOUN	20,647	L-19
CALLAHAN	12,905	E-15
CAMERON	335,227	Q-18
CAMP	11,549	D-22
CARSON	6,516	C-3
CASS	30,438	C-23
CASTRO	8,285	A-9
CHAMBERS	26,031	J-23
CHEROKEE	46,659	E-22
CHILDRESS	7,688	A-14
CLAY	11,006	B-17
COCHRAN	3,730	B-8
COKE	3,864	F-12
COLEMAN	9,235	F-14
COLLIN	491,675	C-19
COLLINGSWORTH	3,206	D-5
COLORADO	20,390	J-20
COMAL	78,021	J-16
COMANCHE	14,026	F-16
CONCHO	3,966	G-14
COOKE	36,363	C-19
CORYELL	74,978	G-17
COTTLE	1,904	A-13
CRANE	3,996	G-9
CROCKETT	4,099	H-10
CROSBY	7,072	B-11
CULBERSON	2,975	F-5
DALLAM	6,222	A-1
DALLAS	2,218,899	D-19
DAWSON	14,985	D-10
DE WITT	20,013	K-18
DEAF SMITH	18,561	D-1
DELTA	5,327	C-21
DENTON	432,976	C-18
DICKENS	2,762	B-12
DIMMIT	10,248	M-14
DONLEY	3,828	D-4
DUVAL	13,120	M-16
EASTLAND	18,297	E-15
ECTOR	121,123	F-9
EDWARDS	2,162	I-12
EL PASO	679,622	E-19
ELLIS	111,360	E-19
ERATH	33,001	E-17
FALLS	18,576	G-19
FANNIN	31,242	B-20
FAYETTE	21,804	I-19
FISHER	4,344	E-13
FLOYD	7,771	A-11
FOARD	1,622	B-14
FORT BEND	354,452	J-21
FRANKLIN	9,458	C-22
FREESTONE	17,867	F-20
FRIO	16,252	K-15
GAINES	14,467	D-9
GALVESTON	250,158	J-22
GARZA	4,872	D-11
GILLESPIE	20,814	I-15
GLASSCOCK	1,406	F-10
GOLIAD	6,928	L-18
GONZALES	18,628	K-18
GRAY	22,744	C-4
GRAYSON	110,595	C-19
GREGG	111,379	E-22
GRIMES	23,552	H-20
GUADALUPE	89,023	J-17
HALE	36,602	A-10
HALL	3,782	E-4
HAMILTON	8,229	F-17
HANSFORD	5,369	A-3
HARDEMAN	4,724	B-14
HARDIN	48,073	H-23
HARRIS	3,400,578	J-22
HARRISON	62,110	E-23
HARTLEY	5,537	B-1
HASKELL	6,093	C-14
HAYS	97,589	I-17
HEMPHILL	3,351	B-5
HENDERSON	73,277	E-21
HIDALGO	569,463	P-17
HILL	32,321	F-19
HOCKLEY	22,716	B-9
HOOD	41,100	E-17
HOPKINS	31,960	C-21
HOUSTON	23,185	G-22
HOWARD	33,627	E-11
HUDSPETH	3,344	F-4
HUNT	76,596	D-20
HUTCHINSON	23,857	B-3
IRION	1,771	G-11
JACK	8,763	C-17
JACKSON	14,391	K-19
JASPER	35,604	G-24
JEFF DAVIS	2,207	H-6
JEFFERSON	252,051	J-24
JIM HOGG	5,281	O-16
JIM WELLS	39,326	N-17
JOHNSON	126,811	E-18
JONES	20,785	D-14
KARNES	15,446	L-17
KAUFMAN	71,313	D-20
KENDALL	23,743	J-16
KENEDY	414	O-18
KENT	859	C-12
KERR	43,653	I-14
KIMBLE	4,468	H-14
KING	356	B-13
KINNEY	3,379	J-12
KLEBERG	31,549	N-18
KNOX	4,253	B-14
LA SALLE	5,866	L-15
LAMAR	48,499	B-21
LAMB	14,709	B-9
LAMPASAS	17,762	G-17
LAVACA	19,210	K-19
LEE	15,657	I-19
LEON	15,335	G-20
LIBERTY	70,154	I-22
LIMESTONE	22,051	F-19
LIPSCOMB	3,057	A-5
LIVE OAK	12,309	L-17
LLANO	17,044	H-16
LOVING	67	F-7
LUBBOCK	242,628	B-10
LYNN	6,550	D-10
MADISON	12,940	H-21
MARION	10,941	D-23
MARTIN	4,746	E-10
MASON	3,738	H-15
MATAGORDA	37,957	L-21
MAVERICK	47,297	K-12
MCCULLOCH	8,205	G-15
MCLENNAN	213,517	F-18
MCMULLEN	851	L-16
MEDINA	39,304	K-15
MENARD	2,360	H-14
MIDLAND	116,009	F-10
MILAM	24,238	H-19
MILLS	5,151	G-16
MITCHELL	9,698	E-12
MONTAGUE	19,117	C-17
MONTGOMERY	293,768	H-21
MOORE	20,121	B-2
MORRIS	13,048	C-22
MOTLEY	1,426	A-12
NACOGDOCHES	59,203	F-23
NAVARRO	45,124	F-20
NEWTON	15,072	G-24
NOLAN	15,802	E-13
NUECES	313,645	N-18
OCHILTREE	9,006	B-4
OLDHAM	2,185	C-1
ORANGE	84,966	I-24
PALO PINTO	27,026	D-16
PANOLA	22,756	E-23
PARKER	88,495	D-17
PARMER	10,016	A-8
PECOS	16,809	G-8
POLK	41,133	H-22
POTTER	113,546	C-2
PRESIDIO	7,304	H-5
RAINS	9,139	D-21
RANDALL	104,312	D-2
REAGAN	3,326	F-10
REAL	3,047	I-14
RED RIVER	14,314	B-22
REEVES	13,137	F-7
REFUGIO	7,828	L-19
ROBERTS	887	B-4
ROBERTSON	16,000	H-20
ROCKWALL	43,080	D-20
RUNNELS	11,495	F-14
RUSK	47,372	E-23
SABINE	10,469	G-24
SAN AUGUSTINE	8,946	G-23
SAN JACINTO	22,246	I-22
SAN PATRICIO	67,138	M-18
SAN SABA	6,186	H-16
SCHLEICHER	2,935	H-12
SCURRY	16,361	D-11
SHACKELFORD	3,302	D-15
SHELBY	25,224	F-23
SHERMAN	3,186	A-2
SMITH	174,706	E-22
SOMERVELL	6,809	E-17
STARR	53,597	P-16
STEPHENS	9,674	D-16
STERLING	1,393	F-11
STONEWALL	1,693	C-14
STONEWALL	1,693	C-13
SUTTON	4,077	H-12
SWISHER	8,378	A-10
TARRANT	1,446,219	D-18
TAYLOR	126,555	E-14
TERRELL	1,081	H-9
TERRY	12,761	C-9
THROCKMORTON	1,850	C-15
TITUS	28,118	C-22
TOM GREEN	104,010	F-12
TRAVIS	812,280	I-18
TRINITY	13,779	G-22
TYLER	20,871	H-23
UPSHUR	35,291	D-22
UPTON	3,404	F-10
UVALDE	25,926	J-14
VAL VERDE	44,856	I-10
VAN ZANDT	48,140	E-21
VICTORIA	84,088	K-19
WALKER	61,758	H-21
WALLER	32,663	I-21
WARD	10,909	F-8
WASHINGTON	30,373	I-20
WEBB	193,117	M-14
WHARTON	41,188	K-20
WHEELER	5,284	C-5
WICHITA	131,664	B-16
WILBARGER	14,676	B-15
WILLACY	20,082	P-18
WILLIAMSON	249,967	H-17
WILSON	32,408	K-17
WINKLER	7,173	F-8
WISE	48,793	C-18
WOOD	36,752	D-22
YOAKUM	7,322	C-9
YOUNG	17,943	D-16
ZAPATA	12,182	O-15
ZAVALA	11,600	K-14
TOTAL	**20,851,820**	

CITIES AND TOWNS

Note: The first name is that of the city or town, second, that of the county in which it is located, then the population and location on the map.

Abernathy, *Lubbock*, 2,839 B-10
Abilene, *Taylor*, 115,930 E-14
• Abram-Perezville, *Hidalgo*, 5,444 L-44
Addison, *Dallas*, 14,166 F-33
Alamo, *Hidalgo*, 14,760 L-46
Alamo Heights, *Bexar*, 7,319 N-23
Albany, *Shackelford*, 1,921 D-15
• Aldine, *Harris*, 13,979 D-43
Aledo, *Parker*, 1,726 G-29
Alice, *Jim Wells*, 19,010 N-17
Allen, *Collin*, 43,554 E-34
Alpine, *Brewster*, 5,786 I-7
Alto, *Cherokee*, 1,190 F-22
Alton, *Hidalgo*, 4,384 K-44
• Alton North, *Hidalgo*, 5,051 P-17
Alvarado, *Johnson*, 3,288 I-31
Alvin, *Brazoria*, 21,413 J-22
Alvord, *Wise*, 1,007 C-18
Amarillo, *Potter*, 173,627 C-3
Ames, *Liberty*, 1,079 C-47
Anahuac, *Chambers*, 2,210 J-23
Anderson, *Grimes*, 257 H-21
• Anderson Mill, *Williamson*, 8,953 O-43
Andrews, *Andrews*, 9,652 E-9
Angleton, *Brazoria*, 18,130 K-22
Anna, *Collin*, 1,225 C-20
Annetta, *Parker*, 1,108 G-29
Anson, *Jones*, 2,556 D-14
Anthony, *El Paso*, 3,850 E-2
Anton, *Hockley*, 1,200 B-10
Aransas Pass, *San Patricio*, 8,138 M-19
Archer City, *Archer*, 1,848 C-16
Arcola, *Fort Bend*, 1,048 F-43
Argyle, *Denton*, 2,365 E-32
Arlington, *Tarrant*, 332,969 D-19
Asherton, *Dimmit*, 1,342 L-14
Aspermont, *Stonewall*, 1,021 C-13
• Atascocita, *Harris*, 35,757 I-22
Athens, *Henderson*, 11,297 E-21
Atlanta, *Cass*, 5,745 C-24
Aubrey, *Denton*, 1,500 C-33
Austin, *Travis*, 656,562 I-18
Azle, *Tarrant*, 9,600 F-29
• Bacliff, *Galveston*, 6,962 F-45
Baird, *Callahan*, 1,623 E-15
Balch Springs, *Dallas*, 19,375 G-35
Balcones Heights, *Bexar*, 3,016 N-23
Ballinger, *Runnels*, 4,243 F-14
Bandera, *Bandera*, 957 J-15
Bangs, *Brown*, 1,620 F-15
• Barrett, *Harris*, 2,872 D-45
Bartlett, *Williamson*, 1,675 H-18
• Barton Creek, *Travis*, 1,589 P-42
Bartonville, *Denton*, 1,093 E-32
Bastrop, *Bastrop*, 5,340 I-18
• Batesville, *Zavala*, 1,298 K-15
Bay City, *Matagorda*, 18,667 K-21
Bayou Vista, *Galveston*, 1,644 G-46
Baytown, *Harris*, 66,430 E-46
Beach City, *Chambers*, 1,645 E-46
Beaumont, *Jefferson*, 113,866 I-24
Bedford, *Tarrant*, 47,152 F-32
Beeville, *Bee*, 13,129 M-18
Bellaire, *Harris*, 15,642 E-43
Bellmead, *McLennan*, 9,214 J-37
Bells, *Grayson*, 1,190 C-20
Bellville, *Austin*, 3,794 I-20
Belton, *Bell*, 14,623 G-18
Benavides, *Duval*, 1,686 N-17
Benbrook, *Tarrant*, 20,208 H-30
Benjamin, *Knox*, 264 C-14
Bertram, *Burnet*, 1,122 H-17
Beverly Hills, *McLennan*, 2,113 K-37
Bevil Oaks, *Jefferson*, 1,346 B-49
Big Lake, *Reagan*, 2,885 G-11
Big Sandy, *Upshur*, 1,288 D-22
Big Spring, *Howard*, 25,233 E-11
Bishop, *Nueces*, 3,305 N-18
Blanco, *Blanco*, 1,505 I-17
• Bloomington, *Victoria*, 2,562 L-19
Blossom, *Lamar*, 1,439 B-22
Blue Mound, *Tarrant*, 2,388 F-31
Boerne, *Kendall*, 6,178 J-16
Bogata, *Red River*, 1,396 C-22
• Boling-Iago, *Wharton*, 1,271 H-40
• Bolivar Peninsula, *Galveston*, 3,853 J-23
Bonham, *Fannin*, 9,990 C-20
Booker, *Lipscomb*, 1,315 A-5
Borger, *Hutchinson*, 14,302 C-3
Boston, *Bowie*, 400 C-23
Bovina, *Parmer*, 1,874 A-9
Bowie, *Montague*, 5,219 C-17
Boyd, *Wise*, 1,099 E-29
Brackettville, *Kinney*, 1,876 K-13
Brady, *McCulloch*, 5,523 G-15
Brazoria, *Brazoria*, 2,787 K-22
Breckenridge, *Stephens*, 5,868 D-16
Brenham, *Washington*, 13,507 I-20
• Briar, *Tarrant*, 5,350 E-29
Bridge City, *Orange*, 8,651 I-24
Bridgeport, *Wise*, 4,309 C-18
Bronte, *Coke*, 1,076 F-13
Brookshire, *Waller*, 3,450 E-40
Brookside Village, *Brazoria*, 1,960 F-44
Brownfield, *Terry*, 9,488 C-10
Brownsville, *Cameron*, 139,722 Q-18
Brownwood, *Brown*, 18,813 F-16
Bruceville-Eddy, *McLennan*, 1,490 L-36
• Brushy Creek, *Williamson*, 15,371 O-43
Bryan, *Brazos*, 65,660 H-20
• Buchanan Dam, *Llano*, 1,688 H-17
Buda, *Hays*, 2,404 Q-42
Buffalo, *Leon*, 1,804 G-21
Bullard, *Smith*, 1,150 E-22
Bulverde, *Comal*, 3,761 M-23
• Buna, *Jasper*, 2,269 H-24
Bunker Hill Village, *Harris*, 3,654 E-43
Burkburnett, *Wichita*, 10,927 B-16
Burleson, *Johnson*, 20,976 E-18
Burnet, *Burnet*, 4,735 H-17
Cactus, *Moore*, 2,538 B-2
Caddo Mills, *Hunt*, 1,149 E-37
Caldwell, *Burleson*, 3,449 H-20
Calvert, *Robertson*, 1,426 H-20
Cameron, *Milam*, 5,634 H-19
• Cameron Park, *Cameron*, 5,961 Q-18
• Camp Swift, *Bastrop*, 4,731 I-19
Canadian, *Hemphill*, 2,233 B-5
Canton, *Van Zandt*, 3,292 E-21
• Canutillo, *El Paso*, 5,129 F-2
Canyon, *Randall*, 12,875 D-3
• Canyon Lake, *Comal*, 16,870 J-17
Carrizo Springs, *Dimmit*, 5,655 L-14
Carrollton, *Dallas*, 109,576 F-33
Carthage, *Panola*, 6,664 E-23
Castle Hills, *Bexar*, 4,202 N-23
Castroville, *Medina*, 2,664 K-16
Cedar Hill, *Dallas*, 32,093 H-33
Cedar Park, *Williamson*, 26,049 O-43
Celina, *Collin*, 1,861 C-19
Center, *Shelby*, 5,678 F-24
Centerville, *Leon*, 903 G-21
• Central Gardens, *Jefferson*, 4,106 C-51
• Cesar Chavez, *Hidalgo*, 1,469 K-46
Chandler, *Henderson*, 2,099 E-21
• Channelview, *Harris*, 29,685 E-45
Channing, *Hartley*, 356 B-2
Charlotte, *Atascosa*, 1,637 L-16
Childress, *Childress*, 6,778 E-5
China, *Jefferson*, 1,112 I-24
China Grove, *Bexar*, 1,247 O-24
Cibolo, *Guadalupe*, 3,035 N-24
• Cienegas Terrace, *Val Verde*, 2,878 K-12
• Cinco Ranch, *Fort Bend*, 11,196 E-41
• Circle D-Kc Estates, *Bastrop*, 2,010 I-19
Cisco, *Eastland*, 3,851 E-16
Clarendon, *Donley*, 1,974 D-4
Clarksville, *Red River*, 3,883 B-22
Claude, *Armstrong*, 1,313 D-3
Clear Lake Shores, *Galveston*, 1,205 F-45
Cleburne, *Johnson*, 26,005 E-18
Cleveland, *Liberty*, 7,605 I-22
Clifton, *Bosque*, 3,542 F-18
• Cloverleaf, *Harris*, 23,508 E-45
Clute, *Brazoria*, 10,424 K-22
Clyde, *Callahan*, 3,345 E-15
Cockrell Hill, *Dallas*, 4,443 G-33
Coldspring, *San Jacinto*, 691 H-22
Coleman, *Coleman*, 5,127 F-15
College Station, *Brazos*, 67,890 H-20
Colleyville, *Tarrant*, 19,636 F-32
Collinsville, *Grayson*, 1,235 B-33
Colorado City, *Mitchell*, 4,281 E-12
Columbus, *Colorado*, 3,916 J-20
Comanche, *Comanche*, 4,482 F-16
Combes, *Cameron*, 2,553 L-48
Combine, *Dallas*, 1,788 H-35
• Comfort, *Kendall*, 2,358 J-16
Commerce, *Hunt*, 7,669 C-21
Conroe, *Montgomery*, 36,811 I-22
Converse, *Bexar*, 11,508 J-17
Cooper, *Delta*, 2,150 C-21
Coppell, *Dallas*, 35,958 F-32
Copper Canyon, *Denton*, 1,216 E-32
Copperas Cove, *Coryell*, 29,592 L-34
Corinth, *Denton*, 11,325 D-32
Corpus Christi, *Nueces*, 277,454 N-18
Corrigan, *Polk*, 1,721 G-23
Corsicana, *Navarro*, 24,485 E-20
Cotulla, *La Salle*, 3,614 L-15
Crandall, *Kaufman*, 2,774 H-36
Crane, *Crane*, 3,191 G-9
Crockett, *Houston*, 7,141 G-22
• Crosby, *Harris*, 1,714 D-45
Crosbyton, *Crosby*, 1,874 C-11
• Cross Mountain, *Bexar*, 1,524 M-22
Cross Plains, *Callahan*, 1,068 E-15
Crowell, *Foard*, 1,141 B-14
Crowley, *Tarrant*, 7,467 H-30
Crystal City, *Zavala*, 7,190 L-14
Cuero, *De Witt*, 6,571 K-19
Cut And Shoot, *Montgomery*, 1,158 A-44
Daingerfield, *Morris*, 2,517 D-23
Daisetta, *Liberty*, 1,034 C-47
Dalhart, *Dallam*, 7,237 B-2
Dallas, *Dallas*, 1,188,580 D-19
Dallas, *Dallas*, 1,188,580 D-19
Dalworthington Gardens, *Tarrant*, 2,186 G-32
Danbury, *Brazoria*, 1,611 H-44
Dayton, *Liberty*, 5,709 I-23
De Kalb, *Bowie*, 1,769 C-23
De Leon, *Comanche*, 2,433 E-16
Decatur, *Wise*, 5,201 C-18
Deer Park, *Harris*, 28,520 E-45
Del Rio, *Val Verde*, 33,867 K-12
Denison, *Grayson*, 22,773 B-20
Denton, *Denton*, 80,537 C-19
Denver City, *Yoakum*, 3,985 D-9
DeSoto, *Dallas*, 37,646 H-33
Devine, *Medina*, 4,140 K-16
• Deweyville, *Newton*, 1,190 I-25
Diboll, *Angelina*, 5,470 G-23
Dickens, *Dickens*, 332 C-12
Dickinson, *Galveston*, 17,093 G-45
Dilley, *Frio*, 3,674 L-15
Dimmitt, *Castro*, 4,375 A-10
• Doffing, *Hidalgo*, 4,256 K-44
Donna, *Hidalgo*, 14,768 L-46
• Doolittle, *Hidalgo*, 2,358 K-46
Double Oak, *Denton*, 2,179 E-32
Dripping Springs, *Hays*, 1,548 I-17
Dublin, *Erath*, 3,754 F-17
Dumas, *Moore*, 13,747 B-2
Duncanville, *Dallas*, 36,081 H-33
Eagle Lake, *Colorado*, 3,664 J-20
• Eagle Mountain, *Tarrant*, 6,599 F-30
Eagle Pass, *Maverick*, 22,413 L-12
Early, *Brown*, 2,588 F-16
Earth, *Lamb*, 1,109 A-9
• East Bernard, *Wharton*, 1,729 F-40
Eastland, *Eastland*, 3,769 E-16
Edcouch, *Hidalgo*, 3,342 K-47
Eden, *Concho*, 2,561 G-14
Edgecliff Village, *Tarrant*, 2,550 H-31
Edgewood, *Van Zandt*, 1,348 G-39
Edinburg, *Hidalgo*, 48,465 Q-17
Edna, *Jackson*, 5,899 K-20
• Eidson Road, *Maverick*, 9,348 L-12
El Campo, *Wharton*, 10,945 K-20
El Cenizo, *Webb*, 3,545 O-15
El Lago, *Harris*, 3,075 F-45
El Paso, *El Paso*, 563,662 F-2
El Paso, *El Paso*, 563,662 F-2
Eldorado, *Schleicher*, 1,951 H-12
Electra, *Wichita*, 3,168 B-16
Elgin, *Bastrop*, 5,700 I-18
Elkhart, *Anderson*, 1,215 F-21
• Elm Creek, *Maverick*, 1,928 L-12
Elsa, *Hidalgo*, 5,549 K-47
Emory, *Rains*, 1,021 D-21
• Encantada-Ranchito El Calaboz, *Cameron*, 2,100 M-49
Ennis, *Ellis*, 16,045 E-20
• Escobares, *Starr*, 1,954 J-40
Euless, *Tarrant*, 46,005 F-32
• Evadale, *Jasper*, 1,430 I-24
Everman, *Tarrant*, 5,836 H-31
• Fabens, *El Paso*, 8,043 F-3
Fair Oaks Ranch, *Bexar*, 4,695 M-22
Fairfield, *Freestone*, 3,094 F-20
Fairview, *Collin*, 2,644 D-35
Falfurrias, *Brooks*, 5,297 O-17
Farmers Branch, *Dallas*, 27,508 F-33
Farmersville, *Collin*, 3,118 D-36
Farwell, *Parmer*, 1,364 A-8
Ferris, *Ellis*, 2,175 H-34
• Fifth Street, *Fort Bend*, 2,059 F-42
Flatonia, *Fayette*, 1,377 J-19
Florence, *Williamson*, 1,054 H-18
Floresville, *Wilson*, 5,868 K-17
Flower Mound, *Denton*, 50,702 D-19
Floydada, *Floyd*, 3,676 B-11
Forest Hill, *Tarrant*, 12,949 H-31
Forney, *Kaufman*, 5,588 G-36
• Fort Bliss, *El Paso*, 8,264 F-3
• Fort Davis, *Jeff Davis*, 1,050 H-7
• Fort Hancock, *Hudspeth*, 1,713 G-3
• Fort Hood, *Bell*, 33,711 L-34
Fort Stockton, *Pecos*, 7,846 H-8
Fort Worth, *Tarrant*, 534,694 D-18
• Four Corners, *Fort Bend*, 2,954 E-42
Franklin, *Robertson*, 1,470 G-20
Frankston, *Anderson*, 1,209 E-21
Fredericksburg, *Gillespie*, 8,911 I-16
Freeport, *Brazoria*, 12,708 K-22
Freer, *Duval*, 3,241 N-16
• Fresno, *Fort Bend*, 6,603 F-43
Friendswood, *Galveston*, 29,037 J-22
Friona, *Parmer*, 3,854 A-9
Frisco, *Collin*, 33,714 D-34
Fritch, *Hutchinson*, 2,235 C-3
Fulton, *Aransas*, 1,553 P-26
Gail, *Borden*, 171 D-11
Gainesville, *Cooke*, 15,538 C-19
Galena Park, *Harris*, 10,592 E-44
Galveston, *Galveston*, 57,247 K-23
Ganado, *Jackson*, 1,915 K-20
• Garceno, *Starr*, 1,438 J-40
Garden City, *Glasscock*, 350 F-11
Garden Ridge, *Comal*, 1,882 M-24
• Gardendale, *Ector*, 1,197 F-9
• Garfield, *Travis*, 1,660 P-44
Garland, *Dallas*, 215,768 D-19
Gatesville, *Coryell*, 15,591 G-18
George West, *Live Oak*, 2,524 M-17
Georgetown, *Williamson*, 28,339 H-18
Giddings, *Lee*, 5,105 I-19
Gilmer, *Upshur*, 4,799 D-22
Gladewater, *Gregg*, 6,078 E-22
Glen Rose, *Somervell*, 2,122 E-18
Glenn Heights, *Dallas*, 7,224 H-34
Goldthwaite, *Mills*, 1,802 G-16
Goliad, *Goliad*, 1,975 L-18
Gonzales, *Gonzales*, 7,202 J-18
Gorman, *Eastland*, 1,236 E-16
Graham, *Young*, 8,716 D-16
Granbury, *Hood*, 5,718 E-18
Grand Prairie, *Dallas*, 127,427 G-33
Grand Saline, *Van Zandt*, 3,028 D-21
Grandview, *Johnson*, 1,358 E-19
Granger, *Williamson*, 1,299 H-18
Granite Shoals, *Burnet*, 2,040 N-40
• Grape Creek, *Tom Green*, 3,138 F-12
Grapeland, *Houston*, 1,451 G-22
Grapevine, *Tarrant*, 42,059 F-32
• Greatwood, *Fort Bend*, 6,640 F-42
Greenville, *Hunt*, 23,960 C-20
Gregory, *San Patricio*, 2,318 P-25
Groesbeck, *Limestone*, 4,291 G-20
Groves, *Jefferson*, 15,733 I-24
Groveton, *Trinity*, 1,107 G-22
Gruver, *Hansford*, 1,162 A-3
Gun Barrel City, *Henderson*, 5,145 E-20

Explanation of symbols: • - Census Designated Place (CDP)

Gunter, *Grayson*, 1,230 ....B-34
Guthrie, *King*, 170 ....C-13
Hale Center, *Hale*, 2,263 ....B-10
Hallettsville, *Lavaca*, 2,345 ....J-19
Hallsville, *Harrison*, 2,772 ....E-23
Haltom City, *Tarrant*, 39,018 ....G-31
Hamilton, *Hamilton*, 2,977 ....F-17
Hamlin, *Jones*, 2,248 ....D-14
Harker Heights, *Bell*, 17,308 ....M-35
Harlingen, *Cameron*, 57,564 ....Q-18
• Harper, *Gillespie*, 1,006 ....I-15
Hart, *Castro*, 1,198 ....A-10
Haskell, *Haskell*, 3,106 ....C-14
Haslet, *Tarrant*, 1,134 ....F-31
Hawkins, *Wood*, 1,331 ....D-22
Hearne, *Robertson*, 4,690 ....H-20
Heath, *Rockwall*, 4,149 ....F-36
• Hebbronville, *Jim Hogg*, 4,498 ....O-16
Hedwig Village, *Harris*, 2,334 ....E-43
• Heidelberg, *Hidalgo*, 1,586 ....L-47
Helotes, *Bexar*, 4,285 ....J-16
Hemphill, *Sabine*, 1,106 ....G-24
Hempstead, *Waller*, 4,691 ....I-21
Henderson, *Rusk*, 11,273 ....E-23
Henrietta, *Clay*, 3,264 ....B-17
Hereford, *Deaf Smith*, 14,597 ....D-2
Hewitt, *McLennan*, 11,085 ....G-19
Hickory Creek, *Denton*, 2,078 ....E-32
Hico, *Hamilton*, 1,341 ....F-17
Hidalgo, *Hidalgo*, 7,322 ....M-45
Highland Park, *Dallas*, 8,842 ....F-34
Highland Village, *Denton*, 12,173 E-32
• Highlands, *Harris*, 7,089 ....D-45
Hill Country Village, *Bexar*, 1,028 N-23
Hillsboro, *Hill*, 8,232 ....F-19
Hitchcock, *Galveston*, 6,386 ....G-45
Holiday Lakes, *Brazoria*, 1,095 ....H-43
Holland, *Bell*, 1,102 ....H-18
Holliday, *Archer*, 1,632 ....B-16
Hollywood Park, *Bexar*, 2,983 ....M-23
• Homestead Meadows North,
El Paso, 4,232 ....P-3
• Homestead Meadows South,
El Paso, 6,807 ....P-3
Hondo, *Medina*, 7,897 ....K-15
Honey Grove, *Fannin*, 1,746 ....B-39
Hooks, *Bowie*, 2,973 ....C-23
Horizon City, *El Paso*, 5,233 ....F-3
• Horseshoe Bay, *Llano*, 3,337 ....H-17
Houston, *Harris*, 1,953,631 ....J-22
Howe, *Grayson*, 2,478 ....C-19
Hubbard, *Hill*, 1,586 ....F-19
Hudson, *Angelina*, 3,792 ....G-23
• Hudson Bend, *Travis*, 2,369 ....O-42
Hudson Oaks, *Parker*, 1,637 ....G-29
Hughes Springs, *Cass*, 1,856 ....D-23
Humble, *Harris*, 14,579 ....C-44
Hunters Creek Village,
Harris, 4,374 ....E-43
Huntington, *Angelina*, 2,068 ....G-23
Huntsville, *Walker*, 35,078 ....H-21
Hurst, *Tarrant*, 36,273 ....G-32
Hutchins, *Dallas*, 2,805 ....H-34
Hutto, *Williamson*, 1,250 ....O-44
Idalou, *Lubbock*, 2,157 ....C-11
• Indian Hills, *Hidalgo*, 2,036 ....L-47
• Inez, *Victoria*, 1,787 ....L-19
Ingleside, *San Patricio*, 9,388 ....P-25
Ingram, *Kerr*, 1,740 ....I-15
Iowa Park, *Wichita*, 6,431 ....B-16
Iraan, *Pecos*, 1,238 ....H-10
Irving, *Dallas*, 191,615 ....G-33
Italy, *Ellis*, 1,993 ....E-19
Itasca, *Hill*, 1,503 ....E-19
Jacinto City, *Harris*, 10,302 ....E-44
Jacksboro, *Jack*, 4,533 ....C-17
Jacksonville, *Cherokee*, 13,868 ....F-22
Jamaica Beach, *Galveston*, 1,075 K-23
Jasper, *Jasper*, 8,247 ....H-24
Jayton, *Kent*, 513 ....C-12
Jefferson, *Marion*, 2,024 ....D-23
Jersey Village, *Harris*, 6,880 ....J-21
Johnson City, *Blanco*, 1,191 ....I-17
• Jollyville, *Williamson*, 15,813 ....O-43
Jones Creek, *Brazoria*, 2,130 ....I-43
Jonestown, *Travis*, 1,681 ....O-42
Joshua, *Johnson*, 4,528 ....I-30
Jourdanton, *Atascosa*, 3,732 ....L-16
Junction, *Kimble*, 2,618 ....I-14
Justin, *Denton*, 1,891 ....E-31
Karnes City, *Karnes*, 3,457 ....L-18
Katy, *Harris*, 11,775 ....J-21
Kaufman, *Kaufman*, 6,490 ....E-20
Keene, *Johnson*, 5,003 ....E-18
Keller, *Tarrant*, 27,345 ....F-31
Kemah, *Galveston*, 2,330 ....F-45
Kemp, *Kaufman*, 1,133 ....E-20
Kempner, *Lampasas*, 1,004 ....G-17
Kenedy, *Karnes*, 3,487 ....L-18
Kennedale, *Tarrant*, 5,850 ....H-31
Kerens, *Navarro*, 1,681 ....E-20
Kermit, *Winkler*, 5,714 ....F-8
Kerrville, *Kerr*, 20,425 ....I-15
Kilgore, *Gregg*, 11,301 ....E-22
Killeen, *Bell*, 86,911 ....G-18
• Kingsland, *Llano*, 4,584 ....H-17
Kingsville, *Kleberg*, 25,575 ....N-18
Kirby, *Bexar*, 8,673 ....K-17
Kirbyville, *Jasper*, 2,085 ....H-24
Knox City, *Knox*, 1,219 ....C-14
Kountze, *Hardin*, 2,115 ....I-24
Krum, *Denton*, 1,979 ....D-31
Kyle, *Hays*, 5,314 ....Q-42
• La Blanca, *Hidalgo*, 2,351 ....K-46
• La Casita-Garciasville, *Starr*, 2,177 K-42
La Coste, *Medina*, 1,255 ....K-16
La Feria, *Cameron*, 6,115 ....L-48
La Grange, *Fayette*, 4,478 ....J-19
La Grulla, *Starr*, 1,211 ....K-42
• La Homa, *Hidalgo*, 10,433 ....Q-17
La Joya, *Hidalgo*, 3,303 ....L-43
La Marque, *Galveston*, 13,682 ....K-23
La Porte, *Harris*, 31,880 ....E-45
• La Pryor, *Zavala*, 1,491 ....L-14
• La Puerta, *Starr*, 1,636 ....K-42
• La Rosita, *Starr*, 1,729 ....K-40
• La Victoria, *Starr*, 1,683 ....K-42
La Villa, *Hidalgo*, 1,305 ....K-47
• Lackland AFB, *Bexar*, 7,123 ....O-23
Lacy-Lakeview, *McLennan*, 5,764 J-37
Lago Vista, *Travis*, 4,507 ....O-42
• Laguna Heights, *Cameron*, 1,990 M-51
Laguna Vista, *Cameron*, 1,658 ....M-51
• Lake Brownwood, *Brown*, 1,694 ....F-16
Lake Dallas, *Denton*, 6,166 ....E-32
Lake Jackson, *Brazoria*, 26,386 ....K-22
• Lake Kiowa, *Cooke*, 1,883 ....B-32
Lake Worth, *Tarrant*, 4,618 ....G-30
• Lakehills, *Bandera*, 4,668 ....J-16
Lakeside, *Tarrant*, 1,040 ....G-30
Lakeway, *Travis*, 8,002 ....I-17
Lamesa, *Dawson*, 9,952 ....D-10
Lampasas, *Lampasas*, 6,786 ....G-17
Lancaster, *Dallas*, 25,894 ....E-19
Laredo, *Webb*, 176,576 ....N-15
• Laredo Ranchettes, *Webb*, 1,845 N-15
• Las Lomas, *Starr*, 2,684 ....K-41
• Las Quintas Fonterizas,
Maverick, 2,030 ....L-13
• Lasara, *Willacy*, 1,024 ....P-18
• Laughlin AFB, *Val Verde*, 2,225 ....K-12
• Laureles, *Cameron*, 3,285 ....M-50
League City, *Galveston*, 45,444 ....J-22
Leakey, *Real*, 387 ....J-14
Leander, *Williamson*, 7,596 ....N-42
Leon Valley, *Bexar*, 9,239 ....N-23
Leonard, *Fannin*, 1,846 ....C-20
Levelland, *Hockley*, 12,866 ....C-9
Lewisville, *Denton*, 77,737 ....D-19
Lexington, *Lee*, 1,178 ....I-19
Liberty, *Liberty*, 8,033 ....I-23
• Liberty City, *Gregg*, 1,935 ....O-30
Liberty Hill, *Williamson*, 1,409 ....N-42
Lindale, *Smith*, 2,954 ....E-22
Linden, *Cass*, 2,256 ....D-23
Lipscomb, *Lipscomb*, 44 ....A-5
Little Elm, *Denton*, 3,646 ....D-33
Little River-Academy, *Bell*, 1,645 M-36
Littlefield, *Lamb*, 6,507 ....B-10
Live Oak, *Bexar*, 9,156 ....J-17
Livingston, *Polk*, 5,433 ....H-22
Llano, *Llano*, 3,325 ....H-16
• Llano Grande, *Hidalgo*, 3,333 ....L-47
Lockhart, *Caldwell*, 11,615 ....J-18
Lockney, *Floyd*, 2,056 ....B-11
Lone Star, *Morris*, 1,631 ....D-23
Longview, *Gregg*, 73,344 ....E-23
• Lopezville, *Hidalgo*, 4,476 ....L-45
Lorena, *McLennan*, 1,433 ....G-19
Lorenzo, *Crosby*, 1,372 ....B-11
• Los Alvarez, *Starr*, 1,434 ....K-41
Los Fresnos, *Cameron*, 4,512 ....M-50
Los Indios, *Cameron*, 1,149 ....M-48
• Lost Creek, *Travis*, 4,729 ....P-42
Lowry Crossing, *Collin*, 1,229 ....D-35
Lubbock, *Lubbock*, 199,564 ....C-10
Lucas, *Collin*, 2,890 ....E-35
Lufkin, *Angelina*, 32,709 ....G-23
Luling, *Caldwell*, 5,080 ....J-18
Lumberton, *Hardin*, 8,731 ....I-24
Lyford, *Willacy*, 1,973 ....J-48
Lytle, *Atascosa*, 2,383 ....K-16
Mabank, *Kaufman*, 2,151 ....E-20
Madisonville, *Madison*, 4,159 ....H-21
Magnolia, *Montgomery*, 1,111 ....I-21
Malakoff, *Henderson*, 2,257 ....E-21
Manor, *Travis*, 1,204 ....O-44
Mansfield, *Tarrant*, 28,031 ....E-19
Manvel, *Brazoria*, 3,046 ....G-44
Marble Falls, *Burnet*, 4,959 ....N-41
Marfa, *Presidio*, 2,121 ....I-6
Marion, *Guadalupe*, 1,099 ....N-25
• Markham, *Matagorda*, 1,138 ....K-21
Marlin, *Falls*, 6,628 ....G-19
Marshall, *Harrison*, 23,935 ....D-23
Mart, *McLennan*, 2,273 ....F-19
Mason, *Mason*, 2,134 ....H-15
Matador, *Motley*, 740 ....B-12
Mathis, *San Patricio*, 5,034 ....M-18
Maud, *Bowie*, 1,028 ....C-23
• Mauriceville, *Orange*, 2,743 ....B-52
McAllen, *Hidalgo*, 106,414 ....Q-17
McCamey, *Upton*, 1,805 ....G-10
McGregor, *McLennan*, 4,727 ....G-18
McKinney, *Collin*, 54,369 ....C-19
• McQueeney, *Guadalupe*, 2,527 ....M-25
Meadowlakes, *Burnet*, 1,293 ....N-41
Meadows Place, *Fort Bend*, 4,912 E-42
• Medina, *Bandera*, 2,960 ....J-15
Melissa, *Collin*, 1,350 ....C-35
Memphis, *Hall*, 2,479 ....D-5
Menard, *Menard*, 1,653 ....H-14
Mentone, *Loving*, 50 ....F-7
Mercedes, *Hidalgo*, 13,649 ....L-47
Meridian, *Bosque*, 1,491 ....F-18
Merkel, *Taylor*, 2,637 ....E-14
Mertzon, *Irion*, 839 ....G-12
Mesquite, *Dallas*, 124,523 ....G-35
Mexia, *Limestone*, 6,563 ....F-20
Miami, *Roberts*, 588 ....B-5
Midland, *Midland*, 94,996 ....F-10
Midlothian, *Ellis*, 7,480 ....I-33
• Midway North, *Hidalgo*, 3,946 ....L-46
• Midway South, *Hidalgo*, 1,711 ....L-46
• Mila Doce, *Hidalgo*, 4,907 ....L-47
• Milam, *Sabine*, 1,329 ....G-24
Mineola, *Wood*, 4,550 ....D-21
Mineral Wells, *Palo Pinto*, 16,946 D-17
Mission, *Hidalgo*, 45,408 ....Q-17
• Mission Bend, *Fort Bend*, 30,831 E-42
Missouri City, *Fort Bend*, 52,913 J-22
Monahans, *Ward*, 6,821 ....F-8
Mont Belvieu, *Chambers*, 2,324 ..D-46
Montague, *Montague*, 1,253 ....B-18
• Monte Alto, *Hidalgo*, 1,611 ....K-47
Moody, *McLennan*, 1,400 ....G-18
Morgan's Point Resort,
Bell, 2,989 ....L-35
Morton, *Cochran*, 2,249 ....B-9
Mount Pleasant, *Titus*, 13,935 ....C-22
Mount Vernon, *Franklin*, 2,286 ....C-22
Muenster, *Cooke*, 1,556 ....C-18
Muleshoe, *Bailey*, 4,530 ....A-9
Munday, *Knox*, 1,527 ....C-15
• Muniz, *Hidalgo*, 1,106 ....L-46
Murphy, *Collin*, 3,099 ....E-35
Nacogdoches,
Nacogdoches, 29,914 ....F-23
Naples, *Morris*, 1,410 ....C-23
Nash, *Bowie*, 2,169 ....N-34
Nassau Bay, *Harris*, 4,170 ....F-45
Natalia, *Medina*, 1,663 ....K-16
Navasota, *Grimes*, 6,789 ....I-21
Nederland, *Jefferson*, 17,422 ....I-24
Needville, *Fort Bend*, 2,609 ....K-21
New Boston, *Bowie*, 4,808 ....N-33
New Braunfels, *Comal*, 36,494 ....J-17
• New Territory, *Fort Bend*, 13,861 .F-42
Newton, *Newton*, 2,459 ....H-24
Nixon, *Gonzales*, 2,186 ....K-18
Nocona, *Montague*, 3,198 ....B-18
Nolanville, *Bell*, 2,150 ....M-35
• North Alamo, *Hidalgo*, 2,061 ....L-46
• North Escobares, *Starr*, 1,692 ....J-40
North Richland Hills,
Tarrant, 55,635 ....F-31
• Northcliff, *Guadalupe*, 1,819 ....M-24
• Nurillo, *Hidalgo*, 5,056 ....K-46
O'Donnell, *Lynn*, 1,011 ....D-10
Oak Leaf, *Ellis*, 1,209 ....I-33
Oak Point, *Denton*, 1,747 ....D-33
Oak Ridge North,
Montgomery, 2,991 ....B-43
• Oak Trail Shores, *Hood*, 2,475 ....I-28
Odem, *San Patricio*, 2,499 ....P-24
Odessa, *Ector*, 90,943 ....F-9
Old River-Winfree,
Chambers, 1,364 ....D-46
• Olivarez, *Hidalgo*, 2,445 ....L-47
• Olmito, *Cameron*, 1,198 ....M-50
Olmos Park, *Bexar*, 2,343 ....N-23
Olney, *Young*, 3,396 ....C-16
Olton, *Lamb*, 2,288 ....A-10
Onalaska, *Polk*, 1,174 ....H-22
• Onion Creek, *Travis*, 2,116 ....P-43
Orange, *Orange*, 18,643 ....I-25
Orange Grove, *Jim Wells*, 1,288 .M-17
Ore City, *Upshur*, 1,106 ....D-23
Overton, *Rusk*, 2,350 ....E-22
Ovilla, *Ellis*, 3,405 ....H-33
Oyster Creek, *Brazoria*, 1,192 ....I-44
• Ozona, *Crockett*, 3,436 ....H-11
Paducah, *Cottle*, 1,498 ....B-13
Paint Rock, *Concho*, 320 ....G-14
Palacios, *Matagorda*, 5,153 ....L-20
Palestine, *Anderson*, 17,598 ....F-21
Palm Valley, *Cameron*, 1,298 ....L-48
Palmer, *Ellis*, 1,774 ....I-34
Palmhurst, *Hidalgo*, 4,872 ....L-44
Palmview, *Hidalgo*, 4,107 ....L-44
• Palmview South, *Hidalgo*, 6,219 .L-44
Palo Pinto, *Palo Pinto*, 350 ....D-17
Pampa, *Gray*, 17,887 ....C-4
Panhandle, *Carson*, 2,589 ....C-3
Panorama Village,
Montgomery, 1,965 ....I-22
Pantego, *Tarrant*, 2,318 ....G-32
Paris, *Lamar*, 25,898 ....B-21
Parker, *Collin*, 1,379 ....E-35
Pasadena, *Harris*, 141,674 ....J-22
Patton Village,
Montgomery, 1,391 ....B-45
Pearland, *Brazoria*, 37,640 ....F-44
Pearsall, *Frio*, 7,157 ....L-15
• Pecan Acres, *Wise*, 2,289 ....E-30
• Pecan Grove, *Fort Bend*, 13,551 .F-42
Pecan Plantation, *Hood*, 3,544 ....E-18
Pecos, *Reeves*, 9,501 ....G-7
Pelican Bay, *Tarrant*, 1,505 ....F-30
Penitas, *Hidalgo*, 1,167 ....L-44
Perryton, *Ochiltree*, 7,774 ....A-4
Petersburg, *Hale*, 1,262 ....B-11
Pflugerville, *Travis*, 16,335 ....O-43
Pharr, *Hidalgo*, 46,660 ....L-45
Pilot Point, *Denton*, 3,538 ....C-19
• Pinehurst, *Montgomery*, 4,266 ....B-42
• Pinehurst, *Orange*, 2,274 ....C-52
• Pinewood Estates, *Hardin*, 1,633 .B-49
Piney Point Village, *Harris*, 3,380 .E-43
Pittsburg, *Camp*, 4,347 ....D-22
Plains, *Yoakum*, 1,450 ....C-9
Plainview, *Hale*, 22,336 ....B-11
Plano, *Collin*, 222,030 ....D-19
Pleasanton, *Atascosa*, 8,266 ....K-17
Port Aransas, *Nueces*, 3,370 ....N-19
Port Arthur, *Jefferson*, 57,755 ....I-24
Port Isabel, *Cameron*, 4,865 ....Q-19
Port Lavaca, *Calhoun*, 12,035 ....L-20
Port Neches, *Jefferson*, 13,601 ....C-51
• Porter Heights,
Montgomery, 1,490 ....B-44
Portland, *San Patricio*, 14,827 ....N-19
Post, *Garza*, 3,708 ....C-11
Poteet, *Atascosa*, 3,305 ....K-16
Poth, *Wilson*, 1,850 ....K-17
• Potosi, *Taylor*, 1,664 ....E-14
Pottsboro, *Grayson*, 1,579 ....B-19
Prairie View, *Waller*, 4,410 ....I-21
Premont, *Jim Wells*, 2,772 ....N-17
Presidio, *Presidio*, 4,167 ....J-6
Primera, *Cameron*, 2,723 ....L-48
Princeton, *Collin*, 3,477 ....D-35
Progreso, *Hidalgo*, 4,851 ....M-47
Prosper, *Collin*, 2,097 ....D-34
Quanah, *Hardeman*, 3,022 ....A-14
Queen City, *Cass*, 1,613 ....O-34
Quinlan, *Hunt*, 1,370 ....F-38
Quitman, *Wood*, 2,030 ....D-21
Ralls, *Crosby*, 2,252 ....B-11
• Rancho Alegre, *Jim Wells*, 1,775 Q-22
Rancho Viejo, *Cameron*, 1,754 ....M-49
Ranger, *Eastland*, 2,584 ....E-16
Rankin, *Upton*, 800 ....G-10
Ransom Canyon, *Lubbock*, 1,011 M-3
Raymondville, *Willacy*, 9,733 ....P-18
Red Oak, *Ellis*, 4,301 ....I-34
• Redwood, *Guadalupe*, 3,586 ....L-26
Refugio, *Refugio*, 2,941 ....M-19
• Rendon, *Tarrant*, 9,022 ....H-31
Reno, *Lamar*, 2,767 ....B-21
Reno, *Parker*, 2,441 ....F-29
Richardson, *Dallas*, 91,802 ....F-34
Richland Hills, *Tarrant*, 8,132 ....G-31
Richmond, *Fort Bend*, 11,081 ....J-21
Richwood, *Brazoria*, 3,012 ....I-43
Rio Bravo, *Webb*, 5,553 ....O-15
Rio Grande City, *Starr*, 11,923 ....P-16
Rio Hondo, *Cameron*, 1,942 ....L-49
River Oaks, *Tarrant*, 6,985 ....G-30
Roanoke, *Denton*, 2,810 ....E-31
Robert Lee, *Coke*, 1,171 ....F-13
Robinson, *McLennan*, 7,845 ....G-19
Robstown, *Nueces*, 12,727 ....N-18
Roby, *Fisher*, 673 ....D-13
Rockdale, *Milam*, 5,439 ....H-19
Rockport, *Aransas*, 7,385 ....M-19
Rocksprings, *Edwards*, 1,285 ....I-13
Rockwall, *Rockwall*, 17,976 ....D-20
Rogers, *Bell*, 1,117 ....H-19
Rollingwood, *Travis*, 1,403 ....P-43
Roma, *Starr*, 9,617 ....P-16
Roman Forest,
Montgomery, 1,279 ....B-45
Roscoe, *Nolan*, 1,378 ....E-12
Rosebud, *Falls*, 1,493 ....G-19
Rosenberg, *Fort Bend*, 24,043 ....F-41
• Rosita North, *Maverick*, 3,400 ....L-13
• Rosita South, *Maverick*, 2,574 ....L-13
Rotan, *Fisher*, 1,611 ....D-13
Round Rock, *Williamson*, 61,136 .I-18
Rowlett, *Dallas*, 44,503 ....F-35
Royse City, *Rockwall*, 2,957 ....F-36
Runaway Bay, *Wise*, 1,104 ....C-17
Runge, *Karnes*, 1,080 ....L-18
Rusk, *Cherokee*, 5,085 ....F-22
Sabinal, *Jefferson*, 1,586 ....K-15
Sachse, *Dallas*, 9,751 ....F-35
Saginaw, *Tarrant*, 12,374 ....F-30
Saint Hedwig, *Bexar*, 1,875 ....N-25
• Salado, *Bell*, 3,475 ....H-18
San Angelo, *Tom Green*, 88,439 .G-13
San Antonio, *Bexar*, 1,144,646 ....K-16
San Augustine,
San Augustine, 2,475 ....F-24
San Benito, *Cameron*, 23,444 ....Q-18
• San Carlos, *Hidalgo*, 2,650 ....K-46
San Diego, *Duval*, 4,753 ....N-17
• San Elizario, *El Paso*, 11,046 ....F-3
San Juan, *Hidalgo*, 26,229 ....Q-17
• San Leon, *Galveston*, 4,365 ....F-46
San Marcos, *Hays*, 34,733 ....J-17
San Saba, *San Saba*, 2,637 ....G-16
Sanderson, *Terrell*, 861 ....I-9
Sanger, *Denton*, 4,534 ....C-19
Sansom Park, *Tarrant*, 4,181 ....G-30
Santa Anna, *Coleman*, 1,081 ....F-15
Santa Fe, *Galveston*, 9,548 ....G-45
Santa Rosa, *Cameron*, 2,833 ....L-48
Sarita, *Kenedy*, 200 ....O-18
• Scenic Oaks, *Bexar*, 3,279 ....M-22
Schertz, *Guadalupe*, 18,694 ....N-24
Schulenburg, *Fayette*, 2,699 ....J-19
• Scissors, *Hidalgo*, 2,805 ....L-46
Seabrook, *Harris*, 9,443 ....F-45
Seadrift, *Calhoun*, 1,352 ....L-20
Seagoville, *Dallas*, 10,823 ....H-35
Seagraves, *Gaines*, 2,334 ....D-9
Sealy, *Austin*, 5,248 ....J-20
• Sebastian, *Willacy*, 1,864 ....K-48
Seguin, *Guadalupe*, 22,011 ....J-17
Seminole, *Gaines*, 5,910 ....D-9
• Serenada, *Williamson*, 1,847 ....H-18
• Seth Ward, *Hale*, 1,926 ....A-11
Seven Points, *Henderson*, 1,145 .E-20
Seymour, *Baylor*, 2,908 ....C-15
• Shady Hollow, *Travis*, 5,140 ....I-18
Shady Shores, *Denton*, 1,461 ....D-32
Shallowater, *Lubbock*, 2,086 ....B-10
Shamrock, *Wheeler*, 2,029 ....C-5
Shavano Park, *Bexar*, 1,754 ....N-23
• Sheldon, *Harris*, 1,831 ....D-45
Shenandoah, *Montgomery*, 1,503 B-43
Shepherd, *San Jacinto*, 2,029 ....H-22
Sherman, *Grayson*, 35,082 ....C-19
Shiner, *Lavaca*, 2,070 ....K-19
Shoreacres, *Harris*, 1,488 ....F-45
Sienna Plantation,
Fort Bend, 1,896 ....F-43
Sierra Blanca, *Hudspeth*, 533 ....G-4
Silsbee, *Hardin*, 6,393 ....I-24
Silverton, *Briscoe*, 771 ....E-4
Sinton, *San Patricio*, 5,676 ....M-18
• Skidmore, *Bee*, 1,013 ....M-18
Slaton, *Lubbock*, 6,109 ....C-11
Smithville, *Bastrop*, 3,901 ....I-19
Snyder, *Scurry*, 10,783 ....D-12
Socorro, *El Paso*, 27,152 ....F-3
Somerset, *Bexar*, 1,550 ....K-16
Somerville, *Burleson*, 1,704 ....I-20
Sonora, *Sutton*, 2,924 ....H-12
Sour Lake, *Hardin*, 1,667 ....B-49
• South Alamo, *Hidalgo*, 3,101 ....L-46
South Houston, *Harris*, 15,833 ....E-44
South Padre Island,
Cameron, 2,422 ....Q-19
South Point, *Cameron*, 1,118 ....Q-19
Southlake, *Tarrant*, 21,519 ....F-32
Southside Place, *Harris*, 1,546 ....E-43
• Sparks, *Bell*, 2,974 ....H-18
Spearman, *Hansford*, 3,021 ....A-4
Splendora, *Montgomery*, 1,275 ....B-45
• Spring, *Harris*, 36,385 ....I-22
Spring Valley, *Harris*, 3,611 ....E-43
Springtown, *Parker*, 2,062 ....F-29
Spur, *Dickens*, 1,088 ....C-12
Stafford, *Fort Bend*, 15,681 ....F-42
Stamford, *Jones*, 3,636 ....D-14
Stanton, *Martin*, 2,556 ....E-10
Stephenville, *Erath*, 14,921 ....E-17
Sterling City, *Sterling*, 1,081 ....F-12
Stinnett, *Hutchinson*, 1,936 ....B-3
Stockdale, *Wilson*, 1,398 ....K-17
• Stowell, *Chambers*, 1,572 ....E-49
Stratford, *Sherman*, 1,991 ....A-2
Sudan, *Lamb*, 1,039 ....B-9
Sugar Land, *Fort Bend*, 63,328 ....J-21
Sullivan City, *Hidalgo*, 3,998 ....K-43
Sulphur Springs, *Hopkins*, 14,551 C-21
Sundown, *Hockley*, 1,505 ....C-9
Sunnyvale, *Dallas*, 2,693 ....G-35
Sunray, *Moore*, 1,950 ....B-3
Sweeny, *Brazoria*, 3,624 ....I-42
Sweetwater, *Nolan*, 11,415 ....E-13
Taft, *San Patricio*, 3,396 ....M-18
• Taft Southwest,
San Patricio, 1,721 ....P-25
Tahoka, *Lynn*, 2,910 ....C-10
Talty, *Kaufman*, 1,028 ....G-36
Tatum, *Rusk*, 1,175 ....E-23
Taylor, *Williamson*, 13,575 ....H-18
Taylor Lake Village, *Harris*, 3,694 F-45
Teague, *Freestone*, 4,557 ....F-20
Temple, *Bell*, 54,514 ....G-18
Tenaha, *Shelby*, 1,046 ....F-24
Terrell, *Kaufman*, 13,606 ....D-20
Terrell Hills, *Bexar*, 5,019 ....N-23
Texarkana, *Bowie*, 34,782 ....C-24
Texas City, *Galveston*, 41,521 ....K-23
The Colony, *Denton*, 26,531 ....E-33
The Hills, *Travis*, 1,492 ....O-42
• The Woodlands,
Montgomery, 55,649 ....I-22
Thorndale, *Milam*, 1,278 ....H-19
Three Rivers, *Live Oak*, 1,878 ....L-17
Throckmorton,
Throckmorton, 905 ....C-15
Tilden, *McMullen*, 450 ....L-16
• Timberwood Park, *Bexar*, 5,889 ....J-17
Timpson, *Shelby*, 1,094 ....F-23
Tomball, *Harris*, 9,089 ....I-21
Tool, *Henderson*, 2,275 ....E-20
• Tornillo, *El Paso*, 1,609 ....F-3
Trinidad, *Henderson*, 1,091 ....E-20
Trinity, *Trinity*, 2,721 ....H-22
Trophy Club, *Denton*, 6,350 ....E-31
Troup, *Smith*, 1,949 ....E-22
Troy, *Bell*, 1,378 ....G-18
Tulia, *Swisher*, 5,117 ....A-10
Tye, *Taylor*, 1,158 ....E-14
Tyler, *Smith*, 83,650 ....E-22
Universal City, *Bexar*, 14,849 ....N-24
University Park, *Dallas*, 23,324 ....F-34
Uvalde, *Uvalde*, 14,929 ....K-14
• Uvalde Estates, *Uvalde*, 1,972 ....K-14
• Val Verde Park, *Val Verde*, 1,945 .K-12
Valley Mills, *Bosque*, 1,123 ....F-18
Van, *Van Zandt*, 2,362 ....E-21
Van Alstyne, *Grayson*, 2,502 ....C-20
Van Horn, *Culberson*, 2,435 ....G-5
• Van Vleck, *Matagorda*, 1,411 ....I-41
Vega, *Oldham*, 936 ....C-2
Vernon, *Wilbarger*, 11,660 ....B-15
Victoria, *Victoria*, 60,603 ....L-19
Vidor, *Orange*, 11,440 ....I-24
Vinton, *El Paso*, 1,892 ....O-1
Waco, *McLennan*, 113,726 ....G-19
Wake Village, *Bowie*, 5,129 ....N-34
Waller, *Waller*, 2,092 ....C-40
Wallis, *Austin*, 1,172 ....E-40
Waskom, *Harrison*, 2,068 ....E-24
Watauga, *Tarrant*, 21,908 ....F-31
Waxahachie, *Ellis*, 21,426 ....E-19
Weatherford, *Parker*, 19,000 ....D-18
Webster, *Harris*, 9,083 ....F-45
Weimar, *Colorado*, 1,981 ....J-19
Wellington, *Collingsworth*, 2,275 ..D-5
• Wells Branch, *Travis*, 11,271 ....O-43
Weslaco, *Hidalgo*, 26,935 ....Q-17
West, *McLennan*, 2,692 ....F-19
West Columbia, *Brazoria*, 4,255 ..K-21
West Lake Hills, *Travis*, 3,116 ....P-43
• West Livingston, *Polk*, 6,612 ....H-22
• West Odessa, *Ector*, 17,799 ....F-9
West Orange, *Orange*, 4,111 ....C-52
• West Sharyland, *Hidalgo*, 2,947 ..K-44
West Tawakoni, *Hunt*, 1,462 ....F-38
West University Place,
Harris, 14,211 ....E-43
• Westway, *El Paso*, 3,829 ....O-1
Westworth Village, *Tarrant*, 2,124 G-30
Wharton, *Wharton*, 9,237 ....K-21
Wheeler, *Wheeler*, 1,378 ....C-5
White Deer, *Carson*, 1,060 ....C-4
White Oak, *Gregg*, 5,624 ....E-22
White Settlement, *Tarrant*, 14,831 G-30
Whitehouse, *Smith*, 5,346 ....E-22
Whitesboro, *Grayson*, 3,760 ....B-19
Whitewright, *Grayson*, 1,740 ....C-20
Whitney, *Hill*, 1,833 ....F-18
Wichita Falls, *Wichita*, 104,197 ...B-16
• Wild Peach Village,
Brazoria, 2,498 ....I-42
Willis, *Montgomery*, 3,985 ....I-22
Willow Park, *Parker*, 2,849 ....G-29
Wills Point, *Van Zandt*, 3,496 ....D-21
Wilmer, *Dallas*, 3,393 ....H-34
• Wimberley, *Hays*, 3,797 ....I-17
Windcrest, *Bexar*, 5,105 ....N-24
• Windemere, *Travis*, 6,868 ....O-43
• Winnie, *Chambers*, 2,914 ....J-24
Winnsboro, *Wood*, 3,584 ....D-22
Winters, *Runnels*, 2,880 ....F-13
Wolfe City, *Hunt*, 1,566 ....C-20
Wolfforth, *Lubbock*, 2,554 ....C-10
Woodbranch, *Montgomery*, 1,305 B-44
Woodcreek, *Hays*, 1,274 ....Q-41
Woodsboro, *Refugio*, 1,685 ....M-19
Woodville, *Tyler*, 2,415 ....H-23
Woodway, *McLennan*, 8,733 ....K-36
Wortham, *Freestone*, 1,082 ....F-20
• Wyldwood, *Bastrop*, 2,310 ....P-44
Wylie, *Collin*, 15,132 ....E-35
Yoakum, *Dewitt*, 5,731 ....K-19
Yorktown, *De Witt*, 2,271 ....K-18
• Zapata, *Zapata*, 4,856 ....O-15

COUNTIES

(29 Counties)

Name of County	Population	Location on Map
BEAVER	6,005	N-1
BOX ELDER	42,745	E-1
CACHE	91,391	F-6
CARBON	20,422	K-8
DAGGETT	921	H-9
DAVIS	238,994	G-5
DUCHESNE	14,371	H-7
EMERY	10,860	K-7
GARFIELD	4,735	O-4
GRAND	8,485	K-9
IRON	33,779	O-1
JUAB	8,238	J-1
KANE	6,046	P-3
MILLARD	12,405	K-1
MORGAN	7,129	G-5
PIUTE	1,435	N-5
RICH	1,961	F-6
SALT LAKE	898,387	H-5
SAN JUAN	14,413	N-9
SANPETE	22,763	J-6
SEVIER	18,842	L-6
SUMMIT	29,736	G-6
TOOELE	40,735	H-1
UINTAH	25,224	H-9
UTAH	368,536	I-5
WASATCH	15,215	I-6
WASHINGTON	90,354	P-1
WAYNE	2,509	N-5
WEBER	196,533	G-6
TOTAL	**2,233,169**	

CITIES AND TOWNS

Note: The first name is that of the city or town, second, that of the county in which it is located, then the population and location on the map.

Alpine, *Utah,* 7,146 ....I-5
American Fork, *Utah,* 21,941 ....G-10
Beaver, *Beaver,* 2,454 ....N-4
•Benjamin, *Utah,* 1,029 ....J-6
•Benson, *Cache,* 1,451 ....E-5
Blanding, *San Juan,* 3,162 ....P-10
Bluffdale, *Salt Lake,* 4,700 ....F-9
Bountiful, *Davis,* 41,301 ....H-5
Brigham City, *Box Elder,* 17,411 ....F-5
•Canyon Rim, *Salt Lake,* 10,428 ....E-10
Castle Dale, *Emery,* 1,657 ....L-7
Cedar City, *Iron,* 20,527 ....P-3
Cedar Hills, *Utah,* 3,094 ....G-10
Centerfield, *Sanpete,* 1,048 ....L-5
Centerville, *Davis,* 14,585 ....C-10
Clearfield, *Davis,* 25,974 ....B-9
Clinton, *Davis,* 12,585 ....B-9
Coalville, *Summit,* 1,382 ....H-6
•Cottonwood Heights, *Salt Lake,* 27,569 ....E-10
•Cottonwood West, *Salt Lake,* 18,727 ....E-10
Delta, *Millard,* 3,209 ....K-4
Draper, *Salt Lake,* 25,220 ....F-10
Duchesne, *Duchesne,* 1,408 ....I-8
•Dugway, *Tooele,* 2,016 ....I-3
Eagle Mountain, *Utah,* 2,157 ....I-5
East Carbon, *Carbon,* 1,393 ....K-8
•East Millcreek, *Salt Lake,* 21,385 ....E-10
Elk Ridge, *Utah,* 1,838 ....D-4
Enoch, *Iron,* 3,467 ....O-3
Enterprise, *Washington,* 1,285 ....P-1
Ephraim, *Sanpete,* 4,505 ....K-6
•Erda, *Tooele,* 2,473 ....E-8
Fairview, *Sanpete,* 1,160 ....K-6
Farmington, *Davis,* 12,081 ....G-5
Farr West, *Weber,* 3,094 ....A-9
Ferron, *Emery,* 1,623 ....L-7
Fillmore, *Millard,* 2,253 ....L-4
Fruit Heights, *Davis,* 4,701 ....C-10
Garland, *Box Elder,* 1,943 ....D-1
•Granite, *Salt Lake,* 2,018 ....E-10
Grantsville, *Tooele,* 6,015 ....H-4
Gunnison, *Sanpete,* 2,394 ....L-5
Harrisville, *Weber,* 3,645 ....A-9
Heber City, *Wasatch,* 7,291 ....I-6
Helper, *Carbon,* 2,025 ....K-7
Herriman, *Salt Lake,* 1,523 ....F-9
Highland, *Utah,* 8,172 ....G-10
Hildale, *Washington,* 1,895 ....Q-3
Holladay, *Salt Lake,* 14,561 ....E-10
Honeyville, *Box Elder,* 1,214 ....D-1
•Hooper, *Weber,* 3,926 ....B-8
Huntington, *Emery,* 2,131 ....L-7
Hurricane, *Washington,* 8,250 ....Q-2
Hyde Park, *Cache,* 2,955 ....E-5
Hyrum, *Cache,* 6,316 ....F-5
Ivins, *Washington,* 4,450 ....Q-1
Junction, *Piute,* 177 ....N-5
Kamas, *Summit,* 1,274 ....H-6
Kanab, *Kane,* 3,564 ....Q-4
Kaysville, *Davis,* 20,351 ....C-9
•Kearns, *Salt Lake,* 33,659 ....E-9
La Verkin, *Washington,* 3,392 ....Q-2
Layton, *Davis,* 58,474 ....G-5
Lehi, *Utah,* 19,028 ....I-5
Lewiston, *Cache,* 1,877 ....E-5
Lindon, *Utah,* 8,363 ....G-10
•Little Cottonwood Creek Valley, *Salt Lake,* 7,221 ....E-10
Loa, *Wayne,* 525 ....N-6
Logan, *Cache,* 42,670 ....F-5
•Maeser, *Uintah,* 2,855 ....I-10
•Magna, *Salt Lake,* 22,770 ....E-9
Manila, *Daggett,* 308 ....G-9
Manti, *Sanpete,* 3,040 ....L-6
Mapleton, *Utah,* 5,809 ....C-5
Marriott-Slaterville, *Weber,* 1,425 ....A-9
Midvale, *Salt Lake,* 27,029 ....E-10
Midway, *Wasatch,* 2,121 ....I-6
Milford, *Beaver,* 1,451 ....N-3
•Millcreek, *Salt Lake,* 30,377 ....E-10
Millville, *Cache,* 1,507 ....D-3
Moab, *Grand,* 4,779 ....M-10
Monroe, *Sevier,* 1,845 ....M-5
Monticello, *San Juan,* 1,958 ....O-10
Morgan, *Morgan,* 2,635 ....G-6
Moroni, *Sanpete,* 1,280 ....K-6
•Mount Olympus, *Salt Lake,* 7,103 ....E-10
Mount Pleasant, *Sanpete,* 2,707 ....K-6
Murray, *Salt Lake,* 34,024 ....E-10
Naples, *Uintah,* 1,300 ....I-10
Nephi, *Juab,* 4,733 ....K-5
Nibley, *Cache,* 2,045 ....D-3
North Logan, *Cache,* 6,163 ....D-3
North Ogden, *Weber,* 15,026 ....A-9
North Salt Lake, *Davis,* 8,749 ....D-10
•North Snydersville Basin, *Summit,* 1,821 ....D-12
Ogden, *Weber,* 77,226 ....G-5
•Oquirrh, *Salt Lake,* 10,390 ....E-9
Orangeville, *Emery,* 1,398 ....L-7
Orem, *Utah,* 84,324 ....I-6
Panguitch, *Garfield,* 1,623 ....O-4
Park City, *Summit,* 7,371 ....H-6
Parowan, *Iron,* 2,565 ....O-3
Payson, *Utah,* 12,716 ....J-6
Perry, *Box Elder,* 2,383 ....F-5
Plain City, *Weber,* 3,489 ....A-9
Pleasant Grove, *Utah,* 23,468 ....G-10
Pleasant View, *Weber,* 5,632 ....G-5
Price, *Carbon,* 8,402 ....K-7
Providence, *Cache,* 4,377 ....D-3
Provo, *Utah,* 105,166 ....I-6
Randolph, *Rich,* 483 ....F-7
Richfield, *Sevier,* 6,847 ....M-5
Richmond, *Cache,* 2,051 ....E-5
River Heights, *Cache,* 1,496 ....D-3
Riverdale, *Weber,* 7,656 ....B-9
Riverton, *Salt Lake,* 25,011 ....I-5
Roosevelt, *Duchesne,* 4,299 ....I-9
Roy, *Weber,* 32,885 ....G-5
Saint George, *Washington,* 49,663 ....Q-2
Salem, *Utah,* 4,372 ....D-4
Salina, *Sevier,* 2,393 ....L-5
Salt Lake City, *Salt Lake,* 181,743 ....H-5
Sandy, *Salt Lake,* 88,418 ....H-5
Santa Clara, *Washington,* 4,630 ....Q-2
Santaquin, *Utah,* 4,834 ....D-4
Saratoga Springs, *Utah,* 1,003 ....G-10
Smithfield, *Cache,* 7,261 ....E-5
South Jordan, *Salt Lake,* 29,437 ....F-9
South Ogden, *Weber,* 14,377 ....B-9
South Salt Lake, *Salt Lake,* 22,038 ....E-10
•South Snydersville Basin, *Summit,* 3,636 ....E-12
South Weber, *Davis,* 4,260 ....B-9
Spanish Fork, *Utah,* 20,246 ....J-6
Springville, *Utah,* 20,424 ....C-5
•Stansbury Park, *Tooele,* 2,385 ....E-8
•Summit Park, *Summit,* 6,597 ....H-6
Sunset, *Davis,* 5,204 ....B-9
Syracuse, *Davis,* 9,398 ....B-9
Taylorsville, *Salt Lake,* 57,439 ....E-9
Tooele, *Tooele,* 22,502 ....I-4
Tremonton, *Box Elder,* 5,592 ....F-5
Uintah, *Weber,* 1,127 ....B-9
Vernal, *Uintah,* 7,714 ....I-10
Washington, *Washington,* 8,186 ....Q-2
Washington Terrace, *Weber,* 8,551 ....B-9
Wellington, *Carbon,* 1,666 ....K-8
Wellsville, *Cache,* 2,728 ....F-5
Wendover, *Tooele,* 1,537 ....H-1
West Bountiful, *Davis,* 4,484 ....C-10
West Haven, *Weber,* 3,976 ....A-9
West Jordan, *Salt Lake,* 68,336 ....E-9
West Point, *Davis,* 6,033 ....B-9
West Valley City, *Salt Lake,* 108,896 ....H-5
•White City, *Salt Lake,* 5,988 ....F-10
Willard, *Box Elder,* 1,630 ....F-5
Woods Cross, *Davis,* 6,419 ....D-10

Explanation of symbols: • - Census Designated Place (CDP)

County-Town
UTAH
American Map

0 20 40 60 Miles
0 20 40 60 Kilometers

Explanation of Symbols

- State Capital
- Vernon — County Seat
- MSA Boundary
- 251 — MSA Number
- UTAH — County Name

Population Key

- 0-999
- 1,000-2,499
- 2,500-4,999
- 5,000-9,999
- 10,000-19,999
- 20,000-24,999
- 25,000-49,999
- 50,000-99,999
- 100,000-249,999

Inset 1: 0 5 Mi; 0 5 Km
Clarkston, Trenton, Richmond, CACHE, BOX ELDER, Newton, Amalga, Cache, Smithfield, Fielding, Hyde Park, Riverside, Benson, North Logan, Petersboro, Garland, Logan, River Heights, Tremonton, Mendon, Providence, Deweyville, Elwood, Nibley, Millville, Honeyville, Wellsville, Hyrum

Inset 2: 0 5 Mi; 0 5 Km
Provo, 227, Springville, Utah Lake, Palmyra, Mapleton, Lake Shore, Spanish Fork, Benjamin, West Mountain, Salem, UTAH, Payson, Woodland Hills, Spring Lake, Elk Ridge, Genola, Santaquin

Inset 3: 0 10 20 Mi; 0 10 20 Km
Pleasant View, North Ogden, WEBER, Plain City, Farr West, Harrisville, Huntsville, Marriott-Slaterville, Ogden, West Haven, South Ogden, Riverdale, Washington Terrace, Hooper, Roy, Uintah, Clinton, Sunset, South Weber, MORGAN, West Point, Clearfield, Syracuse, Layton, Great Salt Lake, Kaysville, Fruit Heights, Morgan, Henefer, Farmington, SUMMIT, DAVIS, Centerville, Coalville, West Bountiful, Woods Cross, Bountiful, North Salt Lake, SALT LAKE, Salt Lake City, Summit Park, North Snydersville Basin, West Valley City, S. Salt Lake, Canyon Rim, Oakley, Magna, Millcreek, East Millcreek, South Snydersville Basin, Stansbury Park, Taylorsville, Mount Olympus, Holladay, Park City, Kamas, Kearns, Murray, Cottonwood West, Oquirrh, Midvale, Cottonwood Hts., Francis, Samak, Erda, West Jordan, Little Cottonwood Creek Valley, Alta, Sandy, Woodland, Tooele, South Jordan, White City, Granite, WASATCH, Riverton, Draper, Midway, Heber City, Herriman, TOOELE, 251, Bluffdale, 227, Charleston, Daniel, Timber Lakes, Alpine, Highland, Cedar Hills, UTAH, Lehi, Wallsburg, Ophir, American Fork, Pleasant Grove, Saratoga Springs, Lindon

Main map:
ID, WY, NV, CO, AZ
BOX ELDER: Snowville, Portage, Cornish, Lewiston, Cove, Garden City, Richmond, Garden, Smithfield, Laketown, Howell, Benson, Hyde Park, Tremonton, Logan, Randolph, Wellsville, Hyrum, Bear River City, Paradise, Corinne, Avon, Woodruff, Brigham City, Mantua, CACHE, Perry, RICH, Willard, South Willard, Great Salt Lake, Pleasant View, WEBER, Ogden, Roy, DAVIS, MORGAN, Layton, Morgan, SUMMIT, Farmington, Coalville
TOOELE, Bountiful, Salt Lake City, Summit Park, Wendover, West Valley City, SALT LAKE, Oakley, Kamas, Samak, Park City, Grantsville, Sandy, 251, Midway, Heber City, Tooele, Riverton, Alpine, Daniel, Timber Lakes, Stockton, Lehi, Rush Valley, Cedar Fort, Vineyard, Orem, WASATCH, Eagle Mountain, Dugway, UTAH, Provo, Benjamin, Spanish Fork, Payson, Vernon, Elberta, Goshen, Eureka, 227, Rocky Ridge, Mona
DAGGETT, Manila, UINTAH, DUCHESNE, Maeser, Vernal, Neola, Whiterocks, Naples, Tabiona, Altamont, Ballard, Roosevelt, Fort Duchesne, Randlett, Duchesne, Myton
JUAB, Nephi, SANPETE, Scofield, CARBON, Helper, Price, Fountain Green, Fairview, Wellington, Sunnyside, Levan, Moroni, Mount Pleasant, East Carbon, Wales, Spring City, MILLARD, Lynndyl, Leamington, Oak City, Ephraim, EMERY, Elmo, Hinckley, Delta, Huntington, Cleveland, GRAND, Manti, Scipio, Fayette, Orangeville, Castle Dale, Gunnison, Sterling, Clawson, Holden, Centerfield, Mayfield, Ferron, Green River, Fillmore, Redmond, SEVIER, Salina, Emery, Meadow, Aurora, Sigurd, Kanosh, Richfield, Glenwood, Castle Valley, Elsinore, Annabella, Moab, Joseph, Monroe, Koosharem
BEAVER, Marysvale, PIUTE, SAN JUAN, Spanish Valley, Loa, Lyman, Milford, Bicknell, La Sal, Torrey, Beaver, Junction, Minersville, Circleville, Kingston, WAYNE, IRON, GARFIELD, Antimony, Boulder, Monticello, Paragonah, Parowan, Panguitch, Escalante, Enoch, Brian Head, Cedar City, Blanding, Hatch, Tropic, Enterprise, Cannonville, Henrieville, Kanarraville, New Harmony, White Mesa, WASHINGTON, KANE, Alton, 93, Halls Crossing, Glendale, Montezuma Creek, Bluff, Aneth, Toquerville, Leeds, La Verkin, Orderville, Ivins, Hurricane, Springdale, Mexican Hat, Tselakai Dezza, Santa Clara, Virgin, Rockville, Halchita, St. George, Washington, Kanab, Big Water, Oljato-Monument Valley, Hildale, Navajo Mountain

COUNTIES

(14 Counties)

Name of County	Population	Location on Map
ADDISON	35,974	F-3
BENNINGTON	36,994	M-2
CALEDONIA	29,702	C-8
CHITTENDEN	146,571	D-3
ESSEX	6,459	A-10
FRANKLIN	45,417	A-3
GRAND ISLE	6,901	A-2
LAMOILLE	23,233	C-5
ORANGE	28,226	G-6
ORLEANS	26,277	A-6
RUTLAND	63,400	J-2
WASHINGTON	58,039	E-6
WINDHAM	44,216	N-6
WINDSOR	57,418	I-5
TOTAL	**608,827**	

CITIES AND TOWNS

Note: The first name is that of the city or town, second, that of the county in which it is located, then the population and location on the map.

▲Addison, *Addison,* 1,393 ... H-2
▲Alburg, *Grand Isle,* 1,952 ... A-2
●Arlington, *Bennington,* 1,199 ... O-3
▲Arlington, *Bennington,* 2,397 ... O-3
▲Bakersfield, *Franklin,* 1,215 ... C-5
▲Barnet, *Caledonia,* 1,690 ... F-9
Barre, *Washington,* 9,291 ... G-6
▲Barre, *Washington,* 7,602 ... G-6
▲Barton, *Orleans,* 2,780 ... C-8
Bellows Falls, *Windham,* 3,165 ... N-7
●Bennington, *Bennington,* 9,168 ... P-3
▲Bennington, *Bennington,* 15,737 ... P-2
▲Benson, *Rutland,* 1,039 ... J-2
▲Berkshire, *Franklin,* 1,388 ... A-5
▲Berlin, *Washington,* 2,864 ... G-6
▲Bethel, *Windsor,* 1,968 ... I-6
▲Bradford, *Orange,* 2,619 ... H-8
▲Braintree, *Orange,* 1,194 ... H-5
●Brandon, *Rutland,* 1,684 ... J-3
▲Brandon, *Rutland,* 3,917 ... J-3
●Brattleboro, *Windham,* 8,289 ... P-6
▲Brattleboro, *Windham,* 12,005 ... P-6
▲Bridport, *Addison,* 1,235 ... H-2
▲Brighton, *Essex,* 1,260 ... B-10
▲Bristol, *Addison,* 3,788 ... G-3
▲Brookfield, *Orange,* 1,222 ... H-6
▲Burke, *Caledonia,* 1,571 ... D-9
Burlington, *Chittenden,* 38,889 ... E-3
▲Cabot, *Washington,* 1,213 ... E-7
▲Calais, *Washington,* 1,529 ... F-7
▲Cambridge, *Lamoille,* 3,186 ... D,,5
▲Canaan, *Essex,* 1,078 ... A-11
▲Castleton, *Rutland,* 4,367 ... K-3
▲Cavendish, *Windsor,* 1,470 ... M-6
▲Charlotte, *Chittenden,* 3,569 ... F-2
▲Chelsea, *Orange,* 1,250 ... H-7
▲Chester, *Windsor,* 3,044 ... M-6
▲Chittenden, *Rutland,* 1,182 ... J-4
▲Clarendon, *Rutland,* 2,811 ... L-4
▲Colchester, *Chittenden,* 16,986 ... D-3
▲Concord, *Essex,* 1,196 ... E-10
▲Corinth, *Orange,* 1,461 ... H-7
▲Cornwall, *Addison,* 1,136 ... H-3
▲Coventry, *Orleans,* 1,014 ... B-8
▲Craftsbury, *Orleans,* 1,136 ... D-7
▲Danby, *Rutland,* 1,292 ... M-4
▲Danville, *Caledonia,* 2,211 ... E-8
▲Derby, *Orleans,* 4,604 ... A-8
▲Dorset, *Bennington,* 2,036 ... M-3
▲Dover, *Windham,* 1,410 ... O-4
▲Dummerston, *Windham,* 1,915 ... P-6
▲Duxbury, *Washington,* 1,289 ... F-5
▲East Montpelier, *Washington,* 2,578 ... F-6
▲Eden, *Lamoille,* 1,152 ... C-6
▲Enosburg, *Franklin,* 2,788 ... B-5
Enosburg Falls, *Franklin,* 1,473 ... B-5
▲Essex, *Chittenden,* 18,626 ... D-3
Essex Junction, *Chittenden,* 8,591 ... E-3
▲Faifax, *Franklin,* 3,765 ... C-4
●Fair Haven, *Rutland,* 2,435 ... K-2
▲Fair Haven, *Rutland,* 2,928 ... K-2
▲Fairfield, *Franklin,* 1,800 ... B-4
▲Fayston, *Washington,* 1,141 ... G-4
▲Ferrisburg, *Addison,* 2,657 ... G-2
▲Franklin, *Franklin,* 1,268 ... A-4
▲Grand Isle, *Grand Isle,* 1,955 ... C-2
●Graniteville-East Barre, *Washington,* 2,136 ... G-7
▲Guilford, *Windham,* 2,046 ... Q-6
▲Hardwick, *Caledonia,* 3,174 ... E-7
▲Hartford, *Windsor,* 10,367 ... K-7
▲Hartland, *Windsor,* 3,223 ... K-7
▲Highgate, *Franklin,* 3,397 ... A-3
▲Hinesburg, *Chittenden,* 4,340 ... F-3
▲Huntington, *Chittenden,* 1,861 ... F-4
▲Hyde Park, *Lamoille,* 2,847 ... D-6
Hyde Park, *Lamoille,* 415 ... D-6
▲Irasburg, *Orleans,* 1,077 ... B-7
Jericho, *Chittenden,* 1,457 ... E-4
▲Jericho, *Chittenden,* 5,015 ... E-4
Johnson, *Lamoille,* 1,420 ... D-5
▲Johnson, *Lamoille,* 3,274 ... D-5
▲Killington, *Rutland,* 1,095 ... K-5
▲Lincoln, *Addison,* 1,214 ... G-4
▲Londonderry, *Windham,* 1,709 ... N-5
▲Ludlow, *Windsor,* 2,449 ... L-5
▲Lunenburg, *Essex,* 1,328 ... E-11
▲Lyndon, *Caledonia,* 5,448 ... E-9
Lyndonville, *Caledonia,* 1,227 ... D-9
▲Manchester, *Bennington,* 4,180 ... N-3
Manchester, *Bennington,* 602 ... N-3
●Manchester Center, *Bennington,* 2,065 ... N-3
▲Marshfield, *Washington,* 1,496 ... F-7
▲Mendon, *Rutland,* 1,028 ... K-4
●Middlebury, *Addison,* 6,252 ... H-3
▲Middlebury, *Addison,* 8,183 ... H-3
▲Middlesex, *Washington,* 1,729 ... F-5
Milton, *Chittenden,* 1,537 ... D-3
▲Milton, *Chittenden,* 9,479 ... D-3
▲Monkton, *Addison,* 1,759 ... F-3
Montpelier, *Washington,* 8,035 ... F-6
▲Moretown, *Washington,* 1,653 ... F-5
▲Morristown, *Lamoille,* 5,139 ... D-6
Morrisville, *Lamoille,* 2,009 ... D-6
▲Mount Holly, *Rutland,* 1,241 ... L-5
▲New Haven, *Addison,* 1,666 ... G-3
▲Newbury, *Orange,* 1,955 ... G-8
Newfane, *Windham,* 116 ... O-5
▲Newfane, *Windham,* 1,680 ... P-5
Newport, *Orleans,* 5,005 ... B-8
▲Newport, *Orleans,* 1,511 ... B-7
North Bennington, *Bennington,* 1,428 ... P-2
Northfield, *Washington,* 3,208 ... G-5
▲Northfield, *Washington,* 5,791 ... G-5
▲Norwich, *Windsor,* 3,544 ... J-7
▲Orwell, *Addison,* 1,185 ... J-2
▲Pawlet, *Rutland,* 1,394 ... M-3
▲Pittsford, *Rutland,* 3,140 ... J-3
▲Plainfield, *Washington,* 1,286 ... F-7
Poultney, *Rutland,* 1,575 ... L-2
▲Poultney, *Rutland,* 3,633 ... L-3
▲Pownal, *Bennington,* 3,560 ... Q-2
Proctor, *Rutland,* 1,877 ... K-3
▲Putney, *Windham,* 2,634 ... P-6
▲Randolph, *Orange,* 4,853 ... I-5
▲Richford, *Franklin,* 2,321 ... A-5
▲Richmond, *Chittenden,* 4,090 ... E-4
▲Rochester, *Windsor,* 1,171 ... I-5
▲Rockingham, *Windham,* 5,309 ... N-6
▲Royalton, *Windsor,* 2,603 ... J-6
Rutland, *Rutland,* 17,292 ... K-4
▲Rutland, *Rutland,* 4,038 ... K-4
▲Ryegate, *Caledonia,* 1,150 ... G-8
Saint Albans, *Franklin,* 7,650 ... B-3
▲Saint Albans, *Franklin,* 5,086 ... B-3
Saint Johnsbury, *Caledonia,* 6,319 ... E-9
▲Saint Johnsbury, *Caledonia,* 7,571 ... E-9
▲Salisbury, *Addison,* 1,090 ... I-3
▲Shaftsbury, *Bennington,* 3,767 ... O-3
▲Sharon, *Windsor,* 1,411 ... J-7
▲Shelburne, *Chittenden,* 6,944 ... E-2
▲Sheldon, *Franklin,* 1,990 ... B-4
▲Shoreham, *Addison,* 1,222 ... I-2
▲Shrewsbury, *Rutland,* 1,108 ... L-4
●South Barre, *Washington,* 1,242 ... G-6
South Burlington, *Chittenden,* 15,814 ... E-3
▲South Hero, *Grand Isle,* 1,696 ... D-2
●Springfield, *Windsor,* 3,938 ... M-6
▲Springfield, *Windsor,* 9,078 ... M-6
▲Starksboro, *Addison,* 1,898 ... G-3
▲Stowe, *Lamoille,* 4,339 ... E-5
▲Strafford, *Orange,* 1,045 ... I-7
▲Sutton, *Caledonia,* 1,001 ... D-9
Swanton, *Franklin,* 2,548 ... B-3
▲Swanton, *Franklin,* 6,203 ... B-3
▲Thetford, *Orange,* 2,617 ... I-8
▲Topsham, *Orange,* 1,142 ... G-8
▲Townshend, *Windham,* 1,149 ... O-5
▲Troy, *Orleans,* 1,564 ... B-7
▲Tunbridge, *Orange,* 1,309 ... I-6
▲Underhill, *Chittenden,* 2,980 ... D-4
Vergennes, *Addison,* 2,741 ... G-2
▲Vernon, *Windham,* 2,141 ... Q-6
▲Waitsfield, *Washington,* 1,659 ... G-5
▲Wallingford, *Rutland,* 2,274 ... L-4
▲Warren, *Washington,* 1,681 ... G-4
▲Washington, *Orange,* 1,047 ... G-7
Waterbury, *Washington,* 1,706 ... E-5
▲Waterbury, *Washington,* 4,915 ... E-5
▲Waterford, *Caledonia,* 1,104 ... F-9
▲Weathersfield, *Windsor,* 2,788 ... M-6
▲Wells, *Rutland,* 1,121 ... L-3
●West Brattleboro, *Windham,* 3,222 ... P-6
●West Rutland, *Rutland,* 2,263 ... K-3
▲West Rutland, *Rutland,* 2,535 ... K-3
▲West Windsor, *Windsor,* 1,067 ... L-6
▲Westford, *Chittenden,* 2,086 ... D-4
▲Westminster, *Windham,* 3,210 ... O-6
●White River Junction, *Windsor,* 2,569 ... K-7
▲Whitingham, *Windham,* 1,298 ... Q-4
●Wilder, *Windsor,* 1,636 ... J-7
▲Williamstown, *Orange,* 3,225 ... G-6
▲Williston, *Chittenden,* 7,650 ... E-3
▲Wilmington, *Windham,* 2,225 ... P-4
Windsor, *Windsor,* 3,756 ... L-7
Winooski, *Chittenden,* 6,561 ... E-3
▲Wolcott, *Lamoille,* 1,456 ... D-7
▲Woodstock, *Windsor,* 3,232 ... K-6
Woodstock, *Windsor,* 977 ... K-6

Explanation of symbols: ● - Census Designated Place (CDP) ▲ - Township

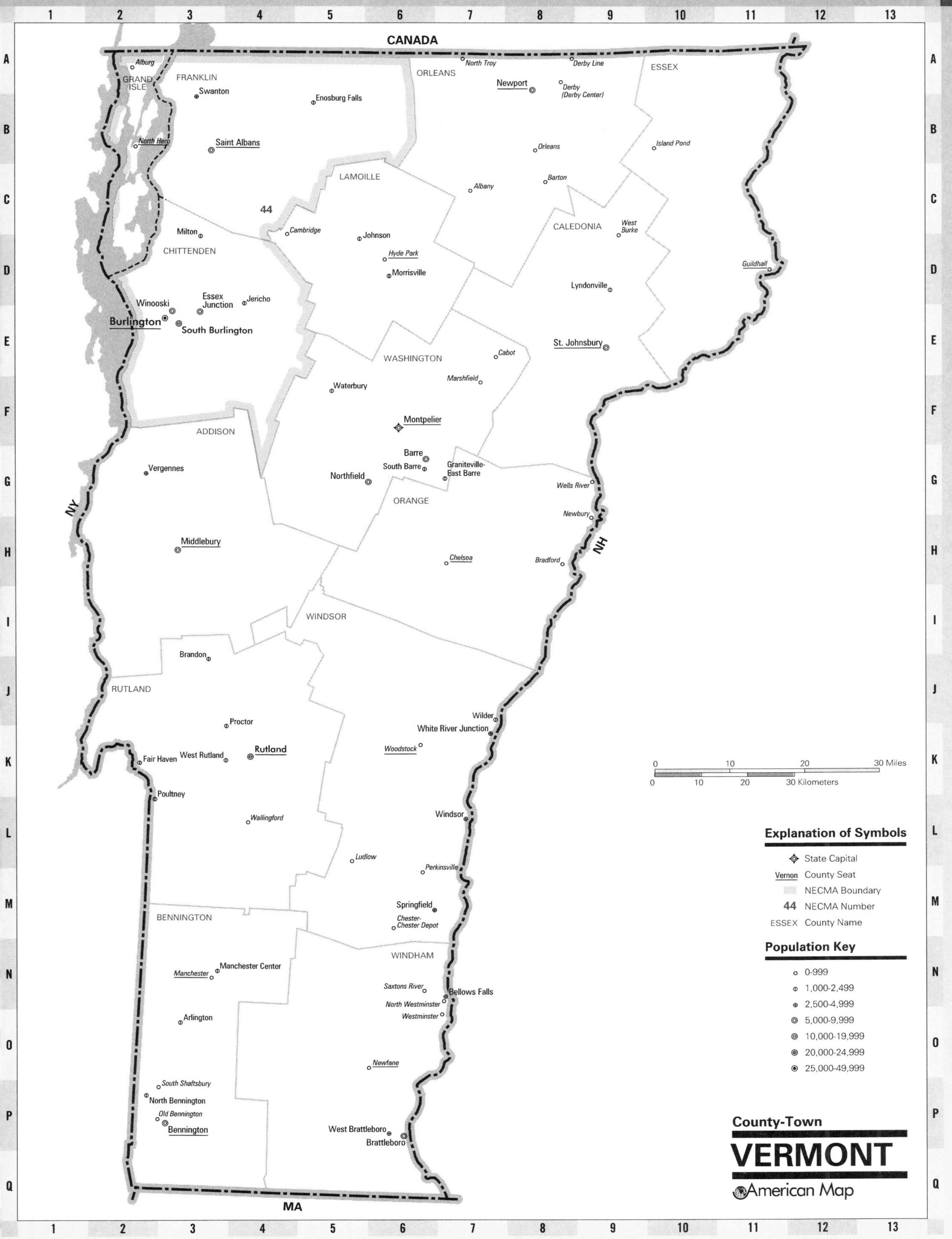
1 2 3 4 5 6 7 8 9 10 11 12 13
A B C D E F G H I J K L M N O P Q
CANADA
Alburg
GRAND ISLE
FRANKLIN
Swanton
Enosburg Falls
ORLEANS
North Troy
Newport
Derby Line
Derby (Derby Center)
ESSEX
North Hero
Saint Albans
Orleans
Island Pond
LAMOILLE
Albany
Barton
44
Cambridge
Johnson
CALEDONIA
West Burke
Milton
CHITTENDEN
Hyde Park
Morrisville
Guildhall
Lyndonville
Winooski
Essex Junction
Jericho
Burlington
South Burlington
St. Johnsbury
Cabot
WASHINGTON
Marshfield
Waterbury
Montpelier
ADDISON
Barre
South Barre
Graniteville-East Barre
Northfield
Vergennes
Wells River
ORANGE
Newbury
NY
Middlebury
NH
Chelsea
Bradford
WINDSOR
Brandon
RUTLAND
Wilder
White River Junction
Proctor
Woodstock
Fair Haven
West Rutland
Rutland
Poultney
Wallingford
Windsor
Ludlow
Perkinsville
Springfield
Chester-Chester Depot
BENNINGTON
WINDHAM
Manchester
Manchester Center
Saxtons River
Bellows Falls
North Westminster
Westminster
Arlington
Newfane
South Shaftsbury
North Bennington
Old Bennington
Bennington
West Brattleboro
Brattleboro
MA
0 10 20 30 Miles
0 10 20 30 Kilometers
Explanation of Symbols
State Capital
Vernon County Seat
NECMA Boundary
44 NECMA Number
ESSEX County Name
Population Key
0-999
1,000-2,499
2,500-4,999
5,000-9,999
10,000-19,999
20,000-24,999
25,000-49,999
County-Town
VERMONT
American Map

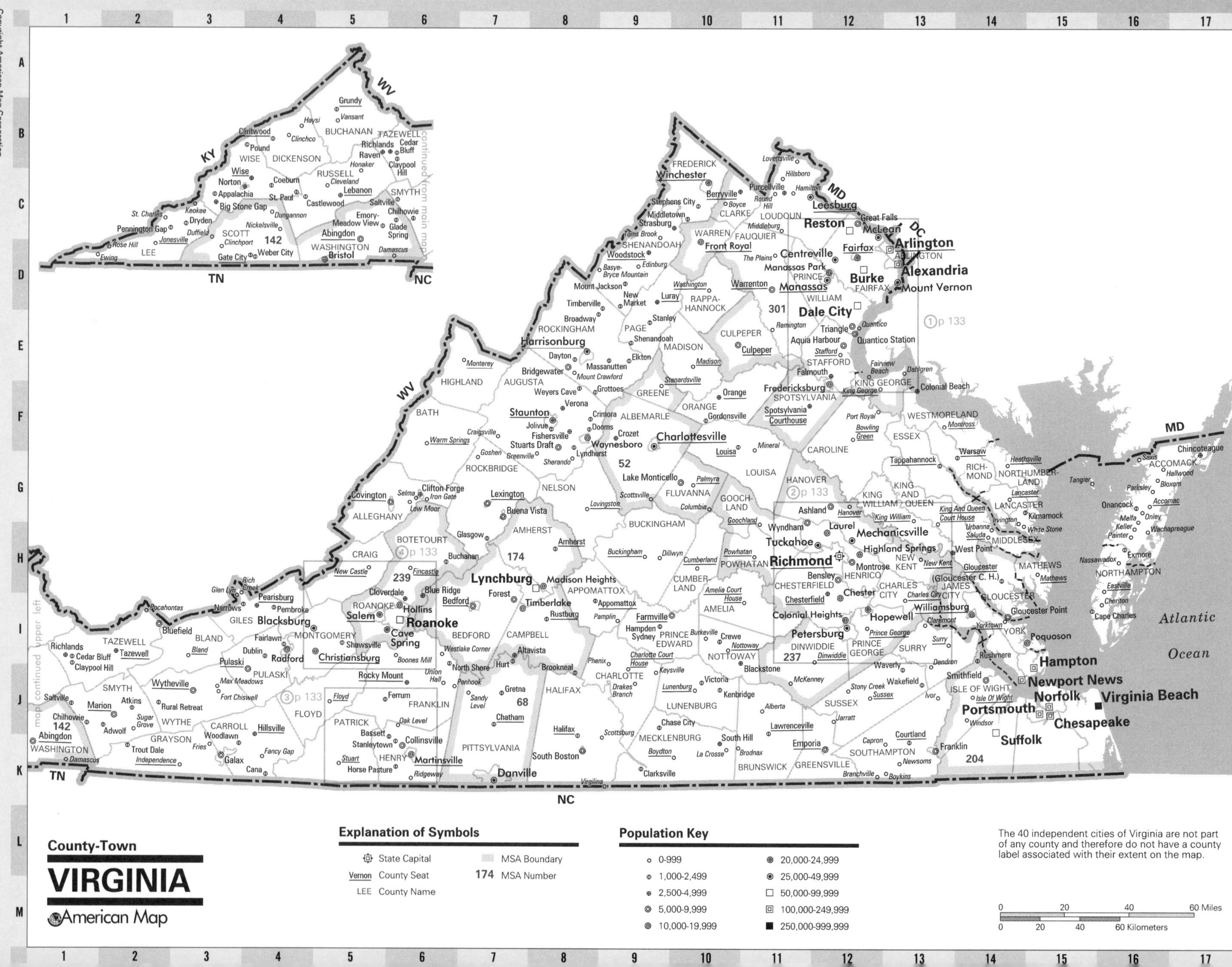

Atlantic Ocean
continued from main map
map continued upper left
1 p 133
2 p 133
3 p 133
4 p 133
Explanation of Symbols
State Capital
Vernon County Seat
LEE County Name
MSA Boundary
174 MSA Number
Population Key
0-999
1,000-2,499
2,500-4,999
5,000-9,999
10,000-19,999
20,000-24,999
25,000-49,999
50,000-99,999
100,000-249,999
250,000-999,999
The 40 independent cities of Virginia are not part of any county and therefore do not have a county label associated with their extent on the map.
60 Miles
60 Kilometers
County-Town
VIRGINIA
American Map

County-Town
VIRGINIA
INSET MAPS
American Map

Explanation of Symbols

⌖	State Capital		MSA Boundary
Vernon	County Seat	174	MSA Number
SURRY	County Name		

Population Key

0-999	20,000-24,999
1,000-2,499	25,000-49,999
2,500-4,999	50,000-99,999
5,000-9,999	100,000-249,999
10,000-19,999	

1
0 5 10 Mi
0 5 10 Km
FAIRFAX
LOUDOUN
PRINCE WILLIAM
FAUQUIER
STAFFORD
CULPEPER
SPOTSYLVANIA
KING GEORGE
ARLINGTON
MD
DC
301
Great Falls
Herndon
Reston
Wolf Trap
McLean
Tysons Corner
Pimmit Hills
Vienna
Idylwood
Chantilly
Oakton
Dunn Loring
Merrifield
Falls Church
Seven Corners
Bailey's Crossroads
Arlington
Jefferson
Fairfax
Mantua
Lake Barcroft
Centreville
Annandale
Lincolnia
North Springfield
Alexandria
Haymarket
Gainesville
Sudley
Loch Lomond
Yorkshire
Bull Run
Manassas Park
West Gate
Clifton
Burke
Springfield
Rose Hill
Huntington
Belle Haven
Franconia
West Springfield
Groveton
Linton Hall
Manassas
Hybla Valley
Fort Hunt
Newington
Mount Vernon
Nokesville
Lorton
Fort Belvoir
Lake Ridge
Occoquan
Woodbridge
Dale City
Montclair
Dumfries
Triangle
Quantico
Quantico Station
Aquia Harbour
Stafford
Potomac
Falmouth
Fredericksburg
Fairview Beach
Dahlgren
King George

2
HANOVER
KING WILLIAM
KING AND QUEEN
HENRICO
NEW KENT
CHESTERFIELD
CHARLES CITY
JAMES CITY
DINWIDDIE
PRINCE GEORGE
SURRY
SUSSEX
237
Ashland
Hanover
Wyndham
Glen Allen
Short Pump
Laurel
Chamberlayne
Dumbarton
Lakeside
Mechanicsville
King William
King And Queen Court House
Tuckahoe
East Highland Park
Richmond
Highland Springs
New Kent
Bon Air
Montrose
Bensley
Bellwood
Chesterfield
Chester
Charles City
Hopewell
Colonial Heights
Ettrick
Matoaca
Fort Lee
Petersburg
Prince George
Claremont
Surry
Dinwiddie
0 5 10 Mi
0 5 10 Km

3
FLOYD
FRANKLIN
PATRICK
HENRY
Floyd
Ferrum
Oak Level
Bassett
Stanleytown
Collinsville
Fieldale
Villa Heights
Laurel Park
Martinsville
Chatmoss
Stuart
Patrick Springs
Horse Pasture
Ridgeway
0 5 10 Mi
0 5 10 Km

4
WV
CRAIG
BOTETOURT
ROANOKE
MONTGOMERY
BEDFORD
FRANKLIN
FLOYD
239
174
New Castle
Fincastle
Daleville
Troutville
Blue Ridge
Cloverdale
Laymantown
Hollins
Salem
Vinton
Roanoke
Blacksburg
Cave Spring
Elliston-Lafayette
Merrimac
Shawsville
Christiansburg
0 10 Mi
0 10 Km

COUNTIES

(95 Counties)

Name of County	Population	Location on Map
ACCOMACK	38,305	G-16
ALBEMARLE	79,236	F-9
ALLEGHANY	12,926	H-5
AMELIA	11,400	I-10
AMHERST	31,894	H-7
APPOMATTOX	13,705	I-8
ARLINGTON	189,453	D-13
AUGUSTA	65,615	F-7
BATH	5,048	F-6
BEDFORD	60,371	I-6
BLAND	6,871	I-2
BOTETOURT	30,496	H-6
BRUNSWICK	18,419	K-10
BUCHANAN	26,978	B-5
BUCKINGHAM	15,623	H-9
CAMPBELL	51,078	I-7
CAROLINE	22,121	G-11
CARROLL	29,245	J-3
CHARLES CITY	6,926	I-12
CHARLOTTE	12,472	J-8
CHESTERFIELD	259,903	H-11
CLARKE	12,652	C-10
CRAIG	5,091	H-5
CULPEPER	34,262	E-10
CUMBERLAND	9,017	H-10
DICKENSON	16,395	B-4
DINWIDDIE	24,533	I-11
ESSEX	9,989	F-13
FAIRFAX	969,749	D-12
FAUQUIER	55,139	D-10
FLOYD	13,874	J-4
FLUVANNA	20,047	G-9
FRANKLIN	47,286	J-6
FREDERICK	59,209	C-10
GILES	16,657	H-4
GLOUCESTER	34,780	I-14
GOOCHLAND	16,863	G-10
GRAYSON	17,917	K-2
GREENE	15,244	F-9
GREENSVILLE	11,560	K-11
HALIFAX	37,355	J-8
HANOVER	86,320	G-11
HENRICO	262,300	H-12
HENRY	57,930	K-5
HIGHLAND	2,536	F-6
ISLE OF WIGHT	29,728	J-13
JAMES CITY	48,102	I-13
KING AND QUEEN	6,630	G-13
KING GEORGE	16,803	F-12
KING WILLIAM	13,146	G-12
LANCASTER	11,567	G-14
LEE	23,589	D-2
LOUDOUN	169,599	C-11
LOUISA	25,627	F-10
LUNENBURG	13,146	J-9
MADISON	12,520	E-9
MATHEWS	9,207	H-14
MECKLENBURG	32,380	K-9
MIDDLESEX	9,932	H-14
MONTGOMERY	83,629	I-4
NELSON	14,445	G-8
NEW KENT	13,462	H-13
NORTHAMPTON	13,093	H-15
NORTHUMBERLAND	12,259	G-14
NOTTOWAY	15,725	I-10
ORANGE	25,881	F-10
PAGE	23,177	E-9
PATRICK	19,407	J-5
PITTSYLVANIA	61,745	K-6
POWHATAN	22,377	H-10
PRINCE EDWARD	19,720	I-9
PRINCE GEORGE	33,047	I-12
PRINCE WILLIAM	280,813	D-11
PULASKI	35,127	J-4
RAPPAHANNOCK	6,983	E-10
RICHMOND	8,809	G-14
ROANOKE	85,778	I-5
ROCKBRIDGE	20,808	G-7
ROCKINGHAM	67,725	E-8
RUSSELL	30,308	C-5
SCOTT	23,403	D-3
SHENANDOAH	35,075	D-9
SMYTH	33,081	J-2
SOUTHAMPTON	17,482	K-12
SPOTSYLVANIA	90,395	F-11
STAFFORD	92,446	E-11
SURRY	6,829	I-13
SUSSEX	12,504	J-12
TAZEWELL	44,598	I-2
WARREN	31,584	C-10
WASHINGTON	51,103	D-4
WESTMORELAND	16,718	F-13
WISE	40,123	B-3
WYTHE	27,599	J-2
YORK	56,297	I-14
TOTAL	**7,078,515**	

INDEPENDENT CITIES

(40 Independent Cities)

Name of Independent City	Population	Location on Map
ALEXANDRIA	128,283	D-13
BEDFORD	6,299	I-7
BRISTOL	17,367	D-5
BUENA VISTA	6,349	H-7
CHARLOTTESVILLE	45,049	G-9
CHESAPEAKE	199,184	J-15
CLIFTON FORGE	4,289	G-6
COLONIAL HEIGHTS	16,897	I-12
COVINGTON	6,303	G-6
DANVILLE	48,411	K-7
EMPORIA	5,665	J-12
FAIRFAX	21,498	D-12
FALLS CHURCH	10,377	P-6
FRANKLIN	8,346	K-13
FREDERICKSBURG	19,279	E-12
GALAX	6,837	K-3
HAMPTON	146,437	I-15
HARRISONBURG	40,468	E-8
HOPEWELL	22,354	I-12
LEXINGTON	6,867	G-7
LYNCHBURG	65,269	H-8
MANASSAS	35,135	D-12
MANASSAS PARK	10,290	D-12
MARTINSVILLE	15,416	K-6
NEWPORT NEWS	180,150	J-14
NORFOLK	234,403	J-15
NORTON	3,904	C-3
PETERSBURG	33,740	I-12
POQUOSON	11,566	I-15
PORTSMOUTH	100,565	J-15
RADFORD	15,859	J-4
RICHMOND	197,790	H-12
ROANOKE	94,911	I-6
SALEM	24,747	I-5
STAUNTON	23,853	F-8
SUFFOLK	63,677	J-14
VIRGINIA BEACH	425,257	J-16
WAYNESBORO	19,520	G-8
WILLIAMSBURG	11,998	I-14
WINCHESTER	23,585	B-10

CITIES AND TOWNS

Note: The first name is that of the city or town, second, that of the county in which it is located, then the population and location on the map.

Explanation of symbols: • - Census Designated Place (CDP)

COUNTIES

(39 Counties)

Name of County	Population	Location on Map
ADAMS	16,428	G-13
ASOTIN	20,551	J-16
BENTON	142,475	I-11
CHELAN	66,616	D-8
CLALLAM	64,525	C-1
CLARK	345,238	K-5
COLUMBIA	4,064	I-14
COWLITZ	92,948	I-4
DOUGLAS	32,603	E-11
FERRY	7,260	A-13
FRANKLIN	49,347	H-12
GARFIELD	2,397	I-15
GRANT	74,698	G-11
GRAYS HARBOR	67,194	F-2
ISLAND	71,558	D-5
JEFFERSON	25,953	E-1
KING	1,737,034	E-8
KITSAP	231,969	F-5
KITTITAS	33,362	F-8
KLICKITAT	19,161	K-7
LEWIS	68,600	H-7
LINCOLN	10,184	E-13
MASON	49,405	F-3
OKANOGAN	39,564	A-9
PACIFIC	20,984	I-3
PEND OREILLE	11,732	B-15
PIERCE	700,820	H-7
SAN JUAN	14,077	C-4
SKAGIT	102,979	B-8
SKAMANIA	9,872	I-6
SNOHOMISH	606,024	D-8
SPOKANE	417,939	F-15
STEVENS	40,066	A-14
THURSTON	207,355	H-5
WAHKIAKUM	3,824	I-3
WALLA WALLA	55,180	J-13
WHATCOM	166,814	A-8
WHITMAN	40,740	G-15
YAKIMA	222,581	H-8
TOTAL	**5,894,121**	

CITIES AND TOWNS

Note: The first name is that of the city or town, second, that of the county in which it is located, then the population and location on the map.

- Aberdeen, *Grays Harbor*, 16,461 ... R-12
- ●Ahtanum, *Yakima*, 4,181 ... U-11
- Airway Heights, *Spokane*, 4,500 ... O-12
- ●Alderwood Manor, *Snohomish*, 15,329 ... R-6
- Algona, *King*, 2,460 ... X-6
- ●Amboy, *Clark*, 2,085 ... K-5
- ●Ames Lake, *King*, 1,435 ... T-8
- Anacortes, *Skagit*, 14,557 ... C-5
- Arlington, *Snohomish*, 11,713 ... O-7
- ●Arlington Heights, *Snohomish*, 2,510 ... O-7
- ●Artondale, *Pierce*, 8,630 ... W-4
- Asotin, *Asotin*, 1,095 ... I-17
- Auburn, *King*, 40,314 ... W-6
- ●Ault Field, *Island*, 2,064 ... C-5
- Bainbridge Island, *Kitsap*, 20,308 ... T-4
- ●Bangor Trident Base, *Kitsap*, 7,253 ... T-3
- ●Barberton, *Clark*, 4,617 ... X-11
- Battle Ground, *Clark*, 9,296 ... K-5
- Bellevue, *King*, 109,569 ... E-6
- Bellingham, *Whatcom*, 67,171 ... B-5
- Benton City, *Benton*, 2,624 ... J-12
- ●Big Lake, *Skagit*, 1,153 ... C-6
- ●Birch Bay, *Whatcom*, 4,961 ... A-5
- Black Diamond, *King*, 3,970 ... F-6
- Blaine, *Whatcom*, 3,770 ... A-5
- Bonney Lake, *Pierce*, 9,687 ... Y-7
- Bothell, *King*, 30,150 ... E-6
- Bremerton, *Kitsap*, 37,259 ... F-5
- Brewster, *Okanogan*, 2,189 ... D-11
- Bridgeport, *Douglas*, 2,059 ... D-11
- Brier, *Snohomish*, 6,383 ... S-6
- ●Brush Prairie, *Clark*, 2,384 ... X-12
- ●Bryn Mawr-Skyway, *King*, 13,977 ... V-6
- Buckley, *Pierce*, 4,145 ... Y-8
- ●Burbank, *Walla Walla*, 3,303 ... J-13
- Burien, *King*, 31,881 ... F-6
- Burlington, *Skagit*, 6,757 ... C-6
- ●Camano, *Island*, 13,347 ... D-5
- Camas, *Clark*, 12,534 ... L-5
- Carnation, *King*, 1,893 ... T-8
- ●Carson River Valley, *Skamania*, 2,116 ... K-7
- ●Cascade Valley, *Grant*, 1,811 ... G-12
- ●Cascade-Fairwood, *King*, 34,580 ... V-7
- Cashmere, *Chelan*, 2,965 ... F-10
- Castle Rock, *Cowlitz*, 2,130 ... J-4
- ●Cathcart, *Snohomish*, 3,015 ... R-7
- Cathlamet, *Wahkiakum*, 565 ... J-3
- ●Central Park, *Grays Harbor*, 2,558 ... R-13
- Centralia, *Lewis*, 14,742 ... H-4
- Chehalis, *Lewis*, 7,057 ... H-4
- Chelan, *Chelan*, 3,522 ... E-10
- Cheney, *Spokane*, 8,832 ... F-16
- Chewelah, *Stevens*, 2,186 ... C-15
- Clarkston, *Asotin*, 7,337 ... I-17
- ●Clarkston Heights-Vineland, *Asotin*, 6,117 ... I-17
- Cle Elum, *Kittitas*, 1,755 ... G-9
- Clyde Hill, *King*, 2,890 ... T-6
- Colfax, *Whitman*, 2,844 ... H-16
- College Place, *Walla Walla*, 7,818 ... J-14
- Colville, *Stevens*, 4,988 ... B-15
- Connell, *Franklin*, 2,956 ... H-13
- Cosmopolis, *Grays Harbor*, 1,595 ... R-12
- ●Cottage Lake, *King*, 24,330 ... S-7
- Coulee Dam, *Okanogan*, 1,044 ... D-13
- ●Country Homes, *Spokane*, 5,203 ... E-16
- Coupeville, *Island*, 1,723 ... C-5
- Covington, *King*, 13,783 ... W-7
- ●Dallesport, *Klickitat*, 1,185 ... L-8
- Darrington, *Snohomish*, 1,136 ... C-7
- Davenport, *Lincoln*, 1,730 ... E-14
- Dayton, *Columbia*, 2,655 ... I-15
- Deer Park, *Spokane*, 3,017 ... D-16
- Des Moines, *King*, 29,267 ... V-6
- ●Desert Aire, *Grant*, 1,124 ... H-11
- ●Dishman, *Spokane*, 10,031 ... O-13
- ●Dollar Corner, *Clark*, 1,039 ... W-11
- Du Pont, *Pierce*, 2,452 ... Y-4
- Duvall, *King*, 4,616 ... S-8
- ●East Hill-Meridian, *King*, 29,308 ... W-7
- ●East Port Orchard, *Kitsap*, 5,116 ... U-4
- ●East Renton Highlands, *King*, 13,264 ... V-7
- East Wenatchee, *Douglas*, 5,757 ... F-10
- ●East Wenatchee Bench, *Douglas*, 13,658 ... F-10
- ●Eastgate, *King*, 4,558 ... U-7
- Eatonville, *Pierce*, 2,012 ... H-6
- Edgewood, *Pierce*, 9,089 ... X-6
- Edmonds, *Snohomish*, 39,515 ... S-5
- ●Elk Plain, *Pierce*, 15,697 ... Z-5
- Ellensburg, *Kittitas*, 15,414 ... G-9
- Elma, *Grays Harbor*, 3,049 ... G-3
- Enumclaw, *King*, 11,116 ... X-8
- Ephrata, *Grant*, 6,808 ... F-11
- ●Erlands Point-Kitsap Lake, *Kitsap*, 2,723 ... U-3
- ●Esperance, *Snohomish*, 3,503 ... S-6
- Everett, *Snohomish*, 91,488 ... D-6
- Everson, *Whatcom*, 2,035 ... A-6
- ●Fairchild AFB, *Spokane*, 4,357 ... E-15
- ●Fairwood, *Spokane*, 6,764 ... E-16
- ●Fall City, *King*, 1,638 ... U-9
- Federal Way, *King*, 83,259 ... F-6
- ●Felida, *Clark*, 5,683 ... K-5
- Ferndale, *Whatcom*, 8,758 ... B-5
- Fife, *Pierce*, 4,784 ... X-6
- ●Finley, *Benton*, 5,770 ... J-13
- Fircrest, *Pierce*, 5,868 ... X-5
- ●Five Corners, *Clark*, 12,207 ... X-12
- ●Fords Prairie, *Lewis*, 1,961 ... H-4
- Forks, *Clallam*, 3,120 ... D-2
- ●Fort Lewis, *Pierce*, 19,089 ... G-5
- ●Fox Island, *Pierce*, 2,803 ... X-4
- ●Frederickson, *Pierce*, 5,758 ... Y-6
- ●Freeland, *Island*, 1,313 ... D-5
- Friday Harbor, *San Juan*, 1,989 ... B-4
- ●Garrett, *Walla Walla*, 1,022 ... J-14
- ●Geneva, *Whatcom*, 2,257 ... B-6
- Gig Harbor, *Pierce*, 6,465 ... W-4
- ●Gleed, *Yakima*, 2,947 ... T-11
- Gold Bar, *Snohomish*, 2,014 ... R-10
- Goldendale, *Klickitat*, 3,760 ... K-9
- ●Graham, *Pierce*, 8,739 ... Z-6
- ●Grand Mound, *Thurston*, 1,948 ... H-4
- Grandview, *Yakima*, 8,377 ... J-11
- Granger, *Yakima*, 2,530 ... I-10
- Granite Falls, *Snohomish*, 2,347 ... P-8
- Grapeview, *Mason*, 2,004 ... W-2
- ●Grayland, *Grays Harbor*, 1,002 ... H-2
- ●Greenacres, *Spokane*, 5,158 ... O-14
- ●Hazel Dell North, *Clark*, 9,261 ... X-11
- ●Hazel Dell South, *Clark*, 6,605 ... X-11
- ●Highland, *Benton*, 3,388 ... J-12
- ●Hobart, *King*, 6,251 ... V-8
- ●Hockinson, *Clark*, 5,136 ... K-5
- Hoquiam, *Grays Harbor*, 9,097 ... G-2
- ●Indianola, *Kitsap*, 3,026 ... S-4
- ●Inglewood-Finn Hill, *King*, 22,661 ... S-6
- Irondale, *Jefferson*, 3,476 ... D-5
- Issaquah, *King*, 11,212 ... U-8
- ●Jordan Road-Canyon Creek, *Snohomish*, 2,326 ... P-8
- Kalama, *Cowlitz*, 1,783 ... J-5
- Kelso, *Cowlitz*, 11,895 ... J-4
- Kenmore, *King*, 18,678 ... S-6
- Kennewick, *Benton*, 54,693 ... J-12
- Kent, *King*, 79,524 ... F-6
- Kettle Falls, *Stevens*, 1,527 ... B-14
- ●Kingsgate, *King*, 12,222 ... S-7
- ●Kingston, *Kitsap*, 1,611 ... S-5
- Kirkland, *King*, 45,054 ... T-6
- Kittitas, *Kittitas*, 1,105 ... G-10
- La Center, *Clark*, 1,654 ... K-5
- Lacey, *Thurston*, 31,226 ... G-5
- Lake Forest Park, *King*, 13,142 ... S-6
- ●Lake Goodwin, *Snohomish*, 3,354 ... O-6
- ●Lake Ketchum, *Snohomish*, 1,173 ... N-6
- ●Lake Marcel-Stillwater, *King*, 1,381 ... T-8
- ●Lake Morton-Berrydale, *King*, 9,659 ... W-7
- ●Lake Shore, *Clark*, 6,670 ... X-11
- Lake Stevens, *Snohomish*, 6,361 ... P-7
- ●Lakeland North, *King*, 15,085 ... W-6
- ●Lakeland South, *King*, 11,436 ... X-6
- Lakewood, *Pierce*, 58,211 ... D-6
- ●Lea Hill, *King*, 10,871 ... W-7
- Leavenworth, *Chelan*, 2,074 ... E-9
- ●Lewisville, *Clark*, 1,688 ... W-12
- ●Liberty Lake, *Spokane*, 4,660 ... O-14
- ●Lochsloy, *Snohomish*, 2,135 ... P-8
- Long Beach, *Pacific*, 1,283 ... I-2
- Longview, *Cowlitz*, 34,660 ... J-4
- ●Longview Heights, *Cowlitz*, 3,513 ... J-4
- Lynden, *Whatcom*, 9,020 ... A-6
- Lynnwood, *Snohomish*, 33,847 ... E-6
- Mabton, *Yakima*, 1,891 ... J-11
- ●Machias, *Snohomish*, 1,015 ... Q-8
- ●Maltby, *Snohomish*, 8,267 ... S-7
- ●Manchester, *Kitsap*, 4,958 ... U-4
- ●Maple Heights-Lake Desire, *King*, 2,569 ... V-7
- Maple Valley, *King*, 14,209 ... V-8
- ●Marietta-Alderwood, *Whatcom*, 3,594 ... B-5
- ●Martha Lake, *Snohomish*, 12,633 ... R-6
- Marysville, *Snohomish*, 25,315 ... D-6
- Mattawa, *Grant*, 2,609 ... H-11
- ●May Creek, *King*, 1,004 ... U-7
- ●McChord AFB, *Pierce*, 4,096 ... Y-5
- McCleary, *Grays Harbor*, 1,454 ... G-4
- ●Meadow Glade, *Clark*, 2,225 ... W-12
- Medical Lake, *Spokane*, 3,758 ... E-15
- Medina, *King*, 3,011 ... T-6
- Mercer Island, *King*, 22,036 ... U-6
- ●Midland, *Pierce*, 7,414 ... Y-5
- Mill Creek, *Snohomish*, 11,525 ... R-7
- ●Mill Plain, *Clark*, 7,400 ... Y-12
- Millwood, *Spokane*, 1,649 ... O-13
- Milton, *Pierce*, 5,795 ... X-6
- ●Minnehaha, *Clark*, 7,689 ... Y-11
- ●Mirrormont, *King*, 3,804 ... V-8
- Monroe, *Snohomish*, 13,795 ... E-6
- Montesano, *Grays Harbor*, 3,312 ... G-3
- Morton, *Lewis*, 1,045 ... I-6
- Moses Lake, *Grant*, 14,953 ... G-12
- ●Moses Lake North, *Grant*, 4,232 ... G-12
- Mount Vernon, *Skagit*, 26,232 ... C-6
- ●Mount Vista, *Clark*, 5,770 ... X-11
- Mountlake Terrace, *Snohomish*, 20,362 ... S-6
- Mukilteo, *Snohomish*, 18,019 ... D-6
- Napavine, *Lewis*, 1,361 ... I-4
- ●Navy Yard City, *Kitsap*, 2,638 ... U-4
- Newcastle, *King*, 7,737 ... U-7
- Newport, *Pend Oreille*, 1,921 ... C-17
- Normandy Park, *King*, 6,392 ... V-6
- North Bend, *King*, 4,746 ... F-7
- ●North Creek, *Snohomish*, 25,742 ... E-6
- ●North Marysville, *Snohomish*, 21,161 ... P-7
- ●North Yelm, *Thurston*, 2,793 ... G-5
- ●Northwest Snohomish, *Snohomish*, 2,061 ... Q-7
- Oak Harbor, *Island*, 19,795 ... N-4
- ●Ocean Park, *Pacific*, 1,459 ... I-2
- Ocean Shores, *Grays Harbor*, 3,836 ... G-2
- Okanogan, *Okanogan*, 2,484 ... C-11
- Olympia, *Thurston*, 42,514 ... G-4
- Omak, *Okanogan*, 4,721 ... C-11
- ●Opportunity, *Spokane*, 25,065 ... E-16
- ●Orchards, *Clark*, 17,852 ... Y-12
- Oroville, *Okanogan*, 1,653 ... A-12
- Orting, *Pierce*, 3,760 ... Y-7
- Othello, *Adams*, 5,847 ... H-12
- ●Otis Orchards-East Farms, *Spokane*, 6,318 ... O-14
- Pacific, *King*, 5,527 ... G-6
- ●Paine Field-Lake Stickney, *Snohomish*, 24,383 ... R-6
- Palouse, *Whitman*, 1,011 ... G-17
- ●Parkland, *Pierce*, 24,053 ... Y-5
- ●Parkwood, *Kitsap*, 7,213 ... U-4
- Pasco, *Franklin*, 32,066 ... J-12
- ●Peaceful Valley, *Whatcom*, 2,448 ... A-6
- ●Picnic Point-North Lynnwood, *Snohomish*, 22,953 ... R-6
- Pomeroy, *Garfield*, 1,517 ... I-16
- Port Angeles, *Clallam*, 18,397 ... D-3
- ●Port Angeles East, *Clallam*, 3,053 ... D-4
- ●Port Ludlow, *Jefferson*, 1,968 ... D-5
- Port Orchard, *Kitsap*, 7,693 ... F-5
- Port Townsend, *Jefferson*, 8,334 ... D-5
- Poulsbo, *Kitsap*, 6,813 ... S-4
- ●Prairie Ridge, *Pierce*, 11,688 ... Y-7
- Prosser, *Benton*, 4,838 ... J-11
- Pullman, *Whitman*, 24,675 ... H-16
- Puyallup, *Pierce*, 33,011 ... G-6
- Quincy, *Grant*, 5,044 ... G-11
- Rainier, *Thurston*, 1,492 ... H-5
- Raymond, *Pacific*, 2,975 ... H-3
- Redmond, *King*, 45,256 ... E-6
- Renton, *King*, 50,052 ... F-6
- Republic, *Ferry*, 954 ... B-13
- Richland, *Benton*, 38,708 ... J-12
- Ridgefield, *Clark*, 2,147 ... W-10
- Ritzville, *Adams*, 1,736 ... G-14
- ●Riverbend, *King*, 2,230 ... V-9
- ●Riverton-Boulevard Park, *King*, 11,188 ... V-6
- ●Rochester, *Thurston*, 1,829 ... H-4
- Roslyn, *Kittitas*, 1,017 ... G-8
- Royal City, *Grant*, 1,823 ... H-11
- ●Salmon Creek, *Clark*, 16,767 ... X-11
- Sammamish, *King*, 34,104 ... T-7
- Sea-Tac, *King*, 25,496 ... V-6
- Seattle, *King*, 563,374 ... E-6
- ●Seattle Hill-Silver Firs, *Snohomish*, 35,311 ... E-6
- Sedro-Woolley, *Skagit*, 8,658 ... C-6
- Selah, *Yakima*, 6,310 ... I-9
- Sequim, *Clallam*, 4,334 ... P-1
- Shelton, *Mason*, 8,442 ... G-4
- Shoreline, *King*, 53,025 ... S-6
- ●Silverdale, *Kitsap*, 15,816 ... T-3
- ●Smokey Point, *Snohomish*, 1,556 ... O-7
- Snohomish, *Snohomish*, 8,494 ... R-7
- Snoqualmie, *King*, 1,631 ... U-9
- Soap Lake, *Grant*, 1,733 ... F-12
- South Bend, *Pacific*, 1,807 ... H-3
- ●South Hill, *Pierce*, 31,623 ... G-6
- ●South Wenatchee, *Chelan*, 1,991 ... F-10
- ●Spanaway, *Pierce*, 21,588 ... Y-5
- Spokane, *Spokane*, 195,629 ... E-16
- Stanwood, *Snohomish*, 3,923 ... C-6
- Steilacoom, *Pierce*, 6,049 ... Y-4
- Stevenson, *Skamania*, 1,200 ... K-7
- ●Sudden Valley, *Whatcom*, 4,165 ... B-6
- Sultan, *Snohomish*, 3,344 ... R-9
- ●Summit, *Pierce*, 8,041 ... Y-6
- Sumner, *Pierce*, 8,504 ... X-6
- Sunnyside, *Yakima*, 13,905 ... J-11
- ●Sunnyslope, *Kitsap*, 2,521 ... F-10
- ●Suquamish, *Kitsap*, 3,510 ... S-4
- Tacoma, *Pierce*, 193,556 ... G-5
- ●Tanglewilde-Thompson Place, *Thurston*, 5,670 ... Z-3
- ●Tanner, *King*, 2,966 ... F-7
- Tenino, *Thurston*, 1,447 ... H-5
- ●Terrace Heights, *Yakima*, 6,447 ... U-12
- ●Three Lakes, *Snohomish*, 2,492 ... Q-8
- Tieton, *Yakima*, 1,154 ... H-9
- Toppenish, *Yakima*, 8,946 ... I-10
- ●Town and Country, *Spokane*, 4,452 ... N-13
- ●Tracyton, *Kitsap*, 3,267 ... T-4
- ●Trentwood, *Spokane*, 4,388 ... O-14
- Tukwila, *King*, 17,181 ... V-6
- ●Tulalip Bay, *Snohomish*, 1,561 ... P-6
- Tumwater, *Thurston*, 12,698 ... Z-2
- Union Gap, *Yakima*, 5,621 ... I-10
- ●Union Hill-Novelty Hill, *King*, 11,265 ... T-7
- University Place, *Pierce*, 29,933 ... G-5
- Vancouver, *Clark*, 143,560 ... L-5
- ●Vashon, *King*, 10,123 ... V-5
- ●Venersborg, *Clark*, 3,274 ... K-5
- ●Veradale, *Spokane*, 9,387 ... O-14
- Waitsburg, *Walla Walla*, 1,212 ... J-14
- Walla Walla, *Walla Walla*, 29,686 ... J-14
- ●Walla Walla East, *Walla Walla*, 2,479 ... J-14
- ●Waller, *Pierce*, 9,200 ... X-5
- ●Walnut Grove, *Clark*, 7,164 ... L-5
- Wapato, *Yakima*, 4,582 ... I-10
- Warden, *Grant*, 2,544 ... G-13
- ●Warm Beach, *Snohomish*, 2,040 ... O-5
- Washougal, *Clark*, 8,595 ... Y-13
- Waterville, *Douglas*, 1,163 ... E-10
- Wenatchee, *Chelan*, 27,856 ... F-10
- ●West Clarkston-Highland, *Asotin*, 4,707 ... I-17
- ●West Lake Sammamish, *King*, 5,937 ... U-7
- ●West Lake Stevens, *Snohomish*, 18,071 ... Q-7
- ●West Longview, *Cowlitz*, 2,882 ... J-4
- ●West Pasco, *Franklin*, 4,629 ... J-12
- West Richland, *Benton*, 8,385 ... J-12
- ●West Side Highway, *Cowlitz*, 4,565 ... J-4
- ●West Valley, *Yakima*, 10,433 ... I-9
- ●West Wenatchee, *Chelan*, 1,681 ... E-10
- Westport, *Grays Harbor*, 2,137 ... H-2
- ●White Center, *King*, 20,975 ... U-6
- White Salmon, *Klickitat*, 2,193 ... K-7
- ●White Swan, *Yakima*, 3,033 ... I-9
- Winlock, *Lewis*, 1,166 ... I-4
- Woodinville, *King*, 9,194 ... S-7
- Woodland, *Cowlitz*, 3,780 ... K-5
- ●Woods Creek, *Snohomish*, 4,502 ... R-8
- Yacolt, *Clark*, 1,055 ... K-5
- Yakima, *Yakima*, 71,845 ... I-9
- Yarrow Point, *King*, 1,008 ... T-6
- Yelm, *Thurston*, 3,289 ... H-5
- Zillah, *Yakima*, 2,198 ... I-10

Explanation of symbols: ● - Census Designated Place (CDP)

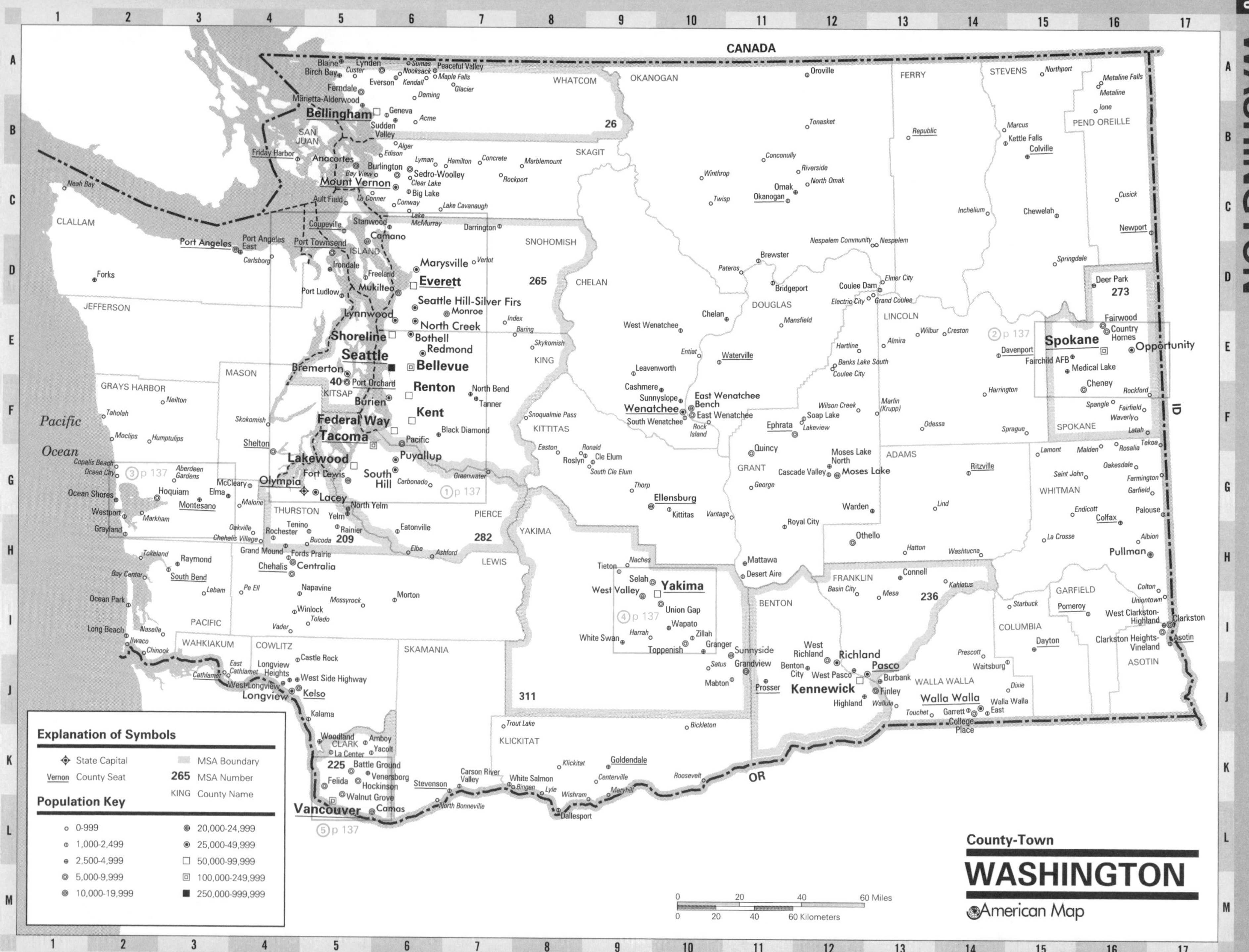
County-Town
WASHINGTON
American Map
Explanation of Symbols
State Capital
Vernon County Seat
MSA Boundary
265 MSA Number
KING County Name
Population Key
0-999
1,000-2,499
2,500-4,999
5,000-9,999
10,000-19,999
20,000-24,999
25,000-49,999
50,000-99,999
100,000-249,999
250,000-999,999
0 20 40 60 Miles
0 20 40 60 Kilometers
CANADA
ID
OR
Pacific Ocean
WHATCOM
OKANOGAN
FERRY
STEVENS
PEND OREILLE
SKAGIT
SAN JUAN
ISLAND
SNOHOMISH
CHELAN
DOUGLAS
LINCOLN
SPOKANE
CLALLAM
JEFFERSON
KITSAP
KING
KITTITAS
GRANT
ADAMS
WHITMAN
GARFIELD
ASOTIN
COLUMBIA
WALLA WALLA
FRANKLIN
BENTON
YAKIMA
KLICKITAT
SKAMANIA
CLARK
COWLITZ
LEWIS
PIERCE
THURSTON
MASON
GRAYS HARBOR
PACIFIC
WAHKIAKUM
Seattle
Spokane
Tacoma
Olympia
Bellevue
Everett
Vancouver
Yakima
Bellingham
Kennewick
Richland
Pasco
Walla Walla
Wenatchee
Ellensburg
Pullman
Port Angeles
Longview
Kelso
Centralia
Chehalis
Mount Vernon
Anacortes
Bremerton
Federal Way
Kent
Renton
Puyallup
Lakewood
Shoreline
Lynnwood
Marysville
Redmond
Moses Lake
Ephrata
Okanogan
Omak
Colville
Newport
Port Townsend
Coupeville
Friday Harbor
Shelton
Montesano
South Bend
Goldendale
Stevenson
Cathlamet
Asotin
Dayton
Pomeroy
Colfax
Ritzville
Davenport
Waterville
Republic
Prosser
Forks
Hoquiam
Ocean Shores
Westport
Long Beach
Ilwaco
Clarkston
Othello
Toppenish
Sunnyside
Grandview
Camas
Battle Ground
p 137

Explanation of Symbols

- State Capital
- Vernon — County Seat
- MSA Boundary
- 265 — MSA Number
- KING — County Name

Population Key

- 0-999
- 1,000-2,499
- 2,500-4,999
- 5,000-9,999
- 10,000-19,999
- 20,000-24,999
- 25,000-49,999
- 50,000-99,999
- 100,000-249,999
- 250,000-999,999

County-Town

WASHINGTON

INSET MAPS

American Map

WEST VIRGINIA

COUNTIES

(55 Counties)

Name of County	Population	Location on Map
BARBOUR	15,557	C-9
BERKELEY	75,905	B-16
BOONE	25,535	H-3
BRAXTON	14,702	E-7
BROOKE	25,447	C-2
CABELL	96,784	G-2
CALHOUN	7,582	E-6
CLAY	10,330	F-6
DODDRIDGE	7,403	C-7
FAYETTE	47,579	H-5
GILMER	7,160	D-6
GRANT	11,299	C-12
GREENBRIER	34,453	I-7
HAMPSHIRE	20,203	B-14
HANCOCK	32,667	A-1
HARDY	12,669	D-13
HARRISON	68,652	C-8
JACKSON	28,000	D-4
JEFFERSON	42,190	C-16
KANAWHA	200,073	G-4
LEWIS	16,919	D-7
LINCOLN	22,108	H-2
LOGAN	37,710	I-2
MARION	56,598	B-8
MARSHALL	35,519	E-1
MASON	25,957	E-3
MCDOWELL	27,329	L-4
MERCER	62,980	K-6
MINERAL	27,078	C-12
MINGO	28,253	I-2
MONONGALIA	81,866	B-8
MONROE	14,583	J-7
MORGAN	14,943	B-15
NICHOLAS	26,562	G-7
OHIO	47,427	C-1
PENDLETON	8,196	E-11
PLEASANTS	7,514	C-5
POCAHONTAS	9,131	G-9
PRESTON	29,334	B-11
PUTNAM	51,589	F-3
RALEIGH	79,220	I-4
RANDOLPH	28,262	D-10
RITCHIE	10,343	D-5
ROANE	15,446	F-5
SUMMERS	12,999	J-6
TAYLOR	16,089	C-9
TUCKER	7,321	C-10
TYLER	9,592	B-7
UPSHUR	23,404	E-8
WAYNE	42,903	G-1
WEBSTER	9,719	F-8
WETZEL	17,693	B-7
WIRT	5,873	D-5
WOOD	87,986	D-4
WYOMING	25,708	J-4
TOTAL	**1,808,344**	

CITIES AND TOWNS

Note: The first name is that of the city or town, second, that of the county in which it is located, then the population and location on the map.

Alderson, *Greenbrier,* 1,091 .... J-7
•Alum Creek, *Kanawha,* 1,839 .... G-4
Amherstdale-Robinette, *Logan,* 1,785 .... J-4
Ansted, *Fayette,* 1,576 .... H-6
Athens, *Mercer,* 1,102 .... K-6
Barboursville, *Cabell,* 3,183 .... G-2
Barrackville, *Marion,* 1,288 .... B-9
•Beaver, *Raleigh,* 1,378 .... J-6
Beckley, *Raleigh,* 17,254 .... J-6
Belington, *Barbour,* 1,788 .... D-10
Belle, *Kanawha,* 1,259 .... H-4
Belmont, *Pleasants,* 1,036 .... C-5
Benwood, *Marshall,* 1,585 .... D-1
Berkley Springs (Bath), *Morgan,* 663 .... A-15
Bethlehem, *Ohio,* 2,651 .... C-1
•Blennerhassett, *Wood,* 3,225 .... C-4
Bluefield, *Mercer,* 11,451 .... L-6
Boaz, *Wood,* 1,345 .... C-5
Bolivar, *Jefferson,* 1,045 .... C-17
•Bradley, *Raleigh,* 2,371 .... I-6
Bridgeport, *Harrison,* 7,306 .... C-9
•Brookhaven, *Monongalia,* 4,734 .... B-10
Buckhannon, *Upshur,* 5,725 .... D-9
Buffalo, *Putnam,* 1,171 .... F-3
Cameron, *Marshall,* 1,212 .... D-2
•Cassville, *Monongalia,* 1,586 .... A-9
Ceredo, *Wayne,* 1,675 .... G-1
Chapmanville, *Logan,* 1,211 .... I-3
Charles Town, *Jefferson,* 2,907 .... C-17
Charleston, *Kanawha,* 53,421 .... G-4
•Chattaroy, *Mingo,* 1,136 .... J-2
•Cheat Lake, *Monongalia,* 6,396 .... A-10
Chesapeake, *Kanawha,* 1,643 .... H-4
Chester, *Hancock,* 2,592 .... A-2
Clarksburg, *Harrison,* 16,743 .... C-8
Clay, *Clay,* 593 .... G-6
Clendenin, *Kanawha,* 1,116 .... G-5
•Coal City, *Raleigh,* 1,905 .... J-6
Coal Fork, *Kanawha,* 1,350 .... G-5
•Crab Orchard, *Raleigh,* 2,761 .... J-5
•Craigsville, *Nicholas,* 2,204 .... G-7
•Cross Lanes, *Kanawha,* 10,353 .... G-4
•Culloden, *Cabell,* 2,940 .... G-3
•Daniels, *Raleigh,* 1,846 .... J-6
•Despard, *Harrison,* 1,039 .... C-9
Dunbar, *Kanawha,* 8,154 .... G-4
Eleanor, *Putnam,* 1,345 .... F-3
Elizabeth, *Wirt,* 994 .... D-5
Elkins, *Randolph,* 7,032 .... E-10
•Elkview, *Kanawha,* 1,182 .... G-5
•Fairlea, *Greenbrier,* 1,706 .... J-8
Fairmont, *Marion,* 19,097 .... B-9
Fayetteville, *Fayette,* 2,754 .... H-6
Follansbee, *Brooke,* 3,115 .... B-2
•Fort Ashby, *Mineral,* 1,354 .... B-14
Franklin, *Pendleton,* 797 .... F-12
•Gilbert Creek, *Mingo,* 1,582 .... K-3
Glen Dale, *Marshall,* 1,552 .... D-1
Glenville, *Gilmer,* 1,544 .... E-7
Grafton, *Taylor,* 5,489 .... C-10
Grantsville, *Calhoun,* 565 .... E-6
Hamlin, *Lincoln,* 1,119 .... G-3
Harrisville, *Ritchie,* 1,842 .... C-6
•Harts, *Lincoln,* 2,361 .... I-3
Hinton, *Summers,* 2,880 .... J-7
•Holden, *Logan,* 1,105 .... I-3
•Hooverson Heights, *Brooke,* 2,909 .... B-2
Huntington, *Cabell,* 51,475 .... G-2
Hurricane, *Putnam,* 5,222 .... G-3
•Inwood, *Berkeley,* 2,084 .... C-16
Kenova, *Wayne,* 3,485 .... G-1
Keyser, *Mineral,* 5,303 .... B-13
Kingwood, *Preston,* 2,944 .... B-11
Lewisburg, *Greenbrier,* 3,624 .... J-8
Logan, *Logan,* 1,630 .... I-3
Lubeck, *Wood,* 1,303 .... C-4
Mabscott, *Raleigh,* 1,403 .... J-6
MacArthur, *Raleigh,* 1,693 .... J-6
Madison, *Boone,* 2,677 .... H-4
•Mallory, *Logan,* 1,143 .... J-3
Mannington, *Marion,* 2,124 .... B-8
Marlinton, *Pocahontas,* 1,204 .... H-9
Marmet, *Kanawha,* 1,693 .... H-4
Martinsburg, *Berkeley,* 14,972 .... B-16
Mason, *Mason,* 1,064 .... D-3
McMechen, *Marshall,* 1,937 .... D-1
Middlebourne, *Tyler,* 870 .... B-7
Milton, *Cabell,* 2,206 .... G-3
Mineralwells, *Wood,* 1,860 .... C-5
Montgomery, *Kanawha,* 1,942 .... H-5
Moorefield, *Hardy,* 2,375 .... D-13
Morgantown, *Monongalia,* 26,809 .... B-10
Moundsville, *Marshall,* 9,998 .... D-1
Mount Gay-Shamrock, *Logan,* 2,623 .... I-3
Mount Hope, *Fayette,* 1,487 .... I-6
Mullens, *Wyoming,* 1,769 .... K-5
New Cumberland, *Hancock,* 1,099 .... A-2
New Haven, *Mason,* 1,559 .... D-3
New Martinsville, *Wetzel,* 5,984 .... B-7
•Newell, *Hancock,* 1,602 .... A-2
Nitro, *Kanawha,* 6,824 .... G-3
Nutter Fort, *Harrison,* 1,686 .... C-9
Oak Hill, *Fayette,* 7,589 .... I-6
Oceana, *Wyoming,* 1,550 .... J-4
Paden City, *Tyler,* 2,860 .... B-7
Parkersburg, *Wood,* 33,099 .... C-4
Parsons, *Tucker,* 1,463 .... D-11
•Pea Ridge, *Cabell,* 6,363 .... G-2
Pennsboro, *Ritchie,* 1,199 .... C-6
Petersburg, *Grant,* 2,423 .... D-13
Philippi, *Barbour,* 2,870 .... D-9
Piedmont, *Mineral,* 1,014 .... B-13
•Pinch, *Kanawha,* 2,811 .... G-5
Pineville, *Wyoming,* 715 .... K-4
•Piney View, *Raleigh,* 1,046 .... I-6
Pleasant Valley, *Marshall,* 3,124 .... D-2
Poca, *Putnam,* 1,013 .... G-4
Point Pleasant, *Mason,* 4,637 .... E-3
•Powellton, *Fayette,* 1,796 .... H-5
Princeton, *Mercer,* 6,347 .... L-6
•Prosperity, *Raleigh,* 1,310 .... I-6
Rainelle, *Greenbrier,* 1,545 .... I-7
Ranson, *Jefferson,* 2,951 .... C-17
Ravenswood, *Jackson,* 4,031 .... E-4
Richwood, *Nicholas,* 2,477 .... H-8
Ripley, *Jackson,* 3,263 .... E-4
Romney, *Hampshire,* 1,940 .... C-14
Ronceverte, *Greenbrier,* 1,557 .... J-8
Saint Albans, *Kanawha,* 11,567 .... G-4
Saint Marys, *Pleasants,* 2,017 .... C-6
Salem, *Harrison,* 2,006 .... C-8
•Shady Spring, *Raleigh,* 2,078 .... J-6
Shinnston, *Harrison,* 2,295 .... C-9
•Sissonville, *Kanawha,* 4,399 .... F-4
Sistersville, *Tyler,* 1,588 .... B-6
Sophia, *Raleigh,* 1,301 .... J-5
South Charleston, *Kanawha,* 13,390 .... K-9
Spencer, *Roane,* 2,352 .... E-5
•Stanaford, *Raleigh,* 1,443 .... J-6
Star City, *Monongalia,* 1,366 .... A-10
Stonewood, *Harrison,* 1,815 .... C-9
Summersville, *Nicholas,* 3,294 .... G-7
Sutton, *Braxton,* 1,011 .... F-7
•Switzer, *Logan,* 1,138 .... J-3
•Teays Valley, *Putnam,* 12,704 .... G-3
Terra Alta, *Preston,* 1,456 .... B-11
•Tornado, *Kanawha,* 1,111 .... G-3
Union, *Monroe,* 548 .... K-8
Vienna, *Wood,* 10,861 .... C-5
•Washington, *Wood,* 1,170 .... C-4
Wayne, *Wayne,* 1,105 .... H-1
Webster Springs (Addison), *Webster,* 808 .... G-8
Weirton, *Hancock,* 20,411 .... B-2
Welch, *McDowell,* 2,683 .... K-4
Wellsburg, *Brooke,* 2,891 .... B-2
West Liberty, *Ohio,* 1,220 .... C-2
West Union, *Doddridge,* 806 .... C-7
Weston, *Lewis,* 4,317 .... D-8
Westover, *Monongalia,* 3,941 .... B-10
Wheeling, *Ohio,* 31,419 .... C-1
White Sulphur Springs, *Greenbrier,* 2,315 .... J-9
•Wiley Ford, *Mineral,* 1,095 .... B-14
Williamson, *Mingo,* 3,414 .... J-2
Williamstown, *Wood,* 2,996 .... C-5
Winfield, *Putnam,* 1,858 .... F-3

Explanation of symbols: • - Census Designated Place (CDP)

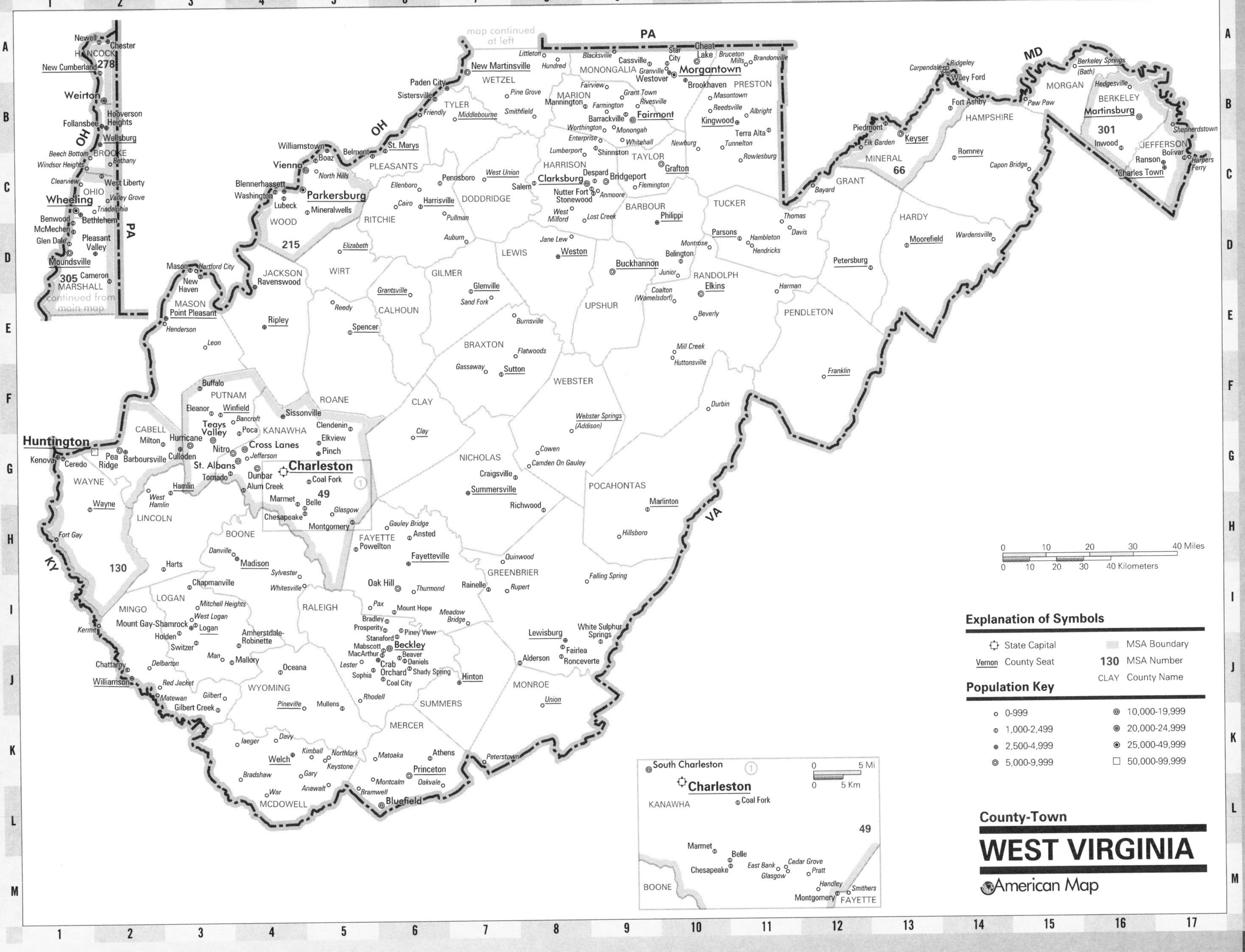
PA
MD
OH
VA
KY
map continued at left
continued from main map
HANCOCK
BROOKE
OHIO
MARSHALL
WETZEL
TYLER
MONONGALIA
MARION
PRESTON
PLEASANTS
WOOD
RITCHIE
DODDRIDGE
HARRISON
TAYLOR
BARBOUR
TUCKER
GRANT
MINERAL
HAMPSHIRE
MORGAN
BERKELEY
JEFFERSON
HARDY
PENDLETON
RANDOLPH
UPSHUR
LEWIS
GILMER
CALHOUN
WIRT
JACKSON
MASON
ROANE
BRAXTON
WEBSTER
POCAHONTAS
CLAY
NICHOLAS
PUTNAM
KANAWHA
CABELL
WAYNE
LINCOLN
BOONE
FAYETTE
GREENBRIER
LOGAN
MINGO
RALEIGH
WYOMING
SUMMERS
MONROE
MERCER
MCDOWELL
Huntington
Charleston
Parkersburg
Wheeling
Weirton
Morgantown
Fairmont
Clarksburg
Martinsburg
Beckley
Bluefield
South Charleston
Coal Fork
Marmet
Belle
Chesapeake
East Bank
Cedar Grove
Glasgow
Pratt
Handley
Montgomery
Smithers
5 Mi
5 Km
0
10
20
30
40 Miles
40 Kilometers
Explanation of Symbols
State Capital
Vernon County Seat
MSA Boundary
130 MSA Number
CLAY County Name
Population Key
0-999
1,000-2,499
2,500-4,999
5,000-9,999
10,000-19,999
20,000-24,999
25,000-49,999
50,000-99,999
County-Town
WEST VIRGINIA
American Map

WISCONSIN

COUNTIES

(72 Counties)

Name of County	Population	Location on Map
ADAMS	18,643	L-8
ASHLAND	16,866	E-5
BARRON	44,963	G-3
BAYFIELD	15,013	D-4
BROWN	226,778	J-11
BUFFALO	13,804	K-3
BURNETT	15,674	G-1
CALUMET	40,631	L-11
CHIPPEWA	55,195	I-4
CLARK	33,557	J-5
COLUMBIA	52,468	N-9
CRAWFORD	17,243	N-5
DANE	426,526	O-8
DODGE	85,897	N-10
DOOR	27,961	J-13
DOUGLAS	43,287	D-2
DUNN	39,858	I-2
EAU CLAIRE	93,142	J-4
FLORENCE	5,088	G-10
FOND DU LAC	97,296	M-11
FOREST	10,024	F-10
GRANT	49,597	P-5
GREEN	33,647	Q-8
GREEN LAKE	19,105	M-9
IOWA	22,780	O-6
IRON	6,861	E-6
JACKSON	19,100	K-6
JEFFERSON	74,021	P-10
JUNEAU	24,316	L-7
KENOSHA	149,577	Q-12
KEWAUNEE	20,187	K-13
LA CROSSE	107,120	L-4
LAFAYETTE	16,137	P-6
LANGLADE	20,740	H-9
LINCOLN	29,641	H-7
MANITOWOC	82,887	M-12
MARATHON	125,834	I-7
MARINETTE	43,384	G-11
MARQUETTE	15,832	M-8
MENOMINEE	4,562	I-10
MILWAUKEE	940,164	P-12
MONROE	40,899	L-5
OCONTO	35,634	H-10
ONEIDA	36,776	G-7
OUTAGAMIE	160,971	K-10
OZAUKEE	82,317	N-12
PEPIN	7,213	J-3
PIERCE	36,804	J-1
POLK	41,319	G-1
PORTAGE	67,182	K-8
PRICE	15,822	F-6
RACINE	188,831	P-11
RICHLAND	17,924	O-6
ROCK	152,307	Q-9
RUSK	15,347	G-4
SAINT CROIX	63,155	I-1
SAUK	55,225	N-7
SAWYER	16,196	F-4
SHAWANO	40,664	J-11
SHEBOYGAN	112,646	N-12
TAYLOR	19,680	H-5
TREMPEALEAU	27,010	L-4
VERNON	28,056	N-5
VILAS	21,033	F-8
WALWORTH	93,759	P-11
WASHBURN	16,036	F-3
WASHINGTON	117,493	O-11
WAUKESHA	360,767	O-11
WAUPACA	51,731	K-9
WAUSHARA	23,154	L-9
WINNEBAGO	156,763	M-10
WOOD	75,555	K-7
TOTAL	**5,363,675**	

CITIES AND TOWNS

Note: The first name is that of the city or town, second, that of the county in which it is located, then the population and location on the map.

Abbotsford, *Clark,* 1,956 ... J-7
Adams, *Adams,* 1,914 ... M-8
Albany, *Green,* 1,191 ... P-9
Algoma, *Kewaunee,* 3,357 ... J-13
Allouez, *Brown,* 15,443 ... K-12
Alma, *Buffalo,* 942 ... K-3
Altoona, *Eau Claire,* 6,698 ... J-4
Amery, *Polk,* 2,845 ... H-2
Antigo, *Langlade,* 8,560 ... I-9
Appleton, *Outagamie,* 70,087 ... L-11
Arcadia, *Trempealeau,* 2,402 ... L-4
Ashland, *Ashland,* 8,620 ... D-5
Ashwaubenon, *Brown,* 17,634 ... K-12
Athens, *Marathon,* 1,095 ... I-7
Augusta, *Eau Claire,* 1,460 ... J-5
Baldwin, *Saint Croix,* 2,667 ... I-2
Balsam Lake, *Polk,* 950 ... H-2
Bangor, *La Crosse,* 1,400 ... M-5
Baraboo, *Sauk,* 10,711 ... N-8
Barneveld, *Iowa,* 1,088 ... P-8
Barron, *Barron,* 3,248 ... H-3
Bayside, *Milwaukee,* 4,518 ... A-12
Beaver Dam, *Dodge,* 15,169 ... N-10
Belgium, *Ozaukee,* 1,678 ... N-12
Belleville, *Dane,* 1,908 ... P-8
• Bellevue, *Brown,* 11,828 ... K-12
Beloit, *Rock,* 35,775 ... Q-10
Berlin, *Green Lake,* 5,305 ... M-10
Big Bend, *Waukesha,* 1,278 ... C-10
Black Creek, *Outagamie,* 1,192 ... K-11
Black Earth, *Dane,* 1,320 ... O-8
Black River Falls, *Jackson,* 3,618 ... L-5
Blair, *Trempealeau,* 1,273 ... L-4
Bloomer, *Chippewa,* 3,347 ... I-4
• Bohners Lake, *Racine,* 1,952 ... E-10
Bonduel, *Shawano,* 1,416 ... J-11
Boscobel, *Grant,* 3,047 ... O-6
Boyceville, *Dunn,* 1,043 ... I-3
• Brice Prairie, *La Crosse,* 1,804 ... M-4
Brillion, *Calumet,* 2,937 ... L-12
Brodhead, *Green,* 3,180 ... Q-9
Brookfield, *Waukesha,* 38,649 ... O-12
Brown Deer, *Milwaukee,* 12,170 ... A-12
• Browns Lake, *Racine,* 1,933 ... D-10
Buffalo City, *Buffalo,* 1,040 ... L-3
Burlington, *Racine,* 9,936 ... D-10
Butler, *Waukesha,* 1,881 ... B-11
Cadott, *Chippewa,* 1,345 ... I-5
Cambridge, *Jefferson,* 1,101 ... P-10
Cameron, *Barron,* 1,546 ... H-3
• Camp Lake, *Kenosha,* 3,255 ... E-11
Campbellsport, *Fond du Lac,* 1,913 ... N-11
Cashton, *Monroe,* 1,005 ... M-6
Cassville, *Grant,* 1,085 ... P-5
Cedar Grove, *Sheboygan,* 1,887 ... N-12
Cedarburg, *Ozaukee,* 10,908 ... O-12
• Chain O'Lakes-King, *Waupaca,* 2,215 ... K-9
Chetek, *Barron,* 2,180 ... H-4
Chilton, *Calumet,* 3,708 ... L-12
Chippewa Falls, *Chippewa,* 12,925 ... J-4
Clear Lake, *Polk,* 1,051 ... H-2
Cleveland, *Manitowoc,* 1,361 ... M-13
Clinton, *Rock,* 2,162 ... Q-10
Clintonville, *Waupaca,* 4,736 ... K-10
Colby, *Clark,* 1,616 ... J-7
Colfax, *Dunn,* 1,136 ... I-3
Columbus, *Columbia,* 4,479 ... O-10
Combined Locks, *Outagamie,* 2,422 ... L-11
• Como, *Walworth,* 1,870 ... E-9
Cornell, *Chippewa,* 1,466 ... I-5
Cottage Grove, *Dane,* 4,059 ... B-8
Crandon, *Forest,* 1,961 ... H-10
Cross Plains, *Dane,* 3,084 ... O-8
Cuba City, *Grant,* 2,156 ... Q-6
Cudahy, *Milwaukee,* 18,429 ... C-12
Cumberland, *Barron,* 2,280 ... H-3
Darien, *Walworth,* 1,572 ... Q-10
Darlington, *Lafayette,* 2,418 ... Q-7
De Forest, *Dane,* 7,368 ... O-9
De Pere, *Brown,* 20,559 ... K-12
Deerfield, *Dane,* 1,971 ... O-10
Delafield, *Waukesha,* 6,472 ... O-11
Delavan, *Walworth,* 7,956 ... Q-11
• Delavan Lake, *Walworth,* 2,352 ... E-8
Denmark, *Brown,* 1,958 ... K-12
Dickeyville, *Grant,* 1,043 ... Q-6
Dodgeville, *Iowa,* 4,220 ... P-7
Dousman, *Waukesha,* 1,584 ... B-9
Durand, *Pepin,* 1,968 ... J-3
Eagle, *Waukesha,* 1,707 ... C-9
• Eagle Lake, *Racine,* 1,320 ... D-11
Eagle River, *Vilas,* 1,443 ... F-9
East Troy, *Walworth,* 3,564 ... D-9
Eau Claire, *Eau Claire,* 61,704 ... J-4
Edgar, *Marathon,* 1,386 ... J-7
Edgerton, *Rock,* 4,933 ... P-10
Elkhart Lake, *Sheboygan,* 1,021 ... M-12
Elkhorn, *Walworth,* 7,305 ... Q-11
Ellsworth, *Pierce,* 2,909 ... J-2
Elm Grove, *Waukesha,* 6,249 ... B-11
Elroy, *Juneau,* 1,578 ... M-7
Evansville, *Rock,* 4,039 ... P-9
• Evergreen, *Marathon,* 3,611 ... J-8
Fall Creek, *Eau Claire,* 1,236 ... J-4
Fall River, *Columbia,* 1,097 ... N-10
Fennimore, *Grant,* 2,387 ... P-6
Fitchburg, *Dane,* 20,501 ... B-6
Florence, *Florence,* 780 ... F-11
Fond du Lac, *Fond du Lac,* 42,203 ... M-11
Fontana-on-Geneva Lake, *Walworth,* 1,754 ... E-9
Fort Atkinson, *Jefferson,* 11,621 ... P-10
Fox Lake, *Dodge,* 1,454 ... N-10
Fox Point, *Milwaukee,* 7,012 ... A-12
Franklin, *Milwaukee,* 29,494 ... P-12
• Franksville, *Racine,* 1,789 ... D-12
Frederic, *Polk,* 1,262 ... G-2
Fredonia, *Ozaukee,* 1,934 ... N-12
• French Island, *La Crosse,* 4,410 ... M-4
Friendship, *Adams,* 698 ... M-8
Galesville, *Trempealeau,* 1,427 ... L-4
Genoa City, *Walworth,* 1,949 ... E-10
Germantown, *Washington,* 18,260 ... A-11
Gillett, *Oconto,* 1,256 ... J-11
Glendale, *Milwaukee,* 13,367 ... A-12
Glenwood City, *Saint Croix,* 1,183 ... I-2
Grafton, *Ozaukee,* 10,312 ... O-12
Grantsburg, *Burnett,* 1,369 ... G-1
Green Bay, *Brown,* 102,313 ... K-12
Green Lake, *Green Lake,* 1,100 ... M-10
Greendale, *Milwaukee,* 14,405 ... C-11
Greenfield, *Milwaukee,* 35,476 ... C-11
Greenwood, *Clark,* 1,079 ... J-6
Hales Corners, *Milwaukee,* 7,765 ... C-11
Hammond, *Saint Croix,* 1,153 ... I-2
Hartford, *Washington,* 10,905 ... O-11
Hartland, *Waukesha,* 7,905 ... B-10
Hayward, *Sawyer,* 2,129 ... F-4
Hazel Green, *Grant,* 1,183 ... Q-6
Hilbert, *Calumet,* 1,089 ... L-12
Hillsboro, *Vernon,* 1,302 ... N-7
Holmen, *La Crosse,* 6,200 ... M-4
Horicon, *Dodge,* 3,775 ... N-11
Hortonville, *Outagamie,* 2,357 ... K-10
Howard, *Brown,* 13,546 ... K-12
Howards Grove, *Sheboygan,* 2,792 ... M-12
Hudson, *Saint Croix,* 8,775 ... I-1
Hurley, *Iron,* 1,818 ... E-7
Hustisford, *Dodge,* 1,135 ... N-11
Independence, *Trempealeau,* 1,244 ... K-4
Iola, *Waupaca,* 1,298 ... K-9
Jackson, *Washington,* 4,938 ... O-12
Janesville, *Rock,* 59,498 ... Q-10
Jefferson, *Jefferson,* 7,338 ... P-10
Johnson Creek, *Jefferson,* 1,581 ... O-10
Juneau, *Dodge,* 2,485 ... N-10
Kaukauna, *Outagamie,* 12,983 ... L-11
Kenosha, *Kenosha,* 90,352 ... Q-13
• Keshena, *Menominee,* 1,394 ... J-10
Kewaskum, *Washington,* 3,274 ... N-11
Kewaunee, *Kewaunee,* 2,806 ... K-13
Kiel, *Manitowoc,* 3,450 ... M-12
Kimberly, *Outagamie,* 6,146 ... L-11
Kohler, *Sheboygan,* 1,926 ... M-13
La Crosse, *La Crosse,* 51,818 ... M-4
• Lac du Flambeau, *Vilas,* 1,646 ... F-8
Ladysmith, *Rusk,* 3,932 ... H-5
Lake Delton, *Sauk,* 1,982 ... N-8
Lake Geneva, *Walworth,* 7,148 ... Q-11
• Lake Koshkonong, *Jefferson,* 1,219 ... P-10
Lake Mills, *Jefferson,* 4,843 ... O-10
Lake Nebagamon, *Douglas,* 1,015 ... E-4
• Lake Ripley, *Jefferson,* 1,603 ... P-10
• Lake Wazeecha, *Wood,* 2,659 ... K-8
• Lake Wisconsin, *Columbia,* 3,493 ... N-8
• Lake Wissota, *Chippewa,* 2,458 ... J-4
Lancaster, *Grant,* 4,070 ... P-6
Lannon, *Waukesha,* 1,009 ... A-11
• Legend Lake, *Menominee,* 1,533 ... J-11
Little Chute, *Outagamie,* 10,476 ... L-11
Lodi, *Columbia,* 2,882 ... O-8
Lomira, *Dodge,* 2,233 ... N-11
Loyal, *Clark,* 1,308 ... J-6
Luck, *Polk,* 1,210 ... G-2
Luxemburg, *Kewaunee,* 1,935 ... K-13
Madison, *Dane,* 208,054 ... B-6
Manawa, *Waupaca,* 1,330 ... K-10
Manitowoc, *Manitowoc,* 34,053 ... L-13
Maple Bluff, *Dane,* 1,358 ... A-7
Marathon City, *Marathon,* 1,640 ... J-8
Marinette, *Marinette,* 11,749 ... I-13
Marion, *Waupaca,* 1,297 ... J-10
Markesan, *Green Lake,* 1,396 ... M-10
Marshall, *Dane,* 3,432 ... O-10
Marshfield, *Wood,* 18,800 ... J-7
Mauston, *Juneau,* 3,740 ... M-7
Mayville, *Dodge,* 4,902 ... N-11
Mazomanie, *Dane,* 1,485 ... O-8
McFarland, *Dane,* 6,416 ... P-9
Medford, *Taylor,* 4,350 ... I-7
Menasha, *Winnebago,* 16,331 ... L-11
Menomonee Falls, *Waukesha,* 32,647 ... O-12
Menomonie, *Dunn,* 14,937 ... J-3
Mequon, *Ozaukee,* 21,823 ... A-12
Merrill, *Lincoln,* 10,146 ... I-8
Merton, *Waukesha,* 1,926 ... A-10
Middleton, *Dane,* 15,770 ... A-6
Milton, *Rock,* 5,132 ... P-10
Milwaukee, *Milwaukee,* 596,974 ... O-12
Mineral Point, *Iowa,* 2,617 ... P-7
Mishicot, *Manitowoc,* 1,422 ... L-13
Mondovi, *Buffalo,* 2,634 ... K-3
Monona, *Dane,* 8,018 ... B-7
Monroe, *Green,* 10,843 ... Q-8
Montello, *Marquette,* 1,397 ... M-9
Monticello, *Green,* 1,146 ... P-8
Mosinee, *Marathon,* 4,063 ... J-8
Mount Horeb, *Dane,* 5,860 ... P-8
Mukwonago, *Waukesha,* 6,162 ... P-11
Muscoda, *Grant,* 1,453 ... O-6
Muskego, *Waukesha,* 21,397 ... C-11
Nashotah, *Waukesha,* 1,266 ... B-9
Neenah, *Winnebago,* 24,507 ... L-11
Neillsville, *Clark,* 2,731 ... K-6
Nekoosa, *Wood,* 2,590 ... K-8
New Berlin, *Waukesha,* 38,220 ... B-11
New Glarus, *Green,* 2,111 ... P-8
New Holstein, *Calumet,* 3,301 ... M-12
New Lisbon, *Juneau,* 1,436 ... M-7
New London, *Waupaca,* 7,085 ... K-10
New Richmond, *Saint Croix,* 6,310 ... I-2
Newburg, *Washington,* 1,119 ... N-12
Niagara, *Marinette,* 1,880 ... G-12
North Fond du Lac, *Fond du Lac,* 4,557 ... M-11
North Hudson, *Saint Croix,* 3,463 ... I-1
North Prairie, *Waukesha,* 1,571 ... C-9
Oak Creek, *Milwaukee,* 28,456 ... P-12
Oakfield, *Fond du Lac,* 1,012 ... M-11
Oconomowoc, *Waukesha,* 12,382 ... B-9
Oconto, *Oconto,* 4,708 ... J-12
Oconto Falls, *Oconto,* 2,843 ... J-12
• Okauchee Lake, *Waukesha,* 3,916 ... B-9
Omro, *Winnebago,* 3,177 ... L-10
Onalaska, *La Crosse,* 14,839 ... M-4
• Oneida, *Brown,* 1,070 ... K-12
Oostburg, *Sheboygan,* 2,660 ... N-12
Oregon, *Dane,* 7,514 ... P-9
Orfordville, *Rock,* 1,272 ... Q-9
Osceola, *Polk,* 2,421 ... H-1
Oshkosh, *Winnebago,* 62,916 ... L-11
Osseo, *Trempealeau,* 1,669 ... K-4
Paddock Lake, *Kenosha,* 3,012 ... E-11
Palmyra, *Jefferson,* 1,766 ... C-9
Pardeeville, *Columbia,* 1,982 ... N-9
Park Falls, *Price,* 2,793 ... F-6
• Pell Lake, *Walworth,* 2,988 ... E-10
Peshtigo, *Marinette,* 3,357 ... I-12
Pewaukee, *Waukesha,* 11,783 ... B-10
Phillips, *Price,* 1,675 ... G-6
Platteville, *Grant,* 9,989 ... P-6
Pleasant Prairie, *Kenosha,* 16,136 ... Q-12
Plover, *Portage,* 10,520 ... K-8
Plymouth, *Sheboygan,* 7,781 ... M-12
Port Edwards, *Wood,* 1,944 ... K-8
Port Washington, *Ozaukee,* 10,467 ... N-12
Portage, *Columbia,* 9,728 ... N-9
• Potter Lake, *Walworth,* 1,099 ... C-10
• Powers Lake, *Kenosha,* 1,500 ... E-10
Poynette, *Columbia,* 2,266 ... N-9
Prairie du Chien, *Crawford,* 6,018 ... O-5
Prairie du Sac, *Sauk,* 3,231 ... O-8
Prescott, *Pierce,* 3,764 ... J-1
Princeton, *Green Lake,* 1,504 ... M-9
Pulaski, *Brown,* 3,060 ... J-11
Racine, *Racine,* 81,855 ... P-13
Randolph, *Dodge,* 1,869 ... N-10
Random Lake, *Sheboygan,* 1,551 ... N-12
Redgranite, *Waushara,* 1,040 ... L-9
Reedsburg, *Sauk,* 7,827 ... N-7
Reedsville, *Manitowoc,* 1,187 ... L-12
Rhinelander, *Oneida,* 7,735 ... G-9
• Rib Mountain, *Marathon,* 6,059 ... J-8
Rice Lake, *Barron,* 8,320 ... H-3
Richland Center, *Richland,* 5,114 ... O-6
Ripon, *Fond du Lac,* 6,828 ... M-10
River Falls, *Pierce,* 12,560 ... J-1
River Hills, *Milwaukee,* 1,631 ... A-12
Rochester, *Racine,* 1,149 ... D-10
Rothschild, *Marathon,* 4,970 ... J-8
Saint Croix Falls, *Polk,* 2,033 ... H-1
Saint Francis, *Milwaukee,* 8,662 ... B-12
Sauk City, *Sauk,* 3,109 ... O-8
Saukville, *Ozaukee,* 4,068 ... N-12
Schofield, *Marathon,* 2,117 ... J-8
• Seymour, *Eau Claire,* 1,474 ... J-4
Seymour, *Outagamie,* 3,335 ... K-11
Sharon, *Walworth,* 1,549 ... Q-10
Shawano, *Shawano,* 8,298 ... J-11
Sheboygan, *Sheboygan,* 50,792 ... M-13
Sheboygan Falls, *Sheboygan,* 6,772 ... M-12
Shell Lake, *Washburn,* 1,309 ... G-3
Sherwood, *Calumet,* 1,550 ... L-11
Shorewood, *Milwaukee,* 13,763 ... O-12
Shorewood Hills, *Dane,* 1,732 ... B-6
Shullsburg, *Lafayette,* 1,246 ... Q-7
Silver Lake, *Kenosha,* 2,341 ... E-11
Slinger, *Washington,* 3,901 ... O-11
Somerset, *Saint Croix,* 1,556 ... I-1
South Milwaukee, *Milwaukee,* 21,256 ... C-12
Sparta, *Monroe,* 8,648 ... M-5
Spencer, *Marathon,* 1,932 ... J-7
Spooner, *Washburn,* 2,653 ... G-3
Spring Green, *Sauk,* 1,444 ... O-7
Spring Valley, *Pierce,* 1,189 ... J-2
Stanley, *Chippewa,* 1,898 ... I-5
Stevens Point, *Portage,* 24,551 ... K-8
Stoughton, *Dane,* 12,354 ... C-8
Stratford, *Marathon,* 1,523 ... J-7
Strum, *Trempealeau,* 1,001 ... K-4
Sturgeon Bay, *Door,* 9,437 ... J-13
Sturtevant, *Racine,* 5,287 ... Q-12
Sun Prairie, *Dane,* 20,369 ... A-8
Superior, *Douglas,* 27,368 ... D-3
Sussex, *Waukesha,* 8,828 ... A-10
• Tainter Lake, *Dunn,* 2,089 ... I-3
Theresa, *Dodge,* 1,252 ... N-11
Thiensville, *Ozaukee,* 3,254 ... A-12
Thorp, *Clark,* 1,536 ... I-5
Tomah, *Monroe,* 8,419 ... M-6
Tomahawk, *Lincoln,* 3,770 ... H-8
Trempealeau, *Trempealeau,* 1,319 ... L-4
Turtle Lake, *Barron,* 1,065 ... H-2
Twin Lakes, *Kenosha,* 5,124 ... Q-11
Two Rivers, *Manitowoc,* 12,639 ... L-13
Union Grove, *Racine,* 4,322 ... D-11
Verona, *Dane,* 7,052 ... B-6
Viroqua, *Vernon,* 4,335 ... N-5
Wales, *Waukesha,* 2,523 ... B-10
Walworth, *Walworth,* 2,304 ... Q-11
Washburn, *Bayfield,* 2,280 ... D-5
Waterford, *Racine,* 4,048 ... P-12
• Waterford North, *Racine,* 4,761 ... D-10
Waterloo, *Jefferson,* 3,259 ... O-10
Watertown, *Jefferson,* 21,598 ... O-10
Waukesha, *Waukesha,* 64,825 ... P-12
Waunakee, *Dane,* 8,995 ... O-9
Waupaca, *Waupaca,* 5,676 ... K-9
Waupun, *Fond du Lac,* 10,718 ... N-10
Wausau, *Marathon,* 38,426 ... J-8
Wautoma, *Waushara,* 1,998 ... L-9
Wauwatosa, *Milwaukee,* 47,271 ... B-11
West Allis, *Milwaukee,* 61,254 ... B-11
West Baraboo, *Sauk,* 1,248 ... N-8
West Bend, *Washington,* 28,152 ... N-12
West Milwaukee, *Milwaukee,* 4,201 ... B-12
West Salem, *La Crosse,* 4,540 ... M-5
Westby, *Vernon,* 2,045 ... N-5
Westfield, *Marquette,* 1,217 ... M-9
Weston, *Marathon,* 12,079 ... J-3
Weyauwega, *Waupaca,* 1,806 ... K-10
Whitefish Bay, *Milwaukee,* 14,163 ... B-12
Whitehall, *Trempealeau,* 1,651 ... K-4
Whitewater, *Walworth,* 13,437 ... P-10
Whiting, *Portage,* 1,760 ... K-8
Williams Bay, *Walworth,* 2,415 ... E-9
• Wind Lake, *Racine,* 5,202 ... P-12
Wind Point, *Racine,* 1,853 ... P-13
• Windsor, *Dane,* 2,533 ... O-9
Winneconne, *Winnebago,* 2,401 ... L-10
Wisconsin Dells, *Columbia,* 2,418 ... N-8
Wisconsin Rapids, *Wood,* 18,435 ... K-8
Wittenberg, *Shawano,* 1,177 ... J-9
Woodville, *Saint Croix,* 1,104 ... I-2
Wrightstown, *Brown,* 1,934 ... K-12

Explanation of symbols: • - Census Designated Place (CDP)

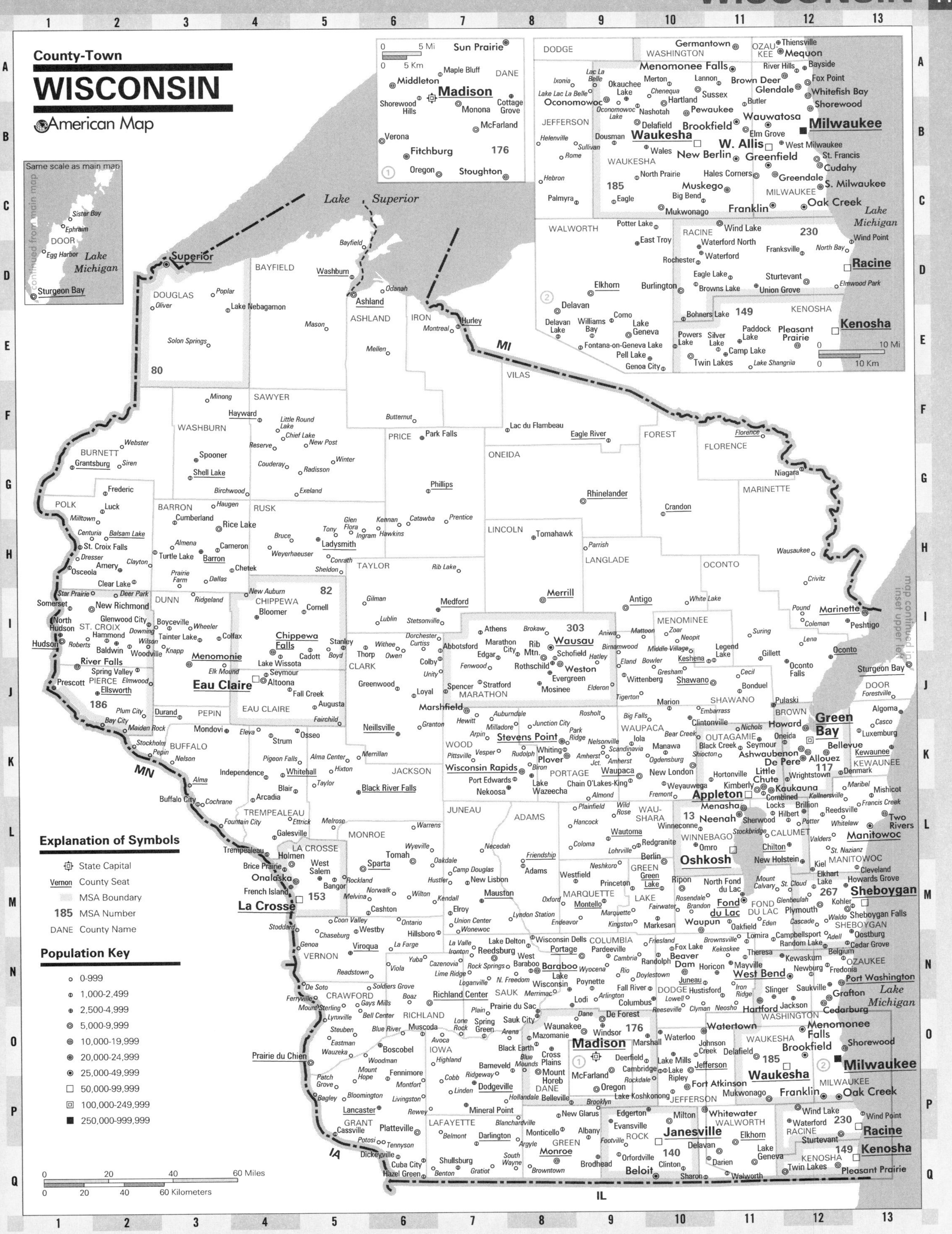
County-Town
WISCONSIN
American Map
Same scale as main map
continued from main map
Sister Bay
Ephraim
DOOR
Egg Harbor
Lake Michigan
Sturgeon Bay
Lake Superior
Explanation of Symbols
State Capital
Vernon County Seat
MSA Boundary
185 MSA Number
DANE County Name
Population Key
0-999
1,000-2,499
2,500-4,999
5,000-9,999
10,000-19,999
20,000-24,999
25,000-49,999
50,000-99,999
100,000-249,999
250,000-999,999
0 20 40 60 Miles
0 20 40 60 Kilometers
0 5 Mi
0 5 Km
Sun Prairie
Maple Bluff
DANE
Middleton
Madison
Shorewood Hills
Monona
Cottage Grove
McFarland
Verona
Fitchburg
176
Oregon
Stoughton
DODGE
WASHINGTON
Germantown
OZAUKEE
Thiensville
Mequon
Menomonee Falls
River Hills
Bayside
Fox Point
Whitefish Bay
Shorewood
Glendale
Brown Deer
Butler
Sussex
Lannon
Merton
Chenequa
Hartland
Okauchee Lake
Lac La Belle
Ixonia
Lake Lac La Belle
Oconomowoc
Oconomowoc Lake
Nashotah
Pewaukee
Wauwatosa
Milwaukee
JEFFERSON
Delafield
Brookfield
Elm Grove
Waukesha
W. Allis
West Milwaukee
Helenville
Sullivan
Dousman
Wales
New Berlin
Greenfield
St. Francis
Cudahy
Rome
WAUKESHA
North Prairie
Hales Corners
Greendale
S. Milwaukee
Hebron
185
Muskego
MILWAUKEE
Eagle
Big Bend
Palmyra
Mukwonago
Franklin
Oak Creek
Lake Michigan
WALWORTH
Potter Lake
Wind Lake
RACINE
230
Wind Point
East Troy
Waterford North
Franksville
North Bay
Rochester
Waterford
Racine
Eagle Lake
Sturtevant
Elmwood Park
Elkhorn
Burlington
Browns Lake
Union Grove
Delavan
Bohners Lake
149
KENOSHA
Delavan Lake
Williams Bay
Como
Lake Geneva
Powers Lake
Silver Lake
Paddock Lake
Pleasant Prairie
Kenosha
Fontana-on-Geneva Lake
Camp Lake
Pell Lake
Twin Lakes
Lake Shangrila
Genoa City
0 10 Mi
0 10 Km
Superior
BAYFIELD
Bayfield
Washburn
Odanah
Ashland
ASHLAND
DOUGLAS
Poplar
Oliver
Lake Nebagamon
Mason
IRON
Montreal
Hurley
MI
Solon Springs
Mellen
80
VILAS
Minong
SAWYER
Hayward
WASHBURN
Little Round Lake
Chief Lake
New Post
Reserve
Butternut
Lac du Flambeau
Eagle River
FOREST
Florence
FLORENCE
PRICE
Park Falls
ONEIDA
BURNETT
Webster
Grantsburg
Siren
Spooner
Couderay
Winter
Radisson
Shell Lake
Birchwood
Exeland
Phillips
Rhinelander
Niagara
MARINETTE
Frederic
POLK
Luck
BARRON
Haugen
RUSK
Crandon
Milltown
Cumberland
Centuria
Balsam Lake
Rice Lake
Glen Flora
Kennan
Catawba
Prentice
Tony
Ingram
Hawkins
LINCOLN
Tomahawk
St. Croix Falls
Almena
Cameron
Bruce
Ladysmith
Parish
Dresser
Turtle Lake
Barron
Weyerhaeuser
Conrath
LANGLADE
OCONTO
Wausaukee
Osceola
Clayton
Amery
Chetek
Sheldon
TAYLOR
Rib Lake
Prairie Farm
Dallas
Clear Lake
Crivitz
Star Prairie
Deer Park
New Auburn
82
Merrill
Somerset
DUNN
Ridgeland
CHIPPEWA
White Lake
New Richmond
Bloomer
Cornell
Gilman
Medford
Antigo
Pound
Marinette
North Hudson
ST. CROIX
Glenwood City
Boyceville
Wheeler
Lublin
Stetsonville
MENOMINEE
Coleman
Peshtigo
Hudson
Hammond
Downing
Tainter Lake
Colfax
Chippewa Falls
Athens
Brokaw
303
Aniwa
Mattoon
Zoar
Suring
Roberts
Wilson
Baldwin
Woodville
Knapp
Menomonie
Stanley
Withee
Thorp
Owen
Dorchester
Curtiss
Abbotsford
Marathon City
Rib Mtn.
Wausau
Birnamwood
Neopit
Middle Village
Legend Lake
Lena
Oconto
River Falls
Cadott
Boyd
Edgar
Schofield
Hatley
Gillett
Spring Valley
Elk Mound
Lake Wissota
CLARK
Colby
Fenwood
Rothschild
Weston
Eland
Bowler
Keshena
Oconto Falls
Sturgeon Bay
Prescott
PIERCE
Elmwood
Eau Claire
Seymour
Altoona
Unity
Evergreen
Gresham
Cecil
Ellsworth
Greenwood
Loyal
Spencer
Stratford
Mosinee
Elderon
Wittenberg
Shawano
Bonduel
DOOR
Forestville
186
Fall Creek
MARATHON
Tigerton
Marion
SHAWANO
Pulaski
Algoma
Plum City
Durand
PEPIN
EAU CLAIRE
Augusta
Marshfield
Auburndale
Rosholt
Big Falls
Embarrass
BROWN
Casco
Bay City
Maiden Rock
Fairchild
Hewitt
Milladore
Junction City
Clintonville
Green Bay
Luxemburg
Stockholm
Pepin
Mondovi
Eleva
Osseo
Neillsville
Granton
Park Ridge
WAUPACA
Bear Creek
Nichols
Howard
Oneida
BUFFALO
Strum
Arpin
Stevens Point
Nelsonville
Iola
OUTAGAMIE
Black Creek
Seymour
Bellevue
Kewaunee
Nelson
Pigeon Falls
Alma Center
Merrillan
WOOD
Vesper
Rudolph
Whiting
Amherst Jct.
Scandinavia
Manawa
Shiocton
Ashwaubenon
De Pere
Allouez
KEWAUNEE
MN
Independence
Whitehall
Hixton
JACKSON
Pittsville
Plover
Amherst
Ogdensburg
Biron
Wisconsin Rapids
PORTAGE
Waupaca
New London
Hortonville
Little Chute
Wrightstown
117
Denmark
Alma
Blair
Taylor
Black River Falls
Port Edwards
Lake Wazeecha
Chain O'Lakes-King
Weyauwega
Kimberly
Kaukauna
Maribel
Mishicot
Buffalo City
Cochrane
Arcadia
Nekoosa
Almond
Fremont
Appleton
Combined Locks
Kellnersville
Francis Creek
TREMPEALEAU
JUNEAU
Plainfield
Wild Rose
Menasha
Brillion
Reedsville
Two Rivers
Fountain City
Ettrick
Melrose
ADAMS
WAUSHARA
13
Neenah
Hilbert
Whitelaw
Galesville
MONROE
Warrens
Hancock
Winneconne
Sherwood
Potter
Manitowoc
Trempealeau
LA CROSSE
Wyeville
Necedah
Wautoma
Stockbridge
CALUMET
Valders
Holmen
Tomah
Coloma
Redgranite
WINNEBAGO
Omro
Chilton
St. Nazianz
Brice Prairie
West Salem
Sparta
Oakdale
Friendship
Lohrville
Berlin
Oshkosh
New Holstein
MANITOWOC
Onalaska
Bangor
Camp Douglas
Adams
Neshkoro
GREEN LAKE
Kiel
Cleveland
Rockland
Hustler
New Lisbon
Westfield
Green Lake
Princeton
Ripon
North Fond du Lac
Mount Calvary
St. Cloud
Elkhart Lake
Howards Grove
French Island
Norwalk
Wilton
Kendall
Mauston
Oxford
MARQUETTE
Rosendale
Glenbeulah
267
Sheboygan
La Crosse
153
Melvina
Cashton
Elroy
Montello
LAKE
Brandon
Fond du Lac
FOND DU LAC
Plymouth
Kohler
Stoddard
Coon Valley
Ontario
Union Center
Wonewoc
Lyndon Station
Endeavor
Marquette
Fairwater
Waupun
Cascade
Waldo
Sheboygan Falls
Westby
Hillsboro
Kingston
Markesan
Oakfield
Eden
SHEBOYGAN
Chaseburg
Genoa
Viroqua
La Farge
La Valle
Ironton
Lake Delton
Reedsburg
Wisconsin Dells
Portage
COLUMBIA
Pardeeville
Friesland
Fox Lake
Brownsville
Lomira
Campbellsport
Random Lake
Adell
Oostburg
Cedar Grove
Belgium
VERNON
Yuba
Cazenovia
Rock Springs
West Baraboo
Baraboo
Wyocena
Cambria
Randolph
Beaver Dam
Kekoskee
Theresa
Kewaskum
OZAUKEE
Viola
Lime Ridge
Lake Wisconsin
Rio
Doylestown
Horicon
Mayville
West Bend
Newburg
Fredonia
Readstown
Loganville
N. Freedom
Poynette
Juneau
Port Washington
De Soto
Soldiers Grove
Merrimac
Fall River
DODGE
Hustisford
Iron Ridge
Slinger
Saukville
Grafton
CRAWFORD
Boaz
Richland Center
SAUK
Lodi
Arlington
Lowell
Lake Michigan
Ferryville
Gays Mills
Prairie du Sac
Columbus
Reeseville
Clyman
Neosho
Hartford
Jackson
Cedarburg
Mount Sterling
Lynxville
Bell Center
RICHLAND
Plain
Dane
De Forest
WASHINGTON
Steuben
Blue River
Muscoda
Lone Rock
Spring Green
Sauk City
Arena
Waunakee
Windsor
176
Watertown
Menomonee Falls
Eastman
Avoca
Mazomanie
Madison
Marshall
Waterloo
Johnson Creek
WAUKESHA
Brookfield
Shorewood
Prairie du Chien
Wauzeka
Boscobel
IOWA
Black Earth
Blue Mounds
Cross Plains
Deerfield
Lake Mills
Delafield
185
Milwaukee
Woodman
Highland
Barneveld
Mount Horeb
McFarland
Cambridge
Jefferson
Waukesha
Patch Grove
Mount Hope
Fennimore
Cobb
Ridgeway
DANE
Oregon
Rockdale
Ripley
Fort Atkinson
MILWAUKEE
Bagley
Montfort
Linden
Dodgeville
Hollandale
Belleville
Lake Koshkonong
Mukwonago
Franklin
Oak Creek
Bloomington
Livingston
Brooklyn
JEFFERSON
Lancaster
Rewey
Mineral Point
New Glarus
Edgerton
Milton
Whitewater
Wind Lake
Wind Point
GRANT
LAFAYETTE
Blanchardville
Evansville
WALWORTH
Waterford
230
Cassville
Platteville
Belmont
Darlington
Monticello
Albany
Janesville
Elkhorn
RACINE
Racine
Potosi
Tennyson
Argyle
GREEN
Footville
ROCK
Sturtevant
Dickeyville
Monroe
Delavan
Lake Geneva
149
Kenosha
Cuba City
Shullsburg
South Wayne
Brodhead
Orfordville
140
KENOSHA
Hazel Green
Benton
Gratiot
Browntown
Beloit
Clinton
Darien
Twin Lakes
Pleasant Prairie
Sharon
Walworth
IA
IL
map continued in inset upper left

COUNTIES

(23 Counties)

Name of County	Population	Location on Map
ALBANY	32,014	H-13
BIG HORN	11,461	A-9
CAMPBELL	33,698	A-13
CARBON	15,639	H-10
CONVERSE	12,052	E-13
CROOK	5,887	A-15
FREMONT	35,804	E-6
GOSHEN	12,538	H-16
HOT SPRINGS	4,882	D-8
JOHNSON	7,075	C-11
LARAMIE	81,607	J-15
LINCOLN	14,573	H-4
NATRONA	66,533	E-10
NIOBRARA	2,407	E-15
PARK	25,786	A-6
PLATTE	8,807	H-15
SHERIDAN	26,560	B-10
SUBLETTE	5,920	F-5
SWEETWATER	37,613	I-6
TETON	18,251	D-4
UINTA	19,742	J-4
WASHAKIE	8,289	E-10
WESTON	6,644	D-15
TOTAL	**493,782**	

CITIES AND TOWNS

Note: The first name is that of the city or town, second, that of the county in which it is located, then the population and location on the map.

Afton, *Lincoln,* 1,818 .... G-4
●Antelope Valley-Crestview, *Campbell,* 1,642 .... C-14
●Arapahoe, *Fremont,* 1,766 .... G-9
Basin, *Big Horn,* 1,238 .... C-9
Buffalo, *Johnson,* 3,900 .... C-12
Casper, *Natrona,* 49,644 .... G-13
Cheyenne, *Laramie,* 53,011 .... L-16
Cody, *Park,* 8,835 .... C-8
Douglas, *Converse,* 5,288 .... G-14
●Ethete, *Fremont,* 1,455 .... G-8
Evanston, *Uinta,* 11,507 .... K-4
Evansville, *Natrona,* 2,255 .... L-2
●Fort Washakie, *Fremont,* 1,477 .... G-8
●Fox Farm-College, *Laramie,* 3,272 .... L-16
Gillette, *Campbell,* 19,646 .... C-14
Glenrock, *Converse,* 2,231 .... G-13
Green River, *Sweetwater,* 11,808 .... K-7
Greybull, *Big Horn,* 1,815 .... C-9
Guernsey, *Platte,* 1,147 .... H-16
●Hoback, *Teton,* 1,453 .... F-4
Jackson, *Teton,* 8,647 .... E-4
Kemmerer, *Lincoln,* 2,651 .... J-5
Lander, *Fremont,* 6,867 .... G-8
Laramie, *Albany,* 27,204 .... K-14
Lovell, *Big Horn,* 2,281 .... B-9
Lusk, *Niobrara,* 1,447 .... G-16
Lyman, *Uinta,* 1,938 .... K-5
Mills, *Natrona,* 2,591 .... G-13
●Moose Wilson Road, *Teton,* 1,439 .... E-4
Mountain View, *Uinta,* 1,153 .... K-5
Newcastle, *Weston,* 3,065 .... D-17
●North Rock Springs, *Sweetwater,* 1,974 .... J-7
Pine Bluffs, *Laramie,* 1,153 .... K-17
Pinedale, *Sublette,* 1,412 .... G-6
Powell, *Park,* 5,373 .... B-8
●Rafter J Ranch, *Teton,* 1,138 .... E-4
●Ranchettes, *Laramie,* 4,869 .... K-16
Rawlins, *Carbon,* 8,538 .... J-11
Riverton, *Fremont,* 9,310 .... G-9
Rock Springs, *Sweetwater,* 18,708 .... J-7
Saratoga, *Carbon,* 1,726 .... K-12
Sheridan, *Sheridan,* 15,804 .... B-11
●Sleepy Hollow, *Campbell,* 1,177 .... C-14
●South Greeley, *Laramie,* 4,201 .... L-16
Sundance, *Crook,* 1,161 .... C-16
Thermopolis, *Hot Springs,* 3,172 .... E-9
Torrington, *Goshen,* 5,776 .... I-17
●Vista West, *Natrona,* 1,008 .... L-1
●Warren AFB, *Laramie,* 4,440 .... K-16
Wheatland, *Platte,* 3,548 .... I-15
●Wilson, *Teton,* 1,294 .... E-4
Worland, *Washakie,* 5,250 .... D-10
Wright, *Campbell,* 1,347 .... E-14

Explanation of symbols: ● - Census Designated Place (CDP)

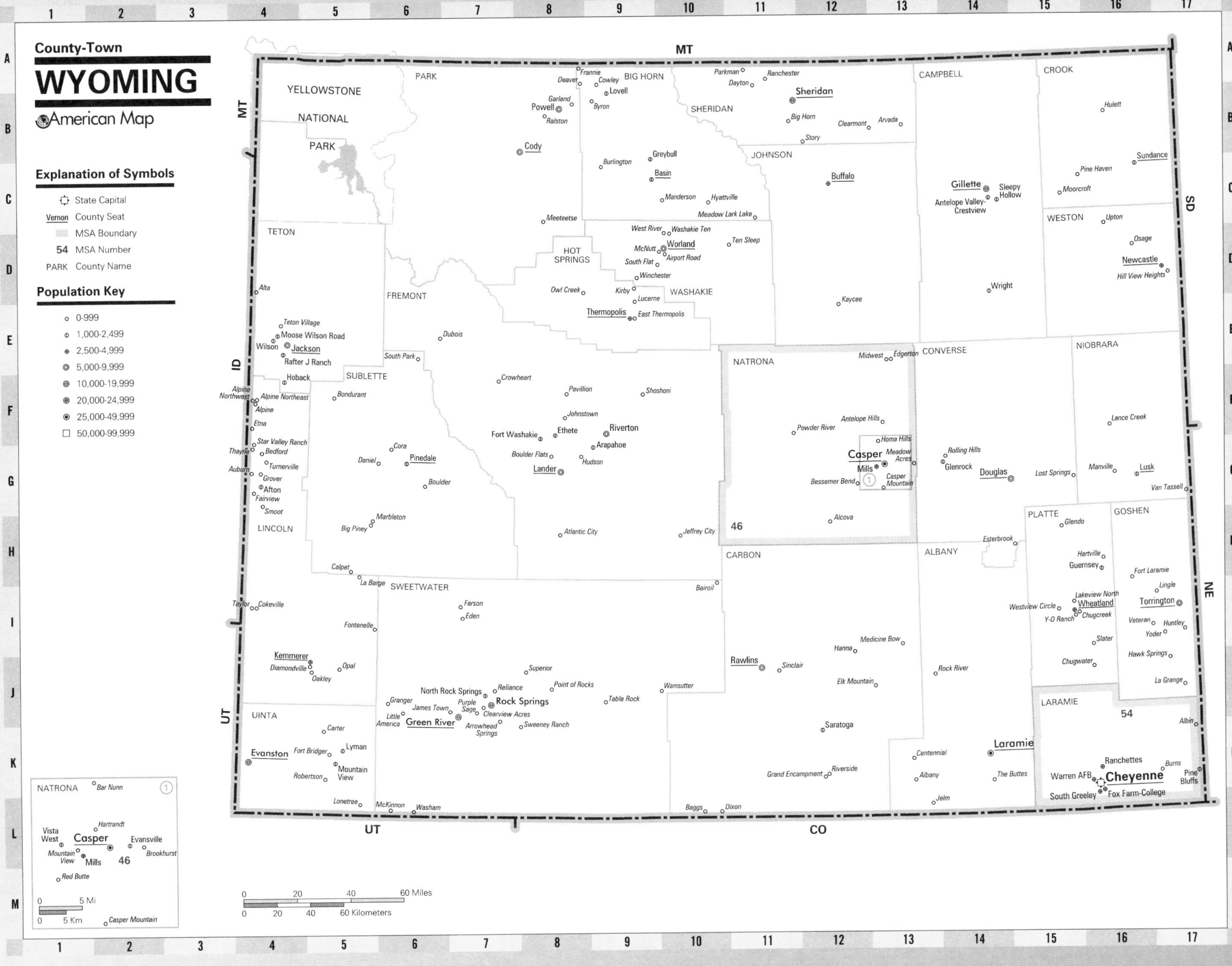
County-Town
WYOMING
American Map
Explanation of Symbols
State Capital
Vernon County Seat
MSA Boundary
54 MSA Number
PARK County Name
Population Key
0-999
1,000-2,499
2,500-4,999
5,000-9,999
10,000-19,999
20,000-24,999
25,000-49,999
50,000-99,999
MT
SD
NE
CO
UT
ID
YELLOWSTONE NATIONAL PARK
PARK
BIG HORN
SHERIDAN
JOHNSON
CAMPBELL
CROOK
WESTON
TETON
HOT SPRINGS
WASHAKIE
FREMONT
SUBLETTE
NATRONA
CONVERSE
NIOBRARA
LINCOLN
PLATTE
GOSHEN
CARBON
ALBANY
SWEETWATER
UINTA
LARAMIE
46
54
Frannie
Deaver
Cowley
Lovell
Byron
Garland
Powell
Ralston
Cody
Burlington
Greybull
Basin
Manderson
Hyattville
Meadow Lark Lake
Meeteetse
Parkman
Ranchester
Dayton
Sheridan
Big Horn
Clearmont
Arvada
Story
Buffalo
Gillette
Sleepy Hollow
Antelope Valley-Crestview
Hulett
Sundance
Pine Haven
Moorcroft
Upton
Osage
Newcastle
Hill View Heights
Wright
Kaycee
West River
Washakie Ten
McNutt
Worland
Airport Road
South Flat
Ten Sleep
Winchester
Owl Creek
Kirby
Lucerne
Thermopolis
East Thermopolis
Alta
Teton Village
Moose Wilson Road
Wilson
Jackson
Rafter J Ranch
Hoback
Alpine Northwest
Alpine Northeast
Alpine
Etna
Star Valley Ranch
Thayne
Bedford
Auburn
Turnerville
Grover
Afton
Fairview
Smoot
Dubois
South Park
Bondurant
Crowheart
Pavillion
Shoshoni
Johnstown
Fort Washakie
Ethete
Riverton
Arapahoe
Boulder Flats
Hudson
Lander
Cora
Daniel
Pinedale
Boulder
Marbleton
Big Piney
Atlantic City
Jeffrey City
Midwest
Edgerton
Antelope Hills
Powder River
Homa Hills
Casper
Meadow Acres
Mills
Bessemer Bend
Casper Mountain
Alcova
Rolling Hills
Glenrock
Douglas
Lost Springs
Lance Creek
Manville
Lusk
Van Tassell
Glendo
Esterbrook
Hartville
Guernsey
Fort Laramie
Lingle
Lakeview North
Wheatland
Westview Circle
Y-O Ranch
Chugcreek
Torrington
Veteran
Huntley
Yoder
Slater
Hawk Springs
Chugwater
La Grange
Calpet
La Barge
Taylor
Cokeville
Farson
Eden
Bairoil
Fontenelle
Kemmerer
Diamondville
Oakley
Opal
Superior
Point of Rocks
North Rock Springs
Reliance
Granger
James Town
Purple Sage
Rock Springs
Little America
Green River
Clearview Acres
Arrowhead Springs
Sweeney Ranch
Table Rock
Wamsutter
Rawlins
Sinclair
Medicine Bow
Hanna
Elk Mountain
Rock River
Saratoga
Carter
Evanston
Fort Bridger
Lyman
Robertson
Mountain View
Lonetree
McKinnon
Washam
Baggs
Dixon
Grand Encampment
Riverside
Centennial
Albany
Jelm
Laramie
The Buttes
Albin
Ranchettes
Burns
Warren AFB
Cheyenne
Pine Bluffs
South Greeley
Fox Farm-College
NATRONA
Bar Nunn
Hartrandt
Vista West
Casper
Evansville
Mountain View
Mills
Brookhurst
46
Red Butte
Casper Mountain
0 5 Mi
0 5 Km
0 20 40 60 Miles
0 20 40 60 Kilometers

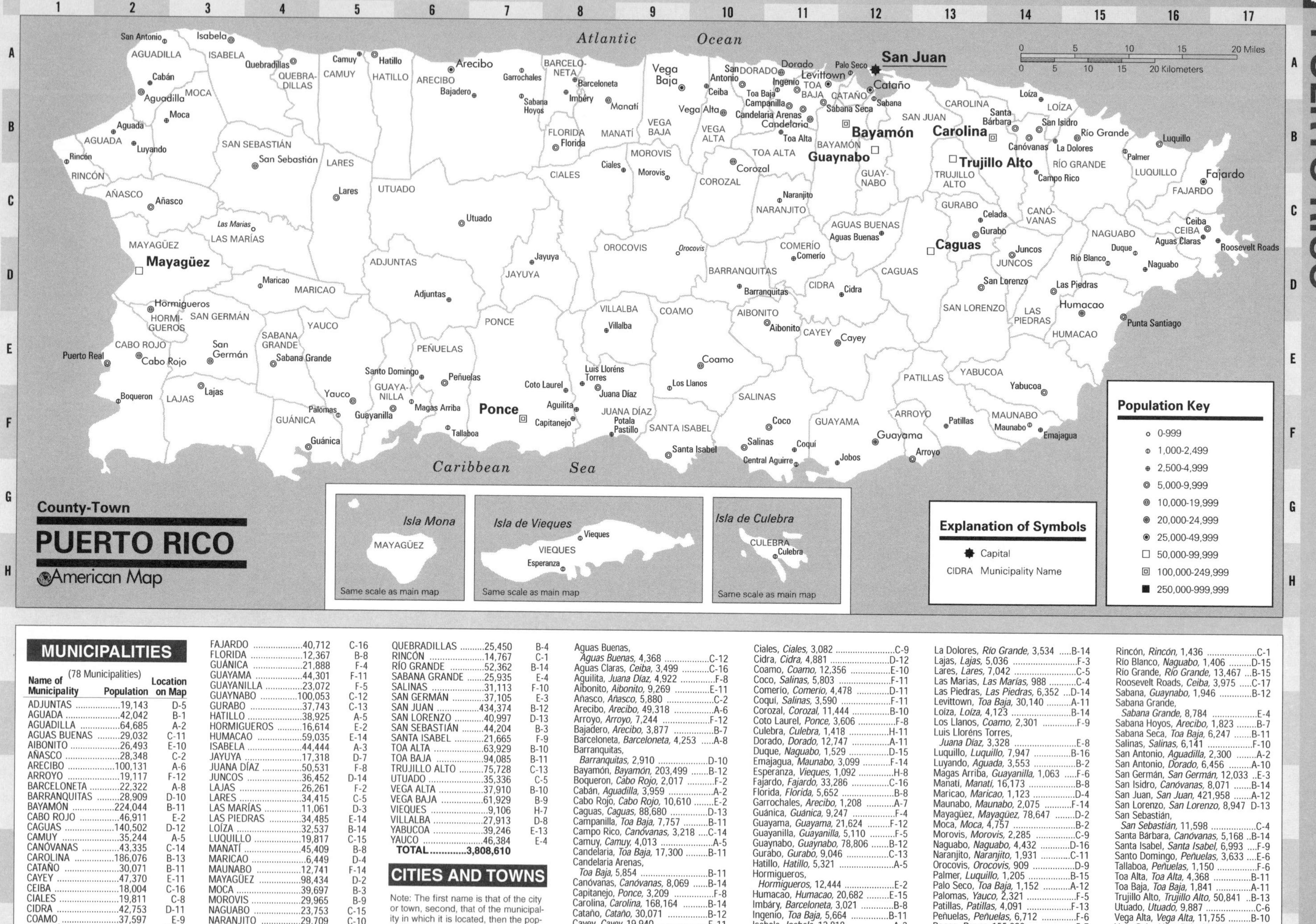

MUNICIPALITIES

(78 Municipalities)

Name of Municipality	Population	Location on Map
ADJUNTAS	19,143	D-5
AGUADA	42,042	B-1
AGUADILLA	64,685	A-2
AGUAS BUENAS	29,032	C-11
AIBONITO	26,493	E-10
AÑASCO	28,348	C-2
ARECIBO	100,131	A-6
ARROYO	19,117	F-12
BARCELONETA	22,322	A-8
BARRANQUITAS	28,909	D-10
BAYAMÓN	224,044	B-11
CABO ROJO	46,911	E-2
CAGUAS	140,502	D-12
CAMUY	35,244	A-5
CANÓVANAS	43,335	C-14
CAROLINA	186,076	B-13
CATAÑO	30,071	B-11
CAYEY	47,370	E-11
CEIBA	18,004	C-16
CIALES	19,811	C-8
CIDRA	42,753	D-11
COAMO	37,597	E-9
COMERÍO	20,002	D-11
COROZAL	36,867	C-10
CULEBRA	1,868	H-10
DORADO	34,017	A-10
FAJARDO	40,712	C-16
FLORIDA	12,367	B-8
GUÁNICA	21,888	F-4
GUAYAMA	44,301	F-11
GUAYANILLA	23,072	F-5
GUAYNABO	100,053	C-12
GURABO	37,743	C-13
HATILLO	38,925	A-5
HORMIGUEROS	16,614	E-2
HUMACAO	59,035	E-14
ISABELA	44,444	A-3
JAYUYA	17,318	D-7
JUANA DÍAZ	50,531	F-8
JUNCOS	36,452	D-14
LAJAS	26,261	F-2
LARES	34,415	C-5
LAS MARÍAS	11,061	D-3
LAS PIEDRAS	34,485	E-14
LOÍZA	32,537	B-14
LUQUILLO	19,817	C-15
MANATÍ	45,409	B-8
MARICAO	6,449	D-4
MAUNABO	12,741	F-14
MAYAGÜEZ	98,434	D-2
MOCA	39,697	B-3
MOROVIS	29,965	B-9
NAGUABO	23,753	C-15
NARANJITO	29,709	C-10
OROCOVIS	23,844	D-8
PATILLAS	20,152	E-12
PEÑUELAS	26,719	E-6
PONCE	186,475	E-7
QUEBRADILLAS	25,450	B-4
RINCÓN	14,767	C-1
RÍO GRANDE	52,362	B-14
SABANA GRANDE	25,935	E-4
SALINAS	31,113	F-10
SAN GERMÁN	37,105	E-3
SAN JUAN	434,374	B-12
SAN LORENZO	40,997	D-13
SAN SEBASTIÁN	44,204	B-3
SANTA ISABEL	21,665	F-9
TOA ALTA	63,929	B-10
TOA BAJA	94,085	B-11
TRUJILLO ALTO	75,728	C-13
UTUADO	35,336	C-5
VEGA ALTA	37,910	B-10
VEGA BAJA	61,929	B-9
VIEQUES	9,106	H-7
VILLALBA	27,913	D-8
YABUCOA	39,246	E-13
YAUCO	46,384	E-4
TOTAL	**3,808,610**	

CITIES AND TOWNS

Note: The first name is that of the city or town, second, that of the municipality in which it is located, then the population and location on the map.

Adjuntas, *Adjuntas,* 4,980 ....D-6
Aguada, *Aguada,* 3,871 ....B-2
Aguadilla, *Aguadilla,* 16,776 ....B-2
Aguas Buenas, *Aguas Buenas,* 4,368 ....C-12
Aguas Claras, *Ceiba,* 3,499 ....C-16
Aguilita, *Juana Díaz,* 4,922 ....F-8
Aibonito, *Aibonito,* 9,269 ....E-11
Añasco, *Añasco,* 5,880 ....C-2
Arecibo, *Arecibo,* 49,318 ....A-6
Arroyo, *Arroyo,* 7,244 ....F-12
Bajadero, *Arecibo,* 3,877 ....B-7
Barceloneta, *Barceloneta,* 4,253 ....A-8
Barranquitas, *Barranquitas,* 2,910 ....D-10
Bayamón, *Bayamón,* 203,499 ....B-12
Boqueron, *Cabo Rojo,* 2,017 ....F-2
Cabán, *Aguadilla,* 3,959 ....A-2
Cabo Rojo, *Cabo Rojo,* 10,610 ....E-2
Caguas, *Caguas,* 88,680 ....D-13
Campanilla, *Toa Baja,* 7,757 ....B-11
Campo Rico, *Canóvanas,* 3,218 ....C-14
Camuy, *Camuy,* 4,013 ....A-5
Candelaria, *Toa Baja,* 17,300 ....B-11
Candelaria Arenas, *Toa Baja,* 5,854 ....B-11
Canóvanas, *Canóvanas,* 8,069 ....B-14
Capitanejo, *Ponce,* 3,209 ....F-8
Carolina, *Carolina,* 168,164 ....B-14
Cataño, *Cataño,* 30,071 ....B-12
Cayey, *Cayey,* 19,940 ....E-11
Ceiba, *Ceiba,* 6,277 ....C-16
Ceiba, *Vega Baja,* 3,698 ....A-10
Celada, *Gurabo,* 4,435 ....C-13
Central Aguirre, *Salinas,* 1,588 ....G-11
Ciales, *Ciales,* 3,082 ....C-9
Cidra, *Cidra,* 4,881 ....D-12
Coamo, *Coamo,* 12,356 ....E-10
Coco, *Salinas,* 5,803 ....F-11
Comerío, *Comerío,* 4,478 ....D-11
Coquí, *Salinas,* 3,590 ....F-11
Corozal, *Corozal,* 11,444 ....B-10
Coto Laurel, *Ponce,* 3,606 ....F-8
Culebra, *Culebra,* 1,418 ....H-11
Dorado, *Dorado,* 12,747 ....A-11
Duque, *Naguabo,* 1,529 ....D-15
Emajagua, *Maunabo,* 3,099 ....F-14
Esperanza, *Vieques,* 1,092 ....H-8
Fajardo, *Fajardo,* 33,286 ....C-16
Florida, *Florida,* 5,652 ....B-8
Garrochales, *Arecibo,* 1,208 ....A-7
Guánica, *Guánica,* 9,247 ....F-4
Guayama, *Guayama,* 21,624 ....F-12
Guayanilla, *Guayanilla,* 5,110 ....F-5
Guaynabo, *Guaynabo,* 78,806 ....B-12
Gurabo, *Gurabo,* 9,046 ....C-13
Hatillo, *Hatillo,* 5,321 ....A-5
Hormigueros, *Hormigueros,* 12,444 ....E-2
Humacao, *Humacao,* 20,682 ....E-15
Imbáry, *Barceloneta,* 3,021 ....B-8
Ingenio, *Toa Baja,* 5,664 ....B-11
Isabela, *Isabela,* 12,818 ....A-3
Jayuya, *Jayuya,* 3,516 ....D-7
Jobos, *Guayama,* 3,475 ....G-11
Juana Díaz, *Juana Díaz,* 9,505 ....F-8
Juncos, *Juncos,* 8,978 ....D-14
La Dolores, *Río Grande,* 3,534 ....B-14
Lajas, *Lajas,* 5,036 ....F-3
Lares, *Lares,* 7,042 ....C-5
Las Marias, *Las Marías,* 988 ....C-4
Las Piedras, *Las Piedras,* 6,352 ....D-14
Levittown, *Toa Baja,* 30,140 ....A-11
Loíza, *Loíza,* 4,123 ....B-14
Los Llanos, *Coamo,* 2,301 ....F-9
Luis Lloréns Torres, *Juana Díaz,* 3,328 ....E-8
Luquillo, *Luquillo,* 7,947 ....B-16
Luyando, *Aguada,* 3,553 ....B-2
Magas Arriba, *Guayanilla,* 1,063 ....F-6
Manatí, *Manatí,* 16,173 ....B-8
Maricao, *Maricao,* 1,123 ....D-4
Maunabo, *Maunabo,* 2,075 ....F-14
Mayagüez, *Mayagüez,* 78,647 ....D-2
Moca, *Moca,* 4,757 ....B-2
Morovis, *Morovis,* 2,285 ....C-9
Naguabo, *Naguabo,* 4,432 ....D-16
Naranjito, *Naranjito,* 1,931 ....C-11
Orocovis, *Orocovis,* 909 ....D-9
Palmer, *Luquillo,* 1,205 ....B-15
Palo Seco, *Toa Baja,* 1,152 ....A-12
Palomas, *Yauco,* 2,321 ....F-5
Patillas, *Patillas,* 4,091 ....F-13
Peñuelas, *Peñuelas,* 6,712 ....F-6
Ponce, *Ponce,* 155,038 ....F-7
Potala Pastillo, *Juana Díaz,* 3,819 ....F-8
Puerto Real, *Cabo Rojo,* 6,166 ....E-2
Punta Santiago, *Humacao,* 5,803 ....E-15
Quebradillas, *Quebradillas,* 5,319 ....A-4
Rincón, *Rincón,* 1,436 ....C-1
Río Blanco, *Naguabo,* 1,406 ....D-15
Río Grande, *Río Grande,* 13,467 ....B-15
Roosevelt Roads, *Ceiba,* 3,975 ....C-17
Sabana, *Guaynabo,* 1,946 ....B-12
Sabana Grande, *Sabana Grande,* 8,784 ....E-4
Sabana Hoyos, *Arecibo,* 1,823 ....B-7
Sabana Seca, *Toa Baja,* 6,247 ....B-11
Salinas, *Salinas,* 6,141 ....F-10
San Antonio, *Aguadilla,* 2,300 ....A-2
San Antonio, *Dorado,* 6,456 ....A-10
San Germán, *San Germán,* 12,033 ....E-3
San Isidro, *Canóvanas,* 8,071 ....B-14
San Juan, *San Juan,* 421,958 ....A-12
San Lorenzo, *San Lorenzo,* 8,947 D-13
San Sebastián, *San Sebastián,* 11,598 ....C-4
Santa Bárbara, *Canóvanas,* 5,168 ....B-14
Santa Isabel, *Santa Isabel,* 6,993 ....F-9
Santo Domingo, *Peñuelas,* 3,633 ....E-6
Tallaboa, *Peñuelas,* 1,150 ....F-6
Toa Alta, *Toa Alta,* 4,368 ....B-11
Toa Baja, *Toa Baja,* 1,841 ....A-11
Trujillo Alto, *Trujillo Alto,* 50,841 ....B-13
Utuado, *Utuado,* 9,887 ....C-6
Vega Alta, *Vega Alta,* 11,755 ....B-10
Vega Baja, *Vega Baja,* 28,811 ....B-9
Vieques, *Vieques,* 2,136 ....H-8
Villalba, *Villalba,* 4,388 ....E-8
Yabucoa, *Yabucoa,* 6,636 ....F-14
Yauco, *Yauco,* 19,609 ....F-5

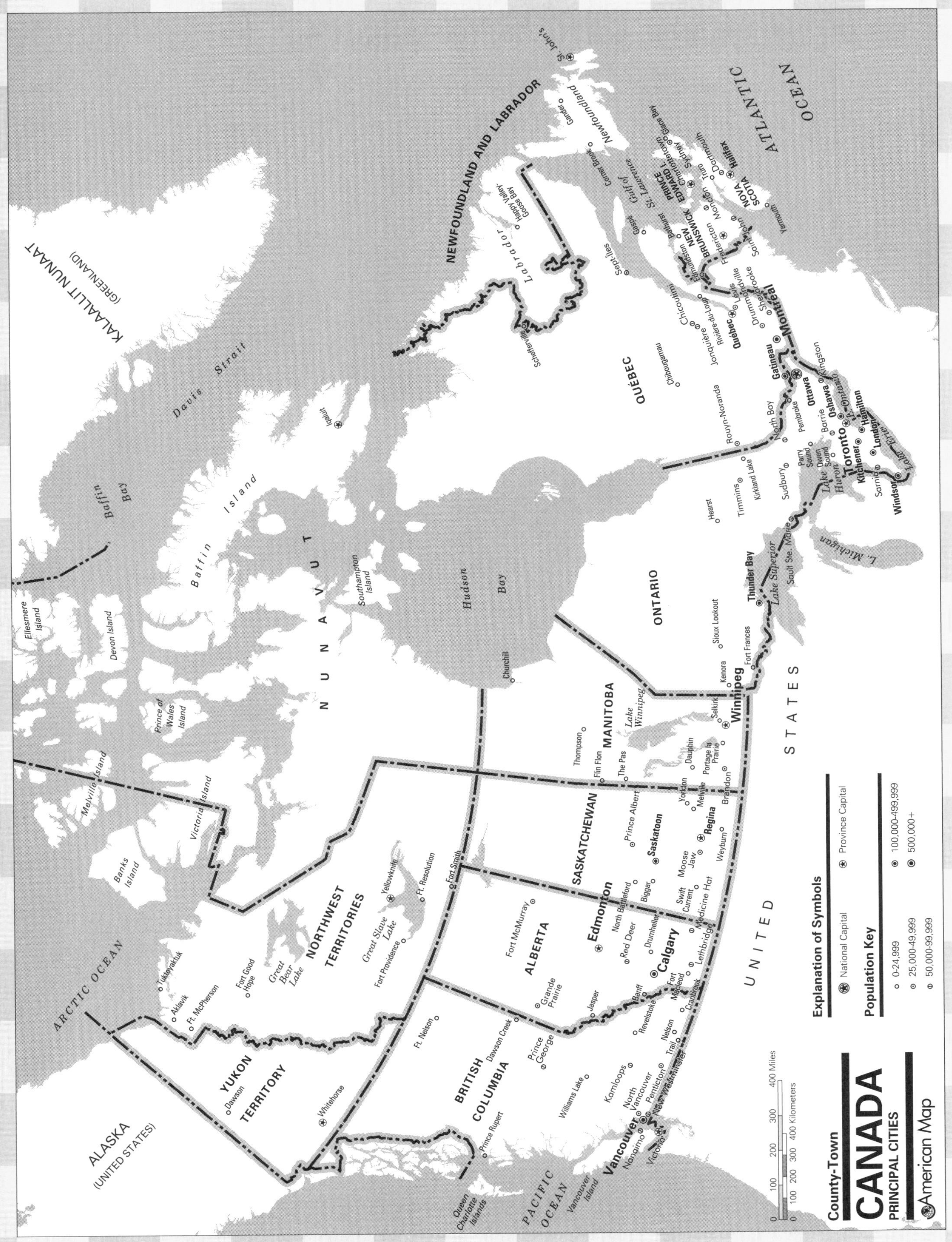

County-Town
CANADA
PRINCIPAL CITIES
American Map
Explanation of Symbols
National Capital
Province Capital
Population Key
0-24,999
25,000-49,999
50,000-99,999
100,000-499,999
500,000+
0 100 200 300 400 Miles
0 100 200 300 400 Kilometers
KALAALLIT NUNAAT
(GREENLAND)
ALASKA
(UNITED STATES)
UNITED STATES
ARCTIC OCEAN
PACIFIC OCEAN
ATLANTIC OCEAN
Baffin Bay
Davis Strait
Hudson Bay
Baffin Island
Ellesmere Island
Devon Island
Prince of Wales Island
Melville Island
Victoria Island
Banks Island
Southampton Island
Queen Charlotte Islands
Vancouver Island
Labrador
Newfoundland
Gulf of St. Lawrence
Great Bear Lake
Great Slave Lake
Lake Winnipeg
Lake Superior
Lake Huron
L. Michigan
L. Ontario
Lake Erie
NUNAVUT
NORTHWEST TERRITORIES
YUKON TERRITORY
BRITISH COLUMBIA
ALBERTA
SASKATCHEWAN
MANITOBA
ONTARIO
QUÉBEC
NEWFOUNDLAND AND LABRADOR
NEW BRUNSWICK
PRINCE EDWARD I.
NOVA SCOTIA
St. John's
Gander
Corner Brook
Happy Valley-Goose Bay
Schefferville
Sept-Îles
Gaspé
Charlottetown
Sydney
Glace Bay
Truro
Dartmouth
Halifax
Yarmouth
Moncton
Bathurst
Fredericton
Saint John
Edmundston
Québec
Lévis
Rivière-du-Loup
Chicoutimi
Jonquière
Chibougamau
Drummondville
Sherbrooke
Montréal
Gatineau
Ottawa
Kingston
Rouyn-Noranda
North Bay
Pembroke
Oshawa
Barrie
Toronto
Hamilton
Kitchener
London
Sarnia
Windsor
Owen Sound
Parry Sound
Sudbury
Kirkland Lake
Timmins
Hearst
Sault Ste. Marie
Thunder Bay
Sioux Lookout
Fort Frances
Kenora
Winnipeg
Selkirk
Portage la Prairie
Brandon
Dauphin
The Pas
Flin Flon
Thompson
Churchill
Iqaluit
Yorkton
Melville
Regina
Weyburn
Moose Jaw
Saskatoon
Prince Albert
Swift Current
Medicine Hat
Biggar
North Battleford
Edmonton
Fort McMurray
Red Deer
Drumheller
Calgary
Lethbridge
Fort Macleod
Banff
Jasper
Grande Prairie
Cranbrook
Nelson
Trail
Revelstoke
Kamloops
Penticton
North Vancouver
New Westminster
Vancouver
Nanaimo
Victoria
Williams Lake
Prince George
Dawson Creek
Ft. Nelson
Prince Rupert
Whitehorse
Dawson
Fort Smith
Ft. Resolution
Yellowknife
Fort Providence
Fort Good Hope
Ft. McPherson
Aklavik
Tuktoyaktuk

DIVISIONS

(19 Divisions)

Name of Division	Population	Location on Map
DIVISION NO. 1	62,330	O-12
DIVISION NO. 2	125,179	P-10
DIVISION NO. 3	37,764	Q-10
DIVISION NO. 4	12,046	M-11
DIVISION NO. 5	43,565	O-10
DIVISION NO. 6	880,859	N-9
DIVISION NO. 7	41,169	L-11
DIVISION NO. 8	133,592	L-9
DIVISION NO. 9	18,196	L-7
DIVISION NO. 10	80,028	K-10
DIVISION NO. 11	898,888	K-8
DIVISION NO. 12	56,499	H-10
DIVISION NO. 13	62,569	I-8
DIVISION NO. 14	27,452	J-5
DIVISION NO. 15	30,800	N-7
DIVISION NO. 16	36,494	B-8
DIVISION NO. 17	54,709	B-5
DIVISION NO. 18	15,022	I-4
DIVISION NO. 19	79,665	G-4
TOTAL	**2,696,826**	

CITIES AND TOWNS

Note: The first name is that of the city or town, second, that of the division in which it is located, then the population and location on the map.

Airdrie, *Division No. 6,* 15,946 ....N-9
Athabasca, *Division No. 13,* 2,313 ....I-10
Banff, *Division No. 15,* 6,098 ....N-8
Barrhead, *Division No. 13,* 4,239 ....J-9
Bassano, *Division No. 2,* 1,272 ....N-10
Beaumont, *Division No. 11,* 5,810 ....N-2
Beaverlodge, *Division No. 19,* 1,997 ....H-5
Black Diamond, *Division No. 6,* 1,811 ....N-9
Blackfalds, *Division No. 8,* 2,001 ....L-9
Bon Accord, *Division No. 11,* 1,493 ....M-2
Bonnyville, *Division No. 12,* 5,100 ....J-12
Bow Island, *Division No. 1,* 1,688 ....P-12
Bowden, *Division No. 8,* 1,014 ....M-9
Brooks, *Division No. 2,* 10,093 ....O-11
Bruderheim, *Division No. 10,* 1,198 ....M-3
Calgary, *Division No. 6,* 768,082 ....N-9
Calmar, *Division No. 11,* 1,797 ....O-2
Camrose, *Division No. 10,* 13,728 ....K-10
Canmore, *Division No. 15,* 8,337 ....N-8
Cardston, *Division No. 3,* 3,417 ....Q-10
Carstairs, *Division No. 6,* 1,887 ....M-9
Claresholm, *Division No. 3,* 3,427 ....O-9
Coaldale, *Division No. 2,* 5,731 ....K-1
Coalhurst, *Division No. 2,* 1,439 ....K-1
Cochrane, *Division No. 6,* 7,424 ....N-9
Coronation, *Division No. 7,* 1,166 ....M-11
Crossfield, *Division No. 6,* 1,899 ....M-9
Devon, *Division No. 11,* 4,496 ....N-2
Didsbury, *Division No. 6,* 3,553 ....M-9
Drayton Valley, *Division No. 11,* 5,883 ....K-8
Drumheller, *Division No. 5,* 5,951 ....M-10
Edmonton, *Division No. 11,* 616,306 ....K-9
Edson, *Division No. 14,* 7,585 ....K-7
Elk Point, *Division No. 12,* 1,403 ....J-12
Fairview, *Division No. 19,* 3,316 ....G-6
Falher, *Division No. 19,* 1,149 ....H-6
Fort Macleod, *Division No. 3,* 2,642 ....P-10
Fort McMurray, *Division No. 16,* 35,213 ....F-11
Fort Saskatchewan, *Division No. 11,* 12,408 ....M-3
Fox Creek, *Division No. 18,* 2,321 ....I-7
Gibbons, *Division No. 11,* 2,748 ....J-10
Grand Centre, *Division No. 12,* 11,708 ....I-12
Grande Cache, *Division No. 18,* 4,380 ....J-5
Grande Prairie, *Division No. 19,* 31,140 ....H-5
Grimshaw, *Division No. 19,* 2,661 ....G-6
Hanna, *Division No. 4,* 3,001 ....M-11
High Level, *Division No. 17,* 3,004 ....D-7
High Prairie, *Division No. 17,* 2,907 ....H-7
High River, *Division No. 6,* 7,359 ....O-9
Hinton, *Division No. 14,* 9,961 ....K-6
Innisfail, *Division No. 8,* 6,116 ....M-9
Jasper, *Division No. 15,* 3,815 ....K-6
Killam, *Division No. 7,* 1,048 ....L-11
La Crete, *Division No. 17,* 1,215 ....D-7
Lac La Biche, *Division No. 12,* 2,611 ....I-11
Lacombe, *Division No. 8,* 8,018 ....L-9
Lake Louise, *Division No. 15,* 1,305 ....M-7
Lamont, *Division No. 10,* 1,581 ....M-4
Leduc, *Division No. 11,* 14,305 ....K-9
Legal, *Division No. 11,* 1,095 ....M-2
Lethbridge, *Division No. 2,* 63,053 ....P-10
Magrath, *Division No. 3,* 1,867 ....P-10
Manning, *Division No. 17,* 1,295 ....F-6
Mayerthorpe, *Division No. 13,* 1,669 ....J-8
Medicine Hat, *Division No. 1,* 46,783 ....O-12
Millet, *Division No. 11,* 1,894 ....K-10
Morinville, *Division No. 11,* 6,226 ....J-9
Nanton, *Division No. 3,* 1,665 ....O-9
Okotoks, *Division No. 6,* 8,510 ....N-9
Olds, *Division No. 6,* 5,815 ....M-9
Oyen, *Division No. 4,* 1,009 ....M-12
Peace River, *Division No. 19,* 6,536 ....G-6
Penhold, *Division No. 8,* 1,625 ....M-9
Picture Butte, *Division No. 2,* 1,669 ....J-1
Pincher Creek, *Division No. 3,* 3,659 ....P-9
Ponoka, *Division No. 8,* 6,149 ....L-9
Provost, *Division No. 7,* 1,904 ....L-12
Rainbow Lake, *Division No. 17,* 1,138 ....D-5
Raymond, *Division No. 2,* 3,056 ....P-10
Red Deer, *Division No. 8,* 60,075 ....L-9
Redcliff, *Division No. 1,* 4,104 ....O-12
Redwater, *Division No. 11,* 2,053 ....M-3
Rimbey, *Division No. 8,* 2,106 ....L-9
Rocky Mountain House, *Division No. 9,* 5,805 ....L-8
Saint Albert, *Division No. 11,* 46,888 ....J-9
Saint Paul, *Division No. 12,* 4,861 ....J-11
Sexsmith, *Division No. 19,* 1,481 ....H-5
Sherwood Park, *Division No. 11,* 64,176 ....K-10
Slave Lake, *Division No. 17,* 6,553 ....H-8
Smoky Lake, *Division No. 12,* 1,087 ....J-10
Spirit River, *Division No. 19,* 1,112 ....G-5
Spruce Grove, *Division No. 11,* 14,271 ....K-9
Stettler, *Division No. 7,* 5,220 ....L-10
Stony Plain, *Division No. 11,* 7,683 ....N-2
Strathmore, *Division No. 5,* 5,282 ....N-10
Sundre, *Division No. 6,* 2,028 ....M-9
Swan Hills, *Division No. 17,* 2,026 ....I-8
Sylvan Lake, *Division No. 8,* 5,178 ....Q-1
Taber, *Division No. 2,* 7,214 ....K-3
Three Hills, *Division No. 5,* 3,022 ....M-10
Tofield, *Division No. 10,* 1,726 ....N-4
Turner Valley, *Division No. 6,* 1,527 ....O-9
Two Hills, *Division No. 10,* 1,040 ....J-11
Valleyview, *Division No. 18,* 1,906 ....H-6
Vauxhall, *Division No. 2,* 1,011 ....O-11
Vègreville, *Division No. 10,* 5,337 ....N-5
Vermilion, *Division No. 10,* 3,744 ....K-12
Viking, *Division No. 10,* 1,081 ....K-11
Vulcan, *Division No. 5,* 1,537 ....O-10
Wabasca, *Division No. 17,* 1,028 ....G-9
Wainwright, *Division No. 7,* 5,079 ....L-12
Wembley, *Division No. 19,* 1,441 ....H-5
Westlock, *Division No. 13,* 4,817 ....J-9
Wetaskiwin, *Division No. 11,* 10,959 ....K-10
Whitecourt, *Division No. 13,* 7,783 ....J-8

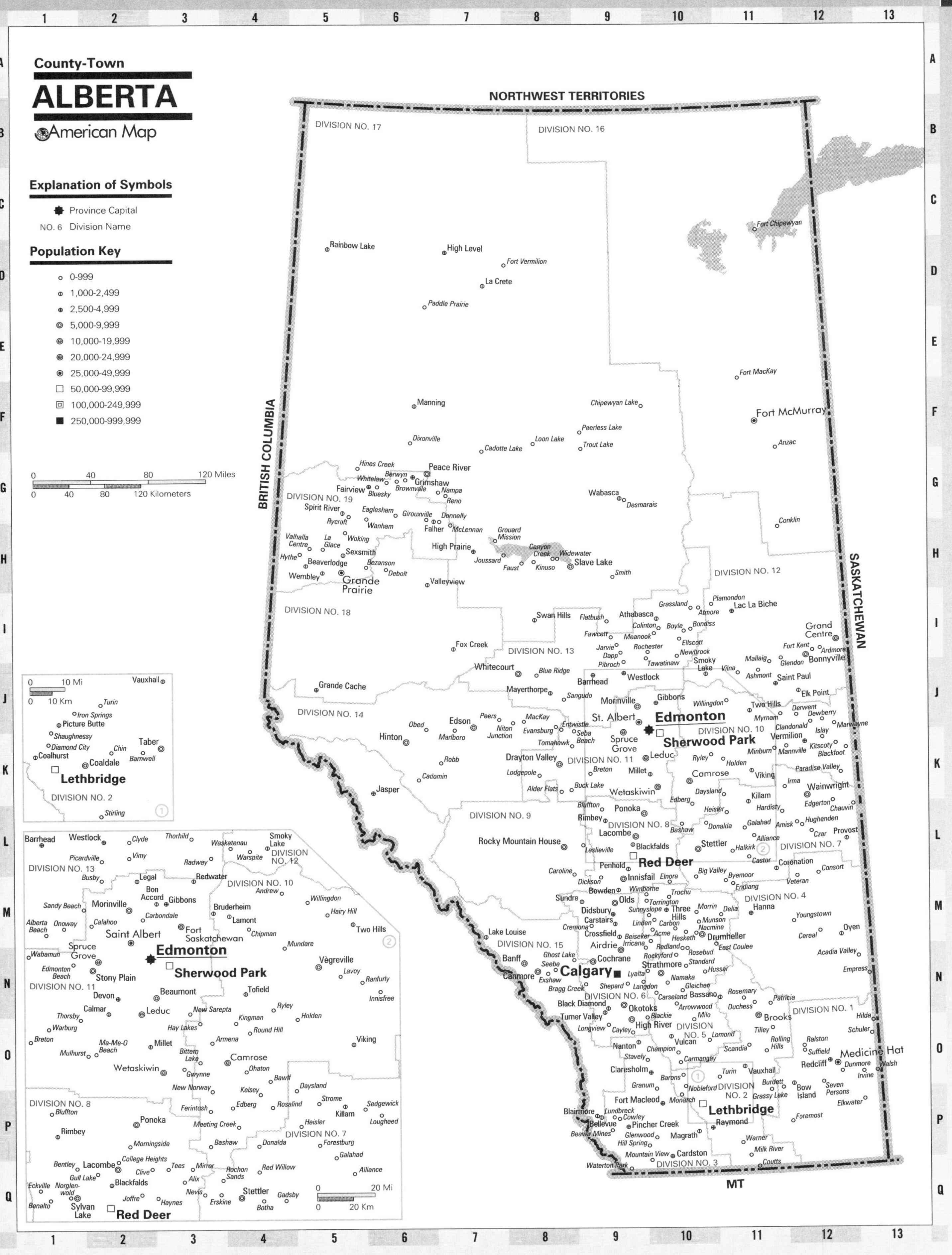
County-Town
ALBERTA
American Map
Explanation of Symbols
Province Capital
NO. 6 Division Name
Population Key
0-999
1,000-2,499
2,500-4,999
5,000-9,999
10,000-19,999
20,000-24,999
25,000-49,999
50,000-99,999
100,000-249,999
250,000-999,999
0 40 80 120 Miles
0 40 80 120 Kilometers
NORTHWEST TERRITORIES
BRITISH COLUMBIA
SASKATCHEWAN
MT
DIVISION NO. 17
DIVISION NO. 16
DIVISION NO. 19
DIVISION NO. 18
DIVISION NO. 12
DIVISION NO. 13
DIVISION NO. 14
DIVISION NO. 10
DIVISION NO. 11
DIVISION NO. 9
DIVISION NO. 8
DIVISION NO. 7
DIVISION NO. 4
DIVISION NO. 15
DIVISION NO. 6
DIVISION NO. 5
DIVISION NO. 1
DIVISION NO. 2
DIVISION NO. 3
Rainbow Lake
High Level
Fort Vermilion
La Crete
Paddle Prairie
Fort Chipewyan
Fort MacKay
Fort McMurray
Anzac
Manning
Chipewyan Lake
Peerless Lake
Trout Lake
Loon Lake
Cadotte Lake
Dixonville
Peace River
Hines Creek
Berwyn
Grimshaw
Whitelaw
Brownvale
Fairview
Bluesky
Nampa
Reno
Spirit River
Eaglesham
Girouxville
Donnelly
Rycroft
Wanham
Falher
McLennan
Grouard Mission
Wabasca
Desmarais
Conklin
Valhalla Centre
La Glace
Woking
Sexsmith
Hythe
Beaverlodge
Bezanson
Debolt
Wembley
Grande Prairie
Valleyview
High Prairie
Joussard
Faust
Canyon Creek
Kinuso
Widewater
Slave Lake
Smith
Grassland
Plamondon
Atmore
Lac La Biche
Swan Hills
Flatbush
Athabasca
Colinton
Boyle
Bondiss
Fawcett
Meanook
Rochester
Jarvie
Dapp
Pibroch
Tawatinaw
Ellscott
Newbrook
Smoky Lake
Vilna
Grand Centre
Fort Kent
Ardmore
Glendon
Bonnyville
Mallaig
Ashmont
Saint Paul
Elk Point
Fox Creek
Whitecourt
Blue Ridge
Barrhead
Westlock
Mayerthorpe
Sangudo
Grande Cache
Morinville
Gibbons
Willingdon
Two Hills
Myrnam
Derwent
Dewberry
Marwayne
St. Albert
Edmonton
Sherwood Park
Clandonald
Islay
Vermilion
Kitscoty
Mannville
Minburn
Blackfoot
Edson
Peers
MacKay
Niton Junction
Evansburg
Entwistle
Seba Beach
Tomahawk
Obed
Marlboro
Hinton
Spruce Grove
Leduc
Drayton Valley
Lodgepole
Breton
Millet
Ryley
Holden
Camrose
Viking
Paradise Valley
Irma
Wainwright
Robb
Cadomin
Jasper
Alder Flats
Buck Lake
Wetaskiwin
Daysland
Killam
Hardisty
Edgerton
Chauvin
Bluffton
Rimbey
Ponoka
Edberg
Heisler
Donalda
Galahad
Amisk
Hughenden
Lacombe
Bashaw
Alliance
Czar
Provost
Rocky Mountain House
Blackfalds
Stettler
Halkirk
Leslieville
Red Deer
Castor
Coronation
Consort
Caroline
Penhold
Innisfail
Elnora
Big Valley
Byemoor
Endiang
Veteran
Dickson
Bowden
Wimborne
Trochu
Sundre
Olds
Torrington
Didsbury
Sunnyslope
Three Hills
Morrin
Delia
Hanna
Carstairs
Linden
Carbon
Munson
Nacmine
Youngstown
Cremona
Crossfield
Beiseker
Acme
Hesketh
Drumheller
Cereal
Oyen
Airdrie
Irricana
Redland
Rosebud
East Coulee
Acadia Valley
Lake Louise
Banff
Ghost Lake
Cochrane
Rockyford
Seebe
Strathmore
Standard
Canmore
Exshaw
Calgary
Lyalta
Hussar
Empress
Bragg Creek
Shepard
Langdon
Namaka
Gleichen
Carseland
Bassano
Rosemary
Patricia
Black Diamond
Okotoks
Arrowwood
Duchess
Turner Valley
Blackie
Milo
Brooks
Hilda
Longview
Cayley
High River
Lomond
Tilley
Schuler
Nanton
Vulcan
Champion
Scandia
Rolling Hills
Ralston
Suffield
Medicine Hat
Stavely
Carmangay
Redcliff
Dunmore
Walsh
Irvine
Claresholm
Barons
Turin
Vauxhall
Granum
Nobleford
Burdett
Bow Island
Seven Persons
Fort Macleod
Monarch
Grassy Lake
Elkwater
Blairmore
Lundbreck
Cowley
Lethbridge
Bellevue
Pincher Creek
Raymond
Foremost
Beaver Mines
Glenwood
Magrath
Hill Spring
Warner
Mountain View
Cardston
Milk River
Waterton Park
Coutts
0 10 Mi
0 10 Km
Turin
Iron Springs
Picture Butte
Shaughnessy
Diamond City
Chin
Taber
Coalhurst
Coaldale
Barnwell
Stirling
Barrhead
Westlock
Clyde
Thorhild
Waskatenau
Smoky Lake
Picardville
Vimy
Radway
Warspite
Busby
Legal
Redwater
Andrew
Willingdon
Sandy Beach
Morinville
Bon Accord
Gibbons
Bruderheim
Hairy Hill
Carbondale
Lamont
Alberta Beach
Onoway
Calahoo
Fort Saskatchewan
Chipman
Two Hills
Saint Albert
Mundare
Spruce Grove
Wabamun
Vegreville
Edmonton Beach
Stony Plain
Sherwood Park
Lavoy
Ranfurly
Tofield
Innisfree
Devon
Beaumont
Calmar
New Sarepta
Ryley
Holden
Thorsby
Leduc
Kingman
Warburg
Hay Lakes
Round Hill
Breton
Ma-Me-O Beach
Armena
Viking
Mulhurst
Millet
Bittern Lake
Camrose
Wetaskiwin
Ohaton
Gwynne
Bawlf
New Norway
Daysland
Kelsey
Edberg
Rosalind
Strome
Sedgewick
Ferintosh
Killam
Bluffton
Ponoka
Meeting Creek
Heisler
Lougheed
Rimbey
Bashaw
Donalda
Forestburg
Morningside
Galahad
College Heights
Bentley
Lacombe
Tees
Mirror
Rochon Sands
Red Willow
Clive
Alliance
Gull Lake
Alix
Eckville
Norglenwold
Blackfalds
Nevis
Stettler
Gadsby
Joffre
Haynes
Erskine
Botha
Benalto
Sylvan Lake
Red Deer
0 20 Mi
0 20 Km

DIVISIONS

(28 Divisions)

Name of Division	Population	Location on Map
ALBERNI-CLAYOQUOT	31,652	L-8
BULKLEY-NECHAKO	41,642	F-8
CAPITAL	317,989	M-10
CARIBOO	66,475	H-10
CENTRAL COAST	3,921	I-8
CENTRAL KOOTENAY	58,099	K-14
CENTRAL OKANAGAN	136,541	K-11
COLUMBIA-SHUSWAP	48,116	I-13
COMOX-STRATHCONA	97,666	K-9
COWICHAN VALLEY	70,978	M-8
EAST KOOTENAY	56,366	K-15
FORT NELSON-LIARD	5,856	B-9
FRASER VALLEY	222,397	L-11
FRASER-FORT GEORGE	98,974	G-10
GREATER VANCOUVER	1,831,665	M-11
KITIMAT-STIKINE	43,618	D-6
KOOTENAY BOUNDARY	32,906	L-13
MOUNT WADDINGTON	14,601	J-8
NANAIMO	121,783	L-10
NORTH OKANAGAN	71,607	K-13
OKANAGAN-SIMILKAMEEN	75,933	L-12
PEACE RIVER	56,477	D-9
POWELL RIVER	19,936	K-10
SKEENA-QUEEN CHARLOTTE	24,795	G-5
SQUAMISH-LILLOOET	29,401	K-11
STIKINE	1,391	B-4
SUNSHINE COAST	24,914	L-10
THOMPSON-NICOLA	118,801	J-11
TOTAL	**3,724,500**	

CITIES AND TOWNS

Note: The first name is that of the city or town, second, that of the division in which it is located, then the population and location on the map.

100 Mile House, *Cariboo,* 1,736 ....J-12
Abbotsford, *Fraser-Fort George,* 105,403 ....M-4
Armstrong, *North Okanagan,* 3,906 ....K-13
Ashcroft, *Thompson-Nicola,* 1,858 ....K-12
Burnaby, *Greater Vancouver,* 179,209 ....L-2
Burns Lake, *Bulkley-Nechako,* 1,793 ....G-9
Cache Creek, *Thompson-Nicola,* 1,115 ....K-12
Campbell River, *Comox-Strathcona,* 31,038 ....K-9
Castlegar, *Central Kootenay,* 7,027 ....L-14
Central Saanich, *Capital,* 14,611 ....I-3
Chase, *Thompson-Nicola,* 2,460 ....J-13
Chetwynd, *Peace River,* 2,980 ....F-11
Chilliwack, *Fraser-Fort George,* 49,126 ....L-6
Coldstream, *North Okanagan,* 8,975 ....K-13
Colwood, *Capital,* 13,848 ....J-3
Comox, *Comox-Strathcona,* 11,069 ....L-10
Coquitlam, *Greater Vancouver,* 101,820 ....L-2
Courtenay, *Comox-Strathcona,* 17,335 ....L-10
Cranbrook, *East Kootenay,* 18,131 ....K-15
Creston, *Central Kootenay,* 4,816 ....L-15
Cultus Lake, *Fraser-Fort George,* 1,091 ....M-6
Cumberland, *Comox-Strathcona,* 2,548 ....L-10
Dawson Creek, *Peace River,* 11,125 ....F-12
Duncan, *Cowichan Valley,* 4,583 ....H-2
Elkford, *East Kootenay,* 2,722 ....K-16
Enderby, *North Okanagan,* 2,754 ....K-13
Esquimalt, *Capital,* 16,151 ....J-3
Fernie, *East Kootenay,* 5,308 ....K-16
Fort Nelson, *Fort Nelson-Liard,* 4,401 ....C-11
Fort Saint James, *Bulkley-Nechako,* 2,028 ....G-10
Fort Saint John, *Peace River,* 15,021 ....E-12
Fraser Lake, *Bulkley-Nechako,* 1,344 ....G-10
Fruitvale, *Kootenay Boundary,* 2,117 ....E-2
Gibsons, *Sunshine Coast,* 5,559 ....L-11
Gold River, *Comox-Strathcona,* 2,041 ....L-9
Golden, *Columbia-Shuswap,* 3,968 ....J-14
Grand Forks, *Kootenay Boundary,* 3,994 ....L-14
Hope, *Fraser-Fort George,* 3,379 ....L-12
Houston, *Bulkley-Nechako,* 2,584 ....G-9
Hudson's Hope, *Peace River,* 1,122 ....F-11
Invermere, *East Kootenay,* 2,687 ....K-15
Kamloops, *Thompson-Nicola,* 76,394 ....K-12
Kaslo, *Central Kootenay,* 1,063 ....K-14
Kelowna, *Central Okanagan,* 89,442 ....K-13
Kent, *Fraser-Fort George,* 2,170 ....L-12
Keremeos, *Okanagan-Similkameen,* 1,167 ....L-13
Kimberley, *East Kootenay,* 5,089 ....K-15
Kitimat, *Kitimat-Stikine,* 11,136 ....G-8
Ladysmith, *Cowichan Valley,* 6,456 ....G-1
Lake Cowichan, *Cowichan Valley,* 2,856 ....H-1
Langley, *Greater Vancouver,* 22,523 ....M-3
Lillooet, *Squamish-Lillooet,* 1,988 ....K-11
Lion's Bay, *Greater Vancouver,* 1,347 ....K-1
Logan Lake, *Thompson-Nicola,* 2,399 ....K-12
Lumby, *North Okanagan,* 1,689 ....K-13
Mackenzie, *Fraser Valley,* 5,629 ....F-11
Maple Ridge, *Greater Vancouver,* 56,173 ....L-3
Masset, *Skeena-Queen Charlotte,* 1,293 ....G-6
Merritt, *Thompson-Nicola,* 7,631 ....K-12
Metchosin, *Capital,* 4,709 ....J-2
Mission, *Fraser-Fort George,* 30,519 ....M-4
Montrose, *Kootenay Boundary,* 1,137 ....F-2
Nakusp, *Central Kootenay,* 1,736 ....K-14
Nanaimo, *Nanaimo,* 70,130 ....F-1
Nelson, *Central Kootenay,* 9,585 ....L-14
New Westminster, *Greater Vancouver,* 49,350 ....L-2
North Cowichan, *Cowichan Valley,* 25,305 ....H-2
North Saanich, *Capital,* 10,411 ....I-3
North Vancouver, *Greater Vancouver,* 41,475 ....L-1
Oak Bay, *Capital,* 17,865 ....J-3
Okanagan Falls, *Okanagan-Similkameen,* 1,874 ....L-13
Oliver, *Okanagan-Similkameen,* 4,468 ....L-13
Osoyoos, *Okanagan-Similkameen,* 4,021 ....L-13
Parksville, *Nanaimo,* 9,472 ....L-10
Peachland, *Central Okanagan,* 4,524 ....K-13
Penticton, *Okanagan-Similkameen,* 30,987 ....L-13
Pitt Meadows, *Greater Vancouver,* 13,436 ....L-3
Port Alberni, *Alberni-Clayoquot,* 18,468 ....L-10
Port Alice, *Mount Waddington,* 1,331 ....K-8
Port Coquitlam, *Greater Vancouver,* 46,682 ....L-3
Port Hardy, *Mount Waddington,* 4,393 ....K-8
Port McNeill, *Mount Waddington,* 2,925 ....K-8
Port Moody, *Greater Vancouver,* 20,847 ....L-2
Powell River, *Powell River,* 13,131 ....K-10
Prince George, *Fraser Valley,* 75,150 ....H-11
Prince Rupert, *Skeena-Queen Charlotte,* 16,714 ....G-7
Princeton, *Okanagan-Similkameen,* 2,838 ....L-12
Quesnel, *Cariboo,* 8,468 ....I-11
Revelstoke, *Columbia-Shuswap,* 8,047 ....J-14
Richmond, *Greater Vancouver,* 148,867 ....M-1
Rossland, *Kootenay Boundary,* 3,781 ....F-1
Salmon Arm, *Columbia-Shuswap,* 8,528 ....K-13
Sechelt, *Sunshine Coast,* 4,388 ....L-10
Sicamous, *Columbia-Shuswap,* 2,827 ....J-13
Sidney, *Capital,* 10,701 ....M-11
Smithers, *Bulkley-Nechako,* 5,624 ....G-8
Spallumcheen, *North Okanagan,* 5,322 ....K-13
Sparwood, *East Kootenay,* 2,343 ....K-16
Squamish, *Squamish-Lillooet,* 10,496 ....L-11
Summerland, *Okanagan-Similkameen,* 4,619 ....L-13
Surrey, *Greater Vancouver,* 304,477 ....M-2
Taylor, *Peace River,* 1,031 ....E-12
Terrace, *Kitimat-Stikine,* 12,779 ....G-8
Tofino, *Alberni-Clayoquot,* 1,170 ....L-9
Trail, *Kootenay Boundary,* 7,896 ....L-14
Ucluelet, *Alberni-Clayoquot,* 1,658 ....L-9
Valemount, *Fraser Valley,* 1,303 ....I-13
Vancouver, *Greater Vancouver,* 514,008 ....L-11
Vanderhoof, *Bulkley-Nechako,* 1,404 ....H-10
Vernon, *North Okanagan,* 31,817 ....K-13
Victoria, *Capital,* 73,504 ....M-11
View Royal, *Capital,* 6,441 ....J-3
Warfield, *Kootenay Boundary,* 1,788 ....E-1
West Vancouver, *Greater Vancouver,* 40,882 ....K-1
Whistler, *Squamish-Lillooet,* 7,112 ....K-11
White Rock, *Greater Vancouver,* 17,210 ....M-2
Williams Lake, *Cariboo,* 10,472 ....I-11

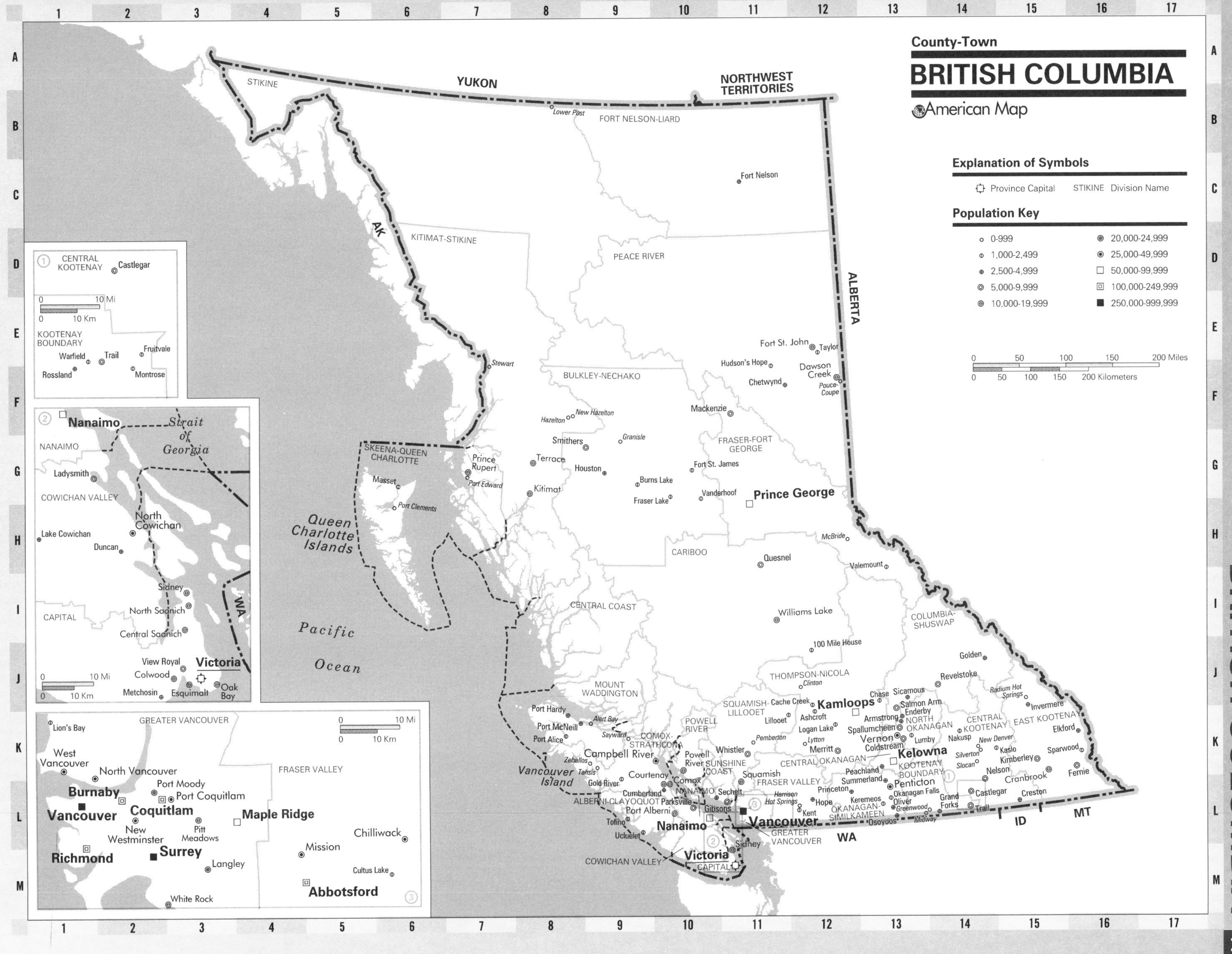
County-Town
BRITISH COLUMBIA
American Map
Explanation of Symbols
Province Capital
STIKINE Division Name
Population Key
0-999
1,000-2,499
2,500-4,999
5,000-9,999
10,000-19,999
20,000-24,999
25,000-49,999
50,000-99,999
100,000-249,999
250,000-999,999
0 50 100 150 200 Miles
0 50 100 150 200 Kilometers
YUKON
NORTHWEST TERRITORIES
ALBERTA
AK
WA
ID
MT
STIKINE
FORT NELSON-LIARD
PEACE RIVER
KITIMAT-STIKINE
BULKLEY-NECHAKO
FRASER-FORT GEORGE
CARIBOO
CENTRAL COAST
MOUNT WADDINGTON
THOMPSON-NICOLA
COLUMBIA-SHUSWAP
SQUAMISH-LILLOOET
POWELL RIVER
COMOX-STRATHCONA
SUNSHINE COAST
NANAIMO
ALBERNI-CLAYOQUOT
COWICHAN VALLEY
CAPITAL
GREATER VANCOUVER
FRASER VALLEY
CENTRAL OKANAGAN
NORTH OKANAGAN
OKANAGAN-SIMILKAMEEN
KOOTENAY BOUNDARY
CENTRAL KOOTENAY
EAST KOOTENAY
SKEENA-QUEEN CHARLOTTE
Queen Charlotte Islands
Vancouver Island
Pacific Ocean
Fort Nelson
Lower Post
Stewart
Fort St. John
Taylor
Dawson Creek
Pouce-Coupe
Hudson's Hope
Chetwynd
Mackenzie
Prince George
McBride
Valemount
Fort St. James
Vanderhoof
Burns Lake
Fraser Lake
Granisle
New Hazelton
Hazelton
Smithers
Houston
Terrace
Kitimat
Prince Rupert
Port Edward
Masset
Port Clements
Quesnel
Williams Lake
100 Mile House
Clinton
Kamloops
Cache Creek
Ashcroft
Logan Lake
Lillooet
Lytton
Merritt
Pemberton
Whistler
Squamish
Harrison Hot Springs
Hope
Kent
Princeton
Keremeos
Oliver
Osoyoos
Summerland
Peachland
Penticton
Okanagan Falls
Kelowna
Vernon
Coldstream
Spallumcheen
Armstrong
Enderby
Lumby
Salmon Arm
Sicamous
Chase
Revelstoke
Golden
Radium Hot Springs
Invermere
Elkford
Sparwood
Fernie
Kimberley
Cranbrook
Creston
Nakusp
New Denver
Kaslo
Silverton
Slocan
Nelson
Castlegar
Trail
Grand Forks
Greenwood
Midway
Vancouver
Sidney
Victoria
Nanaimo
Gibsons
Sechelt
Powell River
Comox
Courtenay
Cumberland
Parksville
Port Alberni
Campbell River
Sayward
Alert Bay
Port McNeill
Port Hardy
Port Alice
Zeballos
Tahsis
Gold River
Tofino
Ucluelet
CENTRAL KOOTENAY
KOOTENAY BOUNDARY
Castlegar
Fruitvale
Montrose
Trail
Warfield
Rossland
0 10 Mi
0 10 Km
Nanaimo
NANAIMO
Ladysmith
COWICHAN VALLEY
Lake Cowichan
Duncan
North Cowichan
Strait of Georgia
CAPITAL
Sidney
North Saanich
Central Saanich
View Royal
Colwood
Metchosin
Esquimalt
Victoria
Oak Bay
WA
GREATER VANCOUVER
FRASER VALLEY
Lion's Bay
West Vancouver
North Vancouver
Burnaby
Vancouver
Richmond
Port Moody
Port Coquitlam
Coquitlam
New Westminster
Pitt Meadows
Surrey
White Rock
Langley
Maple Ridge
Mission
Abbotsford
Chilliwack
Cultus Lake

DIVISIONS

(23 Divisions)

Name of Division	Population	Location on Map
DIVISION NO. 1	16,233	Q-6
DIVISION NO. 2	48,039	Q-5
DIVISION NO. 3	40,485	P-4
DIVISION NO. 4	10,411	Q-3
DIVISION NO. 5	14,766	P-1
DIVISION NO. 6	10,510	P-1
DIVISION NO. 7	57,219	P-2
DIVISION NO. 8	14,891	O-3
DIVISION NO. 9	23,195	P-4
DIVISION NO. 10	8,901	P-4
DIVISION NO. 11	620,064	P-5
DIVISION NO. 12	18,708	O-6
DIVISION NO. 13	39,422	O-5
DIVISION NO. 14	17,054	O-4
DIVISION NO. 15	22,477	O-1
DIVISION NO. 16	10,690	N-1
DIVISION NO. 17	23,975	N-2
DIVISION NO. 18	22,278	N-4
DIVISION NO. 19	14,722	L-3
DIVISION NO. 20	11,446	M-1
DIVISION NO. 21	23,150	H-1
DIVISION NO. 22	35,584	G-4
DIVISION NO. 23	9,678	B-2
TOTAL	**1,113,898**	

CITIES AND TOWNS

Note: The first name is that of the city or town, second, that of the division in which it is located, then the population and location on the map.

Altona, *Division No. 3,* 3,286 ....Q-5
Arborg, *Division No. 18,* 1,012 ....N-5
Argyle, *Division No. 14,* 1,220 ....O-5
Beausejour, *Division No. 12,* 2,712 ....O-6
Boissevain, *Division No. 5,* 1,544 ....Q-2
Brandon, *Division No. 7,* 39,175 ....P-2
Carberry, *Division No. 7,* 1,493 ....P-3
Carman, *Division No. 3,* 2,704 ....P-4
Churchill, *Division No. 23,* 1,073 ....C-7
Dauphin, *Division No. 17,* 8,266 ....N-2
Deloraine, *Division No. 5,* 1,041 ....Q-2
Flin Flon, *Division No. 21,* 6,861 ....I-1
Franklin, *Division No. 15,* 1,724 ....O-3
Gillam, *Division No. 23,* 1,158 ....G-7
Gimli, *Division No. 18,* 1,574 ....O-5
Killarney, *Division No. 5,* 2,208 ....Q-2
La Broquerie, *Division No. 2,* 2,493 ....P-6
Lac du Bonnet, *Division No. 1,* 1,070 ....O-6
Leaf Rapids, *Division No. 23,* 1,500 ....F-3
Lynn Lake, *Division No. 23,* 1,038 ....F-2
MacDonald, *Division No. 9,* 4,900 ....O-4
Melita, *Division No. 5,* 1,152 ....P-1
Miniota, *Division No. 15,* 1,027 ....O-1
Minnedosa, *Division No. 15,* 2,442 ....O-2
Morden, *Division No. 3,* 5,689 ....Q-4
Morris, *Division No. 3,* 1,645 ....P-5
Neepawa, *Division No. 15,* 2,989 ....O-3
Niverville, *Division No. 2,* 1,615 ....P-5
Pinawa, *Division No. 1,* 1,669 ....O-6
Pipestone, *Division No. 6,* 1,710 ....P-1
Portage la Prairie, *Division No. 9,* 13,077 ....P-4
Rivers, *Division No. 7,* 1,117 ....O-2
Roblin, *Division No. 16,* 1,885 ....N-1
Rosser, *Division No. 14,* 1,349 ....P-5
Russell, *Division No. 16,* 1,605 ....N-1
Saint Adolphe, *Division No. 2,* 1,224 ....P-5
Saint Laurent, *Division No. 18,* 1,020 ....O-4
Sainte Anne, *Division No. 2,* 1,511 ....P-5
Sainte Rose du Lac, *Division No. 17,* 1,047 ....N-3
Selkirk, *Division No. 13,* 9,881 ....O-5
Snow Lake, *Division No. 21,* 1,262 ....I-3
Souris, *Division No. 7,* 1,613 ....P-2
Steinbach, *Division No. 2,* 8,478 ....P-5
Stonewall, *Division No. 14,* 3,689 ....O-5
Stony Mountain, *Division No. 14,* 1,744 ....O-5
Strathclair, *Division No. 15,* 1,026 ....O-2
Swan River, *Division No. 20,* 2,907 ....L-1
Teulon, *Division No. 14,* 1,055 ....O-5
The Pas, *Division No. 21,* 6,162 ....J-1
Thompson, *Division No. 22,* 14,385 ....G-4
Virden, *Division No. 6,* 2,956 ....P-1
Westbourne, *Division No. 8,* 2,035 ....O-4
Whitemouth, *Division No. 1,* 1,639 ....P-6
Winkler, *Division No. 3,* 7,241 ....Q-4
Winnipeg, *Division No. 11,* 618,477 ....P-5
Woodlands, *Division No. 14,* 3,457 ....O-4

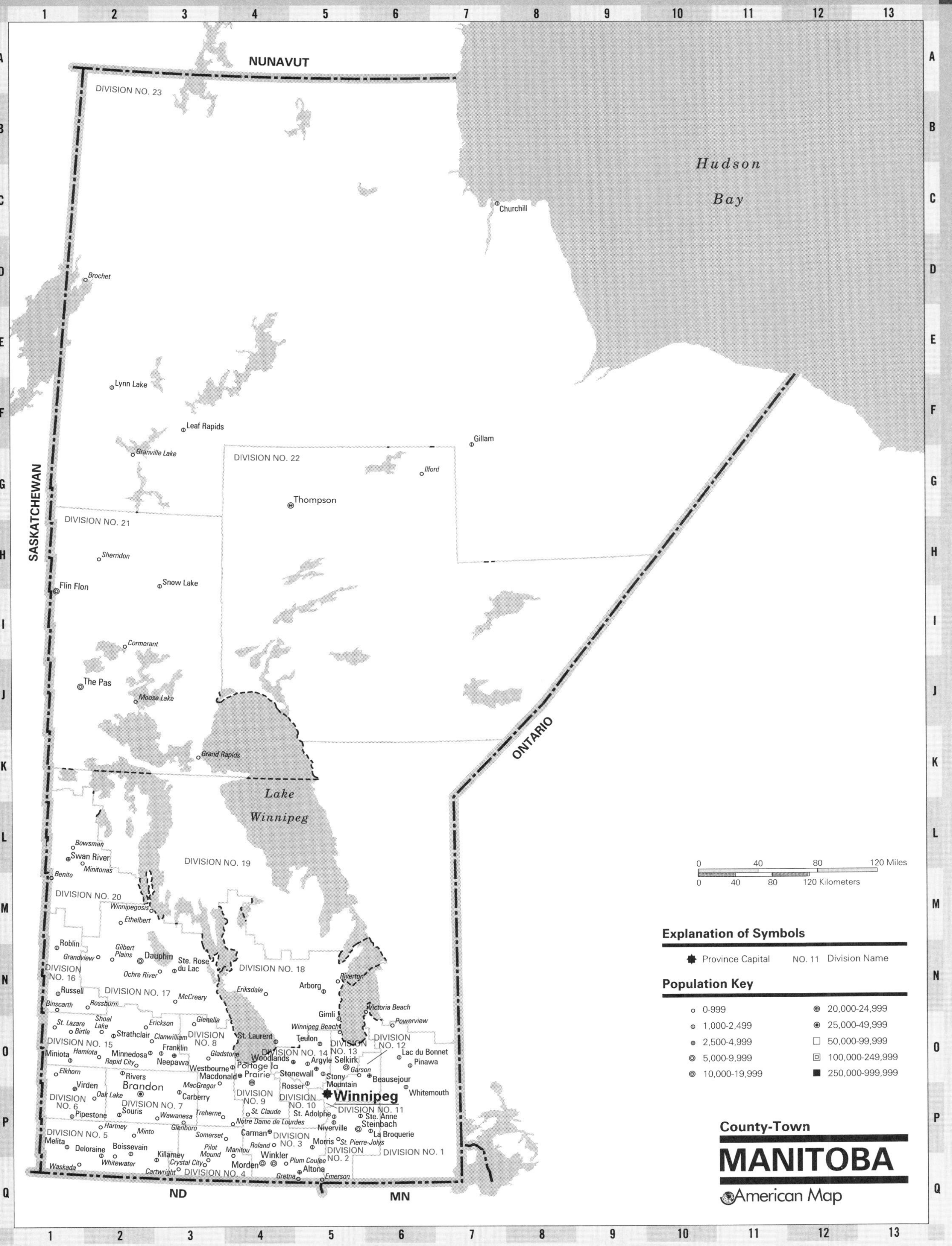
NUNAVUT
DIVISION NO. 23
Hudson
Bay
Churchill
Brochet
Lynn Lake
Leaf Rapids
Granville Lake
Gillam
DIVISION NO. 22
Ilford
Thompson
SASKATCHEWAN
DIVISION NO. 21
Sherridon
Flin Flon
Snow Lake
Cormorant
The Pas
Moose Lake
ONTARIO
Grand Rapids
Lake
Winnipeg
Bowsman
Swan River
Minitonas
Benito
DIVISION NO. 19
DIVISION NO. 20
Winnipegosis
Ethelbert
Roblin
Grandview
Gilbert Plains
Dauphin
Ste. Rose du Lac
Ochre River
DIVISION NO. 16
DIVISION NO. 18
Riverton
Arborg
Eriksdale
Russell
DIVISION NO. 17
McCreary
Binscarth
Rossburn
Victoria Beach
Gimli
Powerview
Winnipeg Beach
St. Lazare
Birtle
Shoal Lake
Strathclair
Erickson
Clanwilliam
Glenella
DIVISION NO. 8
St. Laurent
Teulon
DIVISION NO. 15
Miniota
Hamiota
Minnedosa
Rapid City
Franklin
Neepawa
Gladstone
DIVISION NO. 14
DIVISION NO. 13
DIVISION NO. 12
Lac du Bonnet
Pinawa
Woodlands
Argyle
Selkirk
Westbourne
Portage la Prairie
Macdonald
Stonewall
Stony Mountain
Garson
Beausejour
Elkhorn
Virden
Rivers
Brandon
MacGregor
Rosser
Whitemouth
DIVISION NO. 6
Oak Lake
Carberry
DIVISION NO. 9
DIVISION NO. 10
Winnipeg
DIVISION NO. 7
Souris
Wawanesa
Treherne
St. Claude
St. Adolphe
DIVISION NO. 11
Ste. Anne
Steinbach
Pipestone
Hartney
Glenboro
Notre Dame de Lourdes
Niverville
La Broquerie
DIVISION NO. 5
Minto
Somerset
Carman
DIVISION NO. 3
Morris
St. Pierre-Jolys
Melita
Deloraine
Boissevain
Killarney
Pilot Mound
Manitou
Roland
DIVISION NO. 2
DIVISION NO. 1
Whitewater
Crystal City
Winkler
Plum Coulee
Altona
Waskada
Cartwright
DIVISION NO. 4
Morden
Gretna
Emerson
ND
MN
0 40 80 120 Miles
0 40 80 120 Kilometers
Explanation of Symbols
Province Capital
NO. 11 Division Name
Population Key
0-999
1,000-2,499
2,500-4,999
5,000-9,999
10,000-19,999
20,000-24,999
25,000-49,999
50,000-99,999
100,000-249,999
250,000-999,999
County-Town
MANITOBA
American Map

NEW BRUNSWICK

DIVISIONS

(15 Divisions)

Name of Division	Population	Location on Map
ALBERT	26,492	G-7
CARLETON	26,910	E-3
CHARLOTTE	27,335	H-3
GLOUCESTER	87,601	C-6
KENT	32,094	E-7
KINGS	64,724	G-6
MADAWASKA	36,814	B-2
NORTHUMBERLAND	52,153	C-4
QUEENS	12,470	F-6
RESTIGOUCHE	38,701	B-2
SAINT JOHN	79,302	H-7
SUNBURY	25,358	F-5
VICTORIA	21,929	C-3
WESTMORLAND	120,531	F-7
YORK	85,719	E-4
TOTAL	**738,133**	

CITIES AND TOWNS

Note: The first name is that of the city or town, second, that of the division in which it is located, then the population and location on the map.

NOVA SCOTIA

DIVISIONS

(18 Divisions)

Name of Division	Population	Location on Map
ANNAPOLIS	23,641	J-7
ANTIGONISH	19,554	G-13
CAPE BRETON	117,849	G-15
COLCHESTER	49,262	H-10
CUMBERLAND	33,804	G-8
DIGBY	20,500	J-6
GUYSBOROUGH	10,917	H-13
HALIFAX	342,966	I-11
HANTS	39,483	I-9
INVERNESS	20,919	F-14
KINGS	59,183	I-8
LUNENBURG	47,561	J-8
PICTOU	48,718	G-11
QUEENS	12,417	K-7
RICHMOND	11,022	G-15
SHELBURNE	17,002	L-7
VICTORIA	8,482	F-15
YARMOUTH	27,310	L-6
TOTAL	**909,282**	

CITIES AND TOWNS

Note: The first name is that of the city or town, second, that of the division in which it is located, then the population and location on the map.

PRINCE EDWARD ISLAND

DIVISIONS

(3 Divisions)

Name of Division	Population	Location on Map
KINGS	19,561	E-11
PRINCE	44,566	E-9
QUEENS	70,430	F-10
TOTAL	**134,557**	

CITIES AND TOWNS

Note: The first name is that of the city or town, second, that of the division in which it is located, then the population and location on the map.

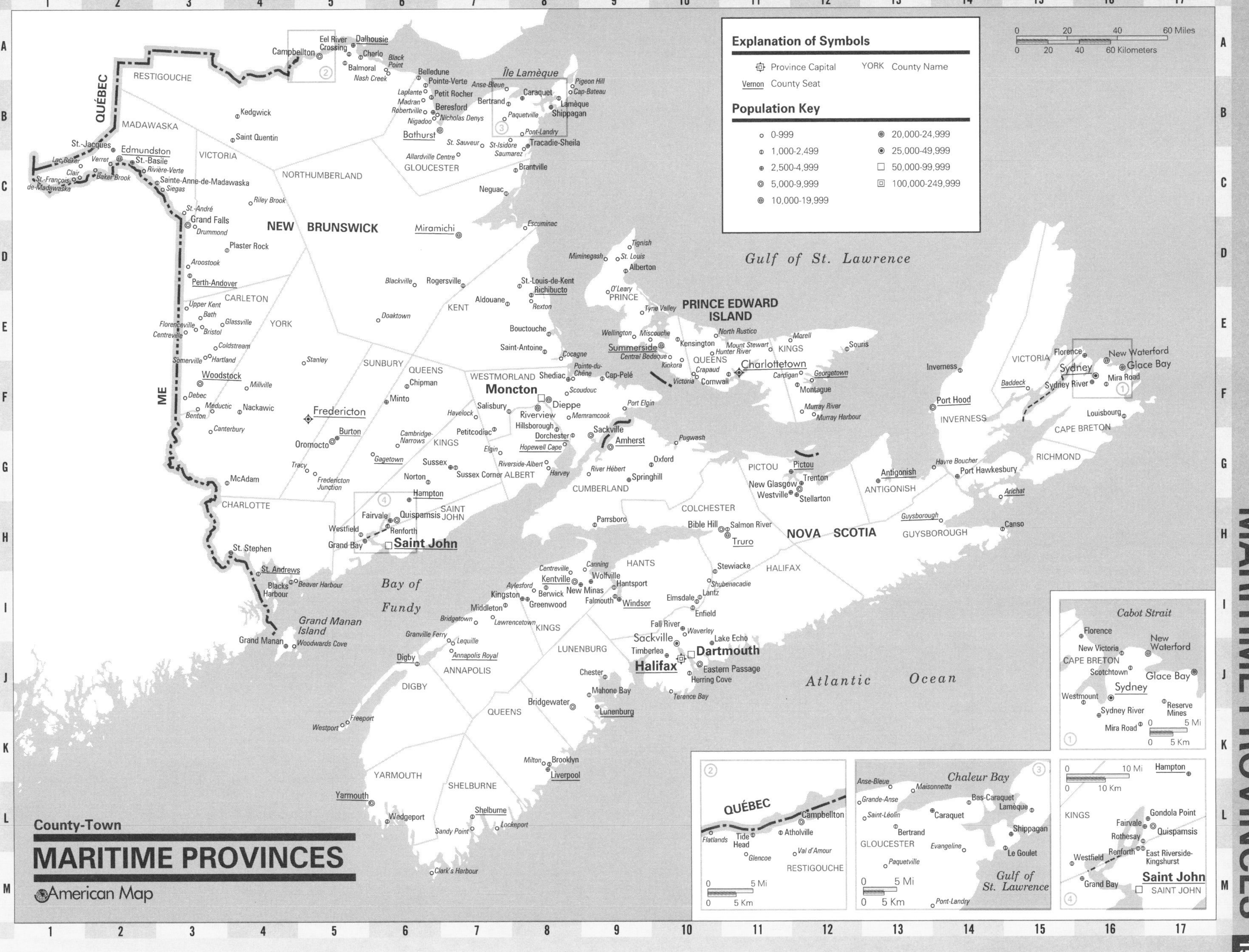
Explanation of Symbols
Province Capital
YORK County Name
Vernon County Seat
Population Key
0-999
1,000-2,499
2,500-4,999
5,000-9,999
10,000-19,999
20,000-24,999
25,000-49,999
50,000-99,999
100,000-249,999
0 20 40 60 Miles
0 20 40 60 Kilometers
QUÉBEC
RESTIGOUCHE
MADAWASKA
VICTORIA
NORTHUMBERLAND
GLOUCESTER
NEW BRUNSWICK
CARLETON
YORK
SUNBURY
QUEENS
KENT
WESTMORLAND
KINGS
ALBERT
SAINT JOHN
CHARLOTTE
ME
Île Lamèque
Gulf of St. Lawrence
PRINCE EDWARD ISLAND
PRINCE
QUEENS
KINGS
Bay of Fundy
Grand Manan Island
CUMBERLAND
COLCHESTER
PICTOU
ANTIGONISH
GUYSBOROUGH
NOVA SCOTIA
HALIFAX
HANTS
KINGS
LUNENBURG
ANNAPOLIS
DIGBY
QUEENS
YARMOUTH
SHELBURNE
INVERNESS
VICTORIA
CAPE BRETON
RICHMOND
Atlantic Ocean
St.-Jacques
Lac Baker
Verret
Clair
St.-François-de-Madawaska
Edmundston
St.-Basile
Baker Brook
Rivière-Verte
Sainte-Anne-de-Madawaska
Siegas
St.-André
Grand Falls
Drummond
Kedgwick
Saint Quentin
Riley Brook
Plaster Rock
Aroostook
Perth-Andover
Upper Kent
Bath
Florenceville
Centreville
Bristol
Glassville
Coldstream
Somerville
Hartland
Woodstock
Millville
Debec
Meductic
Benton
Nackawic
Canterbury
McAdam
St. Stephen
St. Andrews
Blacks Harbour
Beaver Harbour
Grand Manan
Woodwards Cove
Campbellton
Eel River Crossing
Dalhousie
Charlo
Balmoral
Black Point
Nash Creek
Belledune
Pointe-Verte
Laplante
Petit Rocher
Madran
Beresford
Robertville
Nicholas Denys
Nigadoo
Bathurst
Anse-Bleue
Bertrand
Caraquet
Paquetville
Lamèque
Shippagan
Pigeon Hill
Cap-Bateau
St. Sauveur
St-Isidore
Saumarez
Pont-Landry
Tracadie-Sheila
Allardville Centre
Brantville
Neguac
Miramichi
Escuminac
Blackville
Rogersville
Doaktown
Stanley
Chipman
Minto
Fredericton
Burton
Oromocto
Tracy
Fredericton Junction
Gagetown
Cambridge-Narrows
Sussex
Sussex Corner
Norton
Hampton
Fairvale
Quispamsis
Renforth
Westfield
Grand Bay
Saint John
Aldouane
St.-Louis-de-Kent
Richibucto
Rexton
Bouctouche
Saint-Antoine
Cocagne
Shediac
Pointe-du-Chêne
Cap-Pelé
Scoudouc
Moncton
Dieppe
Salisbury
Havelock
Riverview
Memramcook
Hillsborough
Dorchester
Petitcodiac
Hopewell Cape
Elgin
Riverside-Albert
Harvey
Sackville
Amherst
Port Elgin
River Hébert
Springhill
Oxford
Pugwash
Miminegash
Tignish
St. Louis
Alberton
O'Leary
Tyne Valley
Wellington
Miscouche
Summerside
Central Bedeque
Kinkora
Kensington
North Rustico
Hunter River
Mount Stewart
Crapaud
Victoria
Cornwall
Charlottetown
Cardigan
Georgetown
Morell
Souris
Montague
Murray River
Murray Harbour
Parrsboro
Pictou
Trenton
New Glasgow
Westville
Stellarton
Antigonish
Bible Hill
Salmon River
Truro
Stewiacke
Shubenacadie
Lantz
Elmsdale
Enfield
Fall River
Waverley
Lake Echo
Sackville
Timberlea
Dartmouth
Halifax
Eastern Passage
Herring Cove
Terence Bay
Centreville
Canning
Kentville
Wolfville
Hantsport
Aylesford
Kingston
Berwick
New Minas
Falmouth
Windsor
Greenwood
Middleton
Bridgetown
Lawrencetown
Granville Ferry
Lequille
Annapolis Royal
Digby
Chester
Mahone Bay
Lunenburg
Bridgewater
Westport
Freeport
Milton
Brooklyn
Liverpool
Yarmouth
Wedgeport
Shelburne
Sandy Point
Lockeport
Clark's Harbour
Guysborough
Canso
Havre Boucher
Port Hawkesbury
Arichat
Port Hood
Inverness
Baddeck
Florence
Sydney
Sydney River
New Waterford
Glace Bay
Mira Road
Louisbourg
County-Town
MARITIME PROVINCES
American Map
Cabot Strait
Florence
New Victoria
New Waterford
CAPE BRETON
Scotchtown
Glace Bay
Sydney
Westmount
Reserve Mines
Sydney River
Mira Road
0 5 Mi
0 5 Km
QUÉBEC
Campbellton
Tide Head
Flatlands
Atholville
Glencoe
Val d'Amour
RESTIGOUCHE
0 5 Mi
0 5 Km
Chaleur Bay
Anse-Bleue
Maisonnette
Grande-Anse
Bas-Caraquet
Lamèque
Saint-Léolin
Caraquet
Bertrand
Shippagan
GLOUCESTER
Evangeline
Le Goulet
Paquetville
Gulf of St. Lawrence
Pont-Landry
0 5 Mi
0 5 Km
0 10 Mi
0 10 Km
Hampton
KINGS
Gondola Point
Fairvale
Quispamsis
Rothesay
Westfield
Renforth
East Riverside-Kingshurst
Grand Bay
Saint John
SAINT JOHN

DIVISIONS

(10 Divisions)

Name of Division	Population	Location on Map
DIVISION NO. 1	251,523	P-11
DIVISION NO. 2	27,723	P-10
DIVISION NO. 3	22,459	O-8
DIVISION NO. 4	24,824	O-7
DIVISION NO. 5	44,319	N-8
DIVISION NO. 6	39,118	O-8
DIVISION NO. 7	41,534	O-11
DIVISION NO. 8	48,247	N-9
DIVISION NO. 9	22,855	M-8
DIVISION NO. 10	29,190	H-4
TOTAL	**551,792**	

CITIES AND TOWNS

Note: The first name is that of the city or town, second, that of the division in which it is located, then the population and location on the map.

Arnold's Cove, *Division No. 1,* 1,115 ....P-11
Baie Verte, *Division No. 8,* 1,185 ....M-9
Bay Bulls, *Division No. 1,* 1,063 ....E-12
Bay Roberts, *Division No. 1,* 5,472 ....P-11
Bishop's Falls, *Division No. 6,* 3,972 ....N-10
Bonavista, *Division No. 7,* 4,502 ....N-11
Botwood, *Division No. 6,* 3,613 ....N-10
Buchans, *Division No. 6,* 1,056 ....N-9
Burgeo, *Division No. 3,* 2,094 ....P-8
Carbonear, *Division No. 1,* 5,168 ....P-11
Catalina, *Division No. 7,* 1,155 ....O-11
Channel-Port aux Basques, *Division No. 3,* 5,243 ....P-7
Clarke's Beach, *Division No. 1,* 1,244 ....E-11
Corner Brook, *Division No. 5,* 21,893 ....N-8
Deer Lake, *Division No. 5,* 4,638 ....N-8
Dunville, *Division No. 1,* 4,131 ....F-10
Fortune, *Division No. 2,* 1,130 ....P-9
Gambo, *Division No. 7,* 1,980 ....N-11
Gander, *Division No. 6,* 10,119 ....N-10
Glovertown, *Division No. 7,* 2,292 ....A-9
Goulds, *Division No. 1,* 4,674 ....E-12
Grand Bank, *Division No. 2,* 3,275 ....P-9
Grand Falls-Windsor, *Division No. 6,* 14,160 ....N-9
Happy Valley-Goose Bay, *Division No. 10,* 8,655 ....J-6
Harbour Breton, *Division No. 3,* 1,281 ....P-9
Harbour Grace, *Division No. 1,* 3,740 ....D-11
Harbour Main, *Division No. 1,* 1,244 ....E-11
Hare Bay, *Division No. 7,* 1,224 ....N-11
Holyrood, *Division No. 1,* 2,090 ....E-11
Isle aux Morts, *Division No. 3,* 1,203 ....P-7
Joe Batt's Arm-Barr'd Islands-Shoal Bay, *Division No. 8,* 1,028 ....M-10
Kippens, *Division No. 4,* 1,887 ....O-7
La Scie, *Division No. 8,* 1,254 ....M-9
Labrador City, *Division No. 10,* 10,473 ....J-2
Lewisporte, *Division No. 8,* 2,640 ....N-10
Marystown, *Division No. 2,* 6,742 ....P-10
Milltown-Head of Bay d'Espoir, *Division No. 3,* 1,124 O-9
Mount Pearl, *Division No. 1,* 25,519 ....P-12
Musgrave Harbour, *Division No. 8,* 1,051 ....N-11
Norris Arm, *Division No. 6,* 1,007 ....I-12
Paradise, *Division No. 1,* 7,960 ....E-12
Pasadena, *Division No. 5,* 2,468 ....N-8
Port au Choix, *Division No. 9,* 1,146 ....L-8
Pouch Cove, *Division No. 1,* 1,095 ....D-12
Ramea, *Division No. 3,* 1,080 ....P-8
Rocky Harbour, *Division No. 9,* 1,066 ....N-8
Roddickton, *Division No. 9,* 1,103 ....L-9
Saint Alban's, *Division No. 3,* 1,563 ....O-9
Saint Anthony, *Division No. 9,* 2,996 ....L-9
Saint George's, *Division No. 4,* 1,536 ....O-7
Saint John's, *Division No. 1,* 101,936 ....P-12
Saint Lawrence, *Division No. 2,* 1,697 ....Q-10
Spaniard's Bay, *Division No. 1,* 2,771 ....D-11
Springdale, *Division No. 8,* 3,381 ....N-9
Stephenville, *Division No. 4,* 7,764 ....O-7
Stephenville Crossing, *Division No. 4,* 1,476 ....O-7
Summerford, *Division No. 8,* 1,137 ....H-13
Torbay, *Division No. 1,* 2,809 ....D-12
Upper Island Cove, *Division No. 1,* 2,034 ....D-11
Victoria, *Division No. 1,* 1,849 ....D-11
Wabana, *Division No. 1,* 3,136 ....D-12
Wabush, *Division No. 10,* 2,018 ....J-2
Whitbourne, *Division No. 1,* 1,151 ....E-10
Witless Bay, *Division No. 1,* 1,118 ....F-12

1 2 3 4 5 6 7 8 9 10 11 12 13

A B C D E F G H I J K L M N O P Q

Labrador Sea

QUÉBEC

Nain

Davis Inlet

Hopedale

Makkovik

Postville

DIVISION NO. 10

Labrador

Rigolet

Cartwright

North West River

Happy Valley-Goose Bay

Labrador City

Wabush

Port Hope Simpson

Mary's Harbour

QUÉBEC

Red Bay

West St. Modeste

L'Anse-au-Loup

Forteau

L'Anse-au-Clair

Cook's Harbour

St. Lunaire-Griquet

Raleigh

St. Anthony

Goose Cove East

Main Brook

Flowers Cove

Bird Cove

Shoal Cove

Roddickton

Bide Arm

Conche

Port au Choix

Port Saunders

Hawke's Bay

Englee

River of Ponds

Bellburns

DIVISION NO. 9

Daniel's Harbour

Fleur de Lys

Parson's Pond

Baie Verte

La Scie

Cow Head

Seal Cove

Nippers Harbour

Jackson's Arm

Little Bay Islands

Sally's Cove

St. Paul's

Middle Arm

Change Islands

Rocky Harbour

Norris Point

King's Point

Robert's Arm

Trout River

Woody Point

Hampden

Springdale

DIVISION NO. 8

Birchy Bay

Deer Lake

Howley

Botwood

Lewisporte

Cox's Cove

Lark Harbour

DIVISION NO. 5

Bishop's Falls

Gander

Corner Brook

Pasadena

Badger

Grand Falls-Windsor

Buchans

Millertown

Lourdes

Port au Port

Stephenville

DIVISION NO. 6

Kippens

Stephenville Crossing

Heatherton

St. George's

DIVISION NO. 4

DIVISION NO. 3

Newfoundland

Milltown-Head of Bay d'Espoir

St. Alban's

Burnt Islands

Rose Blanche-Harbour Le Cou

Burgeo

Channel-Port aux Basques

Isle aux Morts

Ramea

Rencontre East

Gaultois

Belleoram

Seal Cove

Harbour Breton

Rushoon

Garnish

Grand Bank

Fortune

Lawn

Marystown

Port au Bras

Lamaline

St. Lawrence

Joe Batt's Arm-Barr'd Islands-Shoal Bay

Fogo

Tilting

Seldom-Little Seldom

Musgrave Harbour

Carmanville

Lumsden

Greenspond

St. Brendan's

Gambo

Hare Bay

Bonavista

Catalina

Eastport

Terra Nova

Charlottetown

DIVISION NO. 7

Lethbridge

Milton

Old Perlican

Bay de Verde

Burnt Point

Goobies

Goose Cove

Carbonear

Arnold's Cove

Terrenceville

Bay L'Argent

Parker's Cove

Bay Roberts

St. John's

Mount Pearl

Dunville

DIVISION NO. 2

DIVISION NO. 1

Cape Broyle

Port Kirwan

Point Lance

Renews-Cappahayden

St. Shotts

Gulf of St. Lawrence

Atlantic Ocean

Glovertown

Traytown

Eastport

Happy Adventure

Keels

King's Cove

Bonavista

Elliston

Little Catalina

Catalina

Port Union

Melrose

DIVISION NO. 7

Terra Nova

Charlottetown

Musgravetown

Bloomfield

Lethbridge

Port Blandford

Port Rexton

Atlantic Ocean

Georges Brook

Milton

0 10 20 Mi

0 10 20 Km

Old Perlican

Bay de Verde

Little Heart's Ease

Hant's Harbour

Hodge's Cove

Winterton

Burnt Point

Goobies

New Perlican

Heart's Content

Goose Cove

Sunnyside

Come By Chance

Heart's Desire

DIVISION NO. 2

Victoria

Salmon Cove

Pouch Cove

Arnold's Cove

Carbonear

Bauline

Southern Harbour

Chance Cove

Harbour Grace

Upper Island Cove

Torbay

Riverhead

Wabana

Spaniard's Bay

St. John's

Norman's Cove

Clarke's Beach

Bay Roberts

Paradise

South River

Cupids

Mount Pearl

Chapel Arm

Brigus

Colliers

Goulds

Petty Harbour

Conception Harbour

Whitbourne

Avondale

Harbour Main

Holyrood

Fox Harbour

DIVISION NO. 1

Bay Bulls

Dunville

Witless Bay

Colinet

Mount Carmel-Mitchell's Brook-St. Catherine's

St. Joseph's

Cape Broyle

Ferryland

Fermeuse

Port Kirwan

St. Bride's

St. Mary's

Renews-Cappahayden

Branch

Gaskiers-Point La Haye

Point Lance

St. Vincent's-St. Stephens-Peter's River

Portugal Cove South

0 10 Mi

0 10 Km

Summerford

Point Leamington

Embree

Campbellton

Lewisporte

DIVISION NO. 8

Botwood

Peterview

Norris Arm

DIVISION NO. 6

Bishop's Falls

Glenwood

Grand Falls-Windsor

0 50 100 150 Miles

0 50 100 150 Kilometers

Explanation of Symbols

Province Capital

NO. 5 Division Name

Population Key

0-999	20,000-24,999
1,000-2,499	25,000-49,999
2,500-4,999	50,000-99,999
5,000-9,999	100,000-249,999
10,000-19,999	

County-Town

NEWFOUNDLAND AND LABRADOR

American Map

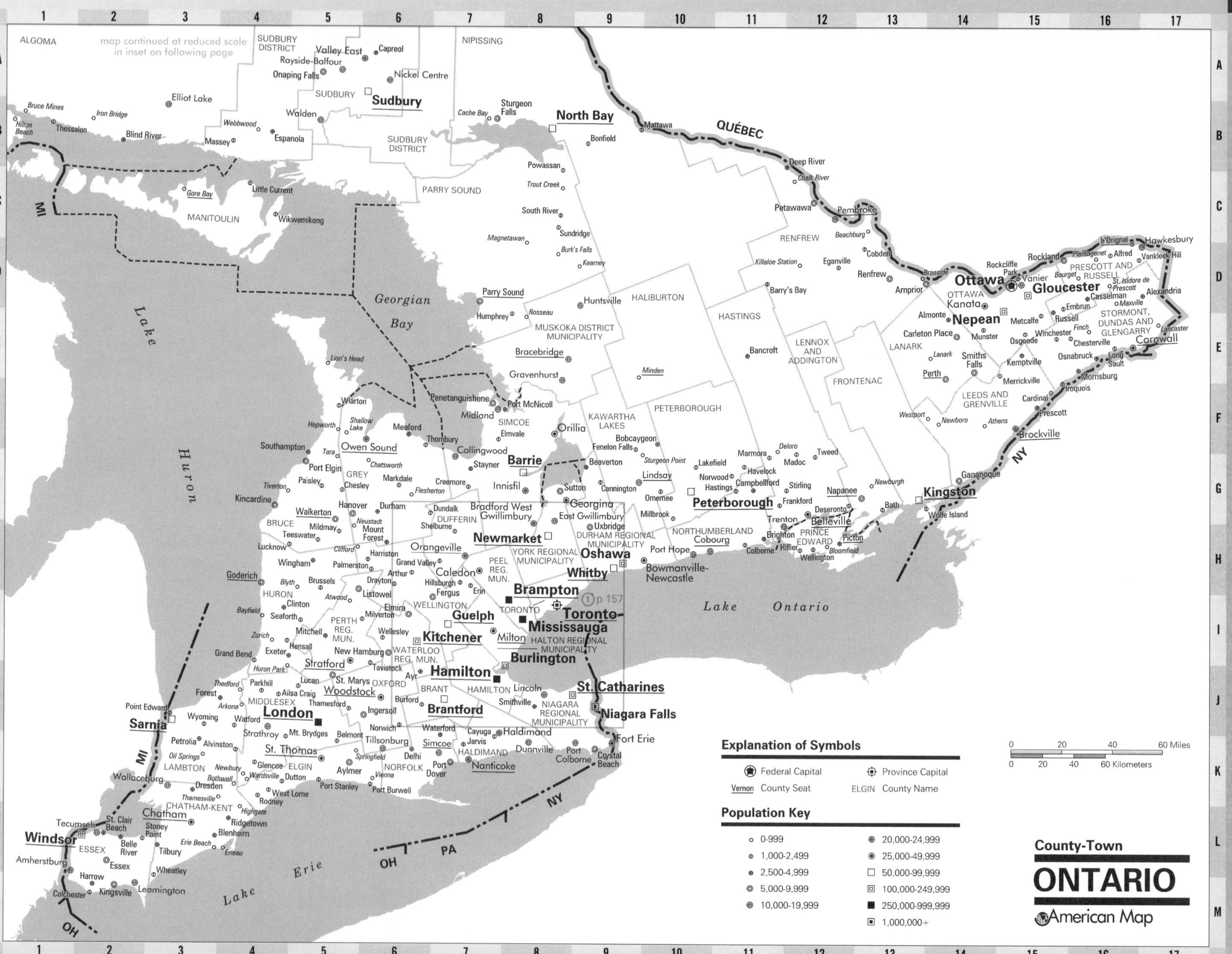
County-Town
ONTARIO
American Map
Explanation of Symbols
Federal Capital
Province Capital
Vernon County Seat
ELGIN County Name
Population Key
0-999
1,000-2,499
2,500-4,999
5,000-9,999
10,000-19,999
20,000-24,999
25,000-49,999
50,000-99,999
100,000-249,999
250,000-999,999
1,000,000+
0 20 40 60 Miles
0 20 40 60 Kilometers
map continued at reduced scale in inset on following page
p 157
QUÉBEC
NY
PA
OH
MI
Lake Huron
Georgian Bay
Lake Ontario
Lake Erie
Ottawa
Toronto
Hamilton
London
Windsor
Kingston
Sudbury
North Bay
Kitchener
Mississauga
Brampton
Oshawa
St. Catharines
Niagara Falls
Sarnia
Peterborough
Barrie
Guelph
Gloucester
Nepean
Burlington
Brantford
Cornwall
Belleville
Chatham
St. Thomas
Woodstock
Stratford
Owen Sound
Orillia
Pembroke
Brockville
Newmarket
Whitby
ALGOMA
NIPISSING
SUDBURY DISTRICT
PARRY SOUND
MANITOULIN
RENFREW
HALIBURTON
HASTINGS
LENNOX AND ADDINGTON
FRONTENAC
LANARK
LEEDS AND GRENVILLE
OTTAWA
PRESCOTT AND RUSSELL
STORMONT, DUNDAS AND GLENGARRY
PETERBOROUGH
KAWARTHA LAKES
MUSKOKA DISTRICT MUNICIPALITY
SIMCOE
DUFFERIN
GREY
BRUCE
HURON
PERTH REG. MUN.
WELLINGTON
WATERLOO REG. MUN.
PEEL REG. MUN.
YORK REGIONAL MUNICIPALITY
DURHAM REGIONAL MUNICIPALITY
NORTHUMBERLAND
PRINCE EDWARD
HALTON REGIONAL MUNICIPALITY
HAMILTON
NIAGARA REGIONAL MUNICIPALITY
HALDIMAND
NORFOLK
BRANT
OXFORD
MIDDLESEX
ELGIN
LAMBTON
CHATHAM-KENT
ESSEX

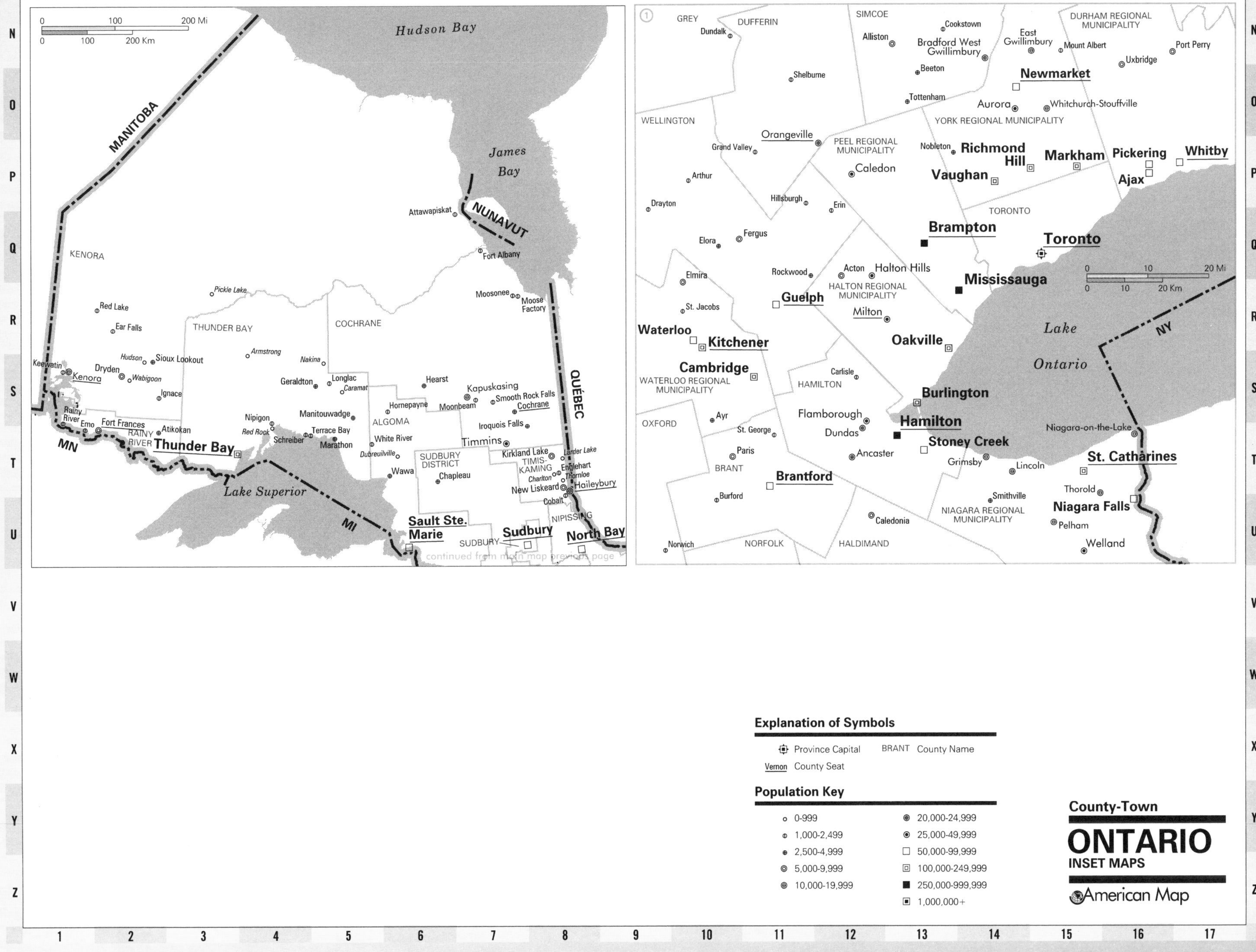
Hudson Bay
James Bay
MANITOBA
NUNAVUT
QUÉBEC
MN
MI
Lake Superior
KENORA
THUNDER BAY
COCHRANE
ALGOMA
SUDBURY DISTRICT
TIMIS-KAMING
NIPISSING
SUDBURY
RAINY RIVER
Attawapiskat
Fort Albany
Moosonee
Moose Factory
Pickle Lake
Red Lake
Ear Falls
Armstrong
Nakina
Keewatin
Kenora
Dryden
Hudson
Sioux Lookout
Wabigoon
Ignace
Geraldton
Longlac
Caramat
Hearst
Kapuskasing
Smooth Rock Falls
Cochrane
Hornepayne
Moonbeam
Iroquois Falls
Rainy River
Emo
Fort Frances
Atikokan
Nipigon
Red Rock
Schreiber
Terrace Bay
Marathon
Manitouwadge
White River
Dubreuilville
Wawa
Timmins
Kirkland Lake
Larder Lake
Englehart
Charlton
Thornloe
New Liskeard
Haileybury
Cobalt
Chapleau
Thunder Bay
Sault Ste. Marie
Sudbury
North Bay
continued from main map previous page
GREY
DUFFERIN
SIMCOE
DURHAM REGIONAL MUNICIPALITY
WELLINGTON
PEEL REGIONAL MUNICIPALITY
YORK REGIONAL MUNICIPALITY
TORONTO
HALTON REGIONAL MUNICIPALITY
WATERLOO REGIONAL MUNICIPALITY
HAMILTON
OXFORD
BRANT
NORFOLK
HALDIMAND
NIAGARA REGIONAL MUNICIPALITY
NY
Lake Ontario
Dundalk
Alliston
Cookstown
Bradford West Gwillimbury
East Gwillimbury
Mount Albert
Uxbridge
Port Perry
Shelburne
Beeton
Newmarket
Tottenham
Aurora
Whitchurch-Stouffville
Orangeville
Grand Valley
Nobleton
Richmond Hill
Markham
Pickering
Whitby
Ajax
Caledon
Vaughan
Arthur
Drayton
Hillsburgh
Erin
Brampton
Toronto
Elora
Fergus
Acton
Halton Hills
Rockwood
Mississauga
Elmira
Guelph
Milton
St. Jacobs
Waterloo
Kitchener
Oakville
Cambridge
Carlisle
Burlington
Ayr
Flamborough
Dundas
Hamilton
St. George
Stoney Creek
Paris
Ancaster
Grimsby
Lincoln
Niagara-on-the-Lake
St. Catharines
Brantford
Burford
Smithville
Thorold
Niagara Falls
Caledonia
Pelham
Norwich
Welland
Explanation of Symbols
Province Capital
BRANT County Name
Vernon County Seat
Population Key
0-999
1,000-2,499
2,500-4,999
5,000-9,999
10,000-19,999
20,000-24,999
25,000-49,999
50,000-99,999
100,000-249,999
250,000-999,999
1,000,000+
County-Town
ONTARIO
INSET MAPS
American Map

DIVISIONS

(50 Divisions)

Name of Division	Population	Location on Map
ALGOMA DISTRICT	125,455	T-5
BRANT COUNTY	114,564	J-6
BRUCE COUNTY	65,680	H-4
CHATHAM-KENT DIVISION	109,650	L-3
COCHRANE DISTRICT	93,240	R-5
DUFFERIN COUNTY	45,657	H-7
DURHAM REGIONAL MUNICIPALITY	458,616	H-9
ELGIN COUNTY	79,159	K-5
ESSEX COUNTY	350,329	L-2
FRONTENAC COUNTY	136,365	F-12
GREY COUNTY	87,632	G-5
HALDIMAND COUNTY	41,028	K-7
HALIBURTON COUNTY	15,321	D-9
HALTON REGIONAL MUNICIPALITY	339,875	I-8
HAMILTON DIVISION	467,799	J-7
HASTINGS COUNTY	118,744	E-11
HURON COUNTY	60,220	I-4
KAWARTHA LAKES DIVISION	67,926	F-9
KENORA DISTRICT	63,335	Q-1
LAMBTON COUNTY	128,975	K-3
LANARK COUNTY	59,845	E-13
LEEDS AND GRENVILLE COUNTIES	96,284	F-14
LENNOX AND ADDINGTON COUNTIES	39,203	E-12
MANITOULIN DISTRICT	11,413	C-3
MIDDLESEX COUNTY	389,616	J-4
MUSKOKA DISTRICT MUNICIPALITY	50,463	E-8
NIAGARA REGIONAL MUNICIPALITY	403,504	J-8
NIPISSING DISTRICT	84,832	A-7
NORFOLK COUNTY	61,547	K-6
NORTHUMBERLAND COUNTY	81,792	H-10
OTTAWA DIVISION	721,136	D-14
OXFORD COUNTY	97,142	J-6
PARRY SOUND DISTRICT	39,906	C-6
PEEL REGIONAL MUNICIPALITY	852,526	H-7
PERTH REGIONAL MUNICIPALITY	72,106	I-5
PETERBOROUGH COUNTY	123,448	F-10
PRESCOTT AND RUSSELL COUNTIES	74,013	D-16
PRINCE EDWARD DIVISION	25,046	H-12
RAINY RIVER DISTRICT	23,163	T-2
RENFREW COUNTY	96,224	D-11
SIMCOE COUNTY	329,865	F-7
STORMONT, DUNDAS AND GLENGARRY COUNTIES	111,301	E-16
SUDBURY DISTRICT	25,457	B-6
SUDBURY DIVISION	164,049	B-5
THUNDER BAY DISTRICT	157,619	R-3
TIMISKAMING DISTRICT	37,807	T-7
TORONTO DIVISION	2,385,421	I-7
WATERLOO REGIONAL MUNICIPALITY	405,435	J-6
WELLINGTON COUNTY	171,395	I-6
YORK REGIONAL MUNICIPALITY	592,445	H-8
TOTAL	**10,753,573**	

CITIES AND TOWNS

Note: The first name is that of the city or town, second, that of the division in which it is located, then the population and location on the map.

COUNTIES

(99 Counties)

Name of County	Population	Location on Map
ABITIBI	25,280	D-2
ABITIBI-OUEST	23,571	E-1
ACTON	15,303	L-11
ANTOINE-LABELLE	33,904	H-6
ARGENTEUIL	28,505	L-7
ARTHABASKA	62,917	K-12
ASBESTOS	15,005	L-12
AVINGNON	15,898	CC-4
BEAUCE-SARTIGAN	46,318	K-14
BEAUHARNOIS-SALABERRY	59,769	X-3
BÉCANCOUR	19,683	J-12
BELLECHASSE	29,674	I-14
BONAVENTURE	19,550	CC-5
BROME-MISSISQUOI	84,359	M-10
CHAMPLAIN	314,306	GG-14
CHARLEVOIX	13,437	G-13
CHARLEVOIX-EST	16,941	F-14
COATICOOK	15,919	M-12
COMMUNAUTÉ-URBAINE-DE-L'OUTAOUAIS	217,609	L-6
COMMUNAUTÉ-URBAINE-DE-QUÉBEC	504,605	O-14
D'AUTRAY	37,553	J-10
DESJARDINS	51,222	P-15
DEUX-MONTAGNES	78,960	L-8
DRUMMOND	84,250	K-11
FRANCHEVILLE	140,541	J-11
JOLIETTE	52,845	K-9
KAMOURASKA	23,215	H-15
LA CÔTE-DE-BEAUPRÉ	21,632	G-12
LA CÔTE-DE-GASPÉ	20,851	BB-6
LA HAUTE-CÔTE-NORD	13,439	D-15
LA HAUTE-GASPÉSIE	13,733	BB-5
LA HAUTE-YAMASKA	77,006	W-9
LA JACQUES-CARTIER	24,819	H-12
LA MATAPÉDIA	20,883	CC-4
LA MITIS	20,160	CC-2
LA NOUVELLE-BEAUCE	25,058	J-13
LA RÉGION-SHERBROOKOISE	132,430	W-11
LA RIVIERE-DU-NORD	83,773	U-4
LA VALLÉE-DE-LA-GATINEAU	20,262	H-5
LA VALLÉE-DU-RICHELIEU	113,832	V-6
LAC-SAINT-JEAN-EST	52,401	F-12
LAJEMMERAIS	95,618	U-6
L'AMIANTE	45,020	J-13
L'ASSOMPTION	102,188	U-5
LAVAL	330,393	EE-12
LE BAS-RICHELIEU	52,288	T-7
LE CENTRE-DE-LA-MAURICIE	67,103	J-10
LE DOMAINE-DU-ROY	33,860	D-9
LE FJORD-DU-SAGUENAY	172,343	A-13
LE GRANIT	21,287	K-13
LE HAUT-RICHELIEU	97,539	X-6
LE HAUT-SAINT-FRANÇOIS	21,946	L-13
LE HAUT-SAINT-LAURENT	22,007	M-7
LE HAUT-SAINT-MAURICE	16,293	E-7
LE ROCHER-PERCÉ	21,340	BB-7
LE VAL-SAINT-FRANÇOIS	33,422	L-11
L'ÉRABLE	24,684	J-12
LES BASQUES	10,204	F-16
LES CHUTES-DE-LA-CHAUDIÈRE	75,598	P-14
LES COLLINES-DE-L'OUTAOUAIS	33,662	L-5
LES ETCHEMINS	18,356	J-14
LES ÎLES-DE-LA-MADELEINE	13,802	MM-7
LES JARDINS-DE-NAPIERVILLE	22,936	Y-5
LES LAURENTIDES	36,335	J-7
LES MASKOUTAINS	78,754	K-10
LES MOULINS	103,213	U-5
LES PAYS-D'EN-HAUT	28,237	U-2
L'ÎLE-D'ORLEANS	6,892	I-13
L'ISLET	19,823	H-15
LOTBINIÈRE	26,921	J-12
MANICOUAGAN	36,271	A-15
MARIA-CHAPDELAINE	28,045	A-10
MASKINONGÉ	23,791	I-10
MATANE	23,723	BB-4
MATAWINIE	41,322	I-9
MÉKINAC	13,480	I-10
MEMPHRÉMAGOG	38,461	M-11
MINGANIE-BASSE-CÔTE-NORD	12,684	KK-5
MIRABEL	22,689	L-9
MONTCALM	38,053	K-9
MONTMAGNY	23,794	I-14
NICOLET-YAMASKA	23,673	K-11
NORD-DU-QUÉBEC	38,395	A-8
PAPINEAU	20,332	K-7
PONTIAC	15,576	H-3
PORTNEUF	45,185	H-11
RIMOUSKI-NEIGETTE	52,677	F-17
RIVIÈRE-DU-LOUP	32,120	G-16
ROBERT-CHICHE	18,712	J-14
ROUSSILLON	132,167	W-5
ROUVILLE	33,090	L-10
ROUYN-NORANDA	42,638	F-1
SEPT-RIVIÈRES-CANIAPISCAU	40,905	KK-4
TÉMISCAMINGUE	18,027	G-1
TÉMISCOUATA	23,082	G-16
THÉRÈSE-DE-BLAINVILLE	119,240	V-3
VALLÉE-DE-L'OR	44,389	E-5
VAUDREUIL-SOULANGES	95,318	M-7
VILLE DE MONTRÉAL	1,783,027	FF-13
TOTAL	**7,138,795**	

CITIES AND TOWNS

Note: The first name is that of the city or town, second, that of the county in which it is located, then the population and location on the map.

Acton Vale, *Acton,* 4,685 .... L-11
Albanel, *Maria-Chapdelaine,* 1,111 .... E-11
Alma, *Lac-Saint-Jean-Est,* 26,127 .... E-12
Amos, *Abitibi,* 13,632 .... E-3
Amqui, *La Matapédia,* 5,207 .... CC-3
Angers, *Les Collines-de-l'Outaouais,* 3,914 .... L-7
Asbestos, *Asbestos,* 6,271 .... L-12
Ascot, *Le Haut-Saint-François,* 8,663 .... L-12
Baie-Comeau, *Manicouagan,* 25,554 .... C-17
Baie-Saint-Paul, *Charlevoix,* 3,569 .... H-14
Barraute, *Abitibi,* 1,159 .... E-4
Beauceville, *Robert-Chiche,* 3,751 .... K-14
Beauharnois, *Beauharnois-Salaberry,* 6,435 .... M-9
Beaupré, *La Côte-de-Beaupré,* 2,799 .... I-14
Bécancour, *Bécancour,* 11,489 .... S-10
Bedford, *Brome-Missisquoi,* 2,748 .... M-11
Bellefeuille, *La Riviere-du-Nord,* 12,803 .... V-3
Beloeil, *La Vallée-du-Richelieu,* 19,294 .... W-7
Bernières-Saint Nicolas,
Les Chutes-de-la-Chaudière, 15,594 .... P-14
Bernierville, *L'Érable,* 1,871 .... T-13
Berthierville, *D'Autray,* 3,952 .... K-10
Black Lake, *L'Amiante,* 4,408 .... K-13
Blainville, *Thérèse-de-Blainville,* 29,603 .... V-4
Boisbriand, *Vaudreuil-Soulanges,* 25,227 .... W-4
Bois-des-Filion, *Les Moulins,* 7,124 .... V-5
Bonaventure, *Bonaventure,* 1,509 .... DD-6
Boucherville, *Lajemmerais,* 34,989 .... W-6
Bromont, *La Haute-Yamaska,* 4,290 .... Y-9
Bromptonville, *Memphrémagog,* 3,426 .... X-12
Brossard, *Champlain,* 65,927 .... X-6
Brownsburg, *Argenteuil,* 2,583 .... V-2
Cabano, *Témiscouata,* 3,086 .... G-17
Campbell's Bay, *Pontiac,* 874 .... K-5
Candiac, *Roussillon,* 11,805 .... X-6
Cantley, *Les Collines-de-l'Outaouais,* 5,425 .... L-6
Cap-aux-Meules, *Les Îles-de-la-Madeleine,* 1,661 .... MM-7
Cap-Chat, *La Haute-Gaspésie,* 2,847 .... AA-4
Cap-de-la-Madeleine, *Francheville,* 33,438 .... J-1
Cap-Santé, *Portneuf,* 2,615 .... I-12
Carignan, *Le Haut-Richelieu,* 5,614 .... X-6
Carleton, *Avingnon,* 2,886 .... DD-5
Causapscal, *La Matapédia,* 2,080 .... CC-3
Chambly, *La Vallée-du-Richelieu,* 19,716 .... X-7
Chandler, *Le Rocher-Percé,* 3,358 .... CC-7
Chapais, *Nord-du-Québec,* 2,030 .... B-8
Charlemagne, *L'Assomption,* 5,739 .... EE-14
Charny, *Les Chutes-de-la-Chaudière,* 10,661 .... Q-14
Châteauguay, *Roussillon,* 41,423 .... X-5
Château-Richer, *Bellechasse,* 3,579 .... I-13
Chelsea, *Les Collines-de-l'Outaouais,* 5,925 .... L-6
Chibougamau, *Nord-du-Québec,* 8,664 .... B-8
Chicoutimi, *Le Fjord-du-Saguenay,* 63,061 .... E-13
Chute-aux-Outardes, *Manicouagan,* 2,155 .... AA-2
Clermont, *Charlevoix-Est,* 3,225 .... G-15
Coaticook, *Coaticook,* 6,653 .... M-12
Coleraine, *L'Amiante,* 1,359 .... K-13
Contrecoeur, *Lajemmerais,* 3,155 .... V-7
Cookshire, *Le Haut-Saint-François,* 1,532 .... L-13
Coteau-du-Lac, *Vaudreuil-Soulanges,* 1,207 .... Y-3
Cowansville, *Brome-Missisquoi,* 12,051 .... M-11
Crabtree, *Joliette,* 2,339 .... U-6
Danville, *Asbestos,* 1,796 .... V-12
Daveluyville, *Arthabaska,* 1,038 .... T-11
Deauville, *La Région-Sherbrookoise,* 2,599 .... X-11
Dégelis, *Témiscouata,* 3,437 .... G-17
Delisle, *Lac-Saint-Jean-Est,* 4,256 .... E-12
Delson, *Roussillon,* 6,703 .... L-10
Desbiens, *Lac-Saint-Jean-Est,* 1,202 .... F-12
Deux-Montagnes, *Deux-Montagnes,* 15,953 .... GG-11
Disraëli, *L'Amiante,* 2,657 .... K-13
Dolbeau, *Maria-Chapdelaine,* 8,310 .... D-11
Donnacona, *Portneuf,* 5,739 .... I-12
Drummondville, *Drummond,* 44,882 .... K-11
Dunham, *Brome-Missisquoi,* 3,370 .... Z-8
East Angus, *Le Haut-Saint-François,* 3,642 .... X-13
East Broughton, *L'Amiante,* 2,489 .... S-15
Farnham, *Brome-Missisquoi,* 6,044 .... M-11
Ferme-Neuve, *Antoine-Labelle,* 2,178 .... I-7
Fermont, *Sept-Rivières-Caniapiscau,* 3,234 .... JJ-5
Fleurimont, *La Région-Sherbrookoise,* 16,262 .... X-12
Forestville, *La Haute-Côte-Nord,* 3,894 .... E-16
Fort-Coulonge, *Pontiac,* 1,716 .... K-5
Gaspé, *La Côte-de-Gaspé,* 16,517 .... BB-7
Gatineau, *Communauté-Urbaine-de-l'Outaouais,* 217,609 .... L-6
Gentilly, *Bécancour,* 2,325 .... J-12
Gracefield, *La Vallée-de-la-Gatineau,* 976 .... K-6
Granby, *La Haute-Yamaska,* 43,316 .... L-11
Grande-Rivière, *Le Rocher-Percé,* 3,888 .... CC-7
Grand-Île, *Beauharnois-Salaberry,* 4,468 .... Y-3
Grand-Mère, *Le Centre-de-la-Mauricie,* 14,223 .... J-11
Greenfield Park, *Champlain,* 17,337 .... HH-14
Grenville, *Argenteuil,* 1,443 .... L-8
Hauterive, *Manicouagan,* 13,626 .... C-17
Havre-Saint-Pierre, *Minganie-Basse-Côte-Nord,* 3,020 .. LL-6
Hébertville, *Lac-Saint-Jean-Est,* 1,514 .... CC-13
Hébertville-Station, *Lac-Saint-Jean-Est,* 1,393 .... BB-13
Hudson, *Vaudreuil-Soulanges,* 4,796 .... X-3
Huntingdon, *Le Haut-Saint-Laurent,* 2,746 .... M-9
Iberville, *Le Haut-Richelieu,* 9,635 .... M-10
Inukjuak, *Nord-du-Québec,* 1,184 .... GG-2
Joliette, *Joliette,* 17,541 .... K-10
Jonquière, *Le Fjord-du-Saguenay,* 56,503 .... F-13
Kingsey Falls, *Arthabaska,* 1,329 .... U-11
Kuujjuaq, *Nord-du-Québec,* 1,726 .... HH-4
La Baie, *Le Fjord-du-Saguenay,* 21,057 .... F-14
La Guadeloupe, *Beauce-Sartigan,* 1,772 .... K-14
La Malbaie, *Charlevoix-Est,* 4,047 .... G-15
La Pêche, *Les Collines-de-l'Outaouais,* 6,160 .... L-6
La Plaine, *Les Moulins,* 14,413 .... V-5
La Pocatière, *Kamouraska,* 4,887 .... H-15
La Prairie, *Roussillon,* 17,128 .... X-6
La Sarre, *Abitibi-Ouest,* 8,345 .... D-1
La Tuque, *Le Haut-Saint-Maurice,* 12,102 .... H-11
Labelle, *Les Laurentides,* 1,170 .... J-8
Lac-au-Saumon, *La Matapédia,* 1,314 .... CC-3
Lac-Beauport, *La Jacques-Cartier,* 3,713 .... I-13
Lac-Brome, *Brome-Missisquoi,* 5,073 .... Y-10
Lac-Etchemin, *Les Etchemins,* 2,488 .... J-14
Lachenaie, *Les Moulins,* 18,489 .... EE-14
Lachute, *Argenteuil,* 11,493 .... L-8
Lac-Mégantic, *Le Granit,* 5,864 .... L-14
Lacolle, *Le Haut-Richelieu,* 1,554 .... M-10
Lafontaine, *La Riviere-du-Nord,* 9,008 .... V-4
L'Annonciation, *Antoine-Labelle,* 2,085 .... J-8
L'Ascension-de-Notre Seigneur,
Lac-Saint-Jean-Est, 1,354 .... E-12
L'Assomption, *L'Assomption,* 11,366 .... K-10
Laterrière, *Le Fjord-du-Saguenay,* 4,815 .... F-13
Laurentides, *Montcalm,* 2,703 .... U-5
Laurier-Station, *Lotbinière,* 2,399 .... Q-13
Laval, *Laval,* 330,393 .... L-9
Lavaltrie, *D'Autray,* 5,821 .... K-10
Le Bic, *Rimouski-Neigette,* 1,354 .... CC-1
Le Gardeur, *L'Assomption,* 16,853 .... EE-14
Lebel-sur-Quévillon, *Nord-du-Québec,* 3,416 .... D-5
Lemoyne, *Champlain,* 5,052 .... HH-14
Lennoxville, *La Région-Sherbrookoise,* 4,036 .... X-12
L'Épiphanie, *L'Assomption,* 4,153 .... U-6
Léry, *Roussillon,* 2,410 .... JJ-11
Les Escoumins, *La Haute-Côte-Nord,* 1,751 .... E-16
Lévis, *Les Chutes-de-la-Chaudière,* 40,407 .... I-13
L'Île-Perrot, *Vaudreuil-Soulanges,* 9,178 .... II-10
Linière, *Beauce-Sartigan,* 1,001 .... K-14
Longueuil, *Champlain,* 127,977 .... W-6
Lorraine, *Thérèse-de-Blainville,* 8,876 .... EE-12
Louiseville, *Maskinongé,* 7,911 .... J-11
Luceville, *La Mitis,* 1,421 .... CC-2
Macamic, *Abitibi-Ouest,* 1,711 .... D-2
Magog, *Memphrémagog,* 14,050 .... M-12
Malartic, *Vallée-de-l'Or,* 4,154 .... F-3
Maniwaki, *La Vallée-de-la-Gatineau,* 4,527 .... J-6
Maple Grove, *Beauharnois-Salaberry,* 2,606 .... JJ-11
Marieville, *Rouville,* 5,510 .... II-17
Mascouche, *Les Moulins,* 28,097 .... V-5
Maskinongé, *Maskinongé,* 1,052 .... S-8
Matagami, *Nord-du-Québec,* 2,243 .... B-4
Matane, *Matane,* 12,364 .... BB-3
McMasterville, *La Vallée-du-Richelieu,* 3,813 .... GG-16
Melocheville, *Beauharnois-Salaberry,* 2,486 .... JJ-10
Metabetchouan, *Lac-Saint-Jean-Est,* 3,474 .... E-12
Mirabel, *Mirabel,* 22,689 .... L-9
Mistassini, *Maria-Chapdelaine,* 6,904 .... D-12
Montebello, *Papineau,* 1,066 .... L-8
Mont-Joli, *La Mitis,* 6,267 .... BB-2
Mont-Laurier, *Antoine-Labelle,* 8,007 .... J-7
Montmagny, *Montmagny,* 11,885 .... I-14
Mont-Rolland, *Les Pays-d'en-Haut,* 2,882 .... U-3
Mont-Saint-Hilaire, *La Vallée-du-Richelieu,* 13,064 .. GG-17
Murdochville, *La Côte-de-Gaspé,* 1,595 .... BB-6

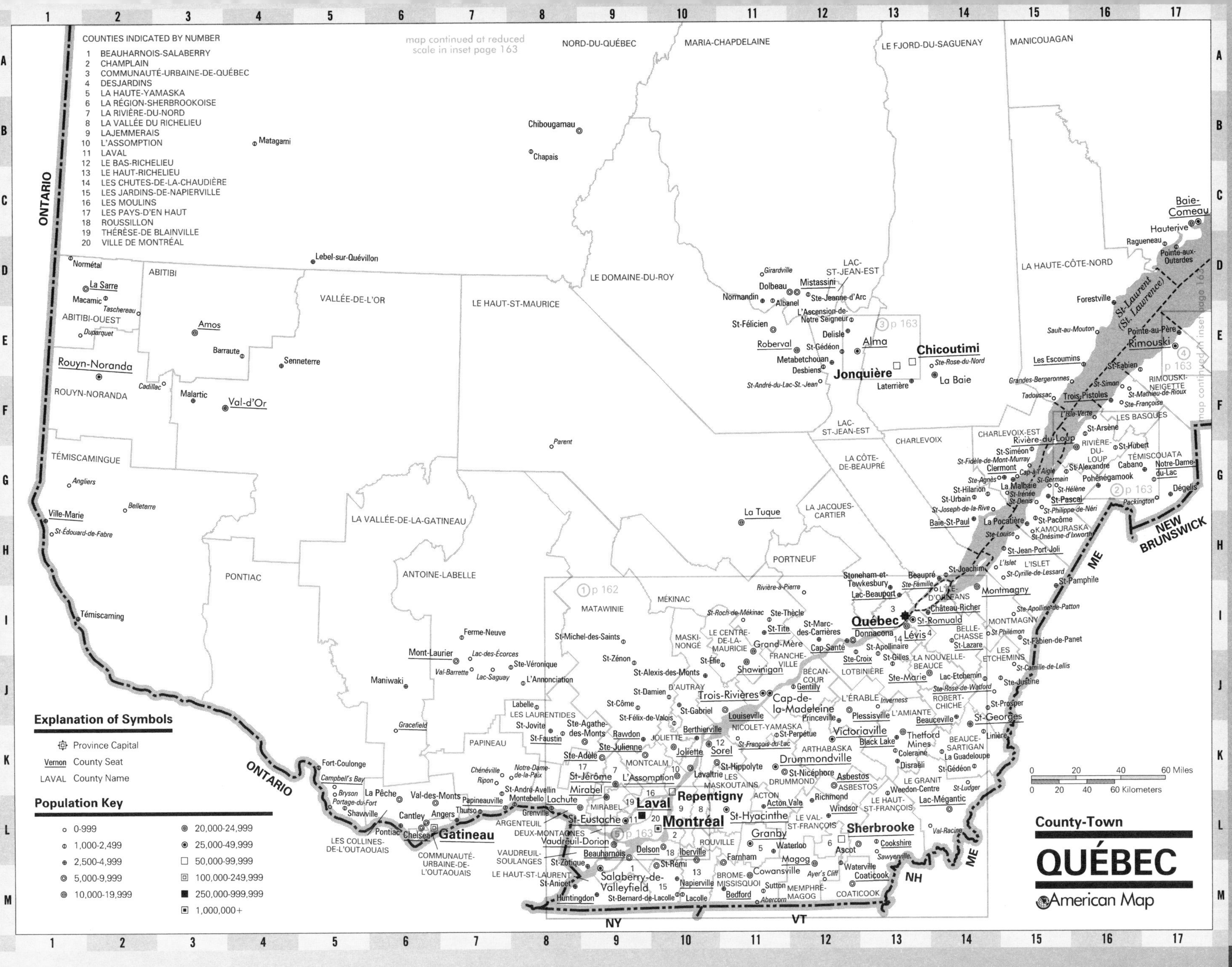
County-Town
QUÉBEC
American Map
0 20 40 60 Miles
0 20 40 60 Kilometers
COUNTIES INDICATED BY NUMBER
1 BEAUHARNOIS-SALABERRY
2 CHAMPLAIN
3 COMMUNAUTÉ-URBAINE-DE-QUÉBEC
4 DESJARDINS
5 LA HAUTE-YAMASKA
6 LA RÉGION-SHERBROOKOISE
7 LA RIVIÈRE-DU-NORD
8 LA VALLÉE DU RICHELIEU
9 LAJEMMERAIS
10 L'ASSOMPTION
11 LAVAL
12 LE BAS-RICHELIEU
13 LE HAUT-RICHELIEU
14 LES CHUTES-DE-LA-CHAUDIÈRE
15 LES JARDINS-DE-NAPIERVILLE
16 LES MOULINS
17 LES PAYS-D'EN HAUT
18 ROUSSILLON
19 THÉRÈSE-DE BLAINVILLE
20 VILLE DE MONTRÉAL
map continued at reduced scale in inset page 163
Explanation of Symbols
Province Capital
Vernon County Seat
LAVAL County Name
Population Key
0-999
1,000-2,499
2,500-4,999
5,000-9,999
10,000-19,999
20,000-24,999
25,000-49,999
50,000-99,999
100,000-249,999
250,000-999,999
1,000,000+
ONTARIO
NEW BRUNSWICK
ME
NH
VT
NY
Québec
Montréal
Laval
Gatineau
Sherbrooke
Trois-Rivières
Chicoutimi
Jonquière
Rimouski
Baie-Comeau
Rouyn-Noranda
Val-d'Or

County-Town

QUÉBEC

MONTRÉAL - QUÉBEC INSET

American Map

For Explanation of Symbols see Québec insets, next page.

County-Town
QUÉBEC
INSET MAPS
American Map

Explanation of Symbols

Symbol	Meaning	Symbol	Meaning
✸	Province Capital	LAVAL	County Name
Vernon	County Seat		

Population Key

0-999	20,000-24,999
1,000-2,499	25,000-49,999
2,500-4,999	50,000-99,999
5,000-9,999	100,000-249,999
10,000-19,999	250,000-999,999
	1,000,000+

MANICOUAGAN
Hauterive
Baie-Comeau
Chute-aux-Outardes
Pointe-Lebel
Ragueneau
Pointe-aux-Outardes
St-Laurent (St. Lawrence)
Cap-Chat
Ste-Anne-des-Monts
Marsoui
Mont-St-Pierre
Petite-Vallée
Rivière-au-Renard
LA HAUTE-GASPÉSIE
Murdochville
LA CÔTE-DE-GASPÉ
Gaspé
Matane
Ste-Félicité
St-Adelme
MATANE
St-Ulric
St-Damase
St-Luc
St-Léandre
Métis-sur-Mer
Mont-Joli
Price
St-Noël
Sayabec
LA MATAPÉDIA
LE ROCHER-PERCÉ
Percé
Grande-Rivière
Luceville
Pointe-au-Père
St-Moïse
Lac-au-Saumon
BONAVENTURE
Rimouski
St-Léon-le-Grand
Causapscal
Chandler
Pabos Mills
Gulf of St. Lawrence
St-Fabien
Le Bic
St-Narcisse-de-Rimouski
St-Charles-Garnier
Amqui
Ste-Marguerite
AVINGNON
St-Simon
St-Valérien
St-Mathieu-de-Rioux
LA MITIS
New Richmond
LES BASQUES
Ste-Françoise
RIMOUSKI-NEIGETTE
Nouvelle
St-Omer
Carleton
St-Siméon
Bonaventure
New Carlisle
St-Jean-de-Dieu
St-Alexis-de-Matapédia
St-Clément
TÉMISCOUATA
NEW BRUNSWICK
Same scale as main map

continued from main map page 161

② St-Laurent (St. Lawrence)
L'Isle-Verte
LES BASQUES
St-Éloi
St-Jean-de-Dieu
St-Georges-de-Cacouna
RIVIÈRE-DU-LOUP
St-Arsène
St-Clément
Rivière-du-Loup
St-Modeste
St-Hubert
Notre-Dame-du-Portage
St-Antonin
TÉMISCOUATA
St-Alexandre
KAMOURASKA
St-Joseph-de-Kamouraska
St-Louis-du-Ha! Ha!
Cabano
Notre-Dame-du-Lac
St-Hélène
Pohénégamook
St-Eusèbe
0 10 Mi / 0 10 Km

③ L'Ascension-de-Notre Seigneur
LAC-ST-JEAN-EST
Delisle
LE FJORD-DU-SAGUENAY
St.-Ambroise
Alma
Saint-Bruno
Hébertville-Station
Hébertville
Chicoutimi
Jonquière
0 10 Mi / 0 10 Km

④ St-Laurent (St. Lawrence)
St-Octave-de-Métis
Price
Mont-Joli
Ste-Luce
Luceville
St-Donat
Pointe-au-Père
St-Anaclet-de-Lessard
Rimouski-Est
Rimouski
LA MITIS
RIMOUSKI-NEIGETTE
Ste-Blandine
0 10 Mi / 0 10 Km

NUNAVUT
Ivujivik
Salluit
Hudson Strait
Kangiqsujuaq
NORD-DU-QUÉBEC
Akulivik
Quaqtaq
Povungnituk
Kangirsuk
Hudson Bay
Inukjuak
Kangiqsualujjuaq
Kuujjuaq
Labrador Sea
Kuujjuarapik
Schefferville
NEWFOUNDLAND AND LABRADOR
James Bay
Wemindji
Fermont
SEPT-RIVIÈRES-CANIAPISCAU
MINGANIE-BASSE-CÔTE-NORD
MANICOUAGAN
ONTARIO
LE FJORD-DU-SAGUENAY
Sept-Îles
Havre-St-Pierre
Matagami
Chapais
Chibougamau
Port-Cartier
Moisie
Île d'Anticosti
MARIA-CHAPDELAINE
Baie-Comeau
St-Laurent
Ste-Anne-des-Monts
Gulf of St. Lawrence
Rouyn-Noranda
VALLÉE-DE-L'OR
LE DOMAINE-DU-ROY
Mistassini
Chicoutimi
Val-d'Or
Roberval
LE HAUT-ST-MAURICE
Jonquière
Îles de la Madeleine
Cap-aux-Meules
LES ÎLES-DE-LA-MADELEINE
La Tuque
Québec
NEW BRUNSWICK
ME
Atlantic Ocean
0 100 200 Mi / 0 100 200 Km

continued from main map page 161

⑤ MIRABEL
THÉRÈSE-DE BLAINVILLE
Mascouche
Le Gardeur
LAJEMMERAIS
St-Canut
Ste-Sophie
Terrebonne
Lachenaie
L'ASSOMPTION
Charlemagne
Répentigny
LA VALLÉE DU RICHELIEU
Mirabel
LES MOULINS
Lorraine
Bois-des-Filion
Varennes
Blainville
THÉRÈSE-DE BLAINVILLE
LAVAL
Rosemère
VILLE DE MONTRÉAL
St-Amable
Ste-Thérèse
Boisbriand
Boucherville
DEUX-MONTAGNES
Laval
Ste-Julie
Mont-St-Hilaire
Beloeil
St-Eustache
McMasterville
St-Joseph-du-Lac
Deux-Montagnes
Longueuil
St-Bruno-de-Montarville
Otterburn Park
Ste-Marthe-sur-le-Lac
CHAMPLAIN
St-Basile-le-Grand
Pointe-Calumet
Montréal
LeMoyne
St-Lambert
Greenfield Park
St-Hubert
ROUVILLE
Brossard
Chambly
Richelieu
Marieville
Vaudreuil-sur-le-Lac
L'Île-Cadieux
La Prairie
Terrasse-Vaudreuil
Ste-Catherine
Candiac
Vaudreuil-Dorion
ROUSSILLON
L'Île-Perrot
Delson
Notre-Dame-de-l'Île-Perrot
St-Constant
St-Luc
VAUDREUIL-SOULANGES
Pointe-des-Cascades
Léry
LE HAUT-RICHELIEU
Pincourt
BEAUHARNOIS-SALABERRY
Beauharnois
Châteauguay
Carignan
Melocheville
Maple Grove
0 5 10 Mi / 0 5 10 Km

DIVISIONS

(18 Divisions)

Name of Division	Population	Location on Map
DIVISION NO. 1	32,291	P-11
DIVISION NO. 2	23,121	O-8
DIVISION NO. 3	16,469	Q-5
DIVISION NO. 4	12,313	P-1
DIVISION NO. 5	35,032	N-10
DIVISION NO. 6	220,602	M-9
DIVISION NO. 7	49,297	M-4
DIVISION NO. 8	31,643	M-2
DIVISION NO. 9	38,562	K-11
DIVISION NO. 10	20,770	K-8
DIVISION NO. 11	231,970	L-6
DIVISION NO. 12	24,454	K-4
DIVISION NO. 13	24,858	J-2
DIVISION NO. 14	40,799	H-8
DIVISION NO. 15	80,666	H-7
DIVISION NO. 16	37,758	H-4
DIVISION NO. 17	38,528	G-2
DIVISION NO. 18	31,104	B-6
TOTAL	**990,237**	

CITIES AND TOWNS

Note: The first name is that of the city or town, second, that of the division in which it is located, then the population and location on the map.

Assiniboia, *Division No. 3,* 2,653 ....P-7
Balgonie, *Division No. 6,* 1,132 ....N-9
Battleford, *Division No. 12,* 3,936 ....J-4
Biggar, *Division No. 12,* 2,312 ....K-4
Buffalo Narrows, *Division No. 18,* 1,053 ....D-6
Cana, *Division No. 5,* 1,014 ....M-11
Canora, *Division No. 9,* 2,208 ....L-11
Carlyle, *Division No. 1,* 1,252 ....P-11
Carnduff, *Division No. 1,* 1,069 ....Q-12
Carrot River, *Division No. 14,* 1,032 ....I-9
Creighton, *Division No. 18,* 1,713 ....F-11
Dalmeny, *Division No. 11,* 1,470 ....K-6
Davidson, *Division No. 11,* 1,105 ....M-7
Esterhazy, *Division No. 5,* 2,602 ....N-12
Estevan, *Division No. 1,* 10,752 ....Q-11
Eston, *Division No. 8,* 1,119 ....M-3
Foam Lake, *Division No. 10,* 1,303 ....L-10
Fort Qu'Appelle, *Division No. 6,* 1,997 ....N-9
Gravelbourg, *Division No. 3,* 1,211 ....O-6
Grenfell, *Division No. 5,* 1,106 ....N-11
Gull Lake, *Division No. 8,* 1,078 ....O-3
Hudson Bay, *Division No. 14,* 1,879 ....J-11
Humboldt, *Division No. 15,* 5,074 ....K-8
Île-à-La-Crosse, *Division No. 18,* 1,403 ....E-6
Indian Head, *Division No. 6,* 1,833 ....N-10
Kamsack, *Division No. 9,* 2,264 ....L-12
Kelvington, *Division No. 14,* 1,046 ....K-10
Kerrobert, *Division No. 13,* 1,109 ....K-3
Kindersley, *Division No. 13,* 4,679 ....L-2
Kipling, *Division No. 5,* 1,004 ....O-11
La Loche, *Division No. 18,* 1,966 ....D-6
La Ronge, *Division No. 18,* 2,964 ....E-7
Lajord, *Division No. 6,* 1,034 ....O-9
Langenburg, *Division No. 5,* 1,119 ....M-12
Langham, *Division No. 11,* 1,104 ....K-5
Lanigan, *Division No. 11,* 1,368 ....L-8
Lloydminster, *Division No. 17,* 18,953 ....I-2
Lumsden, *Division No. 6,* 1,530 ....N-8
Macklin, *Division No. 13,* 1,281 ....J-2
Maple Creek, *Division No. 4,* 2,307 ....O-2
Martensville, *Division No. 11,* 3,477 ....K-6
Meadow Lake, *Division No. 17,* 4,813 ....G-4
Melfort, *Division No. 14,* 5,759 ....J-8
Melville, *Division No. 5,* 4,646 ....M-11
Moose Jaw, *Division No. 7,* 32,973 ....N-7
Moosomin, *Division No. 5,* 2,420 ....O-12
Nipawin, *Division No. 14,* 4,318 ....I-9
North Battleford, *Division No. 16,* 14,051 ....J-4
Outlook, *Division No. 11,* 2,116 ....L-5
Oxbow, *Division No. 1,* 1,263 ....Q-12
Pilot Butte, *Division No. 6,* 1,469 ....N-9
Preeceville, *Division No. 9,* 1,148 ....K-11
Prince Albert, *Division No. 15,* 34,777 ....I-7
Regina, *Division No. 6,* 180,400 ....N-8
Rosetown, *Division No. 12,* 2,496 ....L-4
Rosthern, *Division No. 15,* 1,564 ....J-6
Saskatoon, *Division No. 11,* 193,647 ....K-6
Shaunavon, *Division No. 4,* 1,857 ....P-3
Shellbrook, *Division No. 16,* 1,234 ....I-6
Swift Current, *Division No. 8,* 14,890 ....O-4
Tisdale, *Division No. 14,* 2,966 ....J-9
Unity, *Division No. 13,* 2,200 ....J-3
Uranium City, *Division No. 18, 1,405* A-6
Wadena, *Division No. 10,* 1,477 ....K-9
Warman, *Division No. 11,* 2,839 ....K-6
Watrous, *Division No. 11,* 1,860 ....L-7
Weyburn, *Division No. 2,* 9,723 ....P-9
Wilkie, *Division No. 13,* 1,364 ....J-3
Wynyard, *Division No. 10,* 1,954 ....L-9
Yorkton, *Division No. 9,* 15,154 ....M-11

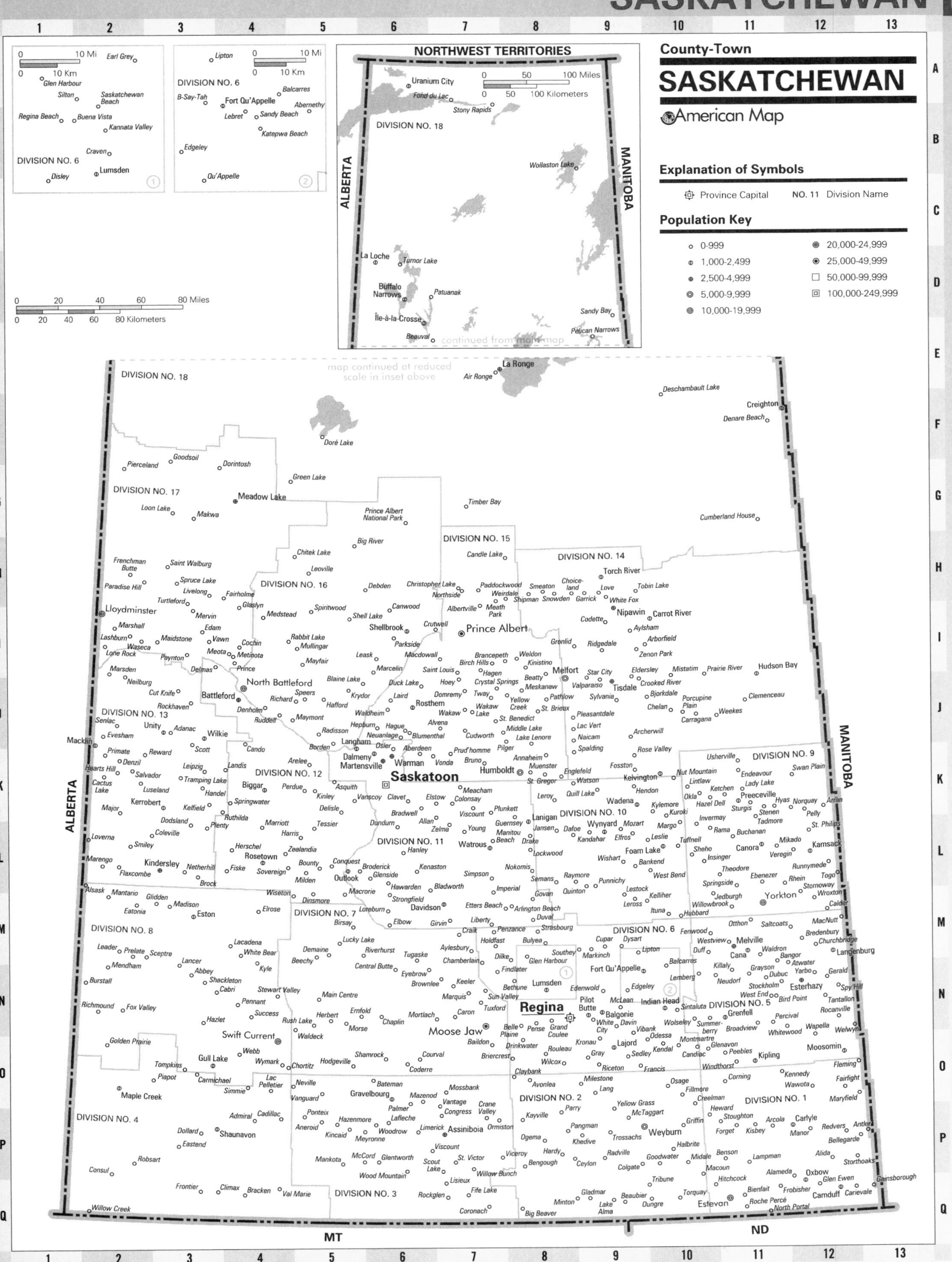
County-Town
SASKATCHEWAN
American Map
Explanation of Symbols
Province Capital
NO. 11 Division Name
Population Key
0-999
1,000-2,499
2,500-4,999
5,000-9,999
10,000-19,999
20,000-24,999
25,000-49,999
50,000-99,999
100,000-249,999
NORTHWEST TERRITORIES
ALBERTA
MANITOBA
MT
ND
0 20 40 60 80 Miles
0 20 40 60 80 Kilometers
0 50 100 Miles
0 50 100 Kilometers
0 10 Mi
0 10 Km
DIVISION NO. 1
DIVISION NO. 2
DIVISION NO. 3
DIVISION NO. 4
DIVISION NO. 5
DIVISION NO. 6
DIVISION NO. 7
DIVISION NO. 8
DIVISION NO. 9
DIVISION NO. 10
DIVISION NO. 11
DIVISION NO. 12
DIVISION NO. 13
DIVISION NO. 14
DIVISION NO. 15
DIVISION NO. 16
DIVISION NO. 17
DIVISION NO. 18
map continued at reduced scale in inset above
continued from main map
Regina
Saskatoon
Prince Albert
Moose Jaw
Swift Current
Yorkton
North Battleford
Battleford
Lloydminster
Estevan
Weyburn
Melfort
Humboldt
Melville
Kindersley
Meadow Lake
Nipawin
Tisdale
La Ronge
Uranium City
La Loche
Buffalo Narrows
Île-à-la-Crosse
Creighton
Fort Qu'Appelle
Lumsden
Maple Creek
Shaunavon
Assiniboia
Kamsack
Canora
Wynyard
Watrous
Rosetown
Biggar
Unity
Wilkie
Outlook
Davidson
Warman
Martensville
Dalmeny
Langham
Esterhazy
Moosomin
Kipling
Carlyle
Gull Lake
Kerrobert
Macklin
Lanigan
Wadena
Kelvington
Preeceville
Foam Lake
Shellbrook
Rosthern
Pilot Butte
White City
Balgonie
Indian Head
Grenfell
Eston
Langenburg
Carrot River
Hudson Bay
Cumberland House
Prince Albert National Park

YUKON

TOTAL POPULATION 30,766

CITIES AND TOWNS

Note: The first name is that of the city or town, second, that of the region in which it is located, then the population and location on the map.

Dawson, Yukon, 1,287 ....K-2
Whitehorse, Yukon, 19,157 ....K-2

NORTHWEST TERRITORIES

REGIONS

(2 Regions)

Name of Region	Population	Location on Map
FORT SMITH	31,967	J-6
INUVIK	10,116	H-5
TOTAL	**40,283**	

CITIES AND TOWNS

Note: The first name is that of the city or town, second, that of the region in which it is located, then the population and location on the map.

Fort Simpson, Fort Smith, 1,257 ....K-5
Fort Smith, Fort Smith, 2,441 ....M-7
Hay River, Fort Smith, 3,611 ....L-6
Inuvik, Inuvik, 3,296 ....H-4
Rae-Edzo, Fort Smith, 1,662 ....K-7
Yellowknife, Fort Smith, 17,275 ....L-7

NUNAVUT

REGIONS

(3 Regions)

Name of Region	Population	Location on Map
BAFFIN	13,218	E-11
KEEWATIN	6,868	E-9
KITKMEOT	5,067	F-10
TOTAL	**25,153**	

CITIES AND TOWNS

Note: The first name is that of the city or town, second, that of the region in which it is located, then the population and location on the map.

Arviat, Keewatin, 1,559 ....L-11
Baker Lake, Keewatin, 1,385 ....K-11
Cambridge Bay, Kitikmeot, 1,351 ....I-9
Cape Dorset, Baffin, 1,118 ....J-14
Igloolik, Baffin, 1,174 ....H-13
Iqaluit, Baffin, 4,220 ....J-16
Kangiqcliniq (Rankin Inlet),
Keewatin, 2,058 ....L-11
Kugluktuk, Kitikmeot, 1,201 ....I-7
Pangnirtung, Baffin, 1,243 ....H-16
Pond Inlet, Baffin, 1,154 ....G-13

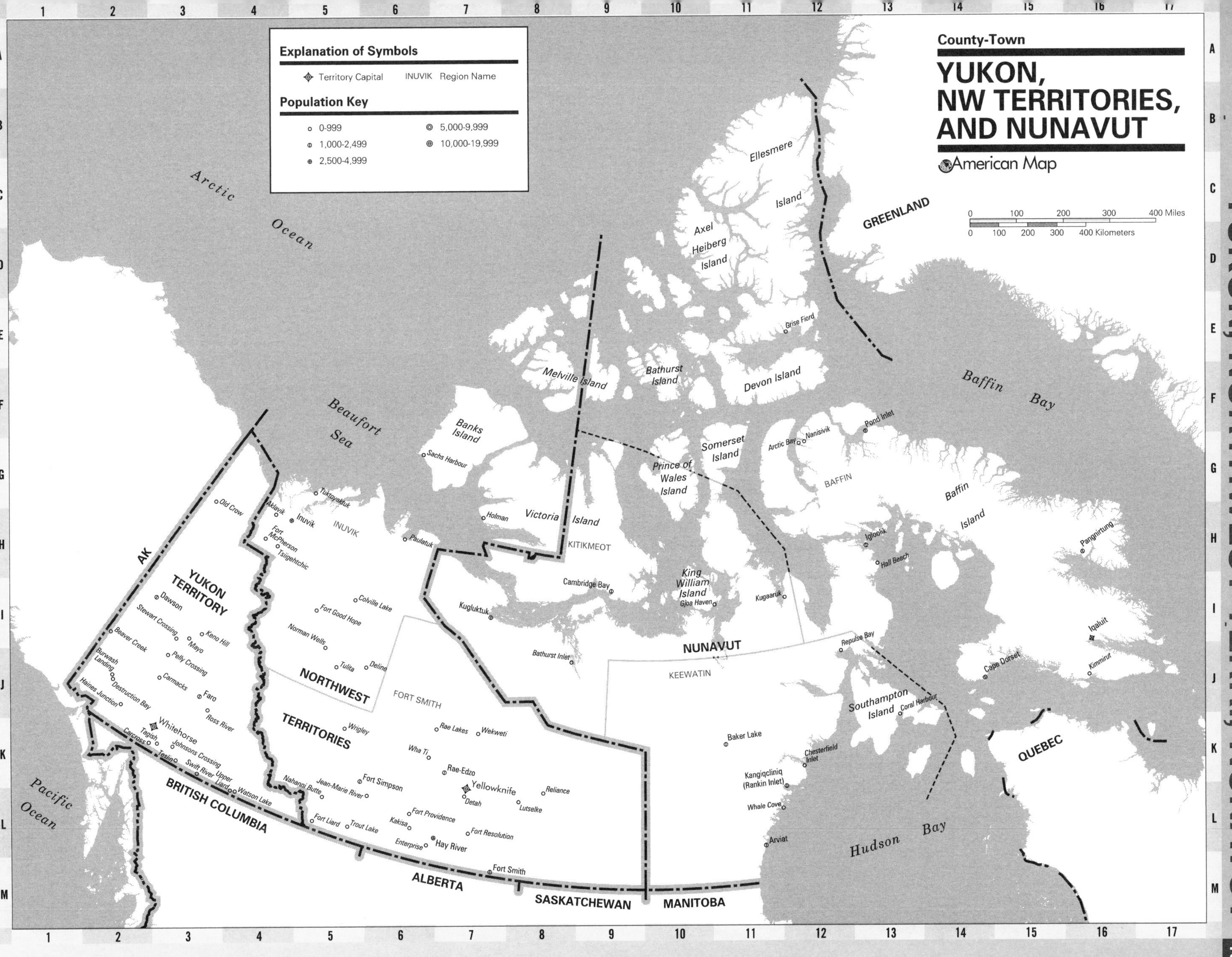
County-Town
YUKON, NW TERRITORIES, AND NUNAVUT
American Map
0 100 200 300 400 Miles
0 100 200 300 400 Kilometers
Explanation of Symbols
Territory Capital
INUVIK Region Name
Population Key
0-999
1,000-2,499
2,500-4,999
5,000-9,999
10,000-19,999
Arctic Ocean
Beaufort Sea
Pacific Ocean
Baffin Bay
Hudson Bay
GREENLAND
Ellesmere Island
Axel Heiberg Island
Grise Fiord
Melville Island
Bathurst Island
Devon Island
Banks Island
Sachs Harbour
Somerset Island
Prince of Wales Island
Victoria Island
King William Island
Baffin Island
Southampton Island
BAFFIN
KITIKMEOT
KEEWATIN
INUVIK
FORT SMITH
NUNAVUT
NORTHWEST TERRITORIES
YUKON TERRITORY
AK
BRITISH COLUMBIA
ALBERTA
SASKATCHEWAN
MANITOBA
QUEBEC
Arctic Bay
Nanisivik
Pond Inlet
Igloolik
Hall Beach
Pangnirtung
Iqaluit
Kimmirut
Cape Dorset
Repulse Bay
Coral Harbour
Chesterfield Inlet
Kangiqcliniq (Rankin Inlet)
Whale Cove
Arviat
Baker Lake
Kugaaruk
Gjoa Haven
Cambridge Bay
Kugluktuk
Bathurst Inlet
Holman
Paulatuk
Tuktoyaktuk
Aklavik
Inuvik
Fort McPherson
Tsiigehtchic
Old Crow
Colville Lake
Fort Good Hope
Norman Wells
Tulita
Deline
Wrigley
Fort Simpson
Jean-Marie River
Nahanni Butte
Fort Liard
Trout Lake
Rae Lakes
Wekweti
Wha Ti
Rae-Edzo
Yellowknife
Detah
Lutselke
Reliance
Fort Providence
Kakisa
Enterprise
Hay River
Fort Resolution
Fort Smith
Dawson
Stewart Crossing
Keno Hill
Mayo
Beaver Creek
Pelly Crossing
Burwash Landing
Destruction Bay
Haines Junction
Carmacks
Faro
Ross River
Whitehorse
Carcross
Tagish
Johnsons Crossing
Teslin
Swift River
Upper Liard
Watson Lake
Copyright American Map Corporation

HIGHWAY AND AIR MILEAGE:

280
223

Top figure: Highway mileage
Bottom figure: Air mileage

Mileage figures are approximate and are taken from various reliable sources.

	ALBUQUERQUE, NM	ATLANTA, GA	BALTIMORE, MD	BIRMINGHAM, AL	BOSTON, MA	BUFFALO, NY	CALGARY, AB	CHICAGO, IL	CINCINNATI, OH	CLEVELAND, OH	COLUMBUS, OH	DALLAS, TX	DENVER, CO	DETROIT, MI	EDMONTON, AB	HALIFAX, NS	HOUSTON, TX	INDIANAPOLIS, IN	JACKSONVILLE, FL	KANSAS CITY, MO	LAS VEGAS, NV	LOS ANGELES, CA	MEMPHIS, TN	MIAMI, FL
ALBUQUERQUE, NM		1400 1269	1890 1637	1260 1137	2197 1972	1770 1579	1513 1161	1301 1123	1378 1249	1583 1419	1456 1336	642 588	430 335	1550 1360	1698 1313	2766 2531	841 752	1270 1168	1641 1487	777 721	586 489	811 675	1030 940	1970 1696
ATLANTA, GA	1400 1269		662 576	151 125	1095 946	915 712	2357 1908	714 597	468 371	709 559	567 446	815 707	1429 1208	729 602	2326 1970	1655 1340	813 692	528 432	318 276	817 681	1979 1747	2218 1934	386 332	670 595
BALTIMORE, MD	1890 1637	662 576		778 693	413 370	355 281	2297 1975	702 613	494 430	358 312	417 336	1357 1196	1672 1503	513 404	2371 1986	982 765	1427 1240	575 515	772 666	1085 961	2401 2106	2671 2317	929 787	1094 946
BIRMINGHAM, AL	1260 1137	151 125	778 693		1202 1052	917 776	2298 1830	657 578	476 408	728 618	577 493	647 580	1209 1095	750 641	2306 1902	1759 1458	685 567	485 433	445 579	712 579	1834 1620	2062 1802	251 217	766 665
BOSTON, MA	2207 1972	1094 946	413 370	1202 1052		458 398	2530 2100	987 856	886 752	653 554	788 640	1807 1547	1985 1768	728 618	2539 2081	588 407	1890 1604	951 812	1189 1013	1442 1253	2752 2381	3051 2598	1350 1138	1541 1257
BUFFALO, NY	1770 1579	912 712	355 281	917 776	470 398		2157 1739	536 461	436 410	190 180	329 296	1383 1197	1548 1296	280 223	2166 1738	1009 773	1500 1288	501 443	1096 878	1000 864	2284 1986	2607 2202	934 808	1435 1183
CALGARY, AB	1513 1161	2357 1908	2297 1975	2298 1830	2530 2100	2157 1739		1664 1401	1967 1648	2006 1670	1995 1675	1937 1536	1109 897	1939 1574	188 171	2980 2341	2184 1758	1845 1552	2690 2193	1618 1254	1305 1026	1578 1189	2099 1628	3041 2494
CHICAGO, IL	1305 1123	692 597	702 613	657 578	981 856	535 461	1664 1401		299 254	346 310	344 287	340 797	1029 914	275 238	1678 1437	1538 1227	1092 936	188 166	1027 860	514 411	1780 1521	2112 1743	548 484	1391 1188
CINCINNATI, OH	1378 1249	468 371	494 430	476 408	886 752	436 410	1967 1648	299 254		247 226	107 96	964 793	1202 1061	260 238	1981 1686	1419 1141	1124 879	110 98	805 619	594 533	2088 1678	2218 1888	490 402	1155 948
CLEVELAND, OH	1583 1419	719 559	358 312	728 618	653 554	190 180	2006 1670	346 310	247 226		140 117	1200 1018	1359 1223	175 92	2020 1686	1193 940	1247 109	311 265	961 761	812 698	2093 1829	2417 2048	745 629	1313 1085
COLUMBUS, OH	1456 1336	567 446	417 336	577 493	788 640	329 296	1995 1675	344 287	107 96	140 117		1061 908	1239 1167	190 161	2010 1703	1319 1042	1176 993	174 182	863 663	665 628	2019 1771	2269 1984	598 517	1110 990
DALLAS, TX	642 588	815 707	1357 1196	647 580	1807 1547	1383 1197	1937 1536	940 797	964 793	1200 1018	1061 908		893 664	1166 991	2078 1652	2345 1954	244 224	893 755	918 897	505 450	1230 1081	1417 1244	468 415	1338 1104
DENVER, CO	430 335	1429 1208	1672 1503	1209 1095	1985 1768	1548 1296	1109 897	1029 914	1202 1081	1359 1223	1239 1167	893 864		1292 1150	1277 1032	2529 2122	1033 877	1061 995	1755 1460	615 555	758 616	1139 835	1062 880	2095 1721
DETROIT, MI	1550 1360	729 602	513 404	750 641	728 618	280 223	1939 1574	275 238	260 238	175 92	190 161	1168 991	1292 1150		1953 1589	1266 991	1315 1095	284 241	1043 824	758 641	2020 1758	2357 1980	730 622	1395 1152
EDMONTON, AB	1698 1313	2326 1970	2371 1986	2306 1902	2539 2081	2166 1738	187 171	1678 1437	1981 1686	2020 1686	2009 1703	2077 1652	1277 1032	1953 1589		2988 2341	2325 1875	1859 1594	2705 2257	1633 1336	1484 1197	1757 1360	2113 1707	3038 2566
HALIFAX, NS	2766 2351	1655 1342	982 765	1759 1458	588 407	1009 773	2980 2341	1538 1227	1419 1141	1193 940	1319 1012	2345 1954	2529 2122	1266 991	2988 2295		2421 2041	1492 1202	1739 1395	1968 1632	3266 2737	3539 2966	1888 1534	2092 1600
HOUSTON, TX	841 752	813 692	1427 1240	685 567	1890 1604	1500 1288	2184 1758	1092 936	1124 879	1247 1109	1176 993	244 224	1033 877	315 1095	2325 1875	2421 2041		1012 860	926 819	766 644	1467 1229	1555 1373	580 480	1237 964
INDIANAPOLIS, IN	1270 1168	528 432	575 515	485 433	951 812	501 443	1845 1552	188 166	110 98	311 265	174 182	893 755	1061 995	284 241	1859 1594	1492 1202	1012 860		846 693	492 450	1840 1591	2115 1806	457 383	1202 1023
JACKSONVILLE, FL	1641 1487	318 276	772 666	445 579	1189 1013	1096 878	2690 2193	1027 860	805 619	961 761	863 663	918 897	1755 1460	1043 824	2705 2257	1739 1395	926 819	846 693		1135 948	2241 1970	2407 2144	693 581	351 329
KANSAS CITY, MO	777 721	817 681	1085 961	712 579	1442 1253	1000 864	1618 1254	514 411	594 533	812 698	865 628	506 450	815 555	758 641	1633 1336	1968 1632	766 644	492 450	1135 948		1365 1145	1615 1357	467 374	1481 1240
LAS VEGAS, NV	586 489	1979 1747	2401 2106	1834 1620	2752 2381	2284 1986	1305 1026	1780 1521	2088 1678	2093 1829	2019 1771	1203 1081	758 616	2020 1758	1484 1197	3266 2737	1467 1229	1840 1591	2241 1970	1365 1145		272 227	1603 1416	2570 2175
LOS ANGELES, CA	811 675	2218 1934	2671 2317	2062 1802	3051 2598	2607 2202	1578 1189	2112 1743	2218 1888	2417 2048	2269 1984	1417 1244	1139 835	2357 1980	1757 1360	3539 2966	1555 1373	2115 1806	2407 2144	1615 1357	272 227		1829 1605	2748 2335
MEMPHIS, TN	1030 940	386 332	929 787	251 217	1350 1138	934 808	2099 1628	548 484	490 402	745 629	598 517	468 415	1062 880	730 662	2113 1707	1888 1543	580 480	457 383	693 581	467 374	1603 1416	1829 1605		1024 867
MIAMI, FL	1970 1696	670 595	1094 946	766 665	1541 1257	1435 1183	3041 2494	1391 1188	1155 946	1313 1085	1110 990	1338 1104	2095 1721	1395 1152	3037 2566	2092 1600	1237 964	1282 1023	351 329	1481 1240	2570 2175	2748 2335	1024 867	
MILWAUKEE, WI	1375 1139	804 669	783 641	744 661	1097 860	592 464	1592 1341	89 74	389 318	436 331	430 331	1025 843	1043 908	362 244	1606 1369	1630 1219	1179 994	276 237	1122 930	575 438	1797 1524	2155 1745	633 556	1471 1259
MINNEAPOLIS, MN	1233 979	1108 906	1105 936	1067 862	1411 1124	951 733	1257 1048	417 340	715 596	761 627	761 627	968 856	871 697	691 539	1271 1083	1909 1951	1202 1051	601 507	1434 1180	463 409	1659 1300	1977 1525	871 699	1779 1506
MONTREAL, PQ	2121 1870	1233 1046	563 460	1300 1084	323 254	393 330	2268 1882	859 742	821 745	577 509	716 623	1761 1508	1855 1654	578 528	2276 1852	715 492	1888 1621	857 753	1354 1139	1333 1146	2583 2274	2917 2488	1302 1135	1693 1320
NASHVILLE, TN	1257 1117	254 214	714 587	200 182	1149 942	725 633	2110 1696	460 401	292 230	537 453	393 337	679 610	1207 1023	549 466	2137 1757	1679 1351	805 663	300 249	574 490	583 480	1811 1581	2036 1785	213 200	923 807
NEW ORLEANS, LA	1147 1033	503 425	1137 998	348 312	1548 1367	1271 1097	2442 1909	941 831	828 701	1077 923	928 806	506 433	1293 1075	1087 938	2456 2004	2105 1753	367 311	829 710	571 516	837 678	1732 1500	1898 1666	407 353	885 672
NEW YORK CITY, NY	1999 1816	865 755	193 179	976 864	215 190	397 286	2466 2055	829 2035	643 579	495 408	553 472	1602 1369	1815 1629	661 486	2480 2032	795 595	1655 995	727 650	974 831	1245 1098	2572 2237	2827 2452	127 957	1333 1092
OKLAHOMA CITY, OK	542 515	859 761	1317 1177	718 626	1709 1505	1272 1135	1743 1356	823 694	873 756	1059 954	946 866	213 185	620 494	1054 911	1873 1467	2232 1891	460 407	761 689	1158 988	354 306	1113 986	1349 1175	479 432	1512 1223
OTTAWA, ON	2044 1770	1143 929	515 425	1221 1011	382 315	324 236	2106 1794	759 651	745 626	508 406	649 528	1669 1422	1759 1530	488 426	2159 1769	831 594	1783 1520	780 660	1264 1090	1223 1058	2488 2145	2761 2374	1221 1037	1616 1378
PHILADELPHIA, PA	1933 1752	770 672	97 96	882 765	309 273	363 283	2418 2010	770 671	699 614	428 363	779 689	1511 1294	1729 1577	594 449	2415 2013	889 673	1568 1339	650 589	872 749	1171 1039	2481 2183	2740 2395	1038 881	1240 1018
PHOENIX, AZ	456 330	1838 1587	2319 2002	1672 1455	2696 2300	2249 1909	1534 1213	1759 1449	1858 1569	2062 1746	1918 1671	1023 890	837 588	2012 1986	1717 1380	3207 2674	1163 1016	1739 1491	2026 1791	1243 1048	285 255	394 258	1473 1263	2362 1977
PITTSBURGH, PA	1629 1498	714 526	238 195	774 608	595 489	221 182	2121 1784	463 407	285 256	131 110	184 144	1239 1060	1444 1311	291 202	2136 1800	1153 884	1370 131	359 328	882 699	875 775	2207 1910	2481 2130	782 626	1236 1012
PORTLAND, OR	1372 1107	279 2172	2807 2358	2701 2065	3166 2537	2693 2156	810 548	2152 1748	2448 1975	2486 2048	2475 2034	2081 1637	1313 985	2422 1959	992 668	3551 2822	2294 1824	2322 1877	3037 2434	1882 1492	996 762	980 831	2371 1853	3350 2700
QUEBEC, QC	2279 2000	1859 1134	689 583	1442 1227	386 305	542 462	2420 1949	994 884	969 854	726 636	867 755	1904 1656	1985 1752	722 661	2428 1907	614 394	2017 1749	1014 894	1447 1264	1468 1291	2773 2365	2996 2595	1455 1266	1800 1529
ST. JOHNS, NF	3612 2872	2486 1890	1829 1314	2606 2007	1434 965	1855 1307	3808 2719	2375 1752	2266 1685	2039 1479	2166 1586	3191 2499	3366 2623	2104 1521	3817 2644	922 550	3267 2563	2339 1741	2586 1926	2815 2159	4104 3232	4377 3463	2735 2090	2938 2102
ST. LOUIS, MO	1041 938	562 484	823 737	496 401	1193 1042	757 668	1836 1441	290 259	341 308	556 492	414 410	656 542	871 788	532 453	1851 1505	1732 1434	797 678	240 230	881 759	255 234	1620 1372	1864 1585	294 248	1232 1065
SALT LAKE CITY, UT	608 486	1937 1589	2093 1864	1786 1468	2422 2103	1945 1705	883 717	1436 1259	1654 1449	1769 1569	1714 1529	1248 1005	520 576	1701 1491	1062 882	2920 2439	1460 1202	1552 1356	2265 1839	1127 927	419 368	723 581	1565 1255	2583 2089
SAN ANTONIO, TX	730 614	995 875	1632 1407	858 745	2018 1764	1625 1432	2040 1694	1209 1041	1206 1025	1453 1246	1313 1140	270 253	946 794	1445 1276	2302 1824	2605 2173	197 192	1191 986	1082 1011	784 697	1287 1069	1387 1198	725 626	1385 1143
SAN DIEGO, CA	811 624	2146 1891	2681 2295	1994 1753	2984 2588	2531 2196	1641 1268	2093 1729	2189 1865	2385 2031	2256 1965	1348 1196	1095 840	2368 1968	1819 1439	3565 2950	1490 1308	2078 1783	2355 2093	1488 1337	336 258	127 101	1805 1567	2678 2267
SAN FRANCISCO, CA	1109 905	2525 2141	2850 2456	2381 2021	3178 2701	2706 2304	1401 1005	2193 1856	2412 2036	2486 2048	2455 2120	1773 1488	1268 949	2450 2089	1583 1168	3658 3041	1947 1646	2303 1947	2789 2374	1884 1507	570 419	397 351	2144 1806	3101 2592
SEATTLE, WA	1468 1184	2722 2182	2748 2334	2576 2083	3060 2494	2599 2119	672 442	2067 1734	2380 1964	2415 2025	2394 2017	2139 1681	1371 989	2344 1935	833 562	3391 2760	2364 1888	2256 1869	3051 2449	1876 1504	1180 869	1157 959	2359 1869	3393 2730
TORONTO, ON	1787 1565	1011 782	457 384	1017 806	609 463	105 69	2087 1689	515 430	543 408	296 187	436 301	1435 1146	1492 1332	240 206	2095 1685	1048 786	1569 1299	524 431	1199 957	1006 822	2251 1952	2523 2175	956 812	1494 1271
VANCOUVER, BC	1578 1285	2764 2239	2854 2364	2688 2146	3115 2509	2688 2139	603 418	2163 1774	2464 2013	2504 2058	2494 1205	2267 1767	1438 1108	2438 1963	764 507	3559 2758	2497 1978	2342 1916	3098 2517	1971 1568	1318 984	1284 1072	2451 1936	3428 2802
WASHINGTON, DC	1844 1651	638 540	38 37	745 660	440 400	2382 291	2351 1974	698 594	500 400	362 322	418 322	1391 1173	1662 1485	519 394	2365 1988	1023 789	1430 1212	568 491	747 635	1054 939	2420 2077	2671 2294	895 759	1096 922
WINNIPEG, MB	1534 1128	1546 1288	1545 1242	1486 1247	1699 1350	1325 975	850 750	852 718	1155 967	1194 944	1183 971	1296 1181	1111 795	1116 848	841 744	2148 1604	1540 1392	1033 881	1880 1572	832 755	1729 1310	2002 1535	1303 1083	2213 1894

280
223

Top figure: Highway mileage
Bottom figure: Air mileage

Mileage figures are approximate and are taken from various reliable sources.

MILWAUKEE, WI	MINNEAPOLIS, MN	MONTREAL, PQ	NASHVILLE, TN	NEW ORLEANS, LA	NEW YORK CITY, NY	OKLAHOMA CITY, OK	OTTAWA, ON	PHILADELPHIA, PA	PHOENIX, AZ	PITTSBURGH, PA	PORTLAND, OR	QUEBEC, QC	ST. JOHNS, NF	ST. LOUIS, MO	SALT LAKE CITY, UT	SAN ANTONIO, TX	SAN DIEGO, CA	SAN FRANCISCO, CA	SEATTLE, WA	TORONTO, ON	VANCOUVER, BC	WASHINGTON, DC	WINNIPEG, MB	
1375 1139	1233 929	2121 1870	1257 1117	1147 1033	1999 1816	542 515	2044 1770	1933 1752	456 330	1629 1498	1372 1107	2279 2000	3612 2872	1041 938	608 486	730 614	811 624	1109 905	1468 1184	1787 1565	1578 1285	1844 1651	1534 1128	ALBUQUERQUE, NM
804 669	1108 906	1233 1046	254 214	503 425	865 755	859 761	1143 929	770 672	1838 1587	714 526	279 2172	1859 1134	2486 1890	562 484	1937 1589	995 875	2146 1891	2525 2141	2722 2182	1011 782	2764 2239	638 540	1546 1288	ATLANTA, GA
783 641	1105 936	563 460	714 587	1137 998	193 179	1317 1177	515 425	97 96	2319 2002	238 195	2807 2358	689 583	1829 1314	823 737	2093 1864	1632 1407	2681 2295	2850 2456	2728 2334	457 384	2856 2364	38 37	1545 1242	BALTIMORE, MD
744 661	1067 862	1300 1084	200 182	348 312	976 864	718 626	1221 1011	882 785	1672 1455	774 608	2701 2065	1442 1227	2606 2007	496 401	1786 1468	858 745	1994 1753	2381 2021	2576 2083	1017 806	2688 2146	745 660	1486 1247	BIRMINGHAM, AL
1097 860	1411 1124	323 254	1149 942	1548 1367	215 190	1709 1505	382 315	309 273	2696 2300	595 489	3166 2537	386 305	1434 965	1193 1042	2422 2103	2018 1764	2984 2588	3178 2701	3060 2494	609 463	3115 2509	440 400	1699 1350	BOSTON, MA
592 464	951 733	393 330	725 633	1271 1097	397 286	1272 1135	324 236	363 283	2249 1909	221 182	2693 2156	542 462	1855 1307	757 668	1945 1705	1625 1432	2531 2196	2706 2304	2599 2119	105 69	2688 2139	382 291	1326 995	BUFFALO, NY
1592 1341	1257 1048	2268 1882	2110 1696	2442 1909	2466 2035	1743 1356	2106 1794	2418 2010	1534 1213	2121 1784	810 548	2420 1949	3808 2719	1836 1441	883 717	2040 1694	1641 1268	1401 1005	672 442	2087 1689	603 418	2351 1974	850 750	CALGARY, AB
89 74	417 340	859 742	460 401	941 831	829 717	823 694	759 651	770 671	1759 1449	463 407	2152 1748	994 884	2375 1752	290 259	1436 1259	1209 1041	2093 1729	2193 1856	2067 1734	515 430	2163 1774	698 594	852 718	CHICAGO, IL
389 318	715 596	821 745	292 230	828 701	643 579	873 756	745 626	699 614	1858 1569	285 256	2448 1975	969 854	2266 1685	341 308	1654 1449	1206 1025	2189 1865	2412 2036	2380 1964	543 408	2464 2013	500 400	1155 967	CINCINNATI, OH
436 331	761 627	577 509	537 453	1077 923	495 408	1059 954	508 406	428 363	2062 1746	131 110	2488 2048	726 636	2039 1479	556 492	1769 1569	1453 1246	2385 2031	2486 2048	2415 2025	296 187	2504 2058	362 294	1194 944	CLEVELAND, OH
430 331	761 27	716 623	393 337	928 806	553 472	946 866	649 528	779 689	1908 1671	184 144	2475 2034	867 755	2166 1586	414 410	1714 1529	1313 1140	2256 1965	2455 2120	2394 2017	436 301	2494 2051	418 322	1183 971	COLUMBUS, OH
1025 843	968 856	1761 1508	679 610	506 433	1602 31369	213 185	1669 1422	1511 1294	1023 890	1239 1060	2081 1637	1904 1656	3191 2499	656 542	1248 1005	270 253	1348 1196	1773 1488	2139 1681	1435 1146	2267 1767	1391 1173	1296 1181	DALLAS, TX
1043 908	871 697	1855 1654	1207 1023	1293 1075	1815 1629	620 494	1759 1530	1729 1577	837 588	1444 1311	1313 985	1985 1752	3366 2623	871 788	520 576	946 794	1095 840	1268 949	1371 989	1492 1332	1438 1108	1662 1485	1111 795	DENVER, CO
362 244	691 539	578 528	549 466	1087 938	661 486	1054 911	488 426	594 449	2012 1986	291 202	2422 1959	722 661	2104 1521	532 453	1701 1491	1445 1276	2368 1966	2450 2089	2344 1935	240 206	2438 1963	519 394	1116 848	DETROIT, MI
1606 1369	1271 1083	2276 1852	2137 1757	2456 2004	2480 2032	1783 1467	2159 1769	2415 2013	1717 1380	2136 1800	992 608	2428 1907	3817 2644	1851 1505	1062 882	2302 1824	1819 1439	1583 1168	833 562	2095 1685	764 507	2365 1988	841 744	EDMONTON, AB
1630 1219	1909 1451	715 492	1679 1351	2105 1753	795 595	2232 1891	831 594	889 673	3207 2674	1153 884	3551 2822	614 394	922 550	1732 1434	2920 2439	2605 2173	3565 2950	3658 3041	3391 2767	1048 786	3559 2758	1023 789	2148 1604	HALIFAX, NS
1179 994	1202 1051	1888 1621	805 663	367 311	1655 1418	460 407	1783 1520	1568 1339	1163 1016	1370 1131	2294 1824	2017 1749	3267 2563	797 678	1460 1202	197 192	1490 1308	1947 1646	2364 1888	1569 1299	2497 1978	1430 1212	1540 1392	HOUSTON, TX
276 237	601 507	857 753	300 249	829 710	727 650	761 689	780 660	650 589	1739 1491	359 328	2322 1877	1014 894	2339 1741	240 230	1552 1356	1191 986	2078 1783	2303 1947	2256 1869	524 431	2343 1916	568 491	1033 881	INDIANAPOLIS, IN
1122 930	1434 1180	1354 1139	574 490	571 516	974 831	1158 988	1264 1090	872 749	2026 1791	882 699	3037 2434	1447 1264	2586 1926	881 759	2265 1839	1082 1011	2355 2093	2789 2374	3051 2449	1199 957	3098 2517	747 635	1880 1572	JACKSONVILLE, FL
575 438	763 409	1333 1146	563 480	837 678	1245 1098	354 306	1223 1058	1171 1039	1243 1048	875 775	1882 1492	1468 1291	2815 2159	255 234	1127 927	784 697	1588 1337	1884 1507	1876 1504	1006 822	1971 1568	1054 939	832 755	KANSAS CITY, MO
1797 1524	1659 1300	2538 2274	1811 1581	1732 1500	2572 2237	1113 986	2488 2145	2481 2183	285 255	2207 1910	996 762	2773 2365	4104 3232	1620 1372	419 368	1287 1069	336 258	570 419	1180 869	2251 1952	1318 984	2420 2077	1729 1310	LAS VEGAS, NV
2155 1745	1977 1525	2917 2488	2036 1785	1898 1666	2827 2452	1349 1175	2761 2374	2740 2395	394 258	2481 2130	980 831	2996 2595	4377 3463	1864 1585	723 581	1387 1198	127 101	397 351	1157 959	2523 2175	1284 1072	2671 2294	2002 1535	LOS ANGELES, CA
633 556	871 699	1302 1135	213 200	407 353	1127 957	479 432	1221 1032	1038 881	1473 1263	782 656	2371 1853	1455 1266	2736 2090	294 248	1565 1255	725 626	1805 1567	2144 1806	2359 1869	956 812	2451 1936	895 759	1303 1083	MEMPHIS, TN
1471 1259	1779 1506	1693 1320	923 807	885 672	1333 1092	1512 1223	1616 1378	1240 1018	2362 1977	1236 1012	3360 2700	1800 1529	2938 2102	1232 1065	2583 2089	1385 1143	2678 2267	3101 2592	3393 2730	1494 1271	3429 2802	1096 922	2213 1894	MIAMI, FL
	338 297	947 756	548 475	1038 903	917 733	896 736	852 631	862 695	1815 1460	561 430	2090 1717	1087 861	2468 1732	372 317	1448 1246	1287 1095	2132 1739	2203 1844	1995 1694	610 434	2091 1722	793 623	775 643	MILWAUKEE, WI
338 297		1248 1102	855 695	1282 1046	1247 1017	816 694	1068 858	1185 985	1664 1278	879 435	1728 1426	1350 1070	2737 1935	577 457	1243 989	1245 1097	2001 1532	2009 1586	1654 1397	906 780	1756 1427	1106 927	446 386	MINNEAPOLIS, MN
947 756	1248 1102		1109 977	1636 1435	385 333	1632 1432	118 102	469 426	2594 2479	601 519	2917 2504	161 144	1543 1002	1095 961	2262 2010	2051 1959	2919 2501	3013 2608	2798 2446	344 322	2847 2295	604 499	1436 1134	MONTREAL, PQ
548 475	855 695	1109 977		535 471	925 758	704 615	1030 863	830 681	1701 1448	570 462	2461 1972	1254 1087	2525 1899	308 271	1723 1403	934 822	1997 1751	2395 1969	2506 1978	776 640	2517 2031	684 552	1299 1081	NASHVILLE, TN
1038 903	1282 1046	1636 1435	535 471		1326 1174	687 567	1564 1311	1257 1092	1523 1309	1119 919	2580 2050	1788 1528	2951 2301	701 601	1762 1431	547 495	1840 1599	2414 1921	2630 2094	1307 1143	2780 2179	1123 964	1655 1418	NEW ORLEANS, LA
917 733	1247 1017	385 333	925 758	1326 1174		1487 1335	423 339	95 84	2464 2144	378 323	2976 2441	516 442	1642 1144	966 879	2245 1975	1820 1580	2803 2435	2998 2573	2895 2408	516 367	2965 2435	228 210	1654 1290	NEW YORK CITY, NY
896 736	816 694	1632 1432	704 615	687 567	1487 1335		1531 1334	1408 1268	988 883	119 1010	1954 1484	1752 1569	3079 2429	521 462	1116 865	477 407	1334 1136	1672 1386	1996 1521	1249 1101	2083 1605	1333 1147	1092 996	OKLAHOMA CITY, OK
852 631	1068 858	118 102	1030 863	1564 1311	423 339	1531 1334		445 375	2485 2089	524 407	2630 2499	271 235	1659 1102	1017 882	2142 1864	1930 1659	2800 2361	2879 2499	2562 2197	261 219	2730 2205	554 455	1319 1044	OTTAWA, ON
862 695	1185 985	469 426	830 681	1257 1092	95 84	1408 1268	445 375		2407 2082	301 274	2900 2411	595 506	1737 1222	890 820	2193 1932	1737 1502	2773 2376	2948 2526	2833 2383	465 348	2917 2405	134 133	1606 1269	PHILADELPHIA, PA
1815 1460	1664 1278	2594 2479	1701 1448	1523 1309	2464 2144	988 883	2485 2089	2407 2082		2119 1821	1345 1009	2720 2317	4063 3190	1500 1267	662 506	1002 843	353 304	787 655	1519 1112	2296 1878	1595 1223	2304 1975	1956 1362	PHOENIX, AZ
561 430	879 735	601 519	570 462	1119 919	378 323	1119 1010	524 407	301 274	2119 1821		2601 2148	742 620	2000 1431	599 576	1916 1779	1476 1277	2440 2106	2655 2453	2537 2321	324 255	2620 2171	236 218	1309 1058	PITTSBURGH, PA
2090 1717	1728 1426	2917 2504	2461 1972	2580 2050	2976 2441	1954 1484	2630 2499	2900 2411	1345 1009	2601 2148		2991 2428	4379 3234	2131 1708	822 630	2095 1714	1086 933	642 540	179 132	2621 2182	315 257	2889 2399	1496 1221	PORTLAND, OR
1087 861	1350 1070	161 144	1254 1087	1788 1528	516 442	1752 1569	271 235	595 506	2720 2317	742 620	2991 2428		1432 872	1252 1117	2377 2057	2164 1891	3034 2585	3114 2656	2830 2367	495 453	2999 2366	730 617	1588 1209	QUEBEC, QC
2468 1732	2737 1935	1543 1002	2525 1899	2951 2301	1642 1144	3079 2429	1659 1102	1737 1222	4063 3190	2000 1431	4379 3234	1432 872		2579 1972	3758 2915	3452 2722	4412 3456	4495 3508	4219 3154	1876 1312	4386 3135	1869 1347	2976 2019	ST. JOHNS, NF
372 317	577 457	1095 961	308 271	701 601	966 879	521 462	1017 882	890 820	1500 1267	599 576	2131 1708	1252 1117	2579 1972		1381 1156	952 786	1833 1557	2138 1736	2163 1710	749 639	2215 1776	826 707	1026 849	ST. LOUIS, MO
1448 1246	1243 989	2262 2010	1723 1403	1762 1431	2245 1975	1116 865	2142 1864	2193 1932	662 506	1916 1779	822 630	2377 2057	3758 2195	1381 1156		1334 1086	755 626	756 600	884 696	1910 1688	960 799	2097 1844	1319 849	SALT LAKE CITY, UT
1287 1095	1245 1097	2051 1959	934 822	547 495	1820 1580	477 407	1930 1659	1737 1502	1002 843	1476 1277	2095 1714	2164 1891	3452 2722	952 786	1334 1086		1297 1129	1740 1487	2180 1775	1646 1481	2329 1880	1587 1371	1566 954	SAN ANTONIO, TX
2132 1739	2001 1532	2919 2501	1997 1751	1840 1599	2803 2435	1334 1136	2730 2361	2773 2376	353 304	2440 2106	1086 933	3034 2585	4412 3456	1833 1557	755 626	1297 1129		514 456	1258 1053	2649 2179	1406 1175	2602 2264	2064 1562	SAN DIEGO, CA
2203 1844	2009 1586	3013 2608	2395 1969	2414 1921	2998 2573	1672 1386	2879 2499	2948 2526	787 655	2655 2453	642 540	3114 2656	4495 3508	2138 1736	756 600	1740 1487	514 456		835 675	2627 2286	954 791	2833 2436	1955 1509	SAN FRANCISCO, CA
1995 1694	1654 1397	2798 2446	2500 1978	2630 2094	2895 2408	1996 1521	2562 2197	2833 2383	1519 1112	2537 2321	179 132	2830 2367	4219 3154	2163 1710	884 696	2180 1775	1258 1053	835 675		2564 2286	142 117	2771 2323	1471 1157	SEATTLE, WA
610 434	906 780	344 322	776 640	1307 1143	516 367	1249 1101	261 219	465 348	2296 1878	324 255	2621 2182	495 453	1876 1312	749 639	1910 1688	1646 1481	2649 2179	2627 2286	2564 2286		2654 2091	571 365	1255 943	TORONTO, ON
2091 1722	1756 1427	2847 2295	2517 2031	2780 2179	2965 2435	2083 1605	2730 2205	2917 2405	1595 1223	2620 2171	315 257	2999 2366	4388 3135	2215 1776	960 799	2329 1880	1406 1175	954 791	142 117	2654 2091		2849 2361	1451 1161	VANCOUVER, BC
793 623	1106 927	604 499	684 552	1123 964	228 210	1333 1147	554 455	134 133	2304 1975	236 218	2889 2339	730 617	1869 1347	826 707	2097 1844	1587 1371	2602 2264	2833 2436	2771 2323	571 365	2849 2361		1539 1245	WASHINGTON, DC
775 643	446 386	1436 1134	1299 1081	1655 1419	1654 1290	1092 996	1319 1044	1606 1269	1956 1362	1309 1058	1496 1221	1588 1209	2976 2019	1026 849	1319 849	1566 954	2064 1562	1955 1509	1471 1157	1255 943	1451 1161	1539 1245		WINNIPEG, MB

PACIFIC
2 PM
MOUNTAIN
3 PM
CENTRAL
4 PM
MANITOBA
604
250
604, 778
Vancouver
Victoria
BRITISH COLUMBIA
Calgary
403
Medicine Hat
Lethbridge
ALBERTA
Saskatoon
306
Swift Current
Moose Jaw
Regina
SASKATCHEWAN
CANADA
Dauphin
204
Winnipeg
Brandon
Bellingham
360
WASHINGTON
206
Everett
Seattle
Aberdeen
Tacoma
425
253
Olympia
Spokane
509
Yakima
Walla Walla
Astoria
503
Vancouver
Portland
971, 503
Salem
OREGON
Eugene
Bend
541
Baker City
Burns
9
Medford
Klamath Falls
Coeur d'Alene
Lewiston
MONTANA
Kalispell
Havre
Great Falls
Missoula
Helena
406
Butte-Silver Bow
Billings
Miles City
NORTH DAKOTA
Williston
Minot
Grand Forks
701
Bismarck
Fargo
5
IDAHO
208
Boise
Idaho Falls
Pocatello
Twin Falls
WYOMING
Cody
Sheridan
307
Casper
Rock Springs
Laramie
Cheyenne
SOUTH DAKOTA
Aberdeen
Rapid City
605
Pierre
Mitchell
Sioux Falls
CALIFORNIA
Redding
530
707
Chico
Ukiah
Santa Rosa
San Francisco
415
Berkeley
925
Oakland
510
Fremont
408
650
Sacramento
916
Stockton
Modesto
209
San Jose
Monterey
Salinas
831
Fresno
559
Visalia
San Luis Obispo
805
Santa Maria
Santa Barbara
661
Bakersfield
760
Lancaster
818
Barstow
Los Angeles
213, 323
310
Pasadena
626
714
Long Beach
562
949
San Bernardino
909
Palm Springs
Pacific Ocean
858
San Diego
619
Tijuana
Mexicali
Ensenada
BAJA CALIFORNIA
NEVADA
Winnemucca
Elko
Reno
775
Carson City
Ely
Las Vegas
702
Needles
UTAH
Logan
Ogden
Salt Lake City
801
385
Provo
8
Richfield
435
Cedar City
Blanding
COLORADO
Greeley
Julesburg
970
Boulder
Denver
Vail
303
720
Grand Junction
Colorado Springs
Pueblo
719
Trinidad
NEBRASKA
Scottsbluff
308
North Platte
Grand Island
Hastings
Sioux City
402
Columbus
Omaha
Lincoln
KANSAS
6
785
Salina
Hutchinson
Dodge City
316
620
Wichita
ARIZONA
Kingman
928
Flagstaff
Winslow
Prescott
602
Phoenix
623
480
Yuma
520
Tucson
Nogales
Douglas
SONORA
Heroica Nogales
Hermosillo
NEW MEXICO
Farmington
Gallup
Santa Fe
Albuquerque
505
Clovis
Roswell
Silver City
Carlsbad
Hobbs
Ciudad Juárez
El Paso
CHIHUAHUA
Chihuahua
MEXICO
OKLAHOMA
Woodward
Enid
Tulsa
918
Oklahoma City
405
Elk City
580
Lawton
Ada
TEXAS
Amarillo
806
Lubbock
Wichita Falls
940
Fort Worth
Dallas
817, 682
214, 469, 972
Abilene
Big Spring
Midland
Odessa
7
903
254
Waco
Pecos
San Angelo
915
Fort Stockton
Alpine
Austin
512
979
Del Rio
210
San Antonio
830
COAHUILA DE ZARAGOZA
Victoria
361
Corpus Christi
Nuevo Laredo
Laredo
Monclova
956
NUEVO LEÓN
Reynosa
Brownsville
Saltillo
Monterrey
TAMAULIPAS
Ciudad Victoria
RUSSIA
Barrow
ALASKA
ALASKA
1 PM
Fort Yukon
Nome
Fairbanks
9
907
Bethel
Anchorage
Seward
Kodiak
YUKON TERR.
867
Dawson
CANADA
PACIFIC
2 PM
Whitehorse
Skagway
B.C.
Juneau
Sitka
Ketchikan
HAWAII
Lihue
Waipahu
Honolulu
Kahului
808
9
HAWAII
12 NOON
Hilo
Kailua

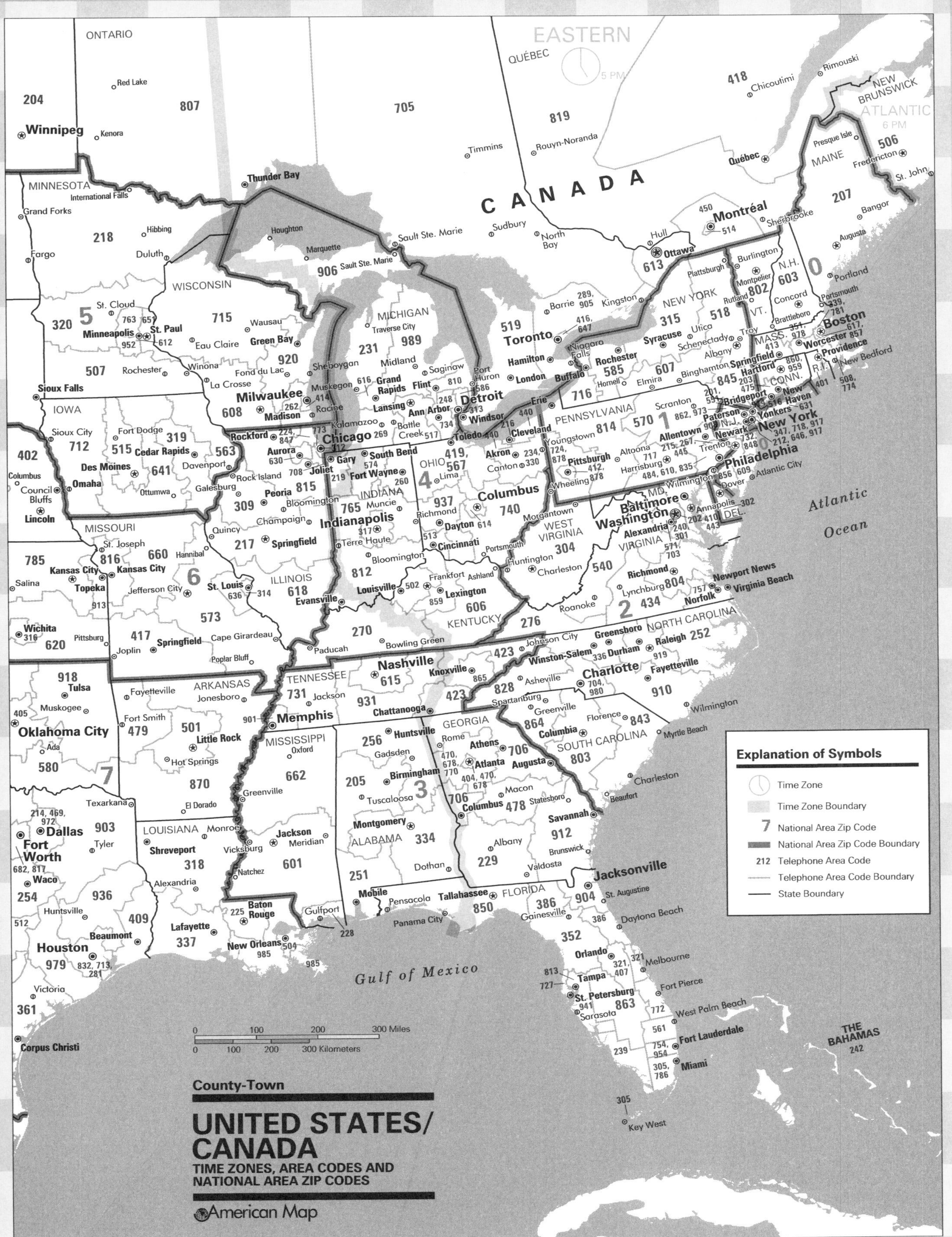

County-Town
UNITED STATES/ CANADA
TIME ZONES, AREA CODES AND NATIONAL AREA ZIP CODES
American Map
Explanation of Symbols
Time Zone
Time Zone Boundary
7 National Area Zip Code
National Area Zip Code Boundary
212 Telephone Area Code
Telephone Area Code Boundary
State Boundary
0 100 200 300 Miles
0 100 200 300 Kilometers
EASTERN
5 PM
ATLANTIC
6 PM
CANADA
ONTARIO
QUÉBEC
NEW BRUNSWICK
Atlantic Ocean
Gulf of Mexico
THE BAHAMAS
242
MINNESOTA
WISCONSIN
MICHIGAN
IOWA
MISSOURI
ILLINOIS
INDIANA
OHIO
KENTUCKY
TENNESSEE
ARKANSAS
MISSISSIPPI
ALABAMA
GEORGIA
FLORIDA
LOUISIANA
SOUTH CAROLINA
NORTH CAROLINA
VIRGINIA
WEST VIRGINIA
PENNSYLVANIA
NEW YORK
MAINE
VT.
N.H.
MASS.
CONN.
R.I.
N.J.
MD.
DEL.
204 Winnipeg
807 Red Lake
Kenora
705 Timmins
819 Rouyn-Noranda
418 Chicoutimi
Rimouski
506 Fredericton
Presque Isle
St. John
Québec
450 Montréal 514
Sherbrooke
Hull
613 Ottawa
Thunder Bay
Sudbury
North Bay
Sault Ste. Marie
Kingston
Barrie 289, 905
519 Toronto 416, 647
Hamilton
London
Windsor
Niagara Falls
207 Bangor
Augusta
Portland
603 Concord
802 Burlington
Montpelier
International Falls
Grand Forks
218 Hibbing
Duluth
Fargo
320 St. Cloud
Minneapolis
St. Paul
507 Rochester
Sioux Falls
715 Wausau
Eau Claire
Green Bay 920
Winona
La Crosse
Fond du Lac
608 Madison
Milwaukee 262 414
Racine
Houghton
Marquette
906
231 Traverse City
989 Midland
Saginaw
616 Grand Rapids
Muskegon
Sheboygan
Flint 810
Lansing
517
Ann Arbor 734
Kalamazoo 269
Battle Creek
Port Huron
Detroit 313 586 248
712 Sioux City
Fort Dodge
515 Des Moines
319 Cedar Rapids
563 Davenport
641
Ottumwa
402 Omaha
Council Bluffs
Lincoln
Columbus
Rockford
Aurora 630
Chicago 312
Joliet
Rock Island
Galesburg
Peoria 309
815
Bloomington
Champaign
217 Springfield
Quincy
Hannibal
Gary
South Bend 574
219
Fort Wayne 260
765 Muncie
Indianapolis 317
Terre Haute
812 Bloomington
Evansville
618
Toledo
Lima
419, 567
937 Dayton
Columbus 614
740
Cincinnati 513
Cleveland 216
Akron 234, 330
Canton
440
Youngstown
Erie
814
724, 878
Pittsburgh 412
Wheeling
Altoona
Harrisburg 717
570 Scranton
Allentown 484, 610, 835
215, 267
Philadelphia
Trenton
Newark
Paterson
New York 347, 718, 917, 212, 646
Yonkers
Buffalo
Rochester 585
716
Syracuse 315
Utica
Schenectady
Albany 518
Troy
Binghamton 607
Elmira
Plattsburgh
Springfield 413
Hartford 860, 959
203, 475
New Haven
Bridgeport
Boston 617
Worcester 857
Providence 401
New Bedford
Atlantic City
Dover 302
Baltimore
Annapolis
Washington 202
Alexandria
240, 301
443, 410
571, 703
304 Charleston
Morgantown
Huntington
Portsmouth
540
Richmond 804
Lynchburg
434
Roanoke
757 Norfolk
Newport News
Virginia Beach
252 Raleigh
919
Durham 336
Greensboro
Winston-Salem
910 Fayetteville
Wilmington
Charlotte 704, 980
828 Asheville
Johnson City
423
Knoxville 865
Nashville 615
731 Jackson
931
Chattanooga
Memphis 901
606 Lexington 859
Frankfort
Ashland
502 Louisville
270 Bowling Green
Paducah
785 Salina
Topeka
Kansas City 816 913
St. Joseph
660
Jefferson City
St. Louis 636 314
573
Cape Girardeau
417 Springfield
Joplin
Poplar Bluff
Wichita 316
620 Pittsburg
918 Tulsa
Muskogee
405 Oklahoma City
Ada
580
479 Fort Smith
Fayetteville
Jonesboro
501 Little Rock
Hot Springs
870
El Dorado
Texarkana
Greenville
662 Oxford
Jackson
601 Meridian
Vicksburg
Natchez
Gulfport 228
256 Huntsville
Gadsden
205 Birmingham
Tuscaloosa
Montgomery 334
Dothan
251 Mobile
Rome
470, 678, 770 Atlanta 404
706 Athens
Augusta
Columbus
478 Macon
Statesboro
912 Savannah
229 Albany
Valdosta
Brunswick
864 Spartanburg
Greenville
803 Columbia
843 Florence
Myrtle Beach
Charleston
Beaufort
Jacksonville 904
St. Augustine
Daytona Beach
386 Gainesville
352
Orlando 321 407
Melbourne
813 Tampa
727 St. Petersburg
941 Sarasota
863
772 Fort Pierce
561 West Palm Beach
754, 954 Fort Lauderdale
305, 786 Miami
239
Key West
Tallahassee
850 Pensacola
Panama City
Shreveport 318
Monroe
Alexandria
337 Lafayette
225 Baton Rouge
New Orleans 504 985
214, 469, 972 Dallas
903 Tyler
Fort Worth 682, 817
254 Waco
936
Huntsville
409 Beaumont
Houston 979 832, 713, 281
512
Victoria
361 Corpus Christi
0 1 2 3 4 5 6 7

FREQUENTLY CALLED CITIES in the United States, Canada, and the Caribbean

Alabama

Birmingham 205
Gadsden 256
Huntsville 256
Mobile 251
Montgomery 334
Tuscaloosa 205

Alaska

all points 907

Arizona

Flagstaff 928
Kingman 928
Page 928
Phoenix 602
Tucson 520
Yuma 928

Arkansas

El Dorado 870
Fort Smith ....479 & 501
Hot Springs 501
Jonesboro 870
Little Rock 501
Pine Bluff 870

California

Anaheim 714
Bakersfield 661
Beverly Hills 818
Burbank 818
Chico 530
El Centro 760
Eureka 707
Fresno 559
Irvine 949
Los Angeles:
Downtown 213
Greater Metro Area 323
Lancaster 661
Modesto 209
Monterey 831
Oakland 510
Oceanside 858
Palo Alto 650
Palm Springs 760
Pasadena 626
Redding 530
Sacramento 916
San Bernardino 909
San Diego 619
San Francisco 415
San Jose 408
Santa Barbara 805
Santa Rosa 707

Colorado

Alamosa 719
Aspen 970
Colorado Springs 719
Denver ....303 & 720
Durango 970
Grand Junction 970
Pueblo 719

Connecticut

Bridgeport ....203 & 475
Hartford ....860 & 959
New Haven ....203 & 475
New London ....860 & 959
Stamford ....203 & 475
Waterbury ....203 & 475

Delaware

all points 302

District of Columbia

Washington, D.C. 202

Florida

Clearwater 727
Daytona Beach 321
Fort Lauderdale ....754 & 954
Fort Myers ....239 & 941
Fort Pierce 772
Gainesville 352
Jacksonville 904
Key West 305
Miami ....305 & 786
Orlando ....321 & 407
Panama City 850
Pensacola 850
St. Petersburg 727
Sarasota 941
Tallahassee 850
Tampa 813
West Palm Beach 561

Georgia

Albany 229
Atlanta:
Central ....404, 678 & 770
Greater Metro Area ....470, 678 & 770
Augusta 706
Columbus 706
Macon 478
Rome 706
Savannah 912

Hawaii

all points 808

Idaho

all points 208

Illinois

Bloomington 309
Carbondale 618
Champaign 217
Chicago:
Inner 312
Outer ....224, 773 & 847
East St. Louis 618
Peoria 309
Rockford 815
Springfield 217

Indiana

Bloomington 812
Evansville 812
Fort Wayne 260
Gary 219
Indianapolis 317
Lafayette 765
Muncie 765
South Bend 574

Iowa

Cedar Rapids 319
Council Bluffs 712
Davenport 563
Des Moines 515
Dubuque 563
Mason City 641
Sioux City 712

Kansas

Garden City 620
Kansas City 913
Salina 785
Topeka 785
Wichita 316

Kentucky

Ashland 606
Covington 859
Lexington-Fayette 859
Louisville 502
Owensboro 270
Paducah 270

Louisiana

Alexandria 318
Baton Rouge 225
Lafayette 337
Lake Charles 337
Monroe 318
New Orleans 504
Shreveport 318

Maine

all points 207

Maryland

Annapolis ....410 & 443
Baltimore ....410 & 443
Bethesda ....240 & 301
Hagerstown ....240 & 301
Salisbury ....410 & 443

Massachusetts

Boston ....617 & 857
Hyannis ....508 & 774
Lawrence ....351 & 978
Lowell ....351 & 978
New Bedford ....508 & 774
Pittsfield 413
Springfield 413
Weymouth ....339 & 781
Worcester ....508 & 774

Michigan

Ann Arbor 734
Detroit 313
Flint 810
Grand Rapids 616
Ironwood 906
Lansing 517
Marquette 906
Pontiac 248
Saginaw 989
Traverse City 231
Warren 586

Minnesota

Bemidji 218
Duluth 218
Minneapolis 612
Rochester 507
St. Cloud 320
St. Paul 651

Mississippi

Gulfport 228
Jackson 601
Meridian 601
Tupelo 662

Missouri

Columbia 573
Kansas City 816
Poplar Bluff 573
St. Joseph 816
St. Louis 314
Suburbs 336
Springfield 417

Montana

all points 406

Nebraska

Lincoln 402
North Platte 308
Omaha 402
Scottsbluff 308

Nevada

Carson City 775
Elko 775
Ely 775
Las Vegas 702
Reno 775

New Hampshire

all points 603

New Jersey

Atlantic City 609
Camden 856
Elizabeth 908
Jersey City ....201 & 551
Middletown ....732 & 848
Morristown ....862 & 973
Newark ....862 & 973
New Brunswick ....732 & 848
Paterson ....862 & 973
Trenton 609

New Mexico

all points 505

New York

Albany 518
Binghamton 607
Buffalo 716
Jamestown 716
Long Island:
- Nassau Co. 516
- Suffolk Co. 631

New York City:
- Bronx ....347, 718 & 917
- Brooklyn ....347, 718 & 917
- Manhattan ....212, 646 & 917
- Queens ....347, 718 & 917
- Staten Island ....347, 718 & 917

Plattsburgh 518
Poughkeepsie 845
Riverhead 631
Rochester 585
Syracuse 315
Watertown 315
White Plains 914
Yonkers 914

North Carolina

Asheville 828
Charlotte ....704 & 980
Durham 919
Fayetteville 910
Greensboro 336
Greenville 252
Raleigh 919
Rocky Mount 252
Wilmington 910
Winston-Salem 336

North Dakota

all points 701

Ohio

Akron ....234 & 330
Athens 740
Cincinnati 513
Cleveland 216
Columbus 614
Dayton 937
Lima ....419 & 567
Lorain 440
Toledo ....419 & 567
Youngstown ....234 & 330

Oklahoma

Ardmore 580
Enid 580
Lawton 580
McAlester 918
Oklahoma City 405
Tulsa 918

Oregon

Astoria 503
Bend 541
Eugene 541
Portland ....503 & 971
Klamath Falls 541
Medford 541
Pendleton 541
Salem ....503 & 971

Pennsylvania

Allentown ....484, 610 & 835
Altoona 814
Bethel Park ....412 & 878
Erie 814
Harrisburg 717
Lancaster 717
New Castle ....724 & 878
Philadelphia ....215, 267 & 445
Pittsburgh ....412 & 878
Scranton 570
State College 814
Williamsport 570

Rhode Island

all points 401

South Carolina

Charleston 843
Columbia 803
Florence 843
Greenville 864
Myrtle Beach 843
Spartanburg 864

South Dakota

all points 605

Tennessee

Chattanooga 423
Jackson 731
Johnson City 423
Knoxville 865
Memphis 901
Nashville 615

Texas

Abilene 915
Amarillo 806
Austin 512
Beaumont 409
Brownsville 956
Corpus Christi 361
Dallas ....214, 469 & 972
Del Rio 830
El Paso 915
Fort Worth ....682 & 817
Galveston 409
Houston ....281, 713 & 832
Laredo 956
Lubbock 806
Lufkin 936
Odessa 915
San Antonio 210
Tyler 903
Waco 254

Utah

Cedar City 435
Moab 435
Ogden 385
Provo 385
Salt Lake City 801

Vermont

all points 802

Virginia

Arlington ....571 & 703
Charlottesville 434
Danville 434
Lynchburg 434
Norfolk 757
Richmond 804
Roanoke 540

Washington

Bellingham 360
Olympia 360
Seattle 206
Spokane 509
Tacoma 253
Walla Walla 509
Yakima 509

West Virginia

all points 304

Wisconsin

Eau Claire 715
Green Bay 920
Madison 608
Milwaukee 414
Superior 715
Wausau 715

Wyoming

all points 307

Canada

Calgary 403
Charlottetown 902
Edmonton 780
Hamilton ....289 & 905
Halifax 902
Kamloops 250
Montreal 450
Ottawa 613
Quebec City 418
Regina 306
St. John 506
St. John's 709
Sherbrooke 819
Sudbury 705
Thunder Bay 807
Timmins 705
Toronto ....416 & 647
Vancouver ....604 & 778
Victoria 250
Whitehorse 867
Windsor 519
Winnipeg 204
Yellowknife 867

Caribbean

Anguilla 264
Antigua & Barbuda 268
Aruba 297
Bahamas 242
Barbados 246
Bermuda 441
British Virgin Islands 284
Cayman Islands 345
Dominica 767
Dominican Republic 809
Grenada 473
Jamaica 876
Montserrat 664
Puerto Rico ....787 & 939
St. Kitts & Nevis 869
St. Lucia 758
St. Vincent & Grenadines 784
Trinidad & Tobago 868
Turks & Caicos 649
U.S. Virgin Islands 340

AREA CODES: Numerical Listing for the United States, Canada, and the Caribbean

200

201 New Jersey - Northeastern (Shared with 551)
202 District of Columbia
203 Connecticut - Southwestern
204 Canada - Manitoba Province
205 Alabama - West Central
206 Washington - Seattle Metro Area
207 Maine
208 Idaho
209 California - Upper Central
210 Texas - San Antonio Metro Area
212 New York - New York City, Manhattan (Shared with 646 & 917)
213 California - Downtown Los Angeles
214 Texas - Dallas Metro & Outlying Area (Shared with 469 & 972)
215 Pennsylvania - Philadelphia Metro Area (Shared with 267)
216 Ohio - Cleveland Metro Area
217 Illinois - Central
218 Minnesota - Northern Third
219 Indiana - Northern
224 Illinois - Northwest (Outer) Chicago & Outlying Area (Shared with 847)
225 Louisiana - Baton Rouge General Area
228 Mississippi - Gulf Coast
229 Georgia - Southeastern (Shared with 912)
231 Michigan - Northwestern
234 Ohio - East Central (Shared with 330)
240 Maryland - Western Half (Shared with 301)
242 Caribbean - Bahamas
246 Caribbean - Barbados
248 Michigan - Detroit Metro Outlying Area
250 Canada - British Columbia Province (Excluding Vancouver Metro Area)
251 Alabama - Mobile Metro and Outlying Area
252 North Carolina - Northeastern
253 Washington - Tacoma Metro Area
254 Texas - Central
256 Alabama - North & East Central
260 Indiana - Northwestern
262 Wisconsin - Southeastern
264 Caribbean - Anguilla
267 Pennsylvania - Philadelphia Metro Area (Shared with 215)
268 Caribbean - Antigua & Barbuda
270 Kentucky - Western Half
276 Virginia - Southwestern
281 Texas - Houston Metro & Outlying Area (Shared with 713 & 832)
284 Caribbean - British Virgin Islands
289 Canada - Lake Ontario Coastal Area (Excluding Toronto Metro area), Ontario Province (Shared with 905)

300

301 Maryland - Western Half (Shared with 240)
302 Delaware
303 Colorado - Denver Metro Area (Shared with 720)
304 West Virginia
305 Florida - Southern (Shared with 786)
306 Canada - Saskatchewan Province
307 Wyoming
308 Nebraska - Western Half
309 Illinois - West Central
310 California - Malibu/Santa Monica Area (Shared with 424)
312 Illinois - Inner Chicago
313 Michigan - Detroit Metro Area
314 Missouri - St. Louis Metro Area
315 New York - North Central
316 Kansas - Wichita Metro Area
317 Indiana - Central
318 Louisiana - Northern & Central
319 Iowa - Eastern
320 Minnesota - Central Third
321 Florida - East Central (Shared with 407)
323 California - Los Angeles Metro Area
330 Ohio - East Central (Shared with 234)
334 Alabama - South Central & Southeastern
336 North Carolina - Northwestern
337 Louisiana - Southwestern
339 Massachusetts - Boston Metro Outlying Area (Shared with 781)
340 Caribbean - United States Virgin Islands
345 Caribbean - Cayman Islands
347 New York - New York City, Outer Boroughs (Shared with 718 & 917)
351 Massachusetts - Northeastern (Shared with 978)
352 Florida - Upper West Central
360 Washington - Western Half (Excluding Seattle-Tacoma Metro Area)
361 Texas - Lower Gulf Coast
386 Florida - Northern

400

401 Rhode Island
402 Nebraska - Eastern Half
403 Canada - Southern Alberta Province
404 Georgia - Central Atlanta (Shared with 678 & 470)
405 Oklahoma - Oklahoma City Metro Area
406 Montana
407 Florida - East Central (Partially Shared with 321)
408 California - San Jose Area (Shared with 669)
409 Texas - Southeastern (Excluding General Houston Area)
410 Maryland - Eastern Half (Shared with 443)
412 Pennsylvania - Pittsburgh Metro Area (Shared with 878)
413 Massachusetts - Western
414 Wisconsin - Milwaukee Metro Area
415 California - San Francisco Metro Area
416 Canada - Toronto Metro Area, Ontario Province (Shared with 647)
417 Missouri - Southwestern
418 Canada - Eastern Quebec Province
419 Ohio - Northwestern (Shared with 567)
423 Tennessee - Northeastern & Southeastern
424 California - Malibu/Santa Monica Area (Shared with 310)
425 Washington - Seattle-Tacoma Metro Outlying Area
434 Virginia - South Central
435 Utah - (Excluding Salt Lake City Metro Area)
440 Ohio - Northeastern
441 Caribbean - Bermuda
443 Maryland - Eastern Half (Shared with 410)
450 Canada - Montreal Metro Area, Quebec Province

469 Texas - Dallas Metro & Outlying Area
(Shared with 214 & 972)
470 Georgia - Central Atlanta
(Shared with 404, 678 & 770)
473 Caribbean - Grenada
478 Georgia - Central
479 Arkansas - Northwestern
480 Arizona - Phoenix Metro Outlying Area
484 Pennsylvania - Philadelphia Metro Outlying Area
(Shared with 610)

500

501 Arkansas - Northwestern
502 Kentucky - North Central
503 Oregon - Portland-Salem Metro Area
(Shared with 971)
504 Louisiana - New Orleans Metro Area
505 New Mexico
506 Canada - New Brunswick Province
507 Minnesota - Southern
508 Massachusetts - Southeastern
(Shared with 774)
509 Washington - Eastern Half
510 California - Oakland-Berkeley Metro Area
512 Texas - Austin General Area
513 Ohio - Southwestern
514 Canada - Montreal Outlying Area
515 Iowa - Central
516 New York - Nassau County, Long Island
517 Michigan - South Central
518 New York - Upstate, Eastern Half
519 Canada - Southwestern Ontario Province
520 Arizona - Southeastern
530 California - Northeastern
540 Virginia - Western
541 Oregon - (Excluding Portland-Salem Metro Area)
551 New Jersey - Northeastern
(Shared with 201)
559 California - Central
561 Florida - Lower East Central
562 California - Long Beach Area
563 Iowa - Eastern
567 Ohio - Northwestern
(Shared with 419)
570 Pennsylvania - Northeastern
571 Virginia - Northeastern
(Shared with 703)
573 Missouri - Eastern
(Excluding Northeast and General St. Louis Area)
574 Indiana - North
580 Oklahoma - Western & Southeastern
585 New York - Southwestern
(Shared with 716)
586 Michigan - East Central
(Shared with 810)

600

601 Mississippi - Southern Half
(Excluding Gulf Coast)
602 Arizona - Phoenix Metro Area
603 New Hampshire
604 Canada - Vancouver Metro Area, British Columbia Province
(Shared with 778)
605 South Dakota
606 Kentucky - Eastern
607 New York - South Central
608 Wisconsin - Southwestern
609 New Jersey - Central & Southeastern
610 Pennsylvania - Philadelphia Metro Outlying Area
(Shared with 484)
612 Minnesota - Western Minneapolis-St. Paul Metro Area
613 Canada - Southeastern Ontario Province
(Excluding Toronto Metro Area)
614 Ohio - Columbus Metro Area
615 Tennessee - Nashville General Area
616 Michigan - Southwestern
617 Massachusetts - Boston Metro Area
(Shared with 857)
618 Illinois - Southern
619 California - San Diego Metro Area
620 Kansas - Southern Half
(Excluding Wichita Metro Area)
623 Arizona - Phoenix Metro Outlying Area
626 California - Pasadena Area
630 Illinois - West Side (Outer) Chicago & Outlying Area
631 New York - Suffolk County, Long Island
636 Missouri - St. Louis Metro Outlying Area
641 Iowa - Central
646 New York - New York City, Manhattan
(Shared with 212 & 917)
647 Canada - Toronto Metro Area, Ontario Province
(Shared with 416)
649 Caribbean - Turks & Caicos Islands
650 California - South Bay Area
651 Minnesota - Eastern Minneapolis-St. Paul Metro Area
660 Missouri - Northwestern
661 California - Bakersfield Area
662 Mississippi - Northern Half
664 Caribbean - Montserrat
669 California - San Jose Area
(Shared with 408)
671 Guam
678 Georgia - Atlanta Metro Outlying Area
(Shared with 470 & 770)
682 Texas - Ft. Worth Metro Area
(Shared with 817)

700

701 North Dakota
702 Nevada - Far Southeastern (Las Vegas General Area)
703 Virginia - Northeastern
(Shared with 571)
704 North Carolina - South Central
(Shared with 980)
705 Canada - Central Southeastern Ontario Province
706 Georgia - Northern Half (Excluding General Atlanta Area)
707 California - Northwestern
708 Illinois - South Side (Outer) Chicago & Outling Area
709 Canada - Newfoundland Province
712 Iowa - Western
713 Texas - Houston Metro & Outlying Area
(Shared with 281 & 832)
714 California - Anaheim & Santa Ana Area
715 Wisconsin - Northern
716 New York - Western
717 Pennsylvania - Southeastern
(Excluding General Philadelphia Area)
718 New York - New York City, Outer Boroughs
(Shared with 347 & 917)
719 Colorado - Southeastern
720 Colorado - Denver Metro Area
(Shared with 303)
724 Pennsylvania - Southwestern
(Excluding Pittsburgh Metro Area)
(Shared with 878)
727 Florida - West Central Coastal Area
731 Tennessee - Eastern Third (Excluding Memphis Metro Area)
732 New Jersey - East Central
(Shared with 848)
734 Michigan - Southeastern
740 Ohio - Southeastern
754 Florida - Ft. Lauderdale Area
(Shared with 954)
757 Virginia - Southeastern
758 Caribbean - St. Lucia
760 California - Southern & Desert Area
(Excluding San Diego Metro Area)

763 Minnesota - Minneapolis - St. Paul Metro Outlying Area
765 Indiana - East Central
767 Caribbean - Dominica
770 Georgia - Atlanta Metro Outlying Area (Shared with 470 & 678)
772 Florida - Lower East Central (Shared with 561)
773 Illinois - Chicago Outer Metro Area
774 Massachusetts - Southeastern (Shared with 508)
775 Nevada - (Excluding Far Southeast, Las Vegas General Area)
778 Canada - Vancouver Metro Area, British Columbia Province (Shared with 604)
780 Canada - Northern Alberta Province
781 Massachusetts - Boston Metro Outlying Area (Shared With 339)
784 Caribbean - St. Vincent & Grenadines
785 Kansas - Northern Half
786 Florida - Southern (Shared with 305)
787 Caribbean - Puerto Rico (Shared with 939)

800

801 Utah - Salt Lake City Metro Area
802 Vermont
803 South Carolina - Central
804 Virginia - East Central
805 California - Santa Barbara Area
806 Texas - Panhandle
807 Canada - Western Ontario Province
808 Hawaii
809 Caribbean - Dominican Republic
810 Michigan - East Central
812 Indiana - Southern
813 Florida - Tampa Area
814 Pennsylvania - Central Western
815 Illinois - Northwestern
816 Missouri - Kansas City Metro Area
817 Texas - Ft. Worth Metro Area (Shared with 682)
818 California - Burbank Area
819 Canada - Southern & Western Quebec Province
828 North Carolina - Southwestern
830 Texas - Southwestern (Excluding San Antonio Metro Area)
831 California - Monterey Area
832 Texas - Houston Metro & Outlying Area (Shared with 281 & 713)
843 South Carolina - Eastern
845 New York- Southeastern (Excluding New York City, Long Island and Westchester County)
847 Illinois - Northwest (Outer) Chicago & Outlying Area (Shared with 224)
848 New Jersey - East Central (Shared with 732)
850 Florida - Panhandle
856 New Jersey - Southwestern
857 Massachusetts - Boston Metro Area (Shared with 617)
858 California - Northwestern San Diego Metro Outlying Area
859 Kentucky - North Central
860 Connecticut - (Excluding Southwestern Corridor)
862 New Jersey - North Central (Shared with 973)
863 Florida - Lower Central
864 South Carolina - Northwestern
865 Tennessee - East Central
867 Canada - Northwest Territories, Nunavut & Yukon Province
868 Caribbean - Trinidad & Tobago
869 Caribbean - St. Kitts & Nevis
870 Arkansas - (Excluding Northwestern)
876 Caribbean - Jamaica
878 Pennsylvania - Southwestern (Shared with 412 & 724)

900

901 Tennessee - Memphis Metro Area
902 Canada - Nova Scotia & Prince Edward Island Provinces
903 Texas - Northeastern
904 Florida - Northeastern
905 Canada - Lake Ontario Coastal Area (Excluding Toronto Metro Area), Ontario Province (Shared with 289)
906 Michigan - Upper Peninsula
907 Alaska
908 New Jersey - Northwestern
909 California - San Bernardino Metro Area
910 North Carolina - Southeastern
912 Georgia - Southeastern
913 Kansas - Kansas City Metro Area
914 New York - Southeastern (Excluding New York City and Long Island)
915 Texas - Central Western
916 California - Upper Central
917 New York - New York City (Shared with 212, 347, 646 & 718)
918 Oklahoma - Northeastern
919 North Carolina - North Central
920 Wisconsin - Eastern
925 California - Fairfield Area
928 Arizona - Excluding Phoenix Metro Area and Southeast
931 Tennessee - Central (Excluding Nashville General Area)
935 California - Southern San Diego Metro Outlying Area
936 Texas - East Central
937 Ohio - South Central
939 Caribbean - Puerto Rico (Shared with 787)
940 Texas - North Central
941 Florida - Southwestern
949 California - Irvine Area, Southern Orange County
952 Minnesota - Minneapolis - St. Paul Metro Outlying Area
954 Florida - Ft. Lauderdale Area/Broward County
956 Texas - Lower Southwestern
970 Colorado - Northern & Western
971 Oregon - Portland - Salem Metro Area (Shared with 503)
972 Texas - Dallas Metro and Outlying Area (Shared with 214 & 469)
973 New Jersey - North Central (Shared with 862)
978 Massachusetts - Northeastern (Shared with 351)
979 Texas - Southeastern
980 North Carolina - South Central (Shared with 704)
985 Louisiana - Southwestern
989 Michigan - Northeastern and Central

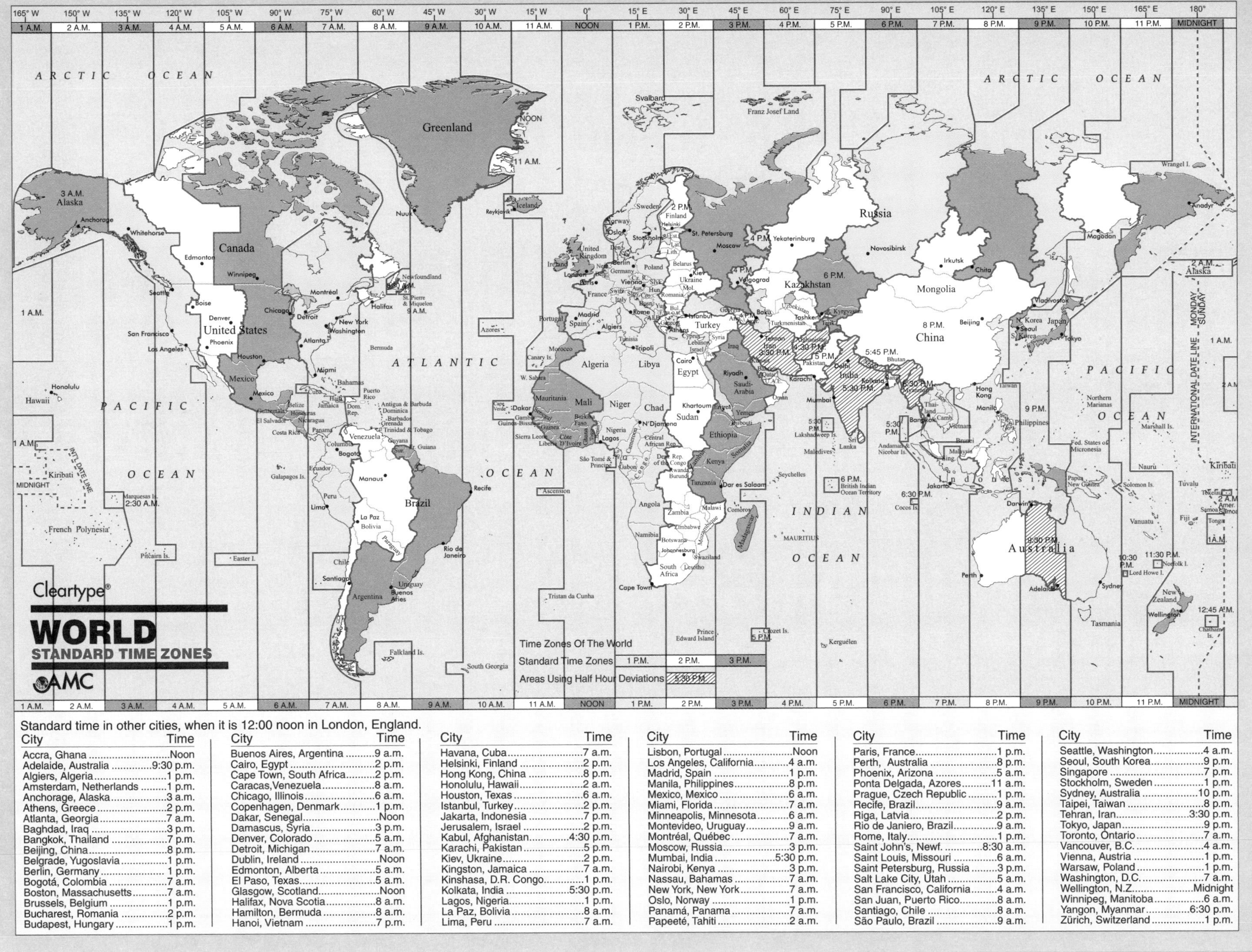

Standard time in other cities, when it is 12:00 noon in London, England.

City	Time
Accra, Ghana	Noon
Adelaide, Australia	9:30 p.m.
Algiers, Algeria	1 p.m.
Amsterdam, Netherlands	1 p.m.
Anchorage, Alaska	3 a.m.
Athens, Greece	2 p.m.
Atlanta, Georgia	7 a.m.
Baghdad, Iraq	3 p.m.
Bangkok, Thailand	7 p.m.
Beijing, China	8 p.m.
Belgrade, Yugoslavia	1 p.m.
Berlin, Germany	1 p.m.
Bogotá, Colombia	7 a.m.
Boston, Massachusetts	7 a.m.
Brussels, Belgium	1 p.m.
Bucharest, Romania	2 p.m.
Budapest, Hungary	1 p.m.
Buenos Aires, Argentina	9 a.m.
Cairo, Egypt	2 p.m.
Cape Town, South Africa	2 p.m.
Caracas,Venezuela	8 a.m.
Chicago, Illinois	6 a.m.
Copenhagen, Denmark	1 p.m.
Dakar, Senegal	Noon
Damascus, Syria	3 p.m.
Denver, Colorado	5 a.m.
Detroit, Michigan	7 a.m.
Dublin, Ireland	Noon
Edmonton, Alberta	5 a.m.
El Paso, Texas	5 a.m.
Glasgow, Scotland	Noon
Halifax, Nova Scotia	8 a.m.
Hamilton, Bermuda	8 a.m.
Hanoi, Vietnam	7 p.m.
Havana, Cuba	7 a.m.
Helsinki, Finland	2 p.m.
Hong Kong, China	8 p.m.
Honolulu, Hawaii	2 a.m.
Houston, Texas	6 a.m.
Istanbul, Turkey	2 p.m.
Jakarta, Indonesia	7 p.m.
Jerusalem, Israel	2 p.m.
Kabul, Afghanistan	4:30 p.m.
Karachi, Pakistan	5 p.m.
Kiev, Ukraine	2 p.m.
Kingston, Jamaica	7 a.m.
Kinshasa, D.R. Congo	1 p.m.
Kolkata, India	5:30 p.m.
Lagos, Nigeria	1 p.m.
La Paz, Bolivia	8 a.m.
Lima, Peru	7 a.m.
Lisbon, Portugal	Noon
Los Angeles, California	4 a.m.
Madrid, Spain	1 p.m.
Manila, Philippines	8 p.m.
Mexico, Mexico	6 a.m.
Miami, Florida	7 a.m.
Minneapolis, Minnesota	6 a.m.
Montevideo, Uruguay	9 a.m.
Montréal, Québec	7 a.m.
Moscow, Russia	3 p.m.
Mumbai, India	5:30 p.m.
Nairobi, Kenya	3 p.m.
Nassau, Bahamas	7 a.m.
New York, New York	7 a.m.
Oslo, Norway	1 p.m.
Panamá, Panama	7 a.m.
Papeeté, Tahiti	2 a.m.
Paris, France	1 p.m.
Perth, Australia	8 p.m.
Phoenix, Arizona	5 a.m.
Ponta Delgada, Azores	11 a.m.
Prague, Czech Republic	1 p.m.
Recife, Brazil	9 a.m.
Riga, Latvia	2 p.m.
Rio de Janiero, Brazil	9 a.m.
Rome, Italy	1 p.m.
Saint John's, Newf.	8:30 a.m.
Saint Louis, Missouri	6 a.m.
Saint Petersburg, Russia	3 p.m.
Salt Lake City, Utah	5 a.m.
San Francisco, California	4 a.m.
San Juan, Puerto Rico	8 a.m.
Santiago, Chile	8 a.m.
São Paulo, Brazil	9 a.m.
Seattle, Washington	4 a.m.
Seoul, South Korea	9 p.m.
Singapore	7 p.m.
Stockholm, Sweden	1 p.m.
Sydney, Australia	10 p.m.
Taipei, Taiwan	8 p.m.
Tehran, Iran	3:30 p.m.
Tokyo, Japan	9 p.m.
Toronto, Ontario	7 a.m.
Vancouver, B.C.	4 a.m.
Vienna, Austria	1 p.m.
Warsaw, Poland	1 p.m.
Washington, D.C.	7 a.m.
Wellington, N.Z.	Midnight
Winnipeg, Manitoba	6 a.m.
Yangon, Myanmar	6:30 p.m.
Zürich, Switzerland	1 p.m.

Dialing International Calls

FOR CODES OF PLACES NOT LISTED, DIAL "0" (OPERATOR)

For example, a call to Cape Town, South Africa, would be dialed:

011 + 27 + 21 + 123456

011	27	21	123456
INTERNATIONAL ACCESS CODE	COUNTRY CODE	CITY ROUTING CODE	LOCAL NUMBER

Place	Code
Algeria	**213**
American Samoa ●	**684**
Argentina	**54**
Buenos Aires	1
Cordoba	51
La Plata	21
Rosario	41
Armenia	**374**
Aruba ●	**297**
Ascension Island ●	**247**
Australia	**61**
Adelaide	8
Brisbane	2
Canberra	2
Melbourne	3
Perth	9
Sydney	2
Austria	**43**
Graz	316
Innsbruck	512
Salzburg	662
Vienna	1
Azerbaijan	**994**
Baku	12
Bahrain ●	**973**
Bangladesh	**880**
Dhaka	2
Belarus	**375**
Minsk	172
Belgium	**32**
Antwerp	3
Brussels	2
Belize	**501**
Belize City	2
Belmopan	8
Bolivia	**591**
La Paz	2
Bosnia & Herzegovina	**387**
Sarajevo	71
Botswana ●	**267**
Brazil	**55**
Brasília	61
Rio de Janeiro	21
São Paulo	11
Brunei	**673**
Bandar Seri Begawan	2
Bulgaria	**359**
Sofia	2
Cameroon ●	**237**
Cape Verde Is. ●	**238**
Caribbean ●	**809**
Chile	**56**
Concepcion	41
Santiago	2
Valparaiso	32
China	**86**
Beijing	10
Fuzhou	591
Guangzhou	20
Hong Kong *	852
Macau *	853
Shanghai	21
Cote D'Ivoire ●	**225**
Colombia	**57**
Barranquilla	2
Bogota	1
Cali	2
Cartegena	5
Medellin	4
Costa Rica ●	**506**
Croatia	**385**
Zagreb	1
Cyprus	**357**
Nicosia	2
Czech Republic	**420**
Brno	5
Prague	2
Dem. Rep. of Congo	**243**
Kinshasa	12
Denmark ●	**45**
Djibouti ●	**253**
Ecuador	**593**
Cuenca	7
Guayaquil	4
Quito	2
Egypt	**20**
Alexandria	3
Cairo	2
Port Said	66
El Salvador ●	**503**
Estonia	**372**
Tallinn	2
Ethiopia	**251**
Addis Ababa	1
Faeroe Islands ●	**298**
Fiji ●	**679**
Finland	**358**
Helsinki	9
France	**33**
Bordeaux	556
Cannes	493
Lyon	478
Marseille	491
Nice	493
Paris	1
Rouen	235
Toulouse	561
French Antilles ●	**596**
French Guiana ●	**594**
French Polynesia ●	**689**
Gabon ●	**241**
Georgia	**995**
T'bilisi	32
Germany	**49**
Berlin	30
Bonn	228
Bremen	421
Cologne	221
Dresden	351
Dusseldorf	211
Frankfurt	69
Hamburg	40
Leipzig	341
Munich	89
Stuttgart	711
Ghana	**233**
Accra	21
Gibraltar ●	**350**
Greece	**30**
Athens	1
Greenland (Kalaallit Nunaat)	**299**
Godthab (Nuuk)	2
Guam ●	**671**
Guantanamo Bay ●	**53**
Guatemala	**502**
Guatemala City	2
All other places	9
Guinea	**224**
Conakry	4
Guyana	**592**
Georgetown	2
Haiti ●	**509**
Honduras ●	**504**
Hungary	**36**
Budapest	1
Iceland ●	**354**
India	**91**
Kolkata (Calcutta)	33
Mumbai (Bombay)	22
New Delhi	11
Indonesia	**62**
Jakarta	21
Iraq	**964**
Baghdad	1
Ireland	**353**
Cork	21
Dublin	1
Israel	**972**
Haifa	4
Jerusalem	2
Tel Aviv	3
Italy	**39**
Bologna	51
Florence	55
Genoa	10
Milan	2
Naples	81
Palermo	91
Rome	6
Venice	41
Japan	**81**
Hiroshima	82
Kobe	78
Kyoto	75
Osaka	6
Sapporo	11
Tokyo	3
Yokohama	45
Jordan	**962**
Amman	6
Kazakhstan	**7**
Almaty	3272
Astana	3172
Kenya	**254**
Nairobi	2
Korea (Rep of)	**82**
Inchon	32
Pusan	51
Seoul	2
Kuwait ●	**965**
Kyrgyz Republic	**996**
Bishkek	312
Latvia ●	**371**
Lesotho ●	**266**
Liberia ●	**231**
Libya	**218**
Tripoli	21
Liechtenstein	**41**
All places	75
Lithuania	**370**
Vilnius	2
Luxembourg ●	**352**
Macedonia	**389**
Skopje	91
Malaysia	**60**
Kuala Lumpur	3
Malta ●	**356**
Marshall Islands	**692**
Majuro	625
Mexico	**52**
Acapulco	744
Guadalajara	33
Mexico City	55
Monterrey	81
Micronesia	**691**
Ponape	320
Moldova	**373**
Kishinev	2
Monaco ●	**377**
Morocco	**212**
Marrakech	4
Tanger	99
Namibia	**264**
Windhoek	61
Nepal	**977**
Kathmandu	1
Netherlands	**31**
Amsterdam	20
Rotterdam	10
The Hague	70
Netherlands Antilles	**599**
Bonaire	7
Curacao	9
St. Maarten	5
New Caledonia ●	**687**
New Zealand	**64**
Auckland	9
Wellington	4
Nicaragua	**505**
Managua	2
Niger ●	**227**
Nigeria	**234**
Lagos	1
Norway	**47**
Oslo	22
Oman ●	**968**
Pakistan	**92**
Islamabad	51
Karachi	21
Palau ●	**680**
Panama ●	**507**
Papua New Guinea ●	**675**
Paraguay	**595**
Asuncion	21
Peru	**51**
Lima	1
Philippines	**63**
Manila	2
Poland	**48**
Krakow	12
Warsaw	22
Portugal	**351**
Lisbon	1
Oatar ●	**974**
Romania ●	**40**
Russia	**7**
Moscow	095
St. Pierre & Miquelon ●	**508**
San Marino ●	**378**
Saudi Arabia	**966**
Jeddah	2
Mecca	2
Medina	4
Riyadh	1
Senegal ●	**221**
Sierra Leone	**232**
Freetown	22
Singapore ●	**65**
Slovakia	**421**
Bratislava	7
Presov	91
Slovenia	**386**
Ljubijana	61
South Africa	**27**
Cape Town	21
Johannesburg	11
Pretoria	12
Spain	**34**
Barcelona	3
Madrid	1
Valencia	6
Sri Lanka	**94**
Colombo	1
Suriname ●	**597**
Sweden	**46**
Stockholm	8
Switzerland	**41**
Berne	31
Geneva	22
Zurich	1
Taiwan	**886**
Taipei	2
Tajikistan	**7**
Dushanbe	3772
Tanzania	**255**
Dar es Salaam	51
Thailand	**66**
Bangkok	2
Togo ●	**228**
Tunisia	**216**
Tunis	1
Turkey	**90**
Ankara	312
Istanbul	212,216
Izmir	232
Turkmenistan	**993**
Ashgabat	312
Uganda	**256**
Entebbe	41
Kampala	42
Ukraine	**380**
Kiev	44
United Arab Emirates	**971**
Abu Dhabi	2
Dubai	4
United Kingdom	**44**
Belfast	1232
Birmingham	121
Edinburgh	131
Glasgow	141
Liverpool	151
London	171 or 181
Manchester	161
Sheffield	114
Southampton	1703
Uruguay	**598**
Montevideo	2
Uzbekistan	**7**
Tashkent	3712
Vatican City	**39**
All places	6
Venezuela	**58**
Caracas	2
Maracaibo	61
Vietnam	**84**
Hanoi	4
Yemen	**967**
Sanaa	1
Yugoslavia	**381**
Belgrade	11
Zambia	**260**
Lusaka	1
Zimbabwe	**263**
Harare	4

*** = No country code required**

● = No city routing code required

METRO MARKET STATISTICAL AREAS

MSA/NECMA	REFERENCE NO.*
Abilene, TX	1
Akron, OH	2
Albany, GA	3
Albany-Schenectady-Troy, NY	4
Albuquerque, NM	5
Alexandria, LA	6
Allentown-Bethlehem-Easton, PA	7
Altoona, PA	8
Amarillo, TX	9
Anchorage, AK	10
Ann Arbor, MI	11
Anniston, AL	12
Appleton-Oshkosh-Neenah, WI	13
Asheville, NC	14
Athens, GA	15
Atlanta, GA	16
Atlantic-Cape May, NJ	17
Augusta-Aiken, GA-SC	18
Austin-San Marcos, TX	19
Bakersfield, CA	20
Baltimore, MD	21
Bangor, ME	22
Barnstable-Yarmouth, MA	23
Baton Rouge, LA	24
Beaumont-Port Arthur, TX	25
Bellingham, WA	26
Benton Harbor, MI	27
Bergen-Passaic, NJ	28
Billings, MT	29
Biloxi-Gulfport-Pascagoula, MS	30
Binghamton, NY	31
Birmingham, AL	32
Bismarck, ND	33
Bloomington, IN	34
Bloomington-Normal, IL	35
Boise City, ID	36
Boston-Worcester-Lawrence-Lowell-Brockton, MA-NH	37
Boulder-Longmont, CO	38
Brazoria, TX	39
Bremerton, WA	40
Brownsville-Harlingen-San Benito, TX	41
Bryan-College Station, TX	42
Buffalo-Niagara Falls, NY	43
Burlington, VT	44
Canton-Massillon, OH	45
Casper, WY	46
Cedar Rapids, IA	47
Champaign-Urbana, IL	48
Charleston, WV	49
Charleston-North Charleston, SC	50
Charlotte-Gastonia-Rock Hill, NC-SC	51
Charlottesville, VA	52
Chattanooga, TN-GA	53
Cheyenne, WY	54
Chicago, IL	55
Chico-Paradise, CA	56
Cincinnati, OH-KY-IN	57
Clarksville-Hopkinsville, TN-KY	58
Cleveland-Lorain-Elyria, OH	59
Colorado Springs, CO	60
Columbia, MO	61
Columbia, SC	62
Columbus, GA-AL	63
Columbus, OH	64
Corpus Christi, TX	65
Cumberland, MD-WV	66
Dallas, TX	67
Danville, VA	68
Davenport-Moline-Rock Island, IA-IL	69
Dayton-Springfield, OH	70
Daytona Beach, FL	71
Decatur, AL	72
Decatur, IL	73
Denver, CO	74
Des Moines, IA	75
Detroit, MI	76
Dothan, AL	77
Dover, DE	78
Dubuque, IA	79
Duluth-Superior, MN-WI	80
Dutchess County, NY	81
Eau Claire, WI	82
El Paso, TX	83
Elkhart-Goshen, IN	84
Elmira, NY	85
Enid, OK	86
Erie, PA	87
Eugene-Springfield, OR	88
Evansville-Henderson, IN-KY	89
Fargo-Moorhead, ND-MN	90
Fayetteville, NC	91
Fayetteville-Springdale-Rogers, AR	92
Flagstaff, AZ-UT	93
Flint, MI	94
Florence, AL	95
Florence, SC	96
Fort Collins-Loveland, CO	97
Fort Lauderdale, FL	98
Fort Myers-Cape Coral, FL	99
Fort Pierce-Port St. Lucie, FL	100
Fort Smith, AR-OK	101
Fort Walton Beach, FL	102
Fort Wayne, IN	103
Fort Worth-Arlington, TX	104
Fresno, CA	105
Gadsden, AL	106
Gainesville, FL	107
Galveston-Texas City, TX	108
Gary, IN	109
Glens Falls, NY	110
Goldsboro, NC	111
Grand Forks, ND-MN	112
Grand Junction, CO	113
Grand Rapids-Muskegon-Holland, MI	114
Great Falls, MT	115
Greeley, CO	116
Green Bay, WI	117
Greensboro-Winston Salem-High Point, NC	118
Greenville, NC	119
Greenville-Spartanburg-Anderson, SC	120
Hagerstown, MD	121
Hamilton-Middletown, OH	122
Harrisburg-Lebanon-Carlisle, PA	123
Hartford, CT	124
Hattiesburg, MS	125
Hickory-Morganton-Lenoir, NC	126
Honolulu, HI	127
Houma, LA	128
Houston, TX	129
Huntington-Ashland, WV-KY-OH	130
Huntsville, AL	131
Indianapolis, IN	132
Iowa City, IA	133
Jackson, MI	134
Jackson, MS	135
Jackson, TN	136
Jacksonville, FL	137
Jacksonville, NC	138
Jamestown, NY	139
Janesville-Beloit, WI	140
Jersey City, NJ	141
Johnson City-Kingsport-Bristol, TN	142
Johnstown, PA	143
Jonesboro, AR	144
Joplin, MO	145
Kalamazoo-Battle Creek, MI	146
Kankakee, IL	147
Kansas City, MO-KS	148
Kenosha, WI	149
Killeen-Temple, TX	150
Knoxville, TN	151
Kokomo, IN	152
La Crosse, WI-MN	153
Lafayette, IN	154
Lafayette, LA	155
Lake Charles, LA	156
Lakeland-Winter Haven, FL	157
Lancaster, PA	158
Lansing-East Lansing, MI	159
Laredo, TX	160
Las Cruces, NM	161
Las Vegas, NV-AZ	162
Lawrence, KS	163
Lawton, OK	164
Lewiston-Auburn, ME	165
Lexington, KY	166
Lima, OH	167
Lincoln, NE	168
Little Rock-North Little Rock, AR	169
Longview-Marshall, TX	170
Los Angeles-Long Beach, CA	171
Louisville, KY-IN	172
Lubbock, TX	173
Lynchburg, VA	174
Macon, GA	175
Madison, WI	176
Mansfield, OH	177
McAllen-Edinburg-Mission, TX	178
Medford-Ashland, OR	179
Melbourne-Titusville-Palm Bay, FL	180
Memphis, TN-AR-MS	181
Merced, CA	182
Miami, FL	183
Middlesex-Somerset-Hunterdon, NJ	184
Milwaukee-Waukesha, WI	185
Minneapolis-St. Paul, MN-WI	186
Missoula, MT	187
Mobile, AL	188
Modesto, CA	189
Monmouth-Ocean, NJ	190
Monroe, LA	191
Montgomery, AL	192
Muncie, IN	193
Myrtle Beach, SC	194
Naples, FL	195
Nashville, TN	196
Nassau-Suffolk, NY	197
New Haven-Bridgeport-Stamford-Danbury-Waterbury, CT	198
New London-Norwich, CT	199
New Orleans, LA	200
New York, NY	201
Newark, NJ	202
Newburgh, NY-PA	203
Norfolk-Virginia Beach-Newport News, VA-NC	204
Oakland, CA	205
Ocala, FL	206
Odessa-Midland, TX	207
Oklahoma City, OK	208
Olympia, WA	209
Omaha, NE-IA	210
Orange County, CA	211
Orlando, FL	212
Owensboro, KY	213
Panama City, FL	214
Parkersburg-Marietta, WV-OH	215
Pensacola, FL	216
Peoria-Pekin, IL	217
Philadelphia, PA-NJ	218
Phoenix-Mesa, AZ	219
Pine Bluff, AR	220
Pittsburgh, PA	221
Pittsfield, MA	222
Pocatello, ID	223
Portland, ME	224
Portland-Vancouver, OR-WA	225
Providence-Warwick-Pawtucket, RI	226
Provo-Orem, UT	227
Pueblo, CO	228
Punta Gorda, FL	229
Racine, WI	230
Raleigh-Durham-Chapel Hill, NC	231
Rapid City, SD	232
Reading, PA	233
Redding, CA	234
Reno, NV	235
Richland-Kennewick-Pasco, WA	236
Richmond-Petersburg, VA	237
Riverside-San Bernardino, CA	238
Roanoke, VA	239
Rochester, MN	240
Rochester, NY	241
Rockford, IL	242
Rocky Mount, NC	243
Sacramento, CA	244
Saginaw-Bay City-Midland, MI	245
St. Cloud, MN	246
St. Joseph, MO	247
St. Louis, MO-IL	248
Salem, OR	249
Salinas, CA	250
Salt Lake City-Ogden, UT	251
San Angelo, TX	252
San Antonio, TX	253
San Diego, CA	254
San Francisco, CA	255
San Jose, CA	256
San Luis Obispo-Antascadro-Paso Robles, CA	257
Santa Barbara-Santa Maria-Lompoc, CA	258
Santa Cruz-Watsonville, CA	259
Santa Fe, NM	260
Santa Rosa, CA	261
Sarasota-Bradenton, FL	262
Savannah, GA	263
Scranton-Wilkes-Barre-Hazleton, PA	264
Seattle-Bellevue-Everett, WA	265
Sharon, PA	266
Sheboygan, WI	267
Sherman-Denison, TX	268
Shreveport-Bossier City, LA	269
Sioux City, IA-NE	270
Sioux Falls, SD	271
South Bend, IN	272
Spokane, WA	273
Springfield, IL	274
Springfield, MO	275
Springfield, MA	276
State College, PA	277
Steubenville-Weirton, OH-WV	278
Stockton-Lodi, CA	279
Sumter, SC	280
Syracuse, NY	281
Tacoma, WA	282
Tallahassee, FL	283
Tampa-St. Petersburg-Clearwater, FL	284
Terre Haute, IN	285
Texarkana, TX-AR	286
Toledo, OH	287
Topeka, KS	288
Trenton, NJ	289
Tucson, AZ	290
Tulsa, OK	291
Tuscaloosa, AL	292
Tyler, TX	293
Utica-Rome, NY	294
Vallejo-Fairfield-Napa, CA	295
Ventura, CA	296
Victoria, TX	297
Vineland-Millville-Bridgeton, NJ	298
Visalia-Tulare-Porterville, CA	299
Waco, TX	300
Washington, DC-MD-VA-WV	301
Waterloo-Cedar Falls, IA	302
Wausau, WI	303
West Palm Beach-Boca Raton, FL	304
Wheeling, WV-OH	305
Wichita, KS	306
Wichita Falls, TX	307
Williamsport, PA	308
Wilmington, NC	309
Wilmington-Newark, DE-MD	310
Yakima, WA	311
Yolo, CA	312
York, PA	313
Youngstown-Warren, OH	314
Yuba City, CA	315
Yuma, AZ	316

NOTE: There are 316 MSAs/NECMAs total, including 12 NECMAs representing the New England states.

* See "MSA/NECMA BOUNDARIES" page 4 for explanation

TOTAL POPULATION

MSA/NECMA	POPULATION	RANK
Los Angeles-Long Beach, CA	9,377,938	1
New York, NY	8,718,045	2
Chicago, IL	7,980,055	3
Boston-Worcester-Lawrence-Lowell-Brockton, MA-NH	5,894,873	4
Philadelphia, PA-NJ	4,946,435	5
Washington, DC-MD-VA-WV	4,714,675	6
Detroit, MI	4,483,071	7
Houston, TX	3,991,691	8
Atlanta, GA	3,824,281	9
Dallas, TX	3,269,983	10
Riverside-San Bernardino, CA	3,108,211	11
Phoenix-Mesa, AZ	2,994,922	12
Minneapolis-St. Paul, MN-WI	2,856,786	13
San Diego, CA	2,798,201	14
Orange County, CA	2,735,375	15
Nassau-Suffolk, NY	2,680,413	16
St. Louis, MO-IL	2,590,981	17
Baltimore, MD	2,490,590	18
Pittsburgh, PA	2,336,230	19
Seattle-Bellevue-Everett, WA	2,330,597	20
Oakland, CA	2,322,512	21
Tampa-St. Petersburg-Clearwater, FL	2,281,537	22
Cleveland-Lorain-Elyria, OH	2,219,856	23
Miami, FL	2,131,916	24
Denver, CO	1,965,781	25
Newark, NJ	1,956,546	26
Portland-Vancouver, OR-WA	1,843,362	27
Kansas City, MO-KS	1,751,214	28
San Francisco, CA	1,717,639	29
San Jose, CA	1,671,121	30
New Haven-Bridgeport-Stamford Danbury-Waterbury,CT	1,633,739	31
Cincinnati, OH-KY-IN	1,624,719	32
Fort Worth-Arlington, TX	1,618,343	33
San Antonio, TX	1,559,558	34
Norfolk-Virginia Beach-Newport News, VA-NC	1,547,085	35
Sacramento, CA	1,535,958	36
Orlando, FL	1,531,635	37
Indianapolis, IN	1,530,570	38
Fort Lauderdale, FL	1,498,581	39
Columbus, OH	1,478,498	40
Milwaukee-Waukesha, WI	1,458,453	41
Charlotte-Gastonia-Rock Hill, NC-SC	1,405,961	42
Las Vegas, NV-AZ	1,367,114	43
Bergen-Passaic, NJ	1,349,797	44
New Orleans, LA	1,310,213	45
Salt Lake City-Ogden, UT	1,281,817	46
Greensboro-Winston Salem-High Point, NC	1,178,495	47
Nashville, TN	1,171,096	48
Buffalo-Niagara Falls, NY	1,146,556	49
Austin-San Marcos, TX	1,132,817	50
Middlesex-Somerset-Hunterdon, NJ	1,131,905	51
Hartford, CT	1,109,946	52
Monmouth-Ocean, NJ	1,104,022	53
Raleigh-Durham-Chapel Hill, NC	1,101,410	54
Memphis, TN-AR-MS	1,100,230	55
Rochester, NY	1,081,365	56
Jacksonville, FL	1,058,981	57
Oklahoma City, OK	1,045,728	58
Grand Rapids-Muskegon-Holland, MI	1,045,268	59
West Palm Beach-Boca Raton, FL	1,038,254	60
Louisville, KY-IN	1,003,148	61
Richmond-Petersburg, VA	964,695	62
Dayton-Springfield, OH	945,669	63
Greenville-Spartanburg-Anderson, SC	926,654	64
Birmingham, AL	913,565	65
Providence-Warwick-Pawtucket, RI	904,809	66
Fresno, CA	888,903	67
Honolulu, HI	872,757	68
Albany-Schenectady-Troy, NY	870,412	69
Tucson, AZ	800,472	70
Tulsa, OK	783,728	71
Ventura, CA	733,036	72
Syracuse, NY	732,039	73
El Paso, TX	713,257	74
Omaha, NE-IA	699,385	75
Akron, OH	690,877	76
Tacoma, WA	689,187	77
Albuquerque, NM	682,848	78
Knoxville, TN	663,880	79
Bakersfield, CA	636,736	80
Gary, IN	625,375	81
Allentown-Bethlehem-Easton, PA	618,269	82
Harrisburg-Lebanon-Carlisle, PA	617,166	83
Scranton-Wilkes-Barre-Hazleton, PA	611,758	84
Toledo, OH	609,243	85
Youngstown-Warren, OH	589,432	86
Springfield, MA	588,063	87
Baton Rouge, LA	578,445	88
Wilmington-Newark, DE-MD	569,635	89
Little Rock-North Little Rock, AR	560,035	90
Jersey City, NJ	558,499	91
Sarasota-Bradenton, FL	557,303	92
Ann Arbor, MI	553,214	93
Stockton-Lodi, CA	550,351	94
Wichita, KS	549,636	95
Charleston-North Charleston, SC	544,103	96
Mobile, AL	536,301	97
McAllen-Edinburg-Mission, TX	534,615	98
Columbia, SC	517,411	99
Vallejo-Fairfield-Napa, CA	503,800	100
Colorado Springs, CO	498,097	101
Fort Wayne, IN	483,652	102
Daytona Beach, FL	471,864	103
Melbourne-Titusville-Palm Bay, FL	470,027	104
Johnson City-Kingsport-Bristol, TN-VA	464,210	105
Lakeland-Winter Haven, FL	462,884	106
Augusta-Aiken, GA-SC	460,338	107
Lancaster, PA	458,907	108
Lexington, KY	453,450	109
Chattanooga, TN-GA	452,198	110
Lansing-East Lansing, MI	449,545	111
Kalamazoo-Battle Creek, MI	446,939	112
Des Moines, IA	440,560	113
Santa Rosa, CA	436,792	114
Flint, MI	436,032	115
Jackson, MS	432,626	116
Modesto, CA	428,970	117
Madison, WI	428,149	118
Spokane, WA	412,358	119
Pensacola, FL	405,930	120
Boise City, ID	405,007	121
Fort Myers-Cape Coral, FL	403,863	122
Canton-Massillon, OH	402,104	123
Saginaw-Bay City-Midland, MI	401,279	124
Santa Barbara-Santa Maria-Lompoc, CA	397,596	125
Corpus Christi, TX	390,241	126
Shreveport-Bossier City, LA	378,708	127
Lafayette, LA	378,517	128
Salinas, CA	376,814	129
Beaumont-Port Arthur, TX	375,954	130
York, PA	375,635	131
Newburgh, NY-PA	372,261	132
Visalia-Tulare-Porterville, CA	359,156	133
Rockford, IL	358,704	134
Davenport-Moline-Rock Island, IA-IL	357,960	135
Reading, PA	357,387	136
Biloxi-Gulfport-Pascagoula, MS	352,155	137
Appleton-Oshkosh-Neenah, WI	346,380	138
Peoria-Pekin, IL	344,948	139
Huntsville, AL	343,820	140
Provo-Orem, UT	340,913	141
Atlantic-Cape May, NJ	337,411	142
Salem, OR	333,946	143
Hamilton-Middletown, OH	332,963	144
Brownsville-Harlingen-San Benito, TX	332,512	145
Trenton, NJ	332,203	146
Hickory-Morganton-Lenoir, NC	325,596	147
Montgomery, AL	323,675	148
Macon, GA	322,093	149
Reno, NV	319,386	150
Eugene-Springfield, OR	316,356	151
Huntington-Ashland, WV-KY-OH	313,439	152
Springfield, MO	307,824	153
Killeen-Temple, TX	303,363	154
Fort Pierce-Port St. Lucie, FL	302,089	155
Utica-Rome, NY	291,615	156
Evansville-Henderson, IN-KY	291,396	157
Savannah, GA	287,349	158
Fayetteville, NC	284,702	159
Fayetteville-Springdale-Rogers, AR	278,016	160
Erie, PA	275,737	161
Tallahassee, FL	274,806	162
Columbus, GA-AL	272,153	163
Boulder-Longmont, CO	270,841	164
Dutchess County, NY	266,269	165
South Bend, IN	258,713	166
Anchorage, AK	256,711	167
Portland, ME	255,078	168
Charleston, WV	253,008	169
Galveston-Texas City, TX	247,932	170
Odessa-Midland, TX	247,274	171
Binghamton, NY	247,060	172
Santa Cruz-Watsonville, CA	246,816	173
Ocala, FL	245,541	174
New London-Norwich, CT	245,304	175
Lincoln, NE	237,337	176
San Luis Obispo-Antascadero-Paso Robles, CA	237,170	177
Duluth-Superior, MN-WI	235,929	178
Johnstown, PA	235,213	179
Fort Collins-Loveland, CO	235,091	180
Brazoria, TX	233,816	181
Bremerton, WA	233,789	182
Lubbock, TX	229,417	183
Roanoke, VA	227,408	184
Wilmington, NC	222,793	185
Green Bay, WI	216,602	186
Yakima, WA	215,705	187
Asheville, NC	215,427	188
Barnstable-Yarmouth, MA	210,806	189
Longview-Marshall, TX	210,534	190
Amarillo, TX	210,292	191
Lynchburg, VA	209,178	192
Naples, FL	209,017	193
Gainesville, FL	206,306	194
Waco, TX	204,796	195
Olympia, WA	204,043	196
Springfield, IL	203,833	197
Clarksville-Hopkinsville, TN-KY	202,665	198
Merced, CA	201,676	199
Chico-Paradise, CA	198,077	200
Fort Smith, AR-OK	195,636	201
Houma, LA	195,114	202
Burlington, VT	194,327	203
Laredo, TX	193,273	204
Racine, WI	186,592	205
Richland-Kennewick-Pasco, WA	184,513	206
Cedar Rapids, IA	183,726	207
Lake Charles, LA	181,438	208
Myrtle Beach, SC	178,658	209
Medford-Ashland, OR	174,918	210
Mansfield, OH	174,320	211
Fort Walton Beach, FL	174,175	212
Elkhart-Goshen, IN	173,805	213
Lafayette, IN	172,920	214
Las Cruces, NM	171,270	215
Tyler, TX	170,615	216
Fargo-Moorhead, ND-MN	169,446	217
Champaign-Urbana, IL	167,570	218
Topeka, KS	165,557	219
Sioux Falls, SD	165,275	220
Redding, CA	164,908	221
St. Cloud, MN	163,298	222
Greeley, CO	162,253	223
Tuscaloosa, AL	161,726	224
Benton Harbor, MI	159,862	225
Bellingham, WA	159,493	226
Jackson, MI	156,597	227
Yolo, CA	155,737	228
Lima, OH	153,867	229
Wheeling, WV-OH	152,124	230
Janesville-Beloit, WI	151,322	231
Charlottesville, VA	150,961	232
Joplin, MO	149,911	233
Parkersburg-Marietta, WV-OH	149,905	234
Panama City, FL	148,422	235
Terre Haute, IN	148,376	236
Rocky Mount, NC	147,210	237
Monroe, LA	147,187	238
Kenosha, WI	145,462	239
Eau Claire, WI	144,180	240
Bloomington-Normal, IL	143,758	241
Decatur, AL	143,653	242
Santa Fe, NM	143,386	243
Jacksonville, NC	142,644	244
Bangor, ME	141,834	245
Vineland-Millville-Bridgeton, NJ	140,097	246
Athens, GA	139,732	247
Yuba City, CA	137,775	248
Florence, AL	137,612	249
Jamestown, NY	137,438	250
Wichita Falls, TX	137,314	251
Pueblo, CO	136,188	252
Punta Gorda, FL	135,815	253
Dothan, AL	134,980	254
Yuma, AZ	134,532	255
Bryan-College Station, TX	134,242	256
Steubenville-Weirton, OH-WV	133,476	257
State College, PA	133,141	258
Pittsfield, MA	132,609	259
Columbia, MO	130,574	260
Altoona, PA	130,310	261
Greenville, NC	128,300	262
Hagerstown, MD	127,695	263
Alexandria, LA	126,953	264
Billings, MT	126,821	265
Florence, SC	125,609	266
Dover, DE	125,058	267
Wausau, WI	123,748	268
Texarkana, TX-AR	123,453	269
Abilene, TX	122,192	270
La Crosse, WI-MN	122,061	271
Sharon, PA	121,848	272
Glens Falls, NY	121,753	273
Flagstaff, AZ-UT	121,437	274
Waterloo-Cedar Falls, IA	120,743	275
Sioux City, IA-NE	120,505	276
Albany, GA	118,442	277
Rochester, MN	117,605	278
Anniston, AL	117,136	279
Williamsport, PA	116,744	280
Muncie, IN	116,324	281
Bloomington, IN	115,627	282
Grand Junction, CO	114,585	283
Decatur, IL	113,185	284
Lawton, OK	112,982	285
Goldsboro, NC	112,688	286
Hattiesburg, MS	112,544	287
Sheboygan, WI	110,580	288
Danville, VA	107,739	289
Sumter, SC	107,295	290
Gadsden, AL	104,326	291
Sherman-Denison, TX	103,883	292
Iowa City, IA	103,232	293
San Angelo, TX	103,197	294
Kankakee, IL	102,307	295
Jackson, TN	101,463	296
Lewiston-Auburn, ME	101,018	297
Kokomo, IN	100,114	298
Grand Forks, ND-MN	99,382	299
Cumberland, MD-WV	97,543	300
St. Joseph, MO	97,300	301
Lawrence, KS	94,151	302
Bismarck, ND	91,845	303
Elmira, NY	91,612	304
Owensboro, KY	91,330	305
Missoula, MT	89,589	306
Rapid City, SD	87,925	307
Dubuque, IA	87,732	308
Victoria, TX	83,275	309
Pine Bluff, AR	81,087	310
Cheyenne, WY	79,067	311
Great Falls, MT	78,833	312
Jonesboro, AR	78,276	313
Pocatello, ID	75,257	314
Casper, WY	63,251	315
Enid, OK	56,906	316

MSA/NECMA Total **218,033,301**
United States Total **272,212,864**
MSA/NECMA (% of U.S.Total) **80.10**

POPULATION BY AGE: 0-4 YEARS

MSA/NECMA	POPULATION	RANK
Los Angeles-Long Beach, CA	750,853	1
Chicago, IL	592,292	2
New York, NY	583,799	3
Boston-Worcester-Lawrence-Lowell-Brockton, MA-NH	387,781	4
Philadelphia, PA-NJ	340,769	5
Houston, TX	326,191	6
Detroit, MI	322,422	7
Washington, DC-MD-VA-WV	321,894	8
Riverside-San Bernardino, CA	284,145	9
Atlanta, GA	279,066	10
Dallas, TX	256,731	11
Phoenix-Mesa, AZ	231,545	12
Minneapolis-St. Paul, MN-WI	216,120	13
San Diego, CA	208,607	14
Orange County, CA	199,011	15
St. Louis, MO-IL	187,152	16
Baltimore, MD	173,312	17
Nassau-Suffolk, NY	167,011	18
Oakland, CA	163,672	19
Seattle-Bellevue-Everett, WA	158,994	20
Cleveland-Lorain-Elyria, OH	150,558	21
Miami, FL	146,748	22
Denver, CO	145,250	23
Pittsburgh, PA	137,241	24
Tampa-St. Petersburg-Clearwater, FL	131,689	25
Newark, NJ	128,728	26
Portland-Vancouver, OR-WA	128,328	27
Fort Worth-Arlington, TX	127,957	28
Kansas City, MO-KS	127,136	29
San Antonio, TX	125,447	30
Norfolk-Virginia Beach-Newport News, VA-NC	122,522	31
Cincinnati, OH-KY-IN	120,798	32
Salt Lake City-Ogden, UT	118,523	33
San Jose, CA	117,065	34
Sacramento, CA	115,444	35
Indianapolis, IN	109,367	36
New Haven-Bridgeport-Stamford-Danbury-Waterbury, CT	106,952	37
Milwaukee-Waukesha, WI	105,391	38
Orlando, FL	103,240	39
Columbus, OH	102,634	40
Las Vegas, NV-AZ	97,888	41
New Orleans, LA	97,847	42
Charlotte-Gastonia-Rock Hill, NC-SC	96,946	43
San Francisco, CA	94,184	44
Fort Lauderdale, FL	89,492	45
Memphis, TN-AR-MS	85,333	46
Grand Rapids-Muskegon-Holland, MI	84,775	47
Austin-San Marcos, TX	83,298	48
Bergen-Passaic, NJ	81,957	49
Fresno, CA	80,763	50
Nashville, TN	79,175	51
Jacksonville, FL	78,776	52
Rochester, NY	76,363	53
Buffalo-Niagara Falls, NY	75,507	54
Oklahoma City, OK	73,840	55
Greensboro-Winston Salem-High Point, NC	73,095	56
Monmouth-Ocean, NJ	72,240	57
Middlesex-Somerset-Hunterdon, NJ	71,164	58
Hartford, CT	70,751	59
Raleigh-Durham-Chapel Hill, NC	70,630	60
Louisville, KY-IN	64,852	61
Richmond-Petersburg, VA	64,781	62
Dayton-Springfield, OH	63,585	63
El Paso, TX	62,516	64
Birmingham, AL	62,454	65
West Palm Beach-Boca Raton, FL	61,580	66
Greenville-Spartanburg-Anderson, SC	60,086	67
Honolulu, HI	59,546	68
Bakersfield, CA	59,050	69
Tucson, AZ	57,931	70
Providence-Warwick-Pawtucket, RI	57,777	71
Ventura, CA	56,900	72
Tulsa, OK	56,313	73
Albany-Schenectady-Troy, NY	56,004	74
Tacoma, WA	54,399	75
Omaha, NE-IA	53,617	76
Albuquerque, NM	53,003	77
Syracuse, NY	51,904	78
McAllen-Edinburg-Mission, TX	49,343	79
Stockton-Lodi, CA	47,510	80
Akron, OH	45,258	81
Charleston-North Charleston, SC	45,089	82
Toledo, OH	43,895	83
Wichita, KS	43,804	84
Baton Rouge, LA	43,268	85
Gary, IN	42,642	86
Vallejo-Fairfield-Napa, CA	39,652	87
Colorado Springs, CO	39,637	88
Mobile, AL	39,454	89
Knoxville, TN	39,452	90
Wilmington-Newark, DE-MD	39,012	91
Little Rock-North Little Rock, AR	38,986	92
Allentown-Bethlehem-Easton, PA	38,728	93
Springfield, MA	38,586	94
Harrisburg-Lebanon-Carlisle, PA	38,378	95
Modesto, CA	38,077	96
Youngstown-Warren, OH	37,909	97
Fort Wayne, IN	36,196	98
Jersey City, NJ	36,032	99
Ann Arbor, MI	35,834	100
Provo-Orem, UT	35,743	101
Scranton-Wilkes-Barre-Hazleton, PA	35,327	102
Lancaster, PA	34,606	103
Augusta-Aiken, GA-SC	34,605	104
Columbia, SC	34,409	105
Visalia-Tulare-Porterville, CA	33,469	106
Salinas, CA	32,514	107
Jackson, MS	32,089	108
Flint, MI	32,047	109
Lakeland-Winter Haven, FL	31,756	110
Kalamazoo-Battle Creek, MI	31,353	111
Lafayette, LA	31,298	112
Corpus Christi, TX	31,175	113
Des Moines, IA	30,951	114
Lansing-East Lansing, MI	30,771	115
Santa Rosa, CA	30,444	116
Boise City, ID	30,321	117
Melbourne-Titusville-Palm Bay, FL	29,734	118
Newburgh, NY-PA	29,407	119
Brownsville-Harlingen-San Benito, TX	29,403	120
Shreveport-Bossier City, LA	28,993	121
Pensacola, FL	28,970	122
Spokane, WA	28,888	123
Chattanooga, TN-GA	28,685	124
Lexington, KY	28,577	125
Saginaw-Bay City-Midland, MI	28,544	126
Santa Barbara-Santa Maria-Lompoc, CA	28,294	127
Sarasota-Bradenton, FL	27,453	128
Madison, WI	27,445	129
Killeen-Temple, TX	27,181	130
Biloxi-Gulfport-Pascagoula, MS	26,549	131
Beaumont-Port Arthur, TX	26,442	132
Canton-Massillon, OH	26,095	133
Daytona Beach, FL	26,039	134
Rockford, IL	25,751	135
Johnson City-Kingsport-Bristol, TN-VA	25,491	136
Appleton-Oshkosh-Neenah, WI	25,120	137
Davenport-Moline-Rock Island, IA-IL	24,828	138
Fayetteville, NC	24,766	139
York, PA	24,661	140
Macon, GA	23,904	141
Salem, OR	23,673	142
Montgomery, AL	23,668	143
Huntsville, AL	23,349	144
Fort Myers-Cape Coral, FL	23,232	145
Hamilton-Middletown, OH	23,046	146
Peoria-Pekin, IL	22,925	147
Reading, PA	22,893	148
Atlantic-Cape May, NJ	22,717	149
Anchorage, AK	22,495	150
Savannah, GA	21,856	151
Odessa-Midland, TX	21,829	152
Reno, NV	21,762	153
Trenton, NJ	21,041	154
Columbus, GA-AL	20,892	155
Merced, CA	20,400	156
Eugene-Springfield, OR	20,012	157
Hickory-Morganton-Lenoir, NC	19,854	158
Springfield, MO	19,533	159
Utica-Rome, NY	19,443	160
Evansville-Henderson, IN-KY	19,221	161
Erie, PA	19,084	162
Laredo, TX	19,044	163
Yakima, WA	18,717	164
Fort Pierce-Port St. Lucie, FL	18,604	165
Fayetteville-Springdale-Rogers, AR	18,430	166
Galveston-Texas City, TX	18,232	167
South Bend, IN	18,132	168
Bremerton, WA	18,091	169
Brazoria, TX	17,978	170
Huntington-Ashland, WV-KY-OH	17,737	171
Dutchess County, NY	17,715	172
Tallahassee, FL	17,476	173
Clarksville-Hopkinsville, TN-KY	17,461	174
New London-Norwich, CT	17,350	175
Boulder-Longmont, CO	17,222	176
Lubbock, TX	17,035	177
Santa Cruz-Watsonville, CA	16,909	178
Portland, ME	16,732	179
Binghamton, NY	16,425	180
Amarillo, TX	16,336	181
Fort Collins-Loveland, CO	16,013	182
Lincoln, NE	15,869	183
Houma, LA	15,864	184
Green Bay, WI	15,762	185
Ocala, FL	15,380	186
Waco, TX	15,296	187
Longview-Marshall, TX	15,180	188
Richland-Kennewick-Pasco, WA	15,153	189
Charleston, WV	14,717	190
San Luis Obispo-Antascadero-Paso Robles,CA	14,648	191
Las Cruces, NM	14,633	192
Duluth-Superior, MN-WI	14,427	193
Elkhart-Goshen, IN	13,888	194
Springfield, IL	13,849	195
Fort Smith, AR-OK	13,770	196
Racine, WI	13,755	197
Olympia, WA	13,731	198
Lake Charles, LA	13,658	199
Burlington, VT	13,551	200
Wilmington, NC	13,489	201
Johnstown, PA	13,452	202
Lynchburg, VA	13,228	203
Chico-Paradise, CA	13,188	204
Roanoke, VA	13,145	205
Fort Walton Beach, FL	12,988	206
Gainesville, FL	12,764	207
Jacksonville, NC	12,666	208
Asheville, NC	12,626	209
Barnstable-Yarmouth, MA	12,524	210
Yuba City, CA	12,467	211
Naples, FL	12,427	212
St. Cloud, MN	12,417	213
Tyler, TX	12,351	214
Greeley, CO	12,341	215
Sioux Falls, SD	12,336	216
Cedar Rapids, IA	12,187	217
Redding, CA	12,108	218
Fargo-Moorhead, ND-MN	11,821	219
Monroe, LA	11,524	220
Myrtle Beach, SC	11,516	221
Topeka, KS	11,499	222
Mansfield, OH	11,478	223
Benton Harbor, MI	11,404	224
Yuma, AZ	11,395	225
Lima, OH	11,329	226
Medford-Ashland, OR	11,281	227
Kenosha, WI	11,083	228
Janesville-Beloit, WI	11,064	229
Yolo, CA	11,013	230
Champaign-Urbana, IL	10,953	231
Jackson, MI	10,919	232
Lafayette, IN	10,691	233
Flagstaff, AZ-UT	10,655	234
Bellingham, WA	10,470	235
Panama City, FL	10,389	236
Tuscaloosa, AL	10,255	237
Dothan, AL	10,247	238
Rocky Mount, NC	10,236	239
Joplin, MO	10,030	240
Vineland-Millville-Bridgeton, NJ	10,018	241
Dover, DE	10,014	242
Wichita Falls, TX	9,977	243
Santa Fe, NM	9,927	244
Eau Claire, WI	9,870	245
Abilene, TX	9,722	246
Decatur, AL	9,620	247
Alexandria, LA	9,602	248
Charlottesville, VA	9,574	249
Albany, GA	9,431	250
Rochester, MN	9,428	251
Pueblo, CO	9,350	252
Lawton, OK	9,242	253
Bloomington-Normal, IL	9,176	254
Terre Haute, IN	9,143	255
Jamestown, NY	9,127	256
Sioux City, IA-NE	9,078	257
Parkersburg-Marietta, WV-OH	9,058	258
Florence, SC	8,970	259
Billings, MT	8,899	260
Bangor, ME	8,876	261
Bryan-College Station, TX	8,842	262
Wausau, WI	8,745	263
Athens, GA	8,741	264
Greenville, NC	8,738	265
Sumter, SC	8,709	266
Wheeling, WV-OH	8,694	267
Texarkana, TX-AR	8,689	268
Columbia, MO	8,630	269
Florence, AL	8,603	270
La Crosse, WI-MN	8,413	271
Hattiesburg, MS	8,236	272
Glens Falls, NY	8,199	273
Goldsboro, NC	8,136	274
Hagerstown, MD	8,045	275
Pittsfield, MA	7,885	276
Altoona, PA	7,828	277
San Angelo, TX	7,818	278
Waterloo-Cedar Falls, IA	7,802	279
Grand Junction, CO	7,795	280
Grand Forks, ND-MN	7,749	281
Rapid City, SD	7,748	282
Williamsport, PA	7,684	283
Sheboygan, WI	7,550	284
Kankakee, IL	7,545	285
Decatur, IL	7,400	286
Anniston, AL	7,373	287
Sharon, PA	7,304	288
Lewiston-Auburn, ME	7,136	289
Steubenville-Weirton, OH-WV	7,095	290
Sherman-Denison, TX	6,901	291
Jackson, TN	6,895	292
State College, PA	6,833	293
St. Joseph, MO	6,773	294
Muncie, IN	6,712	295
Danville, VA	6,596	296
Kokomo, IN	6,578	297
Victoria, TX	6,569	298
Bismarck, ND	6,466	299
Owensboro, KY	6,324	300
Elmira, NY	6,222	301
Great Falls, MT	6,181	302
Gadsden, AL	6,141	303
Missoula, MT	6,088	304
Cheyenne, WY	6,033	305
Iowa City, IA	6,009	306
Bloomington, IN	5,971	307
Pine Bluff, AR	5,965	308
Pocatello, ID	5,959	309
Dubuque, IA	5,835	310
Punta Gorda, FL	5,820	311
Lawrence, KS	5,612	312
Cumberland, MD-WV	5,610	313
Jonesboro, AR	5,215	314
Casper, WY	4,613	315
Enid, OK	3,834	316

MSA/NECMA Total **15,540,187**
United States Total **19,261,317**
MSA/NECMA (% of U.S.Total) **80.68**

POPULATION BY AGE: 5-17 YEARS

MSA/NECMA	POPULATION	RANK
Los Angeles-Long Beach, CA	1,787,012	1
Chicago, IL	1,479,106	2
New York, NY	1,457,234	3
Boston-Worcester-Lawrence-Lowell-Brockton, MA-NH	981,987	4
Philadelphia, PA-NJ	874,679	5
Detroit, MI	824,420	6
Washington, DC-MD-VA-WV	812,567	7
Houston, TX	803,837	8
Atlanta, GA	700,473	9
Riverside-San Bernardino, CA	639,088	10
Dallas, TX	625,092	11
Phoenix-Mesa, AZ	563,259	12
Minneapolis-St. Paul, MN-WI	542,173	13
San Diego, CA	513,521	14
Orange County, CA	489,828	15
St. Louis, MO-IL	489,559	16
Nassau-Suffolk, NY	443,023	17
Baltimore, MD	438,075	18
Oakland, CA	418,779	19
Cleveland-Lorain-Elyria, OH	405,713	20
Seattle-Bellevue-Everett, WA	404,810	21
Pittsburgh, PA	373,295	22
Denver, CO	365,787	23
Miami, FL	361,000	24
Portland-Vancouver, OR-WA	346,300	25
Tampa-St. Petersburg-Clearwater, FL	342,034	26
Kansas City, MO-KS	328,773	27
Newark, NJ	328,667	28
Salt Lake City-Ogden, UT	320,163	29
San Antonio, TX	317,746	30
Cincinnati, OH-KY-IN	310,714	31
Fort Worth-Arlington, TX	306,579	32
San Jose, CA	295,270	33
Norfolk-Virginia Beach-Newport News, VA-NC	292,139	34
Sacramento, CA	289,312	35
Indianapolis, IN	288,290	36
Milwaukee-Waukesha, WI	277,017	37
New Haven-Bridgeport-Stamford-Danbury-Waterbury,CT	275,213	38
Columbus, OH	266,224	39
Orlando, FL	264,530	40
New Orleans, LA	261,883	41
Charlotte-Gastonia-Rock Hill, NC-SC	250,888	42
San Francisco, CA	245,161	43
Las Vegas, NV-AZ	242,653	44
Fort Lauderdale, FL	227,313	45
Memphis, TN-AR-MS	218,669	46
Nashville, TN	217,563	47
Austin-San Marcos, TX	213,970	48
Bergen-Passaic, NJ	212,939	49
Grand Rapids-Muskegon-Holland, MI	206,883	50
Oklahoma City, OK	199,010	51
Jacksonville, FL	197,674	52
Buffalo-Niagara Falls, NY	196,844	53
Rochester, NY	195,834	54
Greensboro-Winston Salem-High Point, NC	194,015	55
Fresno, CA	192,563	56
Monmouth-Ocean, NJ	188,496	57
Hartford, CT	185,078	58
Raleigh-Durham-Chapel Hill, NC	183,416	59
Middlesex-Somerset-Hunterdon, NJ	182,750	60
Louisville, KY-IN	181,946	61
Dayton-Springfield, OH	171,930	62
Richmond-Petersburg, VA	171,562	63
Birmingham, AL	163,479	64
El Paso, TX	161,451	65
Greenville-Spartanburg-Anderson, SC	160,346	66
West Palm Beach-Boca Raton, FL	153,139	67
Tulsa, OK	149,688	68
Providence-Warwick-Pawtucket, RI	149,272	69
Albany-Schenectady-Troy, NY	147,590	70
Honolulu, HI	146,189	71
Tucson, AZ	146,114	72
Ventura, CA	141,728	73
McAllen-Edinburg-Mission, TX	138,137	74
Omaha, NE-IA	136,378	75
Bakersfield, CA	134,986	76
Syracuse, NY	132,657	77
Albuquerque, NM	132,481	78
Tacoma, WA	131,227	79
Gary, IN	124,853	80
Akron, OH	121,009	81
Baton Rouge, LA	118,022	82
Stockton-Lodi, CA	114,491	83
Toledo, OH	112,990	84
Knoxville, TN	108,891	85
Little Rock-North Little Rock, AR	108,731	86
Charleston-North Charleston, SC	107,612	87
Mobile, AL	107,085	88
Wichita, KS	106,163	89
Youngstown-Warren, OH	105,703	90
Harrisburg-Lebanon-Carlisle, PA	102,878	91
Allentown-Bethlehem-Easton, PA	102,113	92
Wilmington-Newark, DE-MD	100,849	93
Ann Arbor, MI	100,209	94
Springfield, MA	99,699	95
Fort Wayne, IN	96,989	96
Vallejo-Fairfield-Napa, CA	96,876	97
Scranton-Wilkes-Barre-Hazleton, PA	95,064	98
Colorado Springs, CO	93,710	99
Columbia, SC	92,963	100
Augusta-Aiken, GA-SC	90,894	101
Modesto, CA	90,812	102
Jersey City, NJ	88,995	103
Provo-Orem, UT	88,357	104
Flint, MI	86,777	105
Jackson, MS	86,522	106
Lancaster, PA	84,929	107
Boise City, ID	84,504	108
Visalia-Tulare-Porterville, CA	83,704	109
Lansing-East Lansing, MI	83,455	110
Kalamazoo-Battle Creek, MI	83,292	111
Corpus Christi, TX	83,287	112
Brownsville-Harlingen-San Benito, TX	82,341	113
Lafayette, LA	81,284	114
Lakeland-Winter Haven, FL	80,998	115
Des Moines, IA	80,107	116
Chattanooga, TN-GA	79,655	117
Santa Rosa, CA	78,980	118
Saginaw-Bay City-Midland, MI	78,831	119
Spokane, WA	77,822	120
Lexington, KY	77,754	121
Melbourne-Titusville-Palm Bay, FL	77,048	122
Shreveport-Bossier City, LA	76,345	123
Salinas, CA	75,451	124
Beaumont-Port Arthur, TX	74,512	125
Pensacola, FL	74,356	126
Canton-Massillon, OH	73,560	127
Johnson City-Kingsport-Bristol, TN-VA	72,075	128
Madison, WI	71,499	129
Biloxi-Gulfport-Pascagoula, MS	71,004	130
Sarasota-Bradenton, FL	70,958	131
Newburgh, NY-PA	70,955	132
Santa Barbara-Santa Maria-Lompoc, CA	69,339	133
Davenport-Moline-Rock Island, IA-IL	68,528	134
Rockford, IL	67,947	135
Daytona Beach, FL	67,864	136
Appleton-Oshkosh-Neenah, WI	65,775	137
Peoria-Pekin, IL	65,409	138
York, PA	65,262	139
Salem, OR	64,161	140
Montgomery, AL	63,208	141
Hamilton-Middletown, OH	62,132	142
Macon, GA	61,989	143
Huntsville, AL	60,403	144
Reading, PA	60,159	145
Fort Myers-Cape Coral, FL	59,176	146
Killeen-Temple, TX	57,616	147
Atlantic-Cape May, NJ	57,453	148
Savannah, GA	57,066	149
Eugene-Springfield, OR	55,768	150
Trenton, NJ	55,101	151
Reno, NV	54,923	152
Huntington-Ashland, WV-KY-OH	54,792	153
Hickory-Morganton-Lenoir, NC	54,702	154
Odessa-Midland, TX	54,132	155
Fayetteville, NC	53,943	156
Evansville-Henderson, IN-KY	53,782	157
Springfield, MO	53,715	158
Utica-Rome, NY	51,465	159
Columbus, GA-AL	51,385	160
Erie, PA	51,280	161
Fayetteville-Springdale-Rogers, AR	49,977	162
Anchorage, AK	49,507	163
Laredo, TX	48,826	164
Brazoria, TX	48,149	165
Galveston-Texas City, TX	48,021	166
Fort Pierce-Port St. Lucie, FL	47,174	167
Merced, CA	47,057	168
Tallahassee, FL	46,862	169
South Bend, IN	46,659	170
Yakima, WA	46,189	171
Bremerton, WA	45,922	172
Dutchess County, NY	45,702	173
Boulder-Longmont, CO	45,523	174
Santa Cruz-Watsonville, CA	43,667	175
Lubbock, TX	43,553	176
Portland, ME	43,424	177
Binghamton, NY	43,154	178
Houma, LA	42,983	179
New London-Norwich, CT	42,561	180
Charleston, WV	42,535	181
Fort Collins-Loveland, CO	42,255	182
Longview-Marshall, TX	42,060	183
Amarillo, TX	41,447	184
Duluth-Superior, MN-WI	41,426	185
Green Bay, WI	41,159	186
Lincoln, NE	40,861	187
Richland-Kennewick-Pasco, WA	40,684	188
Olympia, WA	39,764	189
Johnstown, PA	39,141	190
Ocala, FL	39,035	191
San Luis Obispo-Antascadero-Paso Robles, CA	38,621	192
Fort Smith, AR-OK	38,543	193
Waco, TX	38,365	194
Lake Charles, LA	38,080	195
Clarksville-Hopkinsville, TN-KY	37,880	196
Springfield, IL	37,642	197
Las Cruces, NM	37,331	198
Racine, WI	36,625	199
Roanoke, VA	36,127	200
Wilmington, NC	35,822	201
Lynchburg, VA	35,070	202
Elkhart-Goshen, IN	34,324	203
Chico-Paradise, CA	34,270	204
Asheville, NC	34,108	205
Burlington, VT	34,103	206
Barnstable-Yarmouth, MA	33,424	207
Gainesville, FL	33,143	208
Mansfield, OH	33,048	209
St. Cloud, MN	33,021	210
Cedar Rapids, IA	33,006	211
Greeley, CO	32,481	212
Redding, CA	32,440	213
Tyler, TX	32,135	214
Sioux Falls, SD	31,797	215
Medford-Ashland, OR	31,510	216
Fort Walton Beach, FL	31,261	217
Naples, FL	31,257	218
Benton Harbor, MI	30,924	219
Topeka, KS	30,869	220
Lima, OH	30,687	221
Monroe, LA	30,621	222
Myrtle Beach, SC	30,351	223
Fargo-Moorhead, ND-MN	30,007	224
Yuma, AZ	29,116	225
Jackson, MI	29,034	226
Janesville-Beloit, WI	29,017	227
Bellingham, WA	28,815	228
Lafayette, IN	28,420	229
Yuba City, CA	28,326	230
Joplin, MO	28,272	231
Champaign-Urbana, IL	27,791	232
Yolo, CA	27,647	233
Kenosha, WI	27,332	234
Parkersburg-Marietta, WV-OH	27,219	235
Rocky Mount, NC	27,217	236
Decatur, AL	27,148	237
Eau Claire, WI	27,073	238
Tuscaloosa, AL	26,948	239
Panama City, FL	26,735	240
Dothan, AL	26,613	241
Alexandria, LA	26,533	242
Albany, GA	25,884	243
Flagstaff, AZ-UT	25,859	244
Vineland-Millville-Bridgeton, NJ	25,785	245
Santa Fe, NM	25,760	246
Jacksonville, NC	25,505	247
Wausau, WI	25,318	248
Florence, SC	25,275	249
Jamestown, NY	25,187	250
Wichita Falls, TX	25,182	251
Terre Haute, IN	25,144	252
Wheeling, WV-OH	25,032	253
Sioux City, IA-NE	24,881	254
Bangor, ME	24,872	255
Billings, MT	24,833	256
Pueblo, CO	24,686	257
Texarkana, TX-AR	24,555	258
Charlottesville, VA	24,429	259
Bloomington-Normal, IL	24,086	260
Abilene, TX	23,660	261
Dover, DE	23,584	262
Florence, AL	23,384	263
Athens, GA	22,872	264
Altoona, PA	22,846	265
Greenville, NC	22,618	266
Grand Junction, CO	22,366	267
Rochester, MN	22,211	268
Glens Falls, NY	22,184	269
Columbia, MO	21,991	270
La Crosse, WI-MN	21,959	271
Waterloo-Cedar Falls, IA	21,946	272
Hattiesburg, MS	21,848	273
Pittsfield, MA	21,805	274
Lawton, OK	21,794	275
Bryan-College Station, TX	21,462	276
Sheboygan, WI	21,447	277
Sumter, SC	21,350	278
Steubenville-Weirton, OH-WV	21,330	279
Hagerstown, MD	21,055	280
Williamsport, PA	21,049	281
Decatur, IL	20,858	282
Kankakee, IL	20,841	283
Anniston, AL	20,568	284
Goldsboro, NC	20,478	285
San Angelo, TX	20,177	286
Sharon, PA	20,149	287
Kokomo, IN	19,209	288
Sherman-Denison, TX	18,998	289
Bismarck, ND	18,976	290
Lewiston-Auburn, ME	18,619	291
Grand Forks, ND-MN	18,489	292
Jackson, TN	18,440	293
St. Joseph, MO	18,354	294
State College, PA	18,042	295
Gadsden, AL	17,914	296
Owensboro, KY	17,910	297
Victoria, TX	17,789	298
Muncie, IN	17,747	299
Pocatello, ID	17,557	300
Danville, VA	17,554	301
Dubuque, IA	17,435	302
Rapid City, SD	17,351	303
Elmira, NY	16,810	304
Missoula, MT	16,305	305
Pine Bluff, AR	16,152	306
Cumberland, MD-WV	15,779	307
Bloomington, IN	15,688	308
Iowa City, IA	15,640	309
Cheyenne, WY	15,446	310
Great Falls, MT	15,400	311
Punta Gorda, FL	15,386	312
Lawrence, KS	14,487	313
Jonesboro, AR	13,788	314
Casper, WY	13,253	315
Enid, OK	10,944	316

MSA/NECMA Total **39,672,621**
United States Total **50,021,770**
MSA/NECMA (% of U.S.Total) **79.31**

POPULATION BY AGE: 18-34 YEARS

MSA/NECMA	POPULATION	RANK
Los Angeles-Long Beach, CA	2,371,688	1
New York, NY	2,045,660	2
Chicago, IL	1,885,412	3
Boston-Worcester-Lawrence-Lowell-Brockton, MA-NH	1,437,449	4
Washington, DC-MD-VA-WV	1,162,221	5
Philadelphia, PA-NJ	1,122,838	6
Detroit, MI	1,032,099	7
Houston, TX	997,970	8
Atlanta, GA	964,947	9
Dallas, TX	846,084	10
Riverside-San Bernardino, CA	733,906	11
San Diego, CA	730,696	12
Phoenix-Mesa, AZ	711,184	13
Orange County, CA	699,104	14
Minneapolis-St. Paul, MN-WI	687,221	15
Nassau-Suffolk, NY	600,412	16
St. Louis, MO-IL	576,233	17
Baltimore, MD	570,377	18
Seattle-Bellevue-Everett, WA	540,271	19
Oakland, CA	528,382	20
Pittsburgh, PA	491,081	21
Cleveland-Lorain-Elyria, OH	475,300	22
Miami, FL	471,729	23
Tampa-St. Petersburg-Clearwater, FL	457,667	24
Denver, CO	444,386	25
Newark, NJ	438,818	26
San Jose, CA	421,709	27
Norfolk-Virginia Beach-Newport News, VA-NC	408,973	28
Fort Worth-Arlington, TX	408,789	29
Portland-Vancouver, OR-WA	397,445	30
Kansas City, MO-KS	395,297	31
San Francisco, CA	385,028	32
San Antonio, TX	381,894	33
Columbus, OH	381,874	34
Cincinnati, OH-KY-IN	371,032	35
Orlando, FL	369,691	36
New Haven-Bridgeport-Stamford-Danbury-Waterbury, CT	358,878	37
Indianapolis, IN	356,725	38
Sacramento, CA	351,127	39
Charlotte-Gastonia-Rock Hill, NC-SC	339,141	40
Milwaukee-Waukesha, WI	327,295	41
Austin-San Marcos, TX	319,241	42
New Orleans, LA	306,333	43
Las Vegas, NV-AZ	303,859	44
Raleigh-Durham-Chapel Hill, NC	298,402	45
Fort Lauderdale, FL	292,269	46
Bergen-Passaic, NJ	289,721	47
Salt Lake City-Ogden, UT	284,855	48
Nashville, TN	280,044	49
Greensboro-Winston Salem-High Point, NC	275,742	50
Middlesex-Somerset-Hunterdon, NJ	267,500	51
Memphis, TN-AR-MS	266,941	52
Buffalo-Niagara Falls, NY	257,425	53
Hartford, CT	252,934	54
Rochester, NY	252,822	55
Oklahoma City, OK	250,685	56
Jacksonville, FL	249,648	57
Grand Rapids-Muskegon-Holland, MI	246,018	58
Monmouth-Ocean, NJ	226,505	59
Richmond-Petersburg, VA	226,322	60
Louisville, KY-IN	224,150	61
Greenville-Spartanburg-Anderson, SC	223,618	62
Honolulu, HI	218,393	63
Dayton-Springfield, OH	218,337	64
Providence-Warwick-Pawtucket, RI	214,111	65
Fresno, CA	213,678	66
Birmingham, AL	210,446	67
Albany-Schenectady-Troy, NY	205,597	68
West Palm Beach-Boca Raton, FL	189,334	69
Tucson, AZ	188,895	70
El Paso, TX	184,129	71
Syracuse, NY	178,552	72
Tulsa, OK	175,056	73
Ventura, CA	172,551	74
Tacoma, WA	164,385	75
Omaha, NE-IA	163,839	76
Akron, OH	163,719	77
Albuquerque, NM	158,292	78
Bakersfield, CA	153,675	79
Knoxville, TN	153,643	80
Toledo, OH	149,902	81
Springfield, MA	149,171	82
Ann Arbor, MI	148,983	83
Baton Rouge, LA	147,814	84
Charleston-North Charleston, SC	141,201	85
Harrisburg-Lebanon-Carlisle, PA	140,018	86
Gary, IN	139,609	87
Wilmington-Newark, DE-MD	139,253	88
Jersey City, NJ	138,502	89
Scranton-Wilkes-Barre-Hazleton, PA	136,562	90
Columbia, SC	136,114	91
Allentown-Bethlehem-Easton, PA	134,052	92
McAllen-Edinburg-Mission, TX	132,160	93
Little Rock-North Little Rock, AR	131,250	94
Colorado Springs, CO	128,854	95
Stockton-Lodi, CA	128,298	96
Wichita, KS	125,294	97
Youngstown-Warren, OH	124,307	98
Lansing-East Lansing, MI	122,999	99
Lexington, KY	122,846	100
Madison, WI	121,345	101
Mobile, AL	120,854	102
Vallejo-Fairfield-Napa, CA	117,850	103
Augusta-Aiken, GA-SC	111,542	104
Kalamazoo-Battle Creek, MI	108,275	105
Jackson, MS	107,025	106
Fort Wayne, IN	106,926	107
Johnson City-Kingsport-Bristol, TN-VA	104,859	108
Des Moines, IA	104,006	109
Lancaster, PA	103,829	110
Santa Barbara-Santa Maria-Lompoc, CA	103,316	111
Provo-Orem, UT	101,773	112
Chattanooga, TN-GA	101,751	113
Flint, MI	100,066	114
Lakeland-Winter Haven, FL	98,031	115
Salinas, CA	97,255	116
Modesto, CA	96,794	117
Pensacola, FL	96,584	118
Killeen-Temple, TX	96,239	119
Melbourne-Titusville-Palm Bay, FL	95,589	120
Daytona Beach, FL	95,181	121
Spokane, WA	94,344	122
Sarasota-Bradenton, FL	92,894	123
Santa Rosa, CA	92,442	124
Corpus Christi, TX	91,911	125
Lafayette, LA	91,417	126
Boise City, ID	89,743	127
Saginaw-Bay City-Midland, MI	89,073	128
Fayetteville, NC	87,553	129
Huntsville, AL	87,317	130
Shreveport-Bossier City, LA	86,173	131
Canton-Massillon, OH	86,032	132
Newburgh, NY-PA	84,604	133
Tallahassee, FL	83,432	134
Visalia-Tulare-Porterville, CA	83,217	135
Beaumont-Port Arthur, TX	82,492	136
Biloxi-Gulfport-Pascagoula, MS	82,274	137
Appleton-Oshkosh-Neenah, WI	81,970	138
Brownsville-Harlingen-San Benito, TX	81,761	139
York, PA	81,635	140
Hamilton-Middletown, OH	81,239	141
Montgomery, AL	79,232	142
Trenton, NJ	78,908	143
Davenport-Moline-Rock Island, IA-IL	77,961	144
Reading, PA	77,910	145
Rockford, IL	77,783	146
Springfield, MO	77,782	147
Macon, GA	77,690	148
Peoria-Pekin, IL	75,927	149
Salem, OR	75,511	150
Eugene-Springfield, OR	74,982	151
Atlantic-Cape May, NJ	74,576	152
Hickory-Morganton-Lenoir, NC	73,949	153
Reno, NV	72,946	154
Boulder-Longmont, CO	72,896	155
Columbus, GA-AL	72,323	156
Fort Myers-Cape Coral, FL	71,965	157
Huntington-Ashland, WV-KY-OH	71,275	158
Utica-Rome, NY	69,568	159
Savannah, GA	68,351	160
Gainesville, FL	68,043	161
Anchorage, AK	66,596	162
Fayetteville-Springdale-Rogers, AR	66,198	163
Lincoln, NE	65,992	164
Erie, PA	65,884	165
Lubbock, TX	65,743	166
Dutchess County, NY	63,783	167
South Bend, IN	63,614	168
Evansville-Henderson, IN-KY	63,089	169
San Luis Obispo-Antascadero-Paso Robles, CA	62,949	170
Fort Collins-Loveland, CO	61,580	171
New London-Norwich, CT	59,857	172
Portland, ME	59,227	173
Santa Cruz-Watsonville, CA	59,167	174
Clarksville-Hopkinsville, TN-KY	58,793	175
Binghamton, NY	56,679	176
Lafayette, IN	56,463	177
Galveston-Texas City, TX	56,061	178
Brazoria, TX	55,981	179
Jacksonville, NC	55,956	180
Bryan-College Station, TX	55,475	181
Fort Pierce-Port St. Lucie, FL	55,388	182
Champaign-Urbana, IL	55,230	183
Odessa-Midland, TX	55,198	184
Waco, TX	54,234	185
Charleston, WV	53,022	186
Bremerton, WA	52,911	187
Green Bay, WI	52,572	188
Burlington, VT	52,387	189
Duluth-Superior, MN-WI	52,384	190
Wilmington, NC	52,015	191
State College, PA	51,780	192
Johnstown, PA	50,735	193
Laredo, TX	50,143	194
Chico-Paradise, CA	49,760	195
Roanoke, VA	49,101	196
Lynchburg, VA	49,003	197
Fargo-Moorhead, ND-MN	48,914	198
Amarillo, TX	48,280	199
Yakima, WA	48,193	200
Merced, CA	47,716	201
Ocala, FL	47,684	202
Tuscaloosa, AL	47,412	203
Longview-Marshall, TX	46,970	204
Asheville, NC	46,815	205
Athens, GA	46,626	206
Houma, LA	46,592	207
Yolo, CA	45,925	208
Las Cruces, NM	45,854	209
St. Cloud, MN	45,149	210
Bloomington-Normal, IL	44,237	211
Bloomington, IN	44,216	212
Fort Walton Beach, FL	43,749	213
Olympia, WA	43,675	214
Springfield, IL	43,200	215
Columbia, MO	42,788	216
Cedar Rapids, IA	42,532	217
Charlottesville, VA	42,475	218
Fort Smith, AR-OK	42,446	219
Myrtle Beach, SC	41,533	220
Lake Charles, LA	40,876	221
Greeley, CO	40,619	222
Racine, WI	40,595	223
Bellingham, WA	39,508	224
Sioux Falls, SD	39,485	225
Tyler, TX	39,300	226
Richland-Kennewick-Pasco, WA	38,914	227
Naples, FL	38,871	228
Elkhart-Goshen, IN	38,790	229
Barnstable-Yarmouth, MA	38,515	230
Mansfield, OH	38,343	231
Greenville, NC	37,725	232
Terre Haute, IN	37,702	233
Iowa City, IA	37,686	234
Monroe, LA	37,038	235
Eau Claire, WI	36,839	236
Topeka, KS	36,273	237
Jackson, MI	36,260	238
Medford-Ashland, OR	35,932	239
Muncie, IN	35,743	240
Benton Harbor, MI	35,314	241
Bangor, ME	35,136	242
Wichita Falls, TX	34,999	243
Lawrence, KS	34,876	244
Lima, OH	34,735	245
Flagstaff, AZ-UT	34,561	246
Panama City, FL	34,018	247
Rocky Mount, NC	33,784	248
Vineland-Millville-Bridgeton, NJ	33,752	249
Lawton, OK	33,578	250
Janesville-Beloit, WI	33,390	251
Redding, CA	33,362	252
Kenosha, WI	33,123	253
Joplin, MO	32,920	254
Dothan, AL	32,191	255
Decatur, AL	32,170	256
Jamestown, NY	31,931	257
Wheeling, WV-OH	31,906	258
Parkersburg-Marietta, WV-OH	31,853	259
Abilene, TX	31,650	260
Yuma, AZ	31,580	261
Florence, AL	31,512	262
La Crosse, WI-MN	31,415	263
Hattiesburg, MS	31,283	264
Yuba City, CA	31,112	265
Waterloo-Cedar Falls, IA	30,850	266
Hagerstown, MD	30,826	267
Dover, DE	30,625	268
Pueblo, CO	30,291	269
Santa Fe, NM	30,273	270
Pittsfield, MA	30,088	271
Alexandria, LA	29,756	272
Anniston, AL	29,722	273
Florence, SC	29,677	274
Sumter, SC	29,554	275
Goldsboro, NC	29,286	276
Albany, GA	29,187	277
Grand Forks, ND-MN	28,561	278
Steubenville-Weirton, OH-WV	28,437	279
Glens Falls, NY	28,146	280
Rochester, MN	27,887	281
Altoona, PA	27,767	282
Sharon, PA	27,692	283
Texarkana, TX-AR	27,478	284
Billings, MT	27,014	285
Sioux City, IA-NE	26,256	286
Wausau, WI	26,208	287
Williamsport, PA	26,006	288
San Angelo, TX	25,916	289
Jackson, TN	24,827	290
Decatur, IL	24,585	291
Grand Junction, CO	23,850	292
Sheboygan, WI	23,425	293
Danville, VA	23,404	294
Gadsden, AL	23,261	295
Lewiston-Auburn, ME	23,220	296
Kankakee, IL	22,813	297
Sherman-Denison, TX	22,646	298
Cumberland, MD-WV	22,636	299
Missoula, MT	22,442	300
Punta Gorda, FL	21,621	301
Rapid City, SD	21,522	302
St. Joseph, MO	21,120	303
Elmira, NY	21,082	304
Kokomo, IN	21,016	305
Jonesboro, AR	20,581	306
Pine Bluff, AR	20,541	307
Bismarck, ND	20,147	308
Dubuque, IA	19,853	309
Owensboro, KY	19,833	310
Victoria, TX	18,246	311
Cheyenne, WY	18,006	312
Pocatello, ID	17,252	313
Great Falls, MT	16,952	314
Casper, WY	13,130	315
Enid, OK	12,085	316
MSA/NECMA Total	**51,663,309**	
United States Total	**63,779,309**	
MSA/NECMA (% of U.S.Total)	**81.00**	

POPULATION BY AGE: 35-49 YEARS

MSA/NECMA	POPULATION	RANK
Los Angeles-Long Beach, CA	2,238,370	1
New York, NY	2,096,942	2
Chicago, IL	1,891,482	3
Boston-Worcester-Lawrence-Lowell-Brockton, MA-NH	1,413,624	4
Washington, DC-MD-VA-WV	1,241,858	5
Philadelphia, PA-NJ	1,152,799	6
Detroit, MI	1,051,294	7
Houston, TX	990,368	8
Atlanta, GA	977,959	9
Dallas, TX	793,183	10
Riverside-San Bernardino, CA	711,406	11
Minneapolis-St. Paul, MN-WI	694,974	12
Phoenix-Mesa, AZ	685,706	13
Orange County, CA	670,463	14
San Diego, CA	661,721	15
Nassau-Suffolk, NY	635,458	16
Baltimore, MD	617,037	17
Seattle-Bellevue-Everett, WA	605,135	18
Oakland, CA	604,851	19
St. Louis, MO-IL	601,831	20
Pittsburgh, PA	526,348	21
Denver, CO	515,192	22
Cleveland-Lorain-Elyria, OH	510,143	23
Miami, FL	494,041	24
Tampa-St. Petersburg-Clearwater, FL	485,957	25
Newark, NJ	480,520	26
Portland-Vancouver, OR-WA	471,262	27
San Francisco, CA	469,190	28
San Jose, CA	422,368	29
Kansas City, MO-KS	421,071	30
New Haven-Bridgeport-Stamford-Danbury-Waterbury, CT	393,748	31
Fort Worth-Arlington, TX	382,510	32
Cincinnati, OH-KY-IN	374,973	33
Sacramento, CA	374,767	34
Indianapolis, IN	361,177	35
Norfolk-Virginia Beach-Newport News, VA-NC	359,858	36
Orlando, FL	354,225	37
Fort Lauderdale, FL	349,272	38
San Antonio, TX	348,605	39
Columbus, OH	346,177	40
Milwaukee-Waukesha, WI	343,586	41
Charlotte-Gastonia-Rock Hill, NC-SC	335,553	42
Bergen-Passaic, NJ	323,714	43
Las Vegas, NV-AZ	321,682	44
New Orleans, LA	303,850	45
Nashville, TN	284,194	46
Greensboro-Winston Salem-High Point, NC	283,622	47
Middlesex-Somerset-Hunterdon, NJ	283,484	48
Salt Lake City-Ogden, UT	282,166	49
Raleigh-Durham-Chapel Hill, NC	274,589	50
Austin-San Marcos, TX	274,196	51
Hartford, CT	269,818	52
Memphis, TN-AR-MS	256,076	53
Buffalo-Niagara Falls, NY	255,487	54
Monmouth-Ocean, NJ	252,913	55
Rochester, NY	252,293	56
Jacksonville, FL	249,970	57
Oklahoma City, OK	242,934	58
Richmond-Petersburg, VA	241,853	59
Grand Rapids-Muskegon-Holland, MI	240,565	60
Louisville, KY-IN	239,402	61
West Palm Beach-Boca Raton, FL	225,153	62
Birmingham, AL	213,807	63
Dayton-Springfield, OH	213,562	64
Greenville-Spartanburg-Anderson, SC	212,154	65
Providence-Warwick-Pawtucket, RI	209,155	66
Albany-Schenectady-Troy, NY	202,255	67
Honolulu, HI	200,087	68
Fresno, CA	190,107	69
Tulsa, OK	183,789	70
Ventura, CA	182,005	71
Tucson, AZ	181,231	72
Albuquerque, NM	166,445	73
Syracuse, NY	165,575	74
Omaha, NE-IA	163,115	75
Tacoma, WA	162,500	76
Akron, OH	158,367	77
Knoxville, TN	156,932	78
El Paso, TX	149,586	79
Harrisburg-Lebanon-Carlisle, PA	144,099	80
Bakersfield, CA	142,374	81
Allentown-Bethlehem-Easton, PA	141,930	82
Gary, IN	141,248	83
Toledo, OH	136,155	84
Jersey City, NJ	135,268	85
Ann Arbor, MI	133,725	86
Wilmington-Newark, DE-MD	133,715	87
Baton Rouge, LA	132,150	88
Springfield, MA	131,549	89
Little Rock-North Little Rock, AR	130,868	90
Columbia, SC	126,837	91
Youngstown-Warren, OH	126,798	92
Wichita, KS	126,758	93
Charleston-North Charleston, SC	124,940	94
Scranton-Wilkes-Barre-Hazleton, PA	124,918	95
Stockton-Lodi, CA	123,265	96
Vallejo-Fairfield-Napa, CA	122,537	97
Colorado Springs, CO	119,032	98
Mobile, AL	117,243	99
Santa Rosa, CA	113,679	100
Fort Wayne, IN	111,720	101
Augusta-Aiken, GA-SC	107,268	102
Melbourne-Titusville-Palm Bay, FL	106,618	103
Lexington, KY	106,425	104
Johnson City-Kingsport-Bristol, TN-VA	105,870	105
Madison, WI	105,244	106
Lansing-East Lansing, MI	105,038	107
Chattanooga, TN-GA	104,360	108
Lancaster, PA	104,039	109
Des Moines, IA	103,689	110
Sarasota-Bradenton, FL	102,664	111
Kalamazoo-Battle Creek, MI	100,696	112
Jackson, MS	99,730	113
Flint, MI	99,200	114
McAllen-Edinburg-Mission, TX	98,193	115
Modesto, CA	97,294	116
Spokane, WA	94,955	117
Daytona Beach, FL	94,586	118
Boise City, ID	94,330	119
Santa Barbara-Santa Maria-Lompoc, CA	92,325	120
Lakeland-Winter Haven, FL	92,267	121
Pensacola, FL	91,676	122
York, PA	90,842	123
Saginaw-Bay City-Midland, MI	90,210	124
Canton-Massillon, OH	89,973	125
Newburgh, NY-PA	88,105	126
Salinas, CA	86,746	127
Corpus Christi, TX	85,445	128
Rockford, IL	83,193	129
Lafayette, LA	82,226	130
Reno, NV	82,193	131
Beaumont-Port Arthur, TX	81,620	132
Shreveport-Bossier City, LA	81,430	133
Appleton-Oshkosh-Neenah, WI	80,344	134
Reading, PA	79,971	135
Trenton, NJ	79,960	136
Huntsville, AL	79,449	137
Davenport-Moline-Rock Island, IA-IL	79,354	138
Fort Myers-Cape Coral, FL	78,995	139
Biloxi-Gulfport-Pascagoula, MS	77,645	140
Hickory-Morganton-Lenoir, NC	77,431	141
Hamilton-Middletown, OH	76,562	142
Atlantic-Cape May, NJ	76,203	143
Eugene-Springfield, OR	75,414	144
Peoria-Pekin, IL	75,324	145
Salem, OR	73,635	146
Visalia-Tulare-Porterville, CA	73,277	147
Macon, GA	72,675	148
Montgomery, AL	72,660	149
Boulder-Longmont, CO	72,164	150
Springfield, MO	69,295	151
Anchorage, AK	68,066	152
Evansville-Henderson, IN-KY	67,821	153
Huntington-Ashland, WV-KY-OH	67,340	154
Santa Cruz-Watsonville, CA	66,077	155
Savannah, GA	64,128	156
Dutchess County, NY	63,771	157
Tallahassee, FL	63,738	158
Killeen-Temple, TX	63,530	159
Portland, ME	62,757	160
Fayetteville, NC	62,192	161
Utica-Rome, NY	61,374	162
Brownsville-Harlingen-San Benito, TX	61,209	163
Fort Pierce-Port St. Lucie, FL	60,203	164
Erie, PA	59,864	165
Fayetteville-Springdale-Rogers, AR	59,624	166
Provo-Orem, UT	59,448	167
Charleston, WV	59,218	168
Galveston-Texas City, TX	59,094	169
Columbus, GA-AL	59,020	170
Fort Collins-Loveland, CO	58,185	171
New London-Norwich, CT	57,775	172
South Bend, IN	57,004	173
Bremerton, WA	56,740	174
Brazoria, TX	56,289	175
Lincoln, NE	55,905	176
Odessa-Midland, TX	55,893	177
Binghamton, NY	55,517	178
San Luis Obispo-Antascadero-Paso Robles, CA	54,946	179
Roanoke, VA	54,729	180
Duluth-Superior, MN-WI	51,682	181
Wilmington, NC	51,492	182
Olympia, WA	51,015	183
Green Bay, WI	50,999	184
Lubbock, TX	49,613	185
Asheville, NC	49,117	186
Johnstown, PA	48,852	187
Springfield, IL	48,664	188
Lynchburg, VA	47,447	189
Amarillo, TX	47,232	190
Burlington, VT	46,561	191
Gainesville, FL	46,535	192
Ocala, FL	46,358	193
Longview-Marshall, TX	45,293	194
Barnstable-Yarmouth, MA	45,210	195
Yakima, WA	44,682	196
Clarksville-Hopkinsville, TN-KY	44,282	197
Fort Smith, AR-OK	43,207	198
Cedar Rapids, IA	43,181	199
Racine, WI	42,715	200
Merced, CA	42,619	201
Houma, LA	42,534	202
Richland-Kennewick-Pasco, WA	42,354	203
Naples, FL	41,698	204
Waco, TX	41,374	205
Myrtle Beach, SC	40,470	206
Lake Charles, LA	40,263	207
Chico-Paradise, CA	39,964	208
Fort Walton Beach, FL	39,780	209
Elkhart-Goshen, IN	39,722	210
Santa Fe, NM	38,895	211
Medford-Ashland, OR	38,779	212
Sioux Falls, SD	38,631	213
Topeka, KS	38,597	214
Fargo-Moorhead, ND-MN	38,333	215
Champaign-Urbana, IL	37,994	216
Mansfield, OH	37,445	217
Tyler, TX	37,248	218
Bellingham, WA	37,043	219
Greeley, CO	36,834	220
Redding, CA	36,368	221
Laredo, TX	36,366	222
Jackson, MI	36,215	223
Lafayette, IN	35,723	224
Charlottesville, VA	35,363	225
Las Cruces, NM	35,280	226
St. Cloud, MN	35,042	227
Yolo, CA	34,863	228
Tuscaloosa, AL	34,807	229
Benton Harbor, MI	34,692	230
Rocky Mount, NC	34,494	231
Janesville-Beloit, WI	33,845	232
Panama City, FL	33,777	233
Parkersburg-Marietta, WV-OH	33,622	234
Lima, OH	33,492	235
Kenosha, WI	33,369	236
Decatur, AL	33,059	237
Bangor, ME	32,915	238
Joplin, MO	32,246	239
Wheeling, WV-OH	32,222	240
Bloomington-Normal, IL	31,673	241
Terre Haute, IN	31,538	242
Eau Claire, WI	31,078	243
Monroe, LA	30,606	244
Athens, GA	30,310	245
Vineland-Millville-Bridgeton, NJ	30,109	246
Dothan, AL	29,921	247
Billings, MT	29,868	248
Florence, AL	29,767	249
Columbia, MO	29,742	250
Yuba City, CA	29,687	251
Wichita Falls, TX	29,506	252
Jacksonville, NC	28,806	253
Greenville, NC	28,723	254
Pittsfield, MA	28,713	255
Hagerstown, MD	28,685	256
Pueblo, CO	28,664	257
Wausau, WI	28,655	258
Jamestown, NY	28,476	259
Steubenville-Weirton, OH-WV	28,469	260
Florence, SC	28,104	261
Rochester, MN	27,930	262
Dover, DE	27,754	263
Altoona, PA	27,530	264
Alexandria, LA	27,244	265
Glens Falls, NY	27,134	266
La Crosse, WI-MN	27,115	267
State College, PA	26,617	268
Abilene, TX	26,459	269
Yuma, AZ	26,375	270
Flagstaff, AZ-UT	26,352	271
Texarkana, TX-AR	26,317	272
Sioux City, IA-NE	26,291	273
Bryan-College Station, TX	26,111	274
Albany, GA	25,683	275
Williamsport, PA	25,647	276
Grand Junction, CO	25,629	277
Anniston, AL	25,594	278
Goldsboro, NC	25,300	279
Sheboygan, WI	25,249	280
Waterloo-Cedar Falls, IA	25,161	281
Sharon, PA	24,786	282
Decatur, IL	24,565	283
Bloomington, IN	24,300	284
Lawton, OK	24,047	285
Danville, VA	23,914	286
Iowa City, IA	23,835	287
Sumter, SC	23,720	288
Hattiesburg, MS	23,370	289
Lewiston-Auburn, ME	22,971	290
Kokomo, IN	22,779	291
Muncie, IN	22,294	292
Jackson, TN	22,183	293
San Angelo, TX	22,148	294
Missoula, MT	21,951	295
Sherman-Denison, TX	21,860	296
Kankakee, IL	21,795	297
Gadsden, AL	21,789	298
Bismarck, ND	21,524	299
Grand Forks, ND-MN	21,292	300
St. Joseph, MO	20,961	301
Punta Gorda, FL	20,880	302
Lawrence, KS	20,348	303
Owensboro, KY	20,127	304
Rapid City, SD	20,098	305
Elmira, NY	19,424	306
Cumberland, MD-WV	18,924	307
Dubuque, IA	18,749	308
Cheyenne, WY	18,680	309
Victoria, TX	18,482	310
Great Falls, MT	17,821	311
Jonesboro, AR	16,825	312
Pocatello, ID	16,464	313
Pine Bluff, AR	16,308	314
Casper, WY	14,906	315
Enid, OK	12,580	316

MSA/NECMA Total **51,234,476**
United States Total **62,619,078**
MSA/NECMA (% of U.S.Total) **81.82**

POPULATION BY AGE: 50-64 YEARS

MSA/NECMA	POPULATION	RANK
New York, NY	1,339,744	1
Los Angeles-Long Beach, CA	1,248,778	2
Chicago, IL	1,174,088	3
Boston-Worcester-Lawrence-Lowell-Brockton, MA-NH	876,868	4
Philadelphia, PA-NJ	746,300	5
Washington, DC-MD-VA-WV	704,569	6
Detroit, MI	671,326	7
Atlanta, GA	552,246	8
Houston, TX	530,947	9
Nassau-Suffolk, NY	465,100	10
Dallas, TX	451,710	11
Phoenix-Mesa, AZ	419,730	12
Minneapolis-St. Paul, MN-WI	413,902	13
Pittsburgh, PA	391,590	14
Orange County, CA	391,414	15
Riverside-San Bernardino, CA	387,193	16
St. Louis, MO-IL	387,005	17
Baltimore, MD	379,025	18
San Diego, CA	366,906	19
Tampa-St. Petersburg-Clearwater, FL	359,169	20
Seattle-Bellevue-Everett, WA	348,480	21
Miami, FL	346,321	22
Cleveland-Lorain-Elyria, OH	345,565	23
Oakland, CA	338,867	24
Newark, NJ	315,894	25
Denver, CO	286,895	26
San Francisco, CA	279,404	27
Portland-Vancouver, OR-WA	276,106	28
Kansas City, MO-KS	260,453	29
New Haven-Bridgeport-Stamford-Danbury-Waterbury, CT	260,255	30
San Jose, CA	242,901	31
Bergen-Passaic, NJ	237,100	32
Cincinnati, OH-KY-IN	236,437	33
Fort Worth-Arlington, TX	229,875	34
Indianapolis, IN	225,422	35
Fort Lauderdale, FL	225,194	36
Orlando, FL	223,867	37
Las Vegas, NV-AZ	221,898	38
Sacramento, CA	221,612	39
Columbus, OH	213,900	40
Charlotte-Gastonia-Rock Hill, NC-SC	212,654	41
San Antonio, TX	210,984	42
Milwaukee-Waukesha, WI	209,558	43
Norfolk-Virginia Beach-Newport News, VA-NC	204,806	44
Greensboro-Winston Salem-High Point, NC	191,052	45
New Orleans, LA	184,279	46
Middlesex-Somerset-Hunterdon, NJ	181,993	47
Buffalo-Niagara Falls, NY	179,210	48
Hartford, CT	174,877	49
Nashville, TN	174,493	50
Monmouth-Ocean, NJ	167,227	51
Rochester, NY	161,297	52
Raleigh-Durham-Chapel Hill, NC	158,400	53
Salt Lake City-Ogden, UT	158,302	54
Louisville, KY-IN	156,359	55
West Palm Beach-Boca Raton, FL	155,532	56
Jacksonville, FL	154,743	57
Oklahoma City, OK	154,069	58
Memphis, TN-AR-MS	150,749	59
Dayton-Springfield, OH	149,077	60
Greenville-Spartanburg-Anderson, SC	146,239	61
Austin-San Marcos, TX	144,612	62
Grand Rapids-Muskegon-Holland, MI	143,133	63
Richmond-Petersburg, VA	142,504	64
Birmingham, AL	139,414	65
Honolulu, HI	139,273	66
Providence-Warwick-Pawtucket, RI	131,961	67
Albany-Schenectady-Troy, NY	130,547	68
Tulsa, OK	119,145	69
Tucson, AZ	111,999	70
Fresno, CA	111,340	71
Knoxville, TN	108,615	72
Akron, OH	106,315	73
Syracuse, NY	104,479	74
Ventura, CA	103,906	75
Omaha, NE-IA	100,305	76
Allentown-Bethlehem-Easton, PA	100,266	77
Scranton-Wilkes-Barre-Hazleton, PA	99,672	78
Tacoma, WA	98,761	79
Harrisburg-Lebanon-Carlisle, PA	98,732	80
Youngstown-Warren, OH	97,208	81
Gary, IN	96,555	82
Albuquerque, NM	94,784	83
Sarasota-Bradenton, FL	91,612	84
El Paso, TX	89,524	85
Toledo, OH	85,692	86
Wilmington-Newark, DE-MD	84,715	87
Jersey City, NJ	84,270	88
Springfield, MA	83,825	89
Johnson City-Kingsport-Bristol, TN-VA	82,517	90
Little Rock-North Little Rock, AR	82,345	91
Ann Arbor, MI	80,381	92
Mobile, AL	79,974	93
Bakersfield, CA	79,464	94
Melbourne-Titusville-Palm Bay, FL	79,288	95
Baton Rouge, LA	79,271	96
Daytona Beach, FL	76,948	97
Wichita, KS	76,207	98
Chattanooga, TN-GA	73,999	99
Lakeland-Winter Haven, FL	72,854	100
Stockton-Lodi, CA	72,482	101
Columbia, SC	72,271	102
Charleston-North Charleston, SC	72,127	103
Vallejo-Fairfield-Napa, CA	71,266	104
Fort Wayne, IN	69,515	105
Colorado Springs, CO	69,504	106
Fort Myers-Cape Coral, FL	69,009	107
Lancaster, PA	67,018	108
Flint, MI	66,632	109
Kalamazoo-Battle Creek, MI	66,285	110
Lexington, KY	66,180	111
Des Moines, IA	66,168	112
Augusta-Aiken, GA-SC	65,147	113
Canton-Massillon, OH	64,618	114
Santa Rosa, CA	64,018	115
Pensacola, FL	62,556	116
Lansing-East Lansing, MI	62,260	117
Saginaw-Bay City-Midland, MI	61,694	118
Spokane, WA	60,892	119
York, PA	59,677	120
Madison, WI	59,533	121
McAllen-Edinburg-Mission, TX	59,527	122
Jackson, MS	59,239	123
Boise City, ID	58,679	124
Reading, PA	58,406	125
Modesto, CA	57,547	126
Beaumont-Port Arthur, TX	57,331	127
Davenport-Moline-Rock Island, IA-IL	55,662	128
Newburgh, NY-PA	55,545	129
Shreveport-Bossier City, LA	55,458	130
Huntsville, AL	55,023	131
Rockford, IL	54,986	132
Hickory-Morganton-Lenoir, NC	54,748	133
Peoria-Pekin, IL	54,539	134
Huntington-Ashland, WV-KY-OH	53,698	135
Santa Barbara-Santa Maria-Lompoc, CA	53,323	136
Corpus Christi, TX	53,135	137
Biloxi-Gulfport-Pascagoula, MS	51,922	138
Trenton, NJ	51,479	139
Atlantic-Cape May, NJ	50,740	140
Lafayette, LA	50,308	141
Hamilton-Middletown, OH	49,985	142
Appleton-Oshkosh-Neenah, WI	49,540	143
Reno, NV	49,533	144
Salem, OR	49,031	145
Fort Pierce-Port St. Lucie, FL	48,749	146
Eugene-Springfield, OR	48,064	147
Macon, GA	47,863	148
Salinas, CA	46,133	149
Springfield, MO	45,937	150
Montgomery, AL	45,832	151
Visalia-Tulare-Porterville, CA	45,275	152
Evansville-Henderson, IN-KY	43,872	153
Charleston, WV	43,737	154
Utica-Rome, NY	42,202	155
Dutchess County, NY	41,912	156
Fayetteville-Springdale-Rogers, AR	41,792	157
Ocala, FL	41,732	158
Brownsville-Harlingen-San Benito, TX	40,422	159
Savannah, GA	40,382	160
Boulder-Longmont, CO	39,402	161
Erie, PA	39,078	162
Portland, ME	38,410	163
Binghamton, NY	37,989	164
Johnstown, PA	37,784	165
Roanoke, VA	37,451	166
Wilmington, NC	37,402	167
Galveston-Texas City, TX	37,021	168
Columbus, GA-AL	36,808	169
Tallahassee, FL	36,461	170
Naples, FL	36,409	171
Asheville, NC	36,408	172
New London-Norwich, CT	35,735	173
South Bend, IN	35,682	174
Duluth-Superior, MN-WI	35,467	175
Anchorage, AK	35,223	176
Barnstable-Yarmouth, MA	34,070	177
Bremerton, WA	34,024	178
Fayetteville, NC	33,757	179
Santa Cruz-Watsonville, CA	33,702	180
Odessa-Midland, TX	33,471	181
Lynchburg, VA	33,305	182
Fort Collins-Loveland, CO	33,126	183
Killeen-Temple, TX	32,913	184
Brazoria, TX	32,733	185
San Luis Obispo-Antascadero-Paso Robles, CA	31,776	186
Lincoln, NE	31,724	187
Springfield, IL	31,268	188
Olympia, WA	31,067	189
Green Bay, WI	30,970	190
Longview-Marshall, TX	30,953	191
Provo-Orem, UT	30,916	192
Fort Smith, AR-OK	30,321	193
Amarillo, TX	29,525	194
Myrtle Beach, SC	29,408	195
Yakima, WA	29,401	196
Cedar Rapids, IA	28,656	197
Lubbock, TX	28,619	198
Mansfield, OH	28,521	199
Medford-Ashland, OR	28,300	200
Burlington, VT	28,148	201
Racine, WI	27,900	202
Waco, TX	27,018	203
Houma, LA	26,840	204
Fort Walton Beach, FL	26,627	205
Chico-Paradise, CA	26,597	206
Richland-Kennewick-Pasco, WA	26,470	207
Lake Charles, LA	26,165	208
Redding, CA	25,988	209
Elkhart-Goshen, IN	25,956	210
Wheeling, WV-OH	25,633	211
Gainesville, FL	25,396	212
Punta Gorda, FL	25,350	213
Parkersburg-Marietta, WV-OH	25,226	214
Tyler, TX	25,190	215
Topeka, KS	25,079	216
Clarksville-Hopkinsville, TN-KY	24,600	217
Benton Harbor, MI	24,526	218
Steubenville-Weirton, OH-WV	24,266	219
Merced, CA	23,793	220
Panama City, FL	23,442	221
Florence, AL	23,247	222
Janesville-Beloit, WI	23,233	223
Bellingham, WA	23,198	224
Jackson, MI	23,142	225
Joplin, MO	22,924	226
Decatur, AL	22,867	227
Greeley, CO	22,375	228
Santa Fe, NM	22,095	229
Tuscaloosa, AL	22,054	230
Sioux Falls, SD	21,928	231
Lafayette, IN	21,927	232
Rocky Mount, NC	21,799	233
Laredo, TX	21,782	234
Lima, OH	21,690	235
Pueblo, CO	21,651	236
Fargo-Moorhead, ND-MN	21,608	237
Bangor, ME	21,446	238
Charlottesville, VA	21,364	239
Las Cruces, NM	21,325	240
Kenosha, WI	21,226	241
Altoona, PA	21,116	242
Terre Haute, IN	21,089	243
Pittsfield, MA	20,830	244
Vineland-Millville-Bridgeton, NJ	20,632	245
Yolo, CA	20,297	246
Jamestown, NY	20,292	247
Hagerstown, MD	20,159	248
Sharon, PA	20,047	249
Eau Claire, WI	19,986	250
St. Cloud, MN	19,659	251
Monroe, LA	19,622	252
Champaign-Urbana, IL	19,490	253
Dothan, AL	19,442	254
Yuba City, CA	19,404	255
Billings, MT	19,231	256
Bloomington-Normal, IL	18,555	257
Wichita Falls, TX	18,475	258
Danville, VA	18,428	259
Decatur, IL	18,424	260
Dover, DE	18,417	261
Glens Falls, NY	18,357	262
Wausau, WI	18,336	263
Texarkana, TX-AR	18,298	264
Florence, SC	18,263	265
Anniston, AL	18,032	266
Williamsport, PA	17,882	267
Gadsden, AL	17,740	268
Alexandria, LA	17,640	269
Waterloo-Cedar Falls, IA	17,615	270
Grand Junction, CO	17,558	271
Rochester, MN	17,548	272
Athens, GA	17,518	273
Muncie, IN	17,513	274
Cumberland, MD-WV	16,830	275
Kokomo, IN	16,696	276
Yuma, AZ	16,639	277
La Crosse, WI-MN	16,598	278
Greenville, NC	16,568	279
Sioux City, IA-NE	16,397	280
State College, PA	16,207	281
Goldsboro, NC	16,201	282
Albany, GA	16,101	283
Sherman-Denison, TX	16,059	284
Sheboygan, WI	16,035	285
Columbia, MO	15,845	286
Abilene, TX	15,484	287
Kankakee, IL	14,873	288
Lewiston-Auburn, ME	14,847	289
Flagstaff, AZ-UT	14,675	290
Hattiesburg, MS	14,593	291
Jackson, TN	14,526	292
Owensboro, KY	14,140	293
Bloomington, IN	14,122	294
St. Joseph, MO	13,988	295
Elmira, NY	13,719	296
San Angelo, TX	13,565	297
Lawton, OK	13,248	298
Bismarck, ND	13,161	299
Sumter, SC	13,081	300
Missoula, MT	13,015	301
Bryan-College Station, TX	12,904	302
Dubuque, IA	12,624	303
Iowa City, IA	11,859	304
Great Falls, MT	11,825	305
Cheyenne, WY	11,684	306
Victoria, TX	11,682	307
Jonesboro, AR	11,578	308
Jacksonville, NC	11,562	309
Grand Forks, ND-MN	11,481	310
Rapid City, SD	11,431	311
Pine Bluff, AR	11,133	312
Lawrence, KS	10,649	313
Pocatello, ID	9,962	314
Casper, WY	9,356	315
Enid, OK	8,439	316

MSA/NECMA Total **32,018,132**
United States Total **40,234,435**
MSA/NECMA (% of U.S.Total) **79.58**

GRAY MARKETS: 65+ YEARS

MSA/NECMA	POPULATION	RANK
New York, NY	1,194,666	1
Los Angeles-Long Beach, CA	981,237	2
Chicago, IL	957,675	3
Boston-Worcester-Lawrence-Lowell-Brockton, MA-NH	797,164	4
Philadelphia, PA-NJ	709,050	5
Detroit, MI	581,510	6
Tampa-St. Petersburg-Clearwater, FL	505,021	7
Washington, DC-MD-VA-WV	471,566	8
Pittsburgh, PA	416,675	9
Phoenix-Mesa, AZ	383,498	10
Nassau-Suffolk, NY	369,409	11
Riverside-San Bernardino, CA	352,473	12
Atlanta, GA	349,590	13
St. Louis, MO-IL	349,201	14
Houston, TX	342,378	15
Cleveland-Lorain-Elyria, OH	332,577	16
San Diego, CA	316,750	17
Fort Lauderdale, FL	315,041	18
Baltimore, MD	312,764	19
Miami, FL	312,077	20
Minneapolis-St. Paul, MN-WI	302,396	21
Dallas, TX	297,183	22
Orange County, CA	285,555	23
Seattle-Bellevue-Everett, WA	272,907	24
Oakland, CA	267,961	25
Newark, NJ	263,919	26
West Palm Beach-Boca Raton, FL	253,516	27
San Francisco, CA	244,672	28
New Haven-Bridgeport-Stamford-Danbury-Waterbury, CT	238,693	29
Portland-Vancouver, OR-WA	223,921	30
Kansas City, MO-KS	218,484	31
Orlando, FL	216,082	32
Cincinnati, OH-KY-IN	210,765	33
Denver, CO	208,271	34
Bergen-Passaic, NJ	204,366	35
Monmouth-Ocean, NJ	196,641	36
Milwaukee-Waukesha, WI	195,606	37
Indianapolis, IN	189,589	38
Sacramento, CA	183,696	39
Buffalo-Niagara Falls, NY	182,083	40
Las Vegas, NV-AZ	179,134	41
San Antonio, TX	174,882	42
San Jose, CA	171,808	43
Sarasota-Bradenton, FL	171,722	44
Charlotte-Gastonia-Rock Hill, NC-SC	170,779	45
Columbus, OH	167,689	46
Fort Worth-Arlington, TX	162,633	47
Greensboro-Winston Salem-High Point, NC	160,969	48
Norfolk-Virginia Beach-Newport News, VA-NC	158,787	49
Hartford, CT	156,488	50
New Orleans, LA	156,021	51
Middlesex-Somerset-Hunterdon, NJ	145,014	52
Rochester, NY	142,756	53
Providence-Warwick-Pawtucket, RI	142,533	54
Louisville, KY-IN	136,439	55
Nashville, TN	135,627	56
Dayton-Springfield, OH	129,178	57
Albany-Schenectady-Troy, NY	128,419	58
Jacksonville, FL	128,170	59
Oklahoma City, OK	125,190	60
Greenville-Spartanburg-Anderson, SC	124,211	61
Birmingham, AL	123,965	62
Grand Rapids-Muskegon-Holland, MI	123,894	63
Memphis, TN-AR-MS	122,462	64
Scranton-Wilkes-Barre-Hazleton, PA	120,215	65
Salt Lake City-Ogden, UT	117,808	66
Richmond-Petersburg, VA	117,673	67
Raleigh-Durham-Chapel Hill, NC	115,973	68
Tucson, AZ	114,302	69
Daytona Beach, FL	111,246	70
Honolulu, HI	109,269	71
Fort Myers-Cape Coral, FL	101,486	72
Allentown-Bethlehem-Easton, PA	101,180	73
Fresno, CA	100,452	74
Tulsa, OK	99,737	75
Syracuse, NY	98,872	76
Youngstown-Warren, OH	97,507	77
Austin-San Marcos, TX	97,500	78
Knoxville, TN	96,347	79
Akron, OH	96,209	80
Harrisburg-Lebanon-Carlisle, PA	93,061	81
Lakeland-Winter Haven, FL	86,978	82
Springfield, MA	85,233	83
Omaha, NE-IA	82,131	84
Melbourne-Titusville-Palm Bay, FL	81,750	85
Toledo, OH	80,609	86
Gary, IN	80,468	87
Tacoma, WA	77,915	88
Albuquerque, NM	77,843	89
Ventura, CA	75,946	90
Jersey City, NJ	75,432	91
Johnson City-Kingsport-Bristol, TN-VA	73,398	92
Wilmington-Newark, DE-MD	72,091	93
Fort Pierce-Port St. Lucie, FL	71,971	94
Mobile, AL	71,691	95
Wichita, KS	71,410	96
Little Rock-North Little Rock, AR	67,855	97
Bakersfield, CA	67,187	98
El Paso, TX	66,051	99
Lancaster, PA	64,486	100
Stockton-Lodi, CA	64,305	101
Chattanooga, TN-GA	63,748	102
Fort Wayne, IN	62,306	103
Canton-Massillon, OH	61,826	104
Reading, PA	58,048	105
Baton Rouge, LA	57,920	106
McAllen-Edinburg-Mission, TX	57,255	107
Santa Rosa, CA	57,229	108
Kalamazoo-Battle Creek, MI	57,038	109
Atlantic-Cape May, NJ	55,722	110
Des Moines, IA	55,639	111
Vallejo-Fairfield-Napa, CA	55,619	112
Spokane, WA	55,457	113
Ocala, FL	55,352	114
Columbia, SC	54,817	115
Ann Arbor, MI	54,082	116
York, PA	53,558	117
Beaumont-Port Arthur, TX	53,557	118
Charleston-North Charleston, SC	53,134	119
Saginaw-Bay City-Midland, MI	52,927	120
Pensacola, FL	51,788	121
Lexington, KY	51,668	122
Davenport-Moline-Rock Island, IA-IL	51,627	123
Flint, MI	51,310	124
Santa Barbara-Santa Maria-Lompoc, CA	50,999	125
Augusta-Aiken, GA-SC	50,882	126
Peoria-Pekin, IL	50,824	127
Shreveport-Bossier City, LA	50,309	128
Rockford, IL	49,044	129
Huntington-Ashland, WV-KY-OH	48,597	130
Modesto, CA	48,446	131
Naples, FL	48,355	132
Jackson, MS	48,021	133
Salem, OR	47,935	134
Utica-Rome, NY	47,563	135
Boise City, ID	47,430	136
Colorado Springs, CO	47,360	137
Barnstable-Yarmouth, MA	47,063	138
Punta Gorda, FL	46,758	139
Trenton, NJ	45,714	140
Corpus Christi, TX	45,288	141
Johnstown, PA	45,249	142
Lansing-East Lansing, MI	45,022	143
Hickory-Morganton-Lenoir, NC	44,912	144
Newburgh, NY-PA	43,645	145
Appleton-Oshkosh-Neenah, WI	43,631	146
Evansville-Henderson, IN-KY	43,611	147
Madison, WI	43,083	148
Biloxi-Gulfport-Pascagoula, MS	42,761	149
Eugene-Springfield, OR	42,116	150
Fayetteville-Springdale-Rogers, AR	41,995	151
Lafayette, LA	41,984	152
Springfield, MO	41,562	153
Erie, PA	40,547	154
Duluth-Superior, MN-WI	40,543	155
Visalia-Tulare-Porterville, CA	40,214	156
Hamilton-Middletown, OH	39,999	157
Charleston, WV	39,779	158
Montgomery, AL	39,075	159
Salinas, CA	38,715	160
Huntsville, AL	38,279	161
Reno, NV	38,029	162
Macon, GA	37,972	163
South Bend, IN	37,622	164
Brownsville-Harlingen-San Benito, TX	37,376	165
Binghamton, NY	37,296	166
Roanoke, VA	36,855	167
Asheville, NC	36,353	168
Savannah, GA	35,566	169
Portland, ME	34,528	170
Chico-Paradise, CA	34,298	171
San Luis Obispo-Antascadero-Paso Robles, CA	34,230	172
Dutchess County, NY	33,386	173
Wilmington, NC	32,573	174
New London-Norwich, CT	32,026	175
Columbus, GA-AL	31,725	176
Lynchburg, VA	31,125	177
Longview-Marshall, TX	30,078	178
Galveston-Texas City, TX	29,503	179
Springfield, IL	29,210	180
Medford-Ashland, OR	29,116	181
Wheeling, WV-OH	28,637	182
Yakima, WA	28,523	183
Waco, TX	28,509	184
Amarillo, TX	27,472	185
Fort Smith, AR-OK	27,349	186
Santa Cruz-Watsonville, CA	27,294	187
Lincoln, NE	26,986	188
Tallahassee, FL	26,837	189
Odessa-Midland, TX	26,751	190
Bremerton, WA	26,101	191
Killeen-Temple, TX	25,884	192
Mansfield, OH	25,485	193
Myrtle Beach, SC	25,380	194
Green Bay, WI	25,140	195
Racine, WI	25,002	196
Lubbock, TX	24,854	197
Olympia, WA	24,791	198
Provo-Orem, UT	24,676	199
Redding, CA	24,642	200
Tyler, TX	24,391	201
Cedar Rapids, IA	24,164	202
Fort Collins-Loveland, CO	23,932	203
Steubenville-Weirton, OH-WV	23,879	204
Terre Haute, IN	23,760	205
Boulder-Longmont, CO	23,634	206
Joplin, MO	23,519	207
Pittsfield, MA	23,288	208
Topeka, KS	23,240	209
Altoona, PA	23,223	210
Benton Harbor, MI	23,002	211
Parkersburg-Marietta, WV-OH	22,927	212
Brazoria, TX	22,686	213
Fayetteville, NC	22,491	214
Jamestown, NY	22,425	215
Lake Charles, LA	22,396	216
Lima, OH	21,934	217
Sharon, PA	21,870	218
Pueblo, CO	21,546	219
Elkhart-Goshen, IN	21,125	220
Florence, AL	21,099	221
Sioux Falls, SD	21,098	222
Jackson, MI	21,027	223
Richland-Kennewick-Pasco, WA	20,938	224
Janesville-Beloit, WI	20,773	225
Bellingham, WA	20,459	226
Gainesville, FL	20,425	227
Houma, LA	20,301	228
Tuscaloosa, AL	20,250	229
Merced, CA	20,091	230
Panama City, FL	20,061	231
Vineland-Millville-Bridgeton, NJ	19,801	232
Fort Walton Beach, FL	19,770	233
Lafayette, IN	19,696	234
Rocky Mount, NC	19,680	235
Clarksville-Hopkinsville, TN-KY	19,649	236
Burlington, VT	19,577	237
Yuma, AZ	19,427	238
Eau Claire, WI	19,334	239
Kenosha, WI	19,329	240
Wichita Falls, TX	19,175	241
Hagerstown, MD	18,925	242
Decatur, AL	18,789	243
Fargo-Moorhead, ND-MN	18,763	244
Bangor, ME	18,589	245
Williamsport, PA	18,476	246
Texarkana, TX-AR	18,116	247
St. Cloud, MN	18,010	248
Danville, VA	17,843	249
Monroe, LA	17,776	250
Cumberland, MD-WV	17,764	251
Charlottesville, VA	17,756	252
Glens Falls, NY	17,733	253
Greeley, CO	17,603	254
Sioux City, IA-NE	17,602	255
Gadsden, AL	17,481	256
Sherman-Denison, TX	17,419	257
Grand Junction, CO	17,387	258
Waterloo-Cedar Falls, IA	17,369	259
Decatur, IL	17,353	260
Laredo, TX	17,112	261
Billings, MT	16,976	262
Sheboygan, WI	16,874	263
Las Cruces, NM	16,847	264
Yuba City, CA	16,779	265
Dothan, AL	16,566	266
La Crosse, WI-MN	16,561	267
Wausau, WI	16,486	268
Santa Fe, NM	16,436	269
Muncie, IN	16,315	270
Alexandria, LA	16,178	271
Champaign-Urbana, IL	16,112	272
St. Joseph, MO	16,104	273
Bloomington-Normal, IL	16,031	274
Yolo, CA	15,992	275
Anniston, AL	15,847	276
Florence, SC	15,320	277
Abilene, TX	15,217	278
Anchorage, AK	14,824	279
Dover, DE	14,664	280
Jackson, TN	14,592	281
Kankakee, IL	14,440	282
Elmira, NY	14,355	283
Lewiston-Auburn, ME	14,225	284
Greenville, NC	13,928	285
Kokomo, IN	13,836	286
Athens, GA	13,665	287
State College, PA	13,662	288
San Angelo, TX	13,573	289
Goldsboro, NC	13,287	290
Dubuque, IA	13,236	291
Hattiesburg, MS	13,214	292
Owensboro, KY	12,996	293
Rochester, MN	12,601	294
Albany, GA	12,156	295
Grand Forks, ND-MN	11,810	296
Columbia, MO	11,578	297
Bismarck, ND	11,571	298
Bloomington, IN	11,330	299
Lawton, OK	11,073	300
Pine Bluff, AR	10,988	301
Sumter, SC	10,881	302
Great Falls, MT	10,654	303
Victoria, TX	10,507	304
Jonesboro, AR	10,289	305
Missoula, MT	9,788	306
Rapid City, SD	9,775	307
Bryan-College Station, TX	9,448	308
Flagstaff, AZ-UT	9,335	309
Cheyenne, WY	9,218	310
Enid, OK	9,024	311
Iowa City, IA	8,203	312
Lawrence, KS	8,179	313
Jacksonville, NC	8,149	314
Pocatello, ID	8,063	315
Casper, WY	7,993	316

MSA/NECMA Total **27,904,111**
United States Total **36,296,950**
MSA/NECMA (% of U.S.Total) **76.88**

MSA/NECMA	POPULATION	RANK
New York, NY	2,311,423	1
Chicago, IL	1,535,888	2
Washington, DC-MD-VA-WV	1,184,356	3
Detroit, MI	1,003,576	4
Atlanta, GA	986,217	5
Philadelphia, PA-NJ	971,673	6
Los Angeles-Long Beach, CA	960,655	7
Houston, TX	735,122	8
Baltimore, MD	690,393	9
Dallas, TX	500,061	10
Norfolk-Virginia Beach-Newport News, VA-NC	468,005	11
Memphis, TN-AR-MS	464,350	12
New Orleans, LA	455,730	13
St. Louis, MO-IL	455,596	14
Newark, NJ	434,078	15
Miami, FL	433,764	16
Cleveland-Lorain-Elyria, OH	410,983	17
Oakland, CA	342,356	18
Boston-Worcester-Lawrence-Lowell-Brockton, MA-NH	309,015	19
Richmond-Petersburg, VA	291,164	20
Charlotte-Gastonia-Rock Hill, NC-SC	287,613	21
Fort Lauderdale, FL	271,415	22
Birmingham, AL	264,626	23
Raleigh-Durham-Chapel Hill, NC	263,187	24
Jacksonville, FL	245,214	25
Tampa-St. Petersburg-Clearwater, FL	243,966	26
Kansas City, MO-KS	233,801	27
Greensboro-Winston Salem-High Point, NC	229,747	28
Milwaukee-Waukesha, WI	225,606	29
Nassau-Suffolk, NY	222,391	30
Orlando, FL	219,543	31
Cincinnati, OH-KY-IN	209,382	32
Indianapolis, IN	208,092	33
Riverside-San Bernardino, CA	204,484	34
Pittsburgh, PA	198,911	35
Columbus, OH	197,349	36
Jackson, MS	188,129	37
Nashville, TN	183,357	38
Baton Rouge, LA	181,535	39
Fort Worth-Arlington, TX	177,875	40
New Haven-Bridgeport-Stamford-Danbury-Waterbury, CT	175,789	41
Charleston-North Charleston, SC	170,504	42
San Diego, CA	168,258	43
Greenville-Spartanburg-Anderson, SC	166,651	44
West Palm Beach-Boca Raton, FL	154,585	45
Columbia, SC	154,432	46
Augusta-Aiken, GA-SC	153,028	47
Mobile, AL	150,987	48
Shreveport-Bossier City, LA	139,207	49
Dayton-Springfield, OH	138,610	50
Buffalo-Niagara Falls, NY	134,490	51
Minneapolis-St. Paul, MN-WI	132,893	52
Louisville, KY-IN	130,178	53
Macon, GA	126,785	54
Bergen-Passaic, NJ	126,554	55
Gary, IN	126,526	56
San Francisco, CA	124,834	57
Las Vegas, NV-AZ	122,660	58
Montgomery, AL	118,997	59
Denver, CO	118,553	60
Phoenix-Mesa, AZ	118,248	61
Little Rock-North Little Rock, AR	117,952	62
Lafayette, LA	112,023	63
Oklahoma City, OK	111,812	64
Sacramento, CA	111,136	65
Columbus, GA-AL	109,882	66
Austin-San Marcos, TX	109,266	67
Seattle-Bellevue-Everett, WA	108,900	68
Savannah, GA	108,042	69
Rochester, NY	108,026	70
Hartford, CT	100,903	71
Wilmington-Newark, DE-MD	97,040	72
San Antonio, TX	96,179	73
Tallahassee, FL	95,528	74
Beaumont-Port Arthur, TX	94,043	75
Flint, MI	91,287	76
Fayetteville, NC	87,831	77
Middlesex-Somerset-Hunterdon, NJ	84,949	78
Jersey City, NJ	79,525	79
Akron, OH	76,982	80
Pensacola, FL	75,495	81
Toledo, OH	75,348	82
Grand Rapids-Muskegon-Holland, MI	75,209	83
Lakeland-Winter Haven, FL	75,016	84
Monmouth-Ocean, NJ	73,710	85
Biloxi-Gulfport-Pascagoula, MS	71,088	86
Huntsville, AL	69,293	87
Trenton, NJ	68,595	88
Tulsa, OK	66,560	89
Chattanooga, TN-GA	65,944	90
Youngstown-Warren, OH	61,152	91
Rocky Mount, NC	60,305	92
Killeen-Temple, TX	59,763	93
Omaha, NE-IA	59,632	94
San Jose, CA	58,744	95
Albany, GA	57,913	96
Tacoma, WA	56,208	97
Portland-Vancouver, OR-WA	53,807	98
Atlantic-Cape May, NJ	52,945	99
Vallejo-Fairfield-Napa, CA	52,782	100
Daytona Beach, FL	52,260	101
Florence, SC	49,752	102
Monroe, LA	49,229	103
Gainesville, FL	47,636	104
Sumter, SC	47,523	105
Harrisburg-Lebanon-Carlisle, PA	47,416	106
Syracuse, NY	46,219	107
Longview-Marshall, TX	46,191	108
Melbourne-Titusville-Palm Bay, FL	46,064	109
Tuscaloosa, AL	45,966	110
Lake Charles, LA	45,779	111
Lexington, KY	45,715	112
Galveston-Texas City, TX	45,460	113
Orange County, CA	45,072	114
Fort Pierce-Port St. Lucie, FL	44,903	115
Albany-Schenectady-Troy, NY	44,207	116
Wilmington, NC	44,155	117
Greenville, NC	43,818	118
Kalamazoo-Battle Creek, MI	43,760	119
Wichita, KS	43,564	120
Knoxville, TN	43,005	121
Springfield, MA	42,735	122
Clarksville-Hopkinsville, TN-KY	41,933	123
Lynchburg, VA	41,635	124
Saginaw-Bay City-Midland, MI	40,736	125
Sarasota-Bradenton, FL	39,951	126
Fresno, CA	39,868	127
Ann Arbor, MI	39,712	128
Alexandria, LA	38,974	129
Providence-Warwick-Pawtucket, RI	38,206	130
Tyler, TX	38,141	131
Colorado Springs, CO	37,971	132
Ocala, FL	37,901	133
Pine Bluff, AR	37,861	134
Goldsboro, NC	37,494	135
Danville, VA	37,467	136
Bakersfield, CA	36,824	137
Fort Wayne, IN	35,986	138
Lansing-East Lansing, MI	34,061	139
Waco, TX	33,600	140
Fort Myers-Cape Coral, FL	33,055	141
Athens, GA	33,007	142
Houma, LA	32,046	143
Honolulu, HI	32,004	144
Myrtle Beach, SC	31,899	145
Roanoke, VA	31,152	146
Dothan, AL	30,615	147
Jackson, TN	30,364	148
Texarkana, TX-AR	29,612	149
Hattiesburg, MS	29,529	150
Stockton-Lodi, CA	29,446	151
Canton-Massillon, OH	28,947	152
Tucson, AZ	28,599	153
Peoria-Pekin, IL	28,314	154
South Bend, IN	28,168	155
Rockford, IL	28,031	156
Jacksonville, NC	26,612	157
Newburgh, NY-PA	26,332	158
Dover, DE	26,317	159
Vineland-Millville-Bridgeton, NJ	26,202	160
Benton Harbor, MI	26,153	161
Hickory-Morganton-Lenoir, NC	24,858	162
Charlottesville, VA	24,397	163
Dutchess County, NY	24,004	164
Racine, WI	23,559	165
El Paso, TX	23,209	166
Anniston, AL	22,792	167
Albuquerque, NM	21,909	168
Davenport-Moline-Rock Island, IA-IL	21,733	169
Salinas, CA	21,681	170
Lawton, OK	20,131	171
Brazoria, TX	20,105	172
Panama City, FL	19,682	173
Fort Walton Beach, FL	18,860	174
Lubbock, TX	18,600	175
Des Moines, IA	18,376	176
Evansville-Henderson, IN-KY	18,325	177
Champaign-Urbana, IL	18,281	178
Florence, AL	18,275	179
Decatur, AL	17,688	180
Erie, PA	17,550	181
Springfield, IL	17,287	182
Hamilton-Middletown, OH	17,194	183
Kankakee, IL	17,025	184
Ventura, CA	16,707	185
Asheville, NC	16,567	186
Bryan-College Station, TX	15,948	187
Odessa-Midland, TX	15,750	188
Anchorage, AK	15,660	189
Madison, WI	15,595	190
Gadsden, AL	15,483	191
Salt Lake City-Ogden, UT	15,475	192
Decatur, IL	15,254	193
Utica-Rome, NY	15,204	194
Corpus Christi, TX	14,823	195
Topeka, KS	14,514	196
York, PA	14,141	197
Allentown-Bethlehem-Easton, PA	14,124	198
Lima, OH	13,793	199
Charleston, WV	13,786	200
Jackson, MI	13,054	201
New London-Norwich, CT	12,679	202
Amarillo, TX	12,652	203
Wichita Falls, TX	12,599	204
Lancaster, PA	12,437	205
Reading, PA	12,119	206
Mansfield, OH	12,109	207
Naples, FL	12,072	208
Columbia, MO	11,766	209
Santa Barbara-Santa Maria-Lompoc, CA	10,880	210
Johnson City-Kingsport-Bristol, TN-VA	10,833	211
Hagerstown, MD	9,722	212
Janesville-Beloit, WI	9,528	213
Waterloo-Cedar Falls, IA	9,067	214
Elkhart-Goshen, IN	8,933	215
Merced, CA	8,616	216
Fort Smith, AR-OK	8,354	217
Abilene, TX	8,072	218
Muncie, IN	7,904	219
Reno, NV	7,872	220
Sherman-Denison, TX	7,679	221
Kenosha, WI	7,572	222
Modesto, CA	7,295	223
Huntington-Ashland, WV-KY-OH	7,127	224
Sharon, PA	7,106	225
Bremerton, WA	6,867	226
Spokane, WA	6,854	227
Bloomington-Normal, IL	6,846	228
San Luis Obispo-Antascadero-Paso Robles, CA	6,642	229
Punta Gorda, FL	6,474	230
Terre Haute, IN	6,414	231
Scranton-Wilkes-Barre-Hazleton, PA	6,232	232
Santa Rosa, CA	6,223	233
Steubenville-Weirton, OH-WV	5,733	234
Lincoln, NE	5,709	235
Elmira, NY	5,604	236
Victoria, TX	5,547	237
Johnstown, PA	5,491	238
Kokomo, IN	5,231	239
Springfield, MO	5,178	240
Jonesboro, AR	4,944	241
Binghamton, NY	4,894	242
Visalia-Tulare-Porterville, CA	4,801	243
San Angelo, TX	4,384	244
Olympia, WA	4,303	245
Yuma, AZ	4,109	246
Cedar Rapids, IA	4,040	247
Lawrence, KS	3,997	248
Owensboro, KY	3,985	249
Yuba City, CA	3,750	250
Barnstable-Yarmouth, MA	3,697	251
State College, PA	3,448	252
Yolo, CA	3,431	253
Bloomington, IN	3,323	254
Wheeling, WV-OH	3,228	255
Richland-Kennewick-Pasco, WA	3,214	256
Las Cruces, NM	3,192	257
Lafayette, IN	3,163	258
St. Joseph, MO	3,107	259
Williamsport, PA	3,091	260
Pittsfield, MA	3,069	261
Salem, OR	2,974	262
Jamestown, NY	2,898	263
Santa Cruz-Watsonville, CA	2,811	264
Pueblo, CO	2,806	265
Chico-Paradise, CA	2,653	266
Fayetteville-Springdale-Rogers, AR	2,651	267
Cumberland, MD-WV	2,637	268
Eugene-Springfield, OR	2,617	269
Boulder-Longmont, CO	2,585	270
Yakima, WA	2,476	271
Glens Falls, NY	2,397	272
Iowa City, IA	2,365	273
Cheyenne, WY	2,214	274
Sioux City, IA-NE	2,198	275
Enid, OK	2,081	276
Boise City, ID	2,037	277
Flagstaff, AZ-UT	1,986	278
Rapid City, SD	1,941	279
Portland, ME	1,839	280
Joplin, MO	1,819	281
Parkersburg-Marietta, WV-OH	1,728	282
Burlington, VT	1,627	283
Duluth-Superior, MN-WI	1,581	284
Grand Forks, ND-MN	1,581	285
Fort Collins-Loveland, CO	1,494	286
Sioux Falls, SD	1,411	287
Altoona, PA	1,311	288
Redding, CA	1,309	289
Great Falls, MT	1,284	290
Santa Fe, NM	1,198	291
Rochester, MN	1,192	292
Green Bay, WI	1,122	293
McAllen-Edinburg-Mission, TX	1,005	294
Appleton-Oshkosh-Neenah, WI	993	295
Bellingham, WA	928	296
Brownsville-Harlingen-San Benito, TX	918	297
Pocatello, ID	843	298
Sheboygan, WI	790	299
Greeley, CO	745	300
St. Cloud, MN	693	301
Billings, MT	657	302
Fargo-Moorhead, ND-MN	629	303
Bangor, ME	586	304
Lewiston-Auburn, ME	584	305
La Crosse, WI-MN	583	306
Provo-Orem, UT	541	307
Grand Junction, CO	491	308
Casper, WY	466	309
Medford-Ashland, OR	461	310
Dubuque, IA	356	311
Eau Claire, WI	305	312
Laredo, TX	246	313
Missoula, MT	243	314
Wausau, WI	106	315
Bismarck, ND	91	316

MSA/NECMA Total **29,064,056**
United States Total **34,033,308**
MSA/NECMA (% of U.S.Total) **85.40**

MSA/NECMA	POPULATION	RANK
Los Angeles-Long Beach, CA	4,236,293	1
New York, NY	2,240,785	2
Miami, FL	1,224,304	3
Chicago, IL	1,183,980	4
Riverside-San Bernardino, CA	1,066,057	5
Houston, TX	1,027,676	6
San Antonio, TX	852,415	7
Orange County, CA	812,153	8
San Diego, CA	751,502	9
Phoenix-Mesa, AZ	628,793	10
Dallas, TX	554,600	11
El Paso, TX	538,660	12
McAllen-Edinburg-Mission, TX	473,192	13
San Jose, CA	443,210	14
Oakland, CA	404,195	15
Fresno, CA	387,689	16
Washington, DC-MD-VA-WV	351,936	17
Boston-Worcester-Lawrence-Lowell-Brockton, MA-NH	323,491	18
San Francisco, CA	314,998	19
Austin-San Marcos, TX	295,422	20
Denver, CO	288,189	21
Brownsville-Harlingen-San Benito, TX	285,015	22
Albuquerque, NM	267,602	23
Newark, NJ	252,022	24
Ventura, CA	249,358	25
Tucson, AZ	237,256	26
Fort Worth-Arlington, TX	231,985	27
Philadelphia, PA-NJ	230,682	28
Corpus Christi, TX	230,449	29
Bakersfield, CA	229,825	30
Jersey City, NJ	228,088	31
Las Vegas, NV-AZ	223,250	32
Sacramento, CA	222,984	33
Tampa-St. Petersburg-Clearwater, FL	222,711	34
Nassau-Suffolk, NY	221,505	35
Bergen-Passaic, NJ	214,651	36
Laredo, TX	184,306	37
Fort Lauderdale, FL	183,490	38
Orlando, FL	182,206	39
Visalia-Tulare-Porterville, CA	170,322	40
Stockton-Lodi, CA	162,805	41
Salinas, CA	158,513	42
New Haven-Bridgeport-Stamford-Danbury-Waterbury, CT	156,343	43
Santa Barbara-Santa Maria-Lompoc, CA	136,235	44
Atlanta, GA	135,380	45
Modesto, CA	123,499	46
West Palm Beach-Boca Raton, FL	114,258	47
Detroit, MI	109,945	48
Middlesex-Somerset-Hunterdon, NJ	108,036	49
Salt Lake City-Ogden, UT	105,403	50
Las Cruces, NM	99,966	51
Portland-Vancouver, OR-WA	99,106	52
Seattle-Bellevue-Everett, WA	97,819	53
Hartford, CT	95,389	54
Vallejo-Fairfield-Napa, CA	90,569	55
Merced, CA	81,898	56
Odessa-Midland, TX	80,139	57
Milwaukee-Waukesha, WI	69,986	58
Yakima, WA	69,428	59
Gary, IN	67,876	60
Kansas City, MO-KS	67,649	61
Santa Cruz-Watsonville, CA	66,559	62
New Orleans, LA	66,502	63
Santa Fe, NM	66,335	64
Lubbock, TX	66,116	65
Honolulu, HI	65,360	66
Santa Rosa, CA	64,077	67
Cleveland-Lorain-Elyria, OH	63,868	68
Providence-Warwick-Pawtucket, RI	63,224	69
Yuma, AZ	63,224	70
Minneapolis-St. Paul, MN-WI	62,434	71
Springfield, MA	61,540	72
Monmouth-Ocean, NJ	57,976	73
Pueblo, CO	55,241	74
Colorado Springs, CO	53,773	75
Oklahoma City, OK	53,625	76
Brazoria, TX	51,870	77
Killeen-Temple, TX	49,930	78
Norfolk-Virginia Beach-Newport News, VA-NC	49,828	79
Baltimore, MD	47,550	80
Galveston-Texas City, TX	45,092	81
Reno, NV	44,689	82
Rochester, NY	43,255	83
San Luis Obispo-Antascadero-Paso Robles, CA	42,284	84
Yolo, CA	41,920	85
Grand Rapids-Muskegon-Holland, MI	41,214	86
Greeley, CO	40,159	87
Naples, FL	39,891	88
Allentown-Bethlehem-Easton, PA	39,372	89
Jacksonville, FL	39,201	90
Salem, OR	39,199	91
St. Louis, MO-IL	37,466	92
Tacoma, WA	36,367	93
Amarillo, TX	35,930	94
Omaha, NE-IA	35,573	95
Richland-Kennewick-Pasco, WA	34,461	96
Victoria, TX	34,335	97
Boise City, ID	34,203	98
Wichita, KS	33,133	99
San Angelo, TX	32,988	100
Waco, TX	32,976	101
Buffalo-Niagara Falls, NY	31,599	102
Newburgh, NY-PA	31,474	103
Raleigh-Durham-Chapel Hill, NC	28,144	104
Lakeland-Winter Haven, FL	28,067	105

MSA/NECMA	POPULATION	RANK
Trenton, NJ	27,424	106
Fort Myers-Cape Coral, FL	27,416	107
Daytona Beach, FL	27,409	108
Atlantic-Cape May, NJ	26,781	109
Charlotte-Gastonia-Rock Hill, NC-SC	26,481	110
Yuba City, CA	26,307	111
Sarasota-Bradenton, FL	26,248	112
Fayetteville, NC	26,161	113
Toledo, OH	25,624	114
Reading, PA	25,215	115
Vineland-Millville-Bridgeton, NJ	24,785	116
Bryan-College Station, TX	24,368	117
Lancaster, PA	23,884	118
Tulsa, OK	23,581	119
Abilene, TX	23,090	120
Lansing-East Lansing, MI	22,090	121
Boulder-Longmont, CO	22,080	122
Melbourne-Titusville-Palm Bay, FL	22,039	123
Saginaw-Bay City-Midland, MI	21,770	124
Beaumont-Port Arthur, TX	21,359	125
Wilmington-Newark, DE-MD	20,747	126
Chico-Paradise, CA	20,658	127
Davenport-Moline-Rock Island, IA-IL	20,444	128
Albany-Schenectady-Troy, NY	19,677	129
Fort Pierce-Port St. Lucie, FL	19,307	130
Indianapolis, IN	19,290	131
Pittsburgh, PA	19,103	132
Fort Collins-Loveland, CO	18,805	133
Greensboro-Winston Salem-High Point, NC	18,053	134
Rockford, IL	17,907	135
Wichita Falls, TX	16,880	136
Ann Arbor, MI	16,843	137
Columbus, OH	15,649	138
Nashville, TN	15,590	139
Provo-Orem, UT	15,473	140
Richmond-Petersburg, VA	15,383	141
Harrisburg-Lebanon-Carlisle, PA	14,949	142
Flagstaff, AZ-UT	14,649	143
Memphis, TN-AR-MS	14,355	144
Jacksonville, NC	13,928	145
Racine, WI	13,742	146
Columbus, GA-AL	13,381	147
Anchorage, AK	13,304	148
Tyler, TX	13,249	149
Dutchess County, NY	13,157	150
Syracuse, NY	13,024	151
Des Moines, IA	12,862	152
Eugene-Springfield, OR	12,726	153
Spokane, WA	12,306	154
Topeka, KS	11,969	155
Fort Wayne, IN	11,918	156
Kalamazoo-Battle Creek, MI	11,578	157
Charleston-North Charleston, SC	11,501	158
Augusta-Aiken, GA-SC	11,469	159
Medford-Ashland, OR	11,296	160
Grand Junction, CO	11,248	161
Flint, MI	11,204	162
Bremerton, WA	11,144	163
Pensacola, FL	11,113	164
Cincinnati, OH-KY-IN	11,099	165
New London-Norwich, CT	11,021	166
Ocala, FL	10,995	167
Gainesville, FL	10,768	168
Little Rock-North Little Rock, AR	10,760	169
Greenville-Spartanburg-Anderson, SC	10,439	170
Lawton, OK	10,249	171
Baton Rouge, LA	10,142	172
Columbia, SC	10,117	173
Clarksville-Hopkinsville, TN-KY	10,111	174
Madison, WI	9,746	175
Youngstown-Warren, OH	9,695	176
Olympia, WA	9,312	177
Fayetteville-Springdale-Rogers, AR	9,286	178
Redding, CA	9,260	179
Kenosha, WI	9,233	180
Dayton-Springfield, OH	9,225	181
Tallahassee, FL	8,991	182
Louisville, KY-IN	8,479	183
Lincoln, NE	8,443	184
Cheyenne, WY	8,425	185
Longview-Marshall, TX	8,278	186
Fort Walton Beach, FL	8,166	187
York, PA	8,107	188
Utica-Rome, NY	7,874	189
South Bend, IN	7,872	190
Mobile, AL	7,692	191
Biloxi-Gulfport-Pascagoula, MS	7,306	192
Bellingham, WA	7,201	193
Birmingham, AL	6,768	194
Sioux City, IA-NE	6,753	195
Knoxville, TN	6,425	196
Huntsville, AL	6,263	197
Savannah, GA	6,076	198
Macon, GA	5,950	199
Shreveport-Bossier City, LA	5,891	200
Lafayette, LA	5,789	201
Jamestown, NY	5,536	202
Peoria-Pekin, IL	5,459	203
Fort Smith, AR-OK	5,434	204
Punta Gorda, FL	5,298	205
Akron, OH	5,237	206
Erie, PA	4,920	207
Scranton-Wilkes-Barre-Hazleton, PA	4,913	208
Elkhart-Goshen, IN	4,814	209
Pocatello, ID	4,743	210
Chattanooga, TN-GA	4,741	211
Lexington, KY	4,696	212
Dover, DE	4,334	213
Hickory-Morganton-Lenoir, NC	4,296	214

MSA/NECMA	POPULATION	RANK
Sherman-Denison, TX	4,151	215
Panama City, FL	4,142	216
Billings, MT	4,095	217
Champaign-Urbana, IL	3,956	218
Lafayette, IN	3,949	219
Appleton-Oshkosh-Neenah, WI	3,881	220
Canton-Massillon, OH	3,828	221
Montgomery, AL	3,809	222
Binghamton, NY	3,679	223
Athens, GA	3,660	224
Houma, LA	3,621	225
Lawrence, KS	3,578	226
Barnstable-Yarmouth, MA	3,524	227
Wilmington, NC	3,429	228
Springfield, MO	3,387	229
Grand Forks, ND-MN	3,338	230
Benton Harbor, MI	3,302	231
Fargo-Moorhead, ND-MN	3,161	232
Johnson City-Kingsport-Bristol, TN-VA	3,146	233
Cedar Rapids, IA	3,046	234
Jackson, MI	3,044	235
Kankakee, IL	2,999	236
Asheville, NC	2,993	237
Goldsboro, NC	2,957	238
Jackson, MS	2,868	239
Rapid City, SD	2,826	240
Janesville-Beloit, WI	2,813	241
Dothan, AL	2,784	242
Sheboygan, WI	2,732	243
Glens Falls, NY	2,730	244
Bloomington-Normal, IL	2,713	245
Iowa City, IA	2,701	246
Texarkana, TX-AR	2,633	247
Lake Charles, LA	2,522	248
Green Bay, WI	2,460	249
St. Joseph, MO	2,439	250
Casper, WY	2,404	251
Myrtle Beach, SC	2,367	252
Charlottesville, VA	2,312	253
Greenville, NC	2,276	254
Hamilton-Middletown, OH	2,231	255
Bloomington, IN	2,177	256
Portland, ME	2,166	257
Roanoke, VA	2,149	258
Anniston, AL	2,133	259
Springfield, IL	2,111	260
Burlington, VT	2,108	261
State College, PA	2,065	262
Evansville-Henderson, IN-KY	2,047	263
Pittsfield, MA	1,975	264
Columbia, MO	1,946	265
Lima, OH	1,925	266
Johnstown, PA	1,873	267
Lynchburg, VA	1,853	268
Sumter, SC	1,838	269
Albany, GA	1,821	270
Alexandria, LA	1,814	271
Kokomo, IN	1,779	272
Joplin, MO	1,751	273
Rocky Mount, NC	1,748	274
Huntington-Ashland, WV-KY-OH	1,729	275
Elmira, NY	1,708	276
Great Falls, MT	1,663	277
Duluth-Superior, MN-WI	1,651	278
Tuscaloosa, AL	1,630	279
Rochester, MN	1,620	280
Enid, OK	1,569	281
Waterloo-Cedar Falls, IA	1,528	282
Monroe, LA	1,520	283
Mansfield, OH	1,505	284
Terre Haute, IN	1,485	285
Hagerstown, MD	1,484	286
Sioux Falls, SD	1,393	287
Decatur, AL	1,368	288
Charleston, WV	1,250	289
Missoula, MT	1,246	290
Muncie, IN	1,228	291
St. Cloud, MN	1,211	292
Hattiesburg, MS	1,147	293
Lewiston-Auburn, ME	1,106	294
Jonesboro, AR	1,094	295
La Crosse, WI-MN	1,076	296
Williamsport, PA	952	297
Eau Claire, WI	919	298
Pine Bluff, AR	912	299
Florence, AL	890	300
Bangor, ME	848	301
Steubenville-Weirton, OH-WV	833	302
Florence, SC	771	303
Decatur, IL	760	304
Wausau, WI	736	305
Sharon, PA	735	306
Danville, VA	732	307
Jackson, TN	729	308
Dubuque, IA	726	309
Bismarck, ND	678	310
Wheeling, WV-OH	656	311
Altoona, PA	626	312
Cumberland, MD-WV	601	313
Gadsden, AL	580	314
Parkersburg-Marietta, WV-OH	574	315
Owensboro, KY	487	316

MSA/NECMA Total **28,617,855**
United States Total **31,273,356**
MSA/NECMA (% of U.S.Total) **91.51**

MSA/NECMA	HOUSEHOLDS	RANK
New York, NY	3,319,773	1
Los Angeles-Long Beach, CA	3,112,741	2
Chicago, IL	2,858,123	3
Boston-Worcester-Lawrence-Lowell-Brockton, MA-NH	2,261,788	4
Philadelphia, PA-NJ	1,825,061	5
Washington, DC-MD-VA-WV	1,754,488	6
Detroit, MI	1,703,582	7
Atlanta, GA	1,444,559	8
Houston, TX	1,437,093	9
Dallas, TX	1,245,475	10
Phoenix-Mesa, AZ	1,145,106	11
Minneapolis-St. Paul, MN-WI	1,084,510	12
Riverside-San Bernardino, CA	1,032,903	13
San Diego, CA	999,985	14
St. Louis, MO-IL	999,338	15
Pittsburgh, PA	957,631	16
Tampa-St. Petersburg-Clearwater, FL	950,376	17
Seattle-Bellevue-Everett, WA	942,435	18
Baltimore, MD	941,316	19
Orange County, CA	934,374	20
Nassau-Suffolk, NY	893,700	21
Oakland, CA	886,457	22
Cleveland-Lorain-Elyria, OH	871,590	23
Denver, CO	804,695	24
Miami, FL	756,345	25
Portland-Vancouver, OR-WA	720,214	26
Newark, NJ	702,230	27
San Francisco, CA	690,452	28
Kansas City, MO-KS	681,395	29
Cincinnati, OH-KY-IN	622,108	30
Fort Lauderdale, FL	622,071	31
Fort Worth-Arlington, TX	616,923	32
New Haven-Bridgeport-Stamford-Danbury-Waterbury, CT	611,774	33
Indianapolis, IN	603,014	34
Sacramento, CA	584,784	35
San Jose, CA	581,092	36
Orlando, FL	579,905	37
Columbus, OH	571,917	38
Norfolk-Virginia Beach-Newport News, VA-NC	566,920	39
San Antonio, TX	562,858	40
Milwaukee-Waukesha, WI	554,389	41
Las Vegas, NV-AZ	540,387	42
Charlotte-Gastonia-Rock Hill, NC-SC	533,515	43
New Orleans, LA	491,874	44
Bergen-Passaic, NJ	488,334	45
Greensboro-Winston Salem-High Point, NC	470,850	46
Buffalo-Niagara Falls, NY	456,684	47
Austin-San Marcos, TX	455,341	48
Nashville, TN	452,662	49
West Palm Beach-Boca Raton, FL	435,894	50
Salt Lake City-Ogden, UT	433,796	51
Raleigh-Durham-Chapel Hill, NC	433,147	52
Hartford, CT	422,193	53
Middlesex-Somerset-Hunterdon, NJ	422,083	54
Monmouth-Ocean, NJ	415,437	55
Rochester, NY	409,099	56
Jacksonville, FL	405,441	57
Memphis, TN-AR-MS	403,184	58
Oklahoma City, OK	401,929	59
Louisville, KY-IN	398,583	60
Richmond-Petersburg, VA	381,452	61
Grand Rapids-Muskegon-Holland, MI	374,336	62
Dayton-Springfield, OH	369,030	63
Greenville-Spartanburg-Anderson, SC	361,078	64
Birmingham, AL	352,301	65
Providence-Warwick-Pawtucket, RI	346,579	66
Albany-Schenectady-Troy, NY	340,815	67
Tucson, AZ	330,295	68
Tulsa, OK	310,762	69
Fresno, CA	287,510	70
Honolulu, HI	284,107	71
Syracuse, NY	274,050	72
Akron, OH	271,419	73
Knoxville, TN	268,964	74
Omaha, NE-IA	266,318	75
Albuquerque, NM	263,653	76
Tacoma, WA	253,984	77
Sarasota-Bradenton, FL	243,384	78
Scranton-Wilkes-Barre-Hazleton, PA	241,634	79
Harrisburg-Lebanon-Carlisle, PA	240,650	80
Ventura, CA	239,429	81
Allentown-Bethlehem-Easton, PA	233,141	82
Youngstown-Warren, OH	232,552	83
Toledo, OH	231,275	84
Gary, IN	230,521	85
Springfield, MA	221,311	86
El Paso, TX	217,663	87
Wilmington-Newark, DE-MD	217,093	88
Little Rock-North Little Rock, AR	214,530	89
Baton Rouge, LA	213,448	90
Wichita, KS	212,151	91
Bakersfield, CA	207,631	92
Jersey City, NJ	205,025	93
Charleston-North Charleston, SC	202,311	94
Ann Arbor, MI	201,564	95
Mobile, AL	200,825	96
Melbourne-Titusville-Palm Bay, FL	192,449	97
Columbia, SC	192,394	98
Daytona Beach, FL	191,761	99
Johnson City-Kingsport-Bristol, TN-VA	190,273	100
Colorado Springs, CO	187,195	101
Fort Wayne, IN	181,911	102
Chattanooga, TN-GA	178,783	103
Stockton-Lodi, CA	178,520	104
Lakeland-Winter Haven, FL	178,430	105
Vallejo-Fairfield-Napa, CA	176,100	106
Lexington, KY	175,826	107
Santa Rosa, CA	175,612	108
Des Moines, IA	171,933	109
Flint, MI	171,117	110
Kalamazoo-Battle Creek, MI	170,284	111
Madison, WI	168,918	112
Augusta-Aiken, GA-SC	167,928	113
Fort Myers-Cape Coral, FL	167,676	114
Lansing-East Lansing, MI	167,305	115
Spokane, WA	165,523	116
Lancaster, PA	162,803	117
Canton-Massillon, OH	157,309	118
Jackson, MS	156,027	119
Saginaw-Bay City-Midland, MI	155,503	120
Pensacola, FL	153,378	121
Boise City, ID	149,777	122
McAllen-Edinburg-Mission, TX	144,442	123
Shreveport-Bossier City, LA	144,110	124
Modesto, CA	144,059	125
Davenport-Moline-Rock Island, IA-IL	143,899	126
Beaumont-Port Arthur, TX	143,627	127
York, PA	143,469	128
Lafayette, LA	140,358	129
Rockford, IL	139,694	130
Santa Barbara-Santa Maria-Lompoc, CA	138,946	131
Corpus Christi, TX	136,728	132
Huntsville, AL	136,513	133
Peoria-Pekin, IL	135,395	134
Reading, PA	134,062	135
Appleton-Oshkosh-Neenah, WI	132,516	136
Biloxi-Gulfport-Pascagoula, MS	131,191	137
Atlantic-Cape May, NJ	128,520	138
Reno, NV	127,137	139
Eugene-Springfield, OR	126,800	140
Hickory-Morganton-Lenoir, NC	126,702	141
Newburgh, NY-PA	125,243	142
Huntington-Ashland, WV-KY-OH	123,695	143
Salem, OR	122,527	144
Macon, GA	122,366	145
Hamilton-Middletown, OH	121,671	146
Fort Pierce-Port St. Lucie, FL	120,959	147
Salinas, CA	120,310	148
Trenton, NJ	119,590	149
Springfield, MO	118,545	150
Montgomery, AL	118,083	151
Evansville-Henderson, IN-KY	114,792	152
Visalia-Tulare-Porterville, CA	112,098	153
Utica-Rome, NY	110,170	154
Boulder-Longmont, CO	110,124	155
Savannah, GA	107,841	156
Fayetteville-Springdale-Rogers, AR	106,245	157
Tallahassee, FL	104,800	158
Charleston, WV	104,556	159
Erie, PA	103,992	160
Portland, ME	102,979	161
Killeen-Temple, TX	101,937	162
Ocala, FL	99,677	163
Columbus, GA-AL	98,442	164
Anchorage, AK	98,158	165
South Bend, IN	98,075	166
Duluth-Superior, MN-WI	97,692	167
Galveston-Texas City, TX	96,980	168
Binghamton, NY	95,729	169
Fayetteville, NC	95,468	170
Brownsville-Harlingen-San Benito, TX	95,033	171
Roanoke, VA	93,767	172
Dutchess County, NY	93,697	173
New London-Norwich, CT	92,069	174
Lincoln, NE	91,572	175
Wilmington, NC	91,470	176
Johnstown, PA	91,427	177
Provo-Orem, UT	91,399	178
Barnstable-Yarmouth, MA	90,723	179
Odessa-Midland, TX	89,290	180
Santa Cruz-Watsonville, CA	89,017	181
Fort Collins-Loveland, CO	88,991	182
San Luis Obispo-Antascadero-Paso Robles, CA	87,954	183
Lubbock, TX	87,898	184
Asheville, NC	87,142	185
Bremerton, WA	85,885	186
Green Bay, WI	84,315	187
Naples, FL	84,102	188
Springfield, IL	82,762	189
Lynchburg, VA	82,289	190
Gainesville, FL	81,779	191
Longview-Marshall, TX	81,317	192
Amarillo, TX	81,147	193
Brazoria, TX	80,895	194
Olympia, WA	80,155	195
Chico-Paradise, CA	78,075	196
Waco, TX	77,563	197
Yakima, WA	75,496	198
Burlington, VT	74,740	199
Fort Smith, AR-OK	74,332	200
Myrtle Beach, SC	72,983	201
Cedar Rapids, IA	72,707	202
Medford-Ashland, OR	70,700	203
Clarksville-Hopkinsville, TN-KY	70,303	204
Racine, WI	69,104	205
Richland-Kennewick-Pasco, WA	68,508	206
Lake Charles, LA	67,341	207
Mansfield, OH	67,310	208
Houma, LA	67,206	209
Topeka, KS	66,524	210
Tyler, TX	66,227	211
Redding, CA	65,863	212
Fort Walton Beach, FL	65,779	213
Fargo-Moorhead, ND-MN	64,605	214
Elkhart-Goshen, IN	63,256	215
Champaign-Urbana, IL	63,023	216
Benton Harbor, MI	62,619	217
Wheeling, WV-OH	62,332	218
Sioux Falls, SD	62,279	219
Merced, CA	62,140	220
Lafayette, IN	61,625	221
Bellingham, WA	61,464	222
Tuscaloosa, AL	61,248	223
Parkersburg-Marietta, WV-OH	60,269	224
St. Cloud, MN	58,808	225
Greeley, CO	58,660	226
Joplin, MO	58,566	227
Jackson, MI	58,333	228
Janesville-Beloit, WI	58,146	229
Punta Gorda, FL	58,005	230
Panama City, FL	57,835	231
Santa Fe, NM	57,761	232
Las Cruces, NM	57,585	233
Charlottesville, VA	57,017	234
Yolo, CA	56,676	235
Terre Haute, IN	56,535	236
Florence, AL	55,983	237
Decatur, AL	55,762	238
Lima, OH	55,576	239
Bangor, ME	55,532	240
Rocky Mount, NC	54,701	241
Eau Claire, WI	54,487	242
Kenosha, WI	54,253	243
Pittsfield, MA	54,112	244
Steubenville-Weirton, OH-WV	54,088	245
Pueblo, CO	53,654	246
Monroe, LA	53,155	247
Bloomington-Normal, IL	52,595	248
Jamestown, NY	52,568	249
Athens, GA	51,887	250
Dothan, AL	51,606	251
Billings, MT	51,331	252
Altoona, PA	51,288	253
Wichita Falls, TX	50,474	254
Laredo, TX	50,062	255
Bryan-College Station, TX	49,747	256
Yuba City, CA	49,497	257
Columbia, MO	48,835	258
Greenville, NC	48,808	259
Hagerstown, MD	48,290	260
Waterloo-Cedar Falls, IA	47,627	261
Vineland-Millville-Bridgeton, NJ	47,561	262
Sharon, PA	47,499	263
La Crosse, WI-MN	46,882	264
Texarkana, TX-AR	46,831	265
Yuma, AZ	46,713	266
Dover, DE	46,563	267
Florence, SC	46,171	268
Grand Junction, CO	46,016	269
Wausau, WI	45,843	270
Muncie, IN	45,824	271
State College, PA	45,791	272
Alexandria, LA	45,765	273
Decatur, IL	45,647	274
Abilene, TX	45,066	275
Anniston, AL	45,049	276
Glens Falls, NY	45,029	277
Williamsport, PA	44,875	278
Rochester, MN	44,717	279
Sioux City, IA-NE	44,709	280
Danville, VA	43,361	281
Albany, GA	42,691	282
Bloomington, IN	42,423	283
Sheboygan, WI	41,945	284
Hattiesburg, MS	41,791	285
Gadsden, AL	41,518	286
Sherman-Denison, TX	40,876	287
Kokomo, IN	40,331	288
Lewiston-Auburn, ME	40,035	289
Goldsboro, NC	39,650	290
Jacksonville, NC	39,487	291
Flagstaff, AZ-UT	39,486	292
Cumberland, MD-WV	39,392	293
Lawton, OK	38,474	294
Jackson, TN	38,400	295
St. Joseph, MO	37,840	296
Iowa City, IA	37,824	297
San Angelo, TX	37,513	298
Kankakee, IL	37,459	299
Grand Forks, ND-MN	36,240	300
Missoula, MT	35,782	301
Owensboro, KY	35,498	302
Bismarck, ND	35,202	303
Lawrence, KS	35,189	304
Sumter, SC	35,132	305
Elmira, NY	34,471	306
Rapid City, SD	32,964	307
Dubuque, IA	32,693	308
Cheyenne, WY	31,381	309
Great Falls, MT	31,281	310
Victoria, TX	30,241	311
Jonesboro, AR	30,189	312
Pine Bluff, AR	28,382	313
Pocatello, ID	26,293	314
Casper, WY	25,744	315
Enid, OK	22,779	316

MSA/NECMA Total 81,618,430
United States Total 102,048,200
MSA/NECMA (% of U.S.Total) 79.98

MEDIAN HOUSEHOLD INCOME

MSA/NECMA	EST. INCOME ($)	RANK
San Jose, CA	73,398	1
Nassau-Suffolk, NY	67,853	2
Middlesex-Somerset-Hunterdon, NJ	67,277	3
New Haven-Bridgeport-Stamford-Danbury-Waterbury, CT	62,971	4
Washington, DC-MD-VA-WV	62,953	5
San Francisco, CA	61,104	6
Newark, NJ	59,781	7
Trenton, NJ	59,739	8
Ventura, CA	58,873	9
Bergen-Passaic, NJ	58,477	10
Orange County, CA	57,167	11
Ann Arbor, MI	56,910	12
Anchorage, AK	56,413	13
Santa Cruz-Watsonville, CA	56,383	14
Seattle-Bellevue-Everett, WA	55,890	15
Boulder-Longmont, CO	55,498	16
Oakland, CA	55,288	17
Chicago, IL	54,857	18
Minneapolis-St. Paul, MN-WI	54,564	19
Honolulu, HI	54,215	20
Hartford, CT	52,946	21
Wilmington-Newark, DE-MD	52,845	22
Madison, WI	52,353	23
New London-Norwich, CT	51,701	24
Rochester, MN	51,338	25
Atlanta, GA	51,084	26
Boston-Worcester-Lawrence-Lowell-Brockton, MA-NH	50,755	27
Denver, CO	50,444	28
Dutchess County, NY	50,385	29
Monmouth-Ocean, NJ	50,381	30
Philadelphia, PA-NJ	49,306	31
Salinas, CA	49,233	32
West Palm Beach-Boca Raton, FL	48,933	33
Bloomington-Normal, IL	48,613	34
Baltimore, MD	48,579	35
Grand Rapids-Muskegon-Holland, MI	48,322	36
Portland-Vancouver, OR-WA	48,080	37
Dallas, TX	48,004	38
Milwaukee-Waukesha, WI	47,817	39
Santa Barbara-Santa Maria-Lompoc, CA	47,775	40
Reno, NV	47,765	41
Appleton-Oshkosh-Neenah, WI	47,443	42
Fort Collins-Loveland, CO	47,345	43
Vallejo-Fairfield-Napa, CA	47,274	44
Salt Lake City-Ogden, UT	47,225	45
Santa Rosa, CA	47,138	46
Santa Fe, NM	46,744	47
Raleigh-Durham-Chapel Hill, NC	46,572	48
Nashville, TN	46,532	49
Houston, TX	46,508	50
Detroit, MI	46,277	51
Des Moines, IA	46,272	52
Racine, WI	45,990	53
Charlotte-Gastonia-Rock Hill, NC-SC	45,825	54
Omaha, NE-IA	45,580	55
Naples, FL	45,549	56
Sioux Falls, SD	45,498	57
Kokomo, IN	45,336	58
Provo-Orem, UT	45,322	59
Cedar Rapids, IA	45,289	60
Green Bay, WI	45,277	61
Newburgh, NY-PA	45,271	62
Lancaster, PA	45,222	63
Indianapolis, IN	45,163	64
Lansing-East Lansing, MI	45,071	65
Burlington, VT	44,894	66
Charlottesville, VA	44,832	67
Sheboygan, WI	44,776	68
Kansas City, MO-KS	44,744	69
Elkhart-Goshen, IN	44,659	70
San Diego, CA	44,644	71
Hamilton-Middletown, OH	44,635	72
Harrisburg-Lebanon-Carlisle, PA	44,536	73
Fort Wayne, IN	44,497	74
Allentown-Bethlehem-Easton, PA	44,258	75
Fort Worth-Arlington, TX	44,185	76
Sacramento, CA	44,050	77
Gary, IN	43,928	78
Boise City, ID	43,928	79
St. Louis, MO-IL	43,825	80
Wausau, WI	43,711	81
Richmond-Petersburg, VA	43,707	82
Los Angeles-Long Beach, CA	43,673	83
Columbus, OH	43,650	84
Cincinnati, OH-KY-IN	43,625	85
Lincoln, NE	43,620	86
Iowa City, IA	43,613	87
Reading, PA	43,380	88
Janesville-Beloit, WI	43,106	89
New York, NY	42,913	90
Austin-San Marcos, TX	42,807	91
Portland, ME	42,794	92
Tacoma, WA	42,777	93
Rochester, NY	42,774	94
Kenosha, WI	42,748	95
Fayetteville, NC	42,671	96
Dayton-Springfield, OH	42,616	97
Brazoria, TX	42,430	98
Las Vegas, NV-AZ	42,273	99
Olympia, WA	42,196	100
Rockford, IL	42,054	101
Albany-Schenectady-Troy, NY	41,923	102
Cleveland-Lorain-Elyria, OH	41,875	103
Columbia, SC	41,865	104
York, PA	41,811	105
Flint, MI	41,747	106
Lafayette, IN	41,725	107
Colorado Springs, CO	41,601	108
Phoenix-Mesa, AZ	41,508	109
Richland-Kennewick-Pasco, WA	41,456	110
Fargo-Moorhead, ND-MN	41,452	111
Bremerton, WA	41,418	112
Jersey City, NJ	41,351	113
Atlantic-Cape May, NJ	41,249	114
Wichita, KS	41,206	115
Akron, OH	41,161	116
Jacksonville, FL	40,991	117
Peoria-Pekin, IL	40,429	118
San Luis Obispo-Antascadero-Paso Robles, CA	40,417	119
Toledo, OH	40,374	120
Providence-Warwick-Pawtucket, RI	40,370	121
Fort Walton Beach, FL	40,315	122
Topeka, KS	40,312	123
Little Rock-North Little Rock, AR	40,273	124
Kalamazoo-Battle Creek, MI	40,224	125
Memphis, TN-AR-MS	40,087	126
Dover, DE	39,969	127
Kankakee, IL	39,959	128
Springfield, IL	39,957	129
Norfolk-Virginia Beach-Newport News, VA-NC	39,920	130
Dubuque, IA	39,843	131
Sarasota-Bradenton, FL	39,828	132
South Bend, IN	39,815	133
Jacksonville, NC	39,790	134
Columbia, MO	39,742	135
Roanoke, VA	39,741	136
Birmingham, AL	39,626	137
Saginaw-Bay City-Midland, MI	39,623	138
Jackson, MS	39,537	139
Bellingham, WA	39,529	140
Greensboro-Winston Salem-High Point, NC	39,528	141
Lexington, KY	39,491	142
Albuquerque, NM	39,465	143
Huntsville, AL	39,406	144
Louisville, KY-IN	39,347	145
Charleston-North Charleston, SC	39,337	146
Orlando, FL	39,281	147
Yolo, CA	39,048	148
Casper, WY	39,017	149
Salem, OR	38,977	150
Bismarck, ND	38,887	151
Cheyenne, WY	38,821	152
Decatur, IL	38,746	153
Evansville-Henderson, IN-KY	38,721	154
Fort Lauderdale, FL	38,314	155
Barnstable-Yarmouth, MA	38,301	156
Pittsfield, MA	38,280	157
Jackson, MI	38,231	158
Syracuse, NY	38,210	159
Champaign-Urbana, IL	38,193	160
Greenville-Spartanburg-Anderson, SC	38,133	161
La Crosse, WI-MN	38,076	162
Baton Rouge, LA	38,053	163
Benton Harbor, MI	37,986	164
Rapid City, SD	37,979	165
Pocatello, ID	37,897	166
Canton-Massillon, OH	37,816	167
St. Cloud, MN	37,748	168
Flagstaff, AZ-UT	37,728	169
Sioux City, IA-NE	37,579	170
Lima, OH	37,533	171
Tallahassee, FL	37,509	172
Savannah, GA	37,472	173
Fort Myers-Cape Coral, FL	37,461	174
Eau Claire, WI	37,442	175
Tulsa, OK	37,108	176
Galveston-Texas City, TX	37,087	177
Buffalo-Niagara Falls, NY	37,077	178
Davenport-Moline-Rock Island, IA-IL	36,947	179
Springfield, MA	36,849	180
Montgomery, AL	36,832	181
Hickory-Morganton-Lenoir, NC	36,781	182
State College, PA	36,733	183
Erie, PA	36,725	184
Riverside-San Bernardino, CA	36,702	185
Pittsburgh, PA	36,623	186
Jackson, TN	36,617	187
Bloomington, IN	36,607	188
Stockton-Lodi, CA	36,464	189
Hagerstown, MD	36,439	190
Victoria, TX	36,379	191
Tampa-St. Petersburg-Clearwater, FL	36,296	192
Spokane, WA	36,207	193
Decatur, AL	36,192	194
Vineland-Millville-Bridgeton, NJ	36,095	195
Oklahoma City, OK	36,094	196
Fort Pierce-Port St. Lucie, FL	36,085	197
Myrtle Beach, SC	36,084	198
Springfield, MO	36,079	199
Grand Forks, ND-MN	35,974	200
Albany, GA	35,950	201
Eugene-Springfield, OR	35,933	202
San Antonio, TX	35,930	203
Billings, MT	35,894	204
Asheville, NC	35,872	205
Augusta-Aiken, GA-SC	35,812	206
Lake Charles, LA	35,682	207
Glens Falls, NY	35,665	208
Macon, GA	35,647	209
Missoula, MT	35,559	210
Waterloo-Cedar Falls, IA	35,433	211
Wilmington, NC	35,332	212
Greeley, CO	35,291	213
Fayetteville-Springdale-Rogers, AR	35,288	214
Melbourne-Titusville-Palm Bay, FL	35,276	215
Chattanooga, TN-GA	35,070	216
Lawrence, KS	34,958	217
Knoxville, TN	34,889	218
Pensacola, FL	34,853	219
Tyler, TX	34,803	220
Medford-Ashland, OR	34,735	221
Biloxi-Gulfport-Pascagoula, MS	34,674	222
Odessa-Midland, TX	34,608	223
Parkersburg-Marietta, WV-OH	34,568	224
Panama City, FL	34,337	225
Elmira, NY	34,331	226
Charleston, WV	34,297	227
Mobile, AL	33,947	228
Lynchburg, VA	33,918	229
Mansfield, OH	33,857	230
Modesto, CA	33,813	231
Columbus, GA-AL	33,758	232
Miami, FL	33,758	233
San Angelo, TX	33,750	234
New Orleans, LA	33,726	235
Athens, GA	33,667	236
Amarillo, TX	33,600	237
Duluth-Superior, MN-WI	33,548	238
Goldsboro, NC	33,522	239
Binghamton, NY	33,500	240
Florence, SC	33,481	241
Tucson, AZ	33,421	242
Greenville, NC	33,332	243
Clarksville-Hopkinsville, TN-KY	33,320	244
Youngstown-Warren, OH	33,207	245
Lewiston-Auburn, ME	33,120	246
Lubbock, TX	33,078	247
Lakeland-Winter Haven, FL	33,071	248
Muncie, IN	33,044	249
Utica-Rome, NY	32,997	250
Owensboro, KY	32,984	251
Lawton, OK	32,859	252
Altoona, PA	32,808	253
Yakima, WA	32,801	254
Shreveport-Bossier City, LA	32,732	255
Corpus Christi, TX	32,673	256
Killeen-Temple, TX	32,641	257
Bangor, ME	32,609	258
Grand Junction, CO	32,587	259
Joplin, MO	32,514	260
Great Falls, MT	32,514	261
Tuscaloosa, AL	32,466	262
Jonesboro, AR	32,458	263
Sumter, SC	32,399	264
Dothan, AL	32,292	265
Florence, AL	32,273	266
Bakersfield, CA	32,251	267
Terre Haute, IN	32,213	268
Williamsport, PA	32,102	269
Sherman-Denison, TX	32,078	270
Beaumont-Port Arthur, TX	32,034	271
Sharon, PA	31,931	272
Abilene, TX	31,827	273
Fort Smith, AR-OK	31,789	274
Fresno, CA	31,788	275
Waco, TX	31,774	276
Wichita Falls, TX	31,638	277
Scranton-Wilkes-Barre-Hazleton, PA	31,596	278
Anniston, AL	31,467	279
Punta Gorda, FL	31,441	280
Rocky Mount, NC	31,265	281
Daytona Beach, FL	31,229	282
Houma, LA	31,202	283
St. Joseph, MO	31,183	284
Gainesville, FL	30,848	285
Enid, OK	30,646	286
Monroe, LA	30,587	287
Jamestown, NY	30,585	288
Longview-Marshall, TX	30,525	289
Visalia-Tulare-Porterville, CA	30,390	290
Johnson City-Kingsport-Bristol, TN-VA	30,356	291
Steubenville-Weirton, OH-WV	30,263	292
Chico-Paradise, CA	30,061	293
Pueblo, CO	30,024	294
Merced, CA	29,787	295
Pine Bluff, AR	29,697	296
Alexandria, LA	29,577	297
Texarkana, TX-AR	29,526	298
Ocala, FL	29,399	299
Redding, CA	29,380	300
Gadsden, AL	29,159	301
Wheeling, WV-OH	28,780	302
Yuma, AZ	28,668	303
Bryan-College Station, TX	28,520	304
Lafayette, LA	28,335	305
Hattiesburg, MS	28,123	306
El Paso, TX	28,007	307
Yuba City, CA	27,910	308
Johnstown, PA	27,901	309
Danville, VA	27,795	310
Cumberland, MD-WV	27,007	311
Huntington-Ashland, WV-KY-OH	26,840	312
Laredo, TX	25,766	313
Las Cruces, NM	25,432	314
Brownsville-Harlingen-S Benito, TX	23,032	315
McAllen-Edinburg-Mission, TX	21,477	316

MSA/NECMA Median **38,220**
United States Median **40,926**

MSA/NECMA	EST. INCOME ($)	RANK
San Jose, CA	92,310	1
New Haven-Bridegport-Stamford-Danbury-Waterbury, CT	90,932	2
Nassau-Suffolk, NY	87,388	3
San Francisco, CA	84,224	4
Middlesex-Somerset-Hunterdon, NJ	83,230	5
Newark, NJ	81,928	6
Trenton, NJ	80,028	7
Bergen-Passaic, NJ	80,008	8
Washington, DC-MD-VA-WV	79,423	9
Orange County, CA	75,057	10
Santa Cruz-Watsonville, CA	74,761	11
West Palm Beach-Boca Raton, FL	74,136	12
Ventura, CA	74,094	13
Chicago, IL	72,994	14
Naples, FL	72,757	15
Ann Arbor, MI	71,965	16
Boulder-Longmont, CO	71,570	17
Seattle-Bellevue-Everett, WA	70,968	18
Oakland, CA	70,949	19
Anchorage, AK	70,910	20
Honolulu, HI	70,421	21
Minneapolis-St. Paul, MN-WI	68,248	22
Atlanta, GA	67,771	23
Santa Barbara-Santa Maria-Lompoc, CA	67,262	24
New York, NY	67,245	25
Monmouth-Ocean, NJ	66,982	26
Hartford, CT	66,611	27
Dallas, TX	66,451	28
Wilmington-Newark, DE-MD	65,978	29
Philadelphia, PA-NJ	65,815	30
Salinas, CA	65,600	31
Madison, WI	65,503	32
Houston, TX	65,464	33
Boston-Worcester-Lawrence-Lowell-Brockton, MA-NH	65,290	34
Denver, CO	65,257	35
New London-Norwich, CT	63,933	36
Los Angeles-Long Beach, CA	63,623	37
Santa Fe, NM	63,517	38
Rochester, MN	63,462	39
Reno, NV	63,355	40
Portland-Vancouver, OR-WA	62,289	41
Nashville, TN	62,230	42
Fort Collins-Loveland, CO	61,986	43
Bloomington-Normal, IL	61,779	44
Detroit, MI	61,420	45
Baltimore, MD	61,369	46
Charlottesville, VA	61,197	47
Milwaukee-Waukesha, WI	61,081	48
Grand Rapids-Muskegon-Holland, MI	60,889	49
Raleigh-Durham-Chapel Hill, NC	60,772	50
Dutchess County, NY	60,770	51
Charlotte-Gastonia-Rock Hill, NC-SC	60,643	52
Iowa City, IA	60,447	53
San Diego, CA	60,313	54
Des Moines, IA	59,831	55
Santa Rosa, CA	59,765	56
Salt Lake City-Ogden, UT	59,523	57
Indianapolis, IN	59,359	58
Provo-Orem, UT	59,160	59
Omaha, NE-IA	58,901	60
Sioux Falls, SD	58,460	61
Boise City, ID	58,346	62
Kansas City, MO-KS	58,326	63
Cincinnati, OH-KY-IN	58,222	64
Austin-San Marcos, TX	57,895	65
Vallejo-Fairfield-Napa, CA	57,753	66
Fort Worth-Arlington, TX	57,728	67
Appleton-Oshkosh-Neenah, WI	57,588	68
Elkhart-Goshen, IN	57,508	69
Racine, WI	57,441	70
Columbus, OH	57,424	71
Cedar Rapids, IA	57,060	72
Sacramento, CA	57,004	73
Kokomo, IN	56,992	74
Allentown-Bethlehem-Easton, PA	56,983	75
St. Louis, MO-IL	56,635	76
Hamilton-Middletown, OH	56,555	77
Green Bay, WI	56,464	78
Lansing-East Lansing, MI	56,433	79
Las Vegas, NV-AZ	56,413	80
Fort Wayne, IN	56,367	81
Lancaster, PA	56,287	82
Memphis, TN-AR-MS	56,201	83
Newburgh, NY-PA	55,938	84
Sarasota-Bradenton, FL	55,877	85
Lincoln, NE	55,835	86
Birmingham, AL	55,795	87
Phoenix-Mesa, AZ	55,751	88
Cleveland-Lorain-Elyria, OH	55,715	89
Jackson, MS	55,620	90
Richmond-Petersburg, VA	55,610	91
Harrisburg-Lebanon-Carlisle, PA	55,497	92
Fayetteville, NC	55,424	93
Portland, ME	55,090	94
Dayton-Springfield, OH	54,955	95
Burlington, VT	54,929	96
Akron, OH	54,905	97
Jersey City, NJ	54,828	98
Reading, PA	54,757	99
Gary, IN	54,741	100
Jacksonville, FL	54,630	101
Wausau, WI	54,549	102
Lafayette, IN	54,506	103
Lexington, KY	54,408	104
Yolo, CA	54,351	105
Atlantic-Cape May, NJ	54,211	106
San Luis Obispo-Antascadero-Paso Robles, CA	54,171	107
Colorado Springs, CO	54,067	108
Tacoma, WA	54,062	109
Rochester, NY	53,966	110
Toledo, OH	53,903	111
Flint, MI	53,743	112
Little Rock-North Little Rock, AR	53,737	113
Columbia, MO	53,695	114
Columbia, SC	53,560	115
Wichita, KS	53,512	116
Sheboygan, WI	53,492	117
Fort Lauderdale, FL	53,491	118
Fargo-Moorhead, ND-MN	53,381	119
Janesville-Beloit, WI	53,187	120
Louisville, KY-IN	53,135	121
Albany-Schenectady-Troy, NY	53,104	122
Albuquerque, NM	53,030	123
Kenosha, WI	53,022	124
Rockford, IL	52,878	125
Kalamazoo-Battle Creek, MI	52,862	126
Greensboro-Winston Salem-High Point, NC	52,839	127
Fort Pierce-Port St. Lucie, FL	52,799	128
Orlando, FL	52,759	129
South Bend, IN	52,753	130
Tallahassee, FL	52,631	131
Baton Rouge, LA	52,391	132
Richland-Kennewick-Pasco, WA	52,331	133
Providence-Warwick-Pawtucket, RI	52,290	134
Bellingham, WA	52,253	135
Peoria-Pekin, IL	52,133	136
Saginaw-Bay City-Midland, MI	52,131	137
Brazoria, TX	51,879	138
Fort Walton Beach, FL	51,854	139
Odessa-Midland, TX	51,852	140
Tulsa, OK	51,680	141
Miami, FL	51,672	142
Roanoke, VA	51,643	143
Olympia, WA	51,622	144
Fort Myers-Cape Coral, FL	51,618	145
Bremerton, WA	51,554	146
Springfield, IL	51,496	147
Champaign-Urbana, IL	51,448	148
Evansville-Henderson, IN-KY	51,368	149
Victoria, TX	51,316	150
York, PA	51,195	151
Kankakee, IL	51,161	152
Sioux City, IA-NE	51,098	153
Pittsburgh, PA	51,071	154
Charleston-North Charleston, SC	51,067	155
Rapid City, SD	50,863	156
Salem, OR	50,823	157
Tampa-St. Petersburg-Clearwater, FL	50,722	158
Dubuque, IA	50,716	159
Topeka, KS	50,674	160
Decatur, IL	50,652	161
Huntsville, AL	50,486	162
Casper, WY	50,414	163
Galveston-Texas City, TX	50,395	164
Savannah, GA	50,372	165
State College, PA	50,244	166
Bloomington, IN	50,200	167
Flagstaff, AZ-UT	50,188	168
Montgomery, AL	50,133	169
San Antonio, TX	50,117	170
Jackson, TN	50,050	171
Athens, GA	50,048	172
Greenville-Spartanburg-Anderson, SC	50,043	173
Dover, DE	49,992	174
Norfolk-Virginia Beach-Newport News, VA-NC	49,986	175
Jacksonville, NC	49,810	176
Bismarck, ND	49,798	177
Pittsfield, MA	49,741	178
Barnstable-Yarmouth, MA	49,617	179
Lake Charles, LA	49,607	180
Tyler, TX	49,495	181
Albany, GA	49,446	182
Benton Harbor, MI	49,408	183
Knoxville, TN	49,308	184
Cheyenne, WY	49,264	185
Missoula, MT	49,052	186
Oklahoma City, OK	49,010	187
Wilmington, NC	48,913	188
Myrtle Beach, SC	48,905	189
Canton-Massillon, OH	48,836	190
Syracuse, NY	48,793	191
Stockton-Lodi, CA	48,758	192
Chattanooga, TN-GA	48,723	193
Buffalo-Niagara Falls, NY	48,693	194
Erie, PA	48,668	195
Springfield, MO	48,542	196
La Crosse, WI-MN	48,512	197
Charleston, WV	48,482	198
Riverside-San Bernardino, CA	48,440	199
Spokane, WA	48,439	200
Pocatello, ID	48,388	201
New Orleans, LA	48,351	202
Jackson, MI	48,233	203
Eau Claire, WI	48,201	204
Asheville, NC	48,104	205
Davenport-Moline-Rock Island, IA-IL	48,074	206
Eugene-Springfield, OR	48,052	207
Lubbock, TX	47,870	208
Mobile, AL	47,779	209
Columbus, GA-AL	47,774	210
Lawrence, KS	47,747	211
Waterloo-Cedar Falls, IA	47,688	212
Fayetteville-Springdale-Rogers, AR	47,643	213
Florence, SC	47,493	214
Greenville, NC	47,486	215
Springfield, MA	47,450	216
St. Cloud, MN	47,419	217
Macon, GA	47,273	218
Decatur, AL	47,251	219
Panama City, FL	47,142	220
Medford-Ashland, OR	47,064	221
Pensacola, FL	46,970	222
Lima, OH	46,957	223
Vineland-Millville-Bridgeton, NJ	46,940	224
Muncie, IN	46,933	225
Tuscaloosa, AL	46,826	226
Shreveport-Bossier City, LA	46,790	227
Grand Forks, ND-MN	46,735	228
Augusta-Aiken, GA-SC	46,544	229
Tucson, AZ	46,518	230
Billings, MT	46,443	231
Greeley, CO	46,432	232
Biloxi-Gulfport-Pascagoula, MS	46,338	233
Monroe, LA	46,223	234
Hickory-Morganton-Lenoir, NC	46,196	235
Jonesboro, AR	46,164	236
Corpus Christi, TX	46,054	237
Modesto, CA	46,023	238
Amarillo, TX	46,022	239
San Angelo, TX	45,949	240
Melbourne-Titusville-Palm Bay, FL	45,882	241
Gainesville, FL	45,780	242
Fresno, CA	45,685	243
Yakima, WA	45,456	244
Parkersburg-Marietta, WV-OH	45,266	245
Bryan-College Station, TX	45,236	246
Elmira, NY	45,230	247
Glens Falls, NY	45,100	248
Florence, AL	44,980	249
Waco, TX	44,935	250
Lakeland-Winter Haven, FL	44,859	251
Lynchburg, VA	44,458	252
Joplin, MO	44,250	253
Great Falls, MT	44,218	254
Hagerstown, MD	44,210	255
Bakersfield, CA	44,127	256
Duluth-Superior, MN-WI	44,106	257
Fort Smith, AR-OK	44,072	258
Beaumont-Port Arthur, TX	44,058	259
Abilene, TX	43,965	260
Youngstown-Warren, OH	43,852	261
Owensboro, KY	43,773	262
Dothan, AL	43,690	263
Houma, LA	43,676	264
Visalia-Tulare-Porterville, CA	43,672	265
Grand Junction, CO	43,531	266
Mansfield, OH	43,463	267
Wichita Falls, TX	43,433	268
Binghamton, NY	43,397	269
Altoona, PA	43,394	270
Terre Haute, IN	43,388	271
Sherman-Denison, TX	43,170	272
Alexandria, LA	43,124	273
Killeen-Temple, TX	43,093	274
Scranton-Wilkes-Barre-Hazleton, PA	43,050	275
Utica-Rome, NY	42,951	276
Hattiesburg, MS	42,909	277
Goldsboro, NC	42,802	278
Clarksville-Hopkinsville, TN-KY	42,682	279
Lafayette, LA	42,600	280
Sumter, SC	42,559	281
Chico-Paradise, CA	42,456	282
Daytona Beach, FL	42,425	283
Rocky Mount, NC	42,401	284
Merced, CA	42,354	285
Punta Gorda, FL	42,198	286
Lawton, OK	42,131	287
Longview-Marshall, TX	41,975	288
Pine Bluff, AR	41,922	289
Johnson City-Kingsport-Bristol, TN-VA	41,869	290
Bangor, ME	41,711	291
Lewiston-Auburn, ME	41,042	292
St. Joseph, MO	40,857	293
Sharon, PA	40,719	294
Williamsport, PA	40,668	295
Laredo, TX	40,632	296
Anniston, AL	40,414	297
Texarkana, TX-AR	40,390	298
Jamestown, NY	39,974	299
Redding, CA	39,839	300
Ocala, FL	39,767	301
Pueblo, CO	39,712	302
Enid, OK	39,711	303
Yuba City, CA	39,634	304
Gadsden, AL	39,613	305
Steubenville-Weirton, OH-WV	39,501	306
El Paso, TX	39,375	307
Wheeling, WV-OH	39,049	308
Yuma, AZ	38,428	309
Huntington-Ashland, WV-KY-OH	38,336	310
Danville, VA	37,279	311
Cumberland, MD-WV	36,877	312
Johnstown, PA	36,808	313
Brownsville-Harlingen-San Benito,TX	35,177	314
Las Cruces, NM	34,900	315
McAllen-Edinburg-Mission, TX	32,575	316
MSA/NECMA Average	**52,420**	
United States Average	**56,183**	

TOTAL RETAIL SALES

MSA/NECMA	SALES ($Mil)	RANK
Los Angeles-Long Beach, CA	85,664	1
Chicago, IL	83,211	2
Boston-Worcester-Lawrence-Lowell-Brockton, MA-NH	66,206	3
New York, NY	63,668	4
Philadelphia, PA-NJ	52,718	5
Washington, DC-MD-VA-WV	52,069	6
Detroit, MI	49,082	7
Atlanta, GA	43,631	8
Houston, TX	43,404	9
Dallas, TX	37,974	10
Nassau-Suffolk, NY	33,826	11
Minneapolis-St. Paul, MN-WI	32,615	12
Phoenix-Mesa, AZ	32,468	13
Orange County, CA	30,569	14
Seattle-Bellevue-Everett, WA	27,977	15
St. Louis, MO-IL	27,301	16
San Diego, CA	27,164	17
Riverside-San Bernardino, CA	26,278	18
Tampa-St. Petersburg-Clearwater, FL	26,150	19
Miami, FL	25,517	20
Baltimore, MD	25,076	21
Pittsburgh, PA	23,896	22
Oakland, CA	23,655	23
Denver, CO	23,539	24
Fort Lauderdale, FL	22,081	25
Cleveland-Lorain-Elyria, OH	21,860	26
San Francisco, CA	21,501	27
Portland-Vancouver, OR-WA	21,152	28
New Haven-Bridgeport-Stamford-Danbury-Waterbury, CT	20,083	29
Newark, NJ	19,638	30
San Jose, CA	19,338	31
Orlando, FL	19,209	32
Kansas City, MO-KS	19,055	33
Indianapolis, IN	18,174	34
Fort Worth-Arlington, TX	17,956	35
Cincinnati, OH-KY-IN	17,794	36
Bergen-Passaic, NJ	17,634	37
Columbus, OH	17,502	38
Las Vegas, NV-AZ	16,475	39
Sacramento, CA	16,367	40
Milwaukee-Waukesha, WI	15,572	41
San Antonio, TX	15,325	42
Charlotte-Gastonia-Rock Hill, NC-SC	15,284	43
Norfolk-Virginia Beach-Newport News, VA-NC	14,854	44
Nashville, TN	14,247	45
West Palm Beach-Boca Raton, FL	13,659	46
Middlesex-Somerset-Hunterdon, NJ	13,582	47
Salt Lake City-Ogden, UT	13,569	48
Austin-San Marcos, TX	13,343	49
New Orleans, LA	13,316	50
Greensboro-Winston Salem-High Point, NC	13,010	51
Monmouth-Ocean, NJ	12,218	52
Hartford, CT	12,114	53
Raleigh-Durham-Chapel Hill, NC	12,045	54
Jacksonville, FL	11,857	55
Buffalo-Niagara Falls, NY	11,802	56
Memphis, TN-AR-MS	11,561	57
Honolulu, HI	11,296	58
Oklahoma City, OK	11,149	59
Louisville, KY-IN	10,965	60
Grand Rapids-Muskegon-Holland, MI	10,834	61
Rochester, NY	10,708	62
Richmond-Petersburg, VA	10,190	63
Birmingham, AL	9,790	64
Greenville-Spartanburg-Anderson, SC	9,585	65
Dayton-Springfield, OH	9,279	66
Albany-Schenectady-Troy, NY	9,086	67
Tulsa, OK	8,992	68
Knoxville, TN	8,879	69
Tucson, AZ	8,630	70
Providence-Warwick-Pawtucket, RI	8,227	71
Fresno, CA	7,698	72
Albuquerque, NM	7,664	73
Omaha, NE-IA	7,606	74
Ventura, CA	7,317	75
Syracuse, NY	7,185	76
Akron, OH	7,135	77
Wilmington-Newark, DE-MD	7,071	78
Harrisburg-Lebanon-Carlisle, PA	7,037	79
Tacoma, WA	6,751	80
El Paso, TX	6,742	81
Little Rock-North Little Rock, AR	6,514	82
Sarasota-Bradenton, FL	6,511	83
Toledo, OH	6,444	84
Ann Arbor, MI	6,382	85
Wichita, KS	6,116	86
Baton Rouge, LA	6,115	87
Gary, IN	6,105	88
Melbourne-Titusville-Palm Bay,FL	5,962	89
Allentown-Bethlehem-Easton, PA	5,939	90
Scranton-Wilkes-Barre-Hazleton, PA	5,912	91
Youngstown-Warren, OH	5,646	92
Charleston-North Charleston, SC	5,622	93
Springfield, MA	5,621	94
Columbia, SC	5,577	95
Mobile, AL	5,470	96
Des Moines, IA	5,465	97
Madison, WI	5,434	98
Colorado Springs, CO	5,403	99
Lexington, KY	5,402	100
Bakersfield, CA	5,165	101
Fort Wayne, IN	5,144	102
Chattanooga, TN-GA	5,115	103
Flint, MI	5,095	104
Fort Myers-Cape Coral, FL	5,079	105
Santa Rosa, CA	5,025	106
Johnson City-Kingsport-Bristol, TN-VA	4,976	107
Spokane, WA	4,877	108
Daytona Beach, FL	4,843	109
Lansing-East Lansing, MI	4,842	110
McAllen-Edinburg-Mission, TX	4,806	111
Vallejo-Fairfield-Napa, CA	4,803	112
Kalamazoo-Battle Creek, MI	4,760	113
Boise City, ID	4,689	114
Lakeland-Winter Haven, FL	4,592	115
Augusta-Aiken, GA-SC	4,561	116
Jackson, MS	4,541	117
Lancaster, PA	4,541	118
Saginaw-Bay City-Midland, MI	4,488	119
Jersey City, NJ	4,412	120
Stockton-Lodi, CA	4,372	121
York, PA	4,290	122
Pensacola, FL	4,194	123
Modesto, CA	4,190	124
Reno, NV	4,160	125
Portland, ME	4,154	126
Canton-Massillon, OH	4,143	127
Davenport-Moline-Rock Island, IA-IL	4,093	128
Atlantic-Cape May, NJ	4,088	129
Appleton-Oshkosh-Neenah, WI	4,074	130
Beaumont-Port Arthur, TX	4,063	131
Springfield, MO	3,999	132
Corpus Christi, TX	3,970	133
Macon, GA	3,886	134
Lafayette, LA	3,813	135
Peoria-Pekin, IL	3,809	136
Anchorage, AK	3,796	137
Santa Barbara-Santa Maria-Lompoc, CA	3,765	138
Reading, PA	3,757	139
Newburgh, NY-PA	3,699	140
Shreveport-Bossier City, LA	3,698	141
Eugene-Springfield, OR	3,652	142
Rockford, IL	3,623	143
Huntsville, AL	3,615	144
Trenton, NJ	3,592	145
Salinas, CA	3,484	146
Salem, OR	3,447	147
Montgomery, AL	3,425	148
Boulder-Longmont, CO	3,412	149
Fort Pierce-Port St. Lucie, FL	3,410	150
Hickory-Morganton-Lenoir, NC	3,352	151
Evansville-Henderson, IN-KY	3,255	152
Barnstable-Yarmouth, MA	3,252	153
Savannah, GA	3,125	154
Huntington-Ashland, WV-KY-OH	3,118	155
Naples, FL	3,077	156
Roanoke, VA	3,070	157
Fayetteville-Springdale-Rogers, AR	3,062	158
Tallahassee, FL	3,029	159
Biloxi-Gulfport-Pascagoula, MS	3,021	160
Myrtle Beach, SC	2,963	161
Wilmington, NC	2,925	162
Charleston, WV	2,906	163
Erie, PA	2,859	164
Laredo, TX	2,850	165
Brownsville-Harlingen-San Benito, TX	2,821	166
South Bend, IN	2,769	167
St. Cloud, MN	2,765	168
Lubbock, TX	2,755	169
Fayetteville, NC	2,716	170
Visalia-Tulare-Porterville, CA	2,704	171
Green Bay, WI	2,699	172
Dutchess County, NY	2,682	173
Columbus, GA-AL	2,662	174
Ocala, FL	2,589	175
Provo-Orem, UT	2,586	176
Duluth-Superior, MN-WI	2,573	177
Amarillo, TX	2,566	178
Odessa-Midland, TX	2,565	179
Fort Collins-Loveland, CO	2,559	180
Utica-Rome, NY	2,559	181
Terre Haute, IN	2,557	182
Santa Cruz-Watsonville, CA	2,529	183
New London-Norwich, CT	2,524	184
Lincoln, NE	2,516	185
Burlington, VT	2,495	186
Bellingham, WA	2,474	187
Lynchburg, VA	2,441	188
Longview-Marshall, TX	2,427	189
Asheville, NC	2,416	190
Killeen-Temple, TX	2,395	191
Springfield, IL	2,365	192
Binghamton, NY	2,324	193
San Luis Obispo-Antascadero-Paso Robles, CA	2,318	194
Gainesville, FL	2,296	195
Cedar Rapids, IA	2,294	196
Bremerton, WA	2,289	197
Galveston-Texas City, TX	2,277	198
Sioux Falls, SD	2,273	199
Medford-Ashland, OR	2,255	200
Hamilton-Middletown, OH	2,227	201
Olympia, WA	2,198	202
Richland-Kennewick-Pasco, WA	2,137	203
Fort Smith, AR-OK	2,100	204
Fargo-Moorhead, ND-MN	2,082	205
Yakima, WA	2,045	206
Fort Walton Beach, FL	2,036	207
Santa Fe, NM	2,015	208
Waco, TX	1,999	209
Brazoria, TX	1,995	210
Tyler, TX	1,956	211
Johnstown, PA	1,917	212
Lake Charles, LA	1,914	213
Topeka, KS	1,899	214
Elkhart-Goshen, IN	1,883	215
Panama City, FL	1,872	216
Clarksville-Hopkinsville, TN-KY	1,832	217
Redding, CA	1,824	218
Lafayette, IN	1,822	219
Chico-Paradise, CA	1,817	220
Bangor, ME	1,791	221
Racine, WI	1,791	222
Billings, MT	1,790	223
Houma, LA	1,757	224
Champaign-Urbana, IL	1,720	225
Eau Claire, WI	1,709	226
Mansfield, OH	1,709	227
Charlottesville, VA	1,702	228
Joplin, MO	1,697	229
Monroe, LA	1,691	230
Janesville-Beloit, WI	1,684	231
Bloomington-Normal, IL	1,683	232
Lima, OH	1,660	233
Dover, DE	1,642	234
Columbia, MO	1,628	235
Tuscaloosa, AL	1,606	236
Rochester, MN	1,598	237
Parkersburg-Marietta, WV-OH	1,595	238
Florence, SC	1,561	239
Pittsfield, MA	1,541	240
La Crosse, WI-MN	1,526	241
Flagstaff, AZ-UT	1,511	242
Dothan, AL	1,509	243
Wheeling, WV-OH	1,499	244
Benton Harbor, MI	1,478	245
Rocky Mount, NC	1,475	246
Greenville, NC	1,474	247
Jackson, MI	1,473	248
Florence, AL	1,471	249
Waterloo-Cedar Falls, IA	1,471	250
Athens, GA	1,454	251
Altoona, PA	1,446	252
Kenosha, WI	1,413	253
Glens Falls, NY	1,405	254
Decatur, AL	1,403	255
Yuma, AZ	1,401	256
Wichita Falls, TX	1,391	257
Texarkana, TX-AR	1,371	258
Decatur, IL	1,362	259
Bryan-College Station, TX	1,345	260
Hagerstown, MD	1,326	261
Pueblo, CO	1,319	262
Abilene, TX	1,308	263
Las Cruces, NM	1,297	264
Albany, GA	1,290	265
Wausau, WI	1,290	266
Punta Gorda, FL	1,274	267
State College, PA	1,257	268
Vineland-Millville-Bridgeton, NJ	1,256	269
Grand Junction, CO	1,255	270
Yolo, CA	1,253	271
Sioux City, IA-NE	1,251	272
Merced, CA	1,243	273
Missoula, MT	1,241	274
Alexandria, LA	1,227	275
Rapid City, SD	1,224	276
Yuba City, CA	1,216	277
Greeley, CO	1,214	278
Lewiston-Auburn, ME	1,204	279
Williamsport, PA	1,186	280
Jackson, TN	1,183	281
Jacksonville, NC	1,183	282
Sharon, PA	1,160	283
Kokomo, IN	1,150	284
Grand Forks, ND-MN	1,130	285
Muncie, IN	1,123	286
Steubenville-Weirton, OH-WV	1,120	287
Jamestown, NY	1,115	288
Bismark, MD	1,096	289
Sherman-Denison, TX	1,096	290
Anniston, AL	1,092	291
Bloomington, IN	1,092	292
Sheboygan, WI	1,076	293
Hattiesburg, MS	1,074	294
Iowa City, IA	1,060	295
Kankakee, IL	1,057	296
San Angelo, TX	1,010	297
Danville, VA	994	298
Dubuque, IA	988	299
Cheyenne, WY	982	300
Goldsboro, NC	969	301
Great Falls, MT	951	302
Cumberland, MD-WV	949	303
Jonesboro, AR	943	304
St. Joseph, MO	943	305
Owensboro, KY	941	306
Lawton, OK	931	307
Victoria, TX	929	308
Gadsden, AL	885	309
Elmira, NY	877	310
Sumter, SC	859	311
Lawrence, KS	841	312
Pocatello, ID	760	313
Pine Bluff, AR	746	314
Casper, WY	721	315
Enid, OK	634	316

MSA/NECMA Total **2,327,167**
United States Total **2,800,620**
MSA/NECMA (% of U.S.Total) **83.09**

MSA/NECMA	SALES ($Mil)	RANK
New York, NY	6,106	1
Chicago, IL	4,829	2
Los Angeles-Long Beach, CA	4,688	3
Boston-Worcester-Lawrence-Lowell-Brockton, MA-NH	4,027	4
Washington, DC-MD-VA-WV	3,269	5
Philadelphia, PA-NJ	2,676	6
Detroit, MI	2,421	7
Nassau-Suffolk, NY	2,083	8
Atlanta, GA	2,049	9
Houston, TX	1,998	10
Miami, FL	1,939	11
Dallas, TX	1,750	12
Orange County, CA	1,745	13
San Francisco, CA	1,720	14
Seattle-Bellevue-Everett, WA	1,509	15
San Diego, CA	1,466	16
Bergen-Passaic, NJ	1,387	17
Minneapolis-St. Paul, MN-WI	1,343	18
Baltimore, MD	1,284	19
New Haven-Bridgeport-Stamford-Danbury-Waterbury, CT	1,230	20
Phoenix-Mesa, AZ	1,157	21
Oakland, CA	1,144	22
St. Louis, MO-IL	1,099	23
Riverside-San Bernardino, CA	1,075	24
San Jose, CA	1,068	25
Fort Lauderdale, FL	1,063	26
Pittsburgh, PA	1,026	27
Newark, NJ	1,017	28
Portland-Vancouver, OR-WA	946	29
Cleveland-Lorain-Elyria, OH	943	30
Middlesex-Somerset-Hunterdon, NJ	942	31
Tampa-St. Petersburg-Clearwater, FL	927	32
Orlando, FL	925	33
Honolulu, HI	889	34
Denver, CO	847	35
West Palm Beach-Boca Raton, FL	820	36
San Antonio, TX	813	37
Cincinnati, OH-KY-IN	721	38
Norfolk-Virginia Beach-Newport News, VA-NC	719	39
Monmouth-Ocean, NJ	694	40
Charlotte-Gastonia-Rock Hill, NC-SC	677	41
Las Vegas, NV-AZ	655	42
Sacramento, CA	653	43
Kansas City, MO-KS	648	44
Hartford, CT	630	45
Fort Worth-Arlington, TX	626	46
Columbus, OH	614	47
New Orleans, LA	607	48
Raleigh-Durham-Chapel Hill, NC	596	49
Indianapolis, IN	595	50
Greensboro-Winston Salem-High Point, NC	589	51
Milwaukee-Waukesha, WI	589	52
Salt Lake City-Ogden, UT	588	53
Buffalo-Niagara Falls, NY	574	54
Nashville, TN	566	55
Austin-San Marcos, TX	562	56
Memphis, TN-AR-MS	518	57
Birmingham, AL	503	58
Richmond-Petersburg, VA	485	59
Jersey City, NJ	479	60
Albany-Schenectady-Troy, NY	447	61
Grand Rapids-Muskegon-Holland, MI	438	62
Jacksonville, FL	437	63
Rochester, NY	436	64
Oklahoma City, OK	434	65
Knoxville, TN	427	66
Greenville-Spartanburg-Anderson, SC	383	67
Providence-Warwick-Pawtucket, RI	383	68
El Paso, TX	380	69
McAllen-Edinburg-Mission, TX	373	70
Syracuse, NY	355	71
Portland, ME	349	72
Louisville, KY-IN	346	73
Tulsa, OK	341	74
Tucson, AZ	333	75
Sarasota-Bradenton, FL	332	76
Omaha, NE-IA	316	77
Dayton-Springfield, OH	301	78
Reading, PA	300	79
Laredo, TX	286	80
Myrtle Beach, SC	284	81
Wilmington-Newark, DE-MD	279	82
Springfield, MA	257	83
Akron, OH	256	84
Lexington, KY	256	85
Little Rock-North Little Rock, AR	256	86
Fresno, CA	255	87
Charleston-North Charleston, SC	254	88
Atlantic-Cape May, NJ	250	89
Saginaw-Bay City-Midland, MI	249	90
Mobile, AL	245	91
Scranton-Wilkes-Barre-Hazleton, PA	245	92
Tacoma, WA	244	93
Columbia, SC	243	94
Barnstable-Yarmouth, MA	240	95
Albuquerque, NM	239	96
Lancaster, PA	238	97
Gary, IN	235	98
Ventura, CA	233	99
Santa Barbara-Santa Maria-Lompoc, CA	229	100
Harrisburg-Lebanon-Carlisle, PA	225	101
Allentown-Bethlehem-Easton, PA	221	102
Spokane, WA	220	103
Chattanooga, TN-GA	219	104
Madison, WI	219	105
Anchorage, AK	217	106
Wichita, KS	216	107
Fort Myers-Cape Coral, FL	213	108
Newburgh, NY-PA	213	109
Youngstown-Warren, OH	209	110
Baton Rouge, LA	208	111
Naples, FL	206	112
Des Moines, IA	203	113
Ann Arbor, MI	201	114
Salinas, CA	201	115
Flint, MI	198	116
Brownsville-Harlingen-San Benito, TX	196	117
Toledo, OH	194	118
Augusta-Aiken, GA-SC	192	119
Trenton, NJ	189	120
Vallejo-Fairfield-Napa, CA	183	121
Huntsville, AL	180	122
Kalamazoo-Battle Creek, MI	180	123
Jackson, MS	170	124
Lansing-East Lansing, MI	166	125
Daytona Beach, FL	165	126
Appleton-Oshkosh-Neenah, WI	164	127
Savannah, GA	164	128
Montgomery, AL	160	129
Corpus Christi, TX	156	130
Fort Wayne, IN	156	131
Colorado Springs, CO	154	132
Boise City, ID	153	133
Melbourne-Titusville-Palm Bay, FL	152	134
Reno, NV	150	135
Santa Rosa, CA	148	136
Bakersfield, CA	147	137
Davenport-Moline-Rock Island, IA-IL	147	138
Beaumont-Port Arthur, TX	145	139
Dutchess County, NY	145	140
Lafayette, LA	145	141
Macon, GA	144	142
Lakeland-Winter Haven, FL	140	143
Burlington, VT	138	144
Shreveport-Bossier City, LA	137	145
Johnson City-Kingsport-Bristol, TN-VA	136	146
New London-Norwich, CT	136	147
Fort Pierce-Port St. Lucie, FL	132	148
Evansville-Henderson, IN-KY	131	149
Galveston-Texas City, TX	131	150
Tallahassee, FL	131	151
Asheville, NC	127	152
Columbus, GA-AL	127	153
Lubbock, TX	127	154
Eugene-Springfield, OR	122	155
Stockton-Lodi, CA	122	156
Modesto, CA	121	157
Canton-Massillon, OH	119	158
Pensacola, FL	119	159
Wilmington, NC	119	160
Lincoln, NE	117	161
Boulder-Longmont, CO	115	162
Springfield, MO	114	163
Peoria-Pekin, IL	112	164
York, PA	111	165
Erie, PA	110	166
Amarillo, TX	109	167
Hickory-Morganton-Lenoir, NC	106	168
Fayetteville, NC	103	169
Rockford, IL	103	170
Utica-Rome, NY	103	171
Bellingham, WA	102	172
Santa Fe, NM	102	173
Huntington-Ashland, WV-KY-OH	101	174
Kenosha, WI	101	175
South Bend, IN	100	176
Salem, OR	99	177
Bloomington-Normal, IL	98	178
Odessa-Midland, TX	98	179
Charleston, WV	96	180
Green Bay, WI	91	181
Roanoke, VA	90	182
Santa Cruz-Watsonville, CA	89	183
Pittsfield, MA	89	184
Duluth-Superior, MN-WI	88	185
Fort Collins-Loveland, CO	86	186
Tuscaloosa, AL	86	187
Tyler, TX	83	188
Provo-Orem, UT	81	189
Fayetteville-Springdale-Rogers, AR	80	190
Clarksville-Hopkinsville, TN-KY	78	191
Longview-Marshall, TX	78	192
Gainsville, FL	76	193
Panama City, FL	76	194
Visalia-Tulare-Porterville, CA	76	195
Binghamton, NY	75	196
Fort Walton Beach, FL	75	197
Champaign-Urbana, IL	74	198
Charlottesville, VA	74	199
Yakima, WA	74	200
Monroe, LA	73	201
Glen Falls, NY	71	202
Lake Charles, LA	71	203
Bangor, ME	70	204
Rochester, MN	70	205
Cedar Rapids, IA	69	206
Greenville, NC	68	207
Lynchburg, VA	68	208
Fargo-Moorhead, ND-MN	67	209
Florence, SC	67	210
Biloxi-Gulfport-Pascagoula, MS	66	211
Eau Claire, WI	66	212
Killeen-Temple, TX	65	213
Florence, AL	64	214
Rocky Mount, NC	63	215
Waco, TX	63	216
Texarkana, TX-AR	62	217
Columbia, MO	60	218
Jackson, TN	60	219
Johnstown, PA	60	220
San Luis Obispo-Antascadero-Paso Robles, CA	60	221
Billings, MT	59	222
Bremerton, WA	59	223
Dothan, AL	59	224
Olympia, WA	58	225
Punta Gorda, FL	58	226
Springfield, IL	58	227
Topeka, KS	58	228
Ocala, FL	57	229
Joplin, MO	56	230
Richland-Kennewick-Pasco, WA	56	231
Decatur, IL	55	232
Parkersburg-Marietta, WV-OH	55	233
State College, PA	55	234
Medford-Ashland, OR	54	235
Racine, WI	54	236
Wheeling, WV-OH	54	237
Hattiesburg, MS	53	238
Jonesboro, AR	53	239
Chico-Paradise, CA	52	240
Williamsport, PA	52	241
Brazoria, TX	51	242
Fort Smith, AR-OK	51	243
Sioux Falls, SD	51	244
Alexandria, LA	50	245
Bryan-College Station, TX	50	246
Goldsboro, NC	50	247
Redding, CA	50	248
Sharon, PA	50	249
Lafayette, IN	49	250
Houma, LA	48	251
Las Cruces, NM	47	252
Altoona, PA	46	253
Mansfield, OH	45	254
Albilene, TX	44	255
Bloomington, IN	44	256
Dover, DE	44	257
Flagstaff, AZ-VT	44	258
Witchita Falls, TX	44	259
Rapid City, SD	43	260
Vineland-Millville-Bridgeton, NJ	43	261
La Crosse, WI-MN	42	262
Victoria, TX	41	263
Gadsden, AL	40	264
Lawrence, KS	40	265
Decatur, AL	39	266
Kankakee, IL	39	267
Lima, OH	39	268
San Angelo, TX	39	269
Elmira, NY	38	270
Grand Forks, ND-MN	38	271
Yuma, AZ	38	272
Jacksonville, NC	37	273
Missoula, MT	37	274
Sumter, SC	37	275
Waterloo-Cedar Falls, IA	37	276
Cumberland, MD-WV	36	277
Pine Bluff, AR	36	278
Benton Harbor, MI	35	279
Anniston, AL	34	280
Elkhart-Goshen, IN	33	281
Wausau, WI	33	282
Athens, GA	32	283
Janesville-Beloit, WI	32	284
Bismarck, ND	31	285
Great Falls, MT	31	286
Merced, CA	31	287
Dubuque, IA	30	288
Hagerstown, MD	30	289
Hamilton-Middletown, OH	30	290
Iowa City, IA	30	291
Grand Junction, CO	29	292
Jackson, MI	29	293
Jamestown, NY	29	294
Lawton, OK	28	295
Lewiston-Auburn, ME	28	296
Owensboro, KY	28	297
Pueblo, CO	28	298
Sioux City, IA-NE	28	299
Terre Haute, IN	28	300
St. Cloud, MN	27	301
Steubenville-Weirton, OH-WV	27	302
Yolo, CA	27	303
Albany, GA	26	304
Danville, VA	26	305
Muncie, IN	26	306
Casper, WY	24	307
Cheyenne, WY	24	308
Sherman-Denison, TX	24	309
Yuba City, CA	23	310
Greeley, CO	21	311
Pocatello, ID	21	312
Enid, OK	20	313
Kokomo, IN	20	314
St. Joseph, MO	20	315
Sheboygan, WI	15	316

MSA/NECMA Total **111,445**
United States Total **125,817**
MSA/NECMA (% of U.S.Total) **88.58**

RETAIL SALES: AUTOMOTIVE

MSA/NECMA	SALES ($Mil)	RANK
Chicago, IL	18,851	1
Los Angeles-Long Beach, CA	18,072	2
Boston-Worcester-Lawrence-Lowell-Brockton, MA-NH	13,007	3
Detroit, MI	12,439	4
Philadelphia, PA-NJ	12,110	5
Houston, TX	11,154	6
Dallas, TX	10,048	7
Washington, DC-MD-VA-WV	10,006	8
Atlanta, GA	9,842	9
Fort Lauderdale, FL	8,839	10
Phoenix-Mesa, AZ	8,032	11
Minneapolis-St. Paul, MN-WI	7,542	12
Orange County, CA	6,844	13
New York, NY	6,831	14
Nassau-Suffolk, NY	6,738	15
Tampa-St. Petersburg-Clearwater, FL	6,594	16
St. Louis, MO-IL	6,516	17
Miami, FL	6,262	18
Denver, CO	5,937	19
San Diego, CA	5,554	20
Baltimore, MD	5,396	21
Seattle-Bellevue-Everett, WA	5,354	22
Riverside-San Bernardino, CA	5,306	23
Pittsburgh, PA	5,274	24
Cleveland-Lorain-Elyria, OH	5,031	25
Newark, NJ	5,021	26
Orlando, FL	4,911	27
Kansas City, MO-KS	4,784	28
Portland-Vancouver, OR-WA	4,598	29
Fort Worth-Arlington, TX	4,479	30
Oakland, CA	4,409	31
San Jose, CA	4,247	32
Indianapolis, IN	4,024	33
Charlotte-Gastonia-Rock Hill, NC-SC	3,988	34
Columbus, OH	3,940	35
West Palm Beach-Boca Raton, FL	3,893	36
Bergen-Passaic, NJ	3,828	37
Milwaukee-Waukesha, WI	3,798	38
Nashville, TN	3,712	39
San Antonio, TX	3,697	40
Cincinnati, OH-KY-IN	3,652	41
Las Vegas, NV-AZ	3,480	42
New Haven-Bridgeport-Stamford-Danbury-Waterbury, CT	3,464	43
Salt Lake City-Ogden, UT	3,301	44
Norfolk-Virginia Beach-Newport News, VA-NC	3,281	45
Oklahoma City, OK	3,233	46
Austin-San Marcos, TX	3,157	47
San Francisco, CA	3,120	48
Memphis, TN-AR-MS	3,013	49
Sacramento, CA	3,002	50
Greensboro-Winston Salem-High Point, NC	2,951	51
Monmouth-Ocean, NJ	2,859	52
New Orleans, LA	2,692	53
Grand Rapids-Muskegon-Holland, MI	2,644	54
Raleigh-Durham-Chapel Hill, NC	2,628	55
Hartford, CT	2,591	56
Middlesex-Somerset-Hunterdon, NJ	2,584	57
Jacksonville, FL	2,531	58
Buffalo-Niagara Falls, NY	2,421	59
Rochester, NY	2,417	60
Birmingham, AL	2,401	61
Melbourne-Titusville-Palm Bay, FL	2,356	62
Tulsa, OK	2,285	63
Richmond-Petersburg, VA	2,197	64
Albany-Schenectady-Troy, NY	2,088	65
Greenville-Spartanburg-Anderson, SC	2,088	66
Dayton-Springfield, OH	2,061	67
Ventura, CA	2,011	68
Ann Arbor, MI	1,986	69
Louisville, KY-IN	1,968	70
Omaha, NE-IA	1,841	71
Little Rock-North Little Rock, AR	1,828	72
Tucson, AZ	1,799	73
Sarasota-Bradenton, FL	1,695	74
Fresno, CA	1,670	75
Tacoma, WA	1,653	76
Akron, OH	1,622	77
Harrisburg-Lebanon-Carlisle, PA	1,597	78
Syracuse, NY	1,586	79
Honolulu, HI	1,585	80
Knoxville, TN	1,568	81
Wichita, KS	1,502	82
Wilmington-Newark, DE-MD	1,442	83
Allentown-Bethlehem-Easton, PA	1,405	84
Toledo, OH	1,396	85
Baton Rouge, LA	1,364	86
Charleston-North Charleston, SC	1,347	87
Madison, WI	1,322	88
Fort Myers-Cape Coral, FL	1,297	89
Johnson City-Kingsport-Bristol, TN-VA	1,287	90
Columbia, SC	1,268	91
Youngstown-Warren, OH	1,255	92
Providence-Warwick-Pawtucket, RI	1,249	93
Gary, IN	1,243	94
Fort Wayne, IN	1,222	95
Colorado Springs, CO	1,202	96
Des Moines, IA	1,191	97
Flint, MI	1,190	98
Boise City, ID	1,182	99
Scranton-Wilkes-Barre-Hazleton, PA	1,177	100
Albuquerque, NM	1,175	101
Jackson, MS	1,172	102
Daytona Beach, FL	1,171	103
Macon, GA	1,146	104
El Paso, TX	1,129	105
Pensacola, FL	1,123	106
Mobile, AL	1,122	107
Spokane, WA	1,120	108
Lansing-East Lansing, MI	1,087	109
Lexington, KY	1,085	110
Lakeland-Winter Haven, FL	1,074	111
Vallejo-Fairfield-Napa, CA	1,056	112
Beaumont-Port Arthur, TX	1,033	113
Springfield, MA	1,033	114
Peoria-Pekin, IL	1,025	115
Chattanooga, TN-GA	1,016	116
Lancaster, PA	1,001	117
Kalamazoo-Battle Creek, MI	983	118
Corpus Christi, TX	969	119
Eugene-Springfield, OR	969	120
Augusta-Aiken, GA-SC	937	121
Davenport-Moline-Rock Island, IA-IL	937	122
Bakersfield, CA	898	123
Appleton-Oshkosh-Neenah, WI	897	124
Fort Pierce-Port St. Lucie, FL	880	125
Santa Rosa, CA	880	126
Reading, PA	865	127
York, PA	864	128
Salem, OR	861	129
Stockton-Lodi, CA	858	130
Fayetteville-Springdale-Rogers, AR	845	131
Modesto, CA	844	132
Reno, NV	844	133
Boulder-Longmont, CO	826	134
Atlantic-Cape May, NJ	794	135
Trenton, NJ	766	136
Canton-Massillon, OH	765	137
McAllen-Edinburg-Mission, TX	763	138
Rockford, IL	735	139
Jersey City, NJ	734	140
Hickory-Morganton-Lenoir, NC	732	141
Killeen-Temple, TX	728	142
Saginaw-Bay City-Midland, MI	724	143
Evansville-Henderson, IN-KY	720	144
Lubbock, TX	696	145
Green Bay, WI	695	146
Anchorage, AK	684	147
Santa Cruz-Watsonville, CA	680	148
Erie, PA	672	149
South Bend, IN	656	150
Tallahassee, FL	655	151
Biloxi-Gulfport-Pascagoula, MS	646	152
Huntsville, AL	630	153
Fayetteville, NC	622	154
Shreveport-Bossier City, LA	620	155
Newburgh, NY-PA	615	156
Springfield, MO	609	157
Portland, ME	595	158
Salinas, CA	595	159
Odessa-Midland, TX	592	160
Duluth-Superior, MN-WI	580	161
Lafayette, LA	578	162
Amarillo, TX	577	163
Longview-Marshall, TX	572	164
Savannah, GA	571	165
Naples, FL	564	166
Dutchess County, NY	560	167
Provo-Orem, UT	559	168
Fort Walton Beach, FL	558	169
Santa Barbara-Santa Maria-Lompoc, CA	558	170
Fort Collins-Loveland, CO	557	171
Montgomery, AL	541	172
Huntington-Ashland, WV-KY-OH	538	173
Brazoria, TX	535	174
Burlington, VT	525	175
Utica-Rome, NY	525	176
San Luis Obispo-Antascadero-Paso Robles, CA	519	177
Lincoln, NE	515	178
Elkhart-Goshen, IN	508	179
Columbus, GA-AL	505	180
Hamilton-Middletown, OH	499	181
New London-Norwich, CT	497	182
Cedar Rapids, IA	494	183
Springfield, IL	492	184
Bremerton, WA	486	185
Gainesville, FL	479	186
Ocala, FL	476	187
Billings, MT	470	188
Medford-Ashland, OR	470	189
Myrtle Beach, SC	469	190
Lake Charles, LA	467	191
Binghamton, NY	464	192
Galveston-Texas City, TX	458	193
Roanoke, VA	455	194
Charleston, WV	452	195
Visalia-Tulare-Porterville, CA	445	196
Fort Smith, AR-OK	432	197
Lynchburg, VA	429	198
Waco, TX	424	199
Olympia, WA	417	200
Fargo-Moorhead, ND-MN	416	201
Johnstown, PA	412	202
Columbia, MO	411	203
Wilmington, NC	411	204
Topeka, KS	404	205
Racine, WI	398	206
Sioux Falls, SD	398	207
Janesville-Beloit, WI	392	208
Brownsville-Harlingen-San Benito, TX	391	209
Asheville, NC	389	210
Decatur, IL	387	211
Tyler, TX	386	212
Monroe, LA	379	213
Panama City, FL	379	214
Waterloo-Cedar Falls, IA	378	215
Bangor, ME	375	216
Yakima, WA	375	217
Lima, OH	374	218
Clarksville-Hopkinsville, TN-KY	372	219
Lafayette, IN	365	220
Rochester, MN	361	221
St. Cloud, MN	358	222
Wichita Falls, TX	357	223
Greenville, NC	355	224
Florence, SC	351	225
Champaign-Urbana, IL	349	226
Dover, DE	349	227
Parkersburg-Marietta, WV-OH	343	228
Bloomington-Norma, IL	340	229
Mansfield, OH	340	230
Houma, LA	339	231
Missoula, MT	333	232
Terre Haute, IN	330	233
Richland-Kennewick-Pasco, WA	327	234
Benton Harbor, MI	323	235
Rapid City, SD	320	236
Greeley, CO	317	237
Florence, AL	311	238
Eau Claire, WI	308	239
Texarkana, TX-AR	305	240
Jacksonville, NC	304	241
Wausau, WI	304	242
Williamsport, PA	302	243
Albany, GA	299	244
Chico-Paradise, CA	296	245
Joplin, MO	296	246
Bellingham, WA	295	247
Sherman-Denison, TX	292	248
Kenosha, WI	291	249
Yuba City, CA	283	250
Redding, CA	282	251
Bryan-College Station, TX	281	252
Charlottesville, VA	280	253
Wheeling, WV-OH	279	254
Tuscaloosa, AL	278	255
Yuma, AZ	278	256
Jamestown, NY	275	257
Athens, GA	273	258
Pittsfield, MA	272	259
La Crosse, WI-MN	269	260
Hagerstown, MD	268	261
Vineland-Millville-Bridgeton, NJ	268	262
Abilene, TX	266	263
Jackson, MI	266	264
Anniston, AL	265	265
Santa Fe, NM	263	266
Sioux City, IA-NE	258	267
State College, PA	257	268
San Angelo, TX	256	269
Decatur, AL	255	270
Sheboygan, WI	255	271
Barnstable-Yarmouth, MA	252	272
Muncie, IN	249	273
Hattiesburg, MS	244	274
Rocky Mount, NC	242	275
Great Falls, MT	240	276
Kokomo, IN	240	277
Dothan, AL	234	278
Las Cruces, NM	233	279
Steubenville-Weirton, OH-WV	232	280
Grand Forks, ND-MN	231	281
Bismarck, ND	230	282
Pueblo, CO	230	283
Yolo, CA	228	284
Merced, CA	222	285
Altoona, PA	221	286
Kankakee, IL	220	287
Iowa City, IA	219	288
Glens Falls, NY	218	289
Jackson, TN	218	290
Victoria, TX	216	291
Grand Junction, CO	215	292
Punta Gorda, FL	215	293
Bloomington, IN	210	294
Danville, VA	208	295
Lawton, OK	207	296
Cheyenne, WY	205	297
Sharon, PA	204	298
Pocatello, ID	203	299
Laredo, TX	198	300
Dubuque, IA	197	301
Alexandria, LA	195	302
Pine Bluff, AR	194	303
Flagstaff, AZ-UT	193	304
St. Joseph, MO	190	305
Cumberland, MD-WV	180	307
Goldsboro, NC	177	308
Casper, WY	175	309
Elmira, NY	167	310
Lawrence, KS	165	311
Enid, OK	162	312
Lewiston-Auburn, ME	156	313
Owensboro, KY	151	314
Gadsden, AL	139	315
Jonesboro, AR	123	316
MSA/NECMA Total	**508,514**	
United States Total	**606,478**	
MSA/NECMA (% of U.S.Total)	**83.85**	

MSA/NECMA	SALES ($Mil)	RANK
Chicago, IL	4,661	1
New York, NY	3,666	2
Los Angeles-Long Beach, CA	3,621	3
Boston-Worcester-Lawrence-Lowell-Brockton, MA-NH	3,089	4
Philadelphia, PA-NJ	2,487	5
Detroit, MI	2,481	6
Washington, DC-MD-VA-WV	1,854	7
Nassau-Suffolk, NY	1,509	8
Atlanta, GA	1,476	9
Houston, TX	1,446	10
Cleveland-Lorain-Elyria, OH	1,423	11
Miami, FL	1,400	12
Phoenix-Mesa, AZ	1,275	13
Pittsburgh, PA	1,214	14
Oakland, CA	1,182	15
Orange County, CA	1,180	16
Tampa-St. Petersburg-Clearwater, FL	1,106	17
San Diego, CA	1,090	18
Seattle-Bellevue-Everett, WA	1,085	19
Riverside-San Bernardino, CA	1,073	20
Dallas, TX	1,065	21
San Francisco, CA	1,031	22
St. Louis, MO-IL	1,004	23
Baltimore, MD	956	24
Minneapolis-St. Paul, MN-WI	937	25
Fort Lauderdale, FL	930	26
Newark, NJ	893	27
San Jose, CA	890	28
Indianapolis, IN	821	29
New Haven-Bridgeport-Stamford-Danbury-Waterbury, CT	794	30
Cincinnati, OH-KY-IN	751	31
Bergen-Passaic, NJ	711	32
Milwaukee-Waukesha, WI	701	33
Honolulu, HI	641	34
Sacramento, CA	640	35
Orlando, FL	637	36
New Orleans, LA	623	37
Kansas City, MO-KS	605	38
Buffalo-Niagara Falls, NY	601	39
Charlotte-Gastonia-Rock Hill, NC-SC	592	40
West Palm Beach-Boca Raton, FL	580	41
Hartford, CT	560	42
Greensboro-Winston Salem-High Point, NC	550	43
Fort Worth-Arlington, TX	535	44
Norfolk-Virginia Beach-Newport News, VA-NC	535	45
Las Vegas, NV-AZ	531	46
Columbus, OH	516	47
Memphis, TN-AR-MS	513	48
Portland-Vancouver, OR-WA	507	49
Monmouth-Ocean, NJ	503	50
Providence-Warwick-Pawtucket, RI	498	51
Raleigh-Durham-Chapel Hill, NC	484	52
Louisville, KY-IN	475	53
Nashville, TN	475	54
Denver, CO	466	55
Middlesex-Somerset-Hunterdon, NJ	457	56
Richmond-Petersburg, VA	441	57
Albany-Schenectady-Troy, NY	436	58
Jacksonville, FL	420	59
Rochester, NY	407	60
Fresno, CA	396	61
San Antonio, TX	395	62
Birmingham, AL	385	63
Greenville-Spartanburg-Anderson, SC	385	64
Tucson, AZ	384	65
Gary, IN	353	66
Scranton-Wilkes-Barre-Hazleton, PA	345	67
Dayton-Springfield, OH	344	68
Syracuse, NY	338	69
Oklahoma City, OK	336	70
Ventura, CA	325	71
Albuquerque, NM	323	72
Akron, OH	322	73
Austin-San Marcos, TX	320	74
Sarasota-Bradenton, FL	315	75
Youngstown-Warren, OH	305	76
Knoxville, TN	302	77
Grand Rapids-Muskegon-Holland, MI	299	78
Wilmington-Newark, DE-MD	288	79
Toledo, OH	285	80
Allentown-Bethlehem-Easton, PA	278	81
Harrisburg-Lebanon-Carlisle, PA	277	82
Omaha, NE-IA	274	83
Bakersfield, CA	273	84
Springfield, MA	263	85
Stockton-Lodi, CA	261	86
Santa Rosa, CA	260	87
Tulsa, OK	249	88
Jersey City, NJ	248	89
Mobile, AL	246	90
Ann Arbor, MI	245	91
Fort Wayne, IN	238	92
Flint, MI	237	93
Salt Lake City-Ogden, UT	232	94
Modesto, CA	221	95
Daytona Beach, FL	220	96
Baton Rouge, LA	212	97
Melbourne-Titusville-Palm Bay, FL	208	98
Fort Myers-Cape Coral, FL	206	99
Santa Barbara-Santa Maria-Lompoc, CA	203	100
Charleston-North Charleston, SC	200	101
Canton-Massillon, OH	193	102
Lexington, KY	192	103
Lakeland-Winter Haven, FL	191	104
Tacoma, WA	191	105
Columbia, SC	189	106
Vallejo-Fairfield-Napa, CA	184	107
Trenton, NJ	181	108
Chattanooga, TN-GA	180	109
Atlantic-Cape May, NJ	178	110
Fort Pierce-Port St. Lucie, FL	176	111
Davenport-Moline-Rock Island, IA-IL	175	112
Lancaster, PA	175	113
Saginaw-Bay City-Midland, MI	174	114
Utica-Rome, NY	174	115
Johnson City-Kingsport-Bristol, TN-VA	172	116
Salinas, CA	172	117
Des Moines, IA	169	118
Peoria-Pekin, IL	169	119
Pensacola, FL	167	120
Rockford, IL	164	121
Little Rock-North Little Rock, AR	163	122
Lafayette, LA	162	123
San Luis Obispo-Antascadero-Paso Robles, CA	161	124
Huntington-Ashland, WV-KY-OH	158	125
Visalia-Tulare-Porterville, CA	158	126
Jackson, MS	157	127
Kalamazoo-Battle Creek, MI	157	128
South Bend, IN	154	129
Madison, WI	153	130
El Paso, TX	151	131
Augusta-Aiken, GA-SC	148	132
Newburgh, NY-PA	147	133
Charleston, WV	146	134
Reading, PA	145	135
Shreveport-Bossier City, LA	144	136
Hickory-Morganton-Lenoir, NC	142	137
Erie, PA	140	138
York, PA	140	139
Beaumont-Port Arthur, TX	136	140
Naples, FL	134	141
Santa Cruz-Watsonville, CA	132	142
Barnstable-Yarmouth, MA	131	143
Spokane, WA	130	144
Reno, NV	129	145
Ocala, FL	128	146
Wichita, KS	128	147
Evansville-Henderson, IN-KY	125	148
Montgomery, AL	125	149
Anchorage, AK	124	150
Asheville, NC	123	151
Binghamton, NY	123	152
Lansing-East Lansing, MI	123	153
Macon, GA	122	154
Savannah, GA	119	155
Wilmington, NC	118	156
Dutchess County, NY	116	157
Portland, ME	113	158
Roanoke, VA	113	159
Colorado Springs, CO	112	160
Boise City, ID	110	161
Springfield, IL	104	162
Biloxi-Gulfport-Pascagoula, MS	101	163
Chico-Paradise, CA	101	164
Tallahassee, FL	101	165
Salem, OR	100	166
Hamilton-Middletown, OH	98	167
Johnstown, PA	97	168
Lincoln, NE	97	169
Corpus Christi, TX	96	170
Huntsville, AL	95	171
Sioux Falls, SD	94	172
Appleton-Oshkosh-Neenah, WI	93	173
Cedar Rapids, IA	93	174
Wheeling, WV-OH	93	175
Duluth-Superior, MN-WI	91	176
New London-Norwich, CT	89	177
Odessa-Midland, TX	88	178
Longview-Marshall, TX	87	179
Racine, WI	87	180
Bremerton, WA	84	181
Galveston-Texas City, TX	83	182
Mansfield, OH	83	183
Richland-Kennewick-Pasco, WA	83	184
Altoona, PA	81	185
Bellingham, WA	79	186
Burlington, VT	79	187
Columbus, GA-AL	79	188
Redding, CA	79	189
Springfield, MO	79	190
Houma, LA	77	191
McAllen-Edinburg-Mission, TX	77	192
Myrtle Beach, SC	76	193
Topeka, KS	75	194
Elkhart-Goshen, IN	74	195
Pittsfield, MA	74	196
Eugene-Springfield, OR	73	197
Jackson, MI	73	198
Merced, CA	73	199
Tuscaloosa, AL	73	200
Olympia, WA	71	201
Parkersburg-Marietta, WV-OH	71	202
Bloomington-Normal, IL	70	203
Fayetteville, NC	70	204
Lafayette, IN	70	205
Steubenville-Weirton, OH-WV	69	206
Lima, OH	68	207
Monroe, LA	67	208
Yolo, CA	67	209
Benton Harbor, MI	66	210
Gainesville, FL	65	211
Lake Charles, LA	64	212
Terre Haute, IN	64	213
Vineland-Millville-Bridgeton, NJ	64	214
Champaign-Urbana, IL	63	215
Glens Falls, NY	63	216
Janesville-Beloit, WI	63	217
Punta Gorda, FL	63	218
Sharon, PA	62	219
Charlottesville, VA	61	220
Fort Walton Beach, FL	61	221
Yakima, WA	61	222
Brazoria, TX	60	223
Bangor, ME	59	224
Dover, DE	59	225
Eau Claire, WI	59	226
Lubbock, TX	59	227
Santa Fe, NM	59	228
Tyler, TX	59	229
Boulder-Longmont, CO	58	230
Brownsville-Harlingen-San Benito, TX	58	231
Jamestown, NY	58	232
Clarksville-Hopkinsville, TN-KY	57	233
Decatur, AL	57	234
Fort Collins-Loveland, CO	56	235
Sherman-Denison, TX	56	236
Decatur, IL	55	237
Elmira, NY	55	238
Rocky Mount, NC	55	239
Yuba City, CA	55	240
Florence, SC	54	241
Fort Smith, AR-OK	54	242
Provo-Orem, UT	54	243
Hagerstown, MD	53	244
Fargo-Moorhead, ND-MN	52	245
Williamsport, PA	52	246
Medford-Ashland, OR	50	247
Cumberland, MD-WV	49	248
Fayetteville-Springdale-Rogers, AR	49	249
Kankakee, IL	49	250
Muncie, IN	49	251
Panama City, FL	49	252
Lynchburg, VA	48	253
Waterloo-Cedar Falls, IA	48	254
Yuma, AZ	48	255
Waco, TX	47	256
Amarillo, TX	46	257
Dubuque, IA	46	258
Florence, AL	46	259
Kokomo, IN	46	260
Laredo, TX	46	261
State College, PA	46	262
Abilene, TX	45	263
Green Bay, WI	44	264
Greenville, NC	44	265
Bloomington, IN	43	266
Owensboro, KY	43	267
St. Cloud, MN	43	268
Bismarck, ND	42	269
Alexandria, LA	41	270
Dothan, AL	41	271
Iowa City, IA	41	272
Danville, VA	40	273
Killeen-Temple, TX	40	274
Athens, GA	39	275
Billings, MT	39	276
Anniston, AL	38	277
Hattiesburg, MS	38	278
Rapid City, SD	38	279
Jackson, TN	37	280
Kenosha, WI	37	281
Rochester, MN	37	282
Sioux City, IA-NE	36	283
Albany, GA	35	284
Las Cruces, NM	35	285
Lewiston-Auburn, ME	35	286
Flagstaff, AZ-UT	34	287
Sheboygan, WI	34	288
Gadsden, AL	33	289
Goldsboro, NC	32	290
Joplin, MO	32	291
Columbia, MO	31	292
Jacksonville, NC	30	293
Pueblo, CO	30	294
Texarkana, TX-AR	28	295
Wichita Falls, TX	28	296
Victoria, TX	26	297
Grand Forks, ND-MN	25	298
La Crosse, WI-MN	25	299
San Angelo, TX	21	300
Bryan-College Station, TX	20	301
Great Falls, MT	20	302
Pocatello, ID	20	303
St. Joseph, MO	20	304
Enid, OK	19	305
Grand Junction, CO	19	306
Jonesboro, AR	19	307
Wausau, WI	19	308
Lawton, OK	18	309
Missoula, MT	18	310
Lawrence, KS	17	311
Pine Bluff, AR	17	312
Sumter, SC	17	313
Greeley, CO	16	314
Cheyenne, WY	12	315
Casper, WY	10	316

MSA/NECMA Total **93,546**
United States Total **112,286**
MSA/NECMA (% of U.S.Total) **83.31**

RETAIL SALES: FOOD

MSA/NECMA	SALES ($Mil)	RANK
Los Angeles-Long Beach, CA	22,962	1
Chicago, IL	19,579	2
New York, NY	17,872	3
Boston-Worcester-Lawrence-Lowell-Brockton, MA-NH	16,921	4
Washington, DC-MD-VA-WV	13,574	5
Philadelphia, PA-NJ	12,353	6
Houston, TX	11,063	7
Atlanta, GA	10,769	8
Detroit, MI	10,371	9
Dallas, TX	8,937	10
Phoenix-Mesa, AZ	8,414	11
Orange County, CA	7,848	12
Nassau-Suffolk, NY	7,557	13
Minneapolis-St. Paul, MN-WI	7,308	14
San Diego, CA	7,195	15
Seattle-Bellevue-Everett, WA	7,172	16
Riverside-San Bernardino, CA	6,951	17
Baltimore, MD	6,728	18
St. Louis, MO-IL	6,586	19
Oakland, CA	6,252	20
San Francisco, CA	6,098	21
Pittsburgh, PA	6,078	22
Denver, CO	6,010	23
Tampa-St. Petersburg-Clearwater, FL	6,004	24
Miami, FL	5,660	25
Cleveland-Lorain-Elyria, OH	5,480	26
Newark, NJ	5,138	27
Orlando, FL	5,052	28
Portland-Vancouver, OR-WA	4,749	29
San Jose, CA	4,748	30
New Haven-Bridgeport-Stamford-Danbury-Waterbury, CT	4,687	31
Cincinnati, OH-KY-IN	4,590	32
Fort Lauderdale, FL	4,517	33
Fort Worth-Arlington, TX	4,407	34
Kansas City, MO-KS	4,398	35
Sacramento, CA	4,315	36
Las Vegas, NV-AZ	4,241	37
San Antonio, TX	4,225	38
Indianapolis, IN	4,015	39
Columbus, OH	3,880	40
Bergen-Passaic, NJ	3,855	41
Milwaukee-Waukesha, WI	3,711	42
Charlotte-Gastonia-Rock Hill, NC-SC	3,667	43
New Orleans, LA	3,666	44
Norfolk-Virginia Beach-Newport News, VA-NC	3,643	45
Salt Lake City-Ogden, UT	3,516	46
Austin-San Marcos, TX	3,340	47
Nashville, TN	3,328	48
Middlesex-Somerset-Hunterdon, NJ	3,265	49
Monmouth-Ocean, NJ	3,240	50
Buffalo-Niagara Falls, NY	3,207	51
Honolulu, HI	3,205	52
West Palm Beach-Boca Raton, FL	3,108	53
Greensboro-Winston Salem-High Point, NC	3,034	54
Raleigh-Durham-Chapel Hill, NC	2,980	55
Hartford, CT	2,893	56
Jacksonville, FL	2,890	57
Rochester, NY	2,815	58
Louisville, KY-IN	2,713	59
Oklahoma City, OK	2,636	60
Memphis, TN-AR-MS	2,622	61
Richmond-Petersburg, VA	2,522	62
Greenville-Spartanburg-Anderson, SC	2,429	63
Albany-Schenectady-Troy, NY	2,306	64
Providence-Warwick-Pawtucket, RI	2,255	65
Birmingham, AL	2,212	66
Tucson, AZ	2,128	67
Fresno, CA	2,121	68
Dayton-Springfield, OH	2,109	69
Grand Rapids-Muskegon-Holland, MI	2,064	70
Syracuse, NY	1,952	71
Tulsa, OK	1,944	72
Knoxville, TN	1,938	73
Akron, OH	1,845	74
Omaha, NE-IA	1,833	75
Albuquerque, NM	1,778	76
Ventura, CA	1,752	77
El Paso, TX	1,680	78
Wilmington-Newark, DE-MD	1,677	79
Toledo, OH	1,674	80
Tacoma, WA	1,599	81
Sarasota-Bradenton, FL	1,595	82
Allentown-Bethlehem-Easton, PA	1,563	83
Harrisburg-Lebanon-Carlisle, PA	1,557	84
Wichita, KS	1,532	85
Baton Rouge, LA	1,502	86
Scranton-Wilkes-Barre-Hazleton, PA	1,489	87
Springfield, MA	1,485	88
Gary, IN	1,466	89
Bakersfield, CA	1,399	90
Charleston-North Charleston, SC	1,387	91
Youngstown-Warren, OH	1,377	92
Mobile, AL	1,368	93
Santa Rosa, CA	1,350	94
Lexington, KY	1,334	95
Vallejo-Fairfield-Napa, CA	1,330	96
Des Moines, IA	1,328	97
Little Rock-North Little Rock, AR	1,306	98
Columbia, SC	1,300	99
Daytona Beach, FL	1,284	100
Atlantic-Cape May, NJ	1,224	101
Melbourne-Titusville-Palm Bay, FL	1,215	102
Stockton-Lodi, CA	1,209	103
Fort Myers-Cape Coral, FL	1,205	104
Ann Arbor, MI	1,202	105
Fort Wayne, IN	1,202	106
Spokane, WA	1,189	107
Madison, WI	1,187	108
Chattanooga, TN-GA	1,186	109
McAllen-Edinburg-Mission, TX	1,174	110
Colorado Springs, CO	1,173	111
Johnson City-Kingsport-Bristol, TN-VA	1,165	112
Lancaster, PA	1,159	113
Corpus Christi, TX	1,147	114
Santa Barbara-Santa Maria-Lompoc, CA	1,123	115
Jersey City, NJ	1,113	116
Augusta-Aiken, GA-SC	1,081	117
Anchorage, AK	1,056	118
Boise City, ID	1,056	119
Canton-Massillon, OH	1,053	120
Lakeland-Winter Haven, FL	1,046	121
Modesto, CA	1,044	122
Barnstable-Yarmouth, MA	1,026	123
Jackson, MS	1,016	124
Salinas, CA	1,002	125
Newburgh, NY-PA	996	126
Davenport-Moline-Rock Island, IA-IL	984	127
Flint, MI	978	128
Reno, NV	976	129
Pensacola, FL	965	130
Lansing-East Lansing, MI	962	131
Kalamazoo-Battle Creek, MI	939	132
Lafayette, LA	932	133
Beaumont-Port Arthur, TX	929	134
Trenton, NJ	925	135
Portland, ME	922	136
Saginaw-Bay City-Midland, MI	920	137
Myrtle Beach, SC	913	138
Appleton-Oshkosh-Neenah, WI	882	139
Boulder-Longmont, CO	865	140
Huntsville, AL	865	141
York, PA	860	142
Eugene-Springfield, OR	848	143
Rockford, IL	844	144
Reading, PA	837	145
Shreveport-Bossier City, LA	835	146
Fort Pierce-Port St. Lucie, FL	829	147
Hickory-Morganton-Lenoir, NC	822	148
Tallahassee, FL	822	149
Peoria-Pekin, IL	818	150
Springfield, MO	816	151
Naples, FL	797	152
Biloxi-Gulfport-Pascagoula, MS	795	153
Salem, OR	777	154
Visalia-Tulare-Porterville, CA	767	155
Macon, GA	754	156
Montgomery, AL	752	157
Galveston-Texas City, TX	751	158
Santa Cruz-Watsonville, CA	748	159
Brownsville-Harlingen-San Benito, TX	738	160
Wilmington, NC	737	161
Erie, PA	728	162
Dutchess County, NY	725	163
Huntington-Ashland, WV-KY-OH	723	164
Savannah, GA	721	165
Hamilton-Middletown, OH	713	166
Charleston, WV	712	167
Evansville-Henderson, IN-KY	708	168
Lubbock, TX	684	169
San Luis Obispo-Antascadero-Paso Robles, CA	682	170
Burlington, VT	678	171
South Bend, IN	676	172
Odessa-Midland, TX	663	173
New London-Norwich, CT	660	174
Roanoke, VA	659	175
Utica-Rome, NY	658	176
Binghamton, NY	622	177
Asheville, NC	621	178
Fayetteville-Springdale-Rogers, AR	619	179
Lincoln, NE	614	180
Fayetteville, NC	611	181
Provo-Orem, UT	611	182
Laredo, TX	610	183
Gainesville, FL	605	184
Duluth-Superior, MN-WI	602	185
Fort Collins-Loveland, CO	596	186
Bellingham, WA	590	187
Ocala, FL	586	188
Columbus, GA-AL	585	189
Amarillo, TX	584	190
Green Bay, WI	563	191
Killeen-Temple, TX	558	192
Waco, TX	556	193
Olympia, WA	549	194
Yakima, WA	545	195
Panama City, FL	542	196
Cedar Rapids, IA	541	197
Longview-Marshall, TX	540	198
Bremerton, WA	534	199
Brazoria, TX	526	200
Springfield, IL	515	201
Johnstown, PA	514	202
Santa Fe, NM	502	203
Flagstaff, AZ-UT	494	204
Chico-Paradise, CA	491	205
Richland-Kennewick-Pasco, WA	487	206
Redding, CA	478	207
Houma, LA	477	208
Lynchburg, VA	468	209
Fort Walton Beach, FL	466	210
Medford-Ashland, OR	464	211
Lake Charles, LA	455	212
Fort Smith, AR-OK	452	213
Racine, WI	449	214
Sioux Falls, SD	447	215
Fargo-Moorhead, ND-MN	441	216
Elkhart-Goshen, IN	432	217
Pittsfield, MA	426	218
Bangor, ME	424	219
Yolo, CA	422	220
Clarksville-Hopkinsville, TN-KY	418	221
Tyler, TX	418	222
Champaign-Urbana, IL	417	223
Charlottesville, VA	413	224
St. Cloud, MN	409	225
Lafayette, IN	408	226
Lima, OH	408	227
Billings, MT	407	228
Topeka, KS	406	229
Janesville-Beloit, WI	397	230
Mansfield, OH	393	231
Parkersburg-Marietta, WV-OH	392	232
Wheeling, WV-OH	391	233
Tuscaloosa, AL	389	234
Glens Falls, NY	387	235
Joplin, MO	384	236
Bloomington-Normal, IL	382	237
Terre Haute, IN	376	238
Yuma, AZ	376	239
Monroe, LA	375	240
Greenville, NC	369	241
Benton Harbor, MI	367	242
Rocky Mount, NC	365	243
Pueblo, CO	352	244
Vineland-Millville-Bridgeton, NJ	346	245
Merced, CA	345	246
Bryan-College Station, TX	344	247
Eau Claire, WI	343	248
Florence, AL	341	249
Columbia, MO	340	250
La Crosse, WI-MN	338	251
Florence, SC	336	252
Las Cruces, NM	334	253
Grand Junction, CO	332	254
Altoona, PA	331	255
Waterloo-Cedar Falls, IA	330	256
Dothan, AL	323	257
Abilene, TX	322	258
Decatur, AL	321	259
Punta Gorda, FL	321	260
Kenosha, WI	317	261
Rochester, MN	314	262
Bloomington, IN	313	263
Hagerstown, MD	311	264
Greeley, CO	310	265
Yuba City, CA	310	266
Sioux City, IA-NE	309	267
State College, PA	308	268
Dover, DE	307	269
Athens, GA	306	270
Wichita Falls, TX	306	271
Texarkana, TX-AR	296	272
Steubenville-Weirton, OH-WV	295	273
Sharon, PA	292	274
Williamsport, PA	292	275
Jamestown, NY	290	276
Lewiston-Auburn, ME	286	277
Alexandria, LA	285	278
Wausau, WI	285	279
Muncie, IN	284	280
Decatur, IL	283	281
Jacksonville, NC	283	282
Missoula, MT	283	283
Iowa City, IA	282	284
Jackson, MI	281	285
Kokomo, IN	278	286
San Angelo, TX	275	287
Albany, GA	272	288
Hattiesburg, MS	272	289
Sheboygan, WI	268	290
Anniston, AL	267	291
Rapid City, SD	255	292
Jackson, TN	254	293
Cumberland, MD-WV	251	294
St. Joseph, MO	246	295
Gadsden, AL	242	296
Danville, VA	241	297
Dubuque, IA	241	298
Owensboro, KY	241	299
Grand Forks, ND-MN	237	300
Victoria, TX	237	301
Lawrence, KS	233	302
Great Falls, MT	232	303
Kankakee, IL	227	304
Sherman-Denison, TX	226	305
Bismarck, ND	224	306
Lawton, OK	220	307
Goldsboro, NC	213	308
Sumter, SC	205	309
Elmira, NY	199	310
Cheyenne, WY	192	311
Pocatello, ID	188	312
Casper, WY	177	313
Pine Bluff, AR	174	314
Jonesboro, AR	162	315
Enid, OK	141	316

MSA/NECMA Total **570,985**
United States Total **693,381**
MSA/NECMA (% of U.S.Total) **82.35**

RETAIL SALES: FURNITURE & MAJOR APPLIANCES

MSA/NECMA	SALES ($Mil)	RANK
Los Angeles-Long Beach, CA	7,027	1
Chicago, IL	6,180	2
New York, NY	5,478	3
Washington, DC-MD-VA-WV	4,261	4
Boston-Worcester-Lawrence-Lowell-Brockton, MA-NH	3,763	5
Detroit, MI	3,232	6
Philadelphia, PA-NJ	3,142	7
Houston, TX	2,955	8
Atlanta, GA	2,707	9
Orange County, CA	2,625	10
Dallas, TX	2,566	11
Nassau-Suffolk, NY	2,451	12
Miami, FL	2,333	13
Minneapolis-St. Paul, MN-WI	2,197	14
Seattle-Bellevue-Everett, WA	2,170	15
San Jose, CA	2,161	16
San Diego, CA	2,129	17
San Francisco, CA	2,022	18
Phoenix-Mesa, AZ	2,003	19
Oakland, CA	1,982	20
Denver, CO	1,727	21
St. Louis, MO-IL	1,685	22
Baltimore, MD	1,558	23
Tampa-St. Petersburg-Clearwater, FL	1,530	24
Portland-Vancouver, OR-WA	1,388	25
Cleveland-Lorain-Elyria, OH	1,375	26
Pittsburgh, PA	1,367	27
Newark, NJ	1,357	28
Bergen-Passaic, NJ	1,352	29
Riverside-San Bernardino, CA	1,315	30
Fort Lauderdale, FL	1,271	31
Kansas City, MO-KS	1,259	32
New Haven-Bridgeport-Stamford-Danbury-Waterbury, CT	1,189	33
Milwaukee-Waukesha, WI	1,184	34
Middlesex-Somerset-Hunterdon, NJ	1,169	35
Sacramento, CA	1,158	36
Fort Worth-Arlington, TX	1,127	37
Indianapolis, IN	1,125	38
Orlando, FL	1,071	39
Greensboro-Winston Salem-High Point, NC	1,010	40
Salt Lake City-Ogden, UT	991	41
Columbus, OH	976	42
Las Vegas, NV-AZ	959	43
Charlotte-Gastonia-Rock Hill, NC-SC	927	44
Nashville, TN	921	45
West Palm Beach-Boca Raton, FL	919	46
Austin-San Marcos, TX	886	47
Norfolk-Virginia Beach-Newport News, VA-NC	853	48
Raleigh-Durham-Chapel Hill, NC	795	49
Buffalo-Niagara Falls, NY	787	50
Monmouth-Ocean, NJ	785	51
New Orleans, LA	781	52
San Antonio, TX	779	53
Grand Rapids-Muskegon-Holland, MI	717	54
Hartford, CT	704	55
Omaha, NE-IA	701	56
Cincinnati, OH-KY-IN	692	57
Oklahoma City, OK	660	58
Richmond-Petersburg, VA	649	59
Jacksonville, FL	641	60
Birmingham, AL	620	61
Rochester, NY	603	62
Honolulu, HI	595	63
Louisville, KY-IN	568	64
Dayton-Springfield, OH	564	65
Memphis, TN-AR-MS	551	66
Greenville-Spartanburg-Anderson, SC	537	67
Madison, WI	512	68
Wilmington-Newark, DE-MD	510	69
Albany-Schenectady-Troy, NY	499	70
Tulsa, OK	492	71
Tucson, AZ	481	72
Sarasota-Bradenton, FL	478	73
El Paso, TX	461	74
Knoxville, TN	456	75
Albuquerque, NM	448	76
Ventura, CA	441	77
Tacoma, WA	439	78
Fresno, CA	429	79
Syracuse, NY	422	80
Jersey City, NJ	410	81
Lakeland-Winter Haven, FL	407	82
Providence-Warwick-Pawtucket, RI	393	83
Laredo, TX	391	84
Fort Myers-Cape Coral, FL	377	85
Columbia, SC	358	86
Colorado Springs, CO	356	87
Charleston-North Charleston, SC	354	88
Little Rock-North Little Rock, AR	351	89
Youngstown-Warren, OH	351	90
Toledo, OH	350	91
Naples, FL	346	92
Santa Rosa, CA	341	93
Harrisburg-Lebanon-Carlisle, PA	338	94
Lancaster, PA	334	95
Ann Arbor, MI	332	96
Lansing-East Lansing, MI	327	97
Fort Wayne, IN	322	98
Gary, IN	319	99
Lexington, KY	319	100
Boise City, ID	317	101
Akron, OH	314	102
Allentown-Bethlehem-Easton, PA	310	103
Trenton, NJ	310	104
Wichita, KS	310	105
Hickory-Morganton-Lenoir, NC	308	106
Appleton-Oshkosh-Neenah, WI	305	107
Spokane, WA	303	108
Bakersfield, CA	279	109
McAllen-Edinburg-Mission, TX	277	110
Flint, MI	276	111
Springfield, MA	273	112
Melbourne-Titusville-Palm Bay, FL	272	113
Reno, NV	271	114
Mobile, AL	265	115
Saginaw-Bay City-Midland, MI	264	116
Johnson City-Kingsport-Bristol, TN-VA	258	117
Modesto, CA	258	118
Santa Barbara-Santa Maria-Lompoc, CA	258	119
Davenport-Moline-Rock Island, IA-IL	257	120
Kalamazoo-Battle Creek, MI	257	121
Des Moines, IA	249	122
Daytona Beach, FL	248	123
Scranton-Wilkes-Barre-Hazleton, PA	247	124
Boulder-Longmont, CO	235	125
Chattanooga, TN-GA	232	126
Augusta-Aiken, GA-SC	229	127
Baton Rouge, LA	228	128
Atlantic-Cape May, NJ	226	129
Vallejo-Fairfield-Napa, CA	225	130
Barnstable-Yarmouth, MA	217	131
Peoria-Pekin, IL	217	132
Stockton-Lodi, CA	216	133
Reading, PA	215	134
Roanoke, VA	207	135
Pensacola, FL	204	136
Shreveport-Bossier City, LA	202	137
Lafayette, LA	201	138
Provo-Orem, UT	197	139
Salinas, CA	195	140
Eugene-Springfield, OR	187	141
Fort Pierce-Port St. Lucie, FL	187	142
Jackson, MS	180	143
Canton-Massillon, OH	179	144
Anchorage, AK	172	145
Rockford, IL	172	146
South Bend, IN	172	147
Green Bay, WI	169	148
Huntsville, AL	169	149
Fort Collins-Loveland, CO	165	150
Salem, OR	163	151
Lincoln, NE	160	152
Newburgh, NY-PA	160	153
York, PA	158	154
Amarillo, TX	157	155
Myrtle Beach, SC	157	156
Springfield, IL	155	157
Erie, PA	154	158
Lubbock, TX	152	159
Asheville, NC	151	160
Portland, ME	151	161
Beaumont-Port Arthur, TX	149	162
Cedar Rapids, IA	148	163
Montgomery, AL	145	164
Fayetteville-Springdale-Rogers, AR	144	165
Lynchburg, VA	144	166
Corpus Christi, TX	143	167
Tallahassee, FL	142	168
Olympia, WA	141	169
Huntington-Ashland, WV-KY-OH	140	170
Bremerton, WA	139	171
Burlington, VT	139	172
Utica-Rome, NY	138	173
New London-Norwich, CT	136	174
Ocala, FL	134	175
Evansville-Henderson, IN-KY	132	176
Brownsville-Harlingen-San Benito, TX	130	177
Fayetteville, NC	130	178
Topeka, KS	128	179
Duluth-Superior, MN-WI	127	180
Macon, GA	123	181
Charleston, WV	122	182
Richland-Kennewick-Pasco, WA	121	183
Rochester, MN	121	184
Binghamton, NY	120	185
Chico-Paradise, CA	120	186
Wilmington, NC	120	187
Fort Walton Beach, FL	119	188
Visalia-Tulare-Porterville, CA	118	189
Bloomington-Normal, IL	117	190
Gainesville, FL	117	191
Champaign-Urbana, IL	115	192
Dutchess County, NY	113	193
San Luis Obispo-Antascadero-Paso Robles, CA	112	194
Santa Cruz-Watsonville, CA	109	195
Savannah, GA	109	196
Bellingham, WA	108	197
Killeen-Temple, TX	108	198
Medford-Ashland, OR	108	199
Biloxi-Gulfport-Pascagoula, MS	107	200
Springfield, MO	107	201
Redding, CA	105	202
Charlottesville, VA	104	203
Columbus, GA-AL	103	204
Santa Fe, NM	100	205
Racine, WI	99	206
Billings, MT	98	207
Souix Falls, SD	98	208
Waco, TX	97	209
Odessa-Midland, TX	95	210
Vineland-Millville-Bridgeton, NJ	93	211
Hamilton-Middletown, OH	92	212
Las Cruces, NM	92	213
Columbia, MO	90	214
Tuscaloosa, AL	90	215
Clarksville-Hopkinsville, TN-KY	89	216
Jacksonville, NC	88	217
Monroe, LA	88	218
Altoona, PA	87	219
Fargo-Moorhead, ND-MN	87	220
Johnstown, PA	84	221
Longview-Marshall, TX	84	222
Missoula, MT	82	223
Galveston-Texas City, TX	79	224
Greenville, NC	79	225
Yakima, WA	78	226
Florence, SC	77	227
Lake Charles, LA	77	228
Panama City, FL	77	229
St. Cloud, MN	77	230
Wheeling, WV-OH	77	231
Yuma, AZ	77	232
Eau Claire, WI	76	233
Mansfield, OH	76	234
Jackson, TN	75	235
Punta Gorda, FL	75	236
Kankakee, IL	74	237
Lafayette, IN	74	238
Lima, OH	74	239
Kenosha, WI	73	240
Pueblo, CO	73	241
Wichita Falls, TX	73	242
Rapid City, SD	72	243
Yuba City, CA	72	244
Athens, GA	71	245
Bloomington, IN	71	246
Decatur, AL	70	247
Grand Junction, CO	70	248
Parkersburg-Marietta, WV-OH	69	249
Rocky Mount, NC	69	250
Tyler, TX	69	251
Dover, DE	68	252
Houma, LA	68	253
Waterloo-Cedar Falls, IA	68	254
Bangor, ME	67	255
Florence, AL	67	256
Merced, CA	66	257
Terre Haute, IN	66	258
La Crosse, WI-MN	65	259
Pittsfield, MA	65	260
Wausau, WI	65	261
Fort Smith, AR-OK	64	262
Janesville-Beloit, WI	64	263
State College, PA	64	264
Dothan, AL	62	265
Jackson, MI	62	266
Greeley, CO	61	267
Hagerstown, MD	61	268
Lawrence, KS	61	269
Danville, VA	60	270
Souix City, IA-NE	60	271
Steubenville-Weirton, OH-WV	60	272
Dubuque, IA	59	273
Kokomo, IN	59	274
Elkhart-Goshen, IN	58	275
San Angelo, TX	58	276
Sharon, PA	58	277
Albany, GA	57	278
Decatur, IL	57	279
Glens Falls, NY	56	280
Iowa City, IA	55	281
Anniston, AL	54	282
Muncie, IN	54	283
Bryan-College Station, TX	53	284
Goldsboro, NC	53	285
Alexandria, LA	52	286
Brazoria, TX	51	287
Jamestown, NY	51	288
Joplin, MO	51	289
Benton Harbor, MI	50	290
Gadsden, AL	49	291
Grand Forks, ND-MN	48	292
Owensboro, KY	48	293
Albilene, TX	47	294
Bismarck, ND	47	295
Cumberland, MD-WV	47	296
Jonesboro, AR	47	297
Williamsport, PA	47	298
Lawton, OK	46	299
Texarkana, TX-AR	46	300
Sherman-Denison, TX	45	301
Sheboygan, WI	44	302
Pocatello, ID	43	303
Sumter, SC	40	304
Yolo, CA	40	305
St. Joseph, MO	39	306
Elmira, NY	38	307
Cheyenne, WY	37	308
Lewiston-Auburn, ME	37	309
Hattiesburg, MS	36	310
Flagstaff, AZ-UT	34	311
Casper, WY	33	312
Victoria, TX	32	313
Enid, OK	25	314
Pine Bluff, AR	25	315
Great Falls, MT	24	316

MSA/NECMA Total 149,203
United States Total 167,925
MSA/NECMA (% of U.S.Total) 88.85

MSA/NECMA	SALES ($Mil)	RANK
Los Angeles-Long Beach, CA	10,945	1
Chicago, IL	9,520	2
Boston-Worcester-Lawrence-Lowell-Brockton, MA-NH	7,860	3
Detroit, MI	7,712	4
New York, NY	6,334	5
Houston, TX	6,179	6
Atlanta, GA	6,111	7
Washington, DC-MD-VA-WV	5,979	8
Philadelphia, PA-NJ	5,868	9
Dallas, TX	5,569	10
Minneapolis-St. Paul, MN-WI	4,644	11
Phoenix-Mesa, AZ	4,300	12
Orange County, CA	4,239	13
St. Louis, MO-IL	4,150	14
Riverside-San Bernardino, CA	3,908	15
Portland-Vancouver, OR-WA	3,859	16
San Diego, CA	3,706	17
Seattle-Bellevue-Everett, WA	3,668	18
Nassau-Suffolk, NY	3,449	19
Oakland, CA	3,434	20
Pittsburgh, PA	3,211	21
Kansas City, MO-KS	3,080	22
Baltimore, MD	3,078	23
Denver, CO	3,028	24
Tampa-St. Petersburg-Clearwater, FL	2,957	25
Miami, FL	2,882	26
Cleveland-Lorain-Elyria, OH	2,701	27
Columbus, OH	2,577	28
Cincinnati, OH-KY-IN	2,553	29
San Jose, CA	2,553	30
San Francisco, CA	2,552	31
Indianapolis, IN	2,544	32
Fort Worth-Arlington, TX	2,496	33
Orlando, FL	2,402	34
Honolulu, HI	2,355	35
San Antonio, TX	2,264	36
New Haven-Bridgeport-Stamford-Danbury-Waterbury, CT	2,261	37
Grand Rapids-Muskegon-Holland, MI	2,174	38
Fort Lauderdale, FL	2,108	39
Bergen-Passaic, NJ	2,055	40
Nashville, TN	2,028	41
Milwaukee-Waukesha, WI	2,002	42
New Orleans, LA	1,920	43
Norfolk-Virginia Beach-Newport News, VA-NC	1,920	44
Sacramento, CA	1,919	45
Salt Lake City-Ogden, UT	1,872	46
Dayton-Springfield, OH	1,859	47
Las Vegas, NV-AZ	1,857	48
Charlotte-Gastonia-Rock Hill, NC-SC	1,803	49
Middlesex-Somerset-Hunterdon, NJ	1,783	50
West Palm Beach-Boca Raton, FL	1,778	51
Austin-San Marcos, TX	1,765	52
Jacksonville, FL	1,714	53
Memphis, TN-AR-MS	1,701	54
Louisville, KY-IN	1,697	55
Oklahoma City, OK	1,675	56
Newark, NJ	1,498	57
Greensboro-Winston Salem-High Point, NC	1,483	58
Birmingham, AL	1,476	59
Buffalo-Niagara Falls, NY	1,467	60
Raleigh-Durham-Chapel Hill, NC	1,461	61
Hartford, CT	1,426	62
Richmond-Petersburg, VA	1,405	63
Tucson, AZ	1,370	64
Rochester, NY	1,355	65
El Paso, TX	1,328	66
Monmouth-Ocean, NJ	1,326	67
Little Rock-North Little Rock, AR	1,234	68
Greenville-Spartanburg-Anderson, SC	1,232	69
Albuquerque, NM	1,186	70
Knoxville, TN	1,149	71
Tulsa, OK	1,142	72
Ann Arbor, MI	1,096	73
Kalamazoo-Battle Creek, MI	1,095	74
Albany-Schenectady-Troy, NY	1,077	75
McAllen-Edinburg-Mission, TX	1,075	76
Toledo, OH	1,063	77
Wilmington-Newark, DE-MD	1,043	78
Lansing-East Lansing, MI	1,026	79
Flint, MI	1,009	80
Fresno, CA	1,008	81
Tacoma, WA	994	82
Providence-Warwick-Pawtucket, RI	976	83
Baton Rouge, LA	967	84
Ventura, CA	960	85
Omaha, NE-IA	950	86
Harrisburg-Lebanon-Carlisle, PA	894	87
Scranton-Wilkes-Barre-Hazleton, PA	890	88
Saginaw-Bay City-Midland, MI	870	89
Des Moines, IA	866	90
Lexington, KY	827	91
Fort Wayne, IN	819	92
Youngstown-Warren, OH	813	93
Colorado Springs, CO	792	94
Syracuse, NY	792	95
Gary, IN	787	96
Chattanooga, TN-GA	784	97
Johnson City-Kingsport-Bristol, TN-VA	777	98
Mobile, AL	763	99
Bakersfield, CA	761	100
Jackson, MS	754	101
Wichita, KS	750	102
Melbourne-Titusville-Palm Bay, FL	742	103
Sarasota-Bradenton, FL	742	104
Akron, OH	737	105
Columbia, SC	733	106
Spokane, WA	733	107
Allentown-Bethlehem-Easton, PA	720	108
Santa Rosa, CA	713	109
Augusta-Aiken, GA-SC	707	110
Laredo, TX	696	111
Springfield, MA	695	112
Anchorage, AK	693	113
Modesto, CA	678	114
Reno, NV	676	115
Boise City, ID	674	116
Fort Myers-Cape Coral, FL	664	117
Shreveport-Bossier City, LA	663	118
Charleston-North Charleston, SC	661	119
Lakeland-Winter Haven, FL	658	120
Vallejo-Fairfield-Napa, CA	649	121
Brownsville-Harlingen-San Benito, TX	643	122
Madison, WI	642	123
Davenport-Moline-Rock Island, IA-IL	630	124
Daytona Beach, FL	626	125
Lafayette, LA	623	126
Stockton-Lodi, CA	607	127
Corpus Christi, TX	606	128
Eugene-Springfield, OR	606	129
Salem, OR	602	130
Biloxi-Gulfport-Pascagoula, MS	581	131
Beaumont-Port Arthur, TX	574	132
York, PA	559	133
Green Bay, WI	547	134
Reading, PA	532	135
Appleton-Oshkosh-Neenah, WI	522	136
Pensacola, FL	513	137
Salinas, CA	506	138
Huntsville, AL	492	139
Lubbock, TX	485	140
Tallahassee, FL	485	141
Atlantic-Cape May, NJ	483	142
Fayetteville-Springdale-Rogers, AR	482	143
Huntington-Ashland, WV-KY-OH	477	144
Fort Smith, AR-OK	470	145
Portland, ME	470	146
Charleston, WV	469	147
South Bend, IN	466	148
Fort Collins-Loveland, CO	460	149
Duluth-Superior, MN-WI	458	150
Olympia, WA	458	151
Odessa-Midland, TX	457	152
Fayetteville, NC	453	153
Springfield, MO	453	154
Santa Barbara-Santa Maria-Lompoc, CA	446	155
Lancaster, PA	443	156
Evansville-Henderson, IN-KY	440	157
Rockford, IL	440	158
Wilmington, NC	440	159
Columbus, GA-AL	437	160
Ocala, FL	437	161
Provo-Orem, UT	437	162
Fort Pierce-Port St. Lucie, FL	428	163
Peoria-Pekin, IL	427	164
Roanoke, VA	426	165
Canton-Massillon, OH	423	166
Gainesville, FL	423	167
Montgomery, AL	422	168
Tyler, TX	421	169
Erie, PA	420	170
Jackson, MI	413	171
Trenton, NJ	413	172
Visalia-Tulare-Porterville, CA	413	173
Killeen-Temple, TX	410	174
Richland-Kennewick-Pasco, WA	410	175
Fargo-Moorhead, ND-MN	407	176
Bremerton, WA	406	177
Hickory-Morganton-Lenoir, NC	406	178
Medford-Ashland, OR	401	179
Cedar Rapids, IA	398	180
Macon, GA	386	181
Bellingham, WA	380	182
Topeka, KS	378	183
Boulder-Longmont, CO	377	184
Dover, DE	373	185
Myrtle Beach, SC	370	186
Monroe, LA	364	187
Waco, TX	364	188
Savannah, GA	362	189
Dutchess County, NY	358	190
Yakima, WA	349	191
Jersey City, NJ	346	192
Panama City, FL	345	193
Naples, FL	343	194
Asheville, NC	329	195
Chico-Paradise, CA	329	196
Lynchburg, VA	329	197
Brazoria, TX	328	198
Amarillo, TX	325	199
Longview-Marshall, TX	325	200
Lake Charles, LA	320	201
Fort Walton Beach, FL	315	202
Columbia, MO	306	203
Bangor, ME	304	204
Billings, MT	304	205
Houma, LA	299	206
Galveston-Texas City, TX	297	207
Champaign-Urbana, IL	296	208
Rochester, MN	296	209
Alexandria, LA	290	210
Newburgh, NY-PA	289	211
Redding, CA	288	212
Wichita Falls, TX	288	213
Lincoln, NE	287	214
New London-Norwich, CT	282	215
Bryan-College Station, TX	279	216
Florence, AL	278	217
Elkhart-Goshen, IN	273	218
Abilene, TX	271	219
Lima, OH	269	220
Eau Claire, WI	263	221
Mansfield, OH	262	222
Racine, WI	262	223
Clarksville-Hopkinsville, TN-KY	261	224
Springfield, IL	261	225
Utica-Rome, NY	253	226
Hagerstown, MD	249	227
Parkersburg-Marietta, WV-OH	246	228
Johnstown, PA	244	229
Grand Junction, CO	243	230
Lafayette, IN	241	231
Jonesboro, AR	238	232
Janesville-Beloit, WI	235	233
Wheeling, WV-OH	235	234
Waterloo-Cedar Falls, IA	234	235
Pueblo, CO	229	236
Lawton, OK	225	237
Tuscaloosa, AL	224	238
Missoula, MT	222	239
Decatur, IL	221	240
Binghamton, NY	220	241
Joplin, MO	220	242
Wausau, WI	218	243
Terre Haute, IN	217	244
Benton Harbor, MI	212	245
Jackson, TN	212	246
Grand Forks, ND-MN	212	247
Sherman-Denison, TX	207	248
Burlington, VT	206	249
Florence, SC	206	250
Barnstable-Yarmouth, MA	203	251
Rapid City, SD	203	252
Altoona, PA	202	253
Punta Gorda, FL	202	254
Hamilton-Middletown, OH	201	255
Bloomington-Normal, IL	198	256
Decatur, AL	198	257
Sioux Falls, SD	198	258
Yuma, AZ	195	259
Texarkana, TX-AR	194	260
Muncie, IN	191	261
Flagstaff, AZ-UT	188	262
Las Cruces, NM	184	263
Dothan, AL	183	264
Hattiesburg, MS	182	265
Rocky Mount, NC	181	266
Anniston, AL	180	267
Owensboro, KY	180	268
Sharon, PA	179	269
State College, PA	179	270
Greeley, CO	177	271
Sheboygan, WI	177	272
Athens, GA	176	273
Santa Cruz-Watsonville, CA	176	274
Bloomington, IN	174	275
Yuba City, CA	174	276
Charlottesville, VA	173	277
Santa Fe, NM	173	278
San Angelo, TX	167	279
Jacksonville, NC	166	280
Great Falls, MT	165	281
Lewiston-Auburn, ME	165	282
San Luis Obispo-Antascadero-Paso Robles, CA	161	283
Kankakee, IL	159	284
Iowa City, IA	158	285
Kokomo, IN	157	286
Dubuque, IA	156	287
Steubenville-Weirton, OH-WV	155	288
Elmira, NY	153	289
Cumberland, MD-WV	149	290
Greenville, NC	149	291
Pittsfield, MA	149	292
Gadsden, AL	147	293
Albany, GA	143	294
Cheyenne, WY	142	295
St. Joseph, MO	141	296
Danville, VA	139	297
La Crosse, WI-MN	139	298
Merced, CA	135	299
Goldsboro, NC	134	300
Enid, OK	133	301
Vineland-Millville-Bridgeton, NJ	130	302
St. Cloud, MN	129	303
Williamsport, PA	126	304
Victoria, TX	121	305
Kenosha, WI	118	306
Bismarck, ND	115	307
Sioux City, IA-NE	115	308
Jamestown, NY	114	309
Pine Bluff, AR	113	310
Pocatello, ID	109	311
Sumter, SC	105	312
Glens Falls, NY	103	313
Casper, WY	100	314
Lawrence, KS	99	315
Yolo, CA	94	316
MSA/NECMA Total	**313,425**	
United States Total	**369,526**	
MSA/NECMA (% of U.S.Total)	**84.82**	

MSA/NECMA	SALES ($Mil)	RANK
Chicago, IL	4,612	1
Los Angeles-Long Beach, CA	4,313	2
Boston-Worcester-Lawrence-Lowell-Brockton, MA-NH	3,696	3
Detroit, MI	2,769	4
Atlanta, GA	2,687	5
Washington, DC-MD-VA-WV	2,591	6
Minneapolis-St. Paul, MN-WI	2,507	7
Philadelphia, PA-NJ	2,487	8
Nassau-Suffolk, NY	2,334	9
New York, NY	2,258	10
Houston, TX	2,006	11
Dallas, TX	1,747	12
Phoenix-Mesa, AZ	1,709	13
Riverside-San Bernardino, CA	1,692	14
Orange County, CA	1,681	15
Seattle-Bellevue-Everett, WA	1,674	16
St. Louis, MO-IL	1,618	17
San Diego, CA	1,605	18
Baltimore, MD	1,470	19
Portland-Vancouver, OR-WA	1,452	20
Oakland, CA	1,442	21
Denver, CO	1,416	22
Pittsburgh, PA	1,391	23
Cleveland-Lorain-Elyria, OH	1,281	24
Tampa-St. Petersburg-Clearwater, FL	1,281	25
New Haven-Bridgeport-Stamford-Danbury-Waterbury, CT	1,274	26
Miami, FL	1,248	27
Cincinnati, OH-KY-IN	1,244	28
Sacramento, CA	1,225	29
Charlotte-Gastonia-Rock Hill, NC-SC	1,157	30
Indianapolis, IN	1,135	31
Milwaukee-Waukesha, WI	1,122	32
Orlando, FL	1,101	33
Newark, NJ	1,056	34
San Jose, CA	1,052	35
Fort Lauderdale, FL	1,004	36
San Francisco, CA	1,003	37
Kansas City, MO-KS	996	38
Fort Worth-Arlington, TX	989	39
Raleigh-Durham-Chapel Hill, NC	938	40
Las Vegas, NV-AZ	936	41
Columbus, OH	930	42
Greensboro-Winston Salem-High Point, NC	915	43
Salt Lake City-Ogden, UT	890	44
Bergen-Passaic, NJ	882	45
Grand Rapids-Muskegon-Holland, MI	868	46
Nashville, TN	849	47
Norfolk-Virginia Beach-Newport News, VA-NC	841	48
Middlesex-Somerset-Hunterdon, NJ	838	49
Greenville-Spartanburg-Anderson, SC	789	50
Monmouth-Ocean, NJ	774	51
Hartford, CT	757	52
Austin-San Marcos, TX	733	53
Knoxville, TN	700	54
Louisville, KY-IN	688	55
Jacksonville, FL	683	56
Rochester, NY	678	57
Buffalo-Niagara Falls, NY	648	58
West Palm Beach-Boca Raton, FL	644	59
New Orleans, LA	628	60
Albany-Schenectady-Troy, NY	607	61
Akron, OH	602	62
Richmond-Petersburg, VA	600	63
San Antonio, TX	600	64
Tacoma, WA	570	65
Birmingham, AL	540	66
Tucson, AZ	533	67
Oklahoma City, OK	528	68
Columbia, SC	508	69
Santa Rosa, CA	498	70
Madison, WI	497	71
Memphis, TN-AR-MS	497	72
Dayton-Springfield, OH	496	73
Syracuse, NY	487	74
Fresno, CA	479	75
Ventura, CA	477	76
Des Moines, IA	452	77
Providence-Warwick-Pawtucket, RI	450	78
Wichita, KS	433	79
Albuquerque, NM	432	80
Tulsa, OK	432	81
Augusta-Aiken, GA-SC	431	82
Appleton-Oshkosh-Neenah, WI	425	83
Charleston-North Charleston, SC	417	84
Scranton-Wilkes-Barre-Hazleton, PA	414	85
Ann Arbor, MI	412	86
Little Rock-North Little Rock, AR	407	87
Wilmington-Newark, DE-MD	401	88
Sarasota-Bradenton, FL	397	89
Vallejo-Fairfield-Napa, CA	397	90
Harrisburg-Lebanon-Carlisle, PA	395	91
Allentown-Bethlehem-Easton, PA	394	92
Boise City, ID	394	93
Spokane, WA	393	94
Springfield, MA	390	95
Mobile, AL	388	96
Fort Myers-Cape Coral, FL	385	97
Lancaster, PA	384	98
Gary, IN	381	99
Flint, MI	379	100
Baton Rouge, LA	374	101
Fort Wayne, IN	373	102
Reno, NV	368	103
El Paso, TX	359	104
Johnson City-Kingsport-Bristol, TN-VA	352	105
Kalamazoo-Battle Creek, MI	349	106
Lansing-East Lansing, MI	343	107
Toledo, OH	342	108
Colorado Springs, CO	337	109
Omaha, NE-IA	336	110
Honolulu, HI	335	111
Lakeland-Winter Haven, FL	330	112
Chattanooga, TN-GA	323	113
Bakersfield, CA	318	114
Newburgh, NY-PA	317	115
Springfield, MO	316	116
Youngstown-Warren, OH	315	117
Modesto, CA	307	118
Saginaw-Bay City-Midland, MI	307	119
Lexington, KY	301	120
Rockford, IL	297	121
Daytona Beach, FL	296	122
McAllen-Edinburg-Mission, TX	295	123
Melbourne-Titusville-Palm Bay, FL	286	124
Jackson, MS	285	125
Stockton-Lodi, CA	282	126
Hickory-Morganton-Lenoir, NC	278	127
Green Bay, WI	276	128
Salem, OR	275	129
St. Cloud, MN	272	130
Huntsville, AL	270	131
Portland, ME	264	132
Eugene-Springfield, OR	262	133
Fayetteville-Springdale-Rogers, AR	262	134
York, PA	262	135
Fort Pierce-Port St. Lucie, FL	256	136
Barnstable-Yarmouth, MA	248	137
Fort Collins-Loveland, CO	248	138
Boulder-Longmont, CO	245	139
Anchorage, AK	243	140
Charleston, WV	243	141
Macon, GA	241	142
Bremerton, WA	240	143
Davenport-Moline-Rock Island, IA-IL	238	144
Naples, FL	238	145
Wilmington, NC	237	146
Fayetteville, NC	236	147
Santa Barbara-Santa Maria-Lompoc, CA	236	148
Beaumont-Port Arthur, TX	226	149
Canton-Massillon, OH	226	150
Savannah, GA	224	151
Bellingham, WA	223	152
Cedar Rapids, IA	218	153
Ocala, FL	218	154
Evansville-Henderson, IN-KY	216	155
Lafayette, LA	216	156
Pensacola, FL	213	157
Peoria-Pekin, IL	213	158
Shreveport-Bossier City, LA	213	159
Visalia-Tulare-Porterville, CA	209	160
Huntington-Ashland, WV-KY-OH	206	161
Rochester, MN	206	162
Tallahassee, FL	206	163
Burlington, VT	204	164
Fargo-Moorhead, ND-MN	203	165
Yakima, WA	198	166
Janesville-Beloit, WI	197	167
Reading, PA	197	168
Roanoke, VA	197	169
Utica-Rome, NY	196	170
Dover, DE	195	171
Elkhart-Goshen, IN	195	172
Provo-Orem, UT	195	173
Atlantic-Cape May, NJ	194	174
Myrtle Beach, SC	193	175
Biloxi-Gulfport-Pascagoula, MS	187	176
Redding, CA	187	177
Salinas, CA	186	178
Duluth-Superior, MN-WI	185	179
Clarksville-Hopkinsville, TN-KY	181	180
Montgomery, AL	181	181
Corpus Christi, TX	179	182
Olympia, WA	178	183
Asheville, NC	175	184
Dutchess County, NY	175	185
Richland-Kennewick-Pasco, WA	175	186
Eau Claire, WI	174	187
Rocky Mount, NC	174	188
Lincoln, NE	173	189
South Bend, IN	173	190
Florence, SC	172	191
Racine, WI	171	192
New London-Norwich, CT	170	193
Santa Cruz-Watsonville, CA	169	194
Fort Smith, AR-OK	167	195
Medford-Ashland, OR	167	196
Columbus, GA-AL	166	197
Columbia, MO	162	198
Brownsville-Harlingen-San Benito, TX	161	199
Tyler, TX	161	200
San Luis Obispo-Antascadero-Paso Robles, CA	160	201
Trenton, NJ	154	202
Binghamton, NY	153	203
Chico-Paradise, CA	153	204
Laredo, TX	152	205
Erie, PA	149	206
Gainesville, FL	149	207
Billings, MT	146	208
Hamilton-Middletown, OH	146	209
Lake Charles, LA	145	210
Longview-Marshall, TX	145	211
Dothan, AL	144	212
Bangor, ME	143	213
Greenville, NC	143	214
Houma, LA	141	215
Waterloo-Cedar Falls, IA	140	216
Wausau, WI	139	217
Charlottesville, VA	137	218
Fort Walton Beach, FL	137	219
Tuscaloosa, AL	136	220
Lynchburg, VA	134	221
Amarillo, TX	132	222
Goldsboro, NC	129	223
Killeen-Temple, TX	129	224
Lubbock, TX	128	225
Waco, TX	128	226
La Crosse, WI-MN	127	227
Springfield, IL	127	228
Topeka, KS	127	229
Santa Fe, NM	126	230
Flagstaff, AZ-UT	125	231
Punta Gorda, FL	124	232
Sioux Falls, SD	124	233
Panama City, FL	123	234
Florence, AL	121	235
Athens, GA	118	236
Joplin, MO	118	237
Benton Harbor, MI	116	238
Mansfield, OH	116	239
Odessa-Midland, TX	116	240
Sheboygan, WI	116	241
Jackson, TN	115	242
Johnstown, PA	114	243
Jonesboro, AR	114	244
Sumter, SC	114	245
Lafayette, IN	113	246
Terre Haute, IN	113	247
Galveston-Texas City, TX	112	248
Champaign-Urbana, IL	110	249
Jersey City, NJ	110	250
Bloomington-Normal, IL	107	251
Hattiesburg, MS	107	252
Lima, OH	106	253
Jackson, MI	106	254
Parkersburg-Marietta, WV-OH	104	255
Decatur, AL	103	256
Altoona, PA	102	257
Brazoria, TX	101	258
State College, PA	98	259
Missoula, MT	97	260
Pittsfield, MA	97	261
Glens Falls, NY	96	262
Hagerstown, MD	96	263
Monroe, LA	96	264
Grand Forks, ND-MN	94	265
Jamestown, NY	94	266
Yolo, CA	92	267
Wheeling, WV-OH	91	268
Wichita Falls, TX	91	269
Yuma, AZ	91	270
Las Cruces, NM	90	271
Yuba City, CA	89	272
Dubuque, IA	88	273
Iowa City, IA	88	274
Rapid City, SD	88	275
Sharon, PA	87	276
Jacksonville, NC	86	277
Sioux City, IA-NE	86	278
Grand Junction, CO	85	279
Alexandria, LA	82	280
Kokomo, IN	81	281
Danville, VA	80	282
Bryan-College Station, TX	79	283
Abilene, TX	78	284
Williamsport, PA	76	285
Great Falls, MT	75	286
Owensboro, KY	74	287
Texarkana, TX-AR	74	288
Bloomington, IN	72	289
Sherman-Denison, TX	72	290
Muncie, IN	71	291
Greeley, CO	70	292
Kankakee, IL	70	293
Decatur, IL	69	294
Merced, CA	69	295
Vineland-Millville-Bridgeton, NJ	66	296
Bismarck, ND	65	297
Gadsden, AL	64	298
Lewiston-Auburn, ME	61	299
Pueblo, CO	60	300
Steubenville-Weirton, OH-WV	60	301
Anniston, AL	59	302
Cumberland, MD-WV	59	303
Elmira, NY	56	304
Lawrence, KS	56	305
Victoria, TX	55	306
Lawton, OK	54	307
Albany, GA	53	308
Kenosha, WI	53	309
Pine Bluff, AR	53	310
Pocatello, ID	52	311
San Angelo, TX	45	312
Cheyenne, WY	40	313
St. Joseph, MO	36	314
Casper, WY	31	315
Enid, OK	28	316

MSA/NECMA Total **139,937**
United States Total **177,026**
MSA/NECMA (% of U.S.Total) **79.05**

NOTES